FINLAND

SWEDEN

LAKE LADOGA

Helsingfors

KARELIA

Ingermanland

Volkhov R.

Novgorod

EGNDOM OF

stockholm

Iecarlia

LAKE WETTER

BALTIC SEA

DAGOE

OSEL

GOTLAND

OLAND

BORNHOLM

agen

RG

rlin

Posen

Warsaw

P O L A N D

ESTHONIA

LIVONIA

DOMINION OF TEUTONIC ORDER

SAMOGITIA

Tilsit

Königsberg

PRUSSIA

Danzig

Vistula R.

Breslau

SILESIA

Oder R.

Pskov

Düna R.

L I T H U A N I A

Vilna

Niemen

Pripet R.

Lovat R.

Volga R.

Moscow

M U S C O V Y

Dniepr R.

Desna R.

Kiev

Dnieper R.

the
Habsburgs

Spanish Branch

Austrian Branch

Empire of Charles V,
about 1526
◆
Possessions of the
Bourbons

Hereditary Lands of
Henry of Navarre

Lands of Charles
of Bourbon-Montpensier

Dresden

Prague

EMIA

ANY

MORAVIA

Vienna

AUSTRIA

Styria

inthia

Krakow

Danube R.

Buda

Pest

H U N G A R Y

Drave R.

Theiss R.

Save R.

TRANSYLVANIA

Belgrade

WALLACHIA

Aluta R.

Bucharest

M O L D A V I A

Pruth R.

Dniester R.

Bessarabia

Dobrudja

Bug R.

Yedisan

KHANATE

OF

Crimea

KRIM

BLACK SEA

Constantinople

DALMATIA

OF VENICE

ADRIATIC SEA

REPUBLIC OF RAGUSA

oleto

Benevento

NAPLES

Naples

Taranto

APULIA

CALABRIA

Palermo

SICILY

BOSNIA

SERBIA

MONTENEGRO

ALBANIA

Morava R.

Vardar R.

Danube R.

BULGARIA

Sofia

R U M E L I A

Adrianople

MACEDONIA

Saloniki

Thessaly

Athens

Morea

CORFU
(to Venice)

CEPHALONIA
(to Venice)

ZANTE
(to Venice)

CERIGO
(to Venice)

SEA

E M P I R E

Gallipoli

LEMNOS

MITYLENE

AEGEAN SEA

Angora

Sakaria R.

Kizil Irmak

Smyrna

RHODES

CRETE
(to Venice)

CYPRUS
(to Venice)

Liam Dunne

Judith Miller
W. Strasburg Rd
R.D. #1
West Chester, Pa
Day Room Box # 41

FIFTH
EDITION

WESTERN

CIVILIZATIONS

Their History and Their Culture

FIFTH
EDITION

WESTERN

CIVILIZATIONS

Their History and Their Culture

BY EDWARD McNALL BURNS

Rutgers University

W·W·NORTON & COMPANY·INC·

New York

To the memory of *My Mother*

Who first inspired in me the desire to know

Contents

Part 2. The Classical Civilizations of Greece and Rome

Part 3. The Early Middle Ages

Part 4. The Later Middle Ages and the Renaissance

Part 5. Modern Occidental Civilization, 1517–1789: Commercialism, Absolutism, Rationalism

Part 6. Modern Occidental Civilization, 1789–1914: Democracy, Nationalism, Industrialism

Part 7. The Age of Total War and Revolution, 1914–

Illustrations

Illustrations in Color

Illustrations in the Text

xvii

Maps in Color

Maps and Charts in the Text

ILLUSTRATIONS

Preface

THIS BOOK was published originally in 1941 and revised in 1947, 1949, and 1954. Since the last revision much has occurred to bring into sharper focus the dramatic events of the modern world. We are now able to see more clearly the revolutionary trends of our times. To describe and assess the significance of such developments as the decline of Western Europe, the ascendancy of the Soviet Union and the United States, the power struggle between East and West, the nationalist revolt against imperialism, and the awesome achievements in the fields of atomic and thermonuclear energy, a new edition of *Western Civilizations* becomes necessary. But the present revision is not a mere enlargement of its predecessors. The entire book has been reset. Much new material has been added, but much of the old has been eliminated, and rewriting has been done throughout. Notable changes include: a reduction of the material on philosophy, especially on the less important thinkers; an increase of political history, particularly of the medieval and early modern; a reorganization and enlargement of many chapters; a complete revision of reading lists and their transfer from the end of the book to the concluding page of each chapter; and a thorough study and correction of the maps, with the addition of several new ones. The entire problem of illustrative materials has been re-examined with results which should add immeasurably to their value in the book. With the exception of the color plates, which it is hoped will awaken a new interest in the artistic accomplishments of the past and the present, all photographs, engravings, and drawings are reproduced on pages of the text as close as possible to the subjects they illustrate.

The purpose of this book is to present a compact survey of man's struggles, ideals, and achievements from ancient times to the present. Because of limitations of space, however, the record has had to be confined primarily to western Asia, northern Africa, Europe, and the

Americas. In general, developments in that portion of the world east of Persia have been brought into the picture only in so far as they have been closely related to the history of the West. But within the limits thus described, the object has been to portray the drama of civilization as a whole. No major acts or scenes of that drama have been ignored or slighted. The civilizations before the Greeks have been treated not as a mere prologue but as significant stages in man's unending struggle to solve his problems. If there is any basic philosophic interpretation underlying the narrative, it is the conviction that most of human progress thus far has resulted from the growth of intelligence and respect for the rights of man, and that therein lies the chief hope for a better world in the future.

As its title indicates, this book is not exclusively or even primarily a political history. Political narrative is recognized as important, but it is not the whole substance of history. In the main, the facts of political history are subordinated to the development of institutions and ideas or are presented as the groundwork of cultural, economic, and social movements. The author believes that the effects of the Black Death were no less important than the Hundred Years' War, and that it is of greater value to understand the significance of Newton and Darwin than it is to be able to name the kings of France. In accordance with this broader conception of history, more space has been given to the teachings of Aristotle and the Stoics than to the military exploits of Alexander the Great or Julius Caesar.

In preparing this work the author has profited from the assistance and counsel of many individuals whose services no words of appreciation can adequately measure. He wishes to acknowledge his gratitude especially to Professor Philip L. Ralph of Lake Erie College, who has not only read and criticized the manuscript in its entirety but has written the sections on music. Professor Ross J. S. Hoffman of Fordham University has also criticized most of the manuscript and has made numerous invaluable suggestions for its improvement. Dean Harry M. Orlinsky of the Jewish Institute of Religion and Nathaniel Zimskind of Hebrew Union College have helped with the revision of the chapter on the Hebrews and have saved the author from numerous pitfalls. Professor Peter Charanis of Rutgers University has given expert assistance with the ancient and medieval sections, and Professors Henry R. Winkler, Samuel C. McCulloch, and Norman L. Stamps, and Dr. F. Gunther Eyck with the modern. The chapters on ancient history have been read and criticized by Professor J. W. Swain of the University of Illinois, and those on the medieval world and the Renaissance by Professor Edgar N. Johnson of the University of Nebraska. The sections on modern literature have been examined critically by Professor Rudolf Kirk of the Rutgers Department of English and by Dr. Clara Marburg Kirk, formerly Associate Professor of English at Bryn Mawr. Professor David L. Cowen of Rutgers University has watched with unusual vigilance to eliminate errors and recommend improvements throughout the book. Others who have given valuable aid with one or more chapters include Dr. August Meier, formerly Assistant to the President of Fisk University; Professors Mark M. Heald, Irving S. Kull, L. Ethan Ellis, Sidney Ratner, and George P. Schmidt of Rutgers University; and Professors Oscar J. Falnes and Henry H. B. Noss of New York University. Mrs. Beulah H. Scheer, Secretary of the Rutgers Department of Political Science, has done some of the secretarial work incident to the completion of the book and has helped with the preparation of the chronological charts. The assistance of Professor Albert W. Holzmann and Dr. F. Gunther Eyck with the German pronunciations; of Professor Remigio U. Pane with the Spanish and Italian pronunciations; and of Dr. Madeleine Charanis, Dr. Lucy Huang, and Professor Ardath W. Burks with the French, Chinese and Japanese pronunciations, respectively, is gratefully acknowledged. Most of all, however, the author is indebted to his wife for her arduous labors of research, typing, proofreading, and preparing the index, and for her patience, devotion, and understanding.

EDWARD McNALL BURNS

New Brunswick, N.J.

Picture Acknowledgments

The corporations, public agencies, and individuals listed below have generously provided photographs or other materials to illustrate *Western Civilizations*. Specific contributions are indicated in the list of illustrations by the name of the donor in full or by code letters after the title of the picture furnished.

American Museum of Natural History (AMNH)
American Philosophical Society
American School of Classical Studies, Athens (Agora Excavations)
Arabian-American Oil Company
Arena Chapel, Padua
Baltimore & Ohio Railroad (B&O RR)
Bayeux Public Library
Belgian Government Tourist Bureau (BGTB)
British Information Service (BIS)
British Museum
Chase Manhattan Bank Museum of Moneys of the World (Chase)
Stephen C. Clark
Douglas Aircraft Company
Ford Motor Company
Henry Ford Museum, Dearborn
Foreign Operations Administration
Free Europe Press
French Embassy, Press and Information Division (FEPI)
French Government Tourist Office (FGTO)

Germanic Museum, Nuremberg
German Railroads
German Tourist Information Office (GTIO)
Greek Information Office (GIO)
Henry E. Huntington Library and Art Gallery (Huntington)
Iglesia San Tomé, Toledo, Spain
International Harvester Company
Israeli Government Tourist Office (IGTO)
Italian State Tourist Office (ISTO)
Robert Lehman
Lever Brothers
Marshall MacDuffie
Mauritshuis, The Hague
Metropolitan Museum of Art, New York (MMA)
Minneapolis Institute of Art
Morgan Library, New York (Morgan)
Museum of Modern Art, New York (Modern)
National Archives
National Gallery of Art
National Museum, Naples

Richard J. Neutra

New York Public Library, Picture Collection and Print Collection (NYPL)

Oriental Institute, University of Chicago

Phillips Memorial Gallery

Pitti Palace, Florence

Prado, Madrid

Rutgers University, Department of Art (Rutgers)

Santa Maria della Grazie, Milan

Sistine Chapel

Sperry-Rand Corporation

Standard Oil Company of New Jersey

Spanish Tourist Office (STO)

Swiss National Tourist Office

Tennessee Valley Authority

Trans World Airlines (TWA)

Uffizi Gallery, Florence (Uffizi)

United Nations

United States Army

United States Lines Company

United States Marine Corps

United States Navy

University Prints (UP)

V. W. van Gogh

Whitney Museum of American Art

Yale University Press

FROM SPECIAL COLLECTIONS AND GIFTS IN THE METROPOLITAN MUSEUM OF ART, NEW YORK

BEQUEST OF MRS. H. O. HAVEMEYER, 1929. THE H. O. HAVEMEYER COLLECTION: *Portrait of a Young Man*, Bronzino; *Boy with a Greyhound*, Veronese; *Portrait of a Gentleman*, Ingres; *Pink and Green*, Degas; *Montagne Sainte Victoire with Aqueduct*, Cézanne; *Still Life*, Cézanne.

THE JULES S. BACHE COLLECTION: *Madonna and Child*, Luca della Robbia; *Portrait of a Young Man*, Bellini (1949); *Portrait of a Lady*, Domenico Veneziano (1949).

THE ALFRED STIEGLITZ COLLECTION, 1949: *Sea and Gulls*, John Marin.

BEQUEST OF SAMUEL A. LEWISOHN, 1951: *Ia Orana Maria*, Gauguin.

FROM SPECIAL COLLECTIONS AND GIFTS IN THE MUSEUM OF MODERN ART, NEW YORK

MRS. SIMON GUGGENHEIM FUND: *Piano Lesson*, Henri Matisse; *Three Musicians*, Pablo Picasso; *I and the Village*, Marc Chagall.

ACQUIRED THROUGH THE LILLIE P. BLISS BEQUEST: *The Starry Night*, Vincent van Gogh; *The Table*, Georges Braque.

MRS. JOHN D. ROCKEFELLER, JR., FUND: *Around the Fish*, Paul Klee.

The Dawn of History

No one knows the place of origin of the human species. There is evidence, however, that it may have been south central Africa or possibly central or south central Asia. Here climatic conditions were such as to favor the evolution of a variety of human types from primate ancestors. From their place or places of origin members of the human species wandered to southeastern and eastern Asia, northern Africa, Europe, and eventually to America. For hundreds of centuries they remained primitive, leading a life which was at first little better than that of the higher animals. About 5000 B.C. a few of them, enjoying special advantages of location and climate, developed superior cultures. These cultures, which attained knowledge of writing and considerable advancement in the arts and sciences and in social organization, began in that part of the world known as the Near Orient. This region extends from the western border of India to the Mediterranean Sea and to the farther bank of the Nile. Here flourished, at different periods between 5000 and 300 B.C., the mighty empires of the Egyptians, the Babylonians, the Assyrians, the Chaldeans, and the Persians, together with the smaller states of such peoples as the Cretans, the Sumerians, the Phoenicians, and the Hebrews. In other parts of the world the beginnings of civilization were retarded. There was nothing that could be called civilized life in China until about 2000 B.C. And, except on the island of Crete, there was no civilization in Europe until more than 1000 years later.

THE DAWN OF HISTORY *

	Geological Period			Characteristic Forms of Life	Culture Periods
3 billion— years ago	Precambrian			One-celled organisms First invertebrates: worms, algae	
510 million— years ago	Paleozoic	Cambrian		Mollusks, sponges	
		Ordovician		Insects, first vertebrates Corals, sharks, seaweed	
		Silurian		Lungfish, crustaceans Earliest amphibians	
		Devonian		Large amphibians Ferns	
		Mississippian			
		Pennsylvanian			
180 million— years ago		Permian			
	Mesozoic	Triassic		Giant reptiles Diversified reptiles, birds	
90 million— years ago		Jurassic		Marsupials, bony fishes Trees	
		Cretaceous			
	Cenozoic	Tertiary	Paleocene	Early mammals, first primates	
			Eocene	Primitive apes, ancestors of monkeys	
			Oligocene	Ancestors of great apes Ancestors of man, modern	
			Miocene	mammals	
1 million— years ago			Pliocene	Early human species, other primates	Lower Paleolithic
		Quaternary	Pleistocene	Present day animals and races of men	Upper Paleolithic Neolithic
7,000— years ago			Recent		Civilized man

* Adapted from time scale issued by Geological Names Committee, 1958.

The Stone Age or
Preliterate Cultures

The entire span of human history can be divided roughly into two periods, the Age of Stone and the Age of Metals. The former is sometimes called the Preliterate Age, or the period before the invention of writing. The latter coincides with the period of history based upon written records. The Preliterate Age covered at least 95 per cent of man's existence and did not come to an end until about 5000 B.C. The Age of Metals practically coincides with the history of civilized nations. The Age of Stone is subdivided into the Paleolithic, or Old Stone Age, and the Neolithic, or New Stone Age. Each takes its name from the type of stone tools and weapons characteristically manufactured during the period. Thus during the greater part of the Paleolithic Age implements were commonly made by chipping pieces off a large stone or flint and using the core that remained as a hand ax or "fist hatchet." Toward the end of the period the chips themselves were used as knives or spearheads, and the core thrown away. The Neolithic Age witnessed the supplanting of chipped stone tools by implements made by grinding and polishing stone.

Periods of man's history

The names of the periods mentioned leave much to be desired. They were invented at a time when the study of early cultures was in its infancy. It is now recognized that sharp dividing lines cannot always be drawn between stages of culture on the basis of their methods of making stone tools and weapons. This is particularly true of the later stages. Moreover, types of tools and weapons have not in all cases been the most significant traits distinguishing one culture from another. Nevertheless, the method of naming has been found convenient and will doubtless continue to be used.

Significance of names of the periods

1. The Culture of Lower Paleolithic Men

The Paleolithic period can be dated from roughly 500,000 B.C. to 10,000 B.C. It is commonly divided into two stages, an earlier or Lower Paleolithic and a later or Upper Paleolithic. The Lower Paleolithic was much the longer of the two, covering at least 75 per cent of the entire Old Stone Age. During this time at least four species of men inhabited the earth. One was the famous *Pithecanthropus erectus,* or "erect ape man," whose skeletal remains were found on the island of Java in 1891. Originally only a skull cap, a thigh bone, three teeth, and part of a jaw bone were discovered. But in recent years other fragments, belonging to the same or a similar species, have been unearthed. As a result it is now possible to reconstruct the entire skull of Pithecanthropus. It has been established

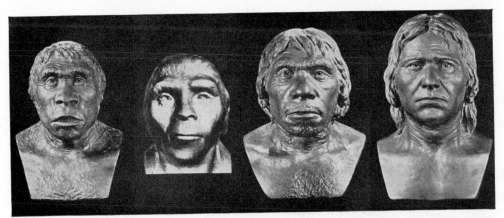

Reconstruction of the Skulls of Four Types of Stone Age Men: Java, Peking, Neanderthal, Cro-Magnon.

that his cranial capacity was nearly double that of a male gorilla, but only two-thirds that of modern man.

A second known inhabitant of the Lower Paleolithic was *Sinanthropus pekinensis,* whose skeletal remains were found in China, about forty miles southwest of Peking (Peiping), between 1926 and 1930. Since the latter date fragments of no fewer than 32 skeletons of the Sinanthropus type have been located, making possible a complete reconstruction of at least the head of this ancient species. Anthropologists generally agree that Sinanthropus and Pithecanthropus are of approximately the same antiquity, and that both probably descended from the same ancestral type. Until recently many scientists believed that the so-called Piltdown man, whose fragmentary "remains" were found in England in 1911, was a contemporary of the Java and Peking species. But in 1953 it was revealed that "Piltdown man" was a hoax. The fragments, which included a skull-cap and a jaw bone, had been skillfully altered. The jaw bone was actually that of an ape, chemically treated to make it appear aged, while the skull-cap was only about 50,000 years old.

Much more dependable evidence exists of another Paleolithic man, although he did not make his appearance until the period was well advanced. This specimen was Fontéchevade man, so called from the cave in which his remains were found in 1947 in Charente, in southwestern France. Although the finds included only fragments of skulls, enough of them were intact to make possible accurate measurements. Moreover, the geological layer in which they were found, and also the one immediately above, was complete and undisturbed, so that little trouble could arise in assigning them to a chronological era. In certain respects Fontéchevade man resembled modern man more closely even than some ancestors of later origin. For example, the skull-cap dimensions were about the same as those of living Europeans. More interesting, the heavy eyebrow ridges, so characteristic of most early men, were lacking, and the construction of the forehead was remarkably similar to that of our own. On the other hand, the brain case was exceptionally thick, and the cranium was low-vaulted. Fontéchevade man derived his large brain capacity from the extraordinary breadth of his cranium, not from its height.

*Fonté-
chevade
man*

During the last 25,000 years of the Lower Paleolithic period a fourth species of ancient man made his appearance. He was *Homo neanderthalensis,* famous as an early cave man. His skeletal fragments were first discovered in the valley of the Neander, near Düsseldorf, northwestern Germany, in 1856. Since then numerous other discoveries have been made, in some cases complete skeletons, in such widely separated regions as Belgium, Spain, Italy, Yugoslavia, Russia, and Palestine. So closely did Neanderthal man resemble modern man that he is classified as a member of the same genus, the genus *Homo.* The resemblance, however, was by no means perfect. Neanderthal men, on the average, were only about five feet, four inches in height. They had receding chins and heavy eyebrow ridges. Although their foreheads sloped back and their brain cases were low-vaulted, their average cranial capacity was slightly greater than that of modern Caucasians. What this may have signified with respect to their intelligence cannot be determined.

*Neanderthal
man*

The knowledge we possess of the culture of Lower Paleolithic men is scanty indeed. The skills they achieved and the learning they acquired must have been pitiful in quantity even when compared with the accomplishments of modern primitive men. Yet Pithecanthropus and his successors were not mere apes, forgetting in a moment the chance triumphs they had made. They undoubtedly had the capacity for speech, which enabled them to communicate with their fellows and to pass on what they had learned to succeeding generations. We are justified in assuming also that they possessed reasoning ability, however crudely it may have been developed. Practically from the beginning, therefore, they were probably tool-

*Lower Paleo-
lithic culture*

using creatures, employing their wits to fashion implements and weapons. Perhaps at first these would be nothing but limbs broken from trees to be used as clubs. Eventually it was discovered that stones could be chipped in such a way as to give them cutting edges. The butt was then held in the palm of the hand. Thus evolved the so-called hand ax or fist hatchet, which appears to have served the combined purposes of a cleaver, saw, scraper, and knife.

Before the end of the Lower Paleolithic period, Neanderthal man seems largely to have abandoned the use of the fist hatchet. Improved methods of chipping stone enabled him to rely primarily upon the flakes themselves. The result was the development of spearheads, borers, and much superior knives and scrapers. Indications have been found also of a degree of advancement in nonmaterial culture. In the entrances to caves where Neanderthal man lived, or at least took refuge, evidence has been discovered of flint-working floors and stone hearths where huge fires appear to have been made. These would suggest the origins of co-operative group life and possibly the crude beginnings of social institutions. More significance may be attached to Neanderthal man's practice of bestowing care upon the bodies of his dead, interring with them in shallow graves tools and other objects of value. Perhaps this practice indicates the development of a religious sense, or at least a belief in some form of survival after death.

2. Upper Paleolithic Culture

About 30,000 B.C. the culture of the Old Stone Age passed from the Lower Paleolithic stage to the Upper Paleolithic. The Upper Paleolithic period lasted for only about 200 centuries, or from 30,000 to 10,000 B.C. A new and superior type of human being dominated the earth in this time. Biologically these men were closely related to modern man. Their foremost predecessors, Neanderthal men, had ceased to exist as a distinct variety. What became of the Neanderthalers is not known. According to one school of opinion, they were probably exterminated by their conquerors or perished through failure of their food supply. According to another school, they lost their identity merely through interbreeding with the newcomers. One branch of them in a remote area of the world may actually have been the ancestors of the new race that now became dominant.

The name used to designate the prevailing breed of Upper Paleolithic men is Cro-Magnon, from the Cro-Magnon cave in Dordogne, France, where some of the most typical remains were discovered. Cro-Magnon men were tall, broad-shouldered, and erect, the males averaging over six feet. They had high foreheads, well-developed chins, and a cranial capacity about equal to the modern average. The heavy eyebrow ridges so typical of earlier species were lacking. Whether Cro-Magnon men left any survivors is a debatable question. They do not seem to have been exterminated but appear to have been driven into mountainous regions and to have been absorbed ultimately into later races.

Upper Paleolithic culture was markedly superior to that which had gone before. Not only were tools and implements better made, but they existed in greater variety. They were not fashioned merely from flakes of stone and an occasional shaft of bone; other materials were used in abundance, particularly reindeer horn and ivory. Examples of the more complicated tools included the bone needle, the fishhook, the harpoon, the dart thrower, and, at the very end, the bow and arrow. That Upper Paleolithic man wore clothing is indicated by the fact that he made buttons and toggles of bone and horn and invented the needle. He did not know how to weave cloth, but animal skins sewn together proved a satisfactory substitute. Large numbers of perforated animal teeth and shells have also been found, suggesting that he made pendants and necklaces to adorn his person. It is certain that he cooked his food, for enormous hearths, evidently used for roasting flesh, have been discovered. In the vicinity of one at Solutré, in southern France, was a mass of charred bones, estimated to contain the remains of 100,000 large animals. Although Cro-Magnon man built no houses, except a few simple huts in regions where natural shelters did not abound, his life was not wholly nomadic. Evidences found in the caves that were his usual homes indicate that he must have used them, seasonally at least, for years at a time.

Upper Paleolithic culture: tools and weapons

With respect to nonmaterial elements there are also indications that Upper Paleolithic culture represented a marked advancement. Group life was now more regular and more highly organized than ever before. The profusion of charred bones at Solutré and elsewhere probably indicates co-operative enterprise in the hunt and sharing of the results in great community feasts. The amazing workmanship displayed in tools and weapons and highly developed techniques in the arts could scarcely have been achieved without some division of labor. It appears certain, therefore, that Upper Paleolithic communities included professional artists and skilled craftsmen. In order to acquire such talents, certain members of the communities must have gone through long periods of training and given all their time to the practice of their specialties. In consequence they would have to be supported by the rest of the group. Thus an aristocracy would arise, and possibly the highest members of it would enjoy enough prestige to become rulers with limited authority.

Evidences of social development

Substantial proof exists that Cro-Magnon man had highly developed notions of a world of unseen powers. He bestowed more care upon the bodies of his dead than did Neanderthal man, painting the corpses, folding the arms over the heart, and depositing pend-

Sympathetic magic

7

ants, necklaces, and richly carved weapons and tools in the graves. He formulated an elaborate system of sympathetic magic designed to increase his supply of food. Sympathetic magic is based upon the principle that imitating a desired result may bring about that result. Applying this principle, Cro-Magnon man made paintings on the walls of his caves depicting the capture of reindeer in the hunt, or he carved images of the cave bear with javelins piercing its side. At other times he fashioned clay models of the bison or mammoth and mutilated them with dart thrusts. The purpose of such representations was quite evidently to facilitate the very results portrayed and thereby to increase the hunter's success and make easier the struggle for existence. Possibly incantations or ceremonies accompanied the making of the pictures or images, and it is likely that the work of producing them was carried on while the actual hunt was in progress.

*Evidences
of intellectual
progress*

The Upper Paleolithic period witnessed some slight intellectual progress. Cro-Magnon man could count, and the first mathematical records in the history of mankind made their appearance. These consisted of various objects: a notched javelin or dart thrower, for example, or a stag tooth scored horizontally with a sharp tool and worn as a pendant. All of them were probably records of animals slain in the hunt. A bare possibility exists that Cro-Magnon man developed a primitive system of writing. Various interesting signs have been discovered which give the appearance of being characters of a written language. They were probably nothing more, however, than conventionalized symbols of natural objects. Plenty of other evidence can be found that the art of this period often showed a tendency toward conventionalization. The possibility that a knowledge of writing existed at this time must therefore be regarded as remote.

*Upper
Paleolithic art*

The supreme achievement of Cro-Magnon man was his art—an achievement so original and resplendent that it ought to be counted

Examples of Upper Paleolithic Engraving and Sculpture. The two objects at the top and upper right are dart throwers. At the lower right is the famous Venus of Willendorf.

among the Seven Wonders of the World. Nothing else illustrates so well the great gulf between his culture and that of his predecessors. Upper Paleolithic art included nearly every branch that the material culture of the time made possible. Sculpture, painting, carving, and engraving were all represented. The ceramic arts and architecture were lacking, for pottery had not yet been invented, and no buildings were erected except of simple design.

The art *par excellence* of Cro-Magnon man was painting. Here were exhibited the greatest number and variety of his talents—his discrimination in the use of color, his meticulous attention to detail, his capacity for the employment of scale in depicting a group, and above all his genius for naturalism. The art of modern primitive folk resembles the art of a child; it portrays things not as they are, but in accordance with naïve preconceptions in the mind. The art of Upper Paleolithic man was remarkably free from such tendencies and showed a firm resolution to copy the world of nature with utmost fidelity. Especially noteworthy was the painter's skill in representing movement. A large proportion of his murals depicted animals running, leaping, browsing, chewing the cud, or facing the hunter at bay. Ingenious devices were often employed to give the impression of motion. Chief among them was the drawing or painting of additional outlines to indicate the areas into which the legs or the head of the animal had moved. But the scheme was so shrewdly executed that no appearance whatever of artificiality resulted.

Cave-man art throws a flood of light on many problems relating to primitive mentality and folkways. To a certain extent it was undoubtedly an expression of a true aesthetic sense. Cro-Magnon man did obviously take some delight in the graceful line or symmetrical pattern or brilliant color. The fact that he painted and tattooed the body and wore ornaments gives evidence of this. But his chief works of art can scarcely have been produced for the sake of creating beautiful objects. Such a possibility must be excluded for several reasons. To begin with, the best of the paintings and drawings are usually to be found on the walls and ceilings of the darkest and most inaccessible parts of the caves. The gallery of paintings at Niaux, for instance, is more than half a mile from the entrance of the cavern. No one could see the artists' creations except in the imperfect light of torches or of primitive lamps which must have smoked and sputtered badly, since the only illuminating fluid was animal fat. Furthermore, there is evidence that Cro-Magnon man was largely indifferent toward his work of art after it was finished. He did not cherish it with the passing of the years, nor did he spend much time in admiring it. On the contrary, he was likely to use the very same surface for a new production. Numerous examples have been found of paintings or drawings superimposed upon earlier ones of the same or of different types. Evidently the important thing was not the finished work itself, but the act of making it.

Painting

Significance of Upper Paleolithic art

Cave Drawings at Lascaux, France. Characteristic examples of the realism of Cro-Magnon man's art.

For Paleolithic man, art was a serious business. The real purpose of nearly all of it was apparently not to delight the senses but to make easier the struggle for existence by increasing the supply of animals useful for food. The artist himself was not an aesthete but a magician, and his art was a form of magic designed to promote the hunter's success. In this purpose lay its chief significance and the foundation of most of its special qualities. It suggests, for example, the real reason why game animals were almost the exclusive subjects of the great murals and why plant life and inanimate objects were seldom represented. It aids us in understanding Cro-Magnon man's neglect of the finished paintings and his predominant interest in the process by which they were made. Finally, magical purposes go far toward explaining the spectacular genius of the artist himself, for the very existence of the community was believed to depend upon the competent performance of his duties, and consequently no effort would be spared in giving him a thorough training.

Upper Paleolithic culture came to an untimely end about 10,000 B.C. Internal decay, exemplified by the decline of art, seems to have been one of the causes. The factors responsible cannot be determined exactly. Impatience with the old methods, a striving after "short cuts" that resulted in standardization and loss of originality, may have been one of them. A more obvious and doubtless more effective cause of the decline of the culture as a whole was partial destruction

Art as a serious business

The end of Upper Paleolithic culture

10

of the food supply. As the last great glacier retreated farther and farther northward, the climate of southern Europe became too warm for the reindeer, and they gradually migrated to the shores of the Baltic. The mammoth, whether for the same or for different reasons, became extinct. Representatives of the magnificent Cro-Magnon race probably followed the reindeer northward, but apparently they did not continue their cultural achievements.

3. *Neolithic Culture*

The last stage of preliterate culture is known as the Neolithic period, or the New Stone Age. The name is applied because stone weapons and tools were now generally made by grinding and polishing instead of by chipping or fracturing as in the preceding periods. *The meaning of the term Neolithic*
The bearers of Neolithic culture were new varieties of modern man who poured into Africa and southern Europe from western Asia. Since no evidence exists of their later extermination or wholesale migration, they must be regarded as the immediate ancestors of most of the peoples now living in Europe.

It is impossible to fix exact dates for the Neolithic period. The culture was not well established in Europe until about 3000 B.C., though it certainly originated earlier. There is evidence that it *The varying dates of the Neolithic stage* existed in Egypt as far back as 5000 B.C., and that it probably began at an equally early date in southwestern Asia. There is also variation in the dates of its ending. It was superseded in the Nile valley by the first historic civilization soon after the year 4000.[1] Except on the island of Crete it did not come to an end anywhere in Europe before 2000, and in northern Europe much later still. In a few regions of the world it has not terminated yet. The natives of some islands of the Pacific, the Arctic regions of North America, and the jungles of Brazil are still in the Neolithic culture stage except for a few customs acquired from explorers and missionaries.

In many respects the New Stone Age was the most significant in the history of the world thus far. The level of material progress rose to new heights. Neolithic man had a better mastery of his *The Neolithic revolution* environment than any of his predecessors. He was less likely to perish from a shift in climatic conditions or from the failure of some part of his food supply. This decided advantage was the result primarily of the development of agriculture and the domestication of animals. Whereas all of the men who had lived heretofore were mere food-gatherers, Neolithic man was a *food-producer*. Tilling the soil and keeping flocks and herds provided him with much more dependable food resources and at times yielded him a surplus. These circumstances made possible a more rapid increase of population,

[1] All dates in Egyptian history prior to 2000 are approximations and may represent a margin of error of several centuries.

promoted a settled existence, and fostered the growth of institutions. Such were the elements of a great social and economic revolution whose importance it would be almost impossible to exaggerate.

*The wide distri-
bution of the
Neolithic cul-
ture*

The new culture also derives significance from the fact that it was the first to be distributed over the *entire* world. Although some earlier cultures, especially those of Neanderthal and Cro-Magnon men, were widely dispersed, they were confined chiefly to the accessible mainland areas of the Old World. Neolithic man penetrated into every habitable area of the earth's surface—from Arctic wastes to the jungles of the tropics. He apparently made his way from a number of centers of origin to every nook and cranny of both hemispheres. He traveled incredible distances by water as well as by land, and eventually occupied every major island of the oceans, no matter how remote. Even Hawaii, situated 4000 miles from the Asiatic mainland, proved not to be beyond his reach. Whether he launched his vessel or raft for some visible goal, and then drifted out of his course and by a lucky accident was washed ashore before he starved to death, or whether he got there by skill or intent, it is certain that he did arrive, for when the white men came the natives of the Hawaiian Islands had essentially the same pattern of culture as Neolithic men everywhere else.

*Factors respon-
sible for wide
distribution*

The factors responsible for this wide distribution cannot be determined with precision. It has been established that Neolithic man invented boats and rafts, without which he could never have escaped the confines of Asia, Africa, and Europe. But why he should have forced his way into steaming jungles, mountain fastnesses, and bleak and barren areas like Labrador and Patagonia remains an impenetrable mystery. We can only conjecture that increasing population required a constant search for new hunting areas and possibly for grazing and agricultural lands. Younger and more venturesome individuals would be forever striking out into new regions in the hope of improving their economic condition.

*Importance of
the Neolithic
migrations*

The historian would have difficulty in overestimating the importance of the Neolithic migrations. The net result was that they distributed a similar pattern of culture over the entire world. The few elements of earlier cultures which had managed to survive were almost completely inundated. Their disappearance means that we now have no way of discovering more than a small part of what went on in Paleolithic man's mind—whether he believed that government is an evil or that private property is sacred or that the world was created out of nothing. The fact that we find particular notions in the primitive mind of today does not prove that they are inseparable from the blood and sinew of the species, for it is necessary to remember that all existing primitive races are the beneficiaries or the victims of a common heritage.

The invention of boats and rafts was not the only example of **12** Neolithic man's mechanical ingenuity. He developed the arts of knitting, of spinning, and of weaving cloth. He made the first pottery and knew how to produce fire artificially by friction. He built houses of wood and sun-dried mud. Toward the end of the period he discovered the possibilities of metals, and a few implements of copper and gold were added to his stock. Since nothing was yet known of the arts of smelting and refining, the use of metals was limited to the more malleable ones occasionally found in the pure state in the form of nuggets.

New tools and technical skills

Neolithic Dwellings. Examples shown are restorations of Swiss lake dwellings. They were commonly erected on poles or stilts for purposes of defense.

But the real foundation stones of the Neolithic culture were the domestication of animals and the development of agriculture. Without these it is inconceivable that the culture would have attained the complexity it did. More than anything else they were responsible for the settled mode of existence, for the growth of villages and social institutions. They stimulated the rise of a division of labor and encouraged the practice of exchange. They compelled man constantly to seek new methods of harnessing nature and thereby led to an increase in his physical equipment and his store of knowledge.

Importance of agriculture and the domestication of animals

The first animal to be domesticated is generally thought to have been the dog, on the assumption that he would be continually hanging around the hunter's camp to pick up bones and scraps of meat. Eventually it would be discovered that he could be put to use in hunting, or possibly in guarding the camp. After achieving success in domesticating the dog, Neolithic man would logically turn his attention to other animals, especially to those he used for food. Before the period ended, at least five species—the cow, the dog, the goat, the sheep, and the pig—had been made to serve his needs. Not all of them in all parts of the world, however. The Neolithic tribes of the New World domesticated no animals at all, except the hairless dog in some parts of Mexico, the llama and the alpaca in the Andean highland, and the guinea pig and the turkey in a few other regions.

Origins of the domestication of animals

The exact spot where agriculture originated has never been positively determined. All we know is that wild grasses which were probably the ancestors of the cereal grains have been found in a number of places. Types of wheat grow wild in Asia Minor, in the Caucasus, and in Mesopotamia. Wild ancestors of barley have been

The beginning of agriculture

13

reported from North Africa, from Persia, from Asia Minor, and from Turkestan. Though it is probable that these were the first crops of Neolithic agriculture, they were by no means the only ones. Millet, vegetables, and numerous fruits were also grown. Flax was cultivated in the Old World for its textile fiber, and in some localities the growing of the poppy for opium had already begun. In the New World maize (Indian corn) was the only cereal crop, but the American Indians cultivated numerous other products, including tobacco, beans, squashes, pumpkins, and potatoes.

Historically, the most important feature of Neolithic culture was probably the development of institutions. An institution may be defined as a combination of group beliefs and activities organized in a relatively permanent fashion for the purpose of fulfilling some group need. It ordinarily includes a body of customs and traditions, a code of rules and standards, and physical extensions such as buildings, punitive devices, and facilities for communication and indoctrination. Since man is a social being, some of these elements probably existed from earliest times, but institutions in their fully developed form seem to have been an achievement of the Neolithic Age.

The nature of institutions

One of the most ancient of human institutions is the family. Sociologists do not agree upon how it should be defined. Historically, however, the family has always meant a more or less permanent unit composed of parents and their offspring, which serves the purposes of care of the young, division of labor, acquisition and transmission of property, and preservation and transmission of beliefs and customs. The family is not now, and never has been, exclusively biological in character. Like most institutions, it has evolved through a long period of changing conventions which have given it a variety of functions and forms.

Definition of the family

The family during Neolithic times appears to have existed in both polygamous and monogamous forms. The term polygamy is used by sociologists to mean any type of plural marriage—either a plurality of husbands or a plurality of wives. The scientific name for the former is *polyandry*, and for the latter *polygyny*. Polyandry seems always to have been rare. At the present time it is confined to a few Eskimo communities, to the Wahuma tribes of East Africa, and to southern India and Tibet. It appears to develop under conditions of extreme poverty where a number of men must pool their resources in order to purchase or support a wife, or where female infanticide is practiced as a means of controlling population growth. The latter custom soon results in an excess of males. Polygyny arises under a variety of conditions. In some cases it results from a preponderance of females. For example, the Arctic seal-hunter's life is so hazardous that in some villages the number of men may be less than half the number of women. In a few instances polygyny has been resorted to as a means of producing a rapid increase in the

Polygamy

population. Since one man can procreate far more offspring than one woman can bear, such peoples as the ancient Hebrews encouraged the taking of extra wives in order that the group might multiply rapidly and thereby protect itself against absorption or annihilation by hostile neighbors. Still a third factor in the origin of polygyny has been the love of display. Rulers and other rich men have maintained a plurality of wives as a form of conspicuous consumption. King Solomon kept a harem of 700 wives and 300 concubines, not necessarily because of a voracious sexual appetite, but in order to impress other monarchs with his ability to support such a large establishment. He was interested also, of course, in political alliances with as many as possible of the surrounding monarchs, and marrying their daughters was a convenient means of establishing these.

A second institution developed in more complex form by Neolithic man was religion. On account of its infinite variations, it is hard to define, but perhaps the following would be accepted as an accurate definition of the institution in at least its basic character: "Religion is everywhere an expression in one form or another of a sense of dependence on a power outside ourselves, a power which

The nature of primitive religion; rites and ceremonies

Megalithic Monuments at Stonehenge, England. The practice of erecting megaliths, or huge stone pillars and structures, was common in Neolithic cultures. Those at Stonehenge are probably the remains of a temple of sun worship.

we may speak of as a spiritual or moral power."[2] Modern anthropologists emphasize the fact that early religion was not so much a matter of belief as a matter of rites. For the most part, the rites came first; the myths, dogmas, and theologies were later rationalizations. Primitive man was universally dependent upon nature—on the regular succession of the seasons, on the rain falling when it

[2] A. R. Radcliffe-Brown, *Structure and Function in Primitive Society,* p. 157.

should, on the growth of plants and the reproduction of animals. Unless he performed sacrifices and rites these natural phenomena, according to his notion, would not occur. For this reason he developed rain-making ceremonies in which water was sprinkled on ears of corn to imitate the falling of the rain. The ceremonial dances of the American Indians often had a similar import. The members of a whole village or even a whole tribe would attire themselves in animal skins and mimic the habits and activities of some species they depended upon for food. They apparently had a vague feeling that by imitating the life pattern of the species they were helping to guarantee its continuance.

*The element of
fear*

But there was also another element conspicuously present in primitive religion. This was the element of fear. Modern primitive men, at least, live in an almost constant state of alarm and dread. As an old Eskimo medicine man said to the explorer Knud Rasmussen: "We do not believe; we fear." [3] Everything strange and unfamiliar is fraught with danger. The savage fears not only sickness and death but also hunger, drought, storms, the spirits of the dead, and the animals he has killed. Every misfortune, loss, or failure is the harbinger of other misfortunes and failures unless the evil influence that caused them is appeased, paralyzed, or annihilated. To accomplish such ends, charms, incantations, and other devices of magic potency seem to be a vital necessity.

*Ceremonies
to ward
off evil*

It follows that a large part of primitive man's religion consists of ceremonial precautions to ward off evil. For example, no savage will risk swimming across a dangerous river without first endeavoring by prayers or incantations to win its favor. An Eskimo who has killed a polar bear must present it with tools and weapons pleasing to it; if the bear is a female, women's knives and needle cases are given. Bestowal of these gifts is considered necessary to appease the wrath of the bear's soul and keep it from wreaking damage. In West Africa, the hunter who has killed a hippopotamus disembowels it, strips himself naked, crawls inside the carcass, and bathes his entire body with the animal's blood. Throughout the procedure he prays to the spirit of the hippo that it will bear him no ill-will for having killed it, and that it will not incite other hippopotami to attack his canoe in revenge.[4]

*Neolithic man's
prelogical mind*

Between the sort of religion just described and the theological religions of Judaism, Christianity, and Islam there seems only the vaguest connection. Most Neolithic men were and still are in a prelogical stage. Their thinking resembles more closely that of a child than it does the thinking of civilized man. They draw no sharp distinction between animate and inanimate objects or between the natural and the supernatural. They recognize no miracles, for nothing is impossible or absurd. In like manner, there are no

[3] Lucien Lévy-Bruhl, *Primitives and the Supernatural*, p. 22.
[4] Lucien Lévy-Bruhl, *How Natives Think*, p. 238.

accidents, for every happening has its mystic significance. Should a child fall into the fire, someone has bewitched him, and the parents will not rest until they have found the culprit. Most primitive men today have little conception of natural cause. Some tribes reject completely the idea of natural death. Others have no notion of natural birth. They see no definite connection between sexual intercourse and reproduction. The union of male and female is merely to prepare the way for a spirit to enter the woman's body and make her pregnant.

Probably the first intellectual revolution in the history of mankind was the transition from the prelogical basis of primitive religion to the type of religious thinking which rests upon a belief in benevolent gods and a philosophical explanation of the universe. How the transition was accomplished, no one knows. Apparently some tribes developed the idea that supernatural beings in manlike form would be more capable of hearing and answering entreaties than disembodied spirits or ghosts. Since prehistoric man almost universally assumed that the spirit of a human being survived the death of his body, and since medicine men were widely revered, it seems possible that the spirits of some of these may have been transferred to mountain tops or to homes in the sky and worshiped as gods. Perhaps in some other cases the awakening of an ethical sense led to a belief in one or more gods as the upholders of righteousness and justice. Such ideas would doubtless come to the minds of exceptional men almost from the beginning, with the result that in particular areas a belief in a single divinity of goodness might well co-exist with the most primitive fears of ghosts and witches. Whatever their origin, personal deities were venerated by the earliest civilizations, and it seems certain that beliefs concerning them did come into existence during the Neolithic culture stage.

The transition to theological religion

Still another of the great institutions to be developed by Neolithic man was the state. By way of definition, the state may be described as an organized society occupying a definite territory and possessing an authoritative government independent of external control. The essence of the state is sovereignty, or the power to make and administer laws and to preserve social order by punishing men for infractions of those laws. A state must not be confused with a nation. The latter is an ethnic concept, used to designate a people bound together by ties of language, customs, or racial origin or by common memories or a belief in a common destiny. A nation may or may not occupy a definite territory and does not possess the element of sovereignty. It may not even have an independent government, as for example the Poles during the long period when they were under Austrian, German, and Russian rule. At the present time most nations are also states, but this condition has resulted largely from the breaking up of the Russian, Austrian, German, and Turkish empires at the end of World War I.

The state defined

*Absence of the
state in many
primitive so-
cieties*

Except in time of crisis, the state does not exist in a very large proportion of primitive societies—a fact which probably indicates that its genesis was rather late in the Neolithic culture stage. Most savage communities have no permanent system of courts, no police agencies, and no governments with coercive power. Custom takes the place of law, the blood-feud is the mode of administering justice, and there is very little conception of crime against the community. To primitive man, offenses are mostly what we call "torts," or private wrongs between individuals or families, in the punishment of which no public authority takes part. The acceptance of *wergeld*, or blood-money, is a common practice, and even felonies such as murder are regarded merely as offenses against the victim's family. Since the family of the victim has been deprived of a valuable member, the proper satisfaction is a money payment. If this is not offered, the family may retaliate in kind by killing the offender or a member of the offender's family. Practically the only wrongs against society are violations of *taboos*, or religious prohibitions, but the punishment for these is religious, not political.

*A variety of
causes of the
origin of the
state*

The origin of the state was probably the consequence of a variety of factors. We are certainly justified in assuming the development of agriculture to have been one of the most important. In sections like the Nile valley, where a numerous population lived by cultivating intensively a limited area of fertile soil, a high degree of social organization was absolutely essential. Ancient customs would not suffice for the definition of rights and duties in such a society, with its high standard of living, its unequal distribution of wealth, and its wide scope for the clash of personal interests. New measures of social control would become necessary, which could scarcely be achieved in any other way than by setting up a government of sovereign authority and submitting to it; in other words, by establishing a state. The result would not be accomplished in a single day or even in a single year. The initial forms of public control would be few and tentative, but they would be gradually extended, until finally a state, not necessarily despotic, but with full authority, would come into being.

A number of ancient states evidently owed their origin to war activities. That is, they were founded for purposes of conquest, for defense against invasion, or to make possible the expulsion of an invader from the country. The Hebrew monarchy seems to have been a product of the first of these reasons. With the war for the conquest of Canaan none too successful, the Hebrew people besought their leader Samuel to give them a king, that they might be "like all the nations" with a powerful ruler to keep them in order and to lead them to victory in battle. One has only to observe the effects of modern warfare, both offensive and defensive, in strengthening and enlarging the powers of government to see how similar influences might have operated to bring the state into existence in the first place.

Some modern anthropologists attach great importance to leadership as a factor in the origin of the state. They point out that in time of crisis an individual of commanding qualities often steps out from the crowd and takes control. In a shipwreck, for example, one of the men in a lifeboat assumes authority, rationing the water and food, if any, and keeping his companions in order. Among the Bushmen of Australia and among the Eskimos, no political institutions exist at all under ordinary circumstances. But when an emergency arises, someone takes the leadership for the duration of the crisis, and what was originally an informal band of hunters takes on the character of a rudimentary state. Among peoples leading a more settled existence the leader has frequently become a sort of political boss, presiding over a "machine," and dispensing feasts and other favors. Sometimes he is revered as almost divine, as a symbol of the unity and interdependence of the group. It is assumed that the members live through him as the body of an individual lives through its head.

Although evidence can be found to support all of the above hypotheses, they should not be regarded as the exclusive explanations. Religion doubtless contributed to the origin of states in some areas. Medicine men, or shamans, frequently exercise a kind of sovereignty. Though they may command no physical force, their power to impose religious penalties and to strike terror into the hearts of their followers gives them a degree of coercive authority. In all probability some of them made themselves kings. It is conceivable that in other cases the state arose from the natural expansion of group life, with its resulting complexities and conflicts. As the population increased in limited areas, customary law and family administration of justice proved inadequate, and political organization became necessary as a substitute. In the domain of politics as in every other sphere concerned with social origins, no one explanation can be made to accommodate all the facts.

Selected Readings

Boas, Franz, *The Mind of Primitive Man*, New York, 1927
Ceram, C. W., *Gods, Graves and Scholars*, New York, 1952
Childe, V. G., *Man Makes Himself*, London, 1936
Dawson, Christopher, *The Age of the Gods*, New York, 1937
Folsom, J. K., *The Family*, New York, 1934
Gillin, John, *The Ways of Men*, New York, 1948
Herskovits, M. J., *Man and His Works*, New York, 1948
Hooton, E. A., *Up from the Ape*, revised edition, New York, 1947

STONE AGE OR PRELITERATE CULTURES

Lévy-Bruhl, Lucien, *How Natives Think*, London, 1926

———, *Primitives and the Supernatural*, New York, 1935

Linton, Ralph, *The Tree of Culture*, New York, 1955

Lowie, R. H., *Primitive Society*, New York, 1925

MacCurdy, G. G., *Human Origins*, New York, 1924, 2 vols.

Malinowski, Bronislaw, *Crime and Custom in Savage Society*, New York, 1951

Nevins, Allan, *The Gateway to History*, New York, 1938

Osborn, H. F., *Men of the Old Stone Age*, New York, 1915

Peake, Harold, and Fleure, H. J., *Hunters and Artists*, New Haven, 1927

Radcliffe-Brown, A. R., *Structure and Function in Primitive Society*, Glencoe, Ill., 1952

Radin, Paul, *Primitive Man as Philosopher*, New York, 1927

———, *Primitive Religion*, New York, 1937

Renard, Georges, *Life and Work in Prehistoric Times*, New York, 1929

Somervell, D. C., ed., A. J. Toynbee, *A Study of History*, New York, 1947–57, 2 vols.

Tyler, J. M., *The New Stone Age in Northern Europe*, New York, 1921

The Nature and Origin
of Civilizations

1. Cultures and Civilizations

The stages of man's advancement described thus far have been
referred to as *cultures*. This word is commonly used to designate
societies or periods which have not yet attained to a knowledge   *Culture defined*
of writing and whose general level of achievement is comparatively
primitive. But the term has other meanings. It is sometimes applied
to intellectual and artistic accomplishments, to literature, art, music,
philosophy, and science. It is employed by some historians to
designate the whole complex pattern of ideas, achievements, traditions, and characteristics of a nation or empire at a particular time.

The term *civilization* also carries a variety of meanings. The
German philosopher of history Oswald Spengler referred to civilizations as decadent phases of highly developed cultures. When a great   *The meaning*
people or empire was in its prime, he characterized its social and   *of civilization*
intellectual pattern as a culture. When it passed its prime and
became ossified and stagnant, he described it as a "civilization." The
noted British historian Arnold J. Toynbee also sees world history as
a succession of cultural units. But he designates each of the primary
ones, throughout its development, as a "civilization." He distinguishes between civilizations and "primitive societies" largely on a
quantitative basis. The latter are "relatively short-lived, are restricted
to relatively narrow geographical areas, and embrace relatively small
numbers of human beings." [1]

The term *civilization* has still another meaning. Since each culture has peculiar features of its own, and since some cultures are
more highly developed than others, we can speak quite properly

[1] *A Study of History* (D. C. Somervell, ed.), Vol. I, p. 35.   **21**

*Civilizations
as
superior
cultures*

of a civilization as a superior culture. We can say that a culture deserves to be called a civilization when it has reached a stage of advancement in which writing has come to be used to a considerable extent, some progress has been made in the arts and sciences, and political, social, and economic institutions have developed sufficiently to conquer at least some of the problems of order, security, and efficiency in a complex society. This is the sense in which the term will be used throughout the remainder of this book.

2. *Factors Responsible for the Origin and Growth of Civilizations*

*Origin and
growth of
civilizations
variously
explained*

What causes contribute to the rise of civilizations? What factors account for their growth? Why do some civilizations reach much higher levels of development than others? Inquiry into these questions is one of the chief pursuits of social scientists. Some decide that factors of geography are the most important. Others stress economic resources, food supply, contact with older civilizations, and so on. Usually a variety of causes is acknowledged, but one is commonly singled out as deserving special emphasis.

*Geographic
theories:
the climatic
hypothesis*

Probably the most popular of the theories accounting for the rise of superior cultures are those which come under the heading of geography. Prominent among them is the hypothesis of climate. The climatic theory, advocated in days past by such notables as Aristotle and Montesquieu, received its most eloquent exposition in the writings of an American geographer, Ellsworth Huntington. Dr. Huntington acknowledged the importance of other factors, but he insisted that no nation, either ancient or modern, rose to the highest cultural status except under the influence of a climatic stimulus. He described the ideal climate as one in which the mean temperature seldom falls below the mental optimum of 38 degrees or rises above the physical optimum of 64 degrees. But temperature is not alone important. Moisture is also essential, and the humidity should average about 75 per cent. Finally, the weather must not be uniform: cyclonic storms, or ordinary storms resulting in weather changes from day to day, must have sufficient frequency and intensity to clear the atmosphere every once in a while and produce those sudden variations in temperature which seem to be necessary to exhilarate and revitalize man.[2]

*Evidence
in favor of
the climatic
hypothesis*

Much can be said in favor of the climatic hypothesis. Certainly some parts of the earth's surface, under existing atmospheric conditions, could never cradle a superior culture. They are either too hot, too humid, too cold, or too dry. Such is the case of regions beyond the Arctic Circle, the larger desert areas, and the jungles of India, Central America, and Brazil. Evidence is available, more-

22   [2] Ellsworth Huntington, *Civilization and Climate*, third edition, pp. 220–23.

over, to show that some of these places have not always suffered under climate so adverse as that now prevalent. Various inhospitable sections of Asia, Africa, and America contain unmistakable traces of more salubrious days in the past. Here and there are the ruins of towns and cities where now the supply of water seems totally inadequate. Roads traverse deserts which at present are impassable. Bridges span river beds which have had no water in them for years. These and similar phenomena, observed by travelers in desert regions, appear to furnish proof that the climatic factor in history cannot be ignored.

The best-known evidences of the cultural importance of climatic change are those pertaining to the civilization of the Mayas. Mayan civilization flourished in Guatemala, Honduras, and on the peninsula of Yucatan in Mexico from about 400 to 1500 A.D. Numbered among its achievements were the making of paper, the invention of the zero, the perfection of a solar calendar, and the development of a system of writing partly phonetic. Great cities were built; marked progress was made in astronomy; and sculpture and architecture were advanced to high levels. At present most of the civilization is in ruins. No doubt many factors conspired to produce its untimely end, including deadly wars between tribes, but climatic change was also probably involved. The remains of most of the great cities are now surrounded by jungles, where malaria is prevalent and agriculture difficult. That the Mayan civilization or any other could have grown to maturity under conditions like these is hard to believe. It seems probable, therefore, that the climate of the Mayan region some five or six centuries ago was different from what it is now.

The Mayan civilization

But the hypothesis is open to criticism on several counts. Evidences of climatic change on a significant scale are still very far from conclusive. There is nothing to indicate, for example, that the climate of Greece and Rome in ancient times was more invigorating than it is at present. Moisture conditions in ancient Greece were undoubtedly more favorable, but there is no proof of alterations in temperature. Nor can the decline of civilization in Egypt and Mesopotamia be accounted for by radical changes in atmospheric conditions. Most of the evidence seems to show that economic and social factors, such as the exhaustion of resources and the growth of slavery and habits of indolence, had far greater effects.

Criticism of the climatic hypothesis

Related to the climatic hypothesis is the soil-exhaustion theory. A group of modern conservationists has hit upon this theory as the sole explanation of the decay and collapse of the great empires of the past and as a universal threat to the nations of the present and future. At best it is only a partial hypothesis, since it offers no theory of the birth or growth of civilizations. But its proponents seem to think that almost any environment not ruined by man is capable of nourishing a superior culture. The great deserts and barren areas of the earth, they maintain, are not natural but artificial, created

The soil-exhaustion theory

23

by man through bad grazing and farming practices. Conservationists discover innumerable evidences of waste and neglect that have wrought havoc in such areas as Mesopotamia, Palestine, Greece, Italy, China, and Mexico. The majestic civilizations that once flourished in these countries were ultimately doomed by the simple fact that their soil would no longer provide sufficient food for the population. As a consequence, the more intelligent citizens migrated elsewhere and left their inferiors to sink slowly into stagnation and apathy. But the fate that overtook the latter was not of their making alone. The whole nation had been guilty of plundering the forests, mining the soil, and pasturing flocks on the land until the grass was eaten down to the very roots. Among the tragic results were floods alternating with droughts, since there were no longer any forests to regulate the run-off of rain or snow. At the same time, much of the top soil on the close-cropped or excessively cultivated hillsides was blown away or washed into the rivers to be carried eventually down to the sea. The damage done was irreparable, since about 300 years are required to produce a single inch of top soil.

*The topograph-
ical theory*

Yet another of the geographic theories is the contention that the topography of the earth's surface has been the main conditioning element in the rise of civilizations. A famous champion of this theory was Karl Ritter, a German who lived in the first half of the nineteenth century. Ritter maintained that the form and shape of continents are of great importance in providing advantages for cultural growth. Continents possessing an irregular coast line and diversified geographic conditions furnish the only favorable environments for the progress of nations. The more compact and homogeneous a continent is, the more backward will be its inhabitants. Over the whole territory their culture will be uniform, and the absence of good harbors will limit contact with the world outside. The result will be stagnation. By contrast, peoples living on a continent such as Europe, with its sharply broken coast line and its varied geographic features, enjoy notable advantages. Their land is accessible by water to its very heart. Numerous bays and harbors and islands off the coast render seafaring easy and break the isolation that would be otherwise inevitable. As a consequence, it is not strange that Europe has been able to develop "the highest of all civilizations." [3]

Even more famous as an exponent of the topographical theory was the English historian Henry Thomas Buckle (1821–1862). Buckle divided the principal environments of man into two classes: (1) those that stimulate the imagination, and (2) those that sharpen the understanding. To illustrate the former he submitted the example

[3] Quoted by Franklin Thomas, "Some Representative Contributions of Anthropogeography to Modern Political Theory," Merriam, Barnes, and others, *A History of Political Theories, Recent Times*, p. 464.

of India, where the works of nature are of "startling magnitude," overawing man and impressing him with a sense of his own insignificance. The natives therefore torture themselves, invent cruel and terrifying gods, and practice a religion of hideous orgies. They are pessimists and fatalists, denying all value to life and repudiating the ability of man to understand and control his world. As an example of the second class of environments, Buckle referred to Greece, where the face of nature is more ordinary and "less threatening to man." Such an environment, he argued, promotes the elevation of man, generates an attitude of optimism, and stimulates a feeling of confidence in the powers of the human mind. He considered it no miracle, therefore, that Greece should have been able to produce one of the world's most distinguished cultures and some of the greatest critical thinkers of all time.[4]

The topographical theory seems to have comparatively little to confirm it. No geologist would agree that coastal indentations and the altitude of mountain ranges have altered much within the range of historic time. Greece has no fewer harbors now than in the age of Pericles, nor has Mount Olympus risen in recent years to any proportions of "startling magnitude." Yet the modern Greeks do not match their ancestors in intellectual accomplishment. If the influence of topography was at one time conducive to rational thinking and to the development of confidence and joy in achievement, why should that influence have ceased to operate? The theory does not explain either how a country like Switzerland could become one of the leading centers of enlightenment of the present day. On the other hand, there is no gainsaying the fact that a long and irregular coast line is an asset in the development of trade, and therefore an important advantage in the diffusion and reception of knowledge.

Criticism of the topographical theory

According to some philosophers of history, most of the great historic cultures were founded by nomads. The foremost exponent of this theory was a German, Franz Oppenheimer. He and his followers contended that nomads were the original conquerors of primitive cultures and the founders of the state and of complex society. Exploitation of the labor of the vanquished and confiscation of their wealth, he asserted, enabled the conquerors to live in ease and luxury. They established themselves as a nobility and bought or commandeered for their own entertainment whatever talent the country afforded. In time they came to encourage actively the progress of learning and the arts as symbols of their life of leisure and their privileged position. They alone had time to enjoy such things, and, besides, patronage of artists and men of letters served as a convenient form of luxurious display.

The nomad theory

Oppenheimer maintained that the diet of the herdsman, consisting

[4] H. T. Buckle, *The History of Civilization in England,* second edition, pp. 93–106.

as it does of meat and milk, is highly nourishing. The nomad, consequently, has boundless energy. He infuses new life into stagnant peoples wherever he goes. Brutal and domineering though he may be, he nevertheless builds the organization, imposes the discipline, and creates the inequalities of rank and class which seem to be necessary as foundations for cultural growth. Moreover, the customs and diet of pastoral folk are conducive to rapid increases of population. The form of marriage is commonly polygamous, and a plentiful supply of the milk of animals "shortens the period of nursing for the mothers, and consequently permits a greater number of children to be born and to grow into maturity." [5] The result is that nomads periodically burst their territorial confines and invade and conquer the lands of more settled peoples.

*Evidence
to confirm the
nomad theory*

Evidence of a sort can be discovered in abundance to corroborate this theory. Not a few of the great cultures of the past appear to have been founded by conquering nomads. Three great reservoirs of humanity seem time after time to have let loose inundations of peoples that poured into the more fertile areas of the Old World. From the grasslands north of the Arabian Desert came the Babylonians, Assyrians, and Chaldeans successively to conquer the Tigris-Euphrates valley. From the steppes of central Asia issued the Medes, Persians, and Indians, and probably most of the ancestors of the nations of Europe. The Arabian Desert itself was the starting point of the Hebrew migrations into the land of Canaan and of the conquests of the Moslems. All of these focal areas are unsuited to agriculture; to this day they are inhabited by nomads. It follows that the peoples mentioned must originally have lived under the pastoral economy, even though some of them had abandoned their flocks and herds at the time they made their principal conquests.

The nomad theory criticized

But the nomad theory has its shortcomings as an explanation of the rise of superior cultures. Certainly it cannot be used to account for the origin of all of them. The Egyptian civilization, for example, appears to have been established by people who derived their livelihood primarily from agriculture. The Phoenicians, who came from Babylonia about 2000 B.C. to found a maritime culture in the Lebanon valley, must have been long accustomed to the peaceful arts of tilling the soil before their migration. Moreover, there is reason to believe that most of the great inventions and discoveries which provided the original basis of civilization were made by peaceful, agricultural peoples. Such folk seem to have originated irrigation, mathematics, and astronomy, and systems of writing. The American economist and philosopher Thorstein Veblen declared that nomadic peoples made no significant contributions whatever, with the exceptions of poetry and religious creeds and cults.[6] But the fact remains that conquering nomads did infuse new energy into the

[5] F. Oppenheimer, *The State*, pp. 42–43.
[6] Thorstein Veblen, *The Instinct of Workmanship*, p. 167.

cultures of settled areas and probably goaded the inhabitants into activity which ultimately resulted in achievements. Moreover, the circumstances surrounding the original expansion of such peoples as the Babylonians, the Assyrians, the Hebrews, and the Moslems leave little doubt that the conditions of nomadic existence were partly responsible for the fact that they founded civilizations.

The most recent hypothesis of the origin of civilizations is the adversity theory of the distinguished British historian, Arnold J. Toynbee. According to this theory, conditions of hardship or adversity are the real causes which have brought into existence superior cultures. Such conditions constitute a challenge which not only stimulates men to try to overcome it but generates additional energy for new achievements. The challenge may take the form of a desert, a jungle area, rugged topography, or a grudging soil. The Hebrews and Arabs were challenged by the first, the Indians of the Andean Highland by the last. The challenge may also take the form of defeat in war or even enslavement. Thus the Carthaginians, as a result of defeat in the First Punic War, were stimulated to conquer a new empire in Spain; while centuries later, Oriental captives enslaved by the Romans strengthened and propagated their religious heritage until Rome herself succumbed to it. In general it is true that the greater the challenge, the greater the achievement; nevertheless, there are limits. The challenge must not be too severe, else it will deal a crushing blow to all who attempt to meet it. Such environments as Greenland, Labrador, and Tierra del Fuego have climate and soil conditions so absolutely bleak and inhospitable that they could never give birth to civilizations.

The adversity theory of Arnold J. Toynbee

The majority of historians believe that the genesis of civilizations cannot be explained except on the basis of a complex of causes. Not any one factor, but a combination of several must be taken into account. Among these factors they place uppermost the geographic and economic elements of favorable climate, fertile soil, access to good harbors, and an abundance of mineral resources. They also accord a high place to opportunities for interchange of ideas with other peoples of a comparable level of advancement. Civilizations do not develop in isolated corners of the world. The backwardness of Australia, New Zealand, and South Africa before the coming of Europeans was probably due to this cause. These sections were favorably situated so far as climate and resources were concerned, but they were too remote to be affected by the stimulus of progress elsewhere. It is common also for historians to emphasize the concentration of population in limited areas and the invention of new skills and processes, such as pictographic writing and the smelting of metals, as factors in the origin of high cultures. Historians also recognize the importance of religion as an influence in the transition from primitive to civilized life. The earliest forms of social regulation were probably for religious purposes. Religion provided

A number of factors must be taken into account in explaining the origin of civilizations

the oldest law codes and systems of morality and perhaps also the
foundations of philosophy and science. Priests constituted the most
ancient class of educated men, and there is reason to believe that
it was they who invented the first systems of writing.

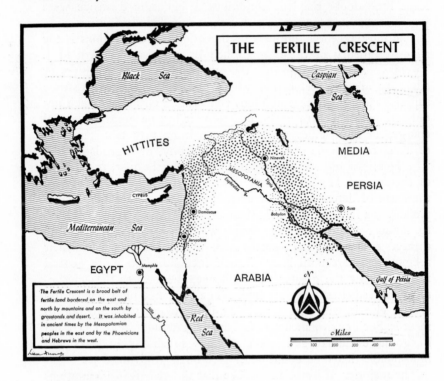

THE FERTILE CRESCENT

The Fertile Crescent is a broad belt of
fertile land bordered on the east and
north by mountains and on the south by
grasslands and desert. It was inhabited
in ancient times by the Mesopotamian
peoples in the east and by the Phoenicians
and Hebrews in the west.

3. Why the Earliest Civilizations Began Where They Did

The Nile and
the Tigris-Eu-
phrates valleys
probably the
centers of the
oldest civiliza-
tions

Which of the great civilizations of antiquity was the oldest is
still a sharply debated question. The judgment of many scholars
inclines toward the Egyptian, though a respectable body of authority supports the claims of the Tigris-Euphrates valley. Still
other experts prefer Elam, a region lying east of the Tigris-Euphrates
valley and bordering on the Persian Gulf. While the opinion of
no competent scholar is to be brushed lightly aside, there is nevertheless stronger warrant for believing that the Nile and Tigris-
Euphrates valleys were the homes of the oldest historic cultures.
These two areas were geographically the most favored sections
in the general region of the so-called Fertile Crescent.[7] Here larger
numbers of artifacts of undoubted antiquity have been found than

[7] The Fertile Crescent is that wide belt of productive land which extends
northwestward from the Persian Gulf and then down the Mediterranean coast
almost to Egypt. It forms a semicircle around the northern part of the Arabian
desert.

in any other sections of the Near Orient. Furthermore, progress in the arts and sciences had reached unparalleled heights in both of these areas as early as 3000 B.C., when most of the rest of the world was steeped in ignorance. If the foundations of this progress were really laid elsewhere, it seems strange that they should have disappeared, although of course there is no telling what the spade of the archaeologist may uncover in the future. The possibility that the world's earliest civilizations may have originated in India or China must be excluded. No evidence exists of anything other than primitive culture in India before 3250 B.C., and the peak of cultural development was not reached until much later. No true civilization flourished in China before 1500 B.C.

Of the several causes responsible for the earliest rise of civilizations in the Nile and Tigris-Euphrates valleys, geographic factors would seem to have been the most important. Both regions had the notable advantage of a limited area of exceedingly fertile soil. Although it extended for a distance of 750 miles, the valley of the Nile was not more than ten miles wide in some places, and its maximum width was thirty-one miles. The total area was less than 10,000 square miles, or roughly the equivalent of the State of Maryland. Through countless centuries the river had carved a vast canyon or trench, bounded on either side by cliffs ranging in height from a few hundred to a thousand feet. The floor of the canyon was covered with a rich alluvial deposit, which in places reached a depth in excess of thirty feet. The soil was of such amazing productivity that as many as three crops per year could be raised on the same land. This broad and fertile canyon constituted the cultivable area of ancient Egypt. Here several million people were concentrated. In Roman times the population of the valley approximated seven million, and probably it was not much smaller in the days of the Pharaohs. Beyond the cliffs there was nothing but desert—the Libyan desert on the west and the Arabian on the east. In the ancient Egyptian language "highlander" was synonymous with foreigner. To "go up" was the equivalent of going abroad, while to "descend" was the popular expression for returning home from the alien world.[8]

A limited area of fertile soil in the Nile valley

In the Tigris-Euphrates valley similar conditions prevailed. As in Egypt, the rivers provided excellent facilities for inland transportation and were alive with fish and waterfowl for a plentiful supply of protein food. The distance between the Tigris and Euphrates rivers at one point was less than twenty miles, while nowhere in the lower valley did it exceed forty-five miles. Since the surrounding country was desert, the people were kept from scattering over too great an expanse of territory. The result, as in Egypt, was the welding of the inhabitants into a compact society, under conditions that facilitated a ready interchange of ideas and discoveries. As the

A similar condition in Mesopotamia

[8] J. H. Breasted, *History of Egypt*, p. 11,

population increased, the need for agencies of social control became ever more urgent. Numbered among such agencies were government, schools, legal and moral codes, and institutions for the production and distribution of wealth. At the same time conditions of living became more complex and artificial and necessitated the keeping of records of things accomplished and the perfection of new techniques. Among the consequences were the invention of writing, the practice of smelting metals, the performance of mathematical operations, and the development of astronomy and the rudiments of physics. With these achievements the first great ordeal of civilization was passed.

Climatic influences also played their part in both regions. The atmosphere of Egypt is dry and invigorating. Even the hottest days produce none of the oppressive discomfort which is often experienced during the summer seasons in more northern countries. The mean temperature in winter varies from 56 degrees in the Delta to 66 degrees in the valley above. The summer mean is 83 degrees and an occasional maximum of 122 is reached, but the nights are always cool and the humidity is extremely low. Except in the Delta, rainfall occurs in negligible quantities, but the deficiency of moisture is counteracted by the annual inundations of the Nile from July to October. Also very significant from the historical standpoint is the total absence of malaria in Upper Egypt, while even in the coastal region it is practically unknown. The direction of the prevailing winds is likewise a favorable factor of more than trivial importance. For more than three-quarters of the year the wind comes from the north, blowing in opposition to the force of the Nile current. The effect of this is to simplify immensely the problem of transportation. Upstream traffic, with the propulsion of the wind to counteract the force of the river, presents no greater difficulty than downstream traffic. This factor in ancient times must have been of enormous advantage in promoting communication among a numerous people, some of whom were separated by hundreds of miles.

Climatic advantages in Egypt

Climatic conditions in Mesopotamia do not seem to have been quite so favorable as in Egypt. The summer heat is more relentless; the humidity is somewhat higher; and tropical diseases take their toll. Nevertheless, the torrid winds from the Indian Ocean, while enervating to human beings, blow over the valley at just the right season to bring the fruit of the date palm to a full ripeness. More than anything else the excellent yield of dates, the dietary staple of the Orient, encouraged the settlement of large numbers of people in the valley of the two rivers. Finally, the melting of the snows in the mountains of the north produced an annual flooding of the Babylonian plain similar to that in Egypt. The effect was to enrich the soil with moisture and to cover it over with a layer of mud of unusual fertility.

Climatic influences in Mesopotamia

Most significant of all of the geographic influences, however, was the fact that the scanty rainfall in both regions provided a spur to initiative and inventive skill. In spite of the yearly floods of the rivers there was insufficient moisture left in the soil to produce abundant harvests. A few weeks after the waters had receded, the earth was baked to a stony hardness. Irrigation was accordingly necessary if full advantage was to be taken of the richness of the soil. As a result, in both Egypt and Mesopotamia elaborate systems of dams and irrigation canals were constructed as long ago as five thousand years. The mathematical skill, engineering ability, and social co-operation necessary for the development of these projects were available for other uses and so fostered the achievement of civilization.

The question remains to be answered, which of the two civilizations, the Egyptian or the Mesopotamian, was the older? This question thus far has defied a satisfactory answer. It is possible to present various facts which seem to suggest the priority of Egypt. Most important of all, the dwellers in the Nile valley enjoyed geographic advantages which were denied to the natives of Mesopotamia: a less enervating atmosphere, a climate comparatively free from disease, and the availability of metals and good building stone. Egypt, moreover, was well protected from invasion and from intermixture with more backward peoples. On the east and west were trackless deserts, on the north was a harborless coast line, and on the south the rocky barriers of a series of cataracts prevented the inroads of African savages. Only at the two northern corners could the valley be penetrated easily. By contrast, Mesopotamia was relatively unprotected. Not one of its boundaries afforded any appreciable degree of security. It stood as a constant temptation to the hungry hordes of nomads in the surrounding mountains and deserts. As a consequence, the progress of cultural evolution was subject to frequent interruptions by the invasions of pillaging tribes.

Until recently most historians appeared to take it for granted that the Egyptian civilization was the older. They based their assumption upon the conclusions of two of the world's most renowned Egyptologists, James H. Breasted and Alexandre Moret. Between the two world wars of the twentieth century, however, facts were unearthed which seemed to prove a substantial Mesopotamian influence in the Nile valley as early as 3500 B.C. This influence was exemplified by the use of cylinder seals, methods of building construction, art motifs, and elements of a system of writing of undoubted Mesopotamian origin. That such achievements could have radiated into Egypt from the Tigris-Euphrates valley at so early a date indicated beyond doubt that the Mesopotamian civilization was one of vast antiquity. It did not necessarily prove, though, that it was older than the Egyptian. For the achievements mentioned were not taken over and copied slavishly. Instead, the Egyptians modified them radically to suit their own culture pattern. On the basis of this evidence, it would seem that the only conclusion which can be safely drawn is that both civilizations were very old, and that for the most part they developed concurrently.

SELECTED READINGS

Baikie, James, *A History of Egypt*, London, 1929, Vol. I

Boas, Franz, *The Mind of Primitive Man*, New York, 1927

Breasted, James H., *The Dawn of Conscience*, New York, 1934

————, *History of Egypt*, New York, 1912

Buckle, Henry T., *History of Civilization in England*, second edition, New York, 1863

Burton, H. E., *The Discovery of the Ancient World*, New Haven, 1932

Butterfield, Herbert, *History and Human Relations*, New York, 1952

Cambridge Ancient History, New York, 1923, Vol. I

Childe, V. G., *The Most Ancient East*, New York, 1929

Clough, Shepard B., *The Rise and Fall of Civilization: An Inquiry into the Relationship Between Economic Development and Civilization*, New York, 1951

Hall, H. R., *Ancient History of the Near East*, New York, 1913

Huntington, Ellsworth, *Civilization and Climate*, third edition, New Haven, 1924

Magoffin, R. V. D., and Davis, E. C., *The Romance of Archaeology*, New York, 1929

Muller, H. J., *The Uses of the Past*, New York, 1952

Myres, J. L., *The Dawn of History*, New York, 1911

Nevins, Allan, *The Gateway to History*, New York, 1938

Smith, G. E., *The Ancient Egyptians and the Origin of Civilization*, revised edition, New York, 1923

Spengler, Oswald, *The Decline of the West*, one-volume edition, New York, 1934

Somervell, D. C., ed., A. J. Toynbee, *A Study of History*, New York, 1947–57, 2 vols.

Trever, A. A., *History of Ancient Civilization*, New York, 1936, Vol. I

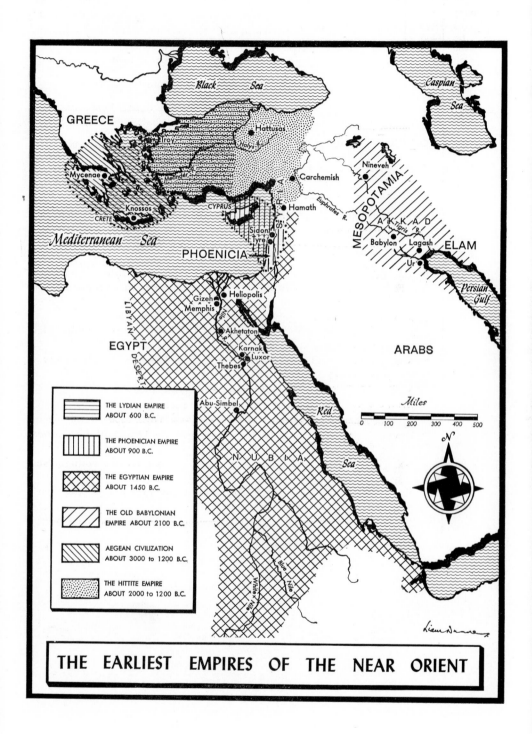

THE EARLIEST EMPIRES OF THE NEAR ORIENT

	Political	Cultural
4000– **B.C.**	Pre-dynastic period in Egypt, *ca.* 4000–3200	Solar calendar in Egypt, *ca.* 4000
	Sumerian supremacy in Mesopotamia, *ca.* 4000–2000	Egyptian hieroglyphic writing, *ca.* 3500
		Development of irrigation, mathematics, rudimentary astronomy in Egypt and Mesopotamia, *ca.* 3500–2500
	Old Kingdom in Egypt, *ca.* 3200–2300	Cuneiform writing, *ca.* 3200 B.C.
3000– **B.C.**	Aegean civilization, *ca.* 3000–1000	Invention of principle of alphabet in Egypt, *ca.* 3000 Construction of great pyramids in Egypt, *ca.* 2700 Philosophy in Egypt, *ca.* 2500
	Middle Kingdom in Egypt, 2100–1788	
2000– **B.C.**	Hittite empire, 2000–1200 Old Babylonian kingdom, 1900–1600 Hyksos conquer Egypt, 1750–1580 Kassites conquer Babylonians, *ca.* 1600	Code of Dungi, *ca.* 2000 Code of Hammurabi, *ca.* 1790
1500– **B.C.**	The Empire in Egypt, 1580–1090	Egyptian temple architecture, 1580–1090 Development of alphabet by Phoenicians, *ca.* 1500
	Hebrew conquest of Canaan, *ca.* 1300–900	Realistic sculpture of Assyrians, 1300–600
1000– **B.C.**	United Hebrew Monarchy, 1025–935 Secession of Ten Tribes of Israel, 935 Kingdom of Israel, 935–722 Kingdom of Judah, 935–586	
	Assyrian empire, 722–612 Assyrian conquest of Egypt, 670	Division of day into hours and minutes, *ca.* 600
	Chaldean empire, 612–539 Babylonian captivity, 586–539 Persian empire, 559–330 Persian conquest of Egypt, 525	Calculation of length of year, *ca.* 600 Deuteronomic Code, *ca.* 600
500– **B.C.**	Persian Empire under Darius, 521–486	Book of Job, *ca.* 500

NEAR ORIENT *Dates are B.C. unless given as A.D.*

Economic	Religious
	Creation and Flood epics in Mesopotamia, *ca.* 4000
Development of serfdom in Mesopotamia and in Egypt, *ca.* 3500	Egyptian sun worship, *ca.* 3500
	Ethical religion in Egypt, *ca.* 3000
	Egyptian belief in personal immortality, *ca.* 2500
Large-scale industry in Egypt and Crete, *ca.* 2000	
	Demon worship and witchcraft in Babylonia, *ca.* 1900
Slavery in Egypt, *ca.* 1580	
Introduction of use of iron by Hittites, *ca.* 1500	
	Religious revolution of Ikhnaton, 1375
World trade of Phoenicians, *ca.* 1000–500	Hebrew worship of Yahweh, *ca.* 1000
	Ten Commandments, *ca.* 700
Slavery in Assyria, *ca.* 750	Prophetic Revolution, 700–500
	Hebrew doctrine of universal monotheism, *ca.* 600
Invention of coinage by Lydians, *ca.* 600	Astral religion of Chaldeans, 600–500
World trade of Chaldeans, 600–500	Divination and astrology, 600–500
	Zoroastrianism, *ca.* 600–300
Royal Road of Persians, *ca.* 500	Babylonian Captivity of Jews, 586–539
	Mithraism, *ca.* 300 B.C.–275 A.D.
	Gnosticism, *ca.* 100 B.C.–100 A.D.
	Rise of Christianity, *ca.* 25 A.D.

The Egyptian Civilization

The rise of civilization in Egypt

The neolithic culture stage came to an end in some parts of the world soon after 5000 B.C. It seems to have disappeared first of all in the Nile valley, but the area watered by the Tigris and Euphrates rivers was not far behind. Progress toward a higher cultural level appears to have been especially rapid in Egypt; not only that, but the achievements of the Egyptians laid the foundation for a great deal of the work of other peoples. It is therefore appropriate that we begin our study of the historic cultures with the rise of civilization on the banks of the Nile.

1. The Pre-Dynastic Period

Meaning of the pre-dynastic period

Since there was no enduring unified state in the valley of the Nile until about 3200 B.C., the centuries from 5000 to 3200 are referred to as the pre-dynastic period.[1] In the early part of this period the country seems to have consisted of a number of "nomes," or city-states each of them independent, although evidently co-operating with others for economic ends. Shortly after the beginning of the fourth millennium a fusion of states took place to form two large kingdoms, one in the north and one in the south. How the consolidations were effected no one knows, but possibly they were accomplished through voluntary agreement or peaceful acquiescence in the rule of some capable prince. There is little evidence of military conquest. These kingdoms endured until the end of the pre-dynastic period, although they seem to have been united for a brief interval soon after their establishment.

The racial complexion of pre-dynastic Egypt was essentially the

[1] Some authorities give the year 3400 as the approximate date for the beginning of the First Dynasty. Although recent research seems to favor about 3200, it should be remembered that all dates prior to 2000 are largely a matter of conjecture.

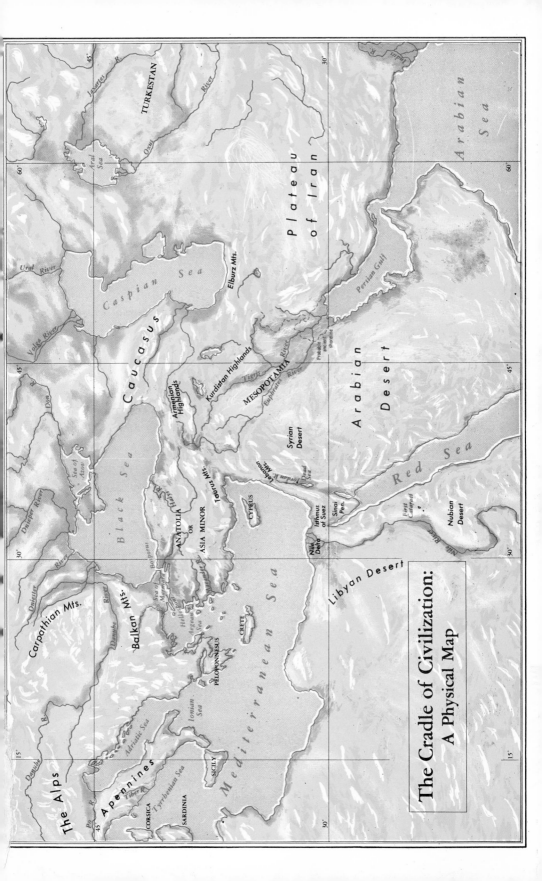

The Cradle of Civilization:
A Physical Map

Egyptian Pottery Jar, with Painted Decoration, *ca.* 3600 B.C. It was filled with food or water and placed in the tomb to provide for the needs of the body in the afterlife.

An Egyptian Official and His Son. Painted limestone, *ca.* 2500 B.C.

Painted limestone figures, *c.* 1300 B.C.

Tomb model of an Egyptian fishing boat, *ca.* 2000 B.C.

Wall painting of an Egyptian house, *ca.* 1400 B.C.

Farm Hand Plowing. Egyptian tomb figures, *ca.* 1900 B.C.

Gold and Inlay Pendant of Princess Sit Hat-Hor Yunet. Egyptian, Twelfth Dynasty.

same as in later epochs. The inhabitants belonged to the Mediterranean branch of the Caucasian race; but they were not a pure strain, and there is nothing to indicate that racial factors as such were of importance in the development of their culture. They were a short, dark, long-headed people, with straight, black hair, deep-set eyes, and slightly aquiline noses. Some of them showed traces of Negroid and Libyan intermixture and possibly of the blood of Semites and other western Asiatic peoples. Their language contained evidences of Semitic elements, which would likewise indicate close relations with some of the natives of Asia.

The pre-dynastic period was by no means insignificant in the cultural history of Egypt. Outstanding progress was made in the arts and crafts and even in some of the sciences. Tools, weapons, and ornaments were expertly fashioned from flint, copper, and gold. New processes of finishing, glazing, and decorating pottery were discovered, with the result that the Egyptians of this period were able to make vessels of as high utility and artistic excellence as any produced by their later descendants. Other important achievements included the development of an efficient system of irrigation, the reclamation of swamp lands, and the weaving of a very superior quality of linen cloth.

But these were not all of their accomplishments. There is evidence that the pre-dynastic Egyptians evolved a system of laws based upon custom, which were held in such high repute that they were later considered binding even upon the Pharaoh himself. A system of writing appears also to have come into use. Although no actual specimen of such writing has ever been found, the examples that have survived from the First Dynasty partake of so complex a nature that they must have originated much earlier. Finally, the Egyptians of this period invented the first solar calendar in the history of man. It seems to have been based upon the annual reappearance of Sirius, the "Dog Star," and it provided for twelve months of thirty days each, with five feast days added at the end of the year. According to the computations of modern Egyptologists, this calendar was put into effect about the year 4200 B.C. The existence of a reasonably accurate calendar at this time argues that a considerable development of mathematics, and possibly the other sciences, had already been attained.

2. Political History under the Pharaohs

About 3200 B.C. the kingdoms of Northern and Southern Egypt were combined into a single political unit, apparently for the second time, although the earlier union was of very brief duration. The traditional founder of the new state was Menes, who therefore became known as the founder of the First Dynasty. Five other dynasties followed in regular order until 2300 B.C. During the first two dynasties the capital was maintained at Thinis in Upper Egypt. The Third Dynasty transferred the seat of government to Memphis on the southern edge of the Delta, in order to secure the advantage of a more central location of administrative functions. Here it remained for approximately five centuries. The period from about 2800 to 2300 B.C. is accordingly called the Memphite period, while the entire age of the first six dynasties is known as the period of the Old Kingdom.

The government of the Old Kingdom

The government of the Old Kingdom did not actually approach the degree of personal absolutism that is commonly believed to have existed. It was nearer a theocracy than an autocracy. The absolutism of the king was exercised not in his own behalf but as the vicar of the god. It was the god as the personification of justice and social order who actually ruled, according to the prevailing conception; the monarch was his agent. It is true, of course, that the king was himself considered divine, the son of the sun god Re. He was held in such high respect that he could not be mentioned by name, but had to be referred to as "Pharaoh," from the Egyptian "per-o" meaning "great house" or "royal house." He was forbidden to marry anyone outside of his immediate family, lest the divine blood be contaminated by an inferior strain. It is to be noted, however, that in all his official actions his authority was limited by the ancient law, which was believed to embody the divine will. He was not above the law, but subject to it. To compare him, therefore, with the divine-right monarchs of more modern times is completely to misunderstand his function.

Union of church and state

No separation of church and state existed in the Old Kingdom. The Pharaoh's chief subordinates were the priests, and he was himself the chief priest. But he had other agents also: a vizier or prime minister, a royal treasurer, a chief architect, a superintendent of public works, a chief justice, and forty-two nomarchs. The last were the governors of the nomes or local districts into which the country was divided. Originally they were appointed by the Pharaoh and were supposed to execute his will, but gradually they made their positions hereditary and usurped for themselves more and more prerogatives of sovereignty. Since the nomes were survivals of the old city-states, sectional feeling lingered and encouraged the local governors to defy the central authority.

Responsibilities of the Pharaoh

The position of Pharaoh was hereditary, but the privilege of succession to the office involved responsibilities. Usually the crown prince served an apprenticeship under his father as superintendent of public works or vizier. He thus came to the throne as an enlightened and educated statesman, familiar with the needs of the country and schooled in the great public enterprises of mining, construction of public works, and irrigation. It was well that he was thus prepared, for as king he was obliged by custom to devote a great deal of his time to inspection and management of the various projects designed to promote the national interest. The divinity that doth hedge a king did not exempt the Pharaoh from arduous service for the public welfare.

The courts and judicial procedure

What has been said already about the importance of Egyptian law suggests that judicial procedure of fairly high quality must have been followed. Such was the case. Although the Old Kingdom had no well-defined class of professional judges, the administrative officials who served at times in a judicial capacity were learned in the law and boasted of their even-handed justice in deciding cases. Altogether six courts, to which different administrative officials were assigned from time to time as judges, composed the judicial branch of the government. Over them all was the chief justice, who sometimes held the position of vizier as well. Appeals could also be taken to the Pharaoh himself under certain circumstances. Apparently no class of cases was excluded from the regular jurisdiction of the courts. Records show that even cases of treason in the king's household were tried with the same scrupulous regard for legal procedure that was exhibited in the trials of petty offenders. The Pharaohs of the Old Kingdom had not yet learned the infamous distinction between political "crimes" and ordinary crimes which has been drawn by the rulers of some modern states.

The non-militaristic character of the Old Kingdom

The government of the Old Kingdom was founded upon a policy of peace and non-aggression. In this respect it was almost unique among ancient states. The Pharaoh had no standing army, nor was there anything that could be called a national militia. Each nome had its local militia, but it was commanded by the civil officials, and when called into active service it generally devoted its energies to labor on the public works. In case of a threat of invasion the various local units were assembled at the call of the Pharaoh and placed under the command of one of his civil subordinates. At no other time did the head of the government have a military force at his disposal. The Egyptians of the Old Kingdom were content for the most part to work out their own destinies and to let other nations alone. The reasons for this attitude are to be found in the protected position of their country, in their possession of land of inexhaustible fertility, and in the fact that their state was a product of co-operative need instead of being grounded in exploitation.

End of the Old Kingdom

After a solid millennium of peace and relative prosperity the Old Kingdom came to an end about 2300 B.C. Several causes appear to have been responsible: the usurpation of power by the nomarchs; the persistence of particularism, or "states' rights" sentiment; the growth of individualism; and the financial burdens imposed upon the people by Pharaohs with grandiose schemes for national development. The period which followed is called the Feudal Age. Save for intervals of order and progress it was marked by anarchy, aggrandizement of the power of the nobles, social revolution of the masses, and invasion by Negroid and Asiatic tribes. It did not end until the rise of the Eleventh Dynasty about 2100—an event which ushered in the next great stage in Egyptian history, which is known as the Middle Kingdom.

The Middle Kingdom (2100–1788 B.C.)

The government of the Middle Kingdom was notably weaker than that of the Old Kingdom. Dynasties of Pharaohs continued a nominal rule, but extensive authority gravitated into the hands of the nomarchs and nobles of lesser rank. The glory of these men was to govern as benevolent despots, performing in their local bailiwicks the functions rightfully belonging to the head of the state. In time they too were assailed by the masses, with the result that after 2000 B.C. the Pharaohs of the Twelfth Dynasty were able to regain a measure of their former power. The people themselves were rewarded by appointments to government positions and by grants of land and vested rights in particular occupations. The whole population, regardless of birth or rank, appears to have been accorded privileges hitherto reserved for the few. For this reason the government of the Twelfth Dynasty is sometimes referred to as the first democratic kingdom in history. The period of its rule was a golden age of social justice and intellectual achievement, although the forms of theocracy still survived.

The invasion of the Hyksos

With the end of the Twelfth Dynasty, Egypt entered another era of internal chaos and foreign invasion which lasted for more than two centuries, or from 1788 to 1580 B.C. The contemporary records are scanty, but they seem to show that the internal disorder was the result of a counter-revolt of the nobles. The Pharaohs were again reduced to impotence, and much of the social progress of the preceding age was destroyed. About 1750 the land was invaded by the Hyksos or "Shepherd Kings," a people of Semitic language from western Asia. They extended a nominal rule over the whole country, although their effective sovereignty was probably confined to the Delta. Their military prowess is commonly ascribed to the fact that they possessed horses and war chariots, but their victory was certainly made easier by the dissension among the Egyptians themselves. Their rule had profound effects upon Egyptian history. Not only did they familiarize the Egyptians with new methods of warfare; but by providing them with a common grievance in the face of foreign tyranny they also enabled them to forget their differences and unite in a common cause. Thus the path was cleared for the restoration of strong government over the whole country.

Expulsion of the Hyksos and founding of the Empire

Near the end of the seventeenth century the rulers of Upper Egypt launched a revolt against the Hyksos, a movement which was eventually joined by most of the natives of the valley. By 1580 all of the conquerors who had not been killed or enslaved had been driven from the country. The hero of this victory, Ahmose I, founder of the Eighteenth Dynasty, now made himself despot of Egypt. The regime he established was much more highly consolidated than any that had hitherto existed. In the great resurgence

of nationalism which had accompanied the struggle against the
Hyksos, local patriotism was annihilated and with it the power of
the nobles. Most of the nomarchs had opposed the rise of Ahmose;
his final triumph made their position untenable and left them with
no alternative but to surrender their claims to sovereignty.

The period which followed the accession of Ahmose is called the
period of the Empire. It lasted from 1580 to 1090 B.C., during which
time the country was ruled by three dynasties of Pharaohs in
succession, the Eighteenth, Nineteenth, and Twentieth. No longer
was the prevailing state policy pacific and isolationist; a spirit of
aggressive imperialism rapidly pervaded the nation. The causes of
this change are not far to seek. The military ardor generated by
the successful war against the Hyksos whetted an appetite for
further victories. A vast military machine had been created to expel
the invader, which proved to be too valuable an adjunct to the
Pharaoh's power to be discarded immediately. Besides, there were
fears, either real or imaginary, of new invasions from western Asia.

*The growth of
imperialism*

The first steps in the direction of the new policy were taken by
the immediate successors of Ahmose in making extensive raids into
Palestine and claiming sovereignty over Syria. The lust for empire
reached its zenith some years later during the reign of Thutmose III,
who came to the throne in 1479 B.C. With one of the most formidable
armies of ancient times he speedily annihilated all opposition in
Syria and eventually made himself master of a vast domain extending from the Euphrates to the farther cataracts of the Nile. Phoenicians, Canaanites, Hittites, and Assyrians acknowledged his suzerainty or paid him tribute. But he never succeeded in welding the
conquered peoples into loyal subjects, and his death was the signal
for widespread revolt in Syria. His successors suppressed the uprising and managed to hold the empire together for some time, but
ultimate disaster could not be averted. More territory had been
annexed than could be managed successfully; the influx of wealth
into Egypt weakened the national fiber by fostering corruption and
luxury; while the constant revolts of the vanquished eventually
sapped the strength of the state beyond all hope of recovery. By
the twelfth century most of the conquered provinces had been
permanently lost.

*Egyptian con-
quests*

The government of the Empire resembled that of the Old Kingdom, except for the fact that it was more absolute. Military power
rather than national unity was now the basis of the Pharaoh's rule.
A professional army was always available with which to overawe his
subjects. His eldest son, who in the Old Kingdom had served an
apprenticeship as vizier, was now the highest ranking officer in
the standing army. Scarcely any vestige of local authority remained.
The nation was divided into more than fifty administrative units,
many of them purely arbitrary, and over each was appointed a
"count" or governor as the direct representative of the monarch's

*The govern-
ment of the
Empire*

41

rule. Most of the former nobles now became courtiers or members of the royal bureaucracy under the complete domination of the king. The Pharaoh was not yet a divine-right monarch, but the actual extent of his power had begun to approach that of more modern despots.

The last of the Pharaohs

The last of the great Pharaohs was Ramses III, who ruled from 1198 to 1167 B.C. He was succeeded by a long line of nonentities who inherited his name but not his ability. By the middle of the twelfth century Egypt had fallen a prey to numerous ills of barbarian invasion and social decadence. Libyans and Nubians were swarming over the country and gradually debasing cultural standards. About the same time the Egyptians themselves appear to have lost their creative talent; their intellects seem to have been led astray by the seductions of magic and superstition; and the inevitable result was domination of the national life by a crude religious formalism. To win immortality by magic devices was now the commanding interest of men of every class. The process of decline was hastened also by the growing power of the priests, who finally usurped the royal prerogatives and dictated the Pharaoh's decrees.

The downfall of Egypt

From the middle of the tenth century to nearly the end of the eighth a dynasty of Libyan barbarians occupied the throne of the Pharaohs. The Libyans were followed by a line of Ethiopians or Nubians, who came in from the desert regions west of the Upper Nile. In 670 Egypt was conquered by the Assyrians, who succeeded in maintaining their supremacy for only eight years. After the collapse of Assyrian rule in 662 the Egyptians regained their independence, and a brilliant renaissance of culture ensued. It was doomed to an untimely end, however, for in 525 B.C. the country was conquered by the Persians. The ancient civilization was never again revived.

3. Egyptian Religion

The importance of religion in Egypt

Religion played a dominant role in the life of the ancient Egyptians. The Greek description of the Egyptians as "the most religious of men" is something of an exaggeration, and yet there is no denying that belief in the supernatural was as important to the culture of the Nile valley as to any other civilization, past or present. Religion left its impress upon almost every department of Egyptian life. The art was an expression of religious symbolism. The literature and philosophy were suffused with religious teachings. The government of the Old Kingdom was to a large extent a theocracy, and even the military Pharaohs of the Empire professed to rule in the name of the god. Economic energy and material resources in considerable amounts were squandered in providing elaborate tombs and in maintaining a costly ecclesiastical system.

The religion of the ancient Egyptians evolved through various stages from simple polytheism to philosophic monotheism. In the beginning each city or district appears to have had its local deities, who were guardian gods of the locality or personifications of nature powers. The unification of the country under the Old Kingdom resulted not only in a consolidation of territory but in a fusion of divinities as well. All of the guardian deities were merged into the great sun god Re or Ra. In later times, with the establishment of a Theban dynasty in control of the government, this deity was commonly called Amon or Ammon-Re from the name of the chief god of Thebes. The gods who personified the vegetative powers of nature were fused into a deity called Osiris, who was also the god of the Nile. Throughout Egyptian history these two great powers who ruled the universe, Re and Osiris, vied with each other for supremacy. Other deities, as we shall see, were recognized also, but they occupied a distinctly subordinate place.

During the period of the Old Kingdom the solar faith, embodied in the worship of Re, was the dominant system of belief. It served as an official religion whose chief function was to give immortality to the state and to the people collectively. The Pharaoh was the living representative of this faith on earth; through his rule the rule of the god was maintained. The belief prevailed also that mummifying the Pharaoh's body and keeping it in an everlasting tomb would contribute to the eternal existence of the nation. But Re was not only a guardian deity. He was in addition the god of righteousness, justice, and truth and the upholder of the moral order of the universe. He offered no spiritual blessings or even material rewards to men as individuals, nor did he concern himself in any other ways with ordinary human welfare. The solar faith was not a religion for the masses as such, except in so far as their welfare coincided with that of the state.

The cult of Osiris, as we have already observed, began its existence as a nature religion. The god personified the growth of vegetation and the life-giving powers of the Nile. The career of Osiris was wrapped about with an elaborate legend. In the remote past, according to belief, he had been a benevolent ruler, who taught his people agriculture and other practical arts and gave them laws. After a time he was treacherously slain by his wicked brother Set, and his body cut into pieces. His wife Isis, who was also his sister, went in search of the pieces, put them together, and miraculously restored his body to life. The risen god regained his kingdom and continued his beneficent rule for a time, but eventually descended to the nether world to serve as judge of the dead. Horus, his posthumous son, finally grew to manhood and avenged his father's death by killing Set.

Originally this legend seems to have been little more than a nature myth. The death and resurrection of Osiris symbolized the recession

The early religious evolution

The solar faith

The Osiris cult

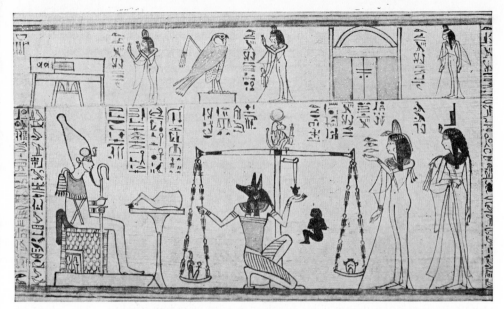

Funerary Papyrus. The scene shows the heart of a princess of the XXIst Dynasty being weighed in a balance before the god Osiris. On the other side of the balance are the symbols for life and truth.

of the Nile in the autumn and the coming of the flood in the spring. But in time the Osiris legend began to take on a deeper significance. The human qualities of the deities concerned—the paternal solicitude of Osiris for his subjects, the faithful devotion of his wife and son—appealed to the emotions of the average Egyptian, who was now able to see his own tribulations and triumphs mirrored in the lives of the gods. More important still, the death and resurrection of Osiris came to be regarded as conveying a promise of personal immortality for man. As the god had triumphed over death and the grave, so might the individual also who followed him faithfully inherit everlasting life. Finally, the victory of Horus over Set appeared to foreshadow the ultimate ascendancy of good over evil.

With the growing perception of these implications, the cult of Osiris gradually became the more popular branch of the Egyptian religion. The worship of the sun god Re required such lofty powers of abstraction that it made little appeal to the average man. Especially during the period of the Middle Kingdom, when individualism rose to its greatest heights, the popular cult received more than its share of attention. The result was not altogether fortunate. Osiris was essentially a god of the dead; he bestowed no rewards upon men in this life. As a consequence of his worship the minds of the Egyptian masses were oriented more and more toward the after-life. Too much emphasis came to be placed upon winning salvation in the world to come, and not enough upon co-operation

44 with Re to promote the reign of righteousness in this world. The solar faith did not die out during the time of the Middle Kingdom, but it was clearly reduced to second place.

Egyptian ideas of the hereafter attained their full development in the later history of the Middle Kingdom. Soon after the beginning of this period the religion had come to include the conception of a *ba*, or "soul," in addition to the idea of a *ka*, or "double." Both were regarded as surviving the death of the individual. The *ba* took flight in the form of a bird. The *ka* wandered off in much the same way that the "other self" might travel to distant places in a dream while the body was locked in sleep. Both the *ba* and the *ka* would eventually return and revivify the body if it were still in existence. For this reason elaborate preparations had to be made to prevent the extinction of one's earthly remains. Not only were bodies mummified but wealthy men left munificent endowments to provide their mummies with food and other essentials. As the religion advanced toward maturity, however, a less naïve conception of the after-life was adopted. The dead were now believed to appear before Osiris to be judged according to their deeds on earth. The process of judgment occupied three stages. In the first, the deceased was required to declare his innocence of forty-two sins, including murder, theft, untruthfulness, greed, adultery, blasphemy, loss of temper, pride, and dishonesty in business transactions. Having thus acquitted himself of this catalogue of vices, the deceased was then obliged to assert his virtues. He must avow that he had satisfied the needs of the gods, that he had given "bread to the hungry, water to the thirsty, clothing to the naked, and a ferry to him who was without a boat." [2] In the third and final stage the heart of the defendant was weighed in the balance against a feather, the symbol of truth, in order to determine the accuracy of his testimony. According to the Egyptian notion, the heart represented the conscience, which would betray the person who testified falsely.

All of the departed who met the tests included in this system of judgment entered a celestial realm of physical delights and simple pleasures. Here in marshes of lilies and lotus-flowers they would hunt wild geese and quail with never-ending success. Or they might build houses in the midst of orchards with luscious fruits of unfailing yield. They would find lily-lakes on which to sail, pools of sparkling water in which to bathe, and shady groves inhabited by singing birds and every manner of gentle creatures. The unfortunate victims whose hearts revealed their vicious lives were condemned to perpetual hunger and thirst in a place of darkness, forever cut off from the glorious light of Re.

The Egyptian religion attained its highest perfection about the end of the Middle Kingdom and the beginning of the Empire. By this time the solar faith and the cult of Osiris had been merged in such a way as to preserve the best features of both. The province of

Egyptian ideas of the hereafter

See color pictures at pages 37, 68, 69

Rewards and punishments

The perfection of the Egyptian religion

[2] J. H. Breasted, *The Dawn of Conscience*, p. 259.

Re as the god of the living, as the champion of good in this world, was accorded almost equal importance with the functions of Osiris, as the giver of personal immortality and the judge of the dead. The religion was now quite clearly an ethical one. Men repeatedly avowed their desire to do justice because such conduct was pleasing to the great sun god.

*Priestcraft
and superstition*

Very soon after the establishment of the Empire the religion which has just been described underwent a serious debasement. Its ethical significance was largely destroyed, and superstition and magic gained the ascendancy. The chief cause seems to have been that the long and bitter war for the expulsion of the Hyksos fostered the growth of irrational attitudes and correspondingly depreciated the intellect. The result was a marked increase in the power of the priests, who preyed upon the fears of the masses to promote their own advantage. Greedy for gain, they inaugurated the practice of selling magical charms, which were supposed to have the effect of preventing the heart of the deceased from betraying his real character. They also sold formulas which, inscribed on rolls of papyrus and placed in the tomb, were alleged to be effective in facilitating the passage of the dead to the celestial realm. The aggregate of these formulas constituted what is referred to as the Book of the Dead. Contrary to the general impression, it was not an Egyptian Bible, but merely a collection of mortuary inscriptions. Some of them proclaimed the moral purity of the deceased; others threatened the gods with disaster unless the persons whose names they bore were granted eternal reward. All of them were purchased in the belief that they guaranteed an entrance into the kingdom of Re. Good deeds and a clear conscience were now considered outmoded.

*See color
pictures at
page 69*

*The religious
revolution of
Ikhnaton*

This degradation of the religion at the hands of the priests into a system of magical fraud finally resulted in a great reformation or religious revolution. The leader of this movement was the Pharaoh Amenhotep IV, who began his reign about 1375 B.C. After some fruitless attempts to correct the most flagrant abuses, he resolved to crush the system entirely. He drove the priests from the temples, hacked the names of the traditional deities from the public monuments, and commanded his people to worship a new god whom he called "Aton," an ancient designation for the physical sun. He changed his own name from Amenhotep ("Amen rests") to Ikhnaton, which meant "Aton is satisfied." Ikhnaton is the name by which he is commonly known in history.

*Ikhnaton's doc-
trines*

More important than these physical changes was the new set of doctrines enunciated by the reforming Pharaoh. According to eminent authorities, he taught first of all a religion of universal monotheism; Aton, he declared, was the only god in existence, the god not merely of Egypt but of the whole universe.[3] He restored

---

[3] J. H. Breasted, *A History of Egypt*, p. 376; see also Alexandre Moret, *From Tribe to Empire*, pp. 298–300.

the ethical quality of the national religion at its best by insisting that
Aton was the author of the moral order of the world and the re-
warder of men for integrity and purity of heart. He envisaged the
new god as an eternal creator and sustainer of all that is of benefit
to man, and as a heavenly father who watches with benevolent care
over all his creatures. Conceptions like these of the unity, righteousness, and benevolence of God were not attained again until the
time of the Hebrew prophets some 600 years later.

The revolution of Ikhnaton was not an enduring success. The
Pharaohs who followed him as rulers of the Empire were not inspired by the same devoted idealism. Such was particularly the
case of the famous Tutenkhamen, who allowed the corrupt and
mercenary priests to regain their power. The result was a revival
and a gradual extension of the same old superstitions which had
prevailed before Ikhnaton's reign. For the great masses of the nation
the ethical significance of the religion was permanently lost, and
they were thrown back once more to ignorance and priestly greed.
Among the educated classes, however, the influence of Ikhnaton's
teachings lingered for some time. Although the god Aton was no
longer recognized, the qualities he represented continued to be held
in high esteem. What happened was that the attributes of Aton were
now transferred by the educated minority to Ammon-Re. The
traditional solar deity was acclaimed as the only god and the embodiment of righteousness, justice, and truth. He was worshiped,
moreover, as a merciful and loving being "who heareth prayers,
who giveth the hand to the poor, who saveth the weary." [4] It should
be noted also that to this religion of ethical monotheism was added
an element of personal salvation through repentance. The religious
philosophers of the time developed the new idea that the god would
refrain from punishing the penitent sinner who humbly implored
forgiveness.

Adherence by the intelligent few to these noble ideas was not
enough to save the religion from complete degeneracy and ruin.
The spread of superstition, the popularity of magic, and the paralyzing grip of a degenerate priesthood were far too deadly in their
effects to be overcome by exalted doctrines. In the end the whole
system of belief and worship was engulfed by formalism and ignorance and by fetishism (worship of magical objects), animal worship, necromancy (black magic: foretelling the future by com-
muning with the dead), and other magical crudities. The commer-
cialism of the priests was more rampant than ever, and the chief
function of the organized religion had come to be the sale of
formulas and charms which would stifle the conscience and trick
the gods into granting eternal salvation. The tragedy was compounded by the fact that as the religion decayed it exerted a baneful
effect upon the rest of the culture. Philosophy, art, and government

*The results of
Ikhnaton's
revolution*

*Decay sets
in once more*

[4] J. H. Breasted, *The Dawn of Conscience*, p. 316.

47

were so closely linked with religion that all of them went down together.

4. Egyptian Intellectual Achievements

The general character of Egyptian philosophy

I. PHILOSOPHY The philosophy of ancient Egypt was chiefly ethical and political, although traces of broader philosophic conceptions are occasionally to be found. The idea that the universe is controlled by mind or intelligence, for example, is a notion that appeared from time to time in the writings of priests and sages. It was first expressed in an inscription known as the *Memphite Drama*, dating from the end of the fourth millennium, and it was revived by Ikhnaton two thousand years later. This idea is so far removed from ordinary anthropomorphic beliefs of ancient peoples that it may seem surprising to find it developed by one of the earliest civilizations; but such was the case. Other philosophic ideas of the ancient Egyptians included the conception of an eternal universe, the notion of constantly recurring cycles of events, and the doctrine of natural cause and effect.

The earliest ethical philosophy

The earliest examples of ethical philosophy are contained in the *Maxims* of Ptahhotep, who served as vizier under one of the Pharaohs of the Fifth Dynasty about 2500 B.C. The work consists of some forty paragraphs of sage advice left by the vizier for the instruction of his son. About half of them are aphorisms of practical wisdom intended for the guidance of the young man in the pursuit of worldly success. Others, however, inculcate morality of a very high order. The son is enjoined to be gracious, tolerant, kindly, and cheerful, but above all to be righteous and just, even to the sacrifice of his own advantage, for "the power of righteousness is that it endures." The author also counsels the avoidance of greed, sensuality, and pride and urges moderation and restraint.[5] Elementary though these maxims are, they are nevertheless highly significant, for they are the first expressions of moral idealism in all the world's literature.

The appearance of disillusionment and skepticism

During the Middle Kingdom ethical philosophy displayed a more sophisticated trend. Indeed, its most prominent characteristics were attitudes of pessimism and disillusionment. One reason was that the ancient faith in the religion of Re had broken down. Men no longer believed that preserving the material remains of the Pharaoh would insure the immortality of the nation. Another was that the collapse of the united kingdom and the prevalence of social disorder and foreign invasion produced a feeling of insecurity and hopelessness. Above all the growth of intellectual maturity made the older conceptions of life and the world appear naïve and groundless. The consequence was a tendency toward the opposite extreme of believing in nothing.

[5] *Ibid.*, pp. 129–39.

A characteristic example of the new philosophic trend was the *Song of the Harp-Player*, which one of the Pharaohs of the Eleventh Dynasty had engraved on the wall of his tomb-chapel about 2100 B.C. It expresses a philosophy of complete skepticism regarding an existence in the after-world: "None cometh from thence that he may tell us how they fare." The gods are not recognized, except that Re is conceived as a blind, impersonal force. No importance is attached to the traditional rewards of virtue and effort; fame, riches, and power are empty delusions. Death is the common fate of Pharaoh and servant alike, and no one knows the day or the hour of its coming. The logical course for man to pursue is therefore to follow desire, to seek his pleasure while he may. But self-indulgence is not enough. One should also strive to gain a good name, by giving "bread to him who hath no field," and by other benevolent works.[6]

The Song of the Harp-Player

The first of a series of Egyptian philosophers whose interests were predominantly political was a priest of Heliopolis who lived during the years that followed the collapse of the Old Kingdom. His name (Khekheperre-soneb) is of such formidable length that he is generally referred to simply as the Priest of Heliopolis. He was the author of the earliest arraignment of society and the first indictment of the upper classes for their injustice to the poor. "The poor man," he declared, "has no strength to save himself from him that is stronger than he." Misery reigns throughout the land. Those who are born to lead are degenerate and cowardly. Society itself is corrupt and complacent. The author recommended no specific reforms, but, as Breasted suggests, many of his reflections would be appropriate in the writings of social critics of our own day.

Political philosophy

With the accession of the Eleventh Dynasty about 2100 B.C., Egypt returned to a semblance of order and prosperity. It was natural that the political philosophy of the time should reflect the welcome change. The most famous specimen of this philosophy is a work which has been given the title of the *Plea of the Eloquent Peasant*. Its authorship is unknown, but it was probably written at the behest of an intelligent Pharaoh who wanted to inculcate high standards of official morality in his subordinates and impress the people with the justice of his rule. It is composed in narrative form and relates the story of a peasant who has been robbed by an unscrupulous official. The victim appeals to the official's superiors, who, at the instance of the Pharaoh, encourage him to unburden himself of all his grievances and to expound his conception of administrative justice. In the course of his pleas the peasant contends that officers of state have the following duties: to act as the father of the orphan, the husband of the widow, and the brother of the forsaken; to ward off the robber and protect the wretched; to execute punishment upon whom it is due; to judge impartially and to speak no falsehood; and to promote such an order of harmony

The Plea of the Eloquent Peasant

[6] *Ibid.*, pp. 163–67.

and prosperity that no one may suffer from hunger or cold or thirst. Few nobler conceptions of the functions of rulers have ever been set forth by political philosophers. We are not to suppose that the sentiments expressed were actually those of the peasant. The story is fictitious. The philosophy it contains reflects the ideals of an enlightened Pharaoh.

II. SCIENCE The branches of science which first absorbed the attention of the Egyptians were astronomy and mathematics. Both were developed for practical ends—to compute the time of the Nile inundations, to lay out the plans for pyramids and temples, and to solve the intricate problems of irrigation and public control of economic functions. The Egyptians were not pure scientists; they had little interest in the nature of the physical universe as such— a fact which probably accounts for their failure to advance very far in the science of astronomy. They perfected a solar calendar, as we have already learned, mapped the heavens, identified the principal fixed stars, and achieved some success in determining accurately the positions of stellar bodies. Nearly all of these accomplishments were made in the pre-dynastic period and in the Old Kingdom. In later times the interest in astronomy waned.

The character of Egyptian science; astronomy

The science of mathematics was more highly developed. The Egyptians laid the foundations for at least two of the common mathematical subjects—arithmetic and geometry. They devised the arithmetical operations of addition, subtraction, and division, although they never discovered how to multiply except through a series of additions. They invented the decimal system, but they had no symbol for zero. Fractions caused them some difficulty: all those with a numerator greater than one had to be broken down into a series, each with *one* as the numerator, before they could be used in mathematical calculations. The only exception was the fraction two-thirds, which the scribes had learned to use as it stood. The Egyptians also achieved a surprising degree of skill in mensuration, computing with accuracy the areas of triangles, rectangles, and hexagons. The ratio of the circumference of a circle to its diameter they calculated to be 3.16. They learned how to compute the volume of the pyramid and the cylinder, and even the volume of the hemisphere.

Achievements in mathematics

See color pictures at page 69

The third branch of science in which the Egyptians did some remarkable work was medicine, although progress was slow until the age of the Middle Kingdom. Early medical practice was conservative and profusely corrupted by superstition, but a document dating from about 1700 B.C. reveals a fairly adequate conception of scientific diagnosis and treatment. Egyptian physicians were frequently specialists: some were oculists; others were dentists, surgeons, specialists in diseases of the stomach, and so on. In the course of their work they made many discoveries of lasting value.

Medicine

50

They recognized the importance of the heart and had some appreciation of the significance of the pulse. They acquired a degree of skill in the treatment of fractures and performed simple operations. Unlike some peoples of later date they ascribed disease to natural causes. They discovered the value of cathartics, noted the curative properties of numerous drugs, and compiled the first *materia medica*, or catalogue of medicines. Many of their remedies, both scientific and magical, were carried into Europe by the Greeks and are still employed by the peasantry of isolated regions.

In other scientific fields the Egyptians contributed little. Although they achieved feats which rival modern engineering, they possessed but the scantiest knowledge of physics. They knew the principle of the inclined plane, but they were ignorant of the pulley. To their credit also must be assigned considerable progress in metallurgy, the invention of the sundial, and the making of paper and glass. With all their deficiencies as pure scientists, they really equaled the Romans in actual accomplishment and went far ahead of anything done by the Hebrews and Persians.

Other scientific accomplishments

III. WRITING AND LITERATURE The Egyptians developed their first form of writing during the pre-dynastic period. This system, known as the *hieroglyphic*, from the Greek words meaning sacred carving, was originally composed of pictographic signs denoting concrete objects. Gradually certain of these signs were conventionalized and used to represent abstract concepts. Other characters were introduced to designate separate syllables which could be combined to form words. Finally, twenty-four symbols, each representing a single consonant sound of the human voice, were added early in the Old Kingdom. Thus the hieroglyphic system of writing had come to include at an early date three separate types of characters, the pictographic, syllabic, and alphabetic.

The hieroglyphic system

The ultimate step in this evolution of writing would have been the complete separation of the alphabetic from the non-alphabetic characters and the exclusive use of the former in written communication. The Egyptians were reluctant to take this step. Their traditions of conservatism impelled them to follow old habits. Although they made frequent use of the consonant signs, they did not commonly employ them as an independent system of writing. It was left for the Phoenicians to do this some 1500 years later. Nevertheless, the Egyptians must be credited with the invention of the principle of the alphabet. It was they who first perceived the value of single symbols for the individual sounds of the human voice. The Phoenicians merely copied this principle, based their own system of writing upon it, and diffused the idea among neighboring nations. In the ultimate sense it is therefore true that the Egyptian alphabet was the parent of every other that has ever been used in the Western world. The Egyptians also devised two other systems of

The principle of the alphabet

writing in addition to the hieroglyphic: the *hieratic*, which was a cursive or running hand employed for business purposes; and the *demotic*, which was a simpler and more popular form of hieratic.

Egyptian literature was largely philosophical and religious. The former type has already been discussed. By far the best specimens

*Egyptian reli-
gious literature*

of the latter were the *Memphite Drama*, the *Royal Sun Hymn* of Ikhnaton, and the hymns of personal piety which have survived from the period of the Empire. The *Memphite Drama*, written about 3000 B.C., was a theological dialogue in which various gods discoursed on the doctrines of the solar religion. The object of the work was apparently to promote the national worship of the sun god Re. Its pervading theme was the idea that Re was the arbiter of human destiny, the author of good, and the giver of life to the "peaceful" and of death to the "guilty." The *Royal Hymn* of Ikhnaton, composed by the great reforming Pharaoh of the fourteenth century B.C., was a stately ode in praise of the majesty, providence, and justice of Aton, "the sole God, beside whom there is no other." It was the supreme embodiment of the Egyptian conception of universal monotheism.

Literature of a deeper emotional quality was exemplified by the hymns of personal piety, written during the two or three hundred

*The hymns of
personal piety*

years that followed the death of Ikhnaton. They likewise avow a belief in one God, but they call him by the more ancient name of Amon, and celebrate his loving kindness rather than his splendor and majesty. He is acclaimed as the "Lord of sweetness who giveth breath to every one he loveth" and bestows his tender care upon his humblest creatures. He is merciful, wise, and just, and forgives those who call upon his name. "Punish me not for my many sins" is a common supplication addressed to him. The following is a typical excerpt from one of these hymns:

> Thou, O Amon, art the lord of the silent
> Who cometh at the cry of the poor.
> When I cry to thee in my affliction,
> Then thou comest and savest me.
> That thou mayest give breath to him who is bowed down,
> And mayest save me lying in bondage.[7]

In addition to the philosophical and religious works, there were many writings of a lighter sort. Folk songs of the common people

*Popular litera-
ture*

at their labors, stories of travel and adventure, odes of victory in battle, and charming love lyrics that suggest the style and imagery of the Biblical Song of Solomon are among the several types which have come down to us. Most famous of the individual compositions was the *Tale of the Two Brothers*, considered by some authorities as the source of the Old Testament narrative of Joseph and Poti-

[7] *Ibid.*, p. 315.

phar's wife. The popular literature of Egypt is especially significant for its influence, since much of its content was copied by later Oriental peoples, and for the light which it throws upon the society of the common man. It portrays the average Egyptian in his prevailing moods of cheerful resignation and joy in the simpler pleasures. It reveals a society comparatively free from the grosser forms of tyranny and ignorance. We are given the impression of a standard of living that was not indescribably poor and mean, in which the middle classes, at least, could acquire the rudiments of an education and thereby escape from a life of drudgery and pain.

5. The Meaning of Egyptian Art

No single interpretation will suffice to explain the meaning of Egyptian art. Its purposes were varied, and the ideals it was supposed to represent changed with the shifting tendencies of political and social history. In general, it expressed the aspirations of a collectivized national life. It was not art for art's sake, nor did it serve to convey the individual's reactions to the problems of his personal world. Yet there were times when the conventions of a communal society were broken down, and the supremacy was accorded to a spontaneous individual art that sensed the beauty of the flower or caught the radiant idealism of a youthful face. Seldom was the Egyptian genius for faithful reproduction of nature entirely suppressed. Even the rigid formalism of the official architecture was commonly relieved by touches of naturalism—columns in imitation of palm trunks, lotus blossom capitals, and occasional statues of Pharaohs which were not conventionalized types but true individual portraits.

The character of Egyptian art

See color pictures at page 69

In most civilizations where the interests of society are exalted above those of its members, architecture is at once the most typical and the most highly developed of the arts. Egypt was no exception. Whether in the Old Kingdom, Middle Kingdom, or Empire it was the problems of building construction which absorbed the talent of the artist. Although painting and sculpture were by no means primitive, they nevertheless had as their primary function the embellishment of temples. Only at times did they rise to the status of independent arts.

Architecture

The characteristic examples of Old Kingdom architecture were the pyramids, the first of which were built at least as early as 2700 B.C. An amazing amount of labor and skill were expended in their construction. The Greek historian Herodotus estimated that 100,000 men must have been employed for twenty years to complete the single pyramid of Khufu at Gizeh. Its total height exceeds 480 feet, and the more than two million limestone blocks it contains are fitted together with a precision which few modern masons could duplicate. Each of the blocks weighs about two and a half tons. They

The pyramids

746 ft. at the base weight 2½ tons

53

The Great Sphinx and Pyramids at Gizeh. For the Egyptian the sphinx, with a human head on the body of a lion, probably represented an attempt to endow the Pharaoh with the strength and courage of the lion.

were evidently hewn out of rock cliffs with drills and wedges and then dragged up earthen ramps by gangs of men and pried into place.

Significance of the pyramids

The significance of the pyramids is not easy to comprehend. They may have been intended for the economic purpose of providing employment opportunities. Such a theory would assume that the population had increased to overcrowding, and that the resources of agriculture, mining, industry, and commerce were no longer adequate to provide a livelihood for all the people. But whatever the validity of this theory, it is hardly a complete explanation. The pyramids also had a political and religious significance. Their construction was an act of faith, the expression of an ambition to endow the state with permanence and stability. As indestructible tombs of the rulers they were believed to guarantee immortality to the people, for the Pharaoh was the embodiment of the national life. It is possible also that they were intended to serve as symbols of sun worship. As the tallest structures in Egypt they would catch the first light of the rising sun and reflect it to the valley below.

The temples

During the Middle Kingdom and the Empire the temple displaced the pyramid as the leading architectural form. No longer was preservation of the material remains of the Pharaoh considered so important, nor was there quite the same credulous faith in the identification of the ruler with the nation. On the other hand, there was the same interest in structures of massive proportions which would express the national strength and the belief in the eternity of the culture. But these structures were not tombs. The most famous examples of them were the great temples at Karnak and Luxor, built during the period of the Empire. Many of their gigantic, richly carved columns still stand as silent witnesses of a splendid architectural talent.

54

THE MEANING
OF EGYPTIAN
ART

Characteristics
of temple arch-
itecture

Egyptian temples were characterized first of all by massive size. The temple at Karnak, with a length of about 1300 feet, covered the largest area of any religious edifice ever built. Its central hall alone could contain almost any of the Gothic cathedrals of Europe. But even its enormous bulk was not enough to satisfy the passion for grandeur. Artificial devices were employed to make the building seem larger than it really was. As an example, the height of the ceiling was progressively diminished from the entrance toward the rear to create the illusion of a long perspective and therefore of a vast expanse of floor. The columns used in the temples had stupendous proportions. The largest of them were seventy feet high, with diameters in excess of twenty feet. It has been estimated that the capitals which surmounted them could furnish standing room for a hundred men.

The Egyptians deliberately chose to give their temples hugeness of size and solidity of construction. They did not completely sacrifice grace and proportion—much of the decoration was instinct with life, and the design frequently bespoke a high regard for symmetry. But impressions of grandeur and massiveness were quite evidently

Hypostyle Hall in the Temple at Karnak. Hugeness, to express the national strength and belief in eternity, was a dominant feature of Egyptian temple architecture. Note also the deeply incised carvings on the columns.

the vital considerations, especially in the temples of the Empire. Such a conclusion is rendered obvious by the fact that the materials used in temple construction were by no means of a flimsy or insubstantial character. Walls several feet thick and columns of enormous diameter were not made necessary by a choice of materials that were likely to crumble; on the contrary, the Egyptians used nothing but the hardest of stone. We are therefore led to the belief that the real purpose of their building style was to symbolize conceptions of national pride, imperial glory, and the strength and permanence of the state. Many other imperialistic peoples, the Assyrians and the Romans for example, have sought to express the majesty of their **55**

*Egyptian sculp-
ture*

accomplishments in buildings of imposing magnitude. Perhaps the tendency in much modern architecture to identify beauty with hugeness is a reflection of a similar pride in conquest.

As already mentioned, Egyptian sculpture and painting served primarily as adjuncts to architecture. The former was heavily laden with conventions which restricted its style and meaning. Statues of Pharaohs were commonly of colossal size. Those produced during the Empire ranged in height from seventy-five to ninety feet. Some of them were colored to resemble life, and the eyes were frequently inlaid with rock crystal. The figures were nearly always rigid, with the arms folded across the chest or fixed to the sides of the body and with the eyes staring straight to the front. Countenances were generally represented as impassive, utterly devoid of emotional expression. Anatomical distortion was frequently practiced: the natural length of the thighs might be increased, the squareness of the shoulders accentuated, or all of the fingers of the hand made equal in length. A familiar example of non-naturalistic sculpture was the Sphinx. This represented the head of a Pharaoh on the body of a lion. The purpose was probably to symbolize the notion that the Pharaoh possessed the lion's qualities of strength and courage. The figures of sculpture in relief were even less in conformity with nature. The

Colossus of Ramses II (XIXth Dynasty). Though almost modern in its sharp, cubist lines, this statue is typically Egyptian in the imperturbable expression of the face and the conventionalized treatment of shoulders, arms, and legs.

Relief Portrait of Seti I (XIXth Dynasty). The face is almost the only individualized part of this portrait. Observe the frontality of the shoulders, the conventionalized position of the feet, and the equal length of the fingers.

head was presented in profile, with the eye fullface; the torso was shown in the frontal position, while the legs were rendered in profile. Such were the general tendencies, but it should be noted that they were not universal. Occasionally the artist succeeded in a partial defiance of conventions, as is evidenced by the production of some highly individual likenesses of the later Pharaohs. The most notable example was a beautiful limestone head of Ikhnaton, found some years ago at Amarna, which clearly portrayed the quality of dreamy mysticism inherent in the soul of the great reformer.

The meaning of Egyptian sculpture is not hard to perceive. The colossal size of the statues of Pharaohs was doubtless intended to symbolize their power and the power of the state they represented. It is significant that the size of these statues increased as the empire expanded and the government became more absolute. The conventions of rigidity and impassiveness, which dominated not only the statues of rulers but even the sculptures of less formal description such as the figure of *The Seated Scribe*, were meant to express the timelessness and stability of the national life. Here was a nation which, according to the ideal, was not to be torn loose from its moorings by the uncertain mutations of fortune but was to remain fixed and imperturbable. The portraits of its chief men consequently must betray no anxiety, fear, or triumph, but an unvarying calmness throughout the ages. In similar fashion, the anatomical distortion can probably be interpreted as a deliberate attempt to express some national ideal. There is certainly no reason to believe that it was practiced through ignorance of the laws of proportion or inability to copy the natural form. Very likely it was intended as a denial of mortality. The eternal existence of the people might very easily be thought to depend upon investing their leaders with attributes which would serve to protest their death as ordinary human beings. The most eloquent device for this purpose was representation of the body of a Pharaoh with the head of a god, but the other examples of non-naturalistic portrayal probably had a similar object.

The meaning of Egyptian sculpture

See color pictures at pages 37, 68, 69

Though most of Egyptian painting has perished, that which survives is largely free from political and religious conventions. Certainly it was not dominated by them to the extent that architecture and sculpture were. The reason is perhaps to be found in the fact that painting developed late and did not have time to become weighted down with a mass of traditions. Religion did exert its influence, but in a positive manner. The best paintings were those created during the reign of Ikhnaton and immediately after. The gospel of the reforming king, with its reverence for nature as the handiwork of God, fostered a revival of naturalism in art which was particularly evident in painting. As a result, the murals of this period exhibit a decided talent for representation of the striking phenomena of the world of experience. They have particular merit as examples of the portrayal of movement. They caught the instant

Painting

57

Fishing and Fowling: Wall Painting Thebes, XVIIIth Dynasty. Most of the women appear to belong to the prosperous classes, while the simple garb and insignificant size of the men indicates that they are probably slaves.

action of the wild bull leaping in the swamp, the headlong flight of the frightened stag, and the effortless swimming of ducks in the pond. Even the paintings in the great temple of Luxor made a similar appeal to the senses; the blue ceiling studded with stars and the flowers and trees emblazoned on the columns and walls bore witness to the artist's appreciation of the beauty of his natural environment.

6. Social and Economic Life

The absence of a caste system

The social organization of Egypt was distinguished by a surprising degree of fluidity. No inflexible caste system ever developed. All men were equal in the sight of the law. Although degrees of economic inequality naturally existed, no man's status was unalterably fixed, unless he was a member of the royal family. Even serfs appear to have been capable of rising above their humble condition. Freemen quite regularly made the transition from one social order to another. Such a structure of society differed in marked degree from the stratified social regimes in other parts of the Orient—in India and Mesopotamia, for example.

The principal classes

During the greater part of the history of Egypt the population was divided into five classes: the royal family; the priests; the nobles; the middle class of scribes, merchants, artisans, and farmers; and the serfs. During the Empire a sixth class, the professional soldiers, was added, ranking immediately below the nobles. Thousands of slaves were captured in this period also, and these formed for a time a seventh class. Despised by freemen and serfs alike, they

58

were forced to labor in the government quarries and on the temple estates. Gradually, however, they were enrolled in the army and even in the personal service of the Pharaoh. With these developments they ceased to constitute a separate class. The position of the various ranks of society shifted from time to time. In the Old Kingdom the nobles and priests among all of the Pharaoh's subjects held the supremacy. During the Middle Kingdom the classes of commoners came into their own. Scribes, merchants, artisans, and serfs rebelled against the nobles and wrested concessions from the government. Particularly impressive is the dominant role played by the merchants and industrialists in this period. The establishment of the Empire, accompanied as it was by the extension of government functions, resulted in the ascendancy of a new nobility, made up primarily of bureaucrats. The priests also waxed in power with the growth of magic and superstition.

The gulf which separated the standards of living of the upper and lower classes of Egypt was just about as wide as it is today in Europe and America. The wealthy nobles lived in splendid villas that opened into fragrant gardens and shady groves. Their food had all the richness and variety of sundry kinds of meat,

The gulf between rich and poor

Making Sun-dried Bricks. Nile mud (generally mixed with chaff or straw) is being worked with a hoe, carried away in buckets and dumped in a pile. Lying on the ground in a row are three bricks, from the last of which a wooden mold, used in shaping them, is being lifted. An overseer with a stick is seated close by. The finished bricks are carried off by means of a yoke across the shoulders. From

a wall-painting at Thebes about 1500 B.C.

Stonecutters Dressing Blocks. Men with mallets and chisels are dressing down blocks to true surfaces. Below, two of them test the accuracy of the dressed surface. After two edges of the block are determined, a cord is stretched between two pegs to help gauge how much remains to be chiseled away.

poultry, cakes, fruit, wine, beer, and sweets. They ate from vessels of alabaster, gold, and silver and adorned their persons with expensive fabrics and costly jewels. By contrast, the life of the poor was wretched indeed. The laborers in the towns inhabited congested slums composed of mud-brick hovels with roofs of thatch. Their only furnishings were stools and boxes and a few crude pottery

*The Egyptian
family*

*The educational
system*

*Agriculture,
trade, and in-
dustry*

jars. The peasants on the great estates enjoyed a less crowded but no more abundant life.

The basic social unit among the Egyptians was the monogamous family. No man, not even the Pharaoh, could have more than one lawful wife. Concubinage, however, was a socially reputable institution. Women occupied an unusually enviable status; in fact, the Egyptian family was almost matriarchal. Descent was traced through the female line, and the authority of the maternal grandfather over the children was greater than that of their own father. Almost alone among Oriental peoples the Egyptians permitted women to succeed to the throne. Another extraordinary social practice was close inbreeding. The ruler as son of the great sun god was required to marry his sister or some other female of his immediate family lest the divine blood be contaminated. The rest of the population commonly followed the identical custom. As yet, historians have been unable to discover any positive traces of racial degeneration produced by this practice, probably for the reason that the Egyptian stock was genetically sound to begin with.

The educational system of this ancient people was about what one would expect in a highly integrated society. Attached to the treasury were a number of public schools equipped for the training of the thousands of scribes whose services were necessary in the keeping of records and accounts and in the administration of government functions. Many of them were also employed in a private capacity by the owners of the landed estates and by the leaders of the business world. Admission to these schools was open to any promising youth regardless of class. Apparently the instruction was provided free of charge by the government because of the vital need for trained men. None but thoroughly utilitarian subjects had any place in the curriculum; the purpose was not education in the broader sense, but practical training. In spite of their limitations, these schools did provide for the poor but talented youth an avenue of escape from a life of hopeless drudgery.

The Egyptian economic system rested primarily upon an agrarian basis. Agriculture was diversified and highly developed, and the soil yielded excellent crops of wheat, barley, millet, vegetables, fruits, flax, and cotton. Theoretically the land was the property of the king, but in the earlier periods he granted most of it to his subjects, so that in actual practice it was largely in the possession of individuals. Commerce did not amount to much before 2000 B.C., but after that date it grew rapidly to a position of first-rate importance. A flourishing trade was carried on with the island of Crete, with Phoenicia, Palestine, and Syria. The chief articles of export consisted of wheat, linen fabrics, and fine pottery. Imports were confined largely to gold, silver, ivory, and lumber. Of no less significance than commerce was manufacturing as a branch of the economic life. As early as 3000 B.C. large numbers of people were already engaged

Sowing Seed and Working It into the Soil. From a bag which he wears over his left shoulder, the sower casts seed under the feet of cattle yoked to a plow. The plow is here used to harrow the soil. While one laborer guides the cows with a stick, another guides the plow straight and keeps the plowshare in the ground by bearing down on the handles. Sheep are then driven across the field to trample in the seed. From wall paintings at Sheikh Saïd, about 2700 B.C.

in industrial pursuits, mostly in separate crafts. In later times factories were established, employing twenty or more persons under one roof, and with some degree of division of labor. The leading industries were quarrying, shipbuilding, and the manufacture of pottery, glass, and textiles.

From an early date the Egyptians made progress in the perfection of instruments of business. They knew the elements of accounting and bookkeeping. Their merchants issued orders and receipts for goods. They invented deeds for property, written contracts, and wills. While they had no system of coinage, they had nevertheless attained a money economy. Rings of copper or gold of definite weight circulated as media of exchange. This Egyptian ring-money is apparently the oldest currency in the history of civilizations. Probably it was not used except for the larger transactions. The simple dealings of the peasants and poorer townsfolk doubtless continued on a basis of barter.

The development of instruments of business

The Egyptian economic system was always collectivistic. From the very beginning the energies of the people had been drawn into socialized channels. The interests of the individual and the interests of society were conceived as identical. The productive activities of the entire nation revolved around the huge state enterprises, and the government remained by far the largest employer of labor. It should be noted, though, that during the Old and Middle Kingdoms this collectivism was not all-inclusive; a considerable sphere was left for private initiative. Merchants conducted their own businesses; many of the craftsmen had their own shops; and as time went on, larger and larger numbers of peasants gained the status of independent farmers. The government continued to operate the quarries and mines, to build pyramids and temples, and to farm the royal estates.

Economic collectivism

The extreme development of state control came with the founding of the Empire. The growth of a military absolutism and the increasing frequency of wars of conquest augmented the need for revenue and for unlimited production of goods. To fulfill this need

*The extreme
development of
state control
under the Em-
pire*

the government extended its control over every department of economic life. The entire agricultural land again became the property of the Pharaoh, in fact as well as in theory. Although large sections of it were granted to favorites of the king, most of it was worked by royal serfs and slaves. The free middle class of earlier days now largely disappeared. The services of craftsmen were conscripted for the erection of magnificent temples and for the manufacture of implements of war, while foreign trade became a state monopoly. As the Empire staggered toward its downfall, the government absorbed more and more of the economic activities of the people.

*Defects
in the economic
system*

Except during the reign of Ikhnaton, a degraded alliance existed between the Pharaohs of the Empire and the priests. Greedy for power and plunder, the members of the ecclesiastical hierarchy supported the kings in their ambitions for despotic rule. As a reward they were granted exemption from taxation and a generous share of the national wealth. War captives were turned over to them in such numbers that they actually held two per cent of the population of the country as temple slaves. In addition, they received from their generous patrons one-seventh of the arable land, hundreds of thousands of cattle, and nearly a hundred ships. They employed a great host of artisans in the manufacture of amulets and funerary equipment, which they sold at tremendous profit to the misguided worshipers. Without question these priestly enterprises meant a serious drain on the national resources and thereby contributed to economic and social decay. Too large a proportion of the wealth of Egypt was being squandered on sterile projects of the church and the state, on otherworldly preparations, and on the conquest of an empire.

7. The Egyptian Achievement and Its Importance to Us

*Egyptian
contributions:
(1) intellectual
and artistic*

Few civilizations of ancient times surpassed the Egyptian in importance to the modern world. Even the influence of the Hebrews was not much greater. From the land of the Pharaohs came the germ and the stimulus for numerous intellectual achievements of later centuries. Important elements of philosophy, mathematics, science, and literature had their beginnings there. The Egyptians also developed one of the oldest systems of jurisprudence and political theory. They perfected the achievements of irrigation, engineering, and the making of pottery, glass, and paper. They were one of the first peoples to have any clear conception of art for other than utilitarian purposes, and they originated architectural principles that were destined for extensive use in subsequent history. Notable among these were the column, the colonnade, the lintel, the obelisk, and the clerestory, or low wall with windows looking out upon the roof of the main part of the building.

More significant still were the Egyptian contributions in the fields of religion and individual and social ethics. Aside from the Persians, the dwellers on the banks of the Nile were the only people of the ancient world to build a national religion around the doctrine of personal immortality. Egyptian priests and sages likewise were the first to preach universal monotheism, the providence of God, forgiveness of sins, and rewards and punishments after death. Finally, Egyptian ethical theory was the source from which various nations derived standards of personal and social morality; for it embraced not only the ordinary prohibitions of lying, theft, and murder, but included also the exalted ideals of justice, benevolence, and the equal rights of all men.

SELECTED READINGS

Baikie, James, *A History of Egypt*, London, 1929
Breasted, James H., *The Dawn of Conscience*, New York, 1934
———, *History of Egypt*, New York, 1912
Engberg, R. M., *The Dawn of Civilization*, Chicago, 1937
Erman, Adolf, *Life in Ancient Egypt*, New York, 1894
Frankfort, Henri, *The Intellectual Adventure of Ancient Man*, Chicago, 1946
Hall, H. R., *Ancient History of the Near East*, New York, 1913
Mason, W. A., *History of the Art of Writing*, New York, 1920
Maspero, G. C. C., *Art in Ancient Egypt*, New York, 1912
Moret, Alexandre, *The Nile and Egyptian Civilization*, New York, 1928
Peet, T. E., *Comparative Study of the Literatures of Egypt, Palestine, and Mesopotamia*, New York, 1931
Petrie, W. M. F., *Social Life in Ancient Egypt*, Boston, 1923
———, *Religious Life in Ancient Egypt*, Boston, 1924
Robinson, Victor, *The Story of Medicine*, New York, 1932
Shorter, A. W., *Everyday Life in Ancient Egypt*, London, 1932
———, *Introduction to Egyptian Religion*, New York, 1932
Smith, G. E., *The Ancient Egyptians and the Origin of Civilization*, New York, 1923
Ullman, B. L., *Ancient Writing*, New York, 1932
Wilson, J. A., *The Burden of Egypt*, Chicago, 1951

SOURCE MATERIALS

Breasted, J. H., *Ancient Records of Egypt*, 5 vols.
———, *Development of Religion and Thought in Ancient Egypt*
Budge, E. A. W., *Osiris and the Egyptian Resurrection*, 2 vols.
Pritchard, J. B., ed., *Ancient Near Eastern Texts*, Princeton, 1950

The Mesopotamian Civilization

*Origin
and comparison
with Egypt*

The other of the most ancient civilizations was that which began in the Tigris-Euphrates valley at least as early as 4000 B.C. For convenience historians refer to this civilization as the Mesopotamian, although the name Mesopotamia is sometimes applied only to the northern portion of the land between the two rivers. The Mesopotamian civilization was distinctly unlike the Egyptian. Its political history was marked by sharper interruptions. Its racial composition was less homogeneous, and its social and economic structure gave wider scope to individual initiative.

*Religious and
social
differences*

The differences in ideals and in religious and social attitudes were perhaps more fundamental. The Egyptian culture was predominantly ethical, the Mesopotamian legalistic. The Egyptian outlook upon life, except during the Middle Kingdom, was generally one of cheerful resignation, comparatively free from the cruder superstitions. By contrast, the Mesopotamian view was gloomy, pessimistic, and enthralled by morbid fears. Where the native of Egypt believed in immortality and dedicated a large part of his energy to preparation for the life to come, his Mesopotamian contemporary lived in the present and regarded his fate beyond the grave with indifference. Finally, the civilization of the Nile valley embodied concepts of monotheism, a religion of love, and social equalitarianism; that of the Tigris-Euphrates was more selfish and cynical. Its religion seldom evolved beyond the stage of primitive polytheism, and its ideal of justice was largely confined to literal observance of the terms of a contract.

1. Political History

The pioneers in the development of the Mesopotamian civilization were a people known as the Sumerians, who settled in the lower

Tigris-Euphrates valley between 5000 and 4000 B.C. Their precise origin is unknown, but they seem to have come from the plateau of central Asia. They spoke a language unrelated to any now known, although their culture bore a certain resemblance to the earliest civilization of India. With little or no difficulty they subjugated the natives already in the lower valley, a mysterious people who were just emerging from the Neolithic stage.

About 2400 B.C. the Sumerians were conquered by Sargon I, the ruler of a nation of Semites who had established themselves in a section of the valley known as Akkad. This was the prelude to the founding of the first great Semitic empire in western Asia, for soon afterward Sargon conquered the Elamites and all of northern Syria to the Mediterranean Sea. But like so many states that have had their roots in conquest, this empire was short-lived. Sargon's death was the signal for the first of a series of Sumerian revolts. Although these revolts were suppressed, they weakened the state and paved the way for its overthrow by the Guti, a fierce barbarian people from the north. Finally, about 2100 B.C., the Sumerians, under the leadership of the city of Ur, rebelled successfully against the rule of the Guti and established their power over all of Sumer and Akkad. The most noted king of the new state was Dungi, who assumed the grandiloquent title of "king of the four regions of the earth" and attempted to duplicate the military accomplishments of Sargon I.

The new Sumerian empire did not survive the death of Dungi. It was annexed by the Elamites in the twenty-first century and about 1800 B.C. was conquered by a Semitic people known as the Amorites, who had come in from the fringes of the Arabian desert. Since they made the village of Babylon the capital of their empire they are commonly called the Babylonians, or the Old Babylonians to distinguish them from the Neo-Babylonians or Chaldeans who occupied the valley much later. The rise of the Old Babylonians inaugurated the second important stage of the Tigris-Euphrates civilization. Although most of the Sumerian culture survived, Sumerian dominance was now at an end. The Babylonians established an autocratic state and during the reign of their most famous king, Hammurabi, extended their dominion north to Assyria. But after his time their empire gradually declined until it was finally overthrown by the Kassites about 1650 B.C.

With the downfall of Old Babylonia a period of retrogression set in which lasted for six hundred years. The Kassites were barbarians with no interest in the cultural achievements of their predecessors. Their lone contribution was the introduction of the horse into the Tigris-Euphrates valley. The old culture would have died out entirely if it had not been for its partial adoption by another Semitic people who as early as 3000 B.C. had founded a tiny kingdom on the plateau of Assur some 500 miles up the Tigris River. These people came to be called the Assyrians, and their ultimate rise to power

The Sumerians

Sumerian political history

The rise and fall of the Old Babylonians

The Kassites and the Assyrians

marked the beginning of the third stage in the development of the Mesopotamian civilization. About 1300 B.C. they began to expand and soon afterward made themselves masters of the whole north-ern valley. In the tenth century they overturned what was left of Kassite power in Babylonia. Their empire reached its height in the eighth and seventh centuries under Sargon II (722–705 B.C.), Sen-nacherib (705–681), and Assurbanipal (668–626). It had now come to include nearly all of the civilized world of that time. One after another, Syria, Phoenicia, the Kingdom of Israel, and Egypt had fallen victims of Assyrian military prowess. Only the little King-dom of Judah was able to withstand the hosts of Nineveh, probably because of an outbreak of pestilence in the ranks of Sennacherib's army.[1]

Brilliant though the successes of the Assyrians were, they did not endure. So rapidly were new territories annexed that the empire soon reached an unmanageable size. The Assyrians' genius for gov-ernment was far inferior to their appetite for conquest. Subjugated nations chafed under the cruel despotism that had been forced upon them and, as the empire gave signs of cracking from within, deter-mined to regain their freedom. The death blow was delivered by the Kaldi or Chaldeans, a nation of Semites who had settled south-east of the valley of the two rivers. Under the leadership of Nabo-polassar, who had served the Assyrian emperors in the capacity of a provincial governor, they organized a revolt and finally captured Nineveh in 612 B.C.

The downfall of the Assyrians and the rise of the Chaldeans

Nabopolassar was succeeded by his son Nebuchadnezzar, who ruled until 562 B.C. During the reign of the latter the Chaldeans rose to the mastery of a new cosmopolitan empire in the Near Orient. The last vestiges of Assyrian authority were annihilated in all of the more valuable sections of the Fertile Crescent. Even the King-dom of Judah, which had successfully defied the Assyrian "wolves," fell an easy victim to the relentless energy of Nebuchadnezzar. The temple at Jerusalem was looted and burned, King Zedekiah was blinded, and he and several thousand of his countrymen were car-ried off into captivity in Babylon.

The Chaldean empire

But the empire of the Chaldeans did not long survive the death of its greatest ruler. During the reigns of his successors the nation turned to the indulgence of antiquarian interests—to the worship of the achievements of the Old Babylonians, whom they ignorantly revered as their ancestors. Jealous contention arose between the kings and the priests; and the Medes, a tributary nation on the eastern border, began to give trouble. But the major reason for the downfall of the Chaldean empire was the insatiable greed of its founder. It was this lust for power and glory that led him to repeat the blunders of the Assyrian monarchs before him in conquering

The downfall of the Chaldeans

---

[1] Hebrew prophets declared that an angel of the Lord visited the camp of the Assyrians by night and slew 185,000 of them. II Kings 19:35.

an unwieldy empire and in humiliating proud peoples. The hand-writing on the wall which Belshazzar is supposed to have seen at his famous feast should have been intended for Nebuchadnezzar.[2]

In 539 B.C. the empire of the Chaldeans fell, after an existence of less than a century. It was overthrown by Cyrus the Persian, as he himself declared, "without a battle and without fighting." The easy victory appears to have been made possible by assistance from the Jews and by a conspiracy of the priests of Babylon to deliver the city to Cyrus as an act of vengeance against the Chaldean king, whose policies they did not like. Members of other influential classes appear also to have looked upon the Persians as deliverers. *The Persian conquest*

Although the Persian state incorporated all of the territories that had once been embraced by the Mesopotamian empires, it included many other provinces besides. It was the vehicle, moreover, of a new and different culture. The downfall of Chaldea must therefore be taken as marking the end of Mesopotamian political history.

2. Sumerian Origins of the Civilization

More than to any other people, the Mesopotamian civilization owed its character to the Sumerians. Much of what used to be ascribed to the Babylonians and Assyrians is now known to have been developed by the nation that preceded them. The system of writing was of Sumerian origin; likewise the religion, the laws, and a great deal of the science and commercial practice. Only in the evolution of government and military tactics and in the develop-ment of the arts was the originating talent of the later conquerors particularly manifest. *The Sumerians the chief originators of Mesopotamian civilization*

Through the greater part of their history the Sumerians lived in a loose confederation of city-states, united only for military pur-poses. At the head of each was a *patesi*, who combined the functions of chief priest, commander of the army, and superintendent of the irrigation system. Occasionally one of the more ambitious of these rulers would extend his power over a number of cities and assume the title of king. Not until the time of Dungi, about 2000 B.C., how-ever, were all of the Sumerian people united under a single authority of the same nationality as themselves. *The Sumerian political system*

The Sumerian economic pattern was relatively simple and per-mitted a wider scope for individual enterprise than was generally allowed in Egypt. The land was never the exclusive property of the king either in theory or in practice. Neither was trade or industry a monopoly of the government. On the other hand, the masses of the people had little they could call their own. Many of them were serfs, but even those who were technically free were little better off, forced as they were to pay high rents and to labor on the public works. Slavery in the strict sense of the word was not an important *The Sumerian economic pat-tern*

[2] Compare the Old Testament account in Daniel 5:24-31.

Diorama of a Part of Ur about 2000 B.C. A modern archaeologist's conception. Walls are omitted to show interiors at left.

institution. Most of those referred to as slaves were really serfs, who had mortgaged their persons for debt. They do not appear to have been an especially degraded class. They could own property, work for wages when their master did not need them, and even marry free women. Doubtless the great majority of them were of Sumerian nationality, a fact which helps to explain their rather liberal treatment.

Agriculture

Agriculture was the chief economic pursuit of most of the citizens, and the Sumerians were excellent farmers. By virtue of their knowledge of irrigation they produced amazing crops of cereal grains and subtropical fruits. Since most of the land was divided into large estates held by the rulers, the priests, and the army officers, the average rural citizen was either a tenant farmer or a serf. Commerce was the second most important source of the nation's wealth. A flourishing trade was established with all of the surrounding countries, revolving around the exchange of metals and timber from the north and west for the agricultural products and manufactured goods from the lower valley. Nearly all of the familiar adjuncts of business were highly developed; bills, receipts, notes, and letters of credit were regularly used. Custom required that deals should be confirmed by written agreements, signed by witnesses. Merchants employed salesmen who traveled to distant regions and sold goods on commission. In all major transactions bars or ingots of gold and silver served as money, the standard unit of exchange being the silver shekel, approximately equal in weight to a modern 50-cent piece but with a purchasing power much greater.

Sumerian law

The most distinctive achievement of the Sumerians was their system of law. It was the product of a gradual evolution out of local usage, but it was finally incorporated into a comprehensive code by Dungi after the middle of the third millennium. Only a few fragments of this law have survived in their original form, but the famous code of Hammurabi, the Babylonian king, is now recognized

Jeweled Headdress of Gold, Carnelian, and Glass. Egyptian, 1475 B.C.

Thutmose III as Amon, 1450 B.C. The Pharaoh wears the crown and the beard of the god, and carries a scimitar and the symbol of "life."

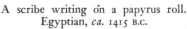

Silversmiths Working on a Stand and a Jar. Egyptian, *ca.* 1450 B.C.

Girl Musicians Playing a Harp, Lute, Pair of Oboes, and Lyre. Egyptian, *ca.* 1410 B.C.

arab or Beetle-Shaped Charm of Pharaoh, *ca.* 1395 B.C. The beetle as sacred in ancient Egypt.

Shawabty ("to answer") Figures, *ca.* 1400 B.C. These were put in the tomb to do any degrading work the rich man might be called upon to do in the next world. Rich men were buried with hundreds of such figures.

Painted Wood Shrine Box for Shawabty Figures. *Ca.* 1200 B.C.

ll pictures courtesy MMA.

Head of Ramses II, 1324–1258 B.C.

Part of the Egyptian "Book of the Dead." A collection of magic formulas to enable the deceased to gain admission to the kingdom of Re and to enjoy its eternal benefits.

Stela or Grave Marker. It shows the deceased being presented to the Sun god on his throne. She is holding her heart in her hand.

A hieroglyphic character for the idea "Millions of Years," 500–330 B.C.

Bronze Bull, Symbol of Strength. Arabian, VI cent. B.C.

A carved sandstone capital, *ca.* 370 B.C., representing a bundle of papyrus reeds.

All pictures courtesy MMA.

to have been nothing more than a revision of the code of Dungi.
Ultimately this code became the basis of the laws of nearly all of
the Semites—Babylonians, Assyrians, Chaldeans, and Hebrews.

The following may be regarded as the essential features of the
Sumerian law:

(1) The *lex talionis,* or law of retaliation in kind—"an eye for
an eye, a tooth for a tooth, a limb for a limb," etc.

(2) Semi-private administration of justice. It was incumbent upon
the victim himself or his family to bring the offender to justice. The
court served principally as an umpire in the dispute between the
plaintiff and defendant, not as an agency of the state to maintain
public security, although constables attached to the court might
assist in the execution of the sentence.

(3) Inequality before the law. The code divided the population
into three classes: patricians or aristocrats; burghers or commoners;
serfs and slaves. Penalties were graded according to the rank of the
victim, but also in some cases according to the rank of the offender.
The killing or maiming of a patrician was a much more serious
offense than a similar crime committed against a burgher or a slave.
On the other hand, when a patrician was the offender he was
punished *more severely* than a man of inferior status would be for
the same crime. The origin of this curious rule was probably to be
found in considerations of military discipline. Since the patricians
were army officers and therefore the chief defenders of the state,
they could not be permitted to give vent to their passions or to
indulge in riotous conduct.

(4) Inadequate distinction between accidental and intentional
homicide. A person responsible for killing another accidentally did
not escape penalty, as he would under modern law, but had to pay
a fine to the family of the victim, apparently on the theory that
children were the property of their fathers and wives the property
of their husbands.

Quite as much as their law the religion of the Sumerians illuminates
their social attitudes and the character of their culture. They did
not succeed in developing a very exalted religion; yet it occupied
an important place in their lives. To begin with, it was polytheistic
and anthropomorphic. They believed in a number of gods and
goddesses, each a distinct personality with human attributes. Shamash, the sun god; Enlil, the lord of the rain and wind; and Ishtar,
the goddess of the female principle in nature, were only a few of
them. Although the Sumerians had a special deity of the plague in
the person of the god Nergal, their religion was really monistic, in
the sense that they regarded all of their deities as capable of both
good and evil. Shamash, for example, as the god of the sun gave
warmth and light for the benefit of man; but he might also send
his burning rays to bake the soil and to wither the tender plants
before they had time to yield their fruits. Religious dualism, in-

The character of Sumerian religion

*A religion for
this world, not
for the next*

volving a belief in entirely separate divinities of good and evil, did
not appear in the Mesopotamian civilization until much later.

The Sumerian religion was a religion for this world exclusively;
it offered no hope for a life to come. The after-life was a mere
temporary existence in a dreary, shadowy place which later came
to be called Sheol. Here the ghosts of the dead lingered for a time,
perhaps a generation or so, and then disappeared. No one could
look forward to resurrection in another world and a joyous eternal
existence as a recompense for the evils of this life; the victory of the
grave was complete. In accordance with these beliefs the Sumerians
bestowed no particular care upon the bodies of their dead. No
mummification was practiced, and no elaborate tombs were built.
Corpses were commonly interred beneath the floor of the house
without a coffin and with very few articles for the use of the ghost.

*A religion
neither ethical
nor spiritual*

Neither spiritual nor ethical content had any place of conspicuous
importance in this religion. As we have seen, the gods were not
spiritual beings but creatures cast in the human mold, with most of
the weaknesses and passions of mortal men. Nor were the purposes
of the religion any more spiritual. It provided no blessings in the
form of solace, uplift of the soul, or oneness with God. If it benefited
man at all, it did so only in the form of material gain—abundant
harvests and prosperity in business. Similarly, the doctrines and
forms of worship were almost devoid of ethical significance. The
religion did not prescribe or enforce standards of morality. The
obligations imposed upon the individual were mainly ritualistic.
Though the gods were often angry with men and vented their wrath
upon them, that wrath was due not to breaches of the divine commandments, but to the failure of men to show proper respect to
the deities and to provide for their needs.

*The Creation
and Flood epics*

The true nature of the Sumerian religion is revealed in the famous
Creation and Flood epics, which provided the framework for the
much later Hebrew stories in the Old Testament. The Creation epic
related the magic triumph of the god Marduk over the jealous and
cowardly gods who had created him, the formation of the world
out of the body of one of his slain rivals, and finally, in order that
the gods might be fed, the making of man out of clay and dragon's
blood. The whole account was crude and revolting, with nothing
in it to appeal to a spiritual or moral sense. Almost as barbarous
was the Sumerian version of the Flood. Grown jealous of man, the
gods decided to destroy the whole race of mortals by drowning.
One of their number, however, betrayed the secret to a favorite
inhabitant of the earth, instructing him to build an ark for the salvation of himself and his kind. The flood raged for seven days, until
the whole earth was covered with water. Even the gods "crouched
like a dog on the wall." Finally the tumult was stilled and the waters
subsided. The favored man and his brothers came forth from the ark
and offered grateful sacrifice. Hungry from their long deprivation

Male Votive Figure, Sumer. This statue of white gypsum, colored with bitumen, shows the conventionalized treatment of hair and beard and the huge, staring eyes common to Mesopotamian art. Observe also the immense thumbs and the fingers of equal length.

of food, the gods "scented the sweet savour, and gathered like flies above the sacrifice," and decided never again to be so foolish as to risk the destruction of man.

In the field of intellectual endeavor the Sumerians achieved no great distinction. They did, however, produce a system of writing which was destined to be used for a thousand years after the downfall of their nation. This was the celebrated *cuneiform* writing, consisting of wedge-shaped characters imprinted on clay tablets with a square-tipped reed. Although at first a pictographic system, it was gradually transformed into an aggregate of syllabic and phonetic signs, some three hundred and fifty in number. No alphabet was ever developed out of it. The Sumerians wrote nothing that could be called philosophy, but they did make some feeble beginnings in science. They discovered the processes of multiplication and division and even the extraction of square and cube root. Their systems of numeration and of weights and measures were duodecimal, with the number sixty as the most common unit. They invented the water clock and the lunar calendar, the latter an inaccurate division of the year into months based upon cycles of the moon. In order to bring it into harmony with the solar year, an extra month had to be added from time to time. Astronomy was little more than astrology, and medicine was a curious compound of herbalism and magic. The repertory of the physician consisted primarily of charms to exorcise the evil spirits which were believed to be the cause of disease.

As artists the Sumerians excelled in metal work, gem carving, and sculpture. They produced some remarkable specimens of naturalistic

Intellectual achievements

71

Fragments of Jewelry Found at Ur in Two Graves of Ladies-in-Waiting to the Queen. The materials used are gold, carnelian, and lapis lazuli. Dating from 3500–2800 B.C., it is the oldest jewelry in the world.

art in their weapons, vessels, jewelry, and human and animal representations, which revealed alike a technical skill and a gift of imagination. Evidently religious conventions had not yet imposed any paralyzing influence, and consequently the artist was still free to follow his own impulses. Architecture, on the other hand, was distinctly inferior, probably because of the limitations enforced by the scarcity of good building materials. Since there was no stone in the valley, the architect had to depend upon sun-dried brick. The characteristic Sumerian edifice, extensively copied by their Semitic successors, was the *ziggurat*, a terraced tower set on a platform and surmounted by a shrine. Its construction was massive, its lines were monotonous, and little architectural ingenuity was exhibited in it. The royal tombs and private houses showed more originality. It was in them that the Sumerian inventions of the arch, the vault, and the dome were regularly employed, and the column was used occasionally.

Sumerian art

3. Old Babylonian "Contributions"

Although the Old Babylonians were an alien nation, they had lived long enough in close contact with the Sumerians to be influenced profoundly by them. They had no culture of their own worthy of the name when they came into the valley, and in general they simply appropriated what the Sumerians had already developed. With so excellent a foundation to build upon, they should have made remarkable progress; but such was not the case. When they ended their history, the state of civilization in the Tigris-Euphrates valley was no more advanced than when they began.

The shortcomings of the Old Babylonians

First among the significant changes which the Old Babylonians made in their cultural inheritance may be mentioned the political and legal. As military conquerors holding in subjection numerous vanquished nations, they found it necessary to establish a consolidated state. Vestiges of the old system of local autonomy were swept away, and the power of the king of Babylon was made supreme. A system of royal taxation was adopted as well as compulsory military service. The system of law was also changed to conform to the new conditions. The list of crimes against the state

Changes in the system of law

was enlarged, and the king's officers assumed a more active role in apprehending and punishing offenders, although it was still impossible for any criminal to be pardoned without the consent of the victim or the victim's family. The severity of penalties was decidedly increased, particularly for crimes involving any suggestion of treason or sedition. Such apparently trivial offenses as "gadding about" and "disorderly conduct of a tavern" were made punishable by death, probably on the assumption that they would be likely to foster disloyal activities. Whereas under the Sumerian law the harboring of fugitive slaves was punishable merely by a fine, the Babylonian law made it a capital crime. According to the Sumerian code, the slave who disputed his master's rights over him was to be sold; the Code of Hammurabi prescribed that he should have his ear cut off. Adultery was also made a capital offense, whereas under the Sumerian law it did not even necessarily result in divorce. In a few particulars the new system of law revealed some improvement. Wives and children sold for debt could not be held in bondage for longer than four years, while a female slave who had borne her master a child could not be sold at all.

The Old Babylonian laws also reflect a somewhat more extensive development of business than that which existed in the preceding culture. That those who traded for profit enjoyed a privileged position in society is evidenced by the fact that the commercial provisions of Hammurabi's code were based upon the principle of "Let the buyer beware." The Babylonian rulers did not believe in a regime of free competition, however. Trade, banking, and industry were subject to elaborate regulation by the state. There were laws regarding partnership, storage, and agency; laws respecting deeds, wills, and the taking of interest on money; and a great host of others. For a deal to be negotiated without a written contract or without witnesses was punishable by death. Agriculture, which was still the occupation of a majority of the citizens, did not escape regulation either. The code provided penalties for failure to cultivate a field and for neglect of dikes and canals. Both government ownership and private tenure of land were permitted; but, regardless of the status of the owner, the tenant farmer was required to pay two-thirds of all he produced as rent.

Economic development

Religion at the hands of the Old Babylonians underwent numerous changes both superficial and profound. Deities that had been venerated by the Sumerians were now neglected, and new ones exalted in their stead. Marduk, originally the local god of the town of Babylon, was elevated to the highest position in the pantheon. Ishtar remained the chief goddess. Tammuz, her brother and lover, who had been of no special significance in the Sumerian religion, now became the third most important divinity. His death in the autumn and resurrection in the spring symbolized the death and rebirth of vegetation. But the death and resurrection of the god had more than a symbolic meaning; vaguely at least they were con-

Changes in the religion

ceived as the real causes of the nature processes themselves, and the god's rites were a form of magic. They carried no spiritual significance, however, conveying no promise of the resurrection of man from the dead or of personal immortality. The Old Babylonians were no more otherworldly in their outlook than the Sumerians.

The increase in
superstition

Equally noteworthy was an increase in superstition. Astrology, divination, and other forms of magic took on added significance. A morbid consciousness of sin gradually displaced the essentially amoral attitude of the Sumerians. In addition, an increased emphasis was placed upon the worship of demons. Nergal, the god of the plague, came to be envisaged as a hideous monster seeking every chance to strike down his victims. Hordes of other demons and malevolent spirits lurked in the darkness and rode through the air bringing terror and destruction to all in their path. Against them there was no defense except sacrifices and magic charms. If the Old Babylonians did not invent witchcraft, they were at least the first "civilized" people to magnify it to serious proportions. Their laws invoked the death penalty against it, and there is evidence that the power of witches was widely feared. Whether the growth of demonology and witchcraft was due to the increasing unhealthfulness of the climate of the Tigris-Euphrates valley, or to the gloomy mentality of the people themselves, is a question which cannot be answered; but it is probable that the former is the chief explanation.

The decline
of intellect and
the arts

There seems to be little doubt that intellectually and artistically the Mesopotamian civilization suffered a partial decline during the period of Babylonian rule. This was not the first instance of cultural retrogression in history, but it was one of the most pronounced. Nothing of any importance was added to the scientific discoveries of the Sumerians, and some of them appear to have been neglected or forgotten. Literature showed some improvement over the earlier writings, especially in the famous Gilgamesh epic, a story of the mighty deeds of a supernatural adventurer. Although most of the legends themselves were of Sumerian origin, it was Babylonian poets who wove them into powerful descriptive style. A kind of prototype of the Book of Job, the so-called *Babylonian Job*, was also written in this period. It relates the story of a pious sufferer who is afflicted he knows not why, and it contains some mature reflections on the helplessness of man and the impenetrable mysteries of the universe.

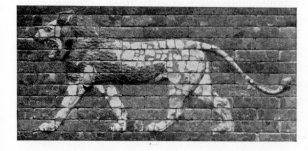

Panel of Glazed Brick, Babylon, Sixth Century B.C. An ornamental relief on a background of earth brown. The lion is in blue, white, and yellow glazes.

As an example of Oriental philosophy it is not without merit. The graphic arts, on the other hand, definitely deteriorated. The Babylonians lacked the creative interest and talent to duplicate the fresh and ingenious carving and engraving of the Sumerians. Moreover, sculpture fell under the domination of religious and political conventions, with the result that originality was stifled.

4. The Metamorphosis under Assyria

Of all the peoples of the Mesopotamian area after the time of the Sumerians, the Assyrians went through the most completely independent evolution. For several centuries they had lived a comparatively isolated existence on top of their small plateau in the upper valley of the Tigris. Eventually they came under the influence of the Babylonians, but not until after the course of their own history had been partially fixed. As a consequence, the period of Assyrian supremacy (from about 1300 B.C. to 612 B.C.) had more nearly a peculiar character than any other era of Mesopotamian history.

The evolution of Assyrian supremacy

The Assyrians were pre-eminently a nation of warriors; not because they were racially different from any of the other Semites, but because of the special conditions of their own environment. Their situation was strikingly similar to that of the modern Japanese, except that they lived on a plateau instead of on a group of islands. The limited resources of their original home and the constant danger of attack from hostile nations around them forced the development of warlike habits and imperial ambitions. It is therefore not strange that their greed for territory should have known no limits. The more they conquered, the more they felt they had to conquer, in order to protect what they had already gained. Every success excited ambition and riveted the chains of militarism more firmly than ever. Disaster was inevitable.

A nation of warriors

The exigencies of war determined the whole character of the Assyrian system. The state was a great military machine. The army commanders were at once the richest and the most powerful class in the country. Not only did they share in the plunder of war, but they were frequently granted huge estates as rewards for victory. At least one of them, Sargon II, dared to usurp the throne. The military establishment itself represented the last word in preparedness. The standing army greatly exceeded in size that of any other nation of the Near Orient. New and improved armaments and techniques of fighting gave to the Assyrian soldiers unparalleled advantages. Iron swords, heavy bows, long lances, battering rams, fortresses on wheels, and metal breastplates, shields, and helmets were only a few examples of their superior equipment.

Features of the Assyrian militarism

But swords and spears and engines of war were not their only instruments of combat. As much as anything else the Assyrians depended upon frightfulness as a means of overcoming their enemies.

Terrorism

75

Upon soldiers captured in battle, and sometimes upon non-combatants as well, they inflicted unspeakable cruelties—skinning them alive, impaling them on stakes, cutting off ears, noses, and sex organs, and then exhibiting the mutilated victims in cages for the benefit of cities that had not yet surrendered. Accounts of these cruelties are not taken from atrocity stories circulated by their enemies; they come from the records of the Assyrians themselves. Their chroniclers boasted of them as evidences of valor, and the people believed in them as guaranties of security and power. It is clear why the Assyrians were the most hated of all the nations of antiquity.

The tragedy of Assyrian militarism

There is much grist for the mill of the pacifist in the military history of Assyria. There has never been a better illustration of the unwisdom of conquest and the folly of brute force. Seldom has the decline of an empire been so swift and so complete; for in spite of her magnificent armaments and her wholesale destruction of her foes, Assyria's period of imperial splendor lasted little more than a century. Nation after nation conspired against her and finally accomplished her downfall. Her enemies took frightful vengeance. The whole land was so thoroughly sacked and the people so completely enslaved or exterminated that it has been difficult to trace any subsequent Assyrian influence upon history. The power and security which military strength was supposed to provide proved a mockery in the end. If Assyria had been utterly defenseless, her fate could not have been worse.

Neglect of the arts of peace

With so complete an absorption in military pursuits, it was inevitable that the Assyrians should have neglected in some measure the arts of peace. Such progress as they did make was largely conditioned by the factors of war. There was no further development of industry and commerce, for the Assyrians scorned such pursuits as beneath the dignity of a soldierly people. As compared with the thousands of business tablets left by the Old Babylonians, only a few hundred have ever been found at Nineveh. The minimum of manufacturing and trade which had to be carried on was left to the Arameans, a people closely related to the Phoenicians and the Hebrews. The Assyrians themselves preferred to derive their living from agriculture. The land system included both public and private holdings. The temples held the largest share of the landed wealth. Although the estates of the crown were likewise extensive, they were constantly being diminished by grants to the army officers. Numerous private citizens were also the owners of freehold estates.

Defects in the economic system

Neither the economic nor the social order was sound. The frequent military campaigns depleted the energies and resources of the nation. In the course of time the army officers became a pampered aristocracy, delegating their duties to their subordinates and devoting themselves to luxurious pleasures. The stabilizing influence of a prosperous and intelligent middle class was precluded by the rule that only foreigners could engage in commercial activities. Yet more

serious was the treatment accorded to the lower classes, the serfs
and the slaves. The former comprised the bulk of the rural population. Some of them cultivated definite portions of their master's
estates and retained a part of what they produced for themselves.
Others were "empty" men, without even a plot to cultivate and
dependent on the need for seasonal labor to provide for their means
of subsistence. All were extremely poor and were subject to the
additional hardships of labor on the public works and compulsory
military service. The slaves, who were chiefly an urban working
class, were really of two different types: the domestic slaves, who
performed household duties and sometimes engaged in business for
their masters; and the war captives. The former were not numerous
and were allowed a great deal of freedom, even to the extent of
owning property. The latter suffered much greater miseries. Bound
by heavy shackles, they were compelled to labor to the point of
exhaustion in building roads, canals, and palaces.

Whether the Assyrians adopted the law of the Old Babylonians
has never been settled. Undoubtedly they were influenced by it, but
several of the features of Hammurabi's code are entirely absent. *Assyrian law*
Notable among these are the *lex talionis* and the system of gradation
of penalties according to the rank of the victim and the offender.
Whereas the Babylonians prescribed the most drastic punishments
for crimes suggestive of treason or sedition, the Assyrians reserved
theirs for such offenses as abortion and unnatural vice, probably
for the military reason of preventing a decline in the birth rate.
Another contrast is the more complete subjection of Assyrian
women. Wives were treated as chattels of their husbands, the right
of divorce was placed entirely in the hands of the male, a plurality
of wives was permitted, and all married women were forbidden
to appear in public with their faces unveiled. Here, according to
Professor Olmstead, was the beginning of the Oriental seclusion
of women.[3]

That a military nation like the Assyrians should not have taken
first rank in intellectual achievement is easily understandable. The
atmosphere of a military campaign is not favorable to reflection or *Scientific*
disinterested research. Yet the demands of successful campaigning *achievements*
may lead to a certain accumulation of knowledge, for practical
problems have to be solved. Under such circumstances the Assyrians
accomplished some measure of scientific progress. They appear to
have divided the circle into 360 degrees and to have estimated locations on the surface of the earth in something resembling latitude
and longitude. They recognized and named five planets and achieved
some success in predicting eclipses. Since the health of armies is
important, medicine received considerable attention. More than five
hundred drugs, both vegetable and mineral, were catalogued and
their uses indicated. Symptoms of various diseases were described
and were generally interpreted as due to natural causes, although

[3] A. T. E. Olmstead, *History of Assyria*, p. 553.

The Lion Hunt. A typical specimen of Assyrian sculpture in relief. The Assyrians were masters in depicting scenes of violence and animal ferocity.

incantations and the prescription of disgusting compounds to drive out demons were still commonly employed as methods of treatment.

In the domain of art the Assyrians surpassed the Old Babylonians and at least equaled the work of the Sumerians, although in different form. Sculpture was the art most highly developed, particularly in the low reliefs. These portrayed dramatic incidents of war and the hunt with the utmost fidelity to nature and a vivid description of movement. The Assyrians delighted in depicting the cool bravery of the hunter in the face of terrific danger, the ferocity of lions at bay, and the death agonies of wounded beasts. Unfortunately this art was limited almost entirely to the two themes of war and sport. Its purpose was to glorify the exploits of the ruling class. Architecture ranked second to sculpture from the standpoint of artistic excellence. Assyrian palaces and temples were built of stone, obtained from the mountainous areas of the north, instead of the mud brick of former times. Their principal features were the arch and the dome. The column was also used but never very successfully. The chief demerit of this architecture was its hugeness, which the Assyrians appeared to regard as synonymous with beauty.

Assyrian culture reached its height in the seventh century during the reign of Assurbanipal. A man of considerable refinement, he was almost the only ruler of the nation to devote any attention to the patronage of learning and the arts. He ordered his scribes to collect all the copies of Babylonian writings that could be found on every conceivable subject and bring them to the royal library at Nineveh. Where necessary he authorized revisions to be made in order to bring the ancient learning into harmony with more recent

The excellence of Assyrian art

Assurbanipal, patron of culture

Assyrian Winged Bull, now in Oriental Institute, University of Chicago. Its precise significance is unknown, but it may have been intended to symbolize the Assyrian militarists' worship of strength and speed.

knowledge. Under Assurbanipal's patronage the royal library came to contain more than 22,000 tablets. Many of them were magic formulas, but included in the lot were thousands of letters, business documents, and military chronicles. The king himself was the author of an autobiography and of numerous letters that displayed some literary talent. But the most important of the original compositions of the Assyrians were their narratives of military campaigns, which, in their highly embellished and deliberately exaggerated form, represent one of the earliest attempts at patriotic historical writing.

5. The Chaldean Renascence

The Mesopotamian civilization entered its final stage with the overthrow of Assyria and the establishment of Chaldean supremacy. This stage is often called the Neo-Babylonian, because Nebuchadnezzar and his followers restored the capital at Babylon and attempted to revive the culture of Hammurabi's time. As might have been expected, their attempt was not wholly successful. The Assyrian metamorphosis had altered that culture in various profound and ineffaceable ways. Besides, the Chaldeans themselves had a history of their own which they could not entirely escape. Nevertheless, they did manage to revive certain of the old institutions and ideals. They restored the ancient law and literature, the essentials of the Old Babylonian form of government, and the economic system of their supposed ancestors with its dominance of industry and trade. Farther than this they were unable to go.

The Chaldean or final stage in Mesopotamian civilization

It was in religion that the failure of the Chaldean renascence was most conspicuous. Although Marduk was restored to his traditional place at the head of the pantheon, the system of belief was little more than superficially Babylonian. What the Chaldeans really did was to develop an astral religion. The gods were divested of their limited human qualities and exalted into transcendent, omnipotent beings. They were actually identified with the planets themselves. Marduk became Jupiter, Ishtar became Venus, and so on. Though

The astral religion of the Chaldeans

79

still not entirely aloof from man, they certainly lost their character as beings who could be cajoled and threatened and coerced by magic. They ruled the universe almost mechanically. While their immediate intentions were sometimes discernible, their ultimate purposes were inscrutable.

The growth of fatalism

Two significant results flowed from these amazing conceptions. The first was an attitude of fatalism. Since the ways of the gods were past finding out, all that man could do was to resign himself to his fate. It behooved him therefore to submit absolutely to the gods, to trust in them implicitly, in the vague hope that the results in the end would be good. Thus arose for the first time in history the conception of piety as submission—a conception which was adopted in several other religions, as we shall see in succeeding chapters. For the Chaldeans it implied no otherworldly significance; one did not resign himself to calamities in this life in order to be justified in the next. The Chaldeans had no interest in a life to come. Submission might bring certain earthly rewards, but in the main, as they conceived it, it was not a means to an end at all. It was rather the expression of an attitude of despair, of humility in the face of mysteries that could not be fathomed.

The development of a spiritual consciousness

The second great result which came from the growth of an astral religion was the development of a stronger spiritual consciousness. This is revealed in the penitential hymns of unknown authors and in the prayers which were ascribed to Nebuchadnezzar and other kings as the spokesmen for the nation. In most of them the gods are addressed as exalted beings who are concerned with justice and righteous conduct on the part of men, although the distinction between ceremonial and genuine morality is not always sharply drawn. It has been asserted by one author that these hymns could have been used by the Hebrews with little modification except for the substitution of the name of Yahweh for that of the Chaldean god.[4]

The abasement of man

With the gods promoted to so lofty a plane, it was perhaps inevitable that man should have been abased. Creatures possessed of mortal bodies could not be compared with the transcendent, passionless beings who dwelt in the stars and guided the destinies of the earth. Man was a lowly creature, sunk in iniquity and vileness, and hardly even worthy of approaching the gods. The consciousness of sin already present in the Babylonian and Assyrian religions now reached a stage of almost pathological intensity. In the hymns the sons of men are compared to prisoners, bound hand and foot, languishing in darkness. Their transgressions are "seven times seven." Their misery is increased by the fact that their evil nature has prompted them to sin unwittingly.[5] Never before had men been

[4] Morris Jastrow, *The Civilization of Babylonia and Assyria*, p. 217.
[5] *Ibid.*, pp. 471-74.

regarded as so hopelessly depraved, nor had religion been fraught
with so gloomy a view of life.

Curiously enough, the pessimism of the Chaldeans does not appear to have affected their morality very much. So far as the
evidence goes, they indulged in no rigors of asceticism. They did *Chaldean*
not mortify the flesh, nor did they even practice self-denial. Ap- *morality*
parently they took it for granted that man could not avoid sinning,
no matter how hard he tried. They seem to have been just as deeply
engrossed in the material interests of life and in the pursuit of the
pleasures of sense as any of the earlier nations. Indeed, it seems
that they were even more greedy and sensual. Occasional references
were made in their prayers and hymns to reverence, kindness, and
purity of heart as virtues, and to oppression, slander, and anger as
vices, but these were intermingled with ritualistic conceptions of
cleanness and uncleanness and with expressions of desire for physical
satisfactions. When the Chaldeans prayed, it was not always that
their gods would make them good, but more often that they would
grant long years, abundant offspring, and luxurious living.

Aside from religion, the Chaldean culture differed from that of
the Sumerians, Babylonians, and Assyrians chiefly in regard to
scientific achievements. Without doubt the Chaldeans were the *Chaldean*
most capable scientists in all of Mesopotamian history, although *science*
their accomplishments were limited primarily to astronomy. They
worked out the most elaborate system for recording the passage of
time which had yet been devised, with their invention of the seven-
day week and their division of the day into twelve double-hours
of 120 minutes each. They kept accurate records of their observation of eclipses and other celestial occurrences for more than 350
years—until long after the downfall of their empire. Two of their
most spectacular achievements were made by individual astronomers
whose names have come down to us. In the sixth century Nabu-
Rimannu calculated the correct length of the year within about
twenty-six minutes, and about a hundred years later Kidinnu discovered and proved the periodic change in the inclination of the
earth's axis.

The motivating force behind Chaldean astronomy was religion.
The chief purpose of mapping the heavens and collecting astronomical data was to discover the future which the gods had prepared for *The religious*
the race of men. Since the planets were gods themselves, that future *basis of Chal-*
could best be divined in the movements of the heavenly bodies. *dean science*
Astronomy was therefore primarily astrology. Sciences other than
astronomy continued in a backward state, probably because they
were not definitely related to religion. Medicine in particular showed
little advance beyond the stage it had reached under the Assyrians.
The same was true of the remaining aspects of Chaldean culture.
Art differed only in its greater magnificence. Literature, dominated

by the antiquarian spirit, revealed a monotonous lack of originality. The writings of the Old Babylonians were extensively copied and re-edited, but they were supplemented by little that was new.

6. The Mesopotamian Legacy

Mesopotamian influence: (1) upon the modern world

Notwithstanding the relatively inferior quality of the Mesopotamian civilization, its influence has been scarcely less than that of Egypt. From one or another of the four Mesopotamian nations we get a considerable number of our most common culture elements: the seven-day week; the fact that the dials on our watches and clocks contain numerals up to twelve, corresponding to the Chaldean division of the day into twelve double-hours; the belief in horoscopes; the superstition of planting crops according to the phases of the moon; the twelve signs of the zodiac; the circle of 360 degrees; and the arithmetical process of multiplication.

(2) upon the Persians, Phoenicians, Canaanites, and Hebrews

The influence exerted upon various nations of antiquity was even more significant. The Persians were profoundly affected by Chaldean culture. The Hittites, who aided the Kassites in overthrowing the Babylonians about 1750 B.C., adopted the clay tablets, the cuneiform writing, the Gilgamesh epic, and much of the religion of the nation they conquered. The Babylonian religion also had its effect upon the Phoenicians, as is evidenced by their worship of Astarte (Ishtar) and Tammuz. From the Sumerians or Old Babylonians the Canaanites derived a large part of their law as well as a good many of their religious beliefs. But the principal heirs of Mesopotamian culture were the Hebrews. Possibly as far back as 1800 B.C. some of their ancestors had lived for a time in the northwestern portion of the valley between the two rivers. Numerous Mesopotamian traits were also acquired indirectly through contact with the Canaanites and Phoenicians. It was probably in this manner that the Hebrews came into possession of the Creation and Flood legends and a system of law which had its ultimate origin in the Mesopotamian civilization. An even greater influence was exerted during the period of the Captivity, from 586 to 539 B.C. During these years the Jews were brought into direct association for the first time with a rich and powerful nation. In spite of their hatred of their captors they unconsciously adopted many of their ways. There is evidence, for example, that they acquired some of the Chaldean penchant for trade. In addition, much of the symbolism, pessimism, fatalism, and demonology of the Chaldeans passed into the religion of Judah, transforming it markedly from the character it had had in the time of the Prophets.[6]

Mesopotamian institutions and beliefs also exerted their influence upon the Greeks and the Romans, although for the most part in-

[6] The Hebrew calendar to this day contains a month named in honor of the god Tammuz.

directly. The Stoic philosophy with its doctrines of determinism and pessimism may have reflected that influence in some measure, since its originator, Zeno, was a Semite, probably a Phoenician. A better case could possibly be made for the Mesopotamian origin of such Roman practices as divination, worship of the planets as gods, and the use of the arch and the vault. Several of these elements were introduced to the Romans by the Etruscans, a people of western Asiatic origin. Others were brought in by the Romans themselves as a result of their military campaigns in Asia Minor. That there were natives of the Mesopotamian region resident in Rome, in the later centuries of her history at least, is evidenced by the fact that the Romans used the name "Chaldeans" as synonymous with "astrologers" and sought the aid of such persons on numerous occasions in divining the future.

Selected Readings

Cambridge Ancient History, Vols. I and III

Contenau, G., *Everyday Life in Babylonia and Assyria*, New York, 1954

Delaporte, L. J., *Mesopotamia: The Babylonian and Assyrian Civilization*, New York, 1925

Frankfort, Henri, *The Birth of Civilization in the Near East*, Bloomington, 1951

———, *The Intellectual Adventure of Ancient Man*, Chicago, 1946

Hall, H. R., and Woolley, C. L., *Ur Excavations*, Philadelphia, 1927–39, 5 vols.

Hogarth, D. G., *The Ancient East*, New York, 1915

Hrozny, Bedrich, *Ancient History of Western Asia, India and Crete*, Prague, 1953

Jastrow, Morris, *The Civilization of Babylonia and Assyria*, Philadelphia, 1915

Johns, C. H. W., *Relations between the Laws of Babylonia and the Laws of the Hebrew Peoples*, New York, 1915

Olmstead, A. T. E., *History of Assyria*, New York, 1923

Woolley, C. L., *The Sumerians*, New York, 1928

Source Materials

Barton, G. A., *The Royal Inscriptions of Sumer and Akkad*

Harper, R. F., ed. and tr., *Assyrian and Babylonian Literature*

———, ed., *The Code of Hammurabi*

Johns, C. H. W., *Assyrian Deeds and Documents*, 4 vols.

Luckenbill, D. D., ed., *Ancient Records of Assyria and Babylonia*, 2 vols.

Rogers, R. W., ed. and tr., *Cuneiform Parallels to the Old Testament*, 2 vols.

The Civilization of Ancient Persia

Persia produces a new civilization

The Chaldeans, as we have seen, were the last of the nations with a culture essentially Mesopotamian. In 539 B.C. the Persians conquered the valley of the two rivers and soon afterward the whole empire of the Chaldean kings. But the Persians established what was really a new civilization. While they adopted much from the Chaldeans, they made no effort to preserve the old culture intact, and they introduced a great many new elements from other sources. Their religion was entirely different, while their art was compounded of elements taken from nearly every people they conquered. Neither did they continue the Chaldean interest in science nor the development of business and industry. Finally, it should be remembered that the empire of the Persians included a great many territories which had never been subject to the Chaldean kings.

1. The Empire and Its History

The Persian background

Comparatively little is known of the Persians before the sixth century B.C. Up to that time they appear to have led an obscure and peaceful existence on the eastern shore of the Persian Gulf. Their homeland afforded only modest advantages. On the east it was hemmed in by high mountains, and its coast line was destitute of harbors. The fertile valleys of the interior, however, were capable of providing a generous subsistence for a limited population. Save for the development of an elaborate religion, the people had made little progress. They had no system of writing, but they did have a spoken language closely related to Sanskrit and to the languages of ancient and modern Europe. It is for this reason alone and not because of race that they are accurately referred to as an Indo-European people. At the dawn of their history they were not an independent nation but were vassals of the Medes, a kindred people who ruled over a great empire north and east of the Tigris River.

In 559 B.C. a prince by the name of Cyrus became king of a southern Persian tribe. About five years later he made himself ruler of all the Persians and then developed an ambition for dominion over neighboring peoples. As Cyrus the Great he has gone down in history as one of the most sensational conquerors of all time. Within the short space of twenty years he founded a vast empire, larger than any that had previously existed. It is impossible to believe that his successes were due entirely to the force of his own personality. To begin with, he was accepted by the Medes as their king soon after he became ruler of the Persians. The reasons for this are not entirely known. According to various traditions he was the grandson or the son-in-law of the Median king. Perhaps a vague feeling of national kinship impelled Medes and Persians to unite under a common leader. At any rate, Cyrus' "conquest" of the Medes was achieved with such slight opposition that it meant little more than a change of dynasties. Cyrus profited also from the dissension within the Chaldean state, as we noted in the preceding chapter, and from the decrepit condition of other Near Eastern empires. Moreover, the geographic conditions of the Persian homeland were particularly conducive to expansion. The limited area of fertile land, the lack of other resources, and the rich bordering countries inviting conquest were factors which made it virtually inevitable that the nation would break through the confines of its original territory just as soon as the pinch of poverty began to be felt.

The rise of Cyrus

The first of the real conquests of Cyrus was the kingdom of Lydia, which occupied the western half of Asia Minor and was separated from the lands of the Medes only by the Halys River, in what is now northern Turkey. Perceiving the ambitions of the Persians, Croesus, the famous Lydian king, determined to wage a preventive war to preserve his own nation from conquest. He formed alliances with Egypt and Sparta and then consulted the Greek oracle at Delphi as to the advisability of an immediate attack. According to Herodotus, the oracle replied that if he would cross the Halys and assume the offensive he would destroy a great army. He did, but that army was his own. His forces were completely overwhelmed, and his prosperous little kingdom was annexed as a province of the Persian state. Seven years later, in 539 B.C., Cyrus took advantage of discontent and conspiracies in the Chaldean empire to capture the city of Babylon. His victory was an easy one, for he had the assistance of the Jews within the city and of the Chaldean priests, who were dissatisfied with the policies of their king. The conquest of the Chaldean capital made possible the rapid extension of control

The conquests of Cyrus

over the whole empire and thereby added the Fertile Crescent to the domains of Cyrus.

The great conqueror died in 529 B.C., apparently as the result of wounds received in a war with barbarian tribes. Soon afterward a succession of troubles overtook the state he had founded. Like so many other empire builders both before and since, he had devoted too much energy to conquest and not enough to internal development. He was succeeded by his son Cambyses, who conquered Egypt in 525 B.C. During the new king's absence revolt spread throughout his Asiatic possessions. Chaldeans, Elamites, and even the Medes strove to regain their independence. The chief minister of the realm, abetted by the priests, organized a movement to gain possession of the throne for a pretender who was one of their puppets. Upon learning of conditions at home, Cambyses set out from Egypt with his most dependable troops, but he was murdered on the way. The most serious of the revolts was finally crushed by Darius, a powerful noble, who killed the pretender and seized the throne for himself.

Darius I, or the Great, as he is somewhat inaccurately called, ruled over the empire from 521 to 486 B.C. The early years of his reign were occupied in suppressing the revolts of subject peoples and in improving the administrative organization of the state. In both of these tasks he achieved considerable success, but his ambitions for power carried him a little too far. Under the pretext of checking the incursions of the Scythians, he crossed the Hellespont, conquered a large part of the Thracian coast, and thereby aroused the hostility of the Athenians. In addition, he increased the oppression of the Ionian Greeks on the shore of Asia Minor, who had fallen under Persian domination with the conquest of Lydia. He interfered with their trade, collected heavier tribute from them, and forced them to serve in his armies. The immediate result was a revolt of the Ionian cities with the assistance of Athens. And when Darius attempted to punish the Athenians for their part in the rebellion, he found himself involved in a war with nearly all the states of Greece.

The decisive defeat of the Persians in this war proved to be the turning point in their history. The offensive power of the empire was now definitely shattered, and since the interests of the people had been centered upon military glory, the one unifying influence was broken. The nation sank slowly into stagnation and decay. The last century and a half of its existence was marked by frequent assassinations, revolts of provincial governors, and barbarian invasions, until finally in 330 B.C. its independence was annihilated by the armies of Alexander the Great.

Much has been written about the liberality and efficiency of the Persian government, but it seems doubtful that it was greatly superior to the governments of some earlier empires. While it is true

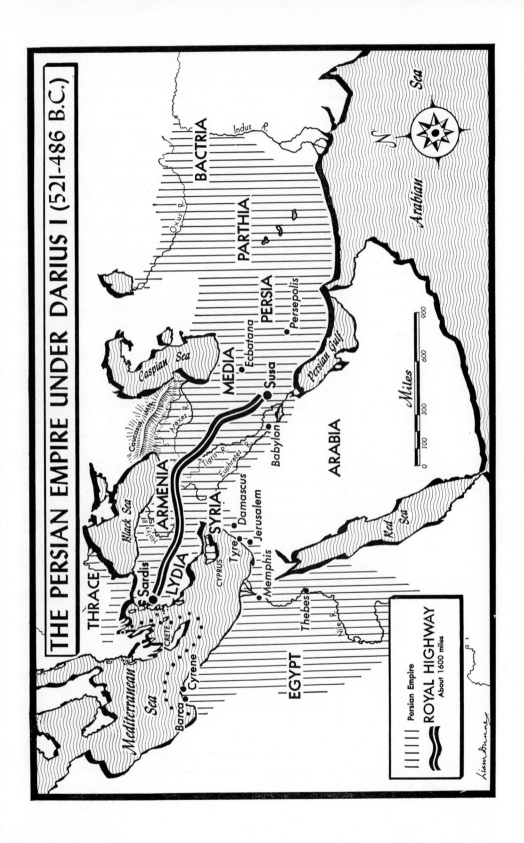

THE PERSIAN EMPIRE UNDER DARIUS I (521-486 B.C.)

BACTRIA

Indus R.

PARTHIA

Oxus R.

PERSIA

Persepolis

MEDIA

Ecbatana

Susa

Caspian Sea

Araxes R.

Persian Gulf

Caucasus Mts.

ARMENIA

Tigris R.

Euphrates R.

Babylon

ARABIA

LYDIA

SYRIA

Damascus

Jerusalem

THRACE

Black Sea

Halys R.

Sardis

CYPRUS

Tyre

Memphis

CRETE

Mediterranean Sea

Barca

Cyrene

Thebes

Nile R.

EGYPT

Red Sea

Arabian Sea

N

Miles
0   100   300   600   900

ROYAL HIGHWAY
About 1600 miles

Persian Empire

Liam Dunne

that neither Cyrus nor any of his successors imitated the terrorism of the Assyrians, the policies of the Persian despots were not free from oppression. Otherwise it would be difficult to account for the frequency of insurrections against them. After all, they did levy tribute upon conquered nations—to the extent of 700 talents of silver annually from Egypt and 1000 talents from Chaldea [1]—to say nothing of forcing their citizens to serve in the army and excluding them from offices of government. Disadvantages like these were scarcely counterbalanced by the privilege of retaining local customs, laws, and religions, which the Persians accorded to the peoples they subjugated.

In theory the Persian king was an absolute monarch ruling by the grace of the god of light. No constitution or principles of justice limited his sovereign authority. In practice he was required to defer to the chief nobles of the realm and to pay some regard to ancient customs, to the traditional laws of the Medes and Persians. For purposes of local government the empire was divided into twenty-one provinces, each under a satrap or civil governor. Although supreme in all matters of civil jurisdiction, the satrap had no military authority. Military powers were entrusted to the commander of the garrisons throughout the province. As an additional safeguard, a secretary for each province was appointed to examine the mail of the satrap and to report any evidences of disloyalty. And, finally, to make assurance doubly sure, the king sent out special inspectors once a year with a powerful guard to visit each province and investigate the conduct of the government. These officials, known as the "Eyes and Ears of the King," were generally members of the royal family or others whom the monarch could especially trust. Elaborate and costly though this system was, it worked so ineffectively that rebellions of the satraps were among the principal causes of Persia's downfall.

Nearly all the activities of the imperial government were directed to the ends of military efficiency and political security. Darius I, in particular, made efforts to train the young men of Persian birth in habits which would fit them for the soldierly life. He sought to instill in the upper classes the virtues of austerity, loyalty, and honor and to keep them from succumbing to luxury and vice. In the end all his efforts were in vain, for the Persians no more than the Assyrians could withstand the temptations of sudden power and wealth. Another of the conspicuous activities of the government was the construction of a marvelous system of roads, the best ever built before the time of the Romans. Most famous was the Royal Road, some 1600 miles in length, which connected Susa near the Persian Gulf

[1] A talent was a unit of weight rather than coinage, and varied from country to country and from time to time. The Persians, if they used the Hebrew-Babylonian talent, were levying about 1.6 million ounces of silver from Chaldea and about 1.1 million ounces from Egypt. Silver in 1957 was selling at about 91 cents per ounce.

with Sardis in Asia Minor. So well kept was this highway that the king's messengers, traveling day and night, could cover its entire length in less than a week. Nearly every province was linked with one or another of the four Persian capitals: Susa, Persepolis, Babylon, and Ecbatana. Although they naturally contributed to ease of trade, the highways were all built primarily to facilitate control over the outlying sections of the empire.

2. Persian Culture

The culture of the Persians, in the narrower sense of intellectual and artistic achievements, was largely derived from that of previous civilizations. Much of it came from Mesopotamia, but a great deal *The eclectic* of it from Egypt, and some from Lydia and northern Palestine. *culture of* Their system of writing was originally the Babylonian cuneiform, *Persia* but in time they devised an alphabet of thirty-nine letters, based upon the alphabet of the Arameans who traded within their borders. In science they accomplished nothing, except to adopt with some slight modifications the solar calendar of the Egyptians and to encourage exploration as an aid to commerce. They deserve credit also for diffusing a knowledge of the Lydian coinage throughout many parts of western Asia.

It was the architecture of the Persians, however, which gave the most positive expression of the eclectic character of their culture. They copied the raised platform and the terraced building style *The eclectic* which had been so common in Babylonia and Assyria. They imitated *character* also the winged bulls, the brilliantly colored glazed bricks, and *of Persian art*

The Great Palace of Darius and Xerxes at Persepolis. Shown here is the Eastern Stairway with the Gate of Xerxes on the right. Persian architects made use of fluted columns, probably copied from the Greeks, and reliefs resembling those of the Assyrians.

other decorative motifs of Mesopotamian architecture. But at least two of the leading features of Mesopotamian construction were not used by the Persians at all—the arch and the vault. In place of them they adopted the column and the colonnade from Egypt. Such matters as interior arrangement and the use of palm and lotus designs at the base of columns also point very distinctly toward Egyptian influence. On the other hand, the fluting of the columns and the volutes or scrolls beneath the capitals were not Egyptian but Greek, adopted not from the mainland of Greece itself but from the Ionian cities of Asia Minor. If there was anything unique about Persian architecture, it was the fact that it was purely secular. The great Persian structures were not temples but palaces. The most famous were the magnificent residences of Darius and Xerxes at

Reliefs from the Staircase at Persepolis. Pictured here are conquered peoples bringing tribute to the Persian king. The various nationalities differ only in styles of dress.

Persepolis. The latter, built in imitation of the temple at Karnak, had an enormous central audience-hall containing a hundred columns and surrounded by innumerable rooms which served as offices and as quarters for the eunuchs and members of the royal harem.

3. The Zoroastrian Religion

The religion of the Persians

By far the most enduring influence left by the ancient Persians was that of their religion. Their system of faith was of ancient origin. It was already highly developed when they began their conquests. And so strong was its appeal, and so ripe were the conditions for its acceptance, that it spread through most of western Asia. Its doctrines turned other religions inside out, displacing beliefs which had been held for ages. The world outlook of nations to this day has been both uplifted and perverted by it.

Although the roots of this religion can be traced as far back as the fifteenth century B.C., its real founder was Zoroaster,[2] who ap-

[2] "Zoroaster" is the corrupt Greek form of the Persian name Zarathustra.

pears to have lived about one hundred years before the Persians
established their empire. From him the religion derives its name of
Zoroastrianism. He seems to have conceived it to be his mission to
purify the traditional beliefs of his people—to eradicate polytheism,
animal sacrifice, and magic and to establish their worship on a more
spiritual and ethical plane. That the movement he led was the
natural accompaniment of the transition to a more civilized agricultural existence is revealed in his teaching of reverence for the cow
and in his prescription of cultivation of the soil as a sacred duty.
In spite of his reforming efforts many of the old superstitions survived (as they usually do), and were gradually fused with the new
ideals.

*The founding of
Zoroastrianism*

In many respects Zoroastrianism had a character unique among
the religions of the world up to that time. First of all, it was dualistic
—not monistic like the Sumerian and Babylonian religions, in which
the same gods were capable of both good and evil; nor did it make
any pretensions to monotheism, or belief in a single divinity, as did
the late Egyptian and Hebrew religions. Two great deities ruled
over the universe: one, Ahura-Mazda,[3] supremely good and incapable of any wickedness, embodied the principles of light, truth,
and righteousness; the other, Ahriman, treacherous and malignant,
presided over the forces of darkness and evil. The two were engaged
in a desperate struggle for supremacy. Although they were about
evenly matched in strength, the god of light would eventually
triumph, and the world would be saved from the powers of darkness.

*Characteristics
of
Zoroastrianism:
(1) dualism*

In the second place, Zoroastrianism was an eschatological religion.
"Eschatology" is the doctrine of last or final things. It includes
such ideas as the coming of a messiah, the resurrection of the dead,
a last judgment, and the translation of the redeemed into a paradise
eternal. According to the Zoroastrian belief the world would endure
for twelve thousand years. At the end of nine thousand years the
second coming of Zoroaster would occur as a sign and a promise
of the ultimate redemption of the good. This would be followed in
due course by the miraculous birth of Saoshyant, the messiah, whose
work would be the perfection of the good as a preparation for the
end of the world. Finally the last great day would arrive when
Ahura-Mazda would overpower Ahriman and cast him down into
the abyss. The dead would then be raised from their graves to be
judged according to their deserts. The righteous would enter into
immediate bliss, while the wicked would be sentenced to the flames
of hell. Ultimately, though, all would be saved; for the Persian
hell, unlike the Christian, did not last forever.

*(2) eschatolog-
ical beliefs*

From what has been said already, the inference will readily be
drawn that the Zoroastrian religion was definitely an ethical one.
Although it contained suggestions of predestination, of the election

*(3) an ethical
religion*

[3] The name was frequently abbreviated to Mazda.

of some from all eternity to be saved, in the main it rested upon the assumption that men possessed free will, that they were free to sin or not to sin, and that they would be rewarded or punished in the after-life in accordance with their conduct on earth. The virtues commended by the religion made an imposing list. Some were obviously of economic or political origin: diligence, the keeping of contracts, obedience to rulers, the begetting of numerous offspring, and tilling the soil ("He who sows corn sows holiness"). Others had a broader significance: Ahura-Mazda commanded that men should be truthful, that they should love and help one another to the best of their power, that they should befriend the poor and practice hospitality. The essence of these broader virtues was perhaps expressed in another of the god's decrees: "Whosoever shall give meat to one of the faithful . . . he shall go to Paradise."

*The principal
sins*

The forms of conduct forbidden were sufficiently numerous and varied to cover the whole list of the Seven Cardinal Sins of medieval Christianity and a great many more. Pride, gluttony, sloth, covetousness, wrathfulness, lust, adultery, abortion, slander, and waste were among the more typical. The taking of interest on loans to others of the same faith was described as the "worst of sins," and the accumulation of riches was strongly discountenanced. The restraints which men were to practice included also a kind of negative Golden Rule: "That nature alone is good which shall not do unto another whatever is not good for its own self." It is pertinent to add that the original Zoroastrianism condemned the ascetic way of life. Self-inflicted suffering, fasting, and even excessive grief were prohibited on the ground that they injured both mind and body and rendered human beings unfit for the duties of agriculture and the begetting of children. Temperance rather than complete abstinence was the traditional Persian ideal.[4]

*(4) a revealed
religion*

Zoroastrianism is especially significant because it was a revealed religion—apparently the first of its type in the history of the Western world. Its followers were believed to be the exclusive possessors of truth; not because they were wiser than other men, but because they shared the secrets of the god. As members of his substance they automatically partook of his wisdom; not in its entirety, of course, but certain portions of it. The truth which they possessed was therefore occult. It could not be deduced by logic or discovered by investigation. Part of it was in the form of sacred writings—the *Avesta*, believed to have been sent down from heaven —but much of it consisted of an oral revelation received by Zoroaster from Mazda and transmitted to his disciples. Contrary to the general opinion, revealed religions have not been so common in the Western world. The Egyptians had no bible or any other Word of God, and neither did the Mesopotamian nations. Likewise, the re-

---

[4] The quotations in the last two paragraphs are taken from J. O. Hertzler, *The Social Thought of the Ancient Civilizations*, pp. 149–158.

ligions of Greece and Rome rested upon no Truth vouchsafed by the gods. Zoroastrianism, Judaism, Christianity, and Islam are the only faiths, with the possible exception of Hinduism, which have had divine revelation as one of their essential elements. Without doubt this has been a factor augmenting their strength, but it has accounted in some measure also for their dogmatism and intolerance.

4. The Mystical and Otherworldly Heritage from Persia

The religion of the Persians as taught by Zoroaster did not long continue in its original state. It was corrupted, first of all, by the persistence of primitive superstitions, of magic and priestcraft. The *The fusion of* farther the religion spread, the more of these relics of barbarism *Zoroastrianism* were engrafted upon it. As the years passed, additional modification *with alien* resulted from the influence of alien faiths, particularly that of the *faiths* Chaldeans. The outcome in the end was the growth of a powerful synthesis in which the primitive priestliness, messianism, and dualism of the Persians were combined with the pessimism and fatalism of the Neo-Babylonians.

Out of this synthesis gradually emerged a profusion of cults, alike in their basic dogmas but according them different emphasis. The oldest of these cults was Mithraism, deriving its name from Mithras, *Mithraism* the chief lieutenant of Mazda in the struggle against the powers of evil. At first only a minor deity in the religion of Zoroastrianism, Mithras finally won recognition in the hearts of many of the Persians as the god most deserving of worship. The reason for this change was probably the emotional appeal made by the incidents of his career. He was believed to have been born of a rock in the presence of a small group of shepherds, who brought him gifts in token of their reverence for his great mission on earth. He then proceeded to subdue all the living creatures around him, taming many of them and rendering them useful to man. The better to accomplish his purpose, he entered into a compact with the sun, obtaining warmth and light that agriculture might flourish. But the most important of his exploits was the capture of the divine bull. Seizing the animal by the horns, he struggled desperately until he had forced him into a cave, where in obedience to a command from the sun he slew him. From the blood and flesh of the bull came all manner of herbs, grain, and other plants valuable to man. No sooner had these things been accomplished than Ahriman produced a drought on the earth; but Mithras thrust his spear into a rock and the waters gushed forth. Next the god of evil sent a flood, but Mithras caused an ark to be built to permit the escape of one man with his flocks. Finally, his work accomplished, Mithras ate a sacramental meal with the sun and ascended into heaven. In due time he would return and bestow immortality upon all of the faithful.

ANCIENT
PERSIAN
CIVILIZATION

*The ritual and
observances of
Mithraism*

The ritual of Mithraism was both elaborate and significant. It included a complicated initiation ceremony of seven stages or degrees, the last of which cemented a mystic fellowship with the god. Prolonged self-denial and laceration of the flesh were necessary accompaniments of the initiation process. Admission to full membership in the cult entitled one to participate in the sacraments, the most important of which were baptism and a sacred meal of bread, water, and possibly wine. Still other observances included lustration (ceremonial cleansing with holy water), the burning of incense, chanting sacred music, and the keeping of sacred days. Of the last, Sunday and the twenty-fifth of December were the specific examples. In imitation of the Chaldean astral religion each day of the week was dedicated to a celestial body. Since the sun as the giver of light and the faithful ally of Mithras was the most important of these bodies, his day was naturally the most sacred. The twenty-fifth of December also possessed its solar significance: as the approximate date of the winter solstice it marked the return of the sun from his long journey south of the Equator. It was in a sense the "birthday" of the sun, since it connoted the revival of his life-giving powers for the benefit of man.

Exactly when the worship of Mithras became a definite cult is unknown, but it was certainly not later than the fourth century B.C. Its characteristics became firmly established during the period of social ferment which followed the collapse of Alexander's empire, and its spread at that time was exceedingly rapid. In the last century B.C. it was introduced into Rome, although it was of little importance in Italy itself until after 100 A.D. It drew its converts especially from the lower classes, from the ranks of soldiers, foreigners, and slaves. Ultimately it rose to the status of one of the most popular religions of the Empire, the chief competitor of Christianity and of the old Roman paganism itself. After 275, however, its strength rapidly waned. How much influence this astonishing cult exerted is impossible to say. Its superficial resemblance to Christianity is certainly not hard to perceive, but this does not mean, of course, that the two were identical, or that one was an offshoot of the other. Nevertheless, it is probably true that Christianity as the younger of the two rivals borrowed a good many of its externals from Mithraism, at the same time preserving its own philosophy virtually untouched.

One of the principal successors of Mithraism in transmitting the legacy from Persia was Manicheism, founded by Mani, a high-born priest of Ecbatana, about 250 A.D. Like Zoroaster he conceived it to be his mission to reform the prevailing religion, but he received scant sympathy in his own country and had to be content with missionary ventures in India and western China. About 276 A.D. he was condemned and crucified by his Persian opponents. Following his death his teachings were carried by his disciples into practically every country of western Asia and finally into Italy about 330 A.D.

Large numbers of western Manicheans, the great Augustine among them, eventually became Christians.

Of all the Zoroastrian teachings, the one which made the deepest impression upon the mind of Mani was dualism. It was therefore natural that it should have become the central doctrine of the new faith. But Mani gave to this doctrine a broader interpretation than it had ever received in the earlier religion. He conceived not merely of two deities engaged in a relentless struggle for supremacy, but of a whole universe divided into two kingdoms, each the antithesis of the other. The first was the kingdom of spirit ruled over by a God eternally good. The second was the kingdom of matter under the dominion of Satan. Only "spiritual" substances like fire, light, and the souls of men were created by God. Darkness, sin, desire, and all things bodily and material owed their origin to Satan. Human nature itself was evil, for the first parents of the race had received their physical bodies from the prince of darkness.

The strict dualism of the Manicheans

The moral implications of this rigorous dualism were readily apparent. Since everything connected with sensation or desire was the work of Satan, man should strive to free himself as completely as possible from enslavement to his physical nature. He should refrain from all forms of sensual enjoyment, the eating of meat, the drinking of wine, the gratification of sexual desire. Even marriage was prohibited, for this would result in the begetting of more physical bodies to people the kingdom of Satan. In addition, man should subdue the flesh by prolonged fasting and the infliction of pain. Recognizing that this program of austerities would be too difficult for ordinary mortals, Mani divided the race of mankind into the "perfect" and the "secular." Only the former would be obliged to adhere to the full program as the ideal of what all should hope to attain. The latter were merely required to eschew idolatry, avarice, fornication, falsehood, and the eating of meat. To aid the children of men in their struggle against the powers of darkness, God had sent prophets and redeemers from time to time to comfort and inspire them. Noah, Abraham, Zoroaster, Jesus, and Paul were all numbered among these divine emissaries; but the last and greatest of them was Mani.

The moral implications of dualism

The influence of Manicheism is very difficult to estimate, but it was undoubtedly considerable. People of all classes in the Roman Empire, including some members of the Christian clergy, embraced its doctrines. In its Christianized form it became one of the principal sects of the early church,[5] and it exerted some influence upon the development of the Albigensian heresy as late as the twelfth and thirteenth centuries. It inspired extravagant Christian speculations upon the dualism between God and the devil and between spirit and matter. Not only did it contribute to the asceticism of Christianity, but it strengthened also the doctrines of original sin and the total depravity of man, as taught by some theologians. Finally, it was a

The influence of Manicheism

[5] See pp. 247, 250.

sovereign source of the famous duality of ethical standards set up by St. Augustine and other Church Fathers: (1) a standard of perfection for the few (the monks and nuns), who would withdraw from the world and lead saintly lives as an example for the rest; and (2) a socially possible standard for the ordinary Christians.

Gnosticism

The third most important cult which developed as an element in the Persian heritage was Gnosticism (from the Greek *gnosis*, meaning knowledge). The name of its founder is unknown, and likewise the date of its origin, but it was certainly in existence as early as the first century A.D. It reached the height of its popularity in the latter half of the second century. Although it gained some followers in Italy, its influence was confined primarily to the Near East.

The mysticism of the Gnostics

The feature which most sharply distinguished this cult from the others was mysticism. The Gnostics denied that the truths of religion could be discovered by reason or could even be made intelligible. They regarded themselves as the exclusive possessors of a secret spiritual knowledge revealed to them directly by God. This knowledge was alone important as a guide to faith and conduct. In like manner, their religious observances were highly esoteric, that is, fraught with hidden meaning known only to the initiated. Sacraments in great profusion, innumerable baptisms, mystic rites, and the use of holy formulas and sacred numbers made up the leading examples.

The combined influence of the several off-shoots of Zoroastrianism

The combined influence of these several Persian religions was enormous. Most of them were launched at a time when political and social conditions were particularly conducive to their spread. The breakup of Alexander's empire about 300 B.C. inaugurated a peculiar period in the history of the ancient world. International barriers were broken down; there was an extensive migration and intermingling of peoples; and the collapse of the old social order gave rise to profound disillusionment and a vague yearning for individual salvation. Men's attentions were centered as never before since the downfall of Egypt upon compensations in a life to come. Under such circumstances religions of the kind described were bound to flourish like the green bay tree. Otherworldly, mystical, and messianic, they offered the very escape that men were seeking from a world of anxiety and confusion.

Other elements in the heritage from Persia

Although not exclusively religious, the heritage left by the Persians contained few elements of a secular nature. Their form of government was adopted by the later Roman monarchs, not in its purely political aspect, but in its character of a divine-right despotism. When such emperors as Diocletian and Constantine I invoked divine authority as a basis for their absolutism and required their subjects to prostrate themselves in their presence, they were really submerging the state in the religion as the Persians had done

from the time of Darius. Traces of Persian influence upon certain

Hellenistic philosophies are also discernible; but here again it was essentially religious, for it was confined almost entirely to the mystical theories of the Neo-Platonists and their philosophical allies.

SELECTED READINGS

Cambridge Ancient History, Vol. IV

Cumont, Franz, *The Mysteries of Mithra*, Chicago, 1903

Hogarth, D. G., *The Ancient East*, New York, 1915

Huart, C. I., *Ancient Persian and Iranian Civilization*, New York, 1927

Jackson, A. W. W., *Zoroaster, the Prophet of Ancient Iran*, New York, 1928

Moore, G. F., *The History of Religions*, New York, 1913, Vol. I

Olmstead, A. T. E., *History of the Persian Empire* (Achaemenid Period), Chicago, 1948

Pavry, J. D. C., *The Zoroastrian Doctrine of a Future Life*, New York, 1929

Rogers, R. W. A., *A History of Ancient Persia from Its Earliest Beginnings to the Death of Alexander*, New York, 1929

Ross, Sir E. D., *The Persians*, New York, 1931

Sykes, Sir P. M., *A History of Persia*, New York, 1921, Vol. I

SOURCE MATERIALS

Darmesteter, James, tr., "The Zend-Avesta," *Sacred Books of the East*, Vol. III

Hertzler, J. O., *The Social Thought of the Ancient Civilizations*, pp. 149–68

The Hebrew Civilization

Of all the peoples of the ancient Orient, none with the possible exception of the Egyptians has been of greater importance to the modern world than the Hebrews. It was the Hebrews, of course, who provided much of the background of the Christian religion—its Commandments, its stories of the Creation and the Flood, its concept of God as lawgiver and judge, and more than two-thirds of its Bible. Hebrew conceptions of morality and political theory have also profoundly influenced modern nations, especially those in which the Calvinist faith has been strong. On the other hand, it is necessary to remember that the Hebrews themselves did not develop their culture in a vacuum. No more than any other people were they able to escape the influence of nations around them. Hebrew religion, as a consequence, contained numerous elements which were quite clearly derived from Egyptian and Mesopotamian sources. Despite all the efforts of prophets to purge the Hebraic faith of foreign corruptions, many of them still remained, and others were added later. As we shall soon discover, Hebrew law was based very largely upon Old Babylonian origins, though of course with modifications. Hebrew philosophy was partly Egyptian and partly Greek; while long before the Book of Job was ever written, there was an Old Babylonian drama of similar character. No one can deny, of course, that the Hebrews were capable of original achievement; at the same time, we cannot overlook the fact that they were influenced greatly by the older civilizations around them.

1. Hebrew Origins and Relations with Other Peoples

The origin of the Hebrew people is still a puzzling problem. Certainly they were not a separate race, nor did they have any physical

characteristics sufficient to distinguish them clearly from other nations around them. The origin of their name is in doubt. According to one account, it was derived from Khabiru or Habiru, a name invented by their enemies and meaning the equivalent of "alien," "outcast," or "nomad." [1] According to other authorities, it is related to the word "Ever" or "Eber," referring to those who came from the other side of the Euphrates. Whatever its origin, it seems to have been applied originally to various immigrant peoples, and was restricted later to the Israelites.

Most scholars agree that the original home of the Hebrews was the Arabian Desert. The first definite appearance of the founders of the nation of Israel, however, was in northwestern Mesopotamia. Apparently as early as 1800 B.C. a group of Hebrews under the leadership of Abraham had settled there. Later Abraham's grandson Jacob led a migration westward and began the occupation of Palestine. It was from Jacob, subsequently called Israel, that the Israelites derived their name. Sometime after 1600 B.C. certain tribes of the Israelites, together with other Hebrews, went down into Egypt to escape the consequences of famine. They appear to have settled in the vicinity of the Delta and to have been enslaved by the Pharaoh's government. Around 1300–1250 B.C. their descendants found a new leader in the indomitable Moses, who freed them from bondage, led them to the Sinai Peninsula, and persuaded them to become worshipers of Yahweh, a god whose name is sometimes written erroneously as Jehovah. Hitherto Yahweh had been the deity of Hebrew shepherd folk in the general locality of Sinai. Making use of a Yahwist cult as a nucleus, Moses welded the various tribes of his followers into a confederation, sometimes called the Yahweh Amphictyony. It was this confederation which played the dominant role in the conquest of Palestine, or the Land of Canaan.

With its scanty rainfall and rugged topography, Palestine as a haven for the Children of Israel left much to be desired. For the most part it was a barren and inhospitable place. But compared with the arid wastes of Arabia it was a veritable paradise, and it is not surprising that the leaders should have pictured it as a "land flowing with milk and honey." Most of it was already occupied by the Canaanites, another people of Semitic speech who had lived there for centuries. Through contact with the Babylonians, Hittites, and Egyptians they had built up a culture which was no longer primitive. They practiced agriculture and carried on trade. They knew the use of iron and the art of writing, and they had adapted the laws of Hammurabi's code to the needs of their simpler existence. Their religion, which was also derived in large part from Babylonia, was cruel and sensual, including human sacrifice and temple prostitution.

The Hebrew conquest of the land of Canaan was a slow and difficult process. Seldom did the tribes unite in a combined attack, and even when they did, the enemy cities were well enough fortified to

[1] A. T. E. Olmstead, *History of Palestine and Syria*, p. 196.

*Efforts
to conquer the
Promised Land*

resist capture. After several generations of sporadic fighting the Hebrews had succeeded in taking only the limestone hills and a few of the less fertile valleys. In the intervals between wars they mingled freely with the Canaanites and adopted no small amount of their culture. Before they had a chance to complete the conquest, they found themselves confronted by a new and more formidable enemy, the Philistines, who had come into Palestine from Asia Minor and from the islands of the Aegean Sea. Stronger than either the Hebrews or Canaanites, the new invaders rapidly overran the country and forced the Hebrews to surrender much of the territory they had already gained. It is from the Philistines that Palestine derives its name.

2. The Record of Political Hopes and Frustrations

*The founding
of the Hebrew
monarchy*

The crisis produced by the Philistine conquests served not to discourage the Hebrews but to unite them and to intensify their ardor for battle. Moreover, it led directly to the founding of the Hebrew monarchy about 1025 B.C. Up to this time the nation had been ruled by "judges," who possessed little more than the authority of religious leaders. But now with a greater need for organization and discipline, the people demanded a king to rule them and to go out before them and fight their battles. The man selected as the first incumbent of the office was Saul, "a choice young man and a goodly," a member of the tribe of Benjamin.

*The reign of
King Saul*

In spite of his popularity at the start, the reign of King Saul was not a happy one, either for the nation or for the ruler himself. Only a few suggestions of the reasons are given in the Old Testament account. Evidently Saul incurred the displeasure of Samuel, the last of the great judges, who had expected to remain the power behind the throne. Before long there appeared on the scene the ambitious David, who, with the encouragement of Samuel, carried on skillful maneuvers to draw popular support from the king. Waging his own military campaigns, he achieved one bloody triumph after another. By contrast, the armies of Saul met disastrous reverses. Finally the king himself, being critically wounded, requested his armor-bearer to kill him. When the latter would not, he drew his own sword, fell upon it, and died.

*The mighty
David*

David now became king and ruled for forty years. His reign was one of the most glorious periods in Hebrew history. He smote the Philistines hip and thigh and reduced their territory to a narrow strip of coast in the south. He united the Twelve Tribes into a consolidated state under an absolute monarch, and he began the construction of a magnificent capital at Jerusalem. But strong government, military glory, and material splendor were not unmixed blessings for the people. Their inevitable accompaniments were high taxation and conscription. As a consequence, before David died,

Entrance to King David's Tomb on Mt. Zion. King David ruled in the tenth century B.C. The entrance to his tomb is obviously of later construction, but the tomb itself is reputed to date from David's death.

rumblings of discontent were plainly to be heard in certain parts of his kingdom.

David was succeeded by his son Solomon, the last of the kings of the united monarchy. As a result of the nationalist aspirations of later times, Solomon has been pictured in Hebrew lore as one of the wisest, justest, and most enlightened rulers in all history. The facts of his career furnish little support for such a belief. About all that can be said in his favor is that he was a shrewd diplomat and an active patron of trade. Most of his policies were oppressive, although of course not deliberately so. Ambitious to copy the luxury and magnificence of other Oriental despots, he established a harem of 700 wives and 300 concubines and completed the construction of sumptuous palaces, stables for 4000 horses, and a costly temple in Jerusalem. Since Palestine was poor in resources, most of the materials for the building projects had to be imported. Gold, silver, bronze, and cedar were brought in in such quantities that the revenues from taxation and from the tolls levied upon trade were insufficient to pay for them. To make up the deficit Solomon ceded twenty towns and resorted to the corvée, or the system of conscripting labor. Every three months 30,000 Hebrews were drafted and sent into Phoenicia to work in the forests and mines of King Hiram of Tyre, from whom the most expensive materials had been purchased.

Solomon aspires to Oriental magnificence

Solomon's extravagance and oppression produced acute discontent among his subjects. His death in 935 B.C. was the signal for open revolt. The ten northern tribes, refusing to submit to his son Rehoboam, seceded and set up their own kingdom. Sectional differences played their part also in the disruption of the nation. The northern Hebrews were sophisticated, accustomed to urban living, and steeped in foreign influences. By contrast, the two southern tribes were composed very largely of pastoral and agricultural folk, loyal to the religion of their fathers, and hating the ways of the foreigner.

The secession of the Ten Tribes

101

Perhaps these differences alone would have been sufficient in time to break the nation asunder.

After the secession the ten northern tribes came to be known as the Kingdom of Israel,[2] while the two southern tribes were called henceforth the Kingdom of Judah. For more than two centuries the two little states maintained their separate existences. But in 722 B.C. the Kingdom of Israel was conquered by the Assyrians. Its inhabitants were scattered throughout the vast empire of their conquerors and were eventually absorbed by the more numerous population around them. They have ever since been referred to as the Lost Ten Tribes of Israel. The Kingdom of Judah managed to survive for more than a hundred years longer, successfully defying the Assyrian menace. But in 586 B.C., as we have already learned, it was overthrown by the Chaldeans under Nebuchadnezzar. Jerusalem was plundered and burned, and its leading citizens were carried off into captivity in Babylon. When Cyrus the Persian conquered the Chaldeans, he freed the Jews and permitted them to return to their native land. Few were willing to go, and considerable time elapsed before it was possible to rebuild the temple. From 539 to 332 B.C. Palestine was a vassal state of Persia. In 332 B.C. it was conquered by Alexander and after his death was placed under the rule of the Ptolemies of Egypt. In 63 B.C. it became a Roman protectorate. Its political history as a Jewish commonwealth was ended in 70 A.D. after a desperate revolt which the Romans punished by destroying Jerusalem and annexing the country as a province. The inhabitants were gradually diffused through other parts of the Empire.

The Diaspora

The destruction of Jerusalem and annexation of the country by the Romans were the principal factors in the so-called *Diaspora*, or dispersion of the Jews from Palestine. Even earlier large numbers of them had fled into various parts of the Greco-Roman world on account of difficulties in their homeland. In their new environment they rapidly succumbed to foreign influences, a fact which was of tremendous importance in promoting a fusion of Greek and Oriental ideas. It was a Hellenized Jew, St. Paul, who was mainly responsible for remolding Christianity in accordance with Greek philosophical doctrines.

3. The Hebrew Religious Evolution

*Reasons for the
varied evolution
of Hebrew
religion*

Few peoples in history have gone through a religious evolution comparable to that of the Hebrews. Its cycle of development ranged all the way from the crudest superstitions to the loftiest spiritual and ethical conceptions. Part of the explanation is doubtless to be found in the peculiar geographic position occupied by the Hebrew people. Located as they were after their conquest of Canaan on the highroad between Egypt and the major civilizations of Asia,

[2] Or the kingdom of Samaria, from the name of its capital city.

they were bound to be affected by an extraordinary variety of influences.

At least five different stages can be distinguished in the growth of the Hebrew religion. The first we can call the pre-Mosaic stage, from the earliest beginnings of the people to approximately 1100 B.C. This stage was characterized at first by animism, the worship of spirits that dwelt in trees, mountains, sacred wells and springs, and even in stones of peculiar shape. Diverse forms of magic were practiced also at this time—necromancy, imitative magic, scapegoat sacrifices, and so on. Numerous relics of these early beliefs and practices are preserved in the Old Testament. For example, the reference in Deuteronomy 33:16 to the Lord as "Him that dwelt in the bush." See also II Kings 6:5-7, in which the story is related of how Elisha made an axehead float by throwing a piece of wood into the water. Under the principle of imitative magic, the floating of the wood on the water brought the axehead to the surface.

The pre-Mosaic stage

[handwritten margin note: not concerned with human form but with spirits.]

Gradually animism gave way to anthropomorphic gods. It would appear that few of the new deities were as yet given names; each was usually referred to merely by the generic name of "El," that is, "God." They were guardian deities of particular places and possibly of separate tribes. No national worship of Yahweh was known at this time.

[handwritten margin note: polytheism ↓]

Anthropomorphic gods

[handwritten margin note: human characteristics & human form]

The second stage, which lasted from the twelfth century B.C. to the ninth, is frequently designated the stage of national monolatry. The term may be defined as the exclusive worship of one god but without any denial that other gods exist. Due chiefly to the influence of Moses, the Hebrews gradually adopted as their national deity during this period a god whose name appears to have been written "Jhwh" or "Yhwh." How it was pronounced no one knows, but scholars generally agree that it was probably uttered as if spelled "Yahweh." The meaning is also a mystery. When Moses inquired of Yahweh what he should tell the people when they demanded to know what god had sent him, Yahweh replied: "I AM THAT I AM: and he said, Thus shalt thou say unto the children of Israel, I AM hath sent me unto you." [3] Neither at this time nor in any other period of ancient history did the Hebrews refer to their god as "Jehovah." The latter name was the result of a blunder committed by Christian Hebraists of the thirteenth century A.D. [4]

The stage of national monolatry

During the time of Moses and for two or three centuries thereafter Yahweh was a somewhat peculiar deity. He was conceived almost exclusively in anthropomorphic terms. He possessed a physical body and the emotional qualities of men. He was capricious, on occasions, and somewhat irascible—as capable of evil and wrathful judgments as he was of good. His decrees were often quite arbitrary,

Characteristics of Yahweh

[3] Exodus 3:13-14.
[4] Adolphe Lods, *Israel from Its Beginnings to the Middle of the Eighth Century*, p. 321.

and he would punish the man who sinned unwittingly just about as readily as him whose guilt was real.[5] Omnipotence was scarcely an attribute that Yahweh could claim, for his power was limited to the territory occupied by the Hebrews themselves. When Naaman the Syrian decided to become a follower of Yahweh, he could solve the problem of territorial dominion only by taking two mules' burden of good Palestinian earth with him.[6] But in spite of these limitations the Hebrews revered their God as their only guide and deliverer, the protector of widows and orphans, and the swift avenger of the nation's wrongs.

The supremacy of law and ritual

The religion of this stage was neither primarily ethical nor profoundly spiritual. Yahweh was revered as a supreme lawgiver and as the stern upholder of the moral order of the universe. According to Biblical account, he issued the Ten Commandments to Moses on top of Mt. Sinai. Old Testament scholars, however, do not generally accept this tradition. They admit that a primitive Decalogue may have existed in Mosaic times, but they doubt that the Ten Commandments in the form in which they are preserved in the Book of Exodus go back any farther than the seventh century. In any event, it is clear that Moses' God was interested just about as much in sacrifice and in ritualistic observances as he was in good conduct or in purity of heart. Moreover, the religion was not vitally concerned with spiritual matters. It offered naught but material rewards in this life and none at all in a life to come. Finally, the belief in monolatry was corrupted by certain elements of fetishism, magic, and even grosser superstitions that lingered from more primitive times or that were gradually acquired from neighboring peoples. These varied all the way from serpent worship to bloody sacrifices and licentious fertility orgies.

The need for reform

By the ninth century the Hebrew faith was badly in need of reform from within. Superstition and idolatry had steadily increased with the passing of the years until the worship of Yahweh was scarcely distinguishable from the worship of the Phoenician and Canaanite Ba'als. First to sense the need for drastic changes were the leaders of ascetic sects like the Nazirites and Rechabites, who denounced the foreign corruptions and clamored for a return to what they thought was the simple piety of their fathers. To emphasize their hatred of everything foreign, they condemned the refinements of civilized life and urged that the people should dwell in tents. Their work was followed by that of the vehement preacher Elijah, who dragged the priests of the Ba'al cults from their altars and slew them with his own hands. Notwithstanding his crusade against the foreign cults, Elijah did not deny the existence of their

---

[5] By way of illustration, he struck Uzza dead merely because that unfortunate individual placed his hand upon the Ark of the Covenant to steady it while it was being transported to Jerusalem. I Chronicles 13:9-10.

[6] II Kings 5:17.

gods; but he insisted that Yahweh was a god of righteousness and
the only deity whom the Hebrews should worship.

The really important work of religious reform, however, was
accomplished by the great prophets—Amos, Hosea, Isaiah,[7] and
Micah. And their achievements represented the third stage in the *The stage of the*
development of the Hebrew religion, the stage of the prophetic *prophetic*
revolution, which occupied the eighth and seventh centuries B.C. *revolution*
The great prophets were men of much broader vision than Elijah
or the leaders of the ascetic sects. Their outlook was progressive;
they did not demand a return to some age of simplicity in the past
but taught that the religion should be infused with a new philosophy
and a new conception of the ends it was supposed to serve. Three
basic doctrines made up the substance of their teachings: (1) monotheism—Yahweh is the lord of the universe; the gods of other nations do not exist; (2) Yahweh is a god of righteousness exclusively;
He is not really omnipotent, but His power is limited by justice and
goodness; the evil in the world comes from man not from God;
(3) the purposes of religion are chiefly ethical; Yahweh cares nothing for ritual and sacrifice, but that men should "seek justice, relieve
the oppressed, judge the fatherless, plead for the widow." Or as
Micah expressed it: "What doth the Lord require of thee, but to
do justly, and to love mercy, and to walk humbly with thy
God?" [8]

In these doctrines was contained a definite repudiation of nearly
everything that the older religion had stood for. Such, however, was
apparently not the intention of the prophets. They conceived it *Contrasts with*
rather as their mission to restore the religion to its ancient purity. *the older reli-*
The crudities within it they regarded as foreign corruptions. But *gion; political*
and social
like many such leaders, they builded better than they knew. Their *aspects*
actual accomplishments went so far beyond their original objectives
that they amounted to a religious revolution. To a considerable
extent this revolution also had its social and political aspects. Wealth
had become concentrated in the hands of a few. Thousands of
small farmers had lost their freedom and had passed under subjection to rich proprietors. If we can believe the testimony of Amos,
bribery was so rife in the law courts that the plaintiff in a suit
for debt had merely to give the judge a pair of shoes and the
defendant would be handed over as a slave.[9] Overshadowing all was
the threat of Assyrian domination. To enable the nation to cope
with that threat, the prophets believed that social abuses should be

[7] Many Old Testament authorities consider the Book of Isaiah the work of
two authors. They ascribe the first part to Isaiah, and the second part, beginning with Chapter 40, to Deutero-Isaiah, or the Second Isaiah. The Second
Isaiah is more emphatic than the first in denying the existence of the gods of
other peoples.

[8] Micah 6:8.

[9] Amos 2:6. This, of course, was poetic propaganda and may have been slightly
exaggerated.

*The religion not
yet otherworld-
ly or mystical*

*The stage
of the Exile or
Babylonian
Captivity*

stamped out and the people united under a religion purged of its alien corruptions.

The results of this revolution must not be misinterpreted. It did eradicate some of the most flagrant forms of oppression, and it rooted out permanently most of the barbarities which had crept into the religion from foreign sources. But the Hebrew faith was not yet a religion which bore much resemblance to modern orthodox Judaism. It contained little of a spiritual character and hardly a trace of the mystical. Instead of being otherworldly, it was oriented toward this life. Its purposes were social and ethical—to promote a just and harmonious society and to abate man's inhumanity to man—not to confer individual salvation in an afterlife. As yet there was no belief in heaven and hell or in Satan as a powerful opponent of God. The shades of the dead went down into Sheol to linger there for a time in the dust and gloom and then disappear.

Nevertheless, the ideals of the prophetic revolution probably represented the highest perfection of the Hebrew religion. After that time it shifted its emphases, responding again to outside influences. The first of these influences made themselves felt during the period of the Babylonian Captivity from 586 to 539 B.C., which constitutes a fourth stage in the evolution of the religion. As a result of association with the Neo-Babylonians, the Jews adopted ideas of pessimism, fatalism, and the transcendence of God. No longer did they conceive of Yahweh as intimately concerned with the social problems of His people, but as an omnipotent, unapproachable being whose essential characteristic was holiness. His thoughts were not men's thoughts nor His ways the ways of mortals. Man's chief duty was to submit absolutely to His inscrutable will.[10] The forms of the religion were also profoundly changed. In a desperate attempt to preserve the identity of the Jews as a nation, their leaders adopted or revived customs and observances which would serve to distinguish them as a peculiar people. The institution of the Sabbath, the forms of synagogal worship, the practice of circumcision, and elaborate distinctions between clean and unclean foods were now given places of fundamental importance. While it is true that most of these observances were of pre-Exilic origin, they had not been regarded as religious essentials for many years. The prophets, moreover, had emphatically denied their importance. The growth of extensive regulations for the conduct of ritual inevitably increased the power of the priests, with the result that Judaism was gradually transformed into an ecclesiastical religion.

The final significant stage in Hebrew religious evolution was the post-Exilic stage or the period of Persian influence. This period may be considered to have covered the years from 539 to about

[10] These ideas are to be found in the Book of Ezekiel and in the writings of Deutero-Isaiah (Isaiah 40-55) which date from the period of the Captivity; also in the Book of Job, written a century or more later.

300 B.C. Perhaps enough has been said already to indicate the character of the influence from Persia. It will be recalled from the preceding chapter that Zoroastrianism was a dualistic, messianic, otherworldly, and esoteric religion. In the period following the Exile these very ideas gained wide acceptance among the Jews. They adopted a belief in Satan as the Great Adversary and the author of evil. They developed an eschatology, including such notions as the coming of a spiritual savior, the resurrection of the dead, and a last judgment. They turned their attention to salvation in an after-world as more important than enjoyment of this life. Lastly, they embraced the conception of a revealed religion. The Book of Ezekiel, for example, was asserted to have been prepared by God in heaven and given to the man whose name it bears with instruction to "eat" it.[11] In time the idea grew that many other books had been dictated directly by Yahweh to certain of His followers. With the adoption of beliefs such as these the Hebrew faith had evolved far from the strict monotheism and the simple ethical religion of the days of the prophets.

4. Hebrew Culture

In certain respects the Hebrew genius was inferior to that of some other great nations of antiquity. In the first place, it revealed no talent for science. Not a single important discovery in any scientific field has ever been traced to the ancient Hebrews. Nor were they particularly adept in appropriating the knowledge of others. They could not build a bridge or a tunnel except of the crudest sort. Whether it was from lack of interest in these things or whether it was because of too deep an absorption in religious affairs is not clear. In the second place, they seem to have been almost entirely devoid of artistic skill. Their only examples of the glyptic arts were engraved seals similar to those made by the Sumerians and Hittites and used for the purpose of affixing signatures. They had no architecture, sculpture, or painting worthy of mention. The famous temple at Jerusalem was not a Hebrew building at all but a product of Phoenician skill, for Solomon imported artisans from Tyre to finish the more complicated tasks.

It was rather in law, literature, and philosophy that the Hebrew genius was most perfectly expressed. Although all of these subjects were closely allied with religion, they did have their secular aspects. The finest example of Jewish law was the Deuteronomic Code, which forms the core of the Book of Deuteronomy. Despite claims of its great antiquity, it was probably an outgrowth of the prophetic revolution. It was based in part upon an older Code of the Covenant, which was derived in considerable measure from the laws of the

---

[11] Ezekiel 3:1-4.

Canaanites and the Old Babylonians.[12] In general, its provisions were more enlightened than those of Hammurabi's code. One of them enjoined liberality to the poor and the stranger. Another commanded that the Hebrew slave who had served six years should be freed; and insisted that he must not be sent away empty. A third provided that judges and other officers should be chosen by the people and forbade them to accept gifts or to show partiality in any form. A fourth condemned witchcraft, divination, and necromancy. A fifth denounced the punishment of children for the guilt of their fathers and affirmed the principle of individual responsibility for sin. A sixth prohibited the taking of interest on any kind of loan made

The Shekel of Ancient Israel. Depicted are the two sides of the silver shekel of 141–137 B.C. This coin weighs 220 grains; a United States silver dollar weighs 412.5 grains. The Chaldeans and Phoenicians also had coins called shekels.

by one Jew to another. A seventh required that at the end of every seven years there should be a "release" of debts. "Every creditor that lendeth aught unto his neighbour shall release it; he shall not exact it of his neighbour, or of his brother . . . save when there shall be no poor among you." [13]

Democratic and equalitarian ideals

As one would expect from the circumstances out of which it grew, a cardinal purpose of the Deuteronomic Code was to infuse into Jewish society a more democratic and equalitarian character. Its authors were not interested in abstract principles. For example, they did not condemn slavery as wrong in itself; they sought merely to prevent the permanent enslavement of Jews. Nevertheless, it is undeniably true that this code did provide for more political and social democracy than the laws of any other Oriental nation except Egypt. Even the king himself was forbidden to accumulate great wealth or to indulge in ostentatious luxury. No military despotism of the Assyrian or Babylonian type was to be tolerated. The king was not above the law but very definitely subject to it; he was

[12] C. F. Kent, *The Message of Israel's Lawgivers*, p. 24.
[13] Deuteronomy 15:1–4.

required to have constantly with him a copy of the code and to "read therein all the days of his life . . . that his heart be not lifted up above his brethren, and that he turn not aside from the commandment." [14] Moreover, his power and that of his officers was strictly limited. The administration of justice was left almost entirely in the hands of the people. In cases of disputed guilt the elders of the city would decide, but the punishment provided in the code would be inflicted by the family of the victim or by the community at large. The conscription of labor for foreign service was also prohibited, and exemption from military duty was required to be granted to the man who had built a new house, planted a new vineyard, or married a new wife; and even to the man who was "fearful and faint-hearted . . . lest his brethren's heart faint as well as his heart." [15]

The literature of the Hebrews was by far the best that the ancient Orient ever produced. Nearly all of it now extant is preserved in the Old Testament and in the books of the so-called Apocrypha. Except for a few fragments like the Song of Deborah in Judges 5 it is not really so ancient as is commonly supposed. Scholars now recognize that the Old Testament was built up mainly through a series of collections and revisions (redactions) in which the old and new fragments were merged and generally assigned to an ancient author, Moses, for example. But the oldest of these redactions was not prepared any earlier than 850 B.C. The majority of the books of the Old Testament were of even more recent origin, with the exception, of course, of certain of the chronicles. As one would logically expect, the philosophical books were of late authorship. Although the bulk of the Psalms were ascribed to King David, a good many of them actually refer to events of the Captivity. It seems certain that the collection as a whole was the work of several centuries. Most recent of all were the books of Ecclesiastes, Esther, and Daniel, composed no earlier than the third century. Likewise, the Apocrypha, or books of doubtful religious authority, did not see the light of day until Hebrew civilization was almost extinct. Some, like Maccabees I and II, relate events of the second century B.C. Others including the Wisdom of Solomon and the Book of Enoch were written under the influence of Greco-Oriental philosophy.

Hebrew literature

Not all of the writings of the Hebrews had high literary merit. A considerable number were dull, repetitious chronicles. Nevertheless, most of them, whether in the form of battle song, prophecy, love lyric, or drama, were rich in rhythm, concrete images, and emotional vigor. Few passages in any language can surpass the scornful indictment of social abuses voiced by the prophet Amos:

Amos' indictment of social abuses

[14] Deuteronomy 17:18–20.
[15] Deuteronomy 20:5–8. It is necessary to remember, however, that there was a strong utopian element in this code. We cannot be sure that all its provisions were actually accepted by the government.

Hear this, O ye that swallow up the needy, even to make the poor
    of the land to fail,
Saying, when will the new moon be gone, that we may sell corn?
And the sabbath that we may set forth wheat,
Making the ephah small, and the shekel great,
And falsifying the balances by deceit?
That we may buy the poor for silver, and the needy for a pair of
    shoes;
Yea, and sell the refuse of the wheat?

*The Song of
Songs*

The most beautiful of Hebrew love lyrics was the Song of Songs
or the Song of Solomon. Its theme was quite probably derived from
an old Canaanite hymn of spring, celebrating the passionate affection of the Shulamith or fertility goddess for her lover, but it had
long since lost its original meaning. The following verses are typical
of its sensuous beauty:

I am the rose of Sharon
and the lily of the valleys.
As the lily among thorns,
so is my love among the daughters.

.   .   .   .

My beloved is white and ruddy,
the chiefest among ten thousand.
His head is as the most fine gold;
his locks are bushy and black as a raven:
His eyes are as the eyes of doves by the rivers of waters,
washed with milk and fitly set.
His cheeks are as a bed of spices, as sweet flowers;
his lips like lilies, dropping sweet smelling myrrh.

.   .   .   .

How beautiful are thy feet with shoes, O prince's daughter!
The joints of thy thighs are like jewels,
the work of the hands of a cunning workman.

*The Book of
Job*

Few authorities would deny that the supreme achievement of the
Hebrew literary genius was the Book of Job. In form the work is a
drama of the tragic struggle between man and fate. Its central theme
is the problem of evil: how it can be that the righteous suffer while
the eyes of the wicked stand out with fatness. The story was an
old one, adapted very probably from a Babylonian writing of similar
content, but the Hebrews introduced into it a much deeper realization of philosophical possibilities. The main character, Job, a man
of unimpeachable virtue, is suddenly overtaken by a series of disasters: he is despoiled of his property, his children are killed, and
his body is afflicted with a painful disease. His attitude at first is

one of stoic resignation; the evil must be accepted along with the
good. But as his sufferings increase he is plunged into despair. He
curses the day of his birth and delivers an apostrophe to death, where
"the wicked cease from troubling and the weary be at rest."

Then follows a lengthy debate between Job and his friends over
the meaning of evil. The latter take the traditional Hebraic view
that all suffering is a punishment for sin, and that those who repent
are forgiven and strengthened in character. But Job is not satisfied
with any of their arguments. Torn between hope and despair, he
strives to review the problem from every angle. He even considers
the possibility that death may not be the end, that there may be some
adjustment of the balance hereafter. But the mood of despair returns, and he decides that God is an omnipotent demon, destroying
without mercy wherever His caprice or anger directs. Finally, in his
anguish he appeals to the Almighty to reveal Himself and make
known His ways to man. God answers him out of the whirlwind
with a magnificent exposition of the tremendous works of nature.
Convinced of his own insignificance and the unutterable majesty of
God, Job despises himself and repents in dust and ashes. In the end
no solution is given of the problem of individual suffering. No
promise is made of recompense in a life hereafter, nor does God
make any effort to refute the hopeless pessimism of Job. Man must
take comfort in the philosophic reflection that the universe is greater
than himself, and that God in the pursuit of His sublime purposes
cannot really be limited by human standards of equity and goodness.

*The problem of
evil*

As philosophers the Hebrews surpassed every other people before
the Greeks with the possible exception of the Egyptians. While
they were not brilliant metaphysicians and constructed no great
theories of the universe, they did concern themselves with most of
the problems relating to the life and destiny of man. Their thought
was essentially personal rather than abstract. Probably the earliest of
their writings of a distinctly philosophical character were the Old
Testament Book of Proverbs and the Apocryphal Book of Ecclesiasticus. In their final form both were of late composition, but much
of the material they contain was doubtless quite ancient. Not all of
it was original, for a considerable portion had been taken from
Egyptian sources, especially from the writings of Amenemope, who
lived about 1000 B.C. The philosophy of Proverbs and Ecclesiasticus
is not very profound and may be considered as representing the
mental adolescence of the Hebrew nation. It is almost entirely
ethical, but its appeal is primarily to prudential considerations, not
to the will of God or to any absolute standards of right and wrong.
It has as its essential teaching: be temperate, diligent, wise, and
honest, and you will surely be rewarded with prosperity, long life,
and a good name among men. Only in such isolated passages as the
following is any recognition given to higher motives of sympathy

*Hebrew
philosophy:
early examples*

or respect for the rights of others: "Whoso mocketh the poor reproacheth his Maker; and he that is glad at calamities shall not be unpunished." [16]

Ecclesiastes

A much more profound and critical philosophy is contained in Ecclesiastes, an Old Testament book, not to be confused with the Apocryphal Ecclesiasticus mentioned above. The author of Ecclesiastes is unknown. In some way it came to be attributed to Solomon, but he certainly did not write it, for it includes doctrines and forms of expression unknown to the Hebrews for hundreds of years after his death. Modern critics date it no earlier than the third century B.C. The basic ideas of its philosophy may be summarized as follows:

(1) Mechanism. The universe is a machine that rolls on forever without evidence of any purpose or goal. There is nothing new under the sun, no progress, merely endless repetition of the past. Sunrise and sunset, birth and death are but separate phases of constantly recurring cycles.

(2) Fatalism. Man is a victim of the whims of fate. There is no necessary relation between effort and success: "The race is not to the swift, nor the battle to the strong, neither yet bread to the wise . . . but time and chance happeneth to them all."

(3) Skepticism. Knowledge of ultimate things is impossible. There is no evidence of any soul or any life after death. Men and beasts are alike: "all are of the dust, and all turn to dust again."

(4) Pessimism. All is vanity and vexation of spirit. Fame, riches, extravagant pleasure are snares and delusions in the end. Although wisdom is better than folly, even it is not a sure key to happiness, for an increase in knowledge brings a keener awareness of suffering. Only a good name and joy in the work of one's hands are much to be prized.

(5) Moderation. Extremes of asceticism and extremes of indulgence are both to be avoided. "Be not righteous over much . . . be not over much wicked: why shouldest thou die before thy time?" [17]

5. The Magnitude of the Hebrew Influence

The nature of the Hebrew influence

The influence of the Hebrews, like that of most other Oriental nations, has been chiefly religious and ethical. While it is true that the Old Testament has served as a source of inspiration for much of the literature and art of the Renaissance and early modern civilizations, this has resulted largely because the Bible was already familiar material as a part of the religious heritage. The same explanation can be applied to the use of the Old Testament as a

---

[16] Proverbs 17:5.
[17] For a more complete analysis of the philosophy of Ecclesiastes see **Morris** Jastrow, *A Gentle Cynic*.

source of law and political theory by the Calvinists in the sixteenth century, and by many other Christians both before and since.

But these facts do not mean that the Hebrew influence has been slight. On the contrary, the history of nearly every Western civilization during the past two thousand years would have been radically different without the heritage from Israel. For it must be remembered that Hebrew beliefs were among the principal foundations of Christianity. The relationship between the two religions is frequently misunderstood. The movement inaugurated by Jesus of Nazareth is commonly represented as a revolt against Judaism; but such was only partly the case. On the eve of the Christian era the Jewish nation had come to be divided into three main sects: a majority sect of Pharisees, and two minority sects of Sadducees and Essenes. The Pharisees represented the middle classes and some of the better educated common folk. They believed in the resurrection, in rewards and punishments after death, and in the coming of a political messiah. Intensely nationalistic, they advocated participation in government and faithful observance of the ancient ritual. They regarded all parts of the law as of virtually equal importance, whether they applied to matters of ceremony or to obligations of social ethics.

Hebrew foundations of Christianity: the beliefs of the Pharisees

Representing altogether different strata of society, the minority sects disagreed with the Pharisees on both religious and political issues. The Sadducees, including the priests and the wealthier classes, were most famous for their denial of the resurrection and of rewards and punishments in an afterlife. Although temporarily at least they favored the acceptance of Roman rule, their attitude toward the ancient law was even more inflexible than that of the Pharisees. The sect of Essenes, the smallest of them all, was possibly the most influential. Its members, who were drawn from the lower classes, practiced asceticism and preached otherworldliness as means of protest against the wealth and power of priests and rulers. They ate and drank only enough to keep themselves alive, held all their goods in common, and looked upon marriage as a necessary evil. Far from being fanatical patriots, they regarded government with indifference and refused to take oaths under any conditions. They emphasized the spiritual aspects of religion rather than the ceremonial and stressed particularly the immortality of the soul, the coming of a religious messiah, and the early destruction of the world. Their most noted member appears to have been John the Baptist, though he later repudiated the sect on the ground that it was preparing only its own followers and not the nation as a whole for the coming of the messiah. It was he who provided an apparent link between the Essenes and the earliest Christians.

The Sadducees and the Essenes

Until recently scholars were dependent for their knowledge of the Essenes almost entirely upon secondary sources. But in 1947 an Arab shepherd unwittingly opened the way to one of the most spectacular discoveries of documentary evidence in world history.

The Dead Sea scrolls

113

Searching for a lost sheep on the western shore of the Dead Sea, he threw a stone that entered a hole in the rocks and made such a peculiar noise that he ran away in fright. He returned, however, with a friend to investigate and discovered a cave in which were stored about fifty cylindrical earthen jars stuffed with writings on leather scrolls. Studied by scholars, the scrolls revealed the existence of a monastic community which flourished from about 130 B.C. to 67 A.D. Its members lived a life of humility and self-denial, holding their goods in common, and devoting their time to prayer and sacraments and to studying and copying Biblical texts. They looked forward confidently to the coming of a messiah, the overthrow of evil, and the establishment of God's kingdom on earth. That they belonged to the sect of Essenes seems almost beyond question.

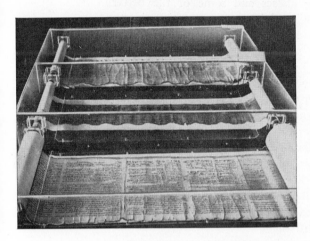

The Dead Sea Scrolls, Now on Display in an Underground Vault at the Hebrew University in Jerusalem. The oldest extant examples of Hebrew religious literature, they furnish us with evidence of the activities of the Essenes, and perhaps other mystical and otherworldly sects, about the beginning of the Christian era.

*Hebrew
influence upon
Christianity*

All branches of Judaism except the Sadducees strongly influenced the development of Christianity. Indeed, many Christians regard their religion as the completion and fulfillment of the religion of the Jews. From Jewish sources Christianity obtained its cosmogony, or theory of the origin of the universe; the Ten Commandments; and a large portion of its theology. Jesus himself, although he condemned the Pharisees for their legalism and hypocrisy, did not repudiate all of their tenets. Like them he revered the prophets, believed in rewards and punishments after death, and considered the Jewish people the chosen of God. Instead of abolishing the ancient law, as he is popularly supposed to have done, he demanded its fulfillment, insisting, however, that it should not be made the essential part of religion. To what extent the beliefs and practices of the Christian religion were molded by the more radical Judaism of the Essenes is a question whose answer must await further research. Perhaps the fundamental influence was slight. Nonetheless, we know that many early Christians practiced asceticism, regarded government with indifference, held all their goods in common, and believed in the imminent end of the world. These parallels do not mean, of course, that Christianity was a mere adaptation of beliefs and practices emanating from Judaism. On account of various factors there was much in it that was unique; but that is a subject which can be discussed more conveniently in another connection.[18]

The ethical and political influence of the Hebrews has also been substantial. Their moral conceptions have been a leading factor in the development of the negative approach toward ethics which has prevailed for so long in Western countries. For the early Hebrews "righteousness" consisted primarily in the observance of taboos. Although a positive morality of charity and social justice made rapid headway during the time of the prophets, this in turn was partly obscured by the revival of priestly influence in the period that followed. As a result, the Torah or Pentateuch (the first five books of the Old Testament), which embraced the code of personal behavior for the Jew, came to be crammed with ritualistic prohibitions. With respect to political influence, the record is more impressive. Hebrew ideals of limited government, the sovereignty of law, and regard for the dignity and worth of the individual have been among the major formative influences which have shaped the growth of modern democracy. It is now almost universally recognized that the traditions of Judaism contributed equally with the influence of Christianity and the Stoic philosophy in fostering recognition of the rights of man and in promoting the development of the free society.

Ethical and political influence of the Hebrews

SELECTED READINGS

Albright, W. F., *From the Stone Age to Christianity*, Baltimore, 1940
———, *Archaeology and the Religion of Israel*, Baltimore, 1942
Anderson, B. W., *Rediscovering the Bible*, New York, 1951
Baron, S. W., *A Social and Religious History of the Jews*, New York, 1937, 3 vols.
Bertholet, Alfred, *A History of Hebrew Civilization*, London, 1926
Burrows, Millar, *Outline of Biblical Theology*, Philadelphia, 1946
Finegan, Jack, *Light from the Ancient Past*, Princeton, 1946
Fowler, H. T., *A History of the Literature of Ancient Israel*, New York, 1914
Fritsch, C. T., *The Qumrān Community*, New York, 1956
Kent, C. F., *The Message of Israel's Lawgivers*, New York, 1902
Klausner, Joseph, *The Messianic Idea in Israel*, New York, 1955
Lods, Adolphe, *Israel from Its Beginnings to the Middle of the Eighth Century*, New York, 1932
———, *The Prophets and the Rise of Judaism*, New York, 1951
Meek, T. J., *Hebrew Origins*, revised edition, New York, 1951
Oesterley, W. O. E., and Robinson, T. H., *Hebrew Religion, Its Origin and Development*, New York, 1932

[18] See chapter on The Civilization of Early Medieval Europe.

Olmstead, A. T. E., *History of Palestine and Syria*, New York, 1931
Orlinsky, H. M., *Ancient Israel*, Ithaca, 1956
Smith, J. M. P., *The Moral Life of the Hebrews*, Chicago, 1923
———, *The Origin and History of Hebrew Law*, Chicago, 1931
Wright, G. E., *The Challenge of Israel's Faith*, Chicago, 1944

SOURCE MATERIALS

The Old Testament, especially the following books and portions of
books: Deuteronomy 5, 12–21; Ecclesiastes; Amos; I Samuel 8–31; II
Samuel; I Kings 1–12; Job; Proverbs; Isaiah 1–12; 40–66; Micah;
Psalms

The Hittite, Aegean, and Lesser Cultures

A few other ancient cultures of the Near Orient require more than passing attention. Chief among them are the Hittite, Aegean, Phoenician, and Lydian cultures. The Hittites are important pri- *Importance of* marily as intermediaries between East and West. They were one *these cultures* of the main connecting links between the civilizations of Egypt, the Tigris-Euphrates valley, and the region of the Aegean Sea. It appears certain also that they were the original discoverers of iron. They introduced that metal to the surrounding peoples, who rapidly adopted it in place of bronze. The Aegean civilization is significant for its remarkable achievements in the arts and for its quality of freedom and courage for experimentation. Though many of its achievements perished, there is evidence that the Greeks owed to the Aegean peoples a considerable debt. The Greek religion, for example, contained numerous Aegean elements. Likewise of Aegean origin were probably such things as the devotion of the Greeks to athletics, their system of weights and measures, their knowledge of navigation, and perhaps also a great many of their artistic traditions. As for the Phoenicians, no one could overlook the importance of their distribution of a knowledge of the alphabet to the surrounding civilized world. The Lydians have gone down in history as the originators of the first system of coinage.

1. The Hittites and the Phrygians

Until about eighty years ago little was known of the Hittites except their name. They were commonly assumed to have played no role of any significance in the drama of history. The slighting references to them in the Bible gave the impression that they were **117**

*The discovery
of remains
of the Hittite
civilization*

little more than a half-barbarian tribe. But in 1870 some curiously inscribed stones were found at Hamath in Syria. This was the beginning of an extensive inquiry which has continued with a few interruptions to the present day. It was not long until scores of other monuments and clay tablets were discovered over most of Asia Minor and through the Near East as far as the Tigris-Euphrates valley. In 1907 certain evidences of an ancient city were unearthed near the village of Boghaz-Keui in the province of Anatolia. Further excavation eventually revealed the ruins of a great fortified capital which was known as Hattusas or Hittite City. Within its walls were discovered more than 20,000 documents and fragments, most of them laws and decrees, of which a good number have since been deciphered.

The Hittite empire

On the basis of these finds and other evidences gradually accumulated, it was soon made clear that the Hittites were once the rulers of a mighty empire covering most of Asia Minor and extending to the upper reaches of the Euphrates. Part of the time it included Syria as well and even portions of Phoenicia and Palestine. The Hittites reached the zenith of their power during the years from 2000 to 1200 B.C. In the last century of this period they waged a long and exhausting war with Egypt which had much to do with the downfall of both empires. Neither was able to regain its strength. After 1200 B.C. Carchemish on the Euphrates River became for a time the leading Hittite city, but as a commercial center rather than as the capital of a great empire. The days of imperial glory were over. Finally, after 717 B.C., all the remaining Hittite territories were conquered and absorbed by the Assyrians, Lydians, and Phrygians.

*The mystery
of the race and
language of the
Hittites*

Where the Hittites came from and what were their relationships to other peoples are problems which still defy a perfect solution. As depicted by the Egyptians, some of them appear to have been of a Mongoloid type. All had enormous hooked noses, receding foreheads, and slanting eyes. Most modern scholars trace their place of origin to Turkestan and consider them related to the Greeks. Their language was Indo-European. Its secret was unlocked during World War I by the Czech scholar Hrozny. Since then thousands of clay tablets making up the laws and official records of the emperors have been deciphered. They reveal a civilization resembling more closely the Old Babylonian than any other.

*The economic
life of the
Hittites*

Hardly enough evidence has yet been collected to make possible an accurate appraisal of Hittite civilization. Some modern historians refer to it as if it were on a level with the Mesopotamian or even with the Egyptian civilization. Such may have been the case from the material standpoint, for the Hittites undoubtedly had an extensive knowledge of agriculture and a highly developed economic life in general. They mined great quantities of silver, copper, and lead, which they sold to surrounding nations. They discovered the mining and use of iron and made that material available for the rest

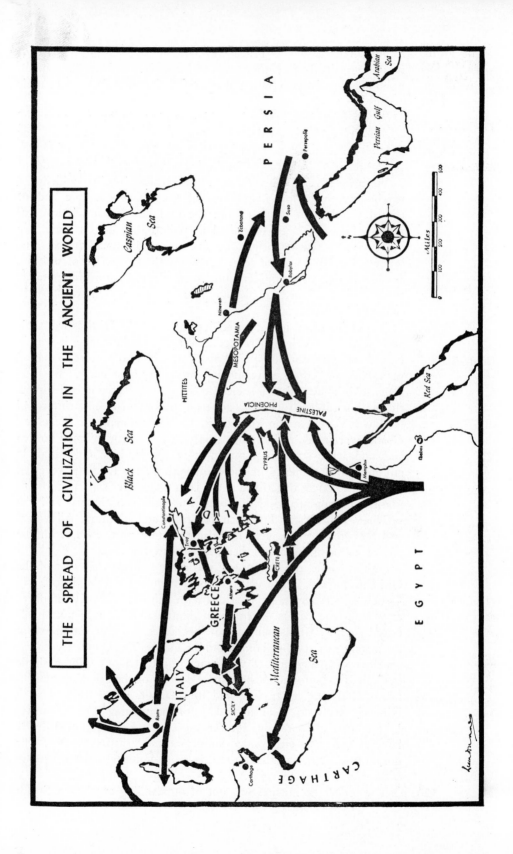

THE SPREAD OF CIVILIZATION IN THE ANCIENT WORLD

of the civilized world. Trade was also one of their principal economic pursuits. In fact, they seem to have depended almost as much upon commercial penetration as upon war for the expansion of their empire.

The intellectual level of Hittite culture

On the other hand, there is nothing as yet to indicate any marked superiority in intellectual attainments, although of course no one can tell what future research may reveal. The thousands of tablets so far recovered appear to be business, legal, and religious documents primarily. The literature of the Hittites consisted chiefly of mythology, including adaptations of the Gilgamesh epic and of creation and flood legends from the Old Babylonians. They had nothing that could be described as philosophy, nor is there any evidence of scientific originality outside of the metallurgical arts. They evidently possessed some talent for the perfection of writing, for in addition to a modified cuneiform adapted from Mesopotamia they also developed a hieroglyphic system which was partly phonetic in character.

Hittite law

One of the most significant achievements of the Hittites was their system of law. Although reflecting Babylonian influence, it was in considerable measure unique. Approximately two hundred separate paragraphs or decrees, covering a great variety of subjects, have been translated. They reflect a society comparatively urbane and sophisticated but subject to minute governmental control. The title to all land was vested in the king or in the governments of the cities. Grants were made to individuals only in return for military service and under the strict requirement that the land be cultivated. If anyone failed to perform these obligations, his holdings reverted to the state. Prices were fixed in the laws themselves for an enormous number of commodities; not only for articles of luxury and the products of industry but even for food and clothing. All wages and fees for services were likewise minutely prescribed, with the pay of women fixed at less than half the rate for men.

Humane character of Hittite law

On the whole, the Hittite law was more humane than that of the Old Babylonians. Death was the punishment for only eight offenses —such as witchcraft, sex relations with animals, and theft of property from the palace. Even premeditated murder was punishable only by a fine. Mutilation was not specified as a penalty at all except for arson or theft when committed by a slave. The contrast with the cruelties of Assyrian law was much more striking. Not a single example is to be found in the Hittite decrees of such fiendish punishments as flaying, castration, and impalement, which the rulers at Nineveh seemed to think necessary for maintaining their authority. Unfortunately the reasons for this more liberal spirit of the Hittite lawgivers remain enshrouded in mystery. Perhaps they had the good sense to realize that justice is more important than force in preserving an orderly society.

120 The art of the Hittites was not of outstanding excellence. So far as we know, it included only sculpture and architecture. The former was generally crude and naïve, but at the same time it revealed a freshness and vigor all too uncommon in the work of Oriental peoples. Most of it was in the form of reliefs depicting scenes of war and mythology. Architecture was ponderous and huge. Temples and palaces were squat, unadorned structures with small, two-columned porches and great stone lions guarding the entrance.

Hittite Sculpture. Perhaps the most highly conventionalized sculpture of the ancient world was that of the Hittite reliefs. Noteworthy are the animal legs and tails with human torsos and heads, the Mesopotamian treatment of the hair and beard, the fingers of even length, and the huge noses. Curious also is the facing position of the king's feet.

Not a great deal is known about the Hittite religion except that it had an elaborate mythology, innumerable deities, and forms of worship of Mesopotamian origin. The name of the chief male deity seems to have been Addu, a god of the storm, who was always represented with a bolt of lightning issuing from his hand. But the chief place in the pantheon was given to a mother goddess of fertility, whose name is unknown. A sun god was also worshiped and a great host of other deities, some of whom appear to have had no particular function at all. The Hittites seem to have welcomed into the divine company practically all of the gods of the peoples they conquered and even of the nations that bought their wares. The practices of the religion included divination, sacrifice, purification ceremonies, and the offering of prayers. Nothing can be found in the records to indicate that the religion was in any sense ethical.

Hittite religion

The chief historical importance of the Hittites probably lies in the role which they played as intermediaries between the Tigris-Euphrates valley and the westernmost portions of the Near East. Doubtless in this way certain culture elements from Mesopotamia were transmitted to such nations as the Canaanites and Hyksos and perhaps to the peoples of the Aegean islands. But the Hittite culture itself appears not to have been without direct influence. It seems to have been reflected in the social customs of the Phrygians, who flourished from about 900 to 300 B.C. Their territory occupied the west central portion of Asia Minor, extending as far east as the Halys River. In language and literature they appear to have been

The Hittites as intermediaries

The Phrygians

121

The Goddess Kybele (Cybele), or Great Mother, on a Processional Car Drawn by Lions. Although this statue was produced by the Romans in the Second Century A.D., the goddess herself was of Phrygian origin. She became one of the most popular deities of the ancient world.

related to the Greeks, and they constituted an important channel for the transmission of culture elements to the Greeks and Romans. Their most widely copied institution was the cult of Cybele, the Great Mother, which spread rapidly and influenced the mystery religions of both Greece and Italy. The chief deities of the cult were Cybele, the Earth Mother, and Sabazius, the Son, who died and rose from the dead each year with the death and rebirth of vegetation. Its ceremonies were characterized by ecstatic frenzy, bloody sacrifices, and wild, orgiastic dances. The Phrygians were conquered by the Lydians about 610 B.C. but recovered their power and enjoyed a semi-independent and relatively prosperous status for another two centuries. Their early kings were all named either Gordius or Midas. The tomb of one of them was discovered in 1957 by a University of Pennsylvania archaeological expedition near Ankara, the capital of modern Turkey.

The Hittites and the Aegean civilization

Some authorities maintain that the Trojans who were attacked by the Greeks in the twelfth century B.C. were allies of the Hittites. If this is true, it would almost certainly follow that Trojan culture would bear the stamp of Hittite influence. And inasmuch as the Trojans maintained close relations with the Cretans, if they were not indeed of the same race, it would be reasonable to assume some cultural interchange between the Hittites and the principal centers of the Aegean civilization.

2. The Aegean Civilization

A long-forgotten civilization

By a strange coincidence the discovery of the existence of the Hittite and Aegean civilizations was made at just about the same time. Before 1870 scarcely anyone dreamed that a great civilization had flourished on the Aegean islands and on the shores of Asia Minor for hundreds of years prior to the rise of the Greeks. Students of the *Iliad* knew of course of the references to a strange people who were supposed to have dwelt in Troy, to have kidnaped the fair Helen, and to have been punished by the Greeks for this act by the siege and destruction of their city; but it was commonly

122

supposed that these accounts were mere figments of a poetical imagination.

The first discovery of an Aegean culture center was made not by a professional archaeologist but by a retired German business-man, Heinrich Schliemann. Fascinated from early youth by the stories of the Homeric epics, he determined to dedicate his life to archaeological research as soon as he had sufficient income to enable him to do so. Luckily for him and for the world he accumulated a fortune in Russian petroleum and then retired from business to spend both time and money in the pursuit of his boyhood dreams. In 1870 he began excavating at Troy. Within a few years he had uncovered portions of nine different cities, each built upon the ruins of its predecessor. The second of these cities he identified as the Troy of the *Iliad*, although it has been proved since that Troy was the sixth. After fulfilling his first great ambition, he started excavations on the mainland of Greece and eventually discovered two other Aegean cities, Mycenae and Tiryns. The work of Schliemann was soon followed by that of other investigators, notably the Englishman, Sir Arthur Evans, who discovered Knossos, the resplendent capital of the kings of Crete. Up to the present time more than half of the ancient Aegean sites have been carefully searched, and a wealth of knowledge has been accumulated about various aspects of the culture.

The discoveries by Schliemann and others

The Aegean civilization appears to have originated on the island of Crete, the settlements on the mainland of Greece and in Asia Minor being evidently due to expansion. In few other cases in history does the geographic interpretation of culture origins fit so neatly. Crete has a benign and equable climate, neither so hot as to make men lazy nor so cold as to require a life of unceasing struggle. While the soil is fertile, it is not of unlimited area; consequently, as the population increased, men were impelled to sharpen their wits and to contrive new means of earning a living. Some emigrated; others took to the sea; but a larger number remained at home and developed articles for export. The latter included, especially, wine and olive oil, pottery, gems and seals, knives and daggers, and objects of skilled craftsmanship. The chief imports were foodstuffs and metals. As a result of such trade, the country became an industrial and commercial nation with prosperous cities and extensive contacts with the surrounding civilized world. Added to these factors of a favorable environment were the beauties of nature, which abounded almost everywhere, stimulating the development of a marvelous art.

Geographic factors in Aegean history

The Aegean civilization was one of the earliest in the history of the world. As far back as 3000 B.C. the natives of Crete had made the transition from the Neolithic stage to the age of metals and probably to the age of writing. The first peak of advancement was attained under the leadership of the cities of Knossos and Phaistos about 1800

The Aegean civilization one of the oldest in the world

B.C. About a hundred years later a frightful calamity occurred. The great palace at Knossos was demolished and the chief buildings in several other cities as well. Exactly what happened has not been determined, but there is evidence that an earthquake followed by revolution accounted for the disaster. At any rate a new dynasty came to the throne, a new system of writing was adopted, and other elements in the life of the past were changed.

The glory and the downfall of the Aegean civilization

After about fifty years of uncertainty the Aegean civilization rose to new heights of brilliance and strength. Troy and the cities of Crete were rebuilt, and other great centers were established at Mycenae and Tiryns. Soon afterward Cretan hegemony was extended over the remaining portions of the Aegean world. But the new age of power and splendor was not destined for long duration. In the sixteenth century B.C. a group of barbarian Greeks known as Achaeans expanded from their original home Achaia in the northern Peloponnesus and eventually conquered Mycenae. Gradually absorbing the material culture of the vanquished, they became rich and powerful sea lords. About 1400 B.C. they overwhelmed the city of Knossos, and soon the whole island of Crete passed under their sway. Although they were no longer a primitive people, they seem never to have appreciated the finer aspects of Aegean culture. As a result this period of Mycenaean supremacy was marked by a decline in Aegean art and probably in intellect as well. In the twelfth century the Achaeans waged their successful war with the Trojans, but less than two hundred years later they fell themselves the victims of barbarian invasion. The new hordes that came in were also Greeks, but they belonged to the group known as Dorians (from Doris in central Greece). Their culture was relatively primitive, except for the fact that they had iron weapons. For centuries they had lived on the mainland of Greece, gradually penetrating farther southward. About 1200 B.C. they began their conquest of the Mycenaean cities. Two hundred years later the Aegean civilization had passed into the limbo of history.

The racial character of the Aegean people

The racial character of the Aegean people has been determined with substantial accuracy. Archaeological data from Crete, at least, have been found in sufficient profusion to leave little doubt that its ancient inhabitants were a composite nation. Their ancestors appear to have come from Syria and Anatolia and were closely related to the Hittites and to the earliest invaders of India. At the same time there is evidence—from the fact that their artists depicted them with long heads, short, slender bodies, and dark, wavy hair—that they bore a relationship to the Egyptians. Although they occupied Greek territory, they were not Greeks at all in the historic meaning of that name. The true Greeks, as we shall presently see, were of altogether different ethnic origin.

The Aegean civilization was probably one of the freest and most

progressive in all the Near Orient. The ruler was known by the title of Minos, which was roughly the equivalent of Pharaoh (hence the name *Minoan* which is sometimes applied to the civilization). That it was a title of divinity is shown by the fact that it was occasionally used as if it referred to a god. But the Minos was no bristling war lord like the Assyrian and Persian kings. His professional army was small; he had no great fortified cities; nor is there any indication of his use of conscription. He did have a large and efficient navy; but this was for defense against external attack and for the protection of trade, not to overawe the citizens at home.

On the other hand, there was some regimentation of industry; whether benevolent or not is unknown. The king was the chief capitalist and entrepreneur in the country. The factories in connection with his palace turned out great quantities of fine pottery, textiles, and metal goods. Some of their products were intended to supply the needs of the court, but plenty were sold at home and abroad for profit. Although private enterprise was not prohibited, the owners of smaller establishments were naturally at some disadvantage in competing with the king. Nevertheless, numerous privately owned factories did flourish, especially in cities other than the capital, and agriculture and trade were also in private hands. Gournia, for example, had its foundries for the manufacture of bronze, Therasia its olive-oil refineries, and Phaistos its potteries. It must be understood that these establishments, both royal and private, were factories in nearly every modern sense of the word. While they did not use power-driven machinery, they were engaged in large-scale production, and there was division of labor and centralized control and supervision of workers. The hundreds of women employed in the royal textile factory worked under the supervision of the queen.

The Aegean people of nearly all classes appear to have led happy and fairly prosperous lives. If slavery existed at all, it certainly occupied a very unimportant place. The houses in the poorest quarters of great industrial towns such as Gournia were substantially built and commodious, often with as many as six or eight rooms, but we do not know how many families resided in them. If we can judge from the number of inscriptions found in the homes of the common people, literacy was well-nigh universal. Women enjoyed complete equality with men. Regardless of class there was no public activity from which they were debarred, and no occupation which they could not enter. Crete had its female bull fighters and even female pugilists. Ladies of the upper strata devoted much time to fashion. Dressed in their tight-fitting bodices and bell-shaped skirts with flounces which would not have been much out of style in nineteenth-century Europe, they vied with each other for attention in the theaters and at public entertainments of numerous kinds.

The natives of the Aegean area delighted in games and sports of

*The love
of sports and
games*

every description. Chess, dancing, running matches, and boxing rivaled each other in their attraction for the people. The Cretans were the first to build stone theaters where processions and music entertained large audiences. But the most popular of all the diversions, as a spectacle at least, was the rodeo or bull-leaping exhibition. This sport was not so cruel as modern bullfighting, since there was no picador to torture the bull or matador to kill him. As soon as the animal was sufficiently infuriated to charge head down, an athlete would seize him by the horns, leap upon his back, turn a few somersaults, and then jump to the ground. No doubt these exhibitions were somewhat lacking in the tragic beauty which Ernest Hemingway sees in the Spanish bullfight, but they were decidedly more humane.

*The Aegean
religion*

The religion of the subjects of Minos was a medley of strange characteristics. First of all it was matriarchal. The chief deity was not a god but a goddess, who was the ruler of the entire universe —the sea and the sky as well as the earth. All existing things were emanations from her. But it was especially as the embodiment of fecundity, and therefore as the source of all life, that she attained her chief significance. In this capacity she was often represented as a madonna with bared breasts, carrying the holy child or tenderly watching over him. The serpent and the dove were her constant companions, possibly as active symbols of her generative power or of her qualities of wisdom and mercy. Originally no male deity appears to have been worshiped, but later a god was associated with the goddess as her son and lover. Although, like the divine sons in several other religions, he died and rose from the dead, he was never regarded by the Cretans as of particular importance.

*The mother
goddess*

In the second place, the Aegean religion was thoroughly monistic. The mother goddess was the source of evil as well as good; but not in any morbid or terrifying sense. Though she brought the storm and spread destruction in her path, these served for the replenishment of nature. Death itself was interpreted as the condition prerequisite for life. Whether the religion had any ethical purposes is unknown. Its followers undoubtedly looked forward to a happy survival in another world, although not necessarily as a reward for good deeds done on earth. The dead were buried with solicitous care and provided with nearly every accessory that would enhance their comfort and pleasure. Food and drink, toilet articles, lamps, razors, mirrors, and games were the principal articles furnished for the deceased of all classes and ages. In addition, the hunter was given his spear, the sailor a miniature of his favorite boat, children their toys, and rich men their servants in effigy. No signs of any belief in a place of future punishment have ever been found.

Other rather curious features included the worship of animals (the bull, the stag, and the minotaur, which was half bull and half man); the worship of sacred trees; the veneration of sacred objects which were probably reproductive symbols (the double-axe, the pillar, and the cross); and the employment of priestesses instead of priests to administer the rites of the cult. By far the most important act of worship was sacrifice. At the great religious festivals hundreds of animals and large quantities of grain and fruit were brought as grateful offerings to the goddess and her son. It is doubtful, however, that these sacrifices represented in any sense an atonement for sin. They were intended rather to provide sustenance for the deities and to bring man into sacramental fellowship with them. The common Oriental idea of the scapegoat sacrifice, or the shedding of blood for the remission of sins, would appear to have been foreign to the Aegean temperament.

Symbols and sacrifices

For nearly eighty years after the discovery of the Aegean civilization, its system of writing remained one of the enigmas of history. About 1950, however, the Czech scholar Bedrich Hrozny, who had already deciphered Hittite writing, succeeded in unlocking the mystery of Cretan inscriptions. He showed that this dominant Aegean people produced not only one system of writing but three— a hieroglyphic script and two linear scripts, which were used in successive periods. In 1953 an English scholar, Michael Ventris, announced that he had discovered a method which would enable him to decipher the second of these scripts, Linear Script B. In 1957 Dr. Cyrus H. Gordon, of Brandeis University, concluded that Linear Script A was Akkadian, written with a Cretan variation. But all of the inscriptions found thus far are records of business transactions, inventories, and the like. No literary texts have yet been unearthed. It is impossible therefore to tell whether any literature or philosophy had been written. The problem of scientific achievements is easier of solution, since we have material remains for our guidance. Archaeological discoveries on the island of Crete indicate that the ancient inhabitants were gifted inventors and engineers. They built excellent roads of concrete about eleven feet wide. Nearly all the basic principles of modern sanitary engineering were known to the designers of the palace of Knossos, with the result that the royal family of Crete in the seventeenth century B.C. enjoyed comforts and conveniences which were not available for the wealthiest rulers of Western countries in the seventeenth century A.D.

Cretan writing and scientific achievements

If there was any one achievement of the Aegean people which appears more than others to emphasize the vitality and freedom of their culture, it was their art. With the exception of the Greek, no other art of the ancient world was quite its equal. Its distinguishing features were delicacy, spontaneity, and naturalism. It served not to glorify the ambitions of an arrogant ruling class or to inculcate the doctrines of a religion, but to express the delight of the ordinary man in the world of beauty around him. As a result, it was remarkably free from the retarding influence of ancient tradition. It was unique, moreover, in the universality of its application, for it ex-

Aegean art

Architecture

Painting

tended not merely to paintings and statues but even to the humblest objects of ordinary use.

Of the major arts, architecture was the least developed. The great palaces were not remarkably beautiful buildings but rambling structures designed primarily for capaciousness and comfort. As more and more functions were absorbed by the state, the palaces were enlarged to accommodate them. New quarters were annexed to those already built or piled on top of them without regard for order or symmetry. The interiors, however, were decorated with beautiful paintings and furnishings. The architecture of Crete may be said to have resembled the modern international style in its subordination of form to utility and in its emphasis upon a pleasing and livable interior as more important than external beauty.

Painting was the art supreme of the Aegean world. Nearly all of it consisted of murals done in fresco, although painted reliefs were occasionally to be found. The murals in the palaces of Crete were by all odds the best that have survived from ancient times. They re-

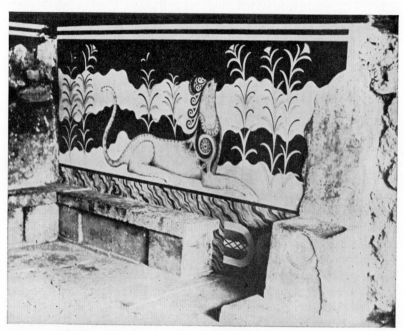

Throne Room in the Palace of Minos. The throne and bench are original; the fresco has been restored in accordance with fragments found on the site which are now in the Candia Museum on the island of Crete. A remarkable grace characterizes the lilies and the body and head of the mythical animal.

vealed almost perfectly the remarkable gifts of the Minoan artist—his instinct for the dramatic, his sense of rhythm, his feeling for nature in her most characteristic moods. He loved to depict the furious gallop of the frightened deer, the stealthy tread of the cat

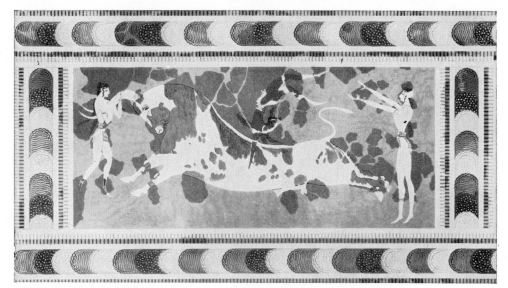

Scenes from the Bull Ring. Cretan painting, about 1500 B.C. Evident are the Cretans' devotion to sport and the skill and agility of their athletes. The body and horns of the bull, however, are exaggerated as are the slenderness of the athletes and their full-face eyes in profile heads.

stalking its prey in the weeds, or the graceful bending of the lily on its slender stem.

Sculpture and the ceramic and gem-carving arts were also developed to a high stage of perfection. The sculpture of the Cretans differed from that of any other people in the ancient Orient. It never relied upon size as a device to convey the idea of power. The Cretans produced no colossi like those of Egypt or reliefs like those of Babylonia depicting a king of gigantic proportions smiting his puny enemies. Instead, they preferred sculpture in miniature. Nearly all of the statues of human beings or of deities that the archaeologists have found are smaller than life-size. Neither was the plastic art of the Aegean essentially propagandistic. Its dominant purpose, as in the case of painting, was to express the individual's delight in the color and drama of his environment. Likewise, the delicately painted pottery, thin as eggshell, the skillfully engraved and inlaid daggers and knives, and the gems and seals of infinitely varied design revealed an almost incredible mastery of materials and respect for the form and beauty of nature.

Sculpture, pottery, and engraving

Much has been written about the significance of the Aegean civilization and its relation to the surrounding cultures. By some historians it is regarded as a mere offshoot of the civilization of Egypt. A number of facts can be adduced to support this view. Both nations were ethnically similar. Their governments were alike in their theocratic character. Both societies contained elements of

Was the Aegean civilization an offshoot of the Egyptian?

129

matriarchy and economic collectivism. But that is about as far as the comparison can be carried. The differences were just as marked. The Aegean people built no great pyramids or magnificent temples. Only in painting did their art resemble that of Egypt very closely. The systems of writing of the two civilizations appear to have been of entirely independent origin, as is evidenced by the fact that a knowledge of Egyptian helps very little in deciphering Cretan. Whereas the Egyptian religion was an elaborate ethical system based upon the worship of a sun god of righteousness and justice, the religion of the Aegean venerated a goddess of nature with no evidence of a concept of ethical purpose. Finally, the two peoples differed in their basic philosophies of life. The Egyptians believed in the sacrifice of personal interests to the glory and eternity of the state and looked to rewards in an after-existence as a just compensation for good deeds on earth. The people of the Aegean were individualists, intent upon living their own lives of pleasurable activity and concerned with the hereafter merely as an extension of their pleasant and satisfying earthly careers.

The influence of the Aegean civilization

The influence of the Aegean civilization is not easy to estimate. The Philistines, who came from some part of the Aegean world, introduced certain aspects of the culture into Palestine and Syria. There is reason to believe that various elements of Phoenician art and the Samson legends of the Old Testament were really acquired from the Philistines. It is probable also that the religious and aesthetic traditions of the Cretans and perhaps something of their spirit of freedom influenced the Greeks. But a considerable part of the Aegean civilization was lost or destroyed. Following the downfall of Knossos a dark age began which lasted for nearly four hundred years. The conquerors were barbarians who were unable to appreciate much of the culture of the people they conquered and consequently allowed it to perish.

Importance of the Aegean civilization for the modern world

Despite its limited influence the Aegean civilization is not without importance for the student of history; for it was one of the few in ancient times which assured to even its humblest citizens a reasonable share of happiness and prosperity, free from the tyranny of a despotic state and a crafty priesthood. The apparent absence of slavery, brutal punishments, forced labor, and conscription, together with the substantial equality of classes and the dignified status accorded to women, all point to a social regime in striking contrast with those of the Asiatic empires. If additional evidence of this contrast is needed, it can be found in the art of the various nations. The Aegean sculptor or painter gloried not in portraying the slaughter of armies or the sacking of cities but in picturing flowery landscapes, joyous festivals, thrilling exhibitions of athletic prowess, and similar scenes of a free and peaceful existence. Last of all, the Aegean civilization is significant for its kinship with what we often think of as the modern spirit. This is clearly exemplified in the devotion of the people to comfort and opulence, in their love of amusement, in their individualism, zest for life, and courage for experimentation.

3. The Lydians and the Phoenicians

When the Hittite empire fell in the eighth century B.C., its successor in its main areas of power was the kingdom of Lydia. The Lydians established their rule in what is now the territory of the Turkish Republic in Anatolia. They quickly secured control of the Greek cities on the coast of Asia Minor and of the entire plateau west of the Halys River. But their power was short-lived. In 550 B.C. their fabulous king, Croesus, fancied he saw a good opportunity to add to his domain the territory of the Medes east of the Halys. The Median king had just been deposed by Cyrus the Persian. Thinking this meant an easy triumph for his own armies, Croesus set out to capture the territory beyond the river. After an indecisive battle with Cyrus, he returned to his own capital (Sardis) for reinforcements. Here Cyrus caught him unprepared in a surprise attack and captured and burned the city. The Lydians never recovered from the blow, and soon afterward all of their territory, including the Greek cities on the coast, passed under the dominion of Cyrus the Great.

The kingdom of Lydia

The Lydians were a people of Indo-European speech, who were probably a mixture of native peoples of Asia Minor with migrant stocks from eastern Europe. Benefiting from the advantages of favorable location and abundance of resources, they enjoyed one of the highest standards of living of ancient times. They were famous for the splendor of their armored chariots and the quantities of gold and articles of luxury possessed by the citizens. The wealth of their kings was legendary, as attested by the simile "rich as Croesus." The chief sources of this prosperity were gold from the streams, wool from the thousands of sheep on the hills, and the profits of the extensive commerce which passed overland from the Tigris-Euphrates valley to the Aegean Sea. But with all their wealth and opportunities for leisure, they succeeded in making only one original contribution to civilization. This was the coinage of money from electrum or "white gold," a natural mixture of gold and silver found in the sands of one of their rivers. Hitherto all systems of money had consisted of weighed rings or bars of metal. The new coins, of varying sizes, were stamped with a definite value more or less arbitrarily given by the ruler who issued them.

The Lydian people and their culture

In contrast with the Lydians, who gained their ascendancy as a result of the downfall of the Hittites, were the Phoenicians, who benefited from the break-up of Aegean supremacy. But the Phoe-

*The Phoenician
cities and con-
federation*

*Achievements
of the Phoe-
nicians*

nicians were neither conquerors nor the builders of an empire. They exerted their influence through the arts of peace, especially through commerce. During most of their history their political system was a loose confederation of city-states, which frequently bought their security by paying tribute to foreign powers. The territory they occupied was the narrow strip between the Lebanon Mountains and the Mediterranean Sea. With good harbors and a central location, it was admirably situated for trade. The great centers of commerce included Tyre, Sidon, and Beirut. Under the leadership of the first, Phoenicia reached the zenith of her cultural brilliance, from the tenth to the eighth century B.C. During the sixth century she passed under the domination of the Chaldeans and then of the Persians. In 332 B.C. Tyre was destroyed by Alexander the Great after a siege of seven months.

The Phoenicians were a people of Semitic language, closely related to the Canaanites. They displayed very little creative genius, but were remarkable adapters of the achievements of others. They produced no original art worthy of the name, and they made but slight contributions to literature. Their religion, like that of the Canaanites, was characterized by human sacrifice to the god Moloch and by licentious fertility rites. They excelled, however, in specialized manufactures and in geography and navigation. They were renowned throughout the ancient world for their glass and metal industries and for their purple dye obtained from a mollusk in the adjacent seas. They developed the art of navigation to such a stage that they could sail by the stars at night. To less venturesome peoples, the North Star was known for some time as the Phoenicians' star. A company of Phoenicians is believed to have circumnavigated Africa. The most lasting achievement of the Phoenicians, however, was the completion and diffusion of an alphabet based upon principles discovered by the Egyptians. The Phoenician contribution was the adoption of a system of signs representing the sounds of the human voice, and the elimination of all pictographic and syllabic characters. The Egyptians, as we have seen, had accomplished the first of these steps but not the second.

Selected Readings

Burn, A. R., *Minoans, Philistines and Greeks*, New York, 1930
Ceram, C. W., *The Secret of the Hittites*, New York, 1956
Childe, V. G., *The Bronze Age*, New York, 1930
Cowley, A. E., *The Hittites*, New York, 1926
Evans, Sir A. J., *The Palace of Minos*, New York, 1921–23, Vols. I–IV
Garstang, John, *The Hittite Empire*, New York, 1929
Glotz, Gustave, *The Aegean Civilization*, New York, 1927
Hall, H. R., *The Civilization of Greece in the Bronze Age*, London, 1928

Hrozny, Bedrich, *Ancient History of Western Asia, India and Crete,*
Prague, 1953
Nilsson, M. P., *The Minoan-Mycenaean Religion and Its Survival in Greek Religion,* New York, 1927
Willetts, R. F., *Aristocratic Society in Ancient Crete,* London, 1955

Source Materials

Evans, Sir Arthur, *Scripta Minoa; the Written Documents of Minoan Crete*
Hertzler, J. O., *The Social Thought of the Ancient Civilizations,* pp. 135-44

The Classical Civilizations
of Greece and Rome

After 600 B.C. the centers of civilization in the Western world were no longer confined to the Near Orient. By that time new cultures were already growing to maturity in Greece and in Italy. Both had started their evolution considerably earlier, but the civilization of Greece did not begin to ripen until about 600 B.C., while the Romans showed little promise of original achievement before 500. About 300 B.C. Greek civilization, properly speaking, came to an end and was superseded by a new culture representing a fusion of elements derived from Greece and from the Near Orient. This was the Hellenistic civilization, which lasted until about the beginning of the Christian era and included not only the Greek peninsula but Egypt and most of Asia west of the Indus River. The outstanding characteristic which serves to distinguish these three civilizations from the ones that had gone before is secularism. No longer does religion absorb the interests of man to the extent that it did in ancient Egypt or in the nations of Mesopotamia. The state is now above the church, and the power of the priests to determine the direction of cultural evolution has been thoroughly shattered. Furthermore, ideals of human freedom and an emphasis upon the welfare of man as an individual have largely superseded the despotism and collectivism of the ancient Near Orient.

Politics	Arts and Letters
Homeric Age, 1200–800	

1000– B.C.

Rome founded, *ca.* 1000	
Beginning of city-states in Greece, *ca.* 800	*Iliad* and *Odyssey, ca.* 800

500– B.C.

Age of the Tyrants in Greece, 650–500	Doric architecture, 650–500
Reforms of Solon, 594–560	
Reforms of Cleisthenes, 508–502	Aeschylus, 525–456
Overthrow of monarchy in Rome and establishment of republic, *ca.* 500	Phidias, 500?–432
Patrician-plebeian struggle in Rome, 500–287	Ionic architecture, *ca.* 500–400
Greco-Persian War, 493–479	Sophocles, 496–406
	Herodotus, 484–425
Delian League, 479–404	Euripides, 480–406
	Thucydides, 471?–400?
Perfection of Athenian democracy, 461–429	Parthenon, *ca.* 460
Law of the Twelve Tables (Rome), *ca.* 450	Aristophanes, 448?–380?
Peloponnesian War, 431–404	

400– B.C.

Decline of democracy in Greece, 400	Corinthian architecture, *ca.* 400–300
Theban supremacy in Greece, 371–362	Praxiteles, 370?–310?
Macedonian conquest of Greece, 338–337	
Conquests of Alexander the Great, 336–323	
Division of Alexander's empire, 323	

300– B.C.

Hortensian Law (Rome), 287	
Punic Wars, 264–146	

200– B.C.

Revolt of the Gracchi, 133–121	

100– B.C.

	Vergil, 70 B.C.–19 A.D.
Dictatorship of Julius Caesar, 46–44	Horace, 65 B.C.–8 A.D.
Principate of Augustus Caesar, 27 B.C.–14 A.D.	
	Tacitus, 55?–117 A.D.
	Colosseum, *ca.* 80 A.D.

Philosophy and Science	Economics	Religion
		Development of worldly, non-ethical religion of the Greeks, 1200–800
	Economic Revolution and colonization in Greece, 750–600 Rise of middle class in Greece, 750–600	
Thales of Miletus, 640–546 Pythagoras, 582?–507		
		Orphic and Eleusinian mystery cults, 500–100
Protagoras, 481?–411 Socrates, 469–399 Hippocrates, 460–377? Democritus, 460?–362? Sophists, *ca.* 450–400 Plato, 427–347		
Aristotle, 384–322 Epicurus, 342–270 Zeno (the Stoic), 336–264 Euclid, 323?–285 Aristarchus, 310–230	Growth of advertising and insurance, 300 B.C.–100 A.D. Hellenistic world trade, 300 B.C.–100 A.D. International money economy, 300 B.C.–100 A.D. Growth of serfdom in Hellenistic empires, 300 B.C.–100 A.D.	
Archimedes, 287?–212 Eratosthenes, 276?–195?	Growth of metropolitan cities, 300 B.C.–400 A.D. Growth of slavery in Rome, 250–100 Rise of middle class in Rome, 250–100	Oriental mystery cults in Rome, 250–50
Herophilus, 220?–150 Polybius, 205?–123?	Decline of small farmer in Rome, 250–100	
	Depressions and unemployment in Hellenistic world, 200 B.C.–100 A.D.	
Skeptics, 200–100	Decline of slavery in Hellenistic world, 200 B.C.–100 A.D.	Development of mysticism and otherworldliness, 200
Introduction of Stoicism into Rome, *ca.* 140 Cicero, 106–43 Lucretius, 98–55		
Seneca, 3 B.C.–65 A.D.	Decline of slavery in Rome, 27 B.C.–476 A.D.	Spread of Mithraism in Rome, 27 B.C.–270 A.D. First persecution of Christians in Rome, *ca.* 65 A.D.

	Politics	Arts and Letters
100— **A.D.**	Barbarian invasions of Rome, *ca.* 100–476 A.D. Completion of Roman law by the great jurists, *ca.* 200 A.D.	
300— **A.D.**	Diocletian, 284–305 A.D. Constantine I, 306–337 A.D.	
476— **A.D.**	Theodosius I, 378–395 A.D. Deposition of last of Roman emperors, 476 A.D.	

GREECE AND ROME (*Continued*)

Philosophy and Science	Economics	Religion
Marcus Aurelius, 121–180 A.D. Galen, 130–200? A.D. Neo-Platonism, 250–600 A.D.		
	Growth of serfdom and extralegal feudalism in Rome, 300–500 A.D.	Beginning of toleration of Christians in Rome, 311 A.D. Christianity made official religion of Roman Empire, 380 A.D.

The Hellenic Civilization

*The character
of Hellenic
civilization*

Among all the peoples of the ancient world, the one whose culture most clearly exemplified the spirit of Western man was the Hellenic or Greek. No other of these nations had so strong a devotion to liberty or so firm a belief in the nobility of human achievement. The Greeks glorified man as the most important creature in the universe and refused to submit to the dictation of priests or despots or even to humble themselves before their gods. Their attitude was essentially secular and rationalistic; they exalted the spirit of free inquiry and made knowledge supreme over faith. It was largely for these reasons that they advanced their culture to the highest stage which the ancient world was destined to reach. But the Greeks did not begin without foundations. It is necessary to remember that the groundwork for many of their achievements had already been laid by certain of the Oriental peoples. The rudiments of their philosophy and science had been prepared by the Egyptians. The Greek alphabet was derived from Phoenicia. And probably to a larger extent than we shall ever realize the Hellenic appreciation of beauty and freedom was a product of Aegean influence.

1. The Homeric Age

*The foundations
of Greek
civilization*

In order to understand the evolution of the Hellenic civilization it is necessary to go back to the first period of its history, the Homeric Age, which extended from approximately 1200 to 800 B.C. It was then that the Greek nation was formed and the foundations laid for many of the social and political developments of subsequent centuries. Not all of the glory that was Greece can be traced to the Homeric Age, but it is nonetheless true that several of the most typical institutions and attitudes of the Greeks in their prime were

140 modifications of forms which had survived from the earliest days.

Probably the original home of the Greeks was somewhere in the Danube valley. When they began their migrations into the Greek peninsula about 2000 B.C., they appear to have been a mixture of Alpine and Nordic stocks, predominantly the former. Later they mingled with the Mediterranean natives who were already established in Greece, especially in the southern portions and on the islands of the Aegean Sea. It is therefore patently absurd to attempt any explanation of the genius of the Greeks on the basis of purity of race, for no one really knows which of the principal admixtures finally came to predominate. About all that it is possible to say is that the Hellenes were a mixed race who spoke a language of Indo-European relationship.

By 1200 B.C. the Greeks had occupied most of the northern sections of the peninsula and a few scattered locations along the coast. At first they filtered in slowly, bringing their herds and flocks with them and settling in the more sparsely populated areas. Many of these early immigrants seem to have belonged to the group which later came to be known as Ionians. Another division, the Achaeans, pushed farther south, conquered Mycenae and Troy, and ultimately gained dominion over Crete. Soon after 1200 the great Dorian invasions began and reached their climax about two centuries later. Some of the Dorians settled in central Greece, but most of them took to the sea, conquering the eastern sections of the Peloponnesus and the southern islands of the Aegean. About 1000 B.C. they captured Knossos, the chief center of the Minoan civilization on the island of Crete.

The early migrations

Whether Achaeans, Ionians, or Dorians, all of the Greeks in the Homeric Age had essentially the same culture, which was comparatively primitive. Not until the very last century of the period was there any general knowledge of writing. Although evidence exists that the Achaeans had a system of writing as early as 1200 B.C., their case was exceptional. We must therefore envisage the Homeric Greeks as a preliterate people during the greater part of their history, with intellectual accomplishments that extended no farther than the development of folk songs, ballads, and short epics sung and embellished by bards as they wandered from one village to another. A large part of this material was finally woven into a great epic cycle by one or more poets and put into written form in the ninth century B.C. Though not all of the poems of this cycle have come down to us, the two most important, the *Iliad* and the *Odyssey*, provide us with our richest store of information about the ideals and customs of the Homeric Age.

The primitive character of Homeric culture

The political institutions of the Homeric Greeks were exceedingly primitive. Each little community of villages was independent of external control, but political authority was so tenuous that it would not be too much to say that the state scarcely existed at all. The king could not make or enforce laws or administer justice. He

Government in the Homeric Age

received no remuneration of any kind, but had to cultivate his farm for a living the same as any other citizen. Practically his only functions were military and priestly. He commanded the army in time of war and offered sacrifices to keep the gods on the good side of the community. Although each little group of villages had its council of nobles and assembly of warriors, neither of these bodies had any definite membership or status as an organ of government. The duties of the former were to advise and assist the king and prevent him from usurping despotic powers. The functions of the latter were to ratify declarations of war and assent to the conclusion of peace. Almost without exception custom took the place of law, and the administration of justice was private. Even willful murder was punishable only by the family of the victim. While it is true that disputes were sometimes submitted to the king for settlement, he acted in such cases merely as an arbitrator, not as a judge. As a matter of fact, the political consciousness of the Greeks of this time was so poorly developed that they had no conception of government as an indispensable agency for the preservation of social order. When Odysseus, king of Ithaca, was absent for twenty years, no regent was appointed in his place, and no session of the council or assembly was held. No one seemed to think that the complete suspension of government, even for so long a time, was a matter of any critical importance.

The rudimentary pattern of social and economic life

The pattern of social and economic life was amazingly simple. Though the general tone of the society portrayed in the epics is aristocratic, there was actually no rigid stratification of classes. Any warrior who displayed unusual bravery in battle could become a noble. Manual labor was not looked upon as degrading, and there were apparently no idle rich. That there were dependent laborers of some kind who worked on the lands of the nobles and served them as faithful warriors seems clear from the Homeric epics, but it is doubtful that they were really slaves, for they were treated as members of the noble's family and could not be sold away from their homes. Agriculture and herding were the basic occupations. Except for a few skilled crafts like those of wagonmaker, swordsmith, goldsmith, and potter, there was no specialization of labor. For the most part every household made its own tools, wove its own clothing, and raised its own food. So far were the Greeks of this time from being a trading people that they had no word in their language for "merchant," and barter was the only method of exchange that was practiced.

Religious conceptions in the Homeric Age

To the Greeks of the Homeric Age religion meant chiefly a system for: (1) explaining the physical world in such a way as to remove its awesome mysteries and give man a feeling of intimate relationship with it; (2) accounting for the tempestuous passions which seized man's nature and made him lose that self-control which the Greeks considered essential for success as a warrior; and (3) obtaining such material benefits as good fortune, long life, skill in craftsmanship, and abundant harvests. Neither at this time nor at any other period of their history did the Greeks expect that their religion would save them from sin or endow them with spiritual blessings. As they conceived it, piety was neither a matter of conduct nor of faith. Their religion, accordingly, had no commandments and no dogmas, no complicated ritual and no sacraments. Every man was at liberty to believe what he pleased and to conduct his own life as he chose without fear of the wrath of the gods. Probably it is no exaggeration to say that this freedom from dogmatism and from fear of the supernatural was one of the most important factors contributing to the intellectual and artistic progress of the Greeks.

As is commonly known, the deities of the Homeric religion were merely human beings writ large. It was really necessary that this should be so if the Greek was to feel at home in the world over which they ruled. Remote, omnipotent beings like the gods of most Oriental religions would have inspired fear rather than a sense of security. What the Greek wanted was not necessarily gods of great power, but deities he could bargain with on equal terms. Consequently he endowed his gods with attributes similar to his own— with human bodies and human weaknesses and wants. He imagined the great company of divinities as frequently quarreling with one another, needing food and sleep, mingling freely with men, and even procreating children occasionally by mortal women. They differed from men only in the fact that they subsisted on ambrosia and nectar, which made them immortal. They dwelt not in the sky or in the stars but on the summit of Mount Olympus, a peak in northern Greece with an altitude of about 10,000 feet.

The deities of the Homeric religion

The religion was thoroughly polytheistic, and no one deity was elevated very high above any of the others. Zeus, the sky god and wielder of the thunderbolt, who was sometimes referred to as the father of the gods and of men, frequently received less attention than Apollo, the sun god, who could reveal the future, or Athena, the goddess of war and patroness of handicrafts. Since the Greeks had no Satan, their religion cannot be described as dualistic. Nearly all of the deities were capable of malevolence as well as good, for they sometimes deceived men and caused them to commit wrongs. The nearest approach to a god of evil was Hades, who presided over the nether world. Although he is referred to in the Homeric poems as "implacable and unyielding" and the most hateful of gods to mortals, he was never assumed to have played an active role in affairs on earth. He was not considered as the source of pestilence, earthquake, or famine. He did not tempt men or work to defeat the benevolent designs of other gods. In short, he was really not regarded as anything more than the guardian of the realm of the dead.

Nature of the gods and goddesses

The Greeks of the Homeric Age were almost completely indifferent to what happened to them after death. Not only did they bestow no care upon the bodies of the dead, but they frequently cremated them. They did assume, however, that the shades or ghosts of men survived for a time after the death of their bodies. All, with a few exceptions, went to the same abode—to the murky realm of Hades situated beneath the earth. This was neither a paradise nor a hell: no one was rewarded for his good deeds, and no one was punished for his sins. Each of the shades appeared to continue the same kind of life its human embodiment had lived on earth. The Homeric poems make casual mention of two other realms, the Elysian Plain and the realm of Tartarus, which seem at first glance to contradict the idea of no rewards and punishments in the hereafter. But the few individuals who enjoyed the ease and comfort of the Elysian Plain had done nothing to deserve such blessings; they were simply persons whom the gods had chosen to favor. The realm of Tartarus was not really an abode of the dead but a place of imprisonment for rebellious deities.

Worship in the Homeric religion consisted primarily of sacrifice. The offerings were made, however, not as an atonement for sin, but merely in order to please the gods and induce them to grant favors. In other words, religious practice was external and mechanical and not far removed from magic. Reverence, humility, and purity of heart were not essentials in it. The worshiper had only to carry out his part of the bargain by making the proper sacrifice, and the gods would fulfill theirs. For a religion such as this no elaborate institutions were required. Even a professional priesthood was unnecessary. Since there were no mysteries and no sacraments, one man could perform the simple rites about as well as another. As a general rule, each head of a family implored the favor of the gods for his own household, and the king performed the same function for the community at large. Although it is true that seers or prophets were frequently consulted because of the belief that they were directly inspired by the gods and could therefore foretell the future, these were not of a priestly class. Furthermore, the Homeric religion included no cult or sacred relics, no holy days, and no system of temple worship. The Greek temple was not a church or place of religious assemblage, and no ceremonies were performed within it. Instead it was a shrine which the god might visit occasionally and use as a temporary house.

As intimated already, the morality of the Greeks in the Homeric period had only the vaguest connection with their religion. While it is true that the gods were generally disposed to support the right, they did not consider it their duty to combat evil and make righteousness prevail. In meting out rewards to men, they appear to have been influenced more by their own whims and by gratitude for sacrifices offered than by any consideration for moral character. The only crime they punished was perjury, and that none too consistently. The conclusion seems justified, then, that Homeric morality rested upon no basis of supernatural sanctions. Perhaps its true foundation was military. Nearly all the virtues extolled in the epics were those which would make the individual a better soldier—bravery, self-control, patriotism, wisdom (in the sense of cunning), love of one's friends, and hatred of one's enemies. There was no conception of sin in the Christian sense of wrongful acts to be repented of or atoned for.

At the end of the Homeric Age the Greek was already well started along the road of social ideals that he was destined to follow in later centuries. He was an optimist, convinced that life was worth living for its own sake, and he could see no reason for looking forward to death as a glad release. He was an egoist, striving for the fulfillment of self. As a consequence he rejected mortification of the flesh and all forms of denial which would imply the frustration of life. He could see no merit in humility or in turning the other cheek. He was a humanist, who worshiped the finite and the natural rather than the otherworldly or sublime. For this reason he refused to invest his gods with awe-inspiring qualities, or to invent any conception of man as a depraved and sinful creature. Finally, he was devoted to liberty in an even more extreme form than most of his descendants in the classical period were willing to accept.

The basic Greek ideals

2. The Evolution of the City-States

About 800 B.C. the village communities of the Homeric Age, which had been founded mainly upon clan organization, began to give way to larger political units. As the need for defense increased, an acropolis or citadel was built on a high location, and a city grew up around it as the seat of government for a whole community. Thus emerged the city-state, the most famous unit of political society developed by the Greeks. Examples were to be found in almost every section of the Hellenic world. Athens, Thebes, and Megara on the mainland; Sparta and Corinth on the Peloponnesus; Miletus on the shore of Asia Minor; and Mitylene and Chalcis on the islands of the Aegean Sea were among the best known. They varied enormously in both area and population. Sparta with more than three thousand square miles and Athens with 1060 had by far the greatest extent; the others averaged less than a hundred. At the peak of their power Athens and Sparta, each with a population of about 400,000, had approximately three times the numerical strength of most of their neighboring states.

The origin and nature of the city-states

With a few exceptions the Greek city-states went through a similar political evolution. They began their histories as monarchies. During the eighth century they were changed into oligarchies. About a hundred years later, on the average, the oligarchies were overthrown by dictators, or "tyrants," as the Greeks called them,

The evolution of the city-states

meaning usurpers who ruled without legal right whether oppressively or not. Finally, in the sixth and fifth centuries, democracies were set up; or in some cases "timocracies," that is, governments based upon a property qualification for the exercise of political rights.

On the whole, it is not difficult to determine the causes of this political evolution. The first change came about as a result of the concentration of landed wealth. As the owners of great estates waxed in economic power, they determined to wrest political authority from the king and vest it in the council, which they generally controlled. In the end they abolished the kingship entirely. Then followed a period of sweeping economic changes and political turmoil. The increasing scarcity of land forced many of the Greeks to emigrate and seek new homes for themselves in unoccupied regions. As a result, numerous colonies were founded, mostly along the shores of the Aegean and Ionian Seas, but some as far east as the Black Sea and as far west as Italy and Spain. The demand for new outlets for trade also prompted some of this expansion. The consequence was a veritable economic revolution in the Greek world. Commerce and industry grew to be leading pursuits, the urban population increased, and wealth assumed new forms. The rising middle class now joined with dispossessed farmers in an attack upon the landholding oligarchy. The natural fruit of the bitter class conflicts that ensued was dictatorship. By encouraging extravagant hopes and promising relief from chaos, ambitious demagogues attracted enough popular support to enable them to ride into power in defiance of constitutions and laws. Ultimately, however, dissatisfaction with tyrannical rule and the increasing economic power and political consciousness of the common citizens led to the establishment of democracies or liberal oligarchies.

*The causes
of the political
cycle*

Unfortunately space does not permit an analysis of the political history of each of the Greek city-states. Except in the more backward sections of Thessaly and the Peloponnesus, it is safe to conclude that the internal development of all of them paralleled the account given above, although minor variations due to local conditions doubtless occurred. The two most important of the Hellenic states, Sparta and Athens, deserve more detailed study.

*The similar
development of
the city-states*

3. The Armed Camp of Sparta

The history of Sparta [1] was the great exception to the political evolution of the city-states. Despite the fact that her citizens were of the purest Dorian strain, she failed to make any progress in the direction of democratic rule. Instead, her government rapidly de-

*The peculiar
development of
Sparta*

[1] Sparta was the leading city of a district called Laconia or Lacedaemonia; sometimes the *state* was referred to by one or the other of these names. The people, also, were frequently called Laconians or Lacedaemonians.

generated into a form more closely resembling the absolutism of the Orient. Culturally, also, the nation stagnated. The causes were due partly to isolation. Hemmed in by mountains on the northeast and west and lacking good harbors, the Spartan people had little opportunity to profit from the advances made in the outside world. Besides, no middle class arose to aid the masses in the struggle for freedom.

The real explanation is to be found, however, in militarism. The Spartans had come into the eastern Peloponnesus as àn invading army. For centuries they had struggled to subdue the Mycenaean natives they found there. By 800 B.C., when they finally succeeded in gaining dominion over all of Laconia, military habits were so firmly fixed that they could not be thrown off. As a consequence, while the other Greek states sated their land hunger through colonization, Sparta, as her population increased, inevitably chose to live by the sword. West of the Taygetus Mountains lay the fertile plain of Messenia. In the late eighth century the Spartans determined to conquer it. The venture was successful, and the Messenian territory was annexed to Laconia. About fifty years later the Messenians enlisted the aid of Argos and launched a revolt. The war that followed was desperately fought, Laconia itself was invaded, and apparently it was only the death of the Argive commander and the patriotic pleas of the fire-eating poet Tyrtaeus that saved the day for the Spartans. This time the victors took no chances. They confiscated the lands of the Messenians, murdered or expelled their leaders, and forced the masses into serfdom.

The origins of Spartan militarism

There was scarcely a feature of the life of the Spartans which was not the result of their martial enterprises. In subduing and despoiling their enemies they unwittingly enslaved themselves; for they lived through the remaining centuries of their history in deadly fear of insurrections. It was this fear which explains their conservatism, their stubborn resistance to change, lest any innovation result in a fatal weakening of the system. Their provincialism can also be attributed to the same cause. Frightened by the prospect that dangerous ideas might be brought into their country, they discouraged travel and prohibited trade with the outside world. The necessity of maintaining the absolute supremacy of the citizen class over an enormous population of serfs required an iron discipline and a strict subordination of the individual; hence the Spartan collectivism, which extended into every branch of the social and economic life. Finally, much of the cultural backwardness of Sparta grew out of the atmosphere of coarseness and hate which inevitably resulted from the bitter struggle to conquer the Messenians and hold them under stern repression.

The results of Spartan militarism

The Spartan constitution, which tradition ascribed to an ancient lawgiver, Lycurgus, provided for a government preserving the forms of the old Homeric system. Instead of one king, however, there were two, representing separate families of exalted rank. The Spartan sovereigns enjoyed but few powers and those chiefly of a military and priestly character. A second and more authoritative branch of the government was the council, composed of the two kings and twenty-eight nobles sixty years of age and over. This body supervised the work of administration, prepared measures for submission to the assembly, and served as the highest court for criminal trials. The third organ of government, the assembly, approved or rejected the proposals of the council and elected all public officials except the kings. But the highest authority under the Spartan constitution was vested in a board of five men known as the ephorate. The ephors virtually were the government. They presided over the council and the assembly, controlled the educational system and the distribution of property, censored the lives of the citizens, and exercised a veto power over all legislation. They had power also to determine the fate of newborn infants, to conduct prosecutions before the council, and even to depose the kings if the religious omens appeared unfavorable. The Spartan government was thus very decidedly an oligarchy. In spite of the fact that the ephors were chosen for one-year terms by the assembly, they were indefinitely re-eligible, and their authority was so vast that there was hardly any ramification of the system which they could not control. Moreover, it should be borne in mind that the assembly itself was not a democratic body. Not even the whole citizen class, which was a small minority of the total population, was entitled to membership in it, but only those males of full political status who had incomes sufficient to qualify them for enrollment in the heavy infantry.

The population of Sparta, which numbered at its peak about 400,000, was divided into three main classes. The ruling element was made up of the Spartiates, or descendants of the original conquerors. Though never exceeding one-twentieth of the total population, the Spartiates alone had political privileges. Next in order of rank were the perioeci, or "dwellers around." The origin of this class is uncertain, but it was probably composed of peoples that had at one time been allies of the Spartans or had submitted voluntarily to Spartan domination. In return for service as a buffer population between the ruling class and the serfs, the perioeci were allowed to carry on trade and to engage in manufacturing. At the bottom of the scale were the helots, or serfs, bound to the soil and despised and persecuted by their masters.

Among these classes only the perioeci enjoyed any appreciable measure of comfort and freedom. While it is true that the economic condition of the helots cannot be described in terms of absolute misery, since they were permitted to keep for themselves a good share of what they produced on the estates of their masters, they were personally subjected to such shameful treatment that they were constantly wretched and rebellious. On occasions they were compelled to give exhibitions of drunkenness and lascivious dances as an example to the Spartan youth of the effects of such practices. At the beginning of each year, if we can believe the testimony of Aristotle, the ephors declared war upon the helots, presumably for the purpose of giving a gloss of legality to the murder of any by the secret police upon suspicion of disloyalty.

Discipline for the benefit of the state

Those who were born into the Spartiate class were doomed to a respectable slavery for the major part of their lives. Forced to submit to the severest discipline and to sacrifice individual interests, they were nothing but cogs in a vast machine. Their education was limited almost entirely to military training, supplemented by exposure and merciless floggings to harden them for the duties of war. Between the ages of twenty and sixty they gave all their time to service to the state. Although marriage was practically compulsory, no family life was permitted. Husbands carried off their wives on the wedding night by a show of force. But they did not live with them. Instead, they were supposed to contrive means of escaping at night to visit them secretly. According to Plutarch, it thus sometimes happened that men "had children by their wives before ever they saw their faces by daylight." [2] No jealousy between marital partners was allowed. The production of vigorous offspring was all-important. Whether they were born within the limits of strict monogamy was a secondary consideration. In any case, children were the property not of their parents but of the state.

Economic regulations

The economic organization of Sparta was designed almost solely for the ends of military efficiency and the supremacy of the citizen class. The best land was owned by the state and was originally divided into equal plots which were assigned to the Spartiate class as inalienable estates. Later these holdings as well as the inferior lands were permitted to be sold and exchanged, with the result that some of the citizens became richer than others. The helots, who did all the work of cultivating the soil, also belonged to the state and were assigned to their masters along with the land. Their masters were forbidden to emancipate them or to sell them outside of the country. The labor of the helots provided for the support of the whole citizen class, whose members were not allowed to be associated with any economic enterprise other than agriculture. Trade and industry were reserved exclusively for the perioeci.

Was the Spartan system communistic?

The Spartan economic system is frequently described by modern historians as communistic. It is true that some of the means of production (the helots and the land) were collectively owned, in theory at least, and that the Spartiate males contributed from their incomes to provide for a common mess in the clubs to which they belonged. But with these rather doubtful exceptions the system was as far removed from communism as it was from anarchy. Essentials of the communist ideal include the doctrines that all the instruments of

[2] Plutarch, "Lycurgus," *Lives of Illustrious Men* (Dryden ed.), Vol. I, p. 81.

production shall be owned by the community, that no one shall live by exploiting the labor of others, and that all shall work for the benefit of the community and share the wealth in proportion to need. In Sparta commerce and industry were in private hands; the helots were forced to contribute a portion of what they produced to provide for the subsistence of their masters; and political privileges were restricted to an hereditary aristocracy, most of whose members performed no socially useful labor whatever. With its militarism, its secret police, its minority rule, and its closed economy, the Spartan system would seem to have resembled fascism more nearly than true communism.

4. The Athenian Triumph and Tragedy

Advantages en-joyed by the Athenians

Athens began her history under conditions quite different from those which prevailed in Sparta. The district of Attica had not been the scene of an armed invasion or of bitter conflict between opposing races. The Ionian penetration of that area was gradual and largely peaceful. As a result, no military caste imposed its rule upon a vanquished people. Furthermore, the wealth of Attica consisted of mineral deposits and splendid harbors rather than agricultural resources. Athens, consequently, never remained a predominantly agrarian state but rapidly developed a prosperous trade and a culture essentially urban.

From monar-chy to oligar-chy in Athens

Until the middle of the eighth century B.C. Athens, like the other Greek states, had a monarchical form of government. During the century that followed, the council of nobles, or Council of the Areopagus, as it came to be called, gradually divested the king of his powers. The transition to rule by the few was both the cause and the result of an increasing concentration of wealth. The introduction of vine and olive culture about this time led to the growth of agriculture as a great capitalistic enterprise. Since vineyards and olive orchards require considerable time to become profitable, only those farmers with abundant resources were able to survive in the business. Their poorer and less thrifty neighbors sank rapidly into debt, especially since grain was now coming to be imported at ruinous prices. The small farmer had no alternative but to mortgage his land, and then his family and himself, in the vain hope that some day a way of escape would be found. Ultimately many of his class became serfs when the mortgages could not be paid.

Threats of revolution and the reforms of Solon

Bitter cries of distress now arose and threats of revolution were heard. The middle classes in the towns espoused the cause of the peasants in demanding liberalization of the government. Finally, in 594 B.C., all parties agreed upon the appointment of Solon as a magistrate with absolute power to carry out reforms. The measures which Solon enacted provided for both political and economic adjustments. The former included: (1) the establishment of a new council, the

Council of Four Hundred, and the admission of the middle classes to membership in it; (2) the enfranchisement of the lower classes by making them eligible for service in the assembly; and (3) the organization of a supreme court, open to all citizens and elected by universal manhood suffrage, with power to hear appeals from the decisions of the magistrates. The economic reforms benefited the poor farmers by canceling existing mortgages, prohibiting enslavement for debt in the future, and limiting the amount of land any one individual could own. Nor did Solon neglect the middle classes. He introduced a new system of coinage designed to give Athens an advantage in foreign trade, imposed heavy penalties for idleness, ordered every man to teach his son a trade, and offered full privileges of citizenship to alien craftsmen who would become permanent residents of the country.

Significant though these reforms were, they did not allay the discontent. The nobles were disgruntled because some of their privileges had been taken away. The middle and lower classes were dissatisfied because they were still excluded from the offices of magistracy, and because the Council of the Areopagus was left with its powers intact. Worse still was the fact that Solon, like certain rulers of modern times, attempted to divert the people from their domestic troubles by persuading them to embark upon military adventures abroad. An old quarrel with Megara was revived, and Athens committed her fate to the uncertainties of war. The chaos and disillusionment that followed paved the way in 560 B.C. for the triumph of Peisistratus, the first of the Athenian tyrants. Although he proved to be a benevolent despot, he nevertheless destroyed many of the liberties the people had previously gained, and Hippias, one of his two sons who succeeded him, was a ruthless and spiteful oppressor.

The rise of dictatorship

In 510 B.C. Hippias was overthrown by a group of nobles with aid from Sparta. Factional conflict raged anew until Cleisthenes, an intelligent aristocrat, enlisted the support of the masses to eliminate his rivals from the scene. Having promised concessions to the people as a reward for their help, he proceeded to reform the government in so sweeping a fashion that he has since been known as the father of Athenian democracy. He greatly enlarged the citizen population by granting full rights to all freemen who resided in the country at that time. He established a new Council of Five Hundred and made it the chief organ of government with power to prepare measures for submission to the assembly and with supreme control over executive and administrative functions. Members of this body were to be chosen by lot from lists of candidates submitted by the demes or townships. Any male citizen over thirty years of age was eligible. Since the Council was so large, it was to be divided into ten committees of fifty, each to manage the affairs of government for a month. Cleisthenes also expanded the authority of the assembly, giving it power to debate and pass or reject the measures submitted

The reforms of Cleisthenes

by the Council, to declare war, to appropriate money, and to audit the accounts of retiring magistrates. Lastly, Cleisthenes is believed to have instituted the device of ostracism, whereby any citizen who might be dangerous to the state could be sent into honorable exile for a ten-year period. The device was quite obviously intended to eliminate men who were suspected of cherishing dictatorial ambitions.

The perfection of Athenian democracy

The Athenian democracy attained its full perfection in the Age of Pericles (461–429 B.C.). It was during this period that the assembly acquired the authority to initiate legislation in addition to its power to ratify or reject proposals of the Council. It was during this time also that the famous Board of Ten Generals rose to a position roughly comparable to that of the British cabinet. The Generals were chosen by the assembly for one-year terms and were eligible for re-election indefinitely. Pericles held the position of Chief Strategus or president of the Board of Generals for more than thirty years. The Generals were not simply commanders of the army but the chief legislative and executive officials in the state, gradually assuming most of the prerogatives which Cleisthenes had given to the Council of Five Hundred. Though wielding enormous power, they could not become tyrants, for their policies were subject to review by the assembly, and they could easily be recalled at the end of their one-year terms or indicted for malfeasance at any time. Finally, it was in the Age of Pericles that the Athenian system of courts was developed to completion. No longer was there merely a supreme court to hear appeals from the decisions of magistrates, but an array of popular courts with authority to try all kinds of cases. At the beginning of each year a list of 6000 citizens was chosen by lot from the various sections of the country. From this list separate juries, varying in size from 201 to 1001, were made up for particular trials. Each of these juries constituted a court with power to decide by majority vote every question involved in the case. Although one of the magistrates presided, he had none of the prerogatives of a judge; the jury itself was the judge, and from its decision there was no appeal. It would be difficult to imagine a system more thoroughly democratic.

Athenian democracy compared with modern democracy

The Athenian democracy differed from the modern form in various ways. First of all, it did not extend to the whole population, but only to the citizen class. While it is true that in the time of Cleisthenes (508–502 B.C.) the citizens probably included a majority of the inhabitants because of his enfranchisement of resident aliens, in the Age of Pericles they were distinctly a minority. It may be well to observe, however, that within its limits Athenian democracy was more thoroughly applied than is the modern form. The choice by lot of nearly all magistrates except the Ten Generals, the restriction of all terms of public officials to one year, and the uncompromising adherence to the principle of majority rule even in judicial trials were examples of a serene confidence in the political capacity of the average man which few modern nations would be willing to accept. The democracy of Athens differed from the contemporary ideal also in the fact that it was direct, not representative. Contrary to the traditional view, the Athenians understood the principle of representation, but they never applied it except in a limited way in the selection of members of the Council of Five Hundred. They were not interested in being governed by men of reputation and ability; what vitally concerned them was the assurance to every citizen of an actual voice in the control of all public affairs. In a word, their ideal was not efficiency in government but democracy.

In the last century of her existence as an independent state Athens fought two great wars. The first, the war with Persia, was an outgrowth of the expansion of that empire into the eastern Mediterranean area. The Athenians resented the conquest of their Ionian kinsmen in Asia Minor and aided them in their struggle for freedom. The Persians retaliated by sending a powerful army and fleet to attack the Greeks. Although all Greece was in danger of conquest, Athens bore the chief burden of repelling the invader. Sparta, especially, rendered but little assistance until the struggle was almost over. The war, which began in 493 B.C. and lasted with interludes of peace for about fourteen years, is commonly regarded as one of the most significant in the history of the world. The decisive victory of the Greeks put an end to the menace of Persian conquest and forestalled at least for a time the submergence of Hellenic ideals of freedom in Oriental despotism. The war also had the effect of strengthening democracy in Athens and making that state the leading power in Greece.

The Persian War and its results

The other of the great struggles, the Peloponnesian War with Sparta, had results of a quite different character. Instead of being another milestone in the Athenian march to power, it ended in tragedy. Athens was so completely humbled that she never again played an eminent role in Greek politics. The causes of this war are of particular interest to the student of the downfall of civilizations. First and most important was the growth of Athenian imperialism. In the last year of the war with Persia, Athens had joined with a number of other Greek states in the formation of an offensive and defensive alliance known as the Delian League. When peace was concluded the League was not dissolved, for many of the Greeks feared that the Persians might come back. As time went on, Athens gradually transformed the League into a naval empire for the advancement of her own interests. She used some of the funds in the common treasury for her own purposes. She tried to reduce all the other members to a condition of vassalage, and when one of them rebelled, she overwhelmed it by force, seized its navy, and imposed tribute upon it as if it were a conquered state. Such high-handed methods aroused the

Athenian imperialism and the Peloponnesian War

153

suspicions of the Spartans, who feared that an Athenian hegemony would soon be extended over all of Greece.

A second major cause was to be found in the social and cultural differences between Athens and Sparta. Athens was democratic, progressive, urban, imperialistic, and intellectually and artistically advanced. Sparta was aristocratic, conservative, agrarian, provincial, and culturally backward. Where such sharply contrasting systems exist side by side, conflicts are almost bound to occur. The attitude of the Athenians and Spartans had been hostile for some time. The former looked upon the latter as uncouth barbarians. The Spartans accused the Athenians of attempting to gain control over the northern Peloponnesian states and of encouraging the helots to rebel. Economic factors also played a large part in bringing the conflict to a head. Athens was ambitious to dominate the Corinthian Gulf, the principal avenue of trade with Sicily and southern Italy. This made her the deadly enemy of Corinth, the chief ally of Sparta.

The war, which broke out in 431 B.C. and lasted until 404, was a record of frightful calamities for Athens. Her trade was destroyed, her democracy overthrown, and her population decimated by a terrible pestilence. Quite as bad was the moral degradation which followed in the wake of the military reverses. Treason, corruption, and brutality were among the hastening ills of the last few years of the conflict. On one occasion the Athenians even slaughtered the whole male population of the state of Melos, and enslaved the women and children, for no other crime than refusing to abandon neutrality. Ultimately, deserted by all her allies except Samos and with her food supply cut off, Athens was left with no alternative but to surrender or starve. The terms imposed upon her were drastic enough: destruction of her fortifications, surrender of all foreign possessions and practically her entire navy, and submission to Sparta as a subject state.

5. Political Debacle—the Last Days

Not only did the Peloponnesian War put an end to the supremacy of Athens; it annihilated freedom throughout the Greek world and sealed the doom of the Hellenic political genius. Following the war Sparta asserted her power over all of Hellas. Oligarchies supported by Spartan troops replaced democracies wherever they existed. Confiscation of property and assassination were the methods regularly employed to combat opposition. Although in Athens the tyrants were overthrown after a time and free government restored temporarily, Sparta was able to dominate the remainder of Greece for more than thirty years. In 371 B.C., however, Epaminondas of Thebes defeated the Spartan army at Leuctra and thereby inaugurated a period of Theban supremacy. Unfortunately Thebes showed little more wisdom and tolerance in governing than Sparta, and nine years later a combination was formed to free the Greek cities from their new oppressor. Failing to break up the alliance, the Thebans gave battle on the field of Mantinea. Both sides claimed the victory, but Epaminondas was slain, and the power of his empire soon afterward collapsed.

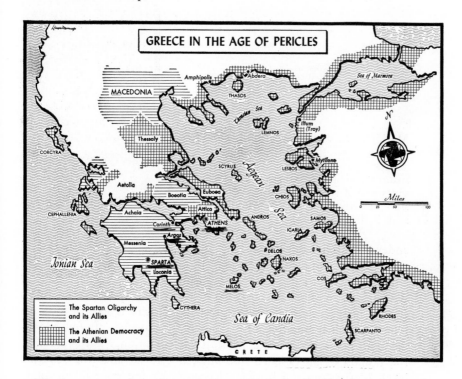

GREECE IN THE AGE OF PERICLES

The Spartan Oligarchy and its Allies

The Athenian Democracy and its Allies

The long succession of wars had now brought the Greek states to the point of exhaustion. Though the glory of their culture was yet undimmed, politically they were prostrate and helpless. Their fate was soon decided for them by the rise of Philip of Macedon. Except for a thin veneer of Hellenic culture, the Macedonians were barbarians; but Philip, before becoming their king, had learned how to lead an army while a hostage at Thebes. Perceiving the weakness of the states to the south, he determined to conquer them. A series of early successes led to the decisive victory at Chaeronea in 338 B.C. and soon afterward to dominion over all of Greece except Sparta. Two years later Philip was murdered as the sequel to a family brawl.

The Macedonian conquest

Rule over Hellas now passed into the hands of his son Alexander, a youth of twenty years. After putting to death all possible aspirants to the throne and quelling some feeble revolts of the Greeks, Alexander conceived the grandiose scheme of conquering Persia. One victory followed another until in the short space of twelve years the whole ancient Near Orient from the Indus River to the Nile had been annexed to Greece as the personal domain of one man. Alex-

Alexander the Great

155

Marble Stele with Law against Tyranny, 338 B.C. The sculptured relief shows a woman (Democracy) crowning an aged man (the People of Athens). The law provides that if anyone establishes a dictatorship in Athens, a person who kills him shall be held guiltless.

ander did not live to enjoy it long. In 323 B.C. he fell ill of Babylonian swamp fever and died at the age of thirty-three.

It is difficult to gauge the significance of Alexander's career. A slave of his emotions and capable of the vilest injustice even to his friends, he scarcely deserves the greatness which has been thrust upon him. Though unquestionably a military genius, he left few monuments of constructive statesmanship. His ambition was to rule after the fashion of an Oriental god-king, not to advance the Hellenic ideals of freedom and justice. Moreover, his influence in spreading Greek culture appears to have been exaggerated considerably. Persia adopted no large number of Hellenic institutions and customs as a result of the Alexandrian conquest. Except for her cities at the mouth of the Nile, Egypt remained Egyptian. The influence of Alexander's conquests was rather in the opposite direction: they opened the way for a stronger infusion of Orientalism into Europe than had ever occurred before—so strong in fact that the days of Hellenic civilization as such were now practically over.

The significance of Alexander's career

6. Hellenic Thought and Culture

I. PHILOSOPHY From what has been said in preceding chapters it should be clear that the popular notion that all philosophy originated with the Greeks is fallacious. Centuries earlier the Egyptians had given much thought to the nature of the universe and to the social and ethical problems of man. The achievement of the Greeks was rather the development of philosophy in a more inclusive mean-

The antecedents of Greek philosophy

156

ing than it had ever possessed before. They attempted to find answers to every conceivable question about the nature of the universe, the problem of truth, and the meaning and purpose of life. The magnitude of their accomplishment is attested by the fact that philosophy ever since has been largely a debate over the validity of their several conclusions.

Greek philosophy had its origins in the sixth century B.C. in the work of the so-called Milesian school, whose members were natives of the great commercial city of Miletus on the shore of Asia Minor. Their philosophy was fundamentally scientific and materialistic. The problem which chiefly engaged their attention was to discover the nature of the physical world. They believed that all things could be reduced to some primary substance or original matter which was the source of worlds, stars, animals, plants, and men, and to which all would ultimately return. Thales, the founder of the school, perceiving that all things contained moisture, taught that the primary substance is water. Anaximander insisted that it could not be any particular thing such as water or fire but some substance "ungendered and imperishable" which "contains and directs all things." He called this substance the Infinite or the Boundless. Evidently what he had in mind was an indeterminate material mass out of which individual things are formed. The third member of the school, Anaximenes, declared that the original material of the universe is air. At first thought this appears to have been a step backward to the idea that some one of the elements is the source from which everything comes. But this is not so, for Anaximenes really chose air as the germinal substance because it made possible a quantitative interpretation of the universe. In other words, he maintained that the essential difference between things consists merely in the *amount* of the basic substance they contain. Air when rarefied becomes fire; when condensed it turns successively to wind, vapor, water, earth, and stone.

The philosophy of the Milesian school

Although seemingly naïve in its conclusions the philosophy of the Milesian school was of real significance. It broke through the mythological beliefs of the Greeks about the origin of the world and substituted a purely rational explanation. It revived and expanded the Egyptian ideas of the eternity of the universe and the indestructibility of matter. It suggested very clearly, especially in the teachings of Anaximander, the concept of evolution in the sense of rhythmic change, of continuing creation and decay. And the conclusion would seem logical that Anaximenes' quantitative interpretation of the universe helped to prepare the way for the atomic conception of matter.

Significance of the teachings of the Milesian school

Before the end of the sixth century Greek philosophy developed a metaphysical turn; that is, it ceased to be occupied solely with problems of the physical world and shifted its attention to abstruse questions about the nature of being, the meaning of truth, and the position of the divine in the scheme of things. First to exemplify the new

The Pythagoreans

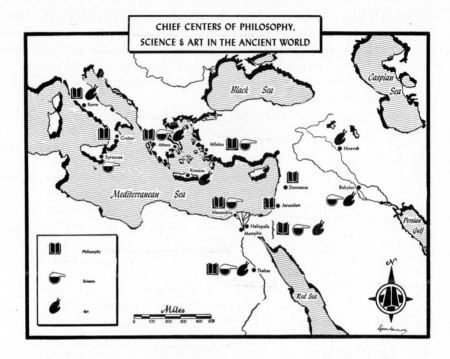

tendency were the Pythagoreans, who interpreted philosophy largely in terms of religion. Little is known about them except that their leader, Pythagoras, migrated from the island of Samos to southern Italy and founded a religious community at Croton. He and his followers apparently taught that the speculative life is the highest good, but that in order to pursue it, man must purify himself from the evil desires of the flesh. They held that the essence of things is not a material substance but an abstract principle, number. Their chief significance lies in the sharp distinctions they drew between spirit and matter, harmony and discord, good and evil. Perhaps it is not inaccurate to regard them as the real founders of dualism in Greek thought.

A consequence of the work of the Pythagoreans was to intensify the debate over the nature of the universe. Some of their contemporaries, notably Parmenides, argued that stability or permanence is the real nature of things; change and diversity are simply illusions of the senses. Parmenides meant by this that underneath all of the surface changes which go on around us there are things which really endure. We cannot perceive them with our senses, but we can discover their existence by reason. Directly opposed to this was the position taken by Heracleitus, who argued that permanence is an illusion, that change alone is real. The universe, he maintained, is in a condition of constant flux, so that it is impossible to step twice into the same stream. Creation and destruction, life and death, are but the obverse and reverse sides of the same picture. In affirming

Renewal of the debate over the nature of the universe

158

such views Heracleitus was really contending that the things we see and hear and feel are all that there is to reality. Evolution or constant change is the law of the universe. The tree or the stone that is here today is gone tomorrow; no underlying substance exists immutable through all eternity.

The eventual answer to the question of the nature of the universe was provided by the atomists. The founder of the atomic theory was Leucippus, but the philosopher chiefly responsible for its development was Democritus, who lived in Abdera on the Thracian coast in the second half of the fifth century. As their name implies, the atomists held that the ultimate constituents of the universe are atoms, infinite in number, indestructible, and indivisible. Although these differ in size and shape, they are exactly alike in composition. Because of the motion inherent in them, they are eternally uniting, separating, and reuniting in different arrangements. Every individual object or organism in the universe is thus the product of a fortuitous concourse of atoms. The only difference between a man and a tree is the difference in the number and arrangement of their atoms. Here was a philosophy which represented the final fruition of the materialistic tendencies of early Greek thought. Democritus denied the immortality of the soul and the existence of any spiritual world. Strange as it may appear to the minds of some people, he was a moral idealist, affirming that "Good means not merely not to do wrong, but rather not to desire to do wrong." [3]

*Solution of the
problem by the
atomists*

About the middle of the fifth century B.C. an intellectual revolution began in Greece. The rise of the common man, the growth of individualism, and the demand for the solution of practical problems produced a reaction against the old ways of thinking. As a result philosophers abandoned the study of the physical universe and turned to consideration of subjects more intimately related to man himself. The first exponents of the new intellectual trend were the Sophists. Originally the term meant "those who are wise," but later it came to be used in the derogatory sense of men who employ specious reasoning. Since most of our knowledge of the Sophists was derived, until comparatively recently, from Plato, one of their severest critics, they were commonly considered to have been the enemies of all that was best in Hellenic culture. Modern research has exposed the fallacy of so extreme a conclusion, even though some members of the group lacked a sense of social responsibility and were quite unscrupulous in "making the worse appear the better cause."

The greatest of the Sophists was undoubtedly Protagoras, a native of Abdera who did most of his teaching in Athens. His famous dictum, "Man is the measure of all things," comprehends the essence of the Sophist philosophy. By this he meant that goodness, truth, justice, and beauty are relative to the needs and interests of man himself. There are no absolute truths or eternal standards of right and

[3] Quoted by Frank Thilly, *History of Philosophy*, p. 40.

justice. Since sense perception is the exclusive source of knowledge, there can be only particular truths valid for a given time and place. Morality likewise varies from one people to another. The Spartans encourage adultery in certain cases on the part of wives as well as husbands; the Athenians seclude their women and refuse even to allow them a normal social life. Which of these standards is right? Neither is right in any absolute sense, for there are no absolute canons of right and wrong eternally decreed in the heavens to fit all cases; yet both are right in the relative sense that the judgment of man alone determines what is good.

The extremist doctrines of the later Sophists

Some of the later Sophists went far beyond the teachings of their great master. Gorgias, for example, perverted the skepticism of Protagoras into the doctrine that the human mind can never know anything except its own subjective impressions. "Nothing exists," he declared; "if anything did exist it could not be known; if a man should chance to apprehend it, it would still be a secret; he would be unable to communicate it to his fellows." [4] The individualism which was necessarily implicit in the teachings of Protagoras was twisted by Thrasymachus into the doctrine that all laws and customs are merely expressions of the will of the strongest and shrewdest for their own advantage, and that therefore the wise man is the "perfectly unjust man" who is above the law and concerned with the gratification of his own desires.

The valuable contributions of the Sophists

Yet there was much that was admirable in the teachings of all the Sophists, even of those who were the most extreme. Without exception they condemned slavery and the racial exclusiveness of the Greeks. They were champions of liberty, the rights of the common man, and the practical and progressive point of view. They perceived the folly of war and ridiculed the silly chauvinism of many of the Athenians. Perhaps their most important work was the extension of philosophy to include not only physics and metaphysics, but ethics, politics, and epistemology, or the science of knowledge, as well. As Cicero expressed it, they "brought philosophy down from heaven to the dwellings of men."

The reaction against Sophism

It was inevitable that the relativism, skepticism, and individualism of the Sophists should have aroused strenuous opposition. In the judgment of the more conservative Greeks these doctrines appeared to lead straight to atheism and anarchy. If there is no final truth, and if goodness and justice are merely relative to the whims of the individual, then neither religion, morality, the state, nor society itself can long be maintained. The result of this conviction was the growth of a new philosophic movement grounded upon the theory that truth is real and that absolute standards do exist. The leaders of this movement were perhaps the three most famous individuals in the history of thought—Socrates, Plato, and Aristotle.

Socrates was born in Athens in 469 B.C. of humble parentage, his

[4] Quoted by A. A. Trever, *History of Ancient Civilization*, Vol. I, p. 348.

father being a sculptor, his mother a midwife. How he obtained an education no one knows, but he was certainly familiar with the teachings of earlier Greek thinkers, presumably from extensive reading. The impression that he was a mere gabbler in the market place is quite unfounded. He became a philosopher on his own account chiefly to combat the doctrines of the Sophists, and he soon gathered around him a circle of admirers, which included the two young aristocrats, Plato and Alcibiades. In 399 B.C. he was condemned to death on a charge of "corrupting the youth and introducing new gods." The real reason for the unjust sentence was the tragic outcome for Athens of the Peloponnesian War. Overwhelmed by resentment and despair, the people turned against Socrates because of his associations with aristocrats, including the traitor Alcibiades, and because of his criticism of popular beliefs.

For the reason that Socrates wrote nothing himself, historians have been faced with a problem in determining the scope of his teachings. He is generally regarded as primarily a teacher of ethics with no interest in abstract philosophy or any desire to found a new school of thought. Certain admissions made by Plato, however, indicate that a large part of the famous doctrine of Ideas was really of Socratic origin. At any rate we can be reasonably sure that Socrates believed in a stable and universally valid knowledge, which man could possess if he would only pursue the right method. This method would consist in the exchange and analysis of opinions, in the setting up and testing of provisional definitions, until finally an essence of truth recognizable by all could be distilled from them. Socrates argued that in similar fashion man could discover enduring principles of right and justice independent of the selfish desires of human beings. He believed, moreover, that the discovery of such rational principles of conduct would prove an infallible guide to virtuous living, for he denied that anyone who truly knows the good can ever choose the evil.

By far the most distinguished of Socrates' pupils was Plato, who was born in Athens in 427 B.C., the son of noble parents. His real name was Aristocles, "Plato" being a nickname supposedly given to him by one of his teachers because of his broad frame. When he was twenty years old he joined the Socratic circle, remaining a member until the tragic death of his teacher. He seems to have drawn inspiration from other sources also, notably from the teachings of Parmenides and the Pythagoreans. Unlike his great master he was a prolific writer, though some of the works attributed to him are of doubtful authorship. The most noted of his writings are such dialogues as the *Apology*, the *Protagoras*, the *Phaedrus*, the *Timaeus*, and the *Republic*. He was engaged in the completion of another great work, the *Laws*, when death overtook him in his eighty-first year.

Plato's objectives in developing his philosophy were similar to those of Socrates although somewhat broader: (1) to combat the

theory of reality as a disordered flux and to substitute an interpretation of the universe as essentially spiritual and purposeful; (2) to
refute the Sophist doctrines of relativism and skepticism; and (3)
to provide a secure foundation for ethics. In order to realize these
objectives he developed his celebrated doctrine of Ideas. He admitted
that relativity and constant change are characteristics of the world
of physical things, of the world we perceive with our senses. But he
denied that this world is the complete universe. There is a higher,
spiritual realm composed of eternal forms or Ideas which only the
mind can conceive. These are not, however, mere abstractions invented by the mind of man, but spiritual things. Each is the archetype
or pattern of some particular class of objects or relation between objects on earth. Thus there are Ideas of man, tree, shape, size, color,
proportion, beauty, and justice. Highest of them all is the Idea of
the Good, which is the active cause and guiding purpose of the whole
universe. The things we perceive with our senses are merely imperfect copies of the supreme realities, Ideas.

Plato's ethical and religious philosophy was closely related to his
doctrine of Ideas. Like Socrates he believed that true virtue has its
basis in knowledge. But the knowledge derived from the senses is
limited and variable; hence true virtue must consist in rational apprehension of the eternal Ideas of goodness and justice. By relegating
the physical to an inferior place, he gave to his ethics a mildly ascetic
tinge. He regarded the body as a hindrance to the mind and taught
that only the rational part of man's nature is noble and good. In contrast with some of his later followers, he did not demand that appetites and emotions should be denied altogether, but urged that
they should be strictly subordinated to the reason. Plato never made
his conception of God entirely clear. Sometimes he referred to the
Idea of the Good as if it were a divine power of subordinate rank;
at other times as if it were the supreme creator and ruler of the universe. Probably the latter is what he really meant. At any rate it is
certain that he conceived of the universe as spiritual in nature and
governed by intelligent purpose. He rejected both materialism and
mechanism. As for the soul, he regarded it not only as immortal but
as pre-existing from all eternity.

As a political philosopher Plato was motivated by the ideal of
constructing a state which would be free from turbulence and self-
seeking on the part of individuals and classes. Neither democracy
nor liberty but harmony and efficiency were the ends he desired to
achieve. Accordingly, he proposed in his *Republic* a famous plan
for society which would have divided the population into three
principal classes corresponding to the functions of the soul. The
lowest class, representing the appetitive function, would include the
farmers, artisans, and merchants. The second class, representing the
spirited element or will, would consist of the soldiers; while the highest class, representing the reason, would include the intellectual aris-

tocracy. Each of these classes would be supposed to perform those tasks for which it was best fitted. The function of the lowest class would be the production and distribution of goods for the benefit of the whole community; that of the soldiers, defense; while the aristocracy by reason of special aptitude for philosophy would enjoy a monopoly of political power. The division of the people into these several ranks would not be made on the basis of birth or wealth, but through a sifting process which would take into account the ability of each individual to profit from education. Thus the farmers, artisans, and merchants would be those who had shown the least intellectual capacity, whereas the philosopher-kings would be those who had shown the greatest.

The last of the great champions of the Socratic tradition was Aristotle, a native of Stagira, born in 384 B.C. At the age of seventeen he entered Plato's Academy,[5] continuing as student and teacher there for twenty years. In 343 he was invited by King Philip of Macedon to serve as tutor to the young Alexander. Perhaps history affords few more conspicuous examples of wasted talent. Seven years later he returned to Athens, where he conducted a school of his own, known as the Lyceum, until his death in 322 B.C. Aristotle wrote even more voluminously than Plato and on a greater variety of subjects. His principal works include treatises on logic, metaphysics, rhetoric, ethics, natural sciences, and politics. A considerable number of the writings credited to him have never been found.

Aristotle

Though Aristotle was as much interested as Plato and Socrates in absolute knowledge and eternal standards, his philosophy differed from theirs in several outstanding respects. To begin with, he had a higher regard for the concrete and the practical. In contrast with Plato, the aesthete, and Socrates, who declared he could learn nothing from trees and stones, Aristotle was a scientist with a compelling interest in biology, medicine, and astronomy. Moreover, he was less inclined than his predecessors to a spiritual outlook. And lastly, he did not share their strong aristocratic sympathies.

*Aristotle
compared with
Plato and
Socrates*

Aristotle agreed with Plato that universals, Ideas (or forms as he called them), are real, and that knowledge derived from the senses is limited and inaccurate. But he refused to go along with his master in ascribing an independent existence to universals and in reducing material things to pale reflections of their spiritual patterns. On the contrary, he asserted that form and matter are of equal importance; both are eternal, and neither can exist inseparable from the other. It is the union of the two which gives to the universe its essential character. Forms are the causes of all things; they are the purposive forces which shape the world of matter into the infinitely varied objects and organisms around us. All evolution, both cosmic and organic, results from the interaction of form and matter upon each

*Aristotle's
conception
of the universe*

[5] So called from the grove of Academus, where Plato and his disciples met to discuss philosophic problems.

other. Thus the presence of the form *man* in the human embryo molds and directs the development of the latter until it ultimately evolves as a human being. While the mechanical motion of the matter itself plays some part in the process also, the determining factor is the purposive action of the form. Aristotle's philosophy may therefore be regarded as a halfway house between the spiritualism and transcendentalism of Plato, on the one hand, and the mechanistic materialism of the atomists on the other. His conception of the universe was *teleological*—that is, governed by purpose; but he refused to regard the spiritual as completely overshadowing its material embodiment.

Aristotle's re-
ligious doc-
trines

That Aristotle should have conceived of God primarily as a First Cause is no more than we should expect from the dominance of the scientific attitude in his philosophy. Unlike Plato's Idea of the Good, Aristotle's God did not fulfill an ethical purpose. His character was that of a Prime Mover, the original source of the purposive motion contained in the forms. In no sense was he a personal God, for his nature was pure intelligence, devoid of all feelings, will, or desire. Aristotle seems to have left no place in his religious scheme for individual immortality: all the functions of the soul, except the creative reason which is not individual at all, are dependent upon the body and perish with it.

Aristotle's
ethical philos-
ophy of the
golden mean

Aristotle's ethical philosophy was less ascetic than Plato's. He did not regard the body as the prison of the soul, nor did he believe that physical appetites are necessarily evil in themselves. He taught that the highest good for man consists in self-realization, that is, in the exercise of that part of man's nature which most truly distinguishes him as a human being. Self-realization would therefore be identical with the life of reason. But the life of reason is dependent upon the proper combination of physical and mental conditions. The body must be kept in good health and the emotions under adequate control. The solution is to be found in the *golden mean*, in preserving a balance between excessive indulgence on the one hand and ascetic denial on the other. This was simply a reaffirmation of the characteristic Hellenic ideal of *sophrosyne* ("nothing too much").

The golden
mean applied to
politics

Although Aristotle included in his *Politics* much descriptive and analytical material on the structure and functions of government, he dealt primarily with the broader aspects of political theory. He considered the state as the supreme institution for the promotion of the good life among men, and he was therefore vitally interested in its origin and development and in the best forms it could be made to assume. Declaring that man is by nature a political animal, he denied that the state is an artificial product of the ambitions of the few or of the desires of the many. On the contrary, he asserted that it is rooted in the instincts of man himself, and that civilized life outside of its limits is impossible. He considered the best state to be neither a monarchy, an aristocracy, nor a democracy, but a *polity*—which

Geometric Horse, VIII cent. B.C.
Greek art of this early period was
[an]gular, formal, and conventionalized.

Geometric Jar, VIII cent.
B.C. Another example of the
stylized decorative patterns
of early Greek art.

Sphinx, *ca.* 540–530 B.C.
Though doubtless of Oriental
derivation, Greek sphinxes had
a softer and more human aspect than the Oriental.

Departure of a Warrior. Gravestone, *ca.* 530 B.C.,
a period when naturalism was the dominant
note of Greek art.

[St]atue of an Amazon, one of
[th]e fabled tribe of women
[w]arriors, V cent. B.C. (Ro-
[m]an copy)

Athena, *ca.* 460 B.C. The
young, graceful patron-
goddess of Athens is about
to send forth an owl as a
sign of victory.

Chorus of Satyrs, *ca.* 420 B.C. The background is black with the figures in red
clay. The satyrs, dressed in fleecy white,
with flowing tails, are the chorus of a
play.

[...]r, 500–490 B.C. The figures
[de]picted in a fine black glaze
[on] the natural red clay show
[ath]letes in the Panathenaic
[ga]mes.

All pictures courtesy MMA.

Bronze Mirror Case, V cent. B.C. Greek articles of everyday use were commonly finished with the same delicacy and precision as major works of art.

Diadoumenos, after Polykleitos, V cent. B.C. An idealized statue of a Greek athlete tying the "diadem," or band of victory, around his head.

Statuette of a Horse, 480–470 B.C. Though an idealized type rather than an individual animal, the detail is almost perfect.

Bracelet Pendant, IV–III cent. B.C. This tiny figure of the god Pan is a masterpiece of detail and expression.

Woman Arranging Her Hair, 400–300 B.C. Sculptors of antiquity took pride in these statuettes of ordinary people in ordinary activities, which were usually made of terra cotta painted soft blue, pink, or yellow.

Head of an Athlete, *ca.* 440–420 The sculptor aimed to express ma beauty in perfect harmony physical and intellectual excelle

Comic Actor, 200–100 B Hellenistic realism often i cluded portrayal of ugly a even deformed individual

Statuette of Hermarchos, III cent. B.C. An example of the realism of Hellenistic sculpture.

Sleeping Eros, 250–150 B.C. Along with a penchant for realism, Hellenistic sculptors were fond of portraying serenity or repose.

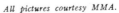

All pictures courtesy MMA.

he defined as a commonwealth intermediate between oligarchy and democracy. Essentially it would be a state under the control of the middle class, but Aristotle intended to make sure that the members of that class would be fairly numerous, for he advocated measures to prevent the concentration of wealth. He defended the institution of private property, but he opposed the heaping up of riches beyond what is necessary for intelligent living. He recommended that the government should provide the poor with money to buy small farms or to "make a beginning in trade and husbandry" and thus promote their prosperity and self-respect.[6]

II. SCIENCE Contrary to a popular belief, the period of Hellenic civilization, strictly speaking, was not a great age of science. The vast majority of the scientific achievements commonly thought of as Greek were made during the Hellenistic period, when the culture was no longer predominantly Hellenic but a mixture of Hellenic and Oriental.[7] The interests of the Greeks in the Periclean age and in the century that followed were chiefly speculative and artistic; they were not deeply concerned with material comforts or with mastery of the physical universe. Consequently, with the exception of some important developments in mathematics, biology, and medicine, scientific progress was relatively slight.

Hellenic science

The founder of Greek mathematics was apparently Thales of Miletus, who is supposed to have originated several theorems which were later included in the geometry of Euclid. Among them were the following: (1) a circle is bisected by any diameter; (2) the angles at the base of an isosceles triangle are equal; (3) if two straight lines cut one another, the vertically opposite angles are equal. Perhaps more significant was the work of the Pythagoreans, who developed an elaborate theory of numbers, classifying them into various categories, such as odd, even, prime, composite, even-times-even, perfect, and so forth. They are also supposed to have discovered the theory of proportion and to have proved for the first time that the sum of the three angles of any triangle is equal to two right angles. But the most famous of their achievements was the discovery of the theorem attributed to Pythagoras himself: the square of the hypotenuse of any right-angled triangle is equal to the sum of the squares on the other two sides. The Greek who first developed geometry as a science is now considered to have been Hippocrates of Chios, not to be confused with the physician, Hippocrates of Cos.[8]

Mathematics

The first of the Greeks to manifest an interest in biology was the philosopher Anaximander, who developed a crude theory of organic evolution based upon the principle of survival through progressive adaptations to the environment. The earliest ancestral animals, he asserted, lived in the sea, which originally covered the whole face of

Biology

[6] *Politics*, Maurice Francis Egan, ed., pp. 158–59.
[7] See the chapter on The Hellenistic Civilization.
[8] George Sarton, *An Introduction to the History of Science*, Vol. I, p. 92.

the earth. As the waters receded, some organisms were able to adjust themselves to their new environment and became land animals. The final product of this evolutionary process was man himself. The real founder of the science of biology, however, was Aristotle. Devoting many years of his life to painstaking study of the structure, habits, and growth of animals, he revealed many facts which were not destined to be discovered anew until the seventeenth century or later. The metamorphoses of various insects, the reproductive habits of the eel, the embryological development of the dog-fish (how the embryo is nourished in the womb by means of a placenta after the fashion of unborn mammals)—these are only samples of the amazing extent of his knowledge. Unfortunately he committed some errors. He denied the sexuality of plants, and he accepted uncritically some ancient myths about goats breathing through their ears and vultures being impregnated by the wind. Although he subscribed to the general theory of evolution, he believed in the spontaneous generation of certain species of worms and insects.

Medicine

Greek medicine also had its origin with the philosophers. The pioneers were Empedocles, exponent of the theory of the four elements (earth, air, fire, and water), and Alcmeon, a member of the Pythagorean school. The former discovered that blood flows to and from the heart, and that the pores of the skin supplement the work of the respiratory passages in breathing. Alcmeon originated the practice of dissecting animal bodies, discovered the optic nerve and the Eustachian tubes, and learned that the brain is the center of the nervous system. More important still was the work of Hippocrates of Cos in the fifth and fourth centuries. If this great physician had made no other contribution than his overthrow of the supernatural explanation of disease, he would still deserve to be called the father of medicine. He dinned into the ears of his pupils the doctrine that "Every disease has a natural cause, and without natural causes, nothing ever happens." In addition, by his methods of careful study and comparison of symptoms he laid the foundations for clinical medicine. He discovered the phenomenon of crisis in disease and improved the practice of surgery. Though he had a wide knowledge of drugs, his chief reliances in treatment were diet and rest. The main fact to his discredit was his development of the theory of the four humors—the notion that illness is due to excesssive amounts of yellow bile, black bile, blood, and phlegm in the system. The practice of bleeding the patient was the regrettable outgrowth of this theory.

III. LITERATURE Generally the most common medium of literary expression in the formative age of a people is the epic of heroic deeds.

*The epic
of heroic deeds*

It is a form well adapted to the pioneering days of battle and lusty adventure when men have not yet had time to be awed by the mystery of things. The most famous of the Greek epics, the *Iliad* and the *Odyssey*, were put into written form just at the end of the Homeric Age. The first has its theme in the love and wrath of

Achilles; the second describes the wanderings and return of Odysseus. Both have supreme literary merit in their carefully woven plots, in the music of their poetry, in the sensuous appeal of their imagery, in the realism of their character portrayals, and in their mastery of the full range of emotional intensity. They exerted an almost incalculable influence upon later writers. Their style and language inspired the fervid emotional poetry of the sixth century, and they were an unfailing source of plots and themes for the great tragedians of the Golden Age.

The three centuries which followed the Homeric Age were distinguished, as we have already seen, by tremendous social changes. The rural pattern of life gave way to an urban society of steadily increasing complexity. The founding of colonies and the growth of commerce provided new interests and new habits of living. Individuals hitherto submerged rose to a consciousness of their power and importance. It was inevitable that these changes should be reflected in new forms of literature, especially of a more personal type. The first to be developed was the elegy, which was probably intended to be declaimed rather than sung to the accompaniment of music. Elegies varied in theme from individual reactions toward love to the idealism of patriots and reformers. Generally, however, they were devoted to melancholy reflection on the disillusionments of life or to bitter lament over loss of prestige. Outstanding among the authors of elegiac verse were Solon the legislator, Mimnermus, and Theognis.

Development of the elegy

In the sixth century and the early part of the fifth, the elegy was gradually displaced by the lyric, which derives its name from the fact that it was sung to the music of the lyre. The new type of poetry was particularly well adapted to the expression of passionate feelings, the violent loves and hates engendered by the strife of classes. It was employed for other purposes also. Both Alcaeus and Sappho used it to describe the poignant beauty of love, the delicate grace of spring, and the starlit splendor of a summer night. Meanwhile other poets developed the choral lyric, intended to express the feelings of the community rather than the sentiments of any one individual. Greatest of all the writers of this group was Pindar of Thebes, who wrote during the first half of the fifth century. The lyrics of Pindar took the form of odes celebrating the victories of athletes and the glories of Hellenic civilization. They are significant also for their religious and moral conceptions. Pindar had accepted the idea that Zeus is a god of righteousness, and that he will punish the wicked with the "direst doom" and reward the good with a life "that knows no tears."

Lyric poetry

The supreme literary achievement of the Greeks was the tragic drama. Like so many of their other great works, it had its roots in religion. At the festivals dedicated to the worship of Dionysus, the god of spring and of wine, a chorus of men dressed as satyrs or goat-men sang and danced around an altar, enacting the various

The origins of tragic drama

parts of a dithyramb or choral lyric which related the story of the god's career. In time a leader came to be separated from the chorus to recite the main parts of the story. The true drama was born about the beginning of the fifth century when Aeschylus introduced a second "actor" and relegated the chorus to the background. The name "tragedy" which came to be applied to this drama was probably derived from the Greek word *tragos* meaning "goat."

Greek Theater in Syracuse on the Island of Sicily. Syracuse was one of the largest and most prosperous of Greek colonial cities. The construction, to take advantage of the slope of the hill, and the arrangement of the stage are of particular interest in this picture. Greek dramas were invariably presented in the open air.

Greek tragedy compared with modern tragedy

Greek tragedy stands out in marked contrast to the tragedies of Shakespeare or Eugene O'Neill. There was, first of all, little action presented on the stage; the main business of the actors was to recite the incidents of a plot which was already familiar to the audience, for the story was drawn from popular legends. Secondly, Greek tragedy devoted little attention to the study of complicated individual personality. There was no unfoldment of personal character as shaped by the vicissitudes of a long career. Those involved in the plot were scarcely individuals at all, but types. On the stage they wore masks to disguise any characteristics which might serve to distinguish them too sharply from the rest of humanity. In addition, Greek tragedies differed from the modern variety in having as their theme the conflict between man and the universe, not the clash of individual personalities, or the conflict of man with himself. The tragic fate which befell the main characters in these plays was external to man himself. It was brought on by the fact that someone had committed a crime against society, thereby offending the moral scheme of the universe. Punishment must follow in order to balance the scale of justice. Finally, the purpose of Greek tragedies was not merely to depict suffering and to interpret human actions, but to portray "the ideal conduct of the ideal Hellene in a painful situation," and to purify the emotions of the audience by representing the triumph of justice.

As already indicated, the founder of Greek tragedy was Aeschylus (525–456 B.C.). Though he is supposed to have written about eighty plays, only seven have survived in complete form, among them *The*

168

Persians, Seven against Thebes, Prometheus Bound, and a trilogy known as *Oresteia*. Guilt and punishment is the recurrent theme of nearly all of them. The second of the dramatists, Sophocles (496–406), is often considered to have been the greatest. His style was more polished and his philosophy more profound than that of his predecessor. He was the author of over a hundred plays, eighteen of which won first or second prize. More than any other writer in Greek history, he personified the Hellenic ideal of "nothing too much." His attitude was distinguished by love of harmony and peace, intelligent respect for democracy, and profound sympathy for human weakness. The most famous of his plays now extant are *Oedipus Rex*, *Antigone*, and *Electra*.

The work of the last of the tragedians, Euripides (480–406), reflects a far different spirit. He was a skeptic, an individualist, a humanist, who took delight in ridiculing the ancient myths and the "sacred cows" of his time. An embittered pessimist who suffered from the barbs of his conservative critics, he loved to humble the proud in his plays and to exalt the lowly. He was the first to give the ordinary man, even the beggar and the peasant, a place in the drama. Euripides is also noted for his sympathy for the slave, for his condemnation of war, and for his protests against the exclusion of women from social and intellectual life. Because of his humanism, his tendency to portray men as they actually were (or even a little worse), and his introduction of the love *motif* into drama, he is often considered a modernist. It must be remembered, however, that in other respects his plays were perfectly consistent with the Hellenic model. They did not exhibit violent action, the evolution of individual character, or the conflict of egos to any more notable extent than did the works of Sophocles or Aeschylus. Among the best-known tragedies of Euripides are *Alcestis*, *Medea*, and *The Trojan Women*.

Hellenic comedy was definitely inferior to tragedy. In common with tragedy it appears to have grown out of the Dionysiac festivals, but it did not attain full development until late in the fifth century B.C. Its only outstanding representative was Aristophanes (448?–380?), a somewhat coarse and belligerent aristocrat who lived in Athens. Most of his plays were written to satirize the political and intellectual ideals of the radical democracy of his time. In *The Knights* he pilloried the incompetent and greedy politicians for their reckless adventures in imperialism. In *The Frogs* he lampooned Euripides for the innovations the latter had made in the drama. *The Clouds* he reserved for ridicule of the Sophists, ignorantly or maliciously classifying Socrates as one of them. While he was undoubtedly a clever poet with a mastery of subtle humor and imaginative skill, his ideas were founded largely upon prejudice.[9]

[9] He is deserving of much credit, however, for his sharp criticisms of the stupid policies of the war-hawks of Athens during the struggle with Sparta.

No account of Greek literature would be complete without some mention of the two great historians of the Golden Age. Herodotus, the "father of history" (484–425), was a native of Halicarnassus in Asia Minor. He traveled extensively through the Persian empire, Egypt, Greece, and Italy, collecting a multitude of interesting data about various peoples. His famous account of the great war between the Greeks and the Persians included so much background that the work seems almost a history of the world. He regarded that war as an epic struggle between East and West, with Zeus giving victory to the Greeks against a mighty host of barbarians.

If Herodotus deserves to be called the father of history, much more does his younger contemporary, Thucydides, deserve to be considered the founder of scientific history. Influenced by the skepticism and practicality of the Sophists, Thucydides chose to work on the basis of carefully sifted evidence, rejecting opinions, legends, and hearsay. The subject of his *History* was the war between Sparta and Athens, which he described scientifically and dispassionately, emphasizing the complexity of causes which led to the fateful clash. His aim was to present an accurate record which could be studied with profit by statesmen and generals of all time, and it must be said that he was in full measure successful. If there was any defect in his historical method, it consisted in overemphasizing political factors to the neglect of the social and economic.

Reconstruction of the Interior of the Parthenon. The statue was a resplendent gold and ivory figure of Athena, protecting goddess of the city state. Like most of the rest of Parthenon sculpture, it was the work of Phidias.

See color pictures at pages 164, 165

7. *The Meaning of Greek Art*

Probably art even more than literature reflected the true character of Hellenic civilization. The Greek was essentially a materialist who conceived his world in physical terms. Plato and the followers of the

The Parthenon. The largest and most famous of Athenian temples, the Parthenon is considered the classic example of Doric architecture. Its columns were made more graceful by tapering them in a slight curve toward the top. Its friezes and pediments were decorated with lifelike sculptures of prancing horses, fighting giants, and benign and confident deities.

mystic religions were, of course, exceptions, but very few other Greeks had much interest in a universe of spiritual realities. It would be natural therefore to find that the material emblems of architecture and sculpture should exemplify best the ideals which the Greek held before him.

The impor- tance of Greek art

What did Greek art express? Above all, it symbolized humanism —the glorification of man as the most important creature in the universe. Though much of the sculpture depicted gods, this did not detract in the slightest from its humanistic quality. The Greek deities existed for the benefit of man, so that in glorifying them he glorified himself. Certainly there was nothing mystical or otherworldly in the religious aspects of Greek art. Both architecture and sculpture embodied the ideals of balance, harmony, order, and moderation. Anarchy and excess were abhorrent to the mind of the Greek, but so was absolute repression. Consequently, his art exhibited qualities of simplicity and dignified restraint—free from decorative extravagance, on the one hand, and from restrictive conventions on the other. Moreover, Greek art was an expression of the national life. Its purpose was not merely aesthetic but political: to symbolize the pride of the people in their city and to enhance their consciousness of unity. The Parthenon at Athens, for example, was the temple of Athena, the protecting goddess who presided over the corporate life of the state. In providing her with a beautiful shrine which she might frequently visit, the Athenians were giving evidence of their love for their city and their hope for its continuing welfare.

The ideals embodied in Greek art

The art of the Hellenes differed from that of nearly every people since their time in an interesting variety of ways. Like most of the tragedies of Aeschylus and Sophocles, it was universal. It included few portraits of personalities either in sculpture or in painting.[10] The human beings depicted were generally types, not individuals. Again, Greek art differed from that of most later peoples in its ethical purpose. It was not art for the sake of mere decoration or for the expression of the artist's individual philosophy, but it was a medium for the ennoblement of man. This does not mean that it was didactic

Greek art compared with that of later peoples

[10] Most of the portraits in sculpture commonly considered Greek really belong to the Hellenistic Age, although a few were produced at the end of the fourth century B.C.

171

in the sense that its merit was determined by the moral lesson it taught; but rather that it was supposed to exemplify qualities of living essentially artistic in themselves. The Athenian, at least, drew no sharp distinction between the ethical and aesthetic spheres; the beautiful and the good were really identical. True morality therefore consisted in rational living, in the avoidance of grossness, disgusting excesses, and other forms of conduct aesthetically offensive. Finally, Greek art may be contrasted with most later forms in the fact that it was not "naturalistic." Although the utmost attention was given to the depiction of beautiful bodies, this had nothing to do with fidelity to nature. The Greek was not interested in interpreting nature for its own sake, but in expressing *human* ideals.

The history of Greek art divides itself naturally into three great periods. The first, which can be called the archaic period, covered the seventh and sixth centuries. During the greater part of this age sculpture was dominated by Egyptian influence, as can be seen in the *frontality and rigidity of the statues*, with their square shoulders and one foot slightly advanced. Toward the end, however, these conventions were thrown aside. The chief architectural styles also had their origin in this period, and several crude temples were built. The second period, which occupied the fifth century, witnessed the full perfection of both architecture and sculpture. The art of this time was completely idealistic. During the fourth century, which was the

Periods in the evolution of Greek art

Marble Statue of the Apollo Type. Probably end of Seventh Century B.C. At this time Greek sculpture was still under Egyptian influence, as can be seen in the headdress, the imperturbable face, and the arms and feet of this statue.

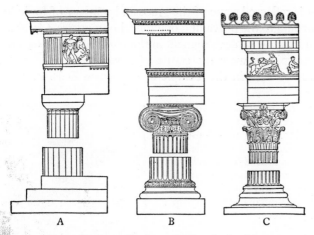

Details of the Three Famous Orders of Greek Architecture. A, Doric; B, Ionic; C, Corinthian.

last period of Hellenic art, architecture declined and sculpture assumed new characteristics. It came to reflect more clearly the reactions of the individual artist, to incorporate traces of realism, and to lose some of its quality as an expression of civic pride.

For all its artistic excellence, Greek temple architecture was one of the simplest of structural forms. Its essential elements were really only five in number: (1) the cella or nucleus of the building, which was a rectangular chamber to house the statue of the god; (2) the columns, which formed the porch and surrounded the cella; (3) the entablature or lintel, which rested upon the columns and supported the roof; (4) the gabled roof itself; and (5) the pediment or triangular section under the gable of the roof. Two different architectural styles were developed, representing modifications of certain of these elements. The more popular was the Doric, which made use of a rather heavy, sharply fluted column surmounted by a plain capital. The other, the Ionic, had more slender and more graceful columns with flat flutings, a triple base, and a scroll or volute capital. The so-called Corinthian style, which was chiefly Hellenistic, differed from the Ionic primarily in being more ornate. The Parthenon, the best example of Greek architecture, was essentially a Doric build-

Architecture

Temple of Athena Nike. This temple, in Athens, is one of the most graceful specimens of the Ionic style. Planned by Pericles in 450 B.C., it was probably not completed until nearly the end of the Fifth Century.

ing, but it reflected some of the grace and subtlety of Ionic influence.
According to the prevailing opinion among critics, Greek sculpture attained its acme of development in the work of Phidias (500?–432?). His masterpieces were the statue of Athena in the Parthenon and the statue of Zeus in the Temple of Olympian Zeus. In addition, he

Hermes with the Infant Dionysus, by Praxiteles, Fourth Century B.C. The god Hermes is represented as a slender, graceful youth, reflecting the humanism of Greek religion. The countenance suggests an attitude of repose and philosophic contentment. Original in the Olympia Museum, Greece.

The *Discobolus,* or Discus Thrower, of Myron. This statue reflects the glorification of the human body characteristic of Athens in the Golden Age. The proportions of the figure, the development and co-ordination of the muscles, and the repose and confidence of the face are perfect. *The Discobolus* is now in the Vatican Museum.

designed and supervised the execution of the Parthenon reliefs. The main qualities of his work are grandeur of conception, patriotism, proportion, dignity, and restraint. Nearly all of his figures are idealized representations of deities and mythological creatures in human form. The second most important fifth-century sculptor was Myron, famous for his statue of the discus thrower and for his glorification of other athletic types. The names of three great sculptors in the fourth century have come down to us. The most gifted of them was Praxiteles, renowned for his portrayal of humanized deities with slender, graceful bodies and countenances of philosophic repose. The best known of his works is the statue of Hermes with the infant Dionysus. His older contemporary, Scopas, gained distinction as an emotional sculptor. One of his most successful creations was the statue of a religious ecstatic, a worshiper of Dionysus, in a condition of mystic frenzy. At the end of the century Lysippus introduced even stronger qualities of realism and individualism into sculpture. He was the first great master of the realistic portrait as a study of personal character.

8. Athenian Life in the Golden Age

The population of Athens in the fifth and fourth centuries was divided into three distinct groups: the citizens, the metics, and the slaves. The citizens, who numbered at the most about 160,000, included only those born of citizen parents, except for the few who were occasionally enfranchised by special law. The metics, who probably did not exceed a total of 100,000, were resident aliens, chiefly non-Athenian Greeks, although some were Phoenicians and Jews. Save for the fact that they had no political privileges and generally were not permitted to own land, the metics had equal opportunities with citizens. They could engage in any occupation they desired and participate in any social or intellectual activities. Contrary to a popular tradition, the slaves in Athens were never a majority of the population. Their maximum number does not seem to have exceeded 140,000. On the whole, they were very well treated and were often rewarded for faithful service by being set free. They could work for wages and own property, and some of them held responsible positions as minor public officials and as managers of banks.

Citizens, metics, and slaves

Life in Athens stands out in rather sharp contrast to that in most other civilizations. One of its leading features was the amazing degree of social and economic equality which prevailed among all the inhabitants. Although there were many who were poor, there were few who were very rich. The average wage was the same for practically all classes of workers, skilled and unskilled alike. Nearly everyone, whether citizen, metic, or slave, ate the same kind of food, wore the same kind of clothing, and participated in the same kind of amusement. This substantial equality was enforced in part by the system of *liturgies*, which were services to the state rendered by wealthy men, chiefly in the form of contributions to support the drama, equip the navy, or provide for the poor.

The amazing degree of social and economic equality

A second outstanding characteristic of Athenian life was its poverty in comforts and luxuries. Part of this was due to the low income of the mass of the people. Teachers, sculptors, masons, carpenters, and common laborers all received the same standard wage of one drachma (about 30 cents) per day. Part of it may have been due also to the mild climate, which made possible a life of simplicity. But whatever the cause, the fact remains that, in comparison with

The poverty of Athenian life

modern standards, the Athenians endured an exceedingly impoverished existence. They knew nothing of such common things as
watches, soap, newspapers, cotton cloth, sugar, tea, or coffee. Their
beds had no springs, their houses had no drains, and their food consisted chiefly of barley cakes, onions, and fish, washed down with
diluted wine. From the standpoint of clothing they were no better
off. A rectangular piece of cloth wrapped around the body and
fastened with pins at the shoulders and with a rope around the waist
served as the main garment. A larger piece was draped around the
body as an extra garment for outdoor wear. No one wore either
stockings or socks, and few had any footgear except sandals.

*Indifference
toward
the business of
making a living*

But lack of comforts and luxuries was a matter of little consequence to the Athenian citizen. He was totally unable to regard these
as the most important things in life. His aim was to live as interest-
ingly and contentedly as possible without spending all his days in
grinding toil for the sake of a little more comfort for his family.
Nor was he interested in piling up riches as a source of power or
prestige. What each citizen really wanted was a small farm or business
which would provide him with a reasonable income and at the same
time allow him an abundance of leisure for politics, for gossip in the
market place, and for intellectual or artistic activities if he had the
talent to enjoy them.

*Attitudes
toward work*

It is frequently supposed that the Athenian was too lazy or too
snobbish to work hard for luxury and security. But such was not
quite the case. It is true that there were some occupations in which
he would not engage, because he considered them degrading or
destructive of moral freedom. He would not break his back digging
silver or copper out of a mine; such work was fit only for slaves
of the lowest intellectual level. On the other hand, there is plenty
of evidence to show that the great majority of Athenian citizens did
not look with disdain upon manual labor. Most of them worked on
their farms or in their shops as independent craftsmen. Hundreds
of others earned their living as hired laborers employed either by
the state or by their fellow Athenians. Cases are on record of citizens,
metics, and slaves working side by side, all for the same wage, in
the construction of public buildings; and in at least one instance the
foreman of the crew was a slave.[11]

*The basic eco-
nomic activities*

In spite of expansion of trade and increase in population, the economic organization of Athenian society remained comparatively simple. Agriculture and commerce were by far the most important enterprises. Even in Pericles' day the majority of the citizens still lived
in the country. Industry was not highly developed. Very few examples of large-scale production are on record, and those chiefly in the
manufacture of pottery and implements of war. The largest establishment that ever existed was apparently a shield factory owned by

176 [11] A. E. Zimmern, *The Greek Commonwealth*, p. 258.

a metic and employing 120 slaves. There was no other more than half as large. The enterprises which absorbed the most labor were the mines, but they were owned by the state and were leased in sections to petty contractors to be worked by slaves. The bulk of industry was carried on in small shops owned by individual craftsmen who produced their wares directly to the order of the consumer.

Religion underwent some notable changes in the Golden Age. The primitive polytheism and anthropomorphism of the Homeric myths were largely supplanted, among intellectuals at least, by a belief in one God as the creator and sustainer of the moral law. Such a doctrine was taught by many of the philosophers, by the poet Pindar, and by the dramatists Aeschylus and Sophocles. Other significant consequences flowed from the mystery cults. These new forms of religion first became popular in the sixth century because of the craving for an emotional faith to make up for the disappointments of life. The more important of them was the Orphic cult, which revolved around the myth of the death and resurrection of Dionysus. The other, the Eleusinian cult, had as its central theme the abduction of Persephone by Pluto, god of the nether world, and her ultimate redemption by Demeter, the great Earth Mother. Both of these cults had as their original purpose the promotion of the life-giving powers of nature, but in time they came to be fraught with a much deeper significance. They expressed to their followers the ideas of vicarious atonement, salvation in an afterlife, and ecstatic union with the divine. Although entirely inconsistent with the spirit of the ancient religion, they made a powerful appeal to certain classes of Greeks and were largely responsible for the spread of the belief in personal immortality. The majority of the people, however, seem to have persisted in their adherence to the worldly, optimistic, and mechanical faith of their ancestors and to have shown little concern about a conviction of sin or a desire for salvation in a life to come.

Changes in religion

It remains to consider briefly the position of the family in Athens in the fifth and fourth centuries. Though marriage was still an important institution for the procreation of children who would become citizens of the state, there is reason to believe that family life had declined. Men of the more prosperous classes, at least, now spent the greater part of their time away from their families. Wives were relegated to an inferior position and required to remain secluded in their homes. Their place as social and intellectual companions for their husbands was taken by alien women, the famous *hetaerae*, many of whom were highly cultured natives of the Ionian cities. Marriage itself assumed the character of a political and economic arrangement, devoid of romantic elements. Men married wives so as to ensure that at least some of their children would be legitimate and in order to obtain property in the form of a dowry. It was important also, of course, to have someone to care for the household.

The family in Athens in the Golden Age

But husbands did not consider their wives as their equals and did not appear in public with them or encourage their participation in any form of social or intellectual activity.

9. The Greek Achievement and Its Significance for Us

The magnitude of the Greek achievement

No careful historian would deny that the achievement of the Greeks was one of the most remarkable in the history of the world. With no great expanse of fertile soil or abundance of mineral resources, they succeeded in developing a higher and more varied civilization than any of the most richly favored nations of the Orient had ever brought forth. With only a limited cultural inheritance from the past to build upon as a foundation, they produced intellectual and artistic achievements which have served ever since as the chief inspiration to man in his quest for wisdom and beauty. It seems reasonable to conclude also that they achieved a more normal and more rational mode of living than most other peoples who have strutted and fretted their hour upon this planet. The absence of violent revolution except in the earlier period, the infrequency of brutal crimes, and the contentment with simple amusements and modest wealth all point to a comparatively happy and satisfied existence. Moreover, the sane moral attitude of the Greek helped to keep him almost entirely free from the nervous instability and emotional conflicts which wreak so much havoc in modern society. Suicide, for example, was exceedingly rare in Greece.[12]

Undesirable features of Greek life

It is necessary to be on our guard, however, against certain uncritical judgments which are sometimes expressed in reference to the achievement of the Greeks. We must not assume that all of the natives of Hellas were as cultured, wise, and free as the citizens of Athens and of the Ionian states across the Aegean. The Spartans, the Arcadians, the Thessalians, and probably the majority of the Boeotians remained untutored and benighted from the beginning to the end of their history. Furthermore, the Athenian civilization itself was not without its defects. It permitted some exploitation of the weak, especially of the ignorant slaves who toiled in the mines. It was based upon a principle of racial exclusiveness which reckoned every man a foreigner whose parents were not both Athenians and consequently denied political rights to the majority of the inhabitants of the country. Its statecraft was not sufficiently enlightened to avoid the pitfalls of imperialism and even of aggressive war. Finally, the attitude of its citizens was not always tolerant and just. Socrates was put to death for his opinions, and two other philosophers, Anaxagoras and Protagoras, were forced to leave the country.[13]

[12] For a discussion of this point see E. A. Westermarck, *The Origin and Development of Moral Ideas*, pp. 247 ff.

[13] It must be conceded, however, that the record of the Athenians for tolerance

Nor is it true that the Hellenic influence has really been as great as is commonly supposed. No intelligent student could accept the sentimental verdict of Shelley: "We are all Greeks; our laws, our literature, our religion, our arts have their roots in Greece." Our laws do not really have their roots in Greece but chiefly in Hellenistic and Roman sources. Much of our poetry is undoubtedly Greek in inspiration, but such is not the case with most of our prose literature. Our religion is no more than partly Greek; except as it was influenced by Plato, Aristotle, and the Romans, it reflects primarily the spirit of the Orient. Even our arts take their form and meaning from Rome as much as from Greece. Actually, modern civilization has been the result of the convergence of several influences coming from a variety of sources. The influence from Greece has been partly overshadowed by heritages from the Near Orient and from the Romans and the Germans. Philosophy appears to have been the only important segment of Greek civilization which has been incorporated into modern culture virtually intact.

In spite of all this, the Hellenic adventure was of profound significance for the history of the world. For the Greeks were the founders of nearly all those ideals which we commonly think of as peculiar to the West. The civilizations of the ancient Orient, with the exception, to a certain extent, of the Hebrew, Egyptian, and Chinese, were dominated by absolutism, supernaturalism, ecclesiasticism, the denial of both body and mind, and the subjection of the individual to the group. Their political regime was the reign of force as expressed in an absolute monarch supported by a powerful priesthood. Their religion was the worship of omnipotent gods who demanded that man should humble and despise himself for the purpose of their greater glory. Culture in these mighty empires served mainly as an instrument to magnify the power of the state and to enhance the prestige of rulers and priests.

By contrast, the civilization of Greece, notably in its Athenian form, was founded upon ideals of freedom, optimism, secularism, rationalism, the glorification of both body and mind, and a high regard for the dignity and worth of the individual man. In so far as the individual was subjected at all, his subjection was to the rule of the majority. Religion was worldly and practical, serving the interests of human beings. Worship of the gods was a means for the ennoblement of man. As opposed to the ecclesiasticism of the Orient, the Greeks had no organized priesthood at all. They kept their priests in the background and refused under any circumstances to allow them to define dogma or to govern the realm of intellect. In addition, they excluded them from control over the sphere of morality.

Hellenic influence sometimes exaggerated

The influence of the Greeks on the West

Contrast of Greek and Oriental ideals

---

was better than that of most other nations, both ancient and modern. There was probably more freedom of expression in Athens during the war with Sparta than there was in the United States during the war of 1917–1918 with Germany.

The Acropolis Today. In the commanding position in the center is the Parthenon. Immediately to the left is the Erechtheum with its Porch of the Maidens facing the Parthenon. Farther to the left is the colonnaded entrance building.

The culture of the Greeks was the first to be based upon the primacy of intellect—upon the supremacy of the spirit of free inquiry. There was no subject they feared to investigate, or any question they regarded as excluded from the province of reason. To an extent never before realized, mind was supreme over faith; logic and science over superstition.[14]

Selected Readings

Abbot, Evelyn, *Pericles and the Golden Age of Athens*, New York, 1925

Agard, Walter, *What Democracy Meant to the Greeks*, Chapel Hill, 1942

Barker, Ernest, *Greek Political Theory: Plato and His Predecessors*, New York, 1919, 2 vols.

Burnet, John, *Early Greek Philosophy*, New York, 1930

Cooper, Lane, ed., *The Greek Genius and Its Influence*, New Haven, 1917

Dickinson, G. L., *The Greek View of Life*, New York, 1927

Fowler, H. N., *A History of Ancient Greek Literature*, New York, 1923

Gardner, Percy, *The Principles of Greek Art*, New York, 1926

Glotz, Gustave, *Ancient Greece at Work*, New York, 1926

Glover, T. R., *Democracy in the Ancient World*, New York, 1927

[14] For further discussion of the contrast between Hellas and the Orient see the admirable study by Edith Hamilton, *The Greek Way*.

Grant, A. J., *Greece in the Age of Pericles*, New York, 1897

Hamilton, Edith, *The Greek Way*, New York, 1930

Larsen, J. A. O., *Representative Government in Greek and Roman History*, Berkeley, 1955

Livingstone, R. W., ed., *The Legacy of Greece*, New York, 1928

Mahaffy, J. P., *Social Life in Greece from Homer to Menander*, New York, 1907

———, *What Have the Greeks Done for Modern Civilization?* New York, 1909

Mitchell, H., *Sparta*, New York, 1952

Moore, C. H., *The Religious Thought of the Greeks*, Cambridge, Mass., 1925

Oakeley, H. D., *Greek Ethical Thought from Homer to the Stoics*, Boston, 1950

Ridder, A. H. P. de, and Deonna, Waldemar, *Art in Greece*, New York, 1927

Robin, Leon, *Greek Thought and the Origins of the Scientific Spirit*, New York, 1928

Ross, W. D., *Aristotle*, New York, 1924

Sarton, George, *A History of Science: Ancient Science through the Golden Age of Greece*, Cambridge, Mass., 1952

———, *An Introduction to the History of Science*, Baltimore, 1927, Vol. I

Sedgwick, W. T., and Tyler, H. W., *A Short History of Science*, New York, 1925

Seymour, T. D., *Life in the Homeric Age*, New York, 1907

Trever, A. A., *History of Ancient Civilization*, New York, 1939, Vol. I

Tucker, T. G., *Life in Ancient Athens*, New York, 1907

Westermann, W. L., *The Slave Systems of Greek and Roman Antiquity*, Philadelphia, 1955

Zimmern, A. E., *The Greek Commonwealth*, New York, 1911

SOURCE MATERIALS

Adams, Francis, *The Genuine Works of Hippocrates*

Aristotle, *Politics; Ethics; History of Animals*

Herodotus, *History*

Hesiod, *Works and Days*

Homer, *The Iliad; The Odyssey*

Plato, *Dialogues*, especially "the Republic," "Phaedo," "the Apology," and "the Sophist"

Plutarch, *Lives of Illustrious Men*, especially "Lycurgus," "Solon," "Pericles," "Aristides," "Themistocles"

Thucydides, *History of the Peloponnesian War*

Xenophon, *Memorabilia*

The Hellenistic Civilization

*A new stage in
world history*

The death of Alexander the Great in 323 B.C. marked the beginning
of a new stage in world history. Hellenic civilization, properly defined, was now at an end. The fusion of cultures and intermingling
of peoples resulting from Alexander's conquests had accomplished
the overthrow of most of the ideals represented by the Greeks in
their prime. Gradually a new pattern of civilization emerged based
upon a mixture of Greek and Oriental elements. To this new civilization, which lasted until about the beginning of the Christian era,
the name Hellenistic is the one most commonly applied.

*Comparison of
the Hellenistic
Age with the
Golden Age of
Greece*

While the Hellenistic Age is sometimes regarded as simply a final
chapter in the history of Greece, this is by no means correct. The
centuries which followed the death of Alexander were so markedly
different from the Golden Age of Greece that they cannot be accurately regarded as a continuation of it. Though the language of the
new era was Greek, and though persons of Greek nationality continued to play an active role in many affairs, the spirit of the culture
was largely the spirit of the Orient. The classical ideal of democracy
was now superseded by despotism perhaps as rigorous as any that
Egypt or Persia had ever produced. The Hellenic devotion to simplicity and the golden mean gave way to extravagance in art and to
a love of luxury and riotous excess. The Athenian economic system
of small-scale production was supplanted by the growth of big business and ruthless competition for profits. Though progress in science continued, the sublime confidence in the power of the mind
which had characterized the teachings of most of the philosophers
from Thales to Aristotle was swallowed up in defeatism and ultimately in the sacrifice of logic to faith. In view of these changes it
seems justifiable to conclude that the Hellenistic Age was really
the era of a new civilization as distinct from the Greek as modern
182 civilization from the culture of the Middle Ages.

1. Political History and Institutions

When Alexander died in 323 B.C., he left no legitimate heir to succeed him. His nearest male relative was a feeble-minded half-brother. Tradition relates that when his friends requested him on his deathbed to designate a successor, he replied vaguely, "To the best man." After his death his highest ranking generals proceeded to divide the empire among them. Some of the younger commanders contested this arrangement, and a series of wars followed which culminated in the decisive battle of Ipsus in 301 B.C. The result of this battle was a new division among the victors. Seleucus took possession of Persia, Mesopotamia, and Syria; Lysimachus assumed control over Asia Minor and Thrace; Cassander established himself in Macedonia; and Ptolemy added Phoenicia and Palestine to his original domain of Egypt. Twenty years later these four states were reduced to three when Seleucus defeated and killed Lysimachus in battle and appropriated his kingdom. In the meantime most of the Greek states had revolted against the attempts of the Macedonian king to extend his power over them. By banding together in defensive leagues several of them succeeded in maintaining their independence for nearly a century. Finally, between 146 and 30 B.C. nearly all of the Hellenistic territory passed under Roman rule.

The Hellenistic states

The dominant form of government in the Hellenistic Age was the despotism of kings who represented themselves as at least semi-divine. Alexander himself was hailed as divine in Egypt. His most powerful successors, the Seleucid kings in Western Asia and the Ptolemies in Egypt, made more systematic attempts to deify themselves. A Seleucid monarch, Antiochus IV, adopted the title "Epiphanes" or "God Manifest." The later members of the dynasty of the Ptolemies signed their decrees "Theos" (God) and revived the practice of sister marriage which had been followed by the Pharaohs as a means of preserving the divine blood of the royal family from contamination. Only in the kingdom of Macedonia was despotism tempered by a modicum of respect for the liberties of the citizens.

Divine monarchy the dominant form of government

Two other political institutions developed as by-products of Hellenistic civilization: the Achaean and Aetolian Leagues. We have already seen that most of the Greek states rebelled against Macedonian rule following the division of Alexander's empire. The better to preserve their independence, several of these states formed alliances among themselves, which were gradually expanded to become confederate leagues. The states of the Peloponnesus, with the exception of Sparta and Elis, were united in the Achaean League, while the Aetolian federation included nearly all of central Greece with the exception of Athens. The organization of these leagues was essentially the same in both cases. Each had a federal council composed of representatives of the member cities with power to enact laws on subjects of general concern. An assembly which all of the

The Achaean and Aetolian Leagues

citizens in the federated states could attend decided questions of war and peace and elected officials. Executive and military authority was vested in the hands of a general, elected for one year and eligible for re-election only in alternate years. Although these leagues are frequently described as federal states, they were scarcely more than confederacies. The central authority, like the government of the American States under the Articles of Confederation, was dependent upon the local governments for contributions of revenue and troops. Furthermore, the powers delegated to the central government were limited primarily to matters of war and peace, coinage, and weights and measures. The chief significance of these Leagues is to be found in the fact that they embodied the principle of representative government and constituted the nearest approach ever made in Greece to voluntary national union.

2. Significant Economic and Social Developments

The economic revolution and its causes

The history of the Hellenistic civilization was marked by economic developments second only in magnitude to the Commercial and Industrial Revolutions of the modern era. Several important causes can be distinguished: (1) the opening up of a vast area of trade from the Indus River to the Nile as a result of the Alexandrian conquests; (2) the rise in prices as a consequence of the release of the enormous Persian hoard of gold and silver into the channels of circulation, resulting in an increase in investment and speculation; and (3) the promotion of trade and industry by governments as a means of augmenting the revenues of the state. The net result of these factors was the growth of a system of large-scale production, trade, and finance, with the state as the principal capitalist and entrepreneur.

Developments in agriculture

Agriculture was as profoundly affected by the new developments as any other branch of the economic life. The most striking phenomena were the concentration of holdings of land and the degradation of the agricultural population. One of the first things which the successors of Alexander did was to confiscate the estates of the chief landowners and add them to the royal domain. The lands thus acquired were either granted to the favorites of the king or leased to tenants under an arrangement calculated to ensure an abundant income for the crown. The tenants were generally forbidden to leave the lands they cultivated until after the harvest and were not allowed to dispose of their grain until after the king had had a chance to sell the share which he received as rent at the highest price the market would bring. When some of the tenants went on strike or attempted to run away, they were all bound to the soil as hereditary serfs. Many of the small independent farmers also became serfs when they got into debt as a result of inability to compete with large-scale production.

In an effort to make all of the resources of the state contribute to

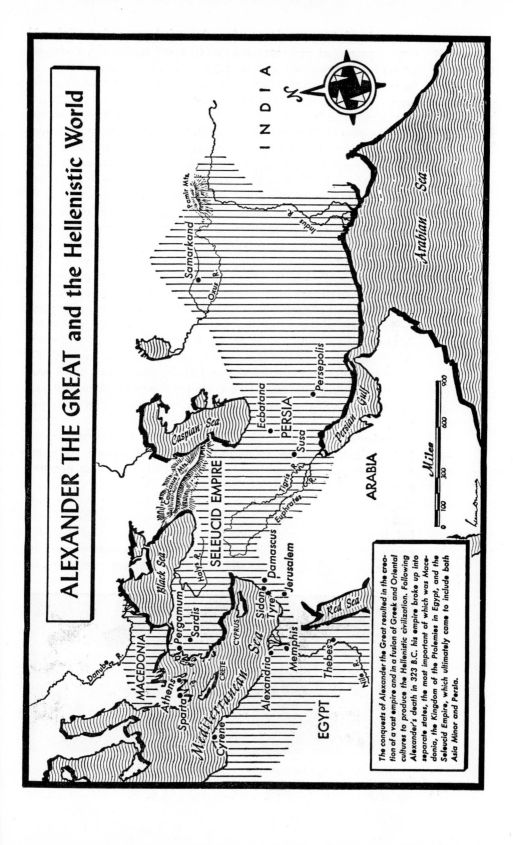

ALEXANDER THE GREAT and the Hellenistic World

INDIA

Pamir Mts.

Samarkand

Oxus R.

Indus

Arabian Sea

Caspian Sea

Persepolis

Ecbatana

PERSIA

Susa

Persian Gulf

Black Sea

Caucasus Mts.

SELEUCID EMPIRE

Tigris R.

Euphrates

Karun R.

ARABIA

Pergamum

Sardis

Halys R.

Damascus

Jerusalem

Sidon

Tyre

CYPRUS

Red Sea

MACEDONIA

Athens

Sparta

CRETE

Mediterranean Sea

Alexandria

Memphis

Cyrene

Thebes

Nile R.

EGYPT

Danube R.

Miles

0   100   300   600   900

The conquests of Alexander the Great resulted in the creation of a vast empire and in a fusion of Greek and Oriental
cultures to produce the Hellenistic civilization. Following
Alexander's death in 323 B.C. his empire broke up into
separate states, the most important of which was Macedonia, the Kingdom of the Ptolemies in Egypt, and the
Seleucid Empire, which ultimately came to include both
Asia Minor and Persia.

*State capitalism
and regimen-
tation of com-
merce*

the profit of the government, the rulers of Egypt and the Seleucid empire promoted and regulated industry and trade. The Ptolemies established factories and shops in nearly every village and town to be owned and operated by the government for its own financial benefit. In addition, they assumed control over all of the enterprises that were privately owned, fixing the prices the owners could charge and manipulating markets for the advantage of the crown. A similar plan of regimentation for industry, though not on quite such an ambitious scale, was enforced by the Seleucid rulers of western Asia. Trade was left by both of these governments very largely in private hands, but it was heavily taxed and regulated in such a way as to make sure that an ample share of the profits would go to the king. Every facility was provided by the government for the encouragement of new trading ventures. Harbors were improved, warships were sent out to police the seas, and roads and canals were built. Moreover, the Ptolemies employed famous geographers to discover new routes to distant lands and thereby gain access to valuable markets. As a result of such methods Egypt developed a flourishing commerce in the widest variety of products. Into the port of Alexandria came spices from Arabia, copper from Cyprus, gold from Abyssinia and India, tin from Britain, elephants and ivory from Nubia, silver from the northern Aegean and Spain, fine carpets from Asia Minor, and even silk from China. Profits for the government and even for some of the merchants were often as high as 20 or 30 per cent.

*The growth of
finance*

Further evidence of the significant economic development of the Hellenistic Age is to be found in the growth of finance. An international money economy, based upon gold and silver coins, now became general throughout the Near East. Banks, usually owned by the government, developed as the chief institutions of credit for business ventures of every description. Because of the abundance of capital, interest rates gradually declined from 12 per cent in the third century to 7 per cent in the second. Speculation, cornering of markets, intense competition, the growth of large business houses, and the de-

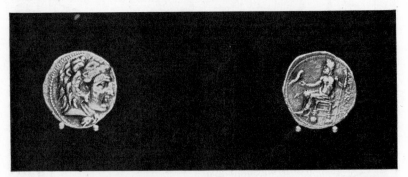

Hellenistic Coins. Obverse and reverse sides of the silver tetradrachma of Macedon, 336–323 B.C. Objects of common use from this period often show as much beauty of design as formal works of art.

velopment of insurance and advertising were other significant phenomena of this remarkable age.

According to the available evidence, the Hellenistic Age, during the first two centuries at least, was a period of prosperity. Although serious crises frequently followed the collapse of speculative booms, they appear to have been of short duration. But the prosperity that existed seems to have been limited chiefly to the rulers, the upper classes, and the merchants. It certainly did not extend to the peasants or even to the workers in the towns. The daily wages of both skilled and unskilled workers in Athens in the third century had dropped to less than half of what they had been in the Age of Pericles. The cost of living, on the other hand, had risen considerably. To make matters worse, unemployment in the large cities was so serious a problem that the government had to provide free grain for many of the inhabitants. Slavery declined in the Hellenistic world, partly because of the influence of the Stoic philosophy, but mainly for the reason that wages were now so low that it was cheaper to hire a free laborer than to purchase and maintain a slave.

Prosperity for the rich, slums and unemployment for the poor

An interesting result of social and economic conditions in the Hellenistic Age was the growth of metropolitan cities. Despite the fact that a majority of the people still dwelt in the country, there was an increasing tendency for men to become dissatisfied with the dullness of rural living and to flock into the cities, where life if not easier was at least more exciting. But the chief reasons are to be found in the expansion of industry and commerce, in the enlargement of governmental functions, and in the desire of former independent farmers to escape the hardships of serfdom. Cities multiplied and grew in the Hellenistic empires almost as rapidly as in nineteenth-century America. Some of them attained metropolitan size virtually overnight. Antioch in Syria quadrupled its population during a single century. Seleucia on the Tigris grew from nothing to a metropolis of several hundred thousand in less than two centuries. The largest and most famous of all the Hellenistic cities was Alexandria in Egypt with over 500,000 inhabitants and possibly as many as 1,000,000. No other city in ancient times, not even Rome, surpassed it in size or in magnificence. Its streets were well paved and laid out in regular order. It had splendid public buildings and parks, a museum, and a library of 750,000 volumes. It was the most brilliant center of Hellenistic cultural achievement, especially in the field of scientific research. The masses of its people, however, were a helpless mob without any share in the brilliant and luxurious life around them, although it was paid for in part out of the fruits of their labor.

The growth of metropolitan cities

3. Hellenistic Culture: Philosophy, Literature, and Art

Hellenistic philosophy went through a peculiar evolution—or retrogression, it might almost be better to say. During the first stage it was still under the influence of Greek thought and consequently showed an elemental regard for reason as the key to the solution of man's problems. During what may be considered a second stage, skepticism concerning all truth and all values resulted in the rejection of reason entirely. Toward the end of the civilization philosophy degenerated into a barren mysticism, with the consequence that the whole intellectual approach, whether based upon reason or experience, was thrown into the discard. Despite the fundamental differences in their teachings, the philosophers of the Hellenistic Age were all agreed upon one thing: the necessity of finding some way of salvation for man from the hardships and evils of his existence.

The first and most important of the Hellenistic philosophies were Epicureanism and Stoicism, both of which originated about 300 B.C. The founders were, respectively, Epicurus and Zeno, who were residents of Athens, though the former was born on the island of Samos, while the latter was a native of Cyprus, probably of Phoenician descent. Epicureanism and Stoicism had several features in common. Both were individualistic, concerned not with the welfare of society primarily, but with the good of the individual. Both were materialistic, denying categorically the existence of any spiritual substances; even divine beings and the soul were declared to be formed of matter. In Stoicism and Epicureanism alike there were definite traces of defeatism, since both of them implied that the efforts of man are futile and suggested a retreat into Oriental quietism as an aim for the wise to pursue. Lastly, the two philosophies were similar in their doctrines that concepts and abstractions are nothing but names, that only particular things are real, and that all knowledge has its basis in sense perception.

But in many ways the two systems were quite different. Zeno and his principal disciples taught that the cosmos is an ordered whole in which all contradictions are resolved for ultimate good. Evil is, therefore, relative; the particular misfortunes which befall human beings are but necessary incidents to the final perfection of the universe. Everything that happens is rigidly determined in accordance with rational purpose. Man is not master of his fate; his destiny is a link in an unbroken chain. He is free only in the sense that he can accept his fate or rebel against it. But whether he accepts or rebels, he cannot overcome it. The supreme duty of man is to submit to the order of the universe in the knowledge that that order is good; in other words, to resign himself as graciously as possible to his fate. Through such an act of resignation he will attain to the highest happiness, which consists in tranquillity of mind. The individual who is most truly happy is therefore the man who by the assertion of his rational nature has accomplished a perfect adjustment of his life to the cosmic purpose and has purged his soul of all bitterness and whining protest against evil turns of fortune.

The Stoics developed an ethical and social theory which accorded well with their general philosophy described above. Believing that the highest good consists in serenity of mind, they naturally emphasized duty and self-discipline as cardinal virtues. Recognizing the prevalence of particular evil, they taught that men should be tolerant and forgiving in their attitudes toward each other. They denied racial exclusiveness and held that all men are brothers under the fatherhood of one God. Unlike their contemporaries, the Cynics, they did not recommend that man should withdraw from society but urged participation in public affairs as a duty for the citizen of rational mind. They condemned slavery and war, but it was far from their purpose to preach any crusade against these evils. They were disposed to think that the results which would flow from violent measures of social change would be worse than the diseases they were supposed to cure. Besides, what difference did it make that the body should be in bondage so long as the mind was free? Despite its negative character the Stoic philosophy was the noblest product of the Hellenistic Age. Its equalitarianism, pacifism, and humanitarianism were important factors in mitigating the harshness not only of that time but of later centuries as well.

The ethical and social teachings of the Stoics

Whereas the Stoics went back to Heracleitus for much of their conception of the universe, the Epicureans derived their metaphysics chiefly from Democritus. Epicurus taught that the basic ingredients of all things are minute, indivisible atoms, and that change and growth are the results of the combination and separation of these particles. Nevertheless, while accepting the materialism of the atomists, Epicurus rejected their absolute mechanism. He denied that an automatic, mechanical motion of the atoms can be the cause of all things in the universe. Though he admitted that the atoms move downward in perpendicular lines because of their weight, he insisted upon endowing them with a spontaneous ability to swerve from the perpendicular and thereby to combine with each other. The chief reason for this peculiar modification of the atomic theory was to make possible a belief in human freedom. If the atoms were capable only of mechanical motion, then man, who is made up of atoms, would be reduced to the status of an automaton; and fatalism would be the law of the universe. In this repudiation of the mechanistic interpretation of life, Epicurus was probably closer to the Hellenic spirit than either Democritus or the Stoics.

Epicurus revives atomism but rules out determinism

The ethical philosophy of the Epicureans was based upon the doctrine that the highest good for man is pleasure. But they did not include all forms of indulgence in the category of genuine pleasure. The so-called pleasures of the debauched man should be avoided, since every excess of carnality must be balanced by its portion of pain. On the other hand, a moderate satisfaction of bodily appetites is permissible and may be regarded as a good in itself. Better than this is mental pleasure, sober contemplation of the reasons for the choice of some things and the avoidance of others, and mature reflection upon satisfactions previously enjoyed. The highest of all

The Epicureans pursue tranquillity of mind through overcoming fear of the supernatural

189

pleasures, however, consists in serenity of soul, in the complete absence of both mental and physical pain. This end can be best achieved
through the elimination of fear, especially fear of the supernatural,
since that is the sovereign source of mental pain. Man must recognize
from the study of philosophy that the soul is material and therefore
cannot survive the body, that the universe operates of itself, and that
the gods do not intervene in human affairs. The gods live remote
from the world and are too intent upon their own happiness to
bother about what takes place on earth. Since they do not reward
or punish men either in this life or in a life to come, there is no
reason why they should be feared. The Epicureans thus came by a
different route to the same general conclusion as the Stoics—the
supreme good is tranquillity of mind.

*The ethical and
political theories
of the Epicu-
reans*

The ethics of the Epicureans as well as their political theory rested
squarely upon a utilitarian basis. In contrast with the Stoics, they did
not insist upon virtue as an end in itself but taught that the only
reason why man should be good is to increase his own happiness.
In like manner, they denied that there is any such thing as absolute
justice; laws and institutions are just only in so far as they contribute
to the welfare of the individual. Certain rules have been found necessary in every complex society for the maintenance of security and
order. Men obey these rules solely because it is to their advantage
to do so. Thus the origin and existence of the state are rooted directly in self-interest. Generally speaking, Epicurus held no high
regard for either political or social life. He considered the state as a
mere convenience and taught that the wise man should take no active
part in public life. Unlike the Cynics, he did not propose that man
should abandon civilization and return to nature; yet his conception
of the happiest life was essentially passive and defeatist. The wise
man will recognize that he cannot eradicate the evils in the world
no matter how strenuous and intelligent his efforts; he will therefore
withdraw to "cultivate his garden," study philosophy, and enjoy
the fellowship of a few congenial friends.

*The defeatist
philosophy
of the Skeptics*

A more radically defeatist philosophy was that propounded by the
Skeptics. Although Skepticism was founded by Pyrrho, a contemporary of Zeno and Epicurus, it did not reach the zenith of its popularity until about a century later under the influence of Carneades
(214–129 B.C.). The chief source of inspiration of the Skeptics was
the Sophist teaching that all knowledge is derived from sense perception and therefore must be limited and relative. From this they
deduced the conclusion that we cannot prove anything. Since the
impressions of our senses deceive us, no truth can be certain. All
we can say is that things *appear* to be such and such; we do not
know what they really *are*. We have no definite knowledge of the
supernatural, of the meaning of life, or even of right and wrong. It
follows that the sensible course to pursue is suspension of judgment;
this alone can lead to happiness. If man will abandon the fruitless

quest for absolute truth and cease worrying about good and evil, he will attain that equanimity of mind which is the highest satisfaction that life affords. The Skeptics were even less concerned than the Epicureans with political and social problems. Their ideal was the typically Hellenistic one of escape for the individual from a world he could neither understand nor reform.

Hellenistic thought reached its lowest point in the philosophies of Philo Judaeus and the Neo-Pythagoreans in the last century B.C. and the first century A.D. The proponents of the two systems were in general agreement as to their basic teachings, especially in their predominantly religious viewpoint. They believed in a transcendent God so far removed from the world as to be utterly unknowable to mortal minds. They conceived the universe as being sharply divided between spirit and matter. They considered everything physical and material as evil; man's soul is imprisoned in his body, from which an escape can be effected only through rigorous denial and mortification of the flesh. Their attitude was mystical and anti-intellectual: truth comes neither from science nor from reason but from revelation; the feeble deductions of the human mind are worthy of nothing but contempt; the ultimate aim in life is to accomplish a mystic union with God, to lose one's self in the divine.

The new religious philosophies

Hellenistic literature is significant mainly for the light which it throws upon the character of the civilization. Most of the writings showed little originality or depth of thought. But they poured forth from the hands of the copyists in a profusion that is almost incredible when we consider that the art of printing by movable type was unknown. The names of at least 1100 authors have been discovered already, and more are being added from year to year. Much of what they wrote was trash, comparable to the Sunday supplements and cheap novels of our own day. Nevertheless, there were several works of more than mediocre quality and a few which met the highest standards ever set by the Greeks.

The profusion of ephemeral literature

The leading types of Hellenistic poetry were the drama, the pastoral, and the mime. Drama was almost exclusively comedy, represented mainly by the plays of Menander. His plays were entirely different from the comedy of Aristophanes. They were distinguished by naturalism rather than by satire, by preoccupation with the seamy side of life rather than with political or intellectual issues. Their dominant theme was romantic love, with its pains and pleasures, its intrigues and seductions, and its culmination in happy marriage. The greatest author of pastorals and mimes was Theocritus of Syracuse, who wrote in the first half of the third century B.C. His pastorals, as the name implies, celebrate the charm of life in the country and idealize the simple pleasures of rustic folk. The mimes, on the other hand, portray in colorful dialogue the squabbles, ambitions, and varied activities of the bourgeoisie in the great metropolitan cities.

Hellenistic poetry

The field of prose literature was dominated by the historians, the biographers, and the authors of utopias. By far the ablest of the writers of history was Polybius of Megalopolis, who lived during the second century B.C. From the standpoint of his scientific approach and his zeal for truth, he probably deserves to be ranked second only to Thucydides among all the historians in ancient times; but he excelled Thucydides in his grasp of the importance of social and economic forces. Although most of the biographies were of a light and gossipy character, their tremendous popularity bears eloquent testimony to the literary tastes of the time. Even more significant was the popularity of the utopias, or descriptive accounts of ideal states. Virtually all of them depicted a life of social and economic equality, free from greed, oppression, and strife, on an imaginary island or in some distant, unfamiliar region. Generally in these paradises money was considered to be unknown, trade was prohibited, all property was held in common, and all men were required to work with their hands in producing the necessaries of life. We are probably justified in assuming that the profusion of this utopian literature was a direct result of the rottenness and injustice of Hellenistic society and a consciousness of the need for reform.

Hellenistic art preserved only a few of the superior qualities of the art of the Greeks. In place of the humanism, balance, and restraint which had characterized the architecture and sculpture of the Golden Age, qualities of exaggerated realism, sensationalism, and voluptuousness now became dominant. The simple and dignified Doric and Ionic temples gave way to luxurious palaces, costly mansions, and elaborate public buildings and monuments symbolical of power and wealth. A typical example was the great lighthouse of Alexandria, which rose to a height of nearly 400 feet, with three diminishing stories and eight columns to support the light at the top. Sculpture likewise exhibited tendencies in the direction of extravagance and sentimentality. Many of the statues and figures in relief were huge and some of them almost grotesque. Violent emotionalism and sordid realism were features common to the majority. Among the examples

*See color
pictures at
page 164*

of this type of sculpture may be mentioned the *Laocoön* and the frieze of the Great Altar of Zeus at Pergamum with its giant gods, ferocious animals, and hybrid monsters mingled in desperate combat to symbolize the struggle of Greeks with Gauls. But by no means all of Hellenistic sculpture was overwrought and grotesque. Some of it was distinguished by a calmness and poise and compassion for human suffering reminiscent of the best work of the great fourth-century artists. Statues which exemplify these superior qualities include the *Aphrodite of Melos* (*Venus de Milo*) and the *Winged Victory of Samothrace*.

The Dying Gaul. A good example of Hellenistic realism in sculpture, which often reflected a preoccupation with the morbid and sensational. Every detail of the warrior's agony is dramatically portrayed. Now in the Capitoline Museum, Rome.

The Winged Victory of Samothrace. In this figure and in the *Venus de Milo,* Hellenistic sculptors preserved some of the calmness and devotion to grace and proportion characteristic of Hellenic art in the Golden Age. Now in the Louvre.

4. The First Great Age of Science

The most brilliant age in the history of science prior to the seventeenth century A.D. was the period of the Hellenistic civilization. Indeed, many of the achievements of the modern age would scarcely have been possible without the discoveries of the scientists of Alexandria, Syracuse, Pergamum, and other great cities of the Hellenistic world. The reasons for the phenomenal development of science in the centuries after the downfall of Alexander's empire are not far to seek. Alexander himself had given some financial encouragement to the progress of research. More important was the stimulus provided for intellectual inquiry by the fusion of Chaldean and Egyptian science with the learning of the Greeks. Possibly a third factor was the new interest in luxury and comfort and the demand for practical knowledge which would enable man to solve the problems of a disordered and unsatisfying existence.

Factors responsible for the remarkable progress of science

The sciences which received the major attention in the Hellenistic Age were astronomy, mathematics, geography, medicine, and physics. Chemistry as a pure science was practically unknown. Except for the work of Theophrastus, who was the first to recognize the sexuality of plants, the biological sciences were also largely neglected. Neither chemistry nor biology bore any definite relationship to trade or to the forms of industry then in existence and apparently they were not regarded as having much practical value.

The most popular sciences

The most famous of the earlier astronomers of this time was

193

Aristarchus of Samos (310–230 B.C.), who is sometimes called the "Hellenistic Copernicus." As a result of his discovery that the apparent immobility of the "fixed" stars is due to their vast distance from the earth, he was the first to have any adequate conception of the enormous size of the universe. But his chief title to fame comes from his deduction that the earth and the other planets revolve around the sun. Unfortunately this deduction was not accepted by his successors. It conflicted with the teachings of Aristotle and with the anthropocentric ideas of the Greeks. Besides, it was not in harmony with the beliefs of the Jews and other Orientals who made up so large a percentage of the Hellenistic population. The only other astronomer of much importance in the Hellenistic Age was Hipparchus, who did his most valuable work in Alexandria in the latter half of the second century B.C. His chief contributions were the invention of the astrolabe, the preparation of the best chart of the heavens known to antiquity, the approximately correct calculation of the diameter of the moon and its distance from the earth, and the discovery of the precession of the equinoxes. His fame was eventually overshadowed, however, by the reputation of Ptolemy of Alexandria, the last of the Hellenistic astronomers. Although Ptolemy made few original discoveries, he systematized the work of others. His principal writing, the *Almagest*, based upon the geocentric theory, was handed down to medieval Europe as the classic summary of ancient astronomy.

Closely allied with astronomy were two other sciences, mathematics and geography. The Hellenistic mathematician of greatest renown was of course Euclid (*ca.* 323–*ca.* 285 B.C.), erroneously considered the founder of geometry. Until the middle of the nineteenth century his *Elements of Geometry* remained the accepted basis for the study of that branch of mathematics. Much of the material in this work was not original but was compiled as a synthesis of the discoveries of others. The most original of the Hellenistic mathematicians was probably Hipparchus, who laid the foundations of both plane and spherical trigonometry. Hellenistic geography owed most of its development to Eratosthenes (*ca.* 276–*ca.* 194 B.C.), astronomer, poet, philologist, and librarian of Alexandria. By means of sun dials placed some hundreds of miles apart, he calculated the circumference of the earth with an error of less than 200 miles. He produced the most accurate map that had yet been devised, with the surface of the earth divided into degrees of latitude and longitude. He propounded the theory that all of the oceans are really one, and he was the first to suggest the possibility of reaching India by sailing west. One of his successors divided the earth into the five climatic zones which are still recognized and explained the ebb and flow of the tides as due to the influence of the moon.

Perhaps none of the Hellenistic advances in science surpassed in importance the progress in medicine. Especially significant was the work of Herophilus of Chalcedon, who conducted his researches in Alexandria about the beginning of the third century. Without question he was the greatest anatomist of antiquity and, according to Galen, the first to practice human dissection. Among his most important achievements were a detailed description of the brain, with an attempt to distinguish between the functions of its various parts; the discovery of the significance of the pulse and its use in diagnosing illness; and the discovery that the arteries contain blood alone, not a mixture of blood and air as Aristotle had taught, and that their function is to carry blood from the heart to all parts of the body. The value of this last discovery in laying the basis for a knowledge of the circulation of the blood can hardly be overestimated.

The ablest of the successors of Herophilus was Erasistratus, who flourished in Alexandria about the middle of the third century. He is considered the founder of physiology as a separate science. Not only did he practice dissection, but he is believed to have gained a great deal of his knowledge of bodily functions from vivisection. He discovered the valves of the heart, distinguished between motor and sensory nerves, and taught that the ultimate branches of the arteries and veins are connected. He was the first to reject absolutely the humoral theory of disease and to condemn excessive blood-letting as a method of cure. Unfortunately this theory was revived by Galen, the great encyclopedist of medicine who lived in the Roman Empire in the second century A.D.

physiology

Prior to the third century B.C. physics had been a branch of philosophy. It was made a separate experimental science by Archimedes of Syracuse. Archimedes discovered the law of floating bodies or specific gravity and formulated with scientific exactness the principles of the lever, the pulley, and the screw. Among his memorable inventions were the compound pulley, the tubular screw for pumping water, the screw propeller for ships, and the burning lens. Although he has been called the "technical Yankee of antiquity," there is evidence that he set no high value upon his ingenious mechanical contraptions and preferred to devote his time to pure scientific research.

Physics

Certain other individuals in the Hellenistic Age were quite willing to give all their attention to applied science. Pre-eminent among them was Hero or Heron of Alexandria, who lived in the last century B.C. The record of inventions credited to him almost passes belief. The list includes a fire engine, a siphon, a force pump, a hydraulic organ, a slot machine, a catapult operated by compressed air, a thermoscope, and even a steam engine. How many of these inventions were really his own is impossible to say, but there appears to be no question that such contrivances were actually in existence in his time or soon thereafter. Nevertheless, the total progress in applied science was com-

Applied science

paratively slight, probably for the reason that human labor continued to be so abundant and cheap that it was not worth while to substitute the labor of machines.

5. Religion in the Hellenistic Age

The new trend in religion

If there was one aspect of the Hellenistic civilization which served more than others to accent the contrast with Hellenic culture, it was the new trend in religion. The civic religion of the Greeks as it was in the age of the city-states had now almost entirely disappeared. For the majority of the intellectuals its place was taken by the philosophies of Stoicism, Epicureanism, and Skepticism. Some who were less philosophically inclined turned to the worship of Fortune or became followers of dogmatic atheism.

The popularity of mystic religions

Among the masses a tendency to embrace the emotional religions of Oriental origin was even more clearly manifest. The Orphic and Eleusinian mystery cults attracted more votaries than ever before. The worship of the Egyptian mother-goddess Isis threatened for a time to reach the proportions of a world religion. The astral religion of the Chaldeans likewise spread rapidly, with the result that its chief product, astrology, was received with fanatical enthusiasm throughout the Hellenistic world. So strong was its appeal that it had much to do with the eclipse of science and reason in the second and first centuries B.C. But the most powerful influence of all came from the offshoots of Zoroastrianism, especially from Mithraism and Gnosticism. While all of the cults of Oriental origin resembled each other in their promises of salvation in a life to come, Mithraism and Gnosticism had a more ethically significant mythology, a deeper contempt for this world, and a more clearly defined doctrine of redemption through a personal savior. These were the ideas which satisfied the emotional cravings of the common people, convinced as they were of the worthlessness of this life and ready to be lured by extravagant promises of better things in a world to come. If we can judge by conditions in our own time, some of the doctrines of these cults must have exerted their influence upon members of the upper classes also. Even the most casual observer of modern society knows that pessimism, mysticism, and otherworldliness are not confined to the downtrodden. In some cases the keenest disgust with this life and the deepest mystical yearnings are to be found among those whose pockets bulge with plenty.

The influence of the Jews

A factor by no means unimportant in the religious developments of the Hellenistic Age was the dispersion of the Jews. As a result of Alexander's conquest of Palestine in 332 B.C. and the Roman conquest about three centuries later, thousands of Jews migrated to various sections of the Mediterranean world. It has been estimated that 1,000,000 of them lived in Egypt in the first century A.D. and 200,000 in Asia Minor. They mingled freely with other peoples, adopt-

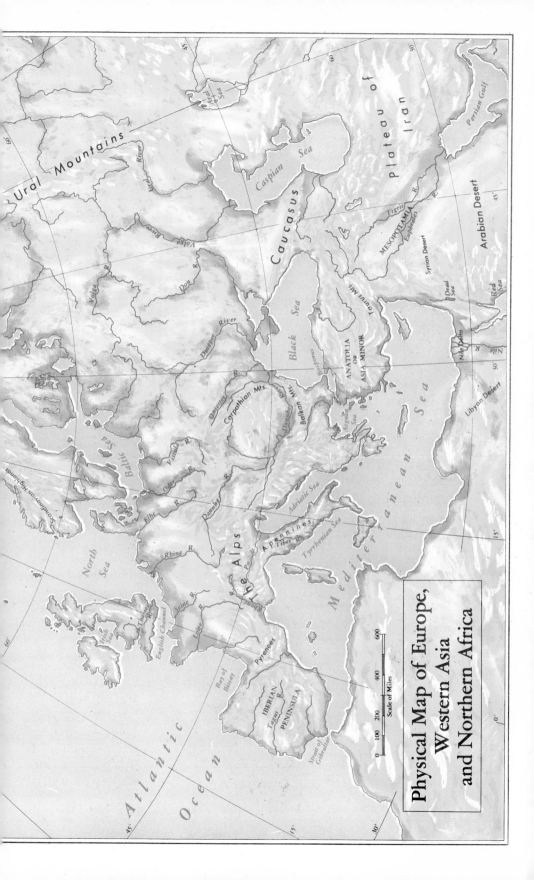

Physical Map of Europe, Western Asia and Northern Africa

Unidentified Man, I cent. B.C. The Romans excelled in portraits of sharp individuality.

Augustus, Reigned 31 B.C.–14 A.D. This portrait suggests the contradictory nature of the genius who gave Rome peace after years of strife.

Constantine, Reig 306–337 A.D. The hea from a statue sixteen in height. Such co marked the decline Roman sculpture.

Wall Painting, I cent. B.C. From a villa near Pompeii.

Mosaic, I cent. A.D. A floor design composed of small pieces of colored marble fitted together to form a picture.

Wall Painting of a Satyr Mask, I cent. B.C. The belief in satyrs, thought to inhabit forests and pastures, was taken over from the Greeks.

Mummy Portrait, II cent. A.D. A Roman woman buried in Egypt.

Architectural Wall Painting f a Pompeiian Villa, I cent. suggesting the Greek origin Roman forms of architecture

ing the Greek language and no small amount of the Hellenic culture which still survived from earlier days. At the same time they played a major part in the diffusion of Oriental beliefs. Their religion had already taken on a spiritual and messianic character as a result of Persian influence. Their leading philosopher of this time, Philo Judaeus of Alexandria, developed a body of doctrine representing the farthest extreme which mysticism had yet attained. Many of the Hellenistic Jews eventually became converts to Christianity and were largely instrumental in the spread of that religion outside of Palestine.

6. A Foretaste of Modernity?

With the possible exception of the Roman, no great culture of ancient times appears to suggest the spirit of the modern age quite so emphatically as does the Hellenistic civilization. Here as in the modern world were to be found a considerable variety of forms of government, the growth of militarism, a decline of respect for democracy, and a trend in the direction of authoritarian rule. Many of the characteristic economic and social developments of the Hel-

Hellenistic civilization compared with that of the modern age

Statue of an Old Market Woman. In the Hellenistic Age the idealism and restraint of Hellenic art were succeeded by a tendency to portray the humble aspects of life and to express compassion for human suffering. Original in the Metropolitan Museum of Art, New York.

lenistic Age are equally suggestive of contemporary experience: the growth of big business, the expansion of trade, the zeal for exploration and discovery, the interest in mechanical inventions, ruthless competition among merchants, the devotion to comfort and the craze for material prosperity, the growth of metropolitan cities with congested slums, and the widening gulf between rich and poor. In the realms of intellect and art the Hellenistic civilization also bore a distinctly modern flavor. This was exemplified by the exaggerated emphasis upon science, the narrow specialization of learning, the penchant for realism and naturalism, the vast production of mediocre literature, and the popularity of mysticism side by side with extreme skepticism and dogmatic unbelief.

Basic differ-
ences

Because of these resemblances there has been a tendency among certain writers to regard our own civilization as decadent. But this is based partly upon the false assumption that the Hellenistic culture was merely a degenerate phase of Greek civilization. Instead, it was a new social and cultural organism born of a fusion of Greek and Oriental elements. Moreover, the differences between the Hellenistic civilization and that of the contemporary world are perhaps just as important as the resemblances. The Hellenistic political outlook was essentially cosmopolitan; nothing comparable to the national patriotism of modern times really prevailed. Despite the remarkable expansion of trade in the Hellenistic Age, no industrial revolution ever took place, for reasons which have already been noted. Finally, Hellenistic science was somewhat more limited than that of the present day. Modern pure science is to a very large extent a species of philosophy—an adventure of the mind in the realm of the unknown. Notwithstanding frequent assertions to the contrary, much of it is gloriously impractical and will probably remain so.

SELECTED READINGS

Bevan, E. R., *Stoics and Skeptics*, New York, 1913
Bury, J. B., and others, *The Hellenistic Age*, New York, 1923
Cary, Max, *The Legacy of Alexander: A History of the Greek World from 323 to 146 B.C.*, New York, 1932.
Ferguson, W. S., *Hellenistic Athens*, New York, 1911
Heath, Sir T. L., *Archimedes*, New York, 1920
———, *Aristarchus of Samos*, New York, 1920
Hicks, R. D., *Stoic and Epicurean*, New York, 1910
Larsen, J. A. O., *Representative Government in Greek and Roman History*, Berkeley, 1955
Mahaffy, Sir J. P., *Greek Life and Thought from the Death of Alexander to the Roman Conquest*, New York, 1896
More, P. E., *Hellenistic Philosophies*, Princeton, 1923
Reymond, Arnold, *History of the Sciences in Greco-Roman Antiquity*, New York, 1927
Sarton, George, *An Introduction to the History of Science,* Baltimore, 1927, Vol. I
Tarn, W. W., *Hellenistic Civilization*, New York, 1952
Taylor, H. O., *Greek Biology and Medicine*, Boston, 1922

Trever, A. A., *History of Ancient Civilization*, New York, 1939, Vol. I
Wenley, R. M., *Stoicism and Its Influence*, New York, 1925

SOURCE MATERIALS

Heath, T. L., *The Works of Archimedes*
Hicks, R. D., ed., *Diogenes Laërtius; Lives of Eminent Philosophers*, Vol. II, Zeno, Cleanthes, Chrysippus, Epicurus
Plutarch, *Lives of Illustrious Men*, "Alexander"
Polybius, *Histories*

Roman Civilization

The rise of Rome

Long before the glory of Greece had begun to fade, another civilization, derived in large measure from that of the Greeks, had started its growth on the banks of the Tiber in Italy. In fact, by the time the Greeks had entered their Golden Age, Rome was already a dominant power on the Italian peninsula. For more than six centuries thereafter her might increased, and she still maintained her supremacy over the civilized world when the glory of Greece was no more than a memory.

Why Roman civilization was generally inferior to that of the Greeks

But the Romans never equaled the Greeks in intellectual or artistic accomplishments. The reasons may have been partly geographic. Except for some excellent marble and small quantities of copper, gold, and iron, Italy has no mineral resources. Her extensive coast line is broken by only two good harbors, Tarentum and Naples. On the other hand, the amount of her fertile land is much larger than that of Greece. As a consequence, the Romans were practically destined to remain a predominantly agrarian people through the greater part of their history. They never enjoyed the intellectual stimulus which comes from trading with other nations. In addition to all this, the topography of Italy is such that the peninsula was more easily accessible to invasion than Greece. The Alps opposed no effectual barrier to the influx of peoples from central Europe, while the low-lying coast in many places invited conquest by sea. As a result, domination of the country by force was more common than peaceful intermingling of immigrants with original settlers. For this reason the Romans became absorbed in military pursuits almost from the moment of their settlement on Italian soil, since they were forced to defend their own conquests against other invaders.

1. From the Beginning to the Overthrow of the Monarchy

Archaeological evidence indicates that Italy was inhabited at least as far back as the Upper Paleolithic age. At this time the territory was occupied by a people closely related to the Cro-Magnon race of southern France. In the Neolithic period people of Mediterranean stock entered the land, some coming in from northern Africa and others from Spain and Gaul. The beginning of the Bronze Age witnessed several new invasions. From the lake country north of the Alps came the first of the immigrants of the Indo-European language group. They were herdsmen and farmers, who brought the horse and the wheeled cart into Italy. Their culture was based upon the use of bronze, although after 1000 B.C. they appear to have acquired a knowledge of iron. These Indo-European invaders seem to have been the ancestors of most of the so-called Italic peoples, including the Romans. Racially they were probably related to the Hellenic invaders of Greece.

The earliest inhabitants of Italy

Between the twelfth and sixth centuries B.C. two other nations of immigrants occupied different portions of the Italian peninsula: the Etruscans and the Greeks. Where the Etruscans came from is a question which has never been satisfactorily answered. Most authorities believe that they were natives of some part of the Near Orient, probably Asia Minor. Although their writing has never been deciphered, enough material evidences survive to indicate the nature of their culture. They had an alphabet based upon the Greek, a high degree of skill in the metallurgical arts, a flourishing trade with the East, and a gloomy religion concerned with the worship of malignant spirits. They bequeathed to the Romans a knowledge of the arch and the vault, the practice of divination, and the cruel amusement of gladiatorial combats. The Etruscans established no great empire but contented themselves with dominating the Italic peoples north and west of the Tiber and exploiting their wealth and labor. The Greeks located mainly along the southern and southwestern shores of Italy and on the island of Sicily. Their most important settlements were Tarentum, Syracuse, and Naples, each of which was an entirely independent city-state. From the Greeks the Romans derived their alphabet, a number of their religious concepts, and much of their art and mythology.

The Etruscans and the Greeks

The actual founders of Rome were Italic peoples who lived in the district of Latium south of the Tiber River. Though the date of the founding of the city is unknown, the event was probably no later than 1000 B.C. The traditional date, 753 B.C., was the invention of later Roman writers. Latium included a number of towns, but Rome by reason of its strategic location soon came to exercise an effective suzerainty over several of the most important of them. One conquest followed another until by the end of the sixth century B.C. the ter-

The founding of Rome

ritory dominated by the Roman state was probably coextensive with the whole Latin plain from the slopes of the Apennines to the Mediterranean Sea.

The political evolution of Rome in this early period resembled in some ways the governmental development of the Greek communities in the formative stage of their history. But it was far from being the same. The Romans appear from the first to have had a much stronger interest in authority and stability than in liberty or democracy. Their state was essentially an application of the idea of the patriarchal family to the whole community, with the king exercising a jurisdiction over his subjects comparable to that of the head of the family over the members of his household. But just as the authority of the father was limited by custom and by the requirement that he respect the wishes of his adult sons, the sovereignty of the king was limited by the ancient constitution, which he was powerless to change without the consent of the chief men of the realm. His prerogatives were not primarily legislative but executive and judicial. He punished men for infractions of order, usually by infliction of the death penalty or by flogging. He judged all civil and criminal cases, but he had no authority to pardon without the consent of the assembly. Although his accession to office had to be confirmed by the people, he could not be deposed, and there was no one who could really challenge the exercise of his regal powers.

In addition to the kingship the Roman government of this time included an assembly and a Senate. The former was composed of all the male citizens of military age. As one of the chief sources of sovereign power, according to the theory, this body had an absolute veto on any proposal for a change in the law which the king might make. Besides, it determined whether pardons should be granted and whether aggressive war should be declared. But it was essentially a ratifying body with no right to initiate legislation or recommend changes of policy. Its members could not even speak except when invited to do so by the king. The Senate, or council of elders, comprised in its membership the heads of the various clans which formed the community. Even more than the common citizens, the rulers of the clans embodied the sovereign power of the state. The king was only one of their number to whom they had delegated the active exercise of their authority. When the royal office became vacant, the powers of the king immediately reverted to the Senate until the succession of a new monarch had been confirmed by the people. In ordinary times the chief function of the Senate was to examine proposals of the king which had been ratified by the assembly and to veto them if they violated rights established by ancient custom. It was thus almost impossible for fundamental changes to be made in the law even when the majority of the citizens were ready to sanction them. This extremely conservative attitude of the ruling classes persisted until the end of Roman history.

The government of Rome under the monarchy; the powers of the king

The Senate and the assembly

Toward the end of the sixth century B.C. senatorial jealousy of the kings increased to such a point that the monarchy was overthrown and an oligarchic republic set up. While the real nature of this revolution was doubtless a movement of the aristocracy to gain supreme power for itself, factors of nationalism may have played some part in it also. Tradition relates that the last of the Roman kings was an Etruscan, whose family, the Tarquins, had usurped the royal office some years before. The Romans of later centuries described in lurid fashion the wicked deeds of these rulers and implied that the overthrow of the monarchy was due primarily to a revolt against alien oppressors. It was probably inevitable, however, that the senatorial class would sooner or later develop ambitions for a monopoly of power, as the nobles in the Greek city-states had done a few centuries before.

The overthrow of the monarchy

2. The Early Republic

The history of the Roman Republic for more than two centuries after its establishment was occupied by almost constant warfare. The causes which led to the series of conflicts are not easy to untangle. It is possible that the overthrow of the Tarquins resulted in acts of reprisal by their kinsmen in neighboring countries. It is conceivable also that other nations on the borders took advantage of the confusion accompanying the revolution to slice off portions of Roman territory. But doubtless the compelling reason was greed for more land. The Romans were already a proud and aggressive people with a rapidly growing population. As the number of the inhabitants increased, the need for outlets into new territory became ever more urgent. Such was the cause which apparently led to the wars with the Volsci and the Aequi at the beginning of the fifth century. Roman expansion at the expense of these peoples aroused the jealousy of other strong nations. First the Republic had to fight the powerful Etruscan city of Veii, located a short distance to the north across the Tiber. After years of siege the city was destroyed, its people sold into slavery, and its territory annexed to the Roman domain. About 390 B.C. ferocious tribes of Gauls took advantage of the temporary exhaustion of Rome to invade the Republic. They captured and sacked the city but were finally bought off with 1000 pounds of gold. Next the Romans had to deal with revolts of some of the peoples previously conquered: the Aequi, the Volsci, and several of the Latin nations. The suppression of these revolts awakened the suspicions of surrounding states and sharpened the appetite of the victors for further triumphs. New wars followed each other in what seemed an unending succession until by 265 B.C. Rome had conquered the entire Italian peninsula.

The origins of Roman imperialism

See color pictures at page 197

This long series of military conflicts had profound effects upon the subsequent history of Rome. It affected adversely the interests of the poorer citizens and furthered the concentration of land in the possession of wealthy proprietors. Long service in the army forced the ordinary farmers to neglect the cultivation of the soil, with the result that they fell into debt and frequently lost their farms. Many of them took refuge in the city, until they were settled later as tenants on great estates in the conquered territories. The wars had the effect also of confirming the agrarian character of the Roman nation. The repeated acquisition of new lands made it possible to absorb the entire population into agricultural pursuits. As a consequence there was no need for the development of industry and commerce as means of earning a livelihood. Lastly, as in the case of Sparta, the Roman wars of conquest enslaved the nation to the military ideal and thereby retarded cultural growth.

*Political
changes follow-
ing the over-
throw of the
monarchy*

During this same period of the early Republic, Rome underwent some significant political changes. These were not due so much to the revolution of the sixth century as to the developments of later years. The revolution which overthrew the monarchy was about as conservative as it is possible for a revolution to be. Its chief effect was to substitute two elected consuls for the king and to exalt the position of the Senate by vesting it with control over the public funds and with a veto on all actions of the assembly. The consuls themselves were usually senators and acted as the agents of their class. They did not rule jointly, but each was supposed to possess the full executive and judicial authority which had previously been wielded by the king. If a conflict arose between them, the Senate might be called upon to decide; or, in time of grave emergency, a dictator might be appointed for a term not greater than six months. In other respects the government remained the same as in the days of the monarchy.

It was not long after the establishment of the Republic until a struggle began by the common citizens for a larger share of political power. Before the end of the monarchy the Roman population had come to be divided into two great classes—the patricians and the plebeians. The former were the aristocracy, wealthy landowners, who were apparently the descendants of the old clan leaders. They monopolized the seats in the Senate and the offices of magistracy. The plebeians were the common people—small farmers, craftsmen, and tradesmen. Many were clients or dependents of the patricians, obliged to fight for them, to render them political support, and to cultivate their estates in return for protection. The grievances of the plebeians were numerous. Compelled to pay heavy taxes and forced to serve in the army in time of war, they were nevertheless excluded from all part in the government except membership in the assembly. Moreover, they felt themselves the victims of discriminatory decisions in judicial trials. They did not even know what legal rights they were supposed to enjoy, for the laws were unwritten, and no one but the consuls had the power to interpret them. In suits for debt the creditor was frequently allowed to sell the debtor into slavery. It was in order to obtain a redress of these grievances that the plebeians rebelled soon after the beginning of the fifth century B.C.

The first victory of the plebeians was gained about 470 B.C., when they forced the patricians to agree to the election of a number of tribunes with power to protect the citizens by means of a veto over unlawful acts of the magistrates. This victory was followed by a successful demand for codification of the laws about 450 B.C. The result was the publication of the famous Law of the Twelve Tables, so called from the fact that it was written on tablets of wood. Although the Twelve Tables came to be revered by the Romans of later times as a kind of charter of the people's liberties, they were really nothing of the sort. For the most part they merely perpetuated ancient custom without even abolishing enslavement for debt. They did, however, enable the people to know where they stood in relation to the law, and they permitted an appeal to the assembly against a magistrate's sentence of capital punishment. About a generation later the plebeians won eligibility to positions as lesser magistrates, and in 362 B.C. the first plebeian consul was elected. Since ancient custom provided that consuls upon completing their term of office should automatically enter the Senate, the patrician monopoly of seats in that body was broken. The final plebeian victory came in 287 B.C. with the passage of the Hortensian Law (named for the dictator Quintus Hortensius), which provided that measures enacted by the assembly should become binding upon the state whether the Senate approved them or not.

The victories of the plebeians

The significance of these changes must not be misinterpreted. They did not constitute a revolution to gain more liberty for the individual but merely to curb the power of the magistrates and to win for the common man a larger share in government. The state as a whole remained as despotic as ever, for its authority over the citizens was not even challenged. As Theodor Mommsen says, the Romans from the time of the Tarquins to that of the Gracchi "never really abandoned the principle that the people were not to govern but to be governed." [1] Because of this attitude the grant of full legislative powers to the assembly seems to have meant little more than a formality; the Senate continued to rule as before. Nor did the admission of plebeians to membership in the Senate have any effect in liberalizing that body. So high was its prestige and so deep was the veneration of the Roman for authority, that the new members were soon swallowed up in the conservatism of the old. Moreover, the fact that the magistrates received no salaries prevented most of the poorer citizens from seeking public office.

Significance of the Plebeian victories

Intellectually and socially the Romans appear to have made but slow advancement as yet. The times were still harsh and crude. Though

[1] *The History of Rome*, Vol. I, p. 313.

*Roman society
and culture still
rather primitive*

writing had been adopted as early as the sixth century, little use was made of it except for the copying of laws, treaties, and funerary inscriptions and orations. Inasmuch as education was limited to instruction imparted by the father in manly sports, practical arts, and soldierly virtues, probably the great majority of the people were still illiterate. War and agriculture continued as the chief occupations for the bulk of the citizens. A few craftsmen were to be found in the cities, and a minor development of trade had occurred, evidenced by the founding of a maritime colony at Ostia on the coast in the fourth century. But the comparative insignificance of Roman commerce at this time is pretty clearly revealed by the fact that the country had no standard system of coinage until 269 B.C.

*The religion
of the Romans
compared with
that of the
Greeks*

The period of the early Republic was the period when the Roman religion assumed the character it was destined to retain through the greater part of the nation's history. In several ways this religion resembled the religion of the Greeks, probably for the reason that the original cultural heritage of both peoples came from the same source. Both religions were worldly and practical with neither spiritual nor ethical content. The relation of man to the gods was external and mechanical, partaking of the nature of a bargain or contract between two parties for their mutual advantage. The deities in both religions performed similar functions: Jupiter corresponded roughly to Zeus as god of the sky, Minerva to Athena as patroness of craftsmen, Venus to Aphrodite as goddess of love, Neptune to Poseidon as god of the sea, and so on. The Roman religion no more than the Greek had any dogmas or sacraments or belief in rewards and punishments in an afterlife.

*Contrasts
with Greek
religion*

But there were significant differences also. The Roman religion was distinctly more political and less humanistic in purpose. It served not to glorify man or to make him feel at home in his world but to protect the state from its enemies and to augment its power and prosperity. The gods were less anthropomorphic; indeed, it was only as a result of Greek and Etruscan influences that they were made personal deities at all, having previously been worshiped as *numina* or animistic spirits. The Romans never conceived of their deities as quarreling among themselves or mingling with human beings after the fashion of the Homeric divinities. Finally, the Roman religion contained a much stronger element of priestliness than the Greek. The priests, or pontiffs as they were called, formed an organized class, a branch of the government itself. They not only supervised the offering of sacrifices, but they were guardians of an elaborate body of sacred traditions and laws which they alone could interpret. It must be clearly understood, however, that these pontiffs were not priests in the sense of intermediaries between the individual Roman and his gods; they heard no confessions, forgave no sins, and administered no sacraments.

The morality of the Romans in this as in later periods had almost no connection with religion. The Roman did not ask his gods to make him good but to bestow upon the community and upon his family material blessings. Morality was a matter of patriotism and of respect for authority and tradition. The chief virtues were bravery, honor, self-discipline, reverence for the gods and for one's ancestors, and duty to country and family. Loyalty to the state took precedence over everything else. For the good of the state the citizen must be ready to sacrifice not only his own life but, if necessary, the lives of his family and friends. The courage of certain consuls who dutifully put their sons to death for breaches of military discipline was a subject of profound admiration. Few peoples in European history with the exception of the Spartans and perhaps the modern Germans have ever taken the problems of national interest so seriously or subordinated the individual so completely to the good of the state.

Morality in the early Republic

3. The Fateful Wars with Carthage

By 265 B.C., as we have already learned, Rome had conquered and annexed the whole of Italy. Proud and confident of her strength, she was almost certain to strike out into new fields of empire. The prosperous island of Sicily was not yet within her grasp, nor could she regard with indifference the situation in other parts of the Mediterranean world. She was now prone to interpret almost any change in the *status quo* as a threat to her own power and security. It was for such reasons that Rome after 264 B.C. became involved in a series of wars with other great nations which decidedly altered the course of her history.

The beginning of imperialism on a major scale

The first and most important of these wars was the struggle with Carthage, a great maritime empire which stretched along the northern coast of Africa from Numidia to the Strait of Gibraltar. Carthage had originally been founded in the ninth century B.C. as a Phoenician colony. In the sixth century it severed its ties with the homeland and gradually developed into a rich and powerful nation. The prosperity of its upper classes was founded upon commerce and upon exploitation of the silver and tin resources of Spain and Britain and the tropical products of north central Africa. Conditions within the country were far from ideal. The Carthaginians appear to have had no conception of free and orderly government. Shameless bribery and cynical oppression of the masses were methods regularly employed by the plutocracy to maintain its dominant position. The form of government itself can best be described as an oligarchy. At the head of the system were two magistrates, or *suffetes*, who exercised powers approximating those of the Roman consuls. The real governors, however, were thirty merchant princes who constituted an inner council of the Senate. By methods constitutional and otherwise these men controlled elections and dominated every other

Carthage

branch of the government. The remaining 270 members of the Senate appear to have been summoned to meet only on special occasions. In spite of these political deficiencies, Carthage had a civilization superior in luxury and scientific attainment to that of Rome when the struggle between the two countries began.

The initial clash with Carthage began in 264 B.C.[2] The primary cause was Roman jealousy over Carthaginian expansion in Sicily.

Causes of the First Punic War

Carthage already controlled the western portion of the island and was threatening the Greek cities of Syracuse and Messana on the eastern coast. If these cities should be captured, all chances of Roman occupation of Sicily would be cut off. Faced with this danger, Rome declared war upon Carthage with the hope of forcing her back into her African domain. Twenty-three years of fighting finally brought victory to the Roman generals. Carthage was compelled to surrender her possessions in Sicily and to pay an indemnity of 3200 talents, or about 2 million dollars at 1957 silver prices.

But the Romans were unable to stand the strain of this triumph. They had had to put forth such heroic efforts to win that when victory was finally secured it made them more arrogant and greedy than ever. As a result, the struggle with Carthage was renewed on two different occasions thereafter. In 218 B.C. the Romans interpreted the Carthaginian attempt to rebuild an empire in Spain as a threat to their interests and responded with a declaration of war. This struggle raged through a period of sixteen years. Italy was ravaged by the armies of Hannibal, the famous Carthaginian commander, whose tactics have been copied by military experts to the present day. Although Rome escaped defeat by the narrowest of margins, the patriotism of her citizens and the leadership of her brilliant general Scipio ultimately saved the day. Carthage was more completely humbled than before. She was compelled to abandon all her possessions except the capital city and its surrounding territory in Africa, and to pay an indemnity of 10,000 talents.

The Second Punic War

Roman vindictiveness and avarice reached their maximum level about the middle of the second century B.C. By this time Carthage had recovered a modicum of her former prosperity—enough to excite the envy and fear of her conquerors. Nothing would now satisfy the senatorial magnates but the complete destruction of Carthage and the expropriation of her land. In 149 B.C. the Senate dispatched an ultimatum demanding that the Carthaginians abandon their city and settle at least ten miles from the coast. Since this demand was tantamount to a death sentence for a nation dependent upon commerce, it was refused—as the Romans probably hoped it would be. The result was the Third Punic War, which was fought between 149 and 146 B.C. Seldom has the world witnessed a more desperate and

The Third Punic War and the destruction of Carthage

[2] The wars with Carthage are known as the Punic Wars. The Romans called the Carthaginians *Poeni*, i.e., Phoenicians, whence is derived the adjective "Punic."

more barbarous struggle. The final assault upon the city was carried into the houses of the natives themselves, and a frightful butchery took place. When the resistance of the Carthaginians was finally broken, the few citizens who were left to surrender were sold into slavery, and their once magnificent city was razed to the ground. The land was organized into a Roman province with the best areas parceled out as senatorial estates.

The wars with Carthage had momentous effects upon Rome. First, they brought her into conflict with eastern Mediterranean powers and thereby paved the way for world dominion. During the Second Punic War, Philip V of Macedon had entered into an alliance with Carthage and had plotted with the king of Syria to divide Egypt between them. In order to punish Philip and to forestall the execution of his plans, Rome sent an army into the East. The result was the conquest of Greece and Asia Minor and the establishment of a protectorate over Egypt. Thus before the end of the second century B.C. virtually the entire Mediterranean area had been brought under Roman dominion. The conquest of the Hellenistic East led to the introduction of semi-Oriental ideas and customs into Rome, changing the whole aspect of cultural life.

Results of the wars with Carthage: (1) conquest of the Hellenistic East

By far the most important effect of the Punic Wars was a great social and economic revolution which swept over Rome in the third and second centuries B.C. The incidents of this revolution may be enumerated as follows: (1) a marked increase in slavery due to the capture and sale of prisoners of war; (2) the decline of the small farmer as a result of the establishment of the plantation system in conquered areas and the influx of cheap grain from the provinces; (3) the growth of a helpless city mob composed of impoverished farmers and workers displaced by slave labor; (4) the appearance of a middle class comprising merchants, moneylenders, and "publicans" or men who held government contracts to operate mines, build roads, or collect taxes; and (5) an increase in luxury and vulgar display, particularly among the *parvenus* who fattened on the profits of war.

(2) a social and economic revolution

As a consequence of this social and economic revolution, Rome was changed from a republic of yeoman farmers into a nation composed very largely of parasites and slaves. Though property had never been evenly distributed, the gulf which separated rich and poor now yawned more widely than before. The old-fashioned ideals of discipline and devotion to the service of the state were sadly weakened, and men began to make pleasure and wealth their gods. A few members of the senatorial aristocracy exerted efforts to check the evil tendencies and to restore the homely virtues of the past. The eminent leader of this movement was Cato the Elder, who inveighed against the new rich for their soft living and strove to set an example to his countrymen by performing hard labor on his farm and dwelling in a house with a dirt floor and no plaster on the walls. But his

Rome transformed into a nation of parasites and slaves

209

efforts had little effect. The rich continued to indulge their expensive tastes and to rival each other in vulgar consumption of wealth. At the same time public morality decayed. Tax gatherers plundered the provinces and used their illicit gains to purchase the votes of the poor. The helpless masses in the city came to expect that politicians would feed them and provide for their amusement with ever more brutal shows. The total effect was so serious that some authorities date the beginning of Rome's decline from this period.[3]

4. The Storm and Stress of the Late Republic

The new period of turbulence

The period from the end of the Punic Wars in 146 B.C. to the accession of Julius Caesar in 46 B.C. was one of the most turbulent in the history of Rome. It was between these years that the nation reaped the full harvest of the seeds of violence sown during the wars of conquest. Bitter class conflicts, assassinations, desperate struggles between rival dictators, wars, and insurrections were the all too common occurrences of this time. Even the slaves contributed their part to the general disorder: first, in 104 B.C. when they ravaged Sicily; and again in 73 B.C. when 70,000 of them under the leadership of Spartacus held the consuls at bay for more than a year. Spartacus was finally slain in battle and six thousand of his followers were captured and crucified.

The revolt of the Gracchi

The first stage in the conflict between classes of citizens began with the revolt of the Gracchi. The Gracchi were mainly spokesmen for the landless farmers against the senatorial aristocracy, but they recruited some support from the middle classes also. In 133 B.C. Tiberius Gracchus, having been elected tribune, persuaded the assembly to enact a law limiting the amount of land which any person might hold to about 310 acres and providing that the excess should be surrendered to the state for lease to poor citizens at a nominal rental. Before the law could be put into effect, Tiberius' term as tribune expired. He thereupon determined to stand for re-election, in defiance of the constitutional provision limiting magistrates' terms to one year. This illegal move gave the senators an excuse for a resort to violence. The elections were accompanied by riots in which Tiberius and three hundred of his followers were slaughtered by clients and slaves of the aristocracy.

Significance of the Gracchan affair

Nine years later Gaius Gracchus, the younger brother of Tiberius, renewed the struggle for the underprivileged orders. Elected tribune for 123 B.C., he procured the enactment of a law providing for a monthly distribution of grain to the people of the city at one-half the market price. Next he prepared an attack upon the powers of the Senate, but he was defeated for re-election as tribune in 121 and was branded as an enemy of the state. When he refused to stand trial be-

[3] See A. J. Toynbee, *A Study of History* (D. C. Somervell ed.), Vol. I, p. 258.

fore the Senate, a state of war was proclaimed against him. After his followers had been routed, Gaius persuaded a faithful slave to kill him. Subsequently three thousand of his adherents were condemned to death. The chief significance of the Gracchan affair is to be found in the extent to which it illustrates the political incapacity of the Romans and the dangers of their narrow conservatism. It is important also for the vicious precedents which were established for the future. The Senate, by its resort to violence, set the example of an appeal to force which the demagogues of later years were not slow to follow.

In spite of all this, the decay of constitutional government was not necessarily inevitable because of the downfall of the Gracchi. The Romans might yet have succeeded in working out a compromise solution of their problems if only they could have kept out of war. But this they were unable to do, for the creation of so vast an empire meant frequent conflicts with bordering nations. In 111 B.C. a great struggle began with Jugurtha, the king of Numidia in northern Africa. This was followed by campaigns to punish the invading Gauls and by a war against Mithradates of Pontus, who was taking advantage of Roman misrule in the East to extend his dominion over Asia Minor. The heroes of these wars invariably returned to Italy to become leaders of one or the other of the great political factions.

The renewal of foreign wars

The first of the conquering heroes to make capital out of his military reputation was Marius, who was elevated to the consulship by the masses in 107 B.C. and re-elected five times thereafter. Unfortunately Marius was no statesman and accomplished nothing for his followers beyond demonstrating the ease with which a military leader with an army at his back could override opposition. Following the death of Marius in 86 B.C. the aristocrats took a turn at government by force. Their champion was Sulla, victor in the war with Mithradates. Appointed dictator in 82 B.C. for an unlimited term, Sulla proceeded to exterminate his opponents and to restore to the Senate its original powers. Even the senatorial veto over acts of the assembly was revived, while the authority of the tribunes was sharply curtailed. After three years of rule Sulla decided to exchange the pomp of power for the pleasures of sense and retired to a life of luxury and ease on his Campanian estate.

The rise of military dictatorships: Marius and Sulla

It was not to be expected that the "reforms" of Sulla would stand unchallenged after he had relinquished his office; for the effect of his decrees was to give control to a bigoted and selfish aristocracy. Several new leaders now emerged to espouse the cause of the people. The most famous of them were Pompey and Julius Caesar. For a time they pooled their energies and resources in a plot to gain control of the government, but later they became rivals and sought to outdo each other in bids for popular support. Pompey won fame as the conqueror of Syria and Palestine, while Caesar devoted his talents to a series of brilliant forays against the Gauls, adding to the Roman state the territory of modern Belgium and France. In 52 B.C.

The struggle between Pompey and Caesar

211

Head of Julius Caesar, showing individuality of Roman portrait
sculpture. In the British Museum.

after a series of mob disorders in Rome the Senate turned to Pompey
and caused his election as sole consul. Caesar was branded an enemy
of the state, and Pompey conspired with the senatorial faction to
deprive him of political power. The result was a deadly war between
the two men. With the famous pronouncement, "The die is cast,"
Caesar crossed the Rubicon (49 B.C.) and began a march on Rome.
Pompey fled to the East in the hope of gathering a large enough
army to regain control of Italy. In 48 B.C. the forces of the two rivals
met at Pharsalus in Thessaly. Pompey was defeated and soon afterward was murdered by agents of the king of Egypt.

*Caesar's
triumph and his
downfall*

After dallying for a season at the court of Cleopatra in Egypt,
Caesar returned to Rome. There was now no one who dared to challenge his power. With the aid of his veterans he cowed the Senate
into granting his every desire. In 46 B.C. he became dictator for ten
years, and in the following year for life. In addition, he assumed nearly
every other magisterial title that would augment his power. He was
consul, tribune, censor, and supreme pontiff. He obtained from the
Senate full authority to make war and peace and to control the
revenues of the state. For all practical purposes he was above the
law, and the other agents of the government were merely his servants.
There seems to be little doubt that he intended to make himself king;
at any rate, it was on such a charge that he was assassinated in 44 B.C.
by a group of conspirators, under the leadership of Brutus and Cassius, representing the old aristocracy.[4]

Through the centuries ever since, students of history have been

[4] During the last few months of his life Caesar became more ill-tempered
and domineering than ever. Perhaps this change was due to the fact that he
was really a sick man, his old affliction of epilepsy having returned. W. E.
Heitland, *The Roman Republic*, Vol. III, p. 355.

blinded by hero worship in estimating Caesar's political career. It is undoubtedly erroneous to acclaim him as the savior of his country or to praise him as the greatest statesman of all time. For he destroyed the essential features of the Republic and made the problem of governing more difficult for those who came after him. What Rome needed at this time was not the rule of force, however efficiently it might be exercised; but an enlightened attempt to correct the inequities of her political and economic regime. Though it is true that Caesar carried out numerous reforms, not all of them were really fundamental. With the aid of a Greek astronomer he revised the official calendar so as to bring it into harmony with the Egyptian solar calendar of 365 days, with an extra day added every fourth year. He investigated extravagance in the distribution of public grain and reduced the number of recipients by more than 50 per cent. He made plans for codification of the law and increased the penalty for criminal offenses. By conferring citizenship upon thousands of Spaniards and Gauls he took an important step toward eliminating the distinction between Italians and provincials. He settled a great many of his veterans and a considerable proportion of the urban poor on unused lands not only in Italy but throughout the empire, and he ordered the proprietors of large estates to employ at least one free citizen to every two slaves. On the other hand, he did nothing to reduce the most glaring inequalities in the distribution of wealth or to enlarge the political rights of the discontented masses. Perhaps if he had lived longer, his record might have been better; but there is nothing to prove that he really had the qualities of statesmanship which the times demanded.

Atrium of an Upper-class House in Pompeii, seen from the Interior. Around the atrium or central court were grouped suites of living rooms. The marble columns and decorated walls still give an idea of the luxury and refinement enjoyed by the privileged minority.

5. *Rome Becomes Sophisticated*

*Rome under
the influence of
Hellenistic civ-
ilization*

During the last two centuries of republican history Rome came under the influence of Hellenistic civilization. The result was a modest
flowering of intellectual activity and a further impetus to social
change beyond what the Punic Wars had produced. The fact must
be noted, however, that several of the components of the Hellenistic
pattern of culture were never adopted by the Romans at all. The
science of the Hellenistic Age, for example, was largely ignored, and
the same was true of some of its art.

*Roman
Epicureanism:
Lucretius*

One of the most notable effects of Hellenistic influence was the
adoption of Epicureanism and Stoicism by numerous Romans of the
upper classes. The most renowned of the Roman exponents of the
Epicurean philosophy was Lucretius (98–55 B.C.), author of a didactic
poem entitled *On the Nature of Things*. In writing this work Lucretius was animated by the desire to explain the universe in such a
way as to liberate man from all fear of the supernatural, which he
regarded as the chief obstacle to peace of soul. Worlds and all things
in them, he taught, are the results of fortuitous combinations of
atoms. Though he admitted the existence of the gods, he conceived
of them as living in eternal peace, neither creating nor governing the
universe. Everything is a product of a mechanical evolution, including
man himself and his habits, institutions, and beliefs. Since mind is
indissolubly linked with matter, death means utter extinction; consequently, no part of the human personality can survive to be rewarded or punished in an after-existence. Lucretius' conception of
the good life was perhaps even more negative than that of Epicurus:
what man needs, he asserted, is not enjoyment but "peace and a pure
heart."

*The Stoic
philosophy of
Cicero*

Stoicism was introduced into Rome by Panaetius of Rhodes about
140 B.C. Although it soon came to include among its converts numerous influential leaders of public life, its most distinguished representative was Cicero (106–43 B.C.), the famous orator and statesman.
While Cicero adopted doctrines from a number of philosophers, including both Plato and Aristotle, the fact remains that he derived far
more of his ideas from the Stoics than from any other source. Certainly his chief ethical writings, *On Duty* and the *Tusculan Disputa-
tions*, reflect substantially the doctrines of Zeno and his school. The
basis of Cicero's ethical philosophy was the premise that virtue is
sufficient for happiness, and that tranquillity of mind is the highest
good. He conceived of the ideal man as one who has been guided
by reason to an indifference toward sorrow and pain. In political
philosophy Cicero went considerably beyond the earlier Stoics. He
was one of the first to deny that the state is superior to the individual
and taught that government had its origin in a compact among men
for their mutual protection. In his *Republic* he set forth the idea of

a higher law of eternal justice which is superior to the statutes and decrees of government. This law is not made by man but is a product of the natural order of things and is discoverable by reason. It is the source of those rights to which all men are entitled as human beings and which governments must not assail. As we shall see presently, this doctrine influenced considerably the development of the Roman law by the great jurists of the second and third centuries A.D. By reason of his contributions to political thought, and by virtue of his urbanity and tolerance, Cicero deserves to be ranked as one of the greatest men Rome ever produced. He typified the genius of the nation at its best.

Hellenistic influence was in large measure responsible for Roman literary progress in the last two centuries of the Republic. It now became the fashion among the upper classes to learn the Greek language and to strive to reproduce in Latin some of the more popular forms of Hellenistic literature. The most noteworthy results were the comedies of Plautus and Terence, written in imitation of the New Comedy of Menander; the passionate lyrics of Catullus; the histories of Sallust, which in spite of their Caesarist bias are among the most scientific ever produced in Rome; and the letters, essays, and orations of Cicero, which are generally regarded as the finest examples of Latin prose.

Roman literary progress

Several of the early Roman writers showed promise at times of equaling the originality and artistry of the Greeks in the classical age. Plautus, for instance, occasionally displayed a freshness of approach, a perception of philosophic implications, and a capacity for social satire. Of humble origin himself, he delighted in ridiculing the mores and institutions which the respectable classes esteemed so highly. He allowed his genius to be thwarted, however, by too slavish a dependence upon the stock characters and themes of Hellenistic comedy. After his time Latin drama degenerated into lifeless formalism. The other of the most original writers of this period was Catullus (84–54 B.C.), one of the greatest lyric poets of all time. He is best known for his passionate love poems written to describe his tortured feelings while infatuated with the dissolute wife of a prominent politician. For years he was unable to free himself from his ardor, though maddened by jealousy of his rivals. But not all of his poetry dealt with the expression of personal emotion. Apparently he was an ardent republican, and in the latter part of his life he wrote coarse lampoons attacking Pompey and Caesar for their demagogic ambitions.

Plautus and Catullus

The conquest of the Hellenistic world accelerated the process of social change which the Punic Wars had begun. The effects were most clearly evident in the growth of luxury, in a widened cleavage between classes, and in a further increase in slavery. The Italian people, numbering about two million at the end of the Republic, had come to be divided into four main castes: the aristocracy, the eques-

Social conditions in the late Republic

215

trians, the common citizens, and the slaves.[5] The aristocracy included the senatorial class with a total membership of three hundred citizens and their families. The majority of them inherited their status, although occasionally a plebeian would gain admission to the Senate through serving a term as consul. Most of the aristocrats gained their living as office holders and as owners of great landed estates. The equestrian order was made up of government contractors, bankers, and the wealthier merchants. Originally this class had been composed of those citizens with incomes sufficient to enable them to serve in the cavalry at their own expense, but the term *equites* had now come to be applied to all outside of the senatorial class who possessed property in substantial amount. The equestrians were the chief offenders in the indulgence of vulgar tastes and in the exploitation of the poor and the provincials. As bankers they regularly charged interest rates of 12 per cent and three or four times that much when they could get it. By far the largest number of the citizens were mere commoners or plebeians. Some of these were independent farmers, a few were industrial workers, but the majority were members of the city mob. When Julius Caesar became dictator, 320,000 citizens were actually being supported by the state.

The status of the slaves

The Roman slaves were scarcely considered people at all but instruments of production like cattle or horses to be worked for the profit of their masters. Notwithstanding the fact that some of them were refined and intelligent foreigners, they had none of the privileges granted to slaves in Athens. The policy of their owners was to get as much work out of them as possible during the years of their prime and then to turn them loose to be fed by the state when they became old and useless. It is a sad commentary on Roman civilization that nearly all of the productive labor in the country was done by slaves. They produced practically all of the nation's food supply, for the amount contributed by the few surviving independent farmers was quite insignificant. At least 80 per cent of the workers employed in factories and shops were slaves or former slaves. But many of the members of the servile population were engaged in nonproductive activities. A lucrative form of investment for the business classes was ownership of slaves trained as gladiators, who could be rented to the government or to aspiring politicians for the amusement of the people. The growth of luxury also required the employment of thousands of slaves in domestic service. The man of great wealth must have his doorkeepers, his litter-bearers, his couriers (for the government of the Republic had no postal service), his valets, and his pedagogues or tutors for his children. In some great mansions there were special servants with no other duties than to rub the master down after his bath or to care for his sandals.

[5] In addition, of course, there were numerous aliens, who really did not constitute a separate class. Many were on about the same level as the common citizens. Others were slaves.

The religious beliefs of the Romans were altered in various ways in the last two centuries of the Republic—again due mainly to the extension of Roman power over most of the Hellenistic states. There was, first of all, a tendency of the upper classes to abandon the traditional religion for the philosophies of Stoicism and Epicureanism. But many of the common people also found worship of the ancient gods no longer satisfying. It was too formal and mechanical and demanded too much in the way of duty and self-sacrifice to meet the needs of the masses, whose lives were now empty and meaningless. Furthermore, Italy had attracted a stream of immigrants from the East, most of whom had a religious background totally different from that of the Romans. The result was the rapid spread of Oriental mystery cults, which satisfied the craving for a more emotional religion and offered the reward of a blessed immortality to the wretched and downtrodden of earth. From Egypt came the cult of Isis and Osiris (or Sarapis, as the god was now more commonly called), while from Phrygia was introduced the worship of the Great Mother, with her eunuch priests and wild, symbolic orgies. So strong was the appeal of these cults that the decrees of the Senate against them proved almost impossible to enforce. In the last century B.C. the Persian cult of Mithraism, which came to surpass all the others in popularity, gained a foothold in Italy.

6. *The Principate or Early Empire* (27 B.C.–284 A.D.)

Shortly before his death in 44 B.C., Julius Caesar had adopted as his sole heir his grandnephew Octavian, then a young man of eighteen quietly pursuing his studies in Illyria across the Adriatic Sea. Upon learning of his uncle's death, Octavian hastened to Rome to take over control of the government. He soon found that he must share his ambition with two of Caesar's powerful friends, Mark Antony and Lepidus. The following year the three men formed an alliance for the purpose of crushing the power of the aristocratic clique responsible for Caesar's murder. The methods employed were not to the new leaders' credit. Prominent members of the aristocracy were hunted down and slain and their property confiscated. The most noted of the victims was Cicero, brutally slain by Mark Antony's soldiers. Though Cicero had taken no part in the conspiracy against Caesar's life, he was feared as the most brilliant defender of the old constitution. The real murderers, Brutus and Cassius, escaped and organized an army of 80,000 republicans, but were finally defeated by Octavian and his colleagues in 42 B.C. About eight years later a quarrel developed among the members of the alliance themselves, inspired primarily by Antony's jealousy of Octavian. The ultimate outcome in 31 B.C. was the triumphant emergence of Caesar's heir as the most powerful man in the Roman state.

The victory of Octavian ushered in a new period in Roman history,

The triumph of Octavian or Augustus Caesar

the most glorious and the most prosperous that the nation experienced. Although problems of peace and order were still far from being completely solved, the deadly civil strife was ended, and the people now had their first decent opportunity to show what their talents could achieve. Unlike his great uncle, Octavian seems to have entertained no monarchical ambitions. He was determined, at any rate, to preserve the forms if not the substance of constitutional government. He accepted the titles of Augustus and Imperator conferred upon him by the Senate and the army.[6] He held the positions of proconsul and tribune permanently; but he refused to make himself dictator or even consul for life, despite the pleas of the populace that he do so. The title by which he preferred to have his authority designated was Princeps, or First Citizen of the State. For this reason the period of his rule and that of his successors is properly called the Principate, or early Empire, to distinguish it from the period of the Republic (sixth century B.C. to 27 B.C.) and from the period of the late Empire (284 A.D. to 476 A.D.).

Octavian, or Augustus as he was now more commonly called, ruled over Italy and the provinces for forty-four years (31 B.C.–14 A.D.). At the beginning of the period he governed by military power and by common consent, but in 27 B.C. the Senate bestowed upon him the series of offices and titles described above. His work as a statesman at least equaled in importance that of his more famous predecessor. Among the reforms of Augustus were the establishment

of new forms of taxation, the creation of a centralized system of courts under his own supervision, and the bestowal of a large measure of local self-government upon cities and provinces. For the nation as a whole he laid the foundations for an elaborate postal service. He insisted upon experience and intelligence as qualifications for appointment to administrative office. By virtue of his proconsular authority he assumed direct control over the provincial governors and punished them severely for graft and extortion. He abolished the old system of farming out the collection of taxes in the provinces, which had led to such flagrant abuses, and appointed his own personal representatives as collectors at regular salaries. But he did not stop with political reforms. He procured the enactment of laws designed to check the more glaring social and moral evils of the time —divorce, race suicide, and adultery. By his own example of temperate living he sought to discourage luxurious habits and to set the precedent for a return to the ancient virtues.

After the death of Augustus in 14 A.D. Rome had few enlightened and capable rulers. Several of his successors were brutal tyrants who squandered the resources of the state and kept the country in an uproar by their deeds of bloody violence. As early as 68 A.D. the army began to take a hand in the selection of the Princeps, with the result

[6] The title Augustus signified "consecrated" and implied the idea that its bearer was specially favored of the gods. Imperator meant "victorious general."

that on several occasions thereafter the head of the government was little more than a military dictator. Between 235 and 284 A.D. sheer anarchy prevailed: of the twenty-six men who were elevated to power in that time only one escaped violent death. As a matter of fact, in the 270 years which followed the demise of Augustus, Rome had scarcely more than four or five rulers of whom much good could be said. The list would include Nerva (96–98 A.D.), Trajan (98–117), Antoninus Pius (138–161), Marcus Aurelius (161–180), and possibly Vespasian (70–79) and Hadrian (117–138).

How can this comparative failure of the political genius of the Romans in the very best period of their history be accounted for? The assertion is frequently made that it was due to the absence of any definite rule of hereditary succession to the office of Princeps. But this answer rests upon a misconception of the nature of the Roman constitution at this time. The government which Augustus established was not intended to be a monarchy. Although the Princeps was virtually an autocrat, the authority he possessed was supposed to be derived exclusively from the Senate and the people of Rome; he could have no inherent right to rule by virtue of royal descent. The explanation must therefore be sought in other factors. The Romans were now reaping the whirlwind which had been sown in the civil strife of the late Republic. They had grown accustomed to violence as the way out when problems did not admit of an easy solution. Furthermore, the long wars of conquest and the suppression of barbarian revolts had cheapened human life in the estimation of the people themselves and had fostered the growth of crime. As a consequence it was practically inevitable that men of vicious character should push their way into the highest political office.

Reasons for the political troubles in Rome

7. Culture and Life in the Period of the Principate

From the standpoint of variety of intellectual and artistic interests the period of the Principate outshone all other ages in the history of Rome. Most of the progress took place, however, in the years from 27 B.C. to 200 A.D. It was between these years that Roman philosophy attained its characteristic form. This period witnessed also the feeble awakening of an interest in science, the growth of a distinctive art, and the production of the best literary works. After 200 A.D. economic and political decay stifled all further cultural growth.

Cultural progress under the Principate

Stoicism was now the prevailing philosophy of the Romans. Much of the influence of Epicureanism lingered and found occasional expression in the writings of the poets, but as a system it had ceased to be popular. The reasons for the triumph of Stoicism are not hard to discover. With its emphasis upon duty, self-discipline, and subjection to the natural order of things, it accorded well with the ancient virtues of the Romans and with their habits of conservatism.

Roman Stoicism

219

Moreover, its insistence upon civic obligations and its doctrine of cosmopolitanism appealed to the Roman political-mindedness and pride in world empire. Epicureanism, on the other hand, was a little too negative and individualistic to agree with the collectivist traditions of Roman history. It seemed not only to repudiate the idea of any purpose in the universe, but even to deny the value of human effort. Since the Romans were men of action rather than speculative thinkers, the Epicurean ideal of the solitary philosopher immersed in the problem of his own salvation could have no permanent attraction for them. It is necessary to observe, however, that the Stoicism developed in the days of the Principate was somewhat different from that of Zeno and his school. The old physical theories borrowed from Heracleitus were now discarded, and in their place was substituted a broader interest in politics and ethics. There was a tendency also for Roman Stoicism to assume a more distinctly religious flavor than that which had characterized the original philosophy.

Seneca, Epictetus, and Marcus Aurelius

Three eminent apostles of Stoicism lived and taught in Rome in the two centuries which followed the rule of Augustus: Seneca (3 B.C.–65 A.D.), millionaire adviser for a time to Nero; Epictetus, the slave (60?–120 A.D.); and the Emperor Marcus Aurelius (121–180 A.D.). All of them agreed that inner serenity is the ultimate goal to be sought, that true happiness can be found only in surrender to the benevolent order of the universe. They preached the ideal of virtue for virtue's sake, deplored the sinfulness of man's nature, and urged obedience to conscience as the voice of duty. Seneca and Epictetus adulterated their philosophy with such deep mystical yearnings as to make it almost a religion. They worshiped the cosmos as divine, governed by an all-powerful Providence who ordains all that happens for ultimate good. Submission to the order of nature is thus equivalent to placing oneself in harmony with the will of God, and is therefore conceived as a religious duty. The last of the Roman Stoics, Marcus Aurelius, was more fatalistic and less hopeful. Although he did not reject the conception of an ordered and rational universe, he shared neither the faith nor the dogmatism of the earlier Stoics. He was confident of no blessed immortality to balance the sufferings of one's earthly career. Living in a melancholy time, he was inclined to think of man as a creature buffeted by evil fortune for which no distant perfection of the whole could fully atone. He urged, nevertheless, that men should continue to live nobly, that they should neither abandon themselves to gross indulgence nor break down in angry protest, but that they should derive what contentment they can from dignified resignation to suffering and tranquil submission to death.

The literary achievements of the Romans bore a definite relation to their philosophy. This was especially true of the works of the most distinguished writers of the Augustan Age. Horace, for ex-

Marcus Aurelius. This mounted figure of the great emperor-philosopher is one of the few equestrian statues produced in the ancient world. It was originally entirely gilded. Now on the Piazza del Campidoglio, Rome.

ample, in his famous *Odes* drew copiously from the teachings of both Epicureans and Stoics. He confined his attention, however, to their doctrines of a way of life, for like most of the Romans he had little curiosity about the nature of the world. He developed a philosophy which combined the Epicurean justification of pleasure with the Stoic bravery in the face of trouble. While he never reduced pleasure to the mere absence of pain, he was sophisticated enough to know that the highest enjoyment is possible only through the exercise of rational control. Perhaps the following lines express about as well as any others the essence of his view of life:

Roman literature: Horace

> Be brave in trouble; meet distress
> With dauntless front; but when the gale
> Too prosperous blows, be wise no less
> And shorten sail.[7]

Vergil likewise reflects a measure of the philosophical temper of his age. Though his *Eclogues* convey something of the Epicurean ideal of quiet pleasure, Vergil was much more of a Stoic. His utopian vision of an age of peace and abundance, his brooding sense of the tragedy of human fate, and his idealization of a life in harmony with nature indicate an intellectual heritage similar to that of Seneca and Epictetus. Vergil's most noted work, the *Aeneid*, like several of the *Odes* of Horace, was a purposeful glorification of Roman imperialism. The *Aeneid* in fact was an epic of empire recounting the toils and triumphs of the founding of the state, its glorious traditions, and

Vergil, Ovid, and Livy

[7] *Odes* (S. Conington trans.), Vol. II, p. 10.

its magnificent destiny. The only other major writers of the Augustan Age were Ovid and Livy. The former, the greatest of Roman elegiac poets, was the chief representative of the cynical and individualist tendencies of his day. His writings, although brilliant and witty, often reflected the dissolute tastes of the time, and their popularity gives evidence of the failure of the efforts of Augustus to regenerate Roman society. The chief title of Livy to fame rests upon his skill as a prose stylist. As a historian he was woefully deficient. His main work, a history of Rome, is replete with dramatic and picturesque narrative, designed to appeal to the patriotic emotions rather than to present the impartial truth.

The literature of the period which followed the death of Augustus also exemplified conflicting social and intellectual tendencies. The *Petronius, Apuleius, Martial, Juvenal, and Tacitus* novels of Petronius and Apuleius and the epigrams of Martial are specimens of individualist writing generally descriptive of the meaner aspects of life. The attitude of the authors is unmoral; their purpose is not to instruct or uplift but chiefly to tell an entertaining story or turn a witty phrase. An entirely different viewpoint is presented in the works of the other most important writers of this age: Juvenal, the satirist, and Tacitus, the historian. Juvenal wrote under the influence of the Stoics but with little intelligence and narrow vision. Laboring under the delusion that the troubles of the nation were due to moral degeneracy, he lashed the vices of his countrymen with the fury of an evangelist. A somewhat similar attitude characterized the writing of his younger contemporary, Tacitus. The best-known of Roman historians, Tacitus described the events of his age not entirely with a view to scientific analysis but largely for the purpose of moral indictment. In his *Annals* and *Histories* he painted a lurid picture of political chaos and social corruption. His description of the customs of the ancient Germans in his *Germania* served to heighten the contrast between the manly virtues of an unspoiled race and the effeminate vices of the decadent Romans. Whatever his

The Colosseum. The Colosseum was built by the Roman emperors as a place of entertainment and public exhibition. It was the scene of gladiatorial combats and of the throwing of Christians to the lions.

The Pantheon, in Rome. Built by the Emperor Hadrian and dedicated to the deities of the seven planets, the Pantheon is a witness to the cosmopolitan religious attitude of the Romans. The distinctive feature of the interior is the dome, 140 feet in diameter, which still stands virtually unimpaired. For upwards of 16 centuries the building has been used as a Christian church.

failings as a historian, he was a master of ironic wit and brilliant aphorism. Referring to the boasted *Pax Romana*, he makes a barbarian chieftain say: "They create a wilderness and call it peace." [8]

Achievements in art

The period of the Principate was the period when Roman art first assumed its distinctive character as an expression of the national life. Before this time what passed for an art of Rome was really an importation from the Hellenistic East. Conquering armies brought back to Italy wagonloads of statues, reliefs, and marble columns as part of the plunder from Greece and Asia Minor. These became the property of wealthy publicans and bankers and were used to embellish their sumptuous mansions. As the demand increased, hundreds of copies were made, with the result that Rome came to have by the end of the Republic a profusion of objects of art which had no more cultural significance than the Rembrandts or Botticellis in the home of some modern broker. The aura of national glory which surrounded the early Principate stimulated the growth of an art more nearly indigenous. Augustus himself boasted that he found Rome a city of brick and left it a city of marble. Nevertheless, much of the old Hellenistic influence remained until the talent of the Romans themselves was exhausted.

Architecture and sculpture

The arts most truly expressive of the Roman character were architecture and sculpture. Both were monumental, designed to symbolize power and grandeur rather than freedom of mind or contentment with life. Architecture contained as its leading elements the round arch, the vault, and the dome, although at times the Corinthian column was employed, especially in the construction of temples. The materials most commonly used were brick, squared stone blocks, and concrete, the last generally concealed with a marble facing. As a further adornment of public buildings, sculptured entablatures and façades, built up of tiers of colonnades or arcades, were frequently added. Copied from Hellenistic sources and bearing little relation to the rest of the structure, many of these decorative devices were

See color pictures at page 197

[8] Tacitus, *Agricola*, p. 30.

showy and unseemly. Roman architecture was devoted primarily to utilitarian purposes. The foremost examples were government buildings, amphitheaters, baths, race courses, and private houses. Nearly all were of massive proportions and solid construction. Among the largest and most famous were the Pantheon, with its dome having a diameter of 142 feet, and the Colosseum, which could accommodate 65,000 spectators at the gladiatorial combats. Roman sculpture included as its main forms triumphal arches and columns, narrative reliefs, altars, and portrait busts and statues. Its distinguishing characteristics were individuality and naturalism. Even more than architecture it served to express the vanity and love of power of the Roman aristocracy, although some of it was marked by unusual qualities of harmony and grace.[9]

Why the Romans accomplished little as scientists

As scientists the Romans accomplished comparatively little either in this period or in any other. Scarcely an original discovery of fundamental importance was made by a man of Latin blood. This fact seems strange when we consider that the Romans had the advantage of Hellenistic science as a foundation upon which to build. But they neglected their opportunity almost completely. Why should this have been so? It was due, first of all, to the circumstance that the Romans were absorbed in problems of government and military conquest. Forced to specialize in law, politics, and military strategy, they had very little time for investigation of nature. A reason of more vital importance was the fact that the Romans were too practical-minded. They had none of that divine fire which impels man to lose himself in the quest for unlimited knowledge. They had no vigorous intellectual curiosity about the world in which they lived. In short, they were not philosophers. Contrary to the popular notion, practical-mindedness is not of itself sufficient to carry scientific progress very far. Modern science would probably have died of undernourishment long ago if it had had to depend solely upon the work of inventors and technologists.

Lack of scientific originality

Mainly because of this lack of talent for pure science, the achievements of the Romans were limited almost entirely to engineering and to the organization of public services. They built marvelous roads, bridges, and aqueducts. They provided the city of Rome with a water supply of 300,000,000 gallons daily. They established the first hospitals in the Western world and the first system of state medicine for the benefit of the poor. But their own writers on scientific subjects were hopelessly devoid of critical intelligence. The most renowned and the most typical of them was Pliny the Elder, who completed about 77 A.D. a voluminous encyclopedia of "science" which he called *Natural History*. This work was admittedly a compilation supposed to have been based upon the writings of nearly 500 different authors. The subjects discussed varied from cosmology to eco-

[9] A great many of the best examples of both architecture and sculpture were produced not by Romans at all but by Greeks resident in Italy.

Roman Aqueduct at Segovia, Spain. Aqueducts for conveying water from the mountains to the larger cities of the empire were among the most splendid engineering accomplishments of the Romans. The picture shows the skill with which large blocks of stone were fitted together to form arches.

nomics. Despite the wealth of material it contains, the work is of limited value. Pliny was totally unable to distinguish between fact and fable. In his estimation, the weirdest tales of wonders and portents were to be accepted as of equal value with the most solidly established facts. He described the marvels of a primitive people whose feet all turned backward, of a country where females conceived at the age of five and died at the age of eight, and of a tiny Mediterranean fish which could cause ships to stand still merely by clinging to them. The other best-known author of an encyclopedia of science was Seneca, the Stoic philosopher, who took his own life at Nero's command in 65 A.D. Seneca was less credulous than Pliny but no more original. Besides, he maintained that the purpose of all scientific study should be to divulge the moral secrets of nature. If there was any Latin who could be considered an original scientist, the title would have to be given to Celsus, who flourished during the reign of Tiberius. Celsus wrote a comprehensive treatise on medicine, including an excellent manual of surgery, but there is a strong suspicion that the entire work was compiled, if not actually translated, from the Greek. Among the operations he described were tonsillectomy, operations for cataracts and goiter, and plastic surgery.

No account of the scientific aspects of Roman civilization would be complete without some mention of the work of Hellenistic scientists who lived in Italy or in the provinces during the period of the Principate. Nearly all of them were physicians. The most distinguished, although apparently not the most original, was Galen of Pergamum, who was active in Rome at various times during the latter half of the second century. While his fame rests primarily upon his medical encyclopedia, systematizing the learning of others, he is deserving of more credit for his own experiments which brought him close to a discovery of the circulation of the blood. He not only taught but proved that the arteries carry blood, and that severance of even a small one is sufficient to drain away all of the blood of the body in little more than half an hour. But Galen was not the only Hellenistic physician who made important contributions in this time. At least two others are entitled to more recognition than is commonly given to them: Soranus of Ephesus, the greatest gynecologist

Hellenistic scientists in Italy

225

of antiquity and inventor of the speculum, and Rufus of Ephesus, who wrote the first accurate description of the liver and of the rhythm of the pulse, and was the first to recommend boiling of suspicious water before drinking it.

Social tendencies under the Principate

Roman society exhibited the same general tendencies under the Principate as in the last days of the Republic. A few significant differences, however, can be noted. Owing in part to the influence of the Stoic philosophy and in part to the abundance of free labor, slavery began to decline. Despite the efforts of Augustus to limit the manumission of slaves, the number of freedmen steadily increased. They crowded into every field of employment, including the civil service. Many succeeded in becoming proprietors of small shops, and some even became rich. Not entirely unconnected with these developments was the growth of the institution of clientage. Members of the citizen class who had lost their property or who had been driven out of business by the competition of enterprising freedmen now frequently became "clients" or dependents of wealthy aristocrats. In return for pittances of food and money these "shabby genteel" served the great magnates by applauding their speeches and fawning before them when they appeared in public. Custom made it practically obligatory for every man of great wealth to maintain a retinue of these miserable flatterers.

Signs of moral decay

Although the evidence has frequently been exaggerated, the period of the Principate was apparently marked by moral decay. Divorce among the upper classes was now so common as to be scarcely a matter of remark. According to the records there were 32,000 prostitutes in Rome during the reign of Trajan, and, if we can judge from the testimony of some of the most noted writers, homosexuality was exceedingly common and even fashionable. While political corruption had been subjected to more stringent control, crimes of violence appear to have increased. But the most serious moral indictment which can be brought against the age would seem to have been a further growth of the passion for cruelty. The great games and spectacles became bloodier and more disgusting than ever. The Romans could no longer obtain a sufficient thrill from mere exhibitions of athletic prowess; pugilists were now required to have their hands wrapped with thongs of leather loaded with iron or lead. The most popular amusement of all was watching the gladiatorial combats in the Colosseum or in other amphitheaters capable of accommodating thousands of spectators. Fights between gladiators were nothing new, but they were now presented on a much more elaborate scale. Not only the ignorant rabble attended them, but wealthy aristocrats also and frequently the head of the government himself. The gladiators fought to the accompaniment of savage cries and curses from the audience. When one went down with a disabling wound, it was the privilege of the crowd to decide whether his life should be spared or whether the weapon of his opponent should be plunged into his heart. One contest after another was staged in the course of a single exhibition. Should the arena become too sodden with blood, it was covered over with a fresh layer of sand, and the revolting performance went on. Most of the gladiators were condemned criminals or slaves, but some were volunteers even from the respectable classes. The Princeps Commodus, the worthless son of Marcus Aurelius, entered the arena several times for the sake of the plaudits of the mob.

Notwithstanding its low moral tone, the age of the Principate was characterized by an even deeper interest in salvationist religions than that which had prevailed under the Republic. Mithraism now gained adherents by the thousands, absorbing most of the followers of the cults of the Great Mother and of Isis and Sarapis. About 40 A.D. the first Christians appeared in Rome. The new sect grew rapidly and eventually succeeded in displacing Mithraism as the most popular of the mystery cults. For some time the Roman government was no more hostile toward Christianity than it was toward the other mystery religions. While it is a fact that some members of the sect were put to death by Nero in response to the demand for a scapegoat for the disastrous fire of 64 A.D., there was no systematic persecution of Christians as such until the reign of Decius nearly two hundred years later. Even then the persecution was inspired by political and social considerations more than by religious motives. Because of their otherworldliness and their refusal to take the customary oaths in the courts or participate in the civic religion, the Christians were regarded as disloyal citizens and dangerous characters. Moreover, their ideals of meekness and non-resistance, their preaching against the rich, and their practice of holding what appeared to be secret meetings made the Romans suspect them as enemies of the established order. In the end, persecution defeated its own purpose. It intensified the zeal of those who survived, with the result that the new faith spread more rapidly than ever.

The spread of Mithraism and Christianity

The establishment of stable government by Augustus ushered in a period of prosperity for Italy which lasted for more than two centuries. Trade was now extended to all parts of the known world, even to Arabia, India, and China. Manufacturing reached more than insignificant proportions, especially in the production of pottery, textiles, and articles of metal and glass. As a result of the development of rotation of crops and the technique of soil fertilization, agriculture flourished as never before. In spite of all this, the economic order was far from healthy. The prosperity was not evenly distributed but was confined primarily to the upper classes. Since the stigma attached to manual labor persisted as strong as ever, production was bound to decline as the supply of slaves diminished. Worse still was the fact that Italy had a decidedly unfavorable balance of trade. The meager industrial development which had occurred was by no means sufficient to provide enough articles of export to meet the demand

Economic prosperity during the first two centuries

for luxuries imported from the provinces and from the outside world. As a consequence, Italy was gradually drained of her supply of precious metals. By the third century signs of economic collapse were already abundant.

8. Roman Law

There is general agreement that the most important legacy which the Romans left to succeeding cultures was their system of law. This system was the result of a gradual evolution which may be considered to have begun with the publication of the Twelve Tables about 450 B.C. In the later centuries of the Republic the law of the Twelve Tables was modified and practically superseded by the growth of new precedents and principles. These emanated from different sources: from changes in custom, from the teachings of the Stoics, from the decisions of judges, but especially from the edicts of the praetors. The Roman praetors were magistrates who had authority to define and interpret the law in a particular suit and issue instructions to the jury for the decision of the case. The jury merely decided questions of fact; all issues of law were settled by the praetor, and generally his interpretations became precedents for the decision of similar cases in the future. Thus a system of judicial practice was built up in somewhat the same fashion as the English common law.

It was under the Principate, however, that the Roman law attained its highest stage of development. This later progress was due in part to the extension of the law over a wider field of jurisdiction, over the lives and properties of aliens in strange environments as well as over the citizens of Italy. But the major reason was the fact that Augustus and his successors gave to certain eminent jurists the right to deliver opinions, or *responsa* as they were called, on the legal issues of cases under trial in the courts. The most prominent of the men thus designated from time to time were Gaius, Ulpian, Papinian, and Paulus. Although most of them held high judicial office, they had gained their reputations primarily as lawyers and writers on legal subjects. The responses of these jurists came to embody a science and philosophy of law and were accepted as the basis of Roman jurisprudence. It was typical of the Roman respect for authority that the ideas of these men should have been adopted so readily even when they upset, as they occasionally did, time-honored beliefs.

The Roman law as it was developed under the influence of the jurists comprised three great branches or divisions: the *jus civile*, the *jus gentium*, and the *jus naturale*. The *jus civile*, or civil law, was essentially the law of Rome and her citizens. As such it existed in both written and unwritten forms. It included the statutes of the Senate, the decrees of the Princeps, the edicts of the praetors, and also certain ancient customs operating with the force of law. The

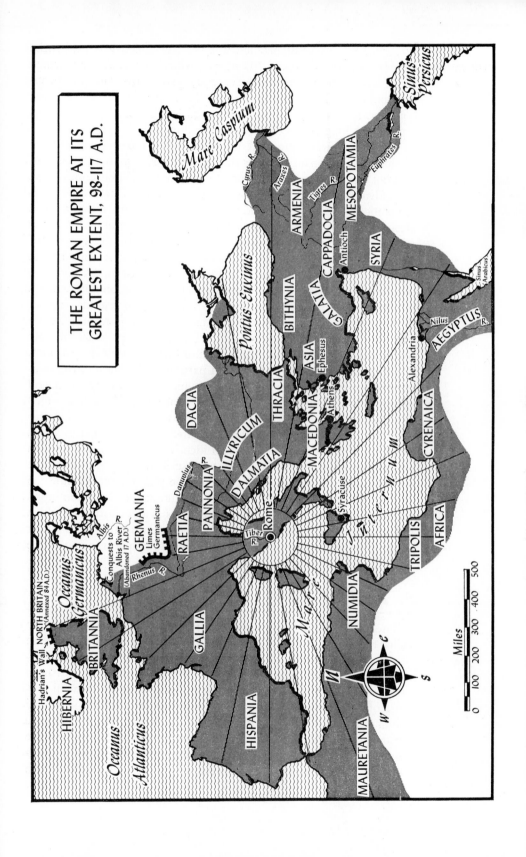

THE ROMAN EMPIRE AT ITS
GREATEST EXTENT, 98–117 A.D.

Mare Caspium

Sinus Persicus

Cyrus R.

Araxes R.

ARMENIA

MESOPOTAMIA

Tigres R.

Euphrates R.

CAPPADOCIA

Antioch

SYRIA

Sinus Arabicus

BITHYNIA

GALATIA

Pontus Euxinus

ASIA

Ephesus

Nilus

AEGYPTUS

R.

Alexandria

DACIA

THRACIA

MACEDONIA

Athens

ILLYRICUM

CYRENAICA

Danubius R.

DALMATIA

PANNONIA

Syracuse

Mare Internum

Rome

RAETIA

Tiber R.

GERMANIA

AFRICA

Limes
Germanicus

TRIPOLIS

Albis

Conquests to
Albis River
(Abandoned 17 A.D.)

Rhenus R.

NUMIDIA

Hadrian's Wall

NORTH BRITAIN
(Annexed 84 A.D.)

Oceanus
Germanicus

BRITANNIA

GALLIA

Mare

HIBERNIA

Oceanus

Atlanticus

HISPANIA

MAURETANIA

N
E
S
W

Miles

0   100   200   300   400   500

jus gentium, or law of peoples, was the law which was held to be common to all men regardless of nationality. It was the law which authorized the institutions of slavery and private ownership of property and defined the principles of purchase and sale, partnership, and contract. It was not superior to the civil law but supplemented it as especially applicable to the alien inhabitants of the empire.

The jus naturale

The most interesting and in many ways the most important branch of the Roman law was the *jus naturale,* or natural law. This was not a product of judicial practice at all but of philosophy. The Stoics had developed the idea of a rational order of nature which is the embodiment of justice and right. They had affirmed that all men are by nature equal, and that they are entitled to certain basic rights which governments have no authority to transgress. The father of the law of nature as a legal principle, however, was none of the Hellenistic Stoics, but Cicero. "True law," he declared, "is right reason consonant with nature, diffused among all men, constant, eternal. To make enactments infringing this law, religion forbids, neither may it be repealed even in part, nor have we power through Senate or people to free ourselves from it." [10] This law is prior to the state itself, and any ruler who defies it automatically becomes a tyrant. Some of the later Stoics—Seneca in particular—elaborated the doctrine of a primordial state of nature in which all men were equal, and no one was exploited by another. In time, the wickedness and greed of some brought slavery and private property into existence; government therefore became necessary for the protection of the weak. With the exception of Gaius, who identified the *jus naturale* with the *jus gentium,* all of the great jurists subscribed to conceptions of the law of nature very similar to those of the philosophers. While the jurists did not regard this law as an automatic limitation upon the *jus civile,* they thought of it nevertheless as a great ideal to which the statutes and decrees of men ought to conform. This development of the concept of abstract justice as a legal principle was one of the noblest achievements of the Roman civilization.

9. *The Late Empire (284–476* A.D.*)*

The last period of Roman history, from 284 to 476 A.D., is properly called the period of the late Empire. With the accession of Diocletian in 284, the government of Rome finally became an undisguised autocracy. It is true, of course, that constitutional government had been little more than a fiction for some time before this, but now all pretense of maintaining the Republic was thrown aside. Both in theory and in practice the change was complete. No longer was the doctrine advanced that the ruler was the mere agent of the Senate and the people; he was now held to be absolutely sovereign on the assumption that the people had surrendered all power to him. Diocletian

Rome becomes a despotic empire during the reign of Diocletian

[10] *The Republic,* Vol. III, p. 22.

adopted the regalia and ceremony of an Oriental despot. In place of the simple military garb of the Princeps he substituted a purple robe of silk interwoven with gold. He required all his subjects who were admitted to an audience with him to prostrate themselves before him. Needless to say, the Senate was now completely excluded from participation in the government. It was not formally abolished, but it was reduced to the status of a municipal council and a social club for the plutocracy. The chief reason for these political changes is undoubtedly to be found in the economic decline of the third century. The people had lost confidence in themselves, as they frequently do under such circumstances, and were ready to sacrifice all of their rights for the faint hope of security.

Diocletian's successors continued his system of absolutism. The most famous of them were Constantine I (306–337), Julian (361–363), and Theodosius I (378–395). Constantine is best known for his establishment of a new capital, called Constantinople, on the site of ancient Byzantium, and for his policy of religious toleration toward Christians. Contrary to a common belief, he did not make Christianity the official religion of the Empire; his various edicts issued in 313 simply gave Christianity an equality of status with the pagan cults, thereby terminating the policy of persecution. Later in his reign he bestowed upon the Christian clergy certain special privileges and caused his sons to be brought up in the new faith, but he continued to maintain the imperial cult. Although he was acclaimed by historians of the church as Constantine the Great, his practice of favoring Christianity was dictated primarily by political motives. A generation after Constantine's death the Emperor Julian attempted to stimulate a pagan reaction. He had come under the influence of the Neo-Platonist philosophy and regarded Christianity as a product of Jewish superstition. The last of the noted pagan emperors, he has been branded by Christian historians as Julian the Apostate. The other most prominent of the rulers of Rome in its dying stage was Theodosius I, who, in spite of his butchery of thousands of innocent citizens on imaginary charges of conspiracy, is also known as "the Great." The chief importance of his reign comes from his decree of 380 commanding all of his subjects to become orthodox Christians. A few years later he classified participation in any of the pagan cults as an act of treason.

From the standpoint of cultural achievement the period of the Empire is of little significance. With the establishment of a despotic state and the degradation of intellect by mystical and otherworldly religions, creative talent was destroyed. The few literary works produced were characterized by an overemphasis upon form and a neglect of content. A barren and artificial rhetoric took the place of the study of the classics in the schools, while science died out completely. Aside from the teachings of the Christian Fathers, which will be discussed later, the prevailing philosophy of the age was Neo-

Diocletian's successors

See color pictures at page 197

Cultural stagnation and the adoption of mystical philosophy

231

Neo-Platonism

Platonism. This philosophy, purporting to be a continuation of the system of Plato, was really an outgrowth of the doctrines of the Neo-Pythagoreans and of Philo Judaeus.[11] The first of its basic teachings was emanationism: everything that exists proceeds from God in a continuing stream of emanations. The initial stage in the process is the emanation of the world-soul. From this come the divine Ideas or spiritual patterns, and then the souls of particular things. The final emanation is matter. But matter has no form or quality of its own; it is simply the privation of spirit, the residue which is left after the spiritual rays from God have burned themselves out. It follows that matter is to be despised as the symbol of evil and darkness. The second major doctrine was mysticism. The soul of man was originally a part of God, but it has become separated from him through its union with matter. The highest goal of life should be mystic reunion with the divine, which can be accomplished through contemplation and through emancipation of the soul from bondage to matter. Man should be ashamed of the fact that he possesses a physical body and should seek to subjugate it in every way possible. Asceticism was therefore the third main teaching of this philosophy.

Plotinus

The real founder of Neo-Platonism was Plotinus, who was born in Egypt about 204 A.D. In the later years of his life he taught in Rome and won many followers among the upper classes. His principal successors diluted the philosophy with more and more bizarre superstitions. In spite of its anti-intellectual viewpoint and its utter indifference to the state, Neo-Platonism became so popular in Rome in the third and fourth centuries A.D. that it almost completely supplanted Stoicism. No fact could have expressed more eloquently the extent of the social and intellectual decline which the Roman nation had experienced.

10. Decay and Decline

The decline and fall of Rome

In 476 A.D. the last of the emperors in the West, the insignificant Romulus Augustulus, was deposed, and a barbarian chieftain assumed the title of King of Rome. Though this event is commonly taken to have marked the end of Roman history, it was really only the final incident in a long process of disintegration. The fall of Rome did not occur with dramatic suddenness, but extended over a period of approximately two centuries. A large part of the civilization was already dead before the Empire collapsed. Indeed, for all practical purposes the pagan culture of Rome from the middle of the third century on could be considered as belonging to the Dark Ages.

Alleged causes of the decline

More has been written on the fall of Rome than on the death of any other civilization. The theories offered to account for the tragedy have been many and various. Moralist historians have found the explanation in the evidences of lechery unearthed at Pompeii or re-

232   [11] See above, p. 191.

vealed in the satires of Juvenal and Martial. They overlook the
fact, however, that nearly all of this evidence comes from the early
Principate, and that in the centuries preceding the collapse of the
Empire, morality became much more austere, due to the influence of
ascetic religions. Historians of a sociological bent have attributed the
downfall to a declining birth rate, a factor which is often alleged
to hold ominous significance for the modern world. But there is
little to indicate that Rome could have been saved by greater numbers. The Athenian civilization reached the height of its glory during
the very centuries when growth of population was most strictly
limited.

If there was one primary factor which operated more than others
to accomplish the downfall of Roman civilization it was imperialism. Nearly all of the troubles which beset the country were traceable in some measure to the conquest of a great empire. It was this
which was largely responsible for the creation of the city mob, for
the growth of slavery, for the strife between classes and the widespread political corruption. It was imperialism also which was partly
responsible for the barbarian invasions, for the exhaustion of the resources of the state to maintain a huge military machine, and for the
influx of alien ideas which the Romans could not readily assimilate.
The idea that Rome became a civilized nation as a result of her conquests is undoubtedly a fallacy. Instead, her repeated victories caused
her ruling population to become greedy and domineering. It is true
that she appropriated much of the Hellenistic culture after her conquest of the Near East; but the really valuable elements of this culture would eventually have been acquired anyway through the
normal expansion of trade, while the evil consequences of domination of vast areas by force would have been avoided.

Actual causes:
(1) imperialism

Another important cause, closely related to imperialism, deserves
analysis: namely, the revolution in economic and social conditions
which swept over Italy in the third and fourth centuries A.D. This
revolution, which differed radically from the one that had occupied
the third and second centuries B.C., had the following features:
(1) the disappearance of money from circulation and the return to
a natural economy; (2) the decline of industry and commerce;
(3) the growth of serfdom and the rise of an extralegal feudalism;
(4) the extension of government control over a large portion of the
economic sphere; and (5) the transition from a regime of individual
initiative to a regime of hereditary status. The primary cause of this
revolution seems to have been the unfavorable balance of trade which
Italy suffered in her commerce with the provinces. In order to
check the withdrawal of precious metals from the country, the
government, instead of encouraging manufactures for export, resorted to the hazardous expedient of debasing the coinage. Nero
began the practice, and his successors continued it until the proportion of baser metal in the Roman coins had increased to 98.5 per cent.

(2) economic
decay

The inevitable result was disappearance of money from circulation. Commerce could no longer be carried on, salaries had to be paid in food and clothing, and taxes collected in produce. The scarcity of money in turn led to a decline in production, until the government intervened with a series of decrees binding peasants to the soil and compelling every townsman to follow the occupation of his father. The great landlords, now that they had control over a body of serfs, entrenched themselves on their estates, defied the central government, and ruled as feudal magnates. The people in the towns, deprived of freedom to live their own lives, sank slowly into wretchedness and despair.

Other causes

No one can present an exhaustive list of causes of Rome's decline. Among others of at least minor significance were the following: (1) the unjust policy of taxation, which rested most heavily upon the middle class and thereby discouraged the development of new economic enterprises; (2) the social stigma attached to work, resulting in the deliberate choice by thousands of the debasing relationship of clientage in preference to useful labor; (3) exhaustion of the soil, resulting in part from unscientific farming and in part from the attempt of too many people to make a living from the land; and (4) the disastrous plagues of Asiatic origin which broke out in 166 and 252 A.D., resulting in depopulating whole sections of Italy and thereby opening the way for barbarian incursions. To the last of these causes should be appended the fact that as lands along the low-lying coast were withdrawn from cultivation, due to the competition of grain from the provinces, malaria spread. The effect of this disease in undermining the vigor of the Italian population is impossible to estimate, but it must have been considerable.

11. The Roman Heritage

Comparison of Rome and the modern world

It is tempting to believe that the modern world owes a vast debt to the Romans: first of all, because Rome is nearer to us in time than any of the other civilizations of antiquity; and secondly, because Rome seems to bear such a close kinship to the modern temper. The resemblances between Roman history and the history of Great Britain or the United States in the nineteenth and twentieth centuries have often been noted. The Roman economic evolution progressed all the way from a simple agrarianism to a complex urban system with problems of unemployment, monopoly, gross disparities of wealth, and financial crises. Roman society likewise exhibited its "modern" phenomena of divorce, declining birth rates, and love of spectacular amusements. The Roman Empire, in common with the British and the American, was founded upon conquest and upon visions of Manifest Destiny. It must not be forgotten, however, that the spirit of Rome was the spirit of classical man, and that, consequently, the similarities between the Roman and modern civilizations are not so important as they seem. As we have noted already, the Romans despised industrial activities, and they were incredibly naïve in matters of science. Neither did they have any idea of the modern national state; the provinces were mere appendages, not integral parts of a body politic. It was largely for this reason that the Romans never developed an adequate system of representative government. Finally, the Roman conception of religion was vastly different from our own. Their system of worship, like that of the Greeks, was external and mechanical, not inward or spiritual in any sense. What Christians consider the highest ideal of piety—an emotional attitude of love for the divine—the Romans regarded as gross superstition.

Nevertheless, the civilization of Rome was not without a definite influence upon later cultures. The form, if not the spirit, of Roman architecture was preserved in the ecclesiastical architecture of the Middle Ages and survives to this day in the design of most of our government buildings. The sculpture of the Augustan Age also lives on in the equestrian statues, the memorial arches and columns, and the portraits in stone of statesmen and generals which adorn our boulevards and parks. Although subjected to new interpretations, the law of the great jurists became an important part of the Code of Justinian and was thus handed down to the later Middle Ages. Mod-

The influence of Roman civilization

The Forum, the civic center of ancient Rome. In addition to public squares, the Forum included triumphal arches, magnificent temples, and government buildings. In the foreground is the Temple of Saturn. Behind it is the Temple of Antoninus and Faustina. The three columns at the extreme right are what is left of the Temple of Castor and Pollux, and in the farthest background is the Arch of Titus.

ern lawyers and especially American judges frequently cite maxims originally invented by Gaius or Ulpian. Furthermore, the legal systems of nearly all Continental European countries today incorporate much of the Roman law. This law has had notable effects in strengthening the right of private ownership of property. It should not be forgotten either that Roman literary achievements furnished much of the inspiration for the revival of learning which spread over Europe in the twelfth century and reached its zenith in the Renaissance. Perhaps not so well known is the fact that the organization of the Catholic Church, to say nothing of part of its ritual, was adapted from the structure of the Roman state and the complex of the Roman religion. For example, the Pope still bears the title of Supreme Pontiff (*Pontifex Maximus*), which was used to designate the authority of the emperor as head of the civic religion. But the most important element in the Roman influence has probably been the idea of the absolute authority of the state. In the judgment of nearly all Romans, with the exception of philosophers like Cicero and Seneca, the state was legally omnipotent. However much the Roman may have detested tyranny, it was really only *personal* tyranny that he feared; the despotism of the Senate as the organ of popular sovereignty was perfectly proper. This conception survives to our own day in the popular conviction that the state can do no wrong, and especially in the doctrines of absolutist political philosophers that the individual has no rights except those which the state confers upon him.

SELECTED READINGS

Arnold, E. V., *Roman Stoicism*, Cambridge, 1911
Bailey, Cyril, ed., *The Legacy of Rome*, New York, 1924
——, ed., *The Mind of Rome*, New York, 1926
Boak, A. E. R., *A History of Rome to 565 A.D.*, New York, 1929
Cowell, F. R., *Cicero and the Roman Republic*, New York, 1948
Cumont, Franz, *The Afterlife in Roman Paganism*, New Haven, 1923
Dill, Samuel, *Roman Society from Nero to Marcus Aurelius*, New York, 1905
Fowler, W. W., *Social Life at Rome in the Age of Cicero*, New York, 1915
——, *The Religious Experience of the Roman People*, London, 1911
Frank, Tenney, *Economic History of Rome*, Baltimore, 1927
——, *A History of Rome*, New York, 1923
Greene, W. C., *The Achievement of Rome*, Cambridge, Mass., 1933
Heitland, W. E., *The Roman Republic*, Cambridge, 1909, 3 vols.
Larsen, J. A. O., *Representative Government in Greek and Roman History*, Berkeley, 1955
Lot, Ferdinand, *The End of the Ancient World*, New York, 1931

Louis, Paul, *Ancient Rome at Work*, New York, 1927

McIlwain, C. H., *The Growth of Political Thought in the West*, New York, 1932

Mackail, J. W., *Latin Literature*, New York, 1895

Mommsen, Theodor, *The History of Rome*, New York, 1908

Rostovtzev, M. I., *Social and Economic History of the Roman Empire*, New York, 1926

————, *History of the Ancient World*, New York, 1927, Vol. II

Thorndike, Lynn, *A History of Magic and Experimental Science in the First Thirteen Centuries of Our Era*, New York, 1923, 2 vols.

Trever, A. A., *History of Ancient Civilization*, New York, 1939, Vol. II

Tucker, T. G., *Life in the Roman World of Nero and St. Paul*, New York, 1915

Westermann, W. L., *The Slave Systems of Greek and Roman Antiquity*, Philadelphia, 1955

Source Materials

Caesar, *Commentaries on the Gallic War*

Cicero, *On the Republic; On the Laws*

Epictetus, *Discourses*

Horace, *Odes; Epodes*

Juvenal, *Satires*

Lucretius, *On the Nature of Things*

Marcus Aurelius, *Meditations*

Tacitus, *Agricola; Germania*

Vergil, *Aeneid*

The Early Middle Ages

During the period from 284 to 476 A.D. Roman civilization was strongly influenced by a revival of Oriental ideals of despotism, otherworldliness, pessimism, and fatalism. In the midst of economic distress and cultural decay men lost interest in earthly achievement and began to yearn for spiritual blessings in a life after death. This change in attitude was due primarily to the spread of Oriental religions, especially Christianity. When the Roman Empire finally collapsed, the victory of Orientalism was almost complete. The result was the evolution of new civilizations, compounded in part of elements taken from Greece and from Rome but with religion as a dominant factor behind most of their achievements. Altogether three new cultures finally emerged: the civilization of western Europe in the early Middle Ages, the Byzantine civilization, and the Saracenic civilization. The periods covered by the history of all three overlapped. The civilization of western Europe in the early Middle Ages extended from about 400 to 800. Although Constantine established his capital on the site of ancient Byzantium in the fourth century A.D., Byzantine civilization did not begin its independent evolution until after 500. It survived until the capture of Constantinople by the Turks in 1453. The Saracenic civilization flourished from the seventh century to the end of the thirteenth.

THE EARLY MIDDLE AGES

Western Europe	Byzantine Empire	The Saracens
Rise of the Papacy, 50–300 Germanic migrations and invasions, 100–600 Growth of the colonate, *ca.* 200–500		
300—	Rise of monasticism, *ca.* 300 Council of Nicaea, 325 Constantinople established as capital, 330	
Invasions of England by Angles and Saxons, 400–600 Decline of industry and commerce, 400–800 Capture of Rome by Visigoths, 410 St. Augustine's *City of God*, 413–426 Origin of Seven Liberal Arts, *ca.* 450 Merovingian dynasty in France, 481–751 Ostrogothic rule in Italy, 493–552	Monophysite movement, 450–565	
500— Boethius' *Consolation of Philosophy*, 523	Justinian's empire, 527–565 Revision and codification of Roman law, 527–535 Construction of church of Santa Sophia, 532–537 Byzantine conquest of Italy, 535–552	
Lombard invasion of Italy, 568		Mohammed, 570?–632
		The Hegira, 622 Capture of Mecca, 630 Conquest of Persia, Egypt, Palestine, Syria, North Africa, Spain, 632–732 Division of Islam into sects—Sunnites, Shiites, and Sufis, *ca.* 640
	Iconoclastic movement, 725–850	
Battle of Tours, 732 Carolingian dynasty, 751–887		
800— Development of feudalism, 800–1300 Charlemagne's empire, 800–814 Treaty of Verdun, 843 Holy Roman Empire, 962–		Development of steel manufacturing, textile manufacturing, leather tooling, and paper making, *ca.* 800–1400

THE EARLY MIDDLE AGES (*Continued*)

	Western Europe	Byzantine Empire	The Saracens
			Hindu-Arabic system of numerals, *ca.* 1000
			Saracenic world trade, *ca.* 1000–1500
		Separation of Eastern and Western churches, 1054	
		Battle of Manzikert, 1071	
1100—	The Crusades, 1096–1204		Cultivation of cotton, sugar, oranges, lemons, bananas, coffee, *ca.* 1100
			Transmission of complete works of Aristotle to Europe, *ca.* 1150
		Capture of Constantinople by Crusaders of Fourth Crusade, 1204	
			Transmission of compass and astrolabe to Europe, *ca.* 1400
	Black Death, 1347		
1453—		Capture of Constantinople by Ottoman Turks, 1453	

The Civilization of
Early Medieval Europe

*Misinterpreta-
tion of the
word
"medieval"*

Sometime during the Renaissance the practice arose of dividing the history of the world into three great epochs: ancient, medieval, and modern. This classification has come to be accepted with almost dogmatic finality. It ties in with the average man's belief that this planet of ours has witnessed only two great periods of progress: the time of the Greeks and the Romans and the age of modern invention. Between these two periods were the Middle Ages, popularly regarded as an interlude of abysmal ignorance and superstition when man lived enveloped in a cowl, oblivious of the wonders of knowledge, and concerned only with escape from the miseries of this world and the torments of hell. The very word "medieval" has an odious meaning in the average mind of today. It has come to be a synonym for reactionary or unprogressive. Thus when a modern reformer wishes to cast reproach upon the ideas of his conservative opponent, all he has to do is to brand them as "medieval." No doubt he would be very much surprised if he should learn that the social and economic doctrines of some medieval thinkers were really quite similar to his own.

*Only the peri-
od from 400 to
800 A.D. really
dark*

The reason for such erroneous judgments lies in the conventional notion that the entire medieval period from the fall of Rome to the beginning of the Renaissance was a cultural unit, that the ideals and institutions of the sixth century, for example, were the same as those of the thirteenth. Nothing could be farther from the truth. The medieval period, in western Europe, really encompassed two civilizations, as different from each other as Greece from Rome or the Renaissance from the nineteenth and twentieth centuries. The first of these civilizations, beginning about 400 A.D., when the process of Roman decay was virtually complete, and extending until 800, was

242

that of the early Middle Ages. It was this period alone which was really distinguished by most of those attributes commonly referred to as "medieval." The culture of the early Middle Ages undoubtedly represented in certain respects a reversion to barbarism. Intellect did not merely stagnate but sank to very low depths of ignorance and credulity. Economic activity declined to primitive levels of barter and ruralism, while morbid asceticism and contempt for this world superseded more normal social attitudes. With the Carolingian Renaissance of the ninth century, however, a new life began in Europe. The human spirit soared to magnificent heights in literature, philosophy, and art. The result was another of the world's great cultures, distinguished alike by intellectual progress and a high degree of prosperity and freedom. Indeed, this later medieval civilization, which endured until the end of the thirteenth century, was more nearly similar to the modern age than most people realize.

1. The Christian Foundation of Early Medieval Culture

Three main factors combined to produce the civilization of early medieval Europe: the Christian religion, the influence of the Germanic barbarians, and the heritage from the classical cultures. The effect of the third was probably less than that of the others. Outside the realm of philosophy the influence of the Greek and Hellenistic civilizations was comparatively slight. While the Roman heritage was still powerful, the men of the early Middle Ages rejected some portions of it as inconsistent with Christianity and barbarized much of the remainder.

Factors influencing early medieval culture

The chief foundation of the new culture was the Christian religion, whose founder, Jesus of Nazareth, was born in a small town of

Nazareth. A modern view of the small town in Judea where Jesus spent his early life, where he worked for a time as a carpenter and began his career of preaching. **243**

*The career of
Jesus of
Nazareth*

Judea some time near the beginning of the Christian era. Judea was then under Roman rule, though the Jews themselves recognized only their own king, Herod I, as their rightful sovereign. The atmosphere of the country was charged with religious emotionalism and political discontent. Some of the people, notably the Pharisees, looked forward to the coming of a political messiah, a son of David, who would rescue the country from foreign rule. Others, for example the Essenes, thought in terms of spiritual deliverance through asceticism, repentance, and mystical union with God. It was this latter sect which prepared the way for the ministry of Jesus. When he was about twenty-eight years old, he was acclaimed by an Essene evangelist, John the Baptist, as one "mightier than I, whose shoes I am not worthy to bear." [1] Thenceforth for about three years the career of Jesus, according to the New Testament accounts, was a continuous course of preaching and teaching and of healing the sick, "casting out devils," restoring sight to the blind, and raising the dead. He not only denounced shame, greed, and licentious living but set the example himself by a life of humility and self-denial. Though the conception he held of himself is somewhat obscure, he apparently believed that he had a divine mission to save mankind from error and sin. His preaching and other activities eventually aroused the antagonism of some of the chief priests and conservative rabbis. They disliked his caustic references to the legalism of the Pharisees, his contempt for form and ceremony, and his scorn for pomp and luxury. They feared also that his claims to being the Messiah would cause trouble with the Romans. Accordingly, they brought him into the highest court in Jerusalem, where he was solemnly condemned for blasphemy and for setting himself up as "King of the Jews" and turned over to Pontius Pilate, the Roman governor, for execution of the sentence. After hours of agony he died on the cross between two thieves on the hill of Golgotha outside Jerusalem.

The crucifixion

The crucifixion of Jesus marked a great climax in Christian history. At first his death was viewed by his followers as the end of their hopes. Their despair soon vanished, however, for rumors began to spread that the Master was alive, and that he had been seen by certain of his faithful disciples. The remainder of his followers were quickly convinced that he had risen from the dead, and that he was truly a divine being. With their courage restored, they reorganized their little band and began preaching and testifying in the name of their martyred leader. In such lowly fashion another of the world's great religions was launched on a career that would ultimately shake the foundations of no less an empire than mighty Rome.

There has never been perfect agreement among Christians as to the precise teachings of Jesus of Nazareth. The only dependable records

[1] Matthew 3:11.

are the four Gospels, but the oldest of these was not written until at least a generation after Jesus' death. According to the beliefs of his orthodox followers, the founder of Christianity revealed himself as the Christ, the divine Son of God, who was sent on this earth to suffer and die for the sins of mankind. They were convinced that after three days in the tomb, he had risen from the dead and ascended into heaven, whence he would come again to judge the world. The Gospels at least make it clear that he included the following among his basic teachings: (1) the fatherhood of God and the brotherhood of man; (2) the Golden Rule; (3) forgiveness and love of one's enemies; (4) repayment of evil with good; (5) self-denial; (6) condemnation of hypocrisy and greed; (7) opposition to ceremonialism as the essence of religion; (8) the imminent approach of the end of the world; and (9) the resurrection of the dead and the establishment of the Kingdom of Heaven.

Christianity was broadened and invested with a more elaborate theology by some of the successors of Jesus. Chief among them was the Apostle Paul, originally known as Saul of Tarsus. Although of Jewish nationality, Paul was not a native of Palestine but a Jew of the Dispersion, born in the city of Tarsus in southeastern Asia Minor. Here he came into contact with the Stoic philosophy, but he was possibly more deeply influenced by Gnosticism. Eventually converted to Christianity, he devoted his limitless energy to propagating that faith throughout the Near East. It would be almost impossible to overestimate the significance of his work. Denying that Jesus was sent merely as the redeemer of the Jews, he proclaimed Christianity to be a universal religion. But this was not all. He gave major emphasis to the idea of Jesus as the Christ, as the God-man who existed from the foundation of the world and whose death on the cross was a propitiation for the sins of mankind. Not only did he reject the works of the Law (i.e., Jewish ritualism) as of primary importance in religion, but he declared them to be utterly worthless in procuring salvation. Man is a sinner by nature, and he can therefore be saved only by faith and by the grace of God "through the redemption that is in Christ Jesus." It follows, according to Paul, that man's fate in the life to come is almost entirely dependent upon the will of God; for "Hath not the potter power over the clay, of the same lump to make one vessel unto honour, and another unto dishonour?" [2] He has mercy "on whom he will have mercy, and whom he will he hardeneth." [3]

By the beginning of the Middle Ages the triumph of Christianity over all its rivals was almost complete. The Emperor Galerius' edict of toleration in 311 was already an admission that the religion was too strong to be stamped out by persecution. By a series of decrees between 380 and 392 Christianity was recognized as the only lawful

The teachings of Jesus

The influence of Paul

Reasons for the triumph of Christianity

[2] Romans 9:21.
[3] Romans 9:18.

faith of the Roman Empire. How is this triumph to be explained? Perhaps as much as anything else it was due to the composite character of Christianity. Here was a religion which ultimately came to embody elements from a wide variety of sources. A large number of them were taken from Judaism: the name of the deity, the cosmogony, the world history, the Ten Commandments, and such doctrines as original sin and the providence of God. In addition, several of the ethical doctrines were really of Jewish origin. Although many of these elements were modified by Jesus and his followers, there can be no doubt that the Hebrew contributions to Christianity were of great importance.

*Persian
and Hellenistic
elements*

But obviously Christianity derived much from other than Jewish sources. Some idea of the debt which it owed to the various religions of Persian origin has been indicated in a preceding chapter.[4] Zoroastrianism had already made the ancient world familiar with such concepts as otherworldliness and an eternal conflict between good and evil. Gnosticism had developed the belief in secret revelation and had taught the notion of a primal man or God-man becoming incarnate in human form. Mithraism had fixed men's attention upon forms of ritual, such as baptism and the use of holy water, and upon the celebration of Sunday and the twenty-fifth of December as sacred days. Supplementing these influences was that of the philosophy of Stoicism which had familiarized the educated classes with ideals of cosmopolitanism and the brotherhood of man. In short, mystery religions and Hellenistic philosophy had already brought into existence a large deposit of doctrines and practices upon which Christianity could draw, at the same time preserving its distinctive character. The early church was an organism that fed upon the whole pagan world, selecting and incorporating a wide variety of ideas and practices which were not inconsistent with its own nature. The appeal of Christianity was therefore more nearly universal than that of any other of the ancient religions.

*Other reasons
for the Chris-
tian triumph*

The other main reasons for the triumph of Christianity may be summarized briefly. It admitted women to full rights of participation in worship, whereas Mithraism, the strongest of its early competitors, excluded them. It enjoyed the advantage for about fifty years of systematic persecution by the Roman government—a factor which enormously strengthened the cohesiveness of the movement, since those who remained in the faith had to be ready to die for their convictions. While most of the other religions revolved around imaginary figures, the creatures of grotesque legends, Christianity possessed as its founder a historic individual of clearly defined personality. Lastly, the triumph of Christianity is partly explained by the fact that it made a stronger appeal to the poor and oppressed than did any of the other mystery religions. Although it included the ideal of the equality of all men in the sight of God, its founder and

[4] See the chapter on The Civilization of Ancient Persia.

some of his followers had condemned the rich and exalted the lowly.
It propagated a new and exceedingly democratic morality, with
meekness, self-effacement, and love of one's enemies as primary virtues. Perhaps these were the qualities most likely to find ready acceptance among the helpless masses who had long since abandoned
all hope of bettering their material condition.

Hardly had Christianity emerged victorious over its rivals than
disaffection developed within its own ranks. This was due partly to
the heterogeneous elements out of which the religion had been *The division of*
formed, and partly also to the compromising attitudes displayed by *Christians into*
the leaders as the success of the movement increased. A more funda- *rival sects:*
mental reason seems to have been the conflict between the intel- *Arians, Athana-*
lectual and emotional tendencies within the religion. Representing *sians, and*
the former were the two most important sects of *subordinationist* *Nestorians*
Christians [5]—the Arians and the Nestorians. Both of them agreed in
their refusal to accept what has since become the orthodox doctrine
of the Trinity. Under the influence of Greek philosophy they rejected the idea that the Christ could be the equal of God. The Arians
maintained that the Son was created by the Father and therefore was
not co-eternal with him or formed of the same substance. Their
chief opponents were the Athanasians, who held that Father, Son,
and Holy Ghost were all absolutely equal and composed of identical
substance. The Nestorians broke away from the rest of the church
with the contention that Mary should be called the mother of Christ
but not the mother of God, implying of course that they considered
the Christ something less than divine.

The most important of the sects that emphasized the emotional
character of Christianity were the Gnostics and the Manicheans. *Gnostics and*
Both were extreme ascetics and mystics. Believing that genuine re- *Manicheans*
ligious truth was a product of revelation exclusively, they were inclined to be strongly suspicious of any attempt to rationalize the
Christian faith. They were opposed also to the tendency toward
worldliness which was making itself evident among many of the
clergy. The Gnostics and the Manicheans were not originally sects
of Christianity at all, but eventually many of them went over to that
faith. Those who became Christians retained their old doctrines of
exaggerated spiritualism and contempt for matter as evil. Naturally
along with these went an abiding distrust of every variety of human
knowledge. The doctrines of all these sects, with the exception of
the Athanasian, were eventually condemned by church councils as
heresies.

Notwithstanding the condemnation of many beliefs as heresies,
the body of Christian doctrine was never very firmly fixed during *The persistence*
the early Middle Ages. Of course, all Christians believed in a God *of doctrinal*
who was the creator and governor of the universe, in salvation from *disputes*

[5] Called "subordinationist" because they insisted upon subordinating Christ to
God the Father.

sin, and in rewards and punishments after death. But as regards many other questions of dogma there was confusion and uncertainty. Even the concept of the Trinity continued to be an issue of debate for several centuries. Many of the Eastern Christians never accepted the extreme Athanasian view of the relation of the Father and the Son adopted by the Council of Nicaea (325). Furthermore, there was no clearly formulated theory at this time of the number and the precise nature of the sacraments, nor was the doctrine of the powers of the priesthood definitely established. In general, there were two main points of disagreement affecting all of these issues. Some very devout believers clung to an ideal of Christianity similar to that of the Apostolic age, when the church was a community of mystics, each of them guided by the Inner Light in matters of faith and conduct. Others envisaged the Christian church as an organized society prescribing its own rules for the government of its members in accordance with the practical requirements of the time.

The importance of Christian organization

The growth of Christian organization was one of the most important developments of the whole medieval era. Even during the first few centuries of that period the church and its related institutions evolved into an elaborate structure which ultimately became the principal framework of society itself. As the Roman Empire in the West decayed, the church took over many of its functions and helped to preserve order amid the deepening chaos. That anything at all was saved out of the wreckage was due in large part to the stabilizing influence of the organized church. It aided in civilizing the barbarians, in promoting ideals of social justice, and in preserving and transmitting the antique learning.

The evolution of church organization

The organization of the church was at first very simple. The early Christian congregations met in the homes of their members and listened to the spiritual testimony of various of the brethren who were believed to have been in direct communication with the Holy Ghost. No distinction between laymen and clergy was recognized. Each independent church had a number of officers, generally known as bishops and elders, whose functions were to preside at the services, discipline members, and dispense charity. Gradually, under the influence of the pagan mystery religions, the ritual of Christianity increased to such a stage of complexity that a professional priesthood seemed to become necessary. The need for defense against persecution and the desire to attain uniformity of belief also favored the development of ecclesiastical organization. The consequence was that about the beginning of the second century one bishop in each important city came to be recognized as supreme over all the clergy in that vicinity. The sphere of his jurisdiction corresponded to the *civitas*, the smallest administrative unit of the Roman state. As the number of congregations multiplied, and as the influence of the church increased due to the adoption of Christianity as the official religion of Rome, distinctions of rank among the bishops themselves began to appear. Those who had their headquarters in the larger cities came to be called metropolitans, with authority over the clergy of an entire province. In the fourth century the still higher dignity of the patriarch was created to designate those bishops who ruled over the oldest and largest of Christian communities—such cities as Rome, Constantinople, Antioch, and Alexandria with their surrounding districts. Thus the Christian clergy by 400 A.D. had come to embrace a definite hierarchy of patriarchs, metropolitans, bishops, and priests.

The climax of all this development was the growth of the primacy of the bishop of Rome, or in other words the rise of the papacy. For several reasons the bishop of Rome enjoyed a pre-eminence over *The rise of the* the other patriarchs of the church. The city in which he ruled was *papacy* venerated by the faithful as a scene of the missionary activities of the Apostles Peter and Paul. The tradition was widely accepted that Peter had founded the bishopric of Rome, and that therefore all of his successors were heirs of his authority and prestige. This tradition was supplemented by the theory that Peter had been commissioned by the Christ as his vicar on earth and had been given the keys of the kingdom of heaven with power to punish men for their sins and even to absolve them from guilt.[6] This theory, known as the doctrine of the Petrine Succession, has been used by Popes ever since as a basis for their claims to authority over the church. The bishops of Rome had an advantage also in the fact that after the transfer of the imperial capital to Constantinople there was seldom any emperor with effective sovereignty in the West. Finally, in 455 the Emperor Valentinian III issued a decree commanding all Western bishops to submit to the jurisdiction of the Pope. It must not be supposed, however, that the church was yet under a monarchical form of government. The patriarchs in the East regarded the extreme assertions of the papal claims as a brazen effrontery, and even many bishops in the West continued to ignore them for some time.

The organization of the church was by no means confined to an ecclesiastical hierarchy. In any study of Christian institutions a prominent place must be given to monasticism. Since monasticism was *Reasons for the* originally an outgrowth of asceticism, it becomes necessary, first of *popularity* all, to examine the relationship between that ideal and the Christian *of asceticism* religion. Original Christianity was only mildly ascetic. Neither Jesus nor his immediate followers practiced any extremes of self-torture. To be sure, Jesus did not marry; he declared that he had no place to lay his head; and he was supposed to have fasted for forty days in the wilderness; but these examples could scarcely have encouraged the pathological excesses of mortification of the flesh indulged in by the hermits of the third and fourth centuries. We must therefore look for additional causes of the growth of this later asceticism. Perhaps the following may be considered fundamental:

[6] See Matthew 16:18–19.

(1) The desire of many pious Christians to protest against the increasing worldliness of the church. The farther they might go to the opposite extreme of the luxurious lives of some of the clergy, for example, the more effective that protest would become.

(2) The choice of morbid self-torture as a substitute for martyrdom. With the abandonment of persecution by the Romans all chances of winning a crown of glory in heaven by undergoing death for the faith were eliminated. But the desire to give evidence of one's religious ardor by self-abasement and suffering was still present and demanded an outlet.

(3) The desire of some Christians who were sincerely devoted to the faith to set an example of exalted piety and unselfishness as an inspiration to their weaker brethren. Even though most men should fail to attain the ideal, the general level of morality and piety would be raised.

(4) The influence of other Oriental religions, especially Gnosticism and Manicheism, with their exaggerated spiritualism, contempt for this world, and degradation of the body.

The asceticism of Christian hermits

The earliest Christian ascetics were hermits, who withdrew from the world to live in seclusion in some wilderness or desert. This form of asceticism seems to have originated in Egypt in the third century. From there it spread into other provinces of the eastern section of the Empire and continued to be popular for more than one hundred years. It developed into a kind of religious mania characterized by morbid excesses. We read of hermits or anchorites grazing in the fields after the manner of animals, rolling naked in thorn bushes, or living in swamps infested with snakes. The famous St. Simeon Stylites passed a whole summer "as a rooted vegetable in a garden" and then began the construction of his celebrated pillar. He built it to a height of sixty feet and spent the remaining thirty years of his life on the top. Such absurdities as these, while certainly not typical of the attitude of the majority of Christians at this time, were probably the natural fruit of too strong an emphasis upon the spiritual way of life.

The rise of monasticism

In time the force of the anchorite hysteria subsided. Certain of the more practical Christian ascetics came to the conclusion that the solitary life of the hermit was not good for the soul, since it sometimes drove men insane. The result of this conclusion was the origin of monasticism. Credit for founding the earliest monastery is commonly assigned to Pachomius, who lived in Egypt in the middle fourth century. The movement he initiated was continued by St. Basil, a bishop of Cappadocia, who was the first to issue a set of rules for the government of a monastic order. Disapproving of extreme self-torture, St. Basil required his monks to discipline themselves by useful labor. They were not to engage in prolonged fasting or in degrading laceration of the flesh, but they were compelled to submit to obligations of poverty and humility and to spend many hours of the day in silent religious meditation. The Basilian type of monasticism came to be adopted universally in the eastern division of Christendom. Many of its units are still to be seen perched on lofty crags to which access can be gained only by climbing long rope ladders or being hauled up in a basket. The history of monasticism in western Europe also began in the fourth century, when ascetic communities on the Egyptian model were established in Rome. There was really no important monasticism in the West, however, until the sixth century, when St. Benedict drafted his famous rule which ultimately became the standard for nearly all the monks of Latin Christendom. The Benedictine rule imposed obligations similar to those of the rule of St. Basil—poverty, obedience, labor, and re-

A Monastery of the Basilian Order on Mt. Athos. The asceticism of the Basilian monks caused them to build their monasteries in almost inaccessible places on lofty crags or on the steep sides of rugged mountains.

ligious devotion. If there was any essential difference, it probably lay in the stronger emphasis of the Benedictine system upon organized control. The abbot of each monastery had practically unlimited authority to discipline the monks under him. The Basilian rule was predicated more upon the assumption that each monk would discipline himself.

The influence of monasticism upon the society of the early Middle Ages would be difficult to exaggerate. The monks were generally the best farmers in Europe; they reclaimed waste lands, drained swamps, and made numerous discoveries relating to the improvement of the soil. They preserved some of the building skill of the Romans and achieved noteworthy progress in many of the industrial arts, especially in wood carving, metal-working, weaving, glass-making, and brewing. Indeed, some modern writers maintain that the foundations of the Industrial Revolution were actually laid in the medieval monasteries. It was monks, furthermore, who wrote most of the

The results of monasticism

251

books, copied the ancient manuscripts, and maintained the majority of the schools and libraries and nearly all of the hospitals that existed during the early Middle Ages. The growth of monasticism also profoundly affected the history of the church. It led to a division in the ranks of the clergy. Living according to a definite rule or *regula*, the monks came to be called the *regular* clergy; while the priests, bishops, and archbishops, who carried on their activities in the midst of the affairs of the world (*saeculum*), were henceforth known as the *secular* clergy. Between the two groups intense rivalry developed, with the monks sometimes organizing reform movements against the worldliness of the priests. The Benedictine monks enjoyed the special favor of the Popes, and it was partly due to an alliance between the papacy and monasticism that the former was able to extend its power over the church.

2. The Germanic Foundations of the New Culture

The ancient Germans

The second most important of the factors which combined to produce the civilization of early medieval Europe was the influence of the Germanic barbarians. They were not the only northern peoples who helped to mold the pattern of early medieval society; the contributions of the Celts in Brittany and Ireland and of the Slavs in central and eastern Europe were by no means insignificant. Nevertheless, the Germanic influence appears to have been the most extensive. The ancient Germans were a long-headed people of predominantly Nordic stock and of Indo-European tongue. Where they came from originally is a problem upon which scholars disagree, but they seem to have migrated into northern Europe from western Asia. By the beginning of the Christian era they had come to be divided into several nations: Scandinavians, Vandals, Goths, Franks, Alemanni, Burgundians, Frisians, Anglo-Saxons, Dutch, and so on. Both in language and in race they originally bore some affinity to the Greeks and the Romans.

The Germanic invasions of the Roman Empire

For centuries different nations of Germanic barbarians had been making incursions into Roman territory. At times they came as invading armies, but generally they filtered in slowly, bringing their families and belongings with them and occupying depopulated or abandoned areas. Many were brought in by Roman commanders and rulers. Julius Caesar was impressed by their value as warriors and enrolled thousands of them in his armies. They were to be found in the bodyguard of nearly every Princeps and emperor. Finally, by the time of Constantine, they formed the bulk of the soldiers in the entire Roman army. Many were also drawn into the civil service and thousands were settled by the government as *coloni* or serfs on the great estates. In view of these conditions it is not surprising that Rome should eventually have been conquered by the Germans. They were a virile and energetic race, constantly increasing in numbers; and as more and more of them gained a foot-hold in Italy, others were bound to be tempted by the opportunities for plunder. In addition, the Romans frequently exploited those who were already in the Empire and thereby provided their kinsmen with an excuse for making an attack. Although armed invasions of Italy began as early as the second century B.C., and were repeated several times thereafter, there were no really disastrous incursions until the fourth and fifth centuries A.D. In 378 the Visigoths, angered by the oppression of imperial governors, raised the standard of revolt. They overwhelmed a Roman army at Adrianople and then marched west-ward into Italy. In 410 under Alaric they captured and plundered Rome, later moving on into southern Gaul. In 455 Rome was sacked by the Vandals, who had migrated from their original home between the Oder and Vistula rivers and established a kingdom in the prov-ince of Carthage. Other Germanic nations also made their way into Italy, and before the end of the fifth century the Roman Empire in the West had passed completely under the domination of the barbarians.

For our knowledge of ancient Germanic society we are dependent primarily upon the *Germania* of Tacitus, written in 98 A.D. The litera-ture and the laws of the Germans themselves also contain much in-formation, but these were not put into written form until after Roman and Christian influences had begun to exert their effect. When Tacitus wrote, the Germanic barbarians had attained a cultural level about equal to that of the Homeric Greeks. They were illiterate and ignorant of any knowledge of the arts. Their houses were built of rough timber plastered over with mud. While they had achieved some development of agriculture, they preferred the risks of plunder-ing expeditions to the prosaic labor of tilling the soil. Nearly all of the work was done by the women and old men and other dependents. When not fighting or hunting, the warriors spent most of their time sleeping and carousing. Gambling and drunkenness were glaring vices, but, if we can believe the testimony of Tacitus, sex morality was singularly pure. Monogamous marriage prevailed, except in those cases where a chief might be permitted to take more than one wife for political reasons. Adultery was rare and was severely pun-ished, while divorce was almost unknown. In some tribes even widows were forbidden to remarry.

Ancient Ger-man society

The economic and political institutions of the Germans were such as befitted a people who were just emerging into a settled existence. The tiny proportion of trade carried on rested solely upon a basis of barter, while cattle were still the main article of wealth. Whether the agricultural land was individually or collectively owned is still a debated question, but there seems little doubt that the forests and pastures were held and used in common. Possibly the com-munity controlled the distribution of new lands as they were ac-quired, allotting the arable portions as individual farms. There is

Economic and political insti-tutions

evidence that a class of wealthy proprietors had grown up as an aristocracy in certain of the tribes. Although Tacitus states that the Germans had slaves, it seems probable that most of their dependents were serfs, since they had houses of their own and paid their masters only a portion of what they produced. Their servitude was a result not only of capture in war but also of indebtedness and especially reckless gambling, in which men staked their own liberty when everything else had been lost. The state scarcely existed at all. Law was a product of custom, and the administration of justice remained very largely in private hands. While the Germans had their tribal courts, the function of these bodies was chiefly to mediate between plaintiff and defendant. It was left to the former to bring the accused to trial and to carry out the penalty prescribed by the customary law. The court merely decided what proofs should be required of each litigant to determine the validity of his plea. Usually these consisted of oaths and ordeals, both of which were considered as appeals to the judgment of the gods. The most important of the remaining political institutions was the primary assembly of the warriors. But this body had no lawmaking powers beyond those involved in the interpretation of custom. Its main function was to decide questions of war and peace and whether the tribe should migrate to some new locality. Originally the German tribes had no kings. They had chiefs elected by the freemen, but these were little more than ceremonial officials. In time of war a military leader was elected and endowed with considerable power, but as soon as the campaign was over his authority lapsed. Nevertheless, as wars increased in frequency and duration, some of the military leaders actually became kings. The formality of election, however, was generally retained.

The influence of the Germans upon medieval history, while not so important as is sometimes imagined, was extensive enough to deserve consideration. Above all, they were largely responsible for several of the elements of feudalism: (1) the conception of law as an outgrowth of custom and not as the expression of the will of a sovereign; (2) the idea of law as a personal possession of the individual which he could take with him wherever he went, in contrast to the Roman conception of law as limited to a definite territory; (3) the notion of a contractual relationship between rulers and subjects, involving reciprocal obligations of protection and obedience; (4) the theory of an honorable relationship between lord and vassal, growing out of the Germanic institution of the *comitatus* or military band, in which the warriors were bound by pledges of honor and loyalty to fight for and serve their leader; (5) trial by ordeal as a prevailing mode of procedure in the feudal courts; and (6) the idea of elective kingship.

The Germanic influence

3. *Political and Economic Developments in Early Medieval Europe*

The political history of western Europe from 476 to 800 has comparatively little interest except for the specialist. A few of the major developments, however, deserve some attention. Following the deposition of the last of the Roman emperors in the West, a Germanic chieftain by the name of Odovacar proclaimed himself king of Italy. But in 493 Italy was conquered by the Ostrogoths under Theodoric, one of the ablest and most intelligent of barbarian leaders. Until nearly the end of his reign of thirty-three years, Theodoric gave Italy a more enlightened rule than the country had known under many of the Caesars. He fostered agriculture and commerce, repaired public buildings and roads, patronized learning, and enforced religious toleration. But in his last years he became querulous and suspicious, accusing some of his faithful subordinates of plotting with the Roman aristocracy to overthrow him. Several of them were put to death, including the philosopher Boethius. Soon after Justinian became emperor at Constantinople in 527 he determined to reconquer Italy and the provinces in the West. Not until 552 was the power of the Ostrogoths finally broken. The long war utterly ruined Italy and opened the way for the Lombard invasion in 568. The Lombards succeeded in holding most of the peninsula under the rule of semi-independent dukes until the conquest of Charlemagne in the late eighth century.

The political history of Italy

The strongest western European state in the early Middle Ages was not established in Italy but in France. In 481 a youth by the name of Clovis became king of an important tribe of the Salian Franks, who dwelt on the left bank of the Rhine. In less than twenty years Clovis conquered nearly all of what is now France and a portion of Germany besides. His adoption of orthodox Christianity won for him the support of the clergy and made possible the subsequent alliance between the Frankish kings and the Popes. The Merovingian dynasty,[7] which he really founded, occupied the throne of the Frankish state until 751. For more than a century the successors of Clovis continued his policy of rigorous despotism, annexing the territory of their enemies, dominating the church, and exploiting the lands of the kingdom as if they were their private possessions. By 639, however, the royal line had begun to degenerate. A series of short-lived weaklings, the so-called do-nothing kings, inherited the crown of their lusty forebears. Absorbed in the pursuit of pleasure, these worthless youths delegated most of their authority to their chief subordinates, the mayors of the palace. Nothing more natural could have happened than the eventual displacement of the Merovingian kings by these very officials to whom they had en-

The kingdom of the Franks

See color pictures at page 260

[7] So called from Meroveus, supposedly the original founder of the family to which Clovis belonged.

trusted their powers. The most capable and aggressive of the mayors of the palace was Charles Martel ("the Hammer"), who may be considered a second founder of the Frankish state. He won fame in 732 by defeating the Moors at Tours, a town only a little more than a hundred miles from Paris. Although his opponents were merely a marauding band, the Battle of Tours is nevertheless important as the high-water mark of Moorish invasion of France. Yet, even after his victory, Charles was content with the substance of power and did not bother to assume the royal title. It was left for his son, Pepin the Short, to have himself elected king of the Franks in 751 and thereby to put an end to Merovingian rule. The new dynasty came to be known as the Carolingian from the name of its most famous representative, Carolus Magnus or Charlemagne.

*The rule
of Charlemagne*

In the minds of most students of history Charlemagne stands out as one of the two or three most important individuals in the whole medieval period. By some of his contemporaries he was acclaimed as a new Augustus who would bring peace and prosperity to western Europe. There can be no question that he established efficient gov-

The Emperor Charlemagne. From a painting by Albrecht Dürer.

ernment, and that he did much to combat the centrifugal tendencies which had gathered momentum during the reigns of the later Merovingians. Not only did he abolish the office of mayor of the palace, but he eliminated the tribal dukes and bestowed all the powers of local government upon his own appointees, the counts. To prevent abuses of authority by the latter he appointed *missi dominici*, or

256 royal messengers, to visit the counties and to report to the king any acts of official injustice. He authorized the *missi* to hold their own courts for the purpose of hearing complaints of oppression and even in extreme cases to remove local officers. He modified the old system of private administration of justice by authorizing the counts to summon accused persons to court and by vesting the magistrates with more control over judicial procedure. He revived the Roman institution of the sworn inquest, in which a number of persons were summoned by agents of the king and bound by oath to tell what they knew of any crimes committed in their locality. This institution survived the downfall of the Carolingian state and was carried by the Normans to England, where it eventually became an important factor in the origin of the grand-jury system. While much of the remainder of the political structure which Charlemagne established perished with the end of his dynasty, the precedent which he set for strong government undoubtedly influenced many of the French kings in the later Middle Ages and the German emperors as well. It should be noted, however, that the glory of Charlemagne's empire rested in large part upon a foundation of slaughter. During the forty-six years of his reign from 768 to 814, he conducted no fewer than fifty-four wars. There was scarcely a people of western Europe against whom he did not fight, except the English. Since most of his campaigns were successful, he annexed to the Frankish domain the greater part of central Europe and northern and central Italy. But some of these conquests were made possible only by a fearful sacrifice of blood and a resort to measures of the harshest cruelty. The campaign against the Saxons met with such stubborn opposition that Charlemagne finally ordered the beheading of forty-five hundred of them. It is typical of the spirit of the times that all of this was done under the pretext of inducing the pagans to adopt Christianity.

As a matter of fact, it was Charlemagne's constant intervention in religious affairs which led to the climax of his whole career—his coronation as Roman Emperor by Pope Leo III. Leo had been in trouble for some time. Accused of being a tyrant and a rake, he so aroused the indignation of the people of Rome that in 799 they gave him a severe beating and forced him to flee from the city. Struggling over the mountains to Germany, he implored the aid of Charlemagne. The great king sent him back to Italy and was instrumental in restoring him to the papal throne. On Christmas day, 800, as Charles knelt in prayer in St. Peter's church the grateful Pope placed a crown on his head while the assembled multitude hailed him as "Augustus, crowned of God, great and pacific Emperor of the Romans." The significance of this event is rather hard to appraise. Charles has been represented as surprised and embarrassed by the honor. But the real cause of his irritation was probably his being made to accept a crown from the Pope. There is evidence that he had already developed some ambitious scheme of his own for reviving imperial power in the

Charlemagne becomes emperor

257

West. Moreover, he regarded his own authority as in no wise limited by any higher sovereignty of the church. He legislated freely on religious matters, controlled all appointments to ecclesiastical offices, and lectured priests and bishops alike on their morals and on what they should preach. Nevertheless, the fact that the coronation was acclaimed by so many of Charlemagne's contemporaries as marking the return to a golden age bears witness to its more than trivial importance. The Carolingian empire thus established was not conceived as the beginning of a new state, but as a revival of the Empire of the Caesars. The grandeur of Rome was now held to be reborn. It would have been more nearly in harmony with the truth if the event had been interpreted as an expression of the cultural and political awakening of the West. Theoretically the Empire with its capital at Constantinople still included Italy and the surrounding areas of Europe. The establishment of an empire in the West was a symbol of the widening gulf between Latin Christendom and Byzantium. Finally, the fact that Charlemagne was crowned by Leo III gave the Popes of the later Middle Ages a bulwark for their claims to supremacy. They could argue that it was they who had really created the empire, acting of course as the vicegerents of God.

See color
pictures at
pages 260,
261

At the beginning of the early Middle Ages a large part of what is now England was still under Roman rule. But in the fifth century the Romans were forced to withdraw on account of increasing trouble with Germanic invasions into Italy. Soon afterward England was overrun by hordes of Saxons, Angles, and Jutes from the Continent. They brought with them the customs and institutions of their homeland, which were similar to those of the other Germanic barbarians. Driving the original Celtic natives into the mountains of Wales and Cornwall, they quickly established their own kingdoms. At one time there were seven—Northumbria, East Anglia, Kent, Essex, Sussex, Wessex, and Mercia—mutually suspicious and hostile. In the ninth century tribes of Danes took advantage of the strife among the Saxon kingdoms and attempted their conquest. Efforts to defeat the new enemy brought the seven kingdoms into a strong confederation under the leadership of Wessex and its celebrated ruler, Alfred the Great. King Alfred reorganized the army, infused new vigor into local government, and revised and broadened the laws. In addition, he founded schools and fostered an interest in literature and other elements of a national culture.

The Saxon kingdoms in England

King Alfred's successors were men of weaker fiber. One of them, Ethelred the Unready, surrendered his kingdom to the powerful Danish King Canute. For eighteen years England was ruled as part of a North Sea empire which also included Norway and Denmark. But in 1035 Canute died, and the Saxon dynasty regained control of England. It was not for long. Ethelred's son, Edward the Confessor, was more interested in cultivating a reputation for piety than he was in statecraft, and allowed affairs of his country to be regulated

The Norman conquest

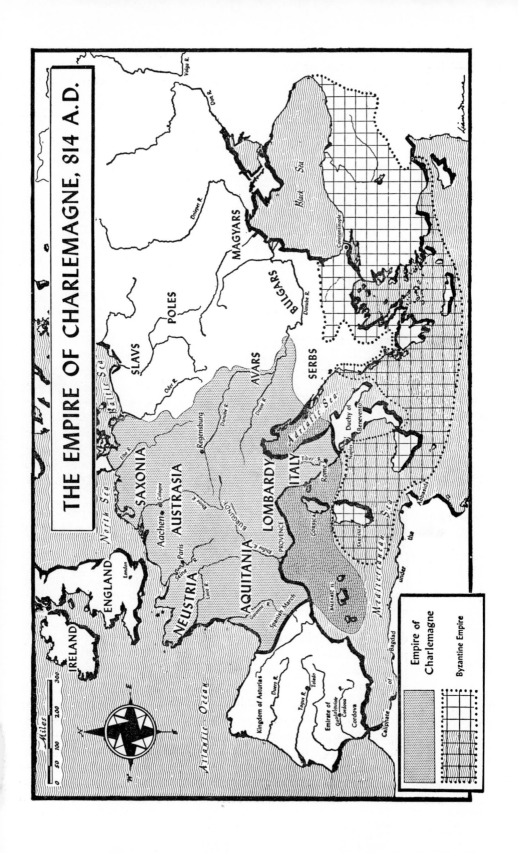

THE EMPIRE OF CHARLEMAGNE, 814 A.D.

IRELAND

ENGLAND

London

North Sea

Atlantic Ocean

Baltic Sea

SLAVS

POLES

MAGYARS

Volga R.

Don R.

Dnieper R.

Oder R.

Black Sea

Constantinople

BULGARS

Danube R.

AVARS

SERBS

SAXONIA

AUSTRASIA

Aachen
Cologne

NEUSTRIA

Paris
Seine R.

Loire R.

AQUITANIA

Regensburg

Danube R.

Theiss R.

Rhine R.

LOMBARDY

PROVENCE

ITALY

Rome
Tiber R.

Naples

Duchy of
Benevento

Adriatic Sea

CORSICA

SARDINIA

BALEARIC Is.

Mediterranean Sea

under the
Abbasids

Caliphate of Bagdad

Kingdom of Asturias

Duero R.

Tagus R.

Toledo

Emirate of
Cordova
Cordova

Spanish March

Burgundy

Rhone R.

Miles
0 50 100 200 300

Empire of Charlemagne

Byzantine Empire

by the Duchy of Normandy, across the Channel. Upon Edward's death the Duke of Normandy, subsequently known as William the Conqueror, laid claim to the crown of England. Landing an army in Sussex in 1066, he caught the English monarch Harold unprepared and defeated him in the Battle of Hastings. Harold fell mortally wounded, and his forces disintegrated. Apparently regarding discretion as the better part of valor, the surviving magnates offered the crown to Duke William. The Battle of Hastings is considered as a turning point in English history, for it ended the period of Anglo-Saxon supremacy and prepared the way for the ultimate establishment of a nation state under William the Norman's successors.

Most of the records of economic life in the early Middle Ages present a mournful picture of return to primitive conditions and in some cases actual misery. The decline of Italy in the second half of the fifth century was especially swift. The forces which were set in motion by the economic revolution of the preceding two hundred years had now attained their full momentum. Commerce and in-

Economic decline in Italy

Duke William of Normandy Crossing the Channel to Conquer England, from the Bayeux Tapestry. The Bayeux Tapestry depicts, in needlework on linen, 72 scenes of the Norman Conquest. It was probably completed under the direction of Bishop Odo of Bayeux, the Conqueror's half-brother.

dustry were rapidly becoming extinct, lands that were formerly productive were growing up in briars and brambles, and the population was declining so noticeably that a law was enacted forbidding any woman under forty years of age to enter a convent. While the proprietors of the great landed estates extended their control over agriculture and over many of the functions of government as well, larger and larger numbers of the masses of the people became serfs. During the reign of Theodoric this process of economic decline was arrested in some measure as a result of the benefits he extended to agriculture and commerce and his reduction of taxes. But Theodoric was unable to eliminate serfdom or to reverse the concentration

Gold Cup, Byzantine, VI–IX cent. The figure is a personification of Constantinople, a queen or goddess holding the scepter and orb of imperial rule. (MMA)

Saint John Writing His Gospel. From an Anglo-Frankish illuminated manuscript, *ca.* 850, produced in a Carolingian monastery. The unknown artist knew nothing of perspective, but excelled in coloring and conveying a sense of vitality and energy. (Morgan Library)

Merovingian Fibula or Brooch, VII cent. A fabulous gold-plated animal set with garnets and colored paste reveals the lively imagination of the early Middle Ages. (MMA)

Enthroned Madonna and Child, Byzantine School, XIII cent. The painters of Siena followed the opulent and brilliant style of Byzantine art. Their madonnas were no earthly mothers, but celestial queens reigning in dignified splendor. (National Gallery)

The Young King, Louis IX, XIII cent. Though Louis was widely revered as a saint, the artist has endowed him with distinctively human features. (Morgan Library)

Aquamanile, German, XII–XIII cent. Aquamaniles were water jugs used for hand washing during church ritual, or at meal times. (MMA)

Ivory Plaque, German, X cent. The plaque shows Otto the Great presenting a church to Christ while St. Peter watches, a reference to Otto's building an empire by cooperating with the Church. (MMA)

Kings in Battle, French, *ca.* 1250. A scene depicting, with the trappings of knighthood, Joshua's fight against the five kings of Canaan. In the center Joshua raises his hand, commanding the sun and moon to stand still to enable him to complete his victory. (Morgan Library)

Chalice, German, XIII cent. A beautifully embellished wine cup used in the sacrament of the Eucharist. (MMA)

of landed wealth, for he felt that he needed the support of the aristocracy. After his death the forces of decay again became operative;
yet if it had not been for Justinian's war of reconquest, Italy might
still have preserved a degree of the prosperity she had gained under
the Ostrogothic king. The long military conflict brought the country to the verge of stark barbarism. Pestilence and famine completed
the havoc wrought by the contending armies. Fields were left untilled, and most of the activities in the towns were suspended. Wolves
penetrated into the heart of the country and fattened on the corpses
that remained unburied. So great was the danger of starvation that
cannibalism appeared in some areas.[8] Only in the larger cities were
the normal functions of civilization continued to any appreciable
extent.

Economic change in what is now France followed a pattern very
similar to that in Italy, but it proceeded at a slower rate. In Roman
times southern Gaul had had a flourishing commerce and considerable industry. By the end of the ninth century, however, stagnation
was almost complete. The streets of the city of Marseille were grown
over with grass and weeds, while the port itself was deserted for
over two hundred years. In some other Mediterranean towns and in
the interior of the country, trade on a petty scale continued to be
carried on, mostly by Jews and Syrians and later by Lombards; but
even the activities of these men became steadily more difficult as
brigandage increased, the roads deteriorated, and money disappeared
from general circulation. The economic history of France was also
characterized by the growth of an irregular feudalism similar to that
which had sprung up in Italy. Several of the causes were closely
related to the policies of the Merovingian and Carolingian kings.
Nearly all of these rulers compensated their officials by grants of
land. Both Pepin the Short and Charlemagne adhered to the example of Charles Martel in expropriating lands of the church and
turning them over to their chief followers as rewards for military
services. More serious than this was the practice of granting _im-
munities, or exemptions from the jurisdiction of the court._ Originally
immunities were given only as favors to bishops and abbots to protect them from unscrupulous officials, but later they were granted
to secular nobles as well. Their legal effect was to make the holder
subject to the exclusive jurisdiction of the king; but as the king was
far away and generally preoccupied with other matters, the nobles
took advantage of the opportunity to increase their own independence. Wars, brigandage, and oppression also contributed to the
growth of a largely feudal structure of society by forcing the weaker
citizens to seek the protection of their more powerful neighbors.
The result was a tendency toward a division of the population into
two distinct classes: a landed aristocracy and serfs.

*Economic
conditions
in France; the
foundations of
feudalism*

[8] J. W. Thompson, *Economic and Social History of the Middle Ages,*
p. 124.

261

4. *Intellectual Attainments of Early Medieval Europe*

Generally speaking, the intellectual culture of early medieval Europe was not of a very high order. Superstition and credulity frequently characterized the work even of many of the outstanding writers. A fondness for compilation rather than for original achievement was also a distinguishing feature of much of the intellectual endeavor. Few men any longer had much interest in philosophy or science, except in so far as those subjects could be made to serve religious purposes. Such an attitude naturally led to mystical interpretations of knowledge and to the acceptance of fables as fact when they appeared to be freighted with symbolical significance for the sphere of religion. In spite of all this, the mind of the times was not hopelessly submerged in darkness. The light of antique learning was never entirely extinguished; even some of the most pious of Church Fathers recognized the value of classical literature. Moreover, there were a few men in the period who, if not creative geniuses, at least had abilities of scholarship which would not have been rated inferior in the best days of Greece.

Nearly all of the philosophers of the early Middle Ages may be classified as either Christians or pagans, although a few seem to have been nominal adherents of the church who wrote in the spirit of pagan thought. The Christian philosophers tended to divide into two different schools: (1) those who emphasized the primacy of authority; and (2) those who believed that the doctrines of the faith should be illumined by the light of reason and brought into harmony with the finest products of pagan thinking. The authoritarian tradition in Christian philosophy stemmed originally from Tertullian, a priest of Carthage who lived about the beginning of the third century. For him, Christianity was a system of sacred law to be accepted entirely upon faith. God was an absolute sovereign, whose decrees no mortal had any right to question. Human knowledge was of no value for religion; indeed, now that the Christ had come, and men had the Gospels, there was no need for any further curiosity. As Tertullian would have it, the wisdom of men was mere foolishness with God, and the more a tenet of the faith contradicted reason the greater was the merit in accepting it.

While few of the Christian Fathers went as far as Tertullian in despising intellectual effort, there were several who adhered to his general principle that the dogmas of the faith were not to be tested by reason. St. Ambrose, the great bishop of Milan in the fourth century, was one of them, in spite of his well-trained mind and his liberal social philosophy. His contemporary, St. Jerome, was another. But the most influential of them all was Pope Gregory I (540–604), known in church history as Gregory the Great. The scion of a rich senatorial family, Gregory scorned the seductions of wealth and power in order that he might dedicate his life to the church.

He turned his father's palace into a convent and gave all of the remainder of the wealth he had inherited to the poor. In his work as a theologian he laid great stress upon the idea of penance as essential to the remission of sins and strengthened the notion of purgatory as a place where even the righteous must suffer for minor offenses in order to be purified for admission to heaven. Perhaps more than anyone else he was responsible for developing the doctrine that the priest in celebrating the mass co-operates with God in performing a miracle which has the effect of repeating and renewing the sacrifice of Christ on the cross.

The most eminent of the Christian philosophers who may be described as representatives of a rationalist tradition were Clement of Alexandria and Origen. Both of them lived in the third century and were deeply influenced by Neo-Platonism and Gnosticism, although they adhered to neither one of those systems very closely. Far from despising all human knowledge, they taught that the best of the Greek thinkers had really anticipated the teachings of Jesus, and that Christianity is improved by being brought into harmony with pagan learning. While Clement and Origen would not qualify as rationalists in the modern sense, inasmuch as they took a great many of their beliefs on faith, they nevertheless recognized the importance of reason as a fundamental basis of knowledge whether religious or secular. They denied the omnipotence of God and taught that God's power is limited by His goodness and wisdom. They rejected the fatalism of many of their opponents and insisted that man by his own free will molds his course of action while on earth. Neither the universe nor anything in it, they declared, was ever created in time; instead, the process of creation is eternal, new things supplanting the old in unending succession. Both Clement and Origen condemned the extreme asceticism of some of their more zealous brethren; in particular, they deplored the tendency of such men as Tertullian to speak of marriage as simply a legalized form of carnality. They avowed, on the contrary, that wedlock and the begetting of children are necessary not only for the good of society but for the perfection of man himself. Finally, they maintained that the purpose of all future punishment is purification and not revenge. Consequently, punishment in hell cannot be eternal, for even the blackest of sinners must eventually be redeemed. If it were not so, God would not be a God of goodness and mercy.

The rationalist Christian philosophers: Clement and Origen

The most erudite and perhaps the most original of all the early Christian philosophers was St. Augustine. In so far as it is possible to classify him at all, he occupied an intermediate position between Clement and Origen, on the one hand, and Tertullian and Gregory on the other. Though contending that truths of revelation were above natural reason, he perceived the need for an intellectual understanding of what he believed. Born in 354, the son of a pagan father and a Christian mother, Augustine was torn by conflicting impulses

The career of St. Augustine

263

throughout the greater part of his life. As a young man he was addicted to sensual pleasures, from which he tried vainly to escape, though he admits in his *Confessions* that his efforts were none too sincere. Even after his engagement to marry he still could not resist the temptation to take a new mistress. Meanwhile, when he was about eighteen years old, he was attracted to philosophy by reading Cicero's *Hortensius*. He passed from one system of thought to another, unable to find spiritual satisfaction in any. For a brief period he considered the possibilities of Christianity, but it impressed him as too crude and superstitious. Then for nine years he was a Manichean, but ultimately he became convinced that that faith was decadent. Next he was attracted to Neo-Platonism, and then, finally, after listening to the preaching of Ambrose, he returned to Christianity. Though already in his thirty-third year when he was baptized, Augustine advanced rapidly in ecclesiastical positions. In 395 he became bishop of Hippo in northern Africa, an office which he held until his death in 430.

The philosophy of St. Augustine

As a philosopher Augustine derived a great many of his theories from the Neo-Platonists. He believed in absolute and eternal truth and in instinctive knowledge which God implants in the minds of men. The supremely important knowledge, however, is knowledge of God and His plan of redemption for mankind. Though most of this knowledge must be derived from the revelation contained in the Scriptures, it is nevertheless the duty of man to understand as much of it as possible in order to strengthen his belief. On the basis of this conclusion St. Augustine developed his famous conception of human history as the unfoldment of the will of God. Everything that has happened or ever will happen represents but an episode in the fulfillment of the divine plan. The whole race of human beings comprises two great divisions: those whom God has predestined to eternal salvation constitute the City of God; all others belong to the Earthly City. The end of the drama of history will come with the Day of Judgment, when the blessed few who compose the City of God will put on the garment of immortality, while the vast multitude in the earthly kingdom will be cast into the fires of hell. This, according to St. Augustine, is the whole meaning of human existence.

St. Augustine's theology

St. Augustine's theology was an integral part of his philosophy. Believing as he did in a deity who controls the operation of the universe down to the smallest detail, he naturally emphasized the omnipotence of God and set limits to the freedom of the will. Since man is sinful by nature, the will has to struggle against an inclination to commit evil. Although man has the power to choose between good and bad, it is God who provides the motive or "inspiration" for the choice. Therefore the virtuous man must thank God for having been able to choose the path of virtue. God created the world in the knowledge that some men would respond to the divine "invitation" to lead holy lives, and that others would resist or refuse to co-operate. In this way God *predestined* a portion of the human race to be saved and left the remainder to perish; or, in other words, He fixed for all time the number of inhabitants of the heavenly city. It was not that He elected some for salvation and denied to all others the opportunity to be saved. Rather, He knew infallibly from all eternity that some would not *wish* to be saved. The influence of St. Augustine was enormous. In spite of the fact that his teachings were modified slightly by the Council of Orange in 529, and still more by the theologians of the later Middle Ages, he is revered to this day as one of the most important Fathers of the Roman Catholic religion. Luther and other Protestant Reformers also held him in the highest esteem, although the interpretations they gave to his teachings frequently differed from those of the Catholics.

Practically the only pagan school of philosophy in early medieval Europe was that of the Neo-Platonists, whose doctrines were discussed in a preceding chapter. There was one other individual thinker, however, who cannot be positively classified as either a pagan or a Christian. It is quite probable that he was a Christian, though he makes no reference to the church or to the name of Christ in his chief work. The name of this man was Boethius. Born about 480 of aristocratic parentage, Boethius eventually became principal adviser to Theodoric, the Ostrogothic king. Later he fell out with that monarch, was accused of treason, and thrown into prison. In 524 he was put to death. The chief philosophical work of Boethius, which he wrote while languishing in prison, is entitled *The Consolation of Philosophy*. Its dominant theme is the relation of man to the universe. The author considers such problems as fate, the divine government of the world, and individual suffering. After carefully weighing the various conceptions of fortune, he comes to the conclusion that true happiness is synonymous with philosophic understanding that the universe is really good, and that evil is only apparent. Pointing out that men who yield to violent impulses either suffer pangs of remorse or find themselves slaves of their passions, he endeavors to show that vice never goes unpunished nor virtue unrewarded. Although he apparently assumes the immortality of the soul, he refers to no definitely Christian belief as a source of consolation. His attitude is essentially that of the Stoics, colored by a trace of Neo-Platonist mysticism. Few treatises on philosophy were more popular in medieval Europe than Boethius' *Consolation of Philosophy*. Not only was it ultimately translated into nearly every vernacular language, but numerous imitations of it also were written.

The history of literature in the early Middle Ages was marked, first of all, by a decline of interest in the classical writings and later by the growth of a crude originality which ultimately paved the way for the development of new literary traditions. By the fifth century the taste for good Latin literature had already begun to decay. Some of the Christian Fathers who had been educated in pagan schools were inclined to apologize for their attachment to the ancient writings; others expressly denounced them; but the attitude which gen-

The Neo-Platonists and Boethius

Literature in the early Middle Ages

erally prevailed was that of St. Augustine. The great bishop of Hippo declared that men should continue to study the pagan classics, not for their aesthetic value or their human appeal, but "with a view to making the wit more keen and better suited to penetrate the mystery of the Divine Word." [9] The Latin language also suffered from the effects of the gradual barbarization of culture. Many theologians appeared to feel that it was almost impious for a Christian to write too well. In composing his commentaries on the Scriptures, Pope Gregory I avowed that he considered it exceedingly inappropriate to "fetter the Heavenly Oracle" to the rules of grammar. As a result, medieval Latin was eventually corrupted by a hopeless confusion of changes in syntax and spelling and by the introduction of new words from colloquial usage. Toward the close of the period, however, the vernacular languages, which had been slowly evolving from a fusion of barbarian dialects, with some admixture of Latin elements, began to be employed for crude poetic expression. The consequence was a new and vigorous literary growth which attained its full momentum about the thirteenth century.

Beowulf and other examples of vernacular literature

The best-known example of this literature in the vernacular is the Anglo-Saxon epic poem *Beowulf*. First put into written form about the eighth century, this poem incorporates ancient legends of the Germanic peoples of northwestern Europe. It is a story of fighting and seafaring and of heroic adventure against deadly dragons and the forces of nature. The background of the epic is heathen, but the author of the work introduced into it some qualities of Christian idealism. *Beowulf* is important, not only as one of the earliest specimens of Anglo-Saxon or Old English poetry, but also for the picture which it gives of the society of the English and their ancestors in the early Middle Ages. Many of the remaining examples of the popular literature of this time were also written in Old English. They include the hymns of Caedmon and numerous elegies describing the rude virtues of early barbarian culture. But no account of the vernacular literature of this time would be complete without some mention of the achievements of the Irish. Ireland in the late sixth and early seventh centuries experienced a brilliant renaissance which made that country one of the brightest spots in the so-called Dark Ages. Without the benefit of any influence from Latin culture, Irish monks and bards wrote stories of fantastic adventure on land and sea and hundreds of poems of gorgeous color and sympathetic understanding of human nature.

The historians

Aside from theological works the leading productions of authors who wrote in Latin during the early Middle Ages were the histories of Orosius, Gregory of Tours, and Bede. At the request of St. Augustine, a Spanish priest by the name of Orosius wrote his *Seven Books against the Pagans*. Distinguished neither by accuracy nor by literary charm, this work was intended to be a history of the world

[9] Quoted by Thompson and Johnson, *An Introduction to Medieval Europe*, p. 221.

showing that the calamities which had befallen ancient nations were due to their wickedness. Bishop Gregory of Tours, a near-contemporary of Clovis, also wrote with a view to defense of the faith. In his *History of the Franks* he condoned the murders of Clovis on the ground that they were committed in the service of the church. Although his work contains interesting information about the events of his time, it is marred by his accounts of the miraculous powers of sacred relics and his tendency to give a supernatural interpretation to every occurrence. By far the best of the historical writings of the early medieval period was the Venerable Bede's *Ecclesiastical History of England.* Bede was an English monk who lived between 673 and 735. Apparently more interested in scholarship than in pious meditation, he pursued his studies so assiduously that he gained a reputation as one of the most learned men of his time. In collecting material for his history he devoted careful attention to sources. He did not hesitate to reject the statements of some of the most respectable authorities when he found them to be in error; and when the evidence was a matter of mere oral tradition, he was honest enough to say so.

No account of intellectual attainments in the early Middle Ages would be complete without some reference to developments in education. After the reign of Theodoric the old Roman system of state schools rapidly disappeared. In some of the Italian cities municipal schools survived even as late as the Renaissance, but throughout the remainder of western Europe the monasteries had a practical monopoly of education. The man who did most to establish the monasteries as institutions of learning was Cassiodorus, formerly chief secretary to Theodoric. Following his retirement from official service, Cassiodorus founded a monastery on his ancestral estate in Apulia and set the monks to work copying manuscripts. The precedent he established was gradually adopted in nearly all the Benedictine institutions. Cassiodorus also insisted that his monks should be trained as scholars, and for this purpose he prepared a curriculum based upon seven subjects, which came to be called the Seven Liberal Arts. These subjects were divided, apparently by Boethius, into the *trivium* and the *quadrivium*. The former included grammar, rhetoric, and logic, which were supposed to be the keys to knowledge; while the *quadrivium* embraced the subjects of more definite content—arithmetic, geometry, astronomy, and music.

Developments in education; the Seven Liberal Arts

The textbooks used in the monastic schools were for the most part elementary. In some of the best schools, however, translations of Aristotle's logical works were studied. But nowhere was any attention given to laboratory science, and history was largely neglected. No professional training of any kind was provided, except for careers in the church. Learning was, of course, a privilege for the few; the masses as a rule received no education, save what they acquired incidentally, and even most members of the secular aristocracy were illiterate. Yet, with all of its shortcomings, this system of education

The value of monastic education

267

did help to save European culture from complete eclipse. And it is worth remembering that the best of the monastic and cathedral schools—notably those at Yarrow and York in England—provided the main impetus for the first of the revivals of learning which occurred in the later Middle Ages.

Selected Readings

Artz, F. B., *The Mind of the Middle Ages*, 1954
Case, S. J., *The Social Origins of Christianity*, Chicago, 1923
———, *Makers of Christianity*, New York, 1934
Coulton, G. G., *Five Centuries of Religion*, New York, 1926
Dawson, C. H., *The Making of Europe*, New York, 1932
Duckett, E. S., *The Gateway to the Middle Ages*, New York, 1938
Edman, Irwin, *The Mind of Paul*, New York, 1935
Flick, A. C., *The Rise of the Medieval Church*, New York, 1909
Glover, T. R., *The Conflict of Religions in the Early Roman Empire*, New York, 1909
Hearnshaw, F. J. C., *The Social and Political Ideas of Some Great Medieval Thinkers*, New York, 1923
Laistner, M. L. W., *Thought and Letters in Western Europe, A.D. 500–900*, New York, 1931
Lamonte, J. L., *The World of the Middle Ages*, New York, 1949
Latourette, K. S., *A History of Christianity*, New York, 1953
McGiffert, A. C., *History of Christian Thought*, New York, 1932, 2 vols.
Moss, H. St. L. B., *The Birth of the Middle Ages, 395–814*, New York, 1935
Patch, R. R., *The Tradition of Boethius*, New York, 1935
Rand, E. K., *Founders of the Middle Ages*, Cambridge, Mass., 1928
Rops, Daniel, *Jesus and His Times*, New York, 1954
Taylor, H. O., *The Classical Heritage of the Middle Ages*, New York, 1925
———, *The Medieval Mind*, New York, 1927, 2 vols.
Thompson, J. W., *Economic and Social History of the Middle Ages*, New York, 1928
———, and Johnson, E. N., *An Introduction to Medieval Europe*, New York, 1937

Source Materials

Boethius, *The Consolation of Philosophy*
Gregory of Tours, *History of the Franks*
King, J. E., ed., *The Historical Works of Bede*, 2 vols.
The New Testament, especially Matthew 5–9; Mark; Romans 3–13
St. Augustine, *The City of God*, especially Books IV, VII, X, XII, XIV, XV, XVII
———, *Confessions*
———, *Enchiridion*, especially Chs. XXVI, XXVII, XXX–XXXIII, XLI, L, LI, XCVIII, XCIX

The Byzantine and Saracenic Civilizations

The so-called medieval period of history does not concern Europe alone. In addition to the cultures of the early European Middle Ages and of the Feudal Age which followed, medieval history includes two other civilizations, the Byzantine and the Saracenic. Although each occupied territory on the European continent, the larger portions of their empires were located in Africa and in Asia. Of greater significance is the fact that the features of both civilizations were largely those of the Orient. While the Saracens were Moslems and the Byzantine people Christians, religion was the dominant factor in the lives of both. The two states were so closely linked with the religious organizations that their governments were mainly theocratic. Moreover, both civilizations were characterized by attitudes of pessimism and fatalism and by a tendency for the mystical point of view to gain supremacy over the rational. It should be noted, however, that the Saracens, especially, made distinctive contributions to philosophy and science, while the Byzantine Empire was exceedingly important for its art and for its work in preserving innumerable achievements of the Greeks and Romans.

The semi-Oriental character of the Byzantine and Saracenic civilizations

1. The Byzantine Empire and Its Culture

In the fourth century the Emperor Constantine established a new capital for the Roman Empire on the site of the old Greek colony of Byzantium. When the western division of the Empire collapsed, Byzantium (or Constantinople as the city was now more commonly called) survived as the capital of a powerful state which included the Near Eastern provinces of the Caesars. Gradually this state came to be known as the Byzantine Empire, although the existence of a

The founding of the Byzantine Empire

269

Byzantine civilization was not clearly recognized before the sixth century. Even after that there were many who believed that Rome had merely shifted its center of gravity to the East.

Byzantine culture more distinctly Oriental than that of Latin Europe

Although Byzantine history covered a period similar to that of the Middle Ages, the cultural pattern was far different from the one which prevailed in western Europe. Byzantine civilization had a much more pronounced Oriental character. Not only did Constantinople face the Orient, but most of the territories of the Empire actually lay outside of Europe. The most important among them were Syria, Asia Minor, Palestine, and Egypt. Furthermore, Greek and Hellenistic elements entered into the formation of Byzantine culture to a greater extent than was ever true in western Europe. The language of the eastern state was predominantly Greek, while the traditions in literature, art, and science were largely Hellenistic. Lastly, the Christianity of the Byzantine Empire differed from that of Latin Europe in being more mystical, abstract, and pessimistic and more completely subject to political control.

Nationalities in the Byzantine Empire

The population of the territories under Byzantine rule comprised a great number of nationalities. The majority of the inhabitants were Greeks and Hellenized Orientals—Syrians, Jews, Armenians, Egyptians, and Persians. In addition, the European sections of the Empire included numerous barbarians, especially Slavs and Mongols. There were some Germans also, but the emperors at Constantinople were generally able to divert the German invasions to the west. The encroachments of the Slavs and the Mongols, on the other hand, proved to be much more difficult to deal with. The original home of the Slavs, a round-headed people of Alpine stock, was apparently the region northeast of the Carpathian Mountains, principally in what is now southwestern Russia. A peaceful agricultural folk, they seldom resorted to armed invasion but gradually expanded into thinly settled territories whenever the opportunity arose. Not only did they move into the vast empty spaces of central Russia, but they occupied many of the regions vacated by the Germans and then slowly filtered through the frontiers of the Eastern Empire. By the seventh century they were the most numerous people in the entire Balkan peninsula, as well as in the whole region of Europe east of the Germans. The Mongolian inhabitants of the Empire included Bulgars and Avars, who had come into Europe from the steppes of what is now Asiatic Russia. Both of these nations were herdsmen, with the furious energy and warlike habits characteristic of that mode of existence. After entering the valley of the Danube, many of them forced their way into Byzantine territory. It was a fusion of some of these Mongolian peoples with Slavs which gave rise to such modern nations as the Bulgarians and the Serbs.

The details of Byzantine political development have little significance for the modern age. The early history of the Empire was marked by struggles to repel the Germanic barbarians. The con-

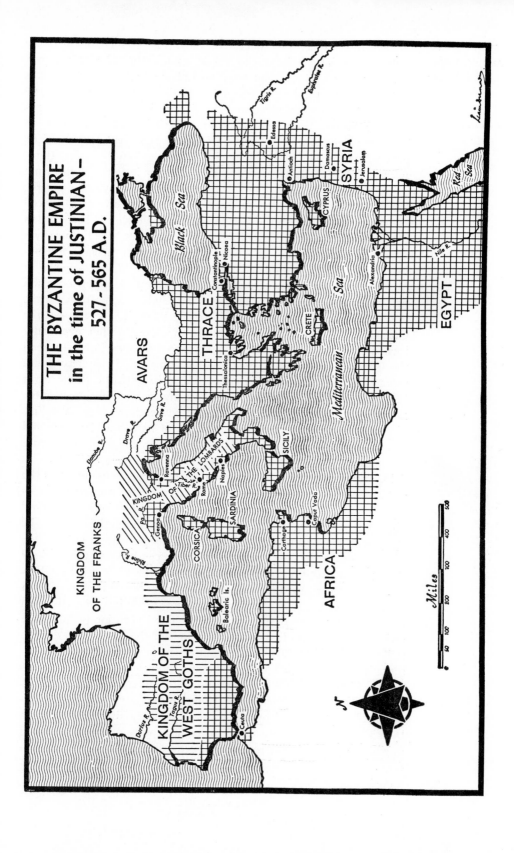

THE BYZANTINE EMPIRE
in the time of JUSTINIAN –
527 - 565 A.D.

KINGDOM
OF THE FRANKS

AVARS

THRACE

Black Sea

Danube R.
Drave R.
Save R.
Rhone R.

KINGDOM OF THE
WEST GOTHS

Douro R.
Tagus R.

Ceuta

KINGDOM

Genoa
Po R.
Ravenna
THE LOMBARDS
Tiber R.
Rome
Naples

CORSICA

SARDINIA

Balearic Is.

SICILY

Caput Vada

Carthage

AFRICA

Constantinople
Nicaea

Thessalonica

CRETE

Mediterranean
Sea

Edessa

Tigris R.
Euphrates R.

Antioch
SYRIA
Damascus
Jerusalem

CYPRUS

Alexandria
Nile R.

EGYPT

Red Sea

Miles
0   50 100   200   300   400   500

N

fidence inspired by the success of these struggles encouraged the Emperor Justinian to begin the reconquest of Italy and North Africa, but most of Italy was soon afterward abandoned to the Lombards and North Africa to the Moslems. In the early seventh century Byzantium became involved in a great war with Persia, which eventually exhausted both empires and laid their territories open to Saracenic conquest. By 750 the Byzantine state had lost all of its possessions outside of Europe with the exception of Asia Minor. After the tide of Saracenic advance had spent its force, Byzantium enjoyed a brief recovery and even regained the province of Syria, the island of Crete, and some portions of the Italian coast, as well as certain territories on the Balkan peninsula which had been lost to the barbarians. In the eleventh century, however, the Empire was attacked by the Seljuk Turks, who rapidly overran the eastern provinces and in 1071 annihilated a Byzantine army of 100,000 men at Manzikert. The Emperor Romanus Diogenes was taken prisoner and held for a ransom of one million pieces of gold. Soon afterward the government sent an appeal for aid to the West. The result was the Crusades, launched originally against the Moslems but eventually turned into plundering attacks upon Byzantine territory. In 1204 the Crusaders captured Constantinople and treated that city "with more barbarity than the barbarian Alaric had treated Rome eight hundred years before." [1] But even these disasters did not prove fatal. During the late thirteenth and early fourteenth centuries the Empire once again recovered some measure of its former strength and prosperity. Its history was finally brought to an end with the capture of Constantinople by the Ottoman Turks in 1453.

*Factors in the
stability of the
Byzantine Em-
pire*

During this long period of approximately one thousand years the stability of Byzantine rule was frequently menaced not only by foreign aggression but also by palace intrigues, mutinies in the army, and violent struggles between political factions. How then can it be explained that the Empire survived so long, especially in view of the rapid decay of the West during the early centuries of this period? Perhaps the first great reason was the fact that Byzantine civilization was largely Oriental and relatively static. Social change did not occur with startling rapidity, and cultural evolution went through no violent cycles of decay and rebirth. The Byzantine people were generally content to live on the traditions of the past rather than to strike out boldly toward new frontiers of achievement. This conservative aspect of their culture helped to preserve the nation from swift decline. Geographic and economic factors were probably much more effective. The location of Constantinople made it almost impregnable. Surrounded on three sides by water and on the fourth by a high wall, the city was able to resist capture practically as long as any will to defend it remained. Furthermore, the Near East suffered no decay of industry and commerce like that which had oc-

[1] J. B. Bury, *History of the Later Roman Empire* (1931 ed.), Vol. I, p. 3.

curred in Italy at the beginning of the Dark Ages. Last of all, the Byzantine government had a well-filled treasury which could always be drawn upon for purposes of defense. The annual revenues of the state have been estimated as high as $100 million (1957 dollars).

The government of the Byzantine Empire was similar to that of Rome after the time of Diocletian, except that it was even more despotic and theocratic. The emperor was an absolute sovereign with unlimited power over every department of national life. His subjects not only fell prostrate before him, but in petitioning his grace they customarily referred to themselves as his slaves. Moreover, the spiritual dignity of the emperor was in no sense inferior to his temporal power. He was the vicar of God with a religious authority supposed to be equal to that of the Apostles. Although some of the emperors were able and hard-working officials, most of the actual functions of the government were performed by an extensive bureaucracy, many of whose members were highly trained. A great army of clerks, inspectors, and spies maintained the closest scrutiny over the life and possessions of every inhabitant.

The government of the Byzantine Empire

The economic system was as strictly regulated as in Hellenistic Egypt. In fact, the Byzantine Empire has been described as a "paradise of monopoly, of privilege, and of paternalism." [2] The state exercised a thorough control over virtually every activity. The wage of every workman and the price of every product were fixed by government decree. In many cases it was not even possible for the individual to choose his own occupation, since the system of guilds which had been established in the late Roman Empire was still maintained. Each worker inherited his status as a member of one guild or another, and the walls which surrounded these organizations were hermetically sealed. Neither did the manufacturer enjoy much greater freedom. He could not choose for himself what quantity or quality of raw materials he would purchase, nor was he permitted to buy them directly. He could not determine how much he would produce or under what conditions he would sell his product. All of these matters were regulated by the trade association to which he belonged, and it in turn was subject to supervision by the government. To provide for cheap administration of the system, the emperors encouraged competing businessmen and workers to act as informers against each other. A number of large industrial enterprises were owned and operated by the state. Chief among them were the murex or purple fisheries, the mines, the armament factories, and the establishments for the weaving of cloth. An attempt was made at one time to extend monopolistic control over the silk industry, but the government factories were unable to supply the demand, and permission had to be given to private manufacturers to resume production.

State control of the economic system

The agricultural regime developed under the late Roman Empire

[2] J. W. Thompson, *Economic and Social History of the Middle Ages*, p. 336.

*The agricultur-
al regime*

was also perpetuated and extended in the Byzantine territories. Most of the land was divided into great estates comparable to the *latifundia* in Italy. Save in the hilly and mountainous regions there were very few independent farmers left. In the richest areas the agricultural population was made up almost entirely of tenant farmers and serfs. The number of the latter was increased in the fifth century when the Emperor Anastasius issued a decree forbidding all peasants who had lived on a particular farm for thirty years ever to remove therefrom. The purpose of the decree was to insure a minimum of agricultural production, but its natural effect was to bind the peasants to the soil and make them actual serfs of their landlords. Another of the significant agricultural developments in the Byzantine Empire was the concentration of landed wealth in the hands of the church. The monasteries, especially, came to be included among the richest proprietors in the country. With the increasing difficulty of making a living from the soil and the growing popularity of asceticism, more and more farmers sought refuge in the cloister and made gifts of their lands to the institutions which admitted them. The estates acquired by the church were cultivated not by the monks or the priests but by serfs. During the seventh and eighth centuries an economic transformation occurred. Many of the serfs gained their freedom and became owners of the lands they cultivated. But by the eleventh century the great estates had reappeared, and the independent peasantry virtually ceased to exist.

*The absorbing
interest in reli-
gion*

No subject appears to have absorbed the interest of the Byzantine people more completely than religion. They fought over religious questions as vehemently as citizens of the modern world quarrel over issues of government control versus private ownership or democracy versus totalitarianism. They took great delight in theological subtleties which would impress most people in our time as barren and trivial. Gregory of Nyssa, one of their own Church Fathers, thus described Constantinople in the fourth century: "Everything is full of those who are speaking of unintelligible things—streets, markets, squares, crossroads. I ask how many oboli I have to pay; in answer they are philosophizing on the born or unborn; I wish to know the price of bread; one answers: 'The Father is greater than the Son'; I inquire whether my bath is ready; one says, 'The Son has been made out of nothing.' "[3]

*Religious con-
troversies; the
Monophysite
movement*

The most crucial of the religious issues, however, were those which grew out of the Monophysite and Iconoclastic movements, although neither of these movements was exclusively religious in character. The Monophysites derived their name from their contention that the Christ was composed of only one nature, and that that nature was divine. This doctrine, which was probably a reflection of the Neo-Platonist contempt for everything physical or material, flatly contradicted the official theology of Christianity. Having begun as early

[3] A. A. Vasiliev, *History of the Byzantine Empire*, Vol. I, pp. 99 f.

as the fifth century, the Monophysite movement reached its height during the reign of Justinian (527–565). Its strength lay chiefly in Syria and in Egypt, where it served as an expression of nationalist resentment against subjection to Constantinople. In dealing with the sect Justinian was caught between two fires. Not only was he ambitious to unite his subjects in allegiance to a single faith, but he was anxious to win the support of Rome. On the other hand, he was reluctant to take any steps for the suppression of the Monophysites partly because of their strength and also because his wife, the popular actress Theodora, was a member of the sect. It was her will that finally prevailed. During the seventh century the Monophysites broke away from the Eastern church. The sect survives to this day as an important branch of Christendom in Egypt, Syria, and Armenia.

The Iconoclastic movement was launched about 725 by a decree of the Emperor Leo III forbidding the use of images in the church. In the Eastern church any image of God, the Christ, or a saint was called an icon. Those who condemned the use of icons in worship were known as Iconoclasts, or image-breakers. The Iconoclastic movement was a product of several factors. First of all, it had a certain affinity with the Monophysite movement in its opposition to anything sensuous or material in religion. Secondly, it was a protest against paganism and worldliness in the church. But perhaps more than anything else it represented a revolt of certain of the emperors against the increasing power of the ecclesiastical system. The monasteries in particular were absorbing so large a proportion of the national wealth and enticing so many men away from service in the army and from useful occupations that they were rapidly undermining the economic vitality of the Empire. Since the monks derived a large part of their income from the manufacture and sale of icons, it was logical that the reforming emperors should center their attacks upon the use of images in the church. Naturally they had the support of many of their pious subjects, who resented what they considered a corruption of their religion by idolatrous practices.

The Iconoclasts

Although the struggle against the worship of images was continued until well into the ninth century, it really accomplished no more than the elimination of sculptured representations; the flat or painted icons were eventually restored. Nevertheless, the Iconoclastic controversy had more than a trivial significance. It may be said to have represented an important stage in the irrepressible conflict between Roman and Oriental traditions, which occupied so large a place in Byzantine history. Those who upheld the use of images generally believed in an ecclesiastical religion in which symbols and ceremony were regarded as indispensable aids to worship. Most of their opponents were mystics and ascetics who condemned any form of institutionalism or veneration of material objects and advocated a return to the spiritualism of primitive Christianity. Many of the ideals

Significance of the Iconoclastic controversy

of the Iconoclasts were similar to those of the Protestant Reformers of the sixteenth century, and the movement itself may be said to have foreshadowed the great revolt of Luther and Calvin against what were considered pagan elements in the Roman Catholic religion. Finally, the Iconoclastic controversy was a potent cause of the separation of the Greek and Roman branches of the church in 1054. Even though the attack upon the use of images was not entirely successful, it went far enough to arouse much antagonism between Eastern and Western Christians. The Pope excommunicated the Iconoclasts and turned from the Byzantine emperors to the Frankish kings for support. From this point on the East and the West drew farther apart.

Social conditions in the Byzantine Empire

Social conditions in the Byzantine Empire presented a marked contrast with western Europe during the early Middle Ages. Whereas large sections of Italy and southern France had sunk to almost primitive levels of ruralism, Byzantine society continued to maintain its essentially urban and luxurious character. Approximately a million people lived in the city of Constantinople alone, to say nothing of

Silver Plate Portraying David and Goliath, and Plaque, in Gold and Enamel, Portraying the Christ. Such objects were among the most appealing examples of Byzantine minor arts.

the thousands who dwelt in Tarsus, Nicaea, Edessa, Thessalonica, and other great urban centers. Merchants, bankers, and manufacturers ranked with the great landlords as members of the aristocracy, for there was no tendency in Byzantium as there had been in Rome to despise the man who derived his income from industry or trade. The rich lived in elegance and ease, cultivating the indulgence of opulent tastes as a fine art. A large part of the industrial activity of the nation was absorbed in the production of articles of luxury to meet the demand of the wealthier classes. Magnificent garments of wool and silk interwoven with gold and silver thread, gorgeously colored tapestries of brocaded or damasked stuffs, exquisite glass and porcelain ware, illuminated gospels, and rare and costly jeweled orna-

ments composed only a small part of the sumptuous output of factories and shops, both public and private.

The life of the lower classes was poor and mean by comparison.
And yet the common man in the Byzantine Empire was probably
better off than the average citizen in most other parts of the Christian
world at that time. The extensive industrial and commercial development and the high degree of economic stability provided opportunities for employment for thousands of urban workers, except during
the period of Moslem invasions, when Constantinople was filled
with refugees who could not be absorbed into the economic system.
Even the lot of the serf who was attached to the estate of some one
of the great secular proprietors was probably superior to that of the
peasants in western Europe, since the landlord's powers of exploitation were at least regulated by law. Nevertheless, the serf's condition
was bad enough, for he was doomed to a life of ignorance and dull
routine within the narrow horizon of the village in which he was
born. His status was unalterably fixed by the mere accident of his
having been born of parents who were serfs. The Byzantine population also included a considerable percentage of slaves, but most
of them were employed in domestic service and doubtless enjoyed
a fairly comfortable existence.

The tone of morality in the Empire exhibited sharp contrasts. The
Byzantine people in spite of their Greek antecedents apparently had
no aptitude for the typical Hellenic virtues of balance and restraint.
In place of the golden mean they seemed always to prefer the extremes. Consequently the most extravagant self-indulgence was frequently to be found side by side with the humblest self-denial or
laceration of the flesh. The contradictory qualities of sensuality and
piety, charity and heartless cruelty, were commonly evident in the
same stratum of society or even in the same individuals. For example, the great reform Emperor, Leo III, tried to improve the lot of
the peasants, but he also introduced mutilation as a punishment for
crime. Life at the imperial court and among some members of the
higher clergy appears to have been characterized by indolence,
luxurious vice, effeminacy, and intrigue. As a consequence, the very
word "Byzantine" has come to be suggestive of elegant sensuality
and refinements of cruelty.

In the intellectual realm the Byzantine people won little distinction
for originality. Comparatively few discoveries or contributions in
any of the fields of knowledge can actually be credited to them. Probably their most noteworthy achievement was the revision and codification of the ancient Roman law. After the time of the great jurists
(second and third centuries A.D.) the creative genius of the Roman
lawyers decayed, and nothing new was added to the philosophy or
the science of law. The volume of statutory enactments, however,
continued to grow. By the sixth century the Roman law had come
to contain numerous contradictory and obsolete provisions. More-

over, conditions had changed so radically that many of the old legal principles could no longer be applied, particularly on account of the establishment of an Oriental despotism and the adoption of Christianity as the official religion. When Justinian came to the throne in 527, he immediately decided upon a revision and codification of the existing law to bring it into harmony with the new conditions and to establish it as an authoritative basis of his rule. To carry out the actual work he appointed a commission of lawyers under the supervision of his minister, Tribonian. Within two years the commission published the first result of its labors. This was the Code, a systematic revision of all of the statutory laws which had been issued from the reign of Hadrian to the reign of Justinian. The Code was later supplemented by the Novels, which contained the legislation of Justinian and his immediate successors. By 532 the commission had completed the Digest, representing a summary of all of the writings of the great jurists. The final product of the work of revision was the Institutes, a textbook of the legal principles which were reflected in both the Digest and the Code. The combination of all four of these results of the program of revision constitutes the *Corpus Juris Civilis*, or the body of the civil law.

The Institutes and the Digest

From the historical standpoint the two most important sections of the *Corpus Juris* were unquestionably the Institutes and the Digest. It was these which contained the philosophy of law and of government which had come to prevail in Justinian's time. There is a popular but somewhat inaccurate belief that this philosophy was the same as that of Ulpian, Papinian, and the other great jurists of three hundred years before. While it is true that most of the old theory was preserved, a few fundamental changes were introduced. First, the *jus civile* was more completely denationalized than it had ever been during Roman times and was now made applicable to citizens of a great many divergent nationalities. The *jus naturale* was now declared to be divine and consequently superior to all of the enactments of men—a conception which was destined to become exceedingly popular in later medieval philosophy. There was a tendency also for Justinian's jurists to speak of the emperor as the sole legislator, on the assumption that the people had surrendered all of their power to him. In other words, the classical Roman law was being revised to make it fit the needs of an Oriental monarch whose sovereignty was limited only by the law of God.

Other Byzantine intellectual achievements

As to the remainder of Byzantine intellectual achievements, comparatively little needs to be said. The nation produced no philosophers of more than secondary rank. But several of them made important contributions to the development of Scholasticism, which emerged as the most popular philosophy of the later Middle Ages. They emphasized the value of reason and attempted to reconcile the teachings of Aristotle with those of the Scriptures and the Christian Fathers. Byzantine literature consisted for the most part of compilations and religious writings, especially encyclopedias, commentaries, hymns, and biographies of saints. Some epic and lyric poetry was also written and numerous histories. By far the most famous of the historians was Procopius, a contemporary of Justinian. Despite his penchant for scandal-mongering in his celebrated *Secret History*, others of his works contain valuable information about the events of his time.

The Byzantine record in science was possibly somewhat better than in most other branches of learning. Most of the progress was made in the early years of the Empire, perhaps on account of the survival of Hellenistic influence. This first golden age was followed by a long period of stagnation until the middle of the tenth century, when a revival began due in large part to Moslem influence and to the patronage of the Emperor Constantine VII. But neither of these eras of progress lasted for more than two centuries. The leading scientists of the early period were John the Grammarian, Aetius, and Alexander of Tralles, all of whom lived in the sixth century. John the Grammarian is far more deserving of credit for his work in physics than for any contributions to grammar. He is especially worthy of attention for having been the first to challenge the traditional theories of motion and gravity. Not only did he anticipate the concept of inertia, but he rejected the notion that the speed of falling bodies is directly proportional to their weight, and he denied the impossibility of creating a vacuum. The other two scientists of the early period were encyclopedists of medicine. Although the influence of Alexander of Tralles surpassed that of Aetius, the work of the latter was more original. Aetius wrote not only the first description of diphtheria but also the best account of diseases of the eye which had been published thus far. The only outstanding scientist of the later period was Symeon Seth, who was also a physician. His chief work was a medical dictionary defining the curative properties of numerous drugs lately discovered by the Hindus and the Saracens.

The record in science

The tastes of the Byzantine people, with their fondness for luxury and splendor, were signally expressed in their art. However, it was not a mere emblem of sensuous delight. It was profoundly conditioned by the peculiar ideals of the civilization itself. For one thing, the strong undercurrent of asceticism prohibited the glorification of man; as a consequence, sculpture was not permitted to develop very far. The art which held the position of pre-eminence was architecture, and it had to be mystical and otherworldly. Furthermore, since the Byzantine civilization was a compound of elements both Roman and Oriental, it was inevitable that its art should combine the love of grandeur and the engineering talent of Rome with the gorgeous coloring and richness of detail characteristic of the Orient.

Byzantine art

The supreme artistic achievement of the Byzantine civilization was the church of Santa Sophia (Holy Wisdom), built at enormous cost by the Emperor Justinian. Although designed by architects of Hel-

*The church of
Santa Sophia*

lenic descent, it was vastly different from any Greek temple. Its purpose was not to express man's pride in himself or his satisfaction with this life, but to symbolize the inward and spiritual character of the Christian religion. It was for this reason that the architects gave little attention to the external appearance of the building. Nothing but plain brick covered with plaster was used for the exterior walls; no marble facings, graceful columns, or sculptured entablatures. The interior, however, was decorated with richly colored mosaics, gold leaf, colored marble columns, and bits of tinted glass set on edge to refract the rays of sunlight after the fashion of sparkling gems.

Mosaic, from the Church of Santa Sophia. The mosaic represents the Emperor Leo VI adoring the Christ seated on the throne.

It was for this reason also that the building was constructed in such a way that no light appeared to come from the outside at all but to be manufactured within.

The structural design of Santa Sophia was something altogether new in the history of architecture. Its central feature was the application of the principle of the dome to a building of square shape.

*Advantages
of structural
design*

The church was designed, first of all, in the form of a cross, and then over the central square was to be erected a magnificent dome, which would dominate the entire structure. The main problem was how to fit the round circumference of the dome to the square area it was supposed to cover. The solution consisted in having four great arches spring from pillars at the four corners of the central square. The rim of the dome was then made to rest on the keystones of the arches, with the curved triangular spaces between the arches filled in with masonry. The result was an architectural framework of marvelous strength, which at the same time made possible a style of im-

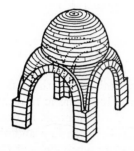

Church of Santa Sophia, in Constantinople. Built by Justinian in the Sixth Century A.D., this church is an outstanding example of Byzantine architectural design. As the accompanying diagram shows, the central dome rests upon four massive arches. The tremendous downward thrust of the dome necessitates the buttressing seen in the photograph in the two enormous masonry piles and half domes. The minarets were added later by the Moslems.

posing grandeur and even some delicacy of treatment. The great dome of Santa Sophia has a diameter of 107 feet and rises to a height of nearly 180 feet from the floor. So many windows are placed around its rim that the dome appears to have no support at all but to be suspended in mid-air.

The other arts of Byzantium included ivory-carving, the making of embossed glassware and brocaded textiles, the illumination of manuscripts, the goldsmith's and jeweler's arts, and considerable painting. The last, however, was not so highly developed as some of the others. In place of painting the Byzantine artist generally preferred mosaics. These were designs produced by fitting together small pieces of colored glass or stone to form a geometric pattern, symbolical figures of plants and animals, or even an elaborate scene of theological significance. Representations of saints and of the Christ were commonly distorted to create the impression of extreme piety.

Other Byzantine arts

See color pictures at pages 260, 261

The importance of the Byzantine civilization is usually underestimated. It was undoubtedly the most powerful factor in determining the course of development of eastern Europe. To a very large extent the civilization of imperial Russia was founded upon the institutions and achievements of Byzantium. The Russian church was an offshoot of the so-called Greek Orthodox or Eastern church, which broke away from Rome in 1054. The Tsar as the head of the religion as well as the state occupied a position analogous to that of the emperor at Constantinople. The architecture of the Russians,

The Byzantine influence in eastern Europe

281

their calendar, and a large part of their alphabet were also of Byzantine origin. Perhaps even the despotism of the Soviet regime can
be traced in some measure to the long-standing tradition of absolute rule in Russia which ultimately goes back to Byzantine influence.

*The Byzantine
influence in the
West*

But the influence of the Byzantine civilization was not limited to
eastern Europe. It would be hard to overestimate the debt of the
West to scholars in Constantinople and the surrounding territory
who copied and preserved manuscripts, prepared anthologies of
Greek literature, and wrote encyclopedias embodying the learning
of the ancient world. Moreover, Byzantine scholars exerted a notable
influence upon the Italian Renaissance. In spite of the fact that the
Eastern emperors eventually lost control of Italy, many of their
former subjects continued to live there, and some others fled to
the Italian cities after the overthrow of the Iconoclastic movement.
The extensive trade between Venice and Constantinople in the late
Middle Ages also fostered cultural relations between East and West.
Consequently, long before the fifteenth century when eminent Greek

Interior of the Church of Sant'
Apollinare, Ravenna. Built in the
Fifth and Sixth Centuries, this
church is a well preserved example
of Byzantine influence.

scholars arrived in Italy, a foundation for the revival of interest in
the Greek classics had already been laid. Likewise, Byzantine art
exerted its effect upon the art of western Europe. Some authorities regard the stained glass windows of the Gothic cathedrals as an
adaptation of the mosaics in Eastern churches. Several of the most
famous churches in Italy, for example St. Mark's in Venice, were
built in close imitation of the Byzantine style. Byzantine painting
also influenced the painting of the Renaissance, especially of the
Venetian school and of El Greco. Finally, it was the *Corpus Juris*
of Justinian which really made possible the transmission of the Roman law to the late Middle Ages and to the modern world.

2. Islam and the Saracenic Civilization

The history of the Saracenic civilization began a little later than
the history of Byzantium and ended a short time earlier. The dates

were roughly 630 A.D. to 1300. In many ways the Saracenic civilization was one of the most important in the Western world—not only because it was the orbit of a new religion, which has attracted converts by the hundreds of millions, but mainly because its impact upon Christian Europe was responsible for social and intellectual changes which can only be described as revolutionary. The term "Saracen" originally meant an Arab, but later it came to be applied to any member of the Moslem faith, regardless of his nationality. Some of the Saracens were Jews, some were Persians, some were Syrians. Nevertheless, the founders of the civilization were Arabs, and it therefore becomes necessary to examine the culture of that people on the eve of their expansion beyond the borders of their homeland.

Toward the end of the sixth century the people of Arabia had come to be divided into two main groups: the urban Arabs and the Bedouins. The former, who dwelt in such cities as Mecca and Yathrib, were traders and petty craftsmen. Many of them were literate, and some were comparatively wealthy. The Bedouins were mostly nomads, subsisting on dates and the flesh and milk of their animals. Ignorant and superstitious, they practiced infanticide and occasional human sacrifice. They were frequently involved in bloody warfare over possession of wells and oases. Neither Bedouins nor urban Arabs had any organized government. The clan and the tribe took the place of the state. When a member of one clan committed a crime against a member of another, the issue was settled by means of the blood feud, which sometimes raged until scores had been killed on each side. The religion was generally polytheistic, although some of the better educated townsmen had adopted a belief in Allah as the only God. From time immemorial Mecca had been a sacred city. Here was the shrine known as the Kaaba, which was supposed to contain a sacred black stone miraculously sent down from heaven. The men who controlled this shrine formed the tribe of the Kuraish, the nearest approach to an Arabian aristocracy that ever existed before the migrations.

Whether the Saracenic civilization would ever have originated without the development of the Moslem religion is a question almost impossible to answer. It is commonly assumed that a new religion was necessary to unite the people and to imbue them with ardor in a common cause. Yet other nations had expanded before this and had accomplished great things without the influence of any particularly inspiring system of belief. Nevertheless, in the case of the Arabs it was a new religion which undoubtedly provided much of the driving force behind the development of their civilization. The origin and nature of that religion must therefore be given careful attention.

The founder of the new faith was born in Mecca about the year 570. The child of parents who belonged to one of the poorest clans of the Kuraish tribe, he was given the common Arabic name of Muhammad or Mohammed. Nothing is known about his early life,

The Saracenic empire not exclusively Arabian

Conditions in Arabia before Mohammed

The Moslem religion as a driving force in the civilization

The early life of Mohammed

283

except that he was left an orphan while still very young and was reared by his grandfather and his uncle. Whether he ever learned to read and write is uncertain, but it is probable that as a member of the leading tribe he would be given some education. When he was about twenty-five years old, he entered the employment of a rich widow and accompanied her caravans perhaps as far north as Syria. Soon afterward he became her husband, thereby acquiring leisure and security to devote all of his time to religious interests.

Mohammed as-sumes the role of social critic

Exactly what influences led Mohammed to become the founder of a new religion, no one knows. He was apparently of a highly emotional nature and may have been an epileptic. At any rate he was subject to fits or convulsive seizures of some kind, during the course of which he believed he heard voices from heaven. Very early in his life he became acquainted with numerous Jews and Christians who lived in the cities of northern Arabia, and he appears to have been deeply impressed by their religious beliefs. In addition, he seems to have developed the idea that social and moral conditions in his country were badly in need of reform. He began to denounce the plutocrats of Mecca for their greed and to reproach his people for their bloody feuds and their practice of infanticide. Gradually he came to conceive of himself as the appointed instrument of God to rescue the Arabian people from the path of destruction.

Founding the new religion

Mohammed's preaching was not at first particularly successful. After almost nine years of communicating the revelations of Allah to all who would listen, he had managed to win very few converts outside of his immediate family. The wealthy Kuraish were naturally against him, and even the common people of Mecca were generally indifferent. As yet he had made no attempt to carry his message to the Bedouins. In 619 he decided to seek a more promising field for the propagation of his teachings. He had learned that the city of Yathrib on the caravan route to the north had been torn for some time by bitter factional strife, and that there might be some chance for a neutral leader to step in and assume control. He sent a number of agents to explore the ground very carefully, and finally in September, 622, he and the remainder of his followers decided to abandon the sacred city of Mecca entirely and to risk their future in the new location. This migration to Yathrib is known to Mohammedans as the Hegira, from the Arabic word meaning "flight," and is considered by them so important that they regard it as the beginning of their era and date all their records from it.

The conquest of Mecca

Mohammed changed the name of Yathrib to Medina (the "city of the Prophet"), and quickly succeeded in establishing himself as ruler of the city. But to obtain means of support for his followers was a somewhat more difficult matter. Besides, the Jews in Medina rejected his leadership. Under these circumstances Mohammed began to enlist the support of the Bedouins for a holy war against his enemies. In a single year approximately six hundred Jews were

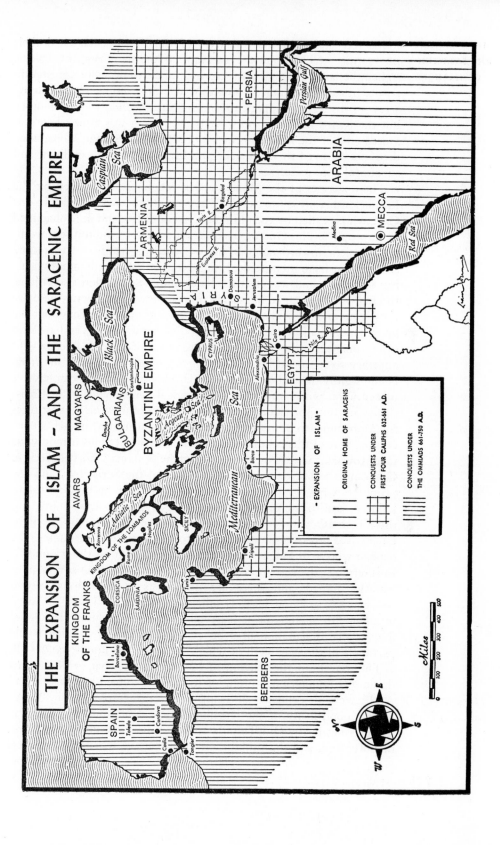

THE EXPANSION OF ISLAM – AND THE SARACENIC EMPIRE

KINGDOM OF THE FRANKS

SPAIN

Toledo
Cordova
Cadiz
Tangier

Barcelona

CORSICA
SARDINIA

KINGDOM OF THE LOMBARDS
Ravenna
Rome
Naples

SICILY

BERBERS

Tunis
Tripoli

Mediterranean Sea

Adriatic Sea

AVARS

MAGYARS

BULGARIANS

BYZANTINE EMPIRE

Constantinople

Black Sea

Aegean Sea

Danube R.

CYPRUS

Borca

Alexandria

Cairo

EGYPT

Nile R.

Caspian Sea

ARMENIA

PERSIA

Bagdad
Tigris R.
Euphrates R.

Persian Gulf

SYRIA
Damascus
Jerusalem

ARABIA

Medina

MECCA

Red Sea

– EXPANSION OF ISLAM –

ORIGINAL HOME OF SARACENS

CONQUESTS UNDER
FIRST FOUR CALIPHS 632-661 A.D.

CONQUESTS UNDER
THE OMMIADS 661-750 A.D.

Miles
0   100   200   300   400   500

N
E
W
S

massacred, and then the followers of the Prophet launched their plundering attacks upon the caravans of the merchants of Mecca. When the latter took up arms to resist, they were badly defeated in battle. In 630 Mohammed entered Mecca in triumph. He murdered a few of his leading opponents and smashed the idols in the temple, but the Kaaba itself was preserved, and Mecca was established as a sacred city of the Mohammedan faith. Two years later Mohammed died, but he lived to see the religion he had founded a militant and successful enterprise.

The doctrines of the Mohammedan religion

The doctrines of the Mohammedan religion as developed by the Prophet are really quite simple. They revolve around a belief in one God, who is called by the old Arabic name Allah, and in Mohammed as his prophet. This God desires that men shall be kind to their neighbors, lenient toward debtors, honest, and forgiving; and that they shall refrain from infanticide, eating swine's flesh, drinking intoxicating beverages, and waging the blood feud. The religion also enjoins the faithful observance of certain obligations. Chief among these are the giving of alms to the poor, fasting during the day throughout the sacred month of Ramadan, praying five times a day, and making a pilgrimage, if possible, at least once in a lifetime to Mecca. But contrary to a general belief, the religion of the Prophet is far from being rigidly formal or mechanical. Almost as much emphasis is placed upon purity of heart and practical benevolence as in Christianity or Judaism. Several passages in the Koran, which constitutes the Mohammedan Scriptures, provide ample warrant for such a conclusion. One of them declares that "There is no piety in turning your faces toward the east or the west, but he is pious who believeth in God, and the last day, and the angels, and the Scriptures, and the prophets; who for the love of God disburseth his wealth to his kindred, and to the orphans, and the needy, and the wayfarer and those who ask, and for ransoming." [4] Another affirms that the highest merit is "to free the captive; or to feed, in a day of famine, the orphan who is of kin, or the poor man who lieth on the ground." [5] Furthermore, there are no sacraments in the system of worship taught by Mohammed, and there are no priests in the Mohammedan church. The religion itself is officially known as "Islam," a word meaning "to submit, or to surrender oneself absolutely to God." The official designation of a believer is a "Moslem," which is the participle of the same verb of which "Islam" is the infinitive.

The probable sources of Islam

The sources of the religion of Islam are somewhat in doubt. Judaism was unquestionably one of them. Mohammed taught that the Arabs were descendants of Ishmael, Abraham's oldest son. Moreover, a good many of the teachings of the Koran are quite similar to doctrines in the Old Testament: strict monotheism, the sanction of polygamy, and the prohibition of usury, the worship of images,

[4] Sura 2:v. 172.
[5] Sura 90:v. 12.

and the eating of pork. Christianity was also an exceedingly important source. Mohammed considered the New Testament as well
as the Old to be a divinely inspired book, and he regarded Jesus as
one of the greatest of a long line of prophets. Besides, the Mohammedan doctrines of the resurrection of the body, the last judgment,
rewards and punishments after death, and the belief in angels were
more probably derived from Christianity than from any other system of belief. On the other hand, it is necessary to remember that
the Christianity with which Mohammed was acquainted was far from
being the orthodox variety. Nearly all of the Christians who lived
in Syria as well as those in Arabia itself were Ebionites or Nestorians.
It is perhaps for this reason that Mohammed always thought of Jesus
as human, the son of Joseph and Mary, and not as a god.

It was not long after the origin of Islam until its followers split
into a number of sects not entirely dissimilar to some of the offshoots
of Christianity. The three most important of the Moslem sects were *The principal*
the Sunnites, the Shiites, and the Sufis. The first two had a political *Mohammedan*
as well as a religious character. The Sunnites maintained that the *sects*
head of the Islamic state and successor to the Prophet should be
elected by representatives of the whole body of believers, in accordance with the ancient Arabian custom of election of tribal chiefs.
In matters of religion they contended that the *sunna*, or traditions
which had grown up outside of the Koran, should be accepted as a
valid source of belief. The Shiites were opposed to the elevation
of anyone to the highest political and religious office who was not
related to the Prophet himself, either by blood or by marriage. In
general, they represented the absolutist ideal in Islam as distinct from
the democratic ideal of the Sunnites. What is more, the Shiites were
against the acceptance of anything but the Koran as a source of religious belief. The Sufis adhered to a mystical and ascetic ideal.
Denying absolutely the validity of rational judgment, they maintained that the only truth worth anything is that which proceeds
from divine revelation. They believed that it is possible for man to
partake of this divine revelation through torturing his body and
thereby releasing the soul for a mystic union with God. Many of
the fakirs and dervishes in India and Persia today are members of
the Sufi sect.

The political history of the Saracenic civilization is closely interwoven with the growth of the religion. As we have already seen,
Mohammed became the founder not merely of a religion but also of *Political history*
an Arabic state with its capital at Medina. Following his death in *of the Islamic*
632 his companions chose as his successor Abu-Bekr, one of the *state: the caliphs*
earliest converts to the faith and the father-in-law of Mohammed.
The new ruler was given the title of *caliph*, that is, successor to the
Prophet. After Abu-Bekr's death two other caliphs were chosen in
succession from among the earlier disciples of Mohammed. In 656,
however, a long struggle began for possession of the supreme power **287**

in Islam. First the Shiites succeeded in deposing a member of the Ommiad family and in electing Ali, the husband of Mohammed's daughter Fatima, as caliph. Five years later Ali was murdered, and the Ommiads came back into power. Soon afterward they transferred the capital to Damascus and established their family as a reigning dynasty with a luxurious court in imitation of the Byzantine model. In 750 the Shiites revolted again, this time under the leadership of a member of the Abbasid family who was a distant relative of the Prophet. The Abbasids seized the throne and moved the capital to the city of Bagdad on the Tigris River, where they ruled as Oriental despots for more than three centuries. A few of them were enlightened patrons of learning, especially Harun-al-Raschid (786–809) and Al-Mamun (813–33).

The Saracenic conquests

In the meantime, a great wave of Saracenic expansion had swept over Asia, Africa, and Europe. When Mohammed died in 632, the authority of his little state probably did not extend over more than one-third of the Arabian peninsula. A hundred years later nearly half of the civilized world was under Moslem domination. The Saracenic empire extended from the borders of India to the Strait of Gibraltar and the Pyrenees Mountains. One after another with startling rapidity, Persia, Syria, Egypt, North Africa, and Spain had been conquered. How can this prodigious expansion be explained? Contrary to common belief, it was not the result primarily of religious ardor. The Saracens were not engaged in a great crusade to impose their beliefs upon the rest of the world. Naturally there were outbreaks of fanaticism from time to time, but as a general rule the Moslems of this period did not really care very much whether the nations they conquered accepted their religion or not. Subject peoples were usually quite leniently treated. As long as they refrained from the possession of arms and paid the tribute levied upon them, they were permitted to retain their own beliefs and customs. Jews and Christians lived unmolested in the Moslem empire for centuries, and some of them rose to positions of prominence in political and intellectual circles.

Reasons for the success of the Saracens as conquerors

In truth, economic and political factors were much more important than religion in causing the Saracenic expansion. First of all, it must be borne in mind that the majority of the Arabs were a prolific race of nomads. Since the men were polygamists, the occasional practice of infanticide was far from sufficient to prevent a rapid increase in population. Arabia, moreover, was suffering from a serious drought, which extended over a number of years shortly after the beginning of the seventh century. Oases which had formerly provided good crops of dates and good pasturage for flocks and herds were gradually being absorbed by the surrounding desert. Discontent among the famished tribes increased to such a point that they would probably have seized upon almost any excuse to plunder neighboring countries. The initial attacks upon Byzantine territory

appear to have grown out of a revolt of Arab mercenaries in Syria.
The leaders of the rebellion appealed to the followers of the Prophet
in Medina, who already had some reputation for military prowess
as a result of their conquest of Mecca. The outcome of this appeal
was a great wave of military invasion which soon made the Arabs
masters not merely of Syria, but also of Persia, Palestine, and Egypt.
Finally, it should be noted that the conquests of the Moslems were
facilitated by the fact that the Byzantine and Persian empires had
fought each other to the point of exhaustion in the previous century,
and their governments were now attempting to replenish their treas-
uries by heavier taxation. As a consequence, many of the inhabitants
of these empires were disposed to welcome the Arabs as deliverers.

The decline of the Saracenic empire was almost as swift as its rise.
The Arabs themselves lacked political experience, and, besides, the
empire they conquered was too vast in extent and composed of too *The decline of*
heterogeneous a mixture of peoples ever to be welded into a strong *the Islamic*
and cohesive political unit. But a more powerful reason for its down- *empire*
fall was sectarian and factional strife. Sunnites and Shiites were never
able to reconcile their differences, and widening cleavages between
the mystics and rationalists also helped to weaken the religion, which
was the basis of the state. In 929 members of the Ommiad family
succeeded in establishing an independent caliphate at Cordova in
Spain. Soon afterward descendants of Ali and Fatima proclaimed
themselves independent rulers of Morocco and Egypt. Meanwhile
the caliphs at Bagdad were gradually succumbing to the debilitating
effects of Oriental customs. Aping the practices of Eastern monarchs,
they retired more and more into the seclusion of the palace and soon
became the puppets of their Persian viziers and later of their Turkish
mercenary troops. In 1057 they surrendered all of their temporal
power to the Sultan of the Seljuk Turks, who two years before had
taken possession of Bagdad. For all practical purposes this marked
the extinction of the Saracenic empire, although much of the territory continued to be ruled by peoples who had adopted the Moslem faith—the Seljuk Turks until the middle of the twelfth century
and the Ottoman Turks from the fifteenth century to 1918.

The intellectual achievements of the Saracens were far superior
to any of which Christian Europe could boast before the twelfth
century. The explanation can be found partly in the energy and con- *The intellectual*
fidence of the Saracens themselves, but it is related also to the fact *achievements of*
that in conquering Persia and Syria they came into possession of a *the Saracens*
brilliant intellectual heritage. In both of these countries traditions of
Greek learning had survived. Numerous physicians of Greek nationality had been attracted to the court of the Persian kings, while
in Syria there were excellent schools of philosophy and rhetoric and
several libraries filled with copies of writings of the Hellenic philosophers, scientists, and poets. Of course, it would be foolish to suppose that very many of the Arabs themselves were able to appreciate **289**

this cultural heritage; their mission was rather to provide the encouragement and the facilities for others to make use of it.

Saracenic philosophy was essentially a compound of Aristotelianism and Neo-Platonism. Its basic teachings may be set forth as follows: Reason is superior to faith as a source of knowledge; the doctrines of religion are not to be discarded entirely, but should be interpreted by the enlightened mind in a figurative or allegorical sense; when thus interpreted they can be made to yield a pure philosophical knowledge which is not in conflict with reason but supplementary to it. The universe never had a beginning in time but is created eternally; it is a series of emanations from God. Everything that happens is predetermined by God; every event is a link in an unbroken chain of cause and effect; both miracles and divine providence are therefore impossible. Although God is the First Cause of all things, He is not omnipotent; His power is limited by justice and goodness. There is no immortality for the individual soul, for no spiritual substance can exist apart from its material embodiment; only the soul of the universe goes on forever, since matter itself is eternal.

The development of Saracenic philosophy was limited to two brief periods of brilliance: the ninth and tenth centuries in the Bagdad caliphate and the twelfth century in Spain. Among the philosophers in the East three great names stand out—Al Kindi, Al Farabi, and Avicenna. The first of them died about 870, and the last was born in 980. All of them seem to have been of Turkish or Persian nationality. In the eleventh century, under the leadership of Algazel, Saracenic philosophy in the East degenerated into religious fundamentalism and mysticism. Like the Sufis, from whom he derived a great many of his doctrines, Algazel denied the competence of reason and urged a reliance upon faith and revelation. After his time philosophy died out in the Bagdad caliphate. The most renowned of the philosophers in the West, and probably the greatest of all the Saracenic thinkers, was Averroës of Cordova (1126–98). His influence upon the Christian Scholastics of the thirteenth century was especially profound.

In no subject were the Saracens farther advanced than in science. In fact, their achievements in this field were the best the world had seen since the end of the Hellenistic civilization. The Saracens were brilliant astronomers, mathematicians, physicists, chemists, and physicians. Despite their reverence for Aristotle, they did not hesitate to criticize his notion of a universe of concentric spheres with the earth at the center, and they admitted the possibility that the earth rotates on its axis and revolves around the sun. Their celebrated poet, Omar Khayyám, developed one of the most accurate calendars ever devised by the mind of man. The Saracens were also capable mathematicians and developed algebra and trigonometry considerably beyond the stage they had reached in Hellenistic times. While they did not invent the celebrated "Arabic" system of numerals, they were nevertheless responsible for adapting it from the Indian system and making it available to the West. Saracenic physicists founded the science of optics and drew a number of significant conclusions regarding the theory of magnifying lenses and the velocity, transmission, and refraction of light. As is commonly known, the chemistry of the Moslems was an outgrowth of alchemy, that famous pseudo-science which was based upon the principle that all the metals were the same in essence, and that baser metals could therefore be transmuted into gold if only the right instrument, the philosopher's stone, could be found. But the efforts of scientists in this field were by no means confined to this fruitless quest. Some even denied the whole theory of transmutation of metals. As a result of innumerable experiments by chemists and alchemists alike, various new substances and compounds were discovered; among them carbonate of soda, alum, borax, bichloride of mercury, nitrate of silver, saltpeter, and nitric and sulphuric acids. In addition, Moslem scientists were the first to describe the chemical processes of distillation, filtration, and sublimation.

The accomplishments in medicine were just as remarkable. Saracenic physicians appropriated the knowledge contained in the medical writings of the Hellenistic Age; but some of them at least were not content with that. Avicenna discovered the contagious nature of tuberculosis, described pleurisy and several varieties of nervous ailments, and pointed out that disease can be spread through contamination of water and soil. His chief medical writing, the *Canon*, was venerated in Europe as an authoritative work until late in the seventeenth century. Avicenna's older contemporary, Rhazes, was the greatest clinical physician of the medieval world. His supreme achievement was the discovery of the true nature of smallpox. Other Moslem physicians discovered the value of cauterization and of styptic agents, diagnosed cancer of the stomach, prescribed antidotes for cases of poisoning, and made notable progress in treatment of diseases of the eyes. In addition, they recognized the highly infectious character of the plague, pointing out that it could be transmitted by garments, by eating utensils and drinking cups, as well as by personal contact. Finally, the Saracens excelled all other medieval peoples in the organization of hospitals and in the control of medical practice. Authentic information is on record of at least thirty-four great hospitals located in the principal cities of Persia, Syria, and Egypt. They appear to have been organized in a strikingly modern fashion. Each had its wards for particular cases, its dispensary, and its library. The chief physicians and surgeons lectured to the students and graduates, examined them, and issued diplomas or licenses to practice. Even the owners of leeches, who in most cases were also barbers, had to submit them for inspection at regular intervals.

Saracenic contributions to medicine

So far as literature was concerned, the Saracens derived their inspiration almost entirely from Persia. If they knew anything about the classic poetry of the Greeks, they evidently found it of little in-

*Saracenic liter-
ature*

terest. As a result, their own writings are colorful, imaginative, sensuous, and romantic; but with a few exceptions they make no very strong appeal to the intellect. The best-known examples of their poetry are the *Book of Kings* by Al-Firdausi (935–1020) and the *Rubáiyát* by Omar Khayyám (*ca.* 1048–*ca.* 1124). The *Book of Kings* is not a work dealing with any theme of Moslem civilization, but is an epic celebrating the glories of the medieval Persian empire. Nevertheless, its 60,000 verses were written under the patronage of Moslem rulers. The *Rubáiyát*, as it is preserved for us in the translation by Edward Fitzgerald, also appears to reflect the qualities of an effete Persian culture much more than the ideals of the Arabs themselves. Its philosophy of mechanism, skepticism, and hedonism is quite similar to that of the Book of Ecclesiastes in the Old Testament. The most famous example of Saracenic literature in prose is the so-called *Arabian Nights*, or *Book of the 1001 Nights*, written mainly during the eighth and ninth centuries. The material of the collection includes fables, anecdotes, household tales, and stories of erotic adventures derived from the literatures of various nations from China to Egypt. The chief significance of the collection of tales is to be found in the picture they present of the sophisticated life of the Moslems in the best days of the Bagdad caliphate.

*The eclectic art
of the Saracens*

Since the Arabs themselves had scarcely any more of an artistic background than the Hebrews, it was necessary that the art of the Moslem civilization should be an eclectic product. Its primary sources were Byzantium and Persia. From the former came many of the structural features of the architecture, especially the dome, the column, and the arch. Persian influence was probably responsible for the intricate, non-naturalistic designs which were used as decorative *motifs* in practically all of the arts. From both Persia and Byzantium came the tendency to subordinate form to rich and sensuous color. Architecture is generally considered the most important of the Saracenic arts, inasmuch as the development of both painting and sculpture was inhibited by religious prejudice against representation

The Court of the Lions in the Alhambra, Granada, Spain. The palace-fortress of the Alhambra is one of the finest monuments to Moslem artistic talent. Notable are the graceful columns, the horseshoe arches, and the delicate tracery in stone which surmounts the arches.

Stained Glass, German, *ca.* 1300. Some stained-glass windows were purely decorative; others told a story. (MMA)

Building Operations. From a French picture Bible, *ca.* 1250. Note the treadmill, with wheel, ropes, and pulley, by means of which a basket of stones is brought to the construction level. (Morgan Library)

Gothic Virgin, French, XIII cent. The Queen of Heaven here is a gentle, understanding mother. (MMA)

Siege of a City. From the *Universal Chronicle* by Jean de Courcy, Flemish, *ca.* 1470. The cannon meant the end of feudal knights and medieval towered fortresses. (Morgan Library)

Vespers of the Holy Ghost, with a View of Paris, Jean Fouquet. From the Book of Hours of Etienne Chevalier, 1461. Demons in the sky are sent flying by the divine light from Heaven. The cathedral is Notre Dame. (Robert Lehman)

A Scholar at Work. From the Flemish manuscript The Golden Legend, 1445–1460. This beautiful book came at the end of the era of costly handwritten, hand-decorated manuscripts. (Morgan Library)

of the human form. By no means all of the examples of this architecture were mosques or churches; many were palaces, schools, libraries, private mansions, and hospitals. Indeed, Saracenic architecture had a much more decidedly secular character than any in medieval Europe. Among its principal elements were bulbous domes, minarets, horseshoe arches, and twisted columns, together with the use of tracery in stone, alternating stripes of black and white, mosaics, and Arabic script as decorative devices. As in the Byzantine style, comparatively little attention was given to exterior ornamentation. The so-called minor arts of the Moslems included the weaving of gorgeous pile carpets and rugs, magnificent leather tooling, and the making of brocaded silks and tapestries, inlaid metal work, enameled glassware, and painted pottery. Most of the products of these arts were embellished with complicated patterns of interlacing geometric designs, plants and fruits and flowers, Arabic script, and fantastic animal creatures. The richness and variety of these works of art, produced in defiance of a religion which often displayed a puritanical trend, afford most convincing proof of the vitality of Moslem civilization.

The economic development of the Saracenic civilization remains to this day one of the marvels of history. In areas which had produced practically nothing for centuries, the Moslems literally made the desert to blossom as the rose. Where only squalid villages encumbered the landscape, they built magnificent cities. The products of their industries were known from China to France and from the interior of Africa to the shores of the Baltic. As the builders of a vast commercial empire, they excelled the Carthaginians. The reasons for this astounding economic development do not lend themselves to easy explanation. Perhaps it was due in some measure to the long experience with trade which many of the Arabs had had in their homeland. When a wider field opened up, they made the most of their skill. The diffusion of the Arabic language over a vast expanse of territory also helped to extend the avenues of trade. In addition, the great variety of resources in the various sections of the empire served to stimulate exchange of the products of one region for those of another. The principal reason, however, was probably the energy of the conquerors themselves, together with their spirit of adventure, which led them to explore every possibility of increasing their wealth and power. They did not hesitate to take risks or to penetrate into unknown regions. They were among the boldest mariners and explorers who had yet appeared on the scene of history.

The economic development of the Islamic empire

Commerce and manufacturing were the main foundations of the national wealth. Both were developed in extraordinary degree. The Saracens made use of a great many of the instruments of commerce familiar to the modern world: checks, receipts, bills of lading, letters of credit, trade associations, joint-stock companies, and various others. Moslem merchants penetrated into southern Russia and even

Commerce and industry

293

into the equatorial regions of Africa. Caravans of thousands of camels traveled overland to the gates of India and China. Moslem ships furrowed new paths across the Indian Ocean, the Persian Gulf, and the Caspian Sea. Except for the Aegean Sea and the route from Venice to Constantinople, the Saracens dominated the Mediterranean almost as if it were a private lake. But so vast an expansion of commerce would scarcely have been possible without a corresponding development of industry; for it was the ability of the people of one region to turn their natural resources into finished products for sale to other regions which provided a basis for a large part of the trade. Nearly every one of the great cities specialized in some particular variety of manufactures. Mosul was a center of the manufacture of cotton cloth; Bagdad specialized in glassware, jewelry, pottery, and silks; Damascus was famous for its fine steel and for its "damask," or woven-figured silk; Morocco was noted for the manufacture of leather; and Toledo for its excellent swords. The products of these cities, of course, did not exhaust the list of Saracenic manufactures. Drugs, perfumes, carpets, tapestries, brocades, woolens, satins, metal products, and a host of others were turned out by the craftsmen of many cities. From the Chinese the Moslems learned the art of paper-making, and the products of that industry were in great demand, not only in the empire itself but in Europe as well. The men engaged in the various industries were organized into guilds, over which the government exercised only a general supervision for the prevention of fraudulent practices. For the most part, the guilds themselves regulated the conduct of business by their own members. Control by the state over economic affairs was much less rigid than in the Byzantine Empire.

Agriculture

From what has been said about commerce and industry, it must not be assumed that agriculture was neglected in the Moslem empire. On the contrary, the Saracens developed farming to as high a level as any other people of the medieval world. They repaired and extended the irrigation systems originally built by the Egyptians, the Sumerians, and the Babylonians. They terraced the slopes of the mountains in Spain in order to plant them with vineyards, and here as elsewhere they converted many barren wastes into highly productive lands by means of irrigation. Experts attached to the imperial palaces and the mansions of the rich devoted much attention to ornamental gardening, to the cultivation of shrubs and flowers of rare beauty and delightful fragrance. The variety of products of the Moslem farms and orchards almost passes belief. Cotton, sugar, flax, rice, wheat, spinach, asparagus, apricots, peaches, lemons, and olives were cultivated as standard crops almost everywhere, while bananas, coffee, and oranges were grown in the warmer regions. Some of the farms were great estates, worked in part by serfs and slaves and in part by free peasants as tenants, but the major portion of the land was divided into small holdings cultivated by the owners themselves.

ISLAM AND
THE SARACENIC
CIVILIZATION

*The intellectual
and artistic in-
fluence of the
Saracenic civ-
ilization*

The influence of the Saracenic civilization upon medieval Europe and upon the Renaissance was almost incalculable; and some of that influence has, of course, persisted until the present time. The philosophy of the Saracens was almost as important as Christianity in providing a basis for the Scholastic thought of the thirteenth century; for it was the Moslems who made available to the West most of the works of Aristotle and indicated more thoroughly than ever before the use to which those writings could be put as a support for religious doctrine. The scientific achievements of the Moslems furnished even more enduring contributions. The list of these contributions includes the Hindu-Arabic system of numerals, the science of algebra, such medical discoveries as the fact of contagion and the nature of smallpox and measles, innumerable drugs and compounds, and the chemical processes of sublimation and filtration. Though the activity of the Saracens in literature was hardly as extensive as in science, their literary influence has been decidedly important. The songs of the troubadours and some other examples of the love poetry of medieval France were directly inspired by Saracenic writings. Some of the stories in the *Book of the 1001 Nights*

Interior of the Great Mosque at Cordoba, Spain. This splendid specimen of Moorish architecture gives an excellent view of the cusped arches and alternating stripes of black and white so commonly used by Moslem architects.

found their way into Boccaccio's *Decameron* and Chaucer's *Canterbury Tales*, while Firdausi's *Book of Kings* furnished the nineteenth-century English writer, Matthew Arnold, with the material for his story of *Sohrab and Rustum*. The art of the Saracens has likewise had an influence of deep significance, especially upon Gothic architecture. A surprisingly large number of the elements in the design of Gothic cathedrals were apparently derived from the mosques and palaces of the Moslems. A partial list would include the cusped arches, the traceried windows, the pointed arch, the use of script and arabesques as decorative devices, and possibly ribbed vaulting. The architecture of late medieval castles was even more closely copied from the design of Moslem buildings, especially the fortresses of Syria.[6]

[6] For a more complete discussion of the influence of Saracenic literature and art, see Arnold and Guillaume, eds., *The Legacy of Islam*.

Finally, the Saracens exerted a profound influence upon the economic development of late medieval and early modern Europe. The revival of trade which took place in western Europe in the eleventh, twelfth, and thirteenth centuries would scarcely have been possible without the development of Moslem industry and agriculture to stimulate the demand for new products in the West. From the Moslems, western Europeans acquired a knowledge of the compass, the astrolabe, the art of making paper, and possibly the production of silk, although knowledge of the last may have been obtained somewhat earlier from the Byzantine Empire. Furthermore, it seems probable that the development by the Moslems of the joint-stock company, checks, letters of credit, and other aids to business transactions had much to do with the beginning of the Commercial Revolution in Europe about 1400. Perhaps the extent of Saracenic economic influence is most clearly revealed in the enormous number of words now in common usage which were originally of Arabic or Persian origin. Among them are "traffic," "tariff," "risk," "check," "magazine," "alcohol," "cipher," "zero," "algebra," "muslin," and "bazaar."

Selected Readings

Ameer Ali, Syed, *The Spirit of Islam*, London, 1922
Arnold, Thomas, and Guillaume, Alfred, eds., *The Legacy of Islam*, New York, 1931
Byron, Robert, *The Byzantine Achievement*, New York, 1929
Dawson, C. H., *The Making of Europe*, New York, 1932
De Boer, T. J., *History of Philosophy in Islam*, London, 1903
Diehl, Charles, *History of the Byzantine Empire*, New Brunswick, N.J., 1956
Goldziher, Ignaz, *Mohammed and Islam*, New Haven, 1917
Hitti, P. K., *The Arabs, A Short History*, Princeton, 1946
Margoliouth, D. S., *Mohammed and the Rise of Islam*, New York, 1927
Pirenne, Henri, *Mohammed and Charlemagne*, New York, 1939
Runciman, Steven, *Byzantine Civilization*, New York, 1933
Sarton, George, *An Introduction to the History of Science*, Baltimore, 1927, Vol. I
Thompson, J. W., *Economic and Social History of the Middle Ages*, New York, 1928, Chs. VI, VII, XIV, XV
Vasiliev, A. A., *History of the Byzantine Empire*, Madison, Wisconsin, 1928-29, 2 vols.

Source Materials

Dewing, H. B., tr., *Procopius: History of the Wars*, 5 vols.
Poole, Lane, ed., *Speeches and Table Talk of the Prophet Mohammed*
Sanders, T. C., tr., *The Institutes of Justinian*
The Koran

The Later Middle Ages
and the Renaissance

By no means all of medieval history in western Europe was characterized by stagnation and barbarism. It cannot be too strongly emphasized that the period which used to be called the Dark Ages did not really extend beyond 800. Soon after that date there were several movements of intellectual awakening which culminated finally in a brilliant flowering of culture in the twelfth and thirteenth centuries. In fact, so remarkable was the progress in western Europe from the ninth century to the end of the thirteenth that the achievements of that period can justifiably be called a new civilization. While some of these achievements were discarded during the subsequent period of the Renaissance, quite a few were preserved and have exerted their influence to the present day. Indeed, the civilization of the later Middle Ages, or the Feudal Age, and that of the Renaissance had more in common than is usually suspected. Both were distinguished by humanism, by a new interest in man as the most important creature in the universe. Both were concerned very largely with affairs of this world as opposed to the other-worldliness of the early Middle Ages. In the Feudal Age and the Renaissance alike there was a tendency to glorify the life of adventure and of conquest in place of the early Christian ideals of humility and self-effacement. Finally, it should be noted that the Renaissance ideal of reverence for the classics of Greek and Latin literature really had its origin in the Feudal Age.

	Europe as a Whole	Southern Europe	Northern Europe
800—	Feudalism develops, 800–1300 Treaty of Verdun, 843 Rise of papal monarchy, 850–1000 Scholasticism, 850–1300 Cluny movement, 950–1100 Romanesque architecture, 1000–1150 Revival of trade with the East, 1050–1150 Struggle between secular and spiritual powers, 1050–1350 Separation between Eastern and Western churches, 1054 Establishment of the College of Cardinals, 1059 The Crusades, 1096–1204 Rise of merchant and craft guilds, 1100–1300 Growth of cities, 1100–1300 Development of the sacramental system of the church, 1100–1300 First universities, *ca.* 1150 Gothic architecture, 1150–1300		Unification of England under Saxon kings, 802– Founding of national monarchy in France, 987 Norman Conquest of England, 1066 Romances of chivalry, 1100–1300 Holy Roman (Hohenstaufen) Empire, 1152–1254
1200—	Orders of friars, 1200– Fourth Lateran Council, 1215	St. Francis of Assisi, 1182–1226 Dante, 1265–1321	Roger Bacon, 1214?–1294 Magna Charta, 1215 St. Thomas Aquinas, 1225?–1274? Origin of Parliament in England, 1265–1295 Hanseatic League, 1300–1500
	Feudalism declines, 1300–1500 Rise of capitalism, 1300–1500 Growth of banking and development of money economy, 1300–1600 Black Death, 1347	Boccaccio, 1313–1375 Savonarola, 1452–1498 Leonardo da Vinci, 1452–1519 Machiavelli, 1469–1527 Michelangelo, 1475–1564 Unification of Spain, 1492 Cervantes, 1547–1616	Establishment of Estates-General in France, 1302 Hundred Years' War, 1337–1453 Christian Renaissance, 1400–1500 War of the Roses in England, 1455–1485 Erasmus, 1466?–1536 Copernicus, 1473–1543 Tudor dynasty in England, 1485–1603 Montaigne, 1533–1592 Sir Francis Bacon, 1561–1626
1600—		Galileo, 1564–1642	Shakespeare, 1564–1616 Sir William Harvey, 1578–1657

The Civilization of the Feudal Age: Political and Economic Institutions

Long before the famous Renaissance of the fourteenth and succeeding centuries, western Europe began slowly to emerge from
the ignorance and barbarism of the Dark Ages. The start of this
gradual awakening can be dated as far back as 800 A.D. During the
five or six centuries that followed, the people of Latin Christendom
cast off at least some of their winter garments of repentance and
otherworldliness and put on the less restrictive attire of the man
who is determined to live in this world and mold his environment to
his own advantage. The causes of this change in attitude were many
and various: the influence of contact with the Saracenic and Byzantine civilizations, the increase in economic security, the revitalizing
effects of the Norse invasions, and the influence of monastic education. Later on, the revival of trade in the eleventh and twelfth centuries and the growth of cities led to an increase in prosperity and
sophistication which greatly stimulated the progress of enlightenment. The results of these several causes were reflected in a brilliant
intellectual and artistic civilization which reached the zenith of its
development in the thirteenth century. Probably the most distinctive
element in the social and political structure of this civilization was
the feudal regime; hence we can justifiably speak of this culture as
the civilization of the Feudal Age. We must not overlook the fact,
however, that from the twelfth century on the role of the commercial and industrial classes in the cities was an exceedingly important one.

*The cultural re-
vival of the
Feudal Age*

299

1. The Origins of the Feudal Regime

Feudalism may be defined as a decentralized structure of society in which the powers of government are exercised by private barons over persons economically dependent upon them. It is a system of overlordship and vassalage in which the right to govern is conceived as a property right belonging to anyone who is the holder of a fief. The relationship between the overlord and his vassals is a contractual relationship involving reciprocal obligations. In return for the protection and economic assistance they receive, the vassals are bound to obey their lord or suzerain, to serve him faithfully, and generally to compensate him by dues or taxes for the services he renders in their interest. Defined in this fashion, feudalism was not limited to the late Middle Ages. Examples of it had existed in several other periods of world history—in many parts of the Roman Empire, for instance, and throughout the early Middle Ages. Late medieval feudalism, however, differed from the earlier specimens in being a legally recognized framework of society. Men did not apologize for it as a crude substitute for centralized government but glorified it as an ideal system, much as we idealize democracy and the national state at the present time.

How did late medieval feudalism originate? To some extent it was the outgrowth of ancient Roman institutions. One of these was

clientage. From very early times Roman citizens who had fallen upon evil days had sought the protection of wealthy patrons, becoming their clients or personal dependents. During the confusion that accompanied the decline of the Empire, clientage was greatly extended. A second of these Roman institutions was the *colonate*. In a desperate attempt to check the decline of agricultural production during the economic revolution of the third and fourth centuries, the government of the Empire bound many of the agricultural laborers and tenants to the soil as *coloni* or serfs, and in effect placed them under the control of the proprietors of large estates. Another institution which developed in the declining stage of the Roman Empire was *precarium*. Originally the *precarium* was a lease of land to a tenant who would cultivate it and pay rent to the owner. If at any time the tenant failed to pay his rent, the owner had the right to evict him. Later the *precarium* frequently assumed the form of the surrender of land by a small owner to a powerful magnate because of indebtedness or need of protection. At the same time the small farmer would bind himself to cultivate the land and to pay rent for its use. The last two of these institutions, the *colonate* and the *precarium*, had much to do with the growth of an extralegal feudalism in late Roman history, since they increased the wealth and importance of the great landed proprietors. As time went on, the tendency of these men was to ignore or defy the central government and to arrogate to themselves the powers of sovereign rulers over their estates. They levied taxes upon their dependents, made laws for the regulation of their affairs, and administered what passed for justice.

Late medieval feudalism was also derived in large part from significant economic and political developments of the early Middle Ages. One of these was the growth of the institution of *beneficium*, which seems to have been developed by the church as a modification of *precarium*. *Beneficium* consisted in the grant of a *benefice*, or the right to use land in return for rent or services. In the seventh century the Merovingian kings adopted the practice of rewarding their counts and dukes with benefices, thereby cementing a bond between public office and landholding. Not long afterward Charles Martel and the Carolingian kings resorted to the granting of benefices to local nobles in return for furnishing mounted troops to fight against the Moors. The result was to increase the dependence of the central government upon the principal landowners throughout the country. The bestowal of *immunities* by the Frankish kings upon some of the holders of benefices also accelerated the growth of a feudal regime. The immunities were exemptions of the lands of a secular or ecclesiastical noble from the jurisdiction of the king's agents. The natural outcome was the exercise of public authority by the noble himself as a virtually independent sovereign, subject only to the nominal overlordship of the king. The other most important development in the early Middle Ages which hastened the growth of a feudal organization of society was the invasions of the Norsemen, the Magyars, and the Moslems. In the eighth and ninth centuries these peoples began making swift incursions into the settled portions of western Europe, plundering the richer areas and occasionally massacring the inhabitants. The attacks of the Norsemen in particular were widely feared. As a consequence, many small farmers who had hitherto maintained their independence now sought the protection of their more powerful neighbors, who frequently had armed retainers and strongholds in which men could take refuge.

Church institutions

Carolingian institutions

The need for defense

But feudalism would never have acquired the special character which it came to possess in the later Middle Ages if it had not been for the Germanic influence. For it was the Germans who provided the ideals of honor, loyalty, and freedom which came to occupy a place of considerable importance in the system. Mention has already been made of the Germanic institution of the *comitatus* as a source of feudal theory and practice. The *comitatus* was a band of warriors and their chief united by mutual obligations of service and loyalty. Though the warriors took a personal oath to protect and defend their chief, and he in return agreed to provide them with horses and weapons, the relationship between the two parties was altogether different from that which existed between the Roman clients and their patron. No element of servility was present in it at all; the warriors were practically the equals of their chief, since all were engaged in the same activities of fighting for glory and plunder.

Germanic institutions

This ideal of a relationship of honor and loyalty in the *comitatus* later found its way into feudalism, so far as the relation between lords and vassals was concerned. The feudal practice of *commendation*, by which vassals swore fealty in a ceremony of homage to their suzerain, was also probably an outgrowth of the *comitatus*. Finally, the feudal conception of law as a product of custom instead of authority, and as the personal possession of the individual which he could take with him wherever he went, is likewise traceable to Germanic influence.

2. Feudalism as a Political and Economic Structure

Feudalism as a system of government

As a system of government, feudalism embodied a number of basic conceptions. First of all, as we have seen, it included the notion that the right to govern was a privilege belonging to any man who was the holder of a fief; but it was a privilege entailing very definite obligations, the violation of which might be followed by loss of the fief. Secondly, it included the notion that all government rests upon contract. Rulers must agree to govern justly in accordance with the laws, both human and divine. Subjects must pledge themselves to obey so long as their rulers govern justly. If either party violates the contract, the other is absolved from his obligations and has the right to take action for redress. In the third place, feudalism was based upon the ideal of limited sovereignty, upon opposition to absolute authority no matter by whom it might be exercised. Feudal government was supposed to be a government of laws and not of men. No ruler, regardless of his rank, had any right to impose his personal will upon his subjects in accordance with the dictates of his own whims. Indeed, under feudal theory, no ruler had the right to make law at all; law was the product of custom or of the will of God. The authority of the king or the baron was limited to the issuance of what might be called administrative decrees to carry the law into effect. Whether the ideals of feudalism were carried out any less successfully in practice than the ideals of political systems generally is a question very hard to answer. Doubtless most people, with their prejudices against everything medieval, would answer it in the affirmative. Yet revolts against oppression were not of very frequent occurrence in the late Middle Ages, notwithstanding the fact that the existence of the *right* to revolt against a ruler who had made himself a tyrant was commonly taught.

Fiefs, vassals, and overlords

Not only in theory but in practice the feudal regime was a system of overlordship and vassalage based upon the granting and holding of fiefs. In the main, a fief was a benefice which had become hereditary. It was not always an area of land, however; it might also be an office or position or the right to collect tolls at a bridge or even the right to coin money or to establish markets and enjoy the profits therefrom. The man who granted the fief was a lord or suzerain,

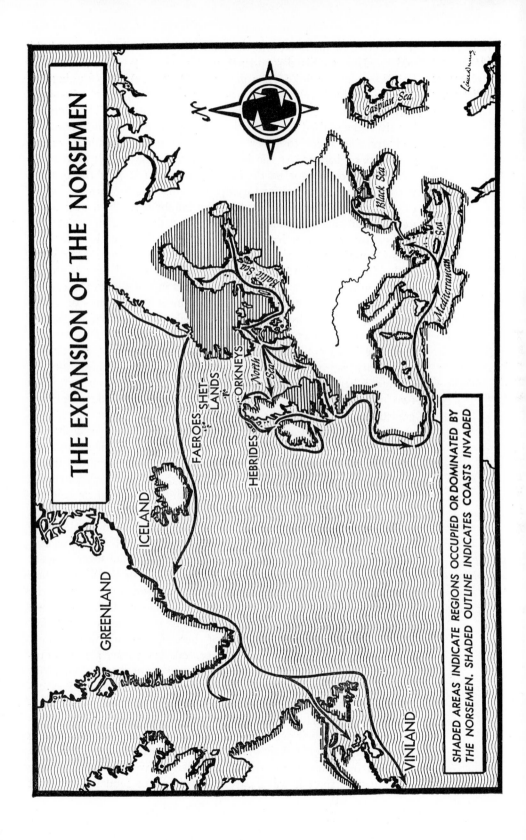

THE EXPANSION OF THE NORSEMEN

GREENLAND

ICELAND

FAEROES

SHET-
LANDS

ORKNEYS

HEBRIDES

North Sea

Baltic Sea

Black Sea

Caspian Sea

Mediterranean

VINLAND

SHADED AREAS INDICATE REGIONS OCCUPIED OR DOMINATED BY
THE NORSEMEN. SHADED OUTLINE INDICATES COASTS INVADED

irrespective of his rank; and the man who received the fief to hold and transmit to his descendants was a vassal, whether he was a knight, count, or duke. As a general rule, the king was the highest suzerain. Immediately below him were the great nobles, who were variously known as dukes, counts, earls, or margraves. These nobles in turn had acquired vassals of their own through dividing their fiefs and granting them to lesser nobles, who were commonly called viscounts or barons. At the bottom of the scale were the knights, whose fiefs could not be divided. Thus, according to the general pattern of things, every lord except the king was the vassal of some other lord, and every vassal except the knight was a lord over other vassals. But this apparently logical and orderly arrangement was broken by numerous irregularities. There were vassals who held fiefs from a number of different lords, not all of them of the same rank. There were lords some of whose vassals held fiefs from the same overlord as they themselves did. And in some cases there were kings who actually held fiefs from certain of their counts or dukes and were therefore to some extent vassals of their own vassals.

*Feudalism not
the same in all
countries*

Moreover, the fact must be borne in mind that feudalism was not the same in all countries of western Europe. Many of its features commonly assumed to have been universal were found only in France, where the system was most fully developed, or in one or two other countries at the most. For example, the rule of primogeniture, under which the fief descended intact to the oldest son, was not in force in Germany; nor were social distinctions so sharply defined there as in France. Furthermore, not all of the lands and not all of the inhabitants of any European country were included under the feudal regime. Most of the farmers in the hilly and mountainous regions of France, Italy, and Germany did not hold their lands as fiefs but owned them outright, as their ancestors had for centuries.

*Feudal rights
and obligations*

Each member of the feudal nobility was involved in an elaborate network of rights and obligations which varied with his status as a suzerain or a vassal. The most important rights of the suzerain were the right to serve as legal guardian in case any of the fiefs he had granted should be inherited by a minor; the right of escheat, or the right to take back the fief of a vassal who had died without heirs; and the right of forfeiture, or the right to confiscate a vassal's fief for violation of contract. The last of these rights could be exercised, however, only after the vassal had been condemned by a court composed of his equals. There were two very important obligations which every suzerain was supposed to perform. First, he was expected to render military assistance to his vassals in warding off attacks by their enemies; and second, he was required to aid his vassals in righting their wrongs, which usually meant the summoning of a court to decide their grievances. The suzerain himself merely presided over this court; the actual decision was rendered by the other vassals, since it was a cardinal principle of feudal justice that no noble could be tried except by his peers. Aside from this privilege of being judged only by his equals, the noble in his capacity as a vassal had only one other important right. That was the right to repudiate his lord for acts of injustice or failure to provide adequate protection. But the obligations of the vassal were more numerous. He must render military service for a certain number of days each year, attend the lord's court, ransom his lord if he were captured, and pay a heavy tax if he inherited or sold a fief.

Feudal society was, of course, highly aristocratic. It was a regime of status, not of individual initiative. In almost all cases the members of the various ranks of the nobility owed their positions to heredity, although occasionally noble rank would be conferred upon a commoner for his services to the king. Seldom was it possible for a man to win advancement under the system by his own efforts or intelligence. Nevertheless, an important exception was to be found in the case of the *ministeriales* in Germany and in the Low Countries. The *ministeriales*, as their name implies, formed a class of administrative officials under feudal rule. They had charge of castles, toll gates, bridges, market places, and so on. Some of the most capable of them rose to be bailiffs or administrators of towns or districts, serving under a great prince or bishop or even under the Emperor himself. Their position was of such high advantage that ultimately they invaded the ranks of the lesser nobility and came to form a subordinate class of knights.

A regime of status, with a few exceptions

The life of the feudal nobility was scarcely the idyllic existence frequently described in romantic novels. While there was undoubtedly plenty of excitement, there was also much hardship, and death took its toll at an early age. From a careful study of medieval skeletons a modern scientist has estimated that the peak of the mortality rate in feudal times came at the age of forty-two,[1] whereas at the present time it occurs at about seventy-five. Moreover, conditions of living even for the richest nobles were comparatively poor. Until almost the end of the eleventh century the feudal castle was nothing but a crude blockhouse of timber. And even the great stone castles of later date were far from being models of comfort and convenience. Rooms were dark and damp, and the bare stone walls were cold and cheerless. Until after the revival of trade with the Orient, which led to the introduction of carpets and rugs, floors were generally covered with rushes or straw, a new layer being put down from time to time as the old became vile from the filth of hunting dogs. The food of the noble and his family, though plentiful and substantial, was neither particularly varied nor appetizing. Meat and fish, cheese, cabbages, turnips, carrots, onions, beans, and peas were the staple articles of diet. The only fruits obtainable in abundance were apples and pears. Coffee and tea were unknown, and so were

The life of the feudal nobles

[1] J. W. Thompson, *An Economic and Social History of the Middle Ages*, p. 718.

spices until after trade with the Orient had continued for some time. Sugar was also eventually introduced, but for a long while it remained so rare and costly that it was often sold as a drug.

Although the nobles did not work for a living, their time was not spent in idleness. The conventions of their society dictated an active life of war, high adventure, and sport. Not only did they wage war on flimsy pretexts for the conquest of neighboring fiefs, but they fought for the sheer love of fighting as an exciting adventure. So much violence resulted that the church intervened with the Peace

Tournament with Lances. Engraving by Lucas Cranach. Tournaments, imitating the conditions of medieval warfare, but with blunted spears and lances, were among the principal recreational pursuits of the feudal aristocracy.

of God in the tenth century and supplemented this with the Truce of God in the eleventh. The Peace of God pronounced the solemn anathemas of the church against any who did violence to places of worship, robbed the poor, or injured members of the clergy. Later the same protection was extended to merchants. The Truce of God prohibited fighting entirely from "vespers on Wednesday to sunrise on Monday" and also from Christmas to Epiphany (January 6) and throughout the greater part of the spring, late summer, and early fall. The purpose of the last regulation was obviously to protect the peasants during the seasons of planting and harvesting. The penalty against any noble who violated this truce was excommunication. Perhaps if rules such as these could have been maintained for a few centuries longer, human beings would eventually have abandoned war as senseless and unprofitable. But the church itself, in launching the Crusades, was really responsible for making the rules a dead letter. And the holy wars against the infidel were fought with a great deal more barbarity than had ever resulted from the petty squabbles of feudal nobles among themselves.

Until comparatively late in the Middle Ages the manners of the feudal aristocracy were anything but refined and gentle. Gluttony was a common vice, and the quantities of wine and beer consumed at a medieval castle brawl would stagger the imagination of a modern toper. At dinner everyone carved his meat with his own dagger and ate it with his fingers. Bones and scraps were thrown on the floor for the omnipresent dogs to fight over. Women were treated with indifference and sometimes with contempt and brutality, for this was a masculine world. In the twelfth and thirteenth centuries, however, the manners of the aristocratic classes were softened and improved considerably by the growth of what is known as chivalry. Chivalry was the social and moral code of feudalism, the embodiment of its highest ideals and the expression of its virtues. The origins of this code were mainly Germanic and Christian, but Saracenic influence played some part in its development also. Chivalry set forth the ideal of a knight who is not only brave and loyal but generous, truthful, reverent, kind to the poor and defenseless, and disdainful of unfair advantage or sordid gain. But perhaps above all, the perfect knight must be the perfect lover. The chivalric ideal made the high love of ladies a veritable cult with an elaborate ceremonial which the hot-blooded young noble must be careful to follow. As a result, women in the late Middle Ages were elevated to a much higher status than they had enjoyed in early medieval Europe. Chivalry also imposed upon the knight the obligation of fighting in defense of noble causes. It was especially his duty to serve as the champion of the church and to further its interests with sword and spear.

The main economic unit of the feudal regime was the manorial estate, although manorialism itself had a political as well as an economic aspect. The manor, or manorial estate, was generally the fief of an individual knight. Lords of higher rank held many manors, the number frequently running into the hundreds or thousands. No one knows even the average size of these economic units, but the smallest appear to have included at least three hundred or four hundred acres. Each manorial estate comprised one or more villages, the lands cultivated by the peasants, the common forest and pasture lands, the land belonging to the parish church, and the lord's demesne, which included the best farm land on the manor. With minor exceptions, all of the arable land was divided into three main blocks: the spring planting ground, the autumn planting ground, and the fallow. These were rotated from year to year, so that the spring planting ground one year would become the autumn planting ground the next, and so on. Such was the famous *three-field system,* which seems to have originated in western Europe toward the end of the eighth century. Manorial agriculture was also conducted very largely under the *open-field system.* The holding allotted to each peasant was not a compact area of the manor, but consisted of a number of strips located in each of the three main blocks of arable land. These strips, averaging about an acre in size, were generally separated only by a narrow band of unplowed turf. The main object of the system was apparently to give to each serf his fair share of the three different kinds of land. In cultivating these strips the peasants worked co-operatively, chiefly because their holdings were scat-

Chivalry

The manorial estate

The three-field system and the open-field system

tered, and it was therefore logical for a number of men to combine their efforts in farming all the strips in a particular area. Besides, no one peasant had enough oxen to draw the crude wooden plows through the stubborn soil.

The servile classes

Except for the noble and his family, the parish priest, and possibly a few administrative officials, the entire population of the manor consisted of persons of servile status. These might be embraced in as many as four different classes: villeins, serfs, crofters and cotters, and slaves. Though villeins and serfs eventually came to be almost indistinguishable, there were at one time several important differences between them. Villeins were originally small farmers who had surrendered their lands as individuals to some powerful neighbor. The ancestors of the serfs had frequently been subjected *en masse*, whole villages of them at once. The villeins were perpetual tenants, not bound in person to the soil; whereas the serfs were bought and sold with the land to which they were attached. As another difference, the villein was liable to obligations only within the definite terms of his customary contract, while the labor of the serf could be exploited virtually as his owner saw fit. Finally, the villein could be taxed only within limits fixed by custom, but the serf was taxable at the lord's mercy. By the thirteenth century, however, most of these differences had disappeared. And it is a notable fact that the villeins were not degraded to the level of serfs; instead, the serfs rose to the level of villeins. While the other dependent classes on the manor were much less numerous than the villeins and serfs, a word or two must be said about them. The crofters and cotters were wretchedly poor men who had no definite status under the feudal regime at all. Unlike even the meanest of the serfs, they had no strips of land which they could cultivate for their living. They occupied small cottages or shanties and hired themselves out to the richer villeins or did odd jobs for the lord of the manor. A few slaves continued to be held throughout the Feudal Age, but in steadily diminishing numbers. They did not fit in well with the manorial type of economy, for the manor was not a plantation but an aggregate of petty farms cultivated under perpetual lease. The few slaves who were to be found were employed mainly as household servants. After the year 1000 slavery as an institution became practically extinct in western Europe.

Obligations of the villeins and serfs

Like all other members of the subject classes under feudalism, the villeins and serfs were liable for numerous obligations. Although these appear at first glance to have been exceedingly oppressive, it is necessary to remember that they took the place of both rent and taxes. The most important of these obligations were the following: the *capitatio*, the *cens*, the *taille*, the *banalités*, the *prestations*, and the *corvée*. The *capitatio* was a head tax imposed only upon serfs. The *cens* was a species of rent paid only by villeins and freemen. The *taille* was a percentage of nearly everything produced on the lands

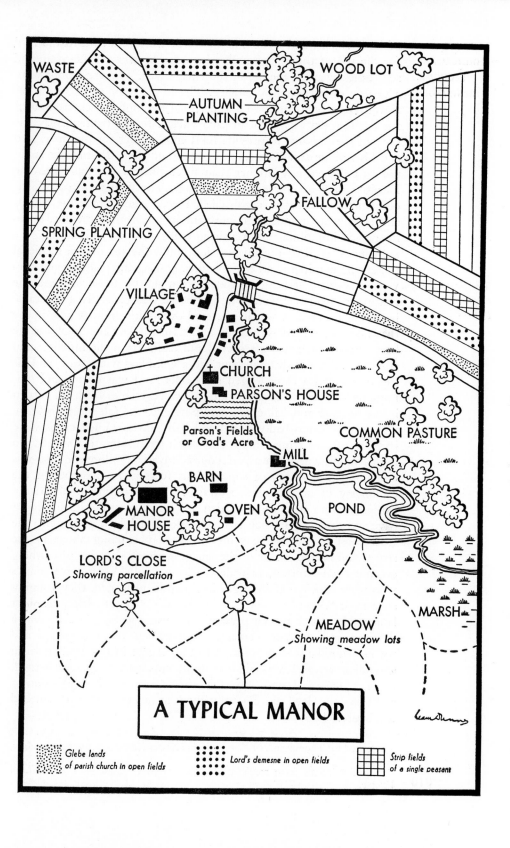

WASTE

WOOD LOT

AUTUMN PLANTING

FALLOW

SPRING PLANTING

VILLAGE

† CHURCH

PARSON'S HOUSE

Parson's Fields or God's Acre

COMMON PASTURE

MILL

BARN

MANOR HOUSE

OVEN

POND

LORD'S CLOSE
Showing parcellation

MEADOW
Showing meadow lots

MARSH

A TYPICAL MANOR

Glebe lands of parish church in open fields

Lord's demesne in open fields

Strip fields of a single peasant

of both villeins and serfs. The *banalités* were fees paid to the lord for the use of the village mill, winepress, brewery, bake-oven, and sometimes even for the use of the village well. The *prestations* were a variety of enforced hospitality. The local count or baron, in his travels from one manor to another, had the right to entertainment for the few days he spent in each village. It was consequently the duty of the peasants to provide food and lodging for the great lord and his retinue and even for his horses and dogs. *Prestations* could not be enforced any oftener than three times a year, and in some localities they became entirely obsolete. The final form of peasant obligations, the *corvée*, consisted of forced labor which the villeins and serfs were required to perform in cultivating the lord's demesne and in building and repairing roads, bridges, and dams.

The lot of the medieval peasant

By no stretch of the imagination could the lot of the medieval peasant be considered an enviable one. During the planting and harvesting seasons, at least, he toiled from sunrise to sunset, and the rewards of his labor were few. His home was generally a miserable hovel constructed of wattle plastered over with mud. A hole in the thatched roof served as the only outlet for smoke. The floor was the bare earth, which was often cold and damp from the infalling rain and snow. For a bed the peasant had a box filled with straw, and his easy chair was a three-legged stool. His food was coarse and monotonous—black or brown bread, a few vegetables from his garden in the summer and fall, cheese and porridge, and salt meats and fish, which were often badly cured and half putrid. When crops were bad, he suffered from famine, and death from starvation was by no means unknown. He was, of course, invariably illiterate and was commonly the victim of superstitious fears and sometimes of the dishonesty of unscrupulous stewards. The hardships of his barren existence were such as to deaden any moral sensibilities he might have possessed. A medieval traveler described how in summer he "saw most of the peasants on market day walking about in the streets and on the square of the village without a vestige of clothing on, not even trousers, in order to keep cool. When some monks who were shocked at the sight indignantly protested, they roughly answered: 'What business is it of yours?'"[2] But perhaps the most lamentable aspect of the peasant's life was the fact that he was a despised and degraded creature. Spokesmen for the nobles and townsmen alike seldom referred to him except in the most scornful and odious terms. It was said that all peasants were shifty, dull-witted, mean, squint-eyed, and ugly; that they were "born of ass's dung," and that "the devil did not want them in hell because they smelled too badly."[3]

[2] Quoted by Thompson, *An Economic and Social History of the Middle Ages*, p. 742.
[3] See illustrations from medieval literature in G. G. Coulton, *The Medieval Village*.

FEUDALISM
AS A
STRUCTURE

*The medieval
peasant and the
modern worker*

Yet the medieval peasant enjoyed some advantages which undoubtedly helped to redress the balance of his miseries. Many of
the fears and uncertainties that plague the lowly in modern times
meant nothing to him. He was in very little danger of loss of employment or of insecurity in old age. It was an established principle
of feudal law that the peasant could not be deprived of his land. If
the land was sold, the serf went with it and retained the right to
cultivate his holdings as before. When he became too old or too
feeble to work, it was the duty of the lord to care for him through
the remainder of his days. Although he worked very hard during
the busiest seasons, he had at least as many holidays as are allowed to
the laborer today. In some parts of Europe these amounted to

Illuminated Manuscript from the
Duc de Berry's *Book of Hours*. Illuminated manuscripts have value
not merely as superlative works of
art but for their portrayals of medieval life and culture. Shown here
are peasants at work in the fields.

Scene in a Medieval Village.
Among the activities shown are
plowing, grinding grain, and
slaughtering a boar for meat. In the
lower right two friars are dispensing bread and soup to the poor.

about sixty out of the year, not counting Sundays. Moreover, it
was customary for the lord of the manor to feast his peasants after
the spring planting was completed and after the harvest was gathered, as well as during the principal religious holidays. Last of all,
the peasant was under no obligation to render military service. His
crops might be trampled and his cattle driven off by the armies of
warring nobles, but at least he could not be compelled to sacrifice his
life for the benefit of some swashbuckling dictator or capitalists
greedy for markets.

No sooner had feudalism reached the height of its development
than it began to show signs of decay. The decline was well along **311**

*The decline of
feudalism: eco-
nomic causes*

on its way in France and Italy by the end of the thirteenth century. The system continued longer in Germany and England, but by 1500 it was almost extinct in all countries of western Europe. Many relics of it, of course, survived until much later—some till the middle of the nineteenth century in central and eastern Europe. The causes of the decline of the feudal regime are not far to seek. Many of them were closely associated with the revolutionary economic changes of the eleventh and succeeding centuries. The revival of trade with the Near East and the growth of cities led to an increased demand for products of the farms. Prices rose, and as a consequence some peasants were able to buy their freedom. Moreover, the expansion of commerce and industry created new opportunities for employment and tempted many serfs to flee to the towns. Once they had made good their escape, it was almost impossible to bring them back. Still another economic cause was the opening up of new lands to agricultural production, mainly on account of the higher prices for products of the soil. In order to get peasants to clear forests and drain swamps, it was frequently necessary to promise them their freedom. The Black Death, which swept over Europe in the fourteenth century, while not exactly an economic factor, had results very similar to those of the causes already mentioned. In other words, it produced a scarcity of labor and thereby enabled the serfs who survived to enforce their demands for freedom. With the peasant a free man, the manorial system was practically impossible, and one of the chief props of the feudal regime had been broken.

Political causes

The political causes of the downfall of feudalism were also of major significance. One was the establishment of professional armies and the inducements offered to the peasants to become mercenary soldiers. Another was the adoption of new methods of warfare which rendered the knights somewhat less indispensable as a military class. A third was the condition of chaos produced by the Hundred Years' War and the peasant insurrections resulting therefrom. A fourth was the influence of the Crusades in eliminating powerful nobles, in promoting the adoption of direct taxation, and in compelling the sale of privileges to communities of serfs as a means of raising money to equip armies. But probably the most important political cause was the rise of strong national monarchies, especially in France and England. By various means the ambitious kings of these countries in the late Feudal Age gradually deprived the nobles of all of their political authority.

3. The Rise of National Monarchies

*The division of
Charlemagne's
Empire*

Soon after the death of Charlemagne in 814 the strong government which he had built up in western Europe collapsed. In 843, by the Treaty of Verdun, his grandsons agreed to divide the Carolingian Empire into three separate parts. The two largest portions

became the kingdoms of East Francia and West Francia, corresponding roughly to the modern states of Germany and France. A wide
belt of land between the two was formed into a middle kingdom
including the territories of modern Belgium, Holland, Alsace, and
Lorraine. Such was the beginning of some of the most important
political divisions in the map of Europe today.

Meanwhile all three of these kingdoms passed rapidly and completely under feudal domination. The real rulers were not the
descendants of the great Carolingian king, but a host of petty *The rise of a national mon- archy in France*
princes, counts, and dukes. The kings themselves sank to the level of
mere feudal overlords, dependent upon the local nobles for their
soldiers and their revenues. While as kings their moral preponderance was still very great, their actual authority over the people was
practically non-existent. Toward the end of the twelfth century,
however, signs of a change in this condition began to appear in
France. In 987 the last of the weak Carolingian monarchs was displaced by the Count of Paris, Hugh Capet. The direct descendants
of this man were to occupy the throne of France for more than
three hundred years. Although neither Hugh nor any of his immediate successors exercised the degree of sovereignty commonly associated with the royal office, several of the later Capetians were
powerful rulers. A number of factors aided these kings in establishing their dominant position. First of all, they were fortunate enough
for hundreds of years to have sons to succeed them, and often an
only son. Consequently there were no deadly quarrels over the
right of succession, nor was there any necessity of dividing the
royal property among disgruntled relatives who might be able to
defend a claim to the throne. In the second place, most of these kings
lived to an advanced age, with the result that their sons were already
mature men when they came to the throne. There were therefore
no regencies to haggle the royal power away during the minority of
a prince. Another factor was the growth of trade, which afforded
the kings new sources of revenue and enabled them to find powerful
allies among the bourgeoisie for their struggle against the nobles.
Finally, considerable credit must be given to the shrewdness and
vigor of several of the kings themselves.

The first of the Capetian kings who may be considered as the
founders of a national monarchy in France was Philip Augustus
(1180–1223). Although Philip may never have conceived of himself *Founders of the French monarchy: Philip Augustus*
as other than the highest feudal overlord, most of his policies had
the effect of seriously weakening the feudal structure. When he
granted fiefs to his vassals he required them to agree that their own
vassals would owe first allegiance to him. Greedy for revenue, he
commuted as many as possible of the feudal reliefs into money payments, sold charters to cities, and levied special taxes on Jews and on
all persons who declined to go on a crusade to reconquer the Kingdom of Jerusalem from the Moslems. He appointed bailiffs and

seneschals to supervise the administration of justice in the feudal courts and to enforce the king's rights as an overlord. While he continued to depend upon his vassals for contributions of troops, he took steps toward the founding of a national army subject to his own control. He hired mercenary soldiers by the thousands and compelled the towns to furnish recruits from among their own citizens. So aggressively did he crowd the nobles into the background that he actually quadrupled the royal domain and transferred many of the functions of the feudality into his own hands.

Enlargement of the kingdom

When the first Capetian monarch ascended the throne, France consisted of only a small territory surrounding the town of Paris. Most of the remainder of the country was held by such powerful nobles as the Duke of Normandy, the Count of Champagne, the Duke of Brittany, the Duke of Burgundy, and the Duke of Aquitaine. Although all of these rulers were technically vassals of the French king, they had become so domineering or acquired so much power that they seldom made more than a pretense of fulfilling their feudal obligations. For example, William the Conqueror and his immediate successors were still Dukes of Normandy and therefore vassals of the king of France, but actually as kings of England they were his powerful rivals and scarcely made even a formal acknowledgment of his overlordship. When Philip Augustus came to the throne of France in 1180 he determined to put an end to such conditions. Taking advantage of the absence of the English kings, he managed by a series of bold strokes to acquire the Duchy of Normandy and a number of adjoining counties, thereby extending the royal domain to the English Channel. By participating in a papal crusade against the Albigenses he also acquired territory in the south. The Albigenses were heretics, and by the standards of the time the lands they inhabited were legitimate plunder. King Philip seized as his share of the booty the County of Toulouse.

Louis IX

The second of the kings most active in consolidating monarchical power in France was Louis IX (1226–1270). Probably few rulers in history have had more interesting personalities. For Louis was a strange mixture of exaggerated piety, shrewd benevolence, and ambitious practicality. At times he imitated the life of a monk, wearing a haircloth shirt next to his skin, fasting punctiliously, and having himself whipped with small chains. He often entertained paupers at his table, considered it his duty to wash the feet of the poor, and sometimes even waited on lepers. Because of his wide reputation for piety and his martyrdom for the faith on a crusade to Tunis, he was canonized only twenty-seven years after his death. But Louis was not merely a saintly ascetic. He found time to establish hospitals, to abolish trial by combat, and to emancipate thousands of serfs on the royal domain, being careful to make each one pay a fee for his freedom. So zealously did he patronize learning and the arts that

314

his reign has been called "the Golden Age of Medieval France." In addition, he labored to increase the power of the monarchy by every shrewd device he could think of. He extended the right of appeal from decisions in the feudal courts to his own court and encouraged his lawyers to draw up a category of cases which would be subject only to the king's jurisdiction. This category was made broad enough to include cases of treason and practically all breaches of the peace. He commanded that his own currency should be accepted in all parts of the kingdom. He made an earnest but not altogether successful attempt to curb the power of the nobles by prohibiting their right of private warfare. Perhaps most significant of all, he assumed for himself the authority to issue ordinances for the entire country without the previous consent of his vassals. Probably nothing could have expressed a more emphatic disavowal of feudal principles than this, since under feudal theory the king could make no departures from customary law without the approval of the chief men of the realm.

The evolution of a national monarchy in medieval France was carried still farther during the reign of Philip IV (1285–1314), or Philip the Fair as he is more commonly called. The policies of this king were determined very largely by an increasing need for revenue, but they were due in some part to the growing popularity of the Roman law with its basic doctrine of the absolute sovereignty of the state. Philip's ambition to raise money led not only to his expulsion of the Jews and the Italian bankers and the confiscation of their property, but prompted him also to change nearly all of the remaining feudal dues into direct taxes. In addition, he devised new levies upon incomes and upon the goods and property of the merchants. But it was Philip's attempt to tax the possessions of the church that was fraught with the deepest significance. This precipitated an angry quarrel with the Pope which had two momentous results: (1) the subjection of the French Catholic church to the king; and (2) the summoning of what has come to be considered the first parliament in the history of France. In order to determine the attitude of his subjects toward his quarrel with the Pope, Philip in 1302 convoked an assembly of the clergy, the lay nobles, and representatives of the towns. Since these were the principal estates or classes of all of his subjects, the assembly came to be known as the Estates-General. It was summoned on two other occasions by Philip to approve new modes of taxation. His successors continued the precedent of convoking it more or less regularly thereafter until 1614. The Estates-General, of course, was not really intended to be an independent legislative assembly but a body of advisers to the king. It was only under the influence of eighteenth-century liberalism that men came to look back upon it as a true parliament. On the other hand, since it included representatives from outside the

Philip the Fair

315

nobility, its establishment may be considered as another stage in the transformation of the French government from a feudal to a national character.

Causes of the Hundred Years' War

Monarchical power in France underwent still further consolidation as a result of the Hundred Years' War (1337-1453). This war grew out of a number of causes. The primary one was probably the long-standing conflict between the French and English kings over territory in France. At the end of the thirteenth century, English monarchs still held part of Guienne and Gascony in southwestern France as vassals of the French crown. The French monarchs resented the presence of a foreign power on their soil. Moreover, they feared that the English interest in the woolen trade of Flanders might lead to an alliance with the Flemish burghers against their sovereign, the King of France. To add fuel to the flames, Edward III, who succeeded to the throne of England in 1327, had a claim to the French crown through his mother, who was a daughter of Philip the Fair. Sensing that war was inevitable, he determined to press this claim in the hope that by so doing he might find a convenient pretext for conquering the Flemish cities.

The course and climax of the conflict

The Hundred Years' War actually covered more than a century, although the fighting was by no means continuous. Hostilities between the royal armies were interrupted by several truces and were accompanied by a number of bloody uprisings of townsmen and peasants. During the greater part of the conflict the English armies were generally victorious. They were better organized, better disciplined, and better equipped. Besides, England did not suffer from the extremes of internal discord which plagued the French. By 1420 the Duke of Burgundy had deserted the French cause, and all of the northern half of France had been occupied by English soldiers. Soon afterward occurred the most dramatic incident of the war, which infused new confidence into the French armies and paved the way for their ultimate victory. A devout but simple peasant girl, Jeanne

Jeanne d'Arc

d'Arc or Joan of Arc, came forward with the declaration that she had been commissioned by God to "drive the English out of the whole kingdom of France." Though she was completely uneducated, "knowing neither A nor B," her piety and sincerity made such a strong impression upon the French soldiers that they firmly believed they were being led by an angel from heaven. In a few months she had liberated most of central France and had brought the dauphin Charles VII to Reims, where he was crowned King of France. But in May, 1430, she was captured by the Burgundians and turned over to the English. The latter regarded her as a witch and set up a special court of the clergy to try her for heresy. Found guilty, she was given over to the secular government on May 30, 1431, and burned in the public square of Rouen.

As is often true of martyrs, Jeanne d'Arc was more powerful dead than alive. Her memory lingers in France to this day as the spiritual embodiment of a patriotic cause. The years that followed her death witnessed a series of uninterrupted triumphs for the French armies. In 1453 the capture of Bordeaux, the last of the English strongholds, brought the war to an end. Only the port of Calais remained of the once extensive English holdings in France. But the Hundred Years' War did more than expel the English from French territory. It added the capstone to the consolidation of royal power in the kingdom of France. The attempts of both the Estates-General and the great nobles to control the government had proved abortive. In spite of the confusion and sufferings of the greater part of the war, France had emerged with enough of a national consciousness to enable her kings to centralize their power in accordance with a pattern of absolute monarchy. The completion of this process marked the final transition from feudalism to something resembling a modern state.

Effects of the Hundred Years' War

The development of a national monarchy in England goes back to the reign of William the Conqueror. His conquest of the island in 1066 resulted in the establishment of a stronger monarchy than had previously existed under the Saxon rulers. The enlargement of power thus effected was not necessarily deliberate. King William made few sweeping changes. For the most part he preserved Anglo-Saxon laws and institutions. He brought over certain elements of feudalism from the Continent, but he took care to prevent too great a degree of decentralization. By the Salisbury Oath he required his vassals to swear allegiance to him directly instead of to their immediate overlords. He prohibited private warfare and retained the right to coin money as a royal prerogative. When he granted lands to his followers, he rarely gave any of them large estates composed of compact territory. He transformed the old *witan*, or advisory council of the Anglo-Saxon kings, into a *curia regis*, or court of the king, composed primarily of his own retainers and administrative subordinates. By the end of his reign the constitution of England had been markedly changed, but the alterations had been so gradual that few were aware of their significance.

Foundations of national monarchy in England

William the Conqueror's immediate successors continued their father's policies, but after the death of Henry I in 1135 a violent quarrel broke out between rival claimants for the throne, and the country was plunged into the depths of anarchy. When Henry II became king in 1154, he found the treasury depleted and the barons entrenched in power. His first objectives, therefore, were to increase the royal revenues and to reduce the power of the nobles. In pursuance of the first, he made a regular practice of commuting the feudal obligation of military service into a money payment known as *scutage*, and levied the first English taxes on personal property and on incomes. In his war against the nobles he demolished hundreds of castles that had been built without authorization and curtailed the jurisdiction of the feudal courts. But he apparently realized that the

The reforms of Henry II

*The Common
Law and jury
system*

power of the barons could not be permanently restricted without thoroughgoing changes in the law and in judicial procedure. Accordingly, he gathered around him a staff of eminent lawyers to advise him regarding the laws which ought to be in force. In addition, he followed a practice already established of appointing itinerant judges to administer justice in the various parts of the realm. These judges, traveling from one region to another, applied a uniform law throughout the kingdom. The precedents laid down by their decisions gradually supplanted local customs and came to be recognized as the Common Law of England. Henry also issued writs commanding the sheriffs to bring before the judges as they went from shire to shire groups of men who were familiar with local conditions. Under oath these men were required to report every case of murder, arson, robbery, or similar crime they knew to have occurred since the judges' last visit. This was the origin of the grand jury. Another of Henry's reforms made it possible for either party to a civil dispute to purchase a writ which would order the sheriff to bring both plaintiff and defendant, together with twelve citizens who knew the facts, before the judge. The twelve were then asked under oath if the plaintiff's statements were true, and the judge rendered his decision in accordance with the answer. Out of this practice grew the institution of the trial jury.

*Henry's quarrel
with Thomas à
Becket*

There was one branch of the administration of justice which Henry failed to bring under royal control, though he made strenuous efforts to do so. This was the judging and punishing of members of the clergy. Priests and other members of the ecclesiastical hierarchy were not tried in ordinary courts but in church courts under the rules of the canon law. Punishment was notoriously lax. A priest, for instance, convicted of murder, was deprived of his clerical status but was rarely given any further penalty. Not only this, but appeals could be taken to the papal court in Rome from decisions in any English courts on ecclesiastical matters. In an effort to eradicate these practices Henry issued the Constitutions of Clarendon in 1164. The Constitutions provided that any clergyman accused of crime must be taken into a royal court first. If the royal court found that a crime had been committed, the defendant would be sent to a church court for trial. If found guilty he would be sent back to the royal court to be sentenced. From such judgments no appeal could be taken to Rome without the king's consent. In attempting to enforce the Constitutions, Henry ran afoul of the Archbishop of Canterbury. The latter, Thomas à Becket, was as devoted to the interests of the church as Henry was to the strengthening of the monarchy. The quarrel reached a tragic climax when the Archbishop was murdered by a band of Henry's knights after the king, in an outburst of anger, had rebuked his followers for doing nothing to rid him of "a turbulent priest." The crime so shocked the English public that the whole program of bringing the ecclesiastical

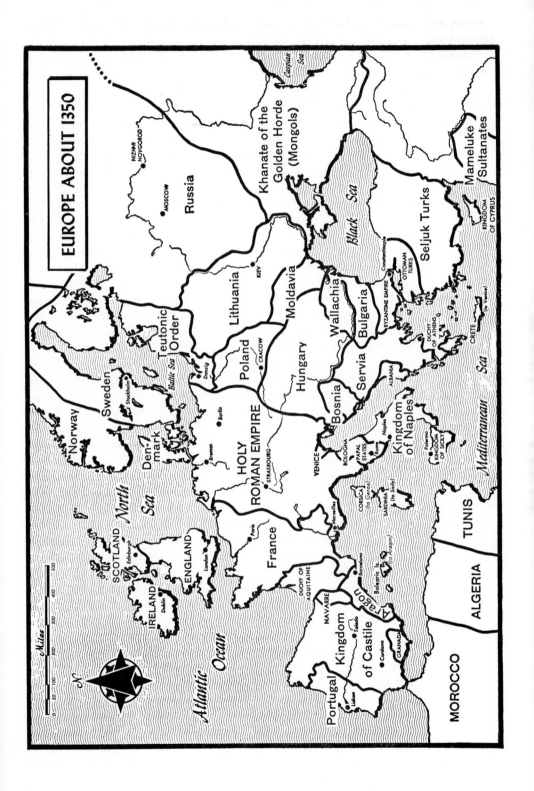

EUROPE ABOUT 1350

*Revolt of the
barons against
King John*

courts under royal control was largely abandoned. The Archbishop
was revered as a martyr and eventually canonized by the Pope.

During the reigns of Henry's sons, Richard I and John, feudalism
enjoyed a partial recovery. For all but six months of his ten-year
reign Richard was absent from England waging the Third Crusade
or defending his possessions on the Continent. Moreover, the heavy
taxation which had to be imposed to defray his military expenses
angered many of the barons. The feudal revolt reached its height
during the reign of King John, who was perhaps not much worse a
tyrant than some of his predecessors. But John had the misfortune
to have two powerful enemies in King Philip Augustus of France
and Pope Innocent III; and when he lost most of his possessions in
France to Philip and suffered a humiliating defeat at the hands of
the Pope, it was inevitable that the barons would take advantage of
the opportunity to regain their power. In 1215 they compelled John
to sign the famous Magna Charta, a document which remains to this
day an important part of the British constitution. The popular interpretation placed upon the Magna Charta is really erroneous. It was
not intended to be a Bill of Rights or a charter of liberties for the
common man. On the contrary, it was a feudal document, a written
feudal contract in which the king as an overlord pledged himself to
respect the traditional rights of his vassals. It was chiefly important
at the time as an expression of the principle of limited government,
of the idea that the king is bound by the law. Some of its feudal
provisions, however, lent themselves to a broader application later
on; for example, the declaration that no man could be imprisoned
or otherwise punished "except by the legal judgment of his peers
or by the law of the land."

*Origin of the
English Parlia-
ment*

The opposition of the barons continued during the reign of
John's son, Henry III. They now drew considerable support from
the middle class and found a new leader in Simon de Montfort.
Civil war broke out, in which the king was taken prisoner. In 1265
Simon de Montfort, wishing to secure popular support for his plans
to limit the powers of the crown, called together an assembly or
parliament which included not only the higher nobles and churchmen but also two knights from each shire and two citizens from
each of the more important towns. Thirty years later this device of
a parliament composed of members of the three great classes became
a regular agency of the government when Edward I in 1295 convoked the so-called Model Parliament. Edward's purpose in summoning this parliament was not to inaugurate democratic reform
but merely to broaden the political structure and thereby make the
king less dependent upon the nobles. Nevertheless, a precedent was
established that representatives of the commons should always
meet with the two higher classes to advise the king. By the end of
the reign of Edward III (1327-77) Parliament had divided for all

practical purposes into two houses, and they had increased their control over taxation and were assuming lawmaking authority. The subsequent evolution of the English Parliament into the sovereign power in the country will be discussed in later chapters.

The extinction of feudalism in England

During the fourteenth century England was profoundly affected by economic changes which had begun somewhat earlier on the Continent. The development of commerce and industry, the growth of cities, the greater use of money, the scarcity of labor—all of these seriously weakened the manorial system and consequently undermined feudal power. In addition, the Hundred Years' War increased the military and financial powers of the kings and tended to make them more independent of baronial support. Feudalism in England was finally extinguished in a great struggle among rival factions for control of the crown. This struggle, known as the War of the Roses, lasted from 1455 to 1485. The death of a great many of the nobles in this war and the disgust of the people with continual disorder enabled the new king, Henry Tudor, or Henry VII, to establish a more highly consolidated rule than the country had known up to this time.

The failure of Germany and Italy to form national states

Although the feudal regime became extinct in Germany by the fifteenth century and in Italy somewhat earlier, in neither of these countries was a national monarchy set up until long after the close of the Middle Ages. The power of the dukes in Germany and the power of the Pope always proved too strong to be overcome. Some of the German Emperors might have succeeded in building up centralized rule if they had been content to remain in their own country, but they persisted in interfering in Italy, thereby antagonizing the Popes and encouraging revolts at home.

The empire of Otto the Great

When the eastern branch of the Carolingian dynasty died out in 911, the Germans returned to their ancient practice of electing a king. Their first choice was Conrad of Franconia. He, in turn, was succeeded by Henry I, the founder of the Saxon dynasty. The most famous member of this dynasty was Henry's son, Otto the Great, who became king in 936. From the beginning of his reign Otto apparently entertained ambitions of becoming something more than a mere king of Germany. He had himself crowned at Aachen, probably to convey the idea that he was the rightful successor of Charlemagne. Soon afterward he intervened in Italian affairs and assumed the title of King of the Lombards. From this it was only a step to becoming involved with the papacy. In 961 Otto responded to appeal from Pope John XII for protection against his enemies, and in January of the following year he was rewarded by being crowned Roman Emperor. Although the empire of Otto the Great was confined to Germany and Italy, there was doubtless the belief in the mind of its founder that it would eventually be enlarged, perhaps to embrace all of Latin Christendom. It was, of course, not

See color
pictures at
page 261

321

*The Holy
Roman Empire
of Frederick
Barbarossa and
Frederick II*

conceived as a new state at all but as a continuation of the Carolingian Empire and the Empire of the Caesars.

In the twelfth century the crown of Otto the Great came into possession of the Hohenstaufen family, whose most distinguished representatives were Frederick Barbarossa and Frederick II. Both of these rulers were outspoken in asserting their claims to imperial dignity. Frederick Barbarossa called the empire of Germany and Italy the Holy Roman Empire on the theory that it was a universal empire established directly by God and co-ordinate in rank with the church. Frederick II, who was king of Sicily and southern Italy as well as Holy Roman Emperor, was much more interested in his southern kingdom than he was in Germany. Nevertheless, he believed just as firmly as did his grandfather Barbarossa in a universal empire as the highest secular power in western Europe. But he considered that the only possible way to make the claims of the Emperor a reality was to build a strong state in Sicily and southern Italy and then extend its power northward. Accordingly, he proceeded to reorganize his southern kingdom into a divine-right despotism. He swept away the vestiges of feudalism almost at a single stroke. Like William the Conqueror he required all nobles, regardless of rank, to swear allegiance to him directly. He established a professional army, introduced direct taxation, and abolished trial by ordeal and by combat. He appointed traveling judges to promote the development of a uniform law and judicial procedure. He decreed it to be an act of sacrilege even to discuss the Emperor's statutes or judgments. He set up a rigid control over commerce and industry and founded government monopolies of the grain trade, the exchange of money, and the manufacture of textiles and other commodities. He even anticipated modern dictators in a campaign for racial purity; for he declared that "When the men of Sicily ally themselves with the daughters of foreigners, the purity of the race becomes besmirched." He seemed to forget the fact that the blood of most of his people was already mixed with Saracenic, Greek, Italian, and Norman infusions, and that he himself was half German and half Norman.

*The crown of
the Holy Ro-
man Emperor
passes to
the Hapsburgs*

Frederick II was no more successful than any of his predecessors in increasing the power of the Holy Roman Empire. His great mistake was his failure to enlist the support of the middle class in the cities as the Capetian monarchs in France had done. Without this it was impossible to break through the wall of papal opposition. After Frederick died in 1250 the Popes proceeded to annihilate the remaining members of the Hohenstaufen line. In 1273 Rudolf of Hapsburg was elected to the imperial throne, but the Holy Roman Empire over which he and his descendants ruled was seldom very powerful. When finally abolished in 1806 by Napoleon, it was little more than a political fiction.

4. *Urban Life in the Feudal Age*

By no means all of the inhabitants of western Europe in the Feudal Age lived in castles, manor houses, or peasant villages. Thousands of others dwelt in cities and towns; and from the eleventh century on, at least, the activities of the urban classes were just as important as the fighting and love-making of nobles or the toiling and roistering of peasants. Indeed, the cities were the real centers of most of the intellectual and artistic progress of the late Middle Ages.

The oldest of the medieval cities in western Europe were undoubtedly those which had survived from Roman times. But outside of Italy these were few indeed. Others came into being from a variety of causes. A great many were towns which had increased in size and importance because of the establishment of bishoprics there. Some had grown out of the expansion of monasteries into centers of trade and industry. Still others had developed from castles or strongholds where people congregated because of the need for protection. But by far the greatest number originated as a result of the revival of trade which began in the eleventh century. The leaders in this revival were the Italian towns of Venice, Genoa, and Pisa. Their merchants rapidly built up a flourishing commerce with the Byzantine Empire and with the great Moslem cities of Bagdad, Damascus, and Cairo. The products brought in by these merchants stimulated a brisk demand not only in Italy but also in Germany, France, and England. As a result, new markets were opened up, and many people turned to manufacturing to imitate products imported from the Near East. Cities and towns multiplied so rapidly that in some regions half the population had been drawn from agriculture into commercial and industrial pursuits by the fourteenth century.

As one would expect, the largest cities of feudal Europe were located in the south. Palermo on the island of Sicily with possibly 300,000 inhabitants surpassed all the others in size and probably in magnificence also. The metropolis of northern Europe was Paris, with a population of about 240,000 in the thirteenth century. The only other cities with a population of 100,000 or over were Venice, Florence, and Milan. Although England doubled the number of her inhabitants between the eleventh century and the fourteenth, only about 45,000 of them lived in London in the thirteenth century. By the end of the Middle Ages nearly all of the cities of western Europe had gained some degree of exemption from feudal control. Their citizens had complete freedom to dispose of their property as they saw fit, to marry whom they pleased, and to go and come as they liked. All feudal dues were either abolished or commuted to monetary payments; and provision was made for cases involving townsmen to be tried in the municipal courts. Some of the largest and wealthiest towns were almost entirely free, having organized governments with elected officials to administer their affairs. This was especially true in northern Italy, Provence, northern France, and Germany. This freedom was secured in a variety of ways—frequently by purchase, occasionally by violence, and sometimes by taking advantage of the weakness of the nobles or their preoccupation with quarrels of their own. The governments of these cities were generally dominated by an oligarchy of merchants, but in some cases democracy prevailed. Annual elections of magistrates were relatively common; universal suffrage was occasionally employed; while in a few towns the rich were disfranchised entirely, and the government was controlled by the masses.

Social problems in the cities

Most of the medieval cities grew so rapidly that it would have been almost impossible to provide optimum standards of healthfulness and comfort for the inhabitants even if there had been sufficient knowledge and inclination to do so. Overcrowding was so bad that sometimes as many as sixteen people lived in three rooms. Part of this congestion was due to the need of the cities for protection against nobles and brigands. To fulfill this need, fortified walls had

The Walls of Carcassonne, a City in Southwestern France. Medieval cities were generally surrounded by fortifications. The massive walls shown here were built in the Eleventh or Twelfth century.

A Section of the Medieval Town of Nordlingen, Germany. The need for protection against invaders led to congested housing conditions inside the walls.

to be built around each city with gates that could be securely barred to shut out marauders. Naturally it was too much trouble to tear down these walls and build new ones with every substantial increase in the population, although eventually this had to be done several times in a great many of the principal towns. Land values within these walls rose to fantastic heights and brought into existence a wealthy rent-collecting class, usually composed of the leading members of the merchant guilds. Because of the high cost of land, houses were built with upper stories that projected over the street, and even space on the walls was utilized for cottages and gardens. Streets were narrow and crooked and generally remained unpaved for centuries. The practice of paving began in Italy in the eleventh century and then gradually spread northward, but no thoroughfare in Paris had a hard surface until 1184 when Philip Augustus paved a single roadway in front of the Louvre. With space in the cities so limited, the streets served as the common playgrounds for boys and young men. Many were the protests voiced by their elders and by the clergy against wrestling, bowling, and pitching of quoits in the streets. "Football was constantly denounced, with good reason, as it was not an orderly game with a fixed number of players . . . but a wild struggle between opposing parties to force the ball through the streets from one end of the town to the other, frequently resulting in broken legs." [4]

Standards of sanitation in most of the medieval cities were distinctly inferior to those of ancient Rome. The great majority of the towns depended upon wells or rivers for their water supply, with the result that outbreaks of typhoid fever were of common occurrence. Although a few cities had underground sewers, none appears to have made provision for the collection of garbage. Refuse was generally thrown into the streets to be removed eventually by the rain or by the pigs and dogs that roamed at large. Conditions in Paris in the twelfth century may be illustrated by the fact that a son of Louis VI was killed when a hog rooting in the offal in the Rue St. Jacques charged between the legs of his horse and threw him to the ground.[5]

Standards of sanitation

The basic economic institutions in the medieval cities were the guilds. Of the two, the merchant and the craft guilds, the merchant organizations were the older, having developed as far back as the eleventh century. At first these included both traders and artisans, and then as industry became more specialized, the original guilds were split up into separate organizations of craftsmen and merchants. The main functions of the merchant guild were to maintain a monopoly of the local market for its own members and to preserve a stable, non-competitive economic system. To accomplish these ends the guild severely restricted trading by foreign merchants in the city, guaranteed to every member the right to participate in every purchase of goods made by any other member, required all of its members to charge uniform prices for the things they sold, drastically punished cornering of the market, and prohibited many forms of advertising. In some cases these rules were enforced by municipal ordinances, since the leading members of the guild were frequently the most powerful officials of the town corporation; but in other instances the methods used were more direct. An English herring merchant complained that "because he sold his merchandise at a less price than other merchants of the town of Yaxley . . . they assaulted him, beat him and ill-treated him and left him there for dead, so that he despaired of his life." [6]

The merchant guilds

[4] L. F. Salzman, *English Life in the Middle Ages*, pp. 82–83.
[5] Thompson, *An Economic and Social History of the Middle Ages*, p. 787.
[6] Quoted by Ephraim Lipson, *Economic History of England*, Vol. I, p. 246.

The craft guilds

Each of the craft guilds had three different classes of members— the master craftsmen, the journeymen, and the apprentices. But only the first two had any voice in the management of guild affairs, and toward the close of the Middle Ages even the journeymen lost most of their privileges. The master craftsmen were always the aristocrats of medieval industry; they owned their shops, employed other workers, and were responsible for the training of apprentices. The whole craft guild system operated very largely for their benefit. The journeymen (from the French *journée*, meaning "day" or "day's work") were craftsmen who worked in the masters' shops for wages. In some parts of Germany it was customary for the young journeyman to spend a year wandering about the country picking up casual employment, the so-called *Wanderjahr*, before settling down in any particular place. But in most other sections of Europe he seems to have lived with the master's family. The industrious and intelligent journeyman could eventually become a master craftsman by accumulating enough money to set up his own shop and by passing an examination, which sometimes included the submission of a masterpiece. As in many specialized trades today, entrance into the medieval craft could be accomplished only through serving an apprenticeship, varying in length from two to seven years, the longer period being more common. The apprentice was entirely under the control of the master craftsman, who was commonly held responsible for the boy's education in elementary subjects, and for the development of his character as well as for teaching him his trade. Usually the apprentice received no compensation except his food, lodging, and clothing. When the period of training was over, he became a journeyman. During the waning of the Middle Ages the craft guilds grew more and more exclusive. Terms of apprenticeship were lengthened, and it was made increasingly difficult for journeymen ever to become masters. The guilds themselves came to be dominated by the richer members, who endeavored to restrict their particular crafts to their own families. As a result, the great mass of the workers were reduced to the level of proletarians, doomed to remain wage earners as long as they lived. Many of the owners of shops now ceased to work with their hands and became capitalists and employers exclusively.

*Functions of
the craft guilds*

The functions of the craft guilds were similar to those of the related organizations of merchants, except for the additional responsibility of maintaining standards of quality. The craftsmen were just as ambitious as the merchants to preserve monopolies in their particular fields and to prevent any real competition among those producing the same article. Consequently they required uniformity of prices and wages, prohibited working after hours, and set up elaborate regulations governing methods of production and the quality of materials used. They even went to the extreme of discouraging new inventions and discoveries unless they were made

326

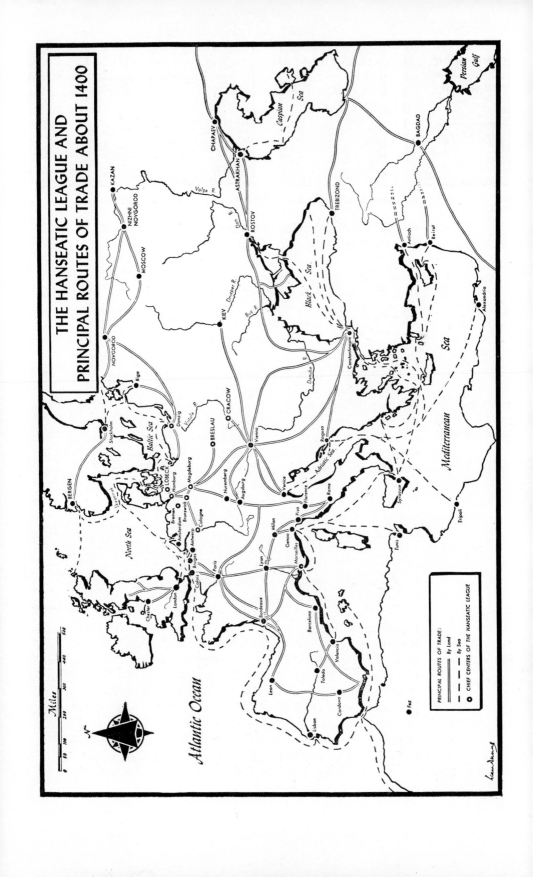

THE HANSEATIC LEAGUE AND
PRINCIPAL ROUTES OF TRADE ABOUT 1400

Miles
0 50 100 200 300 400 500

PRINCIPAL ROUTES OF TRADE:
———————— By Land
– – – – – – By Sea
○ CHIEF CENTERS OF THE HANSEATIC LEAGUE

Atlantic Ocean

North Sea

Baltic Sea

Mediterranean Sea

Black Sea

Caspian Sea

Adriatic Sea

Persian Gulf

BERGEN
Stockholm
Skagerrak
Riga
NOVGOROD
KAZAN
NIZHNI NOVGOROD
MOSCOW
CHAPAEV
ASTRAKHAN
Volga R.
Don R.
ROSTOV
KIEV
Dnieper R.
Bug R.
Danube R.
Vistula R.
Oder R.
Danzig
LÜBECK
Hamburg
Bremen
Magdeburg
BRESLAU
CRACOW
Vienna
Nuremberg
Augsburg
Brunswick
Amsterdam
Antwerp
Cologne
Bruges
Calais
London
Chester
Paris
Lyon
Bordeaux
Marseilles
Genoa
Milan
Pisa
Venice
Florence
Rome
Ragusa
Constantinople
TREBIZOND
Antioch
Beirut
BAGDAD
Alexandria
Tripoli
Tunis
Syracuse
Barcelona
Valencia
Toledo
Leon
Cordova
Lisbon
Fez

Medieval Craftsmen: The tailor, the shoemaker, the baker, and the weaver.

available to all and unless everyone adopted them. Absolutely no one was permitted to practice his trade in a town without first becoming a member of the guild. But in spite of all these regulations there were evidently a good many "chiselers." We read of millers who stole part of their customers' grain, of upholsterers who stuffed their mattresses with thistledown, and of metal-workers who substituted iron for copper and covered it over with gilt. There was a tendency also for some masters to employ workers who were not journeymen at all, having never completed an apprenticeship.

The craft guilds not really labor unions

The medieval craft guilds bore no actual relationship to the labor unions of today, despite a superficial resemblance to those modern unions which are organized on the basis of separate crafts, such as the associations of carpenters, plumbers, and electricians. But the differences are much more fundamental. Unlike the modern labor union, the craft guilds were not strictly confined to the working class; for the master craftsmen were capitalists, owners of the means of production, and employers as well as workers. Furthermore, they included not only men who worked with their hands but some who would now be classified as professional men entirely outside the ranks of labor. For example, there were guilds of notaries, physicians, and pharmacists. Finally, the craft guild had a much greater breadth of purpose. It was really a miniature industrial system in itself, combining the functions of the modern corporation, the trade association, and the labor union.

Social functions of the guilds

Both the craft and merchant guilds performed other functions besides those directly related to production and trade. They served the purposes of religious associations, benevolent societies, and social clubs. Each guild had its patron saint, and its members celebrated together the chief religious holidays and festivals of the church. With the gradual secularization of the drama, the miracle and mystery plays were transferred from the church to the market place, and the guilds assumed charge of presenting them. In addition, each organization ministered to the needs of its members who were sick or in distress of any kind. Money was appropriated to provide for the care of widows and orphans. A member who was no longer

328

able to work or who had been thrown into jail by his enemies could look to his colleagues for assistance. Even an unfortunate brother's debts might be assumed by the guild if his financial plight was serious.

The economic theory upon which the guild system rested was vastly different from that which prevails in capitalist society. It reflected, first of all, some of the ascetic flavor of Christianity. In the eyes of the church the vitally important aim in life should be the salvation of one's soul. Everything else should be kept in a subordinate place. It was not proper that men should expend their energies in the pursuit of luxury, or even that they should strive to become too comfortable. Moreover, the religion had been founded upon the idea that riches are a hindrance to the welfare of the soul. St. Ambrose, one of the most influential of the Christian Fathers, had even referred to private property as "a damnable usurpation." However, the economic theory of the late Middle Ages was influenced not only by Christianity but by Aristotle's doctrines of the golden mean and the just price and by his condemnation of usury. This theory included the following basic assumptions:

The economic theory of the guild system

(1) The purpose of economic activity is to provide goods and services for the community and to enable each member of society to live in security and freedom from want. Its purpose is not to furnish opportunities for the few to get rich at the expense of the many. Men who engage in business with the object of making as much money as possible are no better than pirates or robbers. The only legitimate objects of trade or other business are to provide for the upkeep of a household, for the assistance of the needy, or for some public advantage, lest one's country lack the necessaries of life.[7]

Basic doctrines

(2) Every commodity has its "just price," which is equal to its cost of production. No merchant has a right to sell any article for more than this price plus a small charge for the service he renders in making goods available to the community. To take advantage of scarcity to boost the price or to charge all that the traffic will bear is to commit a mortal sin.

(3) No man is entitled to any larger share of this world's goods than is necessary for his reasonable needs. Any surplus that may come into his possession is not rightfully his but belongs to society. St. Thomas Aquinas, the greatest of all the medieval philosophers, taught that if a rich man refuses to share his wealth with the poor, it is entirely justifiable that his surplus should be taken from him.

(4) No man has a right to financial reward unless he engages in socially useful labor or incurs some actual risk in an economic venture. The taking of interest on loans where no genuine risk is involved constitutes the sin of usury. Medieval economic theory would

[7] Thomas Aquinas, *Summa Theologica*, Fourth Article.

329

therefore conflict with the socially reputable practice today of making investments in high-grade bonds for a safe return, but it would approve a modest return from common stocks.

Exceptions to the ideal

It would be foolish, of course, to suppose that these lofty ideals of an economic system largely devoid of the profit motive were ever carried out to perfection. As we have seen, manifestations of greed were not lacking among many members of the guilds. But more than this, the non-capitalistic guild system did not extend into every sphere of medieval economic activity. For example, it was never successfully applied to international trade. Seldom would an individual merchant or craftsman have sufficient resources to engage in importing or exporting goods. Consequently, companies or associations of merchants had to be formed. The most famous of these associations in the Middle Ages were the Merchants of the Staple and the Teutonic Hanse. The former, organized in the thirteenth century, controlled the exporting of wool from England and the importing of goods from Flemish manufacturing towns such as Bruges and Antwerp. Apparently of somewhat earlier origin, the Teutonic Hanse was an association of German merchants engaged in exchanging the furs, fish, amber, leather, salt, and grain from the Baltic region for the wines, spices, textiles, fruits, and other products of the west and the south. By the fourteenth century this association had developed into the powerful Hanseatic League with a membership of about eighty towns under the leadership of Lübeck, Hamburg, and Bremen. Both the Merchants of the Staple and the Hanse were essentially profit-making organizations, and the activities of their members foreshadowed the growth of a capitalist economy in the Commercial Revolution that was soon to begin.

Selected Readings

Bateson, Mary, *Medieval England*, London, 1904

Boissonnade, Prosper, *Life and Work in Medieval Europe*, New York, 1927

Bryce, James, *The Holy Roman Empire*, New York, 1919

Buchan, Alice, *Joan of Arc and the Recovery of France*, New York, 1948

Henderson, E. F., *A Short History of Germany*, New York, 1931, 2 vols.

Lindsay, P., and Groves, R., *The Peasants' Revolt of 1381*, London, n.d.

Lipson, Ephraim, *Economic History of England*, New York, 5th ed., 1929, Vol. I

Luchaire, A., *Social France in the Time of Philip Augustus*, New York, 1912

Myers, A. R., *England in the Late Middle Ages*, London, 1952

Painter, Sidney, *The Rise of Feudal Monarchies*, Ithaca, 1951

Perroy, Édouard, *The Hundred Years War*, New York, 1951

Pirenne, Henri, *Medieval Cities*, Princeton, 1925

Power, Eileen, *Medieval People*, London, 1924

Runciman, Steven, *A History of the Crusades, The First Crusade and the* *Foundation of the Kingdom of Jerusalem*, New York, 1951, Vol. I

Salzman, L. F., *English Life in the Middle Ages*, Oxford, 1926.

Sayles, G. O., *The Medieval Foundation of England*, London, 1948

Seignobos, Charles, *The Feudal Regime*, New York, 1902

Stephenson, Carl, *Medieval Feudalism*, New York, 1935

Thompson, J. W., *An Economic and Social History of the Middle Ages*, New York, 1928

Tilley, A., *Medieval France*, Cambridge, 1922

Vickers, K. H., *England in the Later Middle Ages*, London, 1913

Source Materials

Coulton, G. G., *Life in the Middle Ages*, 4 vols.

——, *The Medieval Village*

Dante, *De Monarchia* (*On Monarchy*)

John of Salisbury, *Policraticus*

Johnes, Thomas, *Froissart's Chronicles of England, France, Spain, and the Adjoining Countries*, Vol. I, pp. 240–41; Vol. II, 94–95

McKechnie, W. S., *Magna Carta*

Marsiglio of Padua, *Defensor Pacis* (*Defender of the Peace*), especially Book I, Chs. IV, XII, XV

Riley, H. T., *Memorials of London and London Life*

Thatcher, O. J., and McNeal, E. H., *A Source Book for Medieval History*, pp. 283–306, "The Golden Bull of Charles IV"; also documents of feudalism, pp. 341–87

Webster, Hutton, *Historical Selections*, pp. 467–500, documents of the Feudal Regime

The Civilization of the
Feudal Age: Religious and
Intellectual Developments

The change in religious and intellectual attitudes

It has been mentioned more than once already that the civilization of western Europe between 800 and 1300 was vastly different from that which had existed at the beginning of the medieval period. Nowhere was the contrast more striking than in the spheres of religion and the intellect. The religious and intellectual attitudes of the early Middle Ages were products of a time of transition and of considerable chaos. The Roman political and social structure had disintegrated, and no new regime had yet emerged to take its place. As a consequence, the thinking of this time was directed toward pessimism and otherworldly concerns. In the midst of conditions of barbarism and decadence, there did not seem to be much hope for man's earthly future or much reason for confidence in the powers of the mind. But after the ninth century these attitudes gradually gave way to more optimistic sentiments and to an increasing interest in worldly affairs. The original causes were directly related to the progress of monastic education, to the rise of more stable government, and to an increase in economic security. Later such factors as the influence of the Saracenic and Byzantine civilizations and the growth of prosperity in the cities and towns brought the culture of the Feudal Age to a magnificent climax of intellectual achievement in the twelfth and thirteenth centuries. At the same time religion took on a less otherworldly aspect and evolved into an institution more deeply concerned with the affairs of this life.

1. The New Christianity

During the Feudal Age, Christianity underwent so many significant developments from its early medieval character that it seemed
in some respects to be almost a new religion. To be sure, such
cardinal features as faith in one God, the belief in the Trinity, and
the hope for salvation in a world to come continued to be accepted
in their original form; but certain other elements in the religion of
St. Augustine and Gregory the Great were modified or eliminated
and different ones substituted for them. The transformation began
about 850 and reached its zenith in the thirteenth century under the
influence of such leaders as St. Thomas Aquinas, St. Francis, and
Innocent III.

*Late medieval
Christianity*

Perhaps the most important developments were in matters of
doctrine and religious attitudes. The religion of the early Middle
Ages had been pessimistic, fatalistic, and, theoretically at least, opposed to everything worldly as a compromise with the devil. Man
was considered to be inherently wicked and incapable of any good
works except as the beneficiary of God's grace. God Himself was
omnipotent, selecting for reasons of His own those human beings
who would enter His paradise, and leaving the rest to follow the
path to destruction. By the thirteenth century, however, quite different religious conceptions had come to prevail. Life in this world
was now held to be exceedingly important, not only as a preparation for eternity but for its own sake as well. No longer was human
nature regarded as totally evil. Man could therefore co-operate with
God in achieving the salvation of his soul. Instead of emphasizing
the omnipotence of God, philosophers and theologians now stressed
the divine justice and mercy.

*New doctrines
and new atti-
tudes*

The first great summary of late medieval theology was the *Sen-
tences* of Peter Lombard, written during the second half of the
twelfth century. More inclusive statements of doctrine were contained in the *Summary of Theology* of St. Thomas Aquinas and in
the pronouncements issued by church councils, especially the Fourth
Lateran Council of 1215. Probably the most important of the new
elements in this theology were the theory of the priesthood and the
theory of the sacraments. There had, of course, been priests and
sacraments in the church long before the late Feudal Age, but neither
the exact functions of the priests nor the precise nature of the sacraments had ever been clearly formulated. The theory now came to be
held that the priest, by virtue of his ordination by a bishop and the
latter's confirmation by the Pope, was the inheritor of a portion of
the authority conferred by the Christ upon the Apostle Peter. In
effect, this meant that the priest had the power to co-operate with
God in performing certain miracles and in releasing sinners from
the temporal consequences of their wickedness.

*The new theol-
ogy: (1) the
theory of the
priesthood*

It was due primarily to the influence of Peter Lombard that the number of sacraments came to be accepted as seven. The seven were and still are: baptism; confirmation; penance; the Eucharist, or Lord's Supper; marriage; ordination; and extreme unction, or the last rites administered to the dying. The Roman church defines a sacrament as an instrumentality whereby divine grace is communicated to men. The sacramental theory as it came to be accepted during the last centuries of the Feudal Age included a number of separate doctrines. First, there was the doctrine that the sacraments were indispensable means of procuring God's grace, that no individual could be saved without them. Second, there was the principle that the sacraments were automatic in their effects. In other words, it was held that the efficacy of the sacraments did not depend upon the character of the priest who administered them. The priest might be a very unworthy man, but the sacraments in his hands would remain as unpolluted as if they were administered by a saint. Finally, at the Fourth Lateran Council, the doctrine of transubstantiation was made an integral part of the sacramental theory. This doctrine means that the priest, at a given moment in the Eucharistic ceremony, actually co-operates with God in the performance of a miracle whereby the bread and wine of the sacrament are changed or transubstantiated into the body and blood of Christ. The change, of course, is considered a change in essence only; the "accidents" of taste and appearance remain the same.

The adoption of these two fundamental theories, the theory of the priesthood and the theory of the sacraments, had potent effects in exalting the power of the clergy and in strengthening the formal and mechanical elements in the Latin church. However, medieval Catholicism was revitalized and made into a civilizing influence by two other developments which marked the late Feudal Age. One of these was the adoption of a rationalist philosophy by the leading theologians, and the other was the growth of a humanistic attitude. The influence of rationalist philosophy will be discussed farther on in this chapter. The humanizing element in religion expressed itself in a variety of ways—in the revolt against the selfish asceticism of monks and hermits, in the naturalism of St. Francis, but perhaps most of all in the veneration of saints and the Virgin Mary. All through the later medieval period, the veneration or "invocation" of saints was an exceedingly popular practice, especially among the common people. For the average person God and Christ were remote and sublime beings who could hardly be bothered with the petty problems of men. But the saints were human; one could ask them for favors which one would hesitate to request of God. For example, a woman could implore the aid of St. Agnes in helping her find a husband. Even more popular than the invocation of saints was reverence for the Virgin Mary, which came to be almost a religion in itself during the twelfth and thirteenth centuries. Devotion to

334 Mary as the beautiful and compassionate Mother undoubtedly served as one of the strongest expressions of the humanist tendency in medieval religion. For she was venerated not only as the ideal woman but also as Our Lady of Sorrows. The grief that she experienced over the tragic death of her Son was believed to endow her with a special sympathy for the sorrows of mankind. Though revered as the Queen of Heaven, she was, above all, the goddess of this life.

Significant developments in ecclesiastical organization and the adoption of new forms of religious discipline also occurred during the Feudal Age. In 1059 the College of Cardinals was established as *Changes in the* a papal electoral college. Originally the members of this body were *organization of* the deacons, priests, and bishops of certain churches in the city of *the church* Rome. Later high ranking clergy from nearly all countries of the Western world were appointed to membership, although the College included a majority of Italians until 1946. At present there are seventy seats, and a two-thirds vote is necessary to elect the Pope, who is invariably a cardinal himself. Prior to 1059 Popes were chosen in a variety of ways. In the early days they had been elected by the clergy of the diocese of Rome, but later they were often appointed by powerful nobles and frequently by the German emperors. The vesting of the sole right of election in the College of Cardinals was part of a great reform movement to free the church from political control. The other main development in religious organization was the growth of the papal monarchy. The first of the Popes to achieve much success in extending his supremacy over the whole ecclesiastical hierarchy was Nicholas I (858–867). Intervening in disputes between bishops and archbishops, he forced all of them to submit to his own direct authority. Nicholas was followed, however, by a series of weak successors, and the papal monarchy was not revived until the reign of Gregory VII (1073–1085). It reached the highest stage of its medieval development during the pontificate of Innocent III (1198–1216).

During the later centuries of the Feudal Age the church made systematic attempts to extend its moral authority over all of its lay members, whether of high or of low degree. The chief methods *New methods* adopted were excommunication and the requirement of oral con- *of discipline* fession. Excommunication was not used to any extent before the eleventh century. Its effect was to expel an individual from the church and to deprive him of all the privileges of a Christian. His body could not be buried in consecrated ground, and his soul was temporarily consigned to hell. All other Christians were forbidden to associate with him, under penalty of sharing his fate. Sometimes a decree of excommunication against a king or a powerful noble was fortified by placing an *interdict* upon the area over which he ruled. The interdict, by withholding most of the benefits of religion from a ruler's subjects, was intended to kindle their resentment against him and force him to submit to the church. Both excommunication and the interdict proved to be powerful weapons until about the end of the thirteenth century; after that their effectiveness waned. By a decree of the Fourth Lateran Council in 1215 the church adopted the requirement that every individual must make an oral confession of his sins to a priest at least once a year, and then undergo the punishment imposed before becoming eligible to partake of the Eucharist. The result of this decree was to give the priest the authority of a moral guardian over every individual in his parish.

Medieval reform movements: (1) the Cluniac revival

Long before the great Reformation of the sixteenth century, medieval Catholicism went through a series of reformations calculated to restore the institutions of the church to some earlier state of purity or to make them more useful to society. The first of these reform movements was the Cluny movement or the Cluniac revival, which derived its name from the monastery of Cluny, founded in 910. The original purpose of the Cluny movement was simply to reform monasticism. The Benedictine monasteries, which were practically the only ones in existence by the tenth century in western Europe, had grown corrupt and were rapidly passing under the control of feudal nobles. Consequently the Cluniac leaders took as their objectives the enforcement of the rules of piety and chastity upon the monks and the liberation of the monasteries themselves from feudal domination. But by the eleventh century the movement had gained a much broader significance. In fact, its purposes were now so different from the original ones that it is often referred to as the New Cluny movement. No longer were the reformers content merely to purify monasticism and free it from the clutches of the lay feudality; their primary aims were now to eliminate corruption and worldliness from the entire church, to abolish feudal control over the secular clergy as well as over monks, and to establish the absolute supremacy of the Pope in ecclesiastical matters. They centered their attacks, first of all, upon *simony*, which was interpreted to include the buying and selling of church offices, any form of appointment to church offices contrary to the canon law, and the investing of bishops and abbots with the symbols of their spiritual power by secular authorities. In addition, the reformers demanded celibacy for all grades of the clergy. Nearly all of these elements in their program were directed toward making the church entirely independent of the great nobles, especially by depriving them of their power to dictate the appointment of bishops, abbots, and priests. The movement aroused bitter opposition, since it struck at the very basis of the feudal relationship which had been established between secular rulers and the clergy. But most of the program was eventually put into effect, due in large part to the fanatical zeal of such leaders as Hildebrand, the "holy Satan" who in 1073 became Pope Gregory VII.

By the end of the eleventh century the Cluniac monks had begun to sink into the same morass of worldliness as did their older Benedictine brothers whom they had set out to reform. The result was the launching of new movements to set an even stronger example of purity and austerity for the regular clergy. In 1084 the Carthusian order was established with a set of rules more rigorous than any hitherto adopted in the West. The Carthusian monks were required to live in cells, to fast three days each week on bread and water, to wear hair shirts, and to spend all their time in prayer, meditation, and manual labor. A few years later the Cistercian order was founded at Cîteaux in Burgundy and soon proved to be one of the most popular of them all. By the middle of the twelfth century more than three hundred Cistercian monasteries were receiving converts from all over western Europe. Although not so strict in their requirements of individual asceticism as the Carthusians, the founders of the Cistercian order saw to it that the rules would be puritanical enough to constitute an emphatic protest against the luxury and idleness of the Cluniac monks. Only a vegetarian diet was allowed, and manual labor was strictly enforced. Both the Cistercian and Carthusian orders ultimately went down the same road to decline as their predecessors, partly as a result of the accumulation of wealth, but also because monasticism of the old-fashioned type was by the thirteenth century no longer consistent with the ideals of the time.

Undoubtedly the most significant reform movement of the Feudal Age was the rise of the friars in the thirteenth century. Though the friars are often regarded as simply another species of monks, they were really quite different. Originally they were not members of the clergy at all but laymen. Instead of shutting themselves up in monasteries, they devoted all of their time to social welfare work and to preaching and teaching. The growth of the new orders was symptomatic of an attempt to bring religion into harmony with the needs of a world which had completely outgrown the Dark Ages. Men were now coming to realize that the main business of religion was not to enable a few selfish monks to save their own souls at the expense of society, but to help make this world a happier place in which to live and to rescue the great mass of mankind from the slough of ignorance and sin.

The founder of the original order of friars was St. Francis of Assisi (1182–1226). The son of a rich merchant, the young Francis became dissatisfied with the useless life of vanity and pleasure he was expected to lead and determined to become a servant of the poor. Giving away all of his property and donning the rags of a beggar, he set out on his great mission of preaching salvation in the darkest corners of the Italian cities and ministering to the needs of poor, diseased, and helpless outcasts. The philosophy of St. Francis, if such it can be called, was different from that of many other Christian leaders. The major portion of it was founded almost literally upon the teachings of Jesus. St. Francis followed Jesus in his selflessness, in his devotion to poverty as an ideal, in his indifference to doctrine, and in his contempt for form and ceremony. In addition he had a profound love not merely for man but for every creature around him, and even for the objects of inanimate nature. He found God revealed in the sun, the wind, the flowers, and everything that existed for the use or delight of man. His disciples related how he would never put out a fire, but "treated it reverently," and how "he directed the brother who cut and fetched the fire wood never to cut a whole tree, so that some part of it might remain untouched for the love of Him who was willing to work out our salvation upon the wood of the cross." [1] Finally, it should be made clear that St. Francis was not an ascetic in the accurate meaning of that term. Although he denied himself comforts and pleasures, he did not despise the body or practice laceration of the flesh to achieve the salvation of his soul. His abandonment of earthly possessions was done primarily to conquer pride and bring himself down to the level of the people whom he wished to help.

The Dominican order

The second of the orders of friars was the Dominican order, founded about 1215 by St. Dominic, a Castilian noble who lived in southern France. The Dominicans adopted as their principal task the combating of heresy. Believing that the best means to this end was education, they prepared themselves by diligent study to refute the arguments of pagans and skeptics. Many members of the order gained teaching positions in the universities and contributed much to the development of philosophy and theology. By the fourteenth century both the Dominican and Franciscan orders had departed widely from the teachings of their founders, but they continued to exert a strong influence upon late medieval civilization. The majority of the philosophers and scientists of the thirteenth and fourteenth centuries were either Dominicans or Franciscans.

2. The Struggle between the Secular and Spiritual Authorities

The scope of the conflict

As it happened, the growth of the church in the Feudal Age was accompanied by the rise of ambitious political leaders. A conflict between secular and spiritual authorities was practically unavoidable, since the jurisdictions claimed by each frequently overlapped. The struggle began in 1075 and continued with varying intensity until well into the fourteenth century. Two separate stages in the conflict can be distinguished, the first ending in 1122, and the second beginning about twenty years later.

The two great opponents in the first stage were Pope Gregory VII and the German emperor, Henry IV. The quarrel between these powerful rivals was a direct outgrowth of the New Cluny movement, of which Gregory had been the leader for some time before

[1] Quoted by H. O. Taylor, *The Medieval Mind,* Vol. I, pp. 454-55.

he became Pope. As noted previously, one of the fundamental aims of this movement was to free the church from secular control. During a period of many years the practice had been established that a bishop, abbot, or priest who held his position as a fief should be invested with the symbols of his office by the king or noble who granted the fief. This practice, known as lay investiture, was a thorn in the side of such zealous reformers as Gregory; for they feared that as long as the clergy owed allegiance in any degree to secular overlords, papal supremacy would be impossible. But this was not the only issue involved; there was also the question of the Pope's right to exercise temporal authority. Just how much temporal jurisdiction Gregory intended to claim is not quite clear. Sometimes it appears from his decrees that he regarded himself as the supreme ruler of the world and thought of all princes and kings as merely his vassals. But leading scholars of medieval political theory have denied that this was the case. They contend that Gregory's conception of his authority was merely that of *pastor of the Christian flock*, and that he never claimed an unlimited right to create and depose secular rulers or annul their decrees. He would intervene only to protect the interests of the church and the religious rights of Christians.[2] Naturally, this was a rather extensive authority, but it would still fall short of the right to rule as an autocrat over the whole world.

The quarrel between Henry and Gregory was one of the most bitter in the Middle Ages. When Henry refused to obey decrees of the Pope prohibiting lay investiture, Gregory threatened to excommunicate him. The king retaliated by denouncing the Pope as a false monk and ordering him to descend from the throne "to be damned throughout the ages." Whereupon Gregory not only excommunicated Henry but declared his throne vacant and released all his subjects from allegiance to him. Faced with revolt by his vassals, Henry had no alternative but to make peace with the Pope. How he journeyed over the Alps in the depth of winter to Canossa in northern Italy and implored the Pope's forgiveness is a familiar story and need not be recounted here. Later on, Henry had his revenge when he led an army into Italy, set up an anti-pope, and compelled Gregory to flee from Rome. The great apostle of reform died in exile in 1085.

Outcome of the struggle

The first stage of the conflict was brought to an end by the Concordat of Worms, an agreement ratified by a meeting of German princes and clergy and papal legates in 1122. The settlement was a compromise providing that in the future bishops should be invested with the symbols of their political authority by the king and should take an oath of fealty to him as his vassals, but the archbishop was to have the right to invest them with the symbols of their spiritual functions. It was not long, however, until the struggle was re-

The compromise of 1122 and the beginning of the second stage of the struggle

[2] *Cf.* C. H. McIlwain, *The Growth of Political Thought in the West*, pp. 208 ff.

Shrine of the Three Kings, Cologne Cathedral. Richly decorated shrines are one of the principal forms of interior ornamentation in Gothic cathedrals. The cathedral of Cologne (Köln) in western Germany contains the Shrine of the Three Kings, or the Three Wise Men of the East, who are supposed to have brought gifts to the infant Jesus. According to legend, the bones of the Three Kings were brought from Italy in the Twelfth Century by Frederick Barbarossa and buried in Cologne.

newed, this time on a much larger scale. Before it ended in the fourteenth century, nearly all of the monarchs of western Europe had been involved. Among them were the Holy Roman Emperors, Frederick Barbarossa and Frederick II; the French kings, Philip Augustus and Philip the Fair; and the English king, John. The leading contenders on the papal side were Innocent III, Innocent IV, and Boniface VIII. The issues in this second stage of the struggle were more numerous than in the first. They included localism versus centralization in Germany, the right of the Holy Roman Emperors to rule over Italy, the freedom of Italian towns from German domination, and the right of kings to tax the property of the church. Furthermore, the Popes were now extending their claims to temporal authority a degree or two beyond what had been asserted by Gregory VII. Innocent III declared that "It is the business of the pope to look after the interests of the Roman empire, since the empire derives its origin, and its final authority from the papacy." [3] Innocent IV appears to have gone a step further and to have claimed jurisdiction over all temporal affairs and over all human beings, whether Christians or not. Nevertheless, it must be borne in mind that none of these Popes was really demanding absolute power. What they were insisting upon was not a legislative but a judicial authority; in other words, an authority to judge and punish rulers for their sins. The fundamental issue was whether rulers were directly responsible to God for their official acts or indirectly through the Pope.

The second stage of the conflict had momentous results not only for medieval Europe but for subsequent ages as well. For a time the Popes were almost uniformly successful. With the aid of the Lom-

Results of the second stage

[3] O. J. Thatcher and E. H. McNeal, *A Source Book for Medieval History*, p. 220.

bard cities and the rebellious dukes in Germany, they checked the
ambitions of the Holy Roman Emperors and finally broke the power
of the Empire entirely. By means of interdicts Innocent III compelled Philip Augustus to take back the wife he had repudiated and
forced King John to recognize England and Ireland as fiefs of the
papacy. At the beginning of the fourteenth century, however, Boniface VIII went down to humiliating defeat at the hands of King
Philip the Fair of France. As the outcome of a quarrel over Philip's
attempt to tax the property of the church, Boniface was taken prisoner by the king's soldiers, and a month later he died. The Archbishop of Bordeaux was chosen to succeed him, and the papal capital
was transferred to Avignon in France, where it remained for seventy
years. But there were other results also. Many pious Christians now
came to believe that the Popes were carrying their ambitions for
political power too far and were forgetting their spiritual functions.
As a consequence, the papacy lost prestige, and the way was
opened for repudiation of its leadership even in religious affairs.
In like manner, papal meddling in the internal politics of different
countries tended to strengthen the growth of nationalism, particularly in England and France. Finally, the struggle led to a quicken-
ing of intellectual activity. As each side attempted to justify its
position, interest was awakened in ancient writings, an incentive was
provided for the study of the Roman law, and many valuable contributions were made to political theory.

3. The Crusades

It is probably not inaccurate to regard the Crusades as the chief
expression of medieval imperialism. Unfortunately it appears to be
true that nearly every civilization sooner or later develops ex-   *The Crusades*
pansionist tendencies. Certain ones, of course, have been much worse   *an expression*
offenders than others, but imperialism in some degree has been   *of medieval*
characteristic of nearly all of them. It seems to be the natural fruit   *imperialism*
of the increasing complexity of economic life and of the growth
of pride in the real or fancied superiority of a system.

Although the Crusades were by no means a religious movement
exclusively, there can be no denying the importance of the religious
factor in producing them. The century in which they were launched   *The religious*
was an age when religion occupied a predominant place in men's   *causes*
thinking. The medieval Christian had a deep conviction of sin. He   *of the Crusades:*
feared its consequences in the form of eternal damnation and was   *(1) mass pil-*
anxious to avert them by acts of penance. For hundreds of years   *grimages*
the most popular type of penance had been the making of pilgrimages to sacred places. A trip to the Holy Land, if at all possible,
had been the cherished ambition of every Christian. By the eleventh
century the religious revivalism generated by the Cluniac reform
movement, combined with the opening up of trade with the Near

East, had made pilgrimages to Palestine especially appealing. Hundreds of people now joined the roving bands that trailed across central and eastern Europe on their way to the Levant. In 1065 the Bishop of Bamberg led a horde of seven thousand Germans to visit the holy places in and around Jerusalem. Of course, not everyone who joined these mass migrations was inspired by religious ardor. Pilgrimages afforded an opportunity for adventure and sometimes even for profit. Besides, what better chance need one want to escape the responsibilities of life for a season and have a good time in the bargain? Every pilgrim who returned brought back stories of the wonderful sights he had seen and thereby aroused the desire of others to follow his example. Without these mass pilgrimages interest in conquest of the Holy Land would probably never have developed.

(2) religious wars as means of promoting unity

Other religious causes must also be mentioned. For a time during the late eleventh century, prospects for papal supremacy did not look too bright. Gregory VII had been driven from the throne and had died in exile in 1085. His successor was an aged friend who went to his grave after a year of failure. The cardinals then chose a younger and more vigorous man, who adopted the name of Urban II. Urban had been a French noble who had renounced the world to become a monk at Cluny. Subsequently he became the talented assistant of Gregory VII. Elected Pope himself in 1088, he turned his attention to the glorious dream of uniting all classes of Christians in support of the church. Perhaps he might even force a reunion of the Eastern and Western branches of Christendom. At any rate, a war against the infidel, for the rescue of the Holy Places from desecration, would enable Latin Christians to forget their differences and to rally behind the Pope. Already the papacy had inspired or given its blessing to wars on behalf of religion. Predecessors of Urban II had blessed the Norman conquest of England, the campaigns of Robert Guiscard against heretical Greeks in Italy, and the wars of Christians against Moors in Spain. To merge these efforts in a grand enterprise against the whole unbelieving world must have seemed but a logical climax to what had already occurred.

(3) other religious causes

For more than a century the religious leaders in Europe had been disturbed by the prevalence of fighting among the feudal nobles. Despite the Peace of God and the Truce of God, the warfare of barons and knights continued to be a menace to the security of the church. The rights of clergy, peasants, and other noncombatants were often trampled upon, merchants were robbed, and religious edifices pillaged and burned. Against these depredations the penalty of excommunication was of little avail. Small wonder, therefore, that Popes should have turned to the idea of protecting the church and its members by diverting the military ardor of the nobles into a holy war against the heathen. Still another religious cause was surplus idealism left over from the New Cluny movement. Move-

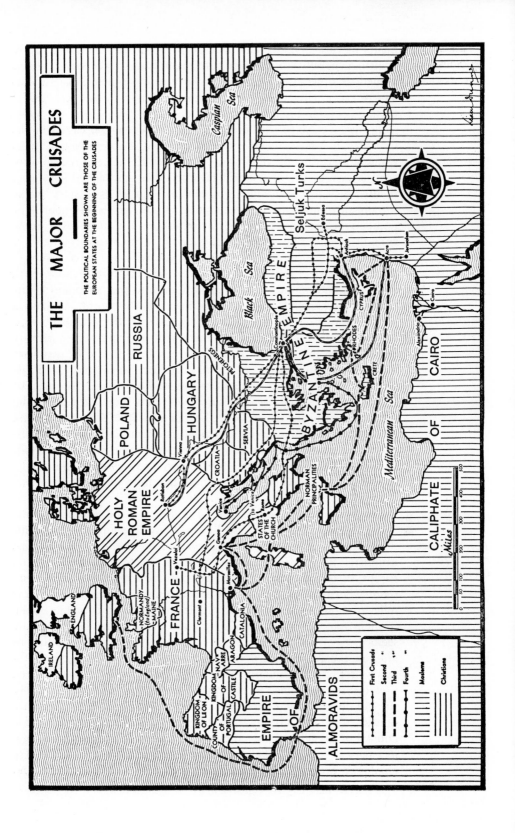

THE MAJOR CRUSADES

THE POLITICAL BOUNDARIES SHOWN ARE THOSE OF THE
EUROPEAN STATES AT THE BEGINNING OF THE CRUSADES

Caspian Sea

RUSSIA

POLAND

HOLY ROMAN EMPIRE

HUNGARY

Black Sea

Seljuk Turks

BYZANTINE EMPIRE

PECHENEGS

Vienna

CROATIA

SERVIA

Regensburg

Venice

Genoa

(to Venice)

STATES OF THE CHURCH

NORMAN PRINCIPALITIES

CRETE

RHODES

CYPRUS

Edessa

Antioch

Acre

Jerusalem

Mediterranean Sea

Alexandria

Cairo

CALIPHATE OF CAIRO

IRELAND

ENGLAND

NORMANDY
(to England)

MAINE

FRANCE

Vézelai

Clermont

Marseilles

KINGDOM OF
NAVARRE

ARAGON

CATALONIA

CASTILE

KINGDOM OF LEON

COUNTY OF PORTUGAL

EMPIRE OF

ALMORAVIDS

First Crusade
Second "
Third "
Fourth "
Moslems
Christians

Miles
0   50 100   200   300   400   500

ments of this kind, which strike deeply into the emotional nature of man, generally stir up more enthusiasm than is necessary for their immediate objectives. Some of this surplus must then find new outlets, just as in later years the fanaticism engendered by the Crusades themselves burst forth into persecution of the Jews.

To discover some of the most important economic causes of the Crusades, one has only to read the speech of Pope Urban II at the Council of Clermont inviting the nobles of France to take up arms for the conquest of Palestine. He urged them to let nothing detain them, "since this land which you inhabit, shut in on all sides by the sea and surrounded by mountain peaks, is too narrow for your large population; nor does it abound in wealth; and it furnishes scarcely enough food for its cultivators. . . . Enter upon the road to the Holy Sepulchre; wrest that land from the wicked race and subject it to yourselves. That land which, as the Scripture says, 'floweth with milk and honey,' was given by God into the possession of the children of Israel. Jerusalem is the navel of the world; the land is fruitful above others, like another paradise of delights." [4] There is evidence also that the manorial system of agriculture was already beginning to impair the fertility of the soil, with the consequence that a good many nobles had fallen into debt. Furthermore, the rule of primogeniture in France and in England created the problem of what to do with the younger sons. New fiefs were hard to obtain, and positions in the church were becoming scarce. As a result, these surplus offspring of the nobles tended to form a rebellious and disorderly class, alert for any opportunity to despoil a weak neighbor of his property. Confronted by such problems as these, the nobles of western Europe needed no second invitation to respond to Pope Urban's plea.

The immediate cause of the Crusades was the advance of the Seljuk Turks in the Near East. In about 1050 these people had come down into western Asia and had gained control over the Bagdad caliphate. Soon afterward they conquered Syria, Palestine, and Egypt. In 1071 they slaughtered a Byzantine army at Manzikert and then swept through Asia Minor and captured Nicaea, within a few miles of Constantinople. After the death of the great Sultan, Malik Shah, in 1092 the Seljuk empire began to disintegrate. The time now seemed ripe for the Byzantine emperor, Alexius Comnenus, to attempt the reconquest of his lost possessions. Realizing the difficulty of this task, since his own government was exhausted from previous struggles, he sent an appeal in 1095 to the Pope, probably for aid in recruiting mercenary soldiers. Urban II, the reigning pontiff, took full advantage of this opportunity. He summoned a council of French nobles and clergy at Clermont and exhorted them in a fiery speech to make war upon the accursed race of Turks. He employed every artful device of eloquence to arouse the fury and

[4] Thatcher and McNeal, *A Source Book for Medieval History*, pp. 519-20.

cupidity of his hearers, emphasizing especially the horrible atrocities which he declared the Turks were committing upon Christians. When he had finished, it is reported that all who were present cried out with one accord, "It is the will of God," and rushed forward to take the crusader's oath. The appeal of Urban II was supplemented soon after the Council of Clermont by the impassioned preaching of Peter the Hermit, who went among the peasants rousing them to a frenzied enthusiasm for the holy cause. In the spring of 1096 he led a great mob of them from France and Germany to Constantinople. Most of his followers were ignorant, poorly equipped, and totally untrained for war. When they began looting in the Byzantine capital, the emperor promptly shipped them across the Bosporus into Asia Minor where the Turks made short work of them.

The first of the organized Crusades was not actually started until late in 1096. The majority of those who participated in it were Frenchmen and Normans, under the leadership of Godfrey of Bouillon, Count Raymond of Toulouse, and Bohemund from the Norman kingdom of Sicily. Altogether, between 1096 and 1244, three other major Crusades and a number of minor ones were launched. Only the first achieved much success in destroying Turkish control over Christian territory. By 1098 most of Syria had been captured, and a year later Jerusalem was taken. But these gains were only temporary. In 1187 Jerusalem was recaptured by the Moslems under Saladin, Sultan of Egypt. Before the end of the thirteenth century every one of the petty states established by the crusaders in the Near East had been wiped out.

The major Crusades

The ultimate failure of the Crusades was due to several causes. To begin with, the expeditions were frequently badly managed; there was seldom any unified command, and rival leaders quarreled among themselves. Further, the victorious armies were always surrounded by an enormous alien population, a fact which increased the difficulty of holding conquered territory. In some of the later expeditions the original purpose of conquering the Holy Land from the Turks was lost sight of altogether. The Fourth Crusade, for example, turned out to be a gigantic plundering foray against Constantinople. But there was also another cause which cannot be overlooked, and that was the conflicting ambitions of the East and the West. According to the evidence, Alexius Comnenus, in appealing to the Pope for aid, professed a desire to protect the Christian churches of the Orient. But this was not his primary objective. He had come to the conclusion that the time was ripe for a major offensive against the Turks. He was not interested simply or even primarily in driving them out of the Holy Land but in reconquering all of the Asiatic provinces of his empire. By contrast, Pope Urban II had the grandiose dream of a holy war of all of Latin Christendom to expel the infidel from Palestine. His underlying purpose was not to rescue the Byzantine Empire but to strengthen Latin

Reasons for the failure of the Crusades

Christianity, to exalt the papacy, and perhaps to restore the union of the Eastern and Western churches. An additional cause of friction between East and West was the ambition of Italian merchants to extend their commercial empire. They coveted the trade that passed through Constantinople and were ready to capture or destroy the city for their own advantage.

The importance of the Crusades not to be exaggerated

In line with a common tendency to overestimate the importance of wars, the Crusades were at one time considered as the primary cause of nearly all of European progress in the late Feudal Age. It was assumed that they led to the growth of cities, to the overthrow of feudalism, and to the introduction of Moslem philosophy and science into Latin Europe. Most historians now regard this assumption as of limited validity, for several reasons. First, the progress of civilization in the Feudal Age was already well under way before the Crusades began. Second, the educated classes in Europe did not generally take part in the military expeditions; as a result, the soldiers who actually went were totally devoid of the intellectual background necessary for an appreciation of Moslem learning. Third, very few of the armies ever reached the real centers of Moslem civilization, which were not Jerusalem or Antioch, but Bagdad, Damascus, Toledo, and Cordova. European intellectual progress in the twelfth and thirteenth centuries was due far more to the revival of trade with the Near East and to the work of scholars and translators in Spain and Sicily than to any influence of holy wars against the Turks. Nor were the Crusades primarily responsible for the political and economic changes at the end of the Middle Ages. The decline of feudalism, for instance, occurred chiefly because of the Black Death, the growth of an urban economy, and the rise of national monarchies; and these in turn were only in minor degree the results of the Crusades.

The actual results of the Crusades

What effects, then, is it possible to ascribe to the great holy wars against Islam? To some extent they hastened the emancipation of the common people. Nobles who were hard pressed for money sold privileges to townsmen and to communities of serfs somewhat earlier than they would otherwise have done. Furthermore, many peasants took advantage of the absence of the nobles to break away from bondage to the soil. Among other economic effects were an increased demand for products of the East, the growth of banking, and the elimination of Constantinople as the middleman in the trade between East and West. Venice, Genoa, and Pisa now gained a virtual monopoly of commerce in the Mediterranean area. In addition, the Crusades had some influence in strengthening the monarchies of France and England by eliminating powerful nobles and providing a pretext for direct taxation; but the political consequences were relatively slight. In the domain of religion, where we would normally expect the most profound results, few except negative effects can be discovered. It is impossible to prove that the Popes enjoyed any increase in power or repute as a result of having launched the Crusades. On the contrary, as the true character of the expeditions became more and more transparent, the papacy seems rather to have suffered a loss of prestige. There was, however, an increase in religious fanaticism, which expressed itself particularly in savage persecution of the Jews. These unfortunate people suffered

French Knights about to Depart on a Crusade. Their chief weapons are the long bow and the spear.

nearly everywhere. They were cruelly beaten and sometimes killed in mob attacks. Naturally, the fury against them was partly economic in origin, since they were the chief moneylenders of the time; nevertheless, it is a significant fact that hostility to Jews had one of its chief sources in the holy wars against Islam. Finally, it is doubtless true that the Crusades had some effect in widening geographic knowledge and in encouraging travel and exploration; but these developments were the result even more of the gradual expansion of trade.

4. The Late Medieval Mind

The beginning of intellectual progress in the Feudal Age dates from the so-called Carolingian Renaissance of the ninth century. This was a movement initiated by Charles the Great when he *The revival of* brought to his court at Aachen the most distinguished scholars he *learning in* could find. In doing this the emperor was prompted partly by his *western Europe* own interest in learning but also by his desire to find uniform standards of orthodoxy which could be imposed upon all of his subjects. Fortunately he seems to have allowed the scholars he imported a generous freedom to pursue their own inclinations. The result was a revival of learning which gathered sufficient momentum to carry over into the reigns of several of Charlemagne's successors. Among the leaders in the movement were Alcuin, director of the palace school; John Scotus Erigena, the rationalist philosopher; and Walafrid Strabo, the poet. After the Carolingian Renaissance intellectual progress in western Europe was comparatively slow for some time. A brief revival under the patronage of the Ottos in Germany in the tenth century was followed by a more virile growth of classical studies in Italy and France after the year 1000. But the **347** climax of intellectual achievement in the Feudal Age was not reached until the twelfth and thirteenth centuries.

I. PHILOSOPHY The outstanding philosophic achievement of the late Middle Ages was the famous system of thought known as Scholasticism. This system is usually defined as the attempt to harmonize reason and faith or to make philosophy serve the interests of theology. But no such definition is sufficient to convey an adequate conception of the Scholastic mind. The great thinkers of the Middle Ages did not limit their interests to problems of religion. On the contrary, they were just as anxious as philosophers in any period to answer the great questions of life, whether they pertained to religion, politics, economics, or metaphysics. Perhaps the best way to explain the true nature of Scholasticism is to define it in terms of its characteristics. In the first place, it was rationalistic, not empirical; in other words, it was based primarily upon logic rather than upon science or experience. The Scholastic philosophers, like the Greek thinkers of the Socratic school, did not believe that the highest truth could be derived from sense perception. They admitted that the senses could provide man with a knowledge of the appearances of things, but they maintained that reality or the essential nature of the universe is discoverable mainly by reason. In the second place, Scholastic philosophy was authoritarian. Even reason was not considered a sufficient instrument for the discovery of all knowledge, but the deductions of logic needed to be buttressed by the authority of the Scriptures, of the Church Fathers, and especially of Plato and Aristotle. Third, Scholastic philosophy had a predominantly ethical approach. Its cardinal aim was to discover how man could improve this life and insure salvation in the life to come. The Scholastic philosopher was a humanist to the extent that he was interested primarily in man. His universe was a compact and ordered whole created for the benefit of the human race. Fourth, Scholastic thought, unlike modern philosophy, was not mainly concerned with causes and underlying relationships; its purpose was rather to discover the attributes of things; the universe was assumed to be static, and therefore it was only necessary to explain the meaning of things and what they were good for, not to account for their origin and evolution.

The primary development of the Scholastic philosophy began with the teachings of Peter Abelard (1079–1142), one of the most significant figures in the history of thought. This handsome and talented Frenchman was educated in the best schools of Paris and gained a wide reputation for dialectical skill before he was out of his twenties. For a number of years he taught in Paris, drawing great crowds to his lectures on philosophy and theology. Despite the fact that he was a monk, his habits of life were far from ascetic. He was proud, belligerent, and egotistical—boastful of his intellectual triumphs and even of his prowess in love. He avowed that he possessed such advantages of comeliness and youth that "he feared no repulse from whatever woman he might deign to honor with his love." His tragic affair with Heloïse, which he poignantly describes in his autobiography, *The Story of My Misfortunes*, finally brought his downfall. But as a philosopher Abelard had accomplishments to his credit for which he had a right to be proud. He was probably the most critical of all the medieval thinkers. In his most famous philosophical work, *Sic et Non* (*Yes and No*), he exposed many of the shabby arguments from authority that were commonly accepted in his time. The preface to this work contains a statement which expresses clearly his conviction of the vital importance of critical reasoning: "For the first key to wisdom is called interrogation, diligent and unceasing. . . . By doubting we are led to inquiry; and from inquiry we perceive the truth."

The heyday of Scholasticism came in the thirteenth century, as a result mainly of the labors of Albertus Magnus and his renowned pupil, St. Thomas Aquinas. These men had the advantage of being able to study most of the works of Aristotle, recently translated from copies in the possession of the Saracens. Albertus Magnus, the only scholar ever to be honored with the title of Great, was born in Germany in 1193. During a long and active career he served as a teacher, especially at Cologne and at the University of Paris. A profound admirer of Aristotle, he strove to emulate the example of that ancient master by taking the whole field of knowledge as his province. His writings included more than twenty volumes on subjects ranging from botany and physiology to the soul and the creation of the universe. He was often skeptical of ancient authorities, and he attempted to found his conclusions upon reason and experience. In referring to hoary myths, such as the one about ostriches eating iron, he would frequently say: "but this is not proved by experience." He defined natural science "as not simply receiving what one is told, but the investigation of causes in natural phenomena." [5]

The heyday of Scholasticism; Albertus Magnus

Thomas Aquinas, the most noted of all the Scholastic philosophers, was born in southern Italy about 1225. Following the example of the great Albert, he entered the Dominican order and devoted his life to teaching. He was a professor at the University of Paris by the time he was twenty-five. His most famous work was his *Summary of Theology*, but he wrote on many other subjects as well, including politics and economics. The fundamental aims of St. Thomas were, first, to demonstrate the rationality of the universe, and second, to establish the primacy of reason. He believed that the universe is an ordered whole governed by intelligent purpose. All things were created in order to make possible the fulfillment of the great Christian plan for the promotion of justice and peace on earth and the salva-

St. Thomas Aquinas

[5] Lynn Thorndike, *A History of Magic and Experimental Science*, Vol. II, ch. 59.

tion of mankind in a world to come. The philosophy of St. Thomas implied a serene confidence in the ability of man to know and understand his world. The great *Summaries* he wrote were attempts to build up out of logic and the wisdom of the past comprehensive systems of knowledge which would leave no mysteries unsolved. Though he leaned very heavily upon the authority of Aristotle, he regarded reason as the primary key to truth. Even his attitude toward religion was essentially intellectual rather than emotional; piety to him was a matter of knowledge much more than of faith. He admitted that a few doctrines of Christianity, such as the belief in the Trinity and the creation of the world in time, could not be proved by the intellect; but he denied that they were contrary to reason, for God Himself is a rational being. As a disciple of Aristotle, St. Thomas taught that the highest good for man is the realization of his true nature; this, he maintained, consists in the knowledge of God, which can be attained in large measure by reason in this life, but will be perfectly realized only in the hereafter. The influence of St. Thomas was not only of cardinal importance in his own time, but it survives to this day. In the late nineteenth century Pope Leo XIII exhorted the bishops of the church "to restore the golden wisdom of St. Thomas and to spread it far and wide for the defense of the faith, for the good of society, and for the advantage of all the sciences." He recommended St. Thomas as a master and guide for everyone interested in scholarly studies.

The decay of Scholasticism

By the end of the thirteenth century Scholasticism had begun to decline. Its decay was due partly to the teachings of the last of the Scholastics, John Duns Scotus. A member of the Franciscan order, Duns Scotus was inclined to emphasize the emotional and practical side of religion in place of the intellectual. He conceived of piety as an act of will rather than an act of intellect. Less confident of the powers of reason than St. Thomas, he excluded a large number of the doctrines of religion from the sphere of philosophy altogether. From this it was only a step to denial that any religious beliefs were capable of rational demonstration; all would have to be accepted on faith or rejected entirely. When this step was finally taken by Duns Scotus' successors, the overthrow of Scholasticism was speedily accomplished.

The growth of nominalism

The other main reason for the decline of Scholasticism was the growing popularity of nominalism. Although nominalism is often considered a branch of Scholasticism, actually the nominalists were fundamentally opposed to nearly everything the Scholastics taught. They denied that concepts or class names have any reality, insisting that they are nothing but abstractions invented by the mind to express the qualities common to a number of objects or organisms. Only individual things are real. Far from accepting the Scholastic confidence in reason, the nominalists contended that all knowledge has its source in experience. Anything beyond the realm of concrete experience must be taken on faith, if it is to be accepted at all; the truths of religion cannot be demonstrated by logic. Although some of the earlier nominalists inclined toward religious skepticism, the majority became mystics. Nominalism flourished in the fourteenth century and for some time was the most popular philosophy in western Europe. Its ablest exponent was the English Franciscan, William of Occam. Nominalism is especially important for having laid the foundations for the scientific progress of the Renaissance and for the mystical religious movements which helped to bring on the Protestant Revolution.

A good many medieval philosophers devoted earnest attention to questions of political authority; a few, in fact, were primarily concerned with such questions. The political theorists of the Feudal Age were in substantial agreement on a large part of their philosophy. Practically all of them had abandoned the idea of the Church Fathers that the state was established by God as a remedy for sin, and that men must therefore render faithful obedience even to the tyrant. It was now commonly held that the state is a product of man's social nature, and that when justice is the guiding principle of the ruler, government is a positive good, not a necessary evil. In the second place, it was generally agreed by the philosophers of the Feudal Age that all of western Europe should constitute a single commonwealth under one supreme ruler. There might be many subordinate kings or princes in the different parts of the continent, but one supreme overlord, either the Pope or the Holy Roman Emperor, should have the highest jurisdiction. The most noted of those who defended the supremacy of the Emperor was Dante in his *De Monarchia*. On the papal side were the Englishman John of Salisbury (*ca.* 1115–1180) and Thomas Aquinas. Virtually without exception the political theorists of the Feudal Age believed in limited government. They had no use for absolutism in any form. John of Salisbury even went so far as to defend the right of the subjects of a tyrant to put him to death. Practically all of late medieval theory was based upon the assumption that the authority of every ruler, whether Pope, Emperor, or king, was essentially judicial in character. His function was merely to apply the law, not to make or alter it in accordance with his will. Indeed, the medievalists did not conceive of law as the command of a sovereign at all, but as the product of custom or of the divine order of nature. On the other hand, the medieval political theorists were not democrats, for not one of them believed in the doctrine of majority rule. The man who came closest to an exposition of the democratic ideal was Marsiglio of Padua in the fourteenth century. He advocated that the people should have the right to elect the monarch and even to depose him if necessary. He believed also in a representative body with power to make laws. But Marsiglio was no champion of unlimited popular sovereignty. In fact, he defined democracy as a

The political theory of the Feudal Age

Opposition to absolutism

351

degraded form of government. His idea of representative government was representation of the citizens according to quality rather than mere numbers, and the law-making powers of his representative body would be confined to the enactment of statutes regulating the structure of the government.

II. SCIENCE The record of scientific achievements in the Feudal Age can scarcely be considered an imposing one. Yet it was probably about all we should expect in view of the absorption of interest in other fields. The names of only a few individual scientists need to be mentioned. One of the most original was Adelard of Bath, who lived in the early years of the twelfth century. Not only did he condemn reliance upon authority, but he devoted many years of his life to direct investigation of nature. He discovered some important facts about the causes of earthquakes, the functions of different parts of the brain, and the processes of breathing and digestion. He was probably the first scientist since the Hellenistic Age to affirm the indestructibility of matter.

The Feudal Age not a great age of science

The toughest-minded of all the medieval scientists was the notorious Holy Roman Emperor, Frederick II, whose reign occupied the first part of the thirteenth century. Frederick was skeptical of almost everything. He denied the immortality of the soul, and he was accused of having written a brochure entitled *Jesus, Moses and Mohammed: the Three Great Impostors.* But he was not satisfied merely to scoff. He performed various experiments of his own to gratify his boundless curiosity, testing the artificial incubation of eggs, for example, and sealing the eyes of vultures to determine whether they found their food by sight or by smell. He was even alleged to have shut a man up in a wine-cask in an effort to prove that the soul dies with the body. His most important scientific contributions were made, however, as a patron of learning. An ardent admirer of Moslem culture, he brought distinguished scholars to Palermo to translate the writings of the Saracens into Latin. He subsidized leading scientists, especially Leonard of Pisa, the most brilliant mathematician of the thirteenth century. In addition, Frederick instituted measures for the improvement of medical practice. He legalized the practice of dissection, established a system of examining and licensing physicians, and founded the University of Naples with one of the best medical schools in Europe.

Frederick II as a scientist

By far the best known of medieval scientists was Roger Bacon (*ca.* 1214–1294), possibly because he predicted certain modern inventions such as horseless carriages and flying machines. In reality, Bacon was much less critical than Frederick II; for he believed that all knowledge must enhance the glory of theology, the queen of the sciences. Moreover, Adelard of Bath preceded him by more than a century in advocating and using the experimental method. Nevertheless, Bacon, by virtue of his strong insistence upon accurate investigation, deserves a high place among medieval scientists. He

Roger Bacon

Alchemists in Their Laboratory. Note the great variety of instru- ments used and the spectacles worn by the experimenter.

denied that either reason or authority could furnish valid knowledge unless supported by experimental research. Besides, he himself did some practical work of great value. His writings on optics remained authoritative for several centuries. He discovered much about magnifying lenses, and it seems more than probable that he invented the simple microscope. Not only was he the best geographer of the Feudal Age, but he was also apparently the first scientist to perceive the inaccuracy of the Julian calendar and to advocate its revision.

III. EDUCATION Much of the advancement in philosophy and science in the late Middle Ages would have been quite impossible without the educational progress which marked the centuries from the ninth to the fourteenth. The Carolingian Renaissance resulted in the establishment of better schools and libraries in several of the monasteries of western Europe. As a consequence of the religious reform movements of the eleventh century, however, the monasteries tended to neglect education, with the result that the monastic educational institutions were gradually overshadowed by the cathedral schools. Some of the latter developed into what would now be considered the equivalent of colleges, providing excellent instruction in the so-called liberal arts. This was notably true of the cathedral schools located at Canterbury, Chartres, and Paris. But by far the most important educational development of the Middle Ages was the rise of the universities.

The transfer of education from the monasteries to the cathedral schools

The term university (from the Latin, *universitas*) originally meant a corporation or guild. In fact, many of the medieval universities were very much like craft guilds, organized for the purpose of training and licensing teachers. Gradually the word came to have the meaning of an educational institution with a school of liberal arts

The rise of the universities

353

and one or more faculties in the professional subjects of law, medicine, and theology. No one knows which of the universities was the
oldest. It may have been Salerno, which was a center of medical
study as far back as the tenth century. The universities of Bologna
and Paris are also very ancient, the former having been established
about 1150 and the latter before the end of the twelfth century. The
next oldest included such famous institutions as the universities of
Oxford, Cambridge, Montpellier, Salamanca, Rome, and Naples.
There were no universities in Germany until the end of the fourteenth century, when schools of this type were organized at Prague,
Vienna, Heidelberg, and Cologne. By the end of the Middle Ages
some eighty universities had been set up in western Europe.

*Organization
of the medieval
universities*

Practically every university in medieval Europe was patterned
after one or the other of two different models. Throughout Italy,
Spain, and southern France the standard was generally the University of Bologna, in which the students themselves constituted the
guild or corporation. They hired the teachers, paid their salaries,
and fined or discharged them for neglect of duty or inefficient
instruction. Nearly all of these southern institutions were secular
in character, specializing in law or medicine. The universities of
northern Europe were modeled after the one at Paris, which was not
a guild of students but of teachers. It included the four faculties of
arts, theology, law, and medicine, each headed by an elected dean.
In the great majority of the northern universities arts and theology
were the leading branches of study. Before the end of the thirteenth
century separate colleges came to be established within the University of Paris. The original college was nothing more than an
endowed home for poor students, but the discovery was soon made
that discipline could best be preserved by having all of the students
live in colleges. Eventually the colleges became centers of instruction as well as residences. While on the Continent of Europe most
of these colleges have ceased to exist, in England the universities of
Oxford and Cambridge still retain the pattern of federal organization copied from Paris. The colleges of which they are composed
are practically independent educational units.

*The course of
study*

Though modern universities have borrowed much of their organization from their medieval prototypes, the course of study has
been radically changed. No curriculum in the Middle Ages included much history or natural science, nor any great amount of
mathematics or classical literature. The conservative educator of
today who believes that mathematics and the classics should form
the backbone of university training can find no support for his
argument in the history of the medieval universities. The student
in the Middle Ages was required, first of all, to spend four or five
years in studying the *trivium*—grammar, rhetoric, and logic, or
dialectic. If he passed his examinations he received the preliminary
degree of bachelor of arts, which conferred no particular distinction.

To assure himself a place in professional life he must devote some additional years to the pursuit of an advanced degree, such as master of arts, doctor of laws, or doctor of medicine. For the master's degree three or four years had to be given to study of the *quadrivium*—arithmetic, geometry, astronomy, and music. These subjects were not quite what their names imply now. Their content was highly philosophical; arithmetic, for example, included primarily a study of the theory of numbers, while music was concerned largely with the properties of sound. The requirements for the doctor's degree were generally more severe and included more specialized training. By the end of the Middle Ages the course for the doctorate of theology at Paris had been extended to fourteen years, and the degree could not be conferred unless the candidate was at least thirty-five years of age. Both the master's and doctor's degrees were teaching degrees; even the title of doctor of medicine meant a teacher of medicine, not a practicing physician.

The life of medieval students differed in many ways from that of their modern descendants. The student body in any one university was not a homogeneous group but was composed of diverse nationalities. The young Frenchman or German who wanted to study law would almost certainly go to Bologna or Padua, just as the young Italian with an interest in theology would probably enroll at Paris. The entire university was usually an independent community, so that the students were exempt from the jurisdiction of the political authorities. A relic of this ancient autonomy is to be found in the fact that some of the German universities still have their own jails. Very few of the medieval students had books, and there was seldom any library from which they could borrow them. As a consequence, the learning process consisted primarily in taking down copious notes on wax tablets from the master's lecture and then analyzing and discussing them afterwards. The young man's education was supposed to be acquired through logic and memory rather than from extensive reading or research. In other respects, however, student life in the Middle Ages was not so far different from what it is now. If the medieval student knew nothing of intercollegiate sports, he at least had his violent fights with the hoodlums of the town to absorb his surplus energy. In the medieval universities as in those of today there were the sharply contrasting types of sincere, intelligent scholars and frank and frivolous loafers. We hear much about radicalism and irreverence in modern colleges, but these tendencies were certainly not absent in the universities of the Middle Ages. Many of these institutions were roundly denounced as breeding places of heresy, paganism, and worldliness. It was said that young men "seek theology at Paris, law at Bologna, and medicine at Montpellier, but nowhere a life that is pleasing to God." The students at Paris even had to be admonished to stop playing dice on the altar of Notre Dame after one of their holiday celebrations.

The university students

IV. LITERATURE No one who has more than a casual acquaintance with the literature of the Feudal Age could ever imagine the whole medieval period to have been an era of darkness and otherworldliness. For much of this literature expresses a humanism, a zest for living, as spontaneous, joyous, and gay as any attitude revealed in the writings of the Renaissance of the fourteenth and succeeding centuries. Indeed, the spirit of late medieval literature was even closer to that of the modern age than most people realize. Probably the actual amount of religious literature in the Feudal Age did not bear a much larger ratio to the total quantity of writings produced than would be true at the present time.

Late medieval writings can be classified, first of all, as either Latin or vernacular literature. The revival of classical studies in the cathedral schools and in the earliest universities led to the production of some excellent Latin poetry. The best examples of this were the secular lyrics, especially those written by a group of poets known as the Goliards or Goliardi. The Goliards derived their name from the fact that they commonly referred to themselves as disciples of Golias. Who Golias was, no one knows, but Professor Haskins thinks that he was probably the devil.[6] Such a choice of a master would undoubtedly have been appropriate enough, for most of the Goliard poets were regarded by the church as lewd fellows of the baser sort for whom nothing was too sacred to be ridiculed. They wrote parodies of the creeds, travesties of the mass, and even burlesques of the Gospels. Their lyrics were purely pagan in spirit, celebrating the beauties of the changing seasons, the carefree life of the open road, the pleasures of drinking and gambling, and especially the joys of love. The authors of these rollicking and satirical songs were mostly wandering students, although some appear to have been men more advanced in years. The names of nearly all of them are unknown. Their poetry is particularly significant as the first emphatic protest against the ascetic ideal of Christianity. The following stanzas taken from *The Confession of Golias* may be considered fairly typical of what they wrote:

*Latin literature
in the Feudal
Age: the po-
etry of the
Goliardi*

> Prelate, most discreet of priests,
> Grant me absolution!
> Dear's the death whereof I die,
> Sweet my dissolution;
> For my heart is wounded by
> Beauty's soft suffusion;
> All the girls I come not nigh
> Mine are in illusion.
>
> 'Tis most arduous to make
> Nature's self-surrender;

356   [6] C. H. Haskins, *The Renaissance of the Twelfth Century*, p. 177.

The Flight into Egypt, Giotto (1276–1337). Giotto is regarded as the founder of the modern tradition in painting. This is one of the frescoes in the Arena Chapel, Padua, depicting scenes from the life of Christ.

e Nativity, Fra Angelico (1387–
5). A Dominican friar, Fra Angelico
oted for his serenely happy religious
atings. (MMA)

Lawrence Enthroned, Fra Lippo
pi (1406–1469). One of the first of
psychological painters, Fra Lippo
pi exhibited in this work his gift
portraying pensive melancholy.
MA)

Spring, Sandro Botticelli (1444–1510). Despite the pagan symbolism, the faces are thoughtful and sober, for Botticelli was a mystic as well as a lover of classical beauty. (Uffizi)

Mona Lisa, Leonardo da Vinci (1452-1519). Unlike most other Renaissance painters who sought to convey an understandable message, Leonardo created questions to which he gave no answer. Nowhere is this more evident than in the enigmatic countenance of Mona Lisa. (Louvre)

The Virgin of the Rocks, Leonardo da Vinci. T painting reveals not only Leonardo's interest human character, but also his absorption in phenomena of nature. (Louvre)

The Last Supper, Leonardo da Vinci. This great fresco depicts the varying reactions of Jesus' disciples when he announces that one of them will betray Him. (Santa Maria della Grazie, Milan)

Seeing girls, to blush and be
Purity's defender!
We young men our longings ne'er
Shall to stern law render,
Or preserve our fancies from
Bodies smooth and tender.[7]

By no means all of medieval literature was written in Latin. As the Feudal Age advanced, the vernacular languages of French, German, Spanish, English, and Italian became increasingly popular as media of literary expression. Until the beginning of the twelfth century nearly all of the literature in the vernacular languages assumed the form of the heroic epic. Among the leading examples were the French *Song of Roland*, the German *Song of the Nibelungs*, the eddas and sagas of the Norsemen, and the Spanish *Poem of My Cid*. These epics picture a virile but unpolished feudal society in its earlier stage of evolution, when valorous deeds in battle on behalf of one's suzerain represented the fulfillment of the highest knightly ideal. Heroism, honor, and loyalty were practically the exclusive themes. The tone of the epics was almost entirely masculine. If women were mentioned at all, it was generally in a condescending fashion. The hero must show the utmost devotion to his superior, but it was not considered inappropriate that he should beat his wife.

The growth of vernacular literature

During the twelfth and thirteenth centuries feudal society in western Europe attained the full flower of its growth. As a result of the progress of learning and of contact with the higher civilization of the Moslems the feudal aristocracy adopted new attitudes and interests. Chivalry, with its glorification of woman and its emphasis upon kindness and refinement of manners, tended to displace the older conception of a feudal ideal limited to the virtues of the battlefield. The first literary works to reflect and in part to inspire this change in ideals were the songs of the troubadours. The original home of the troubadours was southern France, especially the region known as Provence. Here was one of the most highly civilized areas of feudal Europe. It received the full impact of Saracenic influence from Spain, and it seems to have preserved an extensive inheritance from ancient Rome. The prevailing religion of Provence was an outgrowth of Manicheism, embodied in the teachings of an heretical Christian sect called the Albigenses. Perhaps the spirit of religious independence had something to do with the vigor and originality of the culture. Whatever the reasons, there can be no doubt that the troubadours of Provence initiated a movement of profound importance in late medieval literature. The central theme of their songs was romantic love. Woman was idealized now as never before. The virtues of her who had once been condemned by monks

The literature of chivalry: (1) the songs of the troubadours

[7] J. A. Symonds, *Wine, Women and Song*, p. 66.

and church fathers as the very incarnation of evil were extolled to the skies. But the love of the troubadours for the ladies of the feudal courts was not supposed to be sensual; it was a rarefied, almost mystical emotion which could be satisfied by a smile or some trifling memento from the haughty goddesses who were the objects of the singers' affection. The fact must be emphasized also that romantic love was not the only topic in which the troubadours were interested. Many of them wrote acrid satires against the rapacity and hypocrisy of the clergy, and one even addressed a powerful "poem of blame" to God. The literary tradition originated by the troubadours was continued by the *trouvères* in northern France and by the *minne-singers* in Germany.

(2) *the ro-
mances of the
Arthurian cycle*

The most important of all the writings which expressed the ideals of the feudal aristocracy were the romances of the Arthurian cycle. The material of these romances consisted of legends woven about the career of a Celtic chieftain by the name of Arthur, who had been the hero of the struggle against the Anglo-Saxon invaders of Britain. In the twelfth century certain Norman and French writers, especially Marie de France and Chrétien de Troyes, became interested in these legends as a background for the chivalric ideal. The result was the composition of a number of romances of love and adventure, famous alike for their colorful narrative and their poetic beauty. Later the best known of these romances were adapted and completed by German poets. Wolfram von Eschenbach developed what is usually considered the most perfect version of the Parzival legend, while Gottfried von Strassburg gave to the story of Tristram and Iseult its classic medieval form. Although these romances differed in form and in substance, they may yet be said to have had certain features in common. All of them glorified adventure for its own sake, and taught that experience of the deepest and most varied kind is the only sure road to wisdom. All of them strove to inculcate gentleness, protection of the weak, and rescue of those in distress as knightly obligations, in addition to honor, truthfulness, and bravery. The redeeming power of love was another universal element, although not all of the authors agreed as to the form which this love should assume. Some maintained that it ought to be the faithful affection between husband and wife, but others insisted that it must be love unsustained by wedlock. In the minds of the latter group true love was possible only between knight and mistress, never between husband and wife. Finally, in the best of these romances an element of tragedy was nearly always present. Indeed, such a work as Gottfried von Strassburg's *Tristan* might almost be regarded as the prototype of modern tragic literature. He was certainly one of the first to develop the idea of individual suffering as a literary theme and to point out the indistinct dividing line which separates pleasure from pain. For him, to love is to yearn, and suffering and death are integral chapters of the book of life.

By the thirteenth century the merchants and craftsmen of the town had risen to a position of power and influence equal if not superior to that of the feudal nobles. We can therefore logically expect that some literature would be written to appeal to burgher tastes. Among the foremost examples of such writings were the romance of *Aucassin and Nicolette* and the short stories in verse known as the *fabliaux*. The romance of *Aucassin and Nicolette* resembles in some ways the romances of chivalry. The hero Aucassin is a young noble, and the main theme of the romance is the imperious demands of love; but the plot is frequently turned into channels distinctly at variance with the chivalric ideal. Aucassin has fallen desperately in love, not with the high-born wife of some noble, but with Nicolette, a Saracen slave girl. Warned that he will suffer in hell if he does not give up his beloved, the hero replies that he does not mind, for in hell he will enjoy the company of all who have really lived. The story is also quite different from the romances of chivalry in its occasional expression of sympathy for the peasant. But the writings which undoubtedly made the strongest appeal to the urban classes were the *fabliaux*. These were stories written not to edify or instruct but chiefly to amuse. Often richly spiced with indecency, they reveal a contempt for the trappings of chivalry, with its romanticized love and idiotic pursuit of adventure. Most of them are also strongly anti-clerical and indicate no high regard for the religious spirit. Nearly always it is monks and priests who are made the butts of the jokes. The *fabliaux* are significant as expressions of the growing worldliness of the urban classes and as forerunners of the robust realism which was later to appear in the works of such writers as Chaucer and Boccaccio.

The supreme achievements of medieval literary talent were two great masterpieces written in the thirteenth and fourteenth centuries. The first was the *Romance of the Rose* of William of Lorris and John of Meun, and the second was Dante's *Divine Comedy*. Each in its own way is a kind of summary of late medieval civilization. The *Romance of the Rose* consists of two parts: the first four thousand lines were begun by William of Lorris about 1230; the other part, nearly three times as long, was finished by John of Meun about 1265. The two parts are entirely different, the first being an allegory dealing with the cult of chivalric love, while the second is a eulogy of reason. John of Meun was quite skeptical of the value of the feudal aristocracy to medieval society; he hated superstition; and he satirized the monastic orders, the papacy, and many other established institutions of his time. He embodied the mocking, realistic attitude of the bourgeoisie, as his predecessor, William of Lorris, symbolized the romantic, mystical spirit of chivalry. The work of the two men taken together furnishes a kind of guidebook to the late Middle Ages.

Without doubt the most profound of the medieval summaries was

The Romance of the Rose

The Divine
Comedy

the *Divine Comedy* of Dante Alighieri (1265–1321). Not a great deal is known about the life of Dante except that he was the son of a Florentine lawyer and was active during the early part of his career in the political affairs of his city. Despite his absorption in politics he managed to acquire a full mastery of the philosophic and literary knowledge of his time. In 1302 the party to which he belonged was ousted from power in Florence, and he was compelled to live the remainder of his years outside of his native city. Most of his writings were apparently produced during this period of exile. Dante called his chief work simply the *Comedy*, but his admirers during the Italian Renaissance always spoke of it as the *Divine Comedy*, and that is the title which has come down to us. In form the work may be considered a drama of the struggles, temptations, and ultimate redemption of the soul. But of course it is much more than this; for it embraces a complete summation of medieval culture, a magnificent synthesis of the Scholastic philosophy, the science, the religion, and the economic and ethical ideals of the high Feudal Age. Its dominant theme is the salvation of mankind through reason and divine grace, but it includes many other ideas as well. The universe is conceived as a finite world of which the earth is the center and in which everything exists for the benefit of man. All natural phenomena have their meaning in relation to the divine scheme for peace and justice on earth and salvation in the life beyond. Human beings possess free will to choose the good and avoid the evil. The worst of the sins which man can commit is treason or betrayal of trust; the least serious are those which proceed from weakness of the flesh. In many ways Dante was a humanist. He took earnest pleasure in the classical authors, almost worshiping Aristotle, Seneca, and Vergil. He chose Vergil rather than some Christian theologian to personify philosophy, and he admitted certain other distinguished pagans to very comfortable places in purgatory. Furthermore, he did not hesitate to place a number of prominent Popes in hell. By reason of his imaginative power and the warmth and vigor of his style, Dante deserves to be ranked as one of the greatest poets of all time, but he is especially important to the historian for the well-rounded picture he presents of the late medieval mind.

5. Art and Music in the Feudal Age

*The unity of
the arts in the
Feudal Age*

If there was one tendency which medieval man strove to avoid, it was the tendency to specialize in any particular branch of achievement. He conceived of the whole field of knowledge as one, dominated by logic as the key to wisdom. Not only the universe but everything in it was created for a single purpose, the welfare of man. Unity in philosophy, in religion, in government was the prevailing ideal. The same passion for unity carried over into the

Hotel de Ville, Bruges, Belgium. Begun in the Fourteenth Century, this town hall provides a good example of secular Gothic.

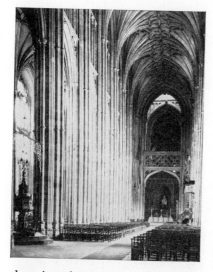

Interior of Canterbury Cathedral, England. This picture provides an excellent impression of the lofty construction of Gothic architecture, and of the ribbed vaulting and pointed arches which helped to make such construction possible.

domain of art, with the result that sculpture and painting were both subordinated to architecture.

The Feudal Age produced two great styles of architecture, the Romanesque and the Gothic. The Romanesque was mainly a product of the monastic revival and attained its full development in the century and a half following the year 1000. Fundamentally it was an ecclesiastical architecture, symbolizing the pride of the monastic orders at the height of their power. Naturally, since the Cluniac revival affected the entire church, the Romanesque style was not confined to monasteries. Nevertheless, it is significant that some of the most impressive Romanesque buildings were houses of the Cluniac order. The essential features of this building style were the round arch, massive walls, enormous piers, small windows, gloomy interiors, and the predominance of horizontal lines. The plainness of interiors was sometimes relieved by mosaics or by frescoing in bright colors, but the style of construction was not such as to encourage elaborate ornamentation. Moreover, the strong religious spirit in which this architecture was conceived did not foster any appeal to the senses. Churches and monasteries should be plain and dark within in order to create the proper atmosphere of piety and of otherworldliness. Some of the architects of southern Europe, however, succeeded in breaking away from this somber monastic tradition and often decorated their churches with an elaborate symbolic sculpture.

Architecture: the Romanesque style

In the late twelfth and thirteenth centuries the Romanesque architecture was superseded in popularity by the Gothic. The in- **361**

The Cathedral of Chartres, France. Regarded by some as the purest and most beautiful example of Gothic design, the Cathedral of Chartres is renowned for the grace and perfect proportions of its towers. The one on the right was built in the Thirteenth Century and reflects the simpler Gothic style of that period. The one on the left was finished in the Sixteenth Century and reveals some of the influence of flamboyant Gothic.

The Romanesque architecture gives way to the Gothic

crease in wealth, the advancement of learning, the growth of secular interests, and the pride of the cities in their newly acquired freedom and prosperity led to a demand for a more elaborate architectural style to express the ideals of the new age. Besides, the monastic revival had now spent its force. Gothic architecture was almost exclusively urban. Its monuments were not monasteries situated on lonely crags but cathedrals, bishops' churches, located in the largest cities and towns. It must be understood, though, that the medieval cathedral was not simply a church but a center of the community life. It generally housed a school and a library and was sometimes used as a town hall. The people of the entire community participated in erecting it, and they rightfully regarded it as civic property. Indeed, many of the Gothic cathedrals were the outcome of town rivalry. For example, the people of Siena became dissatisfied with their modest church after the cathedral at Florence was completed and determined to build a new one on a much more pretentious scale. Frequently the citizens' ambitions got far out of bounds, with the result that many of the buildings were left unfinished. The architects of the cathedral of Chartres, for instance, planned for several more lofty towers than were ever completed.

Gothic architecture was one of the most intricate of building styles. Its basic elements were the pointed arch, groined and ribbed vaulting, and the flying buttress. These devices made possible a much lighter and loftier construction than could ever have been achieved with the round arch and the engaged pier of the Romanesque. In fact, the Gothic cathedral could be described as a skeletal framework of stone enclosed by enormous windows. Other features included lofty spires, rose windows, delicate tracery in stone, elaborately carved façades, multiple columns, and the use of gargoyles, or representations of mythical monsters, as decorative devices. Ornamentation in the best of the cathedrals was generally concentrated on the exterior. Except for the stained glass windows and the intricate carving on woodwork and altars, interiors were kept rather simple and occasionally almost severe. But the inside of the Gothic

The Gothic style

See color pictures at pages 261, 292, 293

Evolution of the Floor Plan of the Medieval Cathedral. *A* is the plan of the Early Christian basilica, the church of Santa Maria Maggiore in Rome, built in the Fourth Century. It is a simple plan of rectangular building with nave flanked by colonnades and side aisles. *B* is the church of San Michele at Pavia, Twelfth Century, Romanesque, with the apse elongated and transepts added, giving the church the form of a Latin cross. *C* is the cathedral at Amiens, Thirteenth Century Gothic. Here the typical Gothic plan shows up—the side aisles continue around the elongated choir and apse, forming the ambulatory, off which radiate the

chapels, and the transepts are fully developed with side aisles.

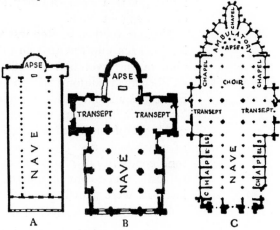

cathedral was never somber or gloomy. The stained glass windows served not to exclude the light but to glorify it, to catch the rays of sunlight and suffuse them with a richness and warmth of color which nature herself could hardly produce even in her gayest moods.

The significance of Gothic architecture is frequently misunderstood. As a matter of fact, its very name, implying that the art was of barbarian origin, was originally a term of reproach given to it by the men of the Renaissance, who wanted to express their contempt for everything medieval. Many people still think of the Gothic cathedral as a product of an ascetic and otherworldly civilization. Nothing could be more inaccurate. In so far as Gothic architecture was spiritual at all, it was the symbol of a religion which had come to recognize the importance of this life. But as we have already seen, the cathedral was more than a church. It was in large part an expression of the new secular spirit which had grown out of the rise of cities and the progress of enlightenment. Many of the scenes depicted on the stained glass windows—a medieval bakeshop in operation, for instance—had no direct religious significance whatever. Moreover, Gothic architecture was in no small degree humanistic. The definite appeal to the senses revealed in the sparkling radiance of colored glass and in the naturalistic sculpture of saints and the Virgin gives positive proof that man's interest in his human self and in the world of natural beauty was no longer considered a sin. Last of all, Gothic architecture was an expression of the medieval intellectual genius. The complicated design, the perfect balance of thrust and counterthrust, and the soaring height of the buildings represented not only the triumph of reasoning skill, but also a desire to burst the confines of limited knowledge and push upward into the highest realms of truth. Each cathedral itself, with its detailed mass of carvings of plant and animal life and symbolic figures, was a kind of encyclopedia of medieval knowledge—a culture epic in stone.

Music in the Feudal Age

Music in the Feudal Age was the product of an evolution extending far back into the early history of medieval Europe. The beginning of this evolution was the development of the plain chant, ascribed by tradition to Pope Gregory the Great. The Gregorian chant was a single unaccompanied melody sung by a solo voice or by a choir in unison. This simple art form provided the basis for nearly all of medieval music. By the tenth century the first signs of a harmonic system had begun to appear, although the original tone combinations chosen were somewhat austere, including most typically successions of fourths and fifths. As time went on, other intervals were added, gradually enriching the color content. It is

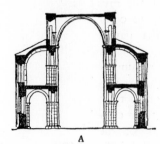

Cross Sections of Medieval Cathedrals: *A,* Romanesque Abbaye-aux-hommes; *B,* French Gothic cathedral of Amiens. Note the round Romanesque arches in *A* as well as the method of buttressing the nave vaulting by the half barrel vault over the triforium gallery. In *B* the pointed Gothic arch makes for a higher nave vaulting and, in all, the frame of the structure is lighter. Here can be seen the typical flying buttresses which take the thrust of the nave vaulting clear of the main structure to the great masonry buttress piers.

A   B

significant, however, that the modern concept of a *harmony* subordinate to a *melody* was entirely lacking. Each new voice that was added was expected to be interesting in itself and not merely part of a tonal background. Thus the new development was along contrapuntal rather than strictly harmonic lines; it was polyphonic rather than monophonic. By the thirteenth century considerable skill had been attained in weaving together two, three, and even four independent voices into a pleasing pattern. As a part of the quadrivium taught in the universities, music was a dryly theoretical and formalized subject, primarily a branch of physics. But as utilized for practical needs by church composers it was a vital, growing thing. Some of the composers in their zeal for freshness and experimentation even chose popular tavern songs, words and all, as the base around which to weave contrapuntally the sacred words of the Mass. In this connection it may be observed that a secular music existed quite apart from that of the church. It too was chiefly vocal, but in contrast to sacred music was emphatically rhythmical, was sung to an instrumental accompaniment, and employed the vernacular languages. It included both folk music of anonymous origin and also, in the late Feudal Age, the songs of the troubadours, trouvères, and minnesingers, some of whom were gifted composers. Ultimately secular music added its influence to the more significant and serious art produced by the church.

SELECTED READINGS

Adams, Henry, *Mont-Saint-Michel and Chartres*, New York, 1913

Artz, F. B., *The Mind of the Middle Ages*, New York, 1954

Barker, Ernest, *The Crusades*, London, 1923

Chaytor, H. J., *The Troubadours*, Cambridge, Mass., 1912

Cheney, E. P., *The Dawn of a New Era, 1250–1453*, New York, 1936

Compayre, Gabriel, *Abelard and the Origin and Early History of Universities*, New York, 1901

Crump, C. G., and Jacob, E. F., *The Legacy of the Middle Ages*, New York, 1926

Easton, Stewart C., *Roger Bacon and His Search for a Universal Science*, New York, 1952

Gilson, E. H., *The Philosophy of St. Thomas Aquinas*, Cambridge, Mass., 1924

———, *Dante the Philosopher*, London, 1948

Haskins, C. H., *Studies in Medieval Culture*, New York, 1929

———, *Studies in the History of Medieval Science*, Cambridge, Mass., 1924

———, *The Renaissance of the Twelfth Century*, Cambridge, Mass., 1928

Hearnshaw, F. J. C., *The Social and Political Ideas of Some Great Medieval Thinkers*, New York, 1923

Hearnshaw, F. J. C., *Medieval Contributions to Modern Civilization*, New York, 1922

Jackson, T. G., *Gothic Architecture*, Cambridge, Mass., 1915, 2 vols.

Jones, Charles W., ed., *Medieval Literature in Translation*, New York, 1950

Krey, A. C., *The First Crusade*, Princeton, 1921

Lang, Paul, *Music in Western Civilization*, New York, 1941

Latourette, K. S., *A History of Christianity*, New York, 1953

McCabe, Joseph, *Peter Abelard*, New York, 1901

McGiffert, A. C., *History of Christian Thought*, New York, 1932, Vol. II

McIlwain, C. H., *The Growth of Political Thought in the West*, New York, 1932

Packard, Sidney, *Europe and the Church under Innocent III*, New York, 1927

Rait, R. S., *Life in the Medieval University*, Cambridge, 1912

Rashdall, Hastings, *The Universities of Europe in the Middle Ages*, New York, 1895, 2 vols.

Reese, Gustave, *Music in the Middle Ages*, New York, 1940

Setton, K. M., ed., *A History of the Crusades*, Philadelphia, 1955, Vol. I

Taylor, H. O., *The Medieval Mind*, New York, 1927, 2 vols.

Thorndike, Lynn, *A History of Magic and Experimental Science during the First Thirteen Centuries of Our Era*, New York, 1923, Vol. II

Ueberweg, Friedrich, *History of Philosophy*, New York, 1876, Vol. I

Vossler, Karl, *Medieval Culture: An Introduction to Dante and His Times*, New York, 1929, 2 vols.

Waddell, Helen, *The Wandering Scholars*, London, 1927

SOURCE MATERIALS

Abelard, Peter, *The Story of My Misfortunes*

Baumer, F. L. V., *Main Currents of Western Thought*, New York, 1952

Coulton, G. G., *A Medieval Garner*

Jones, C. W., ed., *Medieval Literature in Translation*, New York, 1950

Krey, A. C., *The First Crusade; The Accounts of Eyewitnesses and Participants*

Marzialis, F. T., tr., *Memoirs of the Crusades*, for *Villehardouin's Chronicle of the Fourth Crusade* and *Joinville's Chronicle of the Crusade of St. Louis*

Norton, A. O., *Readings in the History of Education: Medieval Universities*

Pegis, A. C., ed., *Basic Writings of St. Thomas Aquinas*, 2 vols.

Polo, Marco, *Travels*

Poole, R. L., *Illustrations of the History of Medieval Thought and Learning*

Robinson, Paschal, tr., *The Writings of St. Francis of Assisi*

Shackford, M. H., *Legends and Satires from Medieval Literature*

Thatcher, O. J., and McNeal, E. H., *A Source Book for Medieval History*, pp. 513–21, Speech of Urban II at Council of Clermont

The Civilization of the
Renaissance: In Italy

Soon after 1300 the majority of the characteristic institutions and ideals of the Feudal Age had begun to decay. Chivalry, feudalism itself, the Holy Roman Empire, the universal authority of the papacy, the guild system of trade and industry were all gradually being weakened and would eventually disappear. The great age of the Gothic cathedrals was practically over, the Scholastic philosophy was beginning to be ridiculed and despised, and the supremacy of the religious and ethical interpretations of life was being slowly but effectively undermined. In place of all these there gradually emerged new institutions and ways of thinking of sufficient importance to stamp the centuries that followed with the character of a different civilization. The traditional name applied to this civilization, which extended from 1300 to approximately 1650, is the Renaissance.

The transition from the Feudal Age to the Renaissance

The term Renaissance leaves much to be desired from the standpoint of historical accuracy. Literally it means rebirth, and it is commonly taken to imply that in the fourteenth century there was a sudden revival of interest in the classical learning of Greece and Rome. But this implication is far from being strictly true. Interest in the classics was by no means rare in the Feudal Age. Such writers as John of Salisbury, Dante, and the Goliard poets were just as enthusiastic admirers of Greek and Latin literature as any who lived in the fourteenth century. Indeed, the so-called Renaissance was in considerable measure simply the culmination of a series of revivals which began as far back as the ninth century. All of these movements were characterized by a reverence for the ancient authors. Even in the cathedral and monastic schools Cicero, Vergil, Seneca,

Meaning of the term Renaissance

367

*The Renais-
sance more than
a revival of
pagan learning*

and, later on, Aristotle frequently received as much worshipful adoration as was given to any of the saints.

The Renaissance was a great deal more than a mere revival of pagan learning. It embraced, first of all, an impressive record of new achievements in art, literature, science, philosophy, politics, education, and religion. While the foundation of many of these was classical, they soon expanded beyond the measure of Greek and Roman influence. Indeed, most of the achievements in painting, science, politics, and religion bore little relation to the classical heritage. Secondly, the Renaissance incorporated a number of dominant ideals and attitudes which are commonly assumed to have set the standard for the modern world. Conspicuous among them were optimism, worldliness, hedonism, naturalism, and individualism; but the most significant of them all was humanism. In its broadest sense humanism may be defined as the glorification of the human and the natural as opposed to the divine or otherworldly. Conceived in this fashion, it was the heart and soul of the Renaissance; for it included practically all of the other ideals already mentioned. Humanism also has the more restricted meaning of enthusiasm for the classical writings because of their human interest. This is the sense in which it was frequently used by the men of the early Renaissance.

Not only was the Renaissance much more than a revival of pagan learning; in some ways it was closely related to the spirit of the late Middle Ages. The pride in human achievement reflected in Gothic architecture, the naturalism of the *fabliaux* and of *Aucassin and Nicolette,* the secularism of the orders of friars, and the striving after knowledge and understanding in the universities all clearly foreshadowed the prevailing ideals of the fourteenth and succeeding centuries. On the other hand, it is hardly correct to think of the Renaissance as only a final chapter in medieval civilization. Many of the new attitudes and achievements were distinctly at variance with the medieval world perspective. No longer did men conceive of the universe as a finite system of concentric spheres revolving around the earth and existing for the glory and salvation of man. The revival of the heliocentric theory as early as the fifteenth century suggested a cosmos of infinitely greater extent, with the earth only one of a number of worlds. The goal of human knowledge was thus pushed much farther into the distance, since the universe according to the new conception could not be so easily reduced to a simple explanation in terms of the Christian epic.

In other ways also the civilization of the Renaissance contrasted sharply with the Middle Ages. Chivalry was now quite generally treated with contempt. The Scholastic philosophy was despised as a stupid mixture of logic and religious dogma. The medieval condemnation of business for the sake of profit no longer received even lip service from the grasping merchants and bankers in every European city. The collectivism of the Middle Ages—the submergence of the individual in the guild, in the church, and in the social order to which he belonged—now gave way to a rabid egoism which glorified almost every form of self-assertiveness and elevated pride from a deadly sin to a cardinal virtue. Perhaps the most striking contrasts were those to be found in the realm of politics. The medieval ideal of a universal commonwealth under the sovereign authority of the Holy Roman Emperor or the Pope had no meaning at all for the political philosophers of the Renaissance. Instead, they maintained that every individual state regardless of its size should be absolutely free from external control. Unfortunately they also rejected the medieval doctrines of limited government and the ethical basis of politics. It was now commonly held that the authority of the ruler was subject to no limitations whatever, and some even asserted that the prince in the exercise of his official functions was not bound by the canons of morality; whatever was necessary to maintain his own power or the power of the state over which he ruled provided its own justification. Scarcely any philosopher in the Middle Ages would have tolerated such doctrines.

1. The Causes of the Renaissance

Most of the causes of the Renaissance have already been indicated. In general they were the very same factors that had stimulated the intellectual and artistic revival of the twelfth and thirteenth centuries: (1) the influence of the Saracenic and Byzantine civilizations; (2) the development of a flourishing commerce; (3) the growth of cities; (4) the revival of an interest in classical studies in the cathedral and monastic schools; (5) the growth of a critical and skeptical attitude exemplified in the philosophies of such men as Abelard; and (6) the gradual escape from the otherworldly and ascetic atmosphere of the early Middle Ages. To these should be added certain other causes which were really elements in the medieval renaissance of the twelfth and thirteenth centuries: first, the revival of the study of the Roman law, with the impetus it gave to the growth of secular interests; second, the expansion of intellectual interests made possible by the rise of the universities; third, the Aristotelianism of the Scholastic philosophy, with its appeal to the authority of a pagan thinker; fourth, the growth of naturalism in literature and art; and fifth, the development of a spirit of scientific inquiry, exemplified in the work of Adelard of Bath, Roger Bacon, and Frederick II. Soon after the Renaissance got under way, its progress was greatly accelerated by the influence of secular and ecclesiastical patrons of learning. Outstanding among the former were the Medici family in Florence, the Sforza family in Milan, the Este lords of Ferrara, and Alfonso the Magnanimous of Naples. Most of these patrons were wealthy merchants who had become despots of the city republics in which they lived. The ecclesiastical patrons included such Popes as Nicholas V,

The real causes of the Renaissance

Patronage of learning

Pius II, Julius II, and Leo X. The attitude of these men was singularly at variance with what is normally expected of occupants of the fisherman's throne. They displayed no interest in theology or in the conversion of the ungodly. They kept on the payroll of the church men who openly attacked fundamental Christian doctrines. Nicholas V, for example, employed as a papal secretary the celebrated Lorenzo Valla, who exposed an important document of the church as a forgery and preached a philosophy of carnal pleasure. Whatever the incongruity of their attitude, the work of these Popes was of inestimable value to cultural progress, for they bestowed their patronage upon some of the most brilliant artists and literary men of the Italian Renaissance.

Alleged causes of the Renaissance: (1) the Crusades

Before leaving this subject of factors responsible for the Renaissance, it will be desirable to dispose of two alleged causes commonly believed to have been of decisive importance. One of these is the Crusades, and the other is the invention of printing. In a preceding chapter we observed that the intellectual influence of the Crusades was slight. The introduction of Moslem learning into Europe came about as a result of the work of scholars in the libraries of Toledo and Cordova and as a consequence of the deliberate attempts of Frederick II to undermine the power of the church by diffusing a pagan culture throughout his domains. Only to the extent that the Crusades weakened feudalism, diminished the prestige of the papacy, and helped to give the Italian cities a monopoly of Mediterranean trade may they be considered as in any way responsible for the beginning of Renaissance civilization. And even these results can be ascribed in large part to other factors.

(2) the invention of printing by movable type

While the invention of printing was an achievement of the utmost importance, it was perhaps even less than the Crusades a direct cause of the Renaissance. For one thing, it came too late. So far as the evidence shows, no printing press was in operation much before the middle of the fifteenth century. The earliest work known to have been printed from movable type actually dates from 1454.[1] By this time the Renaissance in Italy was already well under way, having started about a century and a half before. Furthermore, many of the early humanists were decidedly hostile toward the new invention. They regarded it as a barbarous German contraption and refused to allow their works to be printed lest they obtain too wide a circulation and be misunderstood by the common people. The fact should also be noted that the earliest publishing firms were far more interested in turning out religious books and popular stories than in printing the writings of the new learning. Devotional tracts, service books for the church, writings of the theo-

---

[1] This was an indulgence issued from the press of Johann Gutenberg at Mainz, who is commonly credited with the invention of printing, though it is somewhat doubtful that he did more than perfect the technique developed by others.

logians, and collections of ancient legends were the types of reading matter which really appealed to the public of that day, and were accordingly more profitable to the printers than any of the recondite works of the humanists. The conclusion seems amply justified that the influence of the invention of printing upon the Renaissance extended no farther than to aid slightly in spreading and accelerating the movement in its later stages, particularly in northern Europe. Most of the great benefits of the invention came after the Renaissance had ended.

2. The Renaissance in Italy

Reference has already been made to the fact that the Renaissance had its beginning in Italy. Why should this have been so? As one reason, Italy had a stronger classical tradition than any other country of western Europe. All through the medieval period the Italians had managed to preserve the belief that they were descendants of the ancient Romans. They looked back upon their ancestry with pride, ignoring of course the infiltrations of Lombard, Byzantine, Saracenic, and Norman blood that had been poured into their nation from time to time. In some of the Italian cities traces of the old Roman system of education still survived in the municipal schools. Relics of the ancient pagan spirit were also to be found in the essentially unmoral attitude of the Italians. Ethical considerations did not generally weigh with them so heavily as with northern Europeans. Few Italians appear to have been shocked by the fact that Pope Alexander VI had illegitimate children or that Julius II was a crafty politician and a hard-swearing leader of papal armies. It is likewise true that Italy had a more thoroughly secular culture than most other regions of Latin Christendom. The Italian universities were founded primarily for the study of law or medicine rather than theology, and, with the exception of the University of Rome, few of them had any ecclesiastical connections whatever. In addition to all this, Italy received the full impact of cultural influences from the Byzantine and Saracenic civilizations. Finally, and perhaps most important of all, the Italian cities were the main beneficiaries of the revival of trade with the East. For years the seaport towns of Venice, Naples, Genoa, and Pisa enjoyed a virtual monopoly of the Mediterranean trade, while the merchants of Florence, Bologna, Piacenza, and other cities of the Lombard plain served as the chief middlemen in the commerce between northern and southern Europe. The economic prosperity thus acquired was the principal foundation of the intellectual and artistic progress.

Why the Renaissance began in Italy

I. THE POLITICAL BACKGROUND It is generally assumed that orderly and efficient government is a necessary condition for the development of a superior culture; but such was not the case with the civilization we are now considering. The Renaissance was born in the midst of political turmoil. Not only was Italy not a unified state when the Renaissance began, but throughout the history of the movement the country remained in a turbulent condition. Factional revolts and bitter feuds between petty states followed each other in rapid succession. The reasons for this chaos were several. In the revolt against medieval collectivism, with its condemnation of pride and emphasis upon self-effacement, men went to the opposite extreme and glorified the aggrandizement of self. Almost any form of egoism was now considered justifiable—the pursuit of power or wealth, the quest of physical or artistic pleasure, or the ruthless suppression of one's rivals. It was perhaps inevitable that this change in social attitude should lead to political racketeering, to the rise of adventurers eager to turn every factional difference into angry discord in order to pave the highroad to a seizure of power. Another cause was the fact that the leading citizens were too deeply absorbed in making money to bother very much with affairs of government. Since they were especially reluctant to waste their time in military service, they insisted that their governments should employ mercenary troops. The result was the appearance of bands

of professional soldiers, under leaders known as *condottieri*, who sold their services to the highest bidder. As almost anyone could have predicted, some of these *condottieri* eventually became strong enough to seize control of the governments for which they fought. Much of the turbulence of Italian politics in this period was due also to the intense commercial rivalry among the principal cities. In fact, nearly all of the major wars grew out of attempts by one city or another to gain control of trade routes or to destroy the commerce of a competing city.

At the beginning of the Renaissance, Italy was divided into a host of petty states. Nearly all were independent city republics that had

succeeded during the late Middle Ages in throwing off the domination of the Holy Roman Emperor. In the course of their struggle for freedom many of them had adopted some degree of democratic government. In the midst of the turmoil of the Renaissance, however, practically all traces of this democracy disappeared. One city after another fell under the sway of powerful usurpers. As early as 1311 the government of Milan was transformed into a dictatorship under the head of the Visconti family. When the Visconti died out in 1450, their authority was taken over by one of the most famous of the *condottieri*, Francesco Sforza. In 1434 the republic of Florence passed under the control of the enlightened plutocrat, Cosimo de' Medici. Although Cosimo had no official title, he was accepted by the people of the city as a virtual dictator, mainly because they longed for relief from partisan strife. The Medici family dominated the political life of Florence for sixty years. After the great Cosimo the leading representative of the family was his grandson Lorenzo, styled the "Magnificent." To these two men must be given a large

THE STATES OF ITALY DURING THE RENAISSANCE (about 1494)

MONTFERRAT

Milan

VENICE

SAVOY

MILAN

MANTUA

Venice

Asti

FERRARA

GENOA

MODENA

Bologna

Genoa

LUCCA

Pisa

Florence

FLORENCE

STATES
OF THE
CHURCH

Adriatic

Siena

SIENA

Sea

CORSICA
(to Genoa)

Rome

KINGDOM
OF THE TWO
SICILIES

Naples

SARDINIA
(to Spain)

Mediterranean Sea

Palermo

Miles

0   50   100   200   300   400

part of the credit for the fact that Florence remained for so long a time the most brilliant center of the Italian Renaissance. The republic of Venice also underwent a similar change from modified democracy to despotism. But here the despotic authority was exercised by an oligarchy instead of by a single individual. A small number of the wealthiest families controlled absolutely the elections to the Senate, to the Grand Council, and to the office of Doge, or life president. Even the States of the Church, which included a broad belt stretching across the central portion of the Italian peninsula, presented no contrast to the general pattern of Renaissance government. Except for their greater wealth, the Popes of this time were scarcely distinguishable from the rest of the Italian potentates. They made and broke treaties, hired *condottieri* for wars of conquest, and employed very questionable means of dealing with troublesome opponents.

The expansion of the city-states

Not only was the history of the Italian Renaissance marked by the growth of despotic government; there was also a definite tendency for the larger and more powerful states to absorb the smaller. Under the rule of Gian Galeazzo Visconti (1378–1402) the city-state of Milan reached out and annexed nearly the whole of the Lombard plain. This expansion aroused the apprehension of Venice. As a consequence, the merchants of that city determined to conquer an inland empire which would protect the avenues of trade with central Europe. By 1454 Venice had succeeded in annexing nearly all of northeastern Italy, including the wealthy city of Padua and considerable territory formerly conquered by Milan. Nor did the republic of Florence lag behind in the development of expansionist ambitions. Before the end of the fourteenth century practically all of the district of Tuscany had been taken, and in 1406 the great mercantile city of Pisa succumbed to Florentine domination. The papacy also took part in the general movement of territorial aggrandizement. Under such worldly and aggressive Popes as Alexander VI (1492–1503) and Julius II (1503–1513) the dominion of the Papal States was extended over nearly all of the petty lords of central Italy. As a result of all this expansion, practically the whole of the Italian peninsula by the beginning of the sixteenth century had been brought under the rule of the five most powerful states: the duchy of Milan, the republics of Venice and Florence, the kingdom of Naples, and the States of the Church.

II. THE LITERARY AND ARTISTIC CULTURE No wide gulf separated Italian Renaissance literature from the literature of the late Middle Ages. The vast majority of the literary achievements between 1300 and 1550 were already foreshadowed in one or another of the different trends initiated in the twelfth and thirteenth centuries. The so-called father of Italian Renaissance literature, Francesco Petrarca or Petrarch (1304–1374), was himself very close to the medieval temper. He employed the same Tuscan dialect which Dante had

Petrarch, the father of Italian Renaissance literature

chosen as the basis of an Italian literary language. Moreover, he
believed quite firmly in Christianity as the way of salvation for
man, and he was addicted at times to a monkish asceticism. His
best-known writings, the sonnets he addressed to his beloved Laura,
partook of the same flavor as the chivalrous love poetry of the
thirteenth-century troubadours. Although Petrarch has been widely
acclaimed as the father of humanism, the humanism he founded
differed but slightly from that of many a medieval poet. About all
that was new in Petrarch was his intense absorption in his own
personality and his passionate devotion to the Greek as well as to
the Latin classics.[2] Even here the novelty was primarily a matter of
degree. It is not quite accurate to think of Petrarch as "the first
modern man."

The second of the great figures in the Italian literary Renaissance,
Giovanni Boccaccio (1313–1375), was scarcely much more of an
original genius. Like Petrarch, Boccaccio was a Florentine, the
illegitimate son of a prosperous merchant. His father having planned
for him a business career, he was sent to Naples to serve an apprenticeship in a branch of the great Florentine banking house of
the Bardi. But the young Boccaccio soon displayed more ardor in
worshiping in the temple of the Muses than in computing the
interest on loans. It was perhaps natural that this should be so, for
Naples was a center of gracious living under languorous skies and
of strong poetic traditions emanating from the lands of the Saracens
and the troubadours. It was an environment especially fitted to stimulate the poetic fancies of youth. Boccaccio was also inspired by a
passionate love for the beautiful wife of a Neapolitan citizen. Nearly
all of his earlier works were poems and romances dealing with the
triumphs and tortures of this love. Gradually his skill in the story-
telling art attained perfection, and he eventually found prose a more
suitable medium for his purposes. His first work of merit in the
new style was *Fiammetta*, a forerunner of the psychological novel.
But by far the most notable of Boccaccio's writings was his *Decameron*, which he wrote after his return to Florence about 1348.
The *Decameron* consists of one hundred stories which the author
puts into the mouths of seven young women and three young men.
The stories do not form a novel revolving about a continuous theme
but are united by the artificial plot of having been told by a group
of people who are concerned merely with passing the time during
their sojourn at a villa outside of Florence to escape the ravages
of the Black Death. Though some of the tales were probably invented by Boccaccio, most of them were drawn from the *fabliaux*,

*The more ro-
bust humanism
of Boccaccio*

The Decameron

[2] Curiously enough, Petrarch could not read Greek. His knowledge of Hellenic culture was acquired entirely from what the Romans said about it. His
earnest attempts to learn the language resulted in failure, for he could find no
competent tutor. He therefore contented himself to the end of his life with gaz-
ing admiringly at the pages of Homer but with no more than a vague understanding of what they contained.

from the *Book of the 1001 Nights,* and from other medieval sources. In general they differ from their medieval prototypes in being slightly more ribald, egoistic, and anti-clerical and more deeply concerned with a frank justification of the carnal life; but the *Decameron* certainly does not represent, as many people think, the first emphatic protest against the ascetic and impersonal ideals of the early Middle Ages. Its real significance lies in the fact that it set the pattern for Italian prose and exerted considerable influence upon Renaissance writers in other countries.

The character of literature in the Quattro-cento

The death of Boccaccio in 1375 marks the end of the first period in the Italian Renaissance in literature, a period which is often called the Trecento.[3] The age which followed, known as the Quattrocento, was distinguished by a revival of the Latin language. Enthusiasm for the classics had now attained such force that men could not bear to write in any other language than that of the great masters of ancient Rome. The Italian of Dante and Boccaccio was scorned as the uncouth tongue of butchers and bakers. Naturally such an attitude did not foster the development of the highest talent, for it tended to set as the supreme goal of literary effort the faithful imitation of Latin models. It is therefore not strange that the majority of the writers of this time—such men as Poggio, Beccadelli, Filelfo, and Pontano—should be remembered merely as second-rate figures whose chief claim to distinction is their militant pagan-ism and their delight in erotic themes. Their work represents one of the farthest extremes to which the reaction against Christian belief and morality was destined to go. The Quattrocento was also the period when the passion for Greek studies was at its zenith. Prior to this time the Italian humanists had achieved but indifferent success in their attempts to learn the Greek language and to dis-cover the treasures of Hellenic culture. But in 1393 a famous scholar of Constantinople, Manuel Chrysaloras, arrived in Venice on a mission from the Byzantine emperor to implore the aid of the West in a war against the Turks. Almost immediately acclaimed by the Italians as an apostle of the glorious Hellenic past, he was eventually persuaded to accept a professorship of the Greek classics at the University of Florence. About the beginning of the fifteenth century several other Byzantine scholars, notably Platonist philosophers, migrated to Italy. The influence of these men in providing informa-tion about the achievements of the ancient Greeks seems to have been considerable. At any rate, it was not long until Italian scholars began to make trips to Constantinople and other Byzantine cities in search of manuscripts. Between 1413 and 1423 a certain Giovanni Aurispa, for example, brought back nearly two hundred and fifty

[3] So called from the Italian word for three hundred, *trecento,* used to desig-nate the century which followed 1300. Quattrocento, from the word for four hundred, is applied to the period of the fifteenth century and Cinquecento to the sixteenth.

manuscript books, including works of Sophocles, Euripides, and Thucydides. It was in this way that many of the Hellenic classics, particularly the writings of the dramatists, historians, and earlier philosophers, were first made available to the modern world.

The last great age in the development of Italian Renaissance litera- ture was the Cinquecento, or the period from 1500 to about 1550. Italian was now raised to a full equality with Greek and Latin, classi- cal and modern influences were more perfectly blended, and a deeper originality of both form and content was achieved. But the literary capital of the Renaissance was no longer Florence. In 1494 that city came under the rule of the fanatical reformer Savonarola; and, while the Medici were restored to power about eighteen years later, the brilliant Tuscan metropolis soon afterward fell a victim of factional disputes and foreign invasion. During the first half of the sixteenth century the city of Rome gradually rose to a position of cultural leadership, mainly because of the patronage of the church, especially during the reign of Pope Leo X (Giovanni de' Medici). This gorgeous prelate was the son of Lorenzo the Magnificent. When he was only fourteen years old, his father's in- fluence had been sufficient to procure his appointment as a cardinal. Elevated to St. Peter's throne in 1513, he is reported to have said, "Let us enjoy the papacy since God has given it to us." There can be little doubt that he did enjoy it, for he was a magnificent spend- thrift, lavishing rewards upon artists and writers and financing the construction of beautiful churches.

The chief forms of literature developed in the Cinquecento were epic and pastoral poetry, drama, and history. The most eminent of the writers of epics was Ludovico Ariosto (1474–1533), author of a lengthy poem entitled *Orlando Furioso*. Although woven largely of materials taken from the romances of adventure and the legends of the Arthurian cycle, this work differed radically from any of the medieval epics. It incorporated much that was derived from classical sources; it lacked the impersonal quality of the medieval romances; and it was totally devoid of idealism. Ariosto wrote to make men laugh and to charm them with felicitous descriptions of the quiet splendor of nature and the passionate beauty of love. His work represents the disillusionment of the late Rennaissance, the loss of hope and of faith, and the tendency to seek consolation in the pursuit of aesthetic pleasure. The development of pastoral poetry at this time probably reflects a similar attitude of disenchantment and loss of confidence. As the name implies, the pastoral romance glorifies the simple life amid rustic surroundings and expresses the yearning for a golden age of unspoiled pleasures and freedom from the worries and frustrations of artificial urban society. The chief author of this type of literature in the Italian Renaissance was Jacopo Sannazaro (1458–1530), who gave to his main work the title of *Arcadia*.

In the field of the drama the Italians never achieved more than moderate success. Their failure as writers of tragedy was particularly noticeable, despite the fact that they had considerable knowledge of classical models from which to profit. The Italian was apparently too much of an individualist to be influenced profoundly by the Greek conception of a tragic conflict between man and society and too much of an optimist to brood over personal suffering. His mind was fixed upon the compensations of life rather than upon its grim and terrifying aspects. His real talents lay in naturalistic description, in the development of light and joyous themes, and in the expression of personal egotism. It was natural, therefore, that the best of his dramas should have been comedies, especially satirical comedies, rather than tragedies. The first and the greatest of the Italian comedians was a man who is far better known as a political philosopher—Niccolo Machiavelli (1469–1527). The finest product of his dramatic skill was a work entitled *Mandragola*, which has been called "the ripest and most powerful play in the Italian language." [4] Sparkling with salacious wit and based upon incidents typical of life in the author's native city of Florence, it is a lurid satire of Renaissance society. In this as in his other writings Machiavelli reveals his cynical views of human nature. He appears to believe that all human beings are knaves and fools at heart, with their meanness and stupidity only partly concealed by a thin veneer of refinement and learning.

The historians of the High Renaissance in Italy displayed a critical spirit and a degree of objectivity which had not been seen since the end of the ancient world. First among them in order of time although not in order of greatness was Machiavelli. In his main historical work, an account of the evolution of the Florentine republic to the death of Lorenzo de' Medici, he rigidly excluded all theological interpretations and sought to discover the natural laws which govern the life of a people. More scientific in his methods of analysis was Machiavelli's younger contemporary, Francesco Guicciardini (1483–1540). Having served many years as an ambassador of Florence and as a governor of papal territories, Guicciardini enjoyed a unique advantage in acquiring familiarity with the cynical and tortuous political life of his day. His special gifts as a historian were a capacity for minute and realistic analysis and an uncanny ability in disclosing the springs of human action. His masterpiece was his *History of Italy*, a detailed and dispassionate account of the varying fortunes of that country from 1492 to 1534. No study of Renaissance historians would be complete without some mention of Lorenzo Valla (1406–1457), who may properly be regarded as the father of historical criticism. By careful scrutiny of their literary style he challenged the authenticity of a number of

⁴ J. A. Symonds, "Machiavelli," *Encyclopedia Britannica* (14th edition), Vol. XIV, p. 577.

378

accepted documents. He proved the famous "Donation of Constantine" to be a forgery, thereby demolishing one of the principal
bases of papal supremacy, since this document purported to have
been a grant by the Emperor Constantine of the highest spiritual
and temporal power in the West to the Pope. In addition, Valla
denied that the so-called Apostles' Creed had ever been written by
the Apostles, and he pointed out numerous corruptions in the
Vulgate edition of the New Testament as compared with the earlier
Greek texts. His critical methods served later on to stimulate a
much broader attack by the northern humanists upon the doctrines
and practices of the organized church.

Despite the wealth of brilliant accomplishments in literature, the
proudest achievements of the Italian Renaissance were made in the
realm of art. Of all the arts, painting was undoubtedly supreme. The *Italian painting*
evolution of Italian painting followed a course of development *in the Trecen-*
which roughly paralleled the history of literature. During the initial *to: Giotto the*
period of the Trecento, however, there was only one artist of *naturalist*
distinction worthy to be compared to Petrarch and Boccaccio in
literature. His name was Giotto (1276–1337). With him, painting
definitely took on the status of an independent art, although his
master Cimabue had already made some beginnings in this direction.
Giotto was pre-eminently a naturalist. So skillful was he in depicting *See color*
the semblance of life that, according to the story, one of his drawings *pictures at*
of a fly so completely deceived Cimabue that he attempted to brush *page 356*
the creature away with his hand. Giotto also displayed more than
ordinary talent in the portrayal of action, especially in such frescoes
as *Saint Francis Preaching to the Birds*, *The Massacre of the Innocents*, and his scenes from the life of Christ.

It was not till the Quattrocento, however, that Italian Renaissance
painting really attained its majority. By this time the increase in
wealth and the partial triumph of the secular spirit had freed the *Painting in the*
domain of art to a large extent from the service of religion. The *Quattrocento*
church was no longer the only patron of artists. While subject
matter from Biblical history was still commonly employed, it was
frequently infused with nonreligious themes. The painting of portraits for the purpose of revealing the hidden mysteries of the soul
now became popular. Paintings intended to appeal primarily to the
intellect were paralleled by others whose only purpose was to delight the eye with gorgeous color and beauty of form. The Quattrocento was characterized also by the introduction of painting in oil,
probably from Flanders. The use of the new technique doubtless
had much to do with the artistic advance of this period. Since oil
does not dry so quickly as water, the painter could now work more
leisurely, taking his time with the more difficult parts of the picture
and making corrections if necessary as he went along.

The majority of the painters of the Quattrocento were Florentines. First among them was a precocious youth by the name of **379**

Masaccio, *The Expulsion of Adam and Eve from the Garden of Eden.* As the first of the realists, Masaccio departed from the tradition of Giotto and introduced emotion and psychological study into his paintings. In the Church of Santa Maria del Carmine, Florence.

The Floren-
tine painters:
Masaccio

Masaccio. Although he died at the age of twenty-seven, Masaccio inspired the work of Italian painters for a hundred years. He is commonly considered the first of the realists in Renaissance art. Besides, he introduced an element of universality into his work which profoundly influenced many of his successors. The greatest of his paintings, *The Expulsion of Adam and Eve from the Garden* and *The Tribute Money,* dealt not with specific themes but with the simple emotions common to mankind in all ages. Masaccio was also the first to achieve any notable success in imparting unity of action to groups of figures and in giving the effect of thickness to objects by the use of light and shade.

See color
pictures at
page 356

The best known of the painters who followed directly the paths marked out by Masaccio were Fra Lippo Lippi and Botticelli. As his name indicates, Fra Lippo Lippi was a member of a religious brotherhood. But that did not prevent him from giving his paintings an intensely human appeal. For his portraits of saints and madonnas he chose as models the ordinary men and women of the city of Florence. He was accustomed to depict the Christ child as a lusty infant whom one might expect to pull his mother's hair or fly into an unspiritual tantrum at any minute. Probably his chief contribution to painting was a tradition of psychological analysis. He seems to have been the first to have made the face the mirror of the soul. His most famous pupil, Sandro Botticelli (1444-1510), carried the method of psychological treatment even farther. In spite of his sensitive feeling for nature which led him to paint with such delicate skill the subtle loveliness of youth, the summer sky, and the tender bloom of spring, Botticelli was really more deeply interested in the spiritual beauty of the soul. Like others of his time, he was strongly influenced by Neo-Platonism and dreamed of the reconciliation of pagan and Christian thought. As a consequence many of the countenances he painted reveal a pensive sadness, a mystic yearning for the divine. But by no means all of his work had a religious import. His *Allegory of Spring* and *Birth of Venus* are based entirely upon classical mythology and suggest little more than an absorbing pleasure in the unfolding of life and a romantic longing for the glories of ancient Greece and Rome.

See color pictures at pages 356, 357

Perhaps the greatest of the Florentine painters was Leonardo da Vinci (1452-1519), one of the most talented and versatile geniuses who ever lived. Not only was he a gifted painter but a sculptor, musician, and architect of outstanding ability and a brilliant mathematician, scientist, and philosopher. The son of an illicit union of a prominent lawyer and a woman of humble station, he was placed by his father at an early age under the instruction of Verrocchio, a sculptor and painter of some renown and the most celebrated teacher of art in Florence. By the time he was twenty-five Leonardo was already sufficiently distinguished as a painter to win the favor of Lorenzo the Magnificent. But after five or six years he appears to have become dissatisfied with the intellectual and artistic views of the Medici and gladly accepted an offer of regular employment at the court of the Sforza in Milan. It was under the patronage of the Sforza that he produced some of the finest achievements of his whole career. His work, covering the late years of the fifteenth century and the first two decades of the sixteenth, marks the beginning of the so-called High Renaissance in Italy.

Leonardo da Vinci

As a painter Leonardo da Vinci was impatient with the established tradition of striving to imitate classical models. He believed that all art should have as its basis a scientific study of nature. But he had no intention of confining his interests to the mere surface appearances of things. He was convinced that the secrets of nature are deeply hidden, and that the artist must examine the structure of a plant or probe into the emotions of a human soul as painstakingly as the anatomist would dissect a body. He appears especially to have

Leonardo's artistic approach

been fascinated by the grotesque and unusual in nature. Yawning fissures in the earth, jagged pinnacles of rocks, rare plants and animals, embryos, and fossils—these were the phenomena he loved to ponder, evidently in the belief that this mysterious universe yields more of its secrets in the fantastic and unaccustomed than in the things that are commonplace and obvious. For the same reason he devoted much time to the study of exceptional human types, often wandering the streets for hours in quest of some face which would reveal the beauty and terror, the sincerity and hypocrisy, of the personality behind it. As a result of this deliberate selection of subjects, the paintings of Leonardo have a quality of realism decidedly at variance with the ordinary type. He did not generally portray the aspects of nature as they appear to the casual observer but strove to present them as symbols of his own philosophic reflections. He was one of the most profoundly intellectual of painters.

Leonardo's famous paintings

It is generally agreed that Leonardo da Vinci's masterpieces are his *Virgin of the Rocks*, his *Last Supper*, and his *Mona Lisa*. The first represents not only his marvelous technical skill but also his passion for science and his belief in the universe as a well-ordered place. The figures are arranged in geometric composition with every rock and plant depicted in accurate detail. The *Last Supper*, painted on the walls of the rectory of Santa Maria delle Grazie in Milan, is a study of psychological reactions. A serene Christ, resigned to his terrible fate, has just announced to his disciples that one of them will betray him. The purpose of the artist is to portray the mingled emotions of surprise, horror, and guilt revealed in the faces of the disciples as they gradually perceive the meaning of their master's statement. The third of Leonardo's major triumphs, the *Mona Lisa*, reflects a similar interest in the varied moods of the human soul. Though it is true that the *Mona Lisa* is a portrait of an actual woman, the wife of a Neapolitan by the name of Francesco del Giocondo, it is much more than a mere photographic likeness. A distinguished art critic and philosopher of the nineteenth century has called it a portrait of universal woman—"a perpetual life sweeping together ten thousand experiences." In other words, the famous *Mona Lisa* countenance is not so much that of an individual woman as of feminine humanity. In it are brought together all the thoughts and feelings, the triumphs and defeats, the sympathy and the brutality of womankind through uncounted centuries.[5] The *Mona Lisa* is distinctive also as the supreme embodiment of the artist's skill in depicting the play of light and shade. In place of the old technique of showing a gradual transition from light to dark, Leonardo introduced a new method of punctuating darker areas with little spots of light, and vice versa. The effect was to surround the faces in many of his paintings with a gentle haze, accentuating their tender and pensive look. For him the interplay of light and shadow was

See color pictures at pages 356, 357

[5] Walter Pater, *The Renaissance* (Modern Library edition), pp. 103-4.

an even more significant manifestation of nature than color and outline. His emphasis upon this phenomenon had the result of illuminating some of the figures in the background of his paintings and of
giving a suggestion of dark mystery to others.

The late Quattrocento, or the beginning of the High Renaissance,
was marked by the rise of another celebrated school of Italian
painting, the so-called Venetian school. Its chief representatives included Titian (1477–1576), Giorgione (1478–1510), and Tintoretto
(1518–1594). Of the three, Titian was perhaps the greatest. The
work of all these men reflected the luxurious life and the pleasure-
loving interests of the thriving commercial city of Venice. The
Venetian painters had none of the preoccupation with philosophical
and psychological themes which had characterized the Florentine
school. Their aim was to appeal to the senses rather than to the
mind. They delighted in painting idyllic landscapes and gorgeous
symphonies of color. For their subject matter they chose not merely
the opulent beauty of Venetian sunsets and the shimmering silver
of lagoons in the moonlight but also the man-made splendor of
sparkling jewels, richly colored satins and velvets, and gorgeous
palaces. In this subordination of form and meaning to color and
elegance there were mirrored not only the sumptuous tastes of a
wealthy bourgeoisie but also definite traces of Oriental influence
which had filtered through from Byzantium during the late Middle
Ages.

*The Venetian
painters*

*See color
pictures at
pages 388,
389*

The remaining great painters of the High Renaissance all lived
their active careers in the Cinquecento. It was in this period that
the evolution of art reached its peak, and the first signs of decay
began to appear. Rome was now almost the only artistic center of
importance on the mainland of the Italian peninsula, although the
traditions of the Florentine school still exerted a potent influence.
Among the eminent painters of this period at least two must be
given more than passing attention. One of the most noted of them
was Raphael (1483–1520), a native of Urbino, and perhaps the most
popular artist of the entire Renaissance. The lasting appeal of his
style is due primarily to its charm, its simple humanism, rather
than to any power of thought or emotional fervor behind it. Although Raphael was an ardent admirer of Leonardo da Vinci and
copied many technical features of his work, for the most part he
remained loyal to the ideals of sweetness and piety inherited from
his earlier teachers. He was inclined to glorify form and color for
their own sake and to despise intellectual meaning. Never disturbed
by the mental perplexities of Leonardo da Vinci or the emotional
torments of Michelangelo, he devoted himself to the cultivation of
an ideal type of beauty as an end in itself and to the expression of
religious sentiments. Among his greatest works are the *School of
Athens* and the *Sistine Madonna*.

*The painters of
the late Renais-
sance: Raphael*

The towering giant of the Cinquecento in painting was Michelangelo (1475–1564). Beset by the hardships of poverty, harassed by grasping relatives, and torn by the emotional conflicts of his own tempestuous nature, Michelangelo appears as one of the most tragic figures in the history of art. His dark presentiments were often reflected in his work, with the result that some of his paintings are overwrought and almost morbidly pessimistic. Nevertheless, the sense of tragedy he implanted in the scenes he portrayed was not really personal but universal. After the manner of the Greek dramatists he conceived of the tragic fate of mortals as something external to man himself, a product of the cosmic order of things. If there was any one theme which dominated all of his work, it was humanism in its most intense and eloquent form. He considered the pathos and nobility of man as the only legitimate subjects of art. Rocks and trees and flowers meant nothing to him, not even as background. Michelangelo's grandest achievement as a

Michelangelo, *The Creation of Adam.* One of a series of fresco paintings on the ceiling of the Sistine Chapel in Rome. Suggesting philosophical inquiries into the meaning of life and the universe, it represents Renaissance realism at its height.

painter was the series of frescoes he produced on the ceiling of the Sistine Chapel and on the wall above the altar. The sheer physical labor required to complete the task was prodigious. For four and a half years he toiled on a lofty scaffold, most of the time face upward, covering the six thousand square feet of ceiling with nearly four hundred figures, many of them as much as ten feet in stature. The series embraces a number of scenes in the mighty epic of the human race according to Christian legend. Among them are *God Dividing the Light from the Darkness, God Creating the Earth, The Creation of Adam, The Fall of Man, The Deluge,* and so on. The culminating scene is *The Last Judgment,* which Michelangelo finished some thirty years later on the wall back of the altar. Sometimes referred to as the most famous painting in the world, this scene depicts a Herculean Christ damning the great mass of mankind to perdition. Although the subject matter is Christian, the spirit is thoroughly pagan, as indicated by the naked and muscular

See color pictures at page 388

figures and the suggestion of a ruthless deity who punishes men beyond their deserts. Nowhere else is Michelangelo's conception of universal tragedy more strongly expressed than in this work of his lonely old age.

Medieval sculpture, as we have already seen, was not an independent art but a mere adjunct of architecture. During the Italian Renaissance a gradual evolution began which ultimately had the effect of freeing sculpture from its bondage to architecture and establishing its status as a separate art frequently devoted to secular purposes. Though the work of a number of earlier artists pointed the way to this evolution, the first great master of Renaissance sculpture was Donatello (1386?–1466). He emancipated his art from Gothic mannerisms and introduced a more vigorous note of individualism than did any of his predecessors. His statue of David standing triumphant over the body of the slain Goliath established a precedent of naturalism and of glorification of the nude which sculptors for many years afterward were destined to follow. Donatello also produced the first monumental equestrian statue in bronze since the time of the Romans, a commanding figure of the *condottiere*, Gattamelata.

Italian Renaissance sculpture: Donatello

Gattamelata, by Donatello. This imposing figure of a *condottiere* was probably the first monumental equestrian statue since the time of the Romans. On the Piazza in front of St. Anthony's Church, Padua.

One of the greatest sculptors of the Italian Renaissance, and probably of all time, was Michelangelo. Sculpture, in fact, was the artistic field of Michelangelo's personal preference. Despite his success as a painter he considered himself unfitted for that work. Whether he was ever particularly happy as a sculptor might be open to debate, for he smashed some of the works upon which he had spent months of labor and invested others with the same quality of hopeless pessimism that characterized much of his painting. The dominant purpose which motivated all of his sculpture was the expression of thought in stone. His art was above mere naturalism, for he subordinated nature to the force and sweep of his ideas. Other features of his work included the use of distortion for powerful effect, preoccupation with themes of disillusionment and tragedy, and a tendency to express his philosophical ideas in allegorical form.

Michelangelo, greatest of Renaissance sculptors

385

Most of his great masterpieces were done for the embellishment of tombs, a fact significantly in harmony with his absorbing interest in death, especially in his later career. On the tomb of Pope Julius II, which was never finished, he carved his famous figures of the *Bound Slave* and *Moses*. The first, which is probably in some degree autobiographical, represents tremendous power and talent restrained by the bonds of fate. The statue of Moses is perhaps the leading example of Michelangelo's sculpture showing his use of anatomical distortion to heighten the effect of emotional intensity. Its purpose was evidently to express the towering rage of the prophet on account of the disloyalty of the children of Israel to the faith of their fathers.

Michelangelo's allegorical sculpture

Certain other examples of Michelangelo's work as a plastic artist create an even more striking impression. On the tombs of the Medici in Florence he produced a number of allegorical figures representing such abstractions as sorrow and despair. Two of them are known by the traditional titles of *Dawn* and *Sunset*. The first is that of a female figure, turning and raising her head like someone called from a dreamless sleep to awake and suffer. *Sunset* is the figure of a powerful man who appears to sink under the load of human misery around him. Whether these allegorical figures were intended to symbolize the disasters which had overtaken the republic of Florence or merely to express the artist's own sense of the repletion of disappointment and defeat in the world is unknown. As Michel-

Pietà, by Michelangelo. This portrayal of tragedy was made by the sculptor for his own tomb. Note the distortion for effect exemplified by the elongated body and left arm of the Christ. The figure in the rear is Nicodemus, but was probably intended to stand as a symbol of Michelangelo himself. Original in the Cathedral of Florence.

The Cathedral of Florence. Completed by Filippo Brunelleschi in the Fifteenth Century, the Cathedral of Florence is a prime example of Renaissance architecture. With its majestic dome, massive construction, and horizontal lines, it harks back to the Romans. The bell tower, or campanile, however, begun by Giotto, reflects medieval influence.

angelo's life drew toward its close, he tended to introduce into his sculpture a more exaggerated and spectacular emotional quality. This was especially true of his *Pietà*, intended for his own tomb. The *Pietà* is a statue of the Virgin Mary grieving over the body of the dead Christ. The figure standing behind the Virgin is probably intended to represent Michelangelo himself contemplating the stark tragedy which seemed to epitomize the reality of life. It is perhaps fitting that this profound but overwrought interpretation of human existence should have brought the Renaissance epoch in sculpture to a close.

To a much greater extent than either sculpture or painting, Renaissance architecture had its roots in the past. The new building style was eclectic, a compound of elements derived from the Middle Ages and from pagan antiquity. It was not the Hellenic or the Gothic, however, but the Roman and the Romanesque which provided the inspiration for the architecture of the Italian Renaissance. Neither the Greek nor the Gothic had ever found a congenial soil in Italy. The Romanesque, by contrast, was able to flourish there, since it was more in keeping with Italian traditions, while the per-

Renaissance architecture

sistence of a strong admiration for Latin culture made possible a revival of the Roman style. Accordingly, the great architects of the Renaissance generally adopted their building plans from the Romanesque churches and monasteries and copied their decorative devices from the ruins of ancient Rome. The result was an architecture based upon the cruciform floor plan of transept and nave and embodying the decorative features of the column and arch, or the column and lintel, the colonnade, and frequently the dome. Horizontal lines predominated; and, though many of the buildings were churches, the ideals they expressed were the purely secular ones of joy in this life and pride in human achievement. The finest example of Renaissance architecture is St. Peter's church in Rome, built under the patronage of Popes Julius II and Leo X and designed by the most celebrated architects of the time—Bramante, Raphael, and Michelangelo. Profusely decorated with costly paintings and sculpture, it remains to this day the most magnificent church in the world.

III. PHILOSOPHY AND SCIENCE The Common impression that the Renaissance represented in every way a marked improvement over the Middle Ages is not strictly true. Such was especially not the case in the realm of philosophy. The early philosophers of the Italian Renaissance rejected Scholasticism, which had given a very high place to the exercise of human reason, and wallowed in a mass of childish superstitions and mystical puerilities. Since the Scholastics had made Aristotle their intellectual god, the majority of the early humanists decided to go back to Plato. The leaders in this movement were such men as Marsiglio Ficino (1433–1499), and Pico della Mirandola (1463–1494), both of whom were members of the Platonic Academy founded by Cosimo de' Medici. Unfortunately the Platonism of these men was far from being the pure variety. The bulk of it was made up of the Neo-Platonist teachings of Plotinus together with various mythological accretions which had been accumulated throughout the Middle Ages. The exponents of this philosophy were as blindly uncritical in following what they believed to be the teachings of Plato as any medievalist in his devotion to Aristotle. Indeed, one of the great aims of the Academy was to reconcile Platonism and Christianity and thereby to build a new faith in which worship of the pagan past would hold equal sway with the promise of a life to come. Pico della Mirandola went one step farther and urged a universal religion composed of a mixture of Platonism, Christianity, and the Jewish Kabbala, that fantastic compound of magic, numerology, and mysticism which had been elaborated mainly by followers of Philo and the Neo-Pythagoreans from the pre-Christian era to the end of the Middle Ages.

But not all the Italian humanists were ecstatic worshipers of Plato. Some in their zeal for a revival of pagan culture sought to reawaken an interest in Aristotle for his own sake and not as a bulwark of

Italian Renaissance philosophy: the Neo-Platonists

388

Madonna and Child, Luca della Robbia (1400–1482). This enameled terra cotta plaque is typical of the work of the della Robbia family. (MMA)

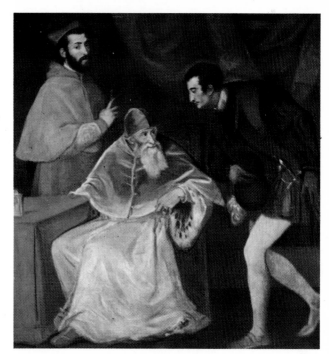

Pope Paul III and His Nephews, Titian (1477–1576). This painting, with its rich harmony of color, is unusual in being both a group portrait and a study of action. (National Museum, Naples)

Portrait of a Young Man, Giovanni Bellini (1430–1516). Though noted for opulence and color, artists of the Venetian school also excelled in portrait painting. (MMA)

The Madonna of the Chair, Raphael (1483–1520). Raphael's art was distinguished by warmth and serenity, and by an uncritical acceptance of the traditions and conventions of his time. (Pitti Palace, Florence)

Portrait of a Girl, Domenico Veneziano (1400–1461). Though born and probably trained in Venice, Domenico was strongly influenced by the technical achievements of the Florentines. (MMA)

"Christ and Madonna." From *The Last Judgment*, Michelangelo (1475–1564). This painting above the altar in the Sistine Chapel, Rome, shows Christ as judge condemning sinners to perdition. Even the Madonna at His side seems to shrink from His wrath.

Young Man, Bronzino (1503–1572). The portrait displays the typical Renaissance spirit of the proud young man who glories in his achievement. (MMA)

Rospigliosi Cup. Attributed to Benvenuto Cellini (1500–1571). Cellini was not only an adventurer and writer, but also a talented goldsmith. The cup shown was intended to hold salt. (MMA)

Boy with a Greyhound, Veronese (1528–1588). Veronese personifies consummate artistic skill with little attention to meaning. (MMA)

The Doge Presented to the Redeemer, Tintoretto (1518–1594). This dramatic painting commemorates a pledge by the Doge in 1576 to build a temple to the Redeemer if Venice were saved from the plague. (MMA)

Four Saints, Correggio (1489–1534). Correggio was noted for his skill in composition and technical detail. He painted the *Four Saints* while still in his teens. (MMA)

Christianity. Others became Stoics, Epicureans, or Skeptics. The most original philosophers of the Italian Renaissance were Lorenzo Valla, Leonardo da Vinci, and Niccolo Machiavelli. The fearless and sensational ventures of Lorenzo Valla into the field of historical criticism have already been noted. He was equally unconventional as a philosopher. Declaring himself a follower of Epicurus, he avowed the highest good to be tranquil pleasure, condemned asceticism as utterly vain and worthless, and insisted that it is irrational to die for one's country. Although Leonardo da Vinci wrote nothing that could be called a philosophical treatise, he may yet be considered a philosopher in the true sense of the word; for he was one of the first to condemn unequivocally the reliance upon authority as a source of truth, and he urged the use of the inductive method. It may be worth while also in these troublous times to take note of his strictures on war, which he called "that most bestial madness." He wrote that "It is an infinitely atrocious thing to take away the life of a man," and he even refused to divulge the secret of one of his inventions for fear it might be used by unscrupulous rulers to increase the barbarity of war.[6]

Lorenzo Valla and Leonardo da Vinci

Niccolo Machiavelli is by far the most famous—and also the most infamous—political philosopher of the Italian Renaissance. No man did more than he to overturn the basic political doctrines of the Middle Ages, especially the ideas of limited government and the ethical basis of politics. He frankly avowed his preference for absolutism as necessary to solidify and strengthen the state, and he expressed his profoundest contempt for the medieval idea of a moral law limiting the authority of the ruler. For him, the state was an end in itself. The supreme obligation of the ruler was to maintain the power and safety of the country over which he ruled. Whatever the means necessary to enable him to fulfill that obligation, the prince should not shrink from adopting them. No considerations of justice or mercy or the sanctity of treaties should be allowed to stand in the way. Cynical in his views of human nature, Machiavelli maintained that all men are prompted exclusively by motives of self-interest, particularly by desires for personal power and material prosperity. The head of the state should therefore take nothing for granted as to the loyalty or affection of his subjects. He should assume that all men are his potential rivals and should endeavor to play them off one against another for his own advantage. Machiavelli also rejected the medieval notion that a static society is desirable. He affirmed, on the contrary, that a state must either expand and develop or undergo the certainty of decay.[7] Notwithstanding the reproaches that have been heaped upon Machiavelli for his unmoral

Machiavelli's political philosophy

[6] Edward MacCurdy, ed., *The Notebooks of Leonardo da Vinci*, Vol. I, p. 24.
[7] Machiavelli's political ideas are found mainly in *The Prince* and in his *Discourses on Livy*. In the latter work he condemned feudalism and defended the republican form of government as preferable to monarchy for most states.

teachings, he remains a significant figure in the history of political theory. Not only his divorce of politics from ethics, but also his suggestion of a positive law created by the state and maintained by physical force, in place of the law of nature, serves to make him the real progenitor of modern conceptions of government. He is significant also as the first important realist in political theory since the time of Polybius. He described the state not in accordance with some lofty ideal but as it actually was in his own day. And it is a deplorable fact that the essential parts of his description would fit the official practices of most rulers ever since.

Science in the Italian Renaissance

Not only did the narrow attitude of the early humanists in Italy retard the progress of philosophy; it also hindered for some time the advancement of science. The early humanists, as we have seen, were not critically minded. They accepted the authority of the Neo-Platonists with a gullibility worthy of the Dark Ages. Moreover, their interests were in art and literature, not in science. Part of this emphasis may undoubtedly be attributed to the fact that the leaders of the Renaissance for some time had only a limited knowledge of Greek achievements. The early pagan revival was predominantly a revival of Latin antiquity. And it will be recalled that the contributions of the Romans to science were exceedingly few and mediocre. But in spite of the unfavorable influence of early humanism, Italy became by the fifteenth century the most important center of scientific discovery in Renaissance Europe. Men from all over the continent came to study in her universities and to profit from the researches of her eminent scholars. The foundations for nearly every major discovery of the fifteenth and sixteenth centuries were laid in Italy. Such was notably the case in the fields of astronomy, mathematics, physics, and medicine.

The revival and proof of the heliocentric theory

The achievement *par excellence* in astronomy was the revival and proof of the heliocentric theory. Contrary to the popular opinion, this was the work not of any one man but of several. It will be remembered that the idea of the sun as the center of our universe had originally been set forth by the Hellenistic astronomer Aristarchus in the third century B.C. But then, some four hundred years later, the theory of Aristarchus had been superseded by the geocentric explanation of Ptolemy. For more than twelve centuries thereafter the Ptolemaic theory was the universally accepted conclusion as to the nature of the physical universe. The Romans seem never to have questioned it, and it was adopted as a cardinal dogma by the Saracenic and Scholastic philosophers. It was first openly challenged about the middle of the fifteenth century by Nicholas of Cusa, who argued that the earth is not the center of the universe. Soon afterward Leonardo da Vinci taught that the earth rotates on its axis and denied that the apparent revolutions of the sun actually occur. In 1496 the now famous Pole, Nicholas Copernicus, came down into Italy to complete his education in civil and canon law. For ten years he studied in the universities of Bologna, Padua, and Ferrara, adding to his course in the law such subjects as mathematics and medicine. He also acquired an interest in astronomy and studied and worked for some years with the leading professors of that science. Upon returning to Poland he established his own observatory and devoted many weary nights to a study of the heavens. Lacking a telescope, he was able to make only a few observations with crude instruments he had devised for measuring the height and position of the sun and various stars. His conclusion that the planets revolve around the sun was based primarily upon mathematical calculations and upon hints received from Italian scientists and from the works of ancient astronomers. Fearing the hostility of the church, he refrained from publishing the results of his work until 1543. The proof sheets of his book, *On the Revolutions of the Heavenly Spheres*, were brought to him on his deathbed.

The most important astronomical evidence for the heliocentric theory was furnished by the greatest of Italian scientists, Galileo Galilei (1564–1642). With a telescope which he had perfected to a magnifying power of thirty times, he discovered the satellites of Jupiter, the rings of Saturn, and spots on the sun.[8] He was able also to determine that the Milky Way is a collection of celestial bodies independent of our solar system and to form some idea of the enormous distances of the fixed stars. Though there were many who held out against them, these discoveries of Galileo gradually convinced the majority of scientists that the main conclusion of Copernicus was true. The final triumph of this idea is commonly called the Copernican Revolution. Few more significant events have occurred in the intellectual history of the world; for it overturned the medieval world-view and paved the way for modern conceptions of mechanism, skepticism, and the infinity of time and space. Unfortunately it contributed also to the decline of humanism and the degradation of man, since it swept man out of his majestic position at the center of the universe and reduced him to a mere particle of dust in an endless cosmic machine.

In the front rank among the physicists of the Renaissance were Leonardo da Vinci and Galileo. If Leonardo da Vinci had failed completely as a painter, his contributions to science would entitle him to everlasting fame. Not the least of these were his achievements in physics. His researches in the fields of hydraulics and hydrostatics went far beyond anything previously attempted. His conclusion that "every weight tends to fall toward the center by the shortest way" contained the kernel of the law of gravitation.[9] In addition to his accomplishments in pure science he worked out

Galileo's achievements in astronomy

The Copernican Revolution

Leonardo da Vinci and Galileo, greatest of Renaissance physicists

[8] Galileo was not the original inventor of the telescope. That honor is usually accorded to Johannes Lippershey, an obscure optician who lived in the Low Countries about the beginning of the seventeenth century. Galileo learned of Lippershey's invention and improved upon it in a single night.

[9] Edward MacCurdy, ed., *The Notebooks of Leonardo da Vinci*, Vol. I, p. 18.

the principles of an astonishing variety of inventions, including a diving boat, a steam engine, an armored fighting car, and a marble saw. Galileo is especially noted as a physicist for his law of falling bodies. Skeptical of the traditional theory that bodies fall with a speed directly proportional to their weight, he demonstrated by actual test from the leaning tower of Pisa that the distance covered in the fall increases as the square of the time involved. Rejecting the Scholastic notions of absolute gravity and absolute levity, he taught that these are purely relative terms, that all bodies have weight, even those which like the air are invisible, and that in a vacuum all objects would fall with equal velocity. Galileo seems to have had a broader conception of a universal force of gravitation than Leonardo da Vinci, for he perceived that the power which holds the moon in the vicinity of the earth and causes the satellites of Jupiter to circulate around that planet is essentially the same as the force which enables the earth to draw bodies to its surface. He never formulated this principle as a law, however, nor did he realize all of its implications as did Newton some fifty years later.

*Progress
in anatomy and
medicine*

The record of Italian achievements in the various sciences related to medicine is also an impressive one. As early as the fourteenth century a physician by the name of Mundinus introduced the practice of dissection at the University of Bologna as the only proper source of anatomical knowledge. Somewhat later Fallopio discovered the human oviducts, or Fallopian tubes, and Eustachio described the anatomy of the teeth and rediscovered the tube which bears his name, leading from the middle ear to the throat. A number of Italian physicians contributed valuable information pertaining to

*The circulation
of the blood*

the circulation of the blood. One of them described the valves of the heart, the pulmonary artery, and the aorta, while another located the valves in the veins. Even more significant was the work of certain foreigners who lived and taught in Italy. Andreas Vesalius, a native of Brussels, issued the first careful description of the human body based upon actual investigation. As a result of his extensive dissections he was able to correct many ancient superstitions, including the one about a single incorruptible bone supposed to be the necessary nucleus of the resurrection of the body. He is commonly considered the father of the modern science of anatomy. Two other physicians of foreign nationality who were heavily indebted to Italian progress in medicine were the Spaniard, Michael Servetus (1511–1553), and the Englishman, William Harvey (1578–1657). Servetus discovered the lesser or pulmonary circulation of the blood. In his work entitled *Errors concerning the Trinity* (his major interest was theology, but he practiced medicine for a living), he described how the blood leaves the left ventricle of the heart, is carried to the lungs to be purified, then returns to the heart and is conveyed from that organ to all parts of the body. But he had no idea of the return of the blood to the heart through the veins. It was left for William Harvey, who had studied under Italian physicians at Padua, to complete the discovery. This he did after his return to England about 1610. In his *Dissertation upon the Movement of the Heart* he described how an artery bound by a ligature would fill with blood in the section nearer the heart, while the portion away from the heart would empty, and how exactly the opposite results would occur when a ligature was placed on a vein. By such experiments he reached the conclusion that the blood is in constant process of circulation from the heart to all parts of the body and back again.

3. The Waning of the Italian Renaissance

Soon after 1550 the Renaissance in Italy came to an end after two and a half centuries of glorious history. The causes of its sudden demise are far from being perfectly clear. Possibly at the head of the list should be placed the loss of economic supremacy. It seems beyond question that the brilliant culture of the Italian cities had rested very largely on a foundation of commercial prosperity resulting from their monopoly of trade with the Near East after the downfall of the Moslem and Byzantine empires. But the discovery of the New World at the end of the fifteenth century led to a rapid shift of the centers of trade from the Mediterranean area to the Atlantic coast. As a result, the life-blood of Italian culture was drained away. Among the other causes of decline may be mentioned the Catholic Reformation and political instability. The effects of the first of these in promoting dogmatism and clerical authority will be discussed in the chapter on The Age of the Reformation. The instability of Italian political life grew out of the unbridled individualism of the time and the jealousy among petty states. Most of the city-republics were governed by despots, who sometimes maintained themselves in power by methods worthy of a modern gangster. Although several of these rulers possessed remarkable ability, they all too frequently bequeathed their authority to weak and incompetent heirs. By way of illustration, the death of Lorenzo the Magnificent in 1492 was followed by the accession of his charming but incredibly stupid son Piero as dictator of Florence.

Reasons for the decline of the Renaissance in Italy

Perhaps still another cause of the decay of Renaissance culture in Italy may be found in the persistence of ignorance and superstition among the masses. Despite the fact that it was possible for men of humble status to push their way upward into the charmed circle of intellectual and artistic genius, few, of course, ever did so. And those who managed to scale the heights were generally inclined to scorn the multitude left behind. With no system of universal education, it was inevitable that the great mass of the common people should have remained benighted. Underneath the proud structure of Italian art and learning were smoldering embers of superstition

The Savonarola affair

393

Palace of the Doge, Venice. Since Venice was the richest city in the world during the Renaissance, it was fitting that her public buildings should be noted for their opulence. The palace of the Doge, or Duke, was built of creamy white Istrian stone and red Verona marble. The style combined Moslem, Byzantine, and Gothic elements.

The Palazzo Vecchio, Florence. The residence of the Medici, the Palazzo Vecchio was built in the Fourteenth and Fifteenth Centuries. The design shows the inspiration of the medieval fortress. Savonarola was burned to death in front of this palace in 1498.

ready to be kindled into flame by the first fanatic who happened along. This fact probably contains the real explanation of the Savonarola affair. Girolamo Savonarola was born in Ferrara in 1452, the son of a shiftless and spendthrift father. Though he lived in a gay and worldly city, his early education, directed by his mother and grandfather, seems to have been chiefly religious. At the age of nineteen he fell passionately in love with the daughter of an aristocratic neighbor. The young lady spurned him contemptuously, and soon afterward he decided to renounce the world and fled to a Dominican monastery at Bologna. In 1482 he was transferred to Florence, where Lorenzo the Magnificent was then at the height of his power. The longer Savonarola remained in Florence, the more he was dismayed by the frivolity and paganism he saw all around him. Within two or three years he began preaching in the cloister garden and in the churches of the city, burning into the hearts of his hearers the terrible wrath that would overtake them if they did not flee from their sins. His fiery eloquence and gaunt and unearthly appearance attracted great hordes of frightened people. By 1494 his power over the mob had reached such proportions that he became virtual dictator of Florence. And then for four long years the gay Tuscan metropolis was subjected to a puritanical rule surpassing in austerity anything that Italy had witnessed since the days of Gregory the Great. Half the year was devoted to Lenten

abstinence, and even marriage was discouraged. Citizens were commanded to surrender their articles of luxury and their books and
paintings alleged to be immoral; all of these works of the devil
were cast into the flames in the public square in the celebrated "burning of the vanities." But in time the people wearied of the rule of
the haggard monk; his enemies plotted against him, and he was
finally condemned to death in 1498 at the instance of the Pope on
trumped-up charges of heresy. While the Savonarola affair was not
in itself a primary cause of the decline of Renaissance civilization,
it is important as an evidence of the uneven diffusion of learning, and therefore of the shaky foundations upon which the civilization was built.

SELECTED READINGS—GENERAL

Burckhardt, Jacob, *The Civilization of the Renaissance in Italy*, new edi-
tion, New York, 1929
Butterfield, Herbert, *The Origins of Modern Science*, New York, 1951
Chubb, T. C., *The Life of Giovanni Boccaccio*, New York, 1930
Ferguson, W. K., *The Renaissance*, New York, 1940
Huizinga, J., *The Waning of the Middle Ages*, London, 1924
Lang, Paul, *Music in Western Civilization*, New York, 1941
Lucas, Henry S., *The Renaissance and the Reformation*, New York, 1934
Owen, John, *The Skeptics of the Italian Renaissance*, London, 1893
Pater, Walter, *The Renaissance*, New York
Randall, J. H., Jr., *The Making of the Modern Mind*, Boston, 1926,
Chs. VI and IX
Roeder, R., *The Man of the Renaissance*, New York, 1933
Schevill, Ferdinand, *The First Century of Italian Humanism*, New York,
1928
Sellery, George Clarke, *The Renaissance: Its Nature and Origins*, Madi-
son, 1950
Shipp, Horace, *The Italian Masters*, New York, 1930
Sichel, Edith, *The Renaissance*, New York, 1914
Smith, Preserved, *A History of Modern Culture*, New York, 1930, Vol. I
Symonds, J. A., *A Short History of the Renaissance in Italy*, New York,
1893
Taylor, H. O., *Thought and Expression in the Sixteenth Century*, Lon-
don, 1920
Thorndike, Lynn, *A History of Magic and Experimental Science in the
Fourteenth and Fifteenth Centuries*, New York, 1934, 2 vols.
——, *Science and Thought in the Fifteenth Century*, New York, 1929
Vallentin, Antonina, *Leonardo da Vinci*, New York, 1938
Van Dyke, Paul, *The Age of the Renascence*, New York, 1912
Wolf, A., *A History of Science, Technology and Philosophy in the XVIth
and XVIIth Centuries*, New York, 1935
Young, G. F., *The Medici*, New York, 1933

SOURCE MATERIALS

Baumer, F. L. V., *Main Currents of Western Thought*, New York, 1952
Galileo Galilei, *The Sidereal Messenger*
MacCurdy, Edward, ed., *The Notebooks of Leonardo da Vinci*, 2 vols.
Machiavelli, Niccolo, *The Prince*, especially Chs. 15–21, 26
———, *Discourses on Livy*, especially Book I, Chs. 3, 4, 6, 9, 11, 12, 25, 32, 33, 34, 47, 53, 55, 58, 59; Book II, Chs. 2, 5, 13, 19, 22
Robinson, J. H., and Rolfe, H. W., *Petrarch, the First Modern Scholar and Man of Letters*
Willis, Robert, tr., *The Works of William Harvey, M.D.*

The Expansion of the Renaissance

That a movement as vigorous as the Italian Renaissance should have spread into other countries was a result no less than inevitable. For years there had been a continuous procession of northern European students coming down into Italy to bask in the genial intellectual climate of Florence, Milan, and Rome. Moreover, the economic and social changes in northern and western Europe had roughly paralleled those of Italy for some time. Everywhere feudalism was being supplanted by a capitalist economy, and a new individualism was superseding the corporate structure of society sanctified by the church in the Middle Ages. Common economic and social interests fostered the growth of a similar culture. But it must not be supposed that the Renaissance in northern and western Europe was exactly the same as that in the south. The Italian and the Teuton differed markedly in temperament and in historical background. Joyous, carefree, and lacking in moral earnestness, the Italian was disposed to find in art and literature the most suitable media of self-expression. Besides, he was the heir of classical traditions, which also enhanced his aesthetic interests. The northern European, on the other hand, by reason of his harder struggle for existence, was inclined toward more serious and more practical pursuits. He tended to view the problems of life from a moral or religious angle. Everything mattered for good or evil; nothing could be esteemed as worthy merely because it was beautiful. As a result of these differences the northern European Renaissance was much less distinctly an artistic movement than the Renaissance in the south. Though painting flourished in the Low Countries, elsewhere it had no more than a limited scope, while sculpture was largely neglected. The

The spread of the Renaissance

397

main efforts of the northern peoples were concentrated in literature and philosophy, often with some religious or practical purpose. Furthermore, the northern humanist did not follow his Italian predecessor down the primrose path of paganism but generally remained loyal to the Christian faith, however sharply he might criticize the organized church.

*The political
background of
the Renaissance
outside of Italy*

The political history of the countries of northern and western Europe during the age of the Renaissance was characterized by developments somewhat similar to those which had occurred in Italy. There was the same transition from the weak and decentralized feudal regime to the concentrated rule of despotic princes. There was also the destruction of the political power of the guilds and the absorption of their prerogatives of sovereignty by the state. The chief difference was to be found in the fact that many of the states outside of Italy were beginning to take on the character of national units. Each of them occupied a territory of considerable size and embraced a population knit together by bonds of language and a vague consciousness of unity as a people. But for the most part these great political organisms were the creations of ambitious monarchs, who broke the power of local nobles and welded their petty principalities into huge dynastic empires. In England this process was abetted by the so-called Wars of the Roses, a series of bloody struggles beginning about 1455 between rival factions of barons. So many were the nobles killed in these wars, and so profound was the disgust with the long period of disorder, that the Tudor dynasty, founded by Henry VII in 1485, was soon able to crush completely the remnants of feudal power. The most noted members of this dynasty, Henry VIII and Queen Elizabeth, were the real founders of despotic government in England—with the support of the middle classes, who desired more protection for their commercial interests than the feudal regime could give.

*The growth
of strong
government in
England*

*Conditions in
France, Spain,
and Germany*

In the case of France it was also a war which led to the establishment of a consolidated state—but an international war rather than an internal squabble. The struggle which enabled the French kings to stamp out feudal sovereignty was the Hundred Years' War (1337–1453), fought primarily to expel the English from France and to break their commercial alliance with the Flemish cities. As a result of this conflict a national consciousness was aroused in the French people, the nobles who had followed their own selfish ambitions were discredited, and the monarchy was extolled for having saved the country from ruin. Within thirty years the shrewd but unscrupulous Louis XI (1461–1483) extended the royal domain over all of France with the exception of Flanders and Brittany. His policies paved the way for the absolute rule of the Bourbons. Still another important country of western Europe began its emergence as a nation-state toward the end of the fifteenth century. This country was Spain, united partly as a result of the marriage of Ferdinand of Aragon

*See color
pictures at
page 261*

and Isabella of Castile in 1469 and partly through the exigencies of the long war against the Moors. Under Philip II (1556–1598) Spain rose to a place in the very front rank of European powers. Aside from Italy, the only major country of western Europe which was not united into a consolidated state during the age of the Renaissance was Germany. Though it is true that political authority in some of the individual German kingdoms was solidified, the country as a whole remained merely a part of the Holy Roman Empire, now headed by the Hapsburg monarchs of Austria. The sovereignty of the Holy Roman Emperors was a mere fiction, mainly because during the Middle Ages they had wasted their energies in a vain attempt to extend their control over Italy, thereby enabling the German dukes to entrench themselves in power.

1. The Intellectual and Artistic Renaissance in Germany

One of the first countries to receive the full impact of the Italian humanist movement was Germany. This was a natural development not only because of the proximity of the two countries, but also *The limited* because of the large-scale migration of German students to the *scope* Italian universities. But the influence of this humanism was short- *of the German* lived and its fruits rather scanty and mediocre. What the results *Renaissance* might have been if Germany had not been hurled so soon into the maelstrom of religious contention cannot be determined. The fact remains, however, that the Protestant Revolution stirred up passions of hate and intolerance which could not be other than inimical to the humanist ideal. A premium was now set upon bigotry and faith, while anything resembling the worship of man or reverence for pagan antiquity was almost certain to be regarded as a work of the devil.

To fix a date for the beginning of the German Renaissance is practically impossible. In such prosperous cities of the south as Augsburg, Nuremberg, Munich, and Vienna there was a lively *German hu-* humanist movement, imported from Italy, as early as 1450. By the *manism: the* beginning of the sixteenth century it had taken firm root in uni- *Letters of Ob-* versity circles, particularly in the cities of Heidelberg, Erfurt, and *scure Men* Cologne. Its most notable representatives were Ulrich von Hutten (1488–1523) and Crotus Rubianus (1480–1539). Both were less interested in the literary aspects of humanism than in its possibilities as an expression of religious and political protest. Von Hutten, especially, made use of his gifts as a writer to satirize the worldliness and greed of the clergy and to indite fiery defenses of the German people against their enemies. He was himself an embittered rebel against almost every institution of the established order. The chief title of von Hutten and Rubianus to fame is their authorship of the *Letters of Obscure Men,* one of the wittiest satires in the history **399** of literature. The circumstances under which it was written are so strikingly like those which frequently occur in the evolution of nations that they deserve to be recounted here. A learned humanist at the University of Heidelberg by the name of Johann Reuchlin had developed a passionate enthusiasm for the study of Hebrew writings. Because he criticized some of the theologians' interpretations of the Old Testament, he was savagely attacked by Christian fanatics and was finally haled before the Inquisitor-General for the Catholic church in Germany. Numerous pamphlets were published on both sides of the controversy, and the issue was soon sharply drawn between freedom and tolerance, on the one hand, and authoritarianism and bigotry on the other. When it became apparent that rational argument was accomplishing nothing, the friends of Reuchlin decided to make use of ridicule. Rubianus and von Hutten published a series of letters purporting to have been written by some of Reuchlin's opponents, with such ridiculous signatures as Ziegenmelker (Goat-milker), Honiglecker (Honey-licker), and Mistlader (Dung-loader). Heinrich Shafmaul (Sheep's mouth), the supposed writer of one of the letters, professed to be worried lest he had sinned grievously by eating an egg which contained a chick on Friday. The author of another of the letters boasted of his brilliant "discovery" that Julius Caesar could not have written the *Commentaries on the Gallic Wars* because he was too busy with his military exploits ever to have learned the Latin language. How much effect these letters had in undermining the influence of the Catholic hierarchy in Germany is impossible to say, but it must have been considerable, for they enjoyed a wide circulation.

The German Renaissance in art was limited entirely to painting and engraving, represented chiefly by the work of Albrecht Dürer (1471–1528) and Hans Holbein (1497–1543). Both of these artists were profoundly influenced by Italian traditions, though much of the Germanic spirit of somber realism is also expressed in their work. Dürer's best-known paintings are his *Adoration of the Magi*, the *Four Apostles*, and *The Crucified Christ*. The last is a study in tragic gloom. It shows the body of the pale Galilean stretched on the cross against a bleak and sinister sky. The glimmer of light on the horizon merely adds to the somber effect of the scene. Some of Dürer's best-known engravings exhibit similar qualities. His *Melancholy* represents a female figure, with wings too small to lift her body, meditating hopelessly on the problems of life, which appear to defy all solution. A compass is in her hand, and various other implements upon which man has relied for the control of his environment lie strewn about the floor. Hans Holbein, the other great artist of the German Renaissance, derives his renown primarily from his portraits and drawings. His portraits of Erasmus, of Henry VIII, of Jane Seymour, and of Anne of Cleves are among the most famous in the world. An impressive example of his drawings is the

German painting: Dürer and Holbein

See color pictures at page 452

400

Portrait of Henry VIII by Hans Holbein the Younger. In the Palazzo Corsini, Rome.

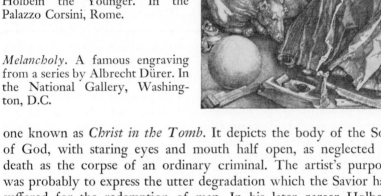

Melancholy. A famous engraving from a series by Albrecht Dürer. In the National Gallery, Washington, D.C.

one known as *Christ in the Tomb*. It depicts the body of the Son of God, with staring eyes and mouth half open, as neglected in death as the corpse of an ordinary criminal. The artist's purpose was probably to express the utter degradation which the Savior had suffered for the redemption of man. In his later career Holbein also drew many religious pictures satirizing the abuses in the Catholic church which were believed to be the chief justification for the Protestant Revolution. He was one of the few prominent artists to devote his talents to the Protestant cause.

The only German during the age of the Renaissance to make any significant contribution to science was Johann Kepler (1571–1630). An ardent adherent of the teachings of Copernicus, he improved the theory of the distinguished Pole by proving that the planets move in elliptical, rather than circular, orbits around the sun. Thus he may be said to have destroyed the last important vestige of the Ptolemaic astronomy, which had assumed the planets to be imbedded in perfect crystalline spheres. In addition, the laws of planetary motion which Kepler formulated were of tremendous value in suggesting to Newton his principle of universal gravitation. There was another scientist of German nationality whose work can be appropriately discussed in this connection, though he was actually born in the vicinity of Zurich, about the end of the fifteenth century. The name of this man was Theophrastus von Hohenheim, but

German science: Kepler and Paracelsus

401

he chose to call himself Paracelsus to indicate his own belief in his superiority to Celsus, the great Roman physician. Although Paracelsus is often referred to as a quack and an impostor, there is really comparatively little evidence that this was the case. He was at least sufficiently skillful as a practitioner of healing to be appointed professor of medicine at the University of Basel and town physician in 1527. Moreover, it is his special merit that he went straight to the book of experience for his knowledge of diseases and their cures. Instead of following the teachings of ancient authorities, he traveled widely, studying cases of illness in different environments and experimenting with innumerable drugs. He denied that the quest for the philosopher's stone should be the function of the chemist and insisted upon the close interrelation of chemistry and medicine. Perhaps his most important specific contribution was his discovery of the relation between cretinism in children and the presence of goiter in their parents.

2. Renaissance Culture in the Low Countries

The derivation and character of Renaissance culture in the Low Countries

Despite the fact that the Low Countries did not win independence of foreign domination until the seventeenth century,[1] they were nevertheless one of the most splendid centers of Renaissance culture on the Continent of Europe outside of Italy. The explanation is to be found primarily in the wealth of the Dutch and Flemish cities and in the important trade connections with southern Europe. As early as 1450 there were significant attainments in art in the Low Countries, including the development of painting in oil. Here also some of the first books were printed. While it is true that the Renaissance in the Low Countries was no broader in scope than in several other areas of northern Europe, its achievements were generally of surpassing brilliance.

Erasmus, the most civilized man of his age

The history of Renaissance literature and philosophy in the Low Countries begins and ends with Desiderius Erasmus, universally acclaimed as the Prince of the Humanists. The son of a priest and a servant girl, Erasmus was born near Rotterdam probably in the year 1466. For his early education he had the benefit of the excellent training given in the school of the Brethren of the Common Life at Deventer.[2] Later, after his father and mother were both dead, his guardians placed him in an Augustinian monastery. Here the young Erasmus found little religion or formal instruction of any kind but plenty of freedom to read what he liked. He devoured all the classics he could get his hands on and the writings of many of the Church Fathers. When he was about thirty years of age, he

---

[1] They were ruled by the Duchy of Burgundy until 1506 when they were inherited by Charles, the young king of Spain, whose grandfather had married the sole heiress of the Burgundian duke.

[2] See The Renaissance in Religion, §7 in this chapter.

obtained permission to leave the monastery and enroll in the University of Paris, where he completed the requirements for the degree of bachelor of divinity. But Erasmus never entered upon the active duties of a priest, choosing rather to make his living by teaching and writing. By extensive reading of the classics he achieved a style of Latin expression so remarkable for its wit and urbanity that everything he wrote was widely read. But Erasmus' love of the classics was not born of pedantic interest. He admired the ancient authors because they gave voice to the very ideals of naturalism, tolerance, and humanitarianism which held so exalted a place in his own mind. He was wont to believe that such pagans as Cicero and Socrates were far more deserving of the title of Saint than many a Christian canonized by the Pope. In 1536 Erasmus died in Basel at the end of a long and unfaltering career in defense of scholarship, high standards of literary taste, and the life of reason. He has rightfully been called the most civilized man of his age.

As a philosopher of humanism Erasmus was the incarnation of the finest ideals of the northern Renaissance. Convinced of the inherent goodness of man, he believed that all misery and injustice would eventually disappear if only the pure sunlight of reason could be allowed to penetrate the noisome caverns of ignorance, superstition, and hate. With nothing of the fanatic about him, he stood for liberality of mind, for reasonableness and conciliation, rather than for fierce intolerance of evil. He shrank from the violence and passion of war, whether between systems, classes, or nations. Much of his teaching and writing was dedicated to the cause of religious reform. The ceremonial, dogmatic, and superstitious extravagances in sixteenth-century Catholic life repelled him. But it was alien to his temper to lead any crusade against them. He sought rather by gentle irony, and occasionally by stinging satire, to expose irrationalism in all of its forms and to propagate a humanist religion of simple piety and noble conduct based upon what he called the "philosophy of Christ." Although his criticism of the Catholic faith had considerable effect in hastening the Protestant Revolution, he recoiled in disgust from the bigotry of the Lutherans. Neither did he have much sympathy for the scientific revival of his time. Like most of the humanists he believed that an emphasis upon science would serve to promote a crude materialism and to detract men's interests from the ennobling influence of literature and philosophy. The chief writings of Erasmus were his *Praise of Folly*, in which he satirized pedantry, the dogmatism of theologians, and the ignorance and credulity of the masses; and his *Familiar Colloquies* and *The Handbook of the Christian Knight*, in which he condemned ecclesiastical Christianity and argued for a return to the simple teachings of Jesus, "who commanded us nothing save love for one another." In a less noted work entitled *The Complaint of Peace*, he expressed his abhorrence of war and his contempt for despotic princes.

The liberal philosophy of Erasmus

The writings of Erasmus

403

The artistic Renaissance in the Low Countries was confined almost entirely to painting; and in this field the outstanding achievements were those of the Flemish school. Flemish painting derived no small measure of its excellence from the fact that it was an indigenous art. Here there were no classical influences, no ancient statues to imitate, and no living traditions from the Byzantine or Saracenic cultures. Until comparatively late, even the Italian influence was of little consequence. The painting of Flanders was rather the spontaneous product of a virile and prosperous urban society dominated by aspiring merchants interested in art as a symbol of luxurious tastes. The work of nearly all the leading painters—the

van Eycks, Hans Memling, and Roger van der Weyden—betrayed this flair for depicting the solid and respectable virtues of their patrons. It was distinguished also by powerful realism, by a relentless attention to the details of ordinary life, by brilliant coloring, and by a deep and uncritical piety. Hubert and Jan van Eyck are noted for their *Adoration of the Lamb,* an altarpiece produced for a church in Ghent soon after the beginning of the fifteenth century.

*See color
pictures at
page 452*

Described by some critics as the noblest achievement of the Flemish school, it portrays a depth of religious feeling and a background of ordinary experience unmatched in Italian art. It was the first great work of the Renaissance to be done by the new method of painting in oil, a process believed to have been invented by the van Eycks. The other two Flemish painters of the fifteenth century, Hans Memling and Roger van der Weyden, are noted, respectively, for naturalism and for the expression of emotional intensity. About a

hundred years later came the work of Peter Breughel, the most independent and the most socially conscious of the northern artists. Spurning the religious and bourgeois traditions of his predecessors, Breughel chose to depict the life of the common man. He loved to portray the boisterous pleasures of peasant folk at their wedding feasts and village fairs or to illustrate proverbs with scenes from the lives of humble people close to the earth. While he was enough of a realist never to idealize the characters in his paintings, his attitude toward them was definitely sympathetic. He employed his talents for the purpose also of condemning the tyranny of the Spanish regime in the Low Countries. One of his paintings, *The Massacre of the Innocents,* pictures the slaughter of women and children by Spanish soldiers. Seldom has great art been used more effectively as a weapon of political protest.

3. *The French Renaissance*

Despite the strong aesthetic interests of the French people, as evidenced by their perfection of Gothic architecture during the Middle Ages, the achievements of their artists in the age of the Renaissance were of comparatively little importance. There was some minor progress in sculpture and a modest advancement in architecture. It was during this time that the Louvre was built, on the site of an earlier structure bearing the same name, while numerous châteaux erected throughout the country represented a more

or less successful attempt to combine the grace and elegance of the Italian style with the solidity of the medieval castle. Nor was science entirely neglected, although the major accomplishments were few. They included the contributions of François Viète (1540–1603) to mathematics and of Ambroise Paré (1517–1590) to surgery. The former invented modern algebraic symbols and elaborated the theory of equations, for which the ground had been prepared by the work of the Italians, Niccolò Tartaglia (1500–1557) and Girolamo Cardan (1501–1576). Paré improved upon the method of treating gunshot wounds by substituting bandages and unguents for applications of boiling oil. He was also responsible for introducing the ligature of arteries as a means of controlling the flow of blood in major amputations.

But the outstanding achievements of the French Renaissance were in literature and philosophy, illustrated especially by the writings of François Rabelais (1490?–1553) and Michel de Montaigne (1533– 1592). Like Erasmus, Rabelais was educated as a monk, but soon after taking holy orders he left the monastery to study medicine at the University of Montpellier. He finished the course for the bachelor's degree in the short space of six weeks and obtained his doctorate about five years later, in the meantime having served for a period as public physician in Lyon in addition to lecturing and editing medical writings. He seems from the start to have interspersed his professional activities with literary endeavors of one sort and another. He wrote almanacs for the common people, satires against quacks and astrologers, and burlesques of popular superstitions. In 1532 Rabelais published his first edition of *Gargantua*, which he later revised and combined with another book bearing the title of *Pantagruel*. Gargantua and Pantagruel were originally the names of legendary medieval giants noted for their prodigious strength and their gross appetites. Rabelais' account of their adventures served as a vehicle for his robust, sprawling wit and for the expression of his philosophy of exuberant humanism. In language far from delicate he satirized the practices of the church, ridiculed Scholasticism, scoffed at superstitions, and pilloried every form of bigotry and repression. No man of the Renaissance was a more uncompromising individualist or exhibited more zeal in glorifying the human and the natural. For him every instinct of man was healthy, provided it was not directed toward tyranny over others. In common with Erasmus he believed in the inherent goodness of man, but unlike the great Prince of the Humanists he was a thoroughgoing pagan, rejecting not only Christian dogma but Christian morality as well. Any degree of restraint, intellectual or moral, was repugnant to Rabelais. His celebrated description of the abbey of Theleme, built by Gargantua, was intended to show the contrast between his conception of freedom and the Christian ascetic ideal. At Theleme there were no clocks summoning to duties and no vows of celibacy or perpetual membership. The inmates could leave when they liked; but while they remained they dwelt together "according to their own free will and pleasure. They rose out of their beds when they thought good; they did eat, drink, labour, sleep, when they had a mind to it, and were disposed for it. None did awake them, none did offer to constrain them . . . for so Gargantua had established it. In all their Rule and strictest tie of their order there was but this one clause to be observed, *Do what thou wilt*." [3]

Montaigne

A man of far different temperament and background was Michel de Montaigne (1533–1592). His father was a Catholic, his mother a Jewess who had become a Protestant. Almost from the day of his birth their son was subjected to an elaborate system of training. Every morning he was awakened by soft music, and he was attended throughout the day by servants who were forbidden to speak any language but Latin. When he was six years old he was ready for the College of Guienne at Bordeaux and at the age of thirteen began the study of law. After practicing law for a time and serving in various public offices, he retired at thirty-seven to his ancestral estate to devote the remainder of his life to study, contemplation, and writing. Always in delicate health, he found it necessary now more than ever to conserve his strength. Besides, he was repelled by the bitterness and strife he saw all around him and for that reason all the more anxious to find a refuge in a world of intellectual seclusion.

*Montaigne's
philosophy of
skepticism and
disenchantment*

Montaigne's ideas are contained in his famous *Essays*, written during his years of retirement. The essence of his philosophy is skepticism in regard to all dogma and final truth. He knew too much about the diversity of beliefs among men, the welter of strange customs revealed by geographic discoveries, and the disturbing conclusions of the new science ever to accept the idea that any one sect had exclusive possession of "the Truth delivered once for all to the saints." It seemed to him that religion and morality were as much the product of custom as styles of dress or habits of eating. He taught that God is unknowable, and that it is as foolish to "weep that we shall not exist a hundred years hence as it would be to weep that we had not lived a hundred years ago." Man should be encouraged to despise death and to live nobly and delicately in this life rather than to yearn piously for an after-existence that is doubtful at best. Montaigne was just as skeptical in regard to any assumption of final truth in philosophy or science. The conclusions of reason, he taught, are sometimes fallacious, and the senses often deceive us. The sooner men come to realize that there is no certainty anywhere the better chance they will have to escape the tyranny which flows from

[3] *Works of Rabelais* (Urquhart and Motteux, trans.), First Book, p. 165.

superstition and bigotry. The road to salvation lies in doubt, not in faith. A second element in Montaigne's philosophy was cynicism. He could see no real difference between the morals of Christians and those of infidels. All sects, he pointed out, fight each other with equal ferocity, except that "there is no hatred so absolute as that which is Christian." Neither could he see any value in crusades or revolutions for the purpose of overthrowing one system and establishing another. All human institutions in his judgment were about equally futile, and he therefore considered it fatuous that man should take them so seriously as to wade through slaughter in order to substitute one for its opposite. No ideal, he maintained, is worth burning your neighbor for. In his attitude toward questions of ethics Montaigne was not such a ribald champion of carnality as Rabelais; yet he had no sympathy for asceticism. He believed it ridiculous that men should attempt to deny their physical natures and pretend that everything connected with sense is unworthy. "Sit we upon the highest throne in the world," he declared, "yet we do but sit upon our own behind." The philosophy of Montaigne, tinctured as it was with escapism and disenchantment, marked a fitting close of the Renaissance in France. But in spite of his negative attitude he did more good in the world than most of his contemporaries who founded new faiths or invented new excuses for absolute monarchs to enslave their subjects. Not only did his ridicule help to quench the flames of the cruel hysteria against witches, but the influence of his skeptical teachings had no small effect in combating fanaticism generally and in paving the way for a more generous tolerance in the future.

Montaigne's tolerance

4. The Spanish Renaissance

During the sixteenth and early seventeenth centuries Spain was at the height of her glory. Her conquests in the Western Hemisphere brought wealth to her nobles and merchants and gave her a proud position in the front rank of European states. Notwithstanding these facts the Spanish nation was not one of the leaders in Renaissance culture. Apparently her citizens were too deeply absorbed in plundering the conquered territories to devote much attention to intellectual or artistic pursuits. Moreover, the long war with the Moors had engendered a spirit of bigotry, the position of the church was too strong, while the expulsion of the Jews at the end of the fifteenth century had deprived the country of talent it could ill afford to lose. For these reasons the Spanish Renaissance was limited to a very few achievements in painting and literature, albeit some of these rank in brilliance with the best that other countries produced.

Reasons for the backwardness of Spain in the Renaissance

Spanish painting bore the deep impression of the bitter struggle between Christian and Moor. As a result it expressed an intense preoccupation with religion and with themes of anguish and tragedy. **407**

Its background was medieval, upon which were engrafted certain influences from Flanders and later from Italy. The first of the eminent Spanish painters was Luis de Morales (1517–1586), frequently called "The Divine." His Madonnas, Crucifixions, and Mater Dolorosas typified that earnest devotion to Catholic orthodoxy regarded by many Spaniards of this time as a duty both religious and patriotic. But the most talented artist of the Spanish Renaissance was not a native of Spain at all, but an immigrant from the island of Crete. His real name was Domenico Theotocopuli, but he is commonly called El Greco. After studying for some time under Titian in Venice, El Greco settled in Toledo about 1575, to live there until his death in 1614. A stern individualist in temperament, he seems to have imbibed but little of the warmth of color and serene joy in satin splendor of the Venetian school. Instead, nearly all of his art is characterized by fevered emotionalism, stark tragedy, or enraptured flights into the supernatural and mystical. His figures are often those of gaunt, half-crazed fanatics; his colors are cold and ashen; while his scenes of suffering and death seem deliberately contrived to produce an impression of horror. Among his famous works are *The Burial of the Count of Orgaz, Pentecost,* and *The Apocalyptic Vision.* Better than any other artist, El Greco expresses the fiery religious zeal of the Spanish people during the heyday of the Jesuits and the Inquisition.

Literature in the Spanish Renaissance displayed tendencies not dissimilar to those in painting. This was notably true of drama, which frequently took the form of allegorical plays depicting the mystery of transubstantiation or appealing to some passion of religious fervor. Others of the dramatic productions dwelt upon themes of political pride or sang the praises of the bourgeoisie and expressed contempt for the dying world of feudalism. The colossus among the Spanish dramatists was Lope de Vega (1562–1635), the most prolific author of plays the literary world has seen. He is supposed to have written no fewer than 1500 comedies and more than 400 religious allegories. Of the total about 500 survive to this day. His secular dramas fall mainly into two classes: (1) the "cloak and sword plays," which depict the violent intrigues and exaggerated ideals of honor among the upper classes; and (2) the plays of national greatness, which celebrate the glories of Spain in her prime and represent the king as the protector of the people against a vicious and degenerate nobility.

Few would deny that the most gifted writer of the Spanish Renaissance was Miguel de Cervantes (1547–1616). His great masterpiece, *Don Quixote,* has even been described as "incomparably the best novel ever written." Composed in the best tradition of Spanish satirical prose, it recounts the adventures of a Spanish gentleman (Don Quixote) who has been slightly unbalanced by constant reading of chivalric romances. His mind filled with all kinds of fantastic adventures, he finally sets out at the age of fifty upon the slippery road of knight-errantry. He imagines windmills to be glowering giants and flocks of sheep to be armies of infidels, whom it is his duty to rout with his spear. In his disordered fancy he mistakes inns for castles and the serving-wenches within them for courtly ladies on fire with love of him. The advances they have no intention of making he must graciously repel in order to prove his devotion to his own Dulcinea. Set off in bold contrast to the ridiculous knight-errant is the figure of his faithful squire, Sancho Panza. The latter represents the ideal of the practical man, with his feet on the ground and content with the substantial pleasures of eating, drinking, and sleeping. The book as a whole is a pungent satire on feudalism, especially on the pretensions of the nobles as the champions of honor and right. Its enormous popularity was convincing proof that medieval civilization was largely extinct even in Spain.

5. The Renaissance in England

In common with Spain, England also enjoyed a golden age in the sixteenth and early seventeenth centuries. Though her vast colonial empire had not yet been established, she was nevertheless reaping big profits from the production of wool and from her trade with the Continent. Her government, recently consolidated under the rule of the Tudors, was making the prosperity of the middle class the object of its special solicitude. Through the elimination of foreign traders, the granting of favors to English shipping, and the negotiation of reciprocal commercial treaties, the English merchant classes were given exceptional advantages over their rivals in other countries. The growth of a national consciousness, the awakening of pride in the power of the state, and the spread of humanism from Italy, France, and the Low Countries also contributed toward the flowering of a brilliant culture in England. Nevertheless, the English Renaissance was confined primarily to philosophy and literature. The arts did not flourish; perhaps because of the Calvinist influence, which began to make itself felt in Britain by the middle of the sixteenth century.

The economic and political foundations of the Renaissance in England

The earliest philosophers of the English Renaissance may best be described simply as humanists. But while they were not unmindful of the value of classical studies, they were interested chiefly in the more practical aspects of humanism. Most of them desired a simpler and more rational Christianity and looked forward to an educational system freed from the dominance of medieval logic. Others were concerned primarily with individual freedom and the correction of social abuses. The greatest of these early thinkers was Sir Thomas More, esteemed by contemporary humanists as "excellent above all his nation." Following a successful career as a lawyer and as Speaker of the House of Commons, More was appointed in 1529

The early English humanists

Lord Chancellor of England. He was not long in this position, however, until he incurred the enmity of his royal master, Henry VIII. More was loyal to Catholic universalism and did not sympathize with the king's design of establishing a national church under subjection to the state. When in 1534 he refused to take the Oath of Supremacy acknowledging the king as the head of the Church of England, he was thrown into the Tower. A year later he was tried before a packed jury, convicted, and beheaded. More's philosophy is contained in his *Utopia*, which he published in 1516. Purporting to describe an ideal society on an imaginary island, the book is really an indictment of the glaring abuses of the time—of poverty undeserved and wealth unearned, of drastic punishments, religious persecution, and the senseless slaughter of war. The inhabitants of Utopia hold all their goods in common, work only six hours a day so that all may have leisure for intellectual pursuits, and practice the natural virtues of wisdom, moderation, fortitude, and justice. Iron is the precious metal "because it is useful," war and monasticism are abolished, and tolerance is granted to all creeds that recognize the existence of God and the immortality of the soul. Despite criticism of the *Utopia* as deficient in wit and originality, the conclusion seems justified that the author's ideals of humanity and tolerance were considerably in advance of those of most other men of his time.

The thinker who has gone down in history as the greatest of all English Renaissance philosophers is Sir Francis Bacon. Born in 1561, the son of a high government official, Bacon was nurtured in the lap of luxury until the age of seventeen when the death of his father compelled him to work for a living. Thereafter the dominating ambition of his life was to obtain some profitable position with the government which would enable him to pursue his intellectual interests. Probably it was this mania for security which accounts for the shady morality of his public career. When occasion arose, he did not shrink from concealing his true beliefs, from disloyalty to his friends, or from sharing in graft. In 1618 he was appointed Lord Chancellor, but after a scant three years in this office he was impeached for accepting bribes. Despite his protestations that the taking of money from litigants had never influenced his decisions, he was convicted and sentenced to pay a fine of $200,000 and to undergo imprisonment in the Tower "at the king's pleasure." King James I remitted the fine and limited the term of imprisonment to four days. Bacon devoted the remaining five years of his life to writing, especially to the completion of the third and enlarged edition of his essays. Among his most valuable works are the *Novum Organum* and *The Advancement of Learning*.

Bacon's monumental contribution to philosophy was the glorification of the inductive method. He was by no means the discoverer of that method, but he trumpeted it forth as the indispensable ground of accurate knowledge. He believed that all seekers of truth in the past had stumbled in darkness because they were slaves of preconceived ideas or prisoners in the dungeons of Scholastic logic. He argued that in order to overcome these obstacles the philosopher should turn to the direct observation of nature, to the accumulation of facts about things and the discovery of the laws that govern them. Induction alone, he believed, was the magic key which would unlock the secrets of truth. Authority, tradition, and syllogistic logic should be as sedulously avoided as the plague. But admirable as these teachings are, they were honored by Bacon himself almost as much in the breach as in the observance. He believed in astrology, divination, and witchcraft. However successful he may have been in clearing his mind of ancient dogma, he was not a good enough scientist to perceive the validity of the Copernican theory. Moreover, the distinction he drew between ordinary knowledge and the truths of religion was hardly in keeping with his stanch defense of induction. "The senses," he wrote, "are like the sun, which displays the face of the earth, but shuts up that of the heavens." For our voyage to the realm of celestial truth, we must "quit the small vessel of human reason and put ourselves on board the ship of the Church, which alone possesses the divine needle for justly shaping the course. The stars of philosophy will be of no further service to us. As we are obliged to obey the divine law, though our will murmur against it, so we are obliged to believe in the word of God, though our reason is shocked at it. The more absurd and incredible any divine mystery is, the greater honor we do God in believing it." It was not such a far cry after all from Roger Bacon in the thirteenth century to Francis Bacon in the seventeenth.

In literature, also, the English followed much more closely in the footsteps of their medieval forerunners than did the Renaissance writers in any other country with the exception of Italy. Indeed, it is difficult to say just when the English Renaissance in literature began. Chaucer's great work, the *Canterbury Tales*, written toward the end of the fourteenth century, is commonly considered medieval; yet it breathed a spirit of earthiness and of lusty contempt for the mystical quite as pronounced as anything to be found in the writings of Shakespeare. If there were any essential differences between the English literature of the Renaissance and that produced during the late Middle Ages, they would consist in a bolder individualism, a stronger sense of national pride, and a deeper interest in themes of philosophic import. The first great poet in England after the time of Chaucer was Edmund Spenser (1552?–1599). His immortal creation, *The Faërie Queene*, is a colorful epic of England's greatness in the days of Queen Elizabeth. Though written as a moral allegory to express the author's desire for a return to the virtues of chivalry, it celebrates also the joy in conquest and much of the gorgeous sensuousness typical of Renaissance humanism. The rich music of its style and its wealth of picturesque incident have endowed the poem with lasting popularity.

But the most splendid achievements of the English in the Eliza-

English Renaissance literature

*The Elizabethan
dramatists*

bethan Age were in the realm of drama. Not since the days of the Greeks had the writing of tragedies and comedies attained such heights as were reached in England during the sixteenth and early seventeenth centuries. Especially after 1580 a galaxy of playwrights appeared whose work outshone that of all their predecessors in nearly two thousand years. Included in this galaxy were such luminaries as Christopher Marlowe, Beaumont and Fletcher, Ben Jonson, and Shakespeare, of whom the first and the last are chiefly significant to the historian. Better than anyone else in his time, Christopher Marlowe embodies the insatiable egoism of the Renaissance—the everlasting craving for the fullness of life, for unlimited knowledge and experience. His brief but stormy career was a succession of scandalous escapades and fiery revolts against the restraints of convention until it was terminated by his death in a tavern brawl before he was thirty years old. The best known of his plays, entitled *Doctor Faustus*, is based upon the legend of Faust, in which the hero sells his soul to the devil in return for the power to feel every possible sensation, experience every possible triumph, and know all the mysteries of the universe.

*The life and
writings of
William
Shakespeare*

William Shakespeare, the most talented genius in the history of drama since Euripides, was born in 1564 into the family of a petty tradesman in the provincial market town of Stratford-on-Avon. His life is enshrouded in more mists of obscurity than the careers of most other great men. It is known that he left his native village when he was about twenty years old, and that ultimately he drifted to London to find employment in the theater. Tradition relates that for a time he earned his living by holding the horses of the more prosperous patrons of the drama. How he eventually became an actor and still later a writer of plays is unknown, but there is evidence that by the time he was twenty-eight he had already acquired a reputation as an author sufficient to excite the jealousy of his rivals. Before he retired to his native Stratford about 1610 to spend the rest of his days in ease, he had written or collaborated in writing nearly forty plays, to say nothing of 150 sonnets and two narrative poems.

*The character
of Shakespeare's
work*

In paying homage to the universality of Shakespeare's genius, we must not lose sight of the fact that he was also a child of the Renaissance. His work bore the deep impression of most of the virtues and defects of Renaissance humanism. Almost as much as Boccaccio or Rabelais, he personified that intense love of things human and earthly which had characterized most of the great writers since the close of the Middle Ages. Moreover, like the majority of the humanists, he showed a limited concern with the problems of politics and the values of science. Virtually the only political theory that interested him greatly was whether a nation had a better chance of prospering under a good king who was weak or under a bad king who was strong. Though his knowledge of the sciences of his time was ex-

William Shakespeare. Portrait made for the First Folio edition of his works, 1623.

tensive, he regarded them as consisting primarily of alchemy, astrology, and medicine.[4] But the force and range of Shakespeare's intellect were far from being bounded by the narrow horizons of the age when he lived. While few of the works of his contemporaries are now widely read, the plays of Shakespeare still hold their rank as a kind of secular Bible wherever the English language is spoken. The reason lies not only in the author's unrivaled gift of expression, but especially in his scintillating wit and his profound analysis of human character assailed by the storms of passion and tried by the whims of fate.

Shakespeare's dramas fall rather naturally into three main groups. Those written during his earlier years conformed to the traditions of existing plays and generally reflected his own confidence in personal success. They include such comedies as *A Midsummer Night's Dream* and *The Merchant of Venice*, a number of historical plays, and the lyrical tragedy, *Romeo and Juliet*. Shortly before 1600 Shakespeare seems to have experienced a change of mood. The restrained optimism of his earlier plays was supplanted by some deep disillusion which led him to distrust human nature and to indict the whole scheme of the universe. The result was a group of dramas characterized by bitterness, overwhelming pathos, and a troubled searching into the mysteries of things. The series begins with the tragedy of intellectual idealism represented by *Hamlet*, goes on to the cynicism of *Measure for Measure* and *All's Well That Ends Well*, and culminates in the cosmic tragedies of *Macbeth* and *King Lear*. Perhaps the famous speech of Gloucester in the last of these plays may be taken to illustrate the depths of the author's pessimism at this time:

Types of Shakespeare's plays

[4] In psychology, however, he gives evidence of being ahead of his time, especially in his treatment of insanity. Perhaps this was natural in view of his profound interest in human emotions, in man's conflict with himself and with the universe of which he is a part.

As flies to wanton boys are we to the gods;
They kill us for their sport.[5]

The final group of dramas includes those written during the closing years of Shakespeare's life, probably after his retirement. Among them are *The Winter's Tale* and *The Tempest*. All of them may be described as idyllic romances. Trouble and grief are now assumed to be only the shadows in a beautiful picture. Despite individual tragedy, the divine plan of the universe is somehow benevolent and just.

6. Renaissance Developments in Music

Music in western Europe in the fifteenth and sixteenth centuries reached such a high point of development that it constitutes, together with painting and sculpture, one of the most brilliant aspects of Renaissance activity. While the visual arts were stimulated by the study of ancient models, music flowered naturally from an independent evolution which had long been in progress in medieval Christendom. As earlier, leadership was supplied by men trained in the service of the church, but the value of folk music was now appreciated, and its principles were combined with those of sacred music to bring a decided gain in color and emotional appeal. The distinction between sacred and profane became less sharp; most composers did not restrict their activities to either field. While the contrapuntal treatment of voices held the center of interest, some writing for instruments was attempted, and the use of instruments for accompaniment steadily increased. Music was no longer regarded merely as a diversion or an adjunct to worship but as an independent art.

Renaissance music compared with its medieval antecedents

Different sections of Europe vied with one another for musical leadership. As with the other arts, advance was related to the increasingly generous patronage made possible by the expansion of commerce, and was centered in the prosperous towns. During the fifteenth century first rank was held by the cities of the Netherlands and Burgundy. The Netherlands school carried vocal counterpoint to a technical perfection. While its members inclined toward a display of excessive ingenuity, they nevertheless rendered a real service by providing models of excellent workmanship. In the sixteenth century the Italians were able to duplicate the skill of their northern masters and far surpassed them in the subordination of technique to artistic effect. In Italy for the first time warmth, color, and sheer beauty became conspicuous features in choral art. In the splendidly Byzantine St. Mark's cathedral of Venice the tendency toward sensuous and brilliant effects was most pronounced, and was emphasized by the use of double choirs singing antiphonally. Thus

The leading schools of composition

[5] *King Lear*, Act IV, scene i.

a similarity is apparent between the Venetian schools of music and painting. At Rome, on the other hand, especially as reflected in the papal choir, there was a stricter adherence to tradition and an emphasis upon the element of worship. The greatest exponent of the Roman school and the composer whose work marks the culmination of the music of the age in its religious aspect was Palestrina (1526– 1594). In his masses and motets technical skill and intensity of purpose are so perfectly blended that the results meet the most exacting artistic standards. Palestrina's music, though employing rich harmonies and sometimes intricate in structure, constantly avoids ex-

Palestrina

Musical Instruments in the Sixteenth Century. In the lower left is shown a small pipe organ, with a bellows operated by the man seated opposite the player. The boxlike instrument on the table is a clavichord. The triangular shaped tube in the lower right corner is a *trumsheit*, or German "drum log."

travagance and possesses a clarity and tonal purity which appeal immediately to the listener. In its restraint, dignity, and moods of devout meditation or elation, it exemplifies not the secular ideals of Renaissance humanism but a profound religious dedication. Comparable developments to those in Italy were taking place in Austria and in southern Germany. Orlandus Lassus, court choirmaster at Munich from 1560 to 1590, was the equal of Palestrina in his handling of the contrapuntal style and exhibited a greater breadth of interests and variety of styles. Progress in England was facilitated by the patronage of the music-loving Tudor monarchs. The commercial ties between England and the Flemish cities may have provided an initial stimulus, but the English composers had enough fertility and originality to keep from being mere imitators of Continental models. The English school takes pre-eminence for the

Orlandus Lassus

415

development of the *madrigal,* in which the subtlety and sustained interest of the perfected contrapuntal technique were applied to secular themes. Because of their vitality and freshness, these madrigals have never ceased to charm. The general level of musical proficiency seems to have been higher in Queen Elizabeth's day than in ours: the singing of part-songs was a popular pastime in homes and at informal social gatherings, and the ability to read a part at sight was expected of a well-bred person.

Renaissance music a magnificent achievement

In conclusion, it may be observed that while counterpoint had matured, our modern harmonic system had been born, and thus a way was opened for fresh experimentation. At the same time one should realize that the music of the Renaissance constitutes not merely a stage in evolution but a magnificent achievement in itself, with masters who rank among the great of all time. The composers Palestrina and Lassus are as truly representative of the artistic triumph of the Renaissance as are the painters Raphael and Michelangelo. The fifteenth and sixteenth centuries, fittingly called the "golden age of song," have never been surpassed in the realization of the possibilities for beauty inherent in the human voice. Their heritage, long neglected except at a few ecclesiastical centers, has within recent years begun to be appreciated, and is now gaining in popularity as interested groups of musicians devote themselves to its revival.

7. The Renaissance in Religion

The Christian Renaissance

No account of the age of the Renaissance would be complete without some attention to the Renaissance in religion, or the Christian Renaissance as it is commonly called. This was a movement almost entirely independent of the Protestant Revolution, which will be discussed in the next chapter. The leaders of the Christian Renaissance were generally humanists, not Protestants. Few of them ever deserted the Catholic faith; their aim was to purify that faith from within, not to overthrow it. Most of them found the bigotry of early Protestantism as repugnant to their religious ideals as any of the abuses in the Catholic church. The original impetus for the Christian Renaissance appears to have come from the Brethren of the Common Life, a group of pious laymen who maintained schools in the Low Countries and in western Germany. Their aim was to propagate a simple religion of practical piety, as free as possible from dogmatism and ritual. The most noted of their early followers was Thomas à Kempis, who wrote or edited about 1425 a book entitled *The Imitation of Christ.* Though profoundly mystical in tone, the book nevertheless repudiated the extreme otherworldliness of medieval mystics and urged a life of simple devotion to the teachings of Jesus. For over a century the *Imitation* was more widely read in Europe than any other book with the exception of the Bible.

By 1500 the Christian Renaissance had become definitely associated with northern humanism. Writers and philosophers in every country lent their support to the movement. Prominent among them were Sebastian Brant in Germany, Sir Thomas More in England, Erasmus in the Low Countries, and figures of lesser renown in France and Spain. The religious teachings of these men were thoroughly in keeping with the humanist ideal as it was understood in northern Europe. Believing that religion should function for the good of man and not for the benefit of an organized church or even for the glory of an ineffable God, they interpreted Christianity primarily in ethical terms. Many of the theological and supernatural elements in it they regarded as superfluous, if not positively harmful. They likewise had little use for ceremonies of any kind, and they ridiculed the superstitions connected with the veneration of relics and the sale of indulgences. While they recognized the necessity of a limited amount of ecclesiastical organization, they denied the absolute authority of the Pope and refused to admit that priests were really essential as intermediaries between man and God. In fine, what most of these Christian humanists really desired was the superiority of reason over faith, the primacy of conduct over dogma, and the supremacy of the individual over the organized system. They believed that this simple and rational religion could best be achieved, not through violent revolt against the Catholic church, but through the gradual conquest of ignorance and the elimination of abuses.

The ideals of the Christian Renaissance

The decline of Renaissance culture in the countries of northern and western Europe came much less abruptly than in Italy. Indeed, the change in some respects was so gradual that there was simply a fusion of the old with the new. The achievements in science, for example, were merely extended, although with a definite shift of emphasis as time went on from the mathematical and physical branches to the biological. The Renaissance art of northern Europe, moreover, gradually evolved into the baroque, which dominated the seventeenth and early eighteenth centuries. On the other hand, humanism, in its Renaissance meaning of the worship of man and indifference to everything else, practically died out after the sixteenth century. In philosophy there has since been a tendency to exalt the universe and to relegate man to a place of insignificance as the helpless victim of an all-powerful destiny. When the end of the northern Renaissance did finally come, it was probably due chiefly to the heritage of bitterness and unreason left by the Protestant Revolt. But that is a subject which can be discussed more appropriately in the chapter that follows.

The decline of the Renaissance outside of Italy

Selected Readings

Allen, P. S., *The Age of Erasmus*, New York, 1914
Elton, G. R., *England under the Tudors*, London, 1955
Gray, Cecil, *The History of Music*, second edition, New York, 1931
Huizinga, J., *The Waning of the Middle Ages*, London, 1924
Hyma, Albert, *The Christian Renaissance*, New York, 1924
———, *Erasmus and the Humanists*, New York, 1930
Lang, Paul, *Music in Western Civilization*, New York, 1941
Lucas, Henry S., *The Renaissance and the Reformation*, New York, 1934
McGinn, D. F., *Shakespeare and the Drama of His Age*, New Brunswick, N.J., 1938
Oxford History of Music, Vols. I–II
Pater, Walter, *The Renaissance*, New York
Randall, J. H., Jr., *The Making of the Modern Mind*, Boston, 1926, Chs. VI and IX
Reese, Gustave, *Music in the Renaissance*, New York, 1954
Sichel, Edith, *The Renaissance*, New York, 1914
Smith, Preserved, *A History of Modern Culture*, New York, 1930, Vol. I
———, *Erasmus, A Study of His Life, Ideals and Place in History*, New York, 1923
Taylor, H. O., *Thought and Expression in the Sixteenth Century*, London, 1920
Thorndike, Lynn, *A History of Magic and Experimental Science in the Fourteenth and Fifteenth Centuries*, New York, 1934, 2 vols.
———, *Science and Thought in the Fifteenth Century*, New York, 1929
Tilley, A. A., *Studies in the French Renaissance*, New York, 1923
Van Dyke, Paul, *The Age of the Renascence*, New York, 1912
Wolf, A., *A History of Science, Technology and Philosophy in the XVIth and XVIIth Centuries*, New York, 1935

Source Materials

Bacon, Sir Francis, *The Great Instauration*, Preface
Erasmus, Desiderius, *The Complaint of Peace*
———, *The Handbook of a Christian Knight*
———, *The Praise of Folly*
Montaigne, Michel de, *Essays*
More, Sir Thomas, *Utopia*, especially Book II
Rabelais, François, *Gargantua and Pantagruel*, especially Book I

Modern Occidental Civilization, 1517-1789: Commercialism, Absolutism, Rationalism

In 1517 a great religious upheaval, known as the Protestant Revolution, began in Germany and eventually spread to many other countries. This religious revolution not only had much to do with terminating the Renaissance, but it was to a large extent the product of such factors as nationalism, individualism, and capitalism, which have come to be recognized as distinctive features of the modern age. For these reasons the Protestant Revolution may properly be considered to have ushered in the initial stage of modern civilization. This stage was characterized also by other developments. The period from 1500 to 1700 was the heyday of the Commercial Revolution, which overthrew the static economy of the medieval guilds and established a dynamic regime of business for profit. The entire era was marked by the growth of absolute governments and by the rise of powerful national states which took the place of the decentralized feudal regime of the Middle Ages. Finally, during the years from 1600 to 1789, there occurred an intellectual revolution, culminating in the enthronement of reason and in the development of the concept of a mechanistic universe governed by inflexible laws.

MODERN OCCIDENTAL CIVILIZATION, 1517–1789

	Europe as a Whole	Western Europe	Central and Eastern Europe
1300—	Rise of a capitalist economy, 1300–1500 Growth of banking, 1300–1600 Development of a money economy, 1300–1600 The Great Schism, 1379–1417 The domestic system, 1400–1750 The enclosure movement, 1400–1800 Voyages of discovery and exploration, 1450–1600	Babylonian Captivity of the Papacy, 1309–1379 Erasmus, 1466?–1536 Machiavelli, 1469–1527 Michelangelo, 1475–1564 Tudor Dynasty in England, 1485–1603 Rabelais, ca. 1490–1553	Copernicus, 1473–1543 Martin Luther, 1483–1546
1500—	Catholic Reformation, 1500–1563		John Calvin, 1509–1564 Beginning of Protestant Revolution, 1517 Zwinglian movement in Switzerland, 1519–1529 Rise of the Anabaptists, ca. 1520 Revolt of the knights, 1522–1523 Peasants' Revolt, 1524–1525
	Founding of Society of Jesus, 1534 Council of Trent, 1545–1563	Montaigne, 1533–1592 Henry VIII establishes Anglican Church, 1534	
1550—		Cervantes, 1547–1616 Sir Francis Bacon, 1561–1626 Shakespeare, 1564–1616 Galileo, 1564–1642 Revolt of the Netherlands, 1565–1609 Monteverdi, 1567–1643 The Elizabethan Compromise, 1570 Massacre of St. Bartholomew's Day, 1572 Rubens, 1577–1640	
	Beginning of International Law: Hugo Grotius, 1583–1645	Sir William Harvey, 1578–1657 Spanish Armada, 1588 Bourbon dynasty in France, 1589–1792 Edict of Nantes, 1598 Velasquez, 1599–1660	
1600—	Joint stock companies, 1600– Baroque architecture, 1600–1750		

	Europe as a Whole	Western Europe	Central and Eastern Europe
	Classicism in literature and the arts, 1600–1750		Cameralism, 1600–1800
	Mercantilism, 1600–1789		
	Chartered companies, 1600–1850		
	Thirty Years' War, 1618–1648	Rembrandt, 1606–1669	
		Colbert, 1619–1683	
	Deism, 1630–1800	Rationalism in philosophy, 1637–1700	
		Puritan Revolution in England, 1640–1649	
	Beginning of modern state system, 1648		
	Treaty of Westphalia, 1648		
		Commonwealth and Protectorate in England, 1649–1659	
		Restoration of the Stuart dynasty, 1660–1688	
		John Milton, *Paradise Lost*, 1667	
	The Enlightenment, 1680–1800	Revocation of Edict of Nantes, 1685	J. S. Bach, 1685–1750
		Newton's law of gravitation, 1687	
1688–	War of the League of Augsburg, 1688–1697	Glorious Revolution in England, 1688–1689	Peter the Great, of Russia, 1682–1725
		John Locke, *Two Treatises of Civil Government*, 1690	
		Voltaire, 1694–1778	
	Agricultural Revolution, 1700–1800	Bank of England, 1694	
	Rococo architecture, 1700–1800		
	War of the Spanish Succession, 1702–1714	Union of England and Scotland, 1707	
	Age of the Enlightened Despots, 1740–1796		Frederick the Great, of Prussia, 1740–1786
	Romanticism, 1750–1800	Rousseau, *The Social Contract*, 1762	
	Seven Years' War, 1756–1763	Beginning of the factory system, *ca.* 1770	Mozart, 1756–1791
			Catherine the Great, of Russia, 1762–1796
		Joseph Priestley discovers oxygen, 1774	
		Adam Smith, *The Wealth of Nations*, 1776	
		Lavoisier discovers indestructibility of matter, 1789	Kant, *The Critique of Pure Reason*, 1781
1789–		Edward Jenner develops vaccination for smallpox, 1796	Goethe, *Faust*, 1790–1808

The Age of the Reformation
(1517-ca. 1600)

Preceding chapters have described the unfolding of a marvelous culture which marked the transition from the Middle Ages to the modern world. It became apparent that this culture, known as the Renaissance, was almost as peculiarly an echo of the past as a herald of the future. Much of its literature, art, and philosophy, and all of its superstitions, had roots which were deeply buried in classical antiquity or in the fabulous centuries of the Middle Ages. Even its humanism breathed veneration for the past. Only in science and politics and in the vigorous assertion of the right of the individual to live as unconventionally and as dangerously as he liked was there much that was really new. But the Renaissance in its later stages was accompanied by the growth of another movement, the Reformation, which somewhat more accurately foreshadowed the modern age. This movement included two principal phases: the Protestant Revolution, which broke out in 1517 and resulted in the secession of most of northern Europe from the Roman faith; and the Catholic Reformation, which reached its height about 1560. Although the latter is not called a revolution, it really was such in nearly every sense of the term; for it effected a profound alteration of some of the notable features of late medieval Catholicism.

In a number of ways the Renaissance and the Reformation were closely related. Both were products of that powerful current of individualism which wrought such havoc to the established order in the fourteenth and fifteenth centuries. Each had a similar background of economic causes in the growth of capitalism and in the rise of a bourgeois society. Both partook of the character of a return to original sources: in the one case, to the literary and artistic achievements of the Greeks and Romans; in the other, to the

The later stages of the Renaissance accompanied by a religious revolution

The relation between the Renaissance and the Reformation

422

Scriptures and the doctrines of the Church Fathers. But in spite of these important resemblances, it is misleading to think of the Reformation as merely the religious aspect of the Renaissance. The guiding principles of the two movements really had little in common. The essence of the Renaissance was enjoyment of this life and indifference to the supernatural. The spirit of the Reformation was otherworldliness and contempt for the things of the flesh as vastly inferior to the spiritual. In the judgment of the humanist, man's nature was inherently good; in the view of the Reformer, it was unspeakably corrupt and depraved. The leaders of the Renaissance believed in reason and tolerance; the followers of Luther and Calvin emphasized faith and conformity. While both the Renaissance and the Reformation aimed at a recovery of the past, each was really oriented in an altogether different direction. The past which the humanists strove to revive was Greek and Roman antiquity, though they actually continued a much larger number of late medieval traditions, especially in literature, than they were willing to admit. The Reformers, by contrast, were interested chiefly in a return to the teachings of St. Paul and St. Augustine; not only did they reject the humanist idea of a revival of pagan achievements, but the Protestants among them, at least, proposed to throw overboard practically the whole body of late medieval institutions and doctrines.

For reasons such as these it seems justifiable to conclude that the Reformation was not really a part of the Renaissance movement. In actual fact, it represented a much sharper break with the civilization of the Feudal Age than ever did the movement led by the humanists. The radical Reformers would have nothing to do with the basic theories and practices of thirteenth-century Christianity. Even the simple religion of love and selflessness for the betterment of man, as taught by St. Francis of Assisi, appeared to repel them almost as much as the mysteries of the sacramental theory or the bombastic claims of Innocent III to spiritual and temporal power. In the main, the religious results of this clash with medieval Christianity have endured to this day. Moreover, the Reformation was intimately bound up with certain political trends which have persisted throughout the modern era. Nationalism, as we shall see, was one of the principal causes of the Protestant Revolution. While it is true that several of the humanists wrote under the influence of national pride, perhaps the majority were swayed by altogether different considerations. Many were scornful of politics, being interested solely in man as an individual; others, the great Erasmus among them, were thoroughly international in their outlook. But the Protestant Reformers could scarcely have gained much of a hearing if they had not associated their cause with the powerful groundswell of national resentment in northern Europe against an ecclesiastical system which had come to be recognized as largely Italian in character. For this

The Reformation not really a part of the Renaissance

*The Christian
Renaissance*

as well as for the reasons mentioned previously, it would seem not unwarranted to regard the Reformation as a gateway to the modern world. And when we speak of the Renaissance in religion, we should think, not of the Reformation, but of the so-called Christian Renaissance, initiated by the Brethren of the Common Life and carried to its highest fulfillment in the teachings of Sir Thomas More and Erasmus. The common assumption that Luther hatched the egg which Erasmus had laid is true only in a very limited sense. The bird which Luther hatched belonged to a much tougher and wilder breed than any that could have descended from the Prince of the Humanists.

1. The Protestant Revolution

The multiplicity of causes of the Protestant Revolution

The Protestant Revolution sprang from a multiplicity of causes, most of them closely related to the political and economic conditions of the age. Nothing could be more grossly inaccurate than to think of the revolt against Rome as exclusively a religious movement. Had it not been for the basic political changes in northern Europe and the growth of new economic interests, Roman Catholicism would probably have undergone no more than a gradual evolution, perhaps in line with the teachings of the Christian Renaissance. Nevertheless, since the religious causes were the most obvious ones, it will be well to consider them first.

Religious causes: abuses in the Catholic church

To the majority of Luther's early followers the movement he launched was chiefly a rebellion against abuses in the Catholic church. That such abuses existed no careful historian would deny, regardless of his religious affiliations. For example, many of the Roman clergy were incredibly ignorant. Some, having obtained their positions through irregular means, were unable to understand the Latin of the mass they were required to celebrate. There were even alleged to be cases of priests who could not repeat the Lord's Prayer or the creed in *any* language. Furthermore, large numbers of the clergy led scandalous lives. While some of the Popes and bishops were living in princely magnificence, the lowly priests occasionally sought to eke out the incomes from their parishes by keeping taverns, gaming houses, or other establishments for profit. Not only did some monks habitually ignore their vows of chastity, but a few indifferent members of the secular clergy surmounted the hardships of the rule of celibacy by keeping mistresses. Alexander VI, one of the most famous Popes on the eve of the Protestant Revolution, was known to have had eight illegitimate children, seven of them born before his election to the papacy. There were numerous evils also in connection with the sale of religious offices and dispensations. As in the case of most civil positions, offices in the church during the Renaissance period were commonly sold to the highest bidder. It is estimated that Pope Leo X enjoyed an income of more than a million dollars a year from the sale of more than two thousand ecclesiastical offices. This abuse was rendered more serious by the fact that the men who bought these positions were under a strong temptation to make up for their investment by levying high fees for their services. The sale of dispensations was a second malodorous form of ecclesiastical graft. A dispensation may be defined as an exemption from a law of the church or from some vow previously taken. On the eve of the Reformation the dispensations most commonly sold were exemptions from fasting and from the marriage laws of the church. By way of illustration, first cousins would be permitted to marry for the payment of a fee of one ducat; while for closer degrees of relationship—for example, uncle and niece—the fee might be as much as thirty times that amount, depending upon ability to pay.

But the abuses which seemed to arouse the most ardent pressure for reform were the sale of indulgences and the superstitious veneration of relics. An indulgence is a remission of all or of part of the temporal punishment due to sin—that is, of the punishment in this life and in purgatory; it is not supposed to have anything to do with the punishment in hell. The theory upon which the indulgence rests is the famous doctrine of the Treasure of Merit developed by Scholastic theologians in the thirteenth century. According to this doctrine, Jesus and the saints, by reason of their "superfluous" virtues on earth, accumulated an excess of merit in heaven. This excess constitutes a treasure of grace upon which the Pope can draw for the benefit of ordinary mortals. Originally indulgences were not issued for payments of money, but only for works of charity, fasting, going on crusades, and the like. It was the Renaissance Popes, with their insatiable greed for revenue, who first embarked upon the sale of indulgences as a profitable business. And the methods they employed were far from scrupulous. The traffic in "pardons" was often turned over to bankers on a commission basis. As an example, the Fuggers in Augsburg had charge of the sale of indulgences for Leo X, with permission to pocket one-third of the proceeds. Naturally, but one motive dominated the business—to raise as much money as possible. As a consequence, the agents of the bankers deluded ignorant people into believing that the indulgences were passports to heaven. By the sixteenth century the nefarious traffic had assumed the proportions of a gigantic scandal.

For centuries before the Reformation the veneration of sacred relics had been an important element in Catholic worship. It was believed that objects used by the Christ, the Virgin, or the saints possessed a miraculous healing and protective virtue for anyone who touched them or came into their presence. But it was inevitable that this belief should have opened the way for innumerable frauds. Superstitious peasants could be easily convinced that almost any ancient splinter of wood was a fragment of the true cross. And there was evidently no dearth of relic-mongers quick to take advantage of such credulity. The results were fantastic beyond belief. According to Erasmus, the churches of Europe contained enough wood of the true cross to build a ship. No fewer than five shinbones of the ass on which Jesus rode to Jerusalem were on exhibition in different places, to say nothing of twelve heads of John the Baptist. Martin Luther declared in a pamphlet lampooning his enemy, the Archbishop of Mainz, that the latter claimed to possess "a whole pound of the wind that blew for Elijah in the cave on Mount Horeb and two feathers and an egg of the Holy Ghost." [1]

Abuses not the primary causes of the Protestant Revolution

Modern historians agree, however, that abuses in the Catholic church were not the primary religious cause of the Protestant Revolution. It was medieval Catholicism itself, not the abuses therein, to which the Reformers objected. Moreover, just before the revolt broke out, conditions had begun to improve. Many pious Catholics themselves had started an agitation for reform, which in time would probably have eliminated most of the glaring evils in the system. But as so often happens in the case of revolutions, the improvement had come too late. Other forces more irresistible in character had been gradually gathering momentum. Chief among these forces of a religious nature was the growing reaction against late medieval theology, with its elaborate sacramental theory, its belief in the necessity of good works to supplement faith, and its doctrine of divine authority in the hands of the priests.

The clash between two different systems of theology: the Augustinian system

From preceding chapters the reader will recall that two different systems of theology had developed within the medieval church.[2] The first was formulated mainly by followers of St. Augustine in the early Middle Ages, on the basis of teachings in the Pauline Epistles. It was predicated on the assumption of an omnipotent God, who sees the whole drama of the universe in the twinkling of an eye. Not even a sparrow falls to the ground except in accordance with the divine decree. Human nature is hopelessly depraved, and it is therefore as impossible for man to perform good works as for thistles to bring forth figs. Man is absolutely dependent upon God not only for grace to keep him from sin but also for his fate after death. Only those mortals can be saved whom God for reasons of His own has predestined to inherit eternal life. Such in its barest outlines was the system of doctrine commonly known as Augustinianism. It was a theology well suited to the age of chaos which followed the breakup of the classical world. Men in this time were prone to fatalism and otherworldliness, for they seemed to be at the mercy of forces beyond their control. But the system never wholly died out. It was preserved intact for centuries in certain areas, especially of Germany, where the progress of late medieval civilization was

---

[1] Preserved Smith, *The Age of the Reformation*, pp. 495–96.
[2] See the chapters on The Civilization of Early Medieval Europe and The Civilization of the Feudal Age: Religious and Intellectual Developments.

426

comparatively slow. To Luther and many of his followers it seemed the most logical interpretation of Christian belief.

With the growth of a more abundant life in the cities of southern and western Europe, it was natural that the pessimistic philosophy of Augustinianism should have been replaced by a system which would restore to man some measure of pride in his own estate. The change was accelerated also by the growth of a dominant church organization. The theology of Augustinianism, by placing man's fate entirely in the hands of God, had seemed to imply that the functions of an organized church were practically unnecessary. Certainly no sinner could rely upon the ministrations of priests to improve his chances of salvation, since those who were to be saved had already been "elected" by God from all eternity. The new system of belief was finally crystallized in the writings of Peter Lombard and St. Thomas Aquinas in the twelfth and thirteenth centuries. Its cardinal premise was the idea that man had been endowed by God with freedom of will, with power to choose the good and avoid the evil. Man could not make this choice, however, entirely unaided, for without the support of heavenly grace he would be likely to fall into sin. It was therefore necessary for him to receive the sacraments, the indispensable means for communicating the grace of God to man. Of the seven sacraments of the church, the three most important for the layman were baptism, penance, and the Eucharist. The first wiped out the stain of previous sin; the second absolved the contrite sinner from guilt; while the third was especially significant for its effect in renewing the saving grace of Christ's sacrifice on the cross. Aside from baptism, none of the sacraments could ever be administered by anyone outside the ranks of the priesthood. The members of the clergy, having inherited the power of the keys from the Apostle Peter, alone had the authority to co-operate with God in forgiving sins and in performing the miracle of the Eucharist, whereby the bread and wine were transubstantiated into the body and blood of the Savior.

The late medieval theology of Peter Lombard and St. Thomas Aquinas

The Protestant Revolution was in very large measure a rebellion against the second of these systems of theology. Although the doctrines of Peter Lombard and St. Thomas Aquinas had really become part of the official theology of the church, they had never been universally accepted. To Christians who had been brought up under Augustinian influence, they seemed to detract from the sovereignty of God and to contradict the plain teachings of Paul that man's will is in bondage and his nature unspeakably vile. Worse still, in the opinion of these critics, was the fact that the new theology greatly strengthened the authority of the priesthood. In sum, what the Reformers wanted was a return to a more primitive Christianity than that which had prevailed since the thirteenth century. Any doctrine or practice not expressly sanctioned in the Scriptures, especially in the Pauline Epistles, or not recognized by

The Protestant Revolution a rebellion against the late medieval system of theology

the Fathers of the Church, they were strongly inclined to reject. It was for this reason that they condemned not only the theory of the priesthood and the sacramental system of the church, but also such medieval additions to the faith as the worship of the Virgin, the belief in purgatory, the invocation of saints, the veneration of relics, and the rule of celibacy for the clergy. Motives of rationalism or skepticism had comparatively little to do with it. While it is true that Luther ridiculed the worship of relics as a form of superstition, in the main the early Protestants were even more suspicious of reason than the Catholics. Their religious ideal rested upon the Augustinian dogmas of original sin, the total depravity of man, predestination, and the bondage of the will—which were certainly more difficult to justify on a rational basis than the liberalized teachings of St. Thomas.

A few remaining religious causes deserve at least passing mention. One was the decline of respect for the papacy in consequence of the so-called "Babylonian Captivity" and the Great Schism. The "Babylonian Captivity" grew out of a quarrel between King Philip IV of France and Pope Boniface VIII at the beginning of the fourteenth century. The soldiers of the king arrested the Pope, and soon afterward Boniface died from the effects of the humiliation. A short

Influence of the "Babylonian Captivity" of the papacy and the Great Schism

St. John Lateran, the Pope's Cathedral in Rome. The "Mother Church" of Catholic Christendom, it derives its name from Plautius Lateranus, a rich nobleman whose property in this area was confiscated by Nero.

time later King Philip's own candidate was elected to St. Peter's throne, and the papal capital was transferred to Avignon in the Rhone valley, where it remained for nearly seventy years. Surrounded by French influences, the Popes who reigned at Avignon were unable to escape the charge of subservience to French interests. In the minds of many Christians the papacy had ceased to be an international institution and had been degraded into the mere plaything of a secular power. In 1378 the head of the church suffered an even greater loss of prestige. An effort to restore the papacy to its original capital led to the election of two Popes, one at Avignon and one at Rome, each loudly proclaiming himself the rightful successor of the Apostle Peter. The resulting division of the church into two factions, supporting respectively the claims of the French and Italian Popes, is known as the Great Schism. Though finally healed by the Council of Constance in 1417, its effect in weakening the position of the papacy could hardly be overestimated.

Still another factor of some importance in hastening the Protestant Revolution was the influence of the mystics and early reformers. For more than two centuries before the time of Luther, mysticism had become one of the most popular forms of religious expression in northern Europe. And it is not without significance that the vast majority of the mystics were Germans or natives of the Low Countries. Pre-eminent among them was Meister Eckhart, who lived in the fourteenth century. Though none of the mystics preached open rebellion against the Catholic system, they were vehemently opposed to the ritualistic route to salvation sponsored by the medieval church. Their version of religion was one in which the individual would attain the highest heaven through extinction of selfish desires and absolute surrender of the soul to God. No sacraments or priestly miracles would be necessary. Faith and a deep emotional piety would accomplish more wonders in reconciling sinful man to God than all the masses in the calendar of the church. Along with the mystics a number of pre-Reformation reformers exerted considerable influence in preparing the ground for the Protestant Revolt. At the end of the fourteenth century an Oxford professor by the name of John Wyclif launched an attack upon the Catholic system which anticipated much of the thunder of Luther and Calvin. He denounced the immorality of the clergy, condemned indulgences and the temporal power of the church, recommended marriage of the clergy, insisted upon the supreme authority of the Scriptures as the source of belief, and denied transubstantiation, though admitting as Luther did later that Christ is actually present in the bread and wine. Most of Wyclif's teachings were ultimately carried to central Europe by Czech students from Oxford. They were actively propagated in Bohemia by John Huss, who was burned at the stake in 1415. Luther acknowledged his deep indebtedness to the Bohemian martyr.

Influence of the mystics and early reformers

Wyclif and Huss

As a political movement the Protestant Revolt was mainly the result of two causes: first, the growth of a national consciousness in northern Europe; and second, the rise of despotic governments. Ever since the late Middle Ages there had been a growing spirit of independence among many of the peoples outside of Italy. They had come to regard their own national life as unique and to resent interference from any external source. The Pope in particular they were inclined to view as a foreigner, who had no right to meddle with local affairs in England, France, or Germany. This feeling was manifested in England as early as the middle of the fourteenth century, when the famous Statutes of Provisors and Praemunire were passed. The first prohibited appointments by the Pope to church offices in England, while the second forbade the appeal of cases from the English courts to Rome. A law more extreme than either of these was issued by the king of France in 1438. The French law, known

The political causes of the Protestant Revolution: the growth of nationalism

as the Pragmatic Sanction of Bourges, practically abolished all papal authority in the country, including the appointive authority and the right to raise revenue. To the civil magistrates was given the power to regulate religious affairs within their own districts. A subsequent decree provided the death penalty for any agent of the Pope who should bring a bull into the country contradicting the Pragmatic Sanction. In Germany, despite the fact that there was no solid political unity, national feeling was by no means absent. It expressed itself in violent attacks upon the clergy by the Imperial Diet and in numerous decrees by the rulers of separate states prohibiting ecclesiastical appointments and the sale of indulgences without their consent.

The rise of despotic governments

The growth of a consciousness of national independence in all of these countries went hand in hand with the rise of despotic governments. Indeed, it would be difficult to say how much of the sense of nationality was spontaneous and how much of it was stimulated by ambitious princes intent upon increasing their power. At any rate it is certain that the claims of rulers to absolute authority were bound to result in defiance of Rome. No despot could long be expected to tolerate the exclusion of religion from his sphere of control. He could not be a despot so long as there was a double jurisdiction within his realm. The appetite of princes for control over the church was whetted originally by the revival of the Roman law, with its doctrine that the people had delegated *all* of their power to the secular ruler. To this must be added the effect of the teaching of Wyclif in England and Pierre Dubois (1250–1312) in France that the temporal power of the Pope should be transferred to the king. From this doctrine it was a comparatively easy step to the idea that all of the Pope's authority could be properly assumed by the head of the state. But whatever the reasons for its growth, there can be no doubt that the ambition of secular princes to establish churches under their own control was a primary cause of the mounting antagonism against Rome.

Economic causes: the desire to confiscate the wealth of the Catholic church

Finally, there were the economic causes of the Protestant Revolution. Foremost among these were the desire to get possession of the wealth of the church and resentment against papal taxation. In the course of its history from the beginning of the Middle Ages, the church had grown into a vast economic empire. It was by far the largest landowner in western Europe, to say nothing of its enormous movable wealth in the form of rich furnishings, jewels, precious metals, and the like. Estimates of the amount of land held by bishoprics and monasteries in the sixteenth century range as high as one-third of the total in Germany and one-fifth in France. Some of these possessions had been acquired by the church through grants by kings and nobles, but most of them came from the gifts and bequests of pious citizens. Legacy-hunting was a favorite occupation of the clergy as early as the twelfth century, as evidenced by a decree of Pope Alexander III declaring that no will could be valid unless made in the presence of a priest.[3] The existence of so much wealth in the hands of the church was a galling grievance not only to the ascetic reformers of the sixteenth century, but to thousands of lay-men as well. Kings, panting for big armies and navies, had an urgent need for more revenue. But Catholic law prohibited the taxing of church property. The exemption of episcopal and monastic property from taxation meant a heavier burden on the possessions of individual owners, especially on the property of merchants and bankers. Moreover, the lesser nobles in Germany were being threat-ened with extinction on account of the collapse of the manorial economy. Many of them looked with covetous eyes upon the lands of the church. If only some excuse could be found for expropriating these, their difficult situation might be relieved.

Papal taxation, by the eve of the Protestant Revolution, had as-sumed a baffling variety of irritating forms. The most nearly uni-versal, if not the most burdensome, was the so-called *Peter's pence,* an annual levy on every household in Christendom.[4] It must be understood that this tax was in addition to the *tithe,* which was supposed to be one-tenth of every Christian's income paid for the support of the parish church. Then there were the innumerable fees paid into the papal treasury for indulgences, dispensations, appeals of judicial decisions, and so on. In a very real sense the moneys collected for the sale of church offices and the *annates,* or com-missions levied on the first year's income of every bishop and priest, were also forms of papal taxation, since the officials who paid them eventually reimbursed themselves through increased collections from the people. But the main objection to these taxes was not that they were so numerous and burdensome. The famous accusation of some modern Catholic writers that the Protestants simply wanted a cheaper religion has no good foundation in fact. The real basis of grievance against the papal levies was their effect in draining the northern countries of so much of their wealth for the enrichment of Italy. Economically the situation was almost exactly the same as if the nations of northern Europe had been conquered by a foreign prince and tribute imposed upon them. Some Germans and English-men were scandalized also by the fact that most of the money col-lected was not being spent for religious purposes, but was being squandered by worldly Popes to maintain a luxurious court. The reason for the resentment, however, was probably as much financial as moral.

Resentment against papal taxation

A third important economic cause of the Protestant Revolt was

[3] J. W. Thompson, *An Economic and Social History of the Middle Ages,* p. 688.
[4] Peter's pence derived its name from the fact that it was a tax of one penny. But the English penny at the end of the Middle Ages was the equivalent in purchasing power of slightly more than one dollar of our money. H. E. Barnes, *An Economic History of the Western World,* p. 121.

Conflicts be-
tween middle-
class ambitions
and the ascetic
ideals of the
church

the conflict between the ambitions of the new middle class and the ascetic ideals of medieval Christianity. It was shown in a preceding chapter that the Catholic philosophers of the late Middle Ages had developed an elaborate theory designed for the guidance of the Christian in matters of production and trade.[5] This theory was founded upon the assumption that business for the sake of profit is essentially immoral. No one has a right to any more than a reasonable wage for the service he renders to society. All wealth acquired in excess of this amount should be given to the church to be distributed for the benefit of the needy. The merchant or craftsman who strives to get rich at the expense of the people is really no better than a common thief. To gain an advantage over a rival in business by cornering the market or beating down wages is contrary to all law and morality. Equally sinful is the damnable practice of usury —the charging of interest on loans where no actual risk is involved. This is sheer robbery, for it deprives the person who uses the money of earnings that are justly his; it is contrary to nature, for it enables the man who lends the money to live without labor.

Effects of the
rise of competi-
tive capitalism

While it is far from true that these doctrines were universally honored even by the church itself, they nevertheless remained an integral part of the Catholic ideal down to the end of the Renaissance period. Even to this day they have not been entirely abandoned, as our study of liberal Catholicism in the nineteenth and twentieth centuries will show.[6] However, the age of the Renaissance was accompanied by the growth of an economic pattern distinctly incompatible with most of these doctrines. A ruthless, dynamic capitalism, based upon the principle of "dog eat dog," was beginning to supplant the old static economy of the medieval guilds. No longer were merchants and manufacturers content with a mere "wage" for the services they rendered to society. They demanded profits, and they could not see that it was any business of the church to decide what a man's earnings should be. Wages were fit only for hirelings, who had neither the wit nor the industry to go after the big rewards. In addition to all this, the growth of banking meant an even more violent conflict with the ascetic ideal of the church. As long as the business of moneylending was in the hands of Jews and Moslems, it mattered little that usury should be branded as a sin. But now that Christians were piling up riches by financing the exploits of kings and merchants, the shoe was on another foot. The new crop of bankers resented being told that their lucrative trade in cash was contrary to the laws of God. This seemed to them like an attempt of spokesmen for an outmoded past to dictate the standards for a new age of progress. But how was it that Italy did not break with

[5] See the chapter on The Civilization of the Feudal Age: Political and Economic Institutions.
[6] See the paragraphs on Christian Socialism at the end of the chapter on the Industrial Revolution of the Nineteenth and Twentieth Centuries.

the Catholic church in view of the extensive development of banking and commerce in such cities as Florence, Genoa, and Milan as early as the fourteenth century? The explanation is probably to be found in the stronger influence of paganism in Renaissance Italy than in any other country of Europe. Great bankers like the Medici of Florence were Christians in nothing but name. Even the Italians who remained something more than nominal Christians did not generally take their beliefs very seriously. Their view of religion was like that of the ancient Romans—external and mechanical, not ethical or spiritual. To the northern European, by contrast, religion had a much deeper significance. He conceived of it very largely as a system of morality ordained by a wrathful God. He was therefore profoundly disturbed by any inconsistency between his worldly life and the doctrines of the faith. When such a conflict arose, he could do only one of two things: either modify his personal conduct to conform to the faith or get a new religion. When the choice was one between ascetic denial and destruction of the system that frowned upon riches, it is not difficult to see which road he would take.

Before leaving this subject of causes, it is important to consider briefly the reasons why the Protestant Revolution began in Germany. First, there was the fact that Germany was somewhat more backward than most other areas of western Europe. The Renaissance had touched her but lightly, and the legacy of the Dark Ages was still very strong. As a consequence, religious-mindedness was more deeply rooted than in Italy, France, or England. Second, Germany was the victim of Catholic abuses to a greater extent than most other countries. The kings of France and England had successfully defied the Pope on appointments to religious offices and on appeals of cases to the Roman *curia*. But Germany had no powerful ruler to defend her interests. It was mainly for this reason that Leo X selected Germany as the most likely field for the sale of indulgences. The evils connected with this traffic would probably have been a stench in the nostrils of any nation. Finally, economic factors were very important. The church in Germany held an enormous proportion of the best agricultural lands, and the country was seething with discontent on account of a too rapid transition from a feudal society to an economy of profits and wages. The grievances of knights and peasants alike made an explosion of some sort inevitable. The petty nobility were threatened with ruin by the concentration of land in large estates, while the peasants were ground between the upper and nether millstones of rising prices and the loss of manorial privileges. Faced with such hardships, both classes turned against the church as their richest and most grievous oppressor. The merchants and bankers, for reasons quite different but just as compelling, were not slow in lending support.

Why the Protestant Revolution began in Germany

I. THE LUTHERAN REVOLT IN GERMANY By the dawn of the sixteenth century Germany was ripe for religious revolution. All **433**

The early career of Martin Luther

that was necessary was to find a leader who could unite the dissatisfied elements and give a suitable theological gloss to their grievances. Such a leader was not long in appearing. His name was Martin Luther, and he was born in Thuringia in 1483. His parents were originally peasants, but his father had left the soil soon after his marriage to work in the mines of Mansfeld. Here he managed to become moderately prosperous and served in the village council. Nevertheless, young Martin's early environment was far from ideal.

A Page from the Bible Translated by Luther into German. The engraving shows several episodes of the story of Jonah in a single composite picture.

Portrait of Martin Luther, by Melchior Lorch, 1548.

He was whipped at home for trivial offenses until the blood came, and his mind was filled with hideous terrors of demons and witches. Some of these superstitions clung to him until the end of his life. His parents intended that he should become a lawyer, and with this end in view they placed him at the age of eighteen in the University of Erfurt. During his first four years at the university, Luther worked hard, gaining more than an ordinary reputation as a scholar. But in 1505, while returning from a visit to his home, he was overtaken by a violent storm and felled to the ground by a bolt of lightning. In terror lest an angry God strike him dead, he vowed to St. Anne to become a monk. Soon afterward he entered the Augustinian monastery at Erfurt. Here he gave himself up to earnest reflection on the state of his soul. Obsessed with the idea that his sins were innumerable, he strove desperately to attain a goal of spiritual peace. He engaged in long vigils and went for days on end without a morsel of food. But the more he fasted and tortured himself, the more his anguish and depression increased. Told that the way of salvation lies in love of God, he was ready to give up in despair. How could he love a Being who is not even just, who saves only those whom it pleases Him to save? "Love Him?" he said to himself, "I do not love Him. I hate Him." But in time, as he pondered the Scriptures, especially the story of the crucifixion, he gained a new insight into the mysteries of the Christian theology. He was profoundly impressed by the humiliation of the Savior's death upon the cross. For the benefit of sinful humanity, the Christ, the God-man, had shared the fate of common criminals. Why had He done so except out of love for His creatures? The God of the storm whose chief attribute appeared to be anger had revealed Himself as a Father who pities His children. Here was a miracle which no human reason could understand. It must be taken on faith; and by faith alone, Luther concluded, can man be justified in the sight of God. This doctrine of justification by faith alone, as opposed to salvation by "good works," quickly became the central doctrine of the Lutheran theology.

Justification by faith alone

But long before Luther had completed his theological system, he was called to lecture on Aristotle and the Bible at the University of Wittenberg, which had recently been founded by Frederick the Wise of Saxony. While serving in this capacity, he was confronted by an event which furnished the spark for the Protestant Revolution. In 1517 an unprincipled Dominican friar by the name of Tetzel appeared in Germany as a hawker of indulgences. Determined to raise as much money as possible for Pope Leo X and the Archbishop of Mainz who had employed him, Tetzel deliberately represented the indulgences as tickets of admission to heaven. Though forbidden to enter Saxony, he came to the borders of that state, and many natives of Wittenberg rushed out to buy salvation at so attractive a price. Luther was appalled by such brazen deception of ignorant people. Accordingly, he drew up a set of ninety-five theses or statements attacking the sale of indulgences, and posted them, after the manner of the time, on the door of the castle church on October 31, 1517. Later he had them printed and sent to his friends in a number of cities. Soon it became evident that the Ninety-five Theses had voiced the sentiments of a nation. All over Germany, Luther was hailed as a leader whom God had raised to break the power of an arrogant and hypocritical clergy. A violent reaction against the sale of indulgences was soon in full swing. Tetzel was mobbed and driven from the country. The revolt against Rome had begun.

Luther's revolt against the sale of indulgences

435

*The condem-
nation and ex-
communication
of Luther*

With the revenue from indulgences cut off, it was inevitable that the Pope should take action. Early in 1518 he commanded the general of the Augustinian order to make the rebellious friar recant. Luther not only refused but published a sermon stating his views more strongly than ever. That no more stringent measures were taken against him at this time was a result of the fact that Leo X was absorbed in the coming imperial election. For more than two years the impetuous friar enjoyed an immunity from persecution, protected by his friend, the Elector Frederick of Saxony. He made use of this time in writing pamphlets to expand his doctrines and to keep the enthusiasm of his supporters from flagging. Forced by his critics to answer questions on many points other than indulgences, he gradually came to realize that his own religion was utterly ir-reconcilable with that of the Roman church. There was no alter-native except to break with the Catholic faith entirely. In 1520 his teachings were formally condemned in a bull promulgated by Leo X, and he was ordered to recant within sixty days or be dealt with as a heretic. Luther replied by publicly burning the Pope's proclama-tion. For this he was excommunicated and ordered to be turned over to the secular arm for punishment. Germany at this time was still under the technical rule of the Holy Roman Empire. Charles V, who had recently been elevated to the throne of this ramshackle state, was anxious to be rid of the insolent rebel at once, but he dared not act without the approval of the Imperial Diet. Accord-ingly, in 1521, Luther was summoned to appear before a meeting of this body at Worms. Since many of the princes and electors who composed the Diet were themselves hostile toward the church, noth-ing in particular was done, despite Luther's stubborn refusal to retract any of the things he had said. Finally, after a number of the members had gone home, the Emperor forced through an edict branding the obstreperous friar as an outlaw. But Luther had already been hidden away in the castle of his friend, the Elector of Saxony. Here he remained until all danger of arrest by the Emperor's soldiers had passed. Charles soon afterward withdrew to conduct his war with France, and the Edict of Worms was never enforced.

*Founding
the Lutheran
church; Lu-
ther's doctrines*

Thenceforth until his death in 1546 Luther was occupied with his work of building an independent German church. Despite the funda-mental conflict between his own beliefs and Catholic theology, he nevertheless retained a good many of the elements of the Roman system. With the passing of the years he became more conservative than many of his own followers and compared some of them to Judas betraying his Master. Though he had originally denounced transubstantiation, he eventually came around to adopting a doctrine which bore at least a superficial resemblance to the Catholic theory. Theologians call this doctrine "consubstantiation," meaning that the body and blood of Christ are really present *along with* the bread and wine. He maintained that the words imputed to the Christ in the New Testament, "This is my body," were literally true, even if contrary to reason. He denied, however, that any change in the substance of the bread and wine occurred as the result of a priestly miracle. The function of the clergyman is simply to *reveal* the presence of God in the bread and wine. In like manner, Luther retained the Catholic practice of elevating the "host," or consecrated wafer of the Eucharist, for the adoration of the faithful. Still, the changes he made were drastic enough to preserve the revolutionary character of the new religion. He substituted German for Latin in the services of the church. He rejected the entire ecclesiastical system of Pope, archbishops, bishops, and priests as custodians of the keys to the kingdom of heaven. By abolishing monasticism and insisting upon the right of priests to marry, he went far toward destroying the barrier which had separated clergy from laity and given the former their special status as representatives of God on earth. He eliminated all of the sacraments with the exception of baptism and the Eucharist, and he denied that even these had any supernatural effect in bringing down grace from heaven. Since he continued to emphasize faith rather than good works as the road to salvation, he naturally discarded such formalized practices as fasts, pilgrimages, the veneration of relics, and the invocation of saints. On the other hand, the doctrines of predestination and the supreme authority of the Scriptures were given in the new religion a higher place than they had ever enjoyed in the old. Last of all, Luther abandoned the Catholic idea that the church should be supreme over the state. Instead of having bishops subject to the Pope as the Vicar of Christ, he organized his church under superintendents who were essentially agents of the government.

Of course, Luther was not alone responsible for the success of the Protestant Revolution. In molding the tenets of the new faith he was ably assisted by Philip Melanchthon, a teacher of Greek and originally a humanist at the University of Wittenberg. It was Melanchthon who drafted the Augsburg Confession (1530), which is still accepted as the creed of the Lutheran church. The overthrow of Catholicism in Germany was also abetted by the outbreak of social revolt. In 1522–1523 there occurred a ferocious rebellion of the knights. These petty nobles, as we have seen, were being impoverished by competition from the great estates and by the change to a capitalist economy. They saw as the chief cause of their misery the concentration of landed wealth in the hands of the great princes of the church. Intensely nationalistic, they dreamed of a united Germany free from the domination of powerful landlords and grasping priests. The leaders of the movement were Ulrich von Hutten, who had turned from a humanist into a fierce partisan of Luther, and Franz von Sickingen, a notorious robber baron and soldier of fortune. To these men the gospel of Luther seemed to provide an excellent program for a war on behalf of German liberty. Although their rebellion was speedily crushed by the armies of the archbishops and richer nobles, it apparently had considerable effect

The outbreak of social revolution; the revolt of the knights

*The uprising
of the lower
classes*

in persuading the pillars of the old regime that too much resistance to the Lutheran movement would scarcely be wise.

The revolt of the knights was followed by a much more violent uprising of the lower classes in 1524–1525. Though most who took part were peasants, a great many poor workmen from the cities were attracted to the movement also. The causes of this second rebellion were somewhat similar to those of the first: the rising cost of living, the concentration of holdings of land, and the religious radicalism inspired by Luther's teachings. But the peasants and urban workers were stirred to action by many other factors as well. The decay of the feudal regime had eliminated the paternal relationship between noble and serf. In its place had grown up a mere cash nexus between employer and worker. The sole obligation now of the upper classes was to pay a wage. When sickness or unemployment struck, the laborer had to make shift with his slender resources as best he could. Furthermore, most of the old privileges which the serf had enjoyed on the manorial estate, of pasturing his flocks on the common lands and gathering wood in the forest, were being rapidly abolished. To make matters worse, landlords were attempting to meet advancing prices by exacting higher rents from the peasants. Finally, the lower classes were angered by the fact that the revival of the Roman law had the effect of bolstering property rights and of strengthening the power of the state to protect the interests of the rich.

The Anabaptists

Many of the downtrodden folk who participated in the so-called Peasants' Revolt belonged to a religious sect known as the Anabaptists. The name means re-baptizers, and was derived from the fact that the members of the sect held infant baptism to be ineffectual and insisted that the rite should be administered only when the individual had reached the age of reason. But a belief in adult baptism was not really their principal doctrine. The Anabaptists were extreme individualists in religion. Luther's teaching that every man has a right to follow the dictates of his own conscience they took exactly as it stood. Not only did they reject the Catholic theory of the priesthood, but they denied the necessity of any clergy at all, maintaining that every individual should follow the guidance of the "inner light." They refused to admit that God's revelation to man had ceased with the writing of the last book of the New Testament, but they insisted that He continues to speak directly to certain of His chosen followers. They attached much importance to literal interpretation of the Bible, even of its most occult portions. They believed that the church should be a community of saints and required of their followers abstention from lying, profanity, gluttony, lewdness, and drinking intoxicating liquors. Many of the members looked forward to the early destruction of this world and the establishment of Christ's kingdom of justice and peace, in which they would have a prominent place. But the Anabaptists were not merely a group of religious extremists; they represented as well the most radical social tendencies of their time. Though it is certainly an exaggeration to call them communists, they did denounce the accumulation of wealth and taught that it was the duty of Christians to share their goods with one another. In addition, they declined to recognize any distinctions of rank or class, declaring all men equal in the sight of God. Many of them also abominated the taking of oaths, condemned military service, and refused to pay taxes to governments that engaged in war. They abstained in general from political life and demanded the complete separation of church and state. Their doctrines represented the extreme manifestation of the revolutionary fervor generated by the Protestant movement.

The Peasants' Revolt of 1524–1525 began in southern Germany and spread rapidly to the north and west until most of the country was involved. At first it had more of the character of a strike than a revolution. The rebels contented themselves with drafting petitions and attempting peaceably to persuade their masters to grant them relief from oppression. But before many months had passed, the movement came under the control of such fanatics as Thomas Münzer, who urged the use of fire and sword against the wicked nobles and clergy. In the spring of 1525 the misguided rustics began plundering and burning cloisters and castles and even murdering some of their more hated opponents. The nobles now turned against them with fiendish fury, slaughtering indiscriminately both those who resisted and those who were helpless. Strange as it may seem, the lords were encouraged in this savagery by several of the Reformers, including the great Luther himself. In a pamphlet *Against the Thievish, Murderous Hordes of Peasants* he urged everyone who could to hunt the rebels down like mad dogs, to "strike, strangle, stab secretly or in public, and let him remember that nothing can be more poisonous, harmful, or devilish than a man in rebellion." [7] To Luther's credit, it should perhaps be added that he feared anarchy more than he did the particular doctrines of the Anabaptists. He believed that the use of force by anyone except the lawful authorities would result in the destruction of the social order.

The Peasants' Revolt of 1524–1525

But the brutal suppression of the Peasants' Revolt did not mark the end of revolutionary activities on the part of the submerged classes. In 1534 a group of Anabaptists gained control of the episcopal city of Münster in Westphalia. Thousands of their fellow believers from the surrounding country came pouring in, and Münster became a New Jerusalem where all of the accumulated vagaries of the lunatic fringe of the movement were put into practice. The property of unbelievers was confiscated, and polygamy was introduced. A certain John of Leyden assumed the title of king, proclaiming himself the successor of David with a mission to conquer

Suppression of the Peasants' Revolt

[7] Quoted by H. S. Lucas, *The Renaissance and the Reformation*, p. 457.

the world and destroy the heathen. But after a little more than a year of this, Münster was recaptured by its bishop, and the leaders of Zion were put to death by horrible tortures. This second disaster proved to be the turning point in the revolt of the have-nots of the sixteenth century. Convinced of the futility of violence, they now abandoned the fanatical dogmas of their fallen leaders and returned to the religious quietism of earlier years. Most of the radical economic teachings were also dropped. Some of the survivors of the persecutions now joined the sect of Mennonites, so called from Menno Simons (1492–1559), whose teachings were partly derived from those of the original Anabaptists. Others fled to England to become the spiritual ancestors of the Quakers.

II. THE ZWINGLIAN AND CALVINIST REVOLTS IN SWITZERLAND

Causes of the Protestant Revolution in Switzerland

The special form of Protestantism developed by Luther did not prove to be particularly popular beyond its native environment. Outside of Germany, Lutheranism became the official religion only in Denmark, Norway, and Sweden. But the force of the Lutheran revolt made itself felt in a number of other lands. Such was especially the case in Switzerland, where nationalism had been gathering strength for centuries. At the close of the Middle Ages the gallant herdsmen and peasants of the Swiss cantons had challenged the right of the Austrians to rule over them, and finally in 1499 had compelled the Emperor Maximilian to recognize their independence, not only of the house of Hapsburg but of the Holy Roman Empire as well. Having thrown off the yoke of a foreign Emperor, the Swiss were not likely to submit indefinitely to an alien Pope. Moreover, the cities of Zurich, Basel, Berne, and Geneva had grown into flourishing centers of trade. Their populations were dominated by solid burghers who were becoming increasingly contemptuous of the Catholic ideal of glorified poverty. Here also northern humanism had found welcome lodgment in cultivated minds, with the effect of creating a healthy distrust of priestly superstitions. Erasmus had lived for a number of years in Basel. Lastly, Switzerland had been plucked by the indulgence peddlers to an extent only less grievous than Germany, while the city of Berne had been the scene of some particularly flagrant monkish frauds.

Ulrich Zwingli

The father of the Protestant Revolution in Switzerland was Ulrich Zwingli. Only a few weeks younger than Luther, he was the son of a well-to-do magistrate, who was able to provide him with an excellent education. He attended the Universities of Vienna and Basel, completing the course for the master's degree at the latter. As a student he devoted nearly all of his time to philosophy and literature, with no interest in religion save in the practical reforms of the Christian humanists. Although he took holy orders at the age of twenty-two, his purpose in entering the priesthood was mainly the opportunity it would give him to cultivate his literary tastes. For some eight years thereafter he continued to accept the patronage of the Pope and to take his vows of celibacy exceedingly lightly. In 1519, however, he experienced one of those sudden conversions so typical of the careers of religious reformers. For this change of heart there seem to have been two main causes: a serious attack of the plague and the influence of Luther. Which of these causes came first is unknown, but both had a powerful effect. From this time on Zwingli became a fervid crusader, not merely for a purer religion but for a break with the Catholic church. He accepted nearly all of the teachings of Luther with the exception of consubstantiation. Zwingli maintained that the bread and wine are mere symbols of the body and blood, and he reduced the sacrament of Holy Communion to a simple memorial service. So ably did he marshal the anti-Catholic forces that by 1528 nearly all of northern Switzerland had deserted the ancient faith. But when he attempted to extend his crusade into the conservative forest cantons, he encountered stiff opposition. In 1529 civil war broke out, resulting after two years in the defeat of the Zwinglian forces and in the death of their leader. By the Peace of Kappel (1531) the Protestants agreed that the choice of a religion for the several areas of Switzerland should be made by the cantonal governments.

From the northern cantons the Protestant Revolt in Switzerland spread to Geneva. This beautiful city, located on a lake of the same name near the French border, had the doubtful advantage of a *The spread of* double government. The people owed allegiance to two feudal *the Protestant* suzerains, the local bishop and the Count of Savoy. When these *Revolt to* high-born chieftains conspired to make their power more absolute, *Geneva* the citizens rebelled against them. The result was their expulsion from the town about 1530 and the establishment of a free republic. But the movement could hardly have been successful without some aid from the northern cantons. Thus it was not long until Protestant preachers from Zurich and Berne began arriving in Geneva. Furthermore, since the leaders of the political revolution were excommunicated for defying their bishop, it was natural that they should be favorably disposed toward a new religion for their city.

It was under this constellation of events that John Calvin arrived in Geneva. Although destined to play so prominent a role in the history of Switzerland, he was not a native of that country but of *John Calvin* France. He was born at Noyon in Picardy in 1509. His mother died when he was very young, and his father, who did not like children, turned him over to the care of an aristocratic friend. For his higher education he was sent to the University of Paris, where, because of his bilious disposition and fault-finding manner, he was dubbed "the accusative case." Later he shifted at his father's wish to the study of law at Orléans. Here he came under the influence of disciples of Luther, evidently to a sufficient extent to cause him to be suspected of heresy. Consequently, in 1534, when the government began an attack on the wavering ones, Calvin fled to Switzerland. He settled for a time in Basel and then moved on to Geneva, which was still in the throes of political revolution. He began preaching and organizing at once, and by 1541 both government and religion had fallen completely under his sway. Until his death from asthma and dyspepsia in 1564 he ruled the city with a rod of iron. History contains few examples of men more dour in temperament and more stubbornly convinced of the rightness of their own ideas.

Calvin's rule at Geneva

Under Calvin's rule Geneva was transformed into a religious oligarchy. The supreme authority was vested in the Congregation of the clergy, who prepared all legislation and submitted it to the Consistory to be ratified. The latter body, composed, in addition to the clergy, of twelve elders representing the people, had as its principal function the supervision of public and private morals. This function was carried out, not merely by the punishment of antisocial conduct but by a persistent snooping into the private life of every individual. The city was divided into districts, and a committee of the Consistory visited each household without warning to conduct an inquisition into the habits of its members. Even the mildest forms of human folly were strictly prohibited. Dancing, card-playing, attending the theater, working or playing on the Sabbath—all were outlawed as major crimes. Innkeepers were forbidden to allow anyone to consume food or drink without first saying grace, or to permit any patron to sit up after nine o'clock unless he was spying on the conduct of others. Needless to say, penalties were severe. Not only murder and treason were classified as capital crimes, but also adultery, witchcraft, blasphemy, and heresy; and the last of these especially was susceptible to a broad interpretation. During the first four years after Calvin became ruler of Geneva, there were no fewer than fifty-eight executions out of a total population of only 16,000.[8] But the good accomplished by all of this harshness seems to have been small indeed. According to Preserved Smith, there were more cases of vice in Geneva after the Reformation than before.[9]

Calvin's theology

The essentials of Calvin's theology are contained in his *Institutes of the Christian Religion*, which was published originally in 1536 and revised and enlarged several times thereafter. His ideas resemble those of St. Augustine more than any other theologian. He conceived of the universe as utterly dependent upon the will of an Almighty God, who created all things for His greater glory. Because of Adam's transgression all men are sinners by nature, bound hand and foot to an evil inheritance they cannot escape. Nevertheless, God for reasons of His own has predestined some for eternal salvation and damned all the rest to the torments of hell. Nothing that human beings may do can alter their fate; their souls are stamped with God's blessing or curse before they are born. But this did not

[8] Preserved Smith, *The Age of the Reformation*, p. 171.
[9] *Ibid.*, p. 174.

mean, in Calvin's opinion, that the Christian could be indifferent to his conduct on earth. If he were among the elect, God would have implanted in him the desire to live right. Abstemious conduct is a sign, though not an infallible one, that he who practices it has been chosen to sit at the throne of glory. Public profession of faith and participation in the sacraments are also presumptive evidences of election to be saved. But most of all, the Calvinists required an active life of piety and good morality as a solemn obligation resting upon members of the Christian Commonwealth. Like the ancient Hebrews, they conceived of themselves as chosen instruments of God with a mission to help in the fulfillment of His purposes on earth. Their duty was not to strive for their souls' salvation but for the glory of God. Thus it will be seen that the Calvinist system did not encourage its followers to sit with folded hands serene in the knowledge that their fate was sealed. No religion has fostered a more abundant zeal in the conquest of nature, in missionary activity, or in the struggle against political tyranny. Doubtless the reason lies in the Calvinist's belief that as the chosen instrument of God he must play a part in the drama of the universe worthy of his exalted status. And with the Lord on his side he was not easily frightened by whatever lions lurked in his path.

The religion of Calvin differed from that of Luther in a number of ways. First, it was more legalistic. Whereas the Wittenberg Reformer had emphasized the guidance of individual conscience, the dictator of Geneva stressed the sovereignty of law. He thought of God as a mighty legislator who had handed down a body of rules in the Scriptures which must be followed to the letter. Secondly, the religion of Calvin was more nearly an Old Testament faith than that of Luther. This can be illustrated in the attitude of the two men toward Sabbath observance. Luther's conception of Sunday was similar to that which prevails in modern Continental Europe. He insisted, of course, that his followers should attend church, but he did not demand that during the remainder of the day they should refrain from all pleasure or work. Calvin, on the other hand, revived the old Jewish Sabbath with its strict taboos against anything faintly resembling worldliness. In the third place, the religion of Geneva was more closely associated with the ideals of the new capitalism. Luther's sympathies lay with the nobles, and on at least one occasion he sharply censured the tycoons of finance for their greed. Calvin sanctified the ventures of the trader and the moneylender and gave an exalted place in his ethical system to the business virtues of thrift and diligence. Finally, Calvinism as compared to Lutheranism represented a more radical phase of the Protestant Revolution. As we have seen, the Wittenberg friar retained a good many features of Roman worship and even some Catholic dogmas. Calvin rejected everything he could think of that smacked of "popery." The organization of his church was con-

The religion of Calvin compared with that of Luther

443

structed in such a way as to exclude all traces of the episcopal system. Congregations were to choose their own elders and preachers, while an association of ministers at the top would govern the entire church. Ritual, instrumental music, stained glass windows, pictures, and images were ruthlessly eliminated, with the consequence that the religion was reduced to "four bare walls and a sermon." Even the observance of Christmas and Easter was sternly prohibited.

The spread of Calvinism

The popularity of Calvinism was not limited to Switzerland. It spread into most countries of western Europe where trade and finance had become leading pursuits. The Huguenots of France, the Puritans of England, the Presbyterians of Scotland, and the members of the Reformed church in Holland were all Calvinists. It was pre-eminently the religion of the bourgeoisie; though, of course, it drew converts from other strata as well. Its influence in molding the ethics of modern times and in bolstering the revolutionary courage of the middle class was enormous. Members of this faith had much to do with the initial revolts against despotism in England and France, to say nothing of their part in overthrowing Spanish tyranny in the Netherlands.

III. THE PROTESTANT REVOLUTION IN ENGLAND The original blow against the Roman church in England was not struck by a religious enthusiast like Luther or Calvin but by the head of the government. This does not mean, however, that the English Reformation was exclusively a political movement. Henry VIII could not have succeeded in establishing an independent English church if such action had not had the endorsement of large numbers of his subjects. And there were plenty of reasons why this endorsement was readily given. Though the English had freed themselves in some measure from papal domination, national pride had reached such a point that any degree of subordination to Rome was resented. Besides, England had been the scene for some time of lively agitation for religious reform. The memory of Wyclif's scathing attacks upon the avarice of the priests, the temporal power of Popes and bishops, and the sacramental system of the church had lingered since the fourteenth century. The influence of the Christian humanists, notably Sir Thomas More, in condemning the superstitions in Catholic worship, had also been a factor of considerable importance. Finally, soon after the outbreak of the Protestant Revolt in Germany, Lutheran ideas were brought into England by wandering preachers and through the circulation of printed tracts. As a result, the English monarch, in severing the ties with Rome, had no lack of sympathy from some of the most influential of his subjects.

Underlying causes of the Protestant Revolution in England

Henry VIII's domestic difficulties

The clash with the Pope was precipitated by Henry VIII's domestic difficulties. For eighteen years he had been married to Catherine of Aragon and had only a sickly daughter to succeed him. The death of all the sons of this marriage in infancy was a grievous disappointment to the king, who desired a male heir to perpetuate the Tudor dynasty. But this was not all, for Henry later became deeply infatuated with the dark-eyed lady-in-waiting, Anne Boleyn, and determined to make her his queen. He therefore appealed in 1527 to Pope Clement VII for an annulment of the marriage to Catherine. The law of the church did not sanction divorce, but it did provide that a marriage could be annulled if proof could be presented that conditions existing at the time of the marriage made it unlawful. Queen Catherine had previously been married to Henry's older brother, Arthur, who had died a few months after the ceremony was performed. Recalling this fact, Henry's lawyers found a passage in the Book of Leviticus which pronounced a curse of childlessness upon the man who should marry his deceased brother's wife. The Pope was now in a difficult position. If he rejected the king's appeal, England would probably be lost to the Catholic faith, for Henry was apparently firmly convinced that the Scriptural curse had blighted his chances of perpetuating his dynasty. On the other hand, if the Pope granted the annulment he would provoke the wrath of the Emperor Charles V, who was a nephew of Catherine. Charles had already invaded Italy and was threatening the Pope with a loss of his temporal power. There seemed nothing for Clement to do but to procrastinate. At first he made a pretense of having the question settled in England, and empowered his own legate and Cardinal Wolsey to hold a court of inquiry to determine whether the marriage to Catherine had been legal. Then after long delay the case was suddenly transferred to Rome. Henry lost patience and resolved to take matters into his own hands. In 1531 he convoked an assembly of the clergy and, by threatening to punish them for violating the Statute of Praemunire in submitting to the papal legate, he induced them to recognize himself as the head of the English church, "as far as the law of Christ allows." Next he persuaded Parliament to enact a series of laws abolishing all payments of revenue to the Pope and proclaiming the Anglican church an independent, national unit, subject to the exclusive authority of the king. By 1534 the last of the bonds uniting the English church to Rome had been cut.

The Anglican church

But the enactments put through by Henry VIII did not really make England a Protestant country. Though the abolition of papal authority was followed by the gradual dissolution of the monasteries and confiscation of their wealth, the church remained Catholic in doctrine. The Six Articles, adopted by Parliament at the king's behest in 1539, left no room for doubt as to official orthodoxy. Auricular confession, masses for the dead, and clerical celibacy were all confirmed, while death by burning was made the penalty for denying the Catholic dogma of the Eucharist. Yet the influence of a minority of Protestants at this time cannot be ignored. Their numbers were steadily increasing, and during the reign of Henry's successor, Edward VI, they actually gained the ascendancy. Since the

Activities of the radical Protestants

new king was only nine years old when he inherited the crown, it was inevitable that the policies of the government should be dictated by powers behind the throne. The men most active in this work were Thomas Cranmer, Archbishop of Canterbury, and the Dukes of Somerset and Northumberland, who successively dominated the council of regency. All three of these officials had strong Protestant leanings. As a result, the creeds and ceremonies of the Church of England were given some drastic revision. Priests were permitted to marry; English was substituted for Latin in the services; the use of images was abolished; and new articles of belief were drawn up repudiating all sacraments except baptism and the Lord's Supper and affirming the Lutheran dogma of justification by faith. When the youthful Edward died in 1553, it looked as if England had definitely entered the Protestant camp.

The Catholic reaction under Mary

Surface appearances, however, are frequently deceiving. They were never more so than in England at the end of Edward's reign. The majority of the people had refused to be weaned away from the usages of their ancient faith, and a reaction had set in against the high-handed methods of the radical Protestants. Moreover, the English during the time of the Tudors had grown accustomed to obeying the will of their sovereign. It was an attitude fostered by nationalism and the desire for order and prosperity. The successor of Edward VI was Queen Mary, the forlorn and graceless daughter of Henry VIII and Catherine. It was inevitable that Mary should have been a Catholic, and that she should have abhorred the revolt against Rome, for the origin of the movement was painfully associated with her mother's sufferings. Consequently, it is not strange that upon coming to the throne she should have attempted to turn the clock back. Not only did she restore the celebration of the mass and the rule of clerical celibacy, but she prevailed upon Parliament to vote the unconditional return of England to papal allegiance. But her policies ended in lamentable failure for several reasons. First of all, she fell into the same error as her predecessors in forcing through changes that were too radical for the temper of the times. The people of England were not ready for a Lutheran or Calvinist revolution, but neither were they in a mood to accept immediate subjection to Rome. Probably a more serious cause of her failure was her marriage to Philip, the ambitious heir to the Spanish throne. Her subjects feared that this union might lead to foreign complications, if not actual domination by Spain. When the queen allowed herself to be drawn into a war with France, in which England was compelled to surrender Calais, her last foothold on the Continent of Europe, the nation was almost ready for rebellion. Death ended Mary's inglorious reign in 1558.

The question whether England was to be Catholic or Protestant was left to be settled by Mary's successor, her half-sister Elizabeth, daughter of the vivacious Anne Boleyn. Though reared as a Protestant, Elizabeth had no deep religious convictions. Her primary interest was statecraft, and she did not intend that her kingdom should be rent in twain by sectarian strife. Therefore she decided upon a policy of moderation, refusing to ally herself with either the extreme Catholics or the fanatical Protestants. So carefully did she hew to this line that for some years she deceived the Pope into thinking that she might turn Catholic. Nevertheless, she was enough of a nationalist to refuse even to consider a revival of allegiance to Rome. One of the first things she did after becoming queen was to order the passage of a new Act of Supremacy declaring the English sovereign to be the "supreme governor" of the independent Anglican church. The final settlement, completed about 1570, was a typical English compromise. The church was made Protestant, but certain articles of the creed were left vague enough so that a moderate Catholic might accept them without too great a shock to his conscience. Moreover, the episcopal form of organization was retained and much of the Catholic ritual. Long after Elizabeth's death in 1603 this settlement remained in effect. Indeed, most elements in it have survived to this day. And it is a significant fact that the modern Church of England is broad enough to include within its ranks such diverse factions as the Anglo-Catholics, who differ from their Roman brethren only in rejecting papal supremacy, and the "low-church" Anglicans, who are as radical in their Protestantism as the Lutherans.

The Elizabethan compromise

While England was engaged in the process of mediating between the extremes of Catholicism and Protestantism, her northern neighbor Scotland was embroiled in a more violent break with the past. The Scottish branch of the Catholic church at the turn of the sixteenth century was one of the most corrupt in Europe. Enjoying the fruits of their vast possessions, the clergy divided their time between luxurious idleness and political intrigue. But this state of affairs could not long continue. Scotland had a greedy and untamed nobility eager to pounce upon the lands of the church at the first convenient opportunity. Besides, the political situation was far from satisfactory to the patriotic elements of the nation. The queen, Mary Stuart, was a mere child when she succeeded to the throne in 1542, and a regency had been assumed by her mother, who belonged to the French family of Guise. Since the Guises were determined Catholics, Catholicism came to be associated in the minds of many people with the Guises and thus with French domination. In 1557 a revolt broke out, and two years later the whole kingdom was ablaze. Leadership of the movement soon fell to a vigorous and stiff-necked preacher by the name of John Knox, who had sat at the feet of Calvin in Geneva. Knox uprooted every vestige of Catholicism in Scotland and established a Presbyterian church on a

The establishment of Presbyterianism in Scotland

radical Calvinist basis.[10] So ripe was the country for a change that upon the death of the regent in 1560 Presbyterianism was proclaimed the official religion of the Scottish nation.

2. The Catholic Reformation

The beginnings of Catholic reform

As noted at the beginning of this chapter, the Protestant Revolution was only one of the phases of the great movement known as the Reformation. The other was the Catholic Reformation, or the Counter Reformation as it used to be called, on the assumption that the primary purpose of its leaders was to cleanse the Catholic church in order to check the growth of Protestantism. Modern historians have shown, however, that the beginnings of the movement for Catholic reform were entirely independent of the Protestant Revolt. In Spain, during the closing years of the fifteenth century, a religious revival inaugurated by Cardinal Ximenes, with the approval of the monarchy, stirred that country to the depths. Schools were established, abuses were eliminated from the monasteries, and priests were goaded into accepting their responsibilities as shepherds of their flocks. Though the movement was launched primarily for the purpose of strengthening the church in the war against heretics and infidels, it nevertheless had considerable effect in regenerating the spiritual life of the nation. In Italy also, since the beginning of the sixteenth century, a number of earnest clerics had been laboring to make the priests of their church more worthy of their Christian calling. The task was a difficult one on account of the paganism of the Renaissance and the example of profligacy set by the papal court. In spite of these obstacles the movement did lead to the founding of several religious orders dedicated to high ideals of piety and social service. Outstanding among them were the Theatine Order and the Capuchin Order. The first was an organization of priests who took monastic vows of poverty, chastity, and obedience, while the second was an order of friars pledged to follow in the footsteps of St. Francis.

The climax of the Catholic Reformation; the reform Popes

But the fires of Catholic reform burned rather low until after the Protestant Revolution began to make serious inroads upon the ancient faith. Not until it appeared that the whole German nation was likely to be swept into the Lutheran orbit did any of the Popes become seriously concerned about the need for reform. The first of the Holy Fathers to attempt a purification of the church was Adrian VI of Utrecht, the only non-Italian to be elected to the papal throne in nearly a century and a half, and the last in history. But his reign of only twenty months was too short to enable him to accomplish much, and in 1523 he was succeeded by a Medici

---

[10] The name Presbyterian comes from "presbytery," the assembly of ministers and lay elders which Knox set up to govern the churches of a particular area in place of a bishop.

(Clement VII), who ruled for eleven years. The campaign against abuses in the church was not renewed until the reign of Paul III (1534–1549). He and three of his successors, Paul IV (1555–1559), Pius V (1566–1572), and Sixtus V (1585–1590), were the most zealous crusaders for reform who had presided over the See of Peter since the days of Gregory VII. They reorganized the papal finances, filled the church offices with priests renowned for austerity, and dealt drastically with those clerics who persisted in idleness and vice. It was under these Popes that the Catholic Reformation reached its height. Unfortunately they were also responsible for reviving the Inquisition, which had fallen into disuse during the Italian Renaissance.

These direct activities of the Popes were supplemented by the decrees of a great church council convoked in 1545 by Paul III, which met in the city of Trent (modern Trento), at intervals be- *The Council of* tween 1545 and 1563. This council was one of the most important *Trent* in the history of the church. The main purpose for which it had been summoned was to re-define the doctrines of the Catholic faith, and several of the steps in this direction were highly significant. Without exception the dogmas challenged by the Protestant Reformers were reaffirmed. Good works were held to be as necessary for salvation as faith. The theory of the sacraments as indispensable means of grace was upheld. Likewise, transubstantiation, the apostolic succession of the priesthood, the belief in purgatory, the invocation of saints, and the rule of celibacy for the clergy were all confirmed as essential elements in the Catholic system. On the much-debated question as to the proper source of Christian belief, the Bible and the traditions of apostolic teaching were held to be of equal authority. Not only was papal supremacy over every bishop and priest expressly maintained, but there was more than a faint suggestion that the authority of the Pope transcended that of the church council itself. By this admission the government of the church was reconstituted as monarchical in form. The great movement of the fourteenth and fifteenth centuries which had attempted to establish the superior authority of the general council was ignored entirely.

The Council of Trent did not confine its attention to matters of dogma. It passed important legislation also for the elimination of abuses and for reinforcing the discipline of the church over its *Reforms of* members. The sale of indulgences was flatly prohibited, and even *the Council of* their issuance for considerations other than money was restricted *Trent* temporarily. Bishops and priests were forbidden to hold more than one benefice, so that none could grow rich from a plurality of incomes. To eliminate the evil of an ignorant priesthood it was provided that a theological seminary must be established in every diocese. Toward the end of its deliberations the Council decided upon a censorship of books to prevent heretical ideas from corrupting the minds of those who still remained in the faith. A commission was appointed to draw up an index or list of writings which ought not to be read. The publication of this list by the Pope in 1564 resulted in the formal establishment of the Index of Prohibited Books as a part of the machinery of the church. Later a permanent agency known as the Congregation of the Index was set up to revise the list from time to time. Altogether more than forty such revisions have been made. The majority of the books condemned have been theological treatises, and probably the effect in retarding the progress of learning has been slight. Nonetheless, the establishment of the Index must be taken as a symptom of the malignant cancer of intolerance which had come to infect both Catholics and Protestants.

Ignatius of Loyola founds the Society of Jesus

The Catholic Reformation would never have been as thorough or as successful as it was if it had not been for the activities of the Jesuits, or members of the Society of Jesus. They did most of the rough political work in the Council of Trent which enabled the Popes to dominate that body in its later and more important sessions. The Jesuits also were largely responsible for winning Poland and southern Germany back into the Catholic fold. The founder of the Society of Jesus was Ignatius of Loyola, a Spanish nobleman from the Basque country. His early career seems not to have been particularly different from that of other Spaniards of his class—a life of philandering and marauding as a soldier of the king. But about the time the Protestant Revolution was getting well under way in Germany, he was painfully wounded in a battle with the French. While waiting for his injuries to heal, he read a pious biography of Jesus and some legends of the saints which profoundly changed his emotional nature. Overwhelmed by a consciousness of his wasted life, he determined to become a soldier of Christ. After a period of morbid self-tortures, in which he saw visions of Satan, Jesus, and the Trinity, he went to the University of Paris to learn more about

Portrait of Ignatius Loyola, Founder of the Society of Jesus. Engraving by Lucas Vorsterman, 1621.

the faith he intended to serve. Here he gathered around him a small group of devoted disciples, with whose aid in 1534 he founded the Society of Jesus. The members took monastic vows and pledged themselves to go on a pilgrimage to Jerusalem. With this aim in view they set out for Italy, intending to embark from Venice. Finding their pilgrimage blocked by a war with the Turks, they enlisted in the crusade for Catholic reform which was just then beginning in Italy. In 1540 their organization was approved by Pope Paul III. From then on it grew rapidly. When Loyola died in 1556, it could boast of no fewer than 1500 members.

The Society of Jesus was by far the most militant of the religious orders fostered by the spiritual zeal of the sixteenth century. It was not merely a monastic society but a company of soldiers sworn *Organization of* to defend the faith. Their weapons were not to be bullets and spears *the Society of* but eloquence, persuasion, instruction in the right doctrines, and *Jesus* if necessary more worldly methods of exerting influence. The organization was patterned after that of a military company, with a general as commander-in-chief and an iron discipline enforced on the members. All individuality was suppressed, and a soldierlike obedience to the general was exacted of the rank and file. Only the highest of the four classes of members had any share in the government of the order. This little group, known as the Professed of the Four Vows, elected the general for life and consulted with him on important matters. But like all the others they were bound to implicit obedience.

As suggested already, the activities of the Jesuits were numerous and varied. First and foremost, they conceived of themselves as the defenders of true religion. For this object they obtained authority *Activities of the* from the Pope to hear confessions and grant absolution. Many of *Jesuits* them became priests in order to gain access to the pulpit and expound the truth as the oracles of God. Still others served as agents of the Inquisition in the relentless war against heresy. In all of this work they followed the leadership of Mother Church as their infallible guide. They raised no questions and attempted to solve no mysteries. Loyola taught that if the church ruled that white was black, it would be the duty of her sons to believe it. But the Jesuits were not satisfied merely to hold the field against the attacks of Protestants and heretics; they were anxious to propagate the faith in the farthest corners of the earth—to make Catholics out of Buddhists, Moslems, the Parsees of India, and even the untutored savages of the newly discovered continents. Long before the Reformation had ended, there were Jesuit missionaries in Africa, in Japan and China, and in North and South America. Yet another important activity of Loyola's soldiers of Christ was education. They founded colleges and seminaries by the hundreds in Europe and America and obtained positions in older institutions as well. Until the Society was suppressed in 1773, they had a monopoly of education in Spain and a near-monopoly in France. That the Catholic church recovered so much of its strength in spite of the Protestant secession was due in large measure to the manifold and aggressive activities of the Jesuits.

3. The Reformation Heritage

The most obvious result of the Reformation was the division of western Christendom into a multitude of hostile sects. No longer was there one fold and one shepherd for the whole of Latin and Teutonic Europe as had been true in the Middle Ages. Instead, northern Germany and the Scandinavian countries had become Lutheran; England had adopted a compromise Protestantism of her own; while Calvinism had triumphed in Scotland, Holland, and French Switzerland. In the vast domain once owing allegiance to the Vicar of Christ only Italy, Austria, France, Spain and Portugal, southern Germany, Poland, and Ireland were left; and even in several of these countries aggressive Protestant minorities were a thorn in the side of the Catholic majority. Strange as it may seem, this splintering of Christianity into rival factions was ultimately a source of some good to man. It worked in the long run to curb ecclesiastical tyranny and thereby to promote religious freedom. As the sects multiplied in various countries, it gradually became evident that no one of them could ever become strong enough to enforce its will upon the rest. Mutual toleration was made necessary in order for any of them to survive. To be sure, this was an incidental and long-delayed result, but its importance cannot be denied. If we follow the reasoning of James Madison, the mutiplication of sects was almost the only cause of religious toleration in the United States.

If there were any other beneficial results of the Reformation, they would probably consist in an added momentum to individualism and in the expansion of popular education. By asserting the right of private judgment and by simplifying ritual and organization, the leaders of the Protestant Revolution liberated man from some of the constraints of medieval ecclesiasticism. It would be a mistake, however, to assume that Lutherans, Calvinists, and Anglicans really believed at this time in genuine religious freedom. They had no interest whatever in tolerating anyone who disagreed with their own respective orthodoxies. About all they did was to set a new and stronger precedent for challenging the authority and beliefs of a universal church. By so doing they promoted self-assertion in the religious sphere in somewhat the same degree as it already existed in the political and economic spheres. A third beneficial consequence of the Reformation was its effect in promoting the education of the masses. The Renaissance, with its absorbing interest in the classics, had had the unfortunate effect of distorting the curricula of the schools into an exaggerated emphasis upon Greek and Latin and of restricting education to the aristocracy. The Lutherans, Cal-

The Harvesters, Pieter Breughel the Elder (1520–1569). Spurning the religious and bourgeois traditions of most of the other Flemish painters, Breughel chose to depict the life of humble people close to the earth. (MMA)

e Virgin and Chancellor Rolin, Jan van Eyck (1390–4). The early Flemish painters loved to present scenes piety in the sumptuous surroundings of wealthy burgh-. (Louvre)

The Betrothal of St. Catherine, Hans Memling (1430–1494). The infant Jesus in the lap of the Virgin is shown placing on the finger of St. Catherine the ring of betrothal to Christ and His Church. (MMA)

Erasmus, Hans Holbein the Younger (1497–1543). This portrait by the German Holbein is generally regarded as the best representation of the character and personality of the Prince of the Humanists. (Louvre)

Burial of the Count of Orgaz, El Greco (1541-1614). El Greco's masterpiece immortalizes the character of the people among whom he dwelt. The elongated figures, gaunt faces, and bold and dramatic colors are typical of his work. (Iglesia S. Tomé, Toledo, Spain)

Queen Mariana of Austria, Diego Velásquez (1599-1660). Velasquez's portraits celebrate the pomp and power of the Spanish court, but also emit the breath and life of real people. (Prado)

The Marchessa Durazzo, Anthony Van Dyck (1599-1641). This portrait of the wife of a Genoese noble conveys a sense of the sophisticated culture of late Renaissance Italy which the Flemish burghers deeply admired. (MMA)

England and Scotland Crowning Charles I, Peter Paul Rubens (1577-1640). This voluptuous scene with classical setting was part of a series painted by Rubens in Whitehall Palace, London, to glorify the Stuart family. (Minneapolis Inst. of Art)

vinists, and Jesuits changed all of this. Ambitious to propagate their respective doctrines, they established schools for the masses, where even the son of the cobbler or peasant might learn to read the Bible and theological tracts. Practical subjects were often introduced in place of Greek and Latin, and it is a significant fact that some of these schools eventually opened their doors to the new science.

A good case can be made for the theory that the Reformation furthered democracy, in the form, at least, of limited government. Every one of the sects, whether Protestant or Catholic, raised arguments against the absolute state. Even the Lutherans, despite their adoption of St. Paul's doctrine that "the powers that be are ordained of God," nevertheless recognized the right of the German princes to rebel against the Holy Roman Empire. Luther wrote that disobedience was a greater sin than murder, unchastity, dishonesty, or theft; but what he meant was the disobedience of ordinary men. He never denied the right of princes and kings to protect their subjects, by armed rebellion if necessary, against a tyrant. A similar attitude, that rebellion can be lawfully waged only by lower magistrates, was the position originally taken by the Calvinists. From such a position, however, it was a comparatively easy step to the doctrine that the people themselves have the right to rebel against intolerable oppression. Calvinists in France, England, and the Low Countries not only asserted the right of revolution but actively practiced it. Jesuit philosophers taught that the authority of the secular ruler is derived from the people, and some even affirmed the right of the ordinary citizen to kill a tyrant. Among the leaders of almost every sect, efforts were made to revive the medieval idea of a higher law of nature, embodying principles of right and justice, which should be recognized as an automatic limitation upon the power of rulers. To this day religious bodies have played an important role in movements to restrict the authority of the omnipotent state.

But we cannot look upon all the results of the Reformation and pronounce them good. One of the evil fruits was a series of religious wars which kept Europe in turmoil for two score years. The first to break out was the Schmalkaldic War (1546–1547), waged by Charles V in an effort to restore the unity of the Holy Roman Empire under the Catholic faith. In a few months he succeeded in cowing the Protestant princes of Germany into submission, but he was unable to force their subjects back into the Roman religion. The strife was ultimately settled by a compromise treaty, the Religious Peace of Augsburg (1555), under which each German prince was to be free to choose either Lutheranism or Catholicism as the faith of his people. The religion of each state was thus made to depend upon the religion of its ruler—a settlement typically in harmony with the despotic traditions of the time. A much more sanguinary struggle took place in France between 1562 and 1593. Here the

The Cities of the Schmalkaldic   Engraving by Hieronymus Cock,
League Surrendering to Charles V.   1560.

Protestants, or Huguenots as they were called, were decidedly in the minority, but they included some of the ablest and most influential members of the commercial and financial classes. Besides, they composed a political party involved in machinations against the Catholics for control of the government. In 1562 a faction of ultra-Catholics under the leadership of the Duke of Guise forced their way into power and, by their threats of persecution of the Huguenots, plunged the country into civil war. The struggle culminated ten years later in the frightful massacre of St. Bartholomew's Day. The regent, Catherine de' Medici, in a desperate effort to put an end to the strife, plotted with the Guises to murder the Protestant chiefs. The conspiracy unloosed the ugly passions of the Paris mob, with the result that in a single night two thousand Huguenots were slain. The war dragged on until 1593 when Henry IV became a Catholic in order to please the majority of his subjects, but the religious issue did not approach a settlement until 1598 when Henry issued the Edict of Nantes guaranteeing freedom of conscience to Protestants.

To a large extent the Revolt of the Netherlands was also an episode in the religious strife stirred up by the Reformation. Long after *The Revolt of the Nether- lands* the Protestant Revolution began in Germany, the countries now known as Belgium and Holland were still being governed as dominions of the Spanish crown. Though Lutheranism and Calvinism had gained a foothold in the cities, the Protestants of the Netherlands were yet but a fraction of the total population. With the passage of time, however, the numbers of Calvinists increased until they included a majority of the townsmen, at least, in the Dutch provinces of the north. Interference by the Spanish government with their freedom of religion led to a desperate revolt in 1565. Religious causes were of course not the only ones. Nationalist feeling was a leading factor also, particularly since the Spanish king, Philip II, persisted in treating the Netherlands as mere subject provinces. In addition, there were serious economic grievances—high taxation and the restriction of commerce for the benefit of Spanish merchants. On the other hand, it was religious hatred that was largely responsible for the bitterness of the struggle. Philip II regarded all Protestants as traitors, and he was determined to root them out of every territory over which he ruled. In 1567 he sent the bigoted Duke of Alva with ten thousand soldiers to quell the revolt in the Netherlands. For six years Alva terrorized the land, putting hundreds of the rebels to death and torturing or imprisoning thousands of others. The Protestants retaliated with almost equal savagery, and the war continued its barbarous course until 1609. It ended in victory for the Protestants, largely through the bravery and self-sacrifice of their original leader, William the Silent. The chief result of the war was the establishment of an independent Dutch Republic comprising the territories now included in Holland. The southern or Belgian provinces, where the majority of the people were Catholics, returned to Spanish rule.

Actual warfare between nations and sects was not the only type of barbarity which the Reformation directly encouraged. For other examples we need only recall the atrocities perpetrated by the Catholic Inquisition, the savage persecution of Anabaptists in Germany, and the fierce intolerance of Calvinists against Catholics. The horrible witchcraft persecution, which will be discussed in the next chapter, was also in large measure the product of the seeds of fanaticism sown by the Reformation. On the whole, the amount of intolerance was now much greater than at any other time in the history of Christianity, not excepting the age of the Crusades. In more than one instance the victims of persecution were distinguished philosophers or scientists, whose talents the world of that day could ill afford to lose. The most eminent of the martyrs to the new learning put to death by the Catholics was Giordano Bruno. Despite his philosophy of mystical pantheism, Bruno set forth in startling fashion a number of the cardinal axioms of modern science. He taught the eternity of the universe, revived the atomic theory of matter, and denied that the heavenly bodies contain any superior element not found in the earth. Partly for these teachings and partly also for his pantheism and for his rejection of miracles, he was haled before the Inquisition and burned at the stake in 1600. One of the victims of Calvinist persecution at Geneva was Michael Servetus, the discoverer of the lesser circulation of the blood. Servetus was convicted of rejecting the doctrines of the Trinity and predestina-

Bigotry, witchcraft, and persecution

tion and of teaching that Palestine is a barren country in defiance of the Old Testament description as a land flowing with milk and honey. In 1553 he was condemned to be burned at the stake by slow fire. Some admirers of Calvin have argued that the Genevan Reformer opposed the burning of Servetus: he wanted him beheaded! But even the evidence for this rather doubtful display of mercy is not conclusive.

The attacks upon reason and science

Aside from the persecution of men of learning, the Reformation was a blow to the progress of enlightenment in still other ways. The aim of the Protestant Reformers was to encourage an absolute reliance upon faith and a belief in the Bible as the final source of religion and truth. This led them to despise intellectual activity as a brazen attempt to assert man's independence of God. Luther blasted against reason as "the devil's harlot" and adjured his followers to "keep to revelation and don't try to understand." [11] Both Luther and Melanchthon condemned the Copernican astronomy on the ground that it was contrary to the Scriptures. The attitude of the leaders of the Catholic Reformation was no better. The Council of Trent included the following in its official decrees: "When God commands us to believe, he does not propose to have us search into his divine judgments, nor to inquire their reasons and causes, but demands an immutable faith. . . . Faith, therefore, excludes not only all doubt, but even the desire of subjecting its truth to demonstration." [12] This seemed to shift the emphasis from one of the cardinal principles of the Catholic philosophy of the late Middle Ages. "Subjecting its truth to demonstration" was the very thing which the great masters of thirteenth-century Scholasticism had considered most essential.

The effects upon art

Finally, the Reformation had a baneful effect upon art. Although Luther had some gifts of aesthetic appreciation, his followers were too deeply absorbed in theological controversy to care whether art survived or perished. Calvin took a more positive stand. Everything that appealed to the senses he utterly deplored as godless and immoral. He believed that the use of any pictures or images in his churches would profane the worship of God. Even the Catholic reformers were only slightly less hostile, despite the splendid traditions of their church as a patron of Renaissance art. The Council of Trent adopted severe restrictions against representation of the human form, and a second-rate artist was employed to paint breeches and skirts on the naked figures in Michelangelo's *Last Judgment*. In view of such attitudes as these, reflecting the bigotry and intolerance of the Reformers, it is rather difficult to believe that the movement they led was a milestone of human progress. If the reforms in the Catholic church could have been accomplished through

[11] Preserved Smith, *The Age of the Reformation*, pp. 625–626.
[12] Catechism of the Council of Trent.

the enlightened philosophy of the Christian humanists instead of by
religious revolution, the tragic aftermath of violence and unreason
might well have been avoided. But the logic of political and economic events in the fifteenth and sixteenth centuries perhaps made
revolution inevitable.

Selected Readings

Bainton, R. H., *The Age of the Reformation*, New York, 1957
———, *Here I Stand: A Life of Martin Luther*, Nashville, 1950
Beard, C., *The Reformation of the Sixteenth Century in Its Relation to Modern Thought and Knowledge*, New York, 1927
Bury, J. B., *History of the Freedom of Thought*, New York, 1913
Harkness, G. E., *John Calvin: the Man and His Ethics*, New York, 1931
Hulme, E. M., *The Renaissance, the Protestant Revolution and the Catholic Reformation in Continental Europe*, New York, 1914
Jenkins, B. A., *The World's Debt to Protestantism*, Boston, 1930
Latourette, K. S., *A History of Christianity*, New York, 1953
Lindsay, T. M., *History of the Reformation*, New York, 1928, 2 vols.
Lucas, H. S., *The Renaissance and the Reformation*, New York, 1934
McGiffert, A. C., *Protestant Thought before Kant*, New York, 1911
Marti, O. A., *The Economic Causes of the Reformation in England*, New York, 1930
Nelson, E. N., *The Idea of Usury*, Princeton, 1949
Randall, J. H., Jr., *The Making of the Modern Mind*, New York, 1926, Ch. VII
Smith, Preserved, *The Age of the Reformation*, New York, 1920
———, *The Life and Letters of Martin Luther*, New York, 1914
Smithson, Robert, *The Anabaptists*, London, 1935
Tawney, R. H., *Religion and the Rise of Capitalism*, New York, 1926
Van Dyke, P., *Ignatius Loyola, The Founder of the Jesuits*, New York, 1926

Source Materials

Baumer, F. L. V., *Main Currents of Western Thought*, New York, 1952
Calvin, John, *Institutes of the Christian Religion*, especially Book II, Chs. 1–3; Book III, Chs. 19, 21–25; Book IV, Chs. 3, 14, 17, 20
Catechism of the Council of Trent
Luther, Martin, *Works* (Jacobs, tr.), "On Trade and Usury," Vol. IV
———, *On Christian Liberty*
———, *Address to the Christian Nobility of the German Nation*

The Commercial Revolution and the New Society (1400-1700)

The meaning of the Commercial Revolution

The last three chapters described in considerable detail the intellectual and religious transition from the medieval to the modern world. It was observed that the Renaissance, despite its kinship in many ways with the Middle Ages, spelled the doom of Scholastic philosophy, undermined the supremacy of Gothic architecture, and overthrew medieval conceptions of politics and the universe. Likewise, it was noted that, before the Renaissance had completed its work, a mighty torrent of religious revolution had swept Christianity from its medieval foundations and cleared the way for spiritual and moral attitudes in keeping with the trends of the new age. That both the Renaissance and the Reformation should have been accompanied by fundamental economic changes goes without saying. Indeed, the intellectual and religious upheavals would scarcely have been possible if it had not been for drastic alterations in the medieval economic pattern. This series of changes, marking the transition from the semi-static, localized, non-profit economy of the late Middle Ages to the dynamic, world-wide, capitalistic regime of the fifteenth and succeeding centuries, is what is known as the Commercial Revolution.

1. The Causes and Incidents of the Commercial Revolution

The causes which led to the beginning of the Commercial Revolution about 1400 are none too clear. This is due to the fact that the initial stage of the movement was more gradual than is commonly

supposed. In so far as it is possible to isolate particular causes, the
following may be said to have been basic: (1) the capture of a
monopoly of Mediterranean trade by the Italian cities; (2) the development of a profitable commerce between the Italian cities and
the merchants of the Hanseatic League in northern Europe; (3) the
introduction of coins of general circulation, such as the ducat of
Venice and the florin of Florence; (4) the accumulation of surplus
capital in trading, shipping, and mining ventures; (5) the demand
for war materials and the encouragement given by the new monarchs to the development of commerce in order to create more
taxable wealth; and (6) the desire for the products of the Far East
stimulated by the reports of travelers, especially the fascinating account of the wealth of China published by Marco Polo upon his return
from a trip to that country toward the end of the thirteenth century. This combination of factors gave to the men of the early
Renaissance new visions of riches and power and furnished them
with some of the equipment necessary for an expansion of business.
Henceforth they were bound to be dissatisfied with the restricted
ideal of the medieval guilds with its ban upon trading for unlimited
profit.

But the Commercial Revolution would never have attained its far-
reaching extent had it not been for the voyages of overseas discovery
which began in the fifteenth century. The reasons why these voyages were undertaken are not hard to perceive. They were due primarily to Spanish and Portuguese ambitions for a share in the trade
with the Orient. For some time this trade had been monopolized
by the Italian cities, with the consequence that the people of the
Iberian peninsula were compelled to pay high prices for the silks,
perfumes, spices, and tapestries imported from the East. It was therefore quite natural that attempts should be made by Spanish and
Portuguese merchants to discover a new route to the Orient independent of Italian control. A second cause of the voyages of discovery was the missionary fervor of the Spaniards. Their successful crusade against the Moors had generated a surplus of religious
zeal, which spilled over into a desire to convert the heathen. To these
causes should be added the fact that advances in geographical
knowledge and the introduction of the compass and the astrolabe [1]
gave mariners more courage to venture into the open sea. But the
effect of these things must not be exaggerated. The popular idea
that all Europeans before Columbus believed that the earth was
flat is simply not true. From the twelfth century on it would be
almost impossible to find an educated man who did not accept the
fact that the earth is a sphere. Furthermore, the compass and the

---

[1] The astrolabe is a device for measuring the altitude or position of heavenly
bodies. It was invented by Hellenistic astronomers and perfected by the Saracens. Especially useful in determining locations at sea, it has since been replaced
by the sextant.

Santa María. A representation of Columbus's flagship, exhibited at the Columbian Exposition of 1893 in Chicago.

A Moslem Astrolabe, Thirteenth Century. Invented by Hellenistic astronomers, the astrolabe was perfected by the Saracens. It became available to European navigators by the beginning of the Commercial Revolution.

astrolabe were known in Europe long before any mariners ever dreamed of sailing the Atlantic, with the exception of the Norsemen. The compass was brought in by the Moslems in the twelfth century, probably from China. The astrolabe was introduced even earlier.

The Spaniards and Portuguese

If we except the Norsemen, who discovered America about 1000 A.D., the pioneers in oceanic navigation were the Portuguese. By the middle of the fifteenth century they had discovered and settled the islands of Madeira and the Azores and had explored the African coast as far south as Guinea. In 1497 their most successful navigator, Vasco da Gama, rounded the tip of Africa and sailed on the next year to India. In the meantime, the Genoese mariner, Christopher Columbus, became convinced of the feasibility of reaching India by sailing west. Rebuffed by the Portuguese, he turned to the Spanish sovereigns, Ferdinand and Isabella, and enlisted their support of his plan. The story of his epochal voyage and its result is a familiar one and need not be recounted here. Though he died ignorant of his real achievement, his discoveries laid the foundations for the Spanish claim to nearly all of the New World. Other discovers representing the Spanish crown followed Columbus, and soon afterward the conquerors, Cortes and Pizarro. The result was the establishment of a vast colonial empire including what is now the southwestern portion of the United States, Florida, Mexico, the West Indies, Central America, and all of South America with the exception of Brazil.

The English and the French were not slow in following the Spanish example. The voyages of John Cabot and his son Sebastian in 1497–1498 provided the basis for the English claim to North America, though there was nothing that could be called a British empire in the New World until after the settlement of Virginia in 1607. Early in the sixteenth century the French explorer Cartier sailed up the St. Lawrence, thereby furnishing his native land with some shadow of a title to eastern Canada. More than a hundred years later the explorations of Joliet, La Salle, and Father Marquette gave the French a foothold in the Mississippi valley and in the region of the Great Lakes. Following their victory in their war for independence the Dutch also took a hand in the struggle for colonial empire. The voyage of Henry Hudson up the river which bears his name enabled them to found New Netherland in 1623, which they were forced to surrender to the English some forty years later. But the most valuable possessions of the Dutch were Malacca, the Spice Islands, and the ports of India and Africa taken from Portugal in the early seventeenth century.

The results of these voyages of discovery and the founding of colonial empires were almost incalculable. To begin with, they expanded commerce from its narrow limits of Mediterranean trade into a world enterprise. For the first time in history the ships of the great maritime powers now sailed the seven seas. The tight little monopoly of Oriental trade maintained by the Italian cities was thoroughly punctured. Genoa, Pisa, and Venice sank henceforth into relative obscurity, while the harbors of Lisbon, Bordeaux, Liverpool, Bristol, and Amsterdam were crowded with vessels and the shelves of their merchants piled high with goods. A second result was a tremendous increase in the volume of commerce and in the variety of articles of consumption. To the spices and textiles from the Orient were now added potatoes, tobacco, and maize from North America; molasses and rum from the West Indies; cocoa, chocolate, quinine, and the cochineal dye from South America; and ivory, slaves, and ostrich feathers from Africa. In addition to these commodities hitherto unknown or obtainable only in limited quantities, the supply of certain older products was greatly increased. This was especially true of sugar, coffee, rice, and cotton, which were brought in in such amounts from the Western Hemisphere that they ceased to be articles of luxury.

The expansion of commerce into a world enterprise

Probably the most significant result of the discovery and conquest of lands overseas was the expansion of the supply of precious metals. When Columbus discovered America, it is estimated that the amount of gold and silver in circulation in Europe was not over $400,000,000. By 1600 the volume of precious metals in Europe had reached about five times this amount. Some of it was plundered by the Spaniards from the treasuries of the Incas and Aztecs, but most of it came from the mines of Mexico, Bolivia, and Peru. The effects of this phenomenal increase in the supply of bullion can only be described as momentous. No other cause was so fully responsible

The increase in the supply of precious metals

for the growth of a capitalistic economy. Men now possessed wealth in a form which could be conveniently stored for future use; and we need scarcely to be reminded that the accumulation of wealth for future investment at a profit is an essential feature of capitalism. Moreover, as gold and silver came to be used primarily as tokens of commodities, and not as commodities themselves, the medieval ideal of trade as an equal exchange was broken down. In place of this ideal there was substituted the modern conception of business for profit. Finally, the rapid inflow of precious metals encouraged speculation. The value of gold and silver fluctuated widely, as new deposits were discovered or as hopes of rich yields were shattered. These fluctuations affected the prices of commodities, with the result that merchants and bankers were tempted to gamble on future trends.

Incidents of the Commercial Revolution: (1) the rise of capitalism

The incidents or features of the Commercial Revolution have been partly suggested by the foregoing discussion of causes. The outstanding one of them was the rise of capitalism. Reduced to its simplest terms, capitalism may be defined as a system of production, distribution, and exchange in which accumulated wealth is invested by private owners for the sake of gain. Its essential features are private enterprise, competition for markets, and business for profit. Generally it involves also the wage system as a method of payment of workers; that is, a mode of payment based not upon the amount of wealth they create, but rather upon their ability to compete with one another for jobs. Further, it is a dynamic system, founded upon the assumption that every producer or merchant has the right to expand his business by stimulating demand for his wares. As indicated already, capitalism is the direct antithesis of the semi-static economy of the medieval guilds, in which production and trade were supposed to be conducted for the benefit of society with only a reasonable charge for the service rendered, instead of unlimited profits. Although capitalism did not come to its full maturity until the nineteenth century, nearly all of its cardinal features were developed during the Commercial Revolution.

(2) the growth of banking

A second important incident of the Commercial Revolution was the growth of banking. Because of the strong disapproval of usury, banking had scarcely been a respectable business during the Middle Ages. For many centuries the little that was carried on was virtually monopolized by Moslems and Jews. During the Crusades the monasteries and the Templars lent money to finance the expeditions or to provide for the needs of the soldiers after they had arrived in the East, but neither of these cases could be regarded as examples of banking in the modern sense. The justification for the loans was not economic but religious, and even then it was considered necessary to evade the ban against usury by accepting gifts in place of charging interest. Not until the fourteenth century was the lending of money as a business enterprise firmly established. The real founders of banking for profit were certain of the great commercial houses

Headquarters of the Fuggers, Augsburg. In these ancient buildings the great banking house of the Fuggers carried on its operations.

of the Italian cities. Notable among them was the Medici firm at Florence, with a capital of about $15,000,000 to support its financial activities. The business insignia of this firm, the cluster of the three golden balls, is still the famous pawnbroker's sign throughout the Western world. By the fifteenth century the banking business had spread to southern Germany, France, and the Low Countries. The leading firm in the north was that of the Fuggers of Augsburg, with a capital of $40,000,000. The Fuggers lent money to kings and bishops, served as brokers for the Pope in the sale of indulgences, and provided the funds that enabled Charles V to buy his election to the throne of the Holy Roman Empire. So shrewdly did they manage their business, and so relentlessly did they pursue their debtors—even browbeating the Emperor himself as if he were a petty trader—that the firm earned an annual profit of 54 per cent for a decade and a half in the sixteenth century. The rise of these private financial houses was followed by the establishment of government banks, intended to serve the monetary needs of the national states. The first in order of time was the Bank of Sweden (1656), but the one which was destined for the role of greatest importance in economic history was the Bank of England, founded in 1694. Although not technically under government control until 1946, it was the bank of issue for the government and the depositary of public funds.

The growth of banking was necessarily accompanied by the adoption of various aids to financial transactions on a large scale. Credit facilities were extended in such a way that a merchant in Amsterdam could purchase goods from a merchant in Venice by **463** means of a bill of exchange issued by an Amsterdam bank. The Venetian merchant would obtain his money by depositing the bill of exchange in his local bank. Later the two banks would settle their accounts by comparing balances. Ultimately a fairly complete system of international clearance was set up making possible the settlement of large numbers of accounts with very little interchange of coin. Among the other facilities for the expansion of credit were the adoption of a system of payment by check in local transactions and the issuance of bank notes as a substitute for gold and silver. Both of these devices were introduced by the Italians and were gradually adopted in northern Europe. The system of payment by check was particularly important in increasing the volume of trade, since the credit resources of the banks could now be expanded far beyond the actual amounts of cash in their vaults.

The Commercial Revolution was not confined, of course, to the growth of trade and banking. Included in it also were fundamental changes in methods of production. The system of manufacture developed by the craft guilds in the late Middle Ages was rapidly becoming defunct. The guilds themselves, dominated by the master craftsmen, had grown selfish and exclusive. Membership in them was commonly restricted to a few privileged families. Besides, they were so completely choked by tradition that they were unable to make adjustments to changing conditions. Moreover, new industries had sprung up entirely outside the guild system. Characteristic examples were mining and smelting and the woolen industry. The rapid development of these enterprises was stimulated by technical advances, such as the invention of the spinning wheel and the stocking frame and the discovery of a new method of making brass, which saved about half of the fuel previously used. In the mining and smelting industries a form of organization was adopted similar to that which has prevailed ever since. The tools and plant facilities belonged to capitalists, while the workers were mere wage laborers subject to hazards of accident, unemployment, and occupational disease.

But the most typical form of industrial production in the Commercial Revolution was the domestic system, developed first of all in the woolen industry. The domestic system derives its name from the fact that the work was done in the homes of individual artisans instead of in the shop of a master craftsman. Since the various jobs in the manufacture of a product were given out on contract in "sweat-shop" fashion, the system is also known as the putting-out system. Notwithstanding the petty scale of production, the organization was basically capitalistic. The raw material was purchased by an entrepreneur (known as a clothier in the woolen industry) and assigned to individual workers, each of whom would complete his allotted task for a stipulated payment. In the case of the woolen industry the yarn would be given out first of all to the spinners, then to the weavers, fullers, and dyers in succession. When

the cloth was finally finished, it would be taken by the clothier and
sold in the open market for the highest price it would bring. The
domestic system was, of course, not restricted to the manufacture
of woolen cloth. As time went on, it was extended into many
other fields of production. It tied in well with the new glorification
of riches and with the conception of a dynamic economy. The
capitalist could now thumb his nose at the old restrictions on profits.
No association of his rivals could judge the quality of his product or
the wages he paid to his workers. Perhaps best of all he could expand his business as he saw fit and introduce new techniques that
would reduce costs or increase the volume of production.

Undoubtedly the domestic system had advantages for the workers themselves, especially as compared to its successor, the factory
system. Though wages were low, there was no regular schedule of
hours, and it was generally possible for the laborer to supplement
his family income by cultivating a small plot of land and raising a
few vegetables at least. Furthermore, conditions of work in the
homes were more healthful than in factories, and the artisan had his
family to assist him with the simpler tasks. Freedom from the supervision of a foreman and from the fear of discharge for petty reasons must also be accounted definite advantages. On the other hand,
it must not be forgotten that the workers were too widely scattered
to organize effectively for common action. As a consequence they
had no means of protecting themselves from dishonest employers,
who cheated them out of part of their wages or forced them to
accept payment in goods. It is also true that toward the end of the
Commercial Revolution the workers became more and more dependent upon the capitalists, who now furnished not only the raw
materials but the tools and equipment as well. In some cases the
laborers were herded into large central shops and compelled to
work under a fixed routine. The difference between this and the
high-pressure methods of the factory system was only a matter
of degree.

That the Commercial Revolution would involve extensive changes
in business organization was practically assured from the start. The
prevailing unit of production and trade in the Middle Ages was the
shop or store owned by an individual or a family. The partnership
was also quite common, in spite of its grave disadvantage of unlimited liability of each of its members for the debts of the entire
firm. Obviously no one of these units was well adapted to business
involving heavy risks and a huge investment of capital. The first
result of the attempt to devise a more suitable business organization
was the formation of *regulated companies*. The regulated company
was an association of merchants banded together for a common
venture. The members did not pool their resources but agreed
merely to co-operate for their mutual advantage and to abide by
certain definite regulations. Usually the purpose of the combination was to maintain a monopoly of trade in some part of the

*Advantages and
disadvantages
of the domestic
system*

*(6) changes in
business or-
ganization; the
growth of
regulated com-
panies*

Coining Money in the Sixteenth Century. These coins were not "milled," and therefore were easily "clipped."

The Spanish Milled Dollar, or "Piece of Eight." It was one of the first coins to have its circumference scored, or "milled." It was cut into halves and quarters to make change.

world. Assessments were often paid by the members for the upkeep of docks and warehouses and especially for protection against "interlopers," as those traders were called who attempted to break into the monopoly. A leading example of this type of organization was an English company known as the Merchant Adventurers, established for the purpose of trade with the Netherlands and Germany.

(7) the joint-stock company

In the seventeenth century the regulated company was largely superseded by a new type of organization at once more compact and broader in scope. This was the *joint-stock company,* formed through the issuance of shares of capital to a considerable number of investors. Those who purchased the shares might or might not take part in the work of the company, but whether they did or not they were joint owners of the business and therefore entitled to share in its profits in accordance with the amount they had invested. The joint-stock company had numerous advantages over the partnership and the regulated company. First, it was a permanent unit, not subject to reorganization every time one of its members died or withdrew. Second, it was eventually established on the basis of limited liability; that is, each member was liable for the debts of the company only in proportion to his own investment. And third, it made possible a much larger accumulation of capital, through a wide distribution of shares. In short, it possessed nearly every advantage of the modern corporation except that it was not a person in the eyes of the law with the rights and privileges guaranteed to individuals. While most of the early joint-stock companies were founded for commercial ventures, some were organized later in industry. A number of the outstanding trading combinations were also *chartered companies.* This means that they held charters from the government granting a monopoly of the trade in a certain

466

locality and conferring extensive authority over the inhabitants. Through a charter of this kind the British East India Company ruled over India as if it were a private estate until 1784, and even in a sense until 1858. Other famous chartered companies were the Dutch East India Company, the Hudson Bay Company, the Plymouth Company, and the London Company. The last of these founded the colony of Virginia and governed it for a time as company property.

The remaining feature of the Commercial Revolution which needs to be considered was the growth of a more efficient money economy. Money, of course, had been in use ever since the revival of trade in the eleventh century. Nevertheless, there were few coins with a value that was recognized other than locally. By 1300 the ducat of Venice and the florin of Florence, each with a value of about $4.00, had come to be accepted rather widely in Italy and also in the international markets of northern Europe. But no country could be said to have had a uniform monetary system. Nearly everywhere there was great confusion. Coins issued by kings circulated side by side with the money of local nobles and even with Moslem currency. Moreover, the types of currency were modified frequently, and the coins themselves were often debased. A common method by which kings expanded their own personal revenues was to increase the proportion of cheaper metals in the coins they minted. But the growth of trade and industry in the Commercial Revolution accentuated the need for more stable and uniform monetary systems. The problem was solved by the adoption of a standard system of money by every important state to be used for all transactions within its borders. Much time elapsed, however, before the reform was complete. England began the construction of a uniform coinage during the reign of Queen Elizabeth, but the task was not finished until late in the seventeenth century. The French did not succeed in reducing their money to its modern standard of simplicity and convenience until the time of Napoleon. In spite of these long delays it appears safe to conclude that national currencies were really an achievement of the Commercial Revolution.

(8) the growth of a more efficient money economy

A Printing Shop in the Seventeenth Century. Engraving by Abraham von Werdt.

2. Mercantilism in Theory and Practice

*The meaning of
mercantilism*

The Commercial Revolution in its later stages was accompanied by the adoption of a new set of doctrines and practices known as mercantilism. In its broadest meaning, mercantilism may be defined as a system of government intervention to promote national prosperity and increase the power of the state. Though frequently considered as a program of economic policy exclusively, its objectives were quite largely political. The purpose of the intervention in economic affairs was not merely to expand the volume of manufacturing and trade, but also to bring more money into the treasury of the king, which would enable him to build fleets, equip armies, and make his government feared and respected throughout the world. Because of this close association with the ambitions of princes to increase their own power and the power of the states over which they ruled, mercantilism has sometimes been called *statism*. Certainly the system would never have come into existence had it not been for the growth of absolute monarchy in place of the weak, decentralized structure of feudalism. But kings alone did not create it. Naturally the new magnates of business lent enthusiastic support, since they would obviously derive great advantages from active encouragement of trade by the state. The heyday of mercantilism was the period between 1600 and 1700, but many of its features survived until the end of the eighteenth century.

*Bullionism and
the favorable
balance of trade*

If there was any one principle which held the central place in mercantilist theory, it was the doctrine of bullionism. This doctrine means that the prosperity of a nation is determined by the quantity of precious metals within its borders. The greater the amount of gold and silver a country contains, the more money the government can collect in taxes, and the richer and more powerful the state will become. The growth of such an idea as this was fostered by knowledge of the prosperity and power of Spain, which seemed to be the direct results of the flood of precious metals pouring in from her American colonies. But what of those countries that owned no bullion-producing colonies? How were *they* to achieve riches and power? For these questions the mercantilists had a ready answer. A nation without access to gold and silver directly should attempt to increase its trade with the rest of the world. If its government took steps to ensure that the value of exports would always exceed the value of imports, more gold and silver would come into the country than would have to be shipped out. This was called maintaining a "favorable balance of trade." To preserve this balance, three main devices would be necessary: first, high tariffs to reduce the general level of imports and to shut out some products entirely; second, bounties on exports; and third, extensive encouragement of manufactures in order that the nation might have as many things to sell abroad as possible.

The theory of mercantilism also included certain elements of economic nationalism, paternalism, and imperialism. By the first is meant the ideal of a self-sufficient nation. The policy of fostering new industries was not intended merely as a device for increasing exports, but also as a means of making the nation independent of foreign supplies. In similar fashion, the mercantilists argued that the government should exercise the functions of a watchful guardian over the lives of its citizens. Marriage should be encouraged and regulated, to the end that the population might steadily increase. Wages, hours of labor, prices, quality of products should be carefully controlled by the government. Generous relief should be provided for the poor, including free medical attention if they were unable to pay for it. These things were to be done, however, not with any view to charity or justice, but mainly in order that the state might rest upon a secure economic foundation and have the support of a numerous and healthy citizenry in case of war. Finally, the mercantilists advocated the acquisition of colonies. Again, the primary purpose was not to benefit individual citizens of the mother country, but to make the nation strong and independent. The types of possessions most ardently desired were such as would enlarge the nation's hoard of bullion. If these could not be obtained, then colonies providing tropical products, naval stores, or any other commodities which the mother country could not produce would be acceptable. The theory which underlay this imperialism was the notion that colonies existed for the benefit of the state that owned them. For this reason they were not allowed to engage in manufacturing or shipping. Their function was to produce raw materials and to consume as large a proportion of manufactured products as possible. In this way they would infuse lifeblood into the industries of the mother country and thus give her an advantage in the struggle for world trade.

imperialism

The majority of those who wrote on mercantilist theory were not professional economists but men of action in the world of business. The best exposition of the subject appears to have been that of Thomas Mun, a leading merchant and for many years a director of the British East India Company. His principal work was published posthumously in 1664 under the title of *England's Treasure by Forraign Trade, or The Ballance of Our Forraign Trade Is the Rule of Our Treasure*. In addition to a host of other champions from the ranks of business, mercantilism had its defenders also in certain of the political philosophers. Included among them were such advocates of absolute monarchy as the Frenchman Jean Bodin (1530–1596) and the Englishman Thomas Hobbes (1588–1679), who were naturally disposed to favor any policy that would increase the wealth and power of the ruler. While most of the apologists for mercantilism were interested in it mainly as a device for promoting a favorable balance of trade, others conceived it as a species of paternalism for increasing prosperity within the country. For example, the Englishman Edward Chamberlayne advocated a policy somewhat similar to contemporary ideas of government spending. He recommended that the state should appropriate a huge fund for the relief of the poor and for the construction of public works as a means of stimulating business.

Attempts to put mercantilist doctrine into practice characterized the history of most of the nations of western Europe in the sixteenth and seventeenth centuries. Obviously Spain had the initial advantage by reason of the flow of bullion from her American empire. And while the Spaniards did not need to resort to artificial devices in order to bring money into their country, their government nevertheless maintained a rigid control over commerce and industry. The policies of most other nations were designed to make up for the lack of bullion-producing colonies by capturing a larger share of export trade. This naturally involved a program of bounties, tariffs, and extensive regulation of manufacturing and shipping. Mercantilist policies were definitely adopted in England during the reign of Queen Elizabeth and were continued by the Stuart monarchs and by Oliver Cromwell. Most of these rulers engaged in a furious scramble for colonies, bestowed monopolistic privileges upon trading companies, and sought in a wide variety of ways to control the economic activities of the citizens. The most interesting examples of mercantilist legislation in England were, first, the Elizabethan laws designed to eliminate idleness and stimulate production and, second, the Navigation Acts. By a series of laws enacted toward the end of the sixteenth century, Queen Elizabeth gave to the justices of the peace the authority to fix prices, regulate hours of labor, and compel every able-bodied citizen to work at some useful trade. The first of the Navigation Acts was passed in 1651 under Oliver Cromwell. With the aim of destroying Dutch predominance in the carrying trade, it required that all colonial exports to the mother country should be carried in English ships. A second Navigation Act was passed in 1660, which provided not merely that colonial exports should be shipped in British vessels but prohibited the sending of certain "enumerated articles," especially tobacco and sugar, directly to Continental European ports. They must be sent first of all to England, whence after the payment of customs duties they could be re-shipped elsewhere. Both of these laws were based upon the principle that colonies should serve for the enrichment of the mother country.

The Germanic states during the Commercial Revolution were too completely occupied with internal problems to take a very active part in the struggle for colonies and overseas trade. As a consequence, German mercantilism was concerned primarily with increasing the strength of the state from within. It partook of the dual character of economic nationalism and a program for a

Mercantilism in practice: in Spain and in England

Mercantilism in Germany: the cameralists

470

planned society. But, of course, the planning was done chiefly for the benefit of the government and only incidentally for that of the people as a whole. Because of their dominant purpose of increasing the revenues of the state, the German mercantilists are known as cameralists (from *Kammer*, a name given to the royal treasury). Most of them were lawyers and professors of finance. Cameralist ideas were put into practice by the Hohenzollern kings of Prussia, notably by Frederick William I (1713–1740) and Frederick the Great (1740–1786). The policies of these monarchs embraced a many-sided scheme of intervention and control in the economic sphere for the purpose of increasing taxable wealth and bolstering the power of the state. Marshes were drained, canals dug, new industries established with the aid of the government, and farmers instructed as to what crops they should plant. In order that the nation might become self-sufficient as soon as possible, exports of raw materials and imports of manufactured products were prohibited. The bulk of the revenues gained from these various policies went for military purposes. The standing army of Prussia was increased by Frederick the Great to 160,000 men.

The most thorough application of mercantilism, in all of its aspects, was probably to be found in France during the reign of Louis XIV (1643–1715). This was due partly to the fact that the French state was the complete incarnation of absolutism and partly to the policies of Jean Baptiste Colbert, chief minister under *le grand monarque* between 1661 and 1683. Contrary to an opinion rather widely held, Colbert was no theorist but a practical politician, ambitious for personal power and intent upon magnifying the opportunities for wealth of the middle class, to which he belonged. He accepted mercantilism, not as an end in itself, but as the most convenient means for increasing the wealth and power of the state and thereby gaining the approval of his sovereign. Nonetheless, the majority of his policies were thoroughly in accord with mercantilist doctrine. He firmly believed that France must acquire as large an amount of the precious metals as possible. To this end he prohibited the export of money, levied high tariffs on foreign manufacturers, and gave liberal bounties to encourage French shipping. It was largely for this purpose also that he fostered imperialism, hoping to increase the favorable balance of trade through the sale of manufactured goods to the colonies. Accordingly, he purchased the islands of Martinique and Guadeloupe in the West Indies, encouraged settlements in Santo Domingo, Canada, and Louisiana, and established trading posts in India and in Africa. Furthermore, he was as devoted to the ideal of self-sufficiency as any of the cameralists in Prussia. He gave subsidies to new enterprises, established a number of state-owned industries, and even had the government purchase goods which were not really needed in order to keep struggling companies on their feet. But he was determined

The application of mercantilism in France; the work of Colbert

to keep the manufacturing industry under strict control, so as to make sure that companies would buy their raw materials only from French or colonial sources and produce the commodities necessary for national greatness. Consequently he clamped upon industry an elaborate set of regulations prescribing nearly every detail of the manufacturing process. Finally, it should be mentioned that Colbert took a number of steps to augment the political strength of the nation directly. He provided France with a navy of nearly 300 ships, drafting citizens from the maritime provinces and even criminals to man them. He sought to promote a rapid growth of population by discouraging young people from becoming monks or nuns and by exempting families with ten or more children from taxation.

3. The Results of the Commercial Revolution

It goes without saying that the Commercial Revolution was one of the most significant developments in the history of the Western world. The whole pattern of modern economic life would have been impossible without it; for it changed the basis of commerce from the local and regional plane of the Middle Ages to the world-wide scale it has occupied ever since. Moreover, it exalted the power of money, inaugurated business for profit, sanctified the accumulation of wealth, and established competitive enterprise as the foundation of production and trade. In a word, the Commercial Revolution was responsible for nearly all of the elements that go to make up the capitalist regime.

Effects of the Commercial Revolution in laying the foundation for modern capitalism

But these were not the only results. The Commercial Revolution was also responsible for the first great orgies of speculation, very similar to those with which the modern world is so unpleasantly familiar. The inflow of precious metals, the rapidly rising prices, and the new emphasis upon riches as the goal of living encouraged a spirit of gambling in business which would never have been possible under the static economy of the Middle Ages. The rapid expansion of business activity in the early days of the Revolution encouraged men to think that fortunes could be made overnight. Innumerable projects were launched for all kinds of curious purposes—to make salt water fresh or to manufacture perpetual-motion machines— and thousands of investors swallowed the bait. A group of wily promoters even managed to sell stock in a company whose purpose was alluringly described as an "undertaking in due time to be revealed." It has been estimated that hundreds of millions of dollars were invested in these schemes in the early years of the eighteenth century.[2]

Orgies of speculation

The South Sea Bubble

The climax of the speculative frenzy was reached in the South Sea Bubble and the Mississippi Bubble about 1720. The first was the result of inflation of the stock of the South Sea Company in

[2] L. B. Packard, *The Commercial Revolution*, p. 81.

England. The promoters of this company agreed to take over a large part of the national debt and in return received from the English government an exclusive right to trade with South America and the Pacific islands. The prospects for profit seemed almost unlimited. The stock of the company rose rapidly in value until it was selling for more than ten times its original price. The higher it rose, the more gullible the public became. But gradually suspicion developed that the possibilities of the enterprise had been overrated. Buoyant hopes gave way to fears, and investors made frantic attempts to dispose of their shares for whatever they would bring. A crash was the inevitable result.

During the very same years when the South Sea Bubble was being inflated in England, the French were going through a similar wave of speculative madness. In 1715 a Scotsman by the name of John Law, who had been compelled to flee from British soil for killing his rival in a love intrigue, settled in Paris, after various successful gambling adventures in other cities. He persuaded the regent of France to adopt his scheme for paying off the national debt through the issuance of paper money and to grant him the privilege of organizing the Mississippi Company for the colonization and exploitation of Louisiana. As the government loans were redeemed, the persons who received the money were encouraged to buy stock in the company. Soon the shares began to soar, ultimately reaching a price forty times their original value. Nearly everyone who could scrape together a few livres of surplus cash rushed forward to participate in the scramble for riches. Stories were told of butchers and tailors who were supposed to have become millionaires by buying a few shares and holding them for a rise in price. But as the realization grew that the company would never be able to pay more than a nominal dividend on the stock at its inflated value, the more cautious investors began selling their holdings. The alarm spread, and soon everyone was as anxious to sell as he had been to buy. In 1720 the Mississippi Bubble burst in a wild panic. Thousands of people who had sold good property to buy the shares at fantastic prices were utterly ruined. The collapse of the South Sea and Mississippi companies gave a temporary chill to the public ardor for gambling. It was not long, however, until the greed for speculative profits revived, and the stock-jobbing orgies that followed in the wake of the Commercial Revolution were repeated many times over during the nineteenth and twentieth centuries.

The Mississippi Bubble

Among other results of the Commercial Revolution were the rise of the bourgeoisie to economic power, the beginning of Europeanization of the world, and the revival of slavery. Each of these requires brief comment. By the end of the seventeenth century the bourgeoisie had become the dominant economic class in nearly every country of western Europe. Its ranks included the merchants, the bankers, the shipowners, the principal investors, and the in-

Europeanization of the world and the revival of slavery

dustrial entrepreneurs. Their rise to power was mainly the result of increasing wealth and their tendency to ally themselves with the king against the remnants of the feudal aristocracy. But as yet their power was purely economic. Not until the nineteenth century did middle-class supremacy in politics become a reality. By the Europeanization of the world is meant the transplanting of European manners and culture in other continents. As a result of the work of traders, missionaries, and colonists, North and South America were rapidly stamped with the character of appendages of Europe. No more than a beginning was made in the transformation of Asia, but enough was done to foreshadow the trend of later times when even Japanese and Chinese would adopt Western locomotives and shell-rimmed spectacles. The most regrettable result of the Commercial Revolution was the revival of slavery. As we learned in our study of the Middle Ages, slavery practically disappeared from European civilization about the year 1000. But the development of mining and plantation-farming in the English, Spanish, and Portuguese colonies led to a tremendous demand for unskilled labor. At first an attempt was made to enslave the American Indians, but they usually proved too hard to manage. The problem was solved in the sixteenth century by the importation of African Negroes. For the next two hundred years and more, Negro slavery was an integral part of the European colonial system, especially in those regions producing tropical products.

Effects of the Commercial Revolution in preparing the way for the Industrial Revolution

Finally, the Commercial Revolution was exceedingly important in preparing the way for the Industrial Revolution. This was true for a number of reasons. First, the Commercial Revolution created a class of capitalists who were constantly seeking new opportunities to invest their surplus profits. Second, the mercantilist policy, with its emphasis upon protection for infant industries and production of goods for export, gave a powerful stimulus to the growth of manufactures. Third, the founding of colonial empires flooded Europe with new raw materials and greatly increased the supply of certain products which had hitherto been luxuries. Most of these required fabrication before they were available for consumption. As a consequence, new industries sprang up wholly independent of any guild regulations that still survived. The outstanding example was the manufacture of cotton textiles, which, significantly enough, was one of the first of the industries to become merchanized. Last of all, the Commercial Revolution was marked by a trend toward the adoption of factory methods in certain lines of production, together with technological improvements such as the invention of the spinning wheel and the stocking frame and the discovery of more efficient processes of refining ores. The connection between these developments and the mechanical progress of the Industrial Revolution is not hard to perceive.

4. *Revolutionary Developments in Agriculture*

To a large extent the sweeping changes which occurred in agriculture between the fifteenth century and the eighteenth may be regarded as effects of the Commercial Revolution. For example, the rise in prices and the increase in urban population made agriculture a profitable business and thus tended to promote its absorption into the capitalist system. In addition, the development of the woolen industry in England caused many landowners of that country to substitute the pasturing of flocks for ordinary farming as their principal source of income. But there were also certain other causes not directly connected with the Commercial Revolution at all. One of them was the reduction of the supply of agricultural labor on account of the Black Death and the influx of peasants into the cities and towns to take advantage of the new opportunities for a living resulting from the revival of trade with the Near East. Another was the opening up of new farms to cultivation under a system of free labor and individual enterprise. A third was the influence of the Crusades and the Hundred Years' War in weakening the power of the nobles and in undermining the structure of the old society. The combined effect of these factors was the destruction of the manorial system and the establishment of agriculture on something like its modern foundations. The transformation was most complete in England, but there were similar developments in other countries also.

The first of the main incidents of the agricultural revolution was the abandonment of the old system of demesne farming. Under the medieval pattern of agriculture the demesne was that part of the manor reserved for the exclusive benefit of the lord himself. The labor of cultivating it had to be done by the serfs as one of the obligations owed to their master. But as more and more serfs ran away or were killed off by the Black Death, this particular obligation, like many of the others, could no longer be enforced. The lords then resorted to the expedient of leasing their demesne lands to the peasants for rent, either in produce or in money. Gradually the system of leasing was extended to the remaining arable portions of the manors, with the result that the erstwhile feudal proprietors became landlords of the modern type. Concurrently with these developments there occurred the gradual elimination of the open-field system. This, it will be recalled, was the system under which the peasants' lands were divided into strips scattered over the different sections of the manor and farmed on a communal basis.[3] The main purpose seems to have been to make sure that the best and the poorer areas of cultivation would be evenly divided. The system began to break down with the advancing prices for agri-

---

[3] See the paragraphs on the manorial estate in the chapter on The Civilization of the Feudal Age: Political and Economic Institutions.

cultural products at the end of the Middle Ages. The shrewder and more ambitious peasants became increasingly dissatisfied with co-operative farming. Impelled by the belief that they could make more money as individual farmers, they traded strips with each other, rented portions of the lord's demesne, and slowly gathered all of their lands into compact blocks. When finally completed, this process, known as the compacting of holdings, went a long way toward the destruction of manorial agriculture.

The enclosure movement

The third important development of the agricultural revolution was the enclosure movement, which was of notable importance in England. This movement had two main aspects: first, the enclosing of the common wood and pasture lands of the manor, thereby abolishing the communal rights which the peasants had enjoyed of pasturing their flocks and gathering wood on the untilled portions of the lord's estate; and second, the eviction of large numbers of peasants from their leaseholds or other rights of tenantry on the arable lands. Both of these forms of enclosure resulted in much hardship for the rural population. For centuries the peasant's rights in the common pasture and woodlot had formed an essential element in his scheme of subsistence, and it was very difficult indeed for him to get along without them. But the fate of those peasants who were dispossessed entirely of their rights of tenantry was much more serious. In most cases they were forced to become landless wage earners or to make their way in the world as helpless beggars. The chief reason for the enclosures was the desire of the former feudal proprietors to convert as large an area of their estates as possible into pasturage for sheep, on account of the high price which could now be obtained for wool. Usually they began by fencing in the common lands as their own property. This was frequently followed by the conversion of many of the grain fields into pastures also, re-sulting in the eviction especially of those peasants whose leaseholds were none too secure. Enclosures began in the fifteenth century and were continued beyond the period of the Commercial Revolution. Even as late as 1819 hundreds of acts were still being passed by the British Parliament authorizing the eviction of tenants and the closing in of great estates. In the eighteenth and nineteenth centuries the process was accelerated by the ambition of capitalists to push their way into the aristocracy by becoming gentleman farmers. The enclosure movement completed the transformation of English agri-culture into a capitalistic enterprise.

The introduc-tion of new crops and im-provements in mechanical equipment

The final stage in the agricultural upheaval which accompanied or followed the Commercial Revolution was the introduction of new crops and improvements in mechanical equipment. Neither of these developments was conspicuous until the beginning of the eighteenth century. It was about this time that Lord Townshend in England discovered the value of raising clover as a means of pre-venting exhaustion of the soil. Not only is the effect of clover in

reducing fertility much less than that of the cereal grains, but it
actually helps to improve the quality of the soil by gathering nitrogen and making the ground more porous. The planting of this crop
from time to time made unnecessary the old system of allowing one-
third of the land to lie fallow each year. Furthermore, the clover
itself provided an excellent winter feed for animals, thereby aiding
the production of more and better livestock. Only a very small number of mechanical improvements were introduced into farming at
this time, but they were of much more than trivial significance.
First came the adoption of the metal plowshare, which made possible a deeper and wider furrow than could ever be accomplished
with the primitive wooden plows handed down from the Middle
Ages. For a time farmers were reluctant to use the new device
in the belief that iron would poison the soil, but this superstition was
eventually abandoned. The other most important mechanical improvement of this period was the drill for planting grain. The
adoption of this invention eliminated the old wasteful method of
sowing grain broadcast by hand, most of it remaining on top of the
ground to be eaten by crows. Significant as these inventions were,
however, the real mechanization of agriculture did not come until
well along in the nineteenth century.

5. The New Society

Profound changes in the texture of society inevitably accompany
economic or intellectual revolutions. The society which was brought
into being by the Renaissance, the Reformation, and the Commercial
Revolution, though retaining characteristics of the Middle Ages,
was really quite different in its underlying features from that which
had gone before. For one thing, the population of Europe was
now considerably larger. The number of inhabitants of both Italy
and England increased by approximately one-third during the single
century from 1500 to 1600. In the same period the estimated population of Germany grew from 12,000,000 to 20,000,000. In 1378 London had a population of about 46,000; by 1605 the total had grown
to about 225,000.[4] The reasons for these increases are closely related
to the religious and economic developments of the time. Undoubtedly in northern countries the overthrow of clerical celibacy
and the encouragement of marriage were factors partly responsible.
But far more important was the increase in means of subsistence
brought about by the Commercial Revolution. Not only were new
products, such as potatoes, maize, and chocolate, added to the food
supply, but older commodities, especially sugar and rice, were now
made available to Europeans in much larger quantities and therefore

*Significant so-
cial changes:
(1) a more
rapid growth
of population*

[4] J. W. Thompson, *Economic and Social History of Europe in the Later
Middle Ages,* p. 461; Preserved Smith, *The Age of the Reformation,* pp. 453–
458.

477

at lower cost. In addition, the growth of new opportunities for making a living in industry and commerce enabled most countries to support a larger population than would ever have been possible under the predominantly agrarian economy of the Middle Ages. It is significant that the bulk of the increases occurred in the cities and towns.

A development of even greater consequence than the growth in population was the increasing equality and fluidity of classes. The Renaissance, the Reformation, and the accompanying Commercial Revolution were all in a sense leveling movements. If there is any one fact that stands out about the social history of the Renaissance, it is the growing indifference of the men of that period toward

(2) an increasing equality and fluidity of classes

A Seventeenth-Century Apothecary Shop.

inherited social status. To be sure, they still prized some of the titles and trappings of the nobility, but entrance into that class was no longer limited by the accident of birth. Almost anyone with sufficient money could become a noble, particularly in Italy. A common expression of the time was "Scratch a knight and you will find a merchant." To a large extent it was personal achievement or wealth, rather than noble birth, which now determined a man's place in public esteem. It is an impressive fact that the majority of the men who rose to positions of leadership in Renaissance culture were not scions of the nobility. Some, like Michelangelo and Shakespeare, sprang from rather humble families. At least three were of illegitimate birth—Boccaccio, Leonardo da Vinci, and Erasmus. The influence of the Renaissance in promoting social equality is illustrated also by the rise of the professions to a higher dignity than they had ever enjoyed in the Middle Ages. The artist, the writer, the lawyer, the university professor, and the physician emerged into a position of importance roughly comparable to that which they hold in modern society. This is confirmed by the incomes which many are known to have received. Michelangelo enjoyed a pension of thousands of dollars a year from the Pope. Raphael left an estate which even by modern standards would be considered princely.[5] Erasmus was able to live in luxury from the gifts and favors received from his patrons. Although few historians would now subscribe wholeheartedly to Nietzsche's dictum that the Reformation was simply a revolt of the ignorant masses against their betters, the influence of that movement in weakening the old aristocracy cannot be ignored. By sanctifying the accumulation of wealth it did much to enthrone the middle class. As for the third of the great leveling movements, the Commercial Revolution, we need only recall its effects in providing the opportunities for any lucky or ambitious burgher to pile up a fortune and thereby to climb the highest rungs of the social ladder.

The condition of the lower classes did not improve at a rate commensurate with that of the bourgeoisie. Some historians deny that there was any improvement at all; but this view is open to debate. It is true that wages remained very low: English masons and carpenters were paid the modern equivalent of not more than a dollar a day about 1550. Attempts were even made to prohibit by law any rise in the level of wages, as in the English Statute of Laborers of 1351. It is also true that there were numerous strikes and insurrections of the lower classes. The most serious were the Great Revolt in England in 1381 and the so-called Peasants' Revolt in Germany in 1524–1525. In both, large numbers of workers from the towns took part along with the peasants. But there were also uprisings of the urban proletariat alone. An example is furnished by the revolt of the workers of Florence between 1379 and 1382 against the denial of their right to form unions and to participate in the government of the city. This revolt like the others was put down with merciless severity. Desperate though these uprisings were, we cannot be sure that they indicate a condition of wretchedness among the lower classes. It must be understood that in a time of transition the spirit of revolution is in the air. There are always many individuals who are unable to adjust themselves to a changing world and consequently become preachers of discontent. Furthermore, if we can judge from what happened in later movements of this kind, the very fact that revolts occurred may perhaps be taken as a sign that the lot of the workers was not so deplorable. Men do not generally rebel unless their economic condition has improved sufficiently to give them some confidence of success. Finally, it is almost impossible to believe that none of the working classes would share in the increasing prosperity of the age. It is probably never strictly true that all of the poor grow poorer while the rich grow richer.

As has been indicated more than once, both the Renaissance and the Reformation were products in large part of a revolt against suppression of the individual. The craving for personal independence was not satisfied with the early successes of these movements, but

(3) the modest gains of the lower classes

(4) rampant individualism

[5] Preserved Smith, *The Age of the Reformation*, p. 472.

instead was renewed with increasing vigor as time went on. During the Renaissance in particular an unquenchable desire to taste all the thrills of power and pleasure swept over Italy and then through the countries of northern Europe. At times the rampant individualism burst all bounds of humility or propriety and soared to fantastic heights of swaggering conceit. The classic example is the unblushing egotism in the *Autobiography* of Benvenuto Cellini (1500–1571). So strong was the revolt against Christian meekness and self-efface-ment that men no longer considered it improper to boast of their accomplishments and even to magnify them beyond their worth. The new desire for an untrammeled assertion of the ego also ex-pressed itself in styles of dress. The age of the Renaissance was a time of unparalleled splendor in personal adornment. The men of the wealthier classes decked themselves out in gorgeous costumes of velvet and lace, competing with one another for the most striking effects of color and variety. For a time every man in Florence was his own dictator of fashion. Needless to say, the women did not lag behind in their attempts to improve upon nature's endowments. The wearing of false hair and the use of an infinite variety of beautifying lotions for the face and even for the teeth and eyelids were common practices. In the sixteenth century Catherine de' Medici introduced the wearing of corsets—which in her case, at least, could be justified on the ground of urgent need. Both sexes indulged in the use of perfumes to an extent which would now be considered disgusting. At festivals in Italy even the mules were scented with sweet-smelling ointments.

*Moral condi-
tions during the
age of
the Renaissance*

The level of morality during the centuries of the Renaissance was not very high, especially when judged by modern Puritanical stand-ards. We do not need to credit all the fabulous stories of the sins of the Borgias in order to understand that in Italy, at least, the age was violent and uncouth. Political assassination and gambling were exceedingly common practices. Even the Popes maintained a huge lottery in Rome. The most lurid vices were probably those in the realm of sex morality and personal vengeance. The decline of feudal ideals of courtly love, together with the glorification of natural im-pulses, led to a marked increase in adultery. Few men of the upper classes—or women either, for that matter—appeared to show much regard for the sanctity of the marriage relation. Young girls were carefully protected by their families, but once a woman had married she was considered legitimate prey for any of her husband's rivals. Prostitution also flourished until virulent epidemics of syphilis in the sixteenth century compelled public authorities to impose restrictions.

*Murder and
vengeance*

But in none of the vices did the Italians show more proficiency than in the fine art of murder. It was taken for granted that the man of spirit would exact a terrible vengeance from anyone who had insulted his honor; and the law would not interfere. The great egoist Cellini boasted that he had murdered a number of his rivals, with perfect immunity from punishment. But acts of personal vengeance were not to be carried out in a clumsy or brutal manner. The code of the gentleman required ingenious refinements of cruelty. The following story related by Burckhardt may be taken to illustrate what is meant:

"In the district of Aquapendente three boys were watching cattle, and one of them said: 'Let us find out the way how people are hung.' While one was sitting on the shoulders of the other, and the third, after fastening the rope around the neck of the first, was tying it to an oak, a wolf came, and the two who were free ran away and left the other hanging. Afterwards they found him dead, and buried him. On the Sunday his father came to bring him bread, and one of the two confessed what had happened, and showed him the grave. The old man then killed him with a knife, cut him up, brought away the liver, and entertained the boy's father with it at home. After dinner, he told him whose liver it was. Hereupon began a series of reciprocal murders between the two families, and within a month thirty-six persons were killed, women as well as men." [6]

In northern Europe political corruption and drunkenness seem to have been the most flagrant evils. When in 1601 the Landgrave of Hesse and the Elector Palatine founded an Order of Temperance *Drunkenness* in a vain attempt to promote sobriety among the nobles, its rules *and profanity* were denounced as excessively severe because they allowed each member only fourteen goblets of wine per day. Manners were coarse, and language richly interlarded with profanity and obscenity was freely used by both sexes. England's "good Queen Bess" could put even her toughest ministers to shame when she unloosed her fish-wife's tongue. More to be deplored was the attitude of heartlessness revealed in the treatment of unfortunates.

The fate of slaves and demented persons was perhaps the most pitiable. For the sake of big profits Negroes were hunted like beasts on the coast of Africa and shipped to the American colonies. It *Slavery and* may be of interest to note that the Englishman who originated *cruelty* this body-snatching business, Captain John Hawkins, called the ship in which he transported the victims the *Jesus*. In view of the fact that insanity was regarded as a form of demonic possession, it is not strange that the sufferers from this disease should have been cruelly treated. They were generally confined in filthy barracks and flogged unmercifully to drive the demons out of their bodies. A favorite diversion of some of our ancestors was to organize parties to visit the madhouses and tease the insane.

The immediate effect of the Reformation in improving conditions of morality appears to have been almost negligible. Perhaps this is explainable in part by the return to the legalism of the Old Testa-

[6] Jacob Burckhardt, *The Civilization of the Renaissance in Italy*, p. 437.

The effect of the Reformation upon moral standards

ment. But probably the chief cause was the fierce antagonism between sects. A condition of war is never favorable to the growth of a high morality. Whatever the reasons, the licentiousness and brutality continued unchecked. Even some of the clergy who were closely identified with the work of religious reform could scarcely be said to have been armored with the breastplate of righteousness. An acquaintance of Luther's seems to have experienced no difficulty in getting a new pastorate after he had been dismissed from an earlier one on charges of seduction. Several of the Protestant Reformers considered polygamy less sinful than divorce, on the ground that the former was recognized in the Old Testament while the latter was prohibited in the New. So doubtful was the quality of moral standards among the Catholic clergy that the Reformers of that faith found it necessary to introduce the closed confessional box for the protection of female penitents. Formerly women as well as men had been required to kneel at the knees of the priest while confessing their sins. The effects of the Reformation upon the virtues of truthfulness and tolerance were woeful indeed. Catholic and Protestant Reformers alike were so obsessed with the righteousness of their own particular cause that they did not hesitate to make use of almost any extreme of falsehood, slander, or repression that seemed to guarantee victory for their side. For example, Luther expressly justified lying in the interests of religion, and the Jesuits achieved a reputation for tortuous reasoning and devious plotting for the advantage of the church. No one seemed to have the slightest doubt that in the sphere of religion the end justified the means.

Manners and customs

Manners and customs were generally about as coarse and brutish as the standards of morality. Life had few of the amenities now taken for granted. Not only were the contemporaries of Erasmus and Shakespeare subject to annoying discomforts, but they lacked even many of the common facilities for privacy. Bathhouses, frequented by both sexes, were the usual equipment for bathing. The solitary traveler who stopped at an inn was almost certain to be asked to share his bed with a stranger. Many of the most popular amusements were distinguished by similar features of indelicacy. The dances of the common people were little more than rowdyish romps accompanied by kissing and embracing. A favorite sport for men of all classes was bear-baiting—a pastime in which savage dogs were turned loose upon a chained bear. Naturally there were other amusements less boisterous and cruel. Tennis, played with wooden balls, enjoyed such popularity that there were 250 courts in Paris alone. Card games also had a strong appeal. One of them known as "triumph" or "trump," invented in England in the sixteenth century, was the forerunner of modern whist and bridge.

The widespread adoption of the tobacco and coffee habits in the seventeenth century ultimately had some effect in softening manners, especially in so far as these milder substances diminished the

Albrecht Dürer, *Dancing Peasants*. Though the condition of the peasants had improved since the Middle Ages, this engraving made in 1514 indicates that there was still room for advancement.

appetite for intoxicating liquors. Although the tobacco plant was brought into Europe by the Spaniards about fifty years after the discovery of America, another half century passed before many Europeans adopted the practice of smoking. At first the plant was believed to possess miraculous healing powers and was referred to as "divine tobacco" and "our holy herb nicotian." [7] The habit of smoking was popularized by English explorers, especially by Sir Walter Raleigh, who had learned it from the Indians of Virginia. It spread rapidly through all classes of European society despite the condemnation of the clergy and the "counterblaste" of King James I against it. The enormous popularity of coffee drinking in the seventeenth century had even more important social effects. Coffee houses or "cafes" sprang up all over Europe and rapidly evolved into leading institutions. They provided not merely an escape for the majority of men from a cribbed and monotonous home life, but they took others away from the sordid excesses of the tavern and the gambling-hell. In addition, they fostered a sharpening of wits and promoted more polished manners, especially inasmuch as they became favorite rendezvous for the literary lions of the time. If we can believe the testimony of English historians, there was scarcely a social or political enterprise which did not have its intimate connections with the establishments where coffee was sold. Some, indeed, were the rallying places of rival factions, which may in time have evolved into political parties. In London, according to Macaulay,

Effects of the coffee and tobacco habits

[7] The word "nicotian" or "nicotine" is derived from Jean Nicot, the French ambassador to Portugal who introduced the tobacco plant into France.

"There were coffee houses where the first medical men might be consulted. . . . There were Puritan coffee houses where no oath was heard and where lank-haired men discussed election and reprobation through their noses; Jew coffee houses where dark-eyed money-changers from Venice and Amsterdam greeted each other; and Popish coffee houses where, as good Protestants believed, Jesuits planned, over their cups, another great fire, and cast silver bullets to shoot the king." [8]

The persistence of superstitions

Despite its remarkable attainments in intellect and the arts, the period was by no means free from crass superstitions. Even at the peak of the Renaissance numerous quaint and pernicious delusions continued to be accepted as valid truths. The illiterate masses clung to their beliefs in goblins, satyrs, and wizards and to their fear of the devil, whose malevolence was assumed to be the cause of diseases, famine, storms, and insanity. But superstition was not harbored alone in the minds of the ignorant. The famous astronomer, Johann Kepler, believed in astrology and depended upon the writing of almanacs, with predictions of the future according to signs and wonders in the heavens, as his chief source of income. Not only did Sir Francis Bacon accept the current superstition of astrology, but he also contributed his endorsement of the witchcraft delusion. Eventually the enlightenment of the Renaissance might have eliminated most of the harmful superstitions, if a reaction had not set in during the Reformation. The emphasis of the Reformers upon faith, their contempt for reason and science, and their incessant harping on the wiles of the devil fostered an attitude of mind decidedly favorable to prejudice and error. Besides, the furor of hate stirred up by religious controversy made it almost impossible for the average man to view his social and individual problems in a calm and intelligent spirit.

The witch-craft delusion

The worst of all the superstitions that flourished in this period was unquestionably the witchcraft delusion. Belief in witchcraft was by no means unknown in the Middle Ages or even in the early Renaissance, but it never reached the proportions of a dangerous madness until after the beginning of the Protestant Revolt. And it is a significant fact that the persecutions attained their most virulent form in the very countries where religious conflict raged the fiercest; that is, in Germany and France. The witchcraft superstition was a direct outgrowth of the belief in Satan which obsessed the minds of so many of the Reformers. Luther maintained that he often talked with the Evil One and sometimes put him to rout after a session of argument by calling him unprintable names.[9] Calvin insisted that the Pope never acted except on the advice of his patron the devil. In general, the tendency of each camp of theologians was

---

[8] Thomas Babington Macaulay, *History of England*, Vol. I, p. 335.

484
[9] Preserved Smith, *The Age of the Reformation*, p. 653.

Sarah Siddons as the Tragic Muse, Sir Joshua Reynolds (1723–1792). Mrs. Siddons, a famous actress of the XVIII cent., is here portrayed as the Queen of Tragedy, in accordance with Reynolds' habit of depicting wealthy patrons in impressive classical poses. (Huntington Library)

The Blue Boy, Thomas Gainsborough (1727–1788). Though the costume suggests the romantic ideal of Prince Charming, the face is a penetrating study of the moodiness and uncertainty of adolescence. (Huntington Library)

Le Mezzetin, Antoine Watteau (1684–1721). Mezzetin was a popular character in Italian comedy who was much liked in France. Watteau enjoyed portraying the make-believe world of the court with its festivals and formalized elegance. (MMA)

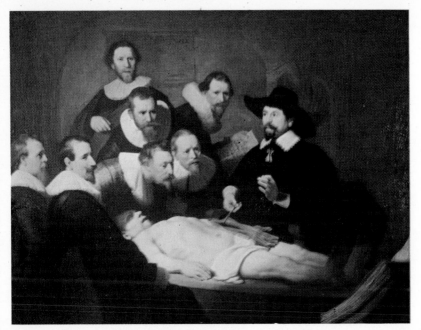

The Anatomy Lesson, Rembrandt van Rijn (1606–1669). Rembrandt scorned the classical themes of most of his contemporaries and turned to character analysis and the portrayal of life. (Mauritshuis, The Hague)

Execution of the Rioters, Francisco Goya (1746–1828). Unlike most artists of his time, Goya dealt unflinchingly with suffering, violence, fear, and death. Depicted here is the execution of Spanish rebels by Napoleon's soldiers in 1808. This harshness caused the rebellion to spread over the whole peninsula. (Prado)

to ascribe all the victories of their opponents to the uncanny powers of the Prince of Darkness. With such superstitions prevailing among religious leaders, it is not strange that the mass of their followers should have harbored bizarre and hideous notions. The belief grew that the devil was really more powerful than God, and that no man's life or soul was safe from destruction. It was assumed that Satan not only tempted mortals to sin, but actually forced them to sin by sending his minions in human form to seduce men and women in their sleep. This was the height of his malevolence, for it jeopardized chances of salvation.

According to the definition of the theologians, witchcraft consisted in selling one's soul to the devil in return for supernatural powers. It was believed that a woman who had concluded such a bargain was thereby enabled to work all manner of spiteful magic against her neighbors—to cause their cattle to sicken and die, their crops to fail, or their children to fall into the fire. But the most valuable gifts bestowed by Satan were the power to blind husbands to their wives' misconduct or to cause women to give birth to idiotic or deformed infants. It is commonly assumed that the so-called witches were toothless old hags whose cranky habits and venomous tongues had made them objects of suspicion and dread to all who knew them. Undoubtedly a good many of the victims of the Salem trials in Massachusetts in 1692 did actually belong to this class. However, the writers on the Continent of Europe generally imagined the witch to be a "fair and wicked young woman," and a large percentage of those put to death in Germany and France were adolescent girls and matrons not yet thirty.[10]

How witch-craft was defined

The earliest persecutions for witchcraft were those resulting from the crusades launched against heretics by the Papal Inquisition in the thirteenth century. With the growth of intolerance of heresy it was probably inevitable that members of sects like the Albigenses should be accused of trafficking with the devil. But the amount of persecution in this period was comparatively small. A second campaign against witches was initiated by Pope Innocent VIII in 1484, who instructed his inquisitors to use torture in procuring convictions. But, as we have already seen, it was not until after the beginning of the Protestant Revolution that witchcraft persecution became a mad hysteria. Luther himself provided some of the impetus by recommending that witches should be put to death with fewer considerations of mercy than were shown to ordinary criminals. Other Reformers quickly followed Luther's example. Under Calvin's administration in Geneva thirty-four women were burned or quartered for the alleged crime in 1545.[11] From this time on the persecutions spread like a pestilence. Women, young girls, and even mere children were tortured by driving needles under their

The persecutions for witchcraft

[10] Preserved Smith, *A History of Modern Culture*, Vol. I, pp. 436–37.
[11] Preserved Smith, *The Age of the Reformation*, p. 656.

nails, roasting their feet in the fire, or crushing their legs under heavy weights until the marrow spurted from their bones, in order to force them to confess filthy orgies with demons. To what extent the persecutions were due to sheer sadism or to the greed of magistrates, who were sometimes permitted to confiscate the property of those convicted, is impossible to say. Certainly there were few people who did not believe that the burning of witches was justifiable. One of the most zealous defenders of the trials was the political philosopher, Jean Bodin. As late as the eighteenth century John Wesley declared that to give up the belief in witchcraft was to give up the Bible.

The peak of the witchcraft persecutions

The witchcraft persecutions reached their peak during the later years of the sixteenth century. The number of victims will never be known, but it was certainly not fewer than 30,000. We read of cities in Germany in which as many as 900 were put to death in a single year, and of whole villages in which practically no women were left alive.

The end of the witchcraft persecutions

After 1600 the mania gradually subsided on the Continent of Europe, though it continued for some years longer in England. The reasons for the decline are not far to seek. In some measure it was due to a recovery of sanity by the people themselves, particularly as the fogs of suspicion and hate produced by religious warfare gradually lifted. But the principal causes were the revival of reason and the influence of scientists and skeptical philosophers. At the very zenith of the witch-burning frenzy certain lawyers began to have doubts as to the value of the evidence admitted at the trials. In 1584 an English jurist by the name of Reginald Scott published a book condemning the belief in witchcraft as irrational and asserting that most of the lurid crimes confessed by accused women were mere figments of disordered minds. Such eminent scientists as Pierre Gassendi (1592–1655) and William Harvey also denounced the persecutions. But the most effective protest of all came from the pen of Montaigne. This distinguished French skeptic directed the shafts of his most powerful ridicule against the preposterous nonsense of the sorcery trials and the cruelty of men like Bodin who would have witches killed on mere suspicion.

The age not one of universal depravity

From what has been said in preceding paragraphs the conclusion must not be drawn that the period of the Renaissance, the Reformation, and the Commercial Revolution was an age of universal depravity. Of course, there were numerous individuals as urbane and tolerant as any who lived in less boisterous times. Such a one was Sir Philip Sidney, who, mortally wounded and tortured with thirst on the battlefield, handed his cup of water to a humble soldier with the simple words, "Thy need is greater than mine." It must be remembered also that this was the age of Sir Thomas More and Erasmus, who were at least as civilized as the majority of men historians have chosen to honor. The enormous popularity of

Castiglione's *Book of the Courtier* may likewise be taken to indicate
that the period was not hopelessly barbarous. This treatise, which
ran through more than a hundred editions, set forth the ideal of a
knight who was not merely brave in battle and accomplished in the
social graces, but courteous, unaffected, and just. In spite of all
this, the dolorous fact remains that for large numbers of men ethics
had lost their true meaning. The cardinal aims were now gratification of self and victory in the struggle to make the whole world
conform to one's own set of dogmas. Perhaps these were inevitable
accompaniments of the chaotic transition from the impersonal society of the Middle Ages.

Selected Readings

Baker, J. N. L., *A History of Geographical Discovery and Exploration*,
New York, 1937

Brebner, John, *The Explorers of North America*, New York, 1933

Burckhardt, Jacob, *The Civilization of the Renaissance in Italy*, London,
1890

Cole, C. W., *Colbert and a Century of French Mercantilism*, New York,
1939

Heaton, Herbert, *Economic History of Europe*, New York, 1936

Heckscher, E. F., *Mercantilism*, New York, 1935, 2 vols.

Hobson, J. A., *The Evolution of Modern Capitalism*, New York, 1926

Morison, S. E., *Admiral of the Ocean Sea: A Life of Christopher Columbus*, Boston, 1942, 2 vols.

Ogg, F. A., and Sharp, W. R., *Economic Development of Modern Europe*,
New York, 1929

Packard, L. B., *The Commercial Revolution*, New York, 1927

Randall, J. H., Jr., *The Making of the Modern Mind*, New York, 1926,
Chs. VI–X

Sée, Henri, *Modern Capitalism: Its Origin and Evolution*, London, 1928

Smith, Preserved, *The Age of the Reformation*, New York, 1920

———, *A History of Modern Culture*, New York, 1930, Vol. I

Tawney, R. H., *Religion and the Rise of Capitalism*, New York, 1926

Thompson, J. W., *Economic and Social History of Europe in the Later
Middle Ages*, New York, 1931

Source Materials

More, Sir Thomas, *Utopia*, Part I, pp. 175–78, the Enclosure Movement

Mun, Thomas, *England's Treasure by Foreign Trade*, Chs. I–IV, XX, XXI

Richter, J. P., *The Literary Works of Leonardo da Vinci*, Vol. II, pp.
304–5, Leonardo da Vinci on Witchcraft

The Age of Absolutism
(1485-1789)

The rise of the new absolutism

It becomes necessary now to go back and attempt to analyze the major political developments which accompanied the birth of modern civilization. During the fourteenth and fifteenth centuries the decentralized feudal regime of the Middle Ages broke down and was gradually replaced by dynastic states with governments of absolute power. For this there were numerous causes, some of which have already been discussed.[1] The position of the nobles was weakened by the growth of an urban economy, by the decay of the manorial system, and by the effects of the Crusades, the Black Death, and the Hundred Years' War. But these factors would not necessarily have laid the foundations for absolute monarchy. They might just as conceivably have resulted in chaos or in the democratic rule of the masses. We must therefore look for other causes to account for the rise of despotic governments. By far the most significant of these was the Commercial Revolution. The founding of colonial empires and the pursuit of mercantilist policies brought the kings an abundance of treasure which they could use for equipping armies and fleets and for an extension of political power. In addition, the expansion of business accentuated the need for strong government. The merchants, bankers, and manufacturers of the fifteenth century were not yet in a position to stand on their own feet. Not only was trade in some danger from the attacks of pirates and brigands, but infant industries needed the nourishment which a powerful state alone could give. As a consequence, the middle class of this early period gave almost unlimited support to the ambitions of despotic rulers. Finally, the Protestant Revolution contributed not a little to

[1] See especially the paragraphs on the decline of feudalism in the chapter on The Civilization of the Feudal Age: Political and Economic Institutions.

the growth of royal omnipotence. It broke the unity of the Christian church, abolished papal overlordship over secular rulers, fostered nationalism, revived the doctrine of the Apostle Paul that "the powers that be are ordained of God," and encouraged the kings of northern Europe to extend their authority over religious as well as over civil affairs. As a result of these several factors the barriers against absolute government were largely removed.

1. The Growth and Decay of Absolute Government in England

The real founders of despotic government in England were the Tudors. The first of the kings of this line, Henry VII, came to the throne in 1485 at the end of the Wars of the Roses, in which rival factions of nobles had fought each other to the point of exhaustion. So great was the disgust on account of the turmoil of these wars that many of the citizens welcomed the establishment of absolute monarchy as an alternative to anarchy. The middle class, especially, desired the protection of consolidated government. This factor more than anything else accounts for the remarkable success of the Tudors in regulating the consciences of their subjects and in binding the nation to their will. It should be added that the most celebrated members of the dynasty, Henry VIII (1509–1547) and Elizabeth I

Absolutism in England founded by the Tudor monarchs

Queen Elizabeth I (1533–1603). In this regal portrait the queen is shown armed with the two symbols of power and justice, the scepter and the orb. A touch of cynicism seems to be revealed in her face.

(1558–1603), gained some of their power through shrewdly maintaining a semblance of popular government. When they desired to enact measures of doubtful popularity, they regularly went through the formality of obtaining parliamentary approval. Or when they wanted more money, they manipulated procedure in such a way as to make the appropriations appear to be voluntary grants by the representatives of the people. But the legislative branch of the government under these sovereigns was little more than a rubber stamp. They convoked Parliament irregularly and limited its sessions to very brief periods;[2] they interfered with elections and packed the two houses with their own favorites; and they cajoled, flattered, or bullied the members as the case might require in order to obtain their support.

James I estab-lishes divine-right monarchy

In 1603 Elizabeth I, the last of the Tudors, died, leaving no direct descendants. Her nearest relative was her cousin, King James VI of Scotland, who now became the sovereign of both England and Scotland under the name of James I. His accession marks the beginning of the troubled history of the Stuarts, the last of the absolute dynasties in England. A curious mixture of stubbornness, vanity, and erudition, King James was appropriately called by Henry IV of France "the wisest fool in Christendom." Though he loved to have his courtiers flatter him as the English Solomon, he did not even have sense enough to emulate his Tudor predecessors in being satisfied with the substance of absolute power; he insisted upon the theory as well. From France he appropriated the doctrine of the divine right of kings, contending that "as it is atheism and blasphemy to dispute what God can do, so it is presumption and high contempt in a subject to dispute what a king can do." In his speech to Parliament in 1609, he declared that "Kings are justly called gods, for they exercise a manner of resemblance of Divine power upon earth."[3]

The high-handed policies of James I

That such ridiculous pretensions to divine authority would arouse opposition among the English people was a result which even James himself should have been able to foresee. Despite the clever machinations of the Tudor sovereigns and the desire of the middle class for stable government, England still had traditions of liberty which could not be ignored. The feudal ideal of limited government expressed in Magna Charta had never been entirely destroyed. Moreover, the policies of the new king were of such a character as to antagonize even some of his most conservative subjects. He insisted upon supplementing his income by modes of taxation which had never been sanctioned by Parliament; and when the leaders of that body remonstrated, he angrily tore up their protests and dissolved the two houses. He interfered with the freedom of business by granting monopolies and extravagant privileges to favored companies. He conducted foreign relations in disregard for the economic interests of some of the most powerful citizens. Ever since the days of Hawkins and Drake, English merchants had been ambitious to destroy the commercial empire of Spain. They openly desired a renewal of the war, begun during Elizabeth's reign, for

[2] During Elizabeth's reign it was in session on the average only three or four weeks out of the year.

[3] Quoted by R. G. Gettell, *History of Political Thought*, p. 201.

that purpose. But James made peace with Spain and entered into negotiations for the marriage of his son to the daughter of the Spanish king. When the Spanish princess rejected him because of his unwillingness to turn Catholic, the English people went wild with joy. Their rejoicing, however, was premature, for a short time later, in accordance with his father's wishes, the prince married the sister of the king of France.

It was not marriage alliances alone that involved King James in religious troubles. The Elizabethan Compromise, which brought the Reformation in England to a close, had not been satisfactory to the more radical Protestants. They believed that it did not depart widely enough from the forms and doctrines of the Roman Church. During the reign of Queen Mary many of them had been in exile in France and had come under the influence of Calvinism. When Elizabeth's compromise policy took shape, they denounced it as representing too great a concession to Catholicism. Gradually they came to be called Puritans from their desire to "purify" the Anglican church of all traces of "Popish" ritual and observances. In addition, they preached an ascetic morality and condemned the episcopal system of church government. However, they did not form a united group. One faction believed that it could transform the Anglican church by working within that organization. The other preferred to withdraw from the Anglican fold and establish separate congregations where they could worship as they pleased. The members of this latter group came to be designated Separatists. They achieved fame in American history as the so-called Pilgrims, who founded Plymouth Colony.

Religious dissension during the reign of James I

Any brand or faction of Puritans was anathema to King James. Though not much interested in theology, he distrusted any religion which did not fit in with his own ideas of relations between church and state. In his estimation the Puritans, by repudiating the episcopal system of church government, were threatening to pull down one of the chief pillars of monarchy itself. Refusal to submit to the authority of bishops appointed by the king was identical in his mind with disloyalty to the sovereign. For this reason he regarded the Puritans as the equivalent of traitors and threatened to "harry them out of the land." He showed little more wisdom or discretion in his dealings with the Catholics. For the most part, he favored them, though he could not resist the temptation to levy fines upon them from time to time for violating the severe code which came down from the Reformation. In 1605 a group of fanatical adherents of the Roman faith organized the Gunpowder Plot. They planned to blow up the Parliament building while the king and the legislators were assembled in it, and in the resulting confusion seize control of the government. The plot was discovered, and Parliament enacted even more stringent laws against the Catholics. James, however, allowed the measures to go unenforced. Needless to say,

Relations with Puritans and Catholics

491

*The revolt
of the judiciary*

his persistent leniency antagonized his Protestant subjects and made him more unpopular than ever.

From 1611 to 1621 King James ruled virtually without Parliament. But this did not mean that his troubles were over. In 1613 the rights of the people found a new champion when Sir Edward Coke was appointed Chief Justice. Coke was no democrat, but he did have a profound reverence for the common law and for the basic liberties inferred from Magna Charta. Moreover, he was a stanch defender of the privileged position of lawyers and judges. When the king insisted that he also had the faculty of reason and could interpret the law as well as the judges, Coke reminded him that he was not learned in the law, and that causes which concerned the lives and fortunes of his subjects were not to be decided by natural reason but only on the basis of long study and experience. Furthermore, the Chief Justice developed a rudimentary concept of judicial review. In the celebrated Dr. Bonham's case, he held that "when an act of Parliament is against common right and reason, or repugnant, or impossible to be performed, the common law will control it, and adjudge such act to be void." [4] There is evidence that this opinion was highly regarded in colonial America, and that it was one of the factors which later gave rise to the idea that the Supreme Court of the United States has the authority to nullify laws of Congress which conflict with the Constitution.

*Charles I and
the Petition of
Right*

The first of the Stuart kings died in 1625 and was succeeded by his son as Charles I. The new monarch was more regal in appearance than his father, but he held the same inflated notions of royal power. As a consequence he was soon in hot water with the Puritans and the leaders of the parliamentary opposition. As in the case of his father, the conflict was precipitated by questions of taxation. Soon after his accession to the throne Charles became involved in a war with France. His need for revenue was desperate. When Parliament refused to make more than the customary grants, he resorted to forced loans from his subjects, punishing those who failed to comply by quartering soldiers upon them or throwing them into prison without a trial. The upshot of this tyranny was the famous Petition of Right, which Charles was compelled by the leaders of Parliament to agree to in 1628. This document, which ranks with Magna Charta as the second great charter of English liberties, declared all taxes not voted by Parliament illegal. It condemned also the quartering of soldiers in private houses and prohibited arbitrary imprisonment and the establishment of martial law in time of peace.

*The continued
tyranny of
Charles I*

But acceptance of the Petition of Right did not end the conflict. Charles soon resumed his old tricks of raising money by various irregular means. He revived obsolete feudal laws and collected fines from all who violated them. He compelled rich burghers to apply for knighthood and then charged them high fees for their titles.

[4] Quoted by George H. Sabine, *A History of Political Theory*, p. 452.

He sold monopolies at exorbitant rates and admonished his judges to increase the fines in criminal cases. But the most unpopular of all his expedients for raising revenue was his collection of ship money. Under an ancient custom the English seaboard towns had been required to contribute ships for the royal navy. Since the needs of the fleet were now provided for in other ways, Charles maintained that the towns should contribute money; and he proceeded to apply the new tax not merely to the coastal cities but to the inland counties as well. The levies of ship money were particularly irritating to the middle class and served to crystallize the opposition of that group to monarchical tyranny. Many refused to pay, and the king's attorney-general finally decided to prosecute. A wealthy squire by the name of John Hampden was haled into court in a test case. When convicted by a vote of seven to five, he acquired a sort of martyrdom. For years he was venerated by the middle class as a symbol of resistance to royal autocracy.

Like his blundering father before him, Charles also aroused the antagonism of the Calvinists. He appointed as Archbishop of Canterbury a clergyman by the name of William Laud, whose sympathies were decidedly high-Anglican. He outraged the Sabbatarianism of the Puritans by authorizing public games on Sunday. Worse still, he attempted to impose the episcopal system of church government upon the Scottish Presbyterians, who were even more radical Calvinists than the Puritans. The result was an armed rebellion by his northern subjects.

Conflict with the Calvinists

In order to get money to punish the Scots for their resistance, Charles was finally compelled in 1640 to summon Parliament, after more than eleven years of autocratic rule. By convoking the legislative body into session he unwittingly placed himself in the power of his opponents. Knowing full well that the king was helpless without money, the leaders of the House of Commons determined to take the government of the country into their own hands. They abolished ship money and the special tribunals which had been used as agencies of tyranny. They impeached and sent to the Tower the king's chief subordinates, Archbishop Laud and the Earl of Strafford. They enacted a law forbidding the monarch to dissolve Parliament and requiring sessions at least every three years. Charles replied to these invasions of his prerogative by a show of force. He marched with his guard into the House of Commons and attempted to arrest five of its leaders. All of them escaped, but the issue was now sharply drawn between king and Parliament, and an open conflict could no longer be averted. Both sides collected troops and prepared for an appeal to the sword.

The outbreak of civil war

These events ushered in a period of civil strife, which lasted from 1642 to 1649. It was a struggle at once political, economic, and religious. Arrayed on the side of the king were most of the chief nobles and landowners, the Catholics, and the stanch Anglicans. The fol-

Cavaliers and Roundheads

493

lowers of Parliament included, in general, the small landholders, tradesmen, and manufacturers. The majority were Puritans and Presbyterians. The members of the king's party were commonly known by the aristocratic name of Cavaliers. Their opponents, who cut their hair short in contempt for the fashionable custom of wearing curls, were called in derision Roundheads. At first the party of the royalists, having obvious advantages of military experience, won most of the victories. In 1644, however, the parliamentary army was reorganized, and soon afterward the fortunes of battle shifted. The Cavalier forces were badly beaten at Marston Moor and at Naseby, and in 1646 the king was compelled to surrender. The struggle would now have ended had not a quarrel developed within the parliamentary party. The majority of its members, who were now Presbyterians, were ready to restore Charles to the throne as a limited monarch under an arrangement whereby the Presbyterian faith would be imposed upon England as the state religion. But a radical minority of Puritans, made up principally of Separatists but now more commonly known as Independents, distrusted Charles and insisted upon religious toleration for themselves and all other Protestants. Their leader was Oliver Cromwell, who had risen to command of the Roundhead army. Taking advantage of the dissension within the ranks of his opponents, Charles renewed the war in 1648 but after a brief campaign was forced to concede that his cause was hopeless.

The defeat and execution of the king

The second defeat of the king gave an indisputable mastery of the situation to the Independents. Cromwell and his friends now resolved to put an end to "that man of blood," the Stuart monarch, and remodel the political system in accordance with their own desires. They conducted a purge of the legislative body by military force, ejecting 143 Presbyterians from the House of Commons; and then with the "Rump Parliament" that remained—numbering about sixty members—they proceeded to eliminate the monarchy. An act was passed redefining treason so as to apply to the offenses of the king. Next a special High Court of Justice was established, and Charles was brought to trial before it. His conviction was a mere matter of form. On January 30, 1649, he was beheaded in front of his palace of Whitehall. A short time later the House of Lords was abolished, and England became an oligarchic republic. The first stage in the so-called Puritan Revolution was now completed.

The Commonwealth and Protectorate

The work of organizing the new state, which was given the name of the Commonwealth, was entirely in the hands of the Independents. Since the Rump Parliament continued as the legislative body, the really fundamental change was in the nature of the executive. In place of the king there was set up a Council of State composed of forty-one members. Cromwell, with the army at his back, soon came to dominate both of these bodies. However, as time went on he became exasperated by the attempts of the legislators to per-

The Trial of Charles I, King of Great Britain and Ireland, 1625–1649. His armies defeated by the forces of Cromwell and himself a prisoner, Charles was tried by a special court in Westminster Hall and convicted of treason "by levying war against the parliament and kingdom of England." Soon afterward he was beheaded. His dignity in his last hours fitted Shakespeare's lines: "Nothing in his Life became him, like the leaving it."

Oliver Cromwell (1599–1658). Except for the military garb, this portrait might well be that of a lawyer, merchant, or man of letters. It shows nothing of the sternness or implacability commonly associated with the English dictator.

petuate themselves in power and to profit from confiscation of the wealth of their opponents. Accordingly, in 1653, he marched a detachment of troops into the Rump and ordered the members to disperse, informing them that the Lord Jehovah had no further use for their services. This action was followed by the establishment of a virtual dictatorship under a constitution drafted by officers of the army. Called the Instrument of Government, it was the nearest approach to a written constitution Britain has ever had. Extensive powers were given to Cromwell as Lord Protector for life, and his office was made hereditary. At first a Parliament exercised limited authority in making laws and levying taxes, but in 1655 its members were abruptly dismissed by the Lord Protector. Thereafter the government was but a thinly disguised autocracy. Cromwell now wielded a sovereignty even more despotic than any the Stuart monarchs would have dared to claim. In declaring his authority to be from God he even revived what practically amounted to the divine right of kings.

That Cromwell's regime would have its difficulties was certainly to be expected, since it rested upon the support of only a small minority of the British nation. He was opposed not only by royalists

495

Cromwell's opponents

and Anglicans but by various dissenters more radical than he. Like all upheavals of a similar character, the Puritan Revolution tended to move farther and farther in an extremist direction. Many of the Puritans became Levellers, who derived their name from their advocacy of equal political rights and privileges for all classes. Expressly disclaiming any intention of equalizing property, they confined their radicalism to the political sphere. They insisted that sovereignty inheres in the people and that government should rest upon the consent of the governed. Long in advance of any other party, they demanded a written constitution, universal manhood suffrage, and the supremacy of Parliament. The Levellers were especially powerful in the army and through it exerted some influence upon the government. Still farther to the left were the Diggers, so called from their attempt to seize and cultivate unenclosed common land and distribute the produce to the poor. Though in common with the Levellers the Diggers appealed to the law of nature as a source of rights, they were more interested in economic than in political equality. They espoused a kind of primitive communism based upon the idea that the land is the "common treasury" of all. Every able-bodied man would be required to work at productive labor, and all persons would be permitted to draw from the common fund of wealth produced in proportion to their needs. The church would be transformed into an educational institution and the clergy would become schoolmasters, giving instruction every seventh day in public affairs, history, and the arts and sciences. "To know the secrets of nature is to know the works of God" was one of the Digger mottoes.

Miscellaneous troubles

But Cromwell's difficulties emanated from numerous sources. Before the Commonwealth had been in existence a year, trouble brewed in Ireland and Scotland. Ireland had been a hotbed of rebellion since 1641, and the dissatisfied elements now refused to recognize Cromwell's government. In Scotland Prince Charles, the oldest son of Charles I, had been proclaimed king, and royalists throughout the British Isles were making his cause their own. Within a few months Cromwell suppressed the revolt of the Irish, declaring upon his return to London in 1650 that the frightful butcheries he had perpetrated at Drogheda and Wexford were "the righteous judgment of God upon the barbarous wretches" who had rebelled. Next he routed the Scottish army and forced Prince Charles to seek refuge on the Continent. Cromwell also had his troubles with religious factions. His policy of granting toleration to all except Anglicans and Catholics continued to be opposed by the majority of the Puritans and the Presbyterians, both of whom desired a state church. That he succeeded in maintaining his regime in power as long as he did was due mainly to three factors: (1) the strength of the army; (2) the commercial advantages he bestowed upon the middle class, especially through the Navigation Act of 1651 and the treaties with

Holland and France; and (3) his victories in wars with the Spaniards and Dutch.

In September, 1658, the stout-hearted Protector died. He was succeeded by his well-meaning but irresolute son Richard, who managed to hold office only until May of the following year. Perhaps even a man of much sterner fiber would also have failed eventually, for the country had grown tired of the austerities of Calvinist rule. Neither the Commonwealth nor the Protectorate had ever had the support of a majority of the English nation. Royalists regarded the Independents as usurpers. Republicans hated the disguised monarchy which Oliver Cromwell had set up. Catholics and Anglicans resented the branding of their acts of worship as criminal offenses. Even some members of the middle class gradually came to suspect that Cromwell's war with Spain had done more harm than good by endangering English commerce with the West Indies. For these and similar reasons there was general rejoicing when in 1660 a newly elected Parliament proclaimed Prince Charles king and invited him to return to England and occupy the throne of his father. The new king had gained a reputation for joyous living and easy morality, and his accession was hailed as a welcome relief from the somber rule of soldiers and zealots. Besides, he pledged himself not to reign as a despot, but to respect Parliament and to observe Magna Charta and the Petition of Right; for he admitted that he was not anxious to "resume his travels." England now entered upon a period known as the Restoration, covered by the reigns of Charles II (1660–1685) and his brother James II (1685–1688). Despite its auspicious beginning, many of the old problems had not really been solved but were simply concealed by the fond belief that the nation had regained its former stability.

Downfall of the Protectorate and restoration of the Stuarts

Toward the end of the seventeenth century England went through a second political upheaval, the so-called Glorious Revolution of 1688–1689. Several of the causes were grounded in the policies of Charles II. That amiable sovereign was extravagant and lazy but determined on occasion to let the country know whose word was law. His strongly pro-Catholic attitude aroused the fears of patriotic Englishmen that their nation might once again be brought into subservience to Rome. Worse still, he showed a disposition, in spite of earlier pledges, to defy the authority of Parliament. In 1672 he suspended the laws against Catholics and other Dissenters and nine years later resolved to dispense with the legislative branch entirely. The policies of Charles II were continued in more insolent form by his brother, who succeeded him in 1685. King James II was an avowed Catholic and seemed bent upon making that faith the established religion of England. He openly violated an act of Parliament requiring that all holders of public office should adhere to the Anglican church, and proceeded to fill important positions in the army and the civil service with his Romanist followers. He continued

The failure of the Puritan Revolution paves the way for the Glorious Revolution of 1688–1689

his brother's practice of exempting Catholics from the disabilities imposed upon them by Parliament, even going so far as to demand that the Anglican bishops should read his decrees for this purpose in their churches. As long as his opponents could expect that James II would be succeeded by one of his two Protestant daughters, they were inclined to tolerate his arbitrary rule, lest the country be plunged again into civil war. But when the king acquired a son by his second wife, who was a Catholic, the die of revolution was cast. It was feared that the young prince would be inoculated with his father's doctrines, and that, as a consequence, England would be fettered with the shackles of despotic and papist rule for an indefinite time to come. To forestall such a result it seemed necessary to depose the king.

*Results
of the Glorious
Revolution*

The "Glorious Revolution" of 1688–1689 was an entirely bloodless affair. A group of politicians from both the upper and middle classes secretly invited Prince William of Orange and his wife Mary, the elder daughter of James II, to become joint rulers of England.[5] William crossed over from Holland with an army and occupied London without firing a shot. Deserted even by those whom he had counted as loyal supporters, King James took refuge in France. The English throne was now declared vacant by Parliament and the crown presented to the new sovereigns. But their enthronement did not complete the revolution. Throughout the year 1689 Parliament passed numerous laws designed to safeguard the rights of Englishmen and to protect its own power from monarchical invasion. First came an act requiring that appropriations should be made for one year only. Next the Toleration Act was passed, granting religious liberty to all Christians except Catholics and Unitarians. Finally, on the sixteenth of December the famous Bill of Rights was enacted into law. It provided for trial by jury and affirmed the right of Englishmen to petition the government for a redress of grievances. It condemned excessive bail, cruel punishments, and exorbitant fines. And it forbade the king to suspend laws or to levy taxes without the consent of Parliament. More sweeping in its provisions than the Petition of Right of 1628, it was backed by a Parliament which now had the power to see that it was obeyed.

*Significance
of the
Glorious
Revolution*

The significance of the revolution of 1688–1689 would be almost impossible to exaggerate. Since it marked the final triumph of Parliament over the king, it therefore spelled the doom of absolute monarchy in England. Never again was any crowned head in Britain able to defy the legislative branch of the government as the Stuart monarchs had done—not even George III, celebrated in American colonial legend as "that royal British brute." The revolution also

---

[5] There is evidence that William himself was a party to the secrets of the dissatisfied Englishmen, and he may even have inspired the invitation. Threatened with war by the king of France, he could make very good use of the resources and military power of England.

dealt the *coup de grâce* to the theory of the divine right of kings.
It would have been impossible for William and Mary to have denied
the fact that they received their crowns from Parliament. And the
authority of Parliament to determine who should be king was made
more emphatic by the passage of the Act of Settlement in 1701. This
law provided that upon the death of the heiress-presumptive Anne,
younger sister of Mary, the crown should go to the Electress Sophia
of Hanover or to the eldest of her heirs who might be Protestant.[6]
There were some forty men or women with a better claim to the
throne than Sophia, but all were eliminated arbitrarily by Parliament on the ground of their being Catholics. Finally, the Glorious
Revolution contributed much to the American and French revolutions at the end of the eighteenth century. The example of the
English in overthrowing absolute rule was a powerful inspiration
to the opponents of despotism elsewhere. It was the British revolutionary ideal of limited government which furnished the substance
of the political theory of Voltaire, Jefferson, and Paine. And a considerable portion of the English Bill of Rights was incorporated in
the French Declaration of the Rights of Man in 1789 and in the
first ten amendments to the American Constitution.

2. *Absolute Monarchy in France and Spain*

The growth of royal despotism in France was the product of a
gradual evolution. Some of its antecedents went back to the reigns
of Philip Augustus, Louis IX, and Philip IV in the thirteenth and   *The origins*
fourteenth centuries. These kings solidified royal power by hiring   *of absolutism in*
mercenary soldiers, substituting national taxation for feudal dues,   *France*
arrogating to themselves the power to administer justice, and restricting the authority of the Pope to regulate ecclesiastical affairs
in their kingdom. The Hundred Years' War (1337–1453) produced
an even further accretion of power for the kings of France. They
were now able to introduce new forms of taxation, to maintain
a huge standing army, and to abolish the sovereignty of the feudal
nobles. The members of this latter class were gradually reduced
to the level of courtiers, dependent mainly upon the monarch for
their titles and prestige.

The trend toward absolutism was interrupted during the sixteenth
century when France was involved in war with Spain and torn
by a bloody struggle between Catholics and Huguenots at home.   *Henry IV*
Ambitious nobles took advantage of the confusion to assert their   *and the Duke of*
power and contested the succession to the throne. Peace was restored *Sully*
to the distracted kingdom in 1593 by Henry of Navarre, who four
years before had proclaimed himself king as Henry IV. Though at

---

[6] In this way the House of Hanover, the ruling dynasty until 1901, came
to the English throne. The first Hanoverian king was Sophia's son, George I
(1714–1727).

one time a leader of the Huguenot faction, Henry perceived that the nation would never accept him unless he renounced the Calvinist religion. Flippantly remarking that Paris was worth a Mass, he formally adopted the Catholic faith. In 1598 he issued the Edict of Nantes, guaranteeing freedom of conscience and political rights to all Protestants. With the grounds for religious controversy thus removed, Henry could turn his attention to rebuilding his kingdom. In this work he had the able assistance of his chief minister, the Duke of Sully. Grim, energetic, and penurious, Sully was a worthy forerunner of Colbert in the seventeenth century. For years the king and his faithful servant labored to repair the shattered fortunes of France. Sully devoted his efforts primarily to fiscal reform, so as to eliminate corruption and waste and bring more revenue into the royal treasury. He endeavored also to promote the prosperity of agriculture by draining swamps, improving devastated lands, subsidizing stock-raising, and opening up foreign markets for the products of the soil. The king gave most of his attention to fostering industry and commerce. He introduced the manufacture of silk into France, encouraged other industries by subsidies and monopolies, and made favorable commercial treaties with England and Spain. But Henry did not stop with economic reforms. He was deeply concerned with crushing the renascent power of the nobility, and so successful were his efforts in this direction that he restored the monarchy to the dominant position it had held at the end of the Hundred Years' War. He was active also in sponsoring the development of a colonial empire in America. During his reign the French acquired a foothold in Canada and began their exploration in the region of the Great Lakes and the Mississippi Valley. His rule was intelligent and benevolent but none the less despotic.

*Cardinal
Richelieu*

The reign of Henry IV was brought to an end by the dagger of a crazed fanatic in 1610. Since the new king, Louis XIII, was only nine years old, the country was ruled by his mother, Marie de Médicis, as regent. In 1624 Louis XIII, no longer under the regency, entrusted the management of his kingdom to a brilliant but domineering cleric, Cardinal Richelieu, whom he made his chief minister. Richelieu dedicated himself to two objectives: (1) to destroy all limitations upon the authority of the king; and (2) to make France the chief power in Europe. In the pursuit of these aims he disciplined both himself and the nation and allowed nothing to stand in his way. He ruthlessly suppressed the nobility, destroying its most dangerous members and rendering the others harmless by attaching them as pensioners to the royal court. Though he fostered education and patronized literature, he neglected the interests of commerce and allowed graft and extravagance to flourish in the government. His main constructive achievements were the creation of a postal service and the establishment of a system under which *intendants*, or agents of the king, took charge of local government. Both were conceived as devices for consolidating the nation under the control of the crown and thereby eradicating surviving traces of feudal authority.

Richelieu's ambitions were not limited to domestic affairs. To make France the most powerful nation in Europe required an aggressive diplomacy and eventual participation in war. France was still surrounded by what Henry IV had referred to as a "Hapsburg ring." On her southern border was Spain, ruled since 1516 by a branch of the Hapsburg family. To the north, less than a hundred miles from Paris, were the Spanish Netherlands. Other centers of Hapsburg power included Alsace, the Franche-Comté, Savoy, Genoa, and Milan, and still farther to the east the great Austrian Empire itself. Cardinal Richelieu eagerly awaited an opportunity to break this ring. As we shall see, he finally found it in the Thirty Years' War. Though engaged in suppressing Protestants at home, he did not hesitate to ally himself with Gustavus Adolphus, king of Sweden and leader of a coalition of Protestant states. Long before his death in 1642 the great cardinal-statesman had forged to the front as the most powerful individual in Europe.

Richelieu's foreign policy

Absolute monarchy in France attained its zenith during the reigns of the last three Bourbon kings before the Revolution.[7] The first of the monarchs of this series was Louis XIV (1643–1715), who epitomized the ideal of absolutism more completely than any other sovereign of his age. Proud, extravagant, and domineering, Louis entertained the most exalted notions of his position as king. Not only did he believe that he was commissioned by God to reign, but he regarded the welfare of the state as intimately bound up with his own personality. The famous phrase imputed to him, *l'état c'est moi* (I am the state), may not represent his exact words, but it expresses very clearly the conception he held of his own authority. He chose the sun as his official emblem to indicate his belief that the nation derived its glory and sustenance from him as the planets do theirs from the actual sun. Perhaps it can be said to the credit of Louis that no man worked harder at the "trade of a king." He gave personal supervision to every department and regarded his ministers as mere clerks with no duty but to obey his orders. There is evidence, however, that the country would have been better off if Louis had been less officious. He interfered with some of Colbert's plans for reform of taxation and wasted the resources that minister had struggled to save. The Sun King himself contributed but little to the improvement of government in France. In general, he followed the policies of Richelieu and Henry IV in consolidating national power at the expense of local officials and in reducing the nobles to mere parasites of the court. But any possible good he may have done was completely overshadowed by his

Louis XIV, the supreme incarnation of absolute rule

[7] The founder of the Bourbon dynasty was Henry IV, originally Henry of Bourbon, King of Navarre.

Portrait of Louis XIV, "Le Grand Monarque." Garbed in resplendent robes of ermine and velvet, with undergarments and stockings of silk.

Philip II, King of Spain, 1556–1598. The famous protruding chin and lower lip which were distinctive marks of the Hapsburgs are clearly evident in this figure.

foolish wars and his reactionary policy in religion. In 1685 he revoked the Edict of Nantes, which had granted freedom of conscience to the Huguenots. As a result, large numbers of his most intelligent and prosperous subjects fled from the country.

Louis XV and Louis XVI

Until the beginning of the Revolution in 1789 the form of the French government remained essentially as Louis XIV had left it. His successors, Louis XV (1715–1774) and Louis XVI (1774–1792), also professed to rule by divine right. But neither of these kings had the desire to emulate the Grand Monarch in his enthusiasm for work and his meticulous attention to the business of state. Louis XV was an indolent rake, who divided his time between gambling and hunting and dalliance with the ladies of his court. Problems of government bored him incredibly, and when obliged to preside at the council table he "opened his mouth, said little, and thought not at all." His grandson, who succeeded him, the ill-fated Louis XVI, was weak in character and mentally dull. Indifferent to politics, he amused himself by shooting deer from the palace window and playing at his hobbies of lock-making and masonry. On the day in 1789 when mobs stormed the Bastille, he wrote in his diary "Nothing." Yet both of these monarchs maintained a government which, if not more despotic, was at least more arbitrary than had ever been the case before. They permitted their ministers to imprison without a trial persons suspected of disloyalty; they suppressed the courts for refusing to approve their decrees; and they brought the country to the verge of bankruptcy by their costly wars and by their reckless extravagance for the benefit of mistresses and worthless favorites. If they had deliberately planned to make revolution inevitable, they could scarcely have succeeded better.

The growth of absolute monarchy in Spain was swifter and less interrupted than was true of its development in France. As late as the thirteenth century what is now Spain was divided into five parts. Four Christian kingdoms—Aragon, Castile, León, and Navarre—maintained a precarious existence in the north, while the southern half of the country was in the possession of the Moors. Before 1250 León had been absorbed by Castile, and some 200 years later further progress toward unification was accomplished by the marriage of Ferdinand of Aragon and Isabella of Castile. Though ruling nominally as independent monarchs, for all practical purposes they were sovereigns of a united Spain. Like their predecessors, they continued the crusade against the Moors, completing as their major achievement the conquest of Granada, last stronghold of Moslem power on the Iberian peninsula. The surviving Moors were expelled from the country, along with the Jews, for in the desperate struggle to drive out an alien invader all forms of non-Christian belief had come to be regarded as treason.

The rise of absolutism in Spain

Queen Isabella died in 1504, and King Ferdinand in 1516. Their entire kingdom was inherited by their daughter Joanna, who had married into the Hapsburg family. Her son succeeded to the throne of Spain as Charles I in 1516. Three years later he was elected Holy Roman Emperor as Charles V, thereby uniting Spain with Central Europe and southern Italy. Charles was interested not merely in the destinies of Spain but in the welfare of the church and in the politics of Europe as a whole. He dreamed that he might be the instrument of restoring the religious unity of Christendom, broken by the Protestant Revolt, and of making the empire over which he presided a worthy successor of Imperial Rome. Though successful in holding his disjointed domain together and in fighting off attempts of the French to conquer his Italian possessions and of the Turks to overrun Europe, he failed in the achievement of his larger objectives. At the age of fifty-six, overcome with a sense of discouragement and futility, he abdicated and retired into a monastery. The German princes chose his brother, Ferdinand I, to succeed him as Holy Roman Emperor. His Spanish and Italian possessions, including the colonies overseas, passed to his son, who became king as Philip II.

The empire of Charles V

Philip II came to the throne of Spain in the heyday of its glory. But he also witnessed, and to a considerable extent was responsible for, the beginning of its decline. His policies were mainly an intensification of those of his predecessors. He was narrow, despotic, and cruel. Determined to enforce a strict conformity in matters of religion upon all of his subjects, he is reputed to have boasted that he would gather faggots to burn his own son if the latter were

Greatness and decay under Philip II

guilty of heresy. Reference has already been made to the horrors of the Spanish Inquisition and of the war for suppression of the revolt in the Netherlands. Philip was equally shortsighted in his colonial policy. Natives were butchered or virtually enslaved. Their territories were greedily despoiled of their gold and silver, which were dragged off to Spain in the mistaken belief that this was the surest means of increasing the nation's wealth. No thought was given to the development of new industries in either the colonies or the mother country. Instead, the gold and silver were largely squandered in furthering Philip's military and political ambitions. It can be said, however, in the king's defense that he was following the accepted theories of the time. Doubtless most other monarchs with a like opportunity would have imitated his example. Philip II's crowning stupidity was probably his war against England. Angered by the attacks of English privateers upon Spanish commerce, and frustrated in his schemes to bring England back into the Catholic faith, he sent a great fleet in 1588, the "Invincible Armada," to

The destruction of the Armada

destroy Queen Elizabeth's navy. But Philip had little knowledge of either the new techniques of naval warfare or of the robust patriotism of the English. A combination of fighting seamanship and disastrous storms sent all but 50 of the 132 ships to the bottom of the Channel. Spain never recovered from the blow. Though a brilliant afterglow, exemplified in the work of the Renaissance artists and dramatists, continued for some years, the greatness of Spain as a nation was approaching its end.

3. Absolutism in Central and Eastern Europe

The other three countries where despotism flourished on its most grandiose scale were Prussia, Austria, and Russia. The founder of

The beginning of absolute monarchy in Prussia

absolute rule in Prussia was the Great Elector, Frederick William, a contemporary of Louis XIV. Not only was he the first member of the Hohenzollern family to acquire full sovereignty over Prussia, but he brought all three of his dominions—Prussia, Brandenburg, and Cleves—under centralized rule, abolishing their local Diets and merging their petty armies into a national military force. The work of the Great Elector was continued and extended by his grandson, known as Frederick William I (1713–1740), since he now had the title of *King* of Prussia.[8] This miserly monarch ruled over his people like a Hebrew patriarch, regulating their private conduct and attending personally to the correction of their shortcomings. His consuming passion was the army, which he more than doubled in size and drilled to a machinelike efficiency. He even sold the furniture in the palace to hire recruits for his famous regiment of Potsdam

[8] Originally the title was King *in* Prussia, probably for the reason that there was another Prussia, West Prussia, which still belonged to Poland.

The Defeat of the Spanish Armada, 1588. From an engraving by John Pine. The situation of the Armada, with some of its ships burning and others dashed on the rocks by a storm, is made to appear hopeless.

Giants. Those whom money could not buy he is alleged to have kidnaped.

The most noted of the Prussian despots was Frederick II (1740–1786), commonly known as Frederick the Great. An earnest disciple of the reformist doctrines of the new rationalist philosophy, Frederick was the leading figure among the "enlightened despots" of the eighteenth century. Declaring himself not the master but merely the "first servant of the state," he wrote essays to prove that Machiavelli was wrong and rose at five in the morning to begin a Spartan routine of personal management of public affairs. He made Prussia in many ways the best-governed state in Europe, abolishing torture of accused criminals, establishing elementary schools, and promoting the prosperity of industry and agriculture. As an admirer of Voltaire, whom he entertained for some time at his court, he tolerated all sorts of religious beliefs. But the benevolence thus applied in internal affairs was not carried over into foreign relations. Frederick robbed Austria of Silesia, conspired with Catherine of Russia to dismember Poland, and contributed somewhat more than his share to the bloody wars of the eighteenth century.

The "enlightened" despotism of Frederick the Great

The full bloom of absolutism in Austria came during the reigns of Maria Theresa (1740–1780) and Joseph II (1780–1790). Under the rule of the beautiful but high-strung empress a national army was established, the powers of the church were curtailed in the interest of consolidated government, and elementary and higher education was greatly expanded. Unlike the despots of most other countries, Maria Theresa was sincerely devoted to Christian morality. Though she participated in the dismemberment of Poland to make

Absolutism in Austria

505

up for the loss of Silesia, she did so with grave misgivings—an attitude which prompted the scornful remark of Frederick the Great: "She weeps, but she takes her share." The reforms of Maria Theresa were vastly extended, at least on paper, by her son Joseph II. Inspired by the teachings of French philosophers, Joseph determined to remake his empire in accordance with the highest ideals of justice and reason. Not only did he plan to reduce the powers of the church by confiscating its lands and abolishing monasteries, but he even gave Jews and heretics equal privileges with Catholics. In addition, he aspired to humble the nobles and improve the condition of the masses. He decreed that the serfs should become free men and promised to relieve them of the feudal obligations owed to their masters. He aimed to make education universal and to force the nobles to pay their proper share of taxes. But most of his magnificent plans ended in failure. He met defeat in his foreign wars. He antagonized not merely the nobles and clergy but also the proud Hungarians, who were deprived of all rights of self-government. He alienated the sympathies of the peasants by making them liable to compulsory military service. He was scarcely any more willing than Louis XIV or Frederick the Great to sacrifice personal power and national glory, even for the sake of his lofty ideals.

*The rise
and expansion
of Russia*

Absolute monarchy in Russia persisted throughout the greater part of that nation's history. Indeed, from the fifteenth century to the twentieth the Russian people knew practically no other form of government. The first of the Russian Tsars was Ivan the Great (1462–1505). In assuming the title of Tsar (Caesar) he proclaimed himself the successor of the last of the Byzantine emperors, who had perished in the capture of Constantinople in 1453. Ivan the Great threw off the yoke of Mongol oppression, united the various principalities, and extended his dominion as far as the Arctic Ocean and the Ural Mountains. Soon afterward Ivan the Terrible (1533–1584) suppressed the boyars, or landed magnates, and pushed the boundaries still farther to the east and south. But Russia was yet only a fraction of the mighty empire which was later established. During the seventeenth century emigrants from the region around Moscow rapidly occupied the fertile plains in the valleys of the Don, the Dnieper, and the Volga. Organized in semi-military bands for protection against hostile natives, the pioneers in this movement were commonly known as Cossacks. Toward the end of the seventeenth century other colonists settled in the vast wilderness of Siberia, thereby extending Russian sway to the Pacific.

*Peter the Great
attempts
to Europeanize
Russia*

But Russia was still almost exclusively an Oriental state. Her expansion had been mainly eastward. Her religion, her alphabet, her calendar had been copied from Byzantium, while the blood of many of her people was mixed with a Tartar strain. The first of the Tsars to give the empire a partial European character was Peter the Great (1682–1725), the most powerful autocrat yet to occupy the Russian throne. With a reckless disregard for ancient customs, Peter endeavored to force his subjects to change their ways of living. He forbade the Oriental seclusion of women and commanded both sexes to adopt European styles of dress. He made the use of tobacco compulsory among the members of his court. He summoned the great nobles before him and clipped their flowing beards with his own hand. In order to make sure of his own absolute power he abolished all traces of local self-government and established a system of national police. For the same reason he annihilated the authority of the patriarch of the Orthodox church and placed all religious affairs under a Holy Synod subject to his own control. Profoundly interested in Western science and technology, he made journeys to Holland and England to learn about shipbuilding and industry. He imitated the mercantilist policies of Western nations by improving agriculture and fostering manufactures and commerce. In order to get "windows to the west" he conquered territory along the Baltic shore and transferred his capital from Moscow to St. Petersburg, his new city at the mouth of the Neva. But the good that he did was greatly outweighed by his extravagant wars and his fiendish cruelty. He put thousands to death for alleged conspiracies against him, and the heads that rolled in the dust of the palace square were frequently chopped off by the arm of the great Tsar himself.

The other most noted of the Russian monarchs in the age of absolutism was Catherine the Great (1762–1796), who before her marriage was a German princess. Frequently classified as one of the "enlightened despots," Catherine corresponded with French philosophers, founded hospitals and orphanages, and even expressed the hope that the Russian serfs might be liberated. But she was shamelessly cruel and unscrupulous. She organized a revolt against her half-insane husband, Peter III, and connived at his murder. She ordered the knout applied to the bare backs of sincere reformers. Her professed sympathy for the peasants did not prevent her from taking their lands in order to give vast estates to her favorites. In short, her rule differed little in practice from that of her half-barbarian predecessors. Her chief significance lies in the fact that she continued the work of Peter the Great in introducing Russia to Western ideas and in making the country a formidable power in European affairs.

Catherine the Great

4. The Wars of the Despots

Between 1485 and 1789 the years of peace in Europe were actually outnumbered by the years of war. The earlier conflicts were largely religious in character and have already been dealt with in the chapter on the Reformation. The majority of the wars after 1600 partook of the nature of struggles for supremacy among the powerful despots of the principal countries. But religion was also a factor in

Character of the wars in the age of the despots

EUROPE AT THE END OF THE
THIRTY YEAR'S WAR, 1648

SWEDEN

Stockholm

Baltic Sea

penhagen

Danzig

EAST
PRUSSIA

RANDENBURG

Berlin

Vistula R.

Warsaw

AXONY

POLAND

AUSTRIA

Vienna

HUNGARY

Budapest

OTTOMAN

Danube R.

Zara (to Venice)

Ragusa (to Venice)

Cattaro (to Venice)

Adriatic Sea

Constantinople

EMPIRE

KINGDOM
THE
SICILIES

Aegean
Sea

Black   Sea

RUSSIA

CRETE
(to Venice)

CYPRUS
(to Ottoman Empire)

Sea

some of them, and so was the greed of the commercial classes. In general, nationalistic motives were much less important than in the wars of the nineteenth and twentieth centuries. Peoples and territories were so many pawns to be moved back and forth in the game of dynastic aggrandizement.

Underlying causes of conflict

The major warfare of the seventeenth century revolved around a titanic duel between Hapsburgs and Bourbons. Originally the rulers of Austria, the Hapsburgs had gradually extended their power over Hungary and Bohemia as well. In addition, the head of the family enjoyed what was left of the distinction of being Holy Roman Emperor. Since the time of Charles V (1519–1556) branches of the Hapsburgs had ruled over Spain, the Netherlands, the Franche-Comté, Alsace, Savoy, Genoa, Milan, and the Kingdom of the Two Sicilies.[9] For many years this expansion of Hapsburg power had been a source of profound disturbance to the rulers of France. They regarded their country as encircled and longed to break through the enclosing ring. But tensions were building up in other parts of Europe also. The princes of Germany looked with alarm upon the growing power of the Holy Roman Emperor and sought opportunities to restrict him in ways that would increase their own stature. The kings of Denmark and Sweden were also developing expansionist ambitions, which could hardly be realized except at the expense of the Hapsburg empire. Finally, the seeds of religious conflict, sown by the Reformation, were about ready to germinate in a new crop of hostilities. In 1608–1609 two opposing alliances had been formed, based upon principles of religious antagonism. The first was the Evangelical Union headed by Frederick, the Calvinist Elector of the Palatinate. The other was an alliance of Catholic princes under the leadership of Maximilian, Duke of Bavaria. The existence of these mutually hostile leagues added to the tension in central Europe and contributed toward making an eventual explosion almost a certainty. The conflict that followed, known as the Thirty Years' War (1618–1648), was one of the most tragic in history.

The Thirty Years' War

The immediate cause of the Thirty Years' War was an attempt of the Holy Roman Emperor, Matthias, to consolidate his power in Bohemia. Though the Hapsburgs had been overlords of Bohemia for a century, the Czech inhabitants of the country had retained their own king. When the Bohemian throne became vacant in 1618, Matthias conspired to obtain the position for one of his kinsmen, Duke Ferdinand of Styria. By exerting pressure he induced the Bohemian Diet to elect Ferdinand king. The Czech leaders re-

[9] Charles V, whose mother was the daughter of Ferdinand and Isabella of Spain, was the grandson of Maximilian I of Austria. Upon the abdication of Charles his empire was divided. The Spanish and Italian dominions and the colonies in America went to his son Philip and his central European possessions to his brother, Ferdinand I.

sented this. Both nationalist and Protestant traditions were strong in the country, and Ferdinand was known to be a stanch champion of militant Catholicism. The upshot was the invasion by Czech noblemen of the Emperor's headquarters in Prague and the tossing of his representatives out of the window. Czech leaders then proclaimed Bohemia an independent state with Frederick, the Calvinist Elector Palatine, as king. The war now began in earnest. The success of the Hapsburgs in suppressing the Bohemian revolt and in punishing Frederick by seizing his lands in the valley of the Rhine galvanized the Protestant rulers of northern Europe into action. Not only the German princes but King Christian IV of Denmark and Gustavus Adolphus of Sweden also joined the crusade against Austrian aggression—with the additional purpose, of course, of expanding their own dominions. In 1630 the French intervened with donations of arms and money to the Protestant allies; and after 1632, when Gustavus Adolphus was killed in battle, France bore the brunt of the struggle. The war was no longer a religious conflict, but essentially a contest between the Bourbon and Hapsburg houses for mastery of the Continent of Europe. The immediate objectives of Cardinal Richelieu, who was directing affairs for Louis XIII, were to wrest the province of Alsace from the Holy Roman Empire and to weaken the hold of the Spanish Hapsburgs on the Netherlands and on Italy. For a time the French armies suffered reverses, but the organizing genius of Richelieu and of Cardinal Mazarin, who succeeded him in 1643, ultimately brought victory to France and her allies. Peace was restored to a distracted Europe by the Treaty of Westphalia in 1648.

Most of the results of the Thirty Years' War were unmitigated evils. By the Treaty of Westphalia France was confirmed in the possession of Alsace and the bishoprics of Metz, Toul, and Verdun; Sweden received territory in Germany; the independence of Holland and Switzerland was formally acknowledged; and the Holy Roman Empire was reduced to a mere fiction, since each of the German princes was now recognized as a sovereign ruler with power to make war and peace and to govern his state as he chose. But most of these changes merely laid the foundations for bitter international squabbles in the future. In addition, the war wrought terrible havoc in central Europe. Probably few military conflicts since the dawn of history had ever caused so much misery to the civilian population. It is estimated that fully one-third of the people in Germany and Bohemia lost their lives as a consequence of famine and disease and the marauding attacks of brutal soldiers. The armies of both sides pillaged, tortured, burned, and killed in such manner as to convert whole regions into veritable desert. In Saxony one-third of the land went out of cultivation, and packs of wolves roamed through areas where thriving villages once had stood. In the midst

Results of the Thirty Years' War

511

of such misery, education and intellectual achievement of every description were bound to decline, with the result that civilization in Germany was retarded by at least a century.

Second stage in the struggle: the War of the League of Augsburg

The Thirty Years' War did not even end the rivalry of Bourbons and Hapsburgs. Though France had made notable gains under the Treaty of Westphalia, she was still confronted on her borders by several possessions of her enemy. Spain on the south, the Belgian Netherlands to the north, the Franche-Comté to the east, and the Kingdom of the Two Sicilies continued to be ruled by the Spanish Hapsburgs, while their Austrian kinsmen had never relinquished title to their provinces in the valley of the Rhine. When Louis XIV took personal charge of affairs in France after the death of Mazarin in 1661, he determined to revise these boundaries. First he made an attempt to conquer the Belgian Netherlands, which involved him in a war not only with Spain but eventually with Holland, the Austrian emperor, and the Elector of Brandenburg. When Louis endeavored to supplement his modest conquests in this war by diplomatic intrigue, a powerful alliance was formed against him by the Emperor Leopold of Austria. The war which followed, known as the War of the League of Augsburg (1688–1697), represented a new stage in the struggle between Hapsburg and Bourbon. In his previous contests Louis XIV had been able to count on the neutrality of England because of the traditional rivalry between that country and Holland. But now, since the Glorious Revolution, England had a new king in the person of William III, erstwhile Stadholder of Holland and implacable enemy of France. William promptly enlisted under the banner of the League of Augsburg, along with Sweden, Austria, Spain, and a number of the German states. With so strong a combination against him, Louis was finally compelled to sue for peace.

Final stage: the War of the Spanish Succession

In 1700 the French king saw what appeared to be a new opportunity. In that year Charles II, king of Spain, died with neither children nor brothers to succeed him, and willed his dominions to the grandson of Louis XIV. The Austrians denounced this settlement, and formed a new alliance with England, Holland, and Brandenburg. The War of the Spanish Succession, which broke out in 1702 when Louis attempted to enforce the claim of his grandson, was the last important stage in the struggle between Bourbons and Hapsburgs.[10] By the Peace of Utrecht (1713–1714) the grandson of Louis XIV was permitted to occupy the Spanish throne, on condition that France and Spain should never be united; Nova Scotia and Newfoundland were transferred to England from France, and

[10] The War of the Austrian Succession (1740–1748), in which France fought on the side of Prussia against Great Britain and Austria, also involved a struggle between Bourbons and Hapsburgs; but the results for France were indecisive. The war was mainly a duel between Prussia and Austria.

Gibraltar from Spain; and the Belgian Netherlands, Naples, and Milan were given to the Austrian Hapsburgs.

The most important of the wars of the despots in the eighteenth century was the Seven Years' War (1756–1763), known in American history as the French and Indian War. The causes of this struggle were closely related to some of the earlier conflicts already discussed. One of the chief factors in the wars of the League of Augsburg and the Spanish Succession had been commercial rivalry between England and France. Each had been striving for supremacy in the development of overseas trade and colonial empires. The Seven Years' War was therefore simply the climax of a struggle which had been going on for nearly a century. Hostilities began, appropriately enough, in America as the result of a dispute over possession of the Ohio valley. Soon the whole question of British or French domination of the North American continent was involved. Eventually nearly every major country of Europe was drawn in on one side or the other. Louis XV of France enlisted the aid of his kinsman, the Bourbon king of Spain. A struggle begun in 1740 between Frederick the Great and Maria Theresa over possession of Silesia was quickly merged with the larger contest. The Seven Years' War thus reached the proportions of what virtually amounted to a world conflict, with France, Spain, Austria, and Russia arrayed against Great Britain and Prussia in Europe and with English and French colonial forces striving for mastery not only in America but also in India.

The outcome of the Seven Years' War was exceedingly significant for the later history of Europe. Frederick the Great won a decisive victory over the Austrians and forced Maria Theresa to surrender all claims to Silesia. The acquisition of this territory increased the area of Prussia by more than a third, thereby raising the Hohenzollern kingdom to the status of a first-rank power. In the struggle for colonial supremacy the British emerged with a sensational triumph. Of her once magnificent empire in America, France lost all but two tiny islands off the coast of Newfoundland, Guadeloupe and a few other possessions in the West Indies, and a portion of Guiana in South America.[11] She was allowed to retain her trading privileges in India, but she was forbidden to build any forts or maintain any troops in that country. France was now crippled almost beyond hope of recovery. Her treasury was depleted, her trade almost ruined, and her chances of dominance on the Continent of Europe completely shattered. These disasters, brought on by the stupid policies of her rulers, had much to do with preparing the ground for the great revolution of 1789. By contrast, Britain was

---

[11] All of the territory given up by the French was acquired by Great Britain, with the exception of Louisiana, which France turned over to Spain as a reward for her part in the war.

now riding the crest of the wave—in a literal as well as a figurative sense, for her triumph in the Seven Years' War was a milestone in her struggle for supremacy on the seas. The wealth from her expanded trade enriched her merchants, thereby enhancing their prestige in political and social affairs. But perhaps most important of all, her victory in the struggle for colonies gave her an abundance of raw materials which enabled her to take the lead in the Industrial Revolution.

5. The Political Theory of Absolutism

The influence of political philosophers in buttressing absolute rule

The autocratic behavior of the despots in the sixteenth, seventeenth, and eighteenth centuries was not all of their own making. As indicated at the beginning of this chapter, they were encouraged by various economic and political factors for which they were not solely responsible. To these causes must be added another: the influence of political theory. Several of the Stuart and Bourbon kings, for example, derived the justification for their policies from philosophers who expressed the prevailing ideas of their time in systematic and forceful writings. These ideas were, of course, not those of the common people, but they did reflect the desires of those whom John Adams used to call "the rich, the well-born, and the able."

Jean Bodin

One of the first of the philosophers to lend encouragement to the absolutist ambitions of monarchs was Jean Bodin (1530–1596), whose zeal in the persecution of witches had earned for him the title of "Satan's Attorney-General." Bodin was not quite so extreme as some of his colleagues in exalting monarchical power. He agreed with the medieval philosophers that rulers were bound by the law of God, and he even acknowledged that the prince had a moral duty to respect the treaties he had signed. But Bodin had no use for parliaments of any description. He emphatically denied the right of a legislative body to impose any limits upon royal power. And while he admitted that princes who violated the divine law or the law of nature were tyrants, he refused to concede that their subjects would have any right of rebellion against them. The authority of the prince is from God, and the supreme obligation of the people is passive obedience. Revolution must be avoided at all costs, for it destroys that stability which is a necessary condition for progress. The main contribution of Bodin, if such it can be called, was his doctrine of sovereignty, which he defined as "supreme power over citizens and subjects, unrestrained by the laws." By this he meant that the prince, who is the only sovereign, is not bound by man-made laws. There is no *legal* restriction upon his authority whatever—nothing except obedience to the natural or moral law ordained by God. Bodin is significant also for his theory of the origin of the state. Rejecting the old feudal doctrine of the contractual basis of political authority, he maintained that the state was an outgrowth of the patriarchal family. The prince stands in the same autocratic relation to his subjects as the father to his children. As sovereign he has a perpetual and humanly unlimited authority to make law and to impose it upon his subjects.

The most noted of all the apostles of absolute government was the Englishman Thomas Hobbes (1588–1679). Writing during the Puritan Revolution and in close association with the royalists, Hobbes was disgusted with the turn which events had taken in his native country and longed for a revival of the monarchy. However, his materialism and his doctrine of the secular origin of the kingship made him none too popular with the Stuarts. For the title of his chief work Hobbes chose the name *Leviathan*, to indicate his conception of the state as an all-powerful monster.[12] All associations within the state, he declared, are mere "worms in the entrails of Leviathan." The essence of Hobbes' political philosophy is directly related to his theory of the origin of government. He taught that in the beginning all men lived in a state of nature, subject to no law but brutal self-interest. Far from being a paradise of innocence and bliss, the state of nature was a condition of universal misery. Every man's hand was against his neighbor. Life for the individual was "solitary, poor, nasty, brutish, and short." [13] In order to escape from this war of each against all, men eventually united with one another to form a civil society. They drew up a contract surrendering all of their rights to a sovereign, who would be strong enough to protect his subjects from violence. Thus the sovereign, while not a party to the contract, was made the recipient of absolute authority. The people gave up *everything* for the one great blessing of security. In contrast with Bodin, Hobbes did not recognize any law of nature or of God as a limitation upon the authority of the prince. Absolute government, he maintained, had been established by the people themselves, and therefore they would have no ground for complaint if their ruler became a tyrant; they had no rights he was bound to respect. On the basis of pure deduction, without any appeal to religion or history, Hobbes arrived at the conclusion that the king is entitled to rule despotically—not because he has been appointed by God, but because the people have *given* him absolute power.

In a sense the great Dutchman, Hugo Grotius (1583–1645), may also be considered an exponent of absolutism; though with him the question of power within the state was more or less incidental to the larger question of relations among the states. Living during the period of religious strife in France, the revolt of the Netherlands, and the Thirty Years' War, Grotius was impressed by the need for

Thomas Hobbes

Hugo Grotius

---

[12] In the Book of Job, Leviathan is the monster that ruled over the primeval chaos. Job 41:1.
[13] *Leviathan* (Routledge ed.), p. 81.

a body of rules which would reduce the dealings of governments with one another to a pattern of reason and order. He wrote his famous *Law of War and Peace* to prove that the principles of elemental justice and morality ought to prevail among nations. Some of these principles he derived from the Roman *jus gentium* and some from the medieval law of nature. So well did he present his case that he has been regarded ever since as one of the chief founders of international law. His central doctrine was the idea that every independent state, regardless of its size, must be treated as fully sovereign and entitled to equal rights. This sovereignty must never be infringed by any other power. Unfortunately this doctrine led to the worship of national honor as something sacred. Almost any affront to a nation's pride—an insult to its flag or the arrest of one of its diplomats—may still be a pretext if not a cause for war. But Grotius' revulsion against turbulence also inspired him to advocate despotic government. He did not see how order could be preserved within the state unless the ruler possessed unlimited authority. He maintained that in the beginning the people had either surrendered to a ruler voluntarily or had been compelled to submit to superior force; but in either case, having once established a government, they were bound to obey it unquestioningly forever.

The significance of philosophers' attempts to justify absolutism

The theories just discussed were not simply those of a few ivory-tower philosophers, but rather the widely accepted ideas of an age when order and security were considered more important than liberty. They reflected the desire of the commercial classes, especially, for the utmost degree of stability and protection in the interest of business. Mercantilism and the policies of the despots went hand in hand with the new theories of absolute rule. The dictum, "I am the state," attributed to Louis XIV, was not just the brazen boast of a tyrant, but it came close to expressing the prevailing conception of government—in Continental Europe at least. Those who had a stake in society really believed that the king *was* the state. They could hardly conceive of a government able to protect and assist their economic activities except in terms of centralized and despotic authority. Their attitude was not so far different from that of some people today who believe that a dictatorship of one form or another is our only means for security and plenty. It seems to be true that despotism flourishes only during difficult times of transition or in periods of uncertainty or danger when men have begun to despair of solving their problems by individual effort. It is not a normal condition of society but an essentially abnormal one, covering but a fraction of human history. And nations generally manage to make short work of their Caesars as soon as the people recover sufficient confidence in their own strength. At any rate, that is what happened in England in the seventeenth century, and also in France about a hundred years later.

Selected Readings—Historical and Biographical

Adams, G. B., *Constitutional History of England*, New York, 1921
Bruun, Geoffrey, *The Enlightened Despots*, New York, 1929
Carston, F. L., *The Origins of Prussia*, London, 1954
Clark, G. N., *The Later Stuarts, 1660–1714*, Oxford, 1934
Gardiner, S. R., *Oliver Cromwell*, New York, 1901
Gipson, L. H., *The Great War for the Empire*, New York, 1954
Hayes, C. J. H., *A Political and Social History of Modern Europe*, New York, 1925, Vol. I
Marriott, J. A. R., and Robertson, C. G., *The Evolution of Prussia*, New York, 1915
Nowak, Frank, *Medieval Slavdom and the Rise of Russia*, New York, 1930
Packard, L. B., *The Age of Louis XIV*, New York, 1929
Schenk, W., *The Concern for Social Justice in the Puritan Revolution*, New York, 1948
Scherger, G. L., *The Evolution of Modern Liberty*, New York, 1904
Sumner, B. H., *Peter the Great and the Emergence of Russia*, London, 1950
Trevelyan, G. M., *England under the Stuarts*, New York, 1904
Vernadsky, George, *Ancient Russia*, New Haven, 1945
Wolf, John B., *The Emergence of the Great Powers, 1685–1715*, New York, 1951
Zeeveld, Gordon, *Foundations of Tudor Policy*, Cambridge, 1948

—Political Theory

Allen, J. W., *History of Political Thought in the Sixteenth Century*, New York, 1928
Burns, C. D., *Political Ideals*, New York, 1932
Dunning, W. A., *Political Theories, from Luther to Montesquieu*, New York, 1902
Figgis, J. N., *The Divine Right of Kings*, Cambridge, 1922
Gettell, R. G., *History of Political Thought*, New York, 1924
Maxey, C. C., *Political Philosophies*, New York, 1938
Walker, T. A., *History of the Law of Nations*, Cambridge, 1899

Source Materials

Bodin, Jean, *Six Books Concerning the State*, especially Book I, Chs. I, VI, VIII, X
Grotius, Hugo, *The Law of War and Peace*, especially Prolegomena and Book I, Ch. I
Hobbes, Thomas, *Leviathan*, Part I, Chs. XIII–XV; Part II, Chs. XIII, XVIII, XIX, XXI, XXVI
James I, *The Trew Law of Free Monarchies*
Webster, Hutton, *Historical Selections*, pp. 640–42, "The Bill of Rights"

The Intellectual Revolution
of the Seventeenth and
Eighteenth Centuries

Causes of intellectual advance in the 17th and 18th centuries

By one of the strangest ironies of history, the period when arrogant despots bestrode the nations of the European continent was a period of stupendous intellectual achievement. To one who understands the underlying forces at work in this and in preceding ages, however, the cultural progress of the seventeenth and eighteenth centuries is not particularly mysterious. The absolute monarchs, of course, had nothing to do with it. Though a few, like Frederick the Great, dabbled in philosophy and science, no one of them could accurately be described as a patron of learning. The intellectual advance of their time was due rather to factors growing out of the principal economic and cultural movements in European history since the end of the Middle Ages. Characteristic examples were the influence of the Renaissance, the increasing prosperity of the middle and lower classes, and the widened intellectual horizons produced by the new knowledge of distant lands and strange peoples.

Character of the Intellectual Revolution

The achievements in philosophy and science in the seventeenth and eighteenth centuries, together with the new attitudes resulting therefrom, constitute what is commonly known as the Intellectual Revolution. But to speak of this revolution as if it were an event without precedent in the records of man leads to an erroneous conception of history. On several occasions before this, developments had occurred which went quite as far in upsetting old habits of thinking as did any of the discoveries of the seventeenth and eighteenth centuries. Illustrations may be found in the radicalism and individualism of the Sophists in fifth-century Athens and in the profoundly disturbing effects of the revival of paganism and worldli-

518

ness in the late Middle Ages. Nevertheless, the Intellectual Revolution of the seventeenth and eighteenth centuries was somewhat broader in scope than any of these earlier upheavals, and its results were perhaps more significant for our own generation.

1. Philosophy in the Seventeenth Century

Perhaps without straining the imagination too much, we can say that the Intellectual Revolution had a triple paternity. Its fathers were René Descartes, Sir Isaac Newton, and John Locke. More will be said later about Newton and Locke. For the present we need to examine the teachings of the renowned Frenchman who initiated the dominant philosophic trend of the seventeenth century. René Descartes (1596–1650), soldier of fortune, mathematician, and physicist, was an unswerving advocate of rationalism in philosophy. He was, of course, not the first exponent of reason as the pathway to knowledge; but his rationalism differed from that of most earlier thinkers—the medieval Scholastics, for instance—in his rigid exclusion of authority. He scorned the use of books, no matter how venerable the reputation of their authors. Convinced that both traditional opinion and the ordinary experiences of mankind are untrustworthy guides, he determined to adopt a new method entirely unprejudiced by either. This method was the mathematical instrument of pure deduction. It would consist in starting with simple, self-evident truths or axioms, as in geometry, and then reasoning from these to particular conclusions. Descartes believed that he had found such an axiom in his famous principle: "I think, therefore I am." From this he maintained that it is possible to deduce a sound body of universal knowledge—to prove, for example, that God exists, that man is a thinking animal, and that mind is distinct from matter. These "truths," he declared, are just as infallible as the truths of geometry, for they are products of the same unerring method.

The rationalism and dualism of René Descartes

But Descartes is important not only as the father of the new rationalism. He was also partly responsible for introducing the conception of a mechanistic universe. He taught that the whole world of matter, organic and inorganic alike, could be defined in terms of extension and motion. "Give me extension and motion," he once boldly declared, "and I will construct the universe." The entire mass of physical substance, he asserted, is continually moving in a series of whirlpools or vortices, some of them infinitely small and others large enough to carry the planets around their suns. Every individual thing—a solar system, a star, the earth itself—is a self-operating machine propelled by a force arising from the original motion given to the universe by God. Descartes did not even exclude the bodies of animals and of men from this general mechanistic pattern. The whole world of physical nature is one. The behavior of animals and the emotional reactions of men flow automatically

Descartes' conception of a mechanistic universe

from internal or external stimuli. He insisted, however, that man is distinct from all other creatures in the possession of a reasoning faculty. Mind is not a form of matter, but an entirely separate substance implanted in the body of man by God. Its seat is the pineal gland, located in the upper region of the skull. Along with this dualism of mind and matter, Descartes also believed in *innate* ideas. He taught that self-evident truths having no relation to sensory experience must be inherent in the mind itself. Man does not learn them through the use of his senses, but perceives them instinctively because they have been part of his mental equipment from birth.

Descartes' intellectual successors: Benedict Spinoza

Of the several teachings of Descartes the new rationalism and mechanism were by far the most influential. In fact, these two doctrines were almost sufficient in themselves to have produced a revolution, for they involved the rejection of nearly all the theological bias of the past. No longer need the philosopher pay homage to revelation as a source of truth; reason was now held to be the solitary fount of knowledge, while the whole idea of spiritual meaning in the universe was cast aside like a worn-out garment. Descartes' principles of rationalism and mechanism were adopted in some form or other by the majority of the philosophers of the seventeenth century. The most noted of his intellectual successors were the Dutch Jew Benedict Spinoza and the Englishman Thomas Hobbes, whom we have already encountered as a political theorist. Benedict (or Baruch) Spinoza was born in Amsterdam in 1632 and died an outcast from his native community forty-five years later. His parents were members of a group of Jewish immigrants who had fled from persecution in Portugal and Spain and had taken refuge in the Netherlands. At an early age Spinoza came under the influence of a disciple of Descartes and as a result grew critical of some of the dogmas of the Hebrew faith. For this he was expelled from the synagogue, cursed by the chief priests and elders, and banished from the community of his people. From 1656 till his death he lived in various cities of Holland, eking out a meager existence by grinding lenses. During these years he developed his philosophy, incorporating the rationalism and mechanism but not the dualism of Descartes. Spinoza maintained that there is only one essential substance in the universe, of which mind and matter are but different aspects. This single substance is God, who is identical with nature itself. Such a conception of the universe was, of course, pure pantheism; but it was grounded upon reason rather than upon faith, and it was intended to express the scientific notions of the unity of nature and the continuity of cause and effect. It is not without significance that one of the greatest of modern scientists, Albert Einstein, declared that his idea of God was the same as that of Spinoza.

Much more than Descartes, Spinoza was interested in ethical questions. Having come to the conclusion early in life that the things men prize most highly—wealth, pleasure, power, and fame—are empty and vain, he set out to inquire whether there was any perfect good which would give lasting and unmitigated happiness to all who attained it. By a process of geometric reasoning he attempted to prove that this perfect good consists in "love of God"—that is, in worship of the order and harmony of nature. If men will but realize that the universe is a beautiful machine, whose operation cannot be interrupted for the benefit of particular persons, they will gain that serenity of mind for which philosophers have yearned through the ages. We can only be delivered from impossible hopes and cringing fears by acknowledging to ourselves that the order of nature is unalterably fixed, and that man cannot change his fate. In other words, we gain true freedom by realizing that we are not free. But with all his determinism, Spinoza was an earnest apostle of tolerance, justice, and rational living. He wrote in defense of religious liberty and, in the face of cruel mistreatment, set a noble example in his personal life of kindliness, humanity, and freedom from vengeful passions.

The third of the great rationalists of the seventeenth century was Thomas Hobbes. Born before either Descartes or Spinoza, he actually outlived both. Hobbes agreed with his two contemporaries in the belief that geometry furnished the only proper method of discovering philosophic truth. But he denied the doctrine of innate ideas, maintaining that the *origin* of all knowledge is in sense perception. He likewise refused to accept either the dualism of Descartes or the pantheism of Spinoza. According to Hobbes, absolutely nothing exists except matter. Mind is simply motion in the brain or perhaps a subtle form of matter, but in no sense a distinct substance. God, also, if we can believe that He exists, must be assumed to have a physical body. There is nothing spiritual anywhere in the universe of which the mind can conceive. This was the most thoroughgoing materialism to make its appearance since the days of Lucretius. Naturally it was combined with mechanism, as materialism usually is. Hobbes contended that not only the universe but man himself can be explained mechanically. All that man does is determined by appetites or aversions, and these in turn are either inherited or acquired through experience. In similar fashion, Hobbes maintained that there are no absolute standards of good and evil. Good is merely that which gives pleasure; evil, that which brings pain. Thus did Hobbes combine with materialism and mechanism a thoroughgoing philosophy of hedonism.

2. The Enlightenment

The climax of the Intellectual Revolution in philosophy was a movement known as the Enlightenment. Beginning in England about 1680, it quickly spread into most of the countries of northern Europe and was not without influence in America. The supreme mani-

*The chief
philosophical
concepts of the
Enlightenment*

festation of the Enlightenment, however, was in France, and the period of its real importance was the eighteenth century. Few other movements in history have had such profound effects in molding men's thoughts or in shaping the course of their actions. The philosophy of the Enlightenment was built around a number of significant concepts, chief among which were the following:

(1) Reason is the only infallible guide to wisdom. All knowledge has its roots in sense perception, but the impressions of our senses are but the raw material of truth, which has to be refined in the crucible of reason before it can have value in explaining the world or in pointing the way to the improvement of life.

(2) The universe is a machine governed by inflexible laws which man cannot override. The order of nature is absolutely uniform and not subject in any way to miracles or to any other form of divine interference.

(3) The simplest and most natural structure of society is the best. The life of the "noble savage" is preferable to that of civilized man with its outworn conventions which serve to perpetuate the tyranny of priests and rulers. Religion, government, and economic institutions should be purged of everything artificial and reduced to a form consistent with reason and natural liberty.[1]

(4) There is no such thing as original sin. Men are not inherently depraved but are driven to acts of cruelty and meanness by scheming priests and war-making despots. The infinite perfectibility of human nature, and therefore of society itself, would become easily realized if men were free to follow the guidance of reason and their own instincts.

*The founders of
the Enlighten-
ment: (1) Sir
Isaac Newton*

The inspiration for the Enlightenment came partly from the rationalism of Descartes, Spinoza, and Hobbes, but the real founders of the movement were Sir Isaac Newton (1642–1727) and John Locke (1632–1704). Although Newton was not a philosopher in the ordinary sense, his work has the deepest significance for the history of thought. His majestic achievement was to bring the whole world of nature under a precise mechanical interpretation. His celebrated principle that "every particle of matter in the universe attracts every other particle with a force varying inversely as the square of the distance between them and directly proportional to the product of their masses" was held to be valid not only on this earth but throughout the endless expanse of solar systems. From this it was an easy step to the conclusion that every event in nature is governed by universal laws, which can be formulated as precisely as mathematical principles. The discovery of these laws is the chief business of science, and the duty of man is to allow them to operate unhindered. Gone was the medieval conception of a universe guided by benevolent purpose; men now dwelt in a world in which the

[1] The political and economic doctrines of the Enlightenment will be treated more fully in the following chapter on The French Revolution.

The Manuscript of Newton's *Philosophia Naturalis Principia Mathematica,* from which the first edition was published in 1687.

procession of events was as automatic as the ticking of a watch. Newton's philosophy did not rule out the idea of a God, but it deprived Him of His power to guide the stars in their courses or to command the sun to stand still.

The influence of John Locke was quite different from that of Newton, but it was scarcely any less important. Locke was the father of a new theory of knowledge, which served as the keynote of the philosophy of the Enlightenment. Rejecting Descartes' doctrine of innate ideas, he maintained that all of man's knowledge originates from sense perception. This theory, known as sensationalism, had already been asserted by Hobbes; but Locke was the first of modern philosophers to develop it in systematic form. He insisted that the human mind at birth is a blank tablet, a "white paper," upon which absolutely nothing is inscribed. It does not even contain the idea of a God or any notions of right and wrong. Not until the newborn child begins to have experiences, to perceive the external world with its senses, is anything registered in its mind. But the simple ideas which result directly from sense perception are merely the foundations of knowledge; no human being could live intelligently on the basis of them alone. These simple ideas must be integrated and fused into *complex ideas.* This is the function of the reason or understanding, which has the power to combine, coordinate, and organize the impressions received from the senses and thus to build a usable body of general truth. Sensation and reason are both indispensable—the one for furnishing the mind with the raw materials of knowledge and the other for working them into meaningful form. It was this combination of sensationalism and rationalism which became one of the basic elements in the philosophy of the Enlightenment. Locke is significant also for his defense of religious toleration and for his liberal political theory, which will be discussed in the chapter on The French Revolution.

(2) John Locke

523

The Enlightenment blossomed forth in its fullest glory in France during the eighteenth century under the leadership of Voltaire and other like-minded critics of the established order. Voltaire, or François Marie Arouet as he was originally named, epitomized the Enlightenment in somewhat the same way as Luther did the Reformation or Leonardo da Vinci the Italian Renaissance. A son of the bourgeoisie, Voltaire was born in 1694 and, despite his delicate physique, lived to within eleven years of the outbreak of the French Revolution. He developed a taste for satiric writing early in his life and got himself into numerous scrapes by his ridicule of noblemen and pompous officials. As a consequence of one of his lampoons he was sent to the Bastille and afterwards exiled to England. Here he remained for three years, acquiring a deep admiration for British institutions, and composing his first philosophic work, which he entitled *Letters on the English.* In this work he popularized the ideas of Newton and Locke, whom he had come to regard as two of the greatest geniuses who ever lived. Most of his later writings—the *Philosophical Dictionary, Candide,* his histories, and many of his poems and essays—were also concerned with exposition of the doctrine that the world is governed by natural laws, and that reason and concrete experience are the only dependable guides for man to follow. Voltaire had contempt for the smug optimism which taught that the ills of each make up the good of all, and that everything is for the best in the best of all possible worlds. He saw, on the contrary, universal misery, hatred, strife, and oppression. Only in his utopia of El Dorado, which he placed somewhere in South America, were freedom and peace conceivable. Here there were no monks, no priests, no lawsuits, and no prisons. The inhabitants dwelt together without malice or greed, worshiping God in accordance with the dictates of reason, and solving their problems by logic and science. But this idyllic life was made possible only by the fact that the land was cut off by impassable mountains from the "regimented assassins of Europe."

Voltaire is best known as a champion of individual freedom. He regarded all restrictions upon liberty of speech and opinion as utterly barbarous. In a letter to one of his opponents he wrote what has often been quoted as the highest criterion of intellectual tolerance: "I do not agree with a word that you say, but I will defend to the death your right to say it." [2] But if there was any one form of repression that Voltaire abhorred more than others, it was the tyranny of organized religion. He blasted with fire and brimstone against the monstrous cruelty of the church in torturing and burning intelligent men who dared to question its dogmas. With reference to the whole system of persecuting and privileged orthodoxy, he adopted as his slogan, "Crush the infamous thing." He was almost as unsparing in his attacks upon political tyranny, especially when

[2] E. B. Hall, *Voltaire in His Letters,* p. 65.

Voltaire, by Jean Antoine Houdon (1741–1828). The noted French sculptor seems to have captured the sardonic attitude of the great foe of superstition and unreason. In front of Théâtre Français, Paris.

it resulted in the slaughter of thousands to glut the ambitions of despots. "It is forbidden to kill," he sarcastically asserted: "therefore all murderers are punished unless they kill in large numbers and to the sound of trumpets." [3]

Among the other philosophers of the Enlightenment in France were Denis Diderot, Jean d'Alembert, Claude Helvetius, and Baron d'Holbach, all of whom lived in the latter part of the eighteenth century. Diderot and d'Alembert were the chief members of a group known as the Encyclopedists, so-called from their contributions to the *Encyclopedia*, which was intended to be a complete summation of the philosophic and scientific knowledge of the age. In general, both of them agreed with the rationalism and liberalism of Voltaire. Diderot, for example, maintained that "men will never be free till the last king is strangled with the entrails of the last priest." D'Alembert, while accepting the rationalist and individualist tendencies of the Enlightenment, differed from most of his associates in advocating a diffusion of the new doctrines among all the people. The general attitude of his contemporaries, notably Voltaire, was to despise the common man, to regard him as a mere clodhopper beyond redemption from ignorance and grossness. But for d'Alembert the only assurance of progress lay in universal enlightenment. Accordingly, he maintained that the truths of reason and science should be taught to the masses in the hope that eventually the whole world might be freed from darkness and tyranny.

Other philosophers of the Enlightenment: the Encyclopedists

The renown of Helvetius and Holbach comes chiefly from their extremist views of materialism and mechanism. They argued that nothing but physical substance exists, and that man differs from the lower animals solely in being more complex. Holding to such

Helvetius and Holbach

[3] *Philosophical Dictionary*, article on "War."

doctrines as these, they inevitably minimized the importance of religion. In their view, faith in a personal God or in rewards and punishments after death serves no useful purpose, either as an explanation of the world or as a basis of good conduct. Helvetius, especially, contended that self-interest, springing from the desire for pleasure and the avoidance of pain, is an ample foundation for morality. He believed that men's evil intentions would be curbed by the fear of retaliation, and that the feeling of pleasure resulting from an unselfish act would outweigh any element of pain. He is often credited with having been the first to use the famous phrase, "the greatest good of the greatest number." Holbach went farther than any of his contemporaries in drawing logical deductions from the theory of mechanism. He taught that the universe is nothing but matter perpetually in motion; it never had a beginning and will never have an end. Every object and organism in it acquires its shape and form from the continuous flux of matter. This was a return to the ancient Greek conception of an eternal universe in constant process of evolution.

*The Enlight-
enment in Ger-
many*

While the Enlightenment was of much less importance in Germany than in France or England, it did give birth to some progressive ideas. The most widely recognized of its German leaders was Gotthold Lessing (1729–1781), primarily a dramatist and critic but also a philosopher of humane and far-sighted views. The essence of his philosophy is tolerance, founded upon a sincere conviction that no one religion has a monopoly of truth. In his play, *Nathan the Wise*, he expounded the idea that nobility of character has no particular relation to theological creeds. He maintained that, historically, men of charitable spirit were as often found among Jews and Moslems as among Christians. Largely for this reason he condemned adherence to any one system of dogma and taught that the development of each of the world's great religions (Christianity included) was simply a step in the spiritual evolution of mankind. One of Lessing's friends and disciples turned out to be the foremost Jewish philosopher of the Enlightenment. His name was Moses Mendelssohn (1729–1786), and he was a sickly product of the ghetto in the German town of Dessau. Agreeing with Lessing that religions should be judged by their effects upon the conduct of their followers, Mendelssohn urged his Jewish brethren to give up their notion of themselves as the Chosen People of God. They should look upon Judaism merely as one of a number of good religions. He recommended also that Jews should renounce their clannishness, that they should cease to long for a return to Zion, and that they should adapt themselves to the civic requirements of the countries in which they lived. His teachings, along with those of Moses Maimonides, the great rationalist Jew of the twelfth century, were among the principal sources of what has since come to be known as Reform Judaism.

Two other philosophers are commonly given a place in the Enlightenment—the Scotsman, David Hume (1711–1776), and the Frenchman, Rousseau (1712–1778).[4] Neither, however, was in full agreement with the majority of his contemporaries. Hume is noted above all for his skepticism. He taught that the mind is a mere bundle of impressions, derived exclusively from the senses and tied together by habits of association. That is, we learn from experience to associate warmth with fire and nourishment with bread. If we had never actually experienced the sensation of warmth, no reasoning faculty in our minds would enable us to draw the conclusion that fire produces heat. But constant repetition of the fact that when we see a flame we generally experience warmth leads to the habit of associating the two in our minds. Impressions and associations are all that there is to knowing. Since every idea in the mind is nothing but a copy of a sense impression, it follows that we can know nothing of final causes, the nature of substance, or the origin of the universe. We cannot be sure of any of the conclusions of reason except those which, like the principles of mathematics, can be verified by actual experience. All others are likely to be the products of feelings and desires, of animal urges and fears. In thus denying the competence of reason, Hume placed himself almost entirely outside the main intellectual trend of the Enlightenment. As a matter of fact, he helped to prepare its death.

David Hume, the foremost skeptic of the Enlightenment

In similar measure Jean Jacques Rousseau repudiated many of the basic assumptions which had stemmed from Newton and Locke. A hopeless misfit wallowing in the mire of his emotions, Rousseau would have been a marvel indeed if he had championed the rationalist doctrines of the Enlightenment. Whole segments of his personality appear to have been out of joint. He failed in nearly every occupation he undertook. He preached lofty ideals of educational reform, but abandoned his own children to a foundling asylum. He quarreled with everybody and reveled in morbid self-disclosures. Undoubtedly it was these qualities of temperament which were largely responsible for his revolt against the coldly intellectual doctrines of his contemporaries. He maintained that to worship reason as the infallible guide to conduct and truth is to lean upon a broken reed. Reason, of course, has its uses, but it is not the whole answer. In the really vital problems of life it is much safer to rely upon feelings, to follow our instincts and emotions. These are the ways of nature and are therefore more conducive to happiness than the artificial lucubrations of the intellect. The "thinking man is a depraved animal." [5] Yet notwithstanding his contempt for reason, Rousseau was in other ways thoroughly in agreement with the viewpoint of the Enlightenment. He extolled the life of the

Rousseau's antirationalism

---

[4] By birth Rousseau was French Swiss, a native of Geneva, but he lived the greater part of his life in France.
[5] *A Discourse on the Origin of Inequality* (Everyman Library ed.), p. 181.

"noble savage" even more fervently than did any of his associates. In his prize-winning essay, the *Discourse on the Arts and Sciences*, he contrasted the freedom and innocence of primitive men with the tyranny and wickedness of civilized society, even insisting that the progress of learning is destructive of human happiness. He shared the impatience of the Enlightenment with every sort of restriction upon individual freedom, though he was much more concerned about the liberty and equality of the masses than were the other reformers of his time. He regarded the origin of private property as the primary source of misery in human society.

The influence of Rousseau

It would be almost impossible to fix limits to the influence of Rousseau. As the first significant writer to uphold the validity of conclusions dictated by emotion and sentiment, he is commonly considered the father of romanticism. For fifty years after his time Europe was bathed in literary tears, and it was difficult to find a philosopher who would boldly assert the inerrancy of reason. His slogan, "Back to nature," furnished the foundation for a veritable cult dedicated to the pursuit of the simple life. The new fashion spread even to the simpering courtiers at Versailles. The queen herself designed a dainty rural village in a corner of the palace grounds and diverted herself by playing milkmaid. But Rousseau's influence was not limited to the founding of romanticism and the encouragement of sentimental devotion to nature. His dogmas of equality and popular sovereignty, though frequently misinterpreted, became the rallying cries of revolutionaries and of thousands of more moderate opponents of the existing regime. And, as the chapter on The French Revolution will show, it was Rousseau's political philosophy which provided the real inspiration for the modern ideal of majority rule.

The religious doctrines of the Enlightenment: deism

The most typical religious philosophy of the Enlightenment was deism. The originator of this philosophy appears to have been an Englishman by the name of Lord Herbert of Cherbury (1583–1648). In the eighteenth century deistic doctrines were propagated by such men as Voltaire, Diderot, and Rousseau in France; Alexander Pope, Lord Bolingbroke, and Lord Shaftesbury in England; and Thomas Paine, Benjamin Franklin, and Thomas Jefferson in America. Not satisfied with condemning the irrational elements in religion, the deists went on to denounce every form of organized faith. Christianity was spared no more than the others. Institutionalized religions were branded as instruments of exploitation, devised by wily scoundrels to enable them to prey upon the ignorant masses. As Voltaire expressed it, "the first divine was the first rogue who met the first fool." [6] But the aims of the deists were not all destructive. They were interested not merely in demolishing Christianity but in constructing a simpler and more natural religion to replace it. The fundamental tenets of this new religion were about as fol-

[6] *Philosophical Dictionary*, article on "Religion."

lows: (1) there is one God who created the universe and ordained the natural laws that control it; (2) God does not intervene in the affairs of men in this world: He is not a capricious deity, like the God of the Christians and Jews, making "one vessel unto honour and another unto dishonour" in accordance with His peculiar whims; (3) prayer, sacraments, and ritual are mere useless mumbo jumbo; God cannot be wheedled or bribed into setting aside natural law for the benefit of particular persons; (4) man is endowed with freedom of will to choose the good and avoid the evil; there is no predestination of some to be saved and others to be damned, but rewards and punishments in the life hereafter are determined solely by the individual's conduct on earth.

Naïve though many of its assumptions were, the influence of the Enlightenment was tremendous. No other movement, with the possible exception of humanism, had done more to dispel the accumulated fogs of superstition and illogical restraint which still enveloped the Western world. The rationalism of the Enlightenment helped to break the shackles of political tyranny and to weaken the power of conscienceless priests. Its ideal of religious freedom was a leading factor in the ultimate separation of church and state and in the liberation of the Jews from ancient restrictions. The humanitarianism implied in the opposition to oppression carried over into agitation for penal reform and for the abolition of slavery. The desire for a natural order of society contributed to a demand for the overthrow of relics of feudalism and for the destruction of monopoly and unearned privilege. If there was any evil result of the Enlightenment, it probably consisted in an exaggerated development of individualism. Liberty of the individual against political and religious tyranny was unfortunately too easily translated into the right of the strong to satisfy economic greed at the expense of the weak.

The influence of the Enlightenment

3. Revolutionary Scientific Discoveries

The major scientific interests of the Intellectual Revolution followed very largely the paths marked out during the late Renaissance. Accordingly, primary attention was given to the physical sciences. The first significant discoveries were made in mathematics and physics. Early in the seventeenth century René Descartes invented analytical geometry, a union of geometry and algebra. Soon afterward came the development of the infinitesimal calculus by Sir Isaac Newton and Gottfried Wilhelm Leibniz (1646–1716). Embracing as it does the mathematical analysis of continuously varying quantities, the calculus is an essential instrument for computation in engineering and in the higher branches of mechanics.

Achievements in the physical sciences: (1) mathematics

Unquestionably the most illustrious physicist of the Intellectual Revolution was Sir Isaac Newton. His conclusions molded men's thinking in philosophy for a hundred years. His influence upon science was even more lasting; the Newtonian physics stood virtually unchallenged until the twentieth century. It was in 1687 that Newton published his renowned law of universal gravitation. Based in part upon the work of Galileo, this law provided a single unifying principle for the entire world of matter. Besides, it removed all doubt as to the validity of the Copernican hypothesis and placed the study of celestial mechanics on a firm scientific foundation. But Newton's researches in physics were not confined to the problem of gravitation. He devised a series of tables, of great value to navigation, by which the changing positions of the moon among the stars could be accurately predicted. He invented the sextant for measuring these positions and thereby determining latitude and longitude. His achievements in spectrum analysis proved of substantial value in paving the way for later discoveries regarding the nature of light. He shares with Galileo the honor of being the father of modern physics.

Some preliminary progress was made during the Intellectual Revolution in connection with the understanding of electrical phenomena. At the beginning of the seventeenth century the Englishman, William Gilbert, discovered the properties of lodestones and introduced the word "electricity" into the language.[7] Other scientists quickly became interested, and sensational results were anticipated from experiments with the marvelous "fluid." A learned Jesuit even suggested that two persons might communicate at a distance by means of magnetized needles which would point simultaneously to identical letters of the alphabet. More substantial work was done by Stephen Gray (d. 1736) and Charles Dufay (1698–1739), who discovered that substances vary in conductivity and distinguished between positive and negative electricity. Late in the eighteenth century Alessandro Volta (1745–1827) constructed the first battery and proved the identity of "animal magnetism" with electricity. Still another important achievement in electrical physics was the invention in 1746 of the Leyden jar for the storage of electric energy. It was mainly as a result of this invention that Benjamin Franklin was able to show that lightning and electricity are identical. In his celebrated kite experiment in 1752 he succeeded in charging a Leyden jar from a thunderstorm.

Almost as spectacular as the progress in physics was the development of chemistry. If any one scientist can be called the founder of modern chemistry, the title must be given to Robert Boyle (1627–1691). The son of an Irish nobleman, Boyle achieved distinction in 1661 with the publication of his *Sceptical Chymist, or Chymico-Physical Doubts and Paradoxes*. In this work he rejected the theories

[7] "Electric" comes from the Greek word for amber. Gilbert and others had observed that amber rubbed on fur will attract paper, hair, straw, and various other things. Preserved Smith, *A History of Modern Culture*, Vol. I, pp. 63–64.

not only of the alchemists but also of the medico-chemists who followed in the footsteps of Paracelsus.[8] He thereby contributed much toward the establishment of chemistry as a pure science. In addition, he distinguished between a mixture and a compound, learned a great deal about the nature of phosphorus, produced alcohol from wood, suggested the idea of chemical elements, and revived the atomic theory. No scientist before his time had foreshadowed so much of the knowledge of modern chemistry.

*The discovery
of hydrogen
and oxygen*

Despite the work of Boyle, little further development of chemistry occurred for almost a hundred years. The reason lay partly in the wide acceptance of errors concerning such matters as heat, flame, air, and the phenomenon of combustion. The most common of these errors was the so-called phlogiston theory. "Phlogiston" was supposed to be the active principle or mystic substance in fire which caused a flame to burn and consume fuel. In the second half of the eighteenth century a number of important discoveries were made which ultimately overthrew this theory and cleared the way for a true understanding of some of the most familiar chemical reactions. First came the discovery by Joseph Black about 1755 that in the burning of limestone to make quicklime a gas is given off, which he proved to have come from the limestone itself, not from the fire. This gas, which he called "fixed air," was later shown to be carbon dioxide. In 1766 Henry Cavendish, one of the richest men in England, reported the discovery of a new kind of gas obtained by treating iron, zinc, and other metals with sulphuric acid. He showed that this gas, now known as hydrogen, would not of itself support combustion, and yet would be rapidly consumed by a fire with access to the air. In 1774 oxygen was discovered by Joseph Priestley, who had managed for some years to squeeze enough time out of his profession of Unitarian minister to perform some extensive experiments in natural science. He found that a candle would burn with extraordinary vigor when placed in the new gas—a fact which indicated clearly that combustion was not caused by any mysterious principle in the flame itself. A few years after this discovery Cavendish demonstrated that air and water, long supposed to be elements, are a mixture and a compound, respectively, the first being composed of oxygen and nitrogen and the second of oxygen and hydrogen.

The final blow to the phlogiston theory was administered by Antoine Lavoisier (1743–1794), one of the greatest of all scientists of the Intellectual Revolution. By some he has been called "the Newton of Chemistry." Lavoisier proved that both combustion and respiration involve oxidation, the one being rapid and the other slow. He provided the names for oxygen and hydrogen, demonstrated that the diamond is a form of carbon, and argued that life itself is essentially a chemical process. But undoubtedly his greatest

Lavoisier

[8] See above, pp. 401–402.

Lavoisier Demonstrating the Principle of Oxidation.

accomplishment was his creation of quantitative chemistry through his discovery of the law of the conservation of mass. He found evidence that "although matter may alter its state in a series of chemical actions, it does not change in amount; the quantity of matter is the same at the end as at the beginning of every operation, and can be traced by its weight." This "law" has, of course, been modified by later discoveries regarding the structure of the atom and the conversion of some forms of matter into energy. It is hardly too much to say that as a result of Lavoisier's genius chemistry became a true science. To the lasting shame of the French Revolutionists, he was put to death on the guillotine at the age of fifty-one, a victim of the Reign of Terror.

Although it was the physical sciences which received the major attention in the Intellectual Revolution, the biological sciences were by no means neglected. One of the greatest of the early biologists was Robert Hooke (1635–1703), the first man to see and describe the cellular structure of plants. This achievement was soon followed by the work of Marcello Malpighi (1628–1694) in demonstrating the sexuality of plants and in comparing the function of vegetable leaves with that of the lungs of animals. About the same time a Dutch manufacturer of microscopes, Anthony van Leeuwenhoek (1632–1723), discovered protozoa and bacteria and wrote the first description of human spermatozoa. The seventeenth century also witnessed some progress in embryology. About 1670 the Dutch physician, Jan Swammerdam, carefully described the life history of certain insects from the caterpillar stage to maturity and compared the change of tadpole into frog with the development of the human embryo.

In many ways the end of the seventeenth century appeared to mark a decline of originality in the sciences which deal with living things. During the next hundred years biologists were inclined more and more to center their efforts upon description and classification of knowledge already in existence. The most brilliant classifier of biological knowledge was the Swedish scientist, Carl von Linné (1707–

The biological scientists: Hooke, Malpighi, Leeuwenhoek, and Swammerdam

Linnaeus

532

1778), more commonly known by his Latinized name of Linnaeus. In his *System of Nature* and in his *Botanical Philosophy* Linnaeus divided all natural objects into three kingdoms: stone, animal, and vegetable. Each of these kingdoms he subdivided into classes, genera, and species. He invented the system of biological nomenclature still in use, by which every plant and animal is designated by two scientific names, the first denoting the genus and the second the species. Thus he called man *Homo sapiens*. Though some people condemned Linnaeus for presuming to rename the animals that Adam had named, his classification was nevertheless widely adopted even in his own time. Despite certain defects which have had to be corrected, it still has its value. Linnaeus is significant also for his contention that the number of species was not necessarily fixed at the time of the Creation. He even suggested that botanists might well devote their talents to the production of new plants by crossing different species.

The second great genius of descriptive biology in the eighteenth century was the Frenchman Buffon (1707–1788). His *Natural History* in forty-four volumes, though intended as a summation of practically all science, dealt mainly with man and other vertebrates. While much of the material in this work was taken from the writings of other scientists and from the accounts of travelers, the author did have a unique ability in reducing a vast body of knowledge to orderly arrangement and in enlivening it with his own brilliant interpretations. The chief importance of Buffon to us lies in his recognition of the close relationship between man and the higher animals. Though he could never quite bring himself to accept the full implications of the evolutionary theory, he was none the less strongly impressed by the striking resemblances among all of the higher species. He thought that man, the horse, the ass, and the apes might all be considered as members of one great family, and he admitted the possibility that the entire range of organic forms had descended from a single species.

Buffon

The development of physiology and medicine progressed rather slowly during the seventeenth century. Among the several reasons, one was the inadequate preparation of physicians, many of whom had begun their professional careers with little more training than a kind of apprenticeship under an older practitioner. Another was the common disrepute in which surgery was held as a mere trade, like that of barber or blacksmith.[9] Perhaps the most serious of all was the prejudice against dissection of human bodies as a basis of anatomical study. As late as 1750 medical schools which engaged in this practice were in danger of destruction by irate mobs. Despite these obstacles some progress was still possible. About 1670 Malpighi and Leeuwenhoek confirmed the famous discovery of Sir William Harvey by observing the actual flow of blood through the

The paucity of medical achievements in the 17th century

[9] As a matter of fact, surgery in northern Europe was very commonly left in the hands of barbers. Surgeons in England are still referred to as "Mr."

network of capillaries connecting the arteries and veins. At approximately the same time an eminent physician of London, Thomas Sydenham, proposed a new theory of fever as nature's attempt to expel diseased material from the system. The substance of this theory is still quite generally accepted; in fact, new evidence has been discovered which strongly confirms it.

Medical progress in the 18th century

Medical progress during the eighteenth century was somewhat more rapid. Among the noteworthy achievements were the discovery of blood pressure, the founding of histology or microscopic anatomy, the development of the autopsy as an aid to the study of disease, and the recognition of scarlet fever as a malady distinct from smallpox and measles. But the chief milestones of medical advancement in this period were the adoption of inoculation and the development of vaccination for smallpox. Knowledge of inoculation came originally from the Near East, where it had long been employed by the Moslems. Information concerning its use was relayed to England in 1717 through the letters of Lady Montagu, wife of the British ambassador to Turkey. The first systematic application of the practice in the Western world, however, was due to the efforts of the great Puritan leaders, Cotton and Increase Mather, who implored the physicians of Boston to inoculate their patients in the hope of curbing an epidemic of smallpox which had broken out in 1721. By the middle of the century inoculation was quite generally employed by physicians in Europe and in America. In 1796 the milder method of vaccination was discovered by Edward Jenner. It was now revealed that direct inoculation of human beings with the deadly virus of smallpox was unnecessary: a vaccine manufactured in the body of an animal would be just as effective and much less likely to have disastrous results. Vast possibilities were thus opened up for the elimination of contagious diseases.

Geology

Among all the major sciences now commonly recognized, the only one actually originated during the Intellectual Revolution was geology. Hitherto theories of the evolution of the earth had been largely incidental to physics and astronomy. The first scientist to devote his exclusive attention to a systematic study of rocks with a view to understanding the history of our planet was James Hutton. In 1785 he reported his conclusions to the Royal Society of Edinburgh in a paper entitled *Theory of the Earth*. In this work he set forth his famous *uniformitarian* hypothesis, which has been the basis of geology ever since. This hypothesis states that the geological processes of the past were essentially the same as those of the present. Just as the earth is now being slowly changed by the action of rivers, winds, internal disturbances, and the like, so it was constantly being altered by similar causes in the remotest epochs of the past. Here was indeed a revolutionary conclusion, for it necessitated the rejection of the Biblical assumption that the earth had been created in its present form in the space of a few days.

4. Classicism in Art and Literature

In so far as there was any one purpose dominating the art and literature of the seventeenth and eighteenth centuries, it was the desire to preserve or recapture the spirit of ancient Greece and Rome. The artists and writers of the Intellectual Revolution strove to imitate classical models. They chose classical titles and themes for many of their works and embellished them wherever possible with allusions to antique mythology. Deploring the destruction of ancient civilization by "Christian barbarians," they were unable to see much value in the cultural achievements of later centuries. In particular, they despised the Middle Ages as a long night of barbaric darkness. Doubtless most of them would have agreed with the dictum of Rousseau that the Gothic cathedrals were "a disgrace to those who had the patience to build them." In all of these attitudes the men of the Intellectual Revolution were following in the footsteps of the humanists. Devotion to the achievements of classical antiquity was at least one important element of Renaissance culture which had not yet died out. Nevertheless, it must not be forgotten that the classicism of the seventeenth and eighteenth centuries was by no means exactly the same as that of the humanists. As a rule, it was much more sentimental, grandiose, and extravagant. Besides, it was less sincere, since it was frequently employed for the glorification of cynical monarchs and their corrupt and frivolous dependents. Finally, classicism was now perhaps even less a universal theme than it had been during the age of the Renaissance. A number of the great artists and writers of the seventeenth and eighteenth centuries sought to escape from its influence entirely.

The leading arts to be developed during the age of the Intellectual Revolution were architecture and painting. Sculpture ceased to be an independent art, as it had been in the Renaissance, and was relegated to its earlier function of a mere aid to the adornment of buildings. The prevailing style of architecture in the seventeenth century was the so-called baroque. Originating in Italy, it spread to France, England, and Spain and was eventually adopted for churches, palaces, opera houses, museums, and government buildings in practically every Western country. In European capitals to this day it meets the eye in every direction. Among its celebrated monuments still standing are the Luxembourg palace and the main palaces at Versailles in France, St. Paul's cathedral in London, the government buildings in Vienna and Brussels, and the palaces of the Tsars at Peterhof near Leningrad in Russia. The most noted of the baroque architects were Giovanni Bernini (1598–1680), who designed the colonnade and square in front of St. Peter's church in Rome, and Sir Christopher Wren (1632–1723), whose masterpiece was St. Paul's cathedral. The baroque style was supposed to be founded upon the architecture of ancient Rome, but it was much more lavish than anything the Romans produced. Its principal features were hugeness, artificiality, extravagance of ornamentation, and the extensive use of such "classical" elements as the column, the dome, and sculptured representations of mythological scenes. So much detail was added to the surface of the buildings that they often give the impression of having been carved, like the altars in medieval churches. A similar passion for splendor and magnificence was reflected in the enrichment of interiors with gilt and silver, flashing

Rembrandt van Rijn, *Old Woman in an Arm Chair.* The most philosophical of Dutch painters, Rembrandt is noted for his profound studies of human nature. His mastery of art was of wide scope and included single and group portraits, landscapes, and etchings. Original in the Metropolitan Museum, New York.

The rococo and the Georgian styles

The High Altar of the Theatine Church in Munich. This gorgeously carved altar alcove is one of the finest examples of a baroque interior.

mirrors, and colored marble. Taken as a whole, baroque architecture may be regarded as a symbol of the rise of powerful dynastic states and the growth of an absorbing interest in luxury engendered by the Commercial Revolution.

During the eighteenth century the heavy and pompous architectural style of the age of Louis XIV gave way to still other adaptations of the classical. The first to be developed was the rococo architecture in France, so called from the fantastic scrolls and shell-like designs which were commonly employed for ornamentation. The rococo differed from the baroque not only in being lighter but also in the impression of grace and sumptuous refinement it was intended to create. In place of a struggle for dynastic power and for colonial empire, it was now the indolent ease and elegant manners of the court of Louis XV which set the standard for French society. A more delicate and effeminate architecture seemed to be necessary to accompany this change. Well-known examples of the rococo style are the Petit Trianon at Versailles (where the machinery is still shown by which the supper table of Louis XV was brought up through the floor) and the palace of Sans Souci at Potsdam, built by Frederick the Great. About the middle of the eighteenth century a reaction set in against both the rococo and the baroque, and efforts were made to produce a truer and less flamboyant imitation of the classical. Perhaps the best results were achieved in England and in the American colonies with the development of the so-called Georgian style,[10] known on this side of the ocean as colonial architecture. Though the Georgian retained certain elements of the baroque—the columns, the dormer windows, and often the cupola or dome—it at least had the classical merit of simplicity.

To a certain extent the evolution of painting during the seventeenth and eighteenth centuries paralleled that of architecture. The greatest of the painters who may be considered to have expressed the baroque tradition were the Flemings, Peter Paul Rubens (1577–1640) and Anthony Van Dyck (1599–1641), and the Spaniard, Diego Velásquez (1599–1660). Rubens was not merely the outstanding genius among these three, but he was the greatest of all the Flemish painters. In such famous works as *The Fates Spinning* and *Venus and Adonis* he combined classical themes with the sumptuous color and richness so pleasing to the affluent burghers and nobles of his own day. The pink and rounded flesh of his full-blown nudes is thoroughly in keeping with the robust vitality of the age. Both Rubens and his gifted pupil, Anthony Van Dyck, are noted for their portraits of rulers and nobles. These were done in highly aristocratic fashion with full attention to the gorgeous details of elegant apparel and opulent furnishings in the background. Van Dyck's best-known portraits are those of the English kings, James I and Charles I, and their families. Velásquez, the third great artist of the baroque tradition, was the court painter to Philip IV of Spain. Most of his work consisted of paintings of royal faces, suffused in soft and silvery light but empty of meaning or emotional expression.

The rococo style of architecture may also be considered to have had its counterpart in painting. This was especially true in France, where a number of artists under the leadership of Antoine Watteau (1684–1721) and François Boucher (1703–1770) carried the tradition of aristocratic elegance to its farthest extreme. Their work was sentimental, decorative, and often frivolous—qualities which made

Classicism in painting: the baroque tradition

See color pictures at page 453

The rococo parallel in painting

[10] Named from the era when the four Georges reigned successively as kings of England. George I became king in 1714. George IV died in 1830.

it admirably suited to adorn the gaudy palaces of kings and nobles. Somewhat similar tendencies were revealed in much of the painting produced in England during the eighteenth century. The portraits of Sir Joshua Reynolds (1723–1792) and Thomas Gainsborough (1727–1788) were not only elegant and sentimental but sometimes artificial to the point of falsification. They strove to represent the most useless members of the English aristocracy as distinguished and high-minded leaders of society and occasionally portrayed ordinary ladies of the court in impressive classical poses—for example, Sir Joshua Reynolds' *Miss Emily Potts as Thaïs* and *Mrs. Siddons as the Tragic Muse*. It must be said, however, to the credit of Gainsborough that he did not confine his efforts to painting likenesses of wealthy patrons; he also excelled in depicting landscapes with considerable feeling for nature's moods.

All of the painters mentioned thus far were exponents in some degree of the classical influence. But there were others in both the seventeenth and eighteenth centuries who refused to be bound by the prevailing artistic conventions. Foremost among them was Rembrandt van Rijn (1606–1669), now universally acclaimed as one of the greatest painters of all time. The son of a well-to-do miller of Leyden, Rembrandt was allowed to begin his artistic education at an early age. Under a series of native masters he learned the technique of subtle coloring and skillful depiction of the unusual in nature. Famous by the time he was twenty-five, he fell upon evil days later in his life, mainly as a consequence of bad investments and the failure of critics to appreciate his more recondite works. In 1656 he was stripped by his creditors of all he possessed, even to his table linen, and driven from his house. Apparently these reverses served mainly to broaden and deepen his philosophy, for in this very same year he produced some of his greatest achievements. As a painter Rembrandt surpassed all the other members of the Dutch school and deserves to be classed with the great masters of the High Renaissance in Italy. No artist had a keener understanding of the problems and trials of human nature or a stronger perception of the mysteries of this life. His portraits, including those of himself, are imbued with an introspective quality and with a suggestion that the half is not being told. The subjects he delighted to paint were not the incidents of classical mythology but solemn rabbis, tattered beggars, and scenes from the Old and New Testaments, rich in drama and in human interest. Some of his best-known works include *The Good Samaritan*, *The Woman Taken in Adultery*, *The Marriage of Samson*, and *The Night Watch*.

The painters who refused to be bound by classical conventions: (1) Rembrandt

See color pictures at page 484

(2) Hals and Goya

Two other noted artists of the period of the Intellectual Revolution also departed widely from the classical tradition. The first was the Dutchman, Frans Hals (1580–1666), and the second was the Spaniard, Francisco Goya (1746–1828). Like his great contemporary Rembrandt, Hals insisted upon choosing the subjects he liked, regardless of whether they conformed to the notions of genteel critics. Most of his works are realistic portraits. He loved to depict the imbecilic grin in the face of the tavern drunkard, the naïve enthusiasm of itinerant singers and players, or the bewildered misery of some beaten and hopeless derelict. Goya was not merely a rebel against accepted artistic standards but a political and social revolutionary as well. He detested the aristocracy, despised the church, and ridiculed the hypocrisy of respectable society. But he reserved his deepest contempt for absolute monarchy. His *Charles IV on*

Frans Hals, *The Merry Company.* The most expressive works of Hals are those illustrating the joys and tragedies of humble folk; but, like other Dutch painters, he also portrayed the life of comfortable burghers. Original in the Metropolitan Museum of Art, New York.

See color pictures at pages 484, 485

Horseback has been called "the most impudent portrait of royalty ever painted." Goya also made use of his talents to indict the cruelty of war, especially during the period when Europe was ravaged by Napoleon's armies.

The history of literature in the seventeenth and eighteenth centuries exhibited tendencies quite similar to those of art. The most popular literary ideal was classicism, which generally meant not only a studied imitation of classical forms but also an earnest devotion to reason as a way of life, on the assumption that the Greeks and Romans had been rationalists above everything else. Although classicism was not confined to any one country, its principal center was France. Here lived during the reign of Louis XIV a distinguished company of poets and dramatists, who gave more genuine luster to their country than had ever been won by the Grand Monarch in his boldest exploits of diplomacy and war. The most noted member of this company was Jean-Baptiste Poquelin (1622–1673), who is much better known by his adopted name of Molière. Much of the work of these writers was marked by qualities similar to those of the baroque in art: it was decorative, turgid, affected, artificial, and in general expressive of a tendency to subordinate

Classicism in literature: the French poets and dramatists

539

content to form. The writings of Molière, however, stand out as a brilliant exception. Less respectful of ancient formalism than any of his associates, Molière was the most original of French comedians. Few keener critics of human nature have ever lived. "The business of comedy," he once declared, "is to represent in general all the defects of men and especially of the men of our time." The mortal weakness he delighted most to ridicule was pretentiousness—the silly conceit of social climbers in affecting a culture beyond their intelligence or the pompous claims of ignorant physicians in professing infallible skill. But with all of his penchant for satire, Molière had a measure of pity for the evil fortunes of men. In a number of his plays sympathy and even melancholy go hand in hand with clever wit and pungent scorn. His genius was probably broader in scope than that of any other dramatist since Shakespeare.

John Milton

England also had a luxuriant growth of literary effort in the classical style. The first great master of this style as applied to English literature was the renowned Puritan poet, John Milton (1608–1674). The leading philosopher of the Puritan Revolution, Milton wrote the official defense of the beheading of Charles I and later on held the position of Secretary for Foreign Tongues under Cromwell's Commonwealth. Nearly all of his writings were phrased in the rich and stately expression of the classical tradition, while many of the lesser ones revolved about themes from Greek mythology. But Milton was as much a Puritan as he was a classicist. He could never quite get away from the idea that the essence of beauty is morality. His *Comus* ends with the stern admonition: "Love Virtue, she alone is free." Moreover, he was deeply interested in theological problems. His greatest work, *Paradise Lost*, is a synthesis of the religious beliefs of his age, a majestic epic of the Protestant faith. But in spite of the fact that Milton was a Puritan, his views in this work departed widely from Calvinist dogma. Its principal themes are the moral responsibility of the individual and the importance of knowledge as an instrument of virtue. Paradise is lost repeatedly in human life to the extent that man allows passion to triumph over reason in determining the course of his actions. Milton also threw Calvinist doctrine to the winds in his *Areopagitica*, perhaps the most eloquent defense of freedom of speech in the English language.

Alexander Pope and the masters of English prose

Classicism in English literature reached its zenith in the eighteenth century in the poetry of Alexander Pope (1688–1744) and in the writings of a score of masters of prose. Pope was the great exponent in verse of the mechanistic and deistic doctrines of the Enlightenment. In such works as his *Essay on Man* and his *Essay on Criticism* he set forth the view that nature is governed by inflexible laws, and that man must study and follow nature if he would bring any semblance of order into human affairs. The chief masters of prose who wrote under classicist influence were the journalist and writer of popular fiction Daniel Defoe (1660–1731); the satirist Jonathan Swift (1667–1745); the skeptical philosopher David Hume (1711–1776), and his idealist contemporary Bishop Berkeley (1685–1753); and the historian Edward Gibbon (1737–1794), author of *The Decline and Fall of the Roman Empire.*

The age of classicism in English prose was also the period which witnessed the origin of the modern novel. To some extent the new literary form was anticipated by Daniel Defoe's *Robinson Crusoe,* a tale based upon the fictional adventures of a shipwrecked sailor who had spent five years on a desolate island off the coast of Chile. But the true modern novel, with its more or less elaborate plot of human behavior and its psychological analysis of life and love, springs from the work of Samuel Richardson (1689–1761) and Henry Fielding (1707–1754). In 1740 Richardson published his *Pamela, or Virtue Rewarded,* an involved and priggish account of the attempts of a Mr. B. to seduce his virtuous serving maid. Nine years later came Fielding's *The History of Tom Jones,* acclaimed by some critics as the greatest novel in the English language. Rich in humor and in colorful description of manners and customs, it is also free from the sentimentality of Richardson's works. The novels of Richardson and Fielding provided the inspiration for innumerable others, not only in England but on the Continent of Europe as well.

The origin of the modern novel

Earlier in this chapter we learned that the rationalistic and mechanistic philosophy of the Enlightenment was followed by a romantic revolt, expressed first of all in the teachings of Rousseau. We have now to observe that an almost identical development took place in literature. Beginning about 1750 a reaction set in against the intellectualism and high-flown formalism involved in the classical tradition. A group of writers now demanded a return to simplicity and naturalism with less attention to man as a rational creature and more to his instincts and feelings. No longer was it considered disgraceful for the poet to show sympathy or pity or to display any other of his deepest emotions; the heart should rule the head, at least in all cases where problems vital to man's happiness were concerned. No longer was nature regarded as a cold, automatic machine but worshiped as the embodiment of beauty, sublimity, and charm, or tenderly revered as a source of protection and solace. God now ceased to be a mere First Cause and came to be identified with the universe itself or mystically adored as the soul of nature. Still another element in the romantic ideal was glorification of the common man, often accompanied by a generous compassion for the weak and oppressed. Although some of this regard for the lowly had been implied in the humanitarianism of the Enlightenment, most of the leaders of that movement had little respect for the masses. Now under the influence of romanticism the humble herdsman and peasant were given a recognition in literature long overdue.

The beginning of romanticism in literature

The early romantic poets in Britain: Gray, Goldsmith, and Burns

Though literary romanticism had its roots in France in such sentimental works as *Émile* and *The New Héloïse* of Rousseau, the movement attained its most vigorous development in Great Britain and Germany. Among the eighteenth-century romantic poets in Britain were Thomas Gray (1716–1771), author of the *Elegy Written in a Country Churchyard;* and, to a certain extent, Oliver Goldsmith (1728–1774), who celebrated the rustic innocence of Auburn, "loveliest village of the plain." The most original of them all, however, was the Scotsman Robert Burns (1759–1796). In his homely dialect verse the romantic feeling for nature and sympathy for the common man received their finest expression. No writer has inspired more tenderness for the humblest things of this earth or filled the world with a deeper respect for those who toil for their bread. Moreover, Burns was unique among poets of his age in combining an extraordinary pathos with a delicate touch of humor. He had the rare gift of being passionately earnest without being solemn. In the very last years of the eighteenth century two other romantic poets began their literary activities on British soil. Their names were William Wordsworth and Samuel Taylor Coleridge. But since most of the work of these men was done in the nineteenth century, they can be discussed more appropriately in a later chapter.

The romantic writers in Germany: (1) Schiller

The romantic movement in German literature developed primarily under the brilliant guidance of Friedrich Schiller (1759–1805) and Johann Wolfgang von Goethe (1749–1832). Schiller grew up during the period of the *Sturm und Drang* (Storm and Stress), when writers all over Germany were denouncing restraints and conventions and attempting to free the culture of their country from foreign domination. As a consequence his romanticism generally embraced as its important elements the idealization of heroic deeds and the glorification of struggles for freedom. While a very strong quality of individualism pervades a number of his plays, especially *The Robbers* and *The Maid of Orleans*, Schiller's conception of liberty seems to have been closely akin to nationalism. This is revealed quite clearly in his *William Tell*, a drama of the struggle of the Swiss against Austrian tyranny. Interest in the personal fate of the hero is here very definitely subordinated to the larger issue of national independence. At times the hero even appears in a distinctly unfavorable light. This nationalistic aspect of Schiller's work was probably the one which had the major influence upon later German writers.

(2) Goethe

The greatest name in the history of German literature is unquestionably that of Schiller's older contemporary, Johann Wolfgang von Goethe. The two men were associated for a number of years at the court of the Duke of Weimar. Born in Frankfurt, the son of a family of ample means, Goethe was educated for the law but soon found the limits of knowledge in that profession unsatisfying. His indefatigable spirit drove him to the study of medicine, and then

of the fine arts and the natural sciences.[11] He even explored the
depths of alchemy and astrology; meanwhile, however, continuing
his literary efforts, which he had begun about the age of sixteen. His
first important literary production was *The Sorrows of Young
Werther*, a romantic novel about a love-sick youth who takes his
own life with the pistol of his rival and friend. Written in dashing
sentimental style, it attained an enormous popularity not only in
Germany but also in England and France. Though the author apparently intended that it should express the idea that weakness of
character is the greatest of sins, it came to be taken as a symbol of
profound dissatisfaction with the world and as a basis of fiery revolt.
In 1790 Goethe published the first part of his drama *Faust*, which
he finally completed in 1831, a year before his death. Universally
acknowledged as his grandest achievement, *Faust* not only epito-
mizes the personal philosophy of the author but expresses the
spirit of the modern age as few other writings have done. Part I
reflects some of the quality of rebellion in the *Sturm und Drang*,
but in Part II the conviction grows that freedom from restraint is
not enough; the individual must go on in an endless quest for
mastery of all knowledge and for enrichment of life through unlimited experience. Considered as a whole, the drama is a symbol
of perpetual unrest, of that ceaseless yearning for the fullness of
life which has come to be one of the most distinctive traits of modern
civilization.

5. Music in the Seventeenth and Eighteenth Centuries

As was observed in a preceding chapter,[12] the sixteenth century
marked the culmination of one era of musical development, illustrated by massive choral works of polyphonic structure. By
contrast, the seventeenth century was primarily a transitional period, *The rise of in-*
exhibiting various experimental tendencies which resulted in a rich *strumental mu-*
fulfillment in the eighteenth century. The first factor of major *sic and the be-*
importance in the new age was the rise of instrumental music. *ginnings of or-*
chestration and
Western music, it should be remembered, had first matured as a *the opera*
vocal art, and it is not surprising that it was some time before there
was a clear realization of the distinct possibilities inherent in the
creation of music by mechanical means. A marked advance was apparent in the keyboard instruments, especially the organ, which
achieved substantially its present form by the end of the seventeenth

[11] Goethe's achievements as a scientist were by no means insignificant. His
studies of the development of plants and animals contributed much to our
knowledge of comparative morphology. About 1785 he discovered that a formation in the human jawbone is analogous to the corresponding formation in the
jaw of the higher apes. Long before Darwin and even before Lamarck, he
convinced himself by his own researches that organic evolution is a fact.

[12] See above, § 6 in the chapter on The Expansion of the Renaissance.

century. The piano, invented early in the following century, was slow to displace its prototypes, the clavier and harpsichord. (Mozart was the first great musician to recognize the possibilities of the piano and to compose for it.) The violin was perfected in the first third of the eighteenth century, and it is remarkable that the best products of this period, from the workshops of the Amati, Stradivari, and Guarneri families in northern Italy, have never been excelled. Meanwhile, the basis for the modern orchestra was being laid by the tendency to group together related instruments; for example, the violin family (stringed instruments played with a bow) and the flute family (wood winds). The beginnings of the opera constitute the second important innovation of this era. Originating in Italy about 1600, the opera represented an attempt to employ music as a vehicle of dramatic expression, and derived its inspiration both from the classical Greek drama and the medieval mystery plays. Though still in a relatively crude state of development, the opera became very popular as a form of entertainment, and its rapid success had the unfortunate effect of hampering its artistic growth. It soon settled into a conventional pattern lacking both musical originality and dramatic sincerity—a degenerate state in which it remained for the most part until subjected to radical reform in the eighteenth century. But even with its limitations the opera deserves attention because it sought to combine several of the arts, was definitely secular in spirit, and offered employment to musicians hitherto almost entirely dependent upon the patronage of the aristocracy and the church.

Outstanding composers of the early 18th century: (1) J. S. Bach

In the forefront of the progress of instrumental music during the first half of the eighteenth century stands the name of Johann Sebastian Bach (1685–1750), one of the greatest figures in all musical history. The Bachs of Thuringia had for several generations been noted throughout Germany as musicians, and the high reputation of the family may partially explain the underestimation of J. S. Bach by his contemporaries. Bach combined an unbounded imagination and a capacious intellect with heroic powers of discipline and an unquenchable zeal for work. By lifelong study he made himself the master of all the existing formulas of expression; and in practically every field of serious music, with the exception of opera, his influence was marked and beneficial. He revolutionized the technique of playing keyboard instruments. Moreover, he was largely responsible for the adoption of the modern "tempered" scale, which makes it possible to play in any desired key or scale without retuning the instrument. It may be observed in this connection that he was the real founder of modern organ music, and he composed much of the best of it. In his hands the organ *fugue*—a contrapuntal form following the strictest rules—became not merely a dazzling technical feat but a vehicle of the profoundest emotion. While he composed a variety of types of instrumental music, his best-known works, aside from organ pieces, are for choral use, devised principally for the liturgy of the Lutheran service. These last range from settings of simple *chorales* of folk-song origin to elaborate masses. In spite of his versatility and unflagging industry, Bach remained to some extent apart from the age in which he lived. His works are suffused more with the spirit of the German Reformation, or even the Gothic era, than with the optimistic philosophy of the Enlightenment. They

Johann Sebastian Bach (1685–1750).

reflect a preoccupation with death and with man's yearning for redemption and contain overtones of medieval mysticism. Nevertheless, the union of perfect symmetry of form with a tender and untrammeled poetic sensitivity gives Bach's music a beauty which is unsurpassed. Ironical but all too typical were the scant recognition and material reward accorded to him. His constant activity as director, performer, and teacher did not suffice to overcome the struggle against poverty, and his widow was forced to end her days in the poorhouse at Leipzig. So eager was he to bring his works before the public that he taught himself the art of engraving upon copper plates; yet most of his compositions remained unpublished for over a century after his death. Since then his influence has grown steadily, until the exaltation of his memory has raised him almost to the rank of a demigod.

Second only to Bach in musical importance among his contemporaries was G. F. Handel (1685–1759). Like Bach, Handel was a splendid organist, but his chief contribution lay in another direction. After winning easy success in the Italian style of opera, he turned to the dramatic treatment of religious themes and thus created the modern *oratorio*. The most esteemed of his oratorios is *The Messiah*, which he composed within the space of three weeks. In contrast with Bach, Handel attained wide popularity during his

(2) G. F. Handel

545

lifetime, especially in England, where he became a naturalized subject. Undoubtedly one reason for Handel's success in his adopted country was the fact that his virile and heroic oratorios, employing chiefly Old Testament subjects, could be interpreted as symbolizing the struggle of the English people for freedom and for the attainment of national greatness. The sale of his works and a generous pension from the Hanoverian court brought him an ample income, and he was one of the few great composers to become prosperous.

Perfection of the symphony and the opera

The operatic and instrumental fields both figured in the important developments of the latter half of the eighteenth century. The opera was at last raised to a level of artistic excellence. Forms of instrumental composition were perfected which have been of fundamental influence ever since—the *sonata, concerto,* and above all the *symphony.* And finally the orchestra was established essentially on its modern basis. So impressive were the achievements of this era, particularly the growth of the symphony orchestra, that it has come to be known as the "classical" period of musical history. The two figures who most truly represented the progress of this age were the Austrians Haydn and Mozart.

Haydn, composer of symphonies

Joseph Haydn (1732–1809), the son of a poor wagon-maker, was early faced with a bitter struggle for a livelihood. He managed to secure a good musical education, largely by self-instruction, but the buffets he received in early youth left a mark of servility upon his personality. The many indignities which both he and Mozart endured from their social superiors speak eloquently of the snobbishness of the eighteenth century and its slight regard for genius divorced from social rank. Haydn's immense gifts, however, brought him wide acclaim in the European musical world and eventually at least a moderate financial security. Through his kindliness of manner he came to be known affectionately as "Papa Haydn" to the musicians who worked under his direction. While he wrote much for voices, his greatness rests principally upon his instrumental works, numbering some 700, most notable of which are the string quartets and the symphonies. He composed more than 100 symphonies and definitely established the classical pattern for this supreme orchestral medium. The Haydn symphonies are remarkably clear-cut and logical in structure; and while sometimes too precise for modern tastes, their warmth, sincerity, and gaiety have enabled them to retain the popularity they deserve.

Mozart, the supreme musical genius of the 18th century

Wolfgang Mozart (1756–1791) is regarded by many as the supreme musical exponent of the ideals of classicism. He is probably also the most striking example on record of a musical prodigy. He composed at the age of five, played in public at six, and published when seven years old. It was well that his career began early, for it was ended at the age of thirty-five, when the composer's powers were still growing. His untimely death may be attributed to the harsh circumstances that surrounded him, for which, however, his own extravagance, characteristic of many Viennese artists, was partly to blame. Heavily in debt at the time of his death, he was buried in a pauper's grave. In spite of his short life he came to surpass all of his contemporaries in the instrumental field, including Haydn, whom he revered. The superiority of his symphonies to those of Haydn consists in their lyric richness, striking harmonic contrasts, and greater boldness of conception. Equally important was his contribution to the opera, a medium which appealed to him strongly. By the later eighteenth century the able C. W. Gluck had done much to vitalize the opera and restore it to its dramatic purpose, and to the same ends Mozart applied his greater genius. Without entirely rejecting the conventional pattern, he wrote a number of operas, both Italian and German, which still rank as masterpieces, not only for the rare quality of their music but for their dramatic insight and integrity. Perhaps most notable among them are *The Magic Flute* and *Don Giovanni*. Although his creative talent was undoubtedly unique, Mozart embodied much of the essence of eighteenth-century aspirations. His art transcended national boundaries; his imagination was broad and uninhibited. His works reveal a lust for life and keen sensibility to the manifold aspects of human experience. Though sometimes melancholy, his music more often speaks the language of hope, exaltation, and triumph.

6. Social Ideals and Realities during the Age of the Enlightenment

A movement as profoundly disturbing to Western society as the Intellectual Revolution was bound to have its effects upon social customs and individual habits. These effects were especially discernible during the bloom of the Enlightenment in the eighteenth century. Of course, not all of the social progress of this time can be traced to intellectual influences; much of it was due to the bulging prosperity induced by the expansion of trade in the Commercial Revolution. Nevertheless, the progress of philosophy and science had more than incidental effects in clearing away the cobwebs of ancient prejudice and in building a more liberal and humane society.

Causes of the social changes of this period

Mention has already been made of the influence of the Enlightenment in promoting the cause of social reform. A characteristic expression of this influence was agitation for revision of drastic criminal codes and for more liberal treatment of prisoners. In regard to both, the need for reform was urgent. Penalties even for minor offenses were exceedingly severe in practically all countries, death being the punishment for stealing a horse or a sheep or for the theft of as little as five shillings in money. During the first half of the eighteenth century no fewer than sixty crimes were added to the capital list in England. The treatment accorded to bankrupts and

Social idealism: (1) the reform of criminal codes

debtors was also a standing disgrace. Beaten and starved by cruel jailers, they died by the thousands in filthy prisons. Conditions such as these eventually challenged the sympathies of several reformers. Foremost among them was Cesare Beccaria, a jurist of Milan, who had been deeply influenced by the writings of French rationalist philosophers. In 1764 he published his famed treatise on *Crimes and Punishments*, in which he condemned the common theory that penalties should be made as horrible as possible in order to deter potential offenders. Insisting that the purpose of criminal codes should be the prevention of crime and the reform of the wayward rather than vengeance, he urged the abolition of torture as unworthy of civilized nations. He likewise condemned capital punishment as contrary to the natural rights of man, since it cannot be revoked in case of error. Beccaria's book created a veritable sensation. It was translated into a dozen languages, and it stimulated efforts to improve conditions in many lands. By the end of the eighteenth century considerable progress had been made in reducing the severity of penalties, in relieving debtors from punishment, and in providing work and better food for prisoners.

(2) opposition to slavery and war

The humanitarian spirit of the Enlightenment found an outlet also in other directions. Several of the scientists and philosophers, notably Buffon and Rousseau, denounced the evils of slavery. Many more condemned the slave trade. The efforts of intellectuals in this regard were warmly seconded by the leaders of certain religious groups, especially by prominent Quakers in America. Even John Wesley, conservative as he was on many social issues, branded slavery as an abomination. Pacifism was another ideal of many of the new liberal thinkers. Voltaire's strictures on war, which have already been related, were by no means the only example of such sentiments. The criticisms of Holbach and Helvetius were just as devastating. Even the sentimental Rousseau could perceive the illogic in Grotius' attempt to draw a distinction between just and unjust wars. From the pens of other *philosophes* emanated various ingenious plans for insuring perpetual peace, including a scheme for a league of nations with power to take concerted action against aggressors.[13]

(3) increase of sympathy for the lower classes

Perhaps it was natural that humanitarian agitation for reform should be accompanied by an increase of sympathy for the lower classes. This was especially true during the final stage of the Enlightenment. With the progress of reason and the increasing emphasis upon the natural rights of man, the strong reaction against the evils of slavery and war was eventually translated into a protest against every form of suffering and oppression. Thus the hardships of the poor came in for a larger share of attention than they had received since the time of the Sophists. Besides, the middle class in the pursuit of its ambition to dethrone the aristocracy needed

[13] This was the famous scheme of the Abbé de Saint-Pierre (1658–1743).

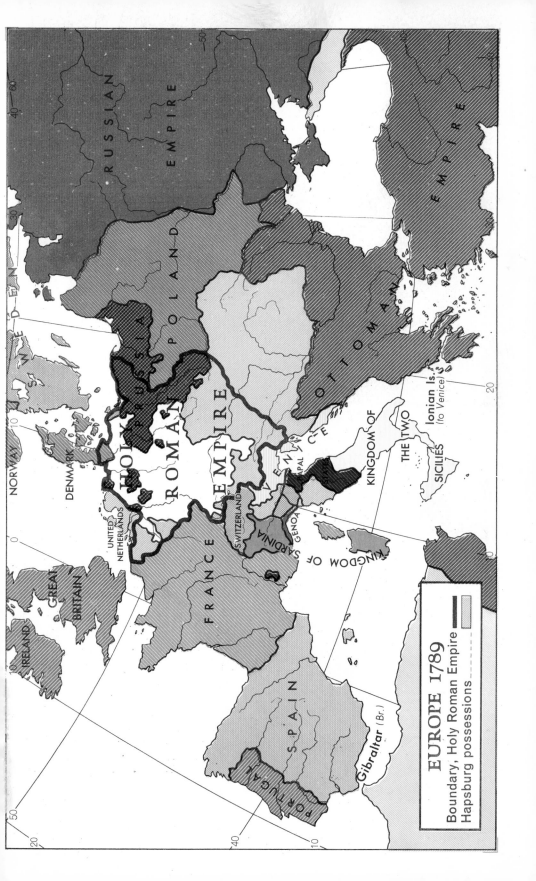

EUROPE 1789
Boundary, Holy Roman Empire
Hapsburg possessions

Portrait of a Gentleman, Jean Auguste Ingres (1780–1867). A student of David, Ingres was a devoted admirer of classical antiquities. But he was also influenced by romanticism. (MMA)

A Woman Reading, Camille Corot (1796–1875). Corot was predominantly a naturalist, a painter of lifelike scenes of innocence and simplicity. He shared the romanticists' sentimental worship of woods and fields. (MMA)

Madame Recamier, Jacques Louis David (1748–1825). David was the exponent of a new classicism during and after the French Revolution. The couch, the lamp, and the costume are copied from Rome and Pompeii. (Louvre)

the support of the peasants and urban workers. Out of such factors there developed a tendency on the part of leading thinkers to espouse the cause of the common man. In particular, it became popular to despise aristocratic lineage or royal birth. Thomas Paine echoed the sentiments of many when he declared that a single honest plowman was worth more than all the crowned ruffians who ever lived. The great Scottish economist, Adam Smith, deplored the habit of feeling more pity for a royal scoundrel like Charles I than for the thousands of common citizens slaughtered in the civil war. Several of the French philosophers of the Enlightenment went considerably farther in professions of sympathy for the masses. Gabriel de Mably (1709–1785), the Marquis de Condorcet (1743–1794), and Rousseau advocated an absolute equality of freedom and privileges for every man. Mably and Condorcet, at least, perceived that this could not be attained except by a redistribution of wealth. While they did not propose socialism, they nevertheless argued that landed property should be held in substantially equal amounts, so that exploitation of the poor by the rich would be practically impossible.

One of the most significant social developments of the Intellectual Revolution was the revolt against Christian morality, particularly its supernatural basis. It was noted in a preceding chapter that a similar revolt had occurred during the Renaissance, exemplified especially by the teachings of such men as Lorenzo Valla, Machiavelli, and Rabelais. The Reformation, however, reversed the trend and established an ethical system in some ways more rigorous than that of the Middle Ages. Now in the late seventeenth and eighteenth centuries the pendulum again swung back. The philosophers of the Enlightenment attempted to separate ethics from religion entirely and to find either a rationalist or a psychological basis for human conduct. Notable among those who followed a rationalist approach was Anthony Ashley Cooper, the third Earl of Shaftesbury (1671–1713). Shaftesbury maintained that every human being is endowed by nature with an innate sense of decency, which is all that is necessary to enable him to distinguish between fundamental issues of right and wrong. This inherent moral sense develops in the mind of the individual before he is mature enough to have any very definite notions about God or a life after death. Consequently there must be a basic morality independent of supernatural sanctions. With the growth of man's reasoning faculties, this basic morality is expanded to embrace the whole field of ethical judgment. But Shaftesbury's ideas of right and wrong were somewhat different from those of traditional moralists. He denied that any act could be truly virtuous if it was motivated by hope of reward or fear of punishment, either in this life or in a life to come. He aimed to revive the Greek conception of virtue as essentially the equivalent of harmony, proportion, and good taste. "Will it not be found," he in-

The revolt against the supernatural basis of Christian morality

quired, "that what is beautiful is harmonious and proportionable; what is harmonious and proportionable is true; and what is at once both beautiful and true is of consequence agreeable and good?"

*The attempt to
discover a new
basis for
morality*

The majority of the philosophers of the Enlightenment inclined to the view that morality is rooted in the psychological instincts of the individual or in considerations of social utility. The doctrine of an instinctive basis was expressed, as we have seen, in the teachings of Helvetius and Holbach, who argued that all human conduct is determined by self-interest, by the pursuit of pleasure and the avoidance of pain. They believed that proper education would enable each individual to perceive that his own self-interest lay in not hurting others, and that ultimately very little restraint would be necessary. David Hume and Adam Smith evolved a somewhat broader theory, contending that morality is determined largely by reflective sympathy. Man, they declared, has a tendency to project himself into the situation of persons around him and to imagine how he would feel under similar circumstances. If the condition of others is wretched, he himself experiences pain, while happiness in others gives rise to sensations of pleasure. Consequently men are impelled by nature to do those things which will promote the happiness of their fellow creatures and especially to avoid those things which will cause suffering. This ethical philosophy was developed most fully in Adam Smith's *Theory of Moral Sentiments* (1759).

*Morality as
exemplified in
the customs
and practices of
the upper
classes*

The revolt against the moral ideals expounded by theologians was reflected not only in the books of the philosophers; it was also revealed in the principal customs and social practices of the time. The eighteenth century, in particular, was an age of pampered elegance and gracious living decidedly at variance with the ascetic taboos of the church. The houses of the nobles were resplendently furnished with shining mirrors, crystal chandeliers, and graceful sofas and chairs richly upholstered in brocaded silk. Men of the upper classes arrayed themselves in powdered wigs, velvet coats with lace at the cuffs, silk stockings, and knee breeches of delicate hue. Not since the days of the Renaissance had fashion played so dominant a part in the lives of both sexes. Habits of personal behavior were also characterized by similar qualities of elegance and artificiality. Form was everything; motive, nothing. The ladies and gentlemen of the best society addressed even those whom they cordially hated with the most fulsome compliments and groveled disgustingly in the presence of higher rank. In a satirical treatise on etiquette, published about 1750, the courtly ceremony of bowing was described, with some measure of truth, as "departing from the perpendicular little by little until the whole spine is presented to the person one is bowing to, as much as to say to him, 'Will your lordship do me the honor of cudgelling me?' " [14]

Actually, among the upper classes, manners very largely took the

[14] Quoted by Preserved Smith, *A History of Modern Culture*, Vol. II, p. 607.

place of morals. The ladies and gentlemen who danced the stately minuet and deported themselves with such charming grace quite commonly ridiculed married love as a relic of a benighted past. Adultery became fashionable and almost a virtue. A husband sometimes lived on friendly terms with his wife's lovers, for no one in this cultivated society would be so uncouth as to display any sentiment of jealousy. Prostitution had not only its apologists but also its defenders, and brothels were quite commonly permitted to remain open on Sundays, though theaters had to be closed. The prevailing attitude toward relations between the sexes appears to have been that of Buffon, who declared that "there is nothing good in love but the physical."

Eighteenth-century society also had its more violent and brutish aspects, which were largely survivals from the turbulent days of the Renaissance. Despite the severity of penal laws, vicious crimes were still very common. In many large cities bands of hooligans roamed the streets at night, while footpads infested the highways in the open country. In London such hoodlums were known as Mohawks, and their favorite diversions, aside from robbery, were beating constables, "turning women upside down," and gouging out the eyes of any who tried to restrain them. Drunkenness continued in much the same measure as before, though the consumption of hard liquor by the poorer classes appears to have increased. About this time gin became popular especially in England as the poor man's drink. Gambling and cruel games and sports likewise survived unabated. Yet another of the prevailing vices of this period was dueling, although it was confined primarily to the upper and middle classes. The gentleman of spirit was still supposed to avenge any real or imaginary insult by challenging the offender to a mortal combat with sword or pistol. Even so prominent a statesman as William Pitt the younger felt obliged to meet an opponent on the so-called field of honor.

It is necessary to observe, however, that the picture of social conditions in the eighteenth century was not altogether dark. For one thing, there was a definite improvement in the standard of living, certainly for the middle classes and probably even for most of the poor. This is evidenced by the increasing per capita consumption of sugar, chocolate, coffee, and tea, which were not merely substituted for other foods and beverages but were additions to the average diet. The growing demand for linen and cotton cloth, and for such articles of luxury as mahogany furniture designed by such masters as Chippendale, Hepplewhite, and Sheraton, may be taken as a further indication of rising prosperity, at least among those who were not hopelessly submerged at the bottom of the heap. The other of the more favorable aspects of social life in this time was a sharp reduction of the death rate. This came about as the result of several causes. Probably the most important was the effective

Canvassing for Votes, by William Hogarth (1697–1764). For our knowledge of social life in the Eighteenth Century we are indebted to the satirical engravings of Hogarth. Bribery seems to be the chief lubricant of the electoral process depicted here.

control of smallpox as a consequence of inoculation and vaccination. A second factor was the establishment of maternity hospitals, which, in combination with improved obstetrical methods, reduced the mortality among infants in the second half of the century by more than 50 per cent and among mothers by an even larger proportion. Finally, advancement in sanitation, together with the adoption of more hygienic habits by people of all classes, contributed not a little to the conquest of various diseases and to lengthening the span of life.

Selected Readings—Philosophy

Becker, C. L., *The Heavenly City of the Eighteenth Century Philosophers*, New Haven, 1932
Brandes, George, *Voltaire*, New York, 1930, 2 vols.
Bury, J. B., *History of the Freedom of Thought*, New York, 1913
Cassirer, Ernest, *Philosophy of the Enlightenment*, Princeton, 1952
Chapman, J. W., *Rousseau—Totalitarian or Liberal?* New York, 1956
Green, F. C., *Jean-Jacques Rousseau: A Critical Study of His Life and Writings*, New York, 1955
Hibben, J. G., *The Philosophy of the Enlightenment*, New York, 1910
Kropotkin, Peter, *Ethics: Origin and Development*, New York, 1924
Lecky, W. E. H., *History of the Rise and Influence of the Spirit of Rationalism in Europe*, New York, 1914, 2 vols.
McGiffert, A. C., *Protestant Thought before Kant*, New York, 1915
Manuel, Frank E., *The Age of Reason*, Ithaca, 1951
Morais, H. M., *Deism in Eighteenth Century America*, New York, 1934
Morley, John, *Rousseau*, New York, 1891, 2 vols.
———, *Voltaire*, New York, 1871
Randall, J. H., Jr., *The Making of the Modern Mind*, New York, 1926, Chs. XI, XII, XVI
Rowe, Constance, *Voltaire and the State*, New York, 1955

Schapiro, J. S., *Condorcet and the Rise of Liberalism in France*, New York, 1934

Smith, Preserved, *A History of Modern Culture*, New York, 1934, Vol. II

Stephen, Leslie, *History of English Thought in the Eighteenth Century*, New York, 1927

Vaughan, C. E., *The Romantic Revolt*, New York, 1930

—Science

Butterfield, Ernest, *The Origins of Modern Science*, New York, 1951

Crew, Henry, *The Rise of Modern Physics*, Baltimore, 1937

Hogben, Lancelot, *Mathematics for the Million*, New York, 1937

Nordenskiöld, Erik, *The History of Biology*, New York, 1928

Sedgwick, W. T., and Tyler, H. W., *A Short History of Science*, New York, 1918

Singer, Charles, *A Short History of Medicine*, New York, 1928

Smith, Preserved, *History of Modern Culture*, New York, 1934, Vol. II

—Literature, Art, and Music

Bukofzer, Manfred F., *Music in the Baroque Era*, New York, 1947

Davenport, Marcia, *Mozart*, New York, 1932

Guérard, A. L., *Life and Death of an Ideal*, New York, 1928

Lang, Paul, *Music in Western Civilization*, New York, 1941

Machlis, Joseph, *The Enjoyment of Music*, New York, 1955

Oxford History of Music, Vol. III

Robertson, J. G., *A History of German Literature*, New York, 1930

Schweitzer, Albert, *J. S. Bach*, London, 1923, 2 vols.

Stephen, Leslie, *English Literature and Society in the Eighteenth Century*, New York, 1907

Vaughan, C. E., *The Romantic Revolt*, New York, 1930

Wright, C. H. C., *French Classicism*, Cambridge, Mass., 1920

Source Materials

Baumer, F. L. V., *Main Currents of European Thought*, New York, 1952

Descartes, René, *Discourse on Method*, Parts I, II, V

Milton, John, *Areopagitica; The Tenure of Kings and Magistrates*

Newton, Sir Isaac, *Principia*, Third Book, Rules of Reasoning in Philosophy

Spinoza, Benedict, *A Theologico-Political Treatise*

Voltaire, *Philosophical Dictionary; Candide; Essay on Toleration*

Modern Occidental Civilization, 1789-1914: Democracy, Nationalism, Industrialism

A second stage in the history of modern Occidental civilization was ushered in by the French Revolution. This event, which occupied the years from 1789 to 1799, had a profound influence upon the modern world. It overthrew mercantilism and the surviving relics of feudalism and contributed to the political supremacy of the middle class. Besides, it was a cardinal source of militant nationalism, of economic individualism, and of the sovereignty of the masses. Several of these results—especially nationalism, democracy, and middle-class supremacy—persisted throughout the nineteenth and early twentieth centuries and were among the dominant characteristics of that era. At the same time, it must not be forgotten that the history of Western nations from the French Revolution to the outbreak of World War I was radically conditioned by other factors. Chief among these was the Industrial Revolution, which began about 1760 and has continued until the present time. Included among its significant results were the urbanization of modern life, the creation of new social classes and new economic and political philosophies, the revival of imperialism, and a general improvement in standards of living. In addition, by enabling countries to support a much larger population than would ever have been possible under an agricultural economy, the Industrial Revolution was partly responsible for the fact that the number of inhabitants of Europe more than doubled between 1789 and 1914.

	America	Britain
	Great Awakening, 1740–1810	Development of steam engine, 1769 William Wordsworth, 1770–1850 Beginning of factory system, *ca.* 1770
1775—	American Revolution, 1775–1783 Declaration of Independence, 1776	Adam Smith, *The Wealth of Nations,* 1776 Classical economics, 1776–1880
	Adoption of the Constitution of the U.S., 1787 John Fitch's steamboat, 1788	
	The Bill of Rights, 1791 Thomas Paine, *The Rights of Man,* 1791	Utilitarianism, 1790–1870 Edward Jenner develops vaccination for smallpox, 1796
1800—	Jeffersonian Revolution, 1800–1801	
		Revival of atomic theory, 1810 Charles Dickens, 1812–1870
1825—	Monroe Doctrine, 1823 Jacksonian Revolution, 1828–1837	First railroad, 1825
		First Reform Act, 1832
	Mechanization of agriculture, 1835– Use of ether as an anesthetic, 1842 Telegraph, 1844	Chartist Movement, 1838–1848 Repeal of Corn Laws, 1846
1850—		Law of dissipation of energy, 1851
	First oil well, 1859 Civil War, 1861–1865	Bessemer process, 1856 Charles Darwin, *Origin of Species,* 1859 J. S. Mill, *On Liberty,* 1859 Antiseptic surgery, 1865 Second Reform Act, 1867
1875—		

CIVILIZATION, 1789–1914

Western Europe	Central and Eastern Europe
Physiocrats, 1750–1800	
	Beethoven, 1770–1827
	Immanuel Kant, *Critique of Pure Reason*, 1781
French Declaration of Rights of Man, 1789 French Revolution, 1789–1799	Friedrich List, 1789–1846
Coup d'état of Napoleon, 1799 Romanticism in literature and arts, 1800–1900 Victor Hugo, 1802–1885 First Empire in France, 1804–1814	F. Schubert, 1797–1828
Battle of Waterloo, 1815	Richard Wagner, 1813–1883 Congress of Vienna, 1814–1815
	Carlsbad Decrees, 1819 Feodor Dostoievski, 1821–1881
Henrik Ibsen, 1828–1906	Leo Tolstoi, 1828–1910 Independence of Greece, 1829
July Revolution in France, 1830 Realism in literature and arts, 1830–1914 Independence of Belgium, 1831	
	Unification of Germany, 1833–1871
Émile Zola, 1840–1902	Tchaikovsky, 1840–1893
February Revolution in France, 1848 Second Republic in France, 1848–1852	Law of conservation of energy, 1847 *Communist Manifesto*, 1848 Unification of Italy, 1848–1870
Second Empire in France, 1852–1870	Crimean War, 1854–1856
	Emancipation of serfs in Russia, 1861
	Austro-Prussian War, 1866 *Ausgleich* establishes Dual Monarchy, 1867
Franco-Prussian War, 1870–1871 Impressionism, 1870–1890 Paris Commune, 1871	Law of Papal Guaranties, 1871 German Empire, 1871–1918 *Kulturkampf*, 1872–1886
Development of dynamo, 1873 Germ theory of disease, 1875	

America	Britain
Telephone, 1876	
	Herbert Spencer, *Data of Ethics,* 1879
Pragmatism, 1880–1930	Third Reform Act, 1884
Beginning of finance capitalism, 1890	
Populism, 1890–1897	
William James, *The Will to Believe,* 1897	
Spanish-American War, 1898	Boer War, 1899–1902
Progressive movement, 1901–1916	
First airplane flight, 1903	
Model T Ford, 1908	
	Parliament Act of 1911

1900—

CIVILIZATION, 1789–1914 (*Continued*)

Western Europe	Central and Eastern Europe
Third Republic in France, 1875–1940	
	Internal-combustion engine, 1876
	Russo-Turkish War, 1877–1878
	Congress of Berlin, 1878
	Triple Alliance, 1882–1914
Post-impressionism, 1890	Berlin-to-Bagdad Railway, 1890–1907
Dreyfus affair, 1894–1905	
Discovery of X-ray, 1895	Ivan Pavlov discovers conditioned reflex, *ca* 1895
	Diesel engine, 1897
First Hague Conference, 1899	Wireless telegraph, 1899
Hugo DeVries, mutation theory, 1901	
Cubism, 1903–	
Entente Cordiale, 1904	Russo-Japanese War, 1904–1905
Separation of church and state in France, 1905	Founding of psychoanalysis, *ca.* 1905
	Russian Revolution of 1905
	Einstein theories, 1905–1910
Second Hague Conference, 1907	
Triple Entente, 1907	Young Turk Revolution, 1908
Discovery of protons and electrons, *ca.* 1910	Bosnian crisis, 1908
	Balkan wars, 1912–1913

The French Revolution (1789-1799)

*The era of rev-
olution*

Profound changes were wrought in the political history of the
Western world in the latter part of the eighteenth century. This
period witnessed the death throes of that peculiar system of government and society which had grown up during the age of the despots.
In England this system had already been largely overthrown by
1689, but in other nations of Europe it lingered on, growing more
and more ossified and corrupt with the passing of the years. It
flourished in every major country of Europe under the combined
influence of militarism and the ambitions of monarchs to consolidate
their power at the expense of the nobles. But scarcely anywhere did
it exist in so abominable a form as in France during the reigns of
the last three Bourbon kings. Louis XIV was the supreme incarnation of absolute rule. His successors, Louis XV and Louis XVI,
dragged the government to the lowest depths of extravagance and
irresponsibility. Moreover, their subjects were sufficiently enlightened to be keenly aware of their disadvantages. For these reasons it is not strange that France should have been the scene of a
violent upheaval to overthrow a regime which had long been
hated and despised by the most intelligent citizens of the country.
And we shall not go far wrong in interpreting the French Revolution as the climax of a century of slowly increasing opposition to
absolutism and to the supremacy of a decadent aristocracy.

1. The Causes of the French Revolution

For convenience we can divide the causes of the French Revolution into three main classes: political, economic, and intellectual.
Naturally this division is somewhat arbitrary, since none of these

classes was entirely distinct. The intellectual causes, for example, and to some extent the political also, were largely economic in origin. Nevertheless, for purposes of simplification it will be best to keep them separate. One of the major political causes has already been mentioned. This was the despotic rule of the Bourbon kings. For nearly two hundred years government in France had been largely a one-man institution. During the fourteenth, fifteenth, and sixteenth centuries a kind of parliament known as the Estates General, composed of representatives of the clergy, the nobility, and the common people, had met at irregular intervals. But after 1614 it was no longer summoned. Henceforth the king was the sole repository of sovereign power. In a very real sense the king was the state. He could do almost anything his imperious will might dictate, without fear of impeachment or legislative restrictions of any kind. No questions of constitutionality or the natural rights of his subjects need trouble him. He could throw men into prison without a trial by means of royal orders, or *lettres de cachet*. He could prevent any criticism of his policies by clamping a rigid censorship on the press or by restricting freedom of speech. It must be conceded, however, that the tyranny of the French kings has often been exaggerated. In actual practice there was comparatively little interference with what men wrote or said, particularly during the reigns of Louis XV and Louis XVI. No action of these monarchs inhibited the mordant wit of Voltaire or suppressed the radical books of Rousseau.[1] On the contrary, the attacks by these and other philosophers increased in virulence the nearer the Revolution approached. The explanation, of course, is not to be found in any liberalism of Louis XV and his dull-witted grandson but rather in their indifference to politics.

A second political cause of the French Revolution was the illogical and unsystematic character of the government. Confusion reigned in nearly every department. The political structure was the product of a long and irregular growth extending back into the Middle Ages. New agencies had been established from time to time to meet some particular condition, with a total disregard for those already in existence. As a result there was much overlapping of functions, and numerous useless officials drew salaries from the public purse. Conflicts of jurisdiction between rival departments frequently delayed action on vital problems for months at a stretch. Almost everywhere inefficiency, waste, and graft were the ruling qualities of the system. Even in financial matters there was no more regularity than in other branches of public policy. Not only did the government have no budget, but accounts were seldom kept; and there was no

---

[1] Voltaire was imprisoned for a time and afterwards exiled to England for one of his vitriolic lampoons, but this was early in his career. Most of his trenchant criticisms of the government and the church were written *after his return* from England.

clear-cut distinction between the income of the king and the income of the state. Worse still was the fact that the collection of public revenues was exceedingly haphazard. Instead of appointing official collectors, the king employed the old Roman system of farming out the collection of taxes to private corporations and individuals, permitting them to retain as profit all that they could gouge from the people in excess of a stipulated amount. Similar disorganized conditions prevailed in the realm of law and judicial procedure. Nearly every province of France had its special code based upon local custom. As a consequence an act punishable as a crime in southern France, where the Roman influence was strongest, might be no concern of the law in a central or northern province. This lack of uniformity was especially galling to the business classes, who were often involved in transactions in distant parts of the country.

(3) the costly wars of the French kings

Probably the most decisive of the political causes was the disastrous wars into which France was plunged during the eighteenth century. Revolutions are not made by sporadic attacks upon a system still in its prime, no matter how oppressive some of its policies may be. Before a great political and social upheaval (which is the way we must define a true revolution) can occur, it seems to be necessary that there shall be a near collapse of the existing order. Something must happen to produce a condition of chaos, to reveal the incompetence and corruption of the government, and to create such disgust and hardship that many of those who formerly supported the old regime shall now turn against it. Nothing could be better calculated to achieve these ends than conflict with foreign powers resulting in humiliating defeat or at least in serious reverses. As a matter of fact, it is almost impossible to conceive of any of the great revolutions of modern times except as a consequence of long and disastrous wars.[2] The first of the wars which prepared the ground for the French Revolution was the Seven Years' War (1756–1763), fought during the reign of Louis XV. In this struggle France was pitted against England and Prussia and, in spite of aid from Austria and also for a time from Russia, went down to overwhelming defeat. As a result, the French were compelled to surrender nearly all of their colonial possessions. It was natural and, on the whole quite justifiable, that the blame for this catastrophe should be placed upon the incompetence of the government. The effects of this blow were made worse when Louis XVI decided in 1778 to intervene in the American War for Independence. Though France was now on the winning side, the cost of maintaining fleets and armies in the Western Hemisphere for more than three years virtually bankrupted the government. As we shall see, it was this condition of financial helplessness in the face of an impossible burden of debt which led

[2] A distinction, of course, must be drawn between true revolutions and those of the palace variety, so common in the Balkans and in Latin America, which are really very little more than substitutes for elections.

directly to the quarrel between the king and the middle class and the consequent outbreak of revolution.

In turning to the economic causes of the French Revolution, we must note first of all that widespread suffering among the mass of the people was not one of them. The popular notion that the Revolution occurred because the majority of the people were starving for want of bread, and because the queen said, "Let them eat cake," is far from historically accurate. Despite the loss of her colonial empire, France on the eve of the Revolution was still a rich and prosperous nation. For more than two centuries her bourgeoisie had been fattening on the profits of expanding trade, while her lower classes had been getting at least some of the crumbs that fell from the tables of the rich. Indeed, it is the opinion of modern scholars that the French peasants in the eighteenth century were better off than the rural folk in any other country of Europe except England.[3] That their condition was actually improving is evidenced by the decline of serfdom during the century preceding the Revolution, and by the fact that a steadily increasing proportion of the peasants were becoming owners of land. No doubt there was a great deal of misery to be found among the dwellers in the slums of Paris, especially during the hard winter of 1788–1789. But these people did not make the Revolution; they merely participated in it after it had been started by others. The fact cannot be emphasized too strongly that the French Revolution was launched as a middle-class movement. Its original objectives were primarily for the benefit of the bourgeoisie. Since the leaders of this class needed the support of a larger percentage of the people, they naturally took some notice of the grievances of the peasants. But the poor proletarians were almost ignored.

The French Revolution not the result of misery and poverty among the people

What then were the real economic causes? Perhaps we should place at the head of the list the rise of the middle class to a position of extraordinary power and prestige. The emergence of a new economic group with a sense of grievances and a consciousness of its own strength and importance seems to be a necessary condition to the outbreak of any revolution. This class is never composed of miserable dregs of humanity—wretched, starving, and hopeless. On the contrary, its ranks must be permeated by a sense of confidence inspired by previous success and strengthened by the belief that additional effort will bring greater gains in the future. During the years of prosperity preceding the Revolution the French bourgeoisie had grown to be the dominant economic class. Aside from the land, nearly all of the productive wealth was in its hands. It controlled the resources of trade, manufacturing, and finance. Moreover, its members appear to have been growing richer year by year. In 1789 the foreign commerce of France reached the unprecedented total

The real economic causes: (1) the rise of the middle class

[3] L. R. Gottschalk, *The Era of the French Revolution*, pp. 30–31.

of 1,153,000,000 francs.[4] But the chief effect of this rising prosperity was to sharpen bourgeois discontent. No matter how much money a merchant, manufacturer, banker, or lawyer might acquire, he was still excluded from political privileges. He had almost no influence at the court; he could not share in the highest honors; and, except in the choice of a few petty local officers, he could not even vote. Besides, he was looked down upon as an inferior by the idle and frivolous nobility. Occasionally some snobbish count or duke would consent to the marriage of his son to the daughter of a wealthy burgher; but one who did often made a practice of referring to the marriage as "manuring [his] land." As the middle class rose in affluence and in consciousness of its own importance, its members were bound to resent such attempts at social discrimination. But above all it was the demand of the commercial, financial, and industrial leaders for political power commensurate with their economic position which made the bourgeoisie a revolutionary class.

A demand for political power was not the only consequence of the growing prosperity of the middle class; there was also an increasing clamor for the abandonment of mercantilist policies. In *(2) opposition to mercantilism* earlier times mercantilism had been welcomed by merchants and manufacturers because of its effects in procuring new markets and fostering trade. But those times were at the beginning of the Commercial Revolution when business was still in its swaddling clothes. As commerce and industry flourished through succeeding centuries, the bourgeoisie became increasingly confident of its ability to stand on its own collective feet. The result was a growing tendency to look upon the regulations of mercantilism as oppressive restrictions. Merchants disliked the special monopolies granted to favored companies and the interference with their freedom to buy in foreign markets. Manufacturers chafed under the laws controlling wages, fixing prices, and restricting the purchase of raw materials outside of France and her colonies. These were only a few of the more annoying regulations enforced by a government operating under the twin objectives of paternalism and economic self-sufficiency. Perhaps it is not strange that the middle class should have come to think of pure economic liberty as a paradise, worthy to be gained at terrific cost. At any rate, it can scarcely be doubted that the desire of businessmen to be rid of mercantilism was one of the principal causes of the French Revolution.

A third factor, mainly economic in character, which contributed much to the outbreak of the French Revolution was the system *(3) the survival of privilege: the First Estate* of privilege entrenched in the society of the Old Regime. Prior to the Revolution the population of France was divided into three great classes or Estates: the first was composed of the clergy; the second, of the nobles; and the third, of the common people. The First Estate really included two different ranks: (1) the higher

[4] *Ibid.*, p. 44.

clergy, made up of cardinals, archbishops, bishops, and abbots; and (2) the lower clergy or parish priests. Though all of these servants of the church were supposed to be members of a privileged group, in actual fact a wide gulf separated the two ranks. The lower clergy were frequently as poor as their humblest parishioners and were generally disposed to sympathize with the common man. By contrast, the higher clergy lived on the fattest fruits of the land and moved in the gay and sophisticated circle of the king and his court. Including no more than 1 per cent of the total population, they nevertheless owned about 20 per cent of all the land, to say nothing of vast wealth in the form of castles, paintings, gold, and jewels. Several of the bishops and archbishops had incomes running into hundreds of thousands of francs. Naturally, most of these gilded prelates gave little attention to religious affairs. Some of them dabbled in politics, aiding the king in maintaining his absolute rule. Others gambled or devoted their energies to more scandalous vices. Though it cannot be assumed that all of them were depraved and neglectful of their professional duties, a sufficient number were corrupt, domineering, and vicious to convince many people that the church was rotten to the core and that its leaders were guilty of robbing the people and wasting the nation's resources.

The Second Estate, comprising the secular nobility, was also divided into two subordinate castes. At the top were the *nobles of the sword*, whose titles went all the way back to the feudal suzerains of the Middle Ages. Beneath them were the *nobles of the robe*, whose immediate ancestors had acquired some judicial office conferring a title of nobility; the "robe" is the magistrate's or judge's gown. Though commonly despised by their brethren of more ancient lineage, the nobles of the robe were by far the most intelligent and progressive members of the upper classes. Several of their number became ardent reformers, while a few played prominent roles in the Revolution itself. Their ranks included such famous critics of the established order as Montesquieu, Mirabeau, and Lafayette. It was the nobles of the sword who really constituted the privileged class in the Second Estate. Together with the higher clergy they monopolized the leading positions in the government, usually delegating the actual work to subordinates. While they owned vast estates, they customarily resided at Versailles and depended upon stewards or bailiffs to extort enough from the peasants to provide for their luxurious needs. Few indeed of these high-born wastrels performed any useful function. They acted as if they believed that their only responsibilities to society were to flatter the king, to cultivate the graces of courtly life, and occasionally to patronize the decadent classical art. In a very real sense, most of them were worthless parasites consuming the wealth which others labored hard to produce.

The Second Estate

Among the most valuable privileges of clerics and nobles were those relating to taxation. And the inequitable system of taxation may well be considered a fourth economic cause of the French Revolution. Taxes in France, long before 1789, had come to consist of two main types. First, there were the direct taxes, which included the *taille*, or tax on real and personal property; the *capitation*, or poll tax; and the *vingtième*, or tax on incomes, originally at the rate of 5 per cent, but in the eighteenth century more commonly 10 or 11 per cent. The indirect taxes, or taxes added to the price of commodities and paid by the ultimate consumer, embraced mainly the tariffs on articles imported from foreign countries and the tolls levied on goods shipped from one province of France to another. In addition, the *gabelle*, or tax on salt, may also be considered a form of indirect tax. For some time the production of salt had been a state monopoly in France, and every individual inhabitant was required to buy at least seven pounds a year from the government works. To the cost of production was added a heavy tax, with the result that the price to the consumer was often as much as fifty or sixty times the actual value of the salt. While exceedingly burdensome, the indirect taxes were not as a rule unfairly distributed. It was difficult, of course, for anyone, regardless of his social status, to avoid paying them. The case of most of the direct taxes, however, was far otherwise. The clergy, by virtue of the medieval rule that the property of the church could not be taxed by the state, escaped payment of both the *taille* and the *vingtième*. The nobles, especially those of higher rank, made use of their influence with the king to obtain exemption from practically all direct levies. As a result, the main task of providing funds for the government fell upon the common people, or members of the Third Estate. And since few of the artisans and laborers had much that could be taxed, the chief burden had to be borne by the peasants and the bourgeoisie.

A final economic cause of the Revolution was the survival of relics of feudalism in France as late as 1789. While the feudal system itself had long since become extinct, vestiges of it remained and served as convenient instruments for maintaining the power of the king and the privileged position of the nobles. In some backward areas of the country serfdom still lingered, but the prevalence of this institution must not be exaggerated. The highest estimate ever given of the number of peasants who were serfs is 1,500,000, out of a total rural population of at least 15,000,000. The vast majority of the peasants were free men. A considerable proportion owned the lands they cultivated. Others were tenants or hired laborers, but the largest percentage appear to have been share-croppers, farming the lands of the nobles for a portion of the harvest, generally ranging from a third to a half. However, even those peasants who were entirely free were still required to perform obligations which had come down from the Feudal Age. One of the most odious of these was the payment of an annual rental to the lord who had formerly controlled the land. Another was the donation to the local noble of a share of the price received whenever a tract of land was sold. In addition, the peasants were still required to contribute the *banalités*, or fees supposedly for the use of various facilities owned by the noble. During the Middle Ages *banalités* had been paid for the use of the lord's flour mill, his wine press, and his bake oven. In spite of the fact that by the eighteenth century many of the peasants owned such equipment themselves and no longer benefited by the services provided by the noble, the *banalités* were still collected in the original amounts.

Probably the most exasperating of all the relics of feudalism were the *corvée* and the hunting privileges of the nobility. The *corvée*, formerly a requirement of labor on the lord's demesne and in the building of roads and bridges on the manorial estate, was now an obligation to the government. For several weeks each year the peasant was forced to put his own work aside and devote his labor to maintaining the public highways. No other class of the population was required to perform this service. Even greater inconvenience was suffered by the rural citizens as a result of the hunting privileges of the nobles. From time immemorial the right to indulge in the diversions of the chase had been regarded as a distinctive badge of aristocracy. The man of gentle birth must have unlimited freedom to pursue this exciting pastime wherever he wished. Naturally, nothing so trivial as the property rights of the peasants should be allowed to stand in the way. In some parts of France the peasants were forbidden to weed or mow in breeding time lest they disturb the nests of the partridges. Rabbits, crows, and foxes could not be killed regardless of how much damage they did to the crops or to domestic fowl and young animals. Furthermore, the peasant was supposed to resign himself to having his fields trampled at any time by the horses of some thoughtless crew of noble hunters.

The corvée *and the hunting privileges of the nobility*

Every great social upheaval of modern times has developed out of a background of intellectual causes. Before a movement can reach the proportions of an actual revolution, it is necessary that it be supported by a body of ideas, providing not only a program of action but a glorious vision of the new order that is finally to be achieved. To a large extent these ideas are the product of political and economic ambitions, but in time they take on the significance of independent factors. Originally secondary or derivative causes, they ultimately become primary causes. Eventually the fulfillment of the ideas is accepted as an end in itself and draws the allegiance of men like the gospel of a new religion. The intellectual causes of the French Revolution were mainly an outgrowth of the Enlightenment. This movement produced two interesting political theories, which have exerted influence ever since. The first was the *liberal* theory of such writers as Locke and Montesquieu; and the second was the *democratic* theory of Rousseau. While the two were funda-

Intellectual causes: liberal and democratic theories

mentally opposed, they nevertheless had elements in common. Both were predicated upon the assumption that the state is a necessary evil and that government rests upon a contractual basis. Each had its doctrine of popular sovereignty, although with contrasting interpretations. And, finally, both upheld in some measure the fundamental rights of the individual.

*The liberal po-
litical theory
of John Locke*

The father of the liberal theory of the seventeenth and eighteenth centuries was John Locke (1632–1704), although several of its doctrines had already been suggested in the writings of John Milton (1608–1674), James Harrington (1611–1677), and Algernon Sydney (1622–1683). Locke's political philosophy is contained chiefly in his *Second Treatise of Civil Government*, published in 1690. In this he developed a theory of limited government intended partly to justify the new system of parliamentary rule set up in England as a result of the Glorious Revolution. He maintained that originally all men had lived in a state of nature in which absolute freedom and equality prevailed, and there was no government of any kind. The only law was the law of nature, which each individual enforced for himself in order to protect his natural rights to life, liberty, and property. It was not long, however, until men began to perceive that the inconveniences of the state of nature greatly outweighed its advantages. With every individual attempting to enforce his own rights, confusion and insecurity were the unavoidable results. Accordingly, the people agreed among themselves to establish a civil society, to set up a government, and to surrender certain powers to it. But they did not make that government absolute. The only power they conferred upon it was the executive power of the law of nature. Since the state is nothing but the joint power of all the members of society, its authority "can be no more than those persons had in a state of nature before they entered into society, and gave it up to the community." [5] All powers not expressly surrendered are reserved to the people themselves. If the government exceeds or abuses the authority explicitly granted in the political contract, it becomes tyrannical; and the people then have the right to dissolve it or to rebel against it and overthrow it.

*Locke's
condemnation
of absolutism*

Locke condemned absolutism in every form. He denounced despotic monarchy, but he was no less severe in his strictures against the absolute sovereignty of parliaments. Though he defended the supremacy of the law-making branch, with the executive primarily an agent of the legislature, he nevertheless refused to concede to the representatives of the people an unlimited power. Arguing that government was instituted among men for the preservation of property (which he generally defined in the inclusive sense of life, liberty, and estate),[6] he denied the authority of any political agency

[5] *Second Treatise of Civil Government* (Everyman Library ed.), p. 184.
[6] *Ibid.*, p. 159.

to invade the natural rights of a single individual. The law of nature, which embodies these rights, is an automatic limitation upon every branch of the government. Regardless of how large a majority of the people's representatives should demand the restriction of freedom of speech or the confiscation and redistribution of property, no such action could legally be taken. If taken illegally it would justify effective measures of resistance on the part of the majority of citizens. Locke was much more concerned with protecting individual liberty than he was with promoting stability or social progress. If forced to make a choice, he would have preferred the evils of anarchy to those of despotism in any form.

The influence of few political philosophers in the history of the world has exceeded that of Locke. Not only were his doctrines of natural rights, limited government, and the right of resistance against *Locke's* tyranny an important source of French Revolutionary theory, but *influence* they found ready acceptance in American thought as well. They furnished most of the theoretical foundation for the colonial revolt against British oppression. They were reflected so clearly in the Declaration of Independence that whole passages of that document might almost have been copied from the *Second Treatise of Civil Government*. Lockian principles also influenced the drafting of the Constitution and especially the arguments advanced by Hamilton, Madison, and Jay in the *Federalist* urging its ratification. Later, when the new government enacted the Alien and Sedition laws, it was mainly on the basis of Lockian theory that Madison and Jefferson in the Virginia and Kentucky Resolutions appealed to the several States to resist the usurpation of power.

In France the foremost exponents of the liberal political theory were Voltaire (1694–1778) and Baron de Montesquieu (1689–1755). As was indicated earlier, Voltaire considered orthodox Christianity *The liberal po-* to be the worst of the enemies of mankind, but he reserved plenty *litical theory* of contempt for tyrannical government. During his exile in England *of Voltaire* he had studied the writings of Locke and had been deeply impressed by their vigorous assertions of individual freedom. Returning to France while still a comparatively young man, he devoted a large part of the remainder of his life to the fight for intellectual, religious, and political liberty. In common with Locke he conceived of government as a necessary evil, with powers which ought to be limited to the enforcement of natural rights. He maintained that all men are endowed by nature with equal rights to liberty, property, and the protection of the laws. But Voltaire was no democrat. He was inclined to think of the ideal form of government as either an enlightened monarchy or a republic dominated by the middle class. To the end of his life he continued to be more than a little afraid of the masses. He was even fearful that his attacks upon organized religion might serve to incite the multitude to deeds of violence. **569**

*The influence
of Montesquieu*

*The separation
of powers and
checks and
balances*

It is related that after he had been robbed by some peasants, he attended church for a season in order to persuade the country bumpkins that he still believed in God.

A more profound and systematic political thinker than Voltaire was his older contemporary, Baron de Montesquieu. Though, like Voltaire, a student of Locke and an ardent admirer of British institutions, Montesquieu was a unique figure among the political philosophers of the eighteenth century. In his celebrated *Spirit of Laws* he brought new methods and new conceptions into the theory of the state. Instead of attempting to found a science of government by pure deduction, he followed the Aristotelian method of studying actual political systems as they were supposed to have operated in the past. He tended to ignore the Lockian ideas of natural rights and the contractual origin of the state and taught that the meaning of the law of nature is to be found in the facts of history. Moreover, he denied that there is any one perfect form of government suitable for all peoples under all conditions. He maintained, on the contrary, that political institutions in order to be successful must harmonize with the physical conditions and the level of social advancement of the nations they are intended to serve. Thus he declared that despotism is best suited to countries of vast domain; limited monarchy to those of moderate size; and republican government to those of small extent. For his own country, France, he was disposed to think that a limited monarchy would be the most appropriate form, since he regarded the nation as too large to be made into a republic unless on some kind of federal plan.

Montesquieu is especially famous for his theory of the separation of powers. He avowed that it is a natural tendency of man to abuse any extent of power entrusted to him, and that consequently every government, regardless of its form, is liable to degenerate into despotism. To prevent such a result he argued that the authority of government should be broken up into its three natural divisions of legislative, executive, and judicial. Whenever any two or more of these are allowed to remain united in the same hands, liberty, he declared, is at an end. The only effective way to avoid tyranny is to enable each branch of the government to act as a check upon the other two. For example, the executive should have the power by means of the veto to curb the encroachments of the lawmaking branch. The legislature, in turn, should have the authority of impeachment in order to restrain the executive. And, finally, there should be an independent judiciary vested with power to protect individual rights against arbitrary acts of either the legislature or the executive. This favorite scheme of Montesquieu was not intended, of course, to facilitate democracy. In fact, its purpose was largely the opposite: to prevent the absolute supremacy of the majority, expressed as it normally would be through the people's representatives in the legislature. It was a typical illustration of that strong dislike which the bourgeoisie had come to have for despotic government in any form, whether of the few or of the many. Montesquieu's principle of the separation of powers was none the less influential. It was incorporated in the first of the governments set up during the French Revolution, and it found its way with very few changes indeed into the Constitution of the United States.[7]

The second of the great political ideals which occupied an important place in the intellectual background of the French Revolution was the ideal of democracy. In contrast with liberalism, democracy was and still is much less concerned with the defense of individual rights than with the enforcement of popular rule. As a matter of fact, in its original, historic meaning, democracy is inseparable from the idea of the sovereignty of the masses. What the majority of the citizens wills is the supreme law of the land, for the voice of the people is the voice of God. It is generally assumed that under democracy the minority will continue to enjoy full liberty of expression, but this assumption does not necessarily hold. The only sovereign right of the minority is the right to become the majority. As long as a particular group remains a minority, its members cannot claim any rights of individual action beyond the control of the state. Many exponents of democracy in the present generation would deny that this statement is true and would stoutly maintain their devotion to freedom of speech and freedom of the press as rights which the government cannot legally infringe. But this attitude springs from the fact that the current ideal is generally combined with liberalism. Indeed, democracy and liberalism have now come to be used as if they were identical in meaning. Originally, however, they were entirely separate ideals. Historic democracy also included a belief in the natural equality of all men, opposition to hereditary privilege, and an abiding faith in the wisdom and virtue of the masses.

The democratic political theory

The founder of democracy as described above was Jean Jacques Rousseau (1712–1778). Since Rousseau was also the father of romanticism, we can expect that sentiment should have deeply colored his political judgments. Consistency, moreover, was not always a crowning virtue of his reasoning. The most significant of his writings on political theory were his *Social Contract* and his *Discourse on the Origin of Inequality*. In both of these he upheld the popular thesis that men had originally lived in a state of nature. But in contrast with Locke he regarded this state of nature as a veritable paradise. No one suffered inconvenience from maintaining his own rights against others. Indeed, there were very few chances of conflict of any sort; for private property did not exist for a long time, and every man was the equal of his neighbor. Eventually, however,

Rousseau, the founder of democracy

---

[7] For the influence of Montesquieu upon the founders of the American government, see E. M. Burns, *James Madison: Philosopher of the Constitution*, pp. 180–83.

evils arose, due primarily to the fact that some men staked off plots of land and said to themselves, "This is mine." It was in such manner that various degrees of inequality developed; and, as a consequence, "cheating trickery," "insolent pomp," and "insatiable ambition" soon came to dominate the relations among men.[8] The only hope of security was now for men to establish a civil society and to surrender all of their rights to the community. This they did by means of a social contract, in which each individual agreed with the whole body of individuals to submit to the will of the majority. Thus the state was brought into existence.

Rousseau developed an altogether different conception of sovereignty from that of the liberals. Whereas Locke and his followers had taught that only a portion of sovereign power is surrendered to the state, the rest being retained by the people themselves, Rousseau contended that sovereignty is indivisible, and that all of it became

Rousseau's conception of sovereignty

Jean-Jacques Rousseau, from a painting by Maurice LaFour (1704–1788).

vested in the community when civil society was formed. He insisted further that each individual in becoming a party to the social contract gave up all of his rights to the people collectively and agreed to submit absolutely to the general will. It follows that the sovereign power of the state is subject to no limitations whatever. The general will, expressed through the vote of the majority, is the court of final appeal. What the majority decides is always right in the political sense and is absolutely binding upon every citizen. The state, which in actual practice means the majority, is legally omnipotent. But this does not really imply, according to Rousseau, that the liberty of the individual is entirely destroyed. On the contrary, subjection to the state has the effect of enhancing *genuine* liberty. Individuals in surrendering their rights to the community merely exchange the animal liberty of the state of nature for the true freedom of reasoning creatures in obedience to law. Compelling an individual to abide by the general will is therefore merely "forcing him to be

[8] *Discourse on the Origin of Inequality* (Everyman Library ed.), p. 207.

free." It must be understood, also, that when Rousseau referred to the state he did not mean the government. He regarded the state as the politically organized community, which has the sovereign function of expressing the general will. The authority of the state cannot be represented, but must be expressed directly through the enactment of fundamental laws by the people themselves. The government, on the other hand, is simply the executive agent of the state. Its function is not to formulate the general will but merely to carry it out. Moreover, the community can set the government up or pull it down "whenever it likes." [9]

The influence of Rousseau's political theory would be hard to exaggerate. His dogmas of equality and the supremacy of the majority were the chief inspiration for the second stage of the French Revolution. Doctrinaire radicals like Robespierre were among his most fervent disciples. But Rousseau's influence was not confined to his own country. Some of his theories made their way to America and found an echo in certain of the principles of Jacksonian Democracy —although, of course, it is extremely improbable that many of Jackson's followers had ever heard of Rousseau. The German Romantic Idealists, who, in the early nineteenth century, glorified the state as "God in history," would also appear to have been indebted in some measure to the philosophy of *The Social Contract*. From Rousseau's doctrines that the state is legally omnipotent, and that true liberty consists in submission to the general will, it was not a very difficult step to exalting the state as an object of worship and reducing the individual to a mere cog in the political machine.[10] Even though Rousseau suggested that the majority would be limited by moral restraints and insisted upon the right of the people to "pull down" their government, these limitations were not enough to counteract the effect of his stress upon absolute sovereignty.

The influence of Rousseau

As a final intellectual cause of the French Revolution, the influence of the new economic theory must be given at least passing attention. In the second half of the eighteenth century a number of brilliant writers began attacking the traditional assumptions in regard to public control over production and trade. Their special target of criticism was mercantilist policy. To a large extent the new economics was founded upon the basic conceptions of the Enlightenment, particularly the idea of a mechanistic universe governed by inflexible laws. The notion now came to prevail that the sphere of the production and distribution of wealth was subject to laws just as irresistible as those of physics and astronomy. The new economic theory may also be regarded as the counterpart of political liberalism. The cardinal aims of the two were quite similar: to reduce the powers of government to the lowest minimum consistent

The influence of the new economic theory

[9] *The Social Contract* (Everyman Library ed.), p. 88.
[10] For a discussion of the political theory of the Romantic Idealists see § 3 in the chapter on The Age of Romanticism and Reaction.

with safety and to preserve for the individual the largest possible measure of freedom in the pursuit of his own devices.

*The doctrines
of the
Physiocrats*

The first of the leading champions of a revised attitude toward economic problems were members of a group known as the Physiocrats. The most eminent among them were François Quesnay (1694–1774), author of the *Tableau Économique*, the bible of Physiocracy; Dupont de Nemours (1739–1817), ancestor of the Dupont family in the United States; and Robert Jacques Turgot (1727–1781), finance minister for a brief period under Louis XVI.[11] From the outset the Physiocrats condemned mercantilist doctrine. One of their chief aims was to prove that the *natural* enterprises of agriculture, mining, and fishing are more important to national prosperity than commerce. Nature, they held, is the real producer of wealth, and therefore those industries which actually exploit the resources of nature and make them yield things of value to man are most to be prized. Trade is essentially sterile, since it merely transfers goods already in existence from one person to another. As time went on, these doctrines were subordinated to another idea which the Physiocrats came to regard as paramount to everything else. This was the liberation of economic activity from the suffocating restraints imposed by the state. The Physiocrats demanded that the government should refrain from all interference with business except in so far as might be necessary for the protection of life and property. Nothing should ever be done to hinder the operation of natural economic laws. This doctrine was neatly summed up in the picturesque maxim, *Laissez faire et laissez passer, le monde va de lui-même* (Let do and let alone, the world goes on of itself). The ideal of *laissez faire* soon came to embody such notions as the sanctity of private property and the rights of freedom of contract and free competition. It was thus the very antithesis of the restrictive policy of mercantilism.

*The economics
of Adam Smith*

The greatest of all the economists of the age of the Enlightenment and one of the most brilliant of all time was Adam Smith (1723–1790). A native of Scotland, Smith began his career as a lecturer on English literature at the University of Edinburgh. From this he was soon advanced to a professorship of logic at Glasgow College. He first won fame in 1759 with the publication of his *Theory of Moral Sentiments*. Although he had been interested for some time in problems of political economy, this interest was effectively stimulated by two years of residence in France while serving as tutor to the young Duke of Buccleuch. Here he became acquainted with the leading members of the Physiocratic school and was delighted to find that some of their theories agreed with his own. He described the economics of Quesnay, "with all its imper-

[11] Another economist, Vincent de Gournay (1712–1759), influenced the Physiocrats, but he was never actually a member of the school. He is commonly credited with having originated the phrase, *laissez faire*.

fections," as "the nearest approximation to truth that has yet been published on the principles of that science." But Smith never enlisted under the standard of the Physiocrats, despite the undoubted influence of many of their doctrines upon him. In 1776 he published his *Inquiry into the Nature and Causes of the Wealth of Nations,* generally considered the most influential treatise on economics ever written. In this work he maintained that labor, rather than agriculture or the bounty of nature, is the real source of wealth. While in general he accepted the principle of *laissez faire,* avowing that the prosperity of all can best be promoted by allowing each individual to pursue his own interest, he nevertheless recognized that certain forms of governmental interference would be desirable. The state should intervene for the prevention of injustice and oppression, for the advancement of education and the protection of public health, and for the maintenance of necessary enterprises which would never be established by private capital. Notwithstanding these rather broad limitations upon the principle of *laissez faire,* Smith's *Wealth of Nations* was adopted as Holy Writ by the economic individualists of the eighteenth and nineteenth centuries. Its influence in causing the French Revolution was indirect but none the less profound. It furnished the final answer to mercantilist argument and thereby strengthened the ambition of the bourgeoisie to have done with a political system which continued to block the path to economic freedom.

2. The Destruction of the Old Regime

In the early summer of 1789 the volcano of discontent in France burst forth into revolution. The immediate cause of the eruption was the near collapse of government finances as a result of costly wars and royal extravagance. By 1786 the public debt had climbed to over a billion dollars and was mounting steadily higher with each succeeding year. Existing revenues were scarcely sufficient to meet the interest payments, to say nothing of reducing the principal. The only chance of relief appeared to be the imposition of new taxes. With this end in view Louis XVI summoned in 1787 an Assembly of Notables in the hope that the chief magnates of the realm might consent to bearing a share of the fiscal burden. The nobles and bishops, however, refused to surrender their privilege of tax exemption. It was then that the demand arose for convocation of the Estates General. This body, composed of representatives of the three great estates or classes of the nation, would advise the king as to the people's will in dealing with the financial emergency. In the summer of 1788 Louis XVI yielded to the popular clamor by summoning the Estates General to meet in May of the following year.

No sooner had the delegations from the three orders met than a controversy developed over the method of voting. In the original

The immediate cause of the French Revolution

**THE FRENCH
REVOLUTION,
1789–1799**

*The triumph of
the Third Es-
tate*

Estates General, established by Philip the Fair in the fourteenth century, each of the classes—the clergy, nobles, and commoners—had voted as a unit. But that was before the Third Estate had amounted to much. In succeeding centuries the bourgeoisie had grown to be the most powerful economic group in the nation. It was therefore inevitable that bourgeois leaders should now be dissatisfied with an arrangement whereby the votes of the two upper classes could negative anything the Third Estate wanted to do. Consequently they demanded that the three orders should sit together and vote by head. Since the commoners had already been granted a number of representatives equal to that of the two other classes combined, it was plain that the Third Estate, by drawing occasional support from disgruntled nobles and clergy, would be able to control the whole body. After a month of wrangling, the Third Estate on June 17 boldly proclaimed itself the National Assembly and invited the

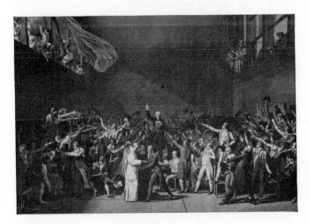

The Oath of the Tennis Court, June 20, 1789. From the painting by Jacques Louis David. On the day mentioned the members of the Third Estate pledged themselves by a solemn oath not to separate until they had adopted a constitution for France. This marked the beginning of the French Revolution.

members of the privileged orders to join in its work. Many of them actually did so. Within two days a majority of the clergy went over and a sprinkling of the nobles also. But then the king intervened. When the rebellious deputies assembled at their hall on the morning of June 20, they found its doors guarded by troops. There were now no alternatives but to submit or to defy the sovereign power of the monarch himself. Confident of the support of a majority of the people, the commoners and their allies withdrew to a near-by hall, variously used as a riding academy and a tennis court. Here under the leadership of Mirabeau and the Abbé Sieyès they bound themselves by a solemn oath not to separate until they had drafted a constitution for France. This Oath of the Tennis Court, on June 20, 1789, was the real beginning of the French Revolution. By claiming the authority to remake the government in the name of the people, the Estates General was not merely protesting against the arbitrary rule of Louis XVI but asserting its right to act as the highest sovereign power in the nation. On June 27 the king virtually conceded this right by ordering the remaining delegates of the privileged classes to meet with the Third Estate as members of a National Assembly.

The course of the French Revolution was marked by three great stages, the first of which extended from June 1789 to August 1792. During most of this period the destinies of France were in the hands of the National Assembly, dominated by the leaders of the Third Estate. In the main, this stage was a moderate, middle-class stage. The masses had not yet gained any degree of political power, nor were they in a position to seize control of the economic system. Aside from the destruction of the Bastille on July 14, 1789, and the murder of a few members of the royal guard, there was comparatively little violence in Paris or Versailles. In certain of the country districts, however, a more unruly spirit prevailed. Many of the

The first stage of the Revolution

The Storming of the Bastille, July 14, 1789. The mob has seized the Governor and has begun the attack on the prison. Though this event is celebrated by the French as their national holiday, it was merely a belated confirmation of the real beginning of the Revolution with the Oath of the Tennis Court on June 20.

peasants grew impatient over the delay in granting reforms and determined to deal with the situation directly. Arming themselves with pitchforks and scythes, they set out to destroy what they could of the Old Regime. They demolished *châteaux* of hated nobles, plundered monasteries and residences of bishops, and murdered some of the miserable lords who offered resistance. Most of this violence occurred during the summer of 1789 and had much to do with frightening the upper classes into surrendering some of their privileges.

The most significant developments of the first stage of the Revolution were the achievements of the National Assembly between 1789 and 1791. The initial one of these achievements was the destruction of the relics of feudalism. This came about largely as a result of the rebellious temper displayed by the peasants. By the beginning of August 1789, such alarming reports of anarchy in the villages had reached the National Assembly that an urgent need for concessions soon came to be recognized by many of the members. On the fourth of August a certain noble proposed in an eloquent speech that all of

Achievements of the first stage: (1) the destruction of feudal privileges

577

his brethren should renounce their feudal privileges. His plea stirred the Assembly to a wild enthusiasm, compounded partly of fear and partly of revolutionary zeal. Nobles, churchmen, and burghers vied with each other in suggesting reforms. Before the night had ended, innumerable remnants of the hoary structure of vested rights had been swept away. Tithes and the feudal dues of the peasants were formally abolished. Serfdom was eliminated. The hunting privileges of the nobles were declared at an end. Exemption from taxation and monopolies of all kinds were sacrificed as contrary to natural equality. While the nobles did not surrender all of their rights, the ultimate effect of these reforms of the "August Days" was to annihilate distinctions of rank and class and to make all Frenchmen citizens of an equal status in the eyes of the law.[12]

*(2) the Dec-
laration of the
Rights of Man*

Following the destruction of privilege the Assembly turned its attention to preparing a charter of liberties. The result was the Declaration of the Rights of Man and of the Citizen, issued in September 1789. Modeled in part after the English Bill of Rights and embodying the teachings of liberal political philosophers, the French Declaration was a typical middle-class document. Property was declared to be a natural right as well as liberty, security, and "resistance to oppression." No one was to be deprived of anything he possessed except in case of public necessity, and then only on condition that he should have been "previously and equitably indemnified." Proper consideration was also to be given to personal rights. Freedom of speech, religious toleration, and liberty of the press were held to be inviolable. All citizens were declared to be entitled to equality of treatment in the courts. No one was to be imprisoned or otherwise punished except in accordance with due process of law. Sovereignty was affirmed to reside in the people, and officers of the government were made subject to deposition if they abused the powers conferred upon them. Nothing was said about any right of the common man to an adequate share of the wealth he produced or even to protection by the state in case of inability to earn a living. The authors of the Declaration of Rights were not socialists, nor were they interested particularly in the economic welfare of the masses.

*(3) the secular-
ization of the
church*

The next of the main accomplishments of the National Assembly was the secularization of the church. Under the Ancient Regime the higher clergy had been a privileged caste, rewarding the king for his favors by a stanch support of absolute rule. As a result, the church had come to be regarded as an instrument of greed and oppression almost as odious as the monarchy itself. Moreover, the ecclesiastical institutions were the possessors of vast estates, and the new Revolutionary government was desperately in need of funds. Accordingly, in November 1789, the National Assembly resolved

---

[12] Along with these reforms in connection with the destruction of monopolies and feudal privileges, the guilds were also abolished and workers were forbidden to form unions.

to confiscate the lands of the church and to use them as collateral for the issue of *assignats*, or paper money. In July of the following year the Civil Constitution of the Clergy was enacted, providing that all bishops and priests should be elected by the people and should be subject to the authority of the state. Their salaries were to be paid out of the public treasury, and they were required to swear allegiance to the new legislation. The secularization of the church also involved a partial separation from Rome. The aim of the Assembly was to make the Catholic church of France a truly national institution with no more than a nominal subjection to the papacy. Since the Pope condemned this arrangement and forbade any bishop or priest to accept it, the result was to divide the clergy of France into two different groups. A minority took the oath of allegiance to the Civil Constitution and were henceforth known as the "juring" clergy. Some of the "non-jurors" fled from the country, but many remained and united with reactionary nobles in stirring up hatred for the whole Revolutionary program.

Not until 1791 did the National Assembly manage to complete its primary task of drafting a new constitution for the nation. Too many other problems of more immediate concern had absorbed its attention. Besides, autocratic government was already a thing of the past. The constitution as it finally emerged gave eloquent testimony to the dominant position now held by the bourgeoisie. France was not made a democratic republic, but the government was converted merely into a limited monarchy, with the supreme power virtually a monopoly of the well-to-do. The privilege of voting was restricted to those who paid a direct tax equal to three days' wages, while eligibility for holding office was limited to citizens of comparative wealth. As to the structure of the government, the principle of the separation of powers was to be the basic feature. For this the founders of the new system went back to Montesquieu's idea of independent legislative, executive, and judicial departments. The lawmaking powers were bestowed upon a Legislative Assembly chosen indirectly by the people through a process somewhat similar to that by which the President of the United States was originally supposed to be selected. The king was deprived of the control he had formerly exercised over the army, the church, and local government. His ministers were forbidden to sit in the Assembly, and he was shorn of all power over the legislative process except a suspensive veto, which could be overridden by the votes of three successive Assemblies. Thus the new system, while far removed from absolute monarchy, was decidedly not a government which the masses could claim as their own.

(4) the Constitution of 1791

In the summer of 1792 the French Revolution entered a second stage, which lasted for about two years. This stage differed from the first in a number of ways. To begin with, France was now a republic. On the tenth of August the Legislative Assembly voted to

579

*The second or
radical stage of
the Revolution*

suspend the king and ordered the election, by universal manhood suffrage, of a National Convention to draft a new constitution. Soon afterward Louis XVI was brought to trial on charges of plotting with foreign enemies of the Revolution, and on January 21, 1793, he was beheaded. In addition to its republican character, the second stage differed from the first in the fact that it was dominated by the lower classes. No longer was the course of the Revolution dictated by relatively conservative members of the bourgeoisie. Instead, it was extremists representing the proletariat of Paris who were largely responsible for determining the nature of the movement. The liberal philosophy of Voltaire and Montesquieu was now replaced by the radical, equalitarian doctrines of Rousseau. Yet another difference

The Execution of Louis XVI. The event took place on what is now the Place de la Concorde in Paris, on January 21, 1793.

was the more violent and bloody character of the second stage. This was the period not only of the execution of the king but also of the September massacres (1792) and of the Reign of Terror from the summer of 1793 to the summer of 1794.

What factors may be taken to explain this spectacular transition from a comparatively moderate, middle-class phase to a stage of radicalism and turmoil? First of all may be mentioned the disappointed hopes of the proletariat. The Revolution in its beginning had held out what appeared to be glorious promises of equality and justice for every citizen. Hope had been built particularly on the Declaration of Rights, in spite of its emphasis upon the sanctity of private property. But now after more than three years of social and political upheaval it was just as hard for the urban worker to earn

*Causes of the
transition to a
radical stage*

Liberty Leading the People, Eugene Delacroix (1798–1863). Delacroix was a colorful painter of dramatic and emotional themes, as exemplified by this imaginary scene from the Revolution of 1830. (Louvre)

Salisbury Cathedral from the Bishop's Garden, John Constable (1776–1837). This British romanticist is best known for his idealizations of nature in her quiet and peaceful moods. (MMA)

The Flight into Egypt, William Blake (1757–1827). A poet as well as a painter, Blake lived in a world of dream and fantasy. He attributed to divine inspiration his talent for expressing delicate simplicity. (MMA)

Lady Lillith, Dante Gabriel Rossetti (1828–1882). The chief figure in the Pre-Raphaelite movement, Rossetti cared more for the expression of ideas than for technical perfection. (MMA)

Grand Canal, Venice, Joseph M. W. Turner (1775–1851). Turner's complete absorption in light, color, and atmosphere helped to prepare the way for the French impressionists. (MMA)

The Guitarist, Edouard Manet. *The Guitarist* is no more impressionistic than is the portrait of Zola. Instead, it reflects the technique of fully modeled figures in somber style which Manet acquired from Hals and Goya. (MMA)

Émile Zola, Édouard Manet (1832–1883). Though Manet is called the "father of impressionism," he was also a rebel against the traditions of sweetness and artificiality that dominated the XIX cent. He liberated painting, as his friend Zola emancipated literature. (Louvre)

Girl Burning Weeds, Jean François Millet (1814–1875). Millet painted the men and women who toiled in the fields and their struggles against poverty and the whims of nature. His sympathies sometimes led him to a romantic idealization. (MMA)

The Third-Class Carriage, Honoré Daumier (1808–1879). Though Daumier was noted for his realistic caricatures and satires, his attitude toward common folk was one of sympathy and understanding. (MMA)

Village Girls, Gustave Courbet (1819–1877). One of the first of the realists, Courbet often portrayed life in a bitter and disparaging light. He eschewed imagination and painted only what he saw. (MMA)

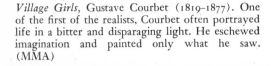

his bread as it had been before. As a matter of fact, it was probably harder on account of the disruption of business. Another disappointment developed when the common man discovered after the adoption of the Constitution of 1791 that he was not even to be allowed to vote. Ever more clearly the realization dawned that he had simply exchanged one set of masters for another. In such a state of mind he was bound to be attracted by the preaching of extremists, who offered to lead him into the Promised Land of security and plenty. A second cause of the transition to a radical stage was the accumulated momentum of the Revolution itself. Every great movement of this kind generates an atmosphere of discontent, which is breathed more deeply by some men than by others. The result is the emergence of a kind of professional revolutionist, who is eternally dissatisfied no matter how much has been accomplished. He denounces the leaders of the revolution in its preliminary stage even more scathingly than he condemns the adherents of the old order. For him, no price of slaughter and chaos is too great to pay in order to purchase the fulfillment of his own ideals. He will murder his closest associates, the moment they disagree with him, just as readily as he will consign the most hated reactionary to outer darkness. He is the political counterpart of the religious fanatic who believes that sword and faggot are proper instruments for hastening the reign of God's righteousness and peace.

But perhaps the most important cause of the triumph of the radicals was the outbreak of war between France and foreign states. In several European countries the progress of the French Revolution was coming to be viewed with increasing alarm by reactionary rulers. The fear was particularly strong in Austria and Prussia, where numerous *émigrés*, or French royalists, had taken refuge and were convincing the monarchs of those countries of the danger that the Revolution might spread. Besides, the French queen, Marie Antoinette, was a member of the Hapsburg family and was making frenzied appeals to the emperor to come to the aid of her husband. In August 1791, the Austrian and Prussian rulers joined in issuing the Declaration of Pillnitz, in which they boldly avowed that the restoration of order and of the rights of the monarch in France was a matter of "common interest to all sovereigns of Europe." Naturally this pronouncement was keenly resented by the French, since it could hardly be interpreted in any other way than as a definite threat of intervention. Moreover, there was a tendency on the part of many of the revolutionists to welcome a conflict with a foreign enemy. While the moderate faction expected that military success would solidify the loyalty of the people to the new regime, many of the radicals were clamoring for war in the secret hope that the armies of France would suffer defeat, and that the monarchy would thereby be discredited. A republic could then be set up, and the heroic soldiers of the people would turn defeat into vic-

The threat of foreign intervention

tory and carry the blessings of freedom to all the oppressed of Europe. With such considerations in mind, the Assembly voted for war on April 20, 1792. As the radicals had hoped, the forces of the French met serious reverses. By August the allied armies of Austria and Prussia had crossed the frontier and were threatening the capture of Paris. A fury of rage and despair seized the capital. The belief prevailed that the military disasters had been the result of treasonable dealings with the enemy on the part of the king and his conservative followers. As a consequence, a vigorous demand arose for drastic action against all who were suspected of disloyalty to the Revolution. It was this situation more than anything else which brought the extremists to the fore and enabled them to gain control of the Legislative Assembly and to put an end to the monarchy.

The government of France during the second stage: the National Convention

From 1792 to 1795—that is, during the second stage of the Revolution and for more than a year longer—the governing power of France was the National Convention. Originally elected as a constituent assembly, this body was supposed to draft a new constitution and then surrender its authority to a regular government. A new constitution was actually drawn up in 1793, but the disordered conditions of the time prevented its being put into effect. With the justification that a national emergency existed, the Convention simply prolonged its life from year to year. After the spring of 1793 it delegated its executive functions to a group of nine (later twelve) of its members, known as the Committee of Public Safety. This agency conducted foreign relations, supervised the command of the armies, and enforced the Reign of Terror. The Convention itself was composed of a number of factions representing various shades of radical opinion. The most important of them were the Girondists and the Jacobins. The Girondists drew their support largely from regions outside of Paris and were inclined to distrust the proletariat. They were republicans but not extreme democrats. Their Jacobin opponents were among the most thoroughgoing radicals of the Revolution.[13] Though most of them sprang from the middle class, they were ardent disciples of Rousseau and militant champions of the urban workers. They accused the Girondists of desiring an "aristocratic republic" and of plotting to destroy the unity of France by putting into effect some kind of federal plan in which the *départements* or provinces would be exalted at the expense of Paris.

The moderate leaders in the National Convention: (1) Thomas Paine

Leadership in the National Convention was furnished by some of the most interesting and dramatic personalities of modern history. Famous among those who usually identified themselves with the Girondists were Thomas Paine (1737–1809) and the Marquis de Condorcet (1743–1794). Following his brilliant work as a pamphleteer in the American Revolution, Paine sailed for England,

[13] The Jacobin Club had not always been radical. During the earlier years of the Revolution it had numbered among its members such well-known moderates

determined to open the eyes of the people of that country "to the madness and stupidity of the government." In 1791 he published his celebrated *Rights of Man,* a blistering attack upon Edmund Burke's *Reflections on the Revolution in France,* issued the previous year. *The Rights of Man* created a sensation, especially after the bungling attempts of the government to suppress it. The author was indicted for treason, but he escaped to France before he could be seized for trial. In 1792 he was elected to the National Convention and immediately began an active career as one of the more moderate leaders of that body. He urged the destruction of the monarchy but opposed the execution of the king on the ground that it would alienate American sympathy. Ultimately he incurred the suspicion of some of the extremists and escaped the guillotine by the sheerest accident.

A man of milder temperament than Paine but of similar philosophic interests was the Marquis de Condorcet. Originally a disciple of Voltaire and Turgot, he eventually went considerably beyond these bourgeois liberals in his demands for reform. He condemned not only the evils of absolutism, mercantilism, slavery, and war, as did many of the enlightened thinkers of his time, but he was one of the first to insist that the elimination of poverty should be a cardinal purpose of statecraft. He thought that this end could be largely attained through the destruction of monopoly and privilege and the abolition of primogeniture and entail. The removal of these obstacles would permit a wide distribution of property, especially land, and thereby enable most individuals to achieve economic independence. He also advocated old-age pensions and co-operative banking to provide cheap credit.[14] At the height of the Terror, Condorcet was outlawed for denouncing the violence of the Jacobins and was compelled to flee for his life. Disguised as a carpenter, he wandered half-starved through the country until one night he was suspected and thrown into prison. The next morning he was found dead on the floor. Whether he collapsed from suffering and exposure or swallowed poison he was supposed to have carried in a ring is unknown.

(2) Condorcet

Foremost among the leaders of the extremist factions were Marat, Danton, and Robespierre. Jean Paul Marat (1743–1793) was educated as a physician and by 1789 had already earned enough distinction in that profession to be awarded an honorary degree by St. Andrew's University in Scotland. Almost from the beginning of the Revolution he stood as a champion of the common people. He opposed nearly all of the dogmatic assumptions of his middle-class colleagues in the Assembly, including the idea that France should pattern her government after that of Great Britain, which he recog-

The extremist leaders: Marat and Danton

---

as Mirabeau, Sieyès, and Lafayette. In 1791, however, it had come under the domination of extremists led by Maximilien Robespierre.

[14] J. S. Schapiro, *Condorcet and the Rise of Liberalism,* pp. 142–55.

nized to be oligarchic in form. He was soon made a victim of persecution and was forced to find refuge in sewers and dungeons, but this did not stop him from his efforts to rouse the people to a defense of their rights. In 1793 he was stabbed through the heart by Charlotte Corday, a young woman who was fanatically devoted to the Girondists. In contrast with Marat, Georges Jacques Danton (1759–1794) did not come into prominence until the Revolution was three years old; but, like Marat, he directed his activities toward goading the masses into rebellion. Elected a member of the Committee of Public Safety in 1793, he had much to do with organizing the Reign of Terror. But as time went on he appears to have wearied of ruthlessness and displayed a fatal tendency to compromise. This gave his opponents in the Convention their opportunity, and in April 1794, he was sent to the guillotine. Upon mounting the scaffold he is reported to have said: "Show my head to the people; they do not see the like every day."

Robespierre

The most famous and perhaps the greatest of all the extremist leaders was Maximilien Robespierre (1758–1794). Born of a family reputed to be of Irish descent, Robespierre was trained for the law and speedily achieved a modest success as an advocate. In 1782 he was appointed a criminal judge, but soon resigned because he could not bear to impose a sentence of death. Of a nervous and timid disposition, he was never able to display much executive ability, but he made up for this lack of talent by fanatical devotion to principle. He had adopted the belief that the philosophy of Rousseau held the one great hope of salvation for all mankind. To put this philosophy into practice he was ready to employ any means that would bring results, regardless of the cost to himself or to others. This passionate loyalty to a gospel which exalted the masses eventually won

Maximilien Robespierre, after a drawing from life by François Gérard (1770–1837).

him a following. Indeed, he was so lionized by the public that he was allowed to wear the knee breeches, silk stockings, and powdered hair of the old society until the end of his life. In 1791 he was accepted as the oracle of the Jacobin Club, now purged of all but its most radical elements. Later he became president of the National Convention and a member of the Committee of Public Safety. Though he had little or nothing to do with originating the Reign of Terror, he was nevertheless responsible for enlarging its scope. He actually came to justify ruthlessness as a necessary and therefore laudable means to revolutionary progress. In the last six weeks of his virtual dictatorship, no fewer than 1285 heads rolled from the scaffold in Paris. But sooner or later such methods were bound to bring his own doom. On July 28, 1794, he and twenty-one of his lieutenants were beheaded, after no more pretense of a trial than Robespierre himself had allowed to his opponents.

The actual extent of violence during the second stage of the Revolution will probably never be known. Many of the stories of horrible butchery that circulated then and later were highly exaggerated. No streets ran red with blood and no rivers were clogged with corpses. Nevertheless, an appalling amount of bloodshed did actually occur. During the period of the Terror, from September 1793 to July 1794, the most reliable estimates place the number of executions at approximately 20,000 in France as a whole. A law of September 17, 1793, made every person who had been identified in any way with the Bourbon government or with the Girondists an object of suspicion; and no one who was a suspect or who was suspected of being a suspect was entirely safe from persecution. When some time later the Abbé Sieyès was asked what he had done to distinguish himself during the Terror, he responded dryly, "I lived." Yet when all is said, it must be conceded that the slaughter during the French Revolution was much less than that which has accompanied most civil and international wars. The 20,000 victims of the Reign of Terror can hardly be compared, for example, to the hundreds of thousands slain during the American War between the States. Napoleon Bonaparte, whom many people worship as a hero, was responsible for at least twenty times as many deaths as all of the members of the Committee of Public Safety. This comparison is not meant to condone the savagery of the Terror, but it may serve to correct a distorted picture.

The extent of violence during the second stage

Despite the violence of the Reign of Terror, the second stage of the French Revolution was marked by some worthy achievements. Such leaders as Robespierre, fanatical though they might be, were nevertheless sincere humanitarians, and it was not to be expected that they would ignore the opportunity to inaugurate reforms. Among their most significant accomplishments were the abolition of slavery in the colonies; the prohibition of imprisonment for debt; the establishment of the metric system of weights and measures;

Achievements of the second stage

and the repeal of primogeniture, so that property might not be inherited exclusively by the oldest son but must be divided in substantially equal portions among all of the immediate heirs. The Convention also attempted to supplement the decrees of the National Assembly in abolishing the remnants of feudalism and in providing for greater freedom of economic opportunity. The property of enemies of the Revolution was confiscated for the benefit of the government and the lower classes. Great estates were broken up and offered for sale to poorer citizens on easy terms. The indemnities hitherto promised to the nobles for the loss of their privileges were abruptly canceled. To curb the rise in the cost of living, maximum prices for grain and other necessities were fixed by law, while merchants who profiteered at the expense of the poor were threatened with the guillotine. Still other measures of reform were those in the sphere of religion. At one time during the Terror an effort was made to abolish Christianity and to substitute the worship of Reason in its place. In accordance with this purpose a new calendar was adopted, dating the year from the birth of the republic (September 22, 1792) and dividing the months in such a way as to eliminate the Christian Sunday. When Robespierre came to power, he supplanted this cult of Reason by a deistic religion dedicated to the worship of a Supreme Being and to the belief in the immortality of the soul. Finally, in 1794, the Convention took the more sensible step of making religion a private concern of the individual. It was decided that church and state should be entirely separate, and that all beliefs not actually hostile to the government should be tolerated.

The end of the second stage: the Thermidorian Reaction

In the summer of 1794 the Reign of Terror came to an end, and soon afterward the Revolution passed into its third and final stage. The event which inaugurated the change was the Thermidorian Reaction, so called from the month of Thermidor (heat month—July 19 to August 18) in the new calendar. The execution of Robespierre on July 28, 1794, represented the completion of a cycle. The Revolution had now devoured its own children. One after another the radical giants had fallen—first Marat, then Hébert and Danton, and now finally Robespierre and Saint-Just. The only remaining leaders in the Convention were men of moderate sympathies. As time went on they inclined toward increasing conservatism and toward any kind of political chicanery which would serve to keep them in power. Gradually the Revolution came once more to reflect the interests of the bourgeoisie. Much of the extremist work of the radicals was now undone. The law of maximum prices and the law against "suspects" were both repealed. Political prisoners were freed, the Jacobins were driven into hiding, and the Committee of Public Safety was shorn of its despotic powers. The new situation made possible the return of priests, royalists, and other *émigrés* from abroad to add the weight of their influence to the conservative trend.

In 1795 the National Convention adopted a new constitution, which lent the stamp of official approval to the victory of the prosperous classes. The new organic law, known as the Constitution of the Year III, granted the suffrage to all adult male citizens who could read and write, but they were permitted to vote only for electors, who in turn would choose the members of the Legislative Body; and in order to be an elector, one had to be the proprietor of a farm or other establishment with an annual income equivalent to at least one hundred days of labor. It was thus made certain that the authority of the government would actually be derived from citizens of considerable wealth. The Legislative Body was to be composed of two houses, a lower house or Council of Five Hundred and a senate or Council of Ancients. Since it was not practicable to restore the monarchy, lest the old aristocracy come back into power, executive authority was vested in a board of five men known as the Directory, to be nominated by the Council of Five Hundred and elected by the Council of Ancients. The new constitution included not only a bill of rights but also a declaration of the *duties* of the citizen. Conspicuous among the latter was the obligation to bear in mind that "it is upon the maintenance of property . . . that the whole social order rests."

That a system so callously defiant of the rights of the masses should be permitted to flourish unopposed was more than anyone should have expected. Scarcely had the Constitution of the Year III been put into effect than a movement to overthrow it was organized by Jacobins under the leadership of "Gracchus" Babeuf. Editor of the *Tribune of the People* and founder of the Society of Equals, Babeuf is often called the first modern socialist. But apparently true socialism was far from his purpose. His real aim did not differ especially from that of other radical Jacobins. He envisaged a society in which all men would be the owners of property in substantially equal amounts. For the attainment of this end he urged the confiscation and redistribution of surplus wealth of the rich. In September 1796, his followers, numbering perhaps 17,000, launched an attack upon the military post at Grenelle, hoping that the garrison would come over to their side and join in a march on Paris. The effort was a pitiful failure. Soon afterward Babeuf and his chief comrade were condemned for treason and were put to death in May of the following year. This ended the last attempt to make the French Revolution a movement for the economic betterment of the lower classes.

The third stage of the French Revolution was of little historical importance as compared with the other two. In general it was a period of stagnation, wholesale corruption, and cynicism. The burning zeal for reform which had characterized the other two stages now disappeared into thin air. The members of the new government were interested much more in opportunities for personal profit

The third stage: the conservative Constitution of the Year III

The radical revolt of "Gracchus" Babeuf

The corrupt and cynical character of the third stage

than in the shining ideals of philosophers for remaking the world. Graft was a familiar accompaniment of the levying and collecting of taxes and the disbursement of public funds. Even some members of the Directory coolly demanded bribes as the price of favors which the duties of their office should normally have required them to bestow. This cynical greed in high places was bound to have its effect upon the tone of society. It is therefore not surprising that the age of the Directory should have been a period of riotous extravagance, dissipation, and frenzied pursuit of wealth. Speculation and gambling tended to crowd legitimate business into a secondary place. While famine stalked the slums of Paris, profiteers accumulated fortunes and flaunted their gains at the expense of the people in senseless display. Thus were the glorious promises of the Revolution trailed in the mud, even by some who had originally sworn to uphold them.

The end of the Revolution: the coup d'état of Napoleon Bonaparte

In the fall of 1799 the Revolution in France came to a close. The event which marked its end was the *coup d'état* of Napoleon Bonaparte on the eighteenth Brumaire (November 9). This, however, was merely the final blow. For some time the regime set up by the Constitution of the Year III had been hovering on the verge of collapse. Though for a while it was bolstered up by victories in the war which was still going on against foreign enemies of the Revolution, eventually even this support was torn away. In 1798–1799 the aggressive policy of the Directory had involved France in a struggle with a new combination of powerful foes—Great Britain, Austria, and Russia. The fortunes of battle soon shifted. One after another the satellite states which the French had erected on their eastern frontier collapsed. The armies of the republic were driven from Italy. Soon it appeared as if all the gains of previous years were to be blotted out. Meanwhile the Directory had been suffering an even greater loss of prestige from its conduct of internal affairs. Thousands of people were disgusted with the shameful corruption of public officials and their heartless indifference to the needs of the poor. To make matters worse, the government was partly responsible for a serious financial crisis. In order to defray the cost of wars and to make up for the extravagance of incompetent officials, the issuance of *assignats* or paper money was increased. The inevitable results were wild inflation and utter chaos. Within a very short time the *assignats* had depreciated until they were actually worth no more than 1 per cent of their face value. By 1797 conditions had grown so hopeless that the only alternative was to repudiate all of the outstanding paper currency. During the period of financial chaos millions of cautious and respectable citizens who had managed to accumulate some property were reduced to the level of proletarians. The effect was naturally to turn them into bitter enemies of the existing government.

It was under these deplorable circumstances that the accession of

Napoleon Bonaparte was rendered comparatively easy. Disgust with
the venality and indifference of the Directory, resentment on account of the hardships suffered from the inflation, the sense of being
humiliated as a result of defeat in the war—these were the factors
which encouraged a widespread conviction that the existing regime
was intolerable, and that only the appearance of a "man on horseback" could save the nation from ruin. In other words, Napoleon
rose to power under conditions quite similar to those which presided
at the birth of more recent dictatorships in Germany and Italy. But,
of course, young Bonaparte was a military hero, as Hitler and Mussolini were not. In 1795 he had endeared himself to the friends of
law and order by defending the National Convention with a "whiff
of grapeshot" against an uprising of Parisian insurgents. Later he
had come trailing clouds of glory from his campaigns in Italy and
in Egypt. True, his reports of success in the latter country were
slightly colored, but they convinced patriotic Frenchmen that here
at last was a general in whose skill they could place absolute trust.
Besides, no one could doubt the fact that he had driven the Austrians
from Italy and had added Savoy and Nice and the Austrian Netherlands to France. It is not much wonder that he should have come to
be regarded as the man of the hour. His name became a symbol of
national greatness and the glorious achievements of the Revolution.
And as the revulsion of feeling against the Directory increased, he
was hailed more than ever as the incorruptible hero who would
deliver the nation from shame and disaster.

The reasons for Napoleon's triumph

3. The Good and Evil Fruits of the Revolution

While the coming to power of Napoleon Bonaparte as a military
dictator marked the beginning of a new era, it by no means erased
the influence of the French Revolution. Indeed, as will subsequently
be shown, Napoleon himself preserved quite a few of the Revolutionary achievements and posed as an embattled champion of Equality and Fraternity, if not of Liberty. But even if he had done none
of these things, the heritage of the Revolution would most certainly
have survived. No movement which had so thoroughly shaken the
foundations of society could ever have passed into history without
leaving a train of momentous results. Its influence reverberated
through most of the years of the nineteenth century and was felt
in a score of nations of the Western world. The new passion for
liberty was the activating force behind numerous insurrections and
so-called revolutions which punctuated the period between 1800 and
1850. First came the uprising of the Spaniards against Joseph Bonaparte in 1808. This was followed by a veritable epidemic of revolutionary disturbances between 1820 and 1831, in such countries as
Greece, Italy, Spain, France, Belgium, and Poland. Finally, the revolutionary movements of 1848 were far from being unrelated to the

The influence of the French Revolution

*The more en-
during results
of the French
Revolution*

*The legacy of
evil results*

great French upheaval of 1789, since most of them were infused with the same nationalist enthusiasm and with similar ideals of political liberty.

The French Revolution also had other results of more enduring character and of greater benefit to mankind as a whole. It dealt, first of all, a powerful blow to absolute monarchy. Thenceforth few kings dared to claim an unlimited authority. Even though a Bourbon was restored to the throne of France in 1814, he made no pretensions to a divine appointment to rule as he liked. Secondly, the French Revolution was responsible for the destruction of nearly all the remnants of a decadent feudalism, including serfdom and the feudal privileges of the nobles. The guilds also were abolished, never to be revived. Though a few of the elements of mercantilism still survived, its days as a recognized policy of governments were definitely numbered. While the separation of church and state, accomplished in 1794, was eventually nullified by Napoleon, it nevertheless furnished a precedent for an ultimate divorce of religion from politics, not only in France but in other countries as well. Among the remaining beneficial results of the Revolution may be mentioned the abolition of slavery in the French colonies, the elimination of imprisonment for debt, the overthrow of the rule of primogeniture, and a wider distribution of land through the breaking up of great estates. Finally, the groundwork of two of Napoleon's most significant achievements, his educational reforms and his codification of the laws, was actually prepared by Revolutionary leaders.

On the other hand, the fact cannot be ignored that the French Revolution bore some bitter fruit. It was largely responsible for the growth of jingoistic nationalism as a dominant ideal. Nationalism, of course, was nothing new. It can be traced almost as far back as the unfoldment of the earliest civilizations. It manifested itself in the Chosen People obsession of the Hebrews and in the racial exclusiveness of the Greeks. Even in its modern European form it has roots that lie buried in the thirteenth century. Nevertheless, nationalism did not really become a virulent and all-pervading force until after the French Revolution. It was the pride of the French people in what they had achieved and their determination to protect those achievements that gave rise to a fanatical patriotism exemplified in the stirring battle song of the *Marseillaise*. Now for the first time in modern history a whole nation was girded for war. In contrast with the relatively small professional armies of former days, the National Convention in 1793 enrolled a force of nearly 800,000 men, while millions behind the lines devoted their energies to the gigantic task of suppressing disaffection at home. Workers, peasants, and bourgeois citizens alike rallied to the slogan of "Liberty, Equality, and Fraternity" as to a holy cause. The cosmopolitanism and pacifism of the philosophers of the Enlightenment were completely forgotten. Later this militant patriotism infected other lands, con- tributing the weight of its influence to exalted notions of national superiority and to racial hatreds. Finally, the French Revolution resulted in a deplorable cheapening of human life. The butchery of thousands during the Reign of Terror, often for no crime at all but merely as a method of striking fear into the hearts of enemies of the Revolution, tended to create the impression that the life of a man was of very small worth compared to the noble aims of the faction in power. Perhaps this impression helps to explain the comparative indifference with which France accepted, a few years later, the sacrifice of hundreds of thousands of her citizens to satisfy the boundless ambitions of Napoleon.

SELECTED READINGS

Barber, E. G., *The Bourgeoisie in Eighteenth-Century France*, Princeton, 1955

Brinton, C. C., *A Decade of Revolution, 1789–1799*, New York, 1934

——, *The Jacobins: An Essay in the New History*, New York, 1930

Funck-Brentano, Frantz, *The Old Regime in France*, New York, 1929

Gershoy, Leo, *The French Revolution, 1789–1799*, New York, 1932

——, *The French Revolution and Napoleon*, New York, 1933

——, *From Despotism to Revolution*, New York, 1944

Gottschalk, L. R., *The Era of the French Revolution*, New York, 1929

——, *Jean Paul Marat; a Study in Radicalism*, New York, 1927

Grant, A. J., and Temperley, H., *Europe: the Revolutionary and Napoleonic Eras*, New York, 1935

Hayes, C. J. H., *The Historical Evolution of Modern Nationalism*, New York, 1931

Kerr, W. B., *The Reign of Terror, 1793–94*, Toronto, 1927

Lefebvre, Georges, *The Coming of the French Revolution*, Princeton, 1947

Lowell, E. J., *The Eve of the French Revolution*, Boston, 1892

Madelin, L., *Figures of the Revolution*, New York, 1929

Martin, Kingsley, *French Liberal Thought in the Eighteenth Century*, Boston, 1929

Mathiez, Albert, *The French Revolution*, New York, 1928

Palmer, R. R., *The Twelve Who Ruled*, Princeton, 1941

Schapiro, J. S., *Condorcet and the Rise of Liberalism in France*, New York, 1934

Sée, Henri, *Economic and Social Conditions in France during the Eighteenth Century*, New York, 1927

Thompson, J. M., *Leaders of the French Revolution*, New York, 1929

SOURCE MATERIALS

Higgins, E. L., *The French Revolution as Told by Contemporaries*, Boston, 1938

Locke, John, *Second Treatise on Civil Government* (Everyman Library ed.), London, 1924

Montesquieu, Baron de, *The Spirit of Laws*, especially Books I, II, III, XI

Rousseau, J. J., *The Social Contract* (Everyman Library ed.), London, 1913

Sieyès, Abbé, *What Is the Third Estate?*

Smith, Adam, *The Wealth of Nations*, Introduction and Books I, IV

University of Pennsylvania Translations and Reprints, Vol. I, No. 5, Declaration of the Rights of Man and of the Citizen

———, *Translations and Reprints*, Vol. I, No. 5, Decree Abolishing the Feudal System

The Age of Romanticism and Reaction (1800-1830)

The century which followed the French Revolution was a period of rapid and tremendous change. By comparison life in preceding ages seems almost static. Never before in so short a time had there been such radical alteration of modes of living or such wholesale destruction of venerable tradition. As a result of a welter of inventions the speed of living was accelerated to a pace which would have startled Leonardo da Vinci or Sir Isaac Newton. The population of Europe increased from 180 million at the close of the French Revolution to the almost incredible total of 460 million by 1914. Never before in little more than a century had anything like such an increase occurred. As a result of these and similar changes, life for modern man took on a degree of complexity and variety hitherto unknown. New political and social ideals multiplied in bewildering confusion. The entire age was an age of flux, of conflicting tendencies and sharp disagreements over the problems of society. We must not suppose, however, that the nineteenth century was totally unrelated to preceding periods. Such was especially not the case of the years between 1800 and 1830. These years were occupied mainly by the aftermath of the French Revolution—by a vigorous reaction against freedom and equality, by a revolt against reason and science, and by an effort to force men back under obedience to authority.

Character of the new age

1. The Significance of Napoleon

We have seen that the *coup d'état* of Napoleon Bonaparte dealt the final blow to the French Revolution. Therefore the period of his rule, from November 1799 to April 1814 and during the Hundred

Napoleon not a
true son of the
French Revo-
lution

Days from March until June 1815 may properly be regarded as the initial stage of the nineteenth-century reaction against the liberal ideals which had made the Revolution possible. To be sure, Napoleon professed to be in sympathy with some of these ideals, but he established a form of government scarcely compatible with any of them. His real aim, so far as it concerned the work of the Revolution, was to preserve those achievements which comported with national greatness and with his own ambitions for military glory. In other words, he fostered and strengthened Revolutionary patriotism and continued those accomplishments of his predecessors which could be adapted to the purposes of concentrated government. But liberty in the sense of the inviolability of personal rights meant nothing to him; in fact, he declared that what the French people needed was not liberty but equality. Moreover, he interpreted equality as meaning little more than a fair opportunity for all regardless of birth. That is, he did not propose to restore serfdom or to give back the land to the old nobility, but neither did he plan any restrictions upon the economic activities of the rich.

The early ca-
reer of Napo-
leon

In order to understand the historical significance of Napoleon, it is necessary to know something of his personal life and of the part which he played in the dramatic events preceding his rise to power. Born in 1769 in a little town in Corsica just a year after the island had been ceded to France, Napoleon was the son of a proud but impoverished family that held a title of nobility from the republic of Genoa. In 1779 he entered a school at Brienne in France and five years later was admitted to the military academy in Paris. As a student he appears to have led an unhappy existence, abstaining from all social pleasures, eating dry bread to save expenses, and growing ever more bitter against the French, whom he accused of enslaving his fellow Corsicans. He achieved no distinction in any academic subject except mathematics, but he applied himself so assiduously to military science that he won a commission as a sub-lieutenant of artillery at the age of sixteen. The progress of the Revolution and the outbreak of foreign war brought rapid promotion, since many of the officers appointed under the Old Regime fled from the country. By 1793 he had become Colonel Bonaparte and had been entrusted with the difficult task of expelling the British from Toulon. Soon afterward he was rewarded with a promotion to brigadier-general. In 1795 he defended the National Convention against an uprising of reactionaries in Paris and was placed in command the following year of the expedition against the Austrians in Italy. His brilliant success in this campaign elevated him to the status of a national hero. His name was on everybody's lips. Politicians feared him and tumbled over one another to grant his every desire. While the comfortable classes adored him as a bulwark against radicalism, many ordinary folk were deceived by his honeyed pledges of devotion to Revolutionary doctrine. To all whose emotions had been set aflame by the new patriotism he loomed as the symbol of victory and of hope for a glorious future.

Had conditions in France been more stable than they were in 1799, it is probable that Napoleon Bonaparte would have lived out his days as no more than a talented army officer. But we have seen that conditions in this and in preceding years were exceedingly chaotic. Corruption, profiteering, and financial ruin added to the woes of a people already bowed down by the miseries of a long revolution. So profound was the mood of despair that thousands welcomed a new despotism as the only hope of relief. Besides, the government of the Directory was shot through with intrigue. One of its members, the Abbé Sieyès, was actually conspiring to overthrow it and was casting about for a popular hero to assist him. But the triumph of Napoleon was also due to certain qualities of his own personality. He was shrewd, egotistical, and unscrupulous. He had the sagacity to perceive that the people were tired of disorder and corruption, and that they longed for the return of stability. Convinced that Destiny had touched his brow, he determined to let nothing stand in the way of fulfillment of his lofty ambitions. He respected no principles or theories, harbored no doubts or perplexities, and suffered no twinges of conscience. He could lie and deceive with the appearance of perfect sincerity. Moreover, he was endowed with an indefatigable energy. He is alleged to have insisted that two hours of sleep were normal for a man, four hours for a woman, and "eight for a fool." He endeared himself to his soldiers by his ability to withstand hardships and by his infinite capacity for personal attention to every detail necessary to the success of a military campaign. Lastly, Napoleon had a keen instinct for the dramatic, a gift of eloquence, and a magnetic ability to exact from his followers the highest measure of devotion. He knew how to make the most of an inspiring setting and to fill the imaginations of all around him with magnificent visions of glory and power.

Napoleon's triumph

The new regime set up by Napoleon after the *coup d'état* of the eighteenth Brumaire was a thinly disguised autocracy. The constitution, drafted by the conspirators themselves, provided for a form of government known as the Consulate. Executive powers were vested in three Consuls, who were to appoint a Senate. The Senate, in turn, was to designate members of the Tribunate and the Legislative Body from lists of candidates chosen by popular vote. The First Consul, who of course was Bonaparte himself, was given authority to propose all laws, in addition to his power to appoint the entire administration and to control the army and the conduct of foreign affairs. The Tribunate was to discuss the laws without voting on them, after which the Legislative Body would accept or reject the laws without the privilege of debating them. Final approval of legislative measures would be determined in many cases by the Senate, which was to decide all questions of constitutionality. Thus the whole sys-

The government of the Consulate

tem depended in last analysis upon the will of the First Consul. But the framers of the constitution made a pretense of deferring to popular sovereignty, since the principle of universal manhood suffrage was revived. In December 1799, the new instrument of government was submitted to a popular referendum and was approved by a stupendous majority. When the votes were finally counted, it was found (or at least it was claimed) that only 1562 out of more than 3,000,000 had been cast in the negative. The constitution thus adopted went into effect on January 1, 1800; but since the Revolutionary calendar was still technically in force, it is known as the Constitution of the Year VIII.

Though Napoleon was now an absolute monarch in nearly everything but name, he still was not satisfied. In 1802 he obtained the consent of the people to extend his term of office as First Consul from ten years to life. All that then remained was to make his position hereditary. In 1804 by another plebiscite he won permission to

The establishment of the empire

Napoleon Crowning Josephine, 1804. Though Napoleon brought Pius VII from Rome to grace his coronation, he took the crown from the Pope's hands and placed it upon his own head, then crowned the Empress. Detail from the painting by Jacques Louis David, in the Louvre.

convert the Consulate into an empire. Soon afterward, in the midst of impressive ceremonies in the cathedral of Notre Dame, he placed a crown upon his own head and assumed the title of Napoleon I, Emperor of the French. His action in making this change was influenced partly by the growth of opposition. Several attempts had recently been made to take his life, and royalist plots were being hatched against him. Napoleon proceeded against the conspirators with characteristic ruthlessness. Scores were arrested upon mere suspicion, and some of the most prominent were singled out for drastic punishment as an example to the rest. The Duc d'Enghien was shot before an open grave after a farce of a trial. General Pichegru was found strangled in his cell. Having thus disposed of his chief enemies, Napoleon evidently concluded that the best way to guard against future trouble of this kind would be to establish a dynasty of his own and thereby cut the ground from under all Bourbon pretenders. Especially if he could obtain for his rule the benediction of the church, there would be few who would dare to oppose him. For this reason, he brought Pope Pius VII all the way from Rome to officiate at his coronation, though he was careful to produce the impression that His Holiness was acting as the mere agent of God and not as an international sovereign who could create and depose the emperor.

It is unfortunately true that most of the fame of Napoleon Bonaparte rests upon his exploits as a soldier; his work as a statesman was much more important. In the latter capacity he made at least a few notable contributions to civilization. He confirmed the redistribution of land accomplished by the Revolution, thereby permitting the average peasant to remain an independent farmer. He eliminated graft and waste from the government, reformed the system of taxation, and established the Bank of France to promote a more efficient control over fiscal affairs. He drained marshes, enlarged harbors, built bridges, and constructed a network of roads and canals. Most of these achievements were completed mainly for military purposes, but partly also in order to win the support of the commercial classes. In addition, he centralized the government of France, dividing the country into uniform districts or *départements*, each under a prefect taking orders from Paris.[1] Perhaps his accomplishment of greatest significance was his completion of the educational and legal reforms begun during the Revolution. He ordered the establishment of public elementary schools in every village, *lycées* or high schools in every important town, and a normal school in Paris for the training of teachers. To supplement these changes, he brought the military and technical schools under control of the state and founded a national university to exercise supervision over the entire system. But he was never willing to allocate more than a small fraction of his budget for educational purposes, with the consequence that less than half of the total number of French children received instruction at the expense of the state. In 1810, with the aid of a staff of jurists, he completed his famous Code Napoléon, a revision and codification of the civil and criminal laws on the basis of plans worked out by the National Convention. Despite its harsh provisions—the death penalty, for example, was retained for theft, and parricides were to have their hands cut off before execution—the Code Napoléon was hailed as the work of a second Justinian. With modifications it remained the law of France and Belgium for more than a century, while substantial portions of it were incorporated in the legal systems of Germany, Italy, Switzerland, Louisiana, and Japan.

Napoleon's work as a statesman included many other changes in the political system of France. For one thing, he restored the union

Napoleon's constructive work as a statesman

---

[1] The *départements* were originally established by the Revolutionary National Assembly, but not under a centralized arrangement. Their officers were to be elected by the people.

*Other results
of Napoleon's
statecraft*

between the Catholic church and the state. In 1801 he signed a Concordat with the Pope, which provided that bishops should be nominated by the First Consul and that the salaries of the clergy should be paid by the government. Even if the Catholic church did not regain the legal monopoly it had enjoyed under the Old Regime, since other religions were also to be tolerated, it was nevertheless placed in a position of decided advantage and was thereby able to increase its power in succeeding years. Not until 1905, when the Concordat of 1801 was finally broken, was Catholicism again reduced to equality with other faiths. Napoleon was responsible also for curtailing the liberties of his subjects almost from the moment he came into power. He abolished trial by jury in certain cases, imposed a strict censorship on the press, and suspended many journals that he suspected of being hostile toward his policies. So effective was his control over the entire nation that not a single French newspaper mentioned the disastrous defeat which Napoleon's navy suffered at Trafalgar until after the collapse of the empire, more than eight years later. In addition to all this, Napoleon perverted education to patriotic purposes and to the glorification of his personal ambitions. He ordered that children should be taught in the schools to love and obey their emperor and to offer "fervent prayers for his safety."

*The beginning
of Napoleon's
wars: the de-
struction of
the Second
Coalition*

It would neither be possible nor desirable in a book of this kind to present a detailed account of Napoleon's exploits as a military commander. Yet the subject cannot be ignored, for the results of his campaigns had considerable effect in shaping the course of history. To his credit it should perhaps be said that the wars in which he engaged were not all of his own making. Upon his accession to power in 1799 he inherited from the Directory the struggle with the Second Coalition, composed of Great Britain, Austria, and Russia.[2] By flattery and intrigue he quickly procured the withdrawal of Russia and then turned against Austria with all the forces he could muster. Leading his choicest battalions through the treacherous passes of the Alps in the spring of 1800, he fell upon the Austrians in the valley of the Po and crushed them as in the jaws of a vise. Soon afterward the Hapsburg emperor sued for peace. By 1801 Great Britain was the only enemy still in the war. Lacking a powerful navy, Bonaparte concluded that the British were beyond his reach and decided to negotiate rather than fight. In 1802 he accepted the Peace of Amiens, whereby Great Britain agreed to give up the colonial possessions seized during the war, exclusive of the islands of Trinidad and Ceylon. Napoleon was now free to devote his time to consolidating his power at home.

But the Peace of Amiens turned out to be no more than a truce.

[2] The First Coalition was the original combination of European powers formed in opposition to the French Revolution. It was organized in 1793 and was made up of Austria, Prussia, Great Britain, Spain, Holland, and some lesser states.

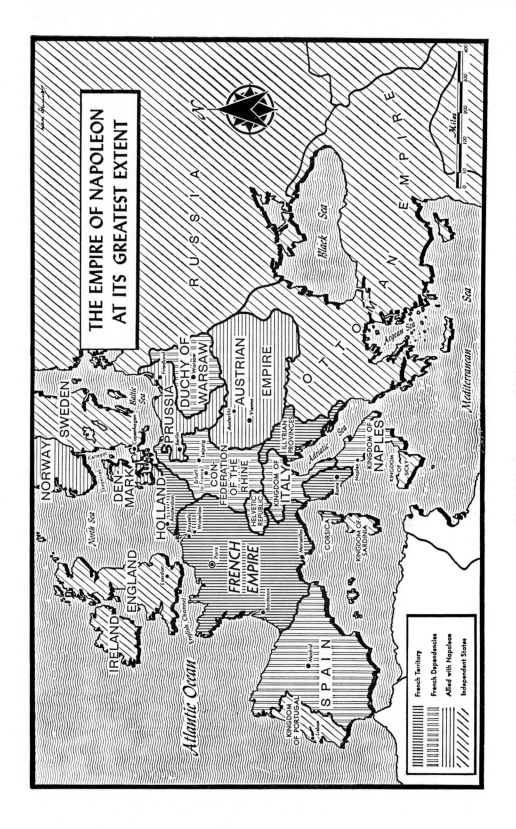

THE EMPIRE OF NAPOLEON
AT ITS GREATEST EXTENT

Miles
0 50 100 200 300 400

NORWAY
SWEDEN
DEN-MARK
North Sea
Kattegat
Skagerrak
Copenhagen
Baltic Sea
RUSSIA
DUCHY OF WARSAW
Warsaw
Friedland
PRUSSIA
Berlin
Leipzig
Austerlitz
AUSTRIAN EMPIRE
Vienna
OTTOMAN EMPIRE
Black Sea
Aegean Sea
Mediterranean Sea
IRELAND
ENGLAND
London
English Channel
Atlantic Ocean
HOLLAND
Amsterdam
Brussels
Waterloo
Paris
Erfurt (to France)
CON-FEDERATION OF THE RHINE
HELVETIC REPUBLIC
FRENCH EMPIRE
Bordeaux
Marseilles
KINGDOM OF ITALY
ILLYRIAN PROVINCES
Adriatic Sea
Rome
CORSICA
KINGDOM OF SARDINIA
KINGDOM OF NAPLES
Naples
KINGDOM OF SICILY
SPAIN
Madrid
KINGDOM OF PORTUGAL
Lisbon

French Territory
French Dependencies
Allied with Napoleon
Independent States

*The renewal of
the war with
Great Britain*

For various reasons England and France again came to grips in 1803. The British were alarmed by Napoleon's extension of influence over Italy and the Netherlands and by his conclusion of an alliance with Spain. Napoleon was irritated by the British refusal to withdraw from Malta in accordance with the Treaty of Amiens. But the chief reason for the renewal of the war was undoubtedly the economic ambitions of both the English and the French. The merchants and manufacturers of Britain feared that Napoleon might soon grow strong enough to reconquer the colonial empire which France had lost in the Seven Years' War. In similar fashion the wily Corsican was counting upon the destruction of British prosperity as the surest way of winning the applause of the French bourgeoisie, whom he reckoned as his most valuable supporters. Though war was declared in May, 1803, hostilities did not actually begin for some time. Both sides spent more than a year in preparation—the French in amassing a fleet for an invasion of England, and the British in acquiring a string of allies. By 1805 the Third Coalition against France had been brought into being—this time composed of Great Britain, Austria, Russia, and Sweden.

Napoleon now resumed his old tactics of attempting to annihilate his Continental enemies first of all. Abandoning for the time being the invasion of England, he hurled an army against the Austrians near the town of Ulm in October, 1805, and soon afterward captured Vienna. In December of the same year he won a decisive victory over a combined army of Austrians and Russians at Austerlitz. The result was the elimination of Austria from the war under the terms of a peace which deprived her of three million of her subjects and reduced her to a second-rate power. Seized with panic lest she meet a similar fate, Prussia now threw down the challenge to France. Napoleon lost no time in accepting, and, before another year had passed, the armies of Frederick William III had been driven from the field. The Corsican marched through Berlin in triumph and subjected the greater part of the country to the rule of his generals. Next he turned his attention to the Russians. Defeating them at Friedland in June, 1807, he impressed upon Tsar Alexander I the wisdom of peace. Napoleon and Alexander met in July at the Prussian town of Tilsit to draft the terms of a settlement. Curiously enough, the two emperors decided to become allies. They drew up what virtually amounted to a partnership to control the destinies of Europe between them. In return for a pledge to co-operate in excluding British trade from the Continent, Napoleon agreed that Alexander should be free to do as he liked with Finland and to take certain territories from Turkey. At the same time Prussia was loaded with a staggering punishment. She was robbed of half her territory, saddled with a huge indemnity, and practically reduced to a vassal state of France.

600   The star of the Little Corporal was now at its zenith. He was master of nearly all of the Continent of Europe west of Russia. He had destroyed what was left of the Holy Roman Empire and had brought most of the German states outside of Austria into a Confederation of the Rhine of which he himself was Protector. He had not only extended the boundaries of France, but he had created as his personal domain a new kingdom of Italy including the valley of the Po and what had once been the republic of Venice. In addition, he had placed relatives and friends on several of the remaining thrones of Europe. His brother Joseph had been made king of Naples, his brother Louis king of Holland, and his brother Jerome king of Westphalia. He had selected his friend, the king of Saxony,

The Battle of Trafalgar, by the English painter Joseph M. W. Turner (1775-1851). This battle is regarded by the British as one of the decisive events in their history, since it destroyed Napoleon's naval power and demolished any hopes he might have had of conquering Britain. The painting hangs in the Royal Maritime Museum at Greenwich.

to be the ruler of the duchy of Warsaw, a new Poland created mainly out of territories taken from Prussia. Not since the days of Charles V had so much of Europe been dominated by any one man. Yet Napoleon's position was far from secure, for he still had the "contemptible nation of shopkeepers" across the English Channel to deal with. Having lost to the British in the great naval battle of Trafalgar (October, 1805), he determined to wear them down by the indirect method of ruining their commerce. In 1806 and the years following he established his famous Continental System, a scheme by which his various puppet states were obliged to co-operate with France in **601** excluding British goods from the whole of Continental Europe. By depriving the English nation of its markets, Napoleon hoped that he could eventually sap its wealth to such a degree that the people would turn against their government and force it to capitulate. By the Treaty of Tilsit, as already noted, he even managed to bring Russia into the scheme.

*The causes
of Napoleon's
downfall*

The story of Napoleon's career from 1808 to 1815 is a record of the gradual decay of his fortunes. From his overthrow of the Directory in 1799 to the Peace of Tilsit in 1807 he had steadily climbed to an eminence which even an Alexander or a Caesar might well have envied. But soon after the latter event his difficulties began to multiply until finally they overwhelmed him in disaster. The explanation for his inexorable decline is to be found in several factors. First of all, with the passage of the years, he grew more egotistical, and therefore less inclined to accept advice even from his most capable subordinates. He kept nurturing the idea that he was a man of destiny until it developed into an obsession, a superstitious fatalism, that destroyed the resiliency of his mind. Second, his aggressive militarism provoked an inevitable reaction among its victims. The more it became evident that Napoleon's conquests were the sordid fruits of a maniacal ambition for power, the stronger was the determination of the vanquished to regain their freedom. Peoples that had at one time mistakenly welcomed him as an apostle of Revolutionary liberty now turned against him as a hated foreign oppressor. In addition, militarism was producing its effect upon France itself. The bones of hundreds of thousands of the best young men of the nation had been strewn in the dust of battlefields all over Europe. The problem not merely of filling their places in the ranks of the army, but also of maintaining the levels of agricultural and industrial production, was becoming more and more serious. Finally, the Continental System proved to be a boomerang. It actually inflicted more damage upon France and her allies than it did upon England. Napoleon found it impossible to enforce the exclusion of British products from the Continent, since most of the countries he dominated were agricultural nations and insisted upon trading the things they produced for manufactured goods from England. Moreover, the British retaliated with a series of Orders in Council making all vessels trading with France or her allies subject to capture. The effect was to cut Napoleon's empire off from sources of supply in neutral countries.

The Spanish revolt

The first episode of Napoleon's downfall was the Spanish revolt which broke out in the summer of 1808. In May of that year Napoleon had tricked the Spanish king and the crown prince into resigning their claims to the throne and had promoted his brother Joseph from king of Naples to king of Spain. But scarcely had the new monarch been crowned than the people rose in revolt. Though Napoleon sent an army against them, he was never able to crush the rebellion entirely. With encouragement and assistance from the

British, the Spaniards kept up a series of guerilla attacks which caused no end of expense and annoyance to the great war-lord of France. Furthermore, the courage of Spain in resisting the invader promoted a spirit of defiance elsewhere, with the result that Napoleon could no longer count upon the docility of any of his victims.

The second stage in the downfall of the Corsican adventurer was the disruption of his alliance with Russia. As a purely agricultural country, Russia had suffered a severe economic crisis when she was no longer able, as a result of the Continental System, to exchange her surplus grain for British manufactures. The consequence was that the Tsar Alexander began to wink at trade with Britain and to ignore or evade the protests from Paris. By 1811 Napoleon decided that he could endure this flouting of the Continental System no longer. Accordingly, he collected an army of 600,000 men and set out in the spring of 1812 to punish the Tsar. The project ended in horrible disaster. The Russians refused to make a stand, thereby leading the French farther and farther into the heart of their country. Not until the enemy was nearing Moscow did they finally give battle at Borodino. Defeated in this engagement, they permitted Napoleon to occupy their ancient capital. But on the very night of his entry, fire of suspicious origin broke out in the city. When the flames subsided, little but the blackened walls of the Kremlin remained to shelter the invading troops. Hoping that the Tsar would eventually surrender, Napoleon lingered amid the ruins for more than a month, finally deciding on October 22 to begin the homeward march. The delay was a fatal blunder. Long before he had reached the border, the terrible Russian winter was upon him. Swollen streams, mountainous drifts of snow, and bottomless mud slowed the retreat almost to a halt. To add to the miseries of bitter cold, disease, and starvation, Cossacks rode out of the blizzard to harry the exhausted troops. Each morning the miserable remnant that pushed on left behind circles of corpses around the campfires of the night before. On December 13 a few thousand broken, starved, and half-demented soldiers crossed the frontier into Germany—a miserable fraction of what had once been proudly styled the *Grande Armée*. The lives of nearly 300,000 men had been sacrificed in the Russian adventure.

The disastrous campaign against Russia

The disastrous outcome of the Russian campaign destroyed the myth that Napoleon was invincible. Soon the Prussians and the Austrians regained their courage and, with Russian aid, joined in a War of Liberation. Napoleon hastily collected a new army and marched to suppress the revolts. He won a few modest victories in the spring and summer of 1813 but was finally cornered at Leipzig by an allied army of 500,000 men. Here on October 16–19 was fought the celebrated Battle of the Nations, in which Napoleon was decisively beaten. His grand empire now collapsed like a house of cards; his vassal states deserted him; and France itself was invaded. On March 31, 1814, the victorious allies entered Paris. Thirteen days later Na-

The Battle of Leipzig

603

poleon signed the Treaty of Fontainebleau, renouncing all of his claims to the throne of France. In return he was granted a pension of two million francs a year and full sovereignty over the island of Elba, located in the Mediterranean Sea within sight of his native Corsica. The victors then took up with the French Senate the problem of reorganizing the government of France. It was agreed that the Bourbon line should be restored in the person of Louis XVIII, brother of the king who had been sent to the guillotine in 1793. It was carefully stipulated, however, that there was not to be a full restoration of the Old Regime. Louis XVIII was made to understand that he must not interfere with the political and economic reforms which still survived as fruits of the Revolution. In accordance with this requirement the new sovereign issued a charter confirming the Revolutionary liberties of the citizen and providing for a limited monarchy.

Napoleon's escape from Elba; the Battle of Waterloo

But the restoration of 1814 proved to be short-lived. The exiled emperor was growing impatient with his tiny island kingdom and eagerly awaiting the first opportunity to escape. His chance came in the spring of 1815. At this time the allies were quarreling among themselves over the disposition of Poland and Saxony. Besides, the French people were showing signs of disgust with the prosaic rule of Louis XVIII and with the effrontery of returning nobles of the Old Regime. Under these circumstances Napoleon slipped away from Elba and landed on the coast of southern France on March 1. Everywhere he was received by peasants and former soldiers in a delirium of joy. Officers sent to arrest him went over to his side with whole regiments of his former comrades in arms. On March 20, after a journey of triumph across the country, Napoleon entered Paris. Louis XVIII, who had sworn that he would die in defense of his throne, was already on his way to Belgium. But Napoleon was not to enjoy his new triumph long. Almost immediately upon learning of the escape from Elba, the allies abandoned their bickerings, proclaimed the Corsican an outlaw, and prepared to depose him by force. On June 12, 1815, Napoleon set out from Paris with the largest army he could gather in the hope of routing the enemy forces before they could invade his country. Six days later at Waterloo in Belgium he suffered a crushing defeat at the hands of the Duke of Wellington in command of an army of British, Dutch, and Germans. With all hope lost, Napoleon returned to Paris, abdicated his throne a second time, and made plans to escape to America. Finding the coast too heavily guarded, he was compelled to take refuge on a British ship. He was subsequently exiled by the British government to the rocky South Atlantic island of St. Helena. There he died, on May 5, 1821, a lonely and embittered man.

The significance of Napoleon

In attempting a final estimate of the significance of Napoleon Bonaparte, we must not lose sight of the fact that his name has been richly embellished with legend. The myth-mongering of patriots and hero-worshipers has raised his reputation almost to supernatural proportions. With the single exception of Jesus of Nazareth, he is actually the most written-about figure in history. But whether he deserves so exalted a fame is at least a debatable question. He was by no means a universal genius with a mastery of all knowledge or a patent on wisdom. Aside from mathematics, he knew little about any of the sciences, and his grasp of economics was too feeble to save him from the colossal errors of the Continental System. Though he was undoubtedly a clever tactician, the blunders of his Russian campaign indicate that even in military affairs he was not infallible. But worse than any other of his shortcomings were his defects of character. He was unscrupulous and unprincipled and capable of the basest trickery even against his friends. Moreover, his boundless egotism made him as coldly indifferent to the shedding of blood as a beast of the jungle crushing the bones of its prey. After sacrificing 300,000 men in the Russian adventure he had the temerity to assuage the grief of their wives and mothers by announcing to the nation that "the Emperor has never felt better in his life." His real significance lies in the fact that he helped to preserve some of the major results of the French Revolution. Though he might easily have done so, he refused to restore the regime of privilege which had flourished in the days of the Bourbons. He confirmed the abolition of serfdom and the repeal of primogeniture, and he allowed the peasants to keep the lands which they had acquired through the breaking up of the great estates. What is more, he was at least indirectly responsible for spreading Revolutionary ideals into other countries. For example, it was his smashing defeat of Prussia in 1806 which finally persuaded the leading men of that nation of the necessity of adopting the main reforms of the French Revolution as the only means by which their state could rise again to smite the oppressor. Under Baron vom Stein and Chancellor Hardenberg, the Prussian government in 1807–1808 abolished serfdom and threw open the various occupations and professions to men in all ranks of society. Unfortunately these measures were accompanied by an outburst of extreme nationalism, which found characteristic expression in the adoption of compulsory military service, one of the tyrannical devices employed by Napoleon himself.

2. The Congress of Vienna and the Concert of Europe

Following the overthrow of Napoleon, an overwhelming desire for peace and order seized the minds of the conservative classes in the victorious countries. Nearly everything that had happened since the hated Corsican had come into power now came to be regarded as a horrible nightmare. In some quarters there was a desire to return to the *status quo* of 1789, to undo the work of the Great Revolution, and to revive the power and the glamour of the Old Regime. The government of the Papal States proceeded to abolish street lighting

The movement to return to the status quo

in Rome as a dangerous novelty, while the Elector of Hesse restored the pigtails to the freshly-powdered heads of his faithful soldiers. The leading statesmen realized, however, that a complete restoration of the old order would not be possible. For example, it was perfectly evident that the French people would not tolerate a revival of serfdom or the return of confiscated lands to the nobles and clergy. Therefore, while the portly Louis XVIII was put back on the throne, it was understood that he would continue to rule in conformity with the Charter of 1814. Furthermore, some of the victorious powers were not ready to give up the conquests they had made at the expense of France. Hence it was found necessary to modify suggestions frequently made for redrawing the map of Europe in accordance with the form it had had in the days of Louis XVI.

The Congress of Vienna

Most of the work of deciding the fate of Europe at the conclusion of the long war which had involved nearly the whole of the Western world was done at the so-called Congress of Vienna. To refer to this body as a "Congress" is to be guilty of a misnomer; for, as a matter of fact, no plenary session of all the delegates was ever held. As in the drafting of the Versailles Treaty more than a hundred years later, the vital decisions were really made by small committees. Nevertheless, the assemblage at Vienna was staged with such pomp and splendor that even the most neglected member was made to feel that he was participating in events of epochal importance. The Austrian government, in the capacity of host, is reputed to have spent some $15,000,000 in providing a gorgeous array of banquets, balls, and military reviews. The chief delegates, however, composed such a galaxy of titled magnificence that the humbler representatives were easily pushed into the background. No less than six monarchs attended: the Tsar of Russia, the emperor of Austria, and the kings of Prussia, Denmark, Bavaria, and Württemberg. Great Britain was represented by Lord Castlereagh and the "Iron Duke" of Wellington. From France came the subtle intriguer Talleyrand, who had served as a bishop under Louis XVI, as foreign minister at the court of Napoleon, and who now stood ready to espouse the cause of reaction.

Alexander I

The dominant roles at the Congress of Vienna were played by Alexander I and Metternich. The dynamic Tsar was one of the most baffling figures in history. Reared at the voluptuous court of Catherine the Great, he imbibed the doctrines of Rousseau from a French Jacobin tutor. In 1801 he succeeded his murdered father as Emperor and for the next two decades disturbed the dreams of his brother-sovereigns by becoming the most liberal monarch in Europe. After the defeat of Napoleon in the Russian campaign, his mind turned more and more into mystical channels. He conceived of a mission to convert the rulers of all countries to the Christian ideals of justice and peace. But the chief effect of his voluble expressions of devotion

606

The Congress of Vienna, 1815. The
figure standing to the left of center
is Prince Metternich.

to "liberty" and "enlightenment" was to frighten conservatives into
suspecting a plot to extend his power over all of Europe. He was
accused of intriguing with Jacobins everywhere to substitute an all-
powerful Russia for an all-powerful France.

The other commanding figure at the Congress was Klemens von
Metternich, born in 1773 at Coblenz in the Rhine valley, where his
father was Austrian ambassador at the courts of three small German   *Metternich*
states. As a student at the University of Strassburg the young Metternich witnessed some excesses of mob violence connected with the
outbreak of the French Revolution, and to these he attributed his
life-long hatred of political innovation. After completing his education he entered the field of diplomacy and served for nearly forty
years as Minister of Foreign Affairs. He was active in fomenting discord between Napoleon and the Tsar Alexander, after the two became allies in 1807, and he played some part in arranging the marriage of Napoleon to the Austrian archduchess, Marie Louise. In
1813 he was made a hereditary prince of the Austrian Empire. At
the Congress of Vienna Metternich distinguished himself for charm
of manner and skillful intrigue. His two great obsessions were hatred
of political and social change and fear of Russia. Actually the two
were related. It was not simply that he feared revolutions as such;
he feared even more revolutions inspired by the "Jacobin" Tsar for
the sake of establishing Russian supremacy in Europe. For this reason
he favored moderate terms for France in her hour of defeat, and
was ready at one time to sponsor the restoration of Napoleon as
Emperor of the French under the protection and overlordship of
the Hapsburg monarchy.

The basic idea which guided the work of the Congress of Vienna
was the principle of *legitimacy*. This principle was invented by
Talleyrand as a device for protecting France against drastic punish-   *Legitimacy*
ment by her conquerors, but it was ultimately adopted by Metter-
nich as a convenient expression of the general policy of reaction.
Legitimacy meant that the dynasties of Europe that had reigned in
pre-Revolutionary days should be restored to their thrones, and that
each country should regain essentially the same territories it had held
in 1789. In accordance with this principle Louis XVIII was recognized as the "legitimate" sovereign of France, and the restoration of
the house of Orange in Holland, of the house of Savoy in Piedmont   **607**

AFTER THE CONGRESS OF VIENNA, 1815

Boundary of the Germanic Confederation	
Austrian Empire	
France	
Prussia	

KINGDOM OF NORWAY AND SWEDEN

KINGDOM OF DENMARK

Baltic Sea

Copenhagen

HOLSTEIN
Hamburg

MECKLENBURG

OVER

PRUSSIA

Berlin

Elbe R.

Oder R.

Vistula R.

Warsaw

SAXONY

REPUBLIC OF CRACOW

Cracow

RUSSIAN EMPIRE

Kiev

Dnieper R.

Main R.

BAVARIA

Danube R.

Munich

Vienna

AUSTRIAN EMPIRE

Budapest

Danube R.

MOLDAVIA

Pruth R.

VENETIA

Sava R.

PO R.

MODENA

WALLACHIA

Adriatic Sea

Danube R.

Black Sea

PAPAL STATES

Rome

MONTENEGRO

OTTOMAN EMPIRE

Naples

Constantinople

KINGDOM OF THE TWO SICILIES

Palermo

and Sardinia, and of the Bourbon rulers of Spain and the Two Sicilies was also confirmed. France was compelled to pay an indemnity of 700,000,000 francs, but her boundaries were to remain essentially the same as in 1789. Other territorial arrangements likewise adhered to the idea of a return to the *status quo*. The Pope was allowed to recover his temporal possessions in Italy; Switzerland was restored as an independent Confederation under guaranties of neutrality by the principal powers; while the Polish kingdom set up by Napoleon was abolished and the country again divided among Russia, Austria, and Prussia.

Violations of legitimacy

But the Congress of Vienna was no less cynical in violating the principle of legitimacy than were the makers of the Versailles Treaty in riding roughshod over the doctrine of the self-determination of nations. In both cases reasons of expediency and national greed played havoc with devotion to ideals. Before the lace-cuffed princes at Vienna had gone very far in restoring the old map of Europe, they diluted the principle of legitimacy with their curious system of compensations. The real purpose of this system was to enable certain of the major powers to gratify their hunger for spoils. For example, Great Britain was permitted to keep the valuable territories she had taken from the Dutch, who had fought for a time on the side of France. Among these rich prizes were South Africa, a portion of Guiana in South America, and the island of Ceylon. Then to compensate the Dutch for the loss of so large a part of their empire, provision was made for transferring the Austrian Netherlands, or Belgium, to Holland. Since this involved a sacrifice on the part of Austria, the Hapsburgs were rewarded with an extensive foothold in Italy. They received the republic of Venice and the duchy of Milan, while members of the family were placed on the thrones of Tuscany, Parma, and Modena. Thus Austria profited by gaining a compact empire occupying a commanding position in central Europe. A similar series of compensations was provided for in order to reward Russia for her part in conquering Napoleon. The Tsar was allowed to retain Finland, which he had seized from Sweden in 1809. Sweden, in turn, was compensated by the acquisition of Norway from Denmark. All of these arrangements were put through with a total disregard for the interests of the peoples concerned. Despite the fact that the Belgians were altogether different in culture and religion from the Dutch, they were nevertheless forced to submit to the rule of Holland. Nor were the interests of the Norwegians considered in the slightest in transferring them to the sovereignty of Sweden. As in the case of the settlement at Versailles in 1919, these offenses against nationality prepared the ground for a rancorous growth of troubles in the future.

One of the cardinal purposes of Metternich and his conservative colleagues was to erect the Vienna settlement into a permanent bulwark of the *status quo*. With this end in view they established the

Quadruple Alliance of Great Britain, Austria, Prussia, and Russia as an instrument for maintaining the settlement intact. In 1818 France was admitted to the combination, thereby making it a Quintuple Alliance. For some years this aggregate of powers functioned as a kind of League of Nations to enforce the system of Metternich. It is also frequently referred to as the Concert of Europe, since its members were pledged to co-operate in suppressing any disturbances which might arise from the attempts of peoples to throw off their "legitimate" rulers or to change international boundaries. In the minds of liberals and nationalists of this period the Quintuple Alliance was often confused with another combination which also grew out of the settlement at Vienna. This was the so-called Holy Alliance, a product of the sentimental idealism of the Tsar Alexander I. In September, 1815, Alexander proposed that the monarchs of Europe should "take as their sole guide . . . the precepts of Justice, Christian Charity, and Peace," and that they should base international relations as well as the treatment of their subjects "upon the sublime truths which the Holy Religion of our Savior teaches . . ." But none of the Tsar's brother-sovereigns took him seriously. Though most of them signed the agreement he proposed, they were inclined to regard it as so much mystical verbiage. As a matter of fact, the Holy Alliance was never anything more than a series of pious pledges. The real weapon for preserving the triumph of reaction was not the Holy Alliance but the Quintuple Alliance.

The system of alliances

The purposes of the Quintuple Alliance were achieved primarily through a series of international congresses which met between 1818 and 1822. Altogether there were four in the series: Aix-la-Chapelle in 1818, Troppau in 1820, Laibach in 1821, and Verona in 1822. It was at the second of these conferences, the Congress of Troppau, that the true character of the Alliance was most clearly revealed. Here the assembled delegates drew up an agreement avowing the intention of the great powers to intervene by force of arms to suppress any revolution that might threaten the stability of Europe. In two different instances the policy of intervention was actually carried out. After an uprising in the Kingdom of the Two Sicilies, in which the Bourbon monarch, Ferdinand I, was compelled to swear allegiance to a liberal constitution, Metternich convoked the Congress of Laibach in 1821. King Ferdinand was summoned before it, commanded to disavow his oath, and persuaded to invite an Austrian army to march into Naples. As a result, the constitution was revoked, and Ferdinand was restored to his position as an autocratic sovereign. In 1822 the Congress of Verona was summoned to deal with an insurrection in Spain, which also had had the effect of forcing the king to subscribe to a liberal constitution. After considerable wrangling among the powers as to the measures which should be taken to crush the revolt, it was finally decided that the king of France should send an army into Spain to support his Bourbon kinsman. Not only was

The activities of the Quintuple Alliance

the revolt speedily crushed, but intervention was followed by the blackest reaction Europe had yet seen. Hundreds of devoted liberals were put to death; even greater numbers were chained in the vilest of prisons. And it is not without interest that some of the ruthless measures of the Spanish king were the result of direct encouragement from the leaders of the Quintuple Alliance.

*The clash
of liberals and
conservatives:
(1) in Great
Britain and
France*

While foreign intervention was confined to Spain and the Kingdom of the Two Sicilies, these were by no means the only countries where violent conflicts occurred between liberals and conservatives. For the system of Metternich involved a regime of stern repression in domestic affairs by the governments of the great powers, as well as the suppression of revolutions in the lesser states. But the more blind and bitter the policy of repression, the greater was the number of uprisings against it. In Great Britain the rule of the Tories for the benefit of the landed aristocracy evoked powerful opposition from intellectual radicals like William Godwin, from the poets Shelley and Byron, and from the new industrial classes. When the protests of these groups were silenced by laws prohibiting public meetings and muzzling the press, some of the more desperate leaders organized the Cato Street Conspiracy in 1820 to murder the whole Tory Cabinet. Discovery of the plot was a foregone conclusion, and five of the conspirators were hanged. In France the modest compromise with progressive ideas which Louis XVIII incorporated in his Charter of 1814 proved to be more than his die-hard followers were willing to stand. As a result, the years between 1815 and 1820 were fraught with savage and sometimes bloody strife between Ultra-Royalists and their liberal and moderate opponents. In 1820 the assassination of the king's nephew by a fanatical liberal so frightened the people that the Ultra-Royalists were swept into control of Parliament. Then followed a series of reactionary laws which pushed France farther back into the mire of the Old Regime. A strict censorship of the press was established and the guaranties of individual liberty revoked. Control over the educational system was vested in the Catholic clergy. The electoral system was so modified as to assure to the rich a majority of the seats in Parliament. In 1824 the victory of the forces of reaction was strengthened still further when Louis XVIII died and was succeeded by his brother, Charles X, the leader of the Ultra-Royalists.

Similar struggles occurred in central and eastern Europe with almost identical results. In Germany students in the universities organized secret societies and participated in stormy agitation against hated regimes. The upshot of these incipient revolts was the assassination by a hot-headed student of the dramatist Kotzebue, a notorious reactionary and Russian spy. This deed convinced Metternich, who dominated the Germanic Confederation, that all of central Europe was about to be engulfed by a radical revolution. Accordingly, he forced through the federal Diet a program of repressive measures known as the Carlsbad Decrees (1819). By the terms of these it was provided that every university should have a government supervisor; rebellious professors were to be removed from their positions; student societies were ordered to be dissolved; and the press was to be subject to a strict censorship. Vigorous enforcement of the Carlsbad Decrees put the liberal movement in Germany under a cloud, from which it did not emerge until 1848.

Meanwhile, the change in the attitude of the Tsar Alexander I had produced some rumblings of discontent in benighted Russia. Time was when Alexander had been one of the most enlightened monarchs of Europe. He had founded schools and universities. He had emancipated a few of the serfs and had considered plans for freeing the remainder. He had even toyed with the idea of granting a written constitution. But after 1818 he turned reactionary and repented the liberal sins of his youth in sackcloth and ashes. This change of heart of the Tsar was the signal for the growth of an opposition movement among officers of the army and the intellectual classes. When Alexander died in 1825, the leaders of this movement determined to prevent the reaction from going any farther. They organized the Dekabrist revolt (from the Russian word for December) to compel the accession to the throne of the liberal Grand Duke Constantine in place of his hard-shell brother, Nicholas. Unfortunately Constantine would have nothing to do with the rebellion, and Nicholas speedily crushed it. The ensuing reign was one of the worst in Russian history. Not only did Nicholas abolish freedom of the press, but he established a system of secret police and converted the nation into a huge military camp where every move of the citizen could be watched and controlled by the government.

(3) in Russia

In spite of what seemed to be enduring victories for the cause of reaction, by 1830 the system of Metternich had begun to break down. The initial step in the process was the withdrawal of Great Britain from the Quintuple Alliance. As early as 1822 the British refused to participate in Metternich's scheme for suppression of the revolution in Spain. Soon afterward they flatly repudiated the entire policy of intervention in the internal affairs of foreign states. It was not that the British of this time were more liberal than their allies on the Continent; it was rather that the Industrial Revolution was forcing Britain to seek new markets for the things she produced. Therefore she was strongly opposed to a foreign policy which would antagonize other nations and cut off her channels of trade. She had developed a lucrative commerce with the states of Central and South America, which had lately thrown off their allegiance to Spain, and she was fearful that the system of Metternich might be used to force these former colonies back under Spanish rule. Motivated by such considerations, she prepared to cut herself loose from the Quintuple Alliance.

Causes of the decline of the system of Metternich: (1) the withdrawal of Great Britain

About the same time that Great Britain was weakening her ties

*(2) the Russo-
Turkish War
of 1828–1829*

with the Concert of Europe, Russia began to develop ambitions which also threatened the supremacy of Metternich's system. For some years the Russians had been greedily awaiting the breakup of the Ottoman Empire in the hope that that would pave the way for an easy expansion into the Balkans. The Russian opportunity came after 1821 when the Greeks launched a rebellion against Turkish rule. Since the Tsar Alexander I was still bound by loyalty to the doctrine of legitimacy, nothing was done until after his death in 1825. His successor, Nicholas I, entertained no such scruples. Especially when he observed in England and France expressions of the profoundest sympathy for the Greeks in their heroic struggle against an infidel oppressor, he determined to go to their rescue. Accordingly, in 1828, he declared war against Turkey. In a little more than a year a Russian army fought its way almost to the gates of the Turkish capital and forced the Sultan to sign the Treaty of Adrianople. By the terms of this treaty Turkey was compelled to acknowledge the independence of Greece, to grant autonomy to Serbia, and to permit the establishment of a Russian protectorate over the provinces which later became the kingdom of Rumania. In thus contributing to the dismemberment of the empire of a "legitimate" ruler, Russia, with considerable encouragement from England and France, dealt a powerful blow to the system of political stagnation which Metternich was striving to maintain. For all practical purposes the empire of the Tsars had ceased to be a member of the Quintuple Alliance.

*(3) the July
Revolution in
France*

The system of Metternich was weakened still further by the series of revolutions which broke out in western Europe in 1830. The first in the series was the July Revolution in France, which resulted in the overthrow of Charles X, the last of the regular line of Bourbon kings. As was indicated previously, Charles X, who had succeeded Louis XVIII in 1824, was the perfect embodiment of the spirit of reaction. His stubborn and vindictive attitude inspired relentless hatred, especially among the ranks of the bourgeoisie, who resented his reduction of the interest on government bonds and his attempt to disfranchise three-fourths of the voters. As evidence accumulated that the king was determined to rule in complete defiance of Parliament, barricades were thrown up in the streets. After futile efforts to quell the insurrection with a remnant of loyal troops, Charles abdicated his throne and fled to England. The leaders of the bourgeoisie then chose as his successor Louis Philippe, a member of the Orleanist branch of the Bourbon family and a former Jacobin who had taken an active part in the revolution of 1789. The new government was proclaimed to be a constitutional monarchy founded upon the principle of popular sovereignty; and the white flag of the Bourbons was replaced by the tricolor originally invented by the apostles of Liberty, Equality, and Fraternity.

Soon after the July Revolution in France a revolt broke out in the

Belgian Netherlands. It will be recalled that in the Vienna settlement of 1815 the Belgian or Austrian Netherlands had been subjected to the rule of Holland in defiance of the obvious differences of language, nationality, and religion between the Belgians and the Dutch. An additional basis of friction was the divergent economic interests of the two peoples. Whereas the Dutch were engaged primarily in commerce and agriculture, the occupations of the Belgians were chiefly industrial. These differences, combined with the stupid tyrannies of the Dutch king, incited the Belgians in the fall of 1830 to strike a blow for independence. The revolt was regarded with favor by the new government in France and also by the British, who hoped that it might benefit their trade. Consequently, the following year, an international agreement was signed in London recognizing the independence of Belgium as a constitutional monarchy. The Dutch had no alternative but to acquiesce in an accomplished fact. In 1839 the independence and neutrality of Belgium were guaranteed by all the great powers.

The revolutionary movement of 1830 spread into a number of other countries, but the results were not so successful. In Italy revolts were staged in the Papal States against Gregory XVI, a zealous reactionary and friend of the Hapsburgs, and also in Parma and Modena against the Austrian puppets who ruled there. But in each of these cases Austrian troops were rushed to the scene and quickly restored the deposed governments. The only permanent results were to stimulate Italian nationalism and to nourish a morbid hate of the Austrians. In the Germanies, uprisings in several of the duchies and lesser kingdoms bore fruit in moderate constitutions, but the governments of the two most important German states—Prussia and Austria —were now so powerful that opposition groups were completely cowed. The only remaining revolt of serious dimensions was the insurrection of the Poles in 1831, a desperate attempt of that harassed people to regain independence from Russia. Had the Poles been as fortunate as the Belgians in obtaining aid from foreign nations, they might have won. But the British and the French were now too busy with affairs in western Europe and gave nothing more than verbal support. As a consequence, the Tsar Nicholas I was able to crush the revolt with murderous severity. Hundreds of the rebellious leaders were shot or exiled to the dreary wastes of Siberia, and Poland was governed henceforth as a conquered province. However, these isolated victories of the reactionaries against such peoples as the Poles and the Italians were not sufficient to keep the regime which Metternich had founded from tottering toward its grave. As an instrument for preserving internal stagnation it lingered in Austria and in parts of Italy until 1848; but as a system of international repression its doom was already sealed by the defection of Great Britain and by the successful uprisings in Belgium and Greece.

3. The Triumph of Conservatism in the Realm of Ideas

The ascendancy of the conservative attitude

Just as there was a struggle in the years from 1800 to 1830 between liberals and conservatives in the political sphere, so there was a similar clash in the realm of ideas. And the outcome of this second struggle was not so far different from that of the first. In general, throughout the period, the doctrines of intellectual conservatives enjoyed the supremacy. Order was exalted above liberty. The interests of groups, of society, and especially of the state were given precedence over those of the individual. An emphasis upon faith, authority, and tradition superseded the eighteenth-century belief in the primacy of reason and science. A group of French philosophers under the leadership of Joseph de Maistre (1754–1821) sought to inaugurate a Catholic revival in which mystical piety, supernaturalism, and the belief in an infallible church would serve as the lamps to guide men's feet from the pitfalls of skepticism and anarchy. For this ascendancy of conservative patterns of thought various factors were responsible. There was first of all the influence of romanticism, founded by Rousseau, with its denial of the competence of reason and its stress upon emotions and feelings. There was also the tendency, common in all ages, of many writers and thinkers to take their cue from the dominant political trend, which in this period, of course, was conservative. But probably the major factor, in the beginning at least, was the strong revulsion of feeling which had set in against the horrors of the French Revolution. All who had been frightened by the violence of that movement were inclined to blame it on the rationalism, materialism, and individualism of the age of the Enlightenment. Hence they were disposed to swing to the opposite extreme of glorifying faith, authority, and tradition. Such in particular was

Edmund Burke

the attitude expressed by Edmund Burke, the renowned British orator and Whig statesman of the late eighteenth century. Although he did not live to see the end of the French Revolution, Burke denounced that movement with all the fiery eloquence he could command. To him the Revolution was an attempt to repudiate the accumulated wisdom of the ages. This world, he averred, cannot be made over in a single night. No one generation has the right to set itself up as the judge of society's future needs. The institutions and traditions which have come down to us from the past have an enduring value. To lay violent hands upon them is to threaten the vital elements of civilization itself.

Romantic Idealism

The body of thought which stands as the most perfect expression of the age of reaction was the German philosophy of Romantic Idealism. This philosophy derives its name from the fact that it was a combination of the romanticist theory of truth with the idealist conception of the universe. That is, it was neither rationalistic nor materialistic in the strict meaning of those terms. Instead it recognized the validity of intuitive or instinctive knowledge in addition to that which comes from reason, and it sought to explain the universe in a sense at least partly spiritual. The Romantic Idealists also deviated sharply from the individualism and humanism of eighteenth-century philosophy. They regarded the individual as totally devoid of significance except in so far as he was a member of some social group. Therefore, they argued, the welfare of the group must come first, and that of the individual will automatically follow. Society and the state are social organisms, products of a *natural* evolution, and not the artificial creations of man himself for his own convenience. No such thing as a state of nature ever existed, nor was political society founded by a social compact. Consequently the individual cannot claim any inviolable sphere of rights beyond the jurisdiction of organized society. His duty is rather to submerge his own interests in those of the group and thereby gain the true liberty which consists in obedience to law and in respect for accumulated tradition.

The philosopher who provided the original inspiration for Romantic Idealism was a methodical little German who lived most of his life in the eighteenth century. His name was Immanuel Kant, and he was born in Königsberg in 1724; there he died in 1804 without once having left his native city, except for a brief period of tutoring in a neighboring village. Devoting most of his life to teaching, he matured his philosophic ideas very slowly. When well along toward middle age he could still refer with scorn to the metaphysicians as those who dwelt on the high towers of abstruse cogitation, "where there is usually a great deal of wind." Not until he was fifty-seven years old did he finish his first great work, the *Critique of Pure Reason*. As a philosopher, Kant owed considerable to the great minds of the Enlightenment. They contributed particularly to his political ideas. Unlike most of his followers, he believed in the natural rights of man and even defended the separation of powers as a necessary protection for the liberty of the citizen. But in the field of general philosophy Kant departed widely from the rationalism of the eighteenth century. He divided the entire universe into two worlds: one, the realm of physical nature, or the world of *phenomena;* and the other, the realm of ultimate reality, or the world of *noumena*. The methods of knowing applicable to these realms are entirely different. Sense perception and reason can give us knowledge only of the realm of *phenomena*, of the world of physical things. But in the higher realm of the spiritual, which is the world of ultimate reality, such methods are of no avail. Since all ordinary knowledge rests in final analysis upon sense perception, we cannot prove by reason or science that God exists, that the human will is free, or that the soul is immortal. Nevertheless, we are justified in assuming that these things are true. For example, we have an irresistible conviction that virtue and happiness are inseparably linked, that the universe is governed by moral law, and that therefore a divine being must preside over the destinies of men. Such a conclusion is altogether outside the jurisdiction of

Romantic Idealism founded by Immanuel Kant

617

science, but it is dictated by feelings entirely too strong to be dismissed as mere illusions. And in the realm of *noumena*, faith, intuition, and deep conviction are just as valid instruments of knowledge as logic and science in the realm of *phenomena*.

Other Romantic Idealist philosophers: Fichte

The immediate disciples of Kant generally inclined toward a more abstract and metaphysical philosophy than that of their master. Such was notably the case of Johann Gottlieb Fichte (1762–1814). Fichte and his associates taught that the world of mind or spirit is the real world, and that the individual realizes his true nature only by bringing himself into harmony with the universal purpose. The human mind can know nothing of reality except in so far as it is informed and guided by the supreme ego or universal intelligence. It is the duty of the individual to allow intuition to discover the demands of this superego, to adjust his own life to them, and thereby to free himself from the slavery of sense. The philosophy of Fichte evolved into a kind of spiritual pantheism with a world-spirit directing all life and activity toward a final goal of sublime perfection. Fichte is also of more than trivial importance as a political philosopher. He was one of the earliest apostles of collectivistic nationalism in Germany. During the years of the Napoleonic invasions he proclaimed to his countrymen the ideal of a united and powerful Germany with a mission to assume the leadership of the civilized world. He taught that this state should rule with an eye single to justice and prosperity for all its subjects. It should therefore regulate prices and insure to each individual his proportionate share of the national wealth. Moreover, the state should be a self-contained economic unit; foreign trade should be reduced to an absolute minimum, and when essential it should be carried on through the government itself. It is hardly necessary to stress the close similarity between some of these ideas and policies adopted by the German nation in the time of Hitler.

Hegel

Undoubtedly the most influential philosopher of the Romantic Idealist movement was Georg Wilhelm Hegel (1770–1831). Professor of philosophy for a considerable period at the University of Berlin, Hegel won a great number of adherents, and through them exerted a potent force in shaping intellectual currents for many years. The central doctrine of Hegel's philosophy is the idea of purposive evolution. He regarded the universe as in a condition of flux, with everything tending to pass over into its opposite. In particular, each institution or social or political organism grows to maturity, fulfills its mission, and then gives way to something different. But the old itself is never entirely destroyed; the clash of opposites results eventually in a fusion, in the creation of a new organism made up of elements taken from the two opposites themselves. Then the process is repeated over and over again with each new stage representing an improvement over that which has gone before. But Hegel's conception of evolution was not mechanistic. He believed the whole process

Georg Wilhelm Friedrich Hegel
(1770–1831).

to be guided by the universal reason or God. Evolution, he maintained, is the unfoldment of God in history. Further, he argued that the war of opposites would ultimately lead to a beneficent goal. This goal he described as the perfect state, in which the interests of every citizen would be perfectly blended with the interests of society. As a matter of fact, Hegel worshiped the state in a much more ecstatic fashion than did any of the other Romantic Idealists. He held that true liberty consists in subjection to political society, and that the individual has no rights which the state is bound to respect; for without the state the individual would be nothing but an animal. "The State is the Divine Idea as it exists on earth." [3]

Romantic Idealism cast its influence in many directions. In one or another of its forms it was adopted as the principal gospel of nearly all in the conservative camp. Churchmen who had been disturbed by the attacks of deists and skeptics were delighted to find a philosophy that recognized the merits of faith and exalted the world of spirit. People with a stake in the maintenance of order rejoiced in the new worship of tradition and authority and in the implied condemnation of revolution. Especially pleasing to the ruling class were the political teachings of Hegel, who enjoyed such prestige at the Prussian court that his enemies called him "the official philosopher." The doctrines of Hegel and Fichte alike strengthened the rising tide of nationalism and ultimately contributed their quota to the devastating flood of fascism.[4] But Romantic Idealism also bore certain other fruits not exactly to the liking of its principal exponents. One

The influence of Romantic Idealism

[3] Hegel, *Philosophy of History* (J. Sibree, trans.), p. 87.
[4] Hegelian ideas influenced the growth of fascism not only in Germany but also in Italy. See H. W. Schneider, *Making the Fascist State*, pp. 20–24.

of their younger contemporaries, Arthur Schopenhauer (1788–1860), developed the notion of a universal force, directing all growth and movement, into a philosophy of stark pessimism. He taught that this force is *will*—a blind, unconscious craving of individuals and species to survive. Since the will to live is present in all animate forms, and since it leads the strong to devour the weak, this world is the worst of all possible worlds. Selfishness, pain, and misery are inseparable from life, and therefore the only road to happiness for man consists in as complete a denial of life as possible after the manner of an Oriental ascetic. Still another of the strange offshoots of Romantic Idealism was the philosophy of history of Karl Marx. For his celebrated doctrine of dialectical materialism, Marx was heavily indebted to Hegel. Both believed in a progressive evolution through a clash of opposing systems, resulting finally in a perfect society. But whereas Hegel assumed that the ultimate goal would be a perfect state, Marx argued that it would be communism. The two men differed also in their conception of the dialectical process—that is, of the war of opposites. Hegel interpreted historical evolution as the unfoldment of the world-spirit or universal reason; Marx contended that historical change is the result of economic factors. It was the proud boast of the great socialist leader that he turned Hegel right side up.

Romantic Idealism was most popular in Germany. In other countries, especially in England and France, where the influence of the Enlightenment had taken deeper root, philosophy was generally more liberal in tone. The leading system of thought in England in the early nineteenth century was Utilitarianism, founded by Jeremy Bentham (1748–1832). Despite a frail and nervous physique, Bentham displayed prodigious intellectual talent throughout the greater part of his long life. He began the study of Latin when he was only three years old and was graduated from Oxford at the age of fifteen. When he was nearly seventy he was still propounding schemes for prison reform and for cutting canals across the Isthmus of Panama and the Isthmus of Suez. His chief philosophical work, the *Principles of Morals and Legislation*, was published in 1789. Bentham's Utilitarianism derives its name from his cardinal teaching that the supreme test to which every belief and institution should be made to conform is the test of utility or usefulness. This test he defined as contributing to the greatest happiness of the greatest number. Any doctrine or practice which fails to meet this requirement should be rejected forthwith, regardless of how much hoary tradition may stand behind it. Despite its social connotations, Bentham's ideal was the acme of individualism. Not only did he maintain that the interest of the community is simply the sum of the interests of the several members who compose it, but he was quite frank in admitting that the motives of individuals are purely selfish. The mainspring of human action is the desire to secure pleasure and to avoid pain. Therefore

Utilitarianism, founded by Jeremy Bentham

society should leave to each of its members complete freedom to follow his own enlightened self-interest. Since every individual knows better than anyone else what constitutes his own good, the welfare of society can best be promoted by allowing to each of its members the maximum liberty of action. Bentham was firmly convinced that granting this concession would not mean a reversion to the ways of the jungle. He insisted that every man would be obliged to respect his neighbor's rights through fear of retaliation; that men would obey the laws for the simple reason that the "probable mischiefs of obedience are less than the probable mischiefs of disobedience." [5]

Bentham's most faithful disciple was James Mill (1773–1836), but the greatest of all the Utilitarian philosophers was James Mill's oldest son, John Stuart Mill (1806–1873). Educated exclusively by his father, John Stuart Mill surpassed even Bentham as an intellectual prodigy. He learned the Greek alphabet at the age of three, and by the time he was eight had read all of Herodotus and a considerable portion of Plato in the original. When scarcely thirteen he had completed a rigorous course of training in history, Scholastic logic, and Aristotelian philosophy. His greatest works are his *Logic*, his *Principles of Political Economy*, his essay *On Liberty*, and his *Representative Government*. As a philosopher, John Stuart Mill summed up nearly all of the major tendencies in English thought initiated by Locke, Hume, and Bentham. That is, he was a sensationalist, a skeptic in regard to final truth, and a champion of the liberal and practical point of view. But he was also an original and independent thinker and made a number of distinct contributions of his own. He founded a new system of logic, based upon experience as the original ground of all knowledge. All of the so-called self-evident truths, even the axioms of mathematics, he argued, are simply inferences derived from the observed facts that nature is uniform and that every effect has a cause. Knowledge comes neither from inborn ideas nor from mystic intuition. Though Mill agreed with the general purport of Bentham's teachings, he rejected the doctrine that the pursuit of pleasure and the avoidance of pain are the sole determinants of human conduct (the "pig philosophy," as Thomas Carlyle once called it). According to Mill the conduct of individuals is often influenced by mere habit and by the desire for unity with their fellow beings. Further, he maintained that pleasures themselves differ in quality, arguing that it is better to be "Socrates dissatisfied than a fool satisfied." In his later years Mill also modified much of Bentham's individualism. While repudiating socialism on the ground that it would involve the destruction of personal liberty, he nevertheless advocated a considerable degree of intervention by the state for the benefit of its less fortunate members. He looked forward to a time "when society will no longer be divided into the idle and

John Stuart Mill

[5] W. A. Dunning, *History of Political Theories,* Vol. III, p. 216.

the industrious; when the rule that they who do not work shall not eat, will be applied not to paupers only, but impartially to all. . . ." [6]

The nearest approach to a liberal and practical philosophy on the Continent of Europe was the Positivism of Auguste Comte (1798–1857). Positivism takes it name from Comte's doctrine that the only knowledge of any value is *positive* knowledge, or knowledge which comes from the sciences. Comte's philosophy may therefore be placed, along with Utilitarianism, in the classification of *empirical* philosophies, which includes those deriving all truth from experience or from observation of the physical world. Comte rejected metaphysics as utterly futile; no man can discover the hidden essences of things—why events happen as they do, or what is the ultimate meaning and goal of existence. All that we know is how things happen, the laws which control their occurrence, and the relations existing between them. Such knowledge may not answer all the questions that pique our curiosity, but it is the limit of which the human mind is capable. Moreover, it is useful and practical knowledge, which can be employed for the betterment of humanity. If there was any one purpose pre-eminent over others in Comte's philosophy, it was to devise means for improving relations among men. He did not agree with Bentham that the actions of individuals are motivated exclusively by self-interest. He avowed, on the contrary, that men are influenced by nobler impulses of *altruism*, or feelings for others, as well as by instincts of selfishness. The great object of all social teaching should be to promote the supremacy of altruism (a word invented by Comte) over egoism. Believing that this purpose could be achieved only through an appeal to the emotions of love and self-sacrifice, Comte developed what he called the Religion of Humanity, which was supposed to bring men together in a common devotion to justice, charity, and benevolence. Although this religion included no belief in the supernatural, it was provided with an extensive ritual and even with a Trinity and a priesthood. Ridiculed by its critics as "Catholicism minus Christianity," it nevertheless represented an attempt to build a system of belief dedicated to the aim of social progress.

4. Romanticism in Literature and the Arts

The nature of the romantic revolt

In the chapter on the Intellectual Revolution it was observed that toward the end of the eighteenth century a romantic revolt set in against the dominant classical tendencies in literature. The essence of romanticism was the glorification of the instincts and emotions as opposed to a worship of the intellect. Included in it also were such elements as a deep veneration for nature, a contempt for formalism, a sentimental love for humble folk, and often a flaming zeal to remake the world. Among the leaders of the new movement in its

[6] J. S. Mill, *Autobiography* (Uniform Library ed.), p. 231.

infancy were Rousseau, Thomas Gray, Oliver Goldsmith, Robert Burns, and Friedrich Schiller. After the beginning of the nineteenth century romanticism flourished apace, attaining the zenith of its growth about 1830. No longer was it confined to literature, but, as we shall presently see, it was a vital force in painting and to a considerable extent also in music. Though it still had to compete in some fields with classicism, especially in France during the era of Napoleon, it was by far the most vigorous literary and artistic influence in the first three decades of the nineteenth century.

Romanticism in literature had its deepest and longest roots in England. Its two great prophets at the beginning of the nineteenth century were the poets William Wordsworth (1770–1850) and Samuel Taylor Coleridge (1772–1834). Wordsworth is noted for his mystical adoration of nature, not alone in its mere surface beauties but especially as the embodiment of a universal spirit which unites all living things in a kinship of divinity. He believed that a sensuous worship of nature would bring man to a deeper awareness of the nobility of life, that it would enable him to hear "the still sad music of humanity" and thereby increase his love and compassion for his fellow creatures. The special gift of Coleridge was an ability to make the weird and fantastic credible. Though he sometimes wandered into the dense jungles of metaphysics, he succeeded in the magic stanzas of *The Ancient Mariner* in producing some of the most colorful imaginative writing in the English language. This work reveals his unusual power of combining tender, almost womanly sentiment with witching descriptions of strange, supernatural terrors, of phantoms and specters that rise out of the murky depths of the emotions to torment man with a sense of his helplessness.

Romanticism in English literature: Wordsworth and Coleridge

Perhaps the most typical of the English romantic poets were John Keats (1795–1821), Percy Bysshe Shelley (1792–1822), and George Gordon, Lord Byron (1788–1824). Keats differed from most of his contemporaries in identifying beauty with intellectual passion in somewhat the same way as the Greeks identified the beautiful with the good. The substance of his creed is expressed in the well-known lines from the *Ode on a Grecian Urn:* "Beauty is truth, truth beauty, —that is all ye know on earth, and all ye need to know." His conception was one of ideal beauty, which endures independently of the fading of the flower or the passing of the loveliness of youth. The other two short-lived poets of the English romantic circle were much more interested in political and social questions. In spite of their upper-class origins, both were rebels against stubborn conservatism and employed their talents in passionate appeals for justice and freedom. Shelley was expelled from Oxford on a charge of atheism and then for some years was a disciple of William Godwin, the philosophical anarchist. Though he eventually modified some of his youthful radicalism and allowed his thoughts to wander more and more into vaporous abstractions, he never relinquished his hatred

Keats, Shelley, and Byron

623

of injustice or his hopes for a golden dawn of happiness and freedom. Lord Byron, who inherited the title of baron at the age of ten, was even more than Shelley a poet of stormy defiance, of romantic daring, and of sardonic laughter at the hypocrisy and arrogance of the human race. Not only in the qualities of his proud personality, but also in the scandals which enveloped his career and in the directness and audacity of his poetic style he typified for the age the spirit of romantic man. His death while aiding the Greeks in their war for independence was a fitting climax to his brief, adventurous life.

Sir Walter Scott

Not all of the romantic writers in Great Britain confined their efforts to poetry. The most noted of those who achieved an enduring reputation in both poetry and prose was the learned but none too subtle Tory, Sir Walter Scott (1771–1832). Nurtured on family pride from his early life and fascinated by the rich legends of his ancestral heritage, Scott never succumbed to the rebellious tendencies which frequently characterized the romantic tradition. So far as political ideals were concerned, he accepted things as they were and even gloried in the advantages of wealth and social position. His interest as a writer was distinctly antiquarian. Both in his poetry and in his prose he sought to revive the heroic and picturesque legends of his Scottish background. His thirty-two Waverly novels deal mainly with the history of medieval Scotland, in an age as remote as the twelfth century. The chief historical importance of Sir Walter Scott consists in the fact that he introduced a new element into literary romanticism—that of worshipful reverence for the past. His novels, which were undoubtedly the most popular and influential fiction of the early nineteenth century, served to cast a glamour upon the Middle Ages, to rescue that epoch from the scorn with which it had been treated as a consequence of the classical prejudices of the Enlightenment.

Romanticism in Germany: Heinrich Heine

Except for the dramas of Schiller and Goethe, discussed in a preceding chapter,[7] romantic literature in Continental countries is scarcely to be compared with that in England. The only other important writer in Germany was Heinrich Heine (1797–1856), born of orthodox Jewish parents but later a convert to Christianity for the sake of expediency. Like Shelley and Byron, Heine was an individualist and a relentless critic of entrenched conservatism. He devoted nearly the whole of his active life to what he loved to call "humanity's war of liberation." But he was not merely a witty satirist and pungent critic of smugness and reaction. In his *Book of Songs* he displayed lyric gifts of tenderness and melancholy and a haunting charm of melody which few other poets of his day could surpass. He has been aptly called "a nightingale nesting in the wig of a Voltaire."

Romanticism in France as in England wavered between a mystic irrationalism, on the one hand, and a gallant defense of individual

[7] See above, pp. 542–543.

liberty and social reform on the other. The chief exponent of the irrational tendency was François de Chateaubriand (1768–1848), a kind of stepfather of French romanticism. Chateaubriand found in the mysteries of Christianity and in the "holy innocence" of simple folk the sublimest beauty in the universe. Along with Joseph de Maistre and others he was the prophet of a Catholic revival designed to guide men back to an age of faith and thus save them from the perils of reason. The libertarian and individualist aspect of French romanticism was best exemplified by the work of George Sand (1804–1876) and Victor Hugo (1802–1885). The former, whose real name was Aurore Dupin, wrote novels of country life with an idyllic charm which has endeared them to countless readers. She was one of the first to make peasants and humble laborers the heroes of fiction. Later she became a zealous advocate of republicanism and of the rights of women to a love untrammeled by marital convention. A novelist of much wider influence was Victor Hugo, who for many years was the living voice of French romanticism. Intensely interested in public affairs, he was an eloquent champion of political freedom and of justice for those who were caught in the web of fate. His best-known work is *Les Miserables*, an epic of the redemption of a soul purified by heroism and suffering and a powerful indictment of social cruelty.

French romantic literature

In attempting to judge the importance of literary romanticism as a factor of social and intellectual progress, we should note, first of all, its grave limitations. The disdain for reason and scientific analysis by even the most liberal of the romanticists was certainly a serious handicap to any permanent solution of humanity's problems. Furthermore, their exaggerated emotionalism occasionally made a mockery of some of their most laudable intentions. Excesses of sentimentality are not easily controlled. To allow free reign to the emotions in one direction is to run the risk of an impairment of judgment in others. Thus we find Victor Hugo hurling bitter invectives against Napoleon III, whom he called "Napoleon the Little," but singing paeans of praise to Napoleon I. It was perhaps for this reason also that the liberalism of so many of the romanticists eventually gave way to nationalism, as in the case of Schiller, or even to hopeless reaction, as in the case of Wordsworth. Yet, notwithstanding these weaknesses, literary romanticism accomplished no small amount of good in combating repression in many of its forms and in proclaiming the nobility of the common man. And probably it is safe to say that it was these elements of strength which really survived to influence the work of such writers as Dickens, George Eliot, and John Ruskin in the middle and later years of the nineteenth century.

The importance of literary romanticism

The growth of a romantic movement in art was scarcely noticeable until after the downfall of Napoleon. This was especially true in France, which has been the most fruitful source of artistic progress in modern times. With the outbreak of the French Revolution a

The revival of classicist art

strong reaction set in against the elegant rococo style of the Old Regime. But instead of launching a new tradition the artists of the Revolution simply went back to what was supposed to be a *pure* classicism, on the assumption that this would be in harmony with the rationalist ideals of the new order. The advent of Napoleon made no perceptible change. The Little Corporal liked to think of himself as a modern Caesar or Alexander the Great. Accordingly, he adopted the Roman imperial eagle as one of his emblems, invested his son with the title of King of Rome, and erected arches, columns, and temples of triumph in the city of Paris. Under such influences it is not surprising that a classicist movement in art of more than ordinary vitality should have crystallized in France in the first two decades of the nineteenth century. It reached its apex in painting under the leadership of Jacques David (1748–1825) and Jean Auguste Ingres (1780–1867). The work of both of these men was characterized by order and restraint, by a strict attention to form, and by a liberal choice of themes from Greek and Roman mythology.

The eventual triumph of romanticism in painting

Notwithstanding the vigor of the classical revival, the force of the romantic influence, overflowing from the channels of literature and philosophy, was not to be denied. After the defeat of Napoleon at Waterloo the period of the Enlightenment and the Revolution was definitely accepted as a closed chapter. There seemed to be no longer any reason for trying to preserve the ideals of a bygone age. As a consequence, classicism in painting was quickly supplanted by romanticism. The foremost champion of the new style in France was Eugene Delacroix (1798–1863), who gloried in portraying struggles for freedom and dramatic scenes from medieval history, illustrated by his *Entrance of the Crusaders into Constantinople*. In place of the sobriety and restraint of classical painting he substituted a lurid emotionalism, the effect of which was often heightened by riotous splashes of color. The work of Delacroix was paralleled to a certain distance by that of the romantic landscape painters. Their chief representative was Camille Corot (1796–1875), leader of the Barbizon school, so called from the village of Barbizon near Paris. Among others who followed the same tradition was the Englishman, J. M. W. Turner (1775–1851). The romantic landscape painters were just as much addicted to effusive displays of emotionalism as Delacroix, but it was an emotionalism of a quieter tone. They were poets of nature who suffused forests and streams and mountains with a gentle haze of tender worship.

See color pictures at pages 549, 580

From what we have learned about the influence of romanticism upon literature and painting, we should normally expect that architecture also would be deeply affected. Such, however, was not the case. While it is true that, under romantic inspirations, a movement was started about 1840 to revive the medieval Gothic, the results were only moderately significant. A large number of churches with soaring spires and pointed arches were actually built, and even some

Architecture not much affected by romanticism

government buildings also; but not infrequently what was supposed to be pure Gothic turned out to be a crude eclecticism made up of elements taken only partly from the Gothic. In general, the classical influence was still too strong to be overcome, with the result that throughout the greater part of the nineteenth century variations of the baroque continued to be the most popular building styles. Not until about 1900 was there much evidence of a desire to create a new and original architecture more truly expressive of our own civilization.

In music, as in painting and in literature, the first three decades of the nineteenth century were pre-eminently an age of romanticism. The romantic spirit in music was evidenced in a number of ways. There was an inclination to rebel against the rigidity of eighteenth-century classicism and a striving for intensity of feeling in preference to elegance of style. The romanticists regarded music not essentially as objective beauty but mainly as a medium for expressing man's inner moods. It must not merely please but must stir a sympathetic vibration in the listener. Attempts were made to capture in tone the various aspects of nature and, above all, human sentiments and passions. To some extent the composers, like the poets, responded to the exciting political drama about them, particularly by fanning the mounting flames of nationalism. All of these traits are illustrated in the development during this period of German opera, which was called romantic opera to distinguish it from its classical Italian counterpart. Discarding artificial nicety for dramatic power, it employed native Germanic material, reveled in an atmosphere of heroic struggle, and sought to inspire love for the German fatherland. C. M. von Weber, the guiding genius of this movement, was a worthy successor of Gluck and Mozart as a vitalizer of the opera. That the spirit of romanticism could be successfully infused into the forms of classicism was evidenced by the two greatest musical giants of the epoch, Beethoven and Schubert.

The beginning of romanticism in music

Ludwig van Beethoven (1770–1827) was born in the west German town of Bonn but spent most of his productive years in Vienna, then regarded as the musical capital of Europe. His life seems to bear out the adage that great art is the product of suffering. Poverty and a harsh father made his childhood unhappy, and his adult life was a succession of difficulties, largely occasioned by his impractical nature and irascible temper. He was not only coarse in manner, careless in dress, and blunt to the point of rudeness, but overly sensitive and suspicious, frequently injuring his closest friends because of resentment toward some imaginary slight. In spite of such traits he was able to retain the loyalty of his friends and to fascinate and humble the Viennese aristocracy, both male and female. The bold independence of thought and action which he carried off successfully in a staid aristocratic society contrasts decidedly with the servility of Haydn and augurs the transition to a new age. The crowning source

Ludwig van Beethoven

of Beethoven's suffering was his deafness, which began to trouble him before he was thirty and became complete in his later years. As a result, he was not only forced to give up playing in public, but many of his greatest works he never heard at all. This affliction, far from diminishing his productivity, drove him more completely into himself. Beethoven began his career as a pianist extraordinary, with unbelievable powers of extemporary playing, and the series of piano sonatas which he composed have ever since been a standard repertory for this instrument. His one opera is occasionally performed, but he was at his best in the fields of chamber music and the symphony. While he made no substantial changes in musical form, he allowed himself complete freedom in method of treatment, effecting a new

Ludwig van Beethoven (1770–1827).

and coherent synthesis of classical elements and enriching them with a passionate idealism. His works affirm the magnificent hopes of the Revolutionary era, undaunted by its reactionary aftermath. A fervent believer in freedom and in the dignity of man, he was not content to be the idol of aristocratic circles but strove to reach a wide popular audience. At the same time he subjected himself to the most rigorous self-discipline, laboring ceaselessly to perfect his own ideas, revising any number of times before considering a composition finished. His stirring *Third Symphony*, completed in 1804, was planned in honor of Napoleon, but when Beethoven learned that his hero was about to make himself emperor, he angrily tore off the title page bearing Bonaparte's name. Subsequently the work became known as the "Heroic Symphony" (*Eroica*). Although Beethoven was criticized by conservatives as an innovator addicted to grating dissonances, general recognition of the soundness of his methods came rapidly, and in contrast to Bach he was widely acclaimed during his lifetime. Changes in taste and idiom with the passing of the years have by no means diminished his stature; he is easily the musical titan of the nineteenth century.

The second of the great composers of this era, Franz Schubert (1797–1828), spent practically all of his life in his native city of Vienna. He is comparable to Mozart both in the brevity of his life, *Franz Schubert* some four years shorter than Mozart's, and in the fluency of his melodic invention; but, as in the case of Beethoven, he utilized the classic forms as a vehicle for romanticism. Whatever Schubert composed—and his output was prodigious—he wrote as if by instinct, and often with incredible speed. He struck off songs so rapidly that his publishers feared to glut the market with the works of one man and refused to give more than a pittance for much of what he produced. Although filled to the brim with the creative gift, Schubert was quite unable to make his way in worldly matters. Shunning bourgeois society, he led a precarious existence amid a small circle of poets and writers until his constitution broke under the strain of privation. Romanticism is the very essence of Schubert's works. His songs reflect every variety of mood and in their gaiety, melancholy, and rich pathos possess an appeal which is poignant and universal. He undertook almost every type of composition, including operas, masses, string quartets, and no fewer than ten symphonies, although not all of these were completed. The instrumental works suffer somewhat from a lack of restraint and from almost a surfeit of melodic abundance. Shortly before his death Schubert came to realize the handicap imposed by his deficient technical training and set himself to correct this fault by earnest study. Some critics assert that he was the most highly endowed by nature of all composers and that if his career had not been cut off so soon he might have outdistanced even Bach and Beethoven. That he was practically allowed to starve to death, with his plans unfulfilled, virtually unknown even in Vienna, is one of the tragedies of musical history.

Selected Readings—The Age of Napoleon

Bruun, Geoffrey, *Europe and the French Imperium*, New York, 1938
Ferrero, Guglielmo, *The Reconstruction of Europe*, New York, 1941
Fisher, H. A. L., *Napoleon*, New York, 1913
Gershoy, Leo, *The French Revolution and Napoleon*, New York, 1933
Geyl, Peter, *Napoleon, For and Against*, New Haven, 1949
Gottschalk, L. R., *The Era of the French Revolution, 1715–1815*, New York, 1929
Guedalla, Philip, *Wellington*, New York, 1931
Kircheisen, F. M., *Napoleon*, New York, 1932
Thompson, J. M., *Napoleon Bonaparte*, New York, 1952

Artz, F. B., *Reaction and Revolution, 1814–1832*, New York, 1934
Gulick, E. V., *Europe's Classical Balance of Power*, Ithaca, 1955
Herman, A., *Metternich*, New York, 1932
May, A. J., *The Age of Metternich, 1814–1848*, New York, 1933
Nicolson, Harold, *The Congress of Vienna*, London, 1946
Webster, C. K., *The Congress of Vienna, 1814–1815*, New York, 1919

—INTELLECTUAL AND ARTISTIC DEVELOPMENTS, 1800–1830

Bell, Clive, *Landmarks in Nineteenth Century Painting*, New York, 1927
Brandes, George, *Main Currents in Nineteenth Century Literature*, New York, 1901–1906
Davidson, W. L., *Political Thought in England from Bentham to Mill*, New York, 1916
Dunning, W. A., *History of Political Theories*, New York, 1905, Vol. III
Einstein, Alfred, *Music in the Romantic Era*, New York, 1947
Gray, Cecil, *The History of Music*, second edition, New York, 1931
Lang, Paul, *Music in Western Civilization*, New York, 1941
Machlis, Joseph, *The Enjoyment of Music*, New York, 1955
Merz, J. T., *History of European Thought in the Nineteenth Century*, New York, 1911–1914
Oxford History of Music, Vol. VI
Randall, J. H., Jr., *The Making of the Modern Mind*, New York, 1926. Chs. XVI and XVII
Wenley, R. M., *Kant and His Philosophical Revolution*, New York, 1911
Wright, C. H. C., *A History of French Literature*, New York, 1925

SOURCE MATERIALS

Bentham, Jeremy, *A Fragment on Government*
———, *Principles of Penal Law*, Part II, Book II, Ch. XII
Burke, Edmund, *Reflections on the Revolution in France*
Fichte, J. G., *Addresses to the German Nation*
Herold, J. C., ed., *The Mind of Napoleon*, New York, 1955
Johnston, R. M., ed., *The Corsican: A Diary of Napoleon in His Own Words*
Kant, Immanuel, *Plan for Perpetual Peace*
Mill, John Stuart, *Autobiography*

The Industrial Revolution of the Nineteenth and Twentieth Centuries

During the period from 1400 to about 1700 modern civilization passed through its first great economic upheaval. This was the Commercial Revolution, which annihilated the semi-static economy of the Middle Ages and replaced it with a dynamic capitalism dominated by merchants, bankers, and shipowners. But the Commercial Revolution was only the beginning of swift and decisive changes in the economic sphere. It was soon followed by an Industrial Revolution, which not only enlarged the scope of giant business in the field of commerce but extended it into the realm of production as well. In so far as it is possible to reduce it to a compact formula, the Industrial Revolution may be said to have embraced the following: (1) the mechanization of industry and agriculture; (2) the application of power to industry; (3) the development of the factory system; (4) a sensational speeding up of transportation and communication; and (5) a marked increase of capitalistic control over nearly all branches of economic activity. Although the Industrial Revolution began as early as 1760, it did not gain its full momentum until the nineteenth century. Many historians divide the movement into two great stages, with the year 1860 marking the approximate boundary line between them. The stage from 1860 to the present is often referred to as the Second Industrial Revolution.

The meaning of the Industrial Revolution

1. The Complex of Causes

The Industrial Revolution sprang from a multitude of causes, some of them much more remote than is usually suspected. It may be well

631

THE
INDUSTRIAL
REVOLUTION

*Early improve-
ments in tech-
nology*

*Other effects of
the Commer-
cial Revolution*

to consider first the early improvements in technology. The marvelous inventions of the late eighteenth century did not spring full-blown like Minerva from the brow of Zeus. On the contrary, there had been a more or less fruitful interest in mechanical innovations for some time. The period of the Commercial Revolution had witnessed the invention of the pendulum clock, the thermometer, the air pump, the spinning wheel, and the stocking frame, to say nothing of improvements in the technique of smelting ores and making brass. About 1580 a mechanical loom was devised, capable of weaving several strands of ribbon at the same time. There were also important technological advances in such industries as glass blowing, clockmaking, wood finishing, and shipbuilding. Several of the early inventions made necessary the use of factory methods. For example, the silk-throwing machine invented in Italy about 1500 had to be housed in a large building and required a considerable corps of workers. In the Temple Mills on the Thames above London, according to a description by Daniel Defoe in 1728, brass was beaten into kettles and pans by enormous hammers operated by water power. These early technological improvements are hardly to be compared in significance with those made after 1760, but they do indicate that the machine age did not burst upon the world out of a clear sky.

Among other causes of paramount importance were certain more direct consequences of the Commercial Revolution. That movement brought into existence a class of capitalists, who were constantly seeking new opportunities to invest their surplus wealth. At first this wealth could be readily absorbed by trade or by mining, banking, and shipbuilding ventures; but as time went on the opportunities in such fields became limited. As a consequence more and more capital was made available for the development of manufacturing. But a rapid development of manufacturing would scarcely have occurred had there not been a growing demand for industrial products. This demand grew largely from the establishment of colonial empires and from the marked increase in the population of Europe. It will be recalled that one of the primary objects in the acquisition of colonies was to expand the market for manufactured goods from the mother country. As one evidence that this object was reasonably well attained, we have the fact that in the single year 1658 no fewer than 24,000 pairs of shoes were shipped to Virginia from England. At the same time the potential markets at home were being rapidly enlarged by the rapid increase of population in western European countries. In England the number of inhabitants rose from 4,000,000 in 1600 to 6,000,000 in 1700 and to 9,000,000 by the end of the eighteenth century. The population of France grew from 17,000,000 in 1700 to 26,000,000 about a hundred years later. How much of this increase was due to the advancement of medicine in the eighteenth century, and how much of it was the product of a more ample food supply resulting from the expansion of trade, is a debatable question; but certainly the influence of the second of these factors cannot be ignored. Finally, the Commercial Revolution gave a stimulus to the growth of manufactures through its basic gospel of mercantilism. The mercantilist policy was designed, as much as for any other purpose, to increase the quantity of manufactured goods available for export and thereby to ensure a favorable balance of trade.

Despite the importance of the causes already mentioned, the Industrial Revolution would undoubtedly have been delayed had it not been for a need for fundamental mechanical improvements in certain fields of production. By 1700 the demand for charcoal for smelting iron had so depleted the resources of timber that several of the nations of western Europe were threatened with deforestation. A partial solution was found about 1709 when Abraham Darby discovered that coke could be used for smelting. But in order to obtain sufficient coke it was necessary that coal be mined in much larger quantities than ever before. Since the chief obstacle to the extraction of coal was the accumulation of water in the mines, the need for the new fuel led to a search for some convenient source of power to drive the pumps. Various experiments in connection with this search finally resulted in the invention of the steam engine. An even more crucial need for mechanization existed in the textile industry. With the increasing popularity of cotton clothing in the seventeenth and eighteenth centuries, it was simply impossible to provide enough yarn with the primitive spinning wheels still in use. Even when every available woman and child was pressed into service, the demand could not be met. In Germany the soldiers in the barracks were actually put to work spinning cotton thread. As the need grew more and more urgent, rewards were offered by scientific societies and business organizations for improved methods of producing yarn. In 1760, for example, the English Society of Arts offered a prize for the invention of a machine which would enable one person to spin six threads at once. The result of all this attention to mechanical needs was the development a few years later of the spinning jenny and the water frame, the forerunners of a series of important inventions in the textile industry. As the practicability of these machines was soon demonstrated, mechanization was bound to be extended to other manufactures.

The need for fundamental mechanical improvements in certain industries

2. Why the Industrial Revolution Began in Britain

At first thought it may seem rather strange that a small island kingdom should not only have become the industrial leader of the world but should have held that leadership for more than a century. A modern philosopher makes the claim that Britain until well into the eighteenth century was "the poorest country in Western Europe." [1] Certainly she had no remarkable variety of products within her

The relative poverty of Britain until well into the 18th century

[1] José Ortega y Gasset, *The Revolt of the Masses*, p. 111 n.

633

borders. She was not nearly so capable of approaching self-sufficiency as France or Germany. Her agricultural resources were no longer adequate to provide for her needs, while the exhaustion of her forests had been noted since the time of the Stuarts. Her coal and iron, generally considered her richest assets, did not assume great industrial importance until the nineteenth century. But side by side with these adverse conditions there were other factors more than sufficient to tip the balance in Britain's favor.

Favorable factors operating in Britain

Possibly we should place at the head of the list of favorable conditions the fact that Britain had profited most from the Commercial Revolution. Though it is true that about 1750 France had a foreign trade 25 per cent larger than that of Britain, it must be remembered that the French population was at least three times as numerous as the British. Moreover, France had reached her limit of imperial aggrandizement, while much of the profit of her world trade was being diverted through loans and taxes to the upkeep of a costly army and a frivolous and extravagant court. Britain, on the other hand, was just on the brink of a golden age of power and prosperity. She had already acquired the most valuable colonies in the Western Hemisphere, and she was soon to clinch her imperial and commercial supremacy by defeating the French in the Seven Years' War. In addition, a much larger proportion of Britain's gains from overseas trade was available for productive investment. Her government was comparatively free from corruption and wasteful expenditure. Her military establishment cost less than that of the French, and her revenues were much more efficiently collected. As a result, her merchants and shipowners were left with a larger share of surplus earnings, which they were eager to invest in any conceivable business venture that might be the source of additional profit.

Britain the leading capitalist nation

In view of these facts it is not strange that Britain should have emerged as the leading capitalist nation in the early eighteenth century. Nowhere was the joint-stock company more highly developed. Trading in securities was organized as a legitimate business when the London Stock Exchange was chartered in 1698. By 1700 London was able to compete with Amsterdam as the financial capital of the world. Britain, moreover, had perhaps the best banking system in Europe. At its apex was the Bank of England, founded in 1694. Though established for the purpose of raising funds for the government, it was organized as a private corporation. Its stock was privately owned, and its management was not subject to any official control by the state. Nevertheless, it always operated in close association with the government, and even in its early days served as an important stabilizing factor in public finance. With the financial stability of the government thus assured, leaders of business enterprise could carry on their activities unhindered by fear of national bankruptcy or ruinous inflation. It may be pertinent to add

634

in this connection that little semblance of order prevailed in French finances until the establishment of the Bank of France during the era of Napoleon.

There is evidence that political and social factors were not unimportant in accounting for the beginning of the Industrial Revolution in Britain. While the British government of the eighteenth century was far from democratic, it was at least more liberal than most of the governments on the Continent. The Glorious Revolution of 1688–1689 had done much to establish the conception of limited sovereignty. The doctrine was now widely accepted that the power of the state should extend no farther than the protection of man's natural right to liberty and to the enjoyment of property. Under the influence of this doctrine Parliament repealed old laws providing for special monopolies and interfering with free competition. Mercantilist principles continued to be applied to trade with the colonies, but in the sphere of domestic business many of the restrictions were gradually abolished. Furthermore, Britain was already coming to be recognized as a haven for refugees from other countries. More than 40,000 Huguenots settled in her villages and cities after being driven from France in 1685 by the revocation of the Edict of Nantes. Thrifty, energetic, and ambitious, these people instilled new vigor into the British nation. Thomas Huxley declared many years later that a drop of Huguenot blood in the veins was worth thousands of pounds sterling. That the influence of these exiles upon industrial progress was not insignificant is revealed by the fact that French names continued to be employed for some time in British cutlery and glass manufactures. Social conditions also were distinctly favorable to the industrial development of Britain. Her nobility had ceased to be a hereditary caste exclusively and was rapidly becoming an aristocracy of wealth. Almost anyone who had made a fortune could rise to the highest levels of social distinction. William Pitt the younger declared that every man with an income of £10,000 a year should have a right to a peerage, no matter how humble his origin. Conditions such as these placed a premium upon business success.

Favorable political and social conditions

A few other causes must be added to complete the picture. First may be mentioned the fact that the damp climate of the British Isles was singularly favorable for the manufacturing of cotton cloth, since the thread would not become brittle and break easily when woven by machines. And it is sufficient to call to mind that it was the mechanization of the textile industry which ushered in the age of machines. Second, the guild system of production, with its elaborate restrictions, had never become as firmly implanted in the soil of Britain as in that of Continental countries. Even the regulations that were established had been thrown off, especially in the northern counties, by the end of the seventeenth century. This, incidentally, was one of the chief reasons why the Industrial Revolu-

Other favorable factors in Britain

635

tion started in northern England rather than in the region nearest the Continent. Lastly, since wealth was more evenly distributed in Britain than in most other nations at that time, her manufacturers could devote their attention to the production of large quantities of cheap and ordinary wares instead of to the making of limited supplies of luxury goods. This factor had considerable influence in promoting the adoption of factory methods in the hope of achieving a larger output. In France, by contrast, the demand was for articles *de luxe* to gratify the tastes of a small class of elegant wastrels. Since quality of workmanship was a primary consideration in this type of goods, there was little incentive to invent machines.

3. Men and Machines in the Early Days

The application of machinery to cotton manufactures

The initial stage of the Industrial Revolution, from about 1760 to 1860, witnessed a phenomenal development of the application of machinery to industry, which laid the foundations for our modern mechanical civilization. As we have seen, the first of the branches of industry to be mechanized was the manufacture of cotton cloth. This was not one of the staple pursuits of Englishmen but was a young enterprise, in which every entrepreneur was free to employ almost any methods he pleased. Furthermore, it was a business in which profits depended upon quantity production. If the industry were to make any progress at all, some means had to be devised of turning out a greater volume of yarn than could ever be accomplished with the primitive implements still in use. The first of the contrivances developed in response to this need was the spinning jenny, invented by James Hargreaves in 1767. The spinning "jenny," so called from the name of the inventor's wife, was really a compound spinning wheel, capable of producing sixteen threads at once. Unfortunately the threads it spun were not strong enough to be used for the longitudinal fibers, or warp, of cotton cloth. It was not until the invention of the water frame by Richard Arkwright about two years later that quantity production of both kinds of cotton yarn became possible. Finally, in 1779, another Englishman, Samuel Crompton, combined features of both the spinning jenny and the water frame in a hybrid contraption which he appropriately called the mule. This machine was gradually improved, until about twenty years later it was capable of spinning simultaneously 400 strands of the finest quality of yarn.

The power loom and the cotton gin

The problems of the cotton industry were still not entirely solved. The invention of spinning machines had more than made up for the deficiency of yarn, but now there was a scarcity of weavers. Those who followed this occupation were able to command such high wages that they were alleged to be strutting about with five-pound notes stuck in their hat bands and to be eating roast goose for their Sunday dinners. It soon became obvious that the only remedy for this shortage of weavers would be the invention of some kind of automatic machine to take the place of the hand loom. Many declared such a contrivance impossible, but a Kentish clergyman, the Reverend Edmund Cartwright, was not to be discouraged so easily. He reasoned that if automatic machinery could be applied to spinning, it could be just as logically extended to weaving. Knowing little about mechanics himself, he hired a carpenter and a smith to put his ideas into effect. The result was the power loom, which Cartwright patented in 1785. A good many years elapsed, however, before it was sufficiently improved to be more than a modest success. Not until about 1820 did it largely displace more primitive methods of weaving. Meanwhile, the invention of a machine for separating the seeds from the cotton fiber made possible a much more abundant supply of raw cotton at a lower price. This was the cotton gin, invented by a Yankee schoolteacher, Eli Whitney, in 1792.

Several of the new inventions in the textile industry contributed to the growth of the factory system. The water frame, the spinning mule, and the automatic loom were large and heavy machines which could not possibly be set up in the cottages of individual workers. All were eventually designed to be driven by power, and, besides, they cost so much that no one but a wealthy capitalist could afford to buy them. It was therefore inevitable that they should be installed in large buildings, and that the workers employed to operate them should be brought under the supervision of the owner or of a manager acting for him. Such were the essentials of the factory system in its original form. Appropriately enough, the real founder of this system was Richard Arkwright, inventor of the water frame. By indomitable perseverance and shrewd management, Arkwright rose from the status of an obscure barber and wigmaker to that of a captain of industry. Commonly working from five in the morning until nine at night, he struggled against obstacles for years. He encountered strenuous opposition from the powerful woolen interests. His shops were gutted by mobs of irate workers who feared that machines would deprive them of their jobs. He was accused, perhaps with some truth, of stealing his ideas for the water frame from others. Altogether he is said to have spent some $60,000 before his plans brought him any profit. He established his first factory, operated by water power, in 1771.

Origin of the factory system

It is difficult to believe that the factory system would ever have assumed much importance had it not been for the perfection of the steam engine. Water wheels were slow, and streams of sufficient force to turn them were not always available. Other sources of power were also tried, but with even less satisfactory results. The original power loom invented by Cartwright was operated by a cow, while some of his successors used horses and even a Newfoundland dog. That steam could be employed as a means of power

Newcomen's steam engine

had been known for centuries. Crude steam engines had been devised by Hero of Alexandria in the first century B.C., by Leonardo da Vinci during the Renaissance, and by various individuals in the early modern period. None of these, however, had been put to any definite use except to turn the spit in royal kitchens and to perform miracles in ancient temples. The first man to apply the power of steam to industrial purposes was Thomas Newcomen, who in 1712 devised a crude but effective engine for pumping water from the British coal mines. By the middle of the century nearly a hundred of his engines were in use. Some were of enormous size and could do the work of more than fifty horses; one had a cylinder six feet in diameter. Even the smallest could generate more power than most water wheels.

Newcomen's engine greatly improved by James Watt

Though of great value to the coal mining industry, Newcomen's engine suffered from defects which prevented its being widely used for general industrial purposes. For one thing, it wasted both fuel and power. It was constructed in such a way that after each stroke of the piston, the steam had to be condensed by spraying cold water into the cylinder. This meant that the cylinder had to be heated again before the next stroke, and this alternate heating and cooling greatly retarded the speed of the engine. In the second place, Newcomen's "Miner's Friend" was adaptable only to the straight-line motion necessary for pumping; the principle of converting the straight-line action of the piston into a rotary motion had not been discovered. Both of these defects were eventually remedied by James Watt, a maker of scientific instruments at the University of Glasgow. In 1763 Watt was asked to repair a model of the Newcomen engine. While engaged in this task he conceived the idea that the machine would be greatly improved if a separate chamber were added to condense the steam, so as to eliminate the necessity of cooling the cylinder. He patented his first engine incorporating this device in 1769. Later he invented a new arrangement of valves which permitted the injection of steam into both ends of the cylinder, thereby making the piston *work* on the backward as well as on the forward stroke. In 1782 he devised a means of converting the action of the piston into a circular motion and thus made the engine available for driving machinery in factories. Unfortunately Watt's genius as an inventor was not matched by his business ability. He admitted that he would "rather face a loaded cannon than settle a disputed account or make a bargain." As a consequence he fell into debt in attempting to place his machines on the market. He was rescued by Matthew Boulton, a wealthy hardware manufacturer of Birmingham. The two men formed a partnership, with Boulton providing the capital. By 1800 the firm had sold 289 engines for use in factories and mines.

Few single inventions have had greater influence upon the history of modern times than the steam engine. Contrary to popular opinion, it was not the initial cause of the Industrial Revolution; instead, it was partly an effect. Watt's engine, at least, would never have become a reality if there had not been a demand for an effective source of power to operate the heavy machines already invented in the textile industry. On the other hand, the perfection of the steam engine was certainly a cause of the more rapid growth of industrialization. It raised the production of coal and iron to a new importance. It made possible, as we shall presently see, a revolution in transportation. It provided almost unlimited opportunities for accelerating the manufacture of goods, thereby making the industrialized nations the richest and most powerful in the world. Before the development of the steam engine, the resources of power were largely at the mercy of the weather. In time of drought, low water in the streams would probably force the mills to curtail operations

The importance of the steam engine

The Steam Engine Invented by James Watt (1736–1819).

or even to shut down entirely. Ships on ocean voyages might be delayed for weeks by lack of wind. Now, however, there was a constant supply of energy, which could be tapped and used when needed. It is therefore not too much to say that the invention of Watt's engine was the real beginning of the age of power.

One of the industries which owed its rapid development to the improvement of the steam engine was the manufacture of iron and iron products. While many of the new machines, such as the spinning jenny and the water frame, could be constructed of wood, steam engines required a more substantial material. Furthermore, the cylinders of these engines needed to be bored as accurately as possible in order to prevent a loss of power. This made necessary a considerable advance in the production of machine tools and in scientific methods of iron manufacture. The pioneer in this work was John Wilkinson, a manufacturer of cannon. In 1774 Wilkinson patented a method of boring cylinders which reduced the percentage of error to a very small amount for that day. Later he turned to the building of iron barges and to the making of plates for iron

Early development of the iron industry

639

bridges. He never wrote a letter without mentioning iron on every page and directed in his will that he should be buried in an iron coffin. Even more important than the achievements of Wilkinson were the accomplishments of another Englishman, Henry Cort, a naval contractor. In 1784 Cort devised the method of puddling, or stirring the molten iron to eliminate a larger percentage of its carbon content. This process made possible the production in quantity of the tougher grade of metal known as wrought iron. Two years later Cort invented the rolling mill for the manufacture of sheet iron. These two achievements revolutionized the industry. Within less than twenty years the production of iron in England quadrupled, and the price dropped to a fraction of what it had been.

Early develop-
ments in trans-
portation: (1)
roads and canals

The fundamental changes in modes of production which have just been described were soon followed by momentous developments in transportation. The first signs of a definite improvement in methods of travel began to appear about 1780. It was about that time that the construction of turnpikes and canals in England was started in earnest. By 1830 nearly all of the highways had been drained and covered with a surface of broken stone, while the principal streams had been linked together by a network of 2500 miles of canals. The improvement of roads made possible a faster stagecoach service. In 1784 the Postmaster General inaugurated a mail service with coaches that ran continuously day and night, covering a distance of 120 miles in twenty-four hours. By the end of the century special stages, known as "flying machines," operated between all of the principal cities, sometimes achieving the sensational speed of nine or ten miles per hour.

(2) the
first railroads

But the really significant progress in transportation did not come until after the steam engine had been generally accepted as a dependable source of power. Attempts were first made to adapt the use of steam to stagecoaches, and several of these ancestors of the modern automobile were actually put on the highways. The most successful was one built about 1800 by Richard Trevithick, which managed to run ninety miles over the road from London to Plymouth. Gradually the opinion grew that it would be more profitable to use the steam engine to draw a train of cars over iron rails. A number of such railroads were already in existence for the purpose of transporting coal, but the cars were drawn by horses. The man primarily responsible for the first steam railway was George Stephenson, a self-made engineer who had never even learned to read until he was seventeen years of age. While employed as an engine-wright at a colliery he devoted his leisure hours to experiments with locomotives. In 1822 he convinced a group of men who were projecting a coal railroad from Stockton to Darlington of the merits of steam traction, and was appointed engineer for the line with full liberty to carry out his plans. The result was the opening three years later of the first railway operated entirely by steam. The locomotives he built for this line attained a speed of fifteen miles an hour, the fastest rate at which human beings had yet traveled. In 1830 he designed his famous *Rocket*, which thundered over the tracks of the Manchester and Liverpool Railroad at nearly twice the speed of the earlier models. Before Stephenson died in 1848, nearly 6000 miles of railroad had been built in England and a similar amount in the United States.

Meanwhile the steam engine was being gradually applied to water transportation. Here it was Americans rather than Englishmen who took the lead. Precisely who should receive credit for inventing the steamboat is a matter of dispute. There is evidence that a number of men had something to do with it. So far as the records go, the earliest operation of a boat propelled exclusively by steam was the achievement of a Virginia mechanic by the name of James Rumsey. In 1785 in the presence of George Washington he drove his craft against the current of the Potomac at the rate of four miles an hour. A short time later another American, John Fitch, constructed a boat which actually carried passengers on the Delaware for several months in 1790. Fitch's steamboat is particularly significant because it embodied a crude screw propeller instead of the paddle wheel universally employed by the other inventors. But Fitch was never able to make his craft a financial success. After vainly attempting to persuade governments to adopt his invention, he committed suicide in 1798. Still a third American, Robert Fulton, is given the credit for having made the steamboat commercially successful. That Fulton was any more ingenious than Rumsey or Fitch is open to doubt, but he was a good enough salesman and promoter to secure the backing of a wealthy capitalist, and he knew how to keep himself in the public eye. In 1807 he was acclaimed as a national hero when his *Clermont*, equipped with a Boulton and Watt engine and a paddle wheel, traveled the entire distance from New York to Albany under its own power. This was the beginning of an era of steam navigation. Soon paddle-wheel craft similar to Fulton's were chugging over rivers and lakes not only in America but in Europe. In April, 1838, the first steamships, the *Sirius* and the *Great Western*, crossed the Atlantic. Two years later Samuel Cunard founded the famous Cunard Line, providing a regular transoceanic service with vessels propelled entirely by steam.

(3) the beginning of steam navigation

The one significant improvement in communications during the first stage of the Industrial Revolution was the invention of the telegraph. As early as 1820 the French physicist Ampère discovered that electromagnetism could be used for sending messages by wire between distant points. About all that remained was to devise effective instruments for transmitting and receiving the messages. Experiments for this purpose were carried on by a number of individuals. Three of them succeeded almost simultaneously. During the year 1837 systems of electric telegraphy were invented by the

The invention of the telegraph

The First Train to Enter the City of Washington. The locomotive was built in 1832 and accumulated a service of 60 years.

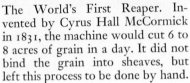

The World's First Reaper. Invented by Cyrus Hall McCormick in 1831, the machine would cut 6 to 8 acres of grain in a day. It did not bind the grain into sheaves, but left this process to be done by hand.

German Karl Steinheil, by the Englishman Charles Wheatstone, and by the American Samuel Morse. It was not until 1844, however, that the first telegraph line, efficient enough for commercial purposes, was established. This was the line between Baltimore and Washington, which Morse succeeded in having built on the strength of improvements in his own invention. Once started, telegraph systems multiplied all over the world. Soon all important cities were linked, and by 1851 a cable had been laid under the English Channel. The crowning achievement of all was the laying of the first Atlantic cable in 1866 under the direction of the American capitalist, Cyrus Field.

In our study of the Commercial Revolution we noted that that movement was accompanied, especially in England, by momentous *Improvements* changes in agriculture, such as the breakdown of manorial farming, *in agriculture* the enclosure of common lands, and the compacting of individual holdings. The Industrial Revolution also had its agricultural aspects. They were especially noticeable in the first sixty years of the nineteenth century. Among them were the production of better breeds of livestock; the introduction of new crops, such as the sugar beet, which was now being extensively cultivated in Germany and France; and the development of agricultural chemistry by Justus von Liebig (1803–1873), which made possible the production of artificial fertilizers. Agriculture in this period also came under the influence of mechanization. Better plows and harrows were designed, and the threshing machine was quite generally adopted. In 1834 the American farmer, Cyrus McCormick, patented his mechanical reaper and soon afterward began its manufacture in Chicago. By 1860 these machines were being sold at the rate of 20,000 a year. As a result of these various improvements, agriculture all over the world rejoiced in an unprecedented prosperity, which lasted until **642** the great depression of 1873.

4. The Second Industrial Revolution

About 1860 the Industrial Revolution entered a new phase so different from what had gone before that some historians are disposed to call it the Second Industrial Revolution. The events which ushered it in were mainly three in number: the development of the Bessemer process of making steel in 1856; the perfection of the dynamo about 1873; and the invention of the internal-combustion engine in 1876. In general, the features which serve to distinguish the Second Industrial Revolution from the first may be stated as follows: (1) the substitution of steel in place of iron as the basic industrial material; (2) the replacement of coal by gas and oil as principal sources of power and the use of electricity as a major form of industrial energy; (3) the development of automatic machinery and a high degree of specialization of labor; (4) the use of alloys and light metals and the products of industrial chemistry; (5) radical changes in transportation and communication; (6) the growth of new forms of capitalist organization; and (7) the spread of industrialization to central and eastern Europe and even to the Far East. A word or two must be said about each of these major developments.

The nature of the Second Industrial Revolution

Methods of making steel have been known for centuries. As early as the year 1000 the Saracens were producing excellent steel swords at Damascus. From the late Middle Ages, Europeans had also known how to manufacture the desirable material. But the methods were slow and difficult and the product expensive. In 1856 Sir Henry Bessemer discovered that the introduction of a jet of air into the molten iron in a blast furnace would eliminate all but the tiniest percentage of carbon and thereby convert the iron into steel. The result was to reduce the price of steel to less than a seventh of its former cost. When it was revealed that the new process could not be applied to any but the higher grades of ores, two English chemists, Sidney Thomas and P. C. Gilchrist, set to work to im-

The discovery of new processes of making steel

The Bessemer Process of Manufacturing Steel. This process, invented in 1856, involved the introduction of a jet of air into the molten iron to reduce its carbon content and thereby toughen it for the production of steel.

prove it. In 1878 they discovered a method whereby even low-grade iron with a heavy content of phosphorus could also be converted into steel. The consequences of this advance were astounding. Not only was the phosphoric iron of England brought into production, but enormous deposits in Lorraine, in Belgium, and in the United States now became immensely valuable. Between 1880 and 1914 the output of steel in Great Britain rose from 2,000,000 tons to 7,000,000, in Germany from 1,000,000 to 15,000,000, and in the United States from 1,600,000 to 28,000,000. Steel almost entirely supplanted iron for railroad rails, for the framework of large buildings, for bridges, and for other purposes where a cheap metal with a high degree of tensile strength was desired.

The displacement of coal as the basic source of power resulted, first of all, from the invention of the dynamo, a machine for converting mechanical energy into electrical energy. Although the principle of the dynamo was formulated by Michael Faraday in 1831, no machine of this kind capable of practical use was available until 1873. From that time on the harnessing of electrical energy to the mechanism of industry went rapidly ahead. The steam engine came to be relegated gradually to the background, to be used primarily for driving dynamos. The electric energy thus generated is converted by electric motors into mechanical energy. In some areas, especially where coal is scarce, the steam engine for driving dynamos has been superseded by water power. By 1929 electricity provided two-thirds of the power required by industry in Great Britain and an even larger proportion in Germany.[2] The German A.E.G. (Allgemeine Elektrizitäts Gesellschaft), manufacturing motors, generators, and other electrical equipment, had evolved into the largest industrial unit in Europe.

The invention of the dynamo

A second revolutionary development making available new sources of power was the utilization of petroleum products to add to the supply of energy. The existence of petroleum had been known for some time before its value was discovered. Until the middle of the nineteenth century it was regarded as a curiosity. Labeled as Indian Oil or Seneca Oil, it was sold in the United States for its alleged medicinal properties. Even after its value for lubricating purposes was revealed, its use was limited by scarcity. In 1859 Edwin L. Drake solved the problem of an adequate supply by drilling the first oil well near Titusville, Pennsylvania. New uses for the product were gradually found, although for many years most of it went into the manufacture of kerosene for lamps. In 1876, however, Nikolaus Otto invented the first successful internal-combustion engine. This was the starting point of a series of developments which heralded the dawn of a motorized age. A few years afterward Gottlieb Daimler adapted the internal-combustion engine to the use of gasoline instead of natural gas, and

The internal-combustion engine

[2] Herbert Heaton, *Economic History of Europe*, p. 518.

Karl Benz equipped it with an electric spark to ignite the fuel. The perfection of the carburetor about 1890 by another German, Wilhelm Maybach, also contributed much to the potentialities of gasoline power. Finally, in 1897, Rudolf Diesel invented an internal-combustion engine using as fuel neither gas nor gasoline but crude oil. Since the 1930's Diesel engines have come into extensive use in ocean liners, locomotives, trucks, and buses. In Europe some motor cars are Diesel-powered.

Among the most typical features of the Second Industrial Revolution have been the introduction of automatic machinery, an enormous increase in mass production, and a division of the tasks of labor into minute segments of the manufacturing process. All three of these things have gone hand in hand, since the years just preceding World War I. A characteristic example of the development of

An Early Assembly Line of the Ford Motor Co., 1913. Bodies were slid down the ramp and attached to the chassis as they passed through the line below. Production amounted to 1000 cars a day.

Men and Machines—a Modern Factory. Interior of the tool and die shop of the River Rouge plant, Ford Motor Co.

*The growth
of mass produc-
tion and the
adoption of
automatic and
highly special-
ized processes
in industry*

automatic machinery has been the invention of the photoelectric cell, or the "electric eye," which can be used to throw switches, to open doors, to sort eggs, to inspect tin cans, to count sheets of paper and measure their thickness, and even to eliminate counterfeit bills. Machines have been invented to direct and operate other machines and to complete whole series of manufacturing processes which formerly required much human labor. Not only has automatic machinery resulted in a marked increase in mass production, but the volume of goods turned out by industry has also been greatly expanded by the adoption of the endless conveyor belt. The idea for this was copied originally by Henry Ford about 1908 from the Chicago packers, who used an overhead trolley to move carcasses of beef along a line of butchers. Ford gradually improved the device to a point where he could assemble a complete chassis of his famous Model T in an hour and thirty-three minutes. In recent years the principle of the conveyor belt and the assembly line, which requires each worker to toil all day at a simple, monotonous task, has been adopted in every automobile factory in the United States and in many other industries as well. It has provided the world with a staggering abundance of goods and has reduced the prices of some articles which were formerly luxuries for the rich; but no one is yet able to foresee how serious may be its effects upon the minds and morale of the workers.

Recent changes in methods of production have come not only from the invention of intricate machines but also from a growing domination of industry by science. As a matter of fact, the significant discoveries of the Second Industrial Revolution have emanated more often from the laboratory of the physicist or chemist than from the brain of the individual inventor. The supremacy of science in the realm of industry was originally foreshadowed in 1856 when William Henry Perkin produced the first aniline or coal-tar dyes. This was the beginning of a marvelous development of synthetic chemistry. From this same coal tar it was discovered that literally hundreds of dyes could be derived, together with an infinite variety of other products, such as aspirin, oil of wintergreen, essence of orange blossoms, saccharine, carbolic acid, and vanilla. As the years passed, many additional substances were added to the list of synthetic products. Methods were devised for manufacturing nitric acid out of the nitrogen in the air, for making glucose from corn, and for producing textile fibers from wood and from minerals. In more recent years remarkable progress has been made in the development of plastics, manufactured from various substances, such as casein, phenol, and coal and petroleum derivatives. The steering wheels on most automobiles are made from such plastics. Good qualities of artificial rubber have also been produced, by various processes based upon the use of either coal or petroleum. Chemists have likewise come to the aid of many of the older industries, discovering methods of utilizing hitherto worthless by-products or of increasing the yield from available supplies of raw materials. For example, cotton seeds have been turned into celluloid, cosmetics, smokeless powder, and salad oil, while the cracking process of refining gasoline has more than doubled the yield from a given quantity of petroleum.

Closely related to the progress in industrial chemistry have been the developments in connection with the light metals and ferro-alloys. The oldest of the light metals, aluminum, though discovered in 1828, did not come into general use until about 1900. It is obtained from a clay known as bauxite which is found in abundance in Dutch and British Guiana, the West Indies, and the United States. Although more expensive to produce than steel, it is now coming to be used extensively for building construction, as well as for automobile engines, airplanes, cooking utensils, and packaging. In a few years it will probably supplant tin-plated steel for the manufacture of "tin" cans. A much rarer metal, magnesium, was applied during World War II to airplane construction and has been adapted since to other limited uses. Originally produced by electrolysis of magnesium chloride, it is now manufactured in larger quantities from sea water. Of at least equal importance with the light metals are the so-called ferro-alloys. These include manganese, chromium, tungsten, vanadium, molybdenum, and a few others. Found mostly in such countries as China, Turkey, Russia, India, and Rhodesia, they are indispensable for modern industry. They alone can give the hardness and toughness to steel which are necessary for the production of machine tools. Together with other widely scattered critical materials, they furnish excellent illustrations of the economic interdependence of the various parts of the contemporary world.

Developments in the light metals and ferro-alloys

The second stage of the Industrial Revolution witnessed perhaps an even greater revolution in transportation and communication than the first. The years after 1860 were marked by feverish activity in railroad building. Before that date there were hardly more than 30,000 miles of railroad in the entire world. By 1890 there were 20,000 miles in Great Britain alone, 26,000 in Germany, and 167,000 in the United States. The service itself was greatly improved by the invention of the air brake in 1868 and by the introduction of the sleeping car, the dining car, and the automatic block-signal system soon afterward. In recent years much attention has been given to increasing the speed of trains. Modern streamlined, Diesel-powered trains race over distances of hundreds of miles at average speeds of eighty or more miles per hour. After 1918, however, the railroads suffered severely under competition from newer forms of transportation. By way of illustration, the number of passengers carried by American railroads dropped from 1,200,000,000 in 1920 to 434,-000,000 in 1933. During the same period the volume of freight declined from 2,400,000,000 tons to 1,300,000,000. By 1954 the number

The revolution in transportation: the extension and improvement of the railroads

The automobile

*Developments
in aviation*

of passengers carried had risen to only 440,000,000, in spite of an estimated increase in population of 30 per cent. The volume of freight transported in 1954 was almost exactly the same as in 1920.

The most important competitor of the railroads is the automobile, together with its offshoots, the bus and the motor truck. It is impossible to assign credit for invention of the automobile to any one person, though various individuals have claimed it. Both Daimler and Benz made gasoline vehicles in Germany as early as the 1880's, but their original inventions were little more than motorized tricycles. The first man to apply the principle of the internal-combustion engine to a carriage seems to have been the Frenchman Levassor. In 1887 he designed a vehicle with the engine in front and with the power transmitted to the rear wheels by means of a clutch, a shaft, and reduction and differential gears. So far as the evidence shows, this was the first true automobile in history. Obviously, many other inventions were necessary in order to ensure the success of the motorcar as a comfortable and efficient means of travel. Not the least of these were the pneumatic tire perfected by J. B. Dunlop in 1888 and the electric self-starter invented by Charles Kettering about 1910. But the automobile might have remained indefinitely a toy for the rich had it not been for the determination of Henry Ford to produce a car which could be bought by persons of moderate incomes. In 1908 he began the manufacture of his Model T on the basis of the theory that he could make more money by selling a great quantity of cheap cars on a small margin of profit than by turning out an expensive product for the wealthy few. Other companies followed his example, with the result that as early as 1928 the automobile industry had grown into the largest single branch of manufacturing in the United States.

Since the 1920's aviation has also developed into a major form of transportation and the production of planes into an important industry. No more than the perfection of the automobile can the invention of the airplane be credited to any one person. The idea that some day man might be able to fly is an old one indeed. Not only was it suggested by Roger Bacon in the thirteenth century, but it was actually embodied in some definite plans for flying machines conceived by the fertile mind of Leonardo da Vinci. Nevertheless, the birth of aviation as a mechanical possibility really dates from the 1890's. It was about that time that Otto Lilienthal, Samuel P. Langley, and others began their experiments with heavier-than-air machines. The work of Langley was carried forward by the Wright brothers, who, in 1903, made the first successful flight in a motor-driven plane. From that point on advancement was rapid. In 1908 the Wright brothers flew nearly a hundred miles. The following year Louis Bleriot crossed the English Channel in the monoplane he had recently invented. During World War I each of the belligerent nations made strenuous efforts to utilize the possibilities of the airplane as a weapon of slaughter. As a consequence, improvements in design and in efficiency came thick and fast. However, it should be remembered that, even without the war, progress would still have been rapid; for, once an invention has been successfully launched, improvements follow in a kind of geometric ratio. At any rate, by 1919 airplane travel was so clearly taken for granted that a regular service was established between London and Paris.

A Commercial Jet Plane. Such planes, flying at altitudes of 40,000 feet, have cruising speeds of 500–600 miles per hour.

A Modern Ocean Liner. The S.S. *United States*, the fastest liner afloat, passing the skyscrapers of lower Manhattan outward bound for Europe.

Now passenger, mail, and express lines connect nearly every important city in the world. During the year 1956 the various companies operating scheduled services in the United States transported a total of more than 40,000,000 passengers.

The early Industrial Revolution, or the age of coal and iron, resulted in but one important advance in communication. This, as we have seen, was the invention of the telegraph, which was already in extensive use by 1860. The age of electricity and the internal-combustion engine has been accompanied by the perfection of a number of devices which have gone far toward annihilating both

Wireless telegraphy, radio, and television

649

time and distance in the dissemination of news and in communicating with far-off places. First came the telephone, for which the credit is commonly given to Alexander Graham Bell; though only a few hours after Bell had applied for a patent in Washington on February 15, 1876, Elisha Gray appeared with practically the same idea.[3] Next came the invention of the wireless telegraph by Guglielmo Marconi, on the basis of discoveries by Heinrich Hertz and others relative to the transmission of electromagnetic waves through the ether. In 1899 Marconi dispatched a wireless message across the English Channel and two years later across the Atlantic. The invention of wireless telegraphy paved the way for the development of radio, the wireless telephone, and television. The first was made possible by the work of Lee DeForest, inventor of the vacuum tube, and the second by the discoveries of Poulsen and Fessenden. Commercial broadcasting began in 1920, and telephone service between England and the United States was inaugurated in 1927. The miracle of television is credited to a Scotsman, J. L. Baird. Originally conceived in 1926, it was not adapted to practical use until about fifteen years later.

Other examples of mechanical progress

The foregoing list of inventions by no means exhausts the record of mechanical progress during the Second Industrial Revolution. Particular reference should be made to the invention of the electric light, which has probably contributed as much to the well-being of the human race as any other invention in history. Not only has it enhanced the comfort and safety of contemporary living, but it has been a boon to miners; while many of the difficult operations of modern surgery would be impossible without it. The electric light was first conceived by Sir Humphry Davy about 1820, but it did not become a commercial success until 1879 when Thomas A. Edison invented the incandescent-filament lamp. Even after that a great many improvements were necessary before it could be widely used. Not until George Westinghouse and Nikola Tesla completed their experiments with the alternating current in 1893 was it possible to provide for the efficient transmission of light and power over long distances. Among other significant mechanical achievements of the period since 1860 have been the invention of type-bar casting (the linotype machine) by Ottmar Mergenthaler, the perfection of artificial refrigeration by J. J. Coleman and others, the invention of the typewriter by Christopher Sholes and Carlos Glidden, and the development of motion-picture photography, originated mainly by Edison.

The growth of finance capitalism

The Second Industrial Revolution has been distinguished from the first not merely by technological advances, but even more strikingly by the development of new forms of capitalist organization. The age of coal and iron was also, generally speaking, the age of small enterprise. Until the middle of the nineteenth century, at least, the

[3] Clive Day, *Economic Development in Modern Europe*, p. 26.

Automation—a High-speed Computer, Univac, Manufactured by Remington Rand. The operator, in the foreground, sits at the Supervisory Control Panel. In the background is the Central Computer. On the right are tape-handling mechanisms that feed information into the computer and take away the finished results.

partnership was still the dominant form of business organization. To be sure, many of these partnerships did business on a considerable scale, but they were hardly to be compared with the giant corporations of more recent years. Their capital came mainly from profits plowed back into the business, and their owners generally took an active part in the work of management. Many joint-stock companies had also been formed, but, except for their attributes of permanence and limited liability, they differed little from the partnerships. All of these types of business organization, in so far as they were concerned with manufacturing, mining, or transportation, may be designated as forms of *industrial capitalism*. During the Second Revolution, especially since 1890, industrial capitalism has been largely superseded by *finance capitalism*, one of the most crucial developments of the modern age. Finance capitalism has four outstanding characteristics: (1) the domination of industry by investment banks and insurance companies; (2) the formation of huge aggregations of capital; (3) the separation of ownership from management; and (4) the growth of holding companies. Each of these requires a brief explanation.

One of the earliest examples of the domination of industry by investment bankers was the formation of the United States Steel Corporation in 1901 with the aid of J. P. Morgan and Company. Since then financial institutions have gained control over an increasing number of American corporations. Of course they do not own all of the stock, or any considerable fraction of it. Several American corporations have hundreds of thousands of stockholders. But these people are chiefly absentee owners; they have little to do with influencing corporate policy, and some of their shares do not even carry voting privileges. Banks and insurance companies wield control in some cases through ownership of a majority of the *voting stock* and in others through floating loans under terms which provide the lenders with extensive powers or with representation on boards of directors.

The domination of industry by investment institutions

The huge aggregations of capital which have come to characterize modern industrial organizations include trusts, mergers, and cartels. All of them are organized for an identical purpose: to restrict

*Trusts, merg-
ers, and cartels*

or prevent competition. Trusts are combinations of all or nearly all of the producers of certain articles in order to control their price and production. Mergers are combinations of companies producing the same or related articles. They differ from trusts in the fact that their constituent units generally lose their identity and are "merged" into a controlling corporation. Their capital stock is exchanged on mutually agreeable terms for shares in the new or controlling company. Cartels may be defined as loose associations of independent companies for the primary purpose of restricting competition in the sale of their products. They differ from both trusts and mergers in not being corporate entities. They issue no capital stock and have no centralized management. They may function on either a domestic or an international scale. During the 1930's some European governments encouraged the formation of domestic cartels for the purpose of strengthening their national industries against foreign competition. But the most interesting and perhaps the most significant types of cartels are those which cut across international boundaries. For example, before World War II, some American corporations had cartel arrangements with similar corporations in Germany, by means of which patents and discoveries were exchanged and the markets of the world divided up to prevent competition.

*The separation
of ownership
from manage-
ment*

A third element in finance capitalism has been the separation of ownership from management. The real owners of industrial enterprises are the millions of men and women who have invested their savings in shares of stock; management is in the hands of a group of officers and directors, chosen by a minority of shareholders who have monopolized the voting stock or collected the proxies of absentee owners. In some cases the officers are little more than salaried employees, owning but a tiny percentage of the company's capital. Indeed, it is not unknown that some of them should prefer to invest their surplus earnings in sounder enterprises than the ones over which they preside.[4] Lastly, finance capitalism has included the growth of the holding company as a basic form of capitalistic organization. The holding company is a device whereby a number of producing units are united under the control of a company which owns their stock. The holding company does not engage in production but receives its income from management fees and from dividends paid by the producing units. Though sometimes justified on the ground that it promotes integration of industry and facilitates business expansion, it is really a symbol of the triumph of the financier over the old-fashioned type of productive capitalist.

Finally, it should be noted that since 1860 industrialization has spread to nearly every country of the civilized world. During the

---

[4] A report of the Securities and Exchange Commission revealed that the president of one of our large steel corporations owned in 1936 only one share of its common stock and thirteen shares of the preferred—in spite of the fact that the company paid him a salary running well into six figures.

age of coal and iron, mechanized production was restricted primarily to Great Britain, France, Belgium, and the United States; and Great Britain was far in advance of the others. After 1860 industrialization spread very rapidly until every one of the major powers had reaped a full harvest of its benefits and evils. The adoption of the new methods was especially conspicuous in Germany. Before 1860 the German states had been predominantly agrarian, with at least 60 per cent of their people obtaining their living from the soil. By 1914 the empire of the Kaisers was the greatest industrial nation in Europe, producing more steel than Great Britain and leading the world in the manufacture of chemicals, aniline dyes, and electrical and scientific equipment. For such remarkable expansion there were several main explanations. In the first place, Germany had no tradition of *laissez faire*. Her economists had been preaching for years that the state should intervene in every way possible to promote the economic strength of the nation. As a consequence it was easy for the government to bolster up feeble industries, to nationalize the railroads and operate them for the benefit of business, and even to encourage the growth of trusts. In the second place, the German people were accustomed to discipline, to the submergence of individual personalities in the groups to which they belonged. Prussia had always been a military state, and her system of inculcating order and obedience through compulsory service in the army was adopted as the foundation of the empire. As a third reason may be mentioned the German emphasis upon applied science in the schools, resulting in an abundant supply of technicians, who could be hired by industrial corporations for a low wage. The famous Krupp munitions works at Essen employed a larger staff of trained scientists than any university in the world. Last, but by no means of least importance, was the fact that Germany acquired, as a result of her victory over France in 1870, the rich iron deposits of Lorraine, which ultimately supplied her with three-fourths of the ore for her basic industry of steel manufacture.

Industrialization did not spread into eastern Europe quite so soon as it did into Germany, nor did it proceed as far. Nevertheless, by 1890 a considerable development of the factory system and of mechanized transportation had begun in Russia. The Industrial Revolution in Russia, like that in Germany, was in part the result of governmental encouragement. Through the influence of Count Serge Witte, distinguished minister under Alexander III and Nicholas II, the government of the Tsars levied prohibitive tariffs and borrowed money from France to subsidize railroads and numerous industrial enterprises. These and other efforts bore some amazing fruit. By 1914 Russia was producing more iron than France; her coal production had more than doubled; and in textiles she ranked fourth in the world. No fewer than 3,000,000 people were engaged directly in manufacturing, while some of her industrial establish-

The spread of industrialization: the Industrial Revolution in Germany

The industrialization of Russia, Italy, and Japan

ments employed as many as 10,000 workers.[5] The Industrial Revolution in Italy and Japan was also advanced very largely by state intervention, at least in its earlier stages. In both countries the movement began about 1880 and completed a cycle of definite progress by the outbreak of World War I. In Italy the government extended the railway system and fostered the growth of silk and cotton manufactures in such measure that Italian exports increased nearly 300 per cent between 1895 and 1914. The achievements of Japan were even more remarkable. By 1914 the little island empire had 6000 miles of railroad, almost entirely owned by the state. Her textile industry almost equaled that of Great Britain, while her foreign commerce had risen in value from virtually nothing to nearly $700,000,000.

5. Society in the Age of the Machine

The phenomenal growth of population

In later chapters there will be occasion to observe some of the political effects of the Industrial Revolution. For the present it is sufficient to take note of the social results. And there is no doubt that most of the important social developments of the nineteenth and early twentieth centuries have sprung from the great economic changes of that period. Perhaps the most obvious and yet one of the most crucial of these developments was an enormous increase in population. Between the French Revolution and World War I the population of nearly every civilized country grew at an unprecedented rate. Some evidences of this phenomenon were noticeable as early as 1800, especially in England, where the increase was about 50 per cent in the second half of the eighteenth century. But in the main the spectacular growth came later. Between the Battle of Waterloo and the outbreak of World War I the population of England and Wales nearly quadrupled. That of Germany rose from about 25,000,000 in 1815 to almost 70,000,000 a hundred years later. The number of inhabitants in France almost doubled between the overthrow of Napoleon and the Franco-Prussian War, while the total of Russians more than doubled in the fifty years preceding 1914. In spite of such adverse factors as famine in Ireland and Russia, emigration to America, and disease resulting from congestion in cities, the population of Europe as a whole mounted from an estimated 190,000,000 in 1800 to 460,000,000 in 1914. During the same period the population of the United States increased from 5,000,000 to almost 100,000,000.

Reasons for the increase in population

To discover the reasons for this unprecedented growth in numbers we must look to several factors. First, it was due in some measure to the effects of the Commercial Revolution in improving the vigor of the race by providing a more abundant and a more varied diet. Second, it was a consequence of the establishment of infant

[5] Clive Day, *Economic Development in Modern Europe*, p. 388.

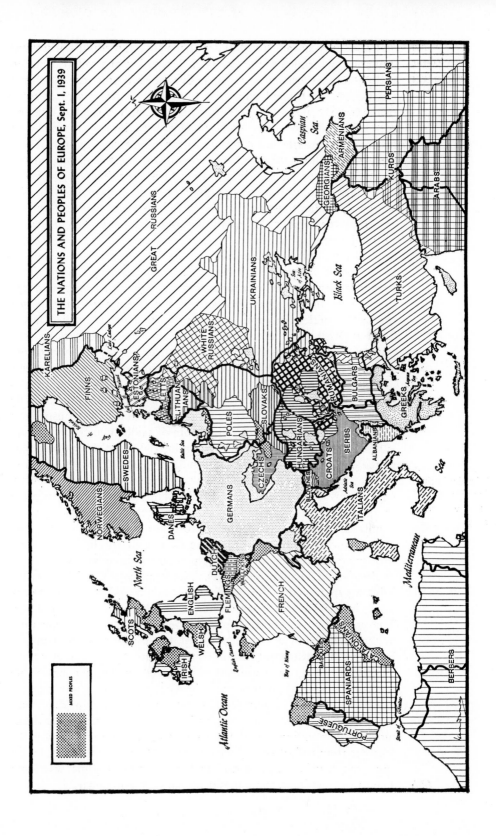

THE NATIONS AND PEOPLES OF EUROPE, Sept. 1, 1939

MIXED PEOPLES

and maternity hospitals and of advancements in medical science and sanitation, which led to the practical elimination of smallpox, scurvy, and cholera, at least from western Europe and America. Possibly a third cause was the influence of nationalism, of the growth of racial pride and the patriotic obsession. Peoples with a solid conviction of their own superiority and buoyant with hopes of victory in future struggles are almost certain to reproduce very rapidly. These were the qualities which characterized most of the nations in the nineteenth century. Like the Hebrews in ancient times, they desired numerous offspring for the purpose of overcoming their enemies or with the hope eventually of spreading their superior culture among all the benighted of earth. But apparently the most important of all the causes, in Europe at least, was the influence of the Industrial Revolution in making it possible for limited areas to support large numbers of people. This increase in population came about not only because the mechanization of agriculture increased the yield from the land, but also because the factory system enlarged the opportunities for earning a living away from the soil. Thus it became possible for countries rich in industrial resources to support several times as many people as ever could be done on an agrarian basis. After World War I this concentration of workers in industry created thorny problems. As a result of the strangulation of international trade, many countries found it almost impossible to keep their industrial systems functioning except by an expansion of armaments and an extensive program of public construction.

Before the second stage of the Industrial Revolution had completed its course, the curve of population growth began to show signs of flattening out. The trend was forecast originally in France, where increase in the number of inhabitants almost ceased as early as 1870. After 1918 a similar tendency became apparent in other countries. Back of this trend there were two chief causes: the curtailment of immigration and the decline of the birth rate. The former prevented the filling up of sparsely settled areas and the relief of congestion in older countries. Time was when the surplus inhabitants of crowded European nations could find homes for themselves in the United States or in the republics of South America. The emigration of these people not only increased the population of the countries in which they settled, but by relieving overcrowding in the homeland fostered an expansion in numbers there as well. The result all through the nineteenth century was a considerable increase in the total population of the Western world. But the major cause of the diminishing rate of growth was a decline in the excess of births over deaths. In western Europe on the average the birth rate was cut in two by the 1930's. In England it dropped from 36.3 per thousand of the population in 1876 to 14.8 in 1934. During approximately the same period in Germany the decline was from 40.9 to 17.5, less than enough to maintain even a stationary level. The

The diminishing rate of growth after 1914

reasons for this precipitous decline were not traceable exclusively
to poverty or hardship but resulted partly from increasing urbanization, which makes children an inconvenience rather than an asset.
During World War II, however, most countries experienced a
marked increase in the rate of births. And twelve years after its
end, no appreciable falling off had taken place.

Closely related to growth of population as an effect of the Industrial Revolution has been an increasing urbanization of Western
society. By 1914 the artificial conditions of city life had come
to be the accepted norm for a large percentage of the inhabitants
of industrialized nations. Growth in urbanization was particularly
striking in such countries as Germany and England. In the former
as late as 1840 there were only two cities of 100,000 inhabitants
or more; in 1910 there were forty-eight. In England during the last
thirty years of the nineteenth century, approximately one-third of
the agricultural population withdrew permanently from the land.
The English census of 1901 revealed that the number of persons
engaged in farming was only about 20 per cent of the number employed in industrial pursuits. In the United States, despite its wealth
of agricultural resources, there was a similar movement away from
the land, albeit at a slower pace. By 1915 the proportion of Americans living in urban areas had risen to about 40 per cent, and by
1920 it was over half. The causes of this drift to the cities and towns
were the increasing attractions of urban life and the steady decline
in need for agricultural labor as a result of mechanized farming.
The effects were a mixture of good and evil. Escape from the soil
freed large numbers of men and women from the isolation of rural
life, from the tyranny of the weather, from the idiocies of primitive
folkways, and from a humdrum existence of lonely toil on stubborn
acres. But at the same time it transformed many of them into pawns
or tools of their employers. It made some of them robots, who
performed their tasks automatically with little sense of responsibility
or comprehension of their place in the economic scheme, and with
nothing to inspire their efforts but the hope of a living wage. If it
rescued them from the hazards of blight and drought, it plunged
them into new dangers of loss of employment from overproduction
and placed them at the mercy of a system beyond their control.

A third great result of the Industrial Revolution was the creation
of two new classes: an industrial bourgeoisie and a proletariat. The
industrial bourgeoisie, composed of the owners of factories, mines,
and railroads, cast in its lot with the old middle class of merchants,
bankers, and lawyers. Thus strengthened in numbers and in influence, the combined bourgeoisie soon ceased to be merely a
middle class and became for all practical purposes the ruling element
in society. In some cases this rise to power was accomplished by
pushing the old landed aristocracy into the background; in others,
by joining with it. But no sooner had the capitalists and entrepreneurs

*The urbaniza-
tion of Western
society*

*The emergence
of the industrial
bourgeoisie*

657

gained the ascendancy than they began to divide among themselves. The great bankers and magnates of industry and commerce came to constitute an upper bourgeoisie with ambitions somewhat distinct from those of the lower bourgeoisie, made up of small merchants, small industrialists, and professional men. The tendency was for the upper bourgeoisie to become more and more deeply absorbed in finance capitalism. Its members were interested in stock-jobbing operations, in launching new ventures for an immediate profit, and in reorganizing businesses already in existence for purposes of monopolistic or speculative control. To the leaders of this class most forms of government intervention, except protective tariffs, were anathema; they insisted that free enterprise was absolutely essential to vigorous economic growth. On the other hand, the lower bourgeoisie began to show signs of a vital concern with stability and security. In many countries the members of this class were to be found advocating measures to curb speculation, to ensure the stability of prices, to eliminate chain stores and monopolies, and even to provide for state ownership of public utilities. It was this group which furnished some of the strongest support for Mussolini and Hitler in the early stages of their rise to power.

The rise of the proletariat

The Industrial Revolution also brought into existence a proletariat, which ultimately attained sufficient strength to challenge the supremacy of the bourgeoisie. In a sense the proletariat has existed since the dawn of civilization, for the term includes all persons who are dependent for their living upon a wage. The free workers in ancient Greece and Rome were proletarians, and so were the journeymen and the crofters and cotters in the Middle Ages. But prior to the Industrial Revolution the wage earners were a small proportion of the working class, since the majority of those who toiled for a living were engaged in agriculture, originally as serfs and later as tenant farmers and share-croppers. Furthermore, the few proletarians who did exist were scarcely conscious of their identity as a class. The Industrial Revolution, by concentrating large numbers of workers in the cities and by subjecting them to common abuses, infused into wage earners a degree of solidarity and imbued them with common aspirations. Nevertheless, their power as an economic class was limited for many years by stringent legislation. The right to strike, for instance, was not granted by any Western nation until after 1850. And not until late in the nineteenth century were the organized workers able to exert much influence upon the policies of governments.

The uneven material benefits of the Industrial Revolution

That the Industrial Revolution has bestowed great material benefits upon the inhabitants of Western nations is a conclusion which even the most bilious of critics would hardly deny. Without question it has supplied contemporary man with tremendous quantities of goods and with an astounding number of appliances to minister to his comfort and convenience. But whether the various classes have participated in these benefits in anything like an equitable ratio is an altogether different question. There seems little doubt that real wages, or wages in terms of purchasing power, rose quite rapidly during the nineteenth century. A leading economist, Sir Josiah Stamp, estimated that the ordinary Englishman in 1913 was four times as well off, in relation to the amount his income would buy, as were his ancestors in 1801. Between 1880 and 1930 real wages in England increased on the average by 50 per cent and the wages of the lowest-paid workers by even more.[6] Similar increases occurred in Germany and France. In the United States average weekly earnings of industrial workers rose by 54 per cent between 1909 and 1940, despite a reduction of the average working week from 51.7 hours to 38.3 hours. Evidences of improvement in standards of living were equally impressive. The average per capita consumption of meat in Germany advanced from 38 pounds in 1816 to 115 pounds in 1912. The figures for consumption of the same commodity in the United States show an increase from 116 pounds per capita in 1935 to 163 pounds in 1956. Between 1918 and 1955 the number of telephones in the United States more than trebled, while the number of automobiles increased more than sixfold. In the last-named year the nation had one telephone for every 3 persons and an automobile for every 3⅙. It would be difficult to prove that the American workers, at least, were not sharing in a generally rising prosperity. On the other hand, there was no gainsaying the fact that the wealth of the United States was far from being evenly distributed. According to a study made by the State of New York, one family out of every eleven in the United States in 1953 had a yearly income of less than $2000, and one out of five had less than $1000.

In addition, it is at least open to doubt that the mechanization of industry has contributed as much to the physical well-being of the laboring classes as is commonly supposed. John Stuart Mill, writing in 1848, declared that it was questionable if all the mechanical inventions made up to that time had lightened the day's toil of a single human being. Perhaps this judgment would not be too extreme if repeated even now. In many cases the common laborer of today seems to be under the necessity of performing about as many backbreaking tasks as ever. Labor-saving devices enable the worker to turn out more goods, but it is doubtful if they really save him much labor. Whatever may be the situation at present, it is certainly true that during the early period of the Industrial Revolution the introduction of machines was not a great boon to the worker. They often meant that able-bodied men were thrown out of employment by the cheap labor of women and children. Moreover, many of the factories, especially those devoted to making textiles, were viler than prisons. Windows were small and were generally

Effects upon the physical well-being of the workers

[6] Heaton, *Economic History of Europe*, p. 746.

kept closed to preserve the moisture desirable for cotton manufacture. Bad air, suffocating heat, and lack of sanitation, combined with intolerable hours, reduced innumerable workers to haggard, consumptive skeletons and drove many to drunkenness and crime. Furthermore, the new industrial towns grew up so rapidly and in such haphazard manner that housing conditions for the poor remained abominable for some time. In Manchester as late as 1840 one-eighth of the working-class families lived in cellars. Others drifted into wretched tenements with as many as a dozen people to a room. So appalling were these conditions that British factory employees in the early nineteenth century were probably worse off than the slaves on American plantations. But against these evils must be reckoned the fact that the Industrial Revolution did facilitate the organization of workers, thus enabling them to use the power of collective action to obtain higher wages and an eventual improvement of working conditions. Besides, the common people undoubtedly benefited from lower prices made possible by mass production.

A Third Industrial Revolution?

Since World War II many observers have pointed to economic changes which seem to suggest that the developed nations of the world are now in the midst of a Third Industrial Revolution. The primary elements of this revolution, if such it can be called, are automation, electronics, nuclear fission, and jet propulsion. The first two are closely related. Automation means the use of machines to tend machines, with human labor completely eliminated or reduced to a minimum. Electronics is that branch of physics which deals with the behavior and effects of electrons, or negative constituents within the atom. Most of the machines used in automation are electronic devices. Examples include high-speed recording and computing machines and machines that inspect and control the output of other machines. Automation has been extended also to entire assembly lines and to other large segments of the manufacturing process. Nuclear fission refers, of course, to the process of splitting the atom and releasing the energy locked within it. One consequence was the production of weapons of unprecedented destructive force. But development of atomic fission as a source of power for peaceful objects is not far in the future. Even earlier will come the perfection of jet engines for purposes other than the propulsion of military aircraft. Nearly all of the commercial airline companies have already ordered jet planes for delivery before 1960. Piston engines will undoubtedly continue in use for some time, but demands for speed and power will make them increasingly obsolete.

Possible effects

The full impact of the revolution described above is impossible to estimate at this time. It has already greatly enhanced the importance of the pure and applied sciences. Engineers and physicists are so much in demand that industrial companies are competing madly for their services and even hoarding them for the future. Vast changes seem also to impend with respect to the materials of modern industry. It has been estimated, for example, that the future development of atomic fission will make possible the extraction of as much power from one gallon of sea water as can now be obtained from 300 gallons of gasoline. Industrial enterprises now worth billions of dollars may shrink in value overnight. Whether advances in knowledge of social problems will keep pace with the drastic changes in production and in business organization is impossible to determine. Equally unpredictable are the possible effects upon the status of the workers. For example, will progress in technology create new jobs rapidly enough to absorb the workers thrown out of employment by automation? Already in the United States the number of sales and service employees exceeds the number of factory workers. Can there be a further increase in the disproportion of nonproducers?

6. New Social and Economic Doctrines

The Industrial Revolution produced its full complement of economic theory—part of it to justify the new order, part of it for critical analysis, and the remainder as a gospel of social reform. No sooner had the factory system been well established and profits begun to flow into the coffers of the new lords of creation than some of the more articulate and belligerent among them rose up to defend their privileges. In doing so they often displayed a coldness toward the plight of the masses and a brazen confidence in their own right to inherit the earth which the nobles of the Old Regime might well have envied. Indeed, some of the apologists for the new system evolved into a type of economic Bourbons, learning nothing from the past and closing their eyes to the dangers of the future. This attitude was expressed in the doctrines that private property is sacred, that every man has a right to do what he will with his own, and that poverty is invariably the result of laziness and incompetence. Several of the high priests of the new capitalism went so far as to declare that poverty was a good thing for the masses since it taught them to respect their superiors and to be grateful to Providence for such blessings as they did receive. An English clergyman, writing about 1830, set forth the view that it was a law of nature that some should be poor in order that the sordid and ignoble offices in the community might be fulfilled. He opined that thereby the stock of human happiness is much increased, for "the more delicate are not only relieved from drudgery and freed from those occasional employments which would make them miserable, but are left . . . to pursue those callings which are suited to their various dispositions and most useful to the state." [7]

Economic Bourbonism

[7] Quoted by Clive Day, *Economic Development in Modern Europe*, p. 55.

*The theory of
the classical
economists*

But some of the economic theory, even in defense of the capitalist ideal, was more disinterested. Of this type were the teachings of the classical economists, or economic liberals, as they are often called. The founder of classical economics was Adam Smith, whose work was discussed in a preceding chapter. Though Smith wrote before industrial capitalism had reached its full stature, and though some of his teachings did not harmonize well with a strict interpretation of *laissez faire*, there was nevertheless enough in the general implications of his theory to cause him to be acclaimed as the prophet of capitalist ideals. The specific doctrines of classical economics, however, were largely the work of Smith's disciples—including such eminent writers as Thomas R. Malthus, David Ricardo, James Mill, and Nassau Senior. The chief elements in the theory subscribed to by most of these men may be summarized as follows:

(1) Economic individualism. Every individual is entitled to use for his own best interests the property he has inherited or acquired by any legitimate method. Each person must be allowed to do what he likes with his own so long as he does not trespass upon the equal right of others to do the same. Since each individual knows best that which will redound to his happiness, society will profit most from allowing every one of its members to follow his own inclinations.

(2) *Laissez faire*. The functions of the state should be reduced to the lowest minimum consistent with public safety. The government should shrink itself into the role of a modest policeman, preserving order and protecting property, but never in any wise interfering with the operation of economic processes.

(3) Obedience to natural law. There are immutable laws operating in the realm of economics as in every sphere of the universe. Examples are the law of supply and demand, the law of diminishing returns, the law of rent, and so on. These laws must be recognized and respected; failure to do so is disastrous.

(4) Freedom of contract. Every individual should be free to negotiate the best kind of contract he can obtain from any other individual. In particular, the liberty of workers and employers to bargain with each other as to wages and hours should not be hampered by laws or by the collective power of labor unions.

(5) Free competition and free trade. Competition serves to keep prices down, to eliminate inefficient producers, and to insure the maximum production in accordance with public demand. Therefore no monopolies should be tolerated, nor any price-fixing laws for the benefit of incompetent enterprisers. Furthermore, in order to force each country to engage in the production of those things it is best fitted to produce, all protective tariffs should be abolished. Free international trade will also help to keep prices down.

Several of the disciples of Adam Smith made distinctive contributions of their own. For example, Thomas R. Malthus (1766–1834) introduced the element of pessimism which caused the new

THE DISTRIBUTION OF PERSONAL INCOME
IN THE UNITED STATES IN 1953

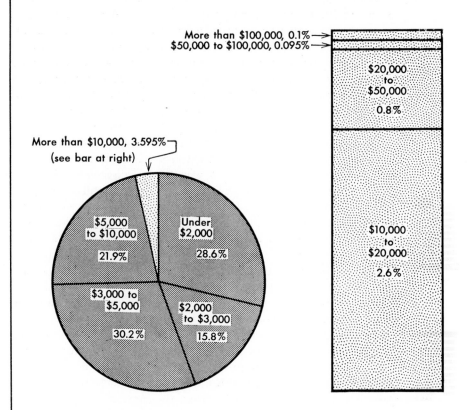

More than $100,000, 0.1%→
$50,000 to $100,000, 0.095%→

$20,000 to $50,000 0.8%

More than $10,000, 3.595%
(see bar at right)

$5,000 to $10,000 21.9%

Under $2,000 28.6%

$10,000 to $20,000 2.6%

$3,000 to $5,000 30.2%

$2,000 to $3,000 15.8%

Percentages refer to the total number of income recipients. The sum of percentages shown is 100.095, in consequence of approximation and rounding.

The year 1953 is the most recent year for which complete income statistics are available. During that year the adjusted gross income of all Americans who filed income tax returns was about $229 billion. This figure includes wages, salaries, rent, interest, and dividends received by individuals and families. It does not include corporate profits. But the personal income of the American people was far from being evenly distributed, despite marked improvement over the past two decades. As the chart shows, about 44 per cent received incomes of less than $3000 annually, while 28 per cent had to struggle along on less than $2000. Fifty-four million persons had incomes large enough to require them to pay a tax, but this represented only slightly more than half of the total population 21 years of age and over. Although many of those who were tax exempt were farmers, whose incomes could not be adequately measured in cash, it was still apparently true that millions of Americans who worked for a living were not receiving a living wage. U. S. Treasury Department, *Statistics of Income for 1953*, p. 10.

economics to be branded as "the dismal science." A clergyman of the Anglican church, rector of a small parish in Surrey, Malthus published his memorable *Essay on Population* in 1798. Issued originally in pamphlet form, the *Essay* grew out of some discussions which the author had with his father concerning the perfectibility of man. The elder Malthus was a disciple of Rousseau, but he was so impressed with his son's arguments against the superficial optimism of the Frenchman that he urged him to put them in writing. The pamphlet created an immediate sensation and provoked discussion for many years afterward. In 1803 it was expanded into a book on the basis of extended researches which the author undertook to refute his critics. The substance of the Malthusian theory is the contention that nature has set stubborn limits to the progress of mankind in happiness and wealth. Because of the voracity of the sexual appetite there is a natural tendency for population to increase more rapidly than the means of subsistence. To be sure, there are certain powerful checks, such as war, famine, disease, and vice; but these, when they operate effectively, augment still further the burden of human misery. It follows that poverty and pain are inescapable. Even if laws were to be passed distributing all wealth equally, the condition of the poor would be only temporarily improved; in a very short time they would begin to raise larger families, with the result that the last state of their class would be as bad as the first. In the second edition of his work Malthus advocated postponement of marriage as a means of relief, but he continued to stress the danger that population would outrun any possible increase in the means of subsistence.

The main teachings of Malthus were taken over and elaborated by David Ricardo (1772–1823), one of the keenest if not one of the broadest intellects of the nineteenth century. Ricardo was an English Jew who embraced Christianity at the age of twenty-one and married a Quaker. By the time he was twenty-five he had accumulated a fortune on the Stock Exchange and soon became one of the richest men in Europe. As an economist Ricardo is famous, first of all, for his subsistence theory of wages. According to this theory, wages tend toward a level which is just sufficient to enable the workers "to subsist and perpetuate their race, without either increase or diminution." This he held to be an iron law, from which there is no escape. If wages should rise temporarily above the subsistence standard, the population would increase, and the ensuing competition for jobs would quickly force the rate of pay down to its former level. Like the Malthusian law upon which it was based, this theory failed to recognize that families with a rising standard of living tend to limit the number of their offspring. Ricardo is noted, in the second place, for his teachings in regard to rent. He maintained that rent is determined by the cost of production on the poorest land that must be brought under cultivation, and that consequently as a country fills up with people an ever-increasing proportion of the social income is taken by the landlords. Though a great proprietor himself, he denounced the recipients of rent as the real enemies of both the capitalists and the workers. Finally, Ricardo is important for his labor theory of value, which influenced one of the main doctrines of the Marxian socialists. However, he attached some significance also to the role of capital in determining value—an idea which was abhorrent to Marx.

In his later years Ricardo frequently associated himself with an interesting group of reformers in England known as the philosophical radicals. Their leaders included such prominent figures as Jeremy Bentham, James Mill, the historian George Grote, and the political scientist John Austin. The foremost economist among them was James Mill (1773–1836), who, as has already been mentioned, enjoyed some reputation as a Utilitarian philosopher. While the teachings of James Mill would now be considered far from radical, they were nevertheless liberal enough to show that the classical economics was not hopelessly benighted and reactionary. The doctrines he incorporated in his *Elements of Political Economy* included the following: (1) the chief object of practical reformers should be to prevent the population from growing too rapidly, on the assumption that the wealth available for productive purposes does not naturally increase as fast as the number of inhabitants; (2) the value of commodities depends entirely upon the quantity of labor necessary to produce them; and (3) the unearned increment of land, or the increase in the value of land which comes exclusively from social causes, such as the building of a new factory in the vicinity, should be heavily taxed by the state. This last doctrine, based upon Ricardo's theory of rent, was destined for a wide popularity in England. In modified form it became part of the gospel of the Liberal party in the early 1900's, and it was a feature of the celebrated Lloyd George budget of 1909.

James Mill

Probably the ablest of the classical economists who came after Ricardo was Nassau William Senior (1790–1864). The first professor of political economy at Oxford, he was also a distinguished lawyer and served on a number of royal commissions. Like most of his predecessors, Senior regarded economics as a deductive science. He maintained that its truths could all be derived from a limited number of great abstract principles. Fortunately he did not always adhere to this method himself, particularly in dealing with questions only partly economic in character. Thus, while he upheld the principle of *laissez faire*, he advocated an increasing amount of governmental interference in such matters as health, housing, and education. His main contribution was his theory that *abstinence* creates a title to wealth. He admitted that labor and natural resources are the primary instruments of value, but he contended that abstinence is a secondary instrument. Therefore he argued that the capitalist

Nassau Senior

665

who has refrained from enjoying all of his wealth in order to accumulate a surplus for investment has a claim on the profits of production. His abstinence involves sacrifice and pain just as does the work of the laborer. Consequently it is unfair to give the entire reward to the latter. The evil reputation of Senior comes primarily from the fact that he condemned the demands of the trade unions for a reduction of the working day. He had an honest but mistaken conviction that the whole net profit of an industrial enterprise is derived from the last hour of operation. Hence to shorten the working day would eliminate profits and thereby result in closing the factories. For this doctrine he was dubbed by his critics "Last Hour" Senior.

*Opponents
of the classical
economics:
(1) John Stuart
Mill*

Most of the leading classical economists or economic liberals were citizens of Great Britain. This was true partly because economic liberalism harmonized well with political liberalism, which was stronger in Britain than in any other European country; and partly because British industrialists were beginning to perceive notable advantages from a policy of free trade with the rest of the world. On the Continent of Europe, however, conditions were entirely different. There the old traditions of strong government still lingered. Moreover, Continental manufacturers were attempting to build up industrial establishments which would be able to compete with the British. To achieve this, it was desirable to have the patronage and protection of the state. Hence we should not be surprised to find that the majority of the opponents of economic liberalism were natives of Continental countries. Nevertheless, at least one of its abler critics was an Englishman—the brilliant Utilitarian philosopher, John Stuart Mill (1806–1873). Though Mill as an economist is often considered a member of the classical school, he actually repudiated a number of its most sacred premises. First, he rejected the universality of natural law. He admitted that there are unchangeable laws governing the field of production, but he insisted that the distribution of wealth can be regulated by society for the benefit of the majority of its members. Second, he advocated more radical departures from *laissez faire* than any recommended by his forerunners. He did not oppose legislation under certain conditions for shortening the working day, and he believed that the state might properly take certain preliminary steps toward the redistribution of wealth by taxing inheritances and by appropriating the unearned increment of land. In the fourth book of his *Principles of Political Economy* he urged the abolition of the wage system and looked forward to a society of producers' co-operatives in which the workers would own the factories and elect the managers to run them. On the other hand, it should not be forgotten that Mill was too much of an individualist ever to go very far in the direction of socialism. He distrusted the state, and his real reason for advocating producers' co-operatives was not to exalt the power of the proletariat but to give to the individual worker the fruits of his labor.

The most noted of the German economists who wrote in direct opposition to the theories of the classical school was Friedrich List (1789–1846), who derived inspiration for some of his ideas from seven years' residence in America. List condemned the doctrines of *laissez faire* and freedom of international trade. Contending that the wealth of a nation is determined less by natural resources than by the productive powers of its citizens, he declared that it is the duty of governments to further the arts and sciences and to see to it that every individual makes the most of his talents in co-operating for the general good. He stressed the well-rounded development of the nation as all-important regardless of the effects upon the immediate fortunes of particular citizens. Holding that manufactures are essential to such a development, he demanded protective tariffs until the new industries should be able to compete with those of any other country. List was the forerunner of a long line of German economists who proposed to make the state the guardian of the production and distribution of wealth. Their object was less that of justice to the individual than the idea of consolidating the unity and increasing the strength of the nation. They believed that the government should not only impose protective tariffs, but should regulate and plan the development of industry so as to balance production and consumption. In general, their ideas represented a mixture of economic nationalism and collectivism, and thereby furnished a basis for some later German developments.

We come next to a group of theorists who were more interested in social justice than in discovering economic laws or in laying the foundations of national prosperity. The earliest exemplars of this more radical attitude were the utopian socialists, who take their name from the fact that they proposed idealistic schemes for co-operative societies, in which all would work at their appropriate tasks and share the results of their common efforts. To a considerable extent the utopian socialists were the heirs of the Enlightenment. Like the philosophers of that movement they believed that all crime and greed were the results of an evil environment. If men could be freed from vicious custom and from a social structure which facilitates enslavement of the weak by the strong, then all might live together in harmony and peace. Accordingly, the utopian socialists recommended the establishment of model communities, largely self-contained, where most of the instruments of production would be collectively owned, and where government would be mainly on a voluntary basis. Among the original propagators of such plans was the Frenchman Charles Fourier (1772–1837),[8] but

[8] Count Henri de Saint-Simon is also commonly considered a founder of utopian socialism, but about all that he actually proposed was the abolition of class distinctions and the control of society by industrial experts. Some of his

the sanest and most realistic of them all was Robert Owen (1771–1858). A native of Wales, Owen rose from an artisan apprentice to co-proprietor and manager of a great cotton mill at New Lanark in Scotland. Here he built new houses for his workers, reduced their hours of work from fourteen to ten, and established free schools for their children. The severe depression which followed in the wake of the Napoleonic wars convinced him that the economic order was in urgent need of reform. Like many others since his day, he concluded that the profit system was the cause of all the trouble. The existence of profit, he maintained, makes it impossible for the worker to buy the things he has produced. The result is overproduction, periodic crises, and unemployment. As a solution, Owen proposed the organization of society into co-operative communities, in which the sole reward to each member would be payment in proportion to his actual hours of labor. A number of such communities were actually set up, the most famous being the ones at Orbiston, Scotland, and New Harmony, Indiana. For a variety of reasons all of them failed within a very short time.

(4) the Marxian socialists

A more influential form of socialism was the so-called "scientific socialism" of Karl Marx (1818–1883). The son of a Jewish lawyer who had turned Christian for professional reasons, Marx was born at Trèves near Coblenz in the Rhineland. His father planned for him a career as a conventional bourgeois lawyer and, with that end in view, sent him to the University of Bonn. But young Marx soon displayed a distaste for the law and abandoned his legal studies for the pursuit of philosophy and history. After a year at Bonn he went to the University of Berlin, where he fell under the influence of a group of disciples of Hegel who were giving the teachings of their master a slightly radical twist. Though Marx earned the degree of doctor of philosophy at the University of Jena in 1841, his critical views prevented him from realizing his ambition of becoming a university professor. He turned to journalism, editing various radical periodicals and contributing articles to others. In 1848 he was arrested on a charge of high treason for participating in the revolutionary movement in Prussia. Though acquitted by a middle-class jury, he was soon afterward expelled from the country. In the meantime he had formed an intimate friendship with Friedrich Engels (1820–1895), who remained his lifelong disciple and *alter ego*. In 1848 the two men issued the *Communist Manifesto*, the "birth cry of modern socialism." From then until his death in 1883 Marx spent nearly all of his years in London, struggling against poverty, occasionally writing a few articles (some of which he sold to the New York *Tribune* for five dollars apiece), but giving most

followers taught that the state should be made the sole inheritor of property, which would then be allotted to individuals in proportion to their ability to use it for the advantage of the community. See Charles Gide and Charles Rist, *A History of Economic Doctrines*, pp. 198–225.

of his time to poring over dusty manuscripts in the British Museum,
from morning until midnight, gathering material for a great work
on political economy. In 1867 he published the first volume of this
work under the title of *Das Kapital*. Two other volumes were issued
after his death from manuscripts revised and edited by some of his
disciples.

Karl Marx (1818–1883). The photograph shows the prophet of socialism at the peak of his career, in
the 1870's.

Not all of the teachings of Karl Marx were entirely original. For
some of his ideas he was indebted to Hegel; for others to the French
socialist, Louis Blanc (1811–1882), and probably to Ricardo. Nevertheless, it was Marx who first combined these ideas into a com- *The doctrines*
prehensive system and gave them full-bodied meaning as an explana- *of Karl Marx*
tion of the facts of political economy. Since Marxist theory has been
one of the most influential bodies of thought in modern times, it is
necessary to understand its doctrines. Fundamental among them are
the following:

(1) The economic interpretation of history. All of the great
political, social, and intellectual movements of history have been
determined by the economic environment out of which they arose. *The economic*
Marx did not insist that the economic motive is the sole explanation *interpretation*
of human behavior, but he did maintain that every fundamental *of history*
historical development, regardless of its character on the surface,
has been the result of alterations in methods of producing and exchanging goods. Thus the Protestant Revolution was essentially an
economic movement; the disagreements over religious belief were
mere "ideological veils," concealing the actual causes.

(2) Dialectical materialism. Every distinct economic system, based
upon a definite pattern of production and exchange, grows to a
point of maximum efficiency, then develops contradictions or weak- *Dialectical ma-*
nesses within it which produce its rapid decay. Meanwhile the *terialism*
foundations of an opposing system are being gradually laid, and
eventually this new system displaces the old, at the same time ab- **669**

sorbing its most valuable elements. This dynamic process of historical evolution will continue by a series of victories of the new over
the old, until the perfect goal of communism has been attained.
After that there will doubtless still be change, but it will be change
within the limits of communism itself.

(3) The class struggle. All history has been made up of struggles
between classes. In ancient times it was a struggle between masters
and slaves and between patricians and plebeians; in the Middle Ages
it was a conflict between guild-masters and journeymen and between lords and serfs; now it has been narrowed down to a struggle
between the class of capitalists and the proletariat. The former includes those who derive their chief income from *owning* the means
of production and from exploiting the labor of others. The proletariat includes those who are dependent for their living primarily
upon a wage, who must sell their labor power in order to exist.

*The class
struggle*

(4) The doctrine of surplus value. All wealth is created by the
worker. Capital creates nothing, but is itself created by labor. The
value of all commodities is determined by the quantity of labor
power necessary to produce them. But the worker does not receive
the full value which his labor creates; instead he receives a wage,
which ordinarily is just enough to enable him to subsist and reproduce his kind. The difference between the value the worker
produces and what he receives is *surplus value*, which goes to the
capitalist. In general, it consists of three different elements: interest,
rent, and profits. Since the capitalist creates none of these things,
it follows that he is a robber, who appropriates the fruits of the
laborer's toil.

Surplus value

(5) The theory of socialist evolution. After capitalism has received
its death blow at the hands of the workers, it will be followed by
the stage of socialism. This will have three characteristics: the
dictatorship of the proletariat; payment in accordance with work
performed; and ownership and operation by the state of all means
of production, distribution, and exchange. But socialism is intended
to be merely a transition to something higher. In time it will be
succeeded by communism, the perfect goal of historical evolution.
Communism will mean, first of all, the classless society. No one
will live by owning, but all men solely by working. The state will
now disappear; it will be relegated to the museum of antiquities,
"along with the bronze ax and the spinning wheel." Nothing will
replace it except voluntary associations to operate the means of
production and provide for social necessities. But the *essence* of
communism is payment in accordance with needs. The wage system
will be completely abolished. Each citizen will be expected to work
in accordance with his faculties and will be entitled to receive from
the total fund of wealth produced an amount in proportion to his
needs. This is the acme of justice according to the Marxist conception.

*Socialist evolu-
tion*

The influence of Karl Marx upon the nineteenth and twentieth centuries can only be compared with that of Voltaire or Rousseau upon the eighteenth. His doctrine of the economic interpretation of history is a popular theory even among historians who are not his own followers. He numbers his disciples in every civilized nation of this planet and in a great many backward countries besides. In Russia he is almost a god, where his dogma of dialectical materialism is accepted not only as a foundation of economics but as a test to which science, philosophy, art, and literature must also conform. In every industrialized nation before World War I there was a socialist political party of considerable importance, the one in Germany having the largest representation in the Reichstag after 1912. Nearly everywhere the growth of socialism was a vital influence in furthering the enactment of social insurance and minimum wage laws and in promoting taxation of incomes and inheritances for the purpose of redistributing wealth. Marx, of course, was not interested in these things as ends in themselves, but the ruling classes were eventually persuaded to adopt them as a convenient tub to be thrown to the socialist whale. Socialists have also quite generally lent their support to the co-operative movement, to government ownership of railroads and public utilities, and to innumerable schemes for protecting workers and consumers against the power of monopoly capitalism.

Toward the end of the nineteenth century the followers of Marx split into two factions. The majority in most countries adhered to the doctrines of a sect known as the revisionists, who, as their name implies, believed that the theories of Marx should be *revised* to bring them into line with changing conditions. The other faction was made up of the strict Marxists, who insisted that not one jot or tittle of the master's teachings should be modified. In addition to this cleavage in general attitude there were also specific differences. Whereas the revisionists advocated the attainment of socialism by peaceful and gradual methods, the strict Marxists were revolutionists. The revisionists concentrated their attention upon immediate reforms, with the slogan, "Less for the better future and more for the better present"; the strict Marxists demanded the dictatorship of the proletariat or nothing. The leaders of the majority faction were willing to recognize the interests of separate nations; they were prone to talk about duty to the fatherland, and they frequently supported the demands of their governments for increased armaments and for lengthened terms of military service. The strict Marxists, on the other hand, were uncompromising internationalists; they held to the contention of Marx that the world proletariat is one great brotherhood, and they frowned upon patriotism and nationalism as capitalist devices to throw dust in the eyes of the workers. On the whole, it was the revisionists who gained control of the socialist parties in the majority of Western nations. The

Social Democratic party in Germany, the Unified Socialist party in France, and the Socialist party in the United States were all very largely dominated by the moderate faction. In Britain leadership of the Labor party was supplied in most cases by the Fabian socialists, so named from their policy of delay in imitation of the tactics of Fabius, a Roman general in the wars against Carthage. About 1918 most of the strict Marxists withdrew altogether from the socialist parties and have since been known generally as communists. But "strict Marxism" in its communist form has often shown a tendency in recent years to abandon the internationalism of Marx and to glorify patriotism and defense of the fatherland. This was particularly true of Russia and some of her satellites during World War II and the years following.

Anarchism

Many of the social idealists of the nineteenth and early twentieth centuries were torn between the desire to improve the welfare of society by collectivist means and the hope of gaining for the individual a maximum of personal freedom. We have seen that even the Marxists proposed eventually to abolish the state. But the collectivist-individualist dilemma received much more attention from the anarchists. Strictly defined, anarchism means opposition to all government based upon force. The followers of this philosophy have generally conceded that some form of social organization would be necessary, but they condemn the coercive state as absolutely incompatible with human liberty. As to the problem of what should be done with the economic system, the anarchists have sharply disagreed. Some have been pure individualists, holding that man's right to acquire and use property should be subject only to the laws of nature. The father of anarchism, William Godwin (1756–1836), believed that if the land were made as free as the air, no further change in the economic structure would be necessary. In the judgment of the French anarchist, Pierre Proudhon (1809–1865), an arrangement whereby society would provide every man with free and unlimited credit would be a sufficient means of insuring economic justice. Such a plan, he thought, would prevent anyone from monopolizing the resources of the earth and would guarantee to the citizen who was thrifty and industrious the full reward of his labors.

The collectivistic anarchists: Bakunin and Kropotkin

But the first of the anarchists to exert much influence were those who combined their hatred of the state with a definite philosophy of collectivism. Foremost among them were the three great Russian aristocrats, Mikhail Bakunin (1814–1876), Peter Kropotkin (1842–1921), and Leo Tolstoi (1828–1910). Though often classified as a communistic anarchist, Bakunin was really much closer to socialism. Indeed, for a time he was associated with the followers of Marx in the International Workingmen's Association, organized in London in 1864. His program for a new society included collective ownership of the means of production, abolition of surplus value, and payment in accordance with work performed. In other words, it was much like that of the socialist stage of the Marxists, except, of course, that it did not involve the preservation of the state. Bakunin is also famous as the father of terroristic anarchism. Advocating the overthrow of the state and of capitalism by violence, he inspired what later came to be called "propaganda by the deed"—that is, attracting attention to the anarchist cause by murdering a few prominent public officials and hated exploiters. It was followers of Bakunin who were alleged to have been responsible for assassinating President McKinley, President Carnot of France, and King Humbert I of Italy. But the more intelligent anarchists of the collectivist school condemned these tactics. For example, Prince Kropotkin denounced the use of individual violence under any conditions. He believed that a final revolutionary effort would be necessary, but he certainly preferred that the state should be weakened by peaceful methods, by gradually convincing people that it is an unnecessary evil, that it breeds wars, and that it exists primarily to enable some men to exploit others. From the standpoint of economic reform, Kropotkin was a communist. He insisted that all property except articles of personal use should be socially owned, and that payment should be on the basis of need.

The most noted of all the collectivistic anarchists, and one of the most interesting figures of modern times, was Count Leo Tolstoi. Best known for his novels, which will be discussed in a later connection, Tolstoi was also one of the greatest of Russian philosophers. *Leo Tolstoi* His ideas were born of strenuous emotional conflict and of an almost despairing search for a way of life which would satisfy his restless intellect. He indulged for a time in fashionable dissipation, attempted to relieve his troubled mind by philanthropic activities, and then finally abandoned it all for the life of a simple peasant. He came to the conclusion that no progress could be made in remedying the ills of society until the upper classes should renounce their privileges and adopt the humble existence of men who toil for their bread. But this would be only a beginning. In addition, all selfish individualism must disappear, all wealth must be surrendered to a common fund, and all agencies of force must be abolished. Tolstoi based much of his philosophy upon the New Testament, especially upon the Sermon on the Mount. He found in Jesus' teachings of meekness, humility, and non-resistance the essential principles of a just society. Above all, he condemned the use of violence, regardless of the purpose for which it is employed. Violence brutalizes man; it places its user in the hands of his enemies; and, as long as force is available as a weapon, reliance upon civilized methods is almost impossible. Some further words of Tolstoi on this subject may well be quoted:

673

"When a government is overthrown by violence and the authority passes into other hands, this new authority is by no means likely to be less oppressive than the former. On the contrary, obliged to defend itself from its exasperated and overthrown enemies, it will be even more cruel and despotic than its predecessor, as has ever been the case in periods of revolution . . . whichever party gains the upper hand, it will be forced in order to introduce and maintain its own system not only to avail itself of all former methods of violence but to invent new ones as well." [9]

Syndicalism

A third of the great radical philosophies produced by the Industrial Revolution was syndicalism, whose chief exponent was Georges Sorel (1847–1922). Syndicalism demands the abolition of both capitalism and the state and the reorganization of society into associations of producers. It resembles anarchism in its opposition to the state; but whereas the anarchist demands the abolition of force, the syndicalist would retain it, even after the state has been destroyed. Syndicalism also resembles socialism in that both would involve collective ownership of the means of production; but instead of making the state the owner and operator of the means of production, the syndicalist would delegate these functions to associations of producers. Thus all the steel mills would be owned and operated by the workers in the steel industry, the coal mines by the workers in the coal industry, and so on. Further, these associations or syndicates would take the place of the state, each one governing its own members in all of their activities as producers. In all other matters the workers would be free from interference. There would, of course, be no laws regulating morals or religion, for syndicalism is a thoroughly materialistic philosophy. On the other hand, its founders entertained no illusions as to the capacity of the masses for self-government. Sorel regarded the average man as very much of a sheep, fit only to be a follower. He believed, therefore, that the ruling authority in the syndicates should be exercised quite frankly by the intelligent few. The other most important ingredient in syndicalist theory is the doctrine of direct action. By this is meant the opposite of political action and may be taken to include the general strike and sabotage, the latter being any kind of crippling activity designed to injure the capitalist employer. The influence of syndicalism has been confined very largely to the Latin countries of Europe and to the United States. In France it was exceedingly popular for a time in the C.G.T. (General Confederation of Labor). In Italy its doctrines of minority rule, direct action, and the organization of society into syndicates were taken over in modified form by the Fascists. In America many elements of the syndicalist philosophy were adopted by the I.W.W. (In-

[9] *The Kingdom of God Is Within You*, p. 183.

dustrial Workers of the World), an organization flourishing from about 1905 to 1920.

Last of all, we must not overlook the Christian socialists, the least radical among all the critics of capitalist economics. The founder of Christian socialism was Robert de Lamennais (1782–1854), a French Catholic priest who sought to revive the Christian religion as an aid to reform and social justice. Similar ideas were expressed by Count Henri de Saint-Simon (1760–1825) in his *New Christianity*. From France the movement spread to England and was adopted by a number of Protestant intellectuals, especially by the novelist Charles Kingsley (1819–1875). In its early days Christian socialism was little more than a demand for application of the teachings of Jesus to the problems created by industry, but in later years it began to assume more tangible form. In 1891 Leo XIII, "the working-man's Pope," issued his famous encyclical *Rerum novarum*, in which he revived with a modern slant the liberal economic attitude of St. Thomas Aquinas. Though the encyclical expressly recognized private property as a natural right and vigorously repudiated the Marxist doctrine of the class war, at the same time it strongly discountenanced unlimited profits. It appealed to employers to respect the dignity of their workers as men and as Christians and not to treat them as "chattels to make money by, or to look upon them merely as so much muscle or physical power." By way of specific proposals to mitigate the harshness of the industrial regime, it recommended factory legislation, the formation of labor unions, an increase in the number of small landowners, and limitation of hours of employment.[10] The issuance of this encyclical gave a mighty impulse to the growth of Christian socialism among liberal Catholics. In European countries before World War I, Catholic parties frequently played an active role, sometimes in combination with the moderate Marxists, in furthering the movement for social legislation. This was especially true of the Center party in Germany, the Christian Socialist party in Austria, and the Liberal Action party in France.

Christian socialism

SELECTED READINGS—THE INDUSTRIAL REVOLUTION

Adams, J. T., *Our Business Civilization*, New York, 1929
Barnes, H. E., *An Economic History of the Western World*, New York, 1937, Chs. X–XVIII
Birnie, Arthur, *An Economic History of the British Isles*, New York, 1936

[10] The substance of Leo's encyclical was reaffirmed in 1931 by Pope Pius XI in a new encyclical, *Quadragesimo Anno*.

Bonbright, J. C., and Means, G. C., *The Holding Company, Its Public Significance and Its Regulation*, New York, 1932

Chase, Stuart, *Men and Machines*, New York, 1933

Clapham, J. H., *The Economic Development of France and Germany*, New York, 1923

Day, Clive, *Economic Development in Modern Europe*, New York, 1933

Dewey, D. R., *Financial History of the United States*, New York, 1922

Dietz, F. C., *The Industrial Revolution*, New York, 1927

Doane, R. R., *The Measurement of American Wealth*, New York, 1933

Heaton, Herbert, *Economic History of Europe*, New York, 1936, Chs. XXI–XXX

Hobson, J. A., *The Evolution of Modern Capitalism*, New York, 1926

Mantoux, Paul, *The Industrial Revolution in the Eighteenth Century*, New York, 1947

Nixon, St. J. C., *The Invention of the Automobile*, London, 1936

Ogg, F. A., and Sharp, W. R., *Economic Development of Modern Europe*, New York, 1929

Polakov, W. N., *The Power Age*, New York, 1933

Reid, W. S., *Economic History of Great Britain*, New York, 1956

Slosson, E. E., *Creative Chemistry*, New York, 1930

Tawney, R. H., *The Acquisitive Society*, New York, 1920

Thompson, W. S., *Population Problems*, New York, 1930

—New Economic Doctrines

Bell, John F., *A History of Economic Thought*, New York, 1956

Cole, G. D. H., *What Marx Really Meant*, New York, 1934

Ferguson, J. M., *Landmarks of Economic Thought*, New York, 1938

Gide, Charles, and Rist, Charles, *A History of Economic Doctrines*, New York

Ginzberg, Eli, *The House of Adam Smith*, New York, 1934

Laidler, H. W., *History of Socialist Thought*, New York, 1927

Russell, Bertrand, *Proposed Roads to Freedom*, New York, 1919

Schumpeter, Joseph, *Capitalism, Socialism, and Democracy*, New York, 1942

Wagner, D. O., ed., *Social Reformers: Adam Smith to John Dewey*, New York, 1934

Source Materials

Malthus, T. R., *An Essay on Population*, especially Books I and IV

Marx, Karl, *Critique of the Gotha Program*

Marx, K., and Engels, F., *The Communist Manifesto*

Owen, Robert, *A New View of Society*

———, *Report to the County of Lanark*

Tolstoi, Count Leo, *The Kingdom of God Is Within You*

Webster, Hutton, *Historical Selections*, pp. 776–80, Children in Factories

The Ascendancy of Democracy and Nationalism (1830-1914)

After the revolutions of 1830 many nations of the Western world experienced a rebirth of democracy. In Europe, Great Britain took the lead, but France, Germany, Switzerland, the Netherlands, Belgium, and Italy did not lag too far behind. Ultimately, even Spain, Turkey, and the Balkan kingdoms adopted at least some of the forms of democratic rule. What most of these countries were interested in was governmental or political democracy, exemplified by parliaments, universal manhood suffrage, and the cabinet system. Not until almost the end of the period was there much concern with social or economic democracy. There was a natural fear that this might constitute a serious threat to the position of the hereditary aristocracy, or force the tycoons of industry and finance to disgorge a portion of their wealth for the benefit of the unprivileged.

The rebirth of democracy

In order to understand the true meaning of democracy, we need to consider its historical origins. As a political ideal democracy had its roots in the philosophy of Rousseau. It was Rousseau's doctrine of the absolute sovereignty of the majority, together with his and the other romanticists' deification of the common man, which more than anything else gave us our ideal of the voice of the people as the voice of God. Historically, political democracy meant, above all, that the majority of the people should be entitled to speak for the entire nation, and that in forming that majority the votes of all the citizens should be equal. The machinery of the democratic state therefore included universal suffrage and such things as frequent elections and adequate popular control over the officers of government. In order that this machinery should operate effectively, the

The meaning of political democracy

677

citizens must have the right to organize political parties and to choose freely among them. Freedom of speech and freedom of the press were also considered essential components of the democratic ideal. But none of these rights was regarded as absolute and beyond the control of the majority. To be sure, if they were destroyed entirely, democracy would cease to exist; but the majority could most certainly limit them when there was a clear and immediate danger to the public safety. Thus it was a common practice for democratic governments to prohibit public speeches advocating violent revolution and to suppress newspapers upholding doctrines alleged to be particularly dangerous. Many prominent persons today who consider themselves good democrats urge that freedom of public expression be denied to fascists and communists. Historically, all that democracy has really required is that all ideas unaccompanied by threat of violence be tolerated and that *peaceful* minorities be allowed to strive to become the majority. The political ideal which affirms the *absolute* right of the citizen to write or speak or live as he pleases, so long as he does no actual harm to his neighbor, is not democracy but individualism.

The meaning of nationalism

The progress of democracy from 1830 to 1914 was accompanied by a vigorous growth of nationalism and its offshoots, imperialism and the struggle for power among nations. Nationalism may be defined as a program or ideal based upon a consciousness of nationhood. The feeling or consciousness of nationhood may depend upon a number of factors. A people may consider themselves a nation because of peculiarities of race, language, religion, or culture. In most cases, however, the factors which weld diverse groups together are a common history and common aspirations for the future or a belief in a common destiny. Only such elements as these can explain the fact that Belgium, Switzerland, Canada, and the United States are nations, since in all four there are major differences in language, in religion, or in both—to say nothing of different ethnic backgrounds. Although nationalism was in some respects a beneficent force, particularly in the early days when it often took the form of struggles for liberty, in the main it was and still is an evil influence. It is especially evil when it expresses itself in jingoism, in militarism, and in ambitions to conquer and dominate.

The evolution of nationalism

Without question nationalism was one of the most powerful forces that molded the history of the Western world between 1830 and 1914. From a vague sentiment during the early centuries of the modern era it grew into a veritable cult. For millions of deluded folk it became a stronger force than religion, surpassing Christianity in its appeal to the emotions and to the spirit of sacrifice in a holy cause. Men died for the honor of the flag as cheerfully as any martyrs had ever laid down their lives for the Cross. Though often co-existent with democracy and liberalism, militant nationalism was more powerful than either, and frequently thwarted or stifled both.

678

Nurtured by the French Revolutionary ideal of Fraternity, modern nationalism evolved through two stages. From 1800 to about 1848 it was little more than an emotional loyalty to a cultural and linguistic group and a yearning for deliverance from foreign oppression. After 1848 it developed into an aggressive movement for national greatness and for the right of each people united by cultural and ethnic ties to determine its own destinies. Its more extreme manifestations were exemplified by a frenzied worship of political power and a slavish devotion to doctrines of racial superiority and illusions of national honor. In such forms it was virtually synonymous with chauvinism, that species of vainglorious patriotism expressed in the sentiment, "My country, right or wrong."

1. The Evolution of Democracy in Great Britain

The evolution of democracy in Great Britain includes primarily three different elements: the extension of the suffrage, the development of the cabinet system of government, and the growth of the *The undemo-* supremacy of the House of Commons. Prior to 1832 the system of *cratic character* voting and representation in England was exceedingly undemocratic. *of the British* Only in a very few boroughs could the majority of the citizens *government in* vote. In the rural areas the franchise was restricted to a mere hand- *the early 19th* ful of the larger proprietors. Out of a total membership of about *century* 650 in the House of Commons no more than a third could be said to have been elected in any proper sense. The rest were appointed by local magnates or selected by petty groups of the richest property-holders or by members of favored guilds. In some cases the positions were openly sold or offered for rent for a term of years. To make matters worse, the distribution of seats had been thrown out of balance by the shift of population to the industrial centers of the north. While many of the new cities, such as Birmingham and Manchester, with more than 100,000 people in each, were denied representation entirely, villages in the south which had been almost depopulated continued to send as many as two and three members to the House of Commons. One of these villages (Old Sarum) was a deserted hill; another (Dunwich) had slipped beneath the waves of the sea; yet both were still represented in Parliament, by that remarkable British capacity for preserving a fiction long after the facts have disappeared.[1]

Despite the smug assurance of the Duke of Wellington that the political system described above was "perfectly satisfactory," there

[1] The prize example of these "rotten boroughs" was the village of Bute in Scotland. Here there was only one inhabitant left who was qualified to vote, but the village retained its right to send a representative to Parliament. On election day this solitary voter regularly appeared at the polling place, "moved and seconded his own nomination, put the question to the vote, and was unanimously elected" to a seat in the House of Commons. W. B. Munro, *The Governments of Europe*, revised edition (1932), p. 134.

The movement for political reform

was much agitation against it. Not only the common people but members of the middle class were thoroughly dissatisfied with an arrangement which gave almost a monopoly of power to the landed aristocracy. Emboldened by the success of the July Revolution of 1830 in France, the British Whigs under the leadership of Lord John Russell and Earl Grey inaugurated a movement for electoral reform. They were greatly aided in their efforts by a group of radicals led by Francis Place, a self-educated tailor who had accumulated a fortune by his wits and then dedicated his life to progressive causes. When the Duke of Wellington, who was now Prime Minister, declined to yield on the question of reform, Place

Interior of the House of Commons. The Government and Opposition members sit on opposite sides of this chamber. Those supporting the Government, or Cabinet, sit to the right of the Speaker, who occupies the canopied throne. His Majesty's Loyal Opposition sits on the Speaker's left. The Cabinet and the "Shadow Cabinet" of the Opposition sit on the front benches.

persuaded his followers to refuse to pay taxes and to withdraw all their money from the banks. He had placards distributed throughout the country bearing the legend, "To stop the Duke, go for Gold." When the run on the Bank of England threatened to become serious, Wellington resigned. Earl Grey then formed a new ministry, and the famous Reform Bill of 1832 became a law. Though its provisions were much more moderate than many of the radicals would have liked, it was still a noteworthy gain. The bill enfranchised most of the adult males of the middle class and nearly all of the smaller landholders and tenant farmers; but the great hordes of agricultural laborers and industrial workers in the cities were still excluded from the suffrage. The proportion of voters was increased from about 1 out of every 100 of the inhabitants to 1 out of 32. In

addition, the bill provided for some sweeping reforms in representation. Villages with a population of less than 2000 were deprived of their right to elect representatives to the House of Commons, while towns of slightly larger size had their representation cut in half. The seats in the Commons thus set free were distributed among the great industrial cities of the north.

The Reform Act of 1832 definitely established the supremacy of the middle class. In the elections which followed soon afterward, the Whigs, who now began to call themselves Liberals, captured a *Results of* majority of seats in the House of Commons. The Tories, hence- *the Reform Act* forth more commonly known as Conservatives, also began to bid *of 1832* for capitalist support. The result was a wave of parliamentary en- actments distinctly favorable to bourgeois interests. One provided for a more liberal franchise in local elections so as to enable the middle class to gain control of the borough governments. A second appropriated money to private societies for the maintenance of schools, to the end that the sons of the poor might be trained in the virtues of diligence. Another, the celebrated Poor Law of 1834, abolished outdoor relief, except for the sick and the aged, and provided that all able-bodied paupers should be compelled to earn their keep in workhouses. This law was based upon the theory that poverty is a man's own fault, and that consequently the poor should be forced to work as a punishment for their shiftlessness. The crowning achievement of all in this period of bourgeois legislation was the repeal of the Corn Laws in 1846. The Corn Laws were a form of protective tariff for the benefit of the landowning class. As revised in 1822, they provided that no foreign grain might be im- ported unless the price of British wheat was at least 70s. per quarter (about $2.19 per bushel). If the price rose above that figure, wheat from foreign countries was allowed to be admitted under a heavy duty. The effect was to give a rich bounty to the British landlords and at the same time to keep the price of bread exceedingly high. For more than twenty years industrial capitalists had clamored for repeal of these tariffs, on the double ground that they necessitated the payment of higher wages and limited the sale of British manu- factures in foreign markets. It was not, however, until 1846 that their efforts were successful. The repeal of the Corn Laws started Britain on the road to her free-trade policy, which was continued in force until after World War I.

None of these results of middle-class supremacy conferred much immediate benefit upon the proletariat. Hours in the factories were still unconscionably long; and, despite the rapid expansion of in- *The Chartist* dustry, periods of hard times still punctuated the rising prosperity. *movement of* Moreover, Parliament was deaf to all of the pleas of the lower *1838–1848* classes for a share in the franchise. The great Liberal statesman, Lord John Russell, flatly declared that the reforms granted in 1832 were final. In the face of such resistance as this, many urban workers decided that the only hope of relief was to strive for a complete **681** democratization of the British government. Accordingly, they enlisted with great enthusiasm under the banner of Chartism, a movement organized in 1838 under the leadership of Feargus O'Connor and William Lovett. Chartism derived its name from its celebrated People's Charter, a program of six points. They included: (1) universal manhood suffrage; (2) equal electoral districts; (3) the secret ballot; (4) annual Parliaments; (5) abolition of property qualifications for members of the House of Commons; and (6) payment of members. Though some of the Chartists advocated violence, most of them confined their activities to mass demonstrations and to the drafting of petitions to be presented to Parliament. In 1848, under the stimulus of the February Revolution in France, the leaders prepared for a giant effort. A procession of 500,000 workers was to march to the Houses of Parliament for the purpose of presenting a monster petition and overawing the members into granting reforms. The ruling classes were badly frightened. The pugnacious old Duke of

The Chartist Procession in London, April 10, 1848.

Wellington was again summoned to command the troops. In addition to the regular army, he was provided with a special force of 170,000 constables—one of whom was Napoleon's slippery nephew, soon to become emperor of France. But on the day scheduled for the demonstration (April 10, 1848) there was a heavy downpour of rain. Instead of the 500,000 workers who were to march in the parade, only a tenth of that number appeared. When the petition was presented to Parliament, it was found to contain less than half of the vaunted 6,000,000 signatures, including such palpably fictitious ones as "Wellington," "the Queen," and "the Prime Minister."

Though Chartism ended in failure, the spirit it represented lived on; and it is significant that all of the six points, with the single exception of the demand for annual Parliaments, have since been incorporated in the British constitution. In the years following the fiasco of 1848 the forces of democracy gradually recouped their strength and succeeded under the guidance of more practical leaders in achieving considerable progress. In 1858 they wrung from the Conservative government of Lord Derby the abolition of property

The Reform Acts of 1867 and 1884

qualifications for members of the House of Commons. By 1866 the democratic movement had gained such headway that the leaders of both parties were ready to compete with each other for popular support. The result was the Reform Act of 1867, maneuvered through Parliament by the Conservative Disraeli when the old generation of Liberals refused to go along with Gladstone in enacting the more moderate bill of the preceding year. The Reform Act of 1867 conferred the franchise upon all men in the towns and cities who occupied separate dwellings regardless of their value and also upon all who occupied tenements with an annual rental of at least £10. Since none but the poorest of the industrial workers were unable to fulfill these conditions, the bulk of the proletariat automatically became entitled to vote. In 1884 the Liberals had a turn at extending the franchise. The Reform Act of that year, the third in the great series of electoral reform measures, was sponsored by Gladstone. Its main provision was to extend the requirements hitherto adopted for the cities and towns to the counties. The result was to enfranchise nearly all of the agricultural laborers.

Democratization of the British electoral system did not reach a stage approaching completion until 1918. True, during the nineteenth century each of the three chief classes of citizens had been granted the suffrage—the middle class by the Act of 1832, the industrial workers by the Act of 1867, and the agricultural laborers by the Act of 1884. Yet Great Britain did not have universal manhood suffrage. After the outbreak of World War I there were still some 2,000,000 adult males who, for one reason or another, were unable to vote. Some were migratory laborers; others were too poor to meet even the minimum property requirements of the second and third Reform Acts. On the other hand, there were about 500,000 wealthy men who still possessed the privilege of plural voting; some were entitled to cast as many as twenty votes apiece, depending upon the number of constituencies in which they owned property. In 1918 an earnest attempt was finally made to remedy the more flagrant of these evils. A statute known as the Representation of the People Act was passed, virtually abolishing all of the old property requirements for voting. Henceforth Britishers were to cast their ballots, not as owners or occupiers of property of such and such value, but almost exclusively as *citizens*. The only exception to this rule was the privilege of a second vote accorded to university graduates and to anyone occupying premises for business purposes in a district other than that of his residence. Finally, it should be noted that the Act of 1918 enfranchised all women, thirty years of age and over, who were occupants of property or wives of occupants. Not for another decade was the age limit reduced to twenty-one years, the same as that for men. But even before the addition of this so-called "flapper vote," nearly 40 per cent of the total inhabitants of Great Britain were entitled to the suffrage in

The Representation of the People Act of 1918

*The British
cabinet system*

*The early evo-
lution of the
cabinet system*

684

national elections, as compared with about 3 per cent in 1832.

The second of the chief factors in the evolution of democracy in Great Britain has been the development of the cabinet system. Without the growth of this system Britain might well have remained simply a limited monarchy. It must be understood that the cabinet is not merely a council of ministers but is the supreme organ of the government. It is a committee of Parliament, responsible to the House of Commons, which exercises in the name of the king the supreme legislative and executive authority. Not only does it decide all questions of general policy, but it originates nearly all legislation; and, as long as it remains in office, it determines what bills shall be passed. If it is defeated in the House of Commons on a fundamental issue, it must either resign forthwith or "go to the country"—that is, dissolve Parliament and order a new election to test the opinion of the voters. In other words, the cabinet has full responsibility for the management of public affairs, subject only to the will of the people and to that of their representatives in the House of Commons. When Englishmen speak of "His Majesty's Government," it is the cabinet they have in mind. When the party in power loses an election and thereby control of the House of Commons, the leader of the opposition party immediately forms a new cabinet. While awaiting his turn to become Prime Minister he receives a salary as leader of His Majesty's Loyal Opposition.

As almost everyone knows, the cabinet system was the product of a slow evolution of precedent. No statute or great charter brought it into being, and to this day it rests solely upon custom. Its history goes back no farther than the Glorious Revolution. True, there was a so-called cabinet during the reign of Charles II, but it was no more than a council of advisers. Not until after the supremacy of the king was superseded by the supremacy of Parliament was the principle established that the chief ministers of the crown should be responsible to Parliament. Upon coming to the throne in 1689, William and Mary acceded to the demand that their choice of advisers should be satisfactory to the legislature. For a time they selected their ministers from both of the major parties, but as the need for harmonious relations with Parliament grew more urgent, they gradually restricted their choice to the party which held the majority. In this way the precedent was set that all of the chief ministers should possess the confidence of the dominant group in Parliament. But the cabinet was not yet a very powerful body. It did not become so until the reign of George I (1714–1727). George was a dull-witted prince from the German state of Hanover. Since he could neither speak nor understand the English language, he entrusted the whole work of governing to his ministers. He stayed away from meetings of the cabinet entirely and allowed that body to pass under the direction of Sir Robert Walpole. Though he persistently disclaimed the title, Walpole was the first Prime Minister in the modern sense. He was the first to perform the double function of head of the cabinet and leader of the majority party in the House of Commons. He established his headquarters at No. 10 Downing Street, which remains to this day the official residence of British prime ministers. When in 1742 he suffered defeat in the House of Commons, he resigned immediately, notwithstanding the fact that he still possessed the full confidence of the king.

Such was the early evolution of the cabinet system. Though most of the precedents upon which it rests had already been set by the middle of the eighteenth century, it still had a rocky road to travel. Some members of Parliament disliked the system, since it appeared to involve a partial surrender of Parliamentary supremacy. During the turbulent reign of George III there was an attempt to do away with cabinet government and return to the days when ministers were responsible to the king. Though George's intentions were generally good, his intellect was not vigorous, and he failed to understand that the era of royal sovereignty was over. Neither, for that matter, did many of his subjects understand the emergence of a system under which the monarch would do nothing but reign, while his ministers would govern the country as leaders of the party that held the majority of seats in the House of Commons. Not until about the middle of the nineteenth century was the cabinet system universally accepted or fully comprehended as an integral part of the British constitution. Its operation was first clearly described by Walter Bagehot in his *English Constitution,* published in 1867. In more recent years a number of new precedents have been added, the most important of them being that when the cabinet is defeated in the House of Commons, the Prime Minister and his colleagues shall have the option of resigning immediately or of dissolving Parliament and appealing to the country in a great national referendum.

The later evolution of the cabinet system

Scarcely less important in the evolution of political democracy in Great Britain has been the emergence of the House of Commons as the more powerful branch of Parliament. Down to the eighteenth century the House of Lords, composed of hereditary peers and the princes of the church, enjoyed much greater dignity and influence. The first step toward the supremacy of the representative chamber was the establishment of the principle, during Walpole's ministry, that the cabinet should be responsible exclusively to the Commons. In the early nineteenth century the precedent became fixed that the lower house should have final authority over matters of finance. But still the Lords had enormous power. They had a veto over general legislation, which was limited only by the fear of public resentment and by the authority of the Prime Minister in an emergency to threaten the creation of new peers.[2] Furthermore, since

The emergence of the House of Commons as the more powerful branch of Parliament

[2] In Britain the king has the authority to elevate an unlimited number of men to the peerage. But since the king acts only upon the advice of the Prime

the upper chamber was invariably a Tory stronghold, the favorite schemes of Liberal cabinets were often balked. Matters reached a crisis in 1909 when the Lords threw out the budget prepared by David Lloyd George, Chancellor of the Exchequer, and backed by the Asquith cabinet. The Prime Minister dissolved Parliament and appealed to the voters. Though his party won but a modest victory, he was convinced that the nation was on his side and began preparation of a bill to clip the wings of the House of Lords. The measure, known as the Parliament Act of 1911, was finally passed after a threat to swamp the upper house with a majority of Liberal peers. The Parliament Act provided that money bills should become laws one month after they had been passed by the House of Commons, whether the Lords approved them or not; in the case of other legislation the House of Lords was given only a suspensive veto: if ordinary bills were passed by the Commons in three consecutive sessions, they became laws at the end of two years, despite the opposition of the upper house. It is therefore accurate to say that the popularly elected branch of Parliament was henceforth, for all practical purposes, the real legislative body in Great Britain.[3]

2. Democracy and Nationalism in France

The insignificant progress of democracy in France before 1848

Following the abortive attempt to establish a regime of equality during the second stage of the great Revolution, France made little progress toward democratic government until 1875. True, the government of Louis Philippe, set up after the July Revolution of 1830, was a considerable improvement over that of his predecessor, Charles X, but it was still far from representing the rule of the masses. Louis Philippe took his cue from the bourgeoisie and systematically ignored the lower classes. Qualifications for the suffrage were indeed reduced, but still only 200,000 Frenchmen were entitled to vote. When leaders of the masses appealed to the Premier, Guizot, for a liberalization of the franchise, he cynically replied, "Get rich." By 1848 the king and his ministers had so aroused the disgust of a large number of their subjects that the latter were ready to incur the risks of a new revolution to overthrow the monarchy.

Causes of the Revolution of 1848

The French revolution of 1848 is known as the February Revolution. Its causes were several. One was the demand of all but a small minority of the people for more democracy. Another was disgust with the corruption of Louis Philippe and his intimate circle; convinced, like Louis XV in an earlier day, that soon would come the deluge, they strove to enrich themselves as fast as possible at public expense. A third cause was discontent of Catholics with the ap-

Minister, it is this official who has the actual power to create new members of the House of Lords. If necessary, he could use this power to pack the upper house with his own followers.

[3] See p. 961 for later revision of the Parliament Act.

parent anti-clerical bias of the Citizen King. He had appointed as his chief minister the Protestant Guizot and had allowed him to discriminate against Catholic schools. A fourth cause was the spread of socialism through the ranks of the industrial proletariat. During the lean months of the depression which began in 1847, many of the workers had been converted to the socialism of Louis Blanc, with its scheme for national workshops to give employment and prosperity to all. But the February Revolution was also a product of nationalism, and in the end this factor was destined to dwarf all the others. As "king of the bourgeoisie" Louis Philippe had placed business above everything else. His chief capitalist supporters were determined that France should not become involved in any war lest their trade and investments be imperiled. Consequently they refused to yield to the clamor for intervention on behalf of the Poles against Russia or of the Italians against Austria. This angered patriotic Frenchmen who thirsted for national glory and for the restoration of France to a position of leadership among the powers of Europe.

By 1847 the government of Louis Philippe had alienated the sympathies of nearly all but a wealthy minority of its subjects. However, the most defiant opposition came from patriotic republicans and monarchists and from the socialists. In 1847 these groups organized a campaign of monster demonstrations and political banquets designed to impress upon the king the need for reform. When the government took alarm and prohibited a demonstration scheduled for February 22, 1848, barricades were thrown up in the streets, and two days later Louis Philippe was forced to abdicate. A provisional government of republicans and socialists took over control of the state, and in April elections were held for a Constituent Assembly. The results of the voting were a disappointment to the socialists, for the reactionaries and middle-class parties had combined to protect the interests of private property. Angry and disillusioned, the radical workers of Paris again tore up the pavements. For three terrible June days there was bloody fighting in the slums of the capital. The insurrection was finally crushed, its leaders were shot, and 4000 of their followers were deported to the colonies. The way was now cleared for the bourgeois majority in the Constituent Assembly to complete a constitution for the Second Republic. The document as it finally emerged was copied in part from that of the United States. It contained a bill of rights and provided for universal manhood suffrage and for the separation of powers. There was to be a President elected by the people for a four-year term, and the people were also to choose a single-chambered Legislative Assembly. Having finished their work, the makers of the constitution set December 10, 1848, as the date for the election of the first President.

Four candidates competed in this election: a moderate republican, a socialist, a Catholic, and a man who had something for everybody

The overthrow of Louis Philippe

*Louis Napoleon
Bonaparte*

—Louis Napoleon Bonaparte. More than 7,000,000 votes were cast; and out of this total the moderate republican received about 1,500,-000, the socialist 370,000, the Catholic 17,000, while the remainder—nearly 5,500,000—went to Louis Napoleon. Who was this man, who enjoyed such amazing popularity that he could poll more than twice as many votes as the other three candidates combined? Louis Napoleon Bonaparte (1808–1873) was the nephew of Napoleon I, his father being Louis Bonaparte, who for a brief period was king of Holland. After his uncle's downfall, Louis Napoleon went into exile, spending most of his time in Germany and in Switzerland. Returning to France after the July Revolution of 1830, he was imprisoned a few years later for attempting to provoke an uprising at Boulogne. But in 1846 he escaped to England, where he was liberally supplied with funds by both British and French reactionaries. By the summer of 1848 the situation in France was such that he knew it was safe to return. In fact, he was welcomed with open arms by men of all classes. Conservatives were looking for a savior to protect their property against the onslaughts of the radicals. Proletarians were beguiled by his glittering schemes for prosperity in his book, *The Extinction of Pauperism,* and by the fact that he had corresponded with Louis Blanc and with Pierre Proudhon, the anarchist. In between these two classes was a great multitude of patriots and hero-worshipers to whom the very name Napoleon was a matchless symbol of glory and greatness. And it was chiefly to this multitude that the nephew of the Corsican owed his astounding triumph. As one old peasant expressed it: "How could I help voting for this gentleman—I whose nose was frozen at Moscow?"

*Louis Napoleon
makes himself
dictator and
then emperor*

With grandiose dreams of emulating his uncle, Louis Napoleon was not long content to be merely *President* of France. Almost from the first he used his position to pave the way for a higher calling. He enlisted the support of the Catholics by permitting them to regain control over the schools and by sending an expedition to Rome to restore the Pope to his temporal power in central Italy. He threw sops to the workers and to the bourgeoisie in the form of old-age insurance and laws for the encouragement of business. In 1851 his first great opportunity came to strike a blow at the republic. The Assembly, dominated by the bourgeoisie, had passed a law restricting the suffrage by approximately one-third. Louis Napoleon perceived his chance to pose as the defender of the rights of the masses. When the legislators refused to comply with his order to restore universal suffrage, he dissolved the Assembly, proclaimed a temporary dictatorship, and invited the people to grant him the power to draw up a new constitution. In the plebiscite held on December 21, 1851, he was authorized by an overwhelming majority (7,500,-000 to 640,000) to proceed as he liked. The new constitution, which he put into effect in January, 1852, made the President an actual dictator. His term of office was lengthened to ten years, and he was

given the exclusive power to initiate legislation and to make war
and peace. While the legislative branch was preserved in name, it
could not initiate or amend bills or even change any specific provisions in the budget. But still the little Caesar was not satisfied; he
would be content with nothing less than the imperial dignity which
had graced the shoulders of his famous uncle. After exactly one year
Louis Napoleon Bonaparte ordered another plebiscite and, with the
approval of over 95 per cent of the voters, assumed the title of
Napoleon III, Emperor of the French. The gullible masses would
soon be able to see where their worship of a magic name and a
tawdry legend would lead them.

The Second Empire in France endured from December, 1852, to
September, 1870. Its creator and preserver ruled by methods not
dissimilar to those of other Caesars both before and since. He *The regime of*
stimulated an imposing prosperity by draining swamps, building *Napoleon III*

Napoleon III, Emperor of the
French, 1852–1870.

roads, improving harbors, subsidizing railroads, and constructing a
magnificent system of boulevards in Paris. He cultivated the favor
of the lower classes by mouthing Revolutionary phrases and by
schemes of pseudosocialism, with government aid for consumers'
co-operatives and for a variety of forms of workers' insurance. At
the same time he strove to make sure that radicals would not become troublesome. He subjected the press to a strict surveillance and
controlled elections by paying the expenses of *official* candidates
and by requiring all others to take an oath of fidelity to the emperor. Nor did he neglect the opportunities to add luster to his regime by an aggressive foreign policy. He annexed Algeria in
northern Africa and established a protectorate over Indo-China. In
1854 he plunged into the Crimean War with Russia under the pretext of protecting Catholic monks in Turkey. Since Napoleon had
the aid of Great Britain and Turkey and also for a time of Sardinia, **689**

he managed to emerge from this war on the victorious side. Though in two years of fighting he had poured out the blood of 75,000 of his soldiers, he could still rejoice in the plaudits of the mob and pose as the arbiter of the destinies of Europe.

The decline and fall of the Second Empire

By 1860 the glamour of Napoleon's reputation had begun to wear thin. The first great blow to his prestige was a result of the sordid outcome of his Italian adventure. In 1858 he had formed an alliance with the Italian nationalists to help them expel the Austrians; but as soon as he saw that his erstwhile friends were bent upon consolidating the whole Italian peninsula into a nation-state and upon destroying the temporal sovereignty of the Pope, he promptly deserted them. By so doing, he antagonized thousands of his more liberal followers, who reproached him with abandoning a gallant people to Austrian oppression. In 1862 Napoleon intervened in Mexico. He sent an army into that country to establish an empire and then offered the throne to the Archduke Maximilian of Austria. But at the conclusion of the American Civil War the government of the United States compelled the withdrawal of the French troops, and soon afterward Maximilian was captured and shot by the Mexicans. As a consequence of this tragic and brutal adventure, opposition to Napoleon's rule markedly increased. After the elections of 1869 he decided that it would be expedient to make some concessions. He agreed that hereafter his ministers should be responsible to the legislature, that the public sale of newspapers should be allowed, and that his policy of subsidizing official candidates in the elections should be abandoned. But in 1870 he resolved to gamble once more upon retrieving his fortunes by a bold stroke of foreign policy. Shortly before this the government had been overturned in Spain, and the revolutionists had offered the crown to Prince Leopold of Hohenzollern, a cousin of the king of Prussia. Pretending to see in this a threat to the security of France, Napoleon informed the Prussian king that he would consider the accession of a Hohenzollern prince to the throne of Spain a cause for war. The sensible decision of Prince Leopold to refuse the crown should have satisfied everybody, but Napoleon was determined to exalt his own prestige by humiliating Prussia in some drastic fashion. He therefore demanded a pledge from King William I that the latter would *never* allow any member of his family to become a candidate for the Spanish throne. The story of how William's refusal was distorted by Bismarck so as to precipitate a war between Prussia and France will be told in another connection. Suffice it to say here that France was badly defeated in a struggle which lasted only a few weeks. After the battle of Sedan (September 2, 1870) Napoleon himself was taken prisoner, and two days later his government was overthrown by a group of republicans in Paris.

Following the collapse of Napoleon's empire a provisional government was organized to rule the country until a new constitution could be drafted. Elections were held in February 1871 for a national constituent assembly, resulting in the choice of some 500 monarchists and only about 200 republicans. The explanation lies in the fact that during the electoral campaign the republicans had urged a renewal of the war, while the monarchists took the attitude that France was already defeated, and that she might as well negotiate with her conquerors for the best terms she could get. It was not that the French people overwhelmingly preferred a monarchy, but rather that they longed for peace. Fortunately the monarchists were hopelessly divided. No sooner had the National Assembly met than they split into three irreconcilable factions. Least numerous were the Imperialists, the dejected followers of Napoleon III, who clung to a waning hope that his government might be restored. Bitterly opposed to them and to each other were the Legitimists and the Orleanists. The former demanded that the crown should be given to the grandson of Charles X, while the latter supported the claims of the grandson of Louis Philippe. Angry discord among the monarchists postponed for almost four years a definite decision as to the permanent form the French government should take. Finally, rather than allow the Legitimists to triumph, the Orleanists cast in their lot with the republicans; and in January 1875 the National Assembly adopted the first of a series of constitutional laws recognizing the government as republican in form. This was the real beginning of the Third Republic in France.

The constitution of the Third Republic consisted of three organic laws adopted by the National Assembly in 1875. Though amendments and precedents effected some changes, its essential form continued until the formal dissolution of the Third Republic on July 9, 1940. The government established by this constitution was about as democratic as any in the world. There was a Parliament, with a lower house elected by universal manhood suffrage, and a President chosen by Parliament. The cardinal feature, however, was the cabinet system, copied in part from Great Britain. The most important powers of the government were exercised by a ministry responsible to Parliament. The President was about the nearest approach to a nonentity that it would be possible to find among heads of states. While an aggressive politician in the office could exert much influence, particularly in the conduct of foreign relations, in general the President of France was little more than a titular ruler. His every official act had to be countersigned—which is to say, approved—by a member of the ministry. On the other hand, there were several important differences between the cabinet system in France and that in Great Britain. While in Britain the cabinet includes only the principal ministers and certain others whom the Prime Minister may designate, in France the ministry and the cabinet were one and the same. The French cabinet was responsible not only to the lower house or Chamber of Deputies but also to the

Senate, which was elected indirectly by the people; the cabinet in Great Britain is responsible exclusively to the House of Commons. The most important difference consists in the fact that the French Premier [4] had no effective authority to dissolve Parliament. It is true that such authority was originally granted by the written constitution, but it was later nullified by precedent. This meant that members of Parliament could overturn cabinets at will, with no risk of being forced to stand for re-election. If defeated on the floor of either house, the Premier and his colleagues had no alternative but to resign. With the possible exception of the multiplicity of parties, nothing contributed so much to the instability of the French system. Cabinets were sometimes unable to hold the support of a majority in Parliament for more than a few weeks or even a few days. Although this instability was often deplored, it was really the product of a natural reaction of the French people against previous dictatorial regimes.[5]

The Boulanger episode

Even after the adoption of a republican constitution in 1875, the victory of democracy in France was by no means complete. For some years the republic had to struggle with reactionary elements determined to restore some form of autocratic rule. Between 1887 and 1889 it was faced with a dangerous crisis in the Boulanger episode. Georges Boulanger was a general in the army and a former minister of war who developed Napoleonic ambitions. Appealing to the injured pride of patriotic Frenchmen, he won enthusiastic applause by clamoring for a war of revenge against Germany. By harping on scandals recently exposed in the republican regime, he endeared himself to the monarchists and also to conservative Catholics, who hated the republic for its anti-clerical program. Soon he was the most popular man in France. Everywhere mobs clamored for their "brave general" under the illusion that a new Bonaparte had risen in their midst. Flattered and emboldened by this adulation, Boulanger determined upon a national plebiscite as more tangible proof of the people's support. He stood for election to the Chamber of Deputies in every available district and won by substantial margins ten times in six months. In January 1889 he crowned his exploits by rolling up a triumphant majority in radical Paris. It seemed now that nothing could stop him from riding into power as a military dictator. But fortunately for the republic, this god who had been worshiped by the rabble and by the ladies in the salons turned out to have feet of clay. When the government finally mustered enough courage to order his arrest on charges of conspiracy, he fled ingloriously to Belgium. Two years later he blew out his brains on the grave of his mistress.

---

[4] The official title of the French Premier was not Prime Minister but President of the Council of Ministers.

[5] See p. 961 for restrictions on the power to overthrow cabinets in the Fourth Republic.

The ignominious collapse of the Boulangist movement did not end the attempts to discredit the republic. In the 1890's the reactionaries adopted anti-Semitism as a spearhead for the advancement of their aims. The fact that certain Jewish bankers had recently been involved in scandalous dealings with politicians lent color to the monarchist charge that the government was shot through with corruption and that money-grabbing Jews were largely to blame. Catholics were persuaded to believe that Jewish politicians had dictated the anti-clerical legislation of the republican regime. With such charges befouling the air, it is not strange that anti-Semitism should have flared into a violent outbreak. In 1894 a Jewish captain of artillery, Alfred Dreyfus, was accused by a clique of monarchist officers of selling military secrets to Germany. Tried by court-martial, he was convicted and sentenced for life to Devil's Island. At first the verdict was accepted as the merited punishment of a traitor; but in 1897 Colonel Picquart, a new head of the Intelligence Division, announced his conclusion that the documents upon which Dreyfus had been convicted were forgeries. A movement for a new trial was launched, which the War Department promptly refused. Soon the whole nation was divided into friends and opponents of the luckless captain. On the side of Dreyfus were the radical republicans, the socialists, people of liberal and humanitarian sympathies, and such prominent literary figures as Émile Zola and Anatole France. The anti-Dreyfusards included the monarchists, the clericals, the Jew-baiters, the militarists, and a considerable number of conservative workingmen and sincere but mistaken patriots. Dreyfus was finally set free by executive order in 1899, and six years later he was cleared of all guilt by the Supreme Court and restored to the army. He was immediately promoted to the rank of major and decorated with the emblem of the Legion of Honor. The outcome of the Dreyfus affair effectively squelched the monarchist movement in France. Since then its adherents have been gradually reduced to political insignificance—a mere "handful of old nuts rattling in a bag."

As already intimated, the Dreyfus affair was an element in a broader struggle over the issue of church and state. From the beginning of its history the Third Republic had been tinctured with anti-clericalism. Its founders were not necessarily atheists, but they did believe that a powerful church with ambitions to extend its political and social influence was a threat to republican government. The aims of the anti-clericals were to curb this influence, to reduce the economic privileges of the Catholic church, and to break the stranglehold which the clergy had gained upon education. The roots of anti-clericalism extended in several directions. In part, it was a result of the Industrial Revolution, which fostered materialistic interests and intensified the struggle between the bourgeoisie and the Old Regime, with which the church was usually identified. It was also a product in some measure of the growth of science and of skeptical and liberal philosophies, which were often employed as primary weapons in fighting religious conservatism. Probably the main cause of its growth was the rise of a militant nationalism. The Catholic church was not only committed to an internationalist outlook, but Popes as late as the 1860's were still asserting their rights to temporal power and pouring out their anathemas upon rulers who would establish omnipotent states. Wherever nationalism gathered powerful momentum, clericalism was almost certain to be regarded as a primary enemy.

The results of anti-clericalism in France

Anti-clericalism in France reached the peak of its fury between 1875 and 1914. The great majority of the leaders of the Third Republic were hostile to the church; and naturally so, for the Catholic hierarchy was aiding the monarchists at every turn. Clericals conspired with monarchists in backing Boulanger and even more actively with militarists and anti-Semites in attempting to discredit the republic during the Dreyfus affair. But in the end they over-reached themselves. The outcome of the Dreyfus affair not only sounded the knell of monarchism but led to a furious attack upon the church. In 1901 the government passed the Associations Act, prohibiting the existence of any religious order in France not authorized by the state. This was followed in 1904 by an act forbidding all members of religious orders to teach in either public or private schools. Finally, in 1905, the Separation Law was passed, which, as its name indicates, dissolved the union of church and state. For the first time since 1801 the adherents of all creeds were placed on an equal basis. No longer were the Catholic clergy to receive their salaries from the public purse. Although some of these measures have been modified in recent years, clericalism remains in the minds of most Frenchmen under a heavy cloud of suspicion.

3. Democracy and Nationalism in Central Europe

The revolution of 1848 in Austria and Hungary

The February Revolution in France touched off a series of revolts in central Europe, beginning with an uprising in Austria on March 13. Mobs of students and workingmen rioted in Vienna and forced the resignation of that last great pillar of the Old Regime, Prince Metternich. Frightened by the refusal of his troops to fire upon the rebels, the emperor promised a constitution for Germanic Austria, excluding Hungary and the Italian possessions. The constitution as finally adopted provided for a cabinet responsible to Parliament and for a liberal franchise, and the assembly which drew it up also abolished the remaining feudal obligations of the peasants. Almost immediately the Hungarians took advantage of the turmoil in Vienna to establish a liberal government, and in April 1849, under the leadership of Louis Kossuth, they proclaimed the independence

694

of the Hungarian Republic. But neither of these revolutions was permanently successful, for the reason that they soon became entangled in the discords of nationalism. The Hungarian liberals were no more willing than the Austrians to grant the privileges to subject nationalities that they claimed for themselves. As a consequence, the Hapsburgs were able to stir up ill feeling among the Slavs and to use them to good advantage in curbing the ambitions of the dominant nationalities. By the summer of 1849 the emperor had succeeded in overthrowing the Hungarian Republic and in revoking the Austrian constitution. All that was saved from the wreckage was the exemption of the peasants from feudal obligations to the nobles. The discontent, however, continued until a compromise known as the *Ausgleich* was finally worked out between the Austrians and the Hungarians in 1867. The *Ausgleich* established a dual monarchy, with the head of the House of Hapsburg serving as both emperor of Austria and king of Hungary. Each of the two parts of the empire was made practically autonomous, with its own cabinet and parliament. Three joint ministers, of war, finance, and foreign affairs, looked after the interests of the state as a whole in their respective spheres. Enabling both the Magyars in Hungary and the Germans in Austria to rule as master races, this arrangement survived until the Dual Empire was broken into fragments in 1918.

Within a week after the revolutionary movement of 1848 began in Vienna, it spread to the states of Germany. Since 1815 the German states together with Austria had constituted the thirty-eight members of the Germanic Confederation. The several princes guarded their semi-independence jealously, but among many of the people there was a growing sentiment in favor of union into a nation-state. Businessmen urged it under the conviction that trade would flourish. Nationalists demanded it on the basis of cultural and racial unity. As a consequence, the revolution of 1848 in Germany had the dual character of a crusade for more liberal government and a movement for unification. Both objectives seemed to hold promise of success at first. During the month of March, 1848, concessions were extorted from nearly every one of the German rulers—in some cases promises of constitutions; in others, liberal ministries or freedom of speech and of press. In May of the same year liberals and nationalists convoked a great national convention at Frankfurt to draft a constitution for a united Germany. This was the celebrated Frankfurt Assembly, composed of high-minded delegates from all the states of the Confederation. The Assembly succeeded in adopting a bill of rights but soon fell into a hopeless tangle over other constitutional issues. When the majority of the delegates agreed that the new Germany should be a limited monarchy, the republicans bolted. There was also heated discussion over the question whether Austria should be included, and over the problem of who should be monarch. When it was decided that only the *German* provinces of Austria should be admitted, the Austrian government commanded

The revolutionary movement in Germany

its delegates to come home. Still hopeful of effecting a union on a less ambitious scale, the Assembly offered the crown to King Frederick William IV of Prussia. But that weak-willed monarch refused to accept for fear of antagonizing Austria and also because he was reluctant to have anything to do with a revolutionary body. The Frankfurt Assembly soon afterward dispersed in disgust, with absolutely nothing to show for its efforts. Most of the reforms which had been secured outside of the Assembly likewise gradually melted away, and thousands of the revolutionaries emigrated from the country and took refuge in the United States.

Bismarck

The unification of Germany was now left to be achieved by the hard realism of Bismarck. Otto von Bismarck (1815–1898) was born into the class of Junkers, or landed aristocrats, who for centuries had furnished the Prussian state with the bulk of its bureaucrats and high army officers. After a session at the Universities of Göttingen and Berlin as an indifferent student but a capable duelist and rake, he entered the government service, only to be dismissed a short time later for his irregular and dissipated habits. For a while his intractable nature found vent in liberalism, but his marriage to the pious daughter of a neighboring squire changed all of that. From a morose and cynical rebel he was converted into a stalwart defender of religion and a roaring reactionary in politics. During the revolutionary movement of 1848 he served in the Prussian Parliament as a stanch upholder of divine-right monarchy. He was one of a group of intransigent aristocrats who urged the Prussian king not to accept a "crown of shame" from the Frankfurt Assembly. Later Bismarck was instrumental in organizing the Conservative party, dedicated to protecting the interests of the Junker class, the established church, and the army, and to the building of a powerful Prussia as the nucleus of a German nation. In 1862 he was summoned by King William I to become Minister-President of his beloved Prussia.

Bismarck's preliminary steps in consolidating German unity

In consolidating the German states into a united nation, Bismarck followed a succession of steps of almost diabolical cleverness. First he plotted to eliminate Austria from her commanding position in the Germanic Confederation. As a preliminary means to this end he entered into a dispute with Denmark over possession of Schleswig and Holstein. Inhabited largely by Germans, these two provinces had an anomalous status. Since 1815 Holstein had been included in the Germanic Confederation, but both were subject to the personal overlordship of the king of Denmark. When in 1864 a Danish king attempted to annex them, Bismarck invited Austria to participate in a war against Denmark. A brief struggle followed, at the end of which the Danish ruler was compelled to renounce all his claims to Schleswig and Holstein in favor of Austria and Prussia. Then the very sequel occurred for which Bismarck ardently hoped: a quarrel between the victors over division of the spoils. The upshot was that in 1866 Prussia and Austria plunged into war. Since Bismarck knew that the Hapsburgs would have the help of the south German states, he formed an alliance with Italy, promising to reward her, in the event of victory, with the cession of Venetia. The conflict which followed, known as the Seven Weeks' War, ended in an easy triumph for Prussia. Austria was forced to give up her claims to Schleswig and Holstein, to surrender Venetia to Italy, and to acquiesce in the dissolution of the Germanic Confederation. Immediately following the war Bismarck proceeded to unite all of the German states north of the Main River into the North German Confederation. The constitution of this union, which the great Minister-President boasted he wrote in a single night, provided that the king of Prussia should be the hereditary President of the Confederation, and that there should be an upper house representing the governments of the several states and a lower house elected by universal manhood suffrage.

The final step in the completion of German unity was the Franco-Prussian War. We have learned of the part played by Napoleon III in provoking a crisis with Prussia over the question of succession to the Spanish throne. But the attitude of Bismarck was just as provocative. He knew that a war with France would be the best thing possible to kindle a *German* nationalism in Bavaria and Württemberg and in the remaining states south of the Main. Consequently when he was informed by King William I at Ems that the demand of the French for perpetual exclusion of the Hohenzollern family from the Spanish throne had been refused, he decided that the time for action had come. He determined to release the telegram received from Ems in such a form as to make it appear that King William had insulted the French ambassador. His own prediction that this would have the effect of "a red rag upon the Gallic bull" was speedily borne out. When the garbled report of what happened at Ems was received in France, the whole nation was immediately in an uproar. On July 15, 1870, when Napoleon's ministers requested the legislative body to approve a declaration of war, there were only ten votes in the negative. No sooner had the struggle begun than the south German states rallied to the side of Prussia in the belief that she was the victim of aggression. Such was the beginning of a war which was destined to have tremendous effects upon the subsequent history of Europe. From the start the Prussians had the advantage. The disciplined efficiency of their military machine stood out in bold contrast to the clumsy ineptitude of the French. Supplies for Napoleon's troops were woefully inadequate, and one of his generals was unable for a time to locate the army he was supposed to command. The result could have been foretold from the beginning. After the capture of Napoleon at Sedan in September, 1870, and the conquest of Paris four months later, the war was officially ended by the Treaty of Frankfurt. France sur-

The Franco-Prussian War

697

DEMOCRACY
AND
NATIONALISM,
1830–1914

The establish-
ment of the
German empire

rendered the major portions of Alsace and Lorraine and agreed to pay an indemnity of one billion dollars.

The Franco-Prussian War destroyed one empire and created another. We have seen that after Napoleon III was captured at Sedan, his government was overthrown in Paris and a provisional republic set up. Beyond the Rhine the great explosion of patriotic enthusiasm made it possible for Bismarck to absorb the south German states into the North German Confederation. Treaties were negotiated during the course of the war stipulating that all of Germany should be united into a Hohenzollern empire. These agreements were given formal effect by an impressive ceremony staged in the palace of

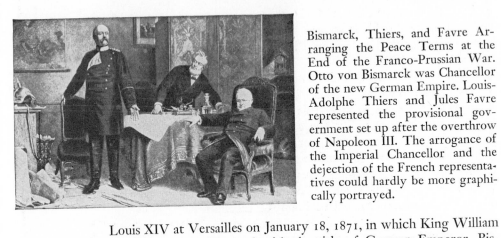

Bismarck, Thiers, and Favre Arranging the Peace Terms at the End of the Franco-Prussian War. Otto von Bismarck was Chancellor of the new German Empire. Louis-Adolphe Thiers and Jules Favre represented the provisional government set up after the overthrow of Napoleon III. The arrogance of the Imperial Chancellor and the dejection of the French representatives could hardly be more graphically portrayed.

Louis XIV at Versailles on January 18, 1871, in which King William I of Prussia was invested with the title of German Emperor. Bismarck, now raised to the dignity of prince, became the first Imperial Chancellor. With no more than the necessary changes, the constitution of the North German Confederation was accepted as the constitution of the new empire. The government thus created had only two features which could positively be considered democratic. First, there was universal manhood suffrage in national elections; and, second, there was a parliament with a lower house, or Reichstag, elected by popular vote. In other respects the system was well adapted to conservative rule. In place of the cabinet system, the Chancellor and the other ministers were responsible solely to the emperor. The emperor himself was no figurehead, but was vested with extensive authority over the army and navy, over foreign relations, and over the enactment and execution of the laws. Besides, he could declare war if the coasts or territory of the empire were attacked, and as king of Prussia he controlled one-third of the votes in the upper house, or Bundesrat, of the imperial parliament.

Conservative character of the German Empire

Limitations on autocracy

Yet the government of the German empire was not a complete autocracy. Although the Kaiser could influence the enactment of legislation, he had no veto power. All treaties he negotiated had to be approved by the Bundesrat, and he could get no money without

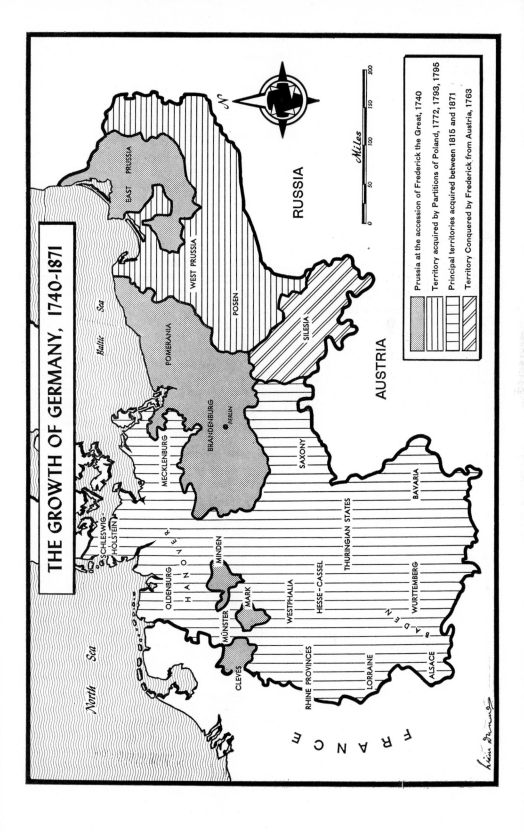

THE GROWTH OF GERMANY, 1740-1871

North Sea

Baltic Sea

RUSSIA

AUSTRIA

FRANCE

SCHLESWIG-HOLSTEIN

MECKLENBURG

POMERANIA

EAST PRUSSIA

WEST PRUSSIA

POSEN

SILESIA

BRANDENBURG

BERLIN

SAXONY

THURINGIAN STATES

BAVARIA

HANOVER

OLDENBURG

MINDEN

MÜNSTER

MARK

CLEVES

WESTPHALIA

HESSE-CASSEL

WURTEMBERG

BADEN

RHINE PROVINCES

LORRAINE

ALSACE

N

Miles

0 50 100 150 200

Prussia at the accession of Frederick the Great, 1740

Territory acquired by Partitions of Poland, 1772, 1793, 1795

Principal territories acquired between 1815 and 1871

Territory Conquered by Frederick from Austria, 1763

the consent of the Reichstag. Indeed, the latter body was far from being a mere debating society, as was so often alleged by Germany's enemies during World War I. On the contrary it had law-making powers virtually the equivalent of those of the Bundesrat, and it was strong enough to extort concessions from several Chancellors. In 1913 the Reichstag almost succeeded in establishing cabinet government. During a quarrel with Chancellor von Bethmann-Hollweg over army tyranny in Alsace, the members of the lower house passed a vote of "no confidence" in the government and demanded that the Chancellor resign. A resolution to withhold appropriations until Bethmann gave up his office failed of adoption by the barest margin.

Anticlerical-
ism in Germa-
ny: the Kultur-
kampf

Like the republic of France, the new German empire also had trouble with the church. The German anti-clerical movement in the nineteenth century was given the pretentious name of *Kulturkampf*, or "struggle for civilization," and it was initiated by Bismarck, with some help from intellectual liberals, in 1872. Bismarck's motives were almost exclusively nationalistic. He was neither a skeptic nor a materialist but a stanch Lutheran. Nevertheless, he perceived in certain Catholic activities a threat to the power and stability of the empire he had just created. He resented, first of all, the support which Catholic priests continued to give to the states'-rights movement in southern Germany and to the grievances of Alsatians and Poles. He was alarmed also by recent assertions of the authority of the Pope to intervene in secular matters and by the promulgation in 1870 of the dogma of papal infallibility. In addition, he was anxious to win the more ardent support of the bourgeois National Liberals in strengthening the foundations of the new empire. For these reasons he resolved to deal such a blow to Catholic influence in Germany that it would never again be a factor in national or local politics. His weapons were a series of laws and decrees issued between 1872 and 1875. First he induced the Reichstag to expel all the Jesuits from the country. Next he forced through the Prussian Landtag the so-called May Laws, which placed theological seminaries under state control and permitted the government to regulate the appointment of bishops and priests. No one was allowed to be appointed to any position in the church unless he was a German citizen and then only after a state examination. At the same time civil marriage was made compulsory, even though a religious ceremony had already been performed. In the enforcement of these measures, six of the ten Catholic bishops in Prussia were imprisoned, and hundreds of priests were driven from the country.

The failure
of the Kultur-
kampf

Although Bismarck won some of the chief battles of the *Kulturkampf*, he lost the war. The causes of his failure were several. First, he antagonized his progressive followers by refusing to consider their demands for ministerial responsibility. Second, the Catholic or Center party appealed so effectively on behalf of the persecuted

clergy and adopted so enlightened an economic program that it grew
into the largest political party in Germany. In the elections of
1874 it captured nearly a fourth of the seats in the Reichstag. Third,
Bismarck was alarmed by the growth of socialism, and he was
even more dismayed when the chief sponsors of this philosophy,
the Social Democrats, formed an alliance with the Centrists. At
their current rate of growth these two parties would soon have a
majority in the Reichstag. In the hope of forestalling such a result,
Bismarck gradually relaxed his persecution of the Catholics. Between 1878 and 1886 nearly all of the obnoxious legislation was
repealed, and the *Kulturkampf* passed into the limbo of statesmen's
blunders. The Catholic church was thus restored practically to its
former position in Germany.

Meanwhile events in Italy had been running a course almost
parallel to those which had led to the unification of Germany. Italy
before 1848, it should be remembered, was a patchwork of petty *The revolution-*
states. The most important of those possessing independence were *ary movement*
the Kingdom of Sardinia in the north, the Papal States in the central *of 1848 in Italy*

Giuseppe Mazzini (1805–1872).
Italian Idealist and Patriot, he
strove in vain for the unification of
his country as a republic.

region, and the Kingdom of the Two Sicilies in the south. The
former republics of Lombardy and Venetia were held by Austria,
while Hapsburg dependents ruled in Tuscany, Parma, and Modena.
As the revolutionary fervor of 1848 swept through the peninsula,
one ruler after another granted democratic reforms. Charles Albert
of Sardinia outdistanced all the others with his celebrated Fundamental Statute providing for civil liberties and a parliamentary form
of government. But it soon became evident that the Italians were
more interested in nationalism than in democracy. For some years
romantic patriots had been dreaming of the *Risorgimento*—the
resurrection of the Italian spirit—which would restore the nation
to the position of glorious leadership it had held in ancient times
and during the age of the Renaissance. To achieve this, it was uni- **701**

versally agreed that Italy must be welded into a single state. But as to the form which the new government should take, there was considerable difference of opinion. Young idealists followed the leadership of Giuseppe Mazzini (1805–1872), who labored with sincere devotion for the founding of a republic. Religious-minded patriots believed that the most practicable solution would be to federate the states of Italy under the presidency of the Pope. The majority of the more moderate nationalists advocated a constitutional monarchy built upon the foundations of the Kingdom of Sardinia. The aims of this third group were gradually crystallized under the leadership of a shrewd Sardinian nobleman, Count Camillo di Cavour (1810–1861). In 1850 he was appointed Minister of Commerce and Agriculture of his native state and in 1852 Prime Minister.

The movement to establish a nation-state in Italy

The campaign for unification of the Italian peninsula began with efforts to expel the Austrians. In 1848 revolts were organized in the territories under Hapsburg domination, and an army of liberation marched from Sardinia to aid the rebels; but the movement ended in failure. It was then that Cavour, as the new leader of the campaign turned to less heroic but more practical methods. In 1855, to attract the favorable attention of Great Britain and France, he entered the Crimean War on their side despite the fact that he had no quarrel with Russia. In 1858 he held a secret meeting with Napoleon III and prepared the stage for an Italian War of Liberation. Napoleon agreed to co-operate in driving the Austrians from Italy for the price of Savoy and Nice to be ceded by Sardinia to France. A war with Austria was duly provoked in 1859, and for a time all went well for the Franco-Italian allies. But after the conquest of Lombardy, Napoleon suddenly withdrew, fearful of ultimate defeat and afraid of antagonizing the Catholics in his own country by aiding an avowedly anti-clerical government. Thus deserted by her ally, Sardinia was unable to expel the Austrians from Venetia. Nevertheless, she did make some extensive gains; for she annexed Lombardy, while the duchies of Tuscany, Parma, and Modena and the northern portion of the Papal States voted in a burst of nationalist enthusiasm for union with her. Sardinia was now more than twice her original size and by far the most powerful state in Italy.

The completion of Italian unification

The second step in consolidating the unity of Italy was the conquest of the Kingdom of the Two Sicilies. This kingdom was ruled by a Bourbon, Francis II, who was thoroughly hated by his Italian subjects. In May 1860 a romantic free-lance adventurer by the name of Giuseppe Garibaldi set out with his famous regiment of 1000 "red shirts" to rescue his fellow Italians from oppression. Within three months he had conquered the island of Sicily and had then marched to the deliverance of Naples, where the people were already in revolt. By November the whole kingdom of Francis II had fallen to the gay buccaneer. Garibaldi at first apparently intended to convert the territory into an independent republic but was finally persuaded to surrender it to the Kingdom of Sardinia. With most of the peninsula now united under a single rule, Victor Emmanuel II, king of Sardinia, assumed the title of King of Italy (March 17, 1861). Venetia was still in the hands of the Austrians, but in 1866 they were forced by the Prussians to cede it to Italy as a reward for her part in the Seven Weeks' War. All that remained to complete the unification of Italy was the annexation of Rome. The Eternal City had resisted conquest thus far largely because of the military protection accorded to the Pope by Napoleon III. But in 1870 the outbreak of the Franco-Prussian War compelled Napoleon to withdraw his troops. The opportunity was too good to be overlooked. In September, 1870, Italian soldiers occupied Rome, and in July of the following year it was made the capital of the united kingdom.

The occupation of Rome brought the kingdom of Italy into conflict with the papacy. Indeed, the whole movement for unification had been characterized by hostility to the church. Such was inevitably the case, with the Pope ruling like a secular prince over the Papal States and hurling the thunders of his wrath against those who would rob him of his domain for the sake of a united Italy. As one after another of these States was annexed, monasteries were gradually closed, and much of the property of the church was confiscated. Following the occupation of Rome in 1870 an attempt was made to solve the problem of relations between the state and the papacy. In 1871 the Italian Parliament enacted the Law of Papal Guaranties purporting to define the status of the Pope as a reigning sovereign. He was to be granted full authority over the Vatican and Lateran buildings and gardens and the right to send and receive ambassadors. In addition, he was to have free use of the Italian postal, telegraph, and railway systems and was to be paid an annual indemnity of about $645,000. This law the reigning pontiff, Pius IX, promptly denounced on the ground that issues affecting the Pope could be settled only by an international treaty to which he himself was a party. Whereupon he shut himself up in the Vatican and refused to have anything to do with a government which had so shamefully treated Christ's Vicar on earth. His successors continued this practice of voluntary imprisonment until 1929, when a series of agreements between the Fascist government and Pius XI effected what appeared to be a satisfactory settlement of the dispute.

Anticlericalism in Italy

Some of the smaller states of central and west central Europe actually made more progress in democracy than did most of their large neighbors. For example, all had the cabinet system of government by the eve of World War I. In addition, universal manhood suffrage had been adopted in Switzerland, in Belgium, and in the Scandinavian countries. Norway and Denmark had taken the next logical step of extending the franchise to women. Belgium, Sweden,

Democracy in the smaller states

and Switzerland had adopted proportional representation, and Switzerland had made extensive use of the initiative and referendum. Proportional representation is a device for guaranteeing representation to minorities as well as to the majority. Each political party is awarded a number of representatives in the legislative body in direct proportion to its voting strength. The initiative and referendum are instruments of direct democracy. Under the initiative a certain percentage of the voters can initiate legislation and compel a legislature or parliament to take action upon it. The referendum is a device for submitting legislation to the people for their final approval or rejection. With the exception of proportional representation, which was adopted for limited use in local elections in Great Britain, none of these devices made much of an appeal in the larger countries.

4. Democracy and Nationalism in Eastern Europe

The period of reform in Russia: the emancipation of the serfs

To speak of democratic progress in the countries of eastern Europe before World War I would be to invite derision. In Russia, for example, the government of the Tsarist empire in 1914 was not much different from what it had been a hundred years earlier. Nevertheless, Russian history after 1850 did witness some remarkable improvements. Though many of them were social and economic rather than political, they did mean a better life for the common people and can justifiably be considered here. The first great period of reform was the reign of Alexander II (1855–1881). In his devotion to duty and in his interest in the welfare of his subjects, Alexander was undoubtedly one of the best of Russian Tsars. He had no intention of surrendering despotic power, but he was at least determined to exercise that power in a benevolent fashion. His reforms were of three main types: economic, political, and educational. The first took the form of freeing the peasants from subjection to the nobles. A tiny beginning in this direction had already been made by Alexander I (1801–1825) in the Baltic provinces, but the vast majority of the Russian peasants remained in a condition of serfdom. On March 3, 1861, the sixth anniversary of his accession to the throne, Alexander II issued a decree which swept the whole system into the dustbin of history. The serfs were made free men, no longer bound to the soil or obligated to work for the nobles. During the next few years the government arranged to purchase from the nobles portions of their estates to be turned over to the peasants. These lands were not given to individuals, but were allotted to the village communities or *mirs* to be parceled out for the use of their members. The *mirs* were required to collect from their members enough money to repay the government in installments over a period of forty-nine years for its purchase of the land. For this reason it is sometimes said that

Alexander liberated the peasants from the nobles and made them
serfs of the state. There is evidence, however, in the increasing yield
of the peasants' holdings (from six bushels of grain per acre in
1861 to ten in 1910) that the *muzhik* had not simply exchanged
one master for another.

Of less significance but by no means unimportant were Alexander's political and educational reforms. In 1862 he abolished the
judicial powers of the old bureaucracy and established a system of
courts on the Western model with professional judges and trial by
jury. In 1864 he accorded to each province the right to elect a
zemstvo, or provincial assembly, to be composed of the chief land-owners and of delegates chosen by the townsfolk and peasants. The
zemstvos were to have authority to legislate on such matters as
roads, education, public health, and the care of the poor. Admirable
in theory as a device for giving the people a share of control over
local affairs, these assemblies were often regrettably handicapped
by the political inexperience of their members and by conflicts of
interests between the peasants and the larger proprietors. Alexander's educational reforms consisted of government aid for the
establishment of elementary schools and technical institutes, the
relaxation of censorship, and the introduction of science into the
curricula of the universities. He planned much more in most of these
directions than he was able to accomplish.

*Alexander II's
political and
educational re-
forms*

After 1865 Alexander II succumbed to reaction and proceeded to
nullify much of his earlier work as a benevolent prince. He subjected the acts of the *zemstvos* to the veto of the imperial governors.
He instilled new vigor into the secret police and restored the old
methods of arbitrary punishment of persons accused of political
crimes. He revived the censorship and ordered the universities to
purge their curricula of the sciences and to direct the attention of
their students toward subjects less provocative of questioning and
doubt. How can this reversal of attitude by the great "Liberating
Tsar" be explained? In part it was an expression of disillusionment
on account of the indifference of many of the people his reforms
were designed to help. Steeped in habits of Oriental fatalism, the
peasants appeared to show little gratitude even for their freedom.
On the other hand, radical intellectuals and leaders of the masses in
the cities scoffed at the Tsar's enlightened endeavors as mere palliatives. But weightier reasons for Alexander's change of heart were
a series of attacks upon his life and the Polish revolt of 1863. Conservatives at his court took advantage of every opportunity to persuade him that these manifestations were the direct results of his
liberal policies. They gradually convinced him that any further concession to rebellious elements would wreck the entire system. It
would be difficult to conceive of advice more stupid. Instead of
frightening malcontents into silence, the revival of the old methods
of repression simply incited revolutionary activity on a wider scale

*Alexander suc-
cumbs to reac-
tion*

than before. As the years passed, Alexander himself became aware that this was true and decided to return once more to the path of reform. But his conversion came too late. On the very day in 1881 when he signed a decree authorizing commissions to prepare new liberal plans, he was killed by a terrorist bomb.

The years which followed the death of Alexander II marked the flood tide of reaction against the entire policy of reform. The new Tsar, Alexander III (1881–1894), governed under the theory that Russia had nothing in common with western Europe, that her people had been nurtured on despotism and mystical piety for centuries and would be utterly lost without them. Such Western ideals as rationalism and individualism would undermine the childlike faith of the Russian masses and would plunge the nation into the dark abyss of anarchy and crime. In like manner, Western institutions of trial by jury, parliamentary government, and free education could never produce other than the most hideous fruits if planted in Russian soil. With such doctrines as these as his guiding principles, Alexander III enforced a regime of stern and vengeful repression. He curtailed in every way possible the powers of the *zemstvos*, increased the authority of the secret police, and even subjected the governments of the *mirs* to wealthy nobles selected by the state. These policies were continued, though in somewhat less rigorous form, by his son, Nicholas II, who was a very much weaker man. Both Tsars were ardent proponents of Russification and used it with a vengeance to strengthen their power. Russification was simply the more ruthless counterpart of similar nationalistic movements in various countries. Its purpose was to extend the language, religion, and culture of Great Russia, or Russia proper, over all of the subjects of the Tsar and thereby to simplify the problem of governing them. It was aimed most of all at the Poles, the Finns, and the Jews, since these were the nationalities considered most dangerous. Inevitably it resulted in some cruel oppression. The Finns were deprived of their constitution; the Poles were compelled to study their own literature in Russian translations; and high officials in the Tsar's government connived at *pogroms* against the Jews. In the worst of these mob attacks—the one at Kishinev in 1903—hundreds of Jews were butchered by fanatical Christians, goaded to a frenzy by foul propaganda.

Alexander III and Nicholas II

The barbarities of Russification had much to do with the outbreak of the revolutionary movement of 1905. But there were also other underlying causes. The Industrial Revolution, which had been under way since about 1890, led to congestion in the cities, to the growth of a militant working class, and to a succession of sharp economic crises. A second cause, closely related to this, was the multiplication of radical parties. The oldest of these parties, if such it can be called, was made up of the nihilists. The nihilists were mainly intellectuals who were so thoroughly disgusted with Rus-

The revolutionary movement of 1905

sian civilization that they believed the whole political and social structure should be razed to the ground. Glorifying reason and science, they professed to believe in nothing which rested upon faith. It was from this that their name was derived—from the Latin *nihil*, nothing. Whereas the nihilists were generally individualists, their successors were mainly collectivists. The most important of the collectivist groups were the anarchists [6]—followers of Bakunin and later of Kropotkin and Tolstoi; the Social Revolutionaries; and the Social Democrats. The last two differed from each other in a number of ways. The Social Revolutionaries were essentially a peasant party, though most of their leaders came from the intelligentsia. With the slogan, "the whole land to the whole people," they demanded that the great estates should be broken up and distributed among the *mirs*. Many of them also advocated terrorism as a means of forcing the upper classes to grant their demands. By

The Russian Revolution of 1905. A painter's conception of a barricade in the streets of Moscow.

contrast, the Social Democrats were a Marxist group, espousing the interests of the proletariat and urging united action by the masses in place of individual terrorism. In 1903 this party broke into two factions: the Bolsheviks, or majority, who believed that Russia was ready for a socialist revolution in the immediate future, and the Mensheviks, or minority, who contended that the completion of a bourgeois capitalist stage was a necessary condition for the establishment of socialism.

The immediate cause of the revolutionary movement was the calamitous outcome of Russia's war with Japan. As reports came in telling how the armies of the Tsar had been routed time after time on the fighting front in Manchuria, it was impressed upon the Russian people as never before that the system of irresponsible tyranny under which they lived was unspeakably rotten and incompetent. Members of the middle class, who had hitherto refrained from

The growth and decline of the revolutionary movement

[6] It will be recalled from the preceding chapter that the great Russian anarchists were invariably collectivists—either socialists or communists—in their economic views. Individualistic anarchism was confined to the West.

association with the revolutionists, now joined in the clamor for change. Radical workingmen organized strikes and held demonstrations in every important city. By the autumn of 1905 nearly the whole urban population had enlisted in a strike of protest. Merchants closed their stores, factory owners shut down their plants, lawyers refused to plead cases in court, and even valets and cooks deserted their wealthy employers. It was soon evident even to the slow-witted Tsar that the government would have to yield. On October 30, he issued his famous October Manifesto pledging guaranties of individual liberties, promising a moderately liberal franchise for the election of a Duma, or national legislature, and affirming that henceforth no law would be valid unless it had the Duma's approval. This was the high-water mark of the revolutionary movement. During the next two years Nicholas issued a series of sweeping decrees which made the October Manifesto virtually a dead letter. In 1906 he deprived the Duma of control over foreign affairs, over the army and navy, and over constitutional questions, and abolished its power to punish the ministers by withholding approval of the budget. In 1907 he decreed that the Duma should be elected indirectly on a class basis by a number of electoral colleges. The wealthier landowners were to choose 60 per cent of the electors, the peasants 22 per cent, the merchants 15 per cent, and the workingmen 3 per cent. Thereafter the legislative body was pretty well packed with obedient followers of the Tsar.

Causes of the decline

The reasons for this setback to the revolutionary movement are not hard to discover. In the first place, the army remained loyal to its commander-in-chief. Consequently, after the termination of the war with Japan in 1905, the Tsar had an enormous body of troops who could be counted upon if necessary to decimate the ranks of the revolutionists. In the second place, Nicholas was able to strengthen his crumbling regime with money borrowed from France. The basis of French aid did not consist in sympathy with autocracy, but rather in the existence of a military alliance between the French and Russian governments. An even more important reason for the decline of the movement was the split in the ranks of the revolutionists themselves. After the issuance of the October Manifesto, large numbers of the bourgeoisie became frightened at threats of the radicals and declared their conviction that the revolution had gone far enough. Withdrawing their support altogether, they became known henceforth as Octobrists. The more liberal merchants and professional men, under the name of Constitutional Democrats or Cadets, maintained that opposition should continue until the Tsar had been forced to establish a government modeled after that of Great Britain. This fatal division rendered the middle class politically impotent. Finally, disaffection appeared within the ranks of the proletariat. Many of the workers lost heart and deserted their

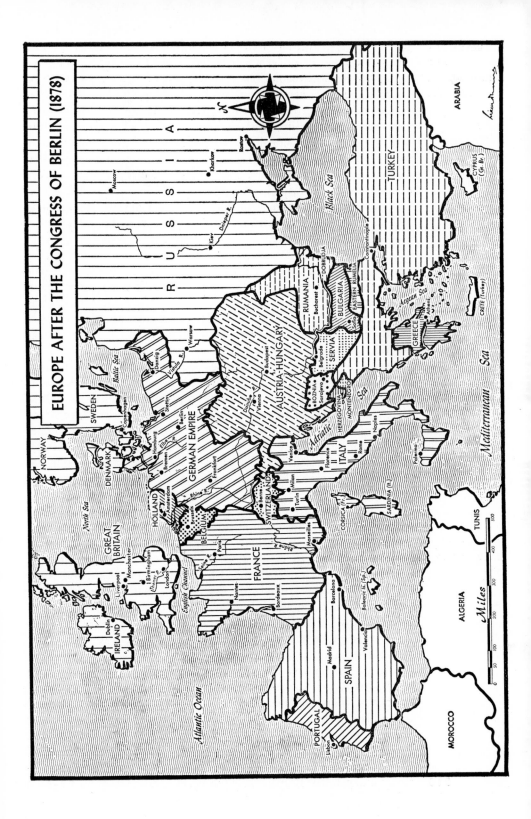

EUROPE AFTER THE CONGRESS OF BERLIN (1878)

*Gains from the
revolutionary
movement*

radical leaders. Further attempts to employ the general strike as a weapon against the government ended in grim disaster.

But the Russian revolutionary movement of 1905 was not a total failure. The cruel vengeance taken by the bloodhounds of the Tsar convinced many people that their government was not a benevolent autocracy, as they had been led to believe, but a stubborn and brutal tyranny. The uprising revealed to the masses their principal mistakes and taught them upon what sources of strength they should rely for success in the future. Even a few of the concessions actually obtained were not wiped out completely. The Duma, for instance, was not abolished. It continued to serve as a means by which at least a scattering remnant of opponents of reaction could make themselves heard. Significantly enough, the revolution of 1917 actually began in the Duma. But this was not all. The revolt of 1905 persuaded some of the more sagacious advisers of the Tsar that last-ditch conservatism was none too safe. The result was the enactment of a number of reforms designed to conciliate the troublesome classes. Among the most significant were the agrarian reforms sponsored by Premier Stolypin between 1906 and 1911. These included: (1) the transfer of 5,000,000 acres of crown lands to the peasants; (2) permission for the peasant to withdraw from the *mir* and set himself up as an independent farmer; and (3) cancellation of the remaining installments owed by the peasants for their land. Nor were the working classes altogether forgotten. Decrees were issued permitting the formation of labor unions, providing for a reduction of the working day (to not more than ten hours in most cases), and establishing sickness and accident insurance. By 1914 it appeared as if Russia might well evolve into a stable and prosperous capitalist nation.

*Nationalism
in the Balkans*

In the lands of the Balkans during the nineteenth century the most dramatic events exemplified nationalism rather than democracy. The few manifestations of the latter that did appear were merely incidental to expressions of the former. Before 1829 the entire Balkan peninsula—bounded by the Aegean, Black, and Adriatic Seas—was controlled by the Turks. But during the next eighty-five years a gradual dismemberment occurred of the Turkish empire in the Balkans. In some instances the slicing away of territories was perpetrated by rival European powers, especially by Russia and Austria; but generally it was the result of nationalist revolts by the Sultan's Christian subjects. In 1829, at the conclusion of the first Russo-Turkish War, the Ottoman Empire was compelled to acknowledge the independence of Greece and to grant autonomy to Serbia and to the provinces of Wallachia and Moldavia under Russian protection. At the end of the Crimean War, Russia was forced to relinquish her domination of Moldavia and Wallachia, with the result that in 1862 the two provinces were united as a virtually independent Rumania. As the years passed, resentment against

Ottoman rule spread through other Balkan territories. In 1875– 1876 there were uprisings in Bosnia, Herzegovina, and Bulgaria, which the Sultan suppressed with murderous vengeance. Reports of atrocities against Orthodox Christians gave Russia an excuse for renewal of her age-long struggle for domination of the Balkans. In this second Russo-Turkish War (1877–1878) the armies of the Tsar won a smashing victory. The Treaty of San Stefano, which terminated the conflict, provided that the Sultan should surrender nearly all of his territory in Europe, except for a remnant around Constantinople. But at this juncture the great powers intervened. Austria and Great Britain, especially, were opposed to letting Russia assume jurisdiction over so large a portion of the Near East. Consequently the Tsar was obliged to submit to a revision of the Treaty of San Stefano at the Congress of Berlin in 1878. The Treaty of Berlin, which was thereupon adopted, returned most of the conquered territory to Turkey, except that Russia was allowed to retain Bessarabia, Thessaly was given to Greece, and Bosnia and Herzegovina were placed under the administrative control of Austria. Seven years later the Bulgars, who had been granted some degree of autonomy by the Treaty of Berlin, seized the province of Eastern Rumelia from Turkey and in 1908 established the independent kingdom of Bulgaria.

In the very year when this last dismemberment occurred, Turkey herself was engulfed by the tidal wave of nationalism. For some time her more enlightened citizens had been growing increasingly *The Young* disgusted with the weakness and incompetence of the Sultan's gov- *Turk revolution* ernment. In particular, those who had been educated in the universities of England and France were becoming more and more convinced that their country should be rejuvenated by the introduction of Western ideas of science, patriotism, and democracy. Organizing themselves into a society known as the Young Turks, they forced the Sultan in 1908 to establish constitutional government. The following year, when a reactionary movement set in, they deposed the reigning Sultan, Abdul Hamid II, and placed on the throne his witless brother, Mohammed V, as a titular sovereign. The real powers of government were now entrusted to a Grand Vizier and ministers responsible to an elected Parliament. Unfortunately this revolution did not mean increased liberty for the non-Turkish inhabitants of the empire. Instead, the Young Turks launched a vigorous movement to Ottomanize all of the Christian subjects of the Sultan. At the same time the disturbances preceding and accompanying the revolution opened the way for still further dismemberment. In 1908 Austria annexed the provinces of Bosnia and Herzegovina, which the Treaty of Berlin had allowed her merely to administer, and in 1911–1912 Italy made war upon Turkey for the conquest of Tripoli.

5. *Movements for Social Reform*

Toward the end of the nineteenth century the idea gained ground that political democracy was not enough. That cabinets should be responsible to parliaments, and that every citizen should be entitled to vote, seemed to be matters of comparatively small moment so long as workers were at the mercy of a ruthlessly competitive industrial system. Consequently, in a number of countries, agitation was begun for what is sometimes called economic democracy. As generally defined, economic democracy implies that all men shall have a substantially equal opportunity to make the most of their latent abilities. It is not synonymous with the old liberal concept of equality before the law, which, as Anatole France scornfully remarked, "forbids the rich man as well as the poor man to sleep under bridges, to beg in the streets, and to steal bread." Economic democracy means that little children shall not be herded into factories to be exploited by selfish employers, that old people shall not be thrown on the human scrap heap when the energy has been drained from their bodies by the soulless machine, and that workers shall not be compelled to bear the whole burden of industrial accident, unemployment, and disease. In short, it involves a somewhat drastic modification of the ideal of *laissez faire*, which appeared to be so firmly entrenched during the second half of the nineteenth century.

*Reasons for the
decline
of* laissez faire

On the other hand, it should be remembered that the decline of *laissez faire* was not exclusively the result of the movement for economic democracy. The original form which modification often took on the Continent of Europe was protectionism, prompted by the desire of the rising industrial bourgeoisie to stave off competition from England. Protectionism was sometimes followed by outright subsidies, illustrated by the bounties given by the Italian and French governments to the silk industry and to various branches of agriculture. In such nations as Germany, Italy, and Russia the railroads and telegraph and telephone lines were either built by the state, or nationalized afterwards, primarily for purposes of military efficiency. In France the tobacco and match manufacturing industries were taken over by the state as sources of public revenue, and were operated as government monopolies. Even a great deal of the social legislation enacted in Continental countries was inspired by reasons of nationalism, militarism, and paternalism. Governments desired to win the loyalty of all classes of their subjects and make sure of a healthy supply of cannon fodder in time of war.

*Bismarck's pro-
gram of social
legislation in
Germany*

The first of the great powers to enact a comprehensive program of social legislation was Germany, under the guidance of her shrewd but domineering Chancellor, Prince von Bismarck. The reasons why Germany should have taken the lead are not difficult to fathom. Unlike Great Britain and France she had never been deeply affected by eighteenth-century liberalism; hence she had no strong traditions of individualism or *laissez faire*. While her political philosophers were persistently affirming the subjection of the individual to the state, her economists were preaching doctrines of national self-sufficiency and paternalism. Bismarck himself maintained that it was the duty of the state to regulate all functions of society in the national interest and to look after the weaker citizens, "that they may not be run over and trampled under foot on the highway of life." But he had other reasons also for engaging in what appeared to be a defense of the workers' rights. He was anxious to undermine the growing popularity of socialism by stealing a portion of its thunder. In a speech in the Reichstag he frankly avowed his purpose of insuring the workingman against sickness and old age so that "these gentlemen [the Social Democrats] will sound their bird call in vain." In addition, he had military purposes in mind. He was desirous of making the German proletarian a loyal soldier and of safeguarding his health in some measure from the debilitating effects of factory labor. Bismarck's program of social legislation was initiated in 1883–1884 with the adoption of laws insuring workmen against sickness and accidents. These acts were soon followed by others providing for rigid factory inspection, limiting the employment of women and children, fixing maximum hours of labor, establishing public employment agencies, and insuring workers against incapacity on account of old age. By 1890, when Bismarck was forced to retire, Germany had adopted nearly all of the elements, with the exception of unemployment insurance, in the pattern of social legislation which has since become familiar in the majority of Western nations.

Other countries on the Continent of Europe soon followed the German example. In 1885 Austria established a maximum day of eleven hours in factories and ten hours in mines, and in 1887–1888 provided for insurance of industrial laborers against illness and accidents. France and Italy did not join the procession until later, but the programs they did adopt were broader in scope. A French law of 1892 not only regulated the employment of women and children but prescribed a maximum day of ten hours for all workers; in 1905 this limit was reduced to nine hours. Other acts of the French Parliament insured free medical attendance for laborers and their families, accorded protection to the activities of labor unions, and compelled employers to compensate workers for injuries. The capstone of this system of legislation was added in 1910 with the passage of a law providing old-age pensions, not only for industrial workers, in accordance with the usual practice, but for domestic servants and farm laborers as well. The series of laws enacted in Italy was much the same, except for the absence of the provision regarding free medical attention. The Italian laws were supplemented, however, by an act of 1912 providing for nationalized life insurance and also by measures encouraging co-operative stores.

Social legislation in France and in Italy

Because of her strong individualist traditions, Great Britain lagged several years behind the other great powers in western Europe. To be sure, there had been some early progress, illustrated by laws prohibiting the employment of women and children in underground labor in the mines; but the British government adopted no extensive measures of social reform until after the rejuvenated Liberal party came into power in 1905. The old generation of Liberals under Gladstone, representing primarily the business classes, had been committed to principles of *laissez faire*. Their energies had been absorbed very largely in problems of political reform and of home rule for Ireland. But in 1898 Gladstone died, and control over his party passed into younger hands. Several of the new leaders— Herbert Asquith, David Lloyd George, John Morley, and Winston Churchill—were enthusiastic idealists, resolved to wage "implacable warfare" against misery and squalor. Upon coming to power in 1905, these ardent reformers determined to throw the old-fashioned doctrines of their party to the winds and transform Britannia into a paradise of fair treatment for all. During the years that followed, down to the beginning of World War I, they succeeded in having written into the statute books the most remarkable schedule of reform legislation since the Glorious Revolution. First came the Workmen's Compensation Act of 1906 and the Old Age Pensions law of 1908. Next came the Trade Boards Act of 1909 authorizing special commissions to fix the minimum pay for workers in sweatshops; three years later the principle that the government could establish minimum wages was extended to the coal-mining industry.

Social insurance

In 1911 the Liberal cabinet procured the passage of the great National Insurance Act introducing a system of contributory insurance against sickness for all wage earners and providing unemployment insurance for workers in the engineering and building trades. The unemployment provisions of the Act applied to more than 2,000,000 workers in industries especially susceptible to the effects of depressions.

*New departures
in economic and
social reform*

To this list of more conventional social reforms of the Liberal government must be added certain others for which there was almost no precedent. In 1901 the House of Lords had rendered its notorious decision in the Taff Vale Railway case, affirming that labor unions could be held liable for damages to property inflicted during the course of a strike. This decision precipitated an angry controversy and led to the formation of the Labor party, pledged to crusade by political action on behalf of the workers. Partly to placate the Labor chieftains the Liberal government put through its Trade Disputes Act of 1906 exempting the funds of labor unions from suits for damages.[7] In 1909 the Liberal Parliament enacted a law permitting the clearance of slum areas and authorizing local

[7] In Britain there is no such thing as judicial review such as that which is exercised by our Federal courts. The House of Lords is the highest court of appeal, but its decisions can be revoked by act of Parliament.

authorities to provide respectable housing for the poor. This law set a precedent for an enormous amount of public housing construction in later years, especially in the period after 1918. Among the most significant of all the social reforms of the Liberal regime were certain provisions incorporated in the Lloyd George budget of 1909. In this remarkable fiscal program David Lloyd George proposed not only to increase the regular income taxes but to levy in addition a super-tax on the incomes of the rich. He recommended also that the government should confiscate 20 per cent of the unearned increment of land values, and that a heavy tax should be imposed upon all undeveloped land appraised in excess of £50 per acre. The object of these measures was twofold: to raise revenue for old-age pensions and for various forms of social insurance and to level down great fortunes. It was hoped that the tax on unearned increment and on undeveloped lands would help to break the land monopoly of the richer nobles—of such magnates as the Duke of Westminster, who owned 600 acres in London, and the Marquess of Bute, who owned one-half of the area of Cardiff, upon which were built some 20,000 houses. Thrown out by the House of Lords, the Lloyd George budget was finally enacted into law after the Liberals were returned to power in the January election of 1910.

6. The New Imperialism

Not long after the beginning of the nineteenth century the type of imperialism fostered by the Commercial Revolution gradually died out. There were few men any longer in public life who rose to defend it; some even roundly condemned it on the ground that colonies were not worth what it cost to acquire and defend them. The causes of this change in attitude are to be found in such factors as the decline of mercantilism and the absorbing interest in internal development which accompanied the early stages of the Industrial Revolution. Following the decay of this early imperialism there was a decided lull in the scramble for external possessions until about 1870, when activity was renewed on a more vigorous and extensive scale. In addition to quantitative differences, the new imperialism bore other striking contrasts with the old. Whereas the struggle for empire during the Commercial Revolution was confined mainly to the Western Hemisphere and the tropical islands, the theaters of imperialism after 1870 were chiefly in Africa and in Asia. The imperialism of mercantilist days was carried on largely to magnify the power and wealth of the state—to bring bullion into the treasury, which would enable the government to maintain armies and equip navies; the new imperialism operated for the benefit of leading *citizens* of the mother country, to provide them with markets for their goods and opportunities for investment of their surplus capital. The raw materials most keenly desired by the imperialists of earlier

The new imperialism contrasted with the old

715

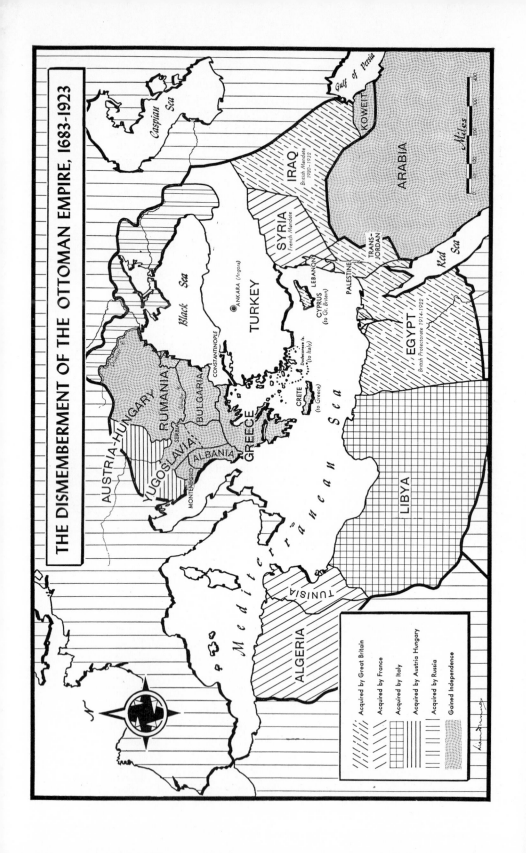

THE DISMEMBERMENT OF THE OTTOMAN EMPIRE, 1683-1923

Caspian Sea

Gulf of Persia

KOWEIT

IRAQ
British Mandate 1920-1932

ARABIA

SYRIA
French Mandate

Black Sea

TRANS-
JORDAN

ANKARA (Angora)

TURKEY

LEBANON

PALESTINE

Red Sea

CONSTANTINOPLE

CYPRUS
(to Gt. Britain)

Dodecanese Is.
(to Italy)

EGYPT
British Protectorate 1914-1922

CRETE
(to Greece)

AUSTRIA-HUNGARY

RUMANIA

BULGARIA

Mediterranean Sea

YUGOSLAVIA

ALBANIA

GREECE

MONTENEGRO

LIBYA

TUNISIA

ALGERIA

Miles

Acquired by Great Britain

Acquired by France

Acquired by Italy

Acquired by Austria Hungary

Acquired by Russia

Gained Independence

days were gold and silver, tropical products, and naval stores; the
later imperialist paid scant regard to any of these but greedily
coveted territories rich in iron, copper, petroleum, manganese, and
wheat. As a final difference, under the old imperialism large-scale
emigration to the colonies was generally discouraged, but a primary
purpose of the new imperialism was to acquire colonies as homes
for surplus inhabitants of the mother country. Although comparatively few could ever be induced to emigrate, the argument continued to be used that colonies were necessary as outlets for the
surplus population of crowded nations.

Undoubtedly the major factors responsible for the revival of imperialism after 1870 were to be found in the Second Industrial Revolution. The spread of industrialization to many other countries in
addition to Great Britain produced an intense competition for
markets and for new sources of raw materials. Despite the problem
of finding outlets for surplus manufactured products, the governments of most countries eventually yielded to capitalist pressure for
protective tariffs. The result was still higher production and a consequent greater demand for colonies as dumping grounds for articles the home market could not absorb. Under such conditions it
became virtually impossible for the regime of international free
trade, which had seemed to promise so much for the peace and
prosperity of the world, to continue. As noted already, some Continental countries adopted protective tariffs during the 1880's. The
United States, also, was closing the door more and more tightly
against foreign manufactures. Perhaps nothing did more to stimulate
the imperialism of European powers than the fear that their accustomed markets in neighboring countries and in America would soon
be lost. But not all of the motives for the new imperialism were
economic. By 1870 or soon after, the population of a number of industrialized nations had begun to expand to uncomfortable limits;
hence there was a desire of governments to acquire territories where
surplus inhabitants might settle and still remain citizens and potential soldiers of the fatherland. Finally, the new imperialism was the
product in considerable measure of nationalism and of the development of an extensive program of missionary activity by the churches
of Europe and America.

*Causes of the
revival of im-
perialism after
1870*

If any one man could be called the father of the new imperialism,
he was probably Leopold II, king of the Belgians. In 1876 Leopold
took possession of the rich Congo River territory in central Africa
(about ten times the size of Belgium) and held it practically as his
personal domain until 1908, when he sold it for a stiff indemnity to
the Belgian government. It was not long after the Belgian king set
the example until Great Britain and France took a deeper interest
than they had ever shown before in the dismemberment of Africa.
The former established a protectorate over Egypt about 1882 and
subsequently took possession of the Egyptian Sudan, Rhodesia,

*The beginning
of the scramble
for African
territory*

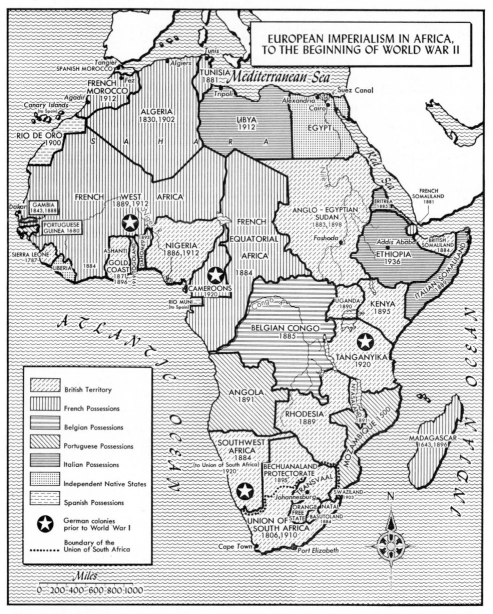

EUROPEAN IMPERIALISM IN AFRICA,
TO THE BEGINNING OF WORLD WAR II

SPANISH MOROCCO
Tangier
Fez
FRENCH MOROCCO 1912
Agadir
Canary Islands (to Spain)
RIO DE ORO 1900
ALGERIA 1830, 1902
S A H A R A
Tunis
Algiers
TUNISIA 1881
Tripoli
Mediterranean Sea
Suez Canal
LIBYA 1912
Alexandria
Cairo
EGYPT
Red Sea

Dakar
GAMBIA 1843, 1888
PORTUGUESE GUINEA 1680
SIERRA LEONE 1787
LIBERIA
FRENCH WEST AFRICA 1889, 1912
ASHANTI 1884
GOLD COAST 1871, 1896
DAHOMEY 1893
TOGOLAND 1919
NIGERIA 1886, 1912
FRENCH EQUATORIAL AFRICA 1884
CAMEROONS 1920
RIO MUNI (to Spain)
ANGLO-EGYPTIAN SUDAN 1883, 1898
Fashoda
ERITREA 1885
FRENCH SOMALILAND 1881
Addis Ababa
ETHIOPIA 1936
BRITISH SOMALILAND 1884
ITALIAN SOMALILAND 1889

ATLANTIC OCEAN

BELGIAN CONGO 1885
Congo
UGANDA 1890
KENYA 1895
TANGANYIKA 1920

ANGOLA 1891
RHODESIA 1889
NYASALAND 1891
MOZAMBIQUE 1500
MADAGASCAR 1643, 1896

SOUTHWEST AFRICA 1884 (to Union of South Africa) 1920
BECHUANALAND PROTECTORATE 1895
TRANSVAAL
Johannesburg
SWAZILAND 1903
ORANGE FREE STATE
NATAL
BASUTOLAND 1884
UNION OF SOUTH AFRICA 1806, 1910
Cape Town
Port Elizabeth

INDIAN OCEAN

N

Legend:
- British Territory
- French Possessions
- Belgian Possessions
- Portuguese Possessions
- Italian Possessions
- Independent Native States
- Spanish Possessions
- ★ German colonies prior to World War I
- Boundary of the Union of South Africa

Miles
0 200 400 600 800 1000

The British captured Cape Colony in
1806. The Union of South Africa was
established in 1910.

Madagascar was a French protectorate
until 1896, when it was taken over as a
colony.

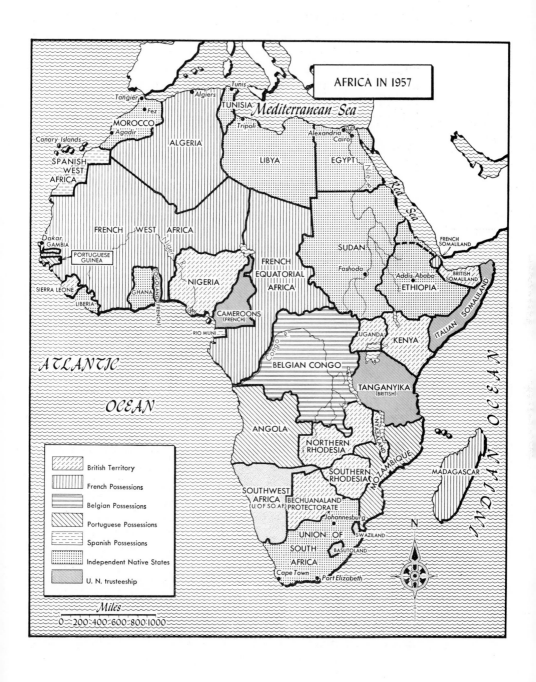

AFRICA IN 1957

Mediterranean Sea

Tangier
Algiers
Tunis
TUNISIA
Fez
MOROCCO
Agadir
Tripoli
Alexandria
Cairo
Canary Islands
ALGERIA
LIBYA
EGYPT
SPANISH
WEST
AFRICA

Dakar
GAMBIA
FRENCH WEST AFRICA
Niger R.
SUDAN
FRENCH
SOMALILAND
PORTUGUESE
GUINEA
Fashoda
Addis Ababa
BRITISH
SOMALILAND
SIERRA LEONE
NIGERIA
FRENCH
EQUATORIAL
AFRICA
ETHIOPIA
GHANA
LIBERIA
TOGOLAND (FRENCH)
CAMEROONS
(FRENCH)
RIO MUNI
UGANDA
KENYA
ITALIAN SOMALILAND

ATLANTIC
Congo R.
BELGIAN CONGO
TANGANYIKA
(BRITISH)

OCEAN
ANGOLA
NORTHERN
RHODESIA
NYASALAND
MOZAMBIQUE
MADAGASCAR
SOUTHWEST
AFRICA
(U.OF SO.AF)
BECHUANALAND
PROTECTORATE
SOUTHERN
RHODESIA

INDIAN OCEAN

Johannesburg
UNION OF
SOUTH
AFRICA
SWAZILAND
BASUTOLAND
Cape Town
Port Elizabeth
N

British Territory
French Possessions
Belgian Possessions
Portuguese Possessions
Spanish Possessions
Independent Native States
U. N. trusteeship

Miles
0 200 400 600 800 1000

Uganda, and British East Africa as colonies. In 1902 the British succeeded after a three-year war in conquering the Boer republics (the
Orange Free State and the Transvaal), which were united in 1909
with the Cape Colony and Natal to form the self-governing dominion of South Africa. Designs of the French upon African territory
were evidenced as early as 1830 when they established control over a
number of Algerian ports. By 1857 they had succeeded in conquering and annexing the remainder of Algeria. But the efforts of the
French to carve out an empire on the Dark Continent did not really
begin on an extensive scale until 1881. In that year they occupied
Tunis and then gradually took possession of the Sahara, the French
Congo, French Guinea, Senegal, and Dahomey. By 1905 nearly all
of the choicest territories in Africa had been monopolized by the
Belgians, the British, and the French.

*Germany and
Italy enter the
African
scramble*

The entrance of Germany and Italy into the scramble for colonies
in Africa was delayed by the complexity of domestic problems. Both
nations had just completed long campaigns for unification and were
still deeply involved in troubles with the papacy. Besides, the rulers
of neither country were much interested in outlying possessions.
Bismarck, for example, was ambitious to consolidate his empire at
home and to hold the position of leadership which Germany had
won in Continental European affairs. He once declared that the
friendship of Great Britain was worth more to him than "twenty
marshy colonies in Africa." [8] However, even Bismarck was eventually persuaded by merchants, industrialists, and shipping magnates
to enter the race for African empire. In 1884 he proclaimed a protectorate over Southwest Africa and then took over in rapid succession German East Africa, the Kamerun, and Togoland. About 1888
the Italians decided that they also must have a share of what was left
of Africa. They established a foothold in Somaliland on the eastern
coast and then attempted to reduce the adjacent country of Abyssinia to a protectorate. The result was one of the most disastrous
defeats ever suffered by a modern nation. The Italian forces were
so badly shattered by the Abyssinians at Adowa in 1896 that Italy
made no further attempts to conquer the Lion of Judah until 1935.
Her only important acquisitions of African territory between 1896
and 1914 were Tripoli and Cyrenaica, which she conquered from
Turkey in 1912 and combined under the new name of Libya.

*Imperialism in
Asia*

Meanwhile European powers were beginning to stake out new
claims for themselves on the continent of Asia. Long before 1870
a number of European nations had engaged in land-grabbing exploits
in the Orient. As early as 1582 the Russians had crossed the Ural
mountains, and in less than a century they had reached the Pacific.
In 1763, after eliminating the French as rivals for possession of India,
the British had begun the subjugation and development of that country, most of which they converted into a possession of the crown in

[8] W. O. Aydelotte, *Bismarck and British Colonial Policy*, p. 21.

1858. At the end of the so-called Opium War in 1842 Great Britain forced the Chinese to cede the island of Hong Kong, and a few years later the French established a protectorate over Indo-China. In 1858 Russia took possession of everything north of the Amur River and soon afterward founded the city of Vladivostok (Ruler of the East), also upon territory wrested from China. But it was not until about 1880 that the chief military and industrialized nations began to dream of carving the whole of Asia into colonies and spheres of influence. The richest prize of all, of course, was the Chinese empire with its 400,000,000 inhabitants and its area as large as that of Europe. Great Britain may be said to have initiated the process by annexing Burma in 1885. Ten years later occurred the first Sino-Japanese War (1894–1895), as a result of which Japan obtained the island of Formosa and the surrender of Chinese claims to Korea, which she eventually annexed and renamed Chosen. During the closing years of the nineteenth century several of the European powers that had recently protested against Japanese aggression proceeded to help themselves to additional slices of the Chinese melon. In 1897 Germany decided that she could avenge the murder of two of her missionaries in China only by seizing the bay of Kiaochow and by exacting the exclusive right to construct railways and exploit the mines of the Shantung peninsula. The very next year Russia extorted the right to build a railway across Chinese Manchuria to Vladivostok, while the British and the French demanded and obtained exclusive control over valuable harbors on the Chinese coast. By 1898 the independence of China appeared to be doomed to early extinction. It was commonly assumed by Europeans, at least, that the southeastern portion of the empire would fall to France as her sphere of influence, that Great Britain and Germany would divide the central portion, and that Russia and Japan would scramble for what was left in the north.

About the turn of the century, imperialism in China was checked temporarily by three extraordinary developments. The first and least important was the proclamation in 1899 of the Open Door policy by the United States. Although this policy was little more than an empty phrase so far as other governments were concerned, it undoubtedly raised the hopes of China that the United States would resent and possibly oppose the imperialist aggressions of other powers. Much more influential was a display of violent resistance by the Chinese themselves. In 1900 the Society of Harmonious Fists, commonly called the Boxers, organized a movement to oust the "foreign devils" from the country. Much property was destroyed, the legations in Peking were besieged, and hundreds of foreigners, including the German minister, were killed. Though supported by the Chinese government, the rebellion was finally suppressed by an expeditionary force of British, Russians, Japanese, Germans, Frenchmen, and Americans. The third and most important cause of the

The temporary decline and subsequent revival of imperialism in China

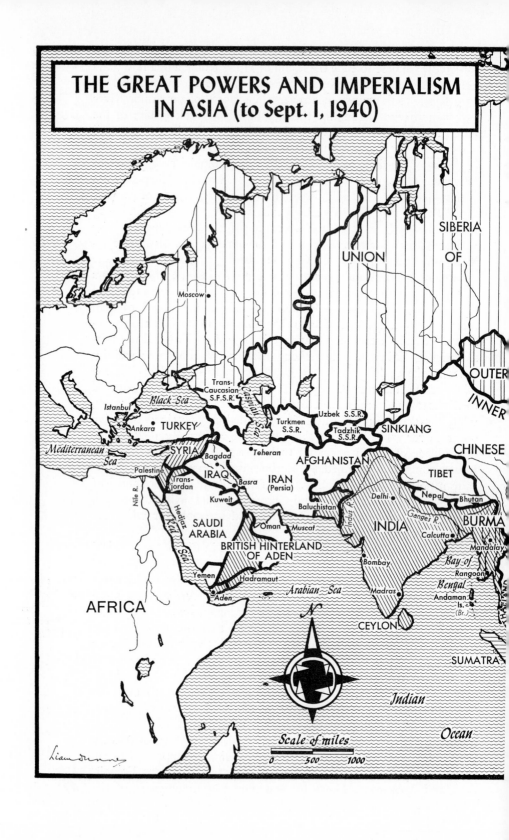

THE GREAT POWERS AND IMPERIALISM IN ASIA (to Sept. 1, 1940)

SIBERIA

OF

UNION

Moscow

OUTER

INNER

Trans-
Caucasian
S.F.S.R.

Black Sea

Caspian Sea

Uzbek S.S.R.

SINKIANG

Istanbul

Ankara

TURKEY

Turkmen
S.S.R.

Tadzhik
S.S.R.

CHINESE

Mediterranean
Sea

SYRIA

Bagdad

Teheran

AFGHANISTAN

TIBET

Palestine

IRAQ

IRAN
(Persia)

Delhi

Nepal

Bhutan

Trans-
jordan

Basra

Baluchistan

Ganges R.

Nile R.

Kuweit

Indus R.

INDIA

BURMA

Hedjaz

Red Sea

SAUDI
ARABIA

Oman

Muscat

Calcutta

Mandalay

BRITISH HINTERLAND
OF ADEN

Bombay

Bay of

Rangoon

Yemen

Hadramaut

Arabian Sea

Madras

Bengal

Andaman
Is.
(Br.)

Aden

AFRICA

CEYLON

SUMATRA

Indian

Scale of miles

Ocean

0   500   1000

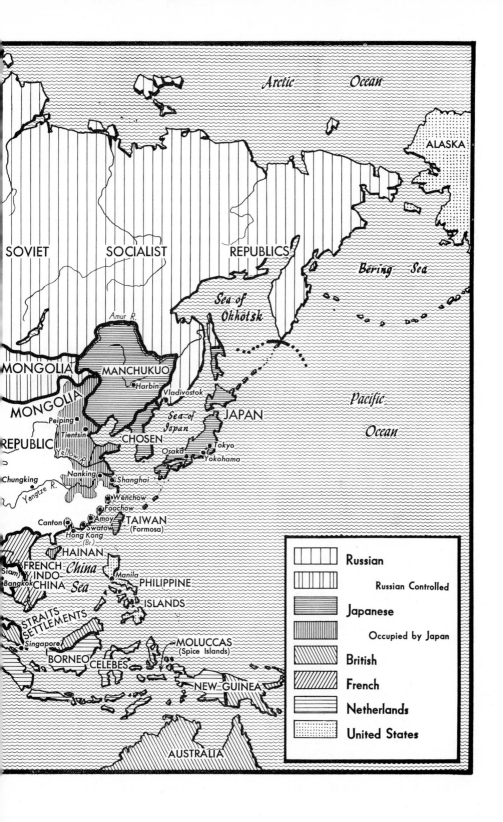

temporary decline of imperialism in China was rivalry among the despoilers themselves. Several of the great powers became suspicious that their competitors were attempting to get more than their proper share of the booty. The distrust was especially keen among Great Britain, Russia, Germany, and Japan. In 1902 the British and the Japanese concluded an alliance to protect certain areas they hoped to develop against the encroachments of the Russians and the Germans. When in 1904 it became evident that Russia intended to swallow Manchuria, the Japanese took up arms. The conflict ended in 1905 in a decisive victory for Japan. Russia was forced to surrender Port Arthur to her rival and to acknowledge Japanese supremacy in Korea. But these developments merely delayed the spoliation of China. In 1912 the same old imperialistic activities were revived

The Boxer Rebellion. The Chicu Mun Gate in Peking, just after the Boxers partially destroyed it.

when Great Britain assumed what virtually amounted to sovereign rights in Tibet. The following year Russia established a protectorate over the enormous province of Outer Mongolia, which the Soviet government still retains in a dependent status. Thus on the eve of World War I the independence of China was still very far from secure against the cupidity of nations professing to represent a superior level of culture.

7. Power Politics and the Armed Peace

National conflicts and struggles for empire are common ingredients of what is known as power politics. The phrase refers to the pursuit of power by sovereign states as an end in itself or a means to the attainment of other ends. The methods employed have traditionally included nearly every form of deceit and trickery invented by the wit of man. Nations in a formal relationship of peace spy upon each other, issue threats and counterthreats, form alliances and counteralliances, and attempt to bluff and hornswoggle each other. Finally, when fear and greed gain the upper hand, they resort to

Power politics defined

war. Though the crudities are frequently glossed over by embassy teas and striped-pants formality, the fundamental rule of power politics is the law of the jungle.

Power politics is not new. It dates back to the origins of the modern state system in the sixteenth and seventeenth centuries. Its methods were followed by Richelieu and by Frederick the Great, to name only two. Its first great peak of development was not reached, however, until after 1830. By that time the international system of Metternich had broken down. Henceforth, in the main, it was each state for itself, and the devil take the hindmost. International struggles for power, prestige, security, and empire made up an increasing proportion of the political history of the Western world until the first great culmination of those struggles in World War I.

The origins of power politics

It would be a mistake, however, to assume that the inhabitants of the Western world were preoccupied exclusively with power rivalries and brutal struggles for national aggrandizement. Strange as it may seem, the period from 1830 to 1914 was distinguished by considerable progress in the development of international law and organization. Various conferences, notably the First and Second Hague Conferences in 1899 and 1907, respectively, succeeded in formulating a number of significant new principles of international law. Among them were rules forbidding the use of explosive bullets and poison gases and outlawing the employment of force for the collection of international debts. In 1885 a convention was signed by fourteen nations pledging themselves to strive for the suppression of slavery and the slave trade, and in 1909 a body of rules known as the Declaration of London was adopted governing the rights and duties of neutrals under conditions of naval warfare.

Progress in the development of international law

The growth of international organization between 1830 and 1914 was exemplified by several developments. In 1874 the Universal Postal Union was created to facilitate the transmission of mails between nations, and the following year an International Telegraphic Union was established. At the First Hague Conference of 1899 the nations represented decided upon the creation of an international arbitration tribunal. Known thereafter as the Hague Permanent Court of Arbitration, it consisted of a panel of judges from which each party to a dispute might choose two arbitrators and those four would choose a fifth. It functioned successfully down to 1914 in the adjustment of fifteen disputes between nations, including a serious controversy between Germany and France over French intervention in Morocco.

The growth of international organization

But the progress in international law and organization, substantial though it was, failed to measure up to the needs of the times. By 1914 the economic and political conditions favorable to the maintenance of peace had almost ceased to exist. The beneficent system of free trade under which Britain had supplied the capital and manufactured goods and the rest of the world the food and raw materials

The failure of internationalism

725

had virtually passed into history. Britain was still interested in pre-serving the *status quo*, from which she had profited for so long, but certain nations on the Continent of Europe were desirous of up-setting it. Germany, in particular, now had a flourishing industry of her own and was eager to find markets in areas hitherto monopolized by the British. The growth of both nationalism and militarism kept pace with the expansion of economic ambitions. Under the cir-cumstances nothing but the strongest and most fully effective inter-national machinery would have been adequate to preserve the peace. But the Hague Court was weak. Actually it was not a court at all but a panel of arbitrators. Since it had no compulsory jurisdiction, gov-ernments could submit their disputes to it or not, just as they chose. Moreover, all of the attempts of the powers to limit armaments by international agreement ended in failure. Competition in armaments magnified fears and transformed the system of independent states into a breeding ground for wars.

The Pax Britan-nica

During the last three-quarters of the nineteenth century Western civilization was built upon a multitude of states. They varied greatly in area and population, but, with a single exception, no one of them was powerful enough to impose its will upon the others. The excep-tion, of course, was Great Britain, with a highly developed industrial system and with a navy equal in strength to the combined navies of any two other powers. By virtue of her industrial and naval might, and also her financial power, Britain was able to hold the rest of the nations of Europe in a kind of balance. As a consequence, no long or exceedingly bloody wars occurred on that continent between the end of the Napoleonic wars and the outbreak of World War I. To attribute this fact exclusively to the influence of Britain is not quite correct, since most of the rest of the nations were too deeply absorbed in problems of internal development to bother very much with foreign affairs. Nevertheless, the so-called Hundred Years' Peace was to a large extent a *Pax Britannica*.

The breakdown of the balance of power

By 1900 the European balance of power had begun to get out of adjustment. Several factors combined to produce the result. Most important was the unification and industrialization of Germany. Prior to 1871 Germany was broken up into a number of states, the largest of which was Prussia. But Prussia had no greater population or economic potential than France. The defeat of France in the Franco-Prussian War and the establishment of the German empire changed this relationship. Germany forged rapidly ahead until by 1900 she had greatly outdistanced France in industrial power and was soon to surpass Great Britain. Meanwhile, her population had grown, while the numbers of the French had virtually stood still. In 1898 the Kaiser decided that Germany must have a navy, to in-crease her prestige as a world power and to protect her expanding commerce. The British soon found themselves unable to maintain their traditional standard of a navy equal in strength to the com-

bined navies of any two other powers. With a powerful navy, a
flourishing industry, and a commanding geographic position, Germany seemed well on the way toward becoming the dominant nation in Europe. Her power and prosperity inspired fear and envy among her neighbors. But Germany, France, and Britain were not the only countries whose status as great powers had undergone a change. Following her unification in 1870, Italy rose to a position almost equal to that of France. Austria, on the other hand, declined on account of the growth of nationalist movements among the numerous Slavs within her borders.

By 1900 six Great Powers in Europe—Germany, France, Russia, Italy, Austria-Hungary, and Great Britain—were competing with each other for power, security, and economic advantage. Each had specific objectives the fulfillment of which it regarded as essential to its national interest. Germany built her ambitions around eastward expansion. After 1890 German capitalists and imperialists dreamed of a *Drang nach Osten* (Drive to the East) and planned the construction of a railway from Berlin to Bagdad to facilitate economic control of the Ottoman Empire. Austria also looked to the east, but to the Balkans rather than to any part of western Asia. Her hold on Trieste and other portions of the Adriatic coast was precarious, since much of this territory was inhabited by Italians. If she could carve a highroad through the Balkans to the Aegean, her access to the sea would be more secure. As time passed, Austria and Germany became more dependent upon each other, the former because of trouble with the Slavs both inside and outside her borders, and the latter because of a growing fear of encirclement. In 1879 Bismarck entered into an alliance with Austria, which was renewed and strengthened in subsequent years. It was an alliance with a corpse, but the Germans clung to it more and more desperately as international tensions deepened.

Ambitions of the Great Powers: Germany and Austria-Hungary

To a large degree the objectives of France were dictated by a desire to curb or counterbalance the growing might of Germany. France hoped to recover Alsace and Lorraine, which had suddenly become very valuable as the result of a discovery by Sidney Thomas and P. C. Gilchrist in 1878 of a method of converting low-grade iron ore into steel. But recovery of the lost provinces was not the only French objective. The French were determined to add Morocco to their African empire regardless of the interests of other powers in that sadly misgoverned country. The motives of the Paris statesmen were a mixture of economic and political. Morocco contained rich mineral deposits, but it would be valuable also for strategic reasons and as a reservoir from which troops might be drawn to offset the manpower shortage at home.

Ambitions of France

A paramount ambition of Russia was to gain control of the Bosporus and the Dardanelles. She had regarded this as her "historic mission" since early in the nineteenth century. Achievement

*Ambitions of
Russia*

of this mission would prevent her fleet from being bottled up in the Black Sea in the event of war with some naval power or powers. Besides, it would give her unquestioned access to the Mediterranean and probably possession of Constantinople. Turkey would be eliminated from Europe, and Russia would fall heir to the Balkans. In addition, if the Tsar's agents could get to Constantinople before the Germans, they could turn the Berlin-to-Bagdad railway into an empty dream. But Imperial Russia had other ambitions. She coveted access to the Persian Gulf and Indian Ocean and tried for years to make Persia a Russian protectorate. She strove also for better outlets to the Pacific and attempted, as previously noted, to extend her control over Manchuria. Finally, through Pan-Slavism she aspired to play the role of guide and protector of all the Slavic peoples of eastern Europe, including those who were under the rule of Austria-Hungary. That each of these ambitions constituted a threat to the *status quo* scarcely needs emphasis.

*Great Britain
and Italy*

The power policies of Great Britain and Italy were somewhat less closely related to the specific actions of other countries. The policy of Britain, in fact, was directed against almost everyone. She was no less suspicious of the Russian ambitions at Constantinople than she was of the German. Until after the beginning of the twentieth century she distrusted France. Her cardinal aims were (1) to maintain the life lines of her empire, (2) to keep open the sea lanes to her sources of imports and her foreign markets, and (3) to preserve a balance among the nations on the European Continent so that no one of them would ever become strong enough to attack her. If the actions of any other country threatened to interfere with these cardinal aims (as they often did), the hostility of Britain would instantly be aroused. She would seek to put the offending nation in its place by diplomatic pressure, forming an alliance against it, or by going to war, as she finally did against Germany in 1914. The ambitions of Italy before 1914 were almost entirely territorial. She had no great empire to defend, nor was her security threatened from any external source. But she did covet Tripoli in northern Africa, which she expected to take from Turkey, and *Italia irredenta*, the "unredeemed Italy," including Trieste and the South Tyrol, which was still in the possession of Austria.

*Japan becomes
a Great Power*

Shortly before 1900 the empire of Japan began to participate actively in power politics. During the second half of the nineteenth century the island kingdom emerged from its Oriental seclusion and went through a transformation that astonished the world. Feudalism was abolished, and a highly centralized state with a constitution modeled after that of Imperial Germany was established. Science, industrialism, universal education, and conscription were imported from the West. Every large city had its streetcars, skyscrapers, and electric lights, although, in the opinion of most authorities, these were nothing but Western trappings on the surface of a culture

still fundamentally Oriental. In 1895, as has been mentioned, Japan
inflicted a decisive defeat upon China, taking from her the island of
Formosa and acquiring a free hand in Korea. In 1904–1905 the
Mikado's generals and admirals surprised the world even more by
defeating Russia. These victories gave Japan a virtually unquestioned
place among the Great Powers. Western diplomats courted her
favor and bowed and scraped in the presence of her rulers.

One of the clearest expressions of the realities of power politics
before 1914 was the growth of militarism. Since the nations of the
world were living in a condition of international anarchy, it was
almost inevitable that their fears and suspicions should lead to competition in armaments. Europe in particular became an armed camp.
After 1870 every one of its chief powers, with the exception of
Great Britain, adopted conscription and universal military training.
Not only that, but they adopted the belief that national security
depended almost entirely upon the extent of military and naval
preparedness. After every war scare the size of armies and navies
increased until, by 1914, all of the important countries, and many of
the smaller ones also, were staggering under a burden which, in a
saner world, would have been regarded as intolerable. There were,
of course, men of humanity and wisdom who recognized the danger
and did all in their power to ward it off. But there were far too
many others who not only denied that any danger existed but
stoutly maintained that militarism was a positive benefit. Theodore
Roosevelt argued that training for war was necessary to preserve
the "manly and adventurous qualities" in a nation. Field Marshal
von Moltke and Heinrich von Treitschke saw in military conflict
one of the divine elements of the universe and a "terrible medicine" for the human race. The French philosopher, Ernest Renan,
justified war as a condition of progress, "the sting which prevents a
country from going to sleep." Although the propagation of such
doctrines was not the chief cause of militarism, it undoubtedly
strengthened the position of those who believed in armaments and
war as the best methods of solving a nation's problems.

*Militarism and
the armed peace*

Selected Readings—Democracy and Social Reform

Beer, Max, *History of British Socialism*, New York, 1942

Brogan, D. W., *France under the Republic*, New York, 1940

Cole, G. D. H., and Postgate, R., *The British People, 1746–1946*, New
York, 1947

Dawson, W. H., *Bismarck and State Socialism*, New York, 1891

Fife, R. H., *The German Empire between Two Wars*, New York, 1916

Hovell, M., *The Chartist Movement*, New York, 1925

Karpovich, M., *Imperial Russia, 1801–1917*, New York, 1932

Lindsay, A. D., *The Essentials of Democracy*, Philadelphia, 1929
Maynard, John, *Russia in Flux*, New York, 1948
Ogg, F. A., *English Government*, New York, 1929
———, *European Government and Politics*, New York, 1934
Orth, S. P., *Socialism and Democracy in Europe*, New York, 1913
Pares, Bernard, *A History of Russia*, New York, 1928
Pipkin, C. W., *The Idea of Social Justice*, New York, 1928
———, *Social Politics and Modern Democracies*, New York, 1931
Postgate, Raymond, *1848: Story of a Year*, London, 1955
Reid, J. H. S., *The Origins of the British Labour Party*, Minneapolis, 1955
Robertson, Priscilla, *Revolutions of 1848: A Social History*, Princeton, 1952
Robinson, G. T., *Rural Russia under the Old Regime*, New York, 1932
Seymour, Charles, *Electoral Reforms in England, 1832–1885*, New Haven, 1915
Smith, T. V., *The Democratic Way of Life*, Chicago, 1926
Somervell, D. C., *Disraeli and Gladstone*, New York, 1926

—NATIONALISM AND IMPERIALISM

Binkley, R. C., *Realism and Nationalism*, New York, 1935
Clark, Grover, *The Balance Sheets of Imperialism*, New York, 1936
Feis, Herbert, *Europe, the World's Banker, 1870–1914*, New Haven, 1930
Fraser, H. F., *Foreign Trade and World Politics*, New York, 1926
Gewehr, W. M., *The Rise of Nationalism in the Balkans, 1800–1930*, New York, 1931
Griffith, G. O., *Mazzini, Prophet of Modern Europe*, New York, 1932
Guérard, A. L., *Napoleon III*, Cambridge, 1943
Harris, N. D., *Europe and Africa*, New York, 1927
———, *Europe and the East*, New York, 1926
Hayes, C. J. H., *The Historical Evolution of Modern Nationalism*, New York, 1931
———, *Essays on Nationalism*, New York, 1933
Hoskins, H. L., *European Imperialism in Africa*, New York, 1930
Kohn, Hans, *The Idea of Nationalism*, New York, 1944
———, *Basic History of Modern Russia*, New York, 1957
Langer, W. L., *The Diplomacy of Imperialism*, New York, 1950
Moon, P. T., *Imperialism and World Politics*, New York, 1926
Noether, E. P., *Seeds of Italian Nationalism, 1700–1815*, New York, 1951
Owen, D. E., *Imperialism and Nationalism in the Far East*, New York, 1929
Siegfried, A., *France, a Study in Nationality*, New Haven, 1930
Simpson, F. A., *The Rise of Louis Napoleon*, New York, 1925
Snyder, L. L., *From Bismarck to Hitler*, Williamsport, Pa., 1935
———, *Basic History of Modern Germany*, New York, 1957
Somervell, D. C., *The British Empire*, London, 1948
Tan, C. C., *The Boxer Catastrophe*, New York, 1955
730 Willcox, W. B., *Star of Empire*, New York, 1950

Dickinson, G. L., *The International Anarchy*, New York, 1926
Langer, W. L., *European Alliances and Alignments*, New York, 1931
Morgenthau, Hans, *Politics among Nations*, 1954
Schuman, F. L., *International Politics*, fourth edition, New York, 1948
Vagts, Alfred, *A History of Militarism*, New York, 1937
Wright, Quincy, *The Causes of War and the Conditions of Peace*, New York, 1935

Source Materials

Angell, Norman, *The Great Illusion*
Bagehot, Walter, *The English Constitution*
Bernhardi, Friedrich von, *Germany and the Next War*
Hayes, C. J. H., *British Social Politics*
Kropotkin, Prince, *Memoirs of a Revolutionist*
Mill, J. S., *Representative Government*
———, *On Liberty*
Renan, Ernest, *What Is a Nation?*
Ruskin, John, *The Crown of Wild Olive*
Schurz, Carl, *Reminiscences*, pp. 163–65, Failure of the Frankfort Assembly
Scott, J. F., and Baltzly, A., *Readings in European History since 1914*, pp. 106–9, The People's Charter
Tocqueville, Alexis de, *Recollections*, pp. 79–89, February Revolution in France
Tolstoi, Count Leo, *Patriotism or Peace*
Treitschke, Heinrich von, *Politics* (Gowan tr.), pp. 9, 23–25, 31
Turgeniev, Ivan, *Fathers and Sons*, Nihilism

The Rise of the United States

Relations with Europe

The country we call the United States of America began its history as an appendage of Europe. Except for the American Indians and the slaves brought over from Africa, all of its original inhabitants were Europeans. They spoke European languages and brought with them European habits, ideas, and achievements. For years many of them thought of America as a place in which to pick up gold and silver or reap a rich harvest from tobacco or indigo plantations and then return to the Old World to live a life of ease and luxury. By the eighteenth century, however, Americans had begun to think of their country as unique, as a nation with a character and destiny of its own. As time went on, the sense of national independence increased, and more and more modifications were made in the European cultural pattern. American civilization was never divorced from its Old World origins, but it acquired an expanding number of unique characteristics as the nation grew and waxed in power. By 1914 America had surpassed most European countries in the achievement of a democratic society and was at least their equal in devotion to concepts of national greatness.

1. The Youth of the Nation

The growth of a spirit of independence

By the middle of the eighteenth century the thirteen British colonies in America, established between 1607 and 1682, had outgrown their swaddling clothes. Their interests were no longer predominantly those of colonists. Their ideals and habits of thinking, in many cases, had diverged from those of the Mother Country. Their economic system had attained a maturity which gave them a feeling of self-reliance and an unwillingness to be tied any longer to the apron strings of British authority. The British, moreover, had abetted this self-reliance by following a policy for a considerable

A New England Town Meeting. The town meeting, dating from the founding of the New England colonies, survives to this day as a major example of direct democracy in the United States.

period of "salutary neglect" with respect to the colonies. Small wonder, therefore, that they should have drifted steadily toward independence. Many years after independence was formally established, John Adams accurately appraised the situation when he wrote that "the revolution was effected before the war commenced. The revolution was in the minds and hearts of the people." [1]

The causes of the American Revolution, or War for Independence, as it is more accurately called, are fairly well known. First and foremost should be placed opposition to the mercantilist policies of the British government. These were exemplified by various acts for the regulation of trade and the raising of revenue passed by the British Parliament. The oldest were the Acts of Trade and Navigation (1651, 1660–1672) which prohibited trade between England and the colonies in other than English-owned or English-built ships, and forbade the exportation of certain "enumerated articles," such as tobacco, sugar, and cotton to any country except England. Much of the time enforcement of these acts remained rather lax and haphazard, but in 1764 Parliament attempted, by means of the so-called Sugar Act, to tighten up the system. The Sugar Act reduced the tariff on certain imports but levied additional duties on sugar, wines, coffee, silks, and linens brought into the colonies from the French and Spanish West Indies. More important, it reformed the customs service and provided more stringent regulations for the collection of duties. New England merchants, who had grown accustomed to lax enforcement, were incensed because they saw their opportunities for bringing in sugar and molasses from the Spanish and French West Indies about to be cut off. A profitable trade had developed in such commodities, which could be sold in large quantities to distillers to be made into rum.

Causes of the American Revolution: (1) mercantilist policies of the mother country

The Sugar Act of 1764 was designed not merely to regulate but also to increase revenues. The Seven Years' War, or French and

[1] Letter to Mr. Niles, January 14, 1818.

Indian War as it was called in America, had left the British treasury
burdened with debt. Since the war had benefited America, many
British statesmen contended that the colonies should pay a share of
the debt. Accordingly, George Grenville, Chancellor of the Exchequer, introduced into Parliament a number of colonial taxation
measures culminating in the fateful Stamp Act of 1765. The Stamp
Act required that revenue stamps costing from a half penny to
twenty shillings be affixed to all newspapers, pamphlets, commercial
bills, legal documents, and similar papers. The tax would not prove
particularly burdensome, although merchants feared a heavy drain
of hard money, since every bill of lading would be taxed and the
stamps could be purchased only for specie. Nevertheless, the Act
aroused a violent storm of opposition participated in by nearly all
classes. Lawyers, bankers, land speculators, and newspapermen
vented their wrath in denunciations and encouraged the boycotting
of British goods. A mob surged through the crooked streets of Boston and gutted the mansion of Lieutenant-Governor Hutchinson.
From New Hampshire to Georgia the Act was flouted, the agents
who sold the stamps were driven from their offices, and the stamps
themselves were publicly burned.

Of capital importance also as a cause of the Revolution was British interference with the interests of land-hungry colonists in the
West. A Royal Proclamation of 1763 organized all territory acquired
by Britain in the French and Indian War into four regions: Gre-
nada (including several West Indian islands), East Florida, West
Florida, and Quebec. More serious, it reserved all the western territory between the Alleghenies and the Mississippi, and between the
Floridas and Quebec, for the exclusive use of the Indians. The colonists were forbidden to make any purchases or settlements whatever
in that region. At a single stroke all the Western land claims which
the colonies had cherished for years were wiped out. In 1774 Parliament sought to amend matters by passing a new Western land act,
the so-called Quebec Act. This law was intended to correct certain
errors in the Proclamation of 1763, but it seemed only to make matters worse by annexing all of the territory north of the Ohio River
to the Province of Quebec. The Western claims of four colonies in
this region were thereby swept away.

(3) interference
with the land-
hunger of the
colonists

Like all revolutions, the one which occurred in America between
1775 and 1781 had its ideological basis. For reasons not altogether
clear, colonial political leaders drew their inspiration from the English philosophers of the seventeenth century rather than from those
of their own time. It was Locke, Sydney, Harrington, Milton, and
to some extent Sir Edward Coke who provided Samuel Adams,
Thomas Paine, and Thomas Jefferson with their sharpest intellectual
weapons. From such sources they drew the idea that Englishmen, no
matter where they might live, had fundamental rights on which the
British government must not infringe. From such sources also came

the doctrines of the state of nature, the social contract, the law of nature, no taxation without representation, and the right of revolution.

Most fundamental of all the ideological causes, perhaps, were the conflicting theories of representation and the sovereignty of Parliament. Colonial leaders maintained that a true representative must be an *actual* representative, that is, he must live in the district whose interests he purported to represent. For the British the prevailing theory was that of "virtual representation," which meant representation of classes rather than of geographical areas. According to this theory every aristocrat in the empire was *virtually* represented by the British nobility, and every commoner by the members of the House of Commons regardless of the location of the districts which happened to elect them. On the issue of the sovereignty of Parliament disagreement was equally sharp. Colonial philosophers, in accordance with seventeenth-century theory, rejected the doctrine of absolute sovereignty, whether of parliaments, kings, or anyone else. British constitutionalists had gradually evolved the theory that Parliament was legally omnipotent. As their noted leader, Sir William Blackstone, expressed it, "The power and jurisdiction of parliament is so transcendent and absolute that it cannot be confined, either for causes or persons, within any bounds. . . . It can, in short, do every thing that is not naturally impossible." [2] This conception was given legal effect in 1766 with the enactment of the Declaratory Act asserting in sweeping terms the authority of Parliament to "make laws and statutes of sufficient force and validity to bind the colonies in all cases whatsoever."

The incidents which precipitated the actual outbreak of the American Revolution are too well known to require much comment. In March 1770, a company of British soldiers stationed in Boston for the protection of British officials became panicky and opened fire on a disorderly mob. When the smoke had cleared away, four Americans lay dead in the snow. This event was the celebrated Boston Massacre. In December 1773 occurred the Boston Tea Party, when a band of citizens disguised as Indians dumped tea into the harbor in resentment against a monopoly in that commodity which the British government had granted to the powerful East India Company. Britain retaliated by closing the port of Boston until the tea was paid for, increasing the power of the king's subordinates in Massachusetts, and ordering the transportation of political offenders to England for trial. General Gage, commander of the British garrison in Boston, was charged with the enforcement of these "Intolerable Acts," as the colonists called them. In the spring of 1775 he learned that Massachusetts patriots were collecting munitions at Concord. On the night of April 18 he sent a detachment of troops to confiscate them. But the patriots learned of the plan and made

(5) conflicting theories of representation and the sovereignty of Parliament

Incidents precipitating the outbreak of war

[2] *Commentaries*, Book I, Ch. II, pp. 160–61.

preparations to defeat it. When the British arrived in Lexington the next morning, they found a determined band of minute-men lined up across the common. In the resulting confusion and panic some-one fired a shot. Soon the firing became general, and the Americans were dispersed, leaving eight of their number dead on the green. The British continued their march to Concord, but on the return to Boston they were assailed by minute-men from behind stone walls, trees, and houses. When the frightened detachment stumbled into Boston, it had lost 247 of its members in killed and wounded. The battles of Lexington and Concord marked the beginning of the Revolution.

The political and social revolution

The American Revolution had a multiple aspect. In the beginning it was a violent protest against the alleged tyrannies of the British government. Scarcely anyone thought as yet of independence, al-though some had visions of reorganizing the empire under a com-mon sovereign, with autonomy for the various regions. In less than a year a demand for independence had become dominant, and a Declaration proclaiming that "these United Colonies are, and of right ought to be, free and independent states" was signed on July 4, 1776. But the Revolution also had something of the character of a political and social upheaval. In many states radicals like Samuel Adams and Thomas Paine had influence enough to accomplish far-reaching reforms. The new constitutions adopted in 1776 did not simply provide for a replacement of British by colonial rule. They deprived the governors of veto power, reduced their terms to one year, and subjected them to the supremacy of the legislature. In some states elaborate checks and balances were erected to prevent any form of despotism. Pennsylvania, Vermont, and Georgia went to the extent of establishing unicameral legislatures. That these po-litical reforms would be accompanied by efforts in the direction of social reform was almost inevitable. A few states attacked the foun-dations of aristocracy—primogeniture, tithes, quit-rents, and en-tails. Others abolished their state churches or wiped out religious qualifications for holding office. Radical economic legislation was also enacted. Several of the states confiscated crown lands and the princely estates of wealthy loyalists and divided them up among small farmers and war veterans. After the war the radicals in some states gained enough power to pass laws for the benefit of the debtor classes. These measures took the form of *stay* laws, suspend-ing the payment of interest and principal on mortgages; *tender* laws, requiring the acceptance of land or produce at fixed prices as legal tender in payment of debts; and paper-money laws. In 1786 an armed rebellion for the benefit of debtors swept over central Massa-chusetts. Led by Daniel Shays, a former army captain, its objective was to prevent the courts from sitting and rendering judgments for the collection of debts. It was finally put down but not until after

736 an infuriated mob had threatened to besiege the state capitol.

The menace of economic radicalism combined with the weakness of both state and central governments led to a demand for drastic revisions in the national constitution. Since 1781 the colonies as a group had been governed under the Articles of Confederation. These, as their name implies, provided for a confederate, not a federal or centralized government. All power was derived from and could be exercised only through the state governments. The central authority could take no action against individuals. Its "great and radical vice," as Alexander Hamilton pointed out, was its power to legislate only for "states or governments in their corporate or collective capacities as contradistinguished from the individuals of which they consist." [3] This resulted in critical handicaps when it came to raising revenue or obtaining soldiers to serve in the army. By 1786 the threat to the security of property and to orderly and stable government was so serious that most of the conservative leaders of the country were ready for drastic changes. In September of that year a convention to consider problems of interstate commerce was convoked at Annapolis. But with only five states represented, Madison and Hamilton induced the delegates to issue a call for a new convention to assemble in May of the following year. The new convention was to deal with the much broader problem of revising the Articles of Confederation to render them "more adequate to the exigencies of the Union."

The movement for a new constitution

The convention of 1787 met in Philadelphia from May to September behind closed doors. Since the leading delegate, James Madison, kept copious notes, we have what seems to be a full and accurate record of what took place. From the outset the majority of the delegates showed an inclination to scrap the Articles of Confederation and write a new instrument. The Constitution which the convention finally produced bore few of the earmarks indeed of a revision of the Articles. The new government was given a sphere of sovereign authority which the states were powerless to invade. The foundations of the system would rest in part on the people themselves, at least in so far as they chose the members of the House of Representatives and participated in the selection of the Electoral College. A powerful executive was created with authority to veto acts of Congress and to use his own agents to enforce the laws. Provision was made also for a federal judiciary, and at least some of the leaders in the convention intended that the Supreme Court should exercise the power of judicial review, that is, nullifying acts of Congress and of the state legislatures allegedly in conflict with the Constitution. Finally, the Constitution itself, and the laws and treaties made in pursuance thereof, were declared to be the supreme law of the land. The judges in every state were to be bound thereby, regardless of any conflicting provisions in the state constitutions or laws.

Adoption of the Constitution

[3] *Federalist* No. 15.

The adoption of the Constitution of 1787 is regarded by some writers as having accomplished a counter-revolution in the United States. True it is that most of the delegates who took a prominent part in the work of the convention were men of substance and conservative views. None of the old firebrands like Samuel Adams, Patrick Henry, Thomas Paine, and John Hancock were present. Thomas Jefferson was absent from the country as minister to France. Of the delegates who attended, the majority seemed to think of democracy as virtually synonymous with mob rule. Edmund Randolph declared that all the evils from which the country had recently suffered were traceable to the "turbulence and follies of democracy." James Madison thought the people were too prone to impetuous and violent impulses ever to be trusted with unlimited power. The primary aim of the fathers of our government was not to enthrone the masses but to establish a *republic* which would promote stability and protect the rights of property against the leveling tendencies of majorities. For this reason they adopted elaborate checks and balances, devised the Electoral College for choosing the President, created a powerful judiciary, and entrusted the selection of Senators to the legislatures of the several states. These principles reflected a definite reaction against the extreme democracy of the Revolutionary period and the years immediately following. No longer dominant were the Revolutionary ideals of glorification of the common people, defense of the rights of man, and distrust of the courts and executive power. Nevertheless, the political system which the fathers created was liberal in comparison with other governments of that time. The President at least was not a monarch, nor was the Senate a chamber of nobles.

The first decades in the history of the United States under its new Constitution were marked by phenomenal growth and expansion. When the first census was taken in 1790, the country had a total population of 3,900,000. By 1830 this had increased to 12,800,000 and by 1860 to 31,000,000. In 1790 the Union comprised 17 states with a total area of 890,000 square miles. By 1830 there were 27 states with more than double the original area. By 1860 the number of states had increased to 33 and the area to more than three times its original size. The period was characterized also by feverish activity in the extension of transportation facilities. First came the era of canal building. New York State set the precedent by beginning the construction of the Erie Canal in 1817 to connect Lake Erie with the Hudson River. Completed in 1825, it reduced the cost of freight from Buffalo to New York from $120 a ton to $14. Soon other states caught the fever. Pennsylvania projected a canal—with horse railroads and inclined planes in the mountainous regions—to link Philadelphia with Pittsburgh. Some states plunged so deeply into the canal-construction business that they went bankrupt. But even if they had been financially successful, inland waterways would

never have provided a complete transportation system. Facilities
for land transportation were also necessary. Recognizing this need,
Congress made a small appropriation in 1806 to start a great National
Road, eventually to extend from Cumberland, Maryland, to St.
Louis. Renewed appropriations were made grudgingly, however,
and the road was not finished for nearly fifty years. Many more
miles of highways were built by the states but never enough to
meet the need. In 1825 a movement was initiated which was destined
to eclipse in importance all other transportation construction projects. This was the building of the Baltimore and Ohio Railroad,
which was opened to horse-drawn railcar traffic in 1830. Throughout the remainder of the nineteenth century railway construction
absorbed as large a proportion of the nation's resources and manpower as did any other economic activity.

Growth and expansion in the early decades were not confined to
material things. There was notable advancement also of democracy.
From 1789 to 1801 the Federalists held the reins of power, repre- *The growth of*
senting the big landowners, the money power, and the conservatives *democracy*

Thomas Jefferson. Portrait by
Thomas Sully of the great apostle
of liberty at the age of 78.

generally. In the latter year the Democratic-Republicans gained
control as a result of the election of Thomas Jefferson to the Presidency in 1800. This event is often referred to as the Jeffersonian
Revolution, on the supposition that Jefferson was the champion of
the masses and of the political power of the underprivileged. There
is danger, however, in carrying this interpretation too far. In several
respects Jefferson's ideas were far removed from democracy in its
historic meaning. Instead of being a follower of Rousseau, he was a
disciple of Locke. He believed that that government is best which
governs least, and he strenuously opposed the unlimited sovereignty
of the majority. His conception of an ideal political system was an
artistocracy of "virtue and talent," in which respect for personal **739**

liberty would be the guiding principle. Furthermore, he compared the mobs of great cities to sores on the human body and despised the mass of industrial workers as "panders of vice, and the instruments by which the liberties of a country are generally overturned." [4]

*The Jefferson-
ian Revolution*

Yet it cannot be denied that the Jeffersonian movement had a number of democratic objectives of cardinal importance. Its leaders were vigorous opponents of special privilege, whether of birth or of wealth. They worked for the repeal of primogeniture and entails and the abolition of established churches. They led the campaign for the addition of a Bill of Rights to the Federal Constitution and were almost exclusively responsible for its success. Although professing devotion to the principle of the separation of powers, they actually believed in the supremacy of the representatives of the people and viewed with abhorrence the attempts of the executive and judicial branches to increase their power. Three of the most typical ideals of Jefferson himself were decentralized government, periodic revisions of constitutions and laws, and the importance of public education. He stressed the value of local government to the extent of advocating primary assemblies similar to the New England town meetings for the exercise of a large proportion of the public powers. He urged that constitutions and laws be submitted to the people for their approval or rejection every nineteen or twenty years, on the theory that no one generation has the right to bind its successors for the indefinite future. In his later life he completed plans for an elaborate system of public education. There was to be free instruction for all children in the elementary schools, and scholarships were to be provided in district colleges and in the state university for a limited number of students selected on the basis of intelligence and achievement. By this method Jefferson sought to ensure opportunity for all, and not simply for the well-born and the rich. The persons thus educated would be available for selection as natural aristocrats by enlightened citizens who had received enough knowledge to recognize good men when they saw them.

*Jeffersonian De-
mocracy gives
way to Jackson-
ian Democracy*

By the end of the War of 1812 the force of Jeffersonian Democracy was almost entirely spent. Any democratic movement of the future would have to proceed from different premises and rest upon new foundations. Not only did the war create new problems and divert men's interests from the need for reform, but the economic aspect of the country had undergone numerous changes. The common people in the cities had grown conscious of their political importance and had begun to demand privileges. More important, the dominance of the Old South, the stronghold of Jeffersonian Democracy, had passed into history. As a result of the Louisiana Purchase and the settlement of the Northwest Territory, a new frontier had come into existence. Life in the new areas was characterized by a rugged freedom and independence which left no room for snobbish-

[4] *Writings of Jefferson* (Washington ed.), Vol. I, p. 403.

Pink and Green, Edgar Degas (1834–1917). Degas was an impressionist to the extent of his interest in fleeting motion. But as an admirer of the classicist, Ingres, he emphasized line and careful composition. (MMA)

Etretat, Claude Monet (1840–1926). Monet loved this part of the Normandy coast for its rugged cliffs and the shimmering light of the sun on rocks and waves. He called some of his paintings *Impressions*, and the name soon came to designate a school. (MMA)

The Japanese Divan, Henri de Toulouse-Lautrec (1864–1901). Toulouse-Lautrec found his chief source of inspiration in the night life of Paris. *Divan Japonais* was a noted Paris café. (MMA)

Balzac, Auguste Rodin (1840–1917). Rodin was the great realist of XIX-cent. sculpture. He concentrated most of his attention upon facial detail, no matter how unflattering the result might be. (MMA)

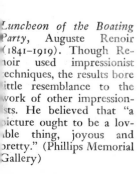

Luncheon of the Boating Party, Auguste Renoir (1841–1919). Though Renoir used impressionist techniques, the results bore little resemblance to the work of other impressionists. He believed that "a picture ought to be a lovable thing, joyous and pretty." (Phillips Memorial Gallery)

Montagne Sainte-Victoire with Aqueduct, Paul Cézanne (1839–1906). This landscape has been a source of inspiration for many of the tendencies of so-called "modern" art. The composition is as structurally balanced and proportioned as a Greek temple. (MMA)

Still Life, Cézanne. It has been said that when the impressionists painted a haystack, there was light, but there was no haystack. When Cézanne painted an apple, there was the play of light; there was also the apple. (MMA)

The Card Players, Cézanne. Here are exemplified Cézanne's skill in composition, his discriminating sense of color, and the sculptured qualities of solidity and depth he gave to his figures. (Stephen C. Clark)

ness or class distinctions. In the struggle to survive, the things that counted most were hard work and sharp wits. Birth and education were of little value. As a consequence, a new democracy, which eventually found its leader in Andrew Jackson, rapidly crystallized around the major principle of equality. The Jacksonian Democrats considered all men politically equal, not merely in rights but in privileges. They therefore stood for universal manhood suffrage, for making all public offices elective, and for rotation in office. Since they considered one man as good as another, they rejected the idea that special knowledge or ability was required for government positions. They even threw open to ordinary citizens such offices as county surveyor and superintendent of schools. Paradoxically, the Jacksonian Democrats approved of a strong executive. They restored the veto power to the state governors, lengthened their terms of office, and acclaimed the President of the United States as the real representative of the people's will. The explanation seems to lie in the fact that they had come to regard legislative bodies as strongholds of "special interests."

2. The Real American Revolution

As was noted earlier, the term American Revolution applied to the events of 1775–1781 was partly a misnomer. The struggle of those years took the form chiefly of a war for independence. True, there were some indications of political and social upheaval manifested especially in the new state constitutions and in the measures against loyalists and aristocrats, but there was no displacement of classes such as occurred during the French Revolution or during the Russian Revolution of 1917. In the main, the same classes continued in power after independence as before. Men of substance like Robert and Gouverneur Morris, John Hancock, and Alexander Hamilton were no less active in the Revolution than impecunious failures like Samuel Adams and Thomas Paine.

The War for Independence a revolution only in part

A much more radical transformation of American society took place in less than a century after independence had become a fact. The event which ushered in this transformation was the Civil War, or War of Secession, or War between the States, as it is variously called. Before the Civil War, as Charles A. Beard has pointed out, the most powerful class in America was the Southern planter aristocracy. Nine of the sixteen Presidents were native Southerners. So were 14 of the 24 Secretaries of State, 15 of the 26 Speakers of the House, and 21 of the 35 justices of the Supreme Court. The Democratic party, dominated generally by Southerners, polled a plurality of the popular vote in 8 of the 10 Presidential elections for which figures are available. Even in 1860 the combined vote of the two branches of the Democratic party exceeded that of the Republican candidate, Abraham Lincoln, by a margin of over

The upheaval wrought by the Civil War

741

350,000. The war and the events which followed reversed the whole picture. A new class of ambitious, self-made men, composed in part of the free farmers of the West and in part of industrial capitalists in the Eastern cities, now captured the reins of power. The Southern agrarians were saddled with disabilities, crippled economically, and deprived of all vestiges of political authority. During the turbulent aftermath of the war, bold enterprisers in the North took advantage of a rich harvest of opportunities in land speculation, railroad building, and exploitation of mineral resources. They also made the most of their political power to strengthen their hold upon the government and to use it to enhance their economic interests.

Causes of the Civil War: (1) slavery

The most obvious cause of the frightful conflict between North and South that raged from 1861 to 1865 was slavery. The first Negro slaves had been brought to Virginia from Africa in 1619. For nearly two centuries thereafter the number increased slowly, and the problem of slavery did not assume serious proportions. By the end of the eighteenth century many Southerners themselves had come to look upon human bondage as undesirable and longed for its early extinction. Increasing numbers of them provided in their wills for the liberation of their slaves and contributed money to various projects for returning the Negroes to Africa. But in 1793 the tables were completely turned by the invention of the cotton gin. The production of cotton was changed overnight from a depressed activity with a doubtful future into a tremendously profitable enterprise. The total output grew from 4000 bales in 1790 to 175,000 in 1810 and 4,000,000 in 1860. In a very real sense Cotton was made King, and the plantation system with its accompaniment of slavery was firmly fixed in the South.

(2) the increasing inequality of North and South

Yet it would be a mistake to suppose that the war grew out of an attempt by the North to coerce the South into abandoning slavery. Until virtually the eve of the struggle sentiment among Northerners was far from unanimous in support of abolition. Abolitionists were commonly regarded as fanatics and disturbers of the peace and were sometimes brutally mistreated for their activities. In 1835 an infuriated crowd attacked William Lloyd Garrison, tied a rope around his neck, and dragged him through the streets of Boston. Two years later a frenzied mob in Illinois lynched the Abolitionist editor, Elijah P. Lovejoy. What most Northerners were chiefly concerned about was the extension of slavery into the territories. They were willing to tolerate its continued existence in the South, but they resented its intrusion into the Louisiana Purchase or into the regions of the Southwest conquered from Mexico in 1848. Such areas they hoped to organize into free states to be settled by land-hungry migrants from New England and the Middle Atlantic region. Perhaps the South would have tolerated such hopes had the two sections remained substantially equal in power and influence. But such was far from the case. Although North and

South each had the same number of states as late as 1840, they differed widely in population. The inhabitants of the North numbered 9,728,000 and those of the South 7,344,000. This gave to the North a total of 135 seats in the House of Representatives compared with only 87 for the South. John C. Calhoun complained that on account of this disparity in numbers, the North would have a perpetual majority in the Electoral College and could therefore prevent a Southerner from ever being chosen President.

As the tides of history moved closer to armed conflict, sectional antagonism loomed ever larger as the real cause of the Civil War. The South was agricultural, the North increasingly industrial. As a *(3) sectional antagonisms* producer of raw materials for export, the former opposed protective tariffs since they would increase the costs of imports. The latter saw in protectionism an indispensable device to enable its new industries to maintain themselves against foreign competition. From the viewpoint of the North a strong central government was necessary to provide internal improvements and to maintain the order and stability essential to the growth of prosperity. Northern statesmen therefore contended that secession and nullification were illegal, that the central government derived its authority from the whole body of the people, and that the Union was older than the states. Deeply conscious of the unique character of their institutions, Southern leaders hoped to keep the activities of the central government down to a minimum. They insisted that sovereignty rested with the separate states, that the states had created the Union, and that the Federal government was merely their agent. Since each state had entered the Union of its own volition, it was free to withdraw therefrom whenever it saw fit. It was free also to nullify any act of the central government which conflicted with its own interests. With the passage of time issues of sectionalism and states' rights became more and more closely linked with the issue of slavery. It seemed to Southerners that the only way they could defend the interests of their section was to insist upon the right to carry slavery into all of the new territories in the hope that they might organize some of them at least as slave states and thereby redress the balance between North and South. Acceptance of this issue by Northerners as fundamental was exemplified by the organization of the Free Soil party in 1848 with its cardinal objective of excluding slavery from the territories. It was exemplified also by a bloody war in Kansas in 1854–1856 between anti-slavery immigrants from New England and pro-slavery partisans who had crossed over from Missouri.

In 1857 the South rejoiced in what seemed a great victory for its contention that slavery could not be outlawed in territories subject to the Federal government. On March 6 of that year the *(4) the Dred Scott decision* Supreme Court, speaking through Chief Justice Taney, issued its decision in the famous case of Scott *v.* Sandford. Dred Scott was a slave owned by a surgeon in the United States Army. His master had taken him from Missouri to Illinois, thence to Minnesota Territory, where slavery had been forbidden by the Missouri Compromise, and finally back to Missouri. There he sued for his freedom on the basis of having twice been a resident on free soil. The Supreme Court rejected his plea on the ground that the Missouri Compromise was unconstitutional. Congress had no right to prohibit slavery in the territories, for this would deprive Southerners who might wish to go there of their property without due process. The Chief Justice also declared that no Negro, whether bond or free, had a right to sue in the Federal Courts. Negroes were not citizens of the United States, and no law of Congress or act of a state legislature could give them that status. When the Constitution was adopted, they were considered as subordinate and inferior beings. It was never the intention of the framers of that instrument that they should enjoy an equality of rights and privileges with members of the Caucasian race. The Chief Justice seems to have been actuated by noble motives. He hoped that a definitive answer from the Supreme Court would settle the question of slavery in the territories, once and for all, and thereby avert civil war. Northerners, however, almost to a man condemned the decision. They admitted the possibility that it might be good constitutional law, but they declared that there was a higher law than the Constitution, and many of them stood ready to uphold that law by force. Instead of averting a civil war, the Dred Scott decision did almost as much as any other factor to make such a war inevitable.

The immediate cause of the outbreak of armed conflict was the election of Abraham Lincoln to the Presidency in 1860. Lincoln was the candidate of the Republican party, founded six years earlier for the express purpose of opposing the extension of slavery. In 1856 it nominated John C. Frémont for President and campaigned on the slogan "Free soil, free speech, and Frémont." Four years later it adopted a broad platform designed to appeal to almost everybody in the North but the radical Abolitionists. It promised internal improvements, high tariffs for the benefit of industry, and a quarter-section of free public land for settlers in the Western territories. On the slavery question it took the clear-cut position of no interference with the institution in the Southern states but absolute exclusion from the territories. Despite the moderation of its platform on the slavery issue, the triumph of the Republican party in the election of 1860 was regarded by the South as almost the equivalent of a declaration of war. The candidate of the party was no Abolitionist; indeed, he had gone so far as to declare himself in favor of a Constitutional amendment protecting slavery in the South. But he had also asserted, just two years before his election, that the nation could not endure "half slave and half free," and he continued his denunciation of the Dred Scott decision, which the South regarded as offering almost the only hope of restoring the balance between

*(5) the election
of Lincoln*

744

the two sections. Without such a balance it would be forever impossible to prevent the North from imposing its costly system of tariffs and internal improvements upon an agrarian South which had no desire for such things.

As soon as it was certain that Lincoln had been elected, South Carolina seceded from the Union. The movement spread like a madness, and more and more states announced their withdrawal. On February 8, 1861, delegates from seven seceded states met at Montgomery, Alabama, and established the Confederate States of America. Jefferson Davis was chosen President and Alexander H. Stephens Vice-President. A month later a new constitution was adopted resembling the Constitution of the United States with a few notable exceptions. The Confederate Constitution limited the President to a single term of six years. It expressly recognized and protected Negro slavery. It gave to Congress the power to appropriate money only upon the specific request of the President. It authorized the President to veto separate items in appropriation bills. It granted to members of the Cabinet the privilege of holding seats in Congress and participating in the discussions. In throwing off their allegiance to the United States and establishing a new government, Southern statesmen contended that they were doing nothing more than exercising the right vouchsafed in the Declaration of Independence to "alter or abolish" a form of government whenever it becomes destructive of "life, liberty, and the pursuit of happiness." To this the North replied, through President Lincoln, that the right of revolution referred to in the Declaration of Independence applied only to tyrannical governments. There could be no right to destroy the freest and most democratic government on earth.

Establishment of the Confederacy

The Civil War followed its tragic course through four horrible years. It began with the attack on Fort Sumter on April 12, 1861, and ended with Robert E. Lee's surrender at Appomattox Court House on April 9, 1865. From the outset the North had decided advantages, with a population of 22,000,000 compared with only 9,000,000 for the Confederacy, and vastly greater financial resources. The North also had a navy, which the South lacked, and a much more diversified and highly developed economic structure. Nearly all the manufacturing establishments were concentrated in the North, while the South was not even self-sufficient in food supplies. On the other hand, the Confederacy had a military tradition, a coast line so long that it almost prevented a blockade, and the even more positive advantage of fighting on its own territory. Its leaders could easily persuade the people that all they needed to do was to hold on until the North became weary and abandoned the struggle. During the first two years the prospects of the South seemed bright. Its armies managed to win or at least to stave off defeat in most of the battles, and possibilities of foreign aid were particularly encouraging. But a turning point came in 1862. In September of that

The military history of the war

year General Lee, hopeful of capturing the railroad bridge at Harrisburg and cutting the Union in two, marched a powerful army across the Potomac. General George B. McClellan, with a Union force twice as large, advanced to meet him. The two armies clashed at Antietam Creek in Maryland. Although not decisively beaten, Lee's troops were sufficiently exhausted that they withdrew across the Potomac. Had they succeeded in attaining their objective, they might well have gone on to capture Philadelphia and probably New York. Lee made one further attempt to invade the North in July 1863, but was again forced to retreat after being checked by the forces of General Meade at Gettysburg. After Antietam the fortunes of the Confederacy steadily waned. The prospects of foreign as-

Lincoln and Staff Officers of General McClellan on the Eve of the Battle of Antietam, 1862. From a photograph by Matthew Brady in the National Archives, Washington, D.C.

sistance faded into oblivion, and Lincoln took advantage of the more favorable turn of events to proclaim the liberation of the slaves in all states and portions of states still in rebellion against the Union. The Emancipation Proclamation transformed the Civil War into a crusade and the crusading fervor helped to guarantee victory for the North.

The results of the Civil War can only be described as climactic. More than 200,000 men were killed in battle or died of wounds, and 413,000 others died of disease, accidents, and other causes. Many Abolitionists doubtless considered this holocaust of lives justifiable, for slavery was permanently destroyed by the addition of the Thirteenth Amendment to the Constitution just before the war ended. Later the Fourteenth Amendment conferred citizenship upon the liberated Negroes, and the Fifteenth forbade the denial of suffrage to them on account of their race, color, or previous con-

Results of the war

dition of servitude. But the Civil War also had other effects. It left
the South prostrate and hagridden by fears and prejudices and incapable for years of taking any part in the democratic evolution of
the country. Southerners who had participated in the rebellion were
deprived by Congress of the privilege of voting or of holding office,
with the result that several of the former Confederate states passed
under the control of illiterate Negroes and "carpetbag" politicians
who had come down from the North. The Fourteenth Amendment
not only bestowed citizenship upon the former slaves, but it contained a provision of tremendous significance for the economic development of the country. The provision referred to forbade any
state to "deprive any person of life, liberty, or property without due
process of law." Representatives of big business contended that the
word "person" in this provision included *corporations* as well as
individuals. By 1886 the Supreme Court had come to accept this
contention. The result was to give an enormous stimulus to the
growth and expansion of corporations, for it made them virtually
immune for several decades from regulation. Almost any act of a
state legislature prescribing maximum hours or minimum wages
could be attacked as depriving corporations of their property without due process. Scarcely anything did more to further the economic
revolution in the United States which stemmed from the Civil War.

3. The Return to Reform

The Civil War and the antecedent controversy over slavery and
states' rights sealed the doom of the Jacksonian Revolution. After
1840 democratic progress and even interest in democracy were relatively slight. Although often acclaimed as a struggle for freedom and
equality, the Civil War ushered in a period of frenzied dollar-
chasing and crude exploitation which Mark Twain aptly called the
Gilded Age. Until about 1890 the popular attitude was to look upon
the natural wealth of America as a Great Barbecue to be shared by
everyone with ambition enough to elbow his way to the front. The
prevailing economic philosophy was that of *laissez faire* and free
competition, or what later came to be known as rugged individualism. Poverty was considered a badge of shiftlessness, and wealth a
sure sign of virtue. Economic competition was regarded as the
counterpart of the struggle for existence and survival of the fittest
in the biological sphere. The more ruthless the competition the
better, in order to ensure the prompt weeding out of the weak and
incompetent. That the prevalence of such doctrines was not favorable to movements for the benefit of the unprivileged masses should
be readily apparent.

Nevertheless, such movements did eventually get under way, and
by the 1890's several had attained a vigorous growth. Though all
had their beginnings as vehicles of class discontent, most of them

*Effects of the
Civil War in
checking de-
mocracy*

747

came in time to be worthy successors of Jeffersonian and Jacksonian Democracy. Their leaders fought for what they considered
the birthright of the great mass of citizens. The first of the post-Civil
War movements of consequence was the Greenback movement of
the 1870's and 1880's. Primarily an expression of the discontent of
debt-ridden farmers, it also had the support of the economist Henry
C. Carey and the industrialist Peter Cooper, who became the
candidate of the Independent National (Greenback) party for President in 1876. The cardinal aim of the movement was to establish
what is now called a managed currency. That is, the government
by issuing greenbacks would expand the supply of currency to keep
pace with the growth of population and the economic development of the country. Much was made of the claim that money in
circulation had shrunk from $58 per capita in 1865 to $17 in 1876.
This shrinkage, it was argued, had meant severe hardship for debtors,
for farmers especially, who had borrowed money to buy land at
inflated prices during or soon after the Civil War. What they needed
was an increase in the volume of money in circulation, which would
produce a rise in prices of the things they had to sell and thereby
enable them to pay off their mortgages. But the Greenbackers also
had other objectives. They advocated income taxes and the restriction of sales of public lands to actual settlers. In 1888, hoping to
win the support of organized labor, they extended their platform to
include demands for government ownership of railroads and tele-
graphs, woman suffrage, and the direct election of United States
Senators.

A broader and more virile movement than Greenbackism was
the Populist movement of the 1890's. Again the most substantial

support came from the farmers. Better prices for agricultural commodities in the late 1880's had allayed the demand for inflation of
the currency, but it flared up again in the 1890's as depression reared
its ugly head. This time it took the form of agitation for the coinage
of silver in the ratio of 16 for silver to 1 of gold. The purpose
would be the same: to increase prices of food and raw commodities,
which had sunk to abnormal levels, and thereby enable producers
to pay their debts. The coinage of silver would also have the advantage of appealing to Western miners as well as to the farmers of
the West and South. In the campaign of 1892 the Populists nominated
James B. Weaver of Iowa for President, on a platform which advocated a graduated income tax, postal savings banks, government
ownership of railroads and telegraph and telephone lines, direct
election of United States Senators, and a single term for the President. General Weaver polled a popular vote of over 1,000,000 and
the electoral votes of four states. Four years later the Populists
repeated their platform, with a few minor additions. In the meantime, free silverites had captured control of the Democratic party

and had nominated for President a facile young orator from Nebraska, William J. Bryan, whose speech denouncing attempts to "crucify mankind upon a cross of gold" had swept the convention off its feet. Since the Democratic convention wrote into its platform nearly everything that the Populists stood for, the latter had no alternative but to endorse Bryan as their candidate. The campaign that followed was one of the most exciting in American history. The Populists were denounced as atheists and communists and Bryan as a dangerous demagogue who was nothing but their instrument. The election resulted in a victory for the Republican candidate, William McKinley, with 7,100,000 votes to 6,500,000 for Bryan.

The election of 1896 marked the high tide of the Populist movement. The party nominated candidates in 1900, but the old fire and fervor were gone. Several factors were responsible. Failure of the wheat crop in India in 1896 was followed by a short European crop in 1897. American farmers who had grain to export benefited from the higher prices. More important were the discovery of rich gold resources in the Klondike and in South Africa and the development of the cyanide process for extracting gold from low-content ores. As a result, the world production of the yellow metal more than doubled in a few years. Prosperity returned, and the silver advocates could no longer make the valid claim that the supply of gold was insufficient to provide for the currency needs of the country. Yet it was too much to expect that the idealism generated by the Greenback and Populist movements would completely die out. In the early years of the twentieth century it rose phoenix-like from the ashes of defeat and gained a sufficient momentum to make it by 1914 one of the most vitalizing forces in the history of the Republic. Crystallizing into the Progressive movement, it differed from its earlier examples in having a broader intellectual and urban appeal and in being concerned with a wider variety of issues. Its leaders included not simply orators and statesmen from the prairies, but philosophers like John Dewey, civic reformers like Tom L. Johnson and Lincoln Steffens, educators like Charles Van Hise of Wisconsin and David Starr Jordan of Stanford, and publicists like Walter Lippmann and Herbert Croly.

The decline of Populism and rise of Progressivism

The earliest formulations of Progressive doctrine seem to have been the Wisconsin Idea and the Oregon System. The former, the work of Charles Van Hise and Robert M. LaFollette, called for the direct primary, tax reform, the regulation of railroads, and especially the use of the facilities of the state university in advancing government by the people. The Oregon System was a collection of proposals for reform which were eventually adopted widely. They included the Australian or secret ballot, registration of voters, the initiative and referendum, the direct primary, the recall, and corrupt practices acts restricting campaign contributions and expenditures with a view to clipping the wings of machine politicians. As time went on, the movement embraced nearly all of the Populist doctrines

Progressive doctrine

except the currency proposals. Many of its leaders also endorsed the short ballot and proportional representation. The former is a plan for restricting popular election to the principal legislative and executive officials, who would be held strictly accountable for their policies and actions. All other officials would be appointed, for the most part under civil-service regulation. The purpose of the short ballot is to relieve the burden of choice on the voter and thereby enable him to express his preferences more intelligently. As was indicated earlier, proportional representation is a scheme for giving representation to political parties in direct proportion to their voting strength. It guarantees seats in the legislative body not merely to the party which has captured a majority of the votes but to each of the minority parties as well.

The growth of Progressivism

The Progressive movement reached the climax of its power between 1910 and 1916. The first of these years witnessed the famous Insurgents' Revolt. A band of Progressive Republican members of the House of Representatives, led by George W. Norris of Nebraska, joined with the Democrats in rebellion against the exercise of autocratic powers by Speaker Joseph G. Cannon. They succeeded in debarring the Speaker from membership on the Committee of Rules and in making it and all other committees elective by the House. Proud and confident as a result of this victory, the Insurgents cast about for new triumphs. In January, 1911, they organized the National Progressive Republican League in combination with such senators as LaFollette of Wisconsin and Jonathan Bourne of Oregon. They adopted a platform combining the chief elements of the Wisconsin Idea and the Oregon System and gave serious consideration to urging the nomination of LaFollette as Republican candidate for President. Some Progressives, however, favored the nomination of Theodore Roosevelt, who had ended his term in the White House in 1909 and had lately returned from a hunting expedition in Africa. It seemed to his admirers that as a popular idol, he would have a much better chance of winning the election than would LaFollette. Their attitude was summed up in the following doggerel:

> Quick and hair-triggerous,
>   Joyous and vigorous,
> Home from the niggerous
>   African shore,
> Bringing a zoo with him,
> Zebra and gnu with him,
> What shall we do with him—
>   Our Theodore?
>
> . . . .
>
> No sweet manorial,
>   Grave professorial,

Staid senatorial
    Honors will do.
Give him the Stick again,
Freedom to kick again,
Raise the Old Nick again!
    "Whoop!" and "Hurroo!" [5]

When Roosevelt failed to win the Republican nomination in 1912, he and his followers bolted the party. Soon afterward they held their own convention and launched the Progressive party with Roosevelt as its candidate. Enthusiasm knew no bounds. The delegates paraded around the hall singing "Onward Christian Soldiers." The nominee himself declared, "We stand at Armageddon, and we battle for the Lord." In the campaign that followed, Roosevelt

The crusade of 1912

The Progressive Movement, 1912. Theodore Roosevelt, candidate for President on the Progressive, or Bull Moose, ticket, addressing a gathering at Morrisville, Vermont.

labeled his program the "New Nationalism." This title was meant to convey the idea of a strong national government exercising positive functions to protect the people against the greedy interests. Such functions would include strict regulation of business by a Federal commission, prohibition of child labor and of injunctions in labor disputes, a minimum wage for women, an eight-hour day for women and children, workmen's compensation, the establishment of a Department of Labor in the Cabinet, and insurance against sickness, unemployment, and old age. To the familiar proposals for universal suffrage, direct election of United States Senators, and the initiative, referendum, and recall, Roosevelt added a demand for the recall of judicial decisions. By far the most radical of his doctrines, this proposal would have given the people the right to overturn the decision of any state court declaring an act of the legislature unconstitutional.

Although Roosevelt was defeated for President in 1912, the outcome of the election was nevertheless a Progressive victory. For

[5] Arthur Guiterman, "His Future," *Collier's*, June 18, 1910.

*The election of
Wilson*

the candidate who did win was a Progressive in everything but name. The victor in the election was Woodrow Wilson, nominee of the Democratic party. As soon as it became evident that the Republicans would split, a triumph for the Democrats was assured, provided only that they could agree upon a progressive candidate. This condition was not easily fulfilled. Champ Clark of Missouri, favorite of the conservatives, had managed to corral the largest number of delegates. Fortunately for the progressives, Bryan was determined to prevent the selection of a candidate backed by either the New York bankers or by Tammany Hall. On the forty-sixth ballot Wilson received the nomination. Governor of New Jersey and erstwhile President of Princeton, Woodrow Wilson was one of the most unusual of American statesmen. In no sense a politician, he had won distinction chiefly as a scholar and an educational leader. He had become Governor of New Jersey in 1910 mainly because the Democrats needed a "respectable" candidate if they hoped to win against their powerful rivals. Once in office he had proceeded to repudiate the bosses and to push through the legislature a series of impressive reforms. His program as candidate for President duplicated many of the Roosevelt proposals. However, he did take a stronger position against the trusts; he demanded lower tariffs; and he declined to advocate the recall of judicial decisions.

The New Freedom

Wilson was inaugurated President on March 4, 1913. For three years thereafter he dedicated almost all his efforts to realization of his progressive program. In large measure he was successful. He fought the tariff lobbyists to a standstill and forced Congress to reduce the duties on over 900 articles. He established the Federal Reserve system designed to provide better regulation of banking and more flexible currency and credit arrangements. He procured the enactment of the Clayton Anti-Trust Act prohibiting interlocking directorates and price discrimination to prevent competition. He established the Federal Trade Commission with power to issue "cease and desist" orders against corporations found to be engaged in unfair business practices. Among his other achievements were an eight-hour law for interstate railways, a child-labor act to prevent the shipment in interstate commerce of products of child labor, and a Federal Farm Loan system to provide for the farmers easier credit than they could obtain from commercial banks. The entire program he proudly named the New Freedom. It came to an untimely end, however, as threats of a war with Germany darkened the skies. After 1916 Wilson's attention was so completely absorbed in problems of international conflict that he had no time or energy left for domestic reform. As a result, Progressivism passed into history in much the same way as did the Jeffersonian and Jacksonian movements of the preceding century. Each was arrested by the outbreak of war—the first by the War of 1812, the second by the Mexican War of 1846–1848 and the Civil War of 1861–1865, and the third by World War I.

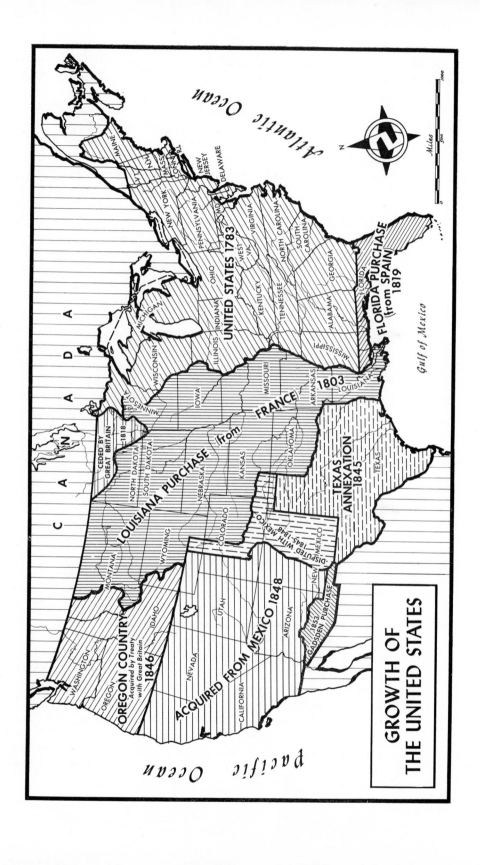

GROWTH OF
THE UNITED STATES

4. *The United States and the World*

No view, perhaps, is more widely held than the theory that the United States, during most of its history, adhered to an isolationist policy. Isolationism was certainly a dream of thousands of Americans. Their ancestors came to this continent in the first place with a determination to shake the dust of Europe off their feet. The oppression many of them had suffered in the Old World and the hardships of their voyage across the Atlantic made America seem like the Promised Land. Europe, by contrast, appeared corrupt and degenerate, perpetually involved in dynastic wars and struggles over the balance of power. On the very eve of our independence, Thomas Paine warned in *Common Sense* that it was the "true interest of America to steer clear of European Contentions." Similar feelings prompted President Washington to counsel the nation in his Farewell Address against "interweaving our destiny with that of any part of Europe." But the classic statement of American isolationism was a slogan often attributed to Washington but actually formulated by Jefferson. In his First Inaugural the third President admonished his countrymen to have "peace, commerce, and honest friendship, with all nations—entangling alliances with none."

Isolationist doctrine continued to be preached throughout the nineteenth and into the twentieth century. Undoubtedly its most noted formulation was the Monroe Doctrine in 1823. This was an expression of America's fear that the reactionary powers of Europe (Austria, Russia, Prussia, and France) might use their combined power to force the republics of the Western Hemisphere which had proclaimed their independence of Spain back under the Spanish yoke. There was concern, also, that having done this, the Alliance might turn upon the United States in order to wipe out the real hotbed of revolutionary ideas. The Doctrine declared that any attempt by European powers to extend their system to the New World would be regarded by the United States as "dangerous to her peace and safety." It also contained the self-denying clause that the United States would refrain from taking part in any of the wars of European powers, "in matters relating to themselves," and would not interfere in the internal concerns of any of these powers. The Monroe Doctrine remained the principal guiding star of United States foreign policy for more than a century. It was used in 1867 to oust the French from Mexico after Napoleon III had taken advantage of the American Civil War to establish a puppet empire south of the Rio Grande. It was invoked against the British in 1895 to compel them to accept United States intervention in a boundary dispute between Venezuela and British Guiana. Fear of its being applied in 1903 induced Germany to abandon a blockade of the coast of Venezuela upon which she had embarked to compel that unfortunate country to acknowledge the claims of some German investors.

Unfortunately, the Monroe Doctrine was also used occasionally as an instrument for the advancement of the "manifest destiny" of the United States. As early as 1820 ardent expansionists like Henry Clay had proclaimed it to be the destiny of the United States to add to its domain the entire North American continent, including the islands off the coast. In 1845 Texas was annexed, soon afterward the Oregon Territory, and in 1848 most of the land now constituting the states of New Mexico, Arizona, and California was taken from Mexico. By the eve of the Civil War there was agitation in the South for the acquisition of Cuba, which the North matched during the war with demands for the annexation of Canada. In 1895 President Cleveland's Secretary of State, Richard Olney, declared that the United States was "practically sovereign on this continent," and that its fiat was law "upon the subjects to which it confines its interposition."

The Monroe Doctrine and Manifest Destiny

The most important uses or misuses of the Monroe Doctrine, in the twentieth century at least, concerned the Panama Canal and internal disorder in the Central American and West Indian republics. In 1901 the United States government obtained the consent of Great Britain to abrogation of the Clayton-Bulwer Treaty of 1850, which had given the British joint rights in any canal that might be constructed on the Isthmus of Panama. But another obstacle stood in the way. The Isthmus of Panama belonged to the republic of Colombia, whose government was not inclined to dispose of its rights on the isthmus short of a stiff indemnity. When the United States offer of $10,000,000 in cash and an annuity of $250,000 was rejected, Panamanian leaders organized a revolt, having received the impression that the United States would give them protection and virtually ensure the success of their enterprise. The revolt was timed to begin on the day when a United States cruiser would arrive in the harbor of Colon. Everything proceeded like clockwork. The revolutionists arrested the Colombian officials on the isthmus and proclaimed the independence of the Republic of Panama. United States marines prevented all effective efforts of the Colombian government to suppress the revolution, and four days later the Department of State in Washington recognized the rebel government as the sovereign authority in Panama. The Colombians nursed their wounded feelings until 1921, when the United States Senate, desirous of obtaining access to Colombian oil, awarded the government an indemnity of $25,000,000.

Acquisition of the Canal Zone

Acquisition of the Canal Zone made the existence of stable governments in the surrounding republics all the more important to the United States. But, in addition, many of these states were rapidly becoming economic colonies of the Colossus of the North. United

The Roosevelt Corollary

States bankers, and some European investors also, had lent large sums of money to Central American and West Indian governments. When these governments defaulted on their debts, the specter of European intervention was likely to loom on the horizon. In 1904 this danger confronted the Dominican Republic, which had passed through an orgy of strife and bloodshed. The situation gave President Theodore Roosevelt an excuse for issuing what has since come to be known as the Roosevelt Corollary to the Monroe Doctrine. In it the wielder of the Big Stick announced that "chronic wrongdoing or impotence" in any of the independent states of the Western Hemisphere might force the United States, "however reluctantly," to exercise an international police power. Since, under the Monroe

Building the Panama Canal. The Pedro Miguel Lock.

Doctrine, European governments were forbidden to intervene, it would be the duty of the government in Washington to go down into the disorderly republics, clean up the messes, and compel the payment of debts. In pursuance of this policy armed intervention was carried out, not only by Theodore Roosevelt in the Dominican Republic, but also by Wilson in Haiti and the Dominican Republic and by Taft and Coolidge in Nicaragua. The Roosevelt Corollary remained in effect until 1930, when it was repudiated by the Clark Memorandum, issued by J. Reuben Clark, Under-Secretary of State in the Hoover administration.

The history of the foreign policy of the United States can be appropriately divided into two periods—from the beginning to 1898, and from 1898 to the present. During the first, the United

States did not commonly intervene in the affairs of the Old World or play for the stakes of international power. To be sure, there were apparent exceptions. Jefferson sent naval vessels to the Mediterranean to wipe out the nests of Barbary pirates, and the United States as a nation participated on a limited scale in the Wars of the French Revolution and much more extensively in the Napoleonic Wars. But the purpose of all these activities was essentially the pursuit of domestic interests. They did not involve efforts to conquer distant colonies or to play any part in the power rivalries of foreign empires.

Beginning with 1898 the United States embarked on a new course with respect to foreign policy. No longer were her interests confined to the Western Hemisphere. The maintenance of a balance of power in Europe and the Asiatic intrigues and rivalries of the great empires were also matters of concern. In the summer of 1898 the government of the United States, acting at the behest of a little group of imperialists, took one of the most fateful steps in its history. This was the destruction of the Spanish fleet in the harbor of Manila, which paved the way for the annexation of the Philippine Islands. The pretext was the fact that the United States was then at war with Spain, but the actual purpose was far different. The men responsible for the venture—Theodore Roosevelt, Assistant Secretary of the Navy; Henry Cabot Lodge, Senator from Massachusetts; Albert J. Beveridge, Senator from Indiana; and Alfred T. Mahan, Admiral in the United States Navy—believed that the Philippines would have economic and strategic value in themselves, but that most of all they would provide a precious entering wedge to exploitation of the China trade. None of these expectations was really fulfilled. Instead, possession of the Philippines served mainly to involve the United States in the power politics of the Far East. Every increase in the might of Japan or of Russia, every enlargement of the German or French sphere of influence in China, seemed like a threat to the interests of the United States.

Between 1898 and 1914 the government of the United States intervened both openly and secretly a number of times in Old World politics. In 1899, when it had become evident that predatory powers, notably Germany, France, Russia, and Japan, were about to carve the whole Chinese Empire into spheres of influence, Secretary of State John Hay, with secret prompting from the British, issued the Open Door Policy. Contrary to popular belief, it did not establish commercial equality in China, but provided merely that the several powers must not discriminate, within their spheres of influence, in favor of their own citizens with regard to commercial privileges. Even in this limited form it failed to receive the definite approval of any of the Great Powers except Britain. In 1905 President Theodore Roosevelt intervened in the Russo-Japanese War to induce the belligerents to lay down their arms and to sign the Treaty of Portsmouth. Although both contestants were nearly exhausted, United

States intervention came at a juncture favorable to Japan. Roosevelt was pro-Japanese and regarded Russia as the primary menace to a balance of power in the Far East. In the same year, with Germany and France at loggerheads over Morocco, Roosevelt took steps to get the two countries to compose their differences at an international conference. The conference met at Algeciras, Spain, in 1906. Two representatives of the United States participated, and Roosevelt, who was strongly pro-French, boasted, with more braggadocio than accuracy, that he stood the Kaiser on his head "with great decision." In succeeding years the same American President authorized agreements with Japan, giving her a free hand in Korea and receiving in return Japanese recognition of the United States title to the Philippines and pious pledges on the independence of China.

Selected Readings

Beard, C. A., *Economic Origins of Jeffersonian Democracy*, New York, 1915
——— and M. R., *The Rise of American Civilization*, New York, 1933
Becker, C. L., *The Declaration of Independence*, New York, 1942
———, *The United States: an Experiment in Democracy*, New York, 1920
Commager, H. S., *The American Mind*, New Haven, 1950
Curti, Merle, *The Growth of American Thought*, New York, 1943
Dorfman, Joseph, *The Economic Mind in American Civilization*, New York, 1949, three vols.
Faulkner, H. U., *The Quest for Social Justice, 1898–1914*, New York, 1931
Filler, Louis, *Crusaders for American Liberalism*, New York, 1939
Gabriel, R. H., *The Course of American Democratic Thought*, New York, 1956
Hicks, Granville, *The Great Tradition, an Interpretation of American Literature since the Civil War*, New York, 1933
Hofstadter, Richard, *The American Political Tradition and the Men Who Made It*, New York, 1948
———, *The Age of Reform: From Bryan to F.D.R.*, New York, 1955
Kelly, Alfred H., and Harbison, W. A., *The American Constitution*, rev. ed., New York, 1955
Latané, J. H., *America as a World Power, 1897–1907*, New York, 1907
Link, A. S., *Wilson: The New Freedom*, Princeton, 1956
Myers, Gustavus, *The History of American Idealism*, New York, 1925
Nettels, C. P., *The Roots of American Civilization*, New York, 1938
Parrington, V. L., *Main Currents in American Thought*, one-volume edition, New York, 1930
Perkins, Dexter, *Hands Off; a History of the Monroe Doctrine*, Boston, 1941
Randall, J. G., *The Civil War and Reconstruction*, Boston, 1937
Rutland, R. A., *The Birth of the Bill of Rights*, Chapel Hill, 1955
Savelle, Max, *The Foundations of American Civilization*, New York, 1942

———, *Seeds of Liberty; the Genesis of the American Mind*, New York,
1948

Schlesinger, A. M., *New Viewpoints in American History*, New York, 1937

Schlesinger, A. M., Jr., *The Age of Jackson*, Boston, 1945

Turner, F. J., *The Frontier in American History*, New York, 1921

Wecter, Dixon, *The Saga of American Society; a Record of Social Aspiration, 1607–1937*, New York, 1937

Weinberg, A. K., *Manifest Destiny; a Study of Nationalist Expansionism in American History*, Baltimore, 1935

Wish, Harvey, *Society and Thought in Early America*, New York, 1950

Source Materials

Commager, H. S., *Documents of American History*, fifth edition, 1949

Hacker, L. M., and Zahler, H. S., *The Shaping of the American Tradition*

Hamilton, Jay, and Madison, *The Federalist*, especially Nos. 10, 16, 39, 47, 48, 62, 69, 78, 84

Heffner, R. D., *A Documentary History of the United States*

MacDonald, William, *Documentary Source Book of American History, 1606–1926*

Padover, S. K., ed., *The Complete Jefferson*, especially pp. 270, 282–93, 1064–69, 1076–85

Tocqueville, Alexis de, *Democracy in America*

Intellectual and Artistic Progress during the Age of Democracy and Nationalism

The character of the new intellectual revolution

Reference is commonly made to the advancement of learning in the seventeenth and eighteenth centuries as the Intellectual Revolution. It would be just as accurate to apply this term to the intellectual progress between 1830 and 1914. Never before in so short a time had the mind of man yielded discoveries and provocative ideas in such profusion. And certainly a large proportion of these were quite as revolutionary in their effects as any that had come down from the past. But in several respects the intellectual revolution from 1830 to 1914 was different from that of the seventeenth and eighteenth centuries. For one thing, the deductive or rationalist tradition was now almost entirely dead. And the decay of rationalism was reflected in a marked decline in the relative importance of philosophy. Indeed, in the new age philosophy was often little more than an echo of science. It was not that the problems of the universe had finally been solved, or that men had lost the ability to think, but rather that the sciences had come to be accepted as the only worthwhile sources of knowledge. To be sure, there were some seekers of wisdom who rebelled against the new tendency; but there were few who had the hardihood to advocate a revival of pure deduction or the viewpoint of the mystic in discovering truth. In other words, the victory of empiricism, or that philosophy which derives its truths from concrete experience rather than from abstract reasoning, was almost complete.

1. The Heyday of Science

As compared with all preceding epochs, the period from 1830 to 1914 marked the zenith of scientific progress. The attainments of this period were not only more numerous, but they probed more deeply into the hidden mysteries of things and revealed the nature of the world and of man in a hitherto unsuspected light. Each of the older branches of science was greatly developed, and a dozen or more new ones were added to the list. The phenomenal scientific progress of this era was the result of various factors. It was due in some measure to the stimulus of the Industrial Revolution, to the rising standard of living, and to the desire for comfort and pleasure. But to think of modern science as essentially a species of practical knowledge is to misunderstand its import. The contemporary pure physicist or chemist is no more concerned with problems of the workaday world than was St. Thomas Aquinas or Albert the Great. In fact, pure science occupies a position in the modern age somewhat similar to that of Scholasticism in the thirteenth century. It is at once a substitute for logic as a discipline for the mind and an expression of an insatiable desire for the conquest of all knowledge, for an intellectual mastery of the universe. The Scholastic philosopher employed altogether different methods, but his aims and his hopes were the same.

The nature and causes of the tremendous scientific progress

While none of the sciences was neglected between 1830 and 1914, it was the biological sciences and medicine which underwent the greatest development. The outstanding achievement in biology was the development of new explanations of the theory of organic evolution. We have seen that this theory was at least as old as Anaximander in the sixth century B.C., and that it was accepted by many of the great minds of antiquity. We have learned also that it was revived in the eighteenth century by the philosopher Holbach, by the poet Goethe, and by the scientists Buffon and Linnaeus. But none of these men offered much proof or explained how the process of evolution works. The first to develop a systematic hypothesis of organic evolution was the French biologist, Jean Lamarck (1744–1829). The essential principle in Lamarck's hypothesis, published in 1809, is the inheritance of acquired characteristics. He maintained that an animal, subjected to a change in environment, acquires new habits, which in turn are reflected in structural changes. These acquired characteristics of body structure, he believed, are transmissible to the offspring, with the result that after a series of generations a new species of animal is eventually produced. Lamarck's successors found little evidence to confirm this hypothesis, but it dominated biological thought for upwards of fifty years. Though still not absolutely discredited, it is admitted to have no more than a partial validity.

Explanations of organic evolution: the hypothesis of Lamarck

A much more scientific hypothesis of organic evolution was that of Charles Darwin, published in 1859. Darwin was born in 1809, the son of a small-town physician. Though he lived to be seventy-three, he was of frail constitution, and during most of his adult life he seems never to have enjoyed a day of the health of ordinary men. In accordance with his father's wish, he began the study of medicine at Edinburgh, but soon withdrew and entered Cambridge to prepare for the ministry. Here he gave most of his time to natural history and was graduated only tenth in his class among those not seeking honors. In 1831 he obtained an appointment as naturalist without pay on H.M.S. *Beagle*, which had been chartered for a scientific expedition around the world. The voyage lasted nearly five years and gave Darwin an unparalleled opportunity to become acquainted at first hand with the manifold variations of animal life. He noted the differences between animals inhabiting islands and related species

Charles Darwin (1809–1882). More than anyone else, Charles Darwin, shown here in his later years, personified the scientific revolution of the Nineteenth Century.

on near-by continents and observed the resemblances between living animals and the fossilized remains of extinct species in the same locality. It was a magnificent preparation for his life's work. Upon returning from the voyage he happened to read Malthus' *Essay on Population* and was struck by the author's contention that throughout the world of nature many more individuals are born than can ever survive, and that consequently the weaker ones must perish in the struggle for food. Finally after twenty more years of careful and extensive research he issued his *Origin of Species*, which has probably done as much to influence modern thinking as any other single book ever written.

The Darwinian hypothesis of natural selection

Darwin's hypothesis as contained in his *Origin of Species* (1859) is known as the hypothesis of natural selection. This involves the idea that it is nature, or the environment, which selects those variants among the offspring that are to survive and reproduce. Darwin

pointed out, first of all, that the parents of every species beget more offspring than can possibly survive. He maintained that, consequently, a struggle takes place among these offspring for food, shelter, warmth, and other conditions necessary for life. In this struggle certain individuals have the advantage because of the factor of *variation*, which means that no two of the offspring are exactly alike. Some are born strong, others weak; some have longer horns or sharper claws than their brothers and sisters or perhaps a coloration of body which enables them better to blend with their surroundings and thus to elude their enemies. It is these favored members of the species that win out in the struggle for existence; the others are eliminated generally before they have lived long enough to reproduce. While Darwin assumed like Lamarck that acquired characteristics could be inherited, he did not consider them of fundamental importance in evolution. He regarded variation and natural selection as the primary factors in the origin of new species. In other words, he taught that individuals with favorable characteristics would transmit their inherited qualities to their descendants through countless generations, and that successive eliminations of the least fit would eventually produce a new species. Finally, it should be noted that Darwin applied his concept of evolution not only to plant and animal species but also to man. In his second great work, *The Descent of Man* (1871), he attempted to show that the human race originally sprang from some apelike ancestor, long since extinct, but probably a common forebear of the existing anthropoid apes and man.

The Darwinian hypothesis was elaborated and improved by several later biologists. About 1890 the German August Weismann (1834–1914) flatly rejected the idea that acquired characteristics could be inherited. He conducted experiments to show that body cells and reproductive cells are entirely distinct, and that there is no way in which changes in the former can affect the latter. He concluded, therefore, that the only qualities transmissible to the offspring are those which have always been present in the germ plasm of the parents.[1] In 1901 the Dutch botanist, Hugo De Vries (1848–1935), published his celebrated mutation hypothesis, based in large part upon laws of heredity discovered by the Austrian monk, Gregor Mendel (1822–1884). De Vries asserted that evolution results not from minor variations, as Darwin had assumed, but from radical differences or mutations, which appear in more or less definite ratio among the offspring. When any of these mutations are favorable to survival in a given environment, the individuals possessing them naturally emerge triumphant in the struggle for existence.

Improvement of the Darwinian hypothesis by Weismann and De Vries

[1] The teachings of Weismann, while generally accepted by scientists of the present day, are taken with certain reservations. It has been shown that germ cells are not entirely insulated from the rest of the body as Weismann taught. It is admitted also that they are not absolutely stable but appear to be subject, under certain conditions, to parallel modifications at the same time that other parts of the body are affected.

Not only do their descendants inherit these qualities, but from time to time new mutants appear, some of which are even better adapted for survival than their parents. Thus in a limited number of generations a new species may be brought into existence. The mutation theory of De Vries corrected one of the chief weaknesses in the Darwinian hypothesis. The variations which Darwin assumed to be the source of evolutionary changes are so small that an incredibly long time would be necessary to produce a new species. De Vries made it possible to conceive of evolution as proceeding by sudden leaps.[2]

The cell theory and the development of embryology

Next to the exposition and proof of organic evolution, the most important biological achievement was probably the development of the cell theory. The cellular structure of plants had already been described by Robert Hooke in the seventeenth century, but it was left for the German biologist, Theodor Schwann (1810–1882), to draw the full implications from Hooke's discovery. Schwann pointed out about 1835 that not only plants but animals also are composed of cells, and that all but the simplest of living things grow and mature by the division and multiplication of these tiny structural units. A few years later it was discovered that all cells are composed of essentially the same combination of matter, to which Hugo von Mohl (1805–1872) gave the name *protoplasm*. Another of the important biological achievements of this period was the development of embryology. The father of the modern science of embryology was the German-Russian Karl Ernst von Baer (1792–1876), who about 1830 set forth his celebrated law of recapitulation. This law, which was subsequently elaborated by Ernst Haeckel (1834–1919), states that during the embryonic period each individual recapitulates or reproduces the various important stages in the life history of the species to which it belongs.

Cytology and bacteriology

Embryology was not the only subdivision of biology to be developed during the nineteenth century. The work of Schwann, von Mohl, and others led to the founding of cytology, or the scientific study of cells. About 1865 Louis Pasteur laid the basis for the science of bacteriology by his epochal attack upon the theory of spontaneous generation. Hitherto it had been commonly supposed that bacteria and other microscopic organisms originated spontaneously from water or from decaying vegetable and animal matter. Pasteur succeeded in convincing the scientific world that all existing forms of life, no matter how small, are reproduced only by living beings. This was his famous law of biogenesis (all known forms of life come from pre-existing life).

Even more spectacular than the achievements in biology was the progress in medicine. Following the discovery of vaccination for smallpox by Jenner in 1796, the next great landmark in the develop-

[2] It must be understood that the hypothesis of De Vries is not complete in itself, but is based upon Darwin's main principle of natural selection.

ment of modern medicine was the introduction of ether as a general anaesthetic. Credit for this achievement was formerly given to William T. G. Morton, a Boston dentist, but it is now known that a Georgia physician, Crawford W. Long, performed the earliest operation with the use of ether in 1842. This discovery not only diminished the anguish of the patient, but enabled the surgeon to take his time and thereby increased the number of successful operations. But still many people died as a consequence of the bungling practice of physicians. Mortality was especially high in obstetrical cases, until methods were discovered of controlling the possibilities of infection. In 1847 the Hungarian physician Ignaz Semmelweiss found out that by washing his hands in antiseptic solutions he could reduce the death rate in obstetrical operations by more than four-fifths. This discovery was extended to the whole field of surgical practice about 1865 by the Englishman Joseph Lister (1827–1912), who is considered the father of antiseptic surgery. Lister achieved sensational results in preventing infection by cleansing wounds and surgical instruments with carbolic acid and by introducing carbolized catgut for surgical sewings. He was rewarded by the British government with a baronetcy in 1883 and was elevated to the peerage in 1897.

The most significant milestone of medical progress during the second half of the nineteenth century was undoubtedly the germ theory of disease. Probably no other single accomplishment has contributed so much to the conquest of the most deadly maladies which afflict mankind. The germ theory of disease was mainly the work of Louis Pasteur and Robert Koch. Pasteur had been practically certain of the germinal origin of disease ever since he had established his biogenetic law, but he was unable to convince the medical profession. Because he was a chemist, physicians were inclined to be scornful of his work, holding that he could know nothing of the sacred precincts of medicine. They admitted the existence of germs, but they regarded them as more probably the results of disease than the cause. The opportunity to prove the validity of the theory came with the spread of an epidemic of anthrax, a disease which was carrying off hundreds of thousands of cattle and sheep in Germany and in France. About 1875 Robert Koch (1843–1910), an obscure country physician of East Prussia, began a series of experiments to prove that anthrax was the result of the tiny rodlike organisms found in the blood of the diseased animals. He inoculated mice with this contaminated blood and noticed that they soon sickened and died. He made cultures of the germs, breeding them on potatoes, and found that the germs alone, when introduced into the bodies of animals, were just as deadly as the blood. Meanwhile Pasteur had also been engaged in researches on anthrax. In 1881 he was challenged by his medical opponents to make a public test on cattle. He divided the animals into two groups. Half of them he inoculated with weakened germs of anthrax, and the remainder he left un-

Landmarks of progress in medicine

The germ theory of disease

treated. A few days later he injected malignant germs into all of the cattle. To the discomfiture of his opponents, every one of the animals that had not been inoculated died, while all of the others survived. The theory that germs were the cause of the disease could no longer be disputed.

The conquest of diseases produced by germs

Once the germ theory was positively established, achievements in medicine multiplied rapidly. The talents of Pasteur and Koch were still by no means exhausted. The former in 1885 evolved a method of treating persons afflicted with hydrophobia, one of the most horrible diseases known to humanity. As a result of this accomplishment, the death rate from a malady hitherto almost always fatal was reduced to less than 1 per cent. In 1882 Robert Koch discovered the bacilli of tuberculosis and of Asiatic cholera. Within a few years the germs of yet other diseases were isolated—of diphtheria, of the bubonic plague, of lockjaw, and of sleeping-sickness. For the prevention and treatment of several of these diseases, antitoxins or serums were developed, the first being the diphtheria antitoxin produced in 1892 by Emil von Behring (1854–1917). About the end of the century effective means of combating malaria and yellow fever were made possible by the discovery that both are spread by particular varieties of mosquitoes. Much advancement was made also in the treatment of syphilis. After the germ had been identified in 1905, August von Wassermann devised a test for revealing its presence in the human body. In 1910 Paul Ehrlich developed a new drug, known as salvarsan, which proved to be an efficient specific for the disease in its primary and secondary stages. Still later the Austrian pathologist Julius Wagner von Jauregg found out that a fever temperature induced by malaria or by other means has remarkable effects in alleviating advanced stages of the disease, such as syphilis of the brain or paresis.

The discovery of hormones and vitamins

Finally, it should be noted that by the outbreak of World War I a beginning had been made in the study of the ductless glands and in the discovery of the vitamins. The first step toward an understanding of the ductless or endocrine glands was taken in 1901 when the Japanese scientist Takamine isolated adrenalin, secreted by the suprarenal glands, and showed that it was useful in regulating the action of the heart. About 1912 it was revealed that the pituitary gland yields a substance vitally necessary for the proper growth of the body. These discoveries paved the way for a considerable development of glandular therapy in more recent years, including methods of curing certain forms of idiocy by supplementing the hormone secretion of the thyroid gland. On the eve of World War I it was demonstrated by a British biochemist that a healthful diet requires not merely starches, fats, sugars, and proteins but "accessory factors" found only in particular foods. These factors were soon named vitamins, and research was begun to determine their character. In 1915 an American scientist at Johns Hopkins, E. V.

McCollum, proved that there are at least two vitamins: Vitamin A,
contained in butter, egg yolks, and fish-liver oils; and Vitamin B,
which is found most abundantly in yeast, lean meats, whole cereals, and green vegetables. Later investigations have disclosed the existence of at least twenty of these mysterious substances, all of them essential to growth or to the prevention of disease. The discovery of the vitamins has been especially significant in the conquest of illnesses of malnutrition, such as beri-beri, scurvy, and rickets.

The record of attainment in the physical sciences is somewhat less impressive until practically the final quarter of the nineteenth century. Nevertheless, three achievements stand out in the earlier period. About 1810 the English Quaker schoolmaster, John Dalton (1766–1844), revived the atomic theory of matter and defended it so assiduously that it was soon adopted as a basic premise of scientific thought. In 1847 Hermann von Helmholtz (1821–1894) formulated the principle of the conservation of energy, or the first law of thermodynamics. This law states that the total energy in the universe is constant, that it can be changed from one form into another but can neither be created nor destroyed. In 1851 came the second law of thermodynamics, or the law of the dissipation of energy. Explained systematically for the first time by William Thomson (Lord Kelvin), this law maintains that, while the total energy of the universe remains constant, the amount of *useful* energy is being steadily diminished. Few discoveries have been more fruitful in influencing the conclusions of astronomers and also of certain philosophers.

Achievements in the physical sciences

Probably it would be safe to say that the period from about 1870 to 1914 surpassed all others since the age of Copernicus in the number of revolutionary developments in the physical sciences. Indeed, it may be doubted whether there was ever a period when so many time-honored scientific conceptions were seriously challenged or overthrown. First of all, there were some extensive revisions of older theories of light, electricity, and energy. About 1865 Clerk Maxwell (1831–1879) showed that light appears to behave in much the same way as electromagnetic waves. In 1887 the German physicist Heinrich Hertz proved the existence of high-frequency electric waves spreading through space with the velocity and other characteristics of light. The discovery of the X-ray by Wilhelm von Röntgen in 1895 led scientists to wonder whether similar rays might not be given off spontaneously in nature. This suspicion was confirmed by the discovery of uranium in 1896 and of the much more active element, radium, by Madame Curie two years later. About 1903 the British physicists, Ernest Rutherford and Frederick Soddy, developed their disintegration theory, explaining how various radioactive elements break down to form less complex elements, giving off at the same time emanations of electrical energy. The net result of these several discoveries was the conclusion that light, electricity,

Revolutionary discoveries in regard to light, electricity, and other forms of energy

*Revisions of
the conception
of matter*

*The Einstein
theories*

the X-ray, and all other forms of energy are essentially the same.

From this conclusion it was a comparatively easy step to fundamental revisions of the conception of matter. As early as 1892 Hendrik Lorentz advanced the contention that matter is not composed of solid, indivisible atoms as the Greeks and John Dalton had assumed, but that the atom itself is made up of smaller units of an electrical nature. About 1910 Ernest Rutherford and the Danish scientist, Niels Bohr, presented a picture of the atom as a kind of miniature solar system, composed of a nucleus containing one or more positively charged *protons* around which revolve a number of negatively charged *electrons*. As we shall see, this conception has been modified in more recent years, but its main implication still stands—that electricity is the fundamental constituent of matter.

The climax of the revolution in the physical sciences was reached with the publication of the Einstein theories. Originally issued in limited form in 1905, they were expanded into a more general application ten years later. Einstein challenged not merely the older conceptions of matter but practically the entire structure of traditional physics. The doctrine for which he is most noted is his principle of relativity. During the greater part of the nineteenth century, physicists had assumed that space and motion were absolute. Space was supposed to be filled with an intangible substance known as *ether*, which provided the medium for the undulations of light. The planets also moved in it like ships sailing in definite courses over the bounding main. The motion of the heavenly bodies was therefore to be measured by reference to this more or less static ether, just as the speed of a vehicle could be measured in terms of the distance traveled on a highway. But elaborate experiments performed by English and American physicists in 1887 virtually exploded the ether hypothesis. Einstein then set to work to reconstruct the scheme of the universe in accordance with an altogether different pattern.

Albert Einstein. From the portrait head by the noted American sculptor, Jo Davidson.

He maintained that space and motion, instead of being absolute, are relative to each other. Objects have not merely three dimensions but four. To the familiar length, breadth, and thickness, Einstein added a new dimension of *time* and represented all four as fused in a synthesis which he called the *space-time continuum*. In this way he sought to explain the idea that mass is dependent upon motion. Bodies traveling at high velocity have different proportions of extension and mass from what they would have at rest. Included also in the Einstein physics is the conception of a finite universe—that is, finite in space. The region of matter does not extend into infinity, but the universe has limits. While these are by no means definite boundaries, there is at least a region beyond which nothing exists. Space curves back upon itself so as to make of the universe a gigantic sphere within which are contained galaxies, solar systems, stars, and planets.

The years from 1830 to 1914 were characterized also by an extensive development of the social sciences. Most of these subjects are of comparatively recent origin. Before the nineteenth century nearly all of man's efforts to analyze his social environment were restricted to history, economics, and philosophy. The first of the new social sciences to be developed was sociology, originated by Auguste Comte (1798–1857) and elaborated by Herbert Spencer (1820–1903). Next came the founding of anthropology by James Prichard (1786–1848) and Sir Edward Burnett Tylor (1832–1917). Though sometimes defined very broadly as "the science of man," anthropology is more commonly restricted to such matters as man's physical evolution, the study of existing human types, and the investigation of prehistoric cultures and of primitive institutions and customs. About 1870 psychology was broken off from philosophy and cultivated as a separate science. Following its origin in Germany under the guidance of Wilhelm Wundt (1832–1920), it was expanded by the Americans William James (1842–1910) and G. Stanley Hall (1846–1924). It was given a new orientation in the 1890's by the work of the Russian Ivan Pavlov (1849–1936). By experiments with animals Pavlov discovered what is known as the conditioned reflex, a form of behavior in which natural reactions are produced by an artificial stimulus. He showed that if dogs were fed immediately following the ringing of a bell, they would eventually respond to the sound of the bell alone and secrete saliva exactly as if confronted by the sight and smell of the food. This discovery suggested the conclusion that the conditioned reflex is an important element in human behavior and encouraged psychologists to center their attention upon physiological experiment as a key to understanding the mind.

After the opening of the twentieth century, psychologists divided into a number of conflicting schools. A group of disciples of Pavlov inaugurated a type of physiological psychology known as behaviorism. Behaviorism is an attempt to study the human being as a purely physiological organism—to reduce all human behavior to a series of physical responses. Such concepts as *mind* and *consciousness* are relegated to the scrap heap as vague and meaningless terms. For the behaviorist nothing is important except the reactions of muscles, nerves, glands, and visceral organs. There is no such thing as an independent psychic behavior; all that man does is physical. Thinking is essentially a form of talking to oneself. Every complex emotion and idea is simply a group of physiological responses produced by some stimulus in the environment. Such was the extremely mechanistic interpretation of human actions offered by followers of Pavlov. Subject to a number of modifications, it still has a strong appeal for those who believe that psychology should be as objective a science as physics or chemistry.

The other most important school of psychology to make its appearance after the turn of the century was psychoanalysis, founded by Sigmund Freud (1856–1939), an Austrian physician. Psychoanalysis interprets human behavior mainly in terms of the subconscious or unconscious mind. Freud admitted the existence of the conscious mind, but he avowed that the subconscious is much more important in determining the actions of the individual. He considered man as exclusively an egoistic creature propelled by basic urges of power, self-preservation, and sex. These urges are much too strong to be overcome; but inasmuch as society has branded their unrestrained fulfillment as sinful, they are commonly driven into the subconscious, where they linger indefinitely as suppressed desires. But they are seldom completely submerged; they rise to the surface in dreams, or they manifest themselves in lapses of memory, in fears and obsessions, and in various forms of abnormal behavior. Freud believed that most cases of mental and nervous disorders result from violent conflicts between natural instincts and the restraints imposed by an unfortunate environment. His investigations and the theories he evolved from them revolutionized the treatment of mental ailments and exerted a profound influence upon literature and the arts.

2. New Philosophic Tendencies

Most of the philosophic movements in the later decades of the nineteenth century and in the early years of the twentieth were deeply influenced by the progress of science. Characteristic examples are to be found in the evolutionary philosophies of Spencer, Huxley, and Haeckel. The first of this trio, Herbert Spencer (1820–1903), was one of the most influential figures of modern times. Born into a family of English Methodists and Quakers of modest means, he refused the offer of relatives to send him to Cambridge and determined to educate himself and live his own life. He worked for a time as a civil engineer on the London and Birmingham railway. Later he became an assistant editor of the *Economist*, but resigned that position upon inheriting $2500 from an uncle. Despite his humble background, he cared little for wealth or power. Moreover, he was inclined to be indolent, reading but haphazardly and neglecting serious books that failed to arouse his interest. For years his life was ill-planned and his ambitions erratic. He spawned ideas for inventions at every turn and cluttered his notebooks with plans for candle-extinguishers, patent saltcellars, wheel-chairs, and other ingenious contraptions. His earliest writings were on political and social problems, the most important of them being his *Social Statics*, published in 1850. Not until he was about forty did he develop a serious interest in philosophy. He completed his three-volume work, *Synthetic Philosophy*, at the age of seventy-six.

The keynote of Spencer's philosophy is his idea of evolution as a universal law. He was deeply impressed by Darwin's *Origin of Species* and enriched the hypothesis of natural selection with a phrase that has clung to it ever since—"the survival of the fittest." He contended that not only species and individuals are subject to evolutionary change, but also planets, solar systems, customs, institutions, and religious and ethical ideas. Everything in the universe completes a cycle of origin, development, decay, and extinction. When the end of the cycle has been reached, the process begins once more and is repeated eternally. Strange as it may seem, Spencer was not a mechanist. He argued that back of the evolutionary process there must be some kind of supernatural Power, and he generally assumed that in the long run evolution is synonymous with progress. But he referred to this Power as the Unknowable and declared that it should be dismissed from scientific consideration. Man's capacity for knowledge is limited to matter and motion, to the facts of sensory experience; these alone should constitute the field of his speculation. As a political philosopher, Spencer was a vigorous champion of individualism. He condemned collectivism as a relic of primitive society, as a feature of the earliest stage of social evolution when individuals had not yet been separated from the undifferentiated mass. He held the state in such great abhorrence that he delivered his manuscripts to his publisher in person rather than entrust them to any such agency of tyranny as the post office.

Spencer's evolutionary philosophy

The other two philosophers of the evolutionist tradition, Huxley and Haeckel, accepted a great many of the fundamental suppositions of Spencer's theory. Thomas Henry Huxley (1825–1895) defended the doctrine of evolution, not only with logical arguments but with a convincing array of scientific facts; for he was a brilliant biologist as well as a philosopher. A "square-jawed man, greedy of controversy," he gloried in the title, "Darwin's bulldog." His celebrated book, *Man's Place in Nature*, was almost as influential in converting the world to evolutionary principles as the *Origin of*

Other evolutionist philosophers: T. H. Huxley

771

Species. But Huxley had broader interests than merely defending organic evolution. Like Spencer, he proposed to extend the evolutionary concept to all of the great problems that trouble man's dreams. He argued that social institutions and moral ideals, instead of being divinely ordained, are simply products of a biological heritage. "The actions we call sinful are part and parcel of the struggle for existence." [3] While he did not reject the possibility of a supernatural power, he averred that "there is no evidence of the existence of such a being as the God of the theologians." [4] He pronounced Christianity to be "a compound of some of the best and some of the worst elements of Paganism and Judaism, moulded in practice by the innate character of certain people of the Western world." [5] A large part of his philosophy is embraced in his famous doctrine of *agnosticism,* a word which he invented to express his contempt for the attitude of dogmatic certainty symbolized by the beliefs of the ancient Gnostics.[6] As propounded by Huxley, agnosticism is the doctrine that neither the existence nor the nature of God nor the ultimate character of the universe is knowable. It is not atheism, but simply an affirmation that man does not know and never can know whether a God exists and whether the universe is governed by purpose or is merely a blind machine.

Ernst Haeckel

The most uncompromising of the evolutionist philosophers was Ernst Heinrich Haeckel (1834–1919). Originally a physician in Berlin, he became disgusted with crotchety patients and soon turned to the more congenial occupation of a professor of zoology. He was the first outstanding scientist on the Continent of Europe to subscribe wholeheartedly to Darwinism. At the age of sixty-five he summarized his conclusions in a book which he entitled *The Riddle of the Universe.* The philosophy of Haeckel comprises three main doctrines: atheism, materialism, and mechanism. He would have nothing to do with Huxley's agnosticism or with Spencer's assumption of an Unknowable Power; on the contrary, he dogmatically affirmed that nothing spiritual exists. The universe, he maintained, is composed of matter alone in a process of constant change from one form into another. This process is as automatic as the ebb and flow of the tides. There is no fundamental difference between living and non-living matter, except that the former is more complex. The first life originated from the spontaneous combination of the essential elements of protoplasm. From these earliest forms of protoplasm all the complex species of the present have gradually evolved through the process of natural selection. Haeckel regarded the mind of man as a product of evolution just as much as his body. The human mind differs only in degree from the minds

[3] Leonard Huxley, *The Life and Letters of Thomas Henry Huxley,* Vol. II, p. 282.
[4] *Ibid.,* Vol. II, p. 162.
[5] T. H. Huxley, *Collected Essays,* Vol. V, p. 142.
[6] See above, p. 96.

Portrait of the Artist, van Gogh. This self-portrait shows a deep seriousness and intense concentration. (V. W. van Gogh)

Ia Orana Maria, Paul Gauguin (1848–1903). Gauguin revolted not only against the complexity and artificiality of European life, but against civilization itself. He finally fled to Tahiti to paint the lush, colorful life of an uncorrupted society. (MMA)

Sunflowers in a Vase, van Gogh. The feverish technique seems to have endowed the flowers with rhythmic motion. (V. W. van Gogh)

The Starry Night, Vincent van Gogh (1853–1890). This painting gives vivid expression to van Gogh's bold conceptions. The landscape is peaceful, but the heavens sputter and churn with vibrant energy. The cypress trees in the foreground are symbols of death. (Mus. Mod. Art)

Portrait of Gertrude Stein, Pab[lo] Picasso (1881–). Picasso seem[s] to have given this portrait of th[e] great experimenter in poetry som[e] elements of the distortion of for[m] characteristic of the work of bot[h]. (MMA)

The Piano Lesson, Henri Matisse (1869–1954). Matisse conveyed a freshness of approach and a vitality of line and color. (Mus. Mod. Art)

Three Musicians, Pablo Picasso. This painting, regarded by many as the masterpiece of cubism, sums up the final stage of the movement. (Mus. Mod. Art)

of the lower animals. Memory, imagination, perception, and thinking are mere functions of matter; psychology should be considered
as a branch of physiology. Such was the compact philosophy of
materialism and determinism which appeared to Haeckel and his
followers to be a logical deduction from the new biology.

The writings of another German—Friedrich Nietzsche—also reveal a decided influence of the idea of evolution. But Nietzsche was
not a scientist, nor was he interested in the nature of matter or in *Friedrich*
the problem of truth. He was essentially a romantic poet glorifying *Nietzsche*
the struggle for existence to compensate for his own life of weakness and misery. Born in 1844, the son of a Lutheran minister, he was
educated in the classics at Leipzig and Bonn and at the age of
twenty-five was made a professor of philology at the University of
Basel. Ten years later he was forced to retire on account of ill
health. He spent the next decade of his life in agony, wandering
from one resort to another in a fruitless quest for relief. If we can
believe his own statement, each year was made up of 200 days of
pain. In 1888 he lapsed into hopeless insanity, which continued until
his death in 1900.

Nietzsche's philosophy is contained in such works as *Thus Spake
Zarathustra*, *A Genealogy of Morals*, and *Beyond Good and Evil*.
His cardinal idea is the notion that natural selection should be per- *Nietzsche's phi-*
mitted to operate unhindered in the case of human beings as it does *losophy*
with plants and animals. He believed that such a constant weeding
out of the unfit would eventually produce a race of supermen—not
merely a race of physical giants but men distinguished above all for
their moral courage, for their strength of character. Those who
should be allowed to perish in the struggle are the moral weaklings,
the ineffective and craven ones, who have neither the strength nor
the courage to battle nobly for a place in the sun. But before any
such process of natural selection could operate, religious obstacles
would have to be removed. Nietzsche therefore demanded that the
moral supremacy of Christianity and Judaism should be overthrown.
Both of these religions, he alleged, are Oriental cults glorifying the
virtues of slaves and of other downtrodden folk. They exalt into
virtues qualities which ought to be considered vices—humility, non-
resistance, mortification of the flesh, and pity for the weak and incompetent. The enthronement of these qualities prevents the elimination of the unfit and preserves them to pour their degenerate
blood into the veins of the race. Nietzsche admired the ancient
Germanic virtues of bravery, strength, loyalty, honor, and cunning.
He defined *good* as "all that heightens in man the feeling of power,
the desire for power, power itself." *Bad* he characterized as "all
that comes from weakness." [7]

Toward the end of the period we are considering, philosophy
began to reflect the uncertainties and confusion of the sciences. The

[7] Quoted by E. A. Singer, *Modern Thinkers and Present Problems*, p. 204. **773**

revolution in physics accomplished by the discoveries regarding the structure of matter caused a number of thinkers to lose confidence in the optimism of Spencer and in the mechanistic universe of Haeckel. Some renounced mechanism and materialism entirely; others embraced attitudes of skepticism and hopelessness or sought refuge in the worship of beauty. Symptomatic of the new trend was a popular American philosophy known as Pragmatism. Founded by Charles Peirce (1839–1914), it was developed in comprehensive form by William James (1842–1910) and John Dewey (1859–1952). Pragmatism takes its name from its central teaching that any idea which meets the pragmatic test—that is, gives practical results— must be accepted as true; provided, of course, it does not conflict with experience. In other words, if a belief in a personal God—or in a multitude of gods—gives mental peace or spiritual satisfaction to any individual, that belief is true for him. The Pragmatists scoffed at all efforts to discover absolute truth or to determine the ultimate nature of reality. They abandoned metaphysics as futile and taught that knowledge should be sought after, not as an end in itself, but as an *instrument* for improving conditions on earth. It should be mentioned also that the Pragmatists rejected all forms of determinism, whether conceived in spiritual or materialistic terms. They denounced interpretations of the universe which reduced man to a slave of some rigid principle or placed him at the mercy of an all-powerful Fate.

The reaction against mechanism and materialism: the doctrines of the Pragmatists

A much more determined protest against the mechanism and materialism of the nineteenth century came from the New Idealists. Among the leaders of this school were the Italian Benedetto Croce (1866–1952), the Englishman F. H. Bradley (1846–1924), and the American Josiah Royce (1855–1916). The New Idealism was essentially a compound of the doctrines of Hegel and of Kant. From the former came the tendency to glorify the state and to subordinate the individual to the group; from the latter was derived the idea of parallel truths in religion and science which never conflict because they belong in two separate realms. The New Idealists admitted that the universe revealed by science is a gigantic machine which grinds on relentlessly, and that man is a helpless atom. But this revelation did not trouble them, for they contended that it is only part of the picture. Science is but a feeble instrument which enables us merely to see as in a glass darkly. We have other methods of knowing which enable us to perceive not merely surface appearances but reality. If we make up our minds to follow the deepest convictions of our being, we shall see the universe as a star-domed city of God, ruled by benevolent purpose and replete with hope for bewildered man. Truths such as these gained by intuition are more valid than any discovered by the telescope of the scientist. Thus did the New Idealists manage to preserve their faith in reli-

The New Idealism

gion and in ultimate perfection against the onslaughts of skeptics and materialists.

Certain other philosophers drew far different conclusions. A group known as the New Realists despised the tendency to seek refuge in faith or in any other form of retreat from reason. They conceded that the evidence from science may not be the complete or final truth; but they argued that it is the only truth substantial enough to be taken as a guide for living. They felt that the divorce of philosophy from science was an unmitigated disaster, and that a large proportion of the world's woes could be traced to the growth of mysticism. Though recognizing that science confronts man with a cold and alien universe, they saw in this no need for clinging to the skirts of faith. Even if man is no more than a bundle of atoms, whose gift of immortality is merely to mingle with the dust of centuries, this does not prevent him from living nobly and from waging a good fight to overcome such evils as are within his power. He can at least preserve his self-respect by striving to direct the forces of nature to the good of himself and his fellows, by avoiding any action which may be the cause of suffering to others, and by cherishing "the lofty thoughts that ennoble his little day; disdaining the coward terrors of the slave of Fate, to worship at the shrine that his own hands have built." [8] Such in particular was the philosophy of the Englishman Bertrand Russell (1872–   ), one of the most prominent of the New Realists and a leading philosophical writer of the twentieth century.

The New Realists

It remains to consider the ideas of those thinkers who took refuge in an ivory tower of aesthetic enjoyment. Conceiving man to be the helpless victim of blind and irresistible forces, they recommended that he should seek what consolation he could find in a sage and discriminating worship of beauty. They recognized, of course, that not everyone could be an artist, but they insisted that most men could learn to live artistically. The new mood was set by Walter Pater, an English essayist and critic of the late nineteenth century, who taught that the highest solace of life consists in discerning the splendor of the passing show and in cramming our brief interval on earth with rich and refined experiences. A slightly different note was sounded by Anatole France (1844–1924), who propounded a gospel of calm despair in the face of an implacable Destiny. The realities of life, he thought, are too hard to be endured unless one can develop a taste for irony. Happiness consists in philosophic reflection on the follies and absurdities of the human spectacle, with a tolerant understanding of why men err. The best-known of all the philosophers of aesthetic enjoyment was probably George Santayana (1863–1952), born in Madrid but resident for most of his life in the United States. Santayana's philosophy is dis-

The philosophers of aesthetic enjoyment

[8] Bertrand Russell, "A Free Man's Worship," *Mysticism and Logic*, p. 57.

tinguished by an urbane skepticism, by a refusal to believe in the God-given authority of any set of ideas or to be swept off his feet by nostrums for a perfect society. He doubted almost everything, even maintaining that the laws of science are no more than observed regularities of phenomena, by no means to be taken as final truths. He saw in disillusionment the beginning of wisdom, for this alone makes it possible to view the issues of life in their just proportions. Acknowledging no absolute certainty in anything, he believed we should seek pleasure in discriminating indulgence of the senses. The part of wisdom is to assume the role of the artist, enjoying in serene detachment whatever color and poetry this world affords.

3. The Age of Realism in Literature

The character of literary realism

The dominant literary trend in the Western world from about 1830 to 1914 was unquestionably *realism*. Classicism was now practically defunct, though romanticism lingered as a secondary trend until late in the century. Still other movements made their appearance from time to time, but none of them attained the sweep and popularity of realism. Literary realism before World War I was distinguished by a number of extraordinary qualities. First, it was a protest against the sentimentality and extravagance of romanticism. The realists portrayed life not in terms of an emotional ideal but in accordance with the hard facts revealed by science and philosophy. Second, realism was distinguished by an absorbing interest in psychological and social problems—in analyzing in detail the conflicting tendencies of human behavior and in depicting the struggles of individuals to overcome the frustrations of their environment. Finally, it should be noted that realists were quite generally governed by one or another of the popular scientific or philosophic conceptions of their time. Perhaps the majority were determinists, holding to the view that mortals are the irresponsible victims of heredity and environment. Others were guided by the evolutionary concept, interpreting man's nature as made up very largely of bestial qualities inherited from his animal ancestors. Still others were swayed by the fervor for social reform and pictured the inequities of the human scene against a sordid background so as to point the need for abolishing poverty, for eliminating war, or for treating those who had broken the laws of society more justly.

Balzac and Flaubert

Realism as a distinct literary movement made its initial appearance in France. Its leading exponents were four great novelists who exerted an influence far beyond the confines of their native land. First in order of time, and possibly also of merit, was Honoré de Balzac (1799–1850). In his stupendous *Human Comedy*, Balzac uncovered with brutal frankness the stupidity, greed, and baseness of men and women, chiefly of the bourgeoisie. He delighted in laying bare the hidden springs of human action and in revealing the rottenness behind the polished exterior of respectable society. An even more precise expression of the realist tradition is to be found in the work of Gustave Flaubert (1821–1880). His foremost novel, *Madame Bovary*, is a cool analysis of human degradation. It is a study of the tragic conflict between romantic dreams and the dreary realities of ordinary existence. Though the book was condemned as salacious, and its author prosecuted for publishing an immoral work, it has been acclaimed by some critics as one of the greatest novels in modern literature.

Realistic writing of a somewhat different brand flowed from the pen of Émile Zola (1840–1902). Indeed, Zola is sometimes classified as a naturalist rather than a realist, to convey the idea that he was interested in an exact, scientific presentation of the facts of nature without any coloring of personal philosophy. But in actual truth Zola did have a definite philosophic viewpoint. His years of wretched poverty in early life imbued him with a deep sympathy for the common man and with a passion for social justice. Though he portrayed human nature as weak and prone to vice and crime, he was not without hope that a decided improvement might come from the creation of a better society. Many of his novels dealt with such social problems as alcoholism, bad heredity, poverty, and disease. He was an aggressive champion of the Third Republic and toward the end of his life took an active part in exposing the monstrous hypocrisy of the Dreyfus affair. The fourth of the great figures in French realism before World War I was Anatole France (1844–1924). In the section on philosophy in this chapter it was noted that Anatole France preached a gospel of wise and tolerant cynicism. Though he satirized human folly, he seldom gave vent to righteous wrath. His goddess was Irony, a gentle and kindly deity who "teaches us to laugh at rogues and fools whom, but for her, we might be so weak as to despise and hate." [9] Yet his tolerance of evil was by no means unlimited. He joined with Zola in a vigorous attack upon the persecutors of Dreyfus and lent his support to many other unpopular causes. In his later years he became so firmly convinced of the injustice of modern society that he allied himself with the socialists. His works included a varied collection of skeptical essays, mischievous short stories, and pungent satires on religion and politics. Among them are *Penguin Island*, *The Revolt of the Angels*, *The Garden of Epicurus*, and *Thaïs*.

Zola and Anatole France

Realist literature in England included the writings of the vast majority of the Victorian novelists and dramatists.[10] Among the first of the novelists to employ the methods of realism were William Makepeace Thackeray (1811–1863) and Charles Dickens (1812–1870). Thackeray was the novelist of the elegant world of the aris-

Thackeray and Dickens

[9] *The Garden of Epicurus* (Alfred Allinson, trans.), p. 94.
[10] The Victorian period is named, of course, from the reign of Queen Victoria (1837–1901).

tocracy, though he was far from admiring all of its qualities. He delighted in exposing the scandals of people in high places and in ridiculing their foibles. Like most of the early Victorians, he was inclined toward a self-satisfied moralizing on the evils of mankind. As Thackeray was the representative of the upper classes, so Dickens was the spokesman for the lower. In such novels as *Oliver Twist, Nicholas Nickleby, Dombey and Son,* and *David Copperfield* he wrote with poignant sympathy of the bitter lot of the poor. He denounced the horrors of the workhouses and scathingly portrayed the delays in the courts and the inhuman treatment of prisoners for debt. Though he was often swept into excesses of sentimentality, his books exerted considerable influence in hastening the progress of social reform.

George Meredith and Thomas Hardy

The writings of Thackeray and Dickens were but pale forerunners of the realism expressed by English novelists toward the end of the Victorian Age. Notable among these later giants were George Meredith (1828–1909) and Thomas Hardy (1840–1928). Meredith began his career as a philosophical and psychological novelist in 1859 when he published his *Ordeal of Richard Feverel,* but another quarter of a century passed before he became famous as a master of realism. Though his language was often obscure and his philosophy somewhat mystical, there can be no denying his genius as an artist of human problems. No theme was too big for his canvas, and no motive too subtle for his analysis. The most renowned of late Victorian realists was undoubtedly Thomas Hardy. In such well-known narratives as *The Return of the Native, Jude the Obscure,* and *Tess of the D'Urbervilles* he expressed his conception that men are the playthings of inexorable fate. The universe is beautiful, he taught, but in no sense friendly, and the struggle of individuals with nature is a pitiable battle against almost impossible odds. If any such being as God exists, He simply watches with indifference while the helpless denizens of the human ant-heap crawl toward suffering and death. It is to be noted that Hardy's attitude was essentially one of pity for his fellow creatures. He regarded man not as a depraved animal but as an atom of dust caught in the wheels of a cosmic machine.

Shaw and Wells

With the beginning of the twentieth century, realism in English literature took a decidedly different turn. The period from 1900 to 1914 was an era of great progress in social reform and of magnificent dreams for the future. It was natural that this spirit of confidence and hope should be reflected in the leading writings. The first literary genius to sound the clarion call of the new age was George Bernard Shaw (1856–1950). Born in Dublin of Anglo-Irish parents, Shaw betook himself to London at the age of twenty, where he earned his living as a journalist-critic of art and the drama. He soon became interested in socialism and emerged as a leader of the Fabian

Society dedicated to the advancement of a modified Marxism. He combined his enthusiasm for socialism with a devotion to materialistic philosophy, an abiding faith in the value of science, and an acid contempt for the artificialities of bourgeois society. By 1900 he had found his true place in literature as the author of realistic dramas. From then on he wrote an amazing number of plays, on subjects ranging from prostitution to socialism and from the Salvation Army to creative evolution. For the most part, his works were not dramas at all in the conventional sense. They were vehicles for the expression of his ideas, in which the plot was completely overshadowed by witty and incisive dialogue. Likewise didactic in tone was the realism of H. G. Wells (1866–1946). The son of a professional cricket player, Wells devoted his early career to teaching science in a private school. As in the case of Shaw, it was a mixture of socialism and faith in the beneficence of science which provided the inspiration for his work as a writer. Most of the novels he published before 1914 depicted scientific utopias, in which toil and poverty would be eliminated by marvelous improvements in technology, while superstition and war would be banished by proper education. His conception of the tragedy of life was not that of a hopeless struggle against nature but the slavery of individuals to outworn institutions and perverted ideals. Among the best-known of his earlier novels are *Tono Bungay, Anne Veronica,* and *The History of Mr. Polly.*

Realism was also a virile movement in many other countries. In Germany it was exemplified in the dramas of Gerhart Hauptmann (1862–1946) and in the first great novel of Thomas Mann (1875–1955). Hauptmann was a social dramatist, who chose his main themes from the age-long struggle of the working classes against poverty and ill treatment at the hands of their masters. He also wrote satires and symbolical plays of psychological conflict. The first great novel of Thomas Mann was published in 1903. Entitled *Buddenbrooks,* it relates the story of the rise and decline of a great merchant family of Lübeck. The narrative is presented with the same lingering fondness for significant detail which distinguishes the author's later works.

Doubtless the most eminent of all the realists of Teutonic nationality was Henrik Ibsen (1828–1906). Though born in Norway, Ibsen was descended from ancestors who were mainly Danish and German. Years of poverty and drudgery in his early life produced a lasting impression upon his mind and left him resentful and bitter. Until the age of twenty-two nearly all of his education had been acquired by assiduous reading. His early dramas were none too favorably received, and while still a young man he decided to abandon his native country. Residing first in Italy and then in Germany, he did not return permanently to Norway until 1891. His writings were characterized most of all by bitter rebellion against the tyranny and ignorance of society. In such plays as *The Pillars of Society,*

Peer Gynt, and *An Enemy of the People* he mercilessly satirized the conventions and institutions of respectable life. Along with this scorn for hypocrisy and social tyranny went a profound distrust of majority rule. He despised democracy as the enthronement of un-principled leaders who would do anything for the sake of votes to perpetuate themselves in power. He makes one of his characters in *An Enemy of the People* say: "A minority may be right—a majority is always wrong."

*Realism
in American
literature*

Notwithstanding the strength of the Puritan tradition in the United States, realism as a literary movement was far from unim-portant in that country. Traces of it were to be found as early as the middle of the nineteenth century in the novels of Hermann Melville (1819–1891). His masterpiece, *Moby Dick,* combined mar-velous description of the wonders and terrors of nature with a pro-found searching into the mysteries of the universe and of man. But realism scarcely became a dominant force until many years later. Toward the end of the nineteenth century a group of young novel-ists began writing frankly of political and social abuses, often in such manner as to awaken a desire for reform. Stephen Crane de-scribed some of the less romantic aspects of war in his *Red Badge of Courage.* Mark Twain pilloried sham and hypocrisy in a series of novels, the most famous of which was *Huckleberry Finn.* The cut-throat speculation of high financiers furnished the theme for Frank Norris's *Octopus.* But the most typical of the realists before 1914 was Theodore Dreiser (1871–1945). His first novel, *Sister Carrie,* was issued in London in 1901 and in New York in 1907, after considerable trouble with timid publishers. It was followed a few years later by two others of similar type—*Jennie Gerhardt* and *The Genius.* Dreiser's novels were characterized by a rigid determinism which recognized neither purpose in the universe nor meaning in life. But he suffused his writings with a quality of sympathy for his puny figures in their hopeless struggles against the forces of disaster.

*Russian
literature:
Turgeniev and
Dostoievski*

Another of the great literatures which came into its own during the age of realism was that of the Russians. However, the bound-aries separating particular movements in Russian literature are far from distinct. Several of the great novelists combined their realism with attitudes essentially romantic, while others were incorrigible idealists. Among the names that stand out are Ivan Turgeniev (1818–1883), Feodor Dostoievski (1821–1881), and Leo Tolstoi (1828–1910). Turgeniev, who spent much of his life in France, was the first of the Russian novelists to become known to western Eu-rope. His chief work, *Fathers and Sons,* describes in brooding and delicate gloom the struggle between the older and younger genera-tions. The hero is a nihilist (a term first used by Turgeniev), who is convinced that the whole social order has nothing in it worth pre-serving. Dostoievski was almost as tragic a figure as any he projected in his novels. Condemned at the age of twenty-eight on a charge of revolutionary activity, he was exiled to Siberia, where he endured four horrible years. His later life was harrowed by poverty, by family troubles, and by epileptic fits. As a novelist, he chose to write of the seamy side, exploring the anguish of miserable creatures driven to shameful deeds by their raw, animal emotions and by the intolerable meanness of their lives. He was a master of psychological analysis, probing into the motives of distorted minds with an intensity that was almost morbid. At the same time he filled his novels with a broad sympathy and with a mystic conviction that the soul of man can be purified only through suffering. His best-known works are *Crime and Punishment* and *The Brothers Karamazov.*

It is generally conceded that the honor of being Russia's greatest novelist must be divided between Dostoievski and Tolstoi. As a communistic anarchist and an earnest champion of the simple life *Leo Tolstoi* of the peasant, Tolstoi was somewhat less deterministic than the author of *Crime and Punishment.* Yet in his *War and Peace,* a majestic epic of Russian conditions during the period of the Napoleonic invasion, he expounds the theme that individuals are at the mercy of Fate when powerful elemental forces are unleashed. His other most celebrated novel, *Anna Karenina,* is a study of the tragedy which lurks in the pursuit of selfish desire. The hero, Levin, is really Tolstoi himself, who eventually finds refuge from doubt and from the vanities of worldly existence in a mystic love of humanity. As Tolstoi grew older he became more and more an evangelist preaching a social gospel. In such novels as *The Kreutzer Sonata* and *Resurrection* he condemned most of the institutions of civilized society and called upon men to renounce selfishness and greed, to earn their living by manual toil, and to cultivate the virtues of poverty, meekness, and non-resistance. He set the example by deeding his property to his wife and by adopting the dress and humble fare of the peasant. His last years were devoted mainly to attacks upon such evils as war and capital punishment and to the defense of victims of persecution.

Realism was by no means the only movement to hold the allegiance of the literary world between 1830 and 1914. Romanticism continued to be exceedingly popular, especially in the realm of *The surviving* poetry. Notable among the poets of this age whose attitudes were *influence of* essentially romantic were Robert Browning (1812–1889) and Alfred *romanticism:* Tennyson (1809–1892). Browning is noted for his sense of the dra- *Browning and* matic and for his penetrating studies of human character; but, like a *Tennyson* true Victorian, he conceived of man as a moral being and the universe as governed by benevolent purpose. His optimism stands out in bold contrast to the fatalism and pessimism of so many of the realists. He understood the baseness of human passions, but he never lost faith in the ultimate triumph of goodness and truth. A poet of much greater fame in his own lifetime was Alfred Tennyson. In 1850 he was made poet laureate, and in 1884 he became Lord Tennyson. His merit, however, consists primarily in his wizardry of words. The majority of his poems are distinguished for their pictures and music rather than for the expression of ideas. His mastery of color and rhythm enabled him to invest the most commonplace thoughts with a power and brilliance that seemed to endow them with lofty and original meaning. Though he tried hard to be a thinker, he seldom did more than reiterate some of the popular ideas of the Victorian Age. He sang the praises of virtue and of patriotism and delved into medieval legends to revive the glories of King Arthur's court. His nearest approach to profundity is *In Memoriam*, written after the death of a beloved friend. It is a series of lyrics in which the author passes from moods of doubt and despair to a final confident hope in "one far-off divine event, To which the whole creation moves."

*The romanti-
cism of Carlyle,
Ruskin, and
Kipling*

Three other English authors may also be considered as representatives of the romantic tradition. The first two, Thomas Carlyle (1795–1881) and John Ruskin (1819–1900), were essayists and critics; the other, Rudyard Kipling (1865–1936), was a poet and a writer of popular stories. Thomas Carlyle is perhaps best known for his theory that heroic individuals are the makers of history and for his trenchant criticisms of nineteenth-century culture. Industrialism, democracy, materialism, science, and Utilitarianism were the objects of his special fury. A victim of chronic dyspepsia, he often appeared to be crabbed and unreasonable. Yet he was not a mere pessimist and faultfinder. He had a keen perception of the real weaknesses of many modern institutions, and he anticipated some contemporary European ideas of the right of the strong to rule. Carlyle and Ruskin had several attributes in common. Both had a tendency to look back to the Middle Ages. Neither had much use for democracy. Ruskin as much as Carlyle detested the factory regime and abhorred the crude materialism of nineteenth-century science. But Ruskin's philosophy was more nearly that of the aesthete and social reformer. He was repelled not only by the poverty and degradation of the industrial system but also by its ugliness. He condemned the ferocious capitalist struggle for profits and urged that workers should be treated as partners in industry, entitled to a more generous share of what they produced. The romanticism of Rudyard Kipling was of an altogether different sort. He had no interest in either the social or the artistic implications of the industrial regime. In his poetry he trumpeted the glories of British imperialism, representing the subjugation of Hindus and Africans as a glamorous missionary enterprise to rescue the heathen from darkness. His prose narratives are mainly stories of adventure, rich in sentimental fondness for the enchantments of India but not very significant from the standpoint of ideas.

4. *The Birth of Modern Art*

From 1830 to about 1860 the leading trend in painting was undoubtedly romanticism. Its most significant expressions were to be found in the work of the Pre-Raphaelites and of Jean François Millet (1814–1875). The chief figure in the Pre-Raphaelite movement was Dante Gabriel Rossetti (1828–1882), an Englishman of Italian ancestry who is better known as a poet than as a painter. Rossetti and his followers aimed to restore painting to the simplicity, directness, and naturalism which they believed it to have possessed in the Middle Ages and in the early Renaissance. All of the artificial and decorative tendencies that had appeared since the time of Raphael they deeply deplored. Repudiating the ideal of pure beauty, they insisted that art, in order to be worthy of the name, must be directly related to life; it must be useful, either in ministering to the needs of man or in conveying intellectual meaning.

Romanticism in painting: the Pre-Raphaelites

A much greater painter than any of the members of the Pre-Raphaelite group was Jean François Millet. Though associated with the Barbizon school,[11] Millet did not always follow the Barbizon tradition of romantic landscape painting. His paramount interest was in depicting the struggles of humble toilers against poverty and the cruel whims of nature. In *The Man with the Hoe* and *The Sower* he interpreted the bitter life of the peasant in a manner quite worthy of his realist successors. But in *The Angelus* and in *The Path through the Wheat* he betrayed the romantic fondness for sentimental piety and for intensity of color.

Millet

The development of realism in nineteenth-century painting is generally associated with the work of Gustave Courbet (1819–1877) and Honoré Daumier (1808–1879). Both were concerned with presenting the facts of life as they saw them, often in a coarse or satirical fashion. They were rebellious against classical and romantic traditions and intensely conscious of the social significance of art. Profoundly sympathetic toward the lower classes, especially the poor of the cities, they delighted in portraying scenes of squalor and misery and in pillorying the vices and foibles of the comfortable bourgeoisie. Daumier, in particular, was a powerful satirist of social and political evils. He ridiculed the corruption of petty officials, the pompous blundering of lawyers and judges, and the hypocritical piety of the rich. Courbet won great popularity by scornfully refusing the cross of the Legion of Honor offered to him by Napoleon III. Both Courbet and Daumier were zealous champions of the victims of oppression and exploitation, performing a function in art somewhat similar to that of Dickens and Zola in literature. Of course, not all of their painting took the form of social indictment. Much of it was mild and sympathetic portrayal of homely scenes from the

See color pictures at pages 580, 581

The realist painters, Courbet and Daumier

[11] See above, p. 626.

lives of the poor. Whatever the subject, they strove to present it without the sentimental embellishments of the romantic schools.

The first completely original movement in nineteenth-century painting was *impressionism*. In a sense, the impressionist was a realist, for he was determined to paint only what he saw, and he was vitally interested in the scientific interpretation of nature. But his technique was different from that of the older realists. He did not depict scenes from the world around him as they would appear after careful study or thoughtful analysis. On the contrary, he sought to present the immediate impressions of his senses, leaving it to the mind of the observer to fill in additional details. This often resulted in a type of work appearing at first glance to be non-naturalistic. Figures were commonly distorted; a few significant details were made to represent an entire object; and dabs of primary color were placed side by side without a trace of blending. Convinced that light is the principal factor in determining the appearance of objects, the impressionists fled from the studio to the woods and fields in an attempt to capture the fleeting alterations of a natural scene with each transitory shift of sunlight and shadow. From science they had learned that light is composed of a fusion of primary colors visible in the spectrum. Accordingly, they decided to use these colors almost exclusively. They chose, for example, to achieve the effect of the green in nature by placing daubs of pure blue and yellow side by side, allowing the eye to mix them. Some of their paintings appear at close view to be nothing but splotches of color, but if studied from across the room, they gradually reduce themselves to a natural design, in which mountains, trees, houses, and the like are more or less clearly discernible.

Like so many of the other artistic movements of modern times, impressionism originated in France. It was founded about 1870 by Édouard Manet (1832–1883), who had been deeply affected by a study of the old Spanish masters, especially Velásquez. Probably the greatest of the impressionists were Claude Monet (1840–1926) and Auguste Renoir (1841–1919). Monet was perhaps the leading exponent of the new mode of interpreting landscapes. His paintings have no structure or design in the conventional sense; they do not depict, but subtly suggest, the outlines of cliffs, trees, mountains, and fields. Intensely interested in the problem of light, he would go out at sunrise with an armful of canvases in order to paint the same subject in a dozen momentary appearances. It has been said of one of his masterpieces that "light is the only important person in the picture." The work of Renoir exhibited a greater variety than that of any of his compeers. His subjects include not only landscapes but portraits and scenes from contemporary life. He is famous most of all for his pink and ivory nudes, done in a manner reminiscent of Titian or Rubens. Renoir made use of the familiar device of spots of sunlight for the purpose of bringing certain parts of a picture into high relief, but he presented his subjects with much more solidity of form than did the other members of his group. To this day he is the most popular of the impressionists.

For upwards of twenty years impressionism flourished as the dominant style of painting in nearly all countries of the Western world. But in the 1890's it yielded its popularity to a new movement, which is called for want of a better name *post-impressionism*. The post-impressionists criticized the formlessness and lack of volume of their predecessors. They contended that the figures of the painter's art should be as solidly and completely molded as statues. They objected also to the impressionist's preoccupation with the casual and momentary aspects of nature, and they deplored his indifference to ideas. The expression of meaning, they argued, should be the fundamental purpose of art; form and method are not ends in themselves but are important only in so far as they contribute to the expression of meaning. Post-impressionism was not only a reaction against impressionism, but in its ultimate tendencies, at least, it was a revolt against all of the hide-bound formulas of the past. It was an expression of the chaos and increasing complexity of the machine age. It symbolized the restlessness and bewilderment which accompanied the emergence of a new society during the closing years of the nineteenth century. It was the beginning of nearly all that we now understand by *modern* art.

The artist who laid the foundations of post-impressionism was Paul Cézanne (1839–1906), now recognized as one of the greatest painters who ever lived. A native of southern France, Cézanne wandered through the world of art as in a dream. Ever hopeful of reaching some higher goal of achievement, he cared little for the works he had finished. His son cut out the windows of some of his masterpieces for amusement, and his servant used others to clean the stove. Cézanne viewed these disasters quite calmly, for he was convinced that he would produce much better work in the future. His aim as a painter was to represent nature in such a way that objects on a flat canvas would appear to have the roundness and depth of sculpture. To accomplish this he practiced mild distortion, applied paint in thick layers, and modeled his figures with meticulous care. So well did he succeed that it has been said that since Cézanne there is no longer any excuse for sculpture.

The influence of Cézanne was reinforced and extended by two other great artists of the post-impressionist manner. One was the half-Peruvian Frenchman, Paul Gauguin (1848–1903), and the other was the Dutchman, Vincent Van Gogh (1853–1890). Both were revolutionary in their methods. Gauguin threw off all the restraints of conventional painting. Declaring that the artist should not be the slave either of nature or of the past, he introduced into his work an exotic symbolism and the most startling adaptations of color. His cardinal purpose was to emotionalize nature, to portray the world in accordance with his own subjective feelings. Gauguin is important also as a symbol of the disillusionment which spread through intellectual and artistic circles toward the end of the nineteenth century. Dismayed by the complexity and artificiality of civilization, he fled to the South Sea islands and spent the last decade of his life painting the hot and luscious colors of an unspoiled, primitive society. He was the forerunner of an extensive primitivist movement in twentieth-century art. For a time Gauguin was a friend of the Netherlands painter Van Gogh, but the friendship abruptly ceased when he awoke one night to find the Dutchman advancing upon him with a knife. Van Gogh was unquestionably insane; he cut off one of his ears and carried it to a woman who had offended him, and he finally took his own life. Yet there can be no denying his genius. The vibrant energy and turbulent emotionalism of his paintings have probably never been equaled. In order to express the intensity of his feelings, he worked with feverish haste, applying directly to his canvas little worms of violent color which he squeezed from his tubes of paint. Van Gogh has been the chief inspiration for nearly all those modern painters who see in the expression of subjective ideas the exclusive function of art.

Cubism

In the years between 1900 and World War I modern art underwent still further revolutionary development. First, Henri Matisse (1869–1954) greatly extended Cézanne's use of distortion and gradually evolved a type of painting which definitely repudiated fixed ideas of aesthetic merit. This tendency was carried much farther by Pablo Picasso (1881–   ), a Catalan Spaniard who came to Paris in 1903 and founded *cubism*. Picasso's art takes its name from his attempt to resolve each figure or object into its underlying geometric elements. It is based upon a doctrine once casually enunciated by Cézanne that the fundamental ideas of form could best be expressed through such shapes as cubes, cones, and cylinders. Picasso took this doctrine literally. But cubism is much more than this. It involves not only distortion but in some cases actual dismemberment. The artist may separate the various parts of a figure and rearrange them in other than their natural pattern. The purpose is partly to symbolize the chaos of modern life but also to express defiance of traditional notions of form—to repudiate the conception of art as mere prettiness. It is for this latter purpose also that the extreme cubists have generally avoided the use of color.

*See color
pictures at
page 773*

Futurism

Another of the main offshoots of post-impressionism which made its appearance before World War I was *futurism*. The spiritual father of futurism was a poet, F. T. Marinetti, who later took an active part in launching Italian Fascism. In 1910 Marinetti and a group of disciples issued a stirring manifesto calling for relentless war against the aesthetic ideals of the past. They condemned the worship of old masters, the slavish devotion to Roman ruins and to the art of the Renaissance, "the erotic obsession," "purism," sentimentality, quietism, and nature-worship. As painters the futurists aspired to glorify the machine and the achievements of modern science. They regarded it as imbecilic that an artist surrounded by the wonders of the modern scientific age should spend his time mooning over pastoral landscapes or attempting to recapture the beauty of classical mythology. Taking their cue from the discovery in physics that the ultimate fact of nature is energy, they insisted that *movement* should be the principal theme of art. Accordingly, they proceeded to break up form in such a manner as to produce the illusion of shimmering and vibration. They loved to depict the motion of a racing animal, the speed of an automobile, or the power and beauty of some complicated machine in a factory. Futurism has exerted a decided influence, especially upon the interior decoration of modern skyscrapers, railroad stations, and government buildings.

Although sculpture flourished in abundance during the age of democracy and nationalism, there was comparatively little that could be considered significant. Most of it was an imitation of the baroque—grandiose, heavy, and exuberantly decorative. It was developed largely for patriotic purposes, to embellish monuments celebrating national greatness. But in the later years of the nineteenth century there was at least one sculptor whose work stands out as original. He was the Frenchman Auguste Rodin (1840–1917), and his achievements have been compared not unfavorably to those of Michelangelo, by whom he was strongly influenced. Rodin was pre-eminently a realist, but he also reflected the currents of romanticism and impressionism. He was interested in psychological analysis and in man's animal origins and his struggle against the forces of nature. His most elaborate work was *The Gate of Hell*, inspired by Dante's *Inferno*. It is a tragedy depicting the sufferings

Sculpture in the age of democracy and nationalism

See color pictures at page 740

Auguste Rodin, *The Thinker*. An example of realism in sculpture apparently suggesting that man's intellectual faculties are inseparable from his animal heritage. The first copy was destroyed by students of conservative sculptors, but the statue was recast by Rodin.

787

of the great mass of mankind, damned by the passions of their animal natures. Rodin is perhaps even better known for his statue, *The Thinker*, which suggests the evolution of man from lower species. Soon after the dawn of the twentieth century, sculpture began to exemplify certain traits of post-impressionist painting. It grew more and more abstract and distorted, indicating the strength of the revolt against prettiness and sentimentality.

Architecture

As in sculpture, so in architecture the influence of the past was exceedingly strong. Until nearly the end of the nineteenth century the builder's art continued to be governed by classical and medieval principles. In general, it was the classical that predominated, exemplified especially by the survival of the ponderous and ornate baroque. Monuments of this style include the National Opera (1864–1871) in Paris and the Reichstag building (1882–1894) and Protestant cathedral (1888–1895) in Berlin. In some cases nineteenth-century baroque buildings were embellished with forms of construction taken from Byzantine, Egyptian, Chinese, Moorish, and Hindu sources. The result was an unparalleled eclecticism bearing testimony to the imperialistic ambitions of European nations. But accompanying this development of the baroque, there was a vigorous revival of the Gothic. The renewal of interest in Gothic architecture was a product of the romantic tendency to glorify everything medieval. Just as old legends of knights in armor had been refurbished by poets, so there must be a return to the building style of the thirteenth century. Consequently Gothic was adopted on a generous scale for churches, universities, and even for some parliament and office buildings. The crowning monstrosity of all was probably the Woolworth skyscraper in New York City, with its pointed arches and ornamental flying buttresses—features having little or no relation to the general purpose of the building.

Development of functional architecture

Between 1880 and 1890 certain architects in Europe and America awoke to the fact that the prevailing styles of building construction were far out of harmony with the facts of modern civilization. The result was the launching of a new architectural movement known as *functionalism*. Its chief pioneers were Otto Wagner (1841–1918) in Germany and Frank Lloyd Wright (1869–   ) in the United States. The basic principle of functionalism is the idea that the appearance of a building shall proclaim its actual use and purpose. There must be no addition of friezes, columns, tracery, or battlements merely because some people consider such ornaments beautiful. True beauty consists in sincerity, in an honest adaptation of materials to the purpose they are intended to serve. Functionalism also includes the idea that architecture shall express either directly or symbolically the distinguishing features of contemporary culture. Ornamentation must therefore be restricted to such elements as will reflect the age of science and the machine. Modern man does not

believe in the Greek ideals of harmony, balance, and restraint or in

A House in the Contemporary Style. The Warren Tremaine residence in Santa Barbara, California, designed by Richard J. Neutra. The pattern of the house is made to blend with the natural surroundings.

The Contemporary Principles Applied in a Skyscraper. Buildings in this style take advantage of the newest materials—stainless steel, aluminum, glass—and make maximum provision for light and ventilation. Lever House, New York; Skidmore, Owings, and Merrill, Architects.

The International Style Applied to a Chapel. Illustrated is the Ronchamp Chapel designed by Charles-Édouard Jeanneret, better known by his pseudonym Le Corbusier. He believes that architecture should approach as closely as possible to sculpture and that a building should be a "machine to live in" providing its occupants with "sun, space, and silence." Unlike Frank Lloyd Wright and his disciples, he designs his structures with a disregard for their natural surroundings.

the medieval virtues of piety and chivalry; but in power, efficiency, speed, and comfort. These are the ideals which should find a place in his art.

There would seem to be little doubt that the functional style of building construction is one of the most significant architectural developments since the Renaissance. Among all of the styles which have been adopted during the last 300 years, it is the only one that is really original. Known also as *modern* architecture or the *international* style, it is the best approach that has yet been made to an efficient use of the tremendous mechanical and scientific resources of the contemporary world. It permits an honest application of new materials—chromium, glass, steel, concrete—and tempts the builder's ingenuity in devising others. Though many people dislike its stark simplicity and its angular, cubist lines, functional architecture has undoubtedly won an established place for the future. It has been adopted for countless new apartment houses, hotels, office buildings, stores, and factories not only in the United States but also in nearly every other civilized nation of the world.

5. *Music in the Age of Democracy and Nationalism*

Romanticism did not die out in music nearly so early as it did in literature and in the other arts. It was at its height during the middle third of the nineteenth century, and it has continued as an important tendency even to the present. Many of the changes in musical expression and ideals in the later nineteenth century are comparable to the trends in literature and the fine arts, but exact parallels can be drawn with difficulty. For example, although realism asserted itself, it could not be pushed to extremes in an art which is essentially neither descriptive nor pictorial. So productive was this period that space will permit discussion of only its most salient features and its most eminent composers.

Romanticism was emphasized in the work of the two contemporary German composers and friends, Robert Schumann (1810–1856) and Felix Mendelssohn (1809–1847). Schumann excelled in songs and in chamber and piano music. While he was one of the most romantic of composers, he was at the same time one of the most intellectual. As an editor and writer he urged the development of musical scholarship and an appreciation of the history of musical achievement. Among his services was the publicizing of the neglected wealth in the songs of Schubert. The insanity which darkened the last two years of Schumann's life was particularly tragic in view of the fineness of his character and influence. Felix Mendelssohn was the grandson of the Jewish philosopher, Moses Mendelssohn. Not the least among his gifts, as in the case of Schumann, were those of his personality. His compositions, although romantic in flavor, are remarkably symmetrical and do not break away from established forms. They convey almost perpetually a sunny mood, perhaps because the composer, born into a prosperous family, was shielded from the stress of life. Among his most valued works are the oratorio *Elijah* and music for *A Midsummer Night's Dream*, the latter written when he was only seventeen.

The other most famous romantic composers were Chopin and Liszt. Born in Poland of a Polish mother and a French father, Frédéric Chopin (1810–1849) spent most of his career in Paris. He wrote almost exclusively for the piano and revealed to the full the emotionally expressive qualities of this instrument. Essentially a tone poet, he was able to invest his short pieces with a tremendous quality of feeling. Although he became popular, his life was a troubled one, evidently too deeply dyed with the moodiness of his creative fancy. A love affair with the novelist George Sand (Aurore Dupin) ended unhappily; and he died of consumption in his fortieth year. Franz Liszt (1811–1886) spent most of his long life in Paris and in the German town of Weimar. He early distinguished himself as a concert pianist, and is commonly regarded as the greatest performer upon that instrument who ever lived. Later he turned intensively to composition, with results which were dazzling if not often of lasting import. Schumann and Mendelssohn had cultivated romanticism with restraint; Chopin brought it to the border of sentimentality; Liszt carried it to the extreme of sensationalism. His flair for exotic effects is most successfully revealed in his treatment of native Hungarian themes. Liszt was acquainted with many French literary figures and showed considerable interest in the revolutionary currents of his day. His chief influence derives from his piano playing and teaching, orchestral conducting, and philanthropic activities on behalf of needy musicians. His kindly assistance to Wagner when the latter was being hounded out of Germany was an incalculable service.

Chopin and Liszt

Richard Wagner (1813–1883), the outstanding musical figure of the later nineteenth century, was a thoroughgoing revolutionary in the world of art. His initial interest was in the drama, and when he turned to music it was primarily for its dramatic possibilities. His musical training came comparatively late and was largely self-administered, but was nonetheless adequate. In his operas—which he preferred to call music-dramas—he applied a technique of blending together action, words, music, and scenic effects; his ideal was really a fusion of all the arts into an integrated whole. The result was something far different from the conventional opera. Wagner dispensed with the arbitrary division of acts into scenes and discarded all artificial trappings; he took wide liberties with harmony and departed from stereotyped melodic patterns. He sought for a continuous flow of music, not subject to the tyranny of form but sensitive to every demand of expression. In several ways his operas, especially the later ones, which include the famous *Ring* cycle, are

The revolutionary achievements of Wagner

reminiscent of ancient Greek drama. His plots deal with the gods and heroes of Teutonic mythology, and the orchestra provides the background and atmosphere somewhat as the chorus did in the Greek theater. However, the lofty idealism of the Greek tragedians is not approached in the *Ring* operas, which, in spite of the magnificence and sensuous beauty of the music, sometimes seem to be glorifying a cult of brutality and egoism. (The philosopher Nietzsche was for a time an ardent admirer of Wagner.) Wagner's revolutionary impulses, which were not confined entirely to aesthetics, brought down a storm upon his head, and he was forced to flee from Germany for a time. The last twenty years of his life, however, saw the triumphal performance of his works, especially at the Bayreuth opera house built under Wagner's own direction, which has ever since been a musical shrine.

Nationalism in music

Such a pervasive force as nationalism could not help making its imprint upon music. In most European countries and even in the United States, folk music came under the scrutiny of scholars or found its way into the compositions of the learned. Many composers were fervent patriots. The early operas of Verdi (d. 1901), dedicated to the cause of Italian liberation, were sufficiently inflammatory to arouse the ire of the Austrian authorities. But Verdi, who lifted the opera to new artistic heights, was no narrow patriot. He drew his mature inspiration from a wide variety of sources, including the plays of Shakespeare. Nationalism is typified in the Bohemians Smetana (d. 1884) and Dvořák (d. 1904) and in the Norwegian Grieg (d. 1907). However, most of the devotees of national music did not deviate widely from accepted idioms of expression, but added their bit to the common European store. César Franck (d. 1890), a Belgian by birth and the founder of a modern French school of composers, is distinguished by a quality of otherworldly mysticism. The Finn, Jean Sibelius (1865–1957), while celebrating national sentiments in his tone poem *Finlandia*, displays capacities too universal to classify him as a mere nationalist. With seven symphonies to his credit, he was one of the most highly regarded of modern composers.

The Russian school

One of the most remarkable of the national schools of music to appear was the Russian. Throughout the greater part of the nineteenth century Russian musicians had been content to follow the lead of the Italians, French, and Germans. Even such a brilliant composer as Tchaikovsky (1840–1893) introduced no real innovations. Finally, however, fresh paths were opened up by Borodin, Moussorgsky, and Rimsky-Korsakov, the last of whom lived into the twentieth century. No one of these men was trained as a professional musician, a fact which makes their achievement all the more impressive. While they did not throw overboard the familiar European scales and harmony, they brought to composition a fresh point of view, an indifference to orthodoxy, and an enthusiastic appreciation of Slavic folk songs and dances. These qualities have won a place for Russia in the very front rank of modern music.

Before the close of the period under consideration, several divergent tendencies were asserting themselves, indicative of the dissatisfaction with old forms which characterized all the arts. Some of these trends constituted new departures and others a return to the ideals of the past. The flowering of romanticism did not mean that the classical tradition had withered away. Not only did the romanticists make continual use of classical devices, but some composers were almost pure classicists. Chief among the latter was the profoundly intellectual and subtle Johannes Brahms (1833–1897). In chamber music and in the symphony Brahms was the successor of Beethoven, and he does not suffer by comparison with the earlier master. Although Richard Strauss (1864–1949) began as a classicist, his fondness for experiment soon became evident and was given free reign, first in his skillfully orchestrated symphonic poems and then in his music-dramas. The latter, in spite of superficial resemblances, are essentially different from the operas of Wagner. While Wagner was romanticism incarnate, Strauss was a realist, who summoned all the resources of the modern orchestra to convert music into a pictorial medium capable of evoking concrete and often commonplace images in the listener. Not content with stimulating intangible emotions, as the romanticists had done, he undertook to paint meticulous pictures, asserting that it should be quite possible to depict even a teaspoon by means of musical sounds. The content of his determined realism ranges all the way from the bleating of sheep and the whirring of windmills in *Don Quixote* to abstract philosophic ideas in *Thus Spake Zarathustra* (based on a text of Nietzsche).

The classicism of Brahms and Richard Strauss

Another manifestation, perhaps of more enduring significance than Strauss's realism, was impressionism, created by the French composer, Claude Debussy (1862–1918). Like the impressionist painters, Debussy abandoned rigidity of design and intellectuality in the attempt to translate into tone the ecstasy or pathos of a particular mood or moment. Also like the impressionists of the brush he moved freely from one tone color to another without modulation (blending). Debussy was probably at his best when he applied his sensitive imagination directly to evoking the imagery implicit in the expanse of the sea, the play of moonlight, or the amorous reverie of a faun on a midsummer afternoon. Rejecting precise form and abstract beauty as artistic imperatives, he sought satisfaction not in the realism of life but in a fantastic world of dreams and shadows.

The impressionism of Debussy

SELECTED READINGS—PHILOSOPHY

Barzun, Jacques, *Darwin, Marx, Wagner*, Boston, 1941
Cushman, H. E., *A Beginner's History of Philosophy*, New York, 1918, Vol. II
Hayes, C. J. H., *A Generation of Materialism*, New York, 1941
Hoffding, Harold, *History of Modern Philosophy*, London, 1900
Hofstadter, Richard, *Social Darwinism in American Thought*, Philadelphia, 1949
Joad, C. E. M., *A Guide to Modern Thought*, New York, 1933
Marvin, F. S., *The Century of Hope*, New York, 1919
Merz, J. T., *History of European Thought in the Nineteenth Century*, Chicago, 1924, 4 vols.
Randall, J. H., Jr., *The Making of the Modern Mind*, New York, 1926, Chs. XVIII–XXI

—SCIENCE

Agar, W. M., *The Dilemma of Science*, London, 1941
De Kruif, Paul, *Microbe Hunters*, New York, 1926
Eddington, A. S., *The Nature of the Physical World*, New York, 1946
Farber, Eduard, *The Evolution of Chemistry*, New York, 1952
Nordenskiöld, Erik, *History of Biology*, New York, 1928
Osborn, H. F., *From the Greeks to Darwin*, New York, 1919
Pillsbury, W. B., *History of Psychology*, New York, 1929
Robinson, Victor, *The Story of Medicine*, New York, 1936
Russell, Bertrand, *The A B C of Relativity*, New York, 1925
Singer, Charles, *A History of Biology*, New York, 1950

—LITERATURE

Brandes, Georg, *Main Currents in Nineteenth Century Literature*, New York, 1901–1906
Brawley, B. G., *A New Survey of English Literature*, New York, 1925
Lalou, René, *Contemporary French Literature*, New York, 1924
Olgin, M. J., *A Guide to Russian Literature*, New York, 1920

—ART

Gardner, Helen, *Art Through the Ages*, New York, 1926
Hitchcock, H. R., *Modern Architecture*, New York, 1929
Wright, W. H., *Modern Painting*, New York, 1927

—MUSIC

Abraham, Gerald, *A Hundred Years of Music*, New York, 1938
Einstein, Alfred, *Music in the Romantic Era*, New York, 1947

Lang, Paul, *Music in Western Civilization*, New York, 1941
Machlis, Joseph, *The Enjoyment of Music*, New York, 1955
Newman, Ernest, *The Life of Richard Wagner*, New York, 1937
Oxford History of Music, Vol. VII
Thompson, Oscar, *Debussy, Man and Artist*, New York, 1937

SOURCE MATERIALS

Baumer, F. L. V., *Main Currents of Western Thought*, New York, 1952
Darwin, Charles, *The Origin of Species*, especially Chs. IV, XV
———, *The Descent of Man*, especially Ch. XXI
Dewey, John, *Human Nature and Conduct*
Freud, Sigmund, *A General Introduction to Psychoanalysis*
Huxley, T. H., *Man's Place in Nature*
James, William, *The Will to Believe*
Mill, J. S., *Autobiography; Utilitarianism*
Spencer, Herbert, *Man versus the State*
———, *Social Statics*

The Age of Total
War and Revolution,
1914-

A large proportion of the distinctive features of the age in which we now live can be traced to the World War of 1914–1918. That war created a multitude of new problems, fostered attitudes of cynicism and disillusionment, and raised grave doubts as to the future of modern civilization. Instead of abating such evils as nationalism and militarism, it intensified them and caused them to fester and grow more malignant than ever. In addition, the war upset the economic equilibrium of industrialized nations, fostered inflation and overexpansion, and paved the way for severe crises and depressions. While the victory of the Allies gave temporary encouragement to democracy, eventually its chief fruit was a crop of dictators, who rode into power in the defeated and dissatisfied nations. Finally, in 1939, the accumulated bitterness of two decades burst forth in a new war, with ultimate consequences which no one can yet predict.

	International	The Americas
	Triple Alliance, 1882–1914 Diplomatic Revolution, 1890–1907 Berlin-to-Bagdad Railway, 1890–1914	
1900—		
	Entente Cordiale, 1904–1923 Algeciras Conference, 1906 Triple Entente, 1907–1917 Bosnian Crisis, 1908 Balkan Wars, 1912–1913 Assassination of Archduke Francis Ferdinand, 1914 World War I, 1914–1918 U.S. enters World War I, 1917	
1919—	Treaty of Versailles, 1919 League of Nations, 1919–1939	John Dewey, *Reconstruction in Philosophy*, 1920 Eugene O'Neill, *Strange Interlude*, 1920 Renaissance of painting in Mexico, *ca.* 1921 Discovery of insulin, 1922
	French invasion of Ruhr Valley, 1923	
	Locarno Agreements, 1925 Pact of Paris, 1928	
1929—		Great Depression, 1929–1934 Regionalism in art, U.S., *ca.* 1930
	Japan invades Manchuria, 1931 Cancellation of German reparations, 1932 Geneva Disarmament Conference, 1932–1934 World Economic Conference, 1933	U.S. abandons gold standard, 1933 NRA, 1933–1935 New Deal, 1933–1939
	Anglo-German naval pact, 1935 Franco-Soviet alliance, 1935 Italy conquers Ethiopia, 1935–1936 Hitler remilitarizes Rhineland, 1936	

CIVILIZATION, 1914–

Britain	Western Europe	Central and Eastern Europe
		Pan-Slavism, 1890–1914 Expressionism in art, 1893 Pan-Germanism, 1895–1914 Greater Serbia movement, 1900–1914 Industrial supremacy of Germany, 1900–1914
A. N. Whitehead, *The Organization of Thought*, 1916		
	Impressionism in music, 1918 Surrealism, 1918	Overthrow of Tsar, 1917 Bolshevik Revolution, 1917 Expressionism in music, 1918 Revolution in Germany, 1918 O. Spengler, *Decline of the West*, 1918 First Communist regime in Hungary, 1919 Weimar Republic, 1919–1933
		NEP in Russia, 1921–1929
		Fascist Revolution in Italy, 1922 Runaway inflation in Germany, 1923
First Labor government, 1924		Death of Lenin, 1924 Thomas Mann, *The Magic Mountain*, 1924
General strike, 1926		Dictatorship of Stalin, 1924–1953
Second Labor government, 1929–1931 Discovery of penicillin, 1930		First Five-year Plan in Russia, 1929–1933
Abandonment of gold standard, 1931 Discovery of neutrons, 1932 Abandonment of free trade, 1932	Overthrow of monarchy in Spain, 1931	
		Nazi Revolution in Germany, 1933
	Development of sulfa drugs, 1935	
	Popular Front in France, 1936–1938	

	International	The Americas
	Rome-Berlin Axis, 1936 Germany absorbs Austria (*Anschluss*), 1938 Appeasement at Munich, 1938	
1939—	Nazi-Soviet Pact, 1939 World War II, 1939–1945	Discovery of streptomycin, *ca.* 1940
	Atlantic Charter, 1941 Attack on Pearl Harbor, 1941 Cairo Conference, 1943 Teheran Conference, 1943 Establishment of United Nations, 1945	Fair Deal in the U.S., 1945– 1953
	Atomic bombs dropped on Japan, 1945 Yalta Conference, 1945 Potsdam Conference, 1945 Cold War of East and West, 1946– Truman Doctrine, 1947	
1949—	European Recovery Program (Marshall Plan), 1948 NATO, 1949 Korean War, 1950–1953	Discovery of cortisone, 1948
	Schuman Plan, 1952	Hydrogen bomb, 1952 Return of Republicans to power in U.S., 1953
	Summit Conference, Geneva, 1955 War in Middle East, 1956	

CIVILIZATION, 1914– (*Continued*)

Britain	Western Europe	Central and Eastern Europe
	Civil War in Spain, 1936–1939 Existentialism, *ca.* 1938	
	Franco regime in Spain, 1939–	Atomic fission, 1939 Neo-Orthodoxy, *ca.* 1940
Third Labor government, 1945–1950		
Dissolution of Empire in India, 1947	Fourth Republic in France, 1946–	Communist coup in Hungary, 1947 Communist coup in Czecho-slovakia, 1948
Return of Conservatives to power, 1950		
		Death of Stalin, 1953 Russia develops hydrogen bomb, 1953

World War I

The glorious age of science, democracy, and social reform discussed in foregoing chapters ended in one of the most frightful wars that had yet occurred. At first thought this fruition may seem paradoxical. But it must be remembered that the period from 1830 to 1914 had features quite unrelated to political, social, or intellectual progress. In addition to being an age of democracy it was also an age of imperialism. While more money was expended for social welfare than ever before, military and naval appropriations were likewise enormously increased. Despite the remarkable advancement in science and in education, cruel and insane superstitions continued to lurk in most unexpected places. Jingoistic nationalism flourished like a pestilence. Intellectual leaders in France, including the novelist Zola, stirred up passionate hatred of Germany. Poets and professors across the Rhine deified the German spirit and cultivated a lofty contempt for the Slavs. Englishmen were taught to believe that they were the most civilized people on earth, and that their right to establish "dominion over palm and pine" came from no less an authority than God Himself. Perhaps it is not strange that young Turks, educated in the universities of western Europe, should have returned home to massacre the Sultan's "Christian cattle" in Macedonia.

1. Underlying Causes of the War

Ever since Thucydides wrote his classic account of the struggle between Sparta and Athens, it has been the custom of historians to divide the factors responsible for wars into immediate and underlying causes. Some of the remote or underlying causes of World War I go back into the history of Europe for more than a century. Most of them, however, date from about 1870. The period after 1870 includes especially the economic causes, which many historians consider to have been the basis of all the others. The economic cause generally placed at the head of the list was industrial and commercial rivalry between Germany and Great Britain. It was shown in the chapter on the Industrial Revolution that Germany, after the founding of the empire in 1871, went through a period of economic growth that was little short of miraculous. By 1914 she was producing more iron and steel than Britain and France combined. In chemicals, in aniline dyes, and in the manufacture of scientific equipment she led the world. The products of her industry were crowding British manufactures in nearly every market of Continental Europe and also in the Far East and in Britain itself. Cutlery bearing the stamp, "Made in Germany," was actually being sold in Sheffield, while Bavarian lead pencils were to be found on the table in the House of Commons. Moreover, the empire of the Kaisers had thrown down a challenge to the supremacy of Britain in the carrying trade. By 1914 the Hamburg-America and the North German Lloyd were among the largest shipping lines in the world. Two of their vessels had successively captured the Atlantic ribbon from the British, and the *Imperator*, launched in 1912, was the largest ship afloat.

There is evidence that certain interests in Great Britain were becoming seriously alarmed over the menace of German competition. The feeling was most acute around the turn of the century, when the *The economic* London *Saturday Review* delivered itself of the following opinion: *warfare* "If Germany were extinguished tomorrow, the day after tomorrow there is not an Englishman in the world who would not be the richer. Nations have fought for years over a city or a right of succession; must they not fight for two hundred and fifty million pounds of commerce? . . . England has at last awakened to what is alike inevitable and her best hope of prosperity. 'Germaniam esse delendam'." [1] While this opinion was neither official nor representative of the sentiments of the nation as a whole, it did reflect the exasperated feelings of some influential citizens. After 1900 the resentment subsided for a time, but it flared up again in the years preceding the outbreak of war. There seemed to be a strong conviction that Germany was waging deliberate and deadly economic warfare upon Britain to capture her markets by unfair methods and drive her ships from the seas. For Britain to allow the Germans to be victorious in this struggle would mean the destruction of her prosperity and a grave threat to her national existence.[2] British citizens who were troubled by such matters thought of their nation as an innocent victim of German aggressiveness and felt fully justified in taking any measures they considered necessary to defend their position.

[1] *The Saturday Review*, Sept. 11, 1897; cited by John Bakeless, *The Economic Causes of Modern Wars*, p. 145n.
[2] For a full account of Anglo-German economic rivalry see R. J. S. Hoffman, *Great Britain and the German Trade Rivalry, 1875–1914.* The author, however, exonerates the British of any intent to make war upon Germany for the purpose of destroying her trade.

There are indications that the French also were alarmed by German industrial expansion. In 1870 France had lost possession of the extensive iron and coal deposits of Lorraine, which had gone to swell the industrial growth of Germany. To be sure, the French had plenty of iron left in the rich Briey fields on their eastern frontier, but they were afraid that their enemy might eventually reach out and grab these too. Besides, France was under the necessity of importing coal, and this galled her pride almost as much as the loss of the iron. Several other instances of economic friction had much to do with causing the war. The Russian ambition to gain control of Constantinople and other portions of Turkish territory conflicted with German and Austrian plans for reserving the Ottoman Empire as their own happy hunting ground of commercial privileges. Russia and Austria were rivals also for a monopoly of trade with the Balkan kingdoms of Serbia, Rumania, Bulgaria, and Greece. Austria was as anxious to prevent these countries from falling into the Russian orbit as Russia was desirous of extending her power over all the Slavs in eastern Europe. Finally, there was sharp economic antagonism between Germany and France over the right to exploit the mineral resources and trading opportunities of Morocco.

To a certain extent the construction of the Berlin-to-Bagdad Railway was likewise an economic cause of the war, though its effects were almost as much political. The establishment of such a railway involved the completion of a line from the Bosporus to Bagdad on the Tigris River, since the road from Berlin to Constantinople was already in existence. From Bagdad it could perhaps be extended to the Persian Gulf and thus open up a shorter route to India. Plans for the railway were conceived by a German company as early as 1890. Considering the risks too great to be undertaken alone, the German capitalists invited British and French bankers to co-operate. All three countries were to receive the same apportionment of capital stock and equal representation on the board of directors. Jealousy and suspicion, however, led to discouragement of the proposal by the governments of Britain and France. The British seem to have feared that their line of empire would be endangered and also their economic interests in Persia and Mesopotamia. The French politicians appear to have yielded to pressure from Russia, who feared that a railroad extending across Turkey would revive "the sick man of the East" and postpone indefinitely the division of his property. In 1913–1914 a series of agreements was concluded by the British, French, and Germans for the construction of Turkish railways on the basis of a division of the Ottoman Empire into spheres of influence. But by this time most of the damage to international amity had been done, especially since Germany had already completed some 375 miles of the line to Bagdad.

It is impossible to say how much weight should be given to the
economic factors back of the war. They were certainly influential,

but perhaps not quite so important as is generally believed. For one thing, the rivalry between Great Britain and Germany has probably been exaggerated. England was in no danger by 1914 of being pushed into the background as a third-rate industrial nation. It is true that her foreign trade was no longer increasing as fast as that of Germany, but still it was increasing. During the forty years following the Franco-Prussian War, the trade of Britain expanded by 130 per cent as compared with 170 per cent for her rival. Even in 1913 the British exported goods to the value of £525,000,000, contrasted with £495,000,000 for the Germans.[3] In like manner, we must guard against assuming too much as to the seriousness of competition between Russia and Germany. Russia was not yet a great capitalist nation with a surplus of products which had to be disposed of abroad. To a much greater extent she was dependent upon imports. In 1912, for instance, her shipments of finished manufactures made up only 2 per cent of her total exports, while the volume of her imports of manufactured goods was more than ten times as great.[4] And it is significant that a considerable proportion of the latter came from Germany. On the other hand, we must remember that there are always powerful individuals who suffer disadvantages from foreign competition. Such persons invariably exert as much pressure as they can to force their own governments into aggressive action. It should not be forgotten either that economic rivalries frequently give birth to political friction. The British feared, for example, that the tremendous industrial development of western Germany would make control of Antwerp and Amsterdam vital to the Kaiser's empire. The ultimate result would be German acquisition of Belgium and the Netherlands with a consequent serious impairment of Britain's strategic position.

The danger of exaggerating the economic causes

Pre-eminent among the political causes of World War I was nationalism. This factor, as previously explained, had roots extending at least as far back as the French Revolution. By the early twentieth century, however, nationalism had come to assume a variety of particularly dangerous forms. Foremost among them were the Greater Serbia scheme, the Pan-Slav movement in Russia, the revenge movement in France, and the Pan-German movement. The first two were closely related. Since the beginning of the twentieth century at least, little Serbia had dreamed of extending her jurisdiction over all the peoples alleged to be similar to her own citizens in race and in culture. Some of these peoples inhabited what were then the two Turkish provinces of Bosnia and Herzegovina. Others included Croatians and Slovenes in the southern provinces of Austria-Hungary. After 1908 when Austria suddenly annexed Bosnia and Herzegovina, the Greater Serbia scheme was directed exclusively against the Hapsburg empire. It took the form of agitation to provoke discontent

Nationalism: the Greater Serbia movement

[3] B. E. Schmitt, *England and Germany*, p. 102.
[4] Clive Day, *Economic Development in Modern Europe*, p. 387.

among the Slav subjects of Austria, in the hope of drawing them away and uniting the territories they inhabited with Serbia. It resulted in a series of dangerous plots against the peace and integrity of the Dual Monarchy. And the fateful climax of these plots was the murder of the heir to the Austrian throne on June 28, 1914.

Pan-Slavism

In many of their activities the Serbian nationalists were aided and abetted by the Pan-Slavists in Russia. The Pan-Slav movement was founded upon the theory that all of the Slavs of eastern Europe constituted one great family. Therefore, it was argued that Russia as the most powerful Slavic state should act as the guide and protector of her little brother nations of the Balkans. The latter were to be encouraged to look to Russia whenever their interests were endangered. Serbs, Bulgarians, and Montenegrins, in their struggles with Austria or with Turkey, were to be made to understand that they always had a powerful and sympathetic friend on the other side of the Carpathians. Pan-Slavism was not merely the wishful sentiment of a few ardent nationalists, but was really a part of the official policy of the Russian government. It goes far toward explaining Russia's aggressive stand in every quarrel that arose between Serbia and Austria.

The revanche *movement in France*

Another of the malignant forms of nationalism contributing to the war of 1914 was the *revanche* (revenge) movement in France. Ever since 1870 fire-eating patriots in France had looked forward to the time when the defeat in the Franco-Prussian War might be avenged. It is almost impossible for non-Europeans to form any adequate notion of the hold which this idea had taken upon the minds of millions of Frenchmen. It was carefully cultivated by sensation-mongering newspapers, and it was fed to the children in the schools as a regular part of their intellectual fare. The noted politician, Raymond Poincaré, declared that he could see no reason for his generation to go on living except to recover the two lost provinces of Alsace and Lorraine. It must be understood, however, that the idea was probably never the opinion of more than a minority of the French people. By 1914 it was strongly opposed by Socialists and by many liberal leaders.

The Pan-German movement

The influence of Pan-Germanism as a species of nationalism before 1914 is difficult to assess. The name of the movement is generally taken to refer to the ideas of the Pan-German League, founded about 1895. Specifically, the League advocated the expansion of Germany to incorporate all of the Teutonic peoples of central Europe. The boundaries of the Empire should be extended to take in Denmark, the Netherlands, Luxemburg, Switzerland, Austria, and Poland as far east as Warsaw. A few of the leaders were not even satisfied with this but demanded a large colonial empire and a vast expansion into the Balkans and western Asia. They insisted that such peoples as the Bulgars and the Turks should at least become satellites of the German Reich. Although the Pan-German League made a great deal of noise, it could scarcely claim to represent the German nation. As late as 1912 it had a membership of only 17,000, and its violent criticism of the government was widely resented. Nevertheless, a large number of its doctrines had been latent in German thinking for upwards of a century. The philosopher Fichte had taught that the Germans, because of their spiritual superiority, had a mission to impose peace upon the rest of Europe. Ideas of Aryanism and of Nordic supremacy also contributed to the notion that the Germans had a divine destiny to persuade or compel "inferior races" to accept their culture. Finally, the efforts of philosophers like Heinrich von Treitschke to deify the great state and to glorify power as the instrument of national policy helped to impregnate the minds of many Germans of the middle and upper classes with an intolerance of other nations and a belief in the right of Germany to dominate her weaker neighbors.

Nationalism of the types described would have been almost sufficient in itself to have plunged a considerable number of European nations into the maelstrom of war. But the conflict would scarcely have assumed the proportions it did, had it not been for the system of entangling alliances. It was this system which transformed a local squabble between Austria and Serbia into a general war. When Russia intervened on behalf of Serbia, Germany felt obliged to come to the defense of Austria. France had close ties to Russia, and Great Britain was drawn in at least partly on account of her commitments to France. Moreover, the system of alliances was a source of suspicion and fear. It was impossible to expect that Europe would continue indefinitely to be divided into opposing camps of substantially equal strength. Conditions were bound to change with the passage of time. Motives which had originally impelled certain nations to enter into partnership with others lost their importance, and the basis for the alliance disappeared. Thus we shall see that Italy practically abandoned her alliance with Germany and Austria, which at first she had been so eager to join. The result was to bind her former partners more closely together and to magnify their obsession of encirclement by a ring of hostile powers.

The effects of the system of entangling alliances

The evolution of the system of entangling alliances goes back to the 1870's, and its original architect was Bismarck. In the main his purposes were peaceful. Prussia and her German allies had emerged victorious in their war with France, and the newly created German empire was the most powerful state on the Continent. Bismarck was anxious, above all, to preserve the fruits of this victory; there is nothing to indicate that he planned any further conquests. However, he was disturbed by fears that the French might start a war of revenge. There was little prospect that they would attempt such a thing singlehanded, but they might with the help of some other power. Therefore Bismarck determined to isolate France by attaching all of her potential friends to Germany. In 1873 he managed to

The evolution of the system of alliances

form an alliance with both Austria and Russia, the so-called League of the Three Emperors. But this combination was of a precarious nature. It went on the rocks after the Congress of Berlin in 1878 when Russia accused Germany and Austria of cheating her out of her gains in the war she had just fought with Turkey. With the League of the Three Emperors defunct, Bismarck cemented a new and much stronger alliance with Austria. In 1882 this partnership was expanded into the celebrated Triple Alliance when Italy was added as a member. The Italians did not join out of love for either Germany or Austria but from motives of anger and fear. They resented the French occupation of Tunisia (1881), a territory which they regarded as properly theirs. Moreover, the Italian politicians were still at odds with the church, and they feared that the clericals in France might gain the upper hand and send a French army to defend the Pope. In the meantime, the Three Emperors' League had been revived. Though it lasted for only six years (1881–1887), Germany managed to hold the friendship of Russia until 1890.

The diplomatic revolution of 1890–1907

Thus after little more than a decade of diplomatic maneuvering, the Iron Chancellor had achieved his ambition. By 1882 France was cut off from nearly every possibility of obtaining aid from powerful friends. Austria and Italy were united with Germany in the Triple Alliance, and Russia after a three-year lapse was back once more in the Bismarckian camp. The only conceivable quarter from which help might come was Great Britain; but, with respect to Continental affairs, the British had returned to their traditional policy of "splendid isolation." Therefore, so far as the danger of a war of revenge was concerned, Germany had little to fear. But if either Bismarck or anyone else imagined that this security would be permanent, he was headed for a sad disillusionment. Between 1890 and 1907, Europe went through a diplomatic revolution which practically annihilated Bismarck's work. To be sure, the Germans had Austria still on their side; but they had lost the friendship of both Russia and Italy, while Britain had abandoned her isolation to enter into agreements with Russia and France. This shift in the balance of power had fateful results. It convinced the Germans that they were surrounded by a ring of enemies, and that consequently they must do everything in their power to retain the loyalty of Austria—even to the extent of supporting her reckless foreign adventures. Scarcely anything could illustrate better the futility of depending upon a system of alliances for the preservation of peace.

Causes of the diplomatic revolution

The causes of this diplomatic revolution are not hard to discover. First, disagreements between Bismarck and the new Kaiser, William II, led to the great Chancellor's retirement in 1890. His successor, Count Caprivi, was interested mainly in an attempt to cultivate the friendship of Great Britain, and consequently he allowed the treaty with Russia to lapse. Second, the growth of Pan-Slavism in Russia brought the empire of the Tsars into conflict with Austria.

Germany, faced with a choice between Russia and Austria, quite
naturally chose the latter. Third, the establishment of financial ties
between Russia and France inevitably paved the way for a political
alliance. In 1888–1889 arrangements had been made for floating
Russian loans to the amount of nearly $500,000,000 on the Paris
Bourse. Offered at an attractive price, the bonds were eagerly
bought by French investors. From then on large numbers of influential citizens of France had a direct interest in the political
fortunes of Russia. A fourth cause was the abandonment of isolation
by Great Britain. The reasons for this change were several. One
was apprehension over the growing economic power of Germany.
Another was the discovery by the British and the French about 1900
of a basis for co-operation in the partitioning of northern Africa.
A final cause of the diplomatic revolution was the shift in Italy's
attitude toward the Triple Alliance. By 1900 the republicans were
firmly in the saddle in France, with the result that Italy no longer
had anything to fear from monarchist-clerical intervention on
behalf of the Pope. Besides, the Italians had largely resigned themselves to the loss of Tunisia and were turning their attention to the
recovery of territories from Austria and to winning the support of
France for the conquest of Tripoli. For these reasons Italy lost
interest in preserving her loyalty to the Triple Alliance.

The first of the major results of the diplomatic revolution was the
formation of the Triple Entente. This came about through a series
of stages. In 1890 Russia and France began a political flirtation which *Results of the*
gradually ripened into a binding alliance. The secret military con- *diplomatic rev-*
vention signed by the two countries in 1894 provided that each *olution; forma-*
should come to the aid of the other in case of an attack by Germany, *tion of the*
or by Austria or Italy supported by Germany; and that in case of *Triple Entente*
mobilization by any of the members of the Triple Alliance, both
Russia and France should immediately mobilize all of their forces
and transport them as close to the frontiers as possible. This Dual
Alliance of Russia and France was followed by the *Entente Cordiale*
between France and Great Britain. During the last two decades of
the nineteenth century the British and the French had frequently
been involved in sharp altercations over colonies and trade. The
two nations almost came to blows in 1898 at Fashoda in the Egyptian
Sudan. But suddenly the French withdrew all of their claims to that
portion of Africa and opened negotiations for a broad compromise
of other disputes. The result was the conclusion in 1904 of the
Entente Cordiale. It was not a formal alliance but a friendly agreement, covering a variety of subjects. Its most important sections
were secret articles respecting the disposition of territories in northern Africa. France agreed to allow Great Britain a free hand in
Egypt, and in return the British gave their consent to the eventual
acquisition by the French of nearly all of Morocco. The final step
in the formation of the Triple Entente was the conclusion of a

mutual understanding between Great Britain and Russia. Again there was no formal alliance. The two powers simply came to an agreement in 1907 concerning their ambitions in Asia. The core of it provided for the division of Persia into spheres of influence. To Russia was assigned the northern portion and to Great Britain the southern. A middle section was to be preserved, temporarily at least, as a neutral area under its legitimate ruler, the Shah.

Thus by 1907 the great powers of Europe had come to be arrayed in two opposing combinations, the Triple Alliance and the Triple Entente. But during the years that the latter was in process of development, the former was being steadily weakened on account of the defection of Italy. We have seen that by 1900 the motives which had impelled Italy to join the Triple Alliance were no longer important. Not only had a decided coolness developed between Italy and Austria, but Italian nationalists were incessantly clamoring for an empire in Africa. Accordingly, in 1900, the government entered into a secret agreement with France providing that, in return for a free rein in Tripoli, Italy would refrain from interference with French ambitions in Morocco. In 1902 Italy and France concluded another secret bargain whereby each agreed to maintain neutrality in case of an attack by a third power. The obligation was to be binding even if one of the two parties, by reason of a threat to its honor or security, should be compelled "to take the initiative of a declaration of war." Since the terms "security" and "honor" are susceptible of a wide interpretation, it is clear that Italy was really pledging herself to remain neutral in almost any kind of war between France and Germany. Her original obligation under the Triple Alliance to aid Germany in case of attack by France was thus rendered practically worthless. The climax of Italy's defection was her Racconigi Agreement of 1909 with Russia. By this she pledged herself to "regard with benevolence" Russia's ambitions to gain control of the Straits and of Constantinople in return for diplomatic support for the conquest of Tripoli.

The fortunes of the Triple Entente were also subject to fluctuations. It was strengthened somewhat between 1905 and 1912 by a series of military "conversations" and informal agreements between Britain and France. These consisted mainly of detailed arrangements by the British and French general staffs for joint action of the two armies in the event that France should be attacked by Germany. Later certain pledges were given of naval co-operation between Britain and France and Britain and Russia. But the coalition was seriously weakened in 1909 as a result of the refusal of Britain and France to support Russia in her dispute with Austria over the latter's annexation of Bosnia and Herzegovina. Still another threat to the integrity of the Triple Entente occurred in 1913 when Britain collaborated with Germany and Austria in forcing Serbia to give up her claim to Albania. Though the Central Powers professed to

Weakening of the Triple Alliance

The instability of the Triple Entente

810

see in the Triple Entente a powerful combination against them, it was really as unstable as the Triple Alliance. Russia's ambitions at Constantinople conflicted with the interests of Britain in the same locality. The British themselves still seemed to entertain the idea at times of playing the Continental powers off against one another. Hence their tendency to vacillate between appeasement of Germany and encouragement of France. Until almost the end of July, 1914, neither Britain's enemies nor her allies could be absolutely certain just what she would do.

The last of the underlying causes of World War I that needs to be considered was the series of international crises which endangered the peace of Europe between 1905 and 1913. Altogether there were five of serious import: three arising out of the Moroccan question, and two concerning disputes in the Near East. While most of these crises were smoothed over by some sort of compromise, all of them left a heritage of suspicion and bitterness. In some cases war was averted only because one of the parties to the dispute was too weak at the time to offer resistance. The result was a sense of humiliation, a smoldering resentment, that was bound to burst into flame on some future occasion. Another effect of the crises was to throw some light on the real sympathies of the major powers. Thus it was made clear during the third Moroccan crisis that Britain recognized a community of interests with France. In like manner, the attitude displayed by Italy indicated that she was far from being a dependable member of the Triple Alliance.

The series of international crises

The Moroccan crises grew out of a clash of economic interests of the French and the Germans. At the beginning of the twentieth century Morocco was an independent country governed by a Sultan. But his territory was comparatively rich in mineral and agricultural wealth which European nations coveted. The cupidity of the French and the Germans was aroused particularly by the iron and manganese deposits and by the excellent trading opportunities. In 1880 the chief powers of the world had signed the Convention of Madrid, which provided that the representatives of all nations should have equal economic privileges in Morocco. But the French were not long satisfied with such an arrangement. By 1903 their Moroccan trade exceeded that of any other country, and they yearned for nothing less than a monopoly. In addition, they desired Morocco as a reservoir from which troops could be drawn and as a bulwark for the defense of Algeria. Accordingly, in 1904, France entered into an agreement with Great Britain to establish a new order in the Sultan's territory. The articles of the agreement made public piously announced the determination of the signatory powers to uphold the independence of Morocco; the secret articles provided for just the opposite. In due time Morocco was to be dismembered. A small section opposite the rock of Gibraltar was to be given to Spain, and the remainder was to be taken over by France. Great Britain,

The clash over Morocco

as we have seen, was to have her reward in the form of a free hand in Egypt.

It was this agreement of 1904 which precipitated the bitter wrangling between France and Germany. By 1905 officials in the German government had learned that some trickery was afoot. They determined either to make France relinquish her claims on Morocco or grant compensations. In 1905 Chancellor von Bülow arranged to have the Kaiser land at the Moroccan port of Tangier and make a speech declaring that Germany stood on her rights. The upshot of this gesture was a crisis which brought Europe to the verge of war. To settle the dispute an international congress was held at Algeciras in Spain in 1906. Though the conference affirmed the sovereign status of the Sultan, it at the same time recognized the special interests of France in his dominions. This outcome suited the French admirably, for now they could penetrate the land of the Moors under the cloak of legality. A second crisis occurred in 1908 and a third in 1911, both resulting from attempts of the Germans to protect what they regarded as their legitimate rights in Morocco. The third crisis is particularly important because of the positive attitude assumed by the British. In July, 1911, David Lloyd George, in his celebrated Mansion House speech, warned Germany that there would be trouble if she attempted to establish a foothold on the Moroccan coast. The Moroccan controversy was settled late in 1911 when France agreed to surrender a portion of the French Congo to Germany. The Kaiser's government thereupon abandoned all claims to Morocco and informed the French that they could do what they liked with the country. Soon afterward all but the narrow strip assigned to Spain was added to the colonial empire of France. But neither of the parties recovered from the bitterness engendered by the dispute. The French maintained that they had been blackmailed into surrendering valuable territory. The Germans argued that the portion of the Congo ceded by France was not a sufficient compensation for the loss of economic privileges in Morocco.

Results of the Moroccan crises

Even more serious than the Moroccan affair were the two Near Eastern crises. The first was the Bosnian crisis of 1908. At the Congress of Berlin in 1878 the two Turkish provinces of Bosnia and Herzegovina had been placed under the administrative control of Austria, although actual possession was still to be vested in the Ottoman Empire. Serbia also coveted the territories, since they would double the size of her kingdom, and give her a possible outlet to the Adriatic. Suddenly on October 5, 1908, Austria annexed the two provinces, in flat violation of the Treaty of Berlin. The Serbs were furious and appealed to Russia. The Tsar's government threatened war, until Germany addressed a sharp note to St. Petersburg announcing her firm intention to back Austria. Since Russia had not yet fully recovered from the war with Japan and was in no position to fight both Germany and Austria, she finally informed the Serbs

The Near Eastern crises: (1) the annexation of Bosnia and Herzegovina

that they would have to wait until a more favorable time. Prevailing opinion in western Europe was sharply critical of Austria. She was reproached with violating international law and recklessly disturbing the balance of power. It was not known at the time that responsibility for the crisis rested to a considerable extent also upon the Foreign Minister of Russia, Alexander Izvolski. In September, 1908, Izvolski had entered into a secret agreement with Count Aerenthal, the Austrian Foreign Minister, at the latter's castle at Buchlau, which provided that Russia would not interfere with the annexation of the two provinces if Austria would lend her support to Russia's ambition to open the Straits. But Izvolski was prevented from carrying out his part of the bargain by opposition from Great Britain and France. When Aerenthal went ahead with the annexation, Izvolski turned against him with an attitude of injured innocence. The Bosnian crisis was unquestionably one of the most important causes of World War I. It created more bad blood between nations than almost any other single factor that could be mentioned. It fanned the flames of Serbian wrath against Austria and encouraged the Serbs to depend upon the support of Russia. It convinced the imperialists in St. Petersburg that they would eventually have to fight not only Austria but Germany. Not the least of its effects was ultimately to bring France into closer *rapport* with Russia. After Izvolski's scheme was frustrated in 1908, he resigned as Foreign Minister and accepted an appointment as ambassador to Paris. Here from 1910 to 1914 he worked with masterly cunning to make France a loyal supporter of the alliance with Russia. He seems to have exerted considerable influence upon Poincaré.

Ill feeling between Austria and Serbia was intensified still further by the Balkan Wars. The first of these wars was in part the out- *(2) the Balkan* growth of the Ottomanization program of the Young Turks. Re- *Wars* ports of atrocities committed by the Sultan's government upon Slavs in Macedonia aroused the sympathies of their kinsmen throughout the Balkans and provided an excuse for an attack upon Turkish territory. In 1912 Serbia, Bulgaria, Montenegro, and Greece, with encouragement from Russia, joined in a Balkan alliance for the conquest of Macedonia. The war was started in October, 1912, and in less than two months the resistance of the Turks was completely shattered. Then came the problem of dividing the spoils. In secret treaties negotiated before hostilities began, Serbia had been promised Albania, in addition to a generous slice of western Macedonia. But now Austria, fearful as always of any increase in Serbian power, intervened at the peace conference and obtained the support of Great Britain and Germany for the establishment of Albania as an independent state. For the Serbs this was the last straw. It seemed that at every turn their path to expansion, at least in a westerly direction, was certain to be blocked by the Hapsburg government. From this time on, anti-Austrian agitation in Serbia and in the

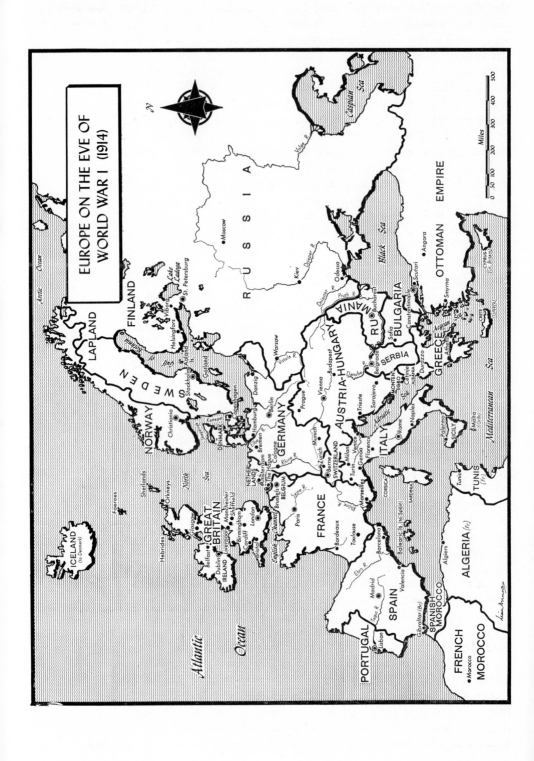

EUROPE ON THE EVE OF
WORLD WAR I (1914)

neighboring province of Bosnia became ever more venomous. While the Serbs did manage to force Bulgaria to share a portion of her gains in Macedonia, this was small compensation for the loss of Albania, which would have provided an outlet to the sea.[5]

2. *The Road to Armageddon*

As almost everyone knows, the immediate cause of World War I was the assassination of Archduke Francis Ferdinand on June 28, 1914. This was the match thrown into the powder-keg of accumulated suspicion and hate. Nevertheless, it was not quite so trivial an event as many people think. Francis Ferdinand was not simply a useless member of the Austrian nobility; he was soon to become emperor. The reigning monarch, Francis Joseph, had reached his eighty-fourth year, and his death was expected momentarily. The murder of the heir to the throne was therefore considered as in a very real sense an attack upon the state. The reaction of the Austrians was somewhat similar to what Americans would feel if an important official of the United States should be assassinated while on a visit to Texas by a band of Mexican nationalists.

The assassination of Francis Ferdinand

June 28, 1914. The Archduke Francis Ferdinand and his wife leaving in the imperial car for their fateful trip to Sarajevo.

The actual murderer of Francis Ferdinand was a Bosnian student by the name of Princip. But this does not tell half of the story. Princip was merely the tool of Serbian nationalists. The murder, though committed in Sarajevo, the capital of Bosnia, was the result of a plot hatched in Belgrade. The conspirators were members of a secret society officially known as Union or Death but commonly called the Black Hand. Considerable evidence has recently been brought to light that the Serbian government knew of the existence of the plot.[6] But neither the Premier nor any of his colleagues took effective measures to prevent its execution or even to warn the Austrian government. This naturally raises the question as to the

Motives of the assassins

[5] The war in which Serbia fought against Bulgaria is known as the Second Balkan War (June–July, 1913). Allied with Serbia were Greece, Montenegro, Rumania, and Turkey. The chief significance of this war lies in the fact that it brought Bulgaria into World War I on the side of the Central Powers in the hope that she might even the score with Serbia.

[6] See S. B. Fay, *The Origins of the World War*, Vol. II, pp. 61 ff.

motives of the assassins. If there is any one answer, it would seem to lie in the plan which Francis Ferdinand was known to be developing for the reorganization of the Hapsburg empire. This plan, designated as *trialism*, involved a proposal for changing the Dual Monarchy into a triple monarchy. In addition to German Austria and Magyar Hungary, already practically autonomous, there was to be a third semi-independent unit composed of the Slavs. This was exactly what the Serb nationalists did not want. They feared that if it were put into effect their Slovene and Croatian kinsmen would be content to remain under Hapsburg rule. Therefore they determined to get Francis Ferdinand out of the way before he could become emperor of Austria-Hungary.

The Austrian ultimatum to Serbia

Until some time after the war was over, it was assumed in western Europe and in the United States that the assassination of the Archduke was the work of disaffected Bosnians. But in the weeks immediately following the tragedy, Austrian officials conducted an investigation which confirmed their suspicions that the plot was of Serbian origin. Consequently, on July 23, they dispatched to the Serbian government a severe ultimatum consisting of eleven demands. Among other things Serbia was to suppress anti-Austrian newspapers, to crush the secret patriotic societies, to eliminate from the government and from the army all persons guilty of anti-Austrian propaganda, and to accept the collaboration of Austrian officials in stamping out the subversive movement against the Hapsburg empire. On July 25, in accordance with the time limit of forty-eight hours, the Serbian government transmitted its reply. It was a document still subject to varying interpretations. Of the total of eleven demands, only one was emphatically refused, and five were accepted without reservations. The German Chancellor regarded it as almost a complete capitulation, and the Kaiser declared that now all reason for war had fallen to the ground. The Austrians, however, pronounced it unsatisfactory, severed diplomatic relations, and mobilized part of their army. The Serbs themselves had been under no illusions about pleasing Austria, since, three hours before transmitting their reply, they had issued an order to mobilize the troops.

Russia and France assume a belligerent attitude

At this point the attitude of other nations becomes extremely important. In fact for some time before this, several of the rulers of the great powers had assumed very positive attitudes. As early as July 18 Sazonov, the Russian Foreign Minister, warned Austria that Russia would not tolerate any effort to humiliate Serbia. Upon learning of the ultimatum to Serbia, the Russian government ordered a series of secret preparations to put the country on a war footing. The furloughs of officers were canceled, troops were recalled to their quarters, stocks of supplies were accumulated, and a "state of war" was proclaimed in the frontier sectors facing Germany and Austria. On July 24 Sazonov exclaimed to the German ambassador: "I do not hate Austria; I despise her. Austria is seeking a pretext to gobble up Serbia; but in that case Russia will make war on Austria." [7] In the adoption of this belligerent attitude, Russia had the support of France. About the twentieth of July, Raymond Poincaré, who was now President of the French republic, paid a visit to St. Petersburg. He kept urging Sazonov to "be firm" and to avoid any compromise which might result in a loss of prestige for the Triple Entente. He warned the Austrian ambassador that "Serbia has very warm friends in the Russian people. And Russia has an ally, France." [8]

The attitude of Germany in these critical days was seemingly more moderate. Although the Kaiser was shocked and infuriated by the assassination, his government did not make any threats or undertake any extensive preparations for war until after the actions of Russia gave cause for alarm. Unfortunately, however, both the Kaiser and the Chancellor, von Bethmann-Hollweg, adopted the premise that stern punishment must be meted out to Serbia without delay. They hoped in this way to confront the Powers with an accomplished fact and thereby to avert a general war. The Kaiser declared on June 30: "Now or never! Matters must be cleared up with the Serbs, *and that soon.*" On July 6 Bethmann-Hollweg gave to the Austrian Foreign Minister, Count Berchtold, a commitment which was interpreted by the latter as a blank check. The Austrian government was informed that the Kaiser would "stand true by Austria's side in accordance with his treaty obligations and old friendship." In giving this pledge Bethmann and his imperial master were gambling on the hope that Russia would not intervene for the protection of Serbia, and that therefore the quarrel would remain a mere local squabble. Later, when they discovered that this hope was in vain, they sought to hold Austria in check. They attempted to persuade their ally to confine her action to a temporary occupation of Belgrade as a pledge that the terms of the ultimatum would be carried out. When this failed, Bethmann even threatened to break Germany's alliance with Austria if Berchtold persisted in disregarding advice. But all of these efforts came too late, for war between Austria and Serbia had already begun.

The attitude of Germany

Austria declared war against Serbia on July 28, 1914. For a fleeting, anxious moment there was a slender possibility that the conflict might be localized. But it was quickly transformed into a war of larger scope by the action of Russia. On July 29 Sazonov and the military clique persuaded the Tsar to issue an order to mobilize all of the troops, not only against Austria but against Germany as well. But before the order could be put into effect, Nicholas changed his mind, having just received an urgent appeal from the Kaiser to help in preserving peace. On July 30 Sazonov and General Tatistchev went to work to induce the Tsar to change his mind again. For more than an hour they sought to convince the reluctant autocrat

Russian mobilization

[7] *Ibid.*, Vol. II, p. 300.
[8] *Ibid.*, Vol. II, p. 281.

that the entire military system should be set in motion. Finally, General Tatistchev remarked: "Yes, it is hard to decide." Nicholas retorted with a show of irritation: "I will decide," and signed an order for immediate mobilization. Sazonov hurried to the telephone to communicate the news to the Chief of Staff. This time every precaution had been taken to avoid any last-minute repentance on the part of the Tsar. It had been arranged that the order should be telegraphed immediately to all parts of the country, and that the Chief of Staff should smash his telephone and disappear for the day. The next morning in a remote Siberian village an English traveler was awakened by a commotion outside his window, followed by the query of an excited peasant: "Have you heard the news? There is war." [9]

The German ultimatums to Russia and France

There was now no drawing back from the abyss. The Germans were alarmed over Russian preparations for war. The latest action of the Tsar's government made the situation far more critical, since in German military circles, and also in French and Russian, general mobilization meant war. Unless the Tsar could somehow halt the process after it had begun, Germany as well as Austria was bound to take up arms against Russia. And with Germany drawn in, France was certain to follow. Upon learning that the Tsar's decree had gone into effect, the Kaiser's government sent an ultimatum to St. Petersburg demanding that mobilization cease within twelve hours. On the afternoon of August 1 the German ambassador requested an interview with the Russian Foreign Minister. He appealed to Sazonov for a favorable answer to the German ultimatum. Sazonov replied that mobilization could not be halted, but that Russia was willing to continue negotiations. The ambassador repeated his question a second and a third time, emphasizing the terrible consequences of a negative answer. Sazonov finally replied: "I have no other answer to give you." The ambassador then handed the Foreign Minister a declaration of war and, bursting into tears, left the room.[10] In the meantime, the Kaiser's ministers had also dispatched an ultimatum to France demanding that she make known her intentions. Premier Viviani replied on August 1 that France would act "in accordance with her interests," and immediately ordered a general mobilization of the army. On August 3 Germany declared war upon France.

The attitude of Britain

All eyes now turned in the direction of Britain. What would she do, now that the other two members of the Triple Entente had rushed headlong into war? For some time after the situation on the Continent had become critical, Britain vacillated. Both the cabinet and the nation were divided. Sir Edward Grey and Winston Churchill advocated a positive stand on the side of France and Russia with an appeal to arms if Britain's interests should be threatened. But

[9] *Ibid.*, Vol. II, pp. 472–73.
[10] G. P. Gooch, *Before the War: Studies in Diplomacy*, Vol. II, p. 368.

August 1, 1914. A German officer reading the declaration of war in the streets of Berlin.

some of their colleagues were much less enthusiastic about intervention in Continental quarrels. Throughout the country there was likewise considerable opposition to mixing in squabbles which were not believed to be of vital concern to England's welfare. Although Grey had on several occasions encouraged the Russians and the French to count upon British aid, it was not until after he received pledges of support from the leaders of the Conservative party that he made any formal commitments. On August 2 he informed the French that "if the German fleet comes into the Channel or through the North Sea to undertake hostile operations against the French coasts or shipping, the British fleet will give all the protection in its power." [11]

In view of this pledge to France, it is difficult to believe that Britain would have long remained out of the war, even if the neutrality of Belgium had never been violated. In fact, as early as July 29, Sir Edward Grey had given the German ambassador in London a "friendly and private" warning that if France were drawn into the war, Great Britain would enter also.[12] Nevertheless, it was the invasion of Belgian territory which provided the immediate cause of Britain's unsheathing the sword. In 1839, along with the other Great Powers, she had signed a treaty guaranteeing the neutrality of Belgium. Moreover, it had been British policy for a century or more to try to prevent domination of the Low Countries, lying directly across the Channel, by any powerful Continental nation. But the

Britain enters the war

[11] S. B. Fay, *The Origins of the World War*, Vol. II, p. 540.
[12] B. E. Schmitt, "July, 1914: Thirty Years After," *Journal of Modern History*, Vol. XVI (1944), p. 193.

famous Schlieffen Plan of the Germans provided for attacking France through Belgium. Accordingly, they demanded of the Belgian government permission to send troops across its territory, promising to respect the independence of the nation and to pay for any damage to property. When Belgium refused, the Kaiser's gray-coated legions began pouring across her frontier. The British Foreign Secretary immediately went before Parliament and presented the idea that his country should rally to the defense of international law and to the protection of small nations. He argued that peace under the circumstances would be a moral crime, and declared that if Britain should fail to uphold her obligations of honor in this matter she would forfeit the respect of the civilized world. The applause which greeted this speech in the House of Commons left him in no doubt as to the attitude of that body. The next day, August 4, the cabinet decided to send an ultimatum to Berlin demanding that Germany respect Belgian neutrality, and that she give a satisfactory reply by midnight. The Kaiser's ministers offered no answer save military necessity, arguing that it was a matter of life and death for Germany that her soldiers should reach France by the quickest and easiest way. As the clock struck twelve, Great Britain and Germany were at war.

The conflagration spreads

Other nations were quickly drawn into the terrible vortex. On August 7 the Montenegrins joined with their kinsmen, the Serbs, in fighting Austria. Two weeks later the Japanese declared war upon Germany, partly because of their alliance with Great Britain, but mainly for the purpose of conquering the German possessions in the Far East. On August 1 Turkey negotiated an alliance with Germany and in October began the bombardment of Russian ports in the Black Sea. Thus most of the nations definitely bound by alliances entered the conflict in its early stages on one side or the other. Italy, however, though still technically a member of the Triple Alliance, proclaimed her neutrality. The Italians insisted that Germany was not fighting a defensive war, and that consequently they were not bound to go to her aid. They said nothing, of course, about their secret agreement of 1902 with France. Italy maintained her neutrality until May, 1915, when she was bribed by secret promises of Austrian and Turkish territory to engage in the war on the side of the Triple Entente.

The question of war guilt

The tumult and excitement which accompanied the beginning of the great holocaust of 1914 have long since died away. But the question of who was responsible for the horrible conflagration is still a vital one. Historians who have examined the evidence are almost unanimously of the opinion that no one nation was solely culpable. The guilt must be shared by Serbia, Austria, Russia, Germany, and France; and perhaps also by Great Britain and Italy. But just how it should be apportioned is a question impossible to answer.

820 It seems accurate to say that none of the Great Powers really wanted a general war, but several of them were disposed to follow policies which made such a war inevitable. Germany, for example, considered it essential to her interest to back up Austria in her reckless determination to punish Serbia, despite the fact that by so doing she would throw down a challenge to Russia. The Germans apparently *hoped* that Russia would ignore the challenge; but they did not *know*, and they were willing to gamble even at the risk of a general war. The Russians themselves probably had no desire to fight Germany or even Austria, but they were ready to threaten the *status quo* by conspiring to control the Straits, and to encourage Serb nationalism to such an extent as to endanger the security of Austria-Hungary. In like manner, France, with respect to her Moroccan policy, was pursuing objectives which doubtless seemed reasonable to her, but which could only be attained at the expense of the interests of Germany. And so it went. Economic ambition and concern for security or national greatness drove too many of the states of Europe to follow courses of action which could lead only to war. War itself was not the objective, but it was the inescapable result when conflicting national ambitions could not be reconciled.

To consider the Great Madness of 1914 as the work of any one individual is even more absurd than to regard it as the diabolical plot of a single nation. It is now abundantly clear that the Kaiser, so often portrayed as the arch-fiend, was less guilty than is commonly believed. True, he was addicted to making vainglorious speeches, boasting of how, during the Bosnian crisis, he had stood by the side of Austria "in shining armor" and referring to himself as "the Most High." But his control over the German government was steadily diminishing. He seldom gave more than two hours a day to public affairs, and much of the time he was only dimly aware of what was going on. The real business of state was conducted by his ministers. But no one of these can be convicted of deliberately plotting the war. Chancellor von Bethmann-Hollweg broke down completely during the final critical days. He had been one of the last of the European statesmen to abandon hope for peace. When he finally realized that the awful catastrophe could not be prevented, he went almost insane. Perhaps a few other statesmen were more successful in retaining their composure, but most of them kept up the pretense at least of trying to prevent the conflict.

The guilt of individuals

In reality the World War of 1914 was much too big a movement ever to have been caused entirely by scheming individuals. While most of the politicians in power at the time were in some measure responsible, their guilt was often of the nature of stupidity rather than of criminal intention. Probably few of them actually wanted war, but they allowed themselves to be drawn into difficult situations and then had to resort to dangerous expedients to avoid a loss of prestige. Most of them believed, as statesmen still do, in bluster and threat as methods of forcing a rival government to give ground.

Dangerous habits and tendencies

At times such tactics worked, as in 1909 when Chancellor von Bülow made Russia retreat from her position in the Bosnian crisis. But even under the most favorable circumstances the game of bluff between nations is fraught with the direst hazards. To a large extent, also, the individuals who occupied the seats of the mighty in 1914 were but the instruments of forces much more powerful than they. Sazonov and Izvolski did not create Pan-Slavism in Russia any more than Poincaré originated the *revanche* movement in France. World War I was the product of chauvinism, of ambitions for national prestige, of capitalist competition for markets and for new fields of investment, of age-old hatreds between nations, and of fears engendered by crises and by the race for superiority in armaments. When such factors combined to rule the constellation of events, prime ministers and foreign secretaries were hardly much more than playthings of fate.

Power politics and international anarchy

In a still broader sense, the conflagration of 1914 was the virtually inevitable consequence of the system of power politics which had cursed the European continent for nearly 300 years. That system was based upon the doctrine that every state is absolutely sovereign and is therefore entitled to pursue whatever foreign policy seems best adapted to its own interest. If a state, in order to obtain raw materials or to improve its defenses, saw fit to pounce upon the territory of a weak neighbor, it did so, and no one would deny it the right. Most of the great nations of Europe sought to attain security for themselves by promoting some sort of balance of power. But unfortunately each attempted to weight the balance in its own favor, usually by creating alliances and then by building them up to maximum strength. This led, among the nations outside the alliance, to fears of encirclement, to the formation of counteralliances, and to efforts to smash anything that faintly resembled a league of enemies. By 1914 the nations of the world were almost in a state of nature, with no effective authority to hold them in check or to adjudicate their quarrels. It was virtually a condition of international anarchy.

3. The Ordeal of Battle

The holy war of the Entente powers

In the prophetic gospel known as *Revelation* it is related that the forces of good and evil shall be gathered together on "the great day of God" to do battle at Armageddon. The unknown author might almost have been thinking of the titanic conflict which engulfed the nations of Europe in 1914. For World War I was seldom admitted to be a struggle between rival imperialist powers or a product of nationalist jealousy. Instead it was represented by spokesmen for both sides as a crusade against the forces of evil. No sooner had the war begun than social and political leaders in England and France

pronounced it a gallant effort to safeguard the rights of the weak and to preserve the supremacy of international law and morality. Prime Minister Asquith on August 6, 1914, declared that England had entered the conflict to vindicate "the principle that smaller nationalities are not to be crushed by the arbitrary will of a strong and overmastering Power." Across the Channel, President Poincaré was pompously assuring his countrymen that France had no other purpose than to stand "before the universe for Liberty, Justice and Reason." Later, as a consequence of the inspiring preaching of such eloquent writers and orators as H. G. Wells, Gilbert Murray, and Woodrow Wilson, the crusade of the Entente powers became a war "to end all wars," to "make the world safe for democracy," and to redeem mankind from the curse of militarism. In the opposing camp the subordinates of the Kaiser were doing all in their power to justify Germany's military efforts. The struggle against the Allies was represented to the German people as a crusade on behalf of a superior *Kultur* and as a battle to protect the Fatherland against the wicked encirclement policy of the Entente nations.[13]

World War I was unique in several respects. Not only were scores of new weapons introduced, but methods of fighting differed quite radically from those in most earlier conflicts. Open warfare disappeared from the Western Front almost at the beginning. After the first few weeks the opposing armies settled down in a vast network

Unique features of World War I

Trench Warfare. After the first few battles, World War I on the Western Front settled into static or position warfare. During the four-year period veritable cities of mud, stone, and timber sprang up behind the trenches.

of trenches, from which attacks were launched usually in the murky hours just before dawn, in efforts to dislodge the enemy. For the most part, the struggle was an endurance contest, in which victory depended mainly upon natural resources and upon the ability of the Entente nations to obtain almost unlimited supplies of money, food, and munitions from across the sea. Probably it is safe to say that World War I was fought with greater savagery than any preceding military engagement of modern times. The use of poison gas, of

---

[13] The quotations in this paragraph are taken from J. S. Ewart, *The Roots and Causes of the Wars*, Vol. I, pp. 16, 104. See also I. C. Willis, *England's Holy War*.

the machine gun, of liquid fire, and of explosive bullets took a toll in lives and in ghastly wounds absolutely unprecedented even in the much longer campaigns of Napoleon. It is an interesting sidelight on this savagery that the number of civilians killed in air raids, in massacres, in famines, and in epidemics exceeded the number of soldiers killed in battle. Finally, the war was unique in the tremendous size of its armies. Altogether about 65,000,000 men fought for longer or shorter periods under the flags of the various belligerents. This was the climax of the steady trend toward mass warfare which had had its beginning during the French Revolution.

Why the United States joined the Allies: cultural reasons

As the conflict dragged on through four appalling years, more and more nations threw down the gage of battle on one side or the other. We have seen that Italy postponed her entrance until the spring of 1915. Bulgaria joined the Central Powers in September, 1915, and Rumania entered on the opposite side about a year later. But the event which finally tipped the scales in favor of an Entente victory was the declaration of war against Germany by the United States on April 6, 1917. The United States entered the war for a variety of reasons. The majority of her prominent citizens were of British extraction. This was true in general of her university presidents, of her leading Protestant ministers, of her newspaper magnates, and of her chief officers of state. Her cultural traditions, her law and political theory, and the foundations of her literature were mainly of English origin. British propaganda agencies took full advantage of these ethnic and cultural ties and skillfully encouraged Americans to believe that the Entente nations were fighting to defend civilization. By contrast, German propaganda was clumsy and inept. And when it failed, German and Austrian representatives in the United States attempted to foment strikes and sabotage in munitions factories. Germany had been feared and distrusted by Americans since the Spanish War of 1898, when one of her admirals was believed to have interfered with Commodore Dewey's capture of Manila. Her methods of waging war in 1914, particularly her violation of the neutrality of Belgium, made her still more an object of suspicion and fear. Hostilities were only a few weeks old when some Americans began to refer to the Germans as "Huns."

Economic causes

Powerful economic forces were also important factors in propelling the American people toward sympathy for the Entente cause. By 1915 the United States had become the chief supplier of munitions and other war materials to Britain, Russia, and France. The traffic reached such proportions as to turn a depression which had begun in 1913 into a glowing prosperity. Most of the commodities sold were not purchased for cash but on credit, or were paid for by means of loans floated in the United States. By April, 1917, at least $1,500,000,000 worth of Allied government bonds had been sold in this country. While there is no proof that the purchasers of these bonds exerted direct pressure upon President Wilson to put the nation into the war, the fact remains that a considerable number of influential citizens had acquired a financial stake in an Entente victory.

Yet another fundamental cause which induced the United States to become a belligerent was President Wilson's eventual decision that his country must play a dominant role in re-shaping the world at the end of the war. He had visions of establishing a new world order based upon a League of Nations which would preserve justice and punish aggressors in the future. Throughout most of the war he had refused to believe in the exclusive righteousness of either side. As late as December, 1916, he had declared that the war aims of both groups of belligerents appeared to be essentially the same. He was still convinced that "peace without victory" and without humiliation or drastic penalties would be the necessary foundation for the new regime of lasting concord among nations. But lurking in the back of his mind for some time had been the conviction that German "autocracy" and German "militarism" were major obstacles to the realization of his ideal. As the German government rejected his efforts for peace and showed an increasing determination to win the war by ruthlessness and disregard for international law, this conviction was greatly strengthened. He still had no quarrel with the German people, but he believed that the recent tendencies of their government left him with no alternative but to destroy it by force.

*Wilson's desire
for a new
world order*

A final underlying cause was the concern of the American government over the maintenance of the balance of power in Europe. For years it had been a cardinal doctrine in the State Department and among military and naval officers that the security of the United States depended upon a balance of forces in the Old World. No one power must be allowed to establish its supremacy over all of Europe. So long as Great Britain was strong enough to prevent that supremacy, the United States was safe. Some authorities believe that American officials had grown so accustomed to thinking of the British Navy as the shield and buckler of American security that they could hardly tolerate the thought of any different situation. Germany, however, presented not merely a challenge to British naval supremacy but threatened to starve the British nation into surrender and make herself dominant over all of Europe.

The direct cause of United States participation in World War I was the submarine warfare of the Germans. But it was much more than an ordinary immediate cause. Some historians regard it as the most important of all the factors, on the ground that without it the United States would not have entered the war at all. When the war began, Germany had only a small fleet of submarines, but she rapidly increased their number. On February 4, 1915, the Kaiser's government announced that neutral vessels headed for British ports would be torpedoed without warning. President Wilson replied to this challenge by declaring that the United States would hold

Germany to "a strict accountability" if any harm should come to American lives or property. The warning had little effect. The Germans were convinced that the U-boat was one of their most valuable weapons, and they considered themselves justified in using it as an answer to the British blockade. They violated pledges to respect American rights and continued occasional sinkings of passenger vessels, in some cases causing the deaths of American citizens. When the Kaiser's ministers announced that, on February 1, 1917, they would launch a campaign of unrestricted submarine warfare, Wilson cut off diplomatic relations with the Berlin government. On April 2 he went before a joint session of the two houses of Congress and requested a declaration of war. The declaration was approved four days later with only six negative votes in the Senate and fifty in the House of Representatives.

In a book of this kind it would be neither possible nor desirable to give a full account of the military history of World War I. The main theater of the conflict, as everyone knows, was the Western Front, which included Belgium and eastern France from the Vosges Mountains to the North Sea. Here for a brief period the Germans swept everything before them, advancing their armies to within fourteen miles of Paris a month after the beginning of the war. But they were unable to capture the city. The French discovered a weak spot in the German line and pushed the Kaiser's hosts back to the valley of the Marne. Here in early September, 1914, occurred a series of engagements known as the First Battle of the Marne. Though neither side could claim a decisive victory, it was clear that the German advance had been checked. The battle is important also in that it marked the end of open warfare. Both armies constructed elaborate trenches and dug themselves in behind barbed wire entanglements. From this point on until the spring of 1918 the war on the Western Front was almost a deadlock. While the British and the French made sizable gains, they could achieve no smashing victory that would bring Germany to sue for peace. But in March, 1918, the Germans launched a powerful attack which threatened for a time to overwhelm the resistance of the Allied armies. It was followed by a counteroffensive of the French, British, and Americans which continued through the summer and fall and finally ended the war.

On the Eastern and Southern Fronts the Central Powers were victorious over a much longer period. At the end of August, 1914, the Russian advance was abruptly halted at Tannenberg in East Prussia, and soon afterward the Tsar's generals began a retreat along the entire Eastern Front. In 1915 the Germans and Austrians captured nearly all of Russian Poland and Lithuania, turning every Russian counterattack into a disastrous rout. After the overthrow of the Tsar in the March revolution of 1917, Russia practically withdrew from the war. Attempts were made by the provisional government to

The war on the Western Front

The war on the Eastern and Southern Fronts

renew the struggle, but the people were so thoroughly disheartened that nothing could be accomplished. In March, 1918, the Bolshevik government concluded a treaty of peace. Meanwhile Rumania had been conquered by the Germans, and Serbia had been reduced to impotence by the Austrians and Bulgarians. On the Southern Front the Italians managed to hold the Austrians at bay for more than two years, and even to conquer small portions of the rugged terrain on the northeastern shore of the Adriatic. But by the middle of 1917 the Italians were beginning to tire of the arduous struggle. Defeatism was rife in the government and among the troops as well. In October the Austrians broke through the frontier defenses and overwhelmed a demoralized Italian army at Caporetto. More than 200,000 prisoners were captured, to say nothing of huge quantities of guns and supplies. It was a staggering blow, from which Italy barely recovered before the end of the war.

While fighting on the several fronts was still going on, various attempts were made to bring about the negotiation of peace. In the spring of 1917 Dutch and Scandinavian socialists decided to summon *Peace proposals* an international socialist conference to meet at Stockholm in the hope of drafting plans for ending the fighting which would be acceptable to all the belligerents. The Petrograd Soviet embraced the idea and on May 15 issued an appeal to socialists of all nations to send delegates to the conference and to induce their governments to agree to a peace "without annexations and indemnities, on the basis of the self-determination of peoples." The socialist parties in all the principal countries on both sides of the war enthusiastically accepted this formula and were eager to send delegates to the conference; but when the British and French governments refused to permit any of their subjects to attend, the project was abandoned. That the rulers of the Entente states were not afraid of these proposals merely because they emanated from socialists is indicated by the fact that a similar formula suggested by the Pope was just as emphatically rejected. On August 1 of this same year Pope Benedict XV appealed to the various governments to agree to the renunciation of claims for indemnities, to the future settlement of international disputes by arbitration, to a reduction of armaments, to the restoration of all occupied areas, and to the holding of plebiscites to determine what should be done with such territories as Alsace-Lorraine, Poland, and the Trentino. Nowhere was there a disposition to take these proposals seriously. Woodrow Wilson, as spokesman for the Allies, declared that negotiation of peace *under any conditions* was impossible so long as Germany was ruled by the Kaiser. The Central Powers professed to regard with favor the general import of the papal suggestions, but they refused to commit themselves on indemnities and restorations, especially the restoration of Belgium.

The most famous of all the peace proposals was President Wilson's program of Fourteen Points, which he incorporated in an   **827** address to Congress on January 8, 1918. Summarized as briefly as possible, this program included: (1) "open covenants openly arrived at," or the abolition of secret diplomacy; (2) freedom of the seas; (3) removal of economic barriers between nations; (4) reduction of national armaments "to the lowest point consistent with safety"; (5) impartial adjustment of colonial claims, with consideration for the interests of the peoples involved; (6) evacuation of Russia; (7) restoration of the independence of Belgium; (8) restoration of Alsace and Lorraine to France; (9) a readjustment of Italian frontiers "along clearly recognizable lines of nationality"; (10) autonomous development for the peoples of Austria-Hungary; (11) restoration of Rumania, Serbia, and Montenegro, with access to the sea for Serbia; (12) autonomous development for the peoples of Turkey, and the Straits from the Black Sea to the Mediterranean "permanently opened"; (13) an independent Poland, "inhabited by indisputably Polish populations," and with access to the sea; (14) a League of Nations. On several other occasions throughout 1918 Wilson reiterated in public addresses that this program would be the basis of the peace for which he would labor. Thousands of copies of the Fourteen Points were scattered by Allied planes over the German trenches and behind the lines in an effort to convince both soldiers and people that the Entente nations were striving for a just and durable peace.

By the close of the summer of 1918 the long nightmare of carnage was approaching its end. The great offensive launched by the British, French, and United States forces in July dealt one shattering blow after another to the German battalions and forced them back almost to the Belgian frontier. By the end of September the cause of the Central Powers was hopeless. Bulgaria withdrew from the war on September 30. Early in October the new Chancellor of Germany, the liberal Prince Max of Baden, appealed to President Wilson for a negotiated peace on the basis of the Fourteen Points. But the fighting went on, for Wilson had returned to his original demand that Germany must drop the Kaiser. Soon afterward Germany's remaining allies were tottering on the verge of collapse. Turkey surrendered at the end of October. The Hapsburg empire was being cracked wide open by the revolts of the Slavs. Moreover, an Austrian offensive against Italy had not only failed but had incited the Italians to a counteroffensive, with the consequent loss to Austria of the city of Trieste and 300,000 prisoners. On November 3 the Emperor Charles, who had succeeded Francis Joseph in 1916, signed an armistice which took Austria out of the war.

Germany was now left with the impossible task of carrying on the struggle alone. The morale of her troops was rapidly breaking. The blockade was causing such a shortage of food that her people were in danger of starving. The revolutionary tremors that had been felt for some time swelled into a mighty earthquake. On

November 8 a republic was proclaimed in Bavaria. The next day nearly all of Germany was in the throes of revolution. A decree was published in Berlin announcing the Kaiser's abdication, and early the next morning the neurotic old gentleman was hustled across the frontier into Holland. In the meantime, the government of the nation had passed into the hands of a provisional council headed by Friedrich Ebert, leader of the socialists in the Reichstag. Ebert and his colleagues immediately took steps to conclude negotiations for an armistice. The terms as now laid down by the Allies provided for acceptance of the Fourteen Points with three amendments. First, the item on freedom of the seas was to be stricken out (in accordance with the request of the British). Second, restoration of invaded areas was to be interpreted in such a way as to include *reparations*. Third, the demand for autonomy for the subject peoples of Austria-Hungary was to be changed into a demand for *independence*. In addition, troops of the Entente nations were to occupy cities in the Rhine valley; the blockade was to be continued in force; and Germany was to hand over 5000 locomotives, 150,000 railway cars, and 5000 motor trucks, all in good condition. Despite the harshness of these terms, there was nothing that the Germans could do but accept. At five o'clock in the morning of November 11, two delegates of the defeated nation met with Marshal Foch in the dark Compiègne forest and signed the papers officially ending the war. Six hours later the order, "cease fire," was given to the troops. That night thousands of people danced through the streets of London, Paris, and Rome in the same delirium of excitement with which they had greeted the declarations of war.

Victory had been won at last, but what a grim tragedy it turned out to be. Of a total of over 42,000,000 men mobilized by the Entente allies, at least 7,000,000 had been slaughtered. Five million of these had been killed in action or had died of wounds; the remainder had been reported "missing" after the battles were over. More than 3,000,000 others had been totally disabled, many with such ghastly wounds that they might have been better off dead. Thus it will be seen that almost one out of every four of the soldiers enlisted in the Allied armies suffered a major casualty. This would have been a terrific price even if all the results which were supposed to flow from an Entente victory had really been achieved. But few indeed were the permanent gains. The war which was to "end all wars" merely sowed the dragon's teeth of a new and more terrible conflict in the future. The autocracy of the Kaiser was indeed destroyed, but the ground was prepared for new despotisms which made the empire of William II look like a haven of liberty. In addition, World War I did nothing to abate either militarism or nationalism. Twenty years after the fighting had ended, there were nearly twice as many men under arms as in 1913; and national rivalries and racial hatreds were more deeply ingrained than ever. These failures were not due

The price of victory

829

to the fact that the Allies won the war, but rather, as we shall see, to the fact that they lost the peace.

4. The Victors' Peace

Character of the peace with Germany and her allies

The so-called peace concluded at the various conferences in 1919 and 1920 was almost without precedent in the annals of modern nations. For it was a dictated peace rather than a negotiated one. Instead of being an agreement between victors and vanquished at a council table, it was designed to be a "sentence from a court." No Germans or Austrians were admitted to the conferences until after

The Big Four in Paris, 1919. From left to right: Prime Minister Lloyd George, Premier Orlando, Premier Clemenceau, and President Wilson.

the documents were completed and were ready for the chastened culprits to affix their signatures. The reason for this almost unprecedented action is to be found in the flood of passion unloosed during the war. The masses had been made to feel that all the righteousness was on one side, and that therefore their enemies should be dealt with as criminals. This feeling was not confined to the Entente countries. Had the Central Powers won a decisive victory, it is scarcely probable that they would have allowed any greater opportunity for a negotiated settlement.

The Paris Conference

The conference convoked in Paris [14] to draft a peace with Germany was technically in session from January until June of 1919. But only six plenary meetings were ever held. Most of the delegates might just as well have stayed at home. All of the important business of the conference was transacted by small committees. At first there was the Council of Ten, made up of the President and Secretary of State of the United States, and the premiers and foreign ministers of Great Britain, France, Italy, and Japan. By the middle of March

[14] The conference did most of its work in Paris. The treaty of peace with Germany, however, takes its name from Versailles, the suburb of Paris in which it was signed.

this body had been found too unwieldy and was reduced to the Council of Four, consisting of the American President and the English, Italian, and French premiers. A month later the Council of Four became the Council of Three when Premier Orlando withdrew from the conference in a huff because Wilson refused to give Italy all she demanded.

The final character of the Treaty of Versailles was determined almost entirely by the so-called Big Three—Wilson, Lloyd George, and Clemenceau. These men were about as different in personality as any three rulers who could ever have been brought together for a common purpose. Wilson was an inflexible idealist, accustomed to dictating to subordinates, and convinced that the hosts of righteousness were on his side. When confronted with unpleasant realities, such as the secret treaties among the Entente governments for division of the spoils, he had a habit of dismissing them as unimportant and eventually forgetting that he had ever heard of them. Though he knew little of the devious trickeries of European diplomacy, his unbending temperament made it difficult for him to take advice or to adjust his views to those of his colleagues. David Lloyd George was a canny little Welsh attorney who had succeeded Asquith as Prime Minister of Britain in 1916. His cleverness and his Celtic humor enabled him to succeed, on occasions, where Wilson failed; but he was above all a politician—shifty, ignorant of European conditions, and careless even of his most critical mistakes. Clemenceau said of him: "I suppose that man can read, but I doubt that he ever does."

The Big Three: Wilson and Lloyd George

The third member of the great triumvirate was the aged and cynical French Premier, Georges Clemenceau. Born when the nineteenth century was still young, Clemenceau had been a journalist in the United States just after the Civil War. Later he had won his nickname of "the Tiger" as a relentless foe of clericals and monarchists. He had fought for the French republic during the stormy days of the Boulangist episode, the Dreyfus affair, and the struggle for separation of church and state. Twice in his lifetime he had seen France invaded and her existence gravely imperiled. Now the tables were turned, and the French, he believed, should take full advantage of their opportunity. Only by keeping a strict control over a prostrate Germany could the security of France be preserved.

Clemenceau

From the beginning two rather embarrassing problems confronted the chief architects of the Versailles Treaty. One was what to do about the Fourteen Points. There could be no doubt that they had been the basis of the German surrender on November 11. It was beyond question also that Wilson had represented them as the Entente program for a permanent peace. Consequently there was every reason for the peoples of the world to expect that the Fourteen Points would be the model for the Versailles settlement—subject only to the three amendments made before the armistice was signed. But what was the result? Not a soul among the highest dig-

Emasculating the Fourteen Points

831

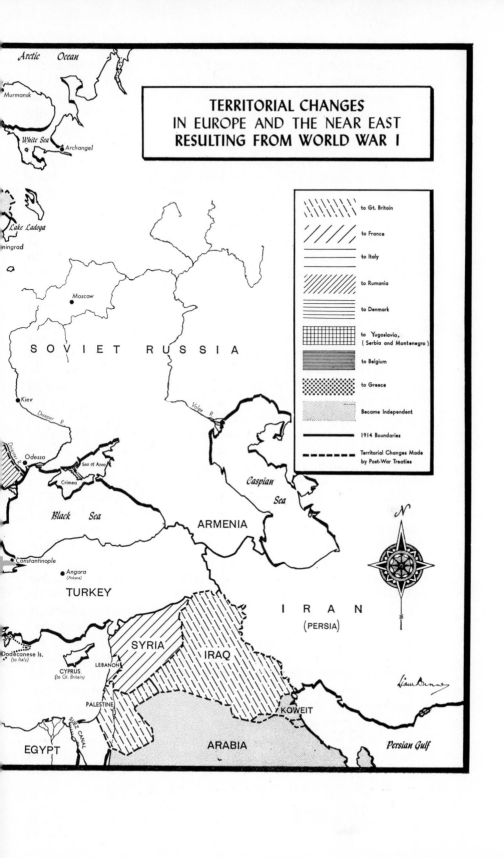

TERRITORIAL CHANGES
IN EUROPE AND THE NEAR EAST
RESULTING FROM WORLD WAR I

to Gt. Britain

to France

to Italy

to Rumania

to Denmark

to Yugoslavia,
(Serbia and Montenegro)

to Belgium

to Greece

Became Independent

1914 Boundaries

Territorial Changes Made
by Post-War Treaties

Arctic Ocean

Murmansk

White Sea

Archangel

Lake Ladoga

ningrad

Moscow

S O V I E T   R U S S I A

Kiev

Dnieper R.

Dniester R.

Odessa

Sea of Azov

Crimea

Volga R.

Caspian Sea

Black Sea

ARMENIA

Constantinople

Angora
(Ankara)

TURKEY

N

I R A N
(PERSIA)

Dodecanese Is.
(to Italy)

CYPRUS
(to Gt. Britain)

LEBANON

SYRIA

IRAQ

PALESTINE

KOWEIT

SUEZ CANAL

EGYPT

ARABIA

Persian Gulf

nitaries at the conference, with the exception of Wilson himself, gave more than lip service to the Fourteen Points. Clemenceau is reported to have sneered: "Even God was satisfied with Ten Commandments, but Wilson must have Fourteen." In the end, the American President was able to salvage, in unmodified form, only four of the parts of his famous program: point seven, requiring the restoration of Belgium; point eight, demanding the return of Alsace and Lorraine to France; point ten, providing for autonomy for the peoples of Austria-Hungary; and the final provision calling for a League of Nations. The others were ignored or modified to such an extent as to change their original meaning. To cite two examples: point four, demanding the reduction of armaments, was applied only to the defeated nations; point eleven, providing for the restoration of Rumania, Serbia, and Montenegro, was modified in such a way as to allow Rumania to double her territory and Serbia to swallow Montenegro!

The second embarrassing question was what disposition should be made of the secret treaties. While the war was being fought, *The secret* sundry clandestine bargains had been negotiated by the Entente *treaties* governments for apportioning the spoils. In March, 1915, it had been agreed that France should recover Alsace-Lorraine and control the left bank of the Rhine, Great Britain and France should divide the colonies of Germany in Africa, while Russia should appropriate German and Austrian Poland and Constantinople. In April of the same year Italy was bribed to enter the war on the side of the Allies by promises of Austrian and Turkish territory, including Trieste, the south Tyrol, and a portion of Dalmatia. Still later there were agreements for giving Armenia to Russia and most of the rest of the Ottoman Empire to Great Britain and France, to say nothing of awarding the German concessions in China and the German islands north of the Equator to Japan. How long these treaties would have remained secret had it not been for the revolution in Russia is impossible to say. Upon coming to power in November, 1917, the Bolsheviks determined to discredit the war in every way possible. Accordingly, they threw open the Tsar's archives, revealing some very interesting documents. Soon afterward the secret treaties were published in the *Manchester Guardian* and in the *New York Evening Post*. It was therefore impossible for Entente statesmen at the Versailles Conference to deny that such treaties existed. Wilson made efforts for a time to have them repudiated, and he did go so far as to refuse to allow Italy to take the Adriatic port of Fiume; but on most of the other agreements he finally gave in. As a result, the distribution of territories taken from the defeated nations followed with remarkable accuracy the lines marked out in the secret treaties. Wilson even permitted Japan to take over the German concessions in China, despite the fact that the Chinese were enlisted **834** in the war on the side of the Allies.

By the end of April, 1919, the terms of the Versailles Treaty were
ready for submission to the enemy, and Germany was ordered to
send delegates to receive them. On April 29 a delegation, headed by
Count von Brockdorff-Rantzau, Foreign Minister of the provisional
republic, arrived in Versailles and was immediately incarcerated in a
hotel and dealt with virtually as prisoners. A week later the members of the delegation were commanded to appear before the Allied
representatives to receive the sentence of their nation. When Brockdorff-Rantzau protested that the terms were too harsh, he was informed by Clemenceau that Germany would have exactly three
weeks in which to make up her mind whether to sign or not to sign.
Eventually the time had to be extended, for the heads of the German government resigned their positions rather than accept the
treaty. Their attitude was summed up by Chancellor Philip Scheide-
mann in the pointed statement: "What hand would not wither that
sought to lay itself and us in those chains?" The Big Three now made
a few minor adjustments, mainly at the instance of Lloyd George,
and Germany was notified that seven o'clock on the evening of
June 23 would bring either acceptance or invasion. Shortly after five
a new government of the provisional republic announced that it
would yield to "overwhelming force" and accede to the victors'
terms. On June 28, the fifth anniversary of the murder of the Austrian Archduke, representatives of the German and Allied governments assembled in the Hall of Mirrors at Versailles and affixed their
signatures to the treaty.

The provisions of the Treaty of Versailles can be outlined briefly.
Germany was required to surrender Alsace and Lorraine to France,

Germany Receives Her Sentence.
Premier Clemenceau, in the Hall of
Mirrors at Versailles, inviting the
Germans to affix their signatures to
the Versailles Treaty.

*The main pro-
visions of the
Treaty of Ver-
sailles*

Eupen and Malmedy to Belgium, northern Schleswig to Denmark, and most of Posen and West Prussia to Poland. The coal mines of the Saar Basin were to be ceded to France, to be exploited by her for fifteen years. At the end of this time the German government would have the privilege of buying them back. The Saar territory itself was to be administered by the League of Nations until 1935 when a plebiscite would be held to determine whether it should remain under the League, return to Germany, or be awarded to France. As a result of these territorial provisions Germany was stripped of one-sixth of her arable land, two-fifths of her coal, two-thirds of her iron, and seven-tenths of her zinc. Her province of East Prussia was cut off from the rest of her territory, and her port of Danzig, almost wholly German, was subjected to the political control of the League of Nations and to the economic domination of Poland. In addition, she was forced to surrender to England, France, and Belgium practically all of her merchant ships of any value, one-eighth of her livestock, and enormous quantities of coal, building materials, and machinery. Germany was, of course, disarmed. She gave up all of her submarines and her navy of surface vessels, with the exception of six small battleships, six light cruisers, six destroyers, and twelve torpedo boats. She was forbidden to have any airplanes, either military or naval, and her army was limited to 100,000 officers and men, to be recruited by voluntary enlistment. To make sure that she would not launch any new attack upon France or Belgium, she was forbidden to keep soldiers or maintain fortifications in the Rhine valley. Lastly, Germany and her allies were held responsible for all the loss and damage suffered by the Entente governments and their citizens, "as a consequence of the war imposed upon them by the aggression of Germany and her allies." This was the so-called war-guilt provision of the treaty (Article 231), but it was also the basis for German reparations.

The problem of how much Germany should pay in reparations was handled with designing shrewdness. The total of loss and damage suffered by the Entente governments and their citizens as a direct result of the war was probably not over $10,000,000,000. But no such amount would have satisfied the Allies. The French in particular were bent upon crippling Germany so completely that she would never be able to regain her economic and military power. Accordingly, it was decided to include under "losses and damages" such items as allowances paid to the families of soldiers, the Belgian war loans, and the cost of maintaining the Allied armies of occupation in the Rhine valley. The problem of fixing the total that Germany should pay was left to a Reparations Commission appointed by the Allied governments. In 1921 the Commission brought in its report, setting the amount at the colossal sum of $33,000,000,000, three times the figure recommended by economic experts at the Versailles Conference. Of course, there was no such amount of

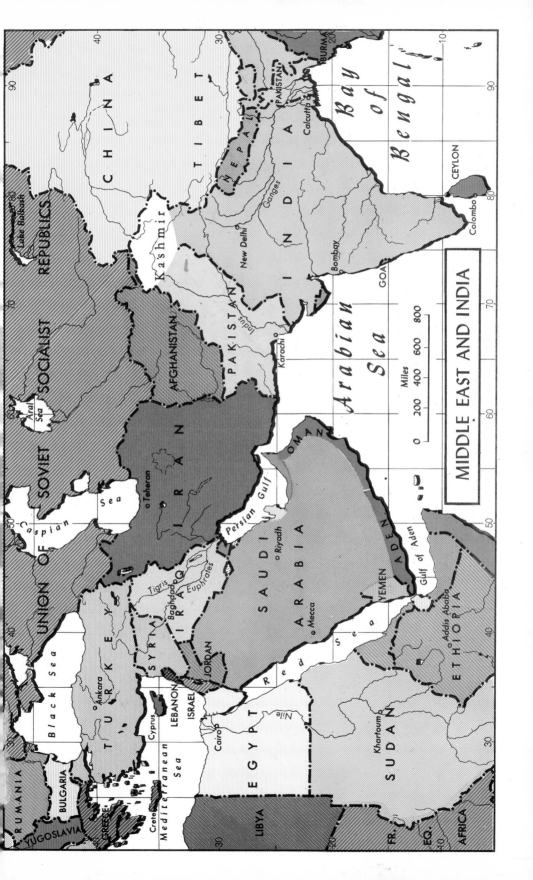

MIDDLE EAST AND INDIA

I and the Village, Marc Chagall (1889–). The subject refers to the artist's childhood and youth in Vitebsk, Russia. The profile on the right is probably that of the artist himself. (Mus. Mod. Art)

The Table, Georges Braque (1881–
An example of later cubism showing t
predominance of curvilinear form and li
instead of geometric structure. (Mus. Mc
Art)

Around the Fish, Paul Klee (1879–1940). Klee is recognized as the most subt
humorist of XX-cent. art. The central motif of a fish on a platter suggests
banquet, but many of the surrounding objects appear to be products of fantas
(Mus. Mod. Art)

money in all of Germany, but the victors expected that over a
period of years most of it could actually be collected.

For the most part, the Treaty of Versailles applied only to Germany. Separate pacts were drawn up to settle accounts with Germany's allies—Austria, Hungary, Bulgaria, and Turkey. The final
form of these minor treaties was determined primarily by a Council
of Five, composed of Clemenceau as chairman and one delegate
each from the United States, Great Britain, France, and Italy. The
settlement with Austria, completed in September, 1919, is known as
the Treaty of St. Germain. Austria was required to recognize the
independence of Hungary, Czechoslovakia, Yugoslavia, and Poland
and to cede to them large portions of her territory. In addition, she
was compelled to surrender Trieste, the south Tyrol, and the Istrian
peninsula to Italy. Altogether the Austrian portion of the Dual
Monarchy was deprived of three-fourths of its area and three-
fourths of its people. In several of the territories surrendered the
inhabitants were largely German-speaking—for example, the Tyrol,
and the region of the Sudeten Mountains awarded to Czechoslovakia.
The Austrian nation itself was reduced to a small, land-locked state,
with nearly one-third of its population concentrated in the city of
Vienna. The only hope of prosperity for the country lay in a union
with Germany; but this was strictly prohibited by the treaty. The
provisions of the peace of St. Germain might well have been
summed up in a single sentence: "Austria renounces her existence."

The second of the minor treaties was that of Neuilly with Bulgaria, which was signed in November, 1919. Doubtless on the assumption that she had had little to do with causing the war, Bulgaria was treated the most leniently of any of the Central Powers.
Nevertheless, she was forced to give up nearly all of the territory
she had gained since the First Balkan War. The Dobrudja went back
to Rumania, western Macedonia to the new kingdom of Yugoslavia, and western Thrace to Greece. All of these regions were inhabited by large Bulgarian minorities. Since Hungary was now an
independent state, it was necessary that a separate treaty be imposed
upon her. This was the Treaty of the Trianon Palace, signed in
June, 1920. It required that Slovakia should be ceded to the republic
of Czechoslovakia, Transylvania to Rumania, and Croatia-Slavonia to
Yugoslavia. In few cases was the principle of self-determination of
peoples more flagrantly violated. Numerous sections of Transylvania had a population that was more than half Hungarian. Included
in the region of Slovakia were not only Slovaks but almost a million
Magyars and about 500,000 Ruthenians. As a consequence, a fanatical irredentist movement flourished in Hungary after the war, directed toward the recovery of these lost provinces. It may be pertinent to add that the Treaty of the Trianon Palace slashed the area
of Hungary from 125,000 square miles to 35,000, and her population
from 22,000,000 to 8,000,000.

*The Treaties of
Sèvres and
Lausanne with
Turkey*

The settlement with Turkey was a product of unusual circumstances. The secret treaties had contemplated the transfer of Constantinople and Armenia to Russia and the division of most of the remainder of Turkey between England and France. But Russia's withdrawal from the war after the Bolshevik revolution, together with insistence by Italy and Greece upon fulfillment of promises made to them, necessitated considerable revision of the original scheme. Finally, in August, 1920, a treaty was signed at Sèvres, near Paris, and submitted to the government of the Sultan. It provided that Armenia should be organized as a Christian republic, that most of Turkey in Europe should be given to Greece, that Palestine and Mesopotamia should become British mandates, that Syria should become a mandate of France, and that southern Anatolia should be set apart as a sphere of influence for Italy. About all that would be left of the Ottoman Empire would be the city of Constantinople and the northern and central portions of Asia Minor. The decrepit government of the Sultan, overawed by Allied military forces, agreed to accept this treaty. But a revolutionary government of Turkish nationalists, which had been organized at Ankara under the leadership of Mustapha Kemal, determined to prevent the settlement of Sèvres from being put into effect. The forces of Kemal obliterated the republic of Armenia, frightened the Italians into withdrawing from Anatolia, and conquered most of the territory in Europe which had been given to Greece. At last, in November, 1922, they occupied Constantinople, deposed the Sultan, and proclaimed Turkey a republic. The Allies now consented to a revision of the peace. A new treaty was concluded at Lausanne in Switzerland in 1923, which permitted the Turks to retain practically all of the territory they had conquered. Though much reduced in size as compared with the old Ottoman Empire, the Turkish republic still had an area of about 300,000 square miles and a population of 13,000,000.

*The League of
Nations*

Incorporated in each of the five treaties which liquidated the war with the Central Powers was the Covenant of the League of Nations. The establishment of a League in which the states of the world, both great and small, would co-operate for the preservation of peace had long been the cherished dream of President Wilson. Indeed, that had been one of his chief reasons for taking the United States into the war. He believed that the defeat of Germany would mean the deathblow of militarism, and that the road would thenceforth be clear for setting up the control of international relations by a *community of power* instead of by the cumbersome and ineffective balance of power. But in order to get the League accepted at all, he felt himself compelled to make numerous compromises. He permitted his original idea of providing for a reduction of armaments "to the lowest point consistent with domestic safety" to be changed into the altogether different phrasing of "consistent with *national* safety." To induce the Japanese to accept the League he allowed them to keep the former German concessions in China. To please the French he sanctioned the exclusion of both Germany and Rus- sia from his proposed federation, despite his long insistence that it should be a combination of all the nations. These handicaps were serious enough. But the League received an even more deadly blow when it was repudiated by the very nation whose President had fathered it.

Established under such unfavorable auspices, the League was never a brilliant success in achieving the aims of its founder. In only a few cases did it succeed in allaying the specter of war, and in each *Successes and* of these the parties to the dispute were small nations. It settled a *failures of the* quarrel between Finland and Sweden in 1920 over the Åland Islands. *League* In 1925 it forestalled a Greek attack on Bulgaria by threat of an economic boycott. In 1932 it prevented a war between Colombia and Peru over the province of Leticia. But in every dispute involving one or more major powers, the League failed. It did nothing about the seizure of Vilna by Poland in 1920, because Lithuania, the victimized nation, was friendless, while Poland had the powerful backing of France. When, in 1923, war threatened between Italy and Greece, the Italians refused to submit to the intervention of the League, and the dispute had to be settled by direct mediation of Great Britain and France. Thereafter, in every great crisis the League was either defied or ignored. Its authority was flouted by Japan in seizing Manchuria in 1931 and by Italy in conquering Ethiopia in 1936. By September, 1938, when the Czechoslovakian crisis arose, the prestige of the League had sunk so low that scarcely anyone thought of appealing to it. On the other hand, the point must be made that Wilson's great project justified its existence in other, less spectacular, ways. It checked the international opium traffic and aided poor and backward countries in controlling the spread of disease. Its agencies collected invaluable statistics on labor and business conditions throughout the world. It conducted plebiscites in disputed areas, supervised the administration of internationalized cities, helped in finding homes for racial and political refugees, and made a notable beginning in codifying international law. Such achievements must certainly be regarded as having provided a substantial groundwork for future co-operation among nations.

Selected Readings—World War I

Albertini, Luigi, *Origins of the War of 1914*, New York, 1952

Bakeless, John, *The Economic Causes of Modern Wars*, New York, 1921

Buehrig, E. H., *Woodrow Wilson and the Balance of Power*, Bloomington, Ind., 1955

Dickinson, G. L., *The International Anarchy*, New York, 1926

Earle, E. M., *Turkey, the Great Powers and the Bagdad Railway*, New York, 1924

Ewart, J. S., *The Roots and Causes of the Wars, 1914–1918*, New York, 1925, 2 vols.

Fay, S. B., *The Origins of the World War*, New York, 1928, 2 vols.

Feis, Herbert, *Europe: The World's Banker, 1870–1914*, New Haven, 1930

Gooch, G. P., *Before the War*, 1936

Hoffman, R. J. S., *Great Britain and the German Trade Rivalry*, Philadelphia, 1933

Lasswell, H. D., *Propaganda Technique in the World War*, New York, 1927

Liddell Hart, B. H., *The Real War, 1914–1918*, Boston, 1930

Lutz, Hermann, *Lord Grey and the World War*, New York, 1928

Millis, Walter, *The Road to War; America 1914–1917*, New York, 1935

Ponsonby, A., *Falsehood in War Time*, New York, 1928

Read, J. M., *Atrocity Propaganda, 1914–1919*, New Haven, 1941

Schmitt, B. E., *The Coming of the War*, New York, 1930, 2 vols.

Stieve, Friedrich, *Izvolsky and the World War*, New York, 1926

Tansill, C. C., *America Goes to War*, Boston, 1938

Willis, I. C., *England's Holy War*, New York, 1928

—THE PEACE OF 1919–1920

Bailey, T. A., *Woodrow Wilson and the Lost Peace*, New York, 1944

Baker, Ray Stannard, *Woodrow Wilson and the World Settlement*, New York, 1922

Birdsall, Paul, *Versailles Twenty Years After*, New York, 1941

Dillon, E. J., *The Inside Story of the Peace Conference*, New York, 1920

Keynes, John Maynard, *The Economic Consequences of the Peace*, New York, 1920

Nicolson, Harold, *Peacemaking, 1919*, New York, 1946

SOURCE MATERIALS

Baker, Ray Stannard, and W. E. Dodd, eds., *The Public Papers of Woodrow Wilson*, 6 vols.

Baker, Ray Stannard, ed., *The Life and Letters of Woodrow Wilson*, 2 vols.

Bethmann-Hollweg, T. von, *Reflections on the World War*

Carnegie Endowment for International Peace, *The Treaties of Peace, 1919–23*, 2 vols.

Gooch and Temperley, eds., *British Documents on the Origins of the War, 1898–1914*

Hendrick, B. J., ed., *The Life and Letters of Walter Hines Page*, 2 vols.

Lichnowsky, Prince, *Heading for the Abyss*

Seymour, Charles, ed., *The Intimate Papers of Colonel House*, 4 vols.

Viscount Grey of Fallodon, *Twenty-five Years*, 2 vols.

Dictatorship and Democracy between Two Wars

Not the least of the tragic consequences of World War I was the degradation of the liberal and democratic ideals. For a time many people were deceived into thinking that the reverse would be true. Ardent defenders of the Entente cause were proclaiming the struggle against Germany to be a holy crusade on behalf of the rights of mankind and for the overthrow of militarism and "irresponsible government." The war itself did actually appear to have accomplished some of these purposes. Not only was militarism destroyed in the defeated countries, but the list of republics in Europe was greatly enlarged by the addition of Germany, Austria, Poland, Finland, Turkey, and Czechoslovakia. Even absolutist Russia appeared for a time to have adopted a liberal government. It was not long, however, until most of these visions of democratic progress were revealed as illusions. The legacy of hysteria, resentment, and hate bequeathed by the war was the worst atmosphere imaginable for the survival of respect for the individual or of confidence in popular rule. Broken by the harshness of the peace, the vanquished nations despaired of the value of liberty and succumbed to the glittering appeal of strong government as a way of escape from what they considered enslavement. But democracy and freedom were none too secure even in the lands of the victors. The frightful years of conflict so completely disrupted the economic order that the governments of Great Britain and France were shaken to their very foundations. Moreover, the chaos and hardships resulting from the war quickly encompassed the downfall of the liberal regime in Russia and prepared the way for the triumph of Fascism in Italy and Nazism in Germany. For more than twenty years after the armistice, the fate of democracy hung in a more delicate balance than in almost any other period since the middle of the nineteenth century.

The effects of the war upon democracy and liberalism

841

1. The Fascist Revolution in Italy

The first of the nations of western Europe to repudiate liberal and democratic ideals was Italy. This may seem strange in view of the fact that the Italians fought in the war on the winning side. But the point must be kept in mind that Italy had been the victim of a frustrated nationalism for many years. Time after time her aspirations for power and for empire had been rudely shattered. In 1881 her hope of acquiring Tunisia had been brought suddenly to an end by the French occupation of that country. Her effort to conquer Abyssinia in the 1890's had been terminated by a crushing defeat at the hands of uncivilized natives in the Battle of Adowa. The effect of these reverses was to produce a sense of humiliation and shame, especially in the minds of the younger generation, and to foster an attitude of contempt for the existing political regime. Blame for Italy's failures was placed not so much upon foreign nations as upon her own governing class. Members of this class were held up to the scorn of the people as degenerate old men—cynical, vacillating, defeatist, and corrupt. Long before World War I there was talk of revolution, of the need for a drastic housecleaning which would deliver the country from its incompetent rulers.

This species of morbid nationalism gained wide popularity. It received much support from a group of intellectuals who had adopted and perverted the philosophy of Hegel. Among the leaders of this group were Giovanni Gentile and Giuseppe Prezzolini, who later gained recognition as philosophers of Fascism. Taking as their fundamental proposition the Hegelian idea that the state is the supreme manifestation of God on earth, they demanded that Italians should submerge their individual and class interests in a united endeavor to revive the greatness of their nation. Italy, they avowed, had a glorious mission to give light to the civilized world as she had done under the Roman Empire and in the age of the great Renaissance. Their slogan was "Nothing for the individual, all for Italy." An even more frenzied and irrational gospel was propagated by the futurists, whose vociferous leader was F. T. Marinetti. Futurism originated as a literary and artistic movement, but it soon took on political significance. Its wild-eyed apostles condemned every form of enslavement to the past. They denounced liberalism, democracy, pacifism, quietism, and all other ideals which they alleged were the special favorites of Italy's elder statesmen. In addition, they glorified war as "the world's only hygiene," the necessary instrument for rejuvenating the nation and for giving "a thousand flavors to life and a little genius to imbeciles." [1]

But the establishment of a Fascist dictatorship in Italy would never have been possible without the demoralizing and humiliating

[1] Quoted by H. W. Schneider, *Making the Fascist State*, p. 8.

effects of World War I. The chief business of the Italian armies had been to keep the Austrians occupied on the Southern Front while the British, French, and Americans hammered Germany into submission along the battle lines in Flanders. To accomplish her purpose Italy had to mobilize more than 5,500,000 men, and of these nearly 700,000 were killed. The direct financial cost of her participation in the struggle was over $15,000,000,000. These sacrifices, of course, were no greater than those made by the British and the French; but Italy was a poor country. Moreover, in the division of the spoils after the fighting was over, the Italians got less than they expected. Not only were they deprived of Fiume by Wilson's insistence that Yugoslavia should have a modern port on the Adriatic, but they were not permitted to share in the distribution of Germany's colonies in Africa. While Italy did receive most of the Austrian territories promised her in the secret treaties, she maintained that this was an inadequate reward for her sacrifices and for her valuable contribution to an Entente victory. At first the nationalists vented their spleen for the "humiliation of Versailles" upon President Wilson, but after a short time they returned to their old habit of castigating Italy's rulers. They alleged that such men as Premier Orlando had been so cravenly weak and inept that they had allowed their own country to be cheated. This revival of contempt for the old ruling generation, the members of which were denounced as "filthy parasites on the better blood of the nation," had much to do with the growth of revolutionary sentiment.

The war contributed to the revolution in a multitude of other ways. It resulted in inflation of the currency, with consequent high prices, speculation, and profiteering. Normally wages would have risen also, but the labor market was glutted on account of the return to civilian life of millions of soldiers. Furthermore, business was demoralized, owing to the extensive and frequent strikes and to the closing of foreign markets. Perhaps the most serious consequence of the war, to the upper and middle classes at least, was the growth of economic radicalism. As hardship and chaos increased, the Socialists embraced a philosophy akin to Bolshevism. In 1918 they voted as a party to join the Moscow International. In the elections of November, 1919, they won about a third of the seats in the Chamber of Deputies. During the following winter socialist workers took over about a hundred factories and attempted to run them for the benefit of the proletariat. Radicalism also spread through the rural areas, where the so-called Red Leagues were organized to break up large estates and to force landlords to reduce their rents. But by 1921 the danger that Italy would go Bolshevik was practically over. Revolutionary radicalism subsided after the return of a socialist delegation from a study of conditions in Russia and after the failure of workers' attempts to operate the factories. Nevertheless, the

(3) *the demoralizing and humiliating effects of the war*

(4) *inflation, radicalism, and economic chaos*

owning classes had been badly frightened and were therefore ready to support the growth of Fascism in the hope that it might save at least part of their property from confiscation.

The immediate cause of the Fascist revolution was the breakdown of parliamentary government. The paralysis of business and the condition of near-anarchy prevailing in many parts of the country made the collection of adequate revenue impossible. As a consequence, budgetary deficits mounted higher and higher. To this difficulty was added a parliamentary deadlock. In the elections of 1921 four different parties gained strong representation in the Chamber of Deputies; but no one of them had a majority. The two largest, the Socialist party and the Popular (Catholic) party, were constantly at swords' points; neither would support a cabinet headed by a member of the other. As a result, it was almost impossible for the government to function. Seldom could a cabinet remain in office long enough to get anything done. The wheels of the legislative machinery practically stopped. As time went on, disgust with the endless squabbling of parties rapidly increased. By the fall of 1922 Parliament had scarcely a friend in the entire country. The newspapers were denouncing not only the deadlock of parties but the whole system of government by majorities. This was nothing new for Italy, for there had been many in prewar years who regarded the parliamentary regime as an alien importation. Nonetheless, the propagation of the idea on an extensive scale did much to encourage the militant proponents of one-man rule.

How much the Fascist movement depended for its success upon the leadership of Mussolini is impossible to say. Undoubtedly his fiery eloquence, his Napoleonic poses, and his Machiavellian ruthlessness proved potent attractions to weaklings in mind and body who had been nurtured on romantic worship of Julius Caesar and Garibaldi. Benito Mussolini was born in 1883, the son of a socialist blacksmith. His mother was a schoolteacher, and in deference to her wishes he entered a normal school and eventually became a teacher. But he was restless and dissatisfied and soon left Italy for further study in Switzerland. Here he gave part of his time to his books and the rest of it to begging his bread and writing articles for socialist newspapers. He was finally expelled from the country for fomenting strikes in factories. Upon returning to Italy he took up journalism as a definite career and eventually became editor of *Avanti*, the leading socialist daily. His ideas at this time were a mixture of contradictory forms of radicalism. He professed to be a Marxian socialist, but he mingled his socialism with doctrines taken from the syndicalists. In fact, the great syndicalist leader Sorel once referred to him as his most promising disciple. Mussolini was influenced also by chauvinism and for a time was a vocal champion of a struggle against Austria for the recovery of the "unredeemed" provinces. On the other hand, he opposed the war against Turkey

Mussolini Addressing a Crowd of His Followers from the Balcony of the
Palazzo Venezia in Rome.

for the conquest of Tripoli and was thrown into jail for attempting
to prevent the departure of troops.

Probably it is safe to say that Mussolini was never a radical by
sincere and reasoned conviction but was simply following the inclinations of a rebellious nature. No man with a definite philosophy *Mussolini's*
could have reversed himself so often. He not only condemned the *contradictory*
imperialism which he later practiced so zealously, but at one time *ideas*
or another before the war he defamed the church, vilified the king,
and called the Italian flag "a rag to be planted on a dung hill." [2]
When World War I broke out in August, 1914, Mussolini insisted
that Italy should remain neutral. But he had scarcely adopted this
position when he began urging participation on the Entente side.
As early as October, 1914, he had gone over bag and baggage to
the interventionist camp. Deprived of his position as editor of
Avanti, he founded a new paper, *Il Popolo d'Italia*, and dedicated
its columns to whipping up enthusiasm for war. The decision of the
government the following spring to go in on the side of the Entente
allies he regarded as a personal victory. He entered the army as a
private in September, 1915, and eventually rose to be a corporal. In
February, 1917, he was wounded by the explosion of a trench
mortar and was allowed to return to his position as editor of *Il
Popolo* in the hope that he might stimulate the flagging enthusiasm
of the Italian people. From then on he worked zealously for a Fascist
revolution.

The word Fascism has a dual origin. It derives in part from the
Latin *fasces*, the ax surrounded by a bundle of rods representing
the authority of the Roman state; it comes also from the Italian

[2] For these and other contradictions between his earlier and later teachings, see
Gaudens Megaro, *Mussolini in the Making.*

The early evo-
lution of Fas-
cism

fascio, meaning group or band. *Fasci* were organized as early as October, 1914, as units of agitation to swing Italy over to the Entente cause. Their membership was made up of young idealists, futurists, fanatical nationalists, bored white-collar workers, and misfits of every description. Mussolini became the leader of the Milan *fascio*. After Italy entered the war, the Fascist bands devoted their attention to combating defeatism. Then came the period of *squadrism*, from 1919 to 1921. Squadrist activities included a campaign of terrorization against all who were considered enemies of the people. The methods consisted of such brutal tactics as clubbing the victim into unconsciousness, pulling his teeth, or administering large doses of castor oil. Kidnaping and murder were also far from unknown. Most of the attacks were perpetrated against radicals, but in some cases the victims were profiteers or landlords who refused to reduce their rents. In Florence a few stubborn shopkeepers were beaten and their stores padlocked and labeled with signs, "Closed for continued robbery."[3] Mussolini himself declared on one occasion that "A few food-hogs hanging from the lamp posts would be a good example." But these attempts to appeal to the poorer classes did not awaken a very eager response from the proletariat, for in most areas the sons of wealthy industrialists and of landed proprietors were far too conspicuous as Mussolini's disciples.

The original platform of the Fascist movement was prepared by Mussolini in 1919. It was a surprisingly radical document, which demanded, among other things, universal suffrage; abolition of the Senate; the establishment by law of an eight-hour day; a heavy capital levy; a heavy tax on inheritances; confiscation of 85 per cent of war profits; acceptance of the League of Nations; "opposition to all imperialisms"; and annexation of Fiume and Dalmatia. This platform was accepted more or less officially until May, 1920, when it was supplanted by another of a much more conservative character. Indeed, the new program omitted all reference to economic reform and consisted of nothing but condemnation of "politicians' so-socialism" and some vague assertions about "revindicating" the principles for which the war had been fought. On neither of these platforms did the Fascists achieve much political success. Even after the elections of 1921 they had only thirty-five representatives in the Chamber of Deputies.

But the Fascists made up for their lack of numbers by disciplined aggressiveness and strong determination. And when the old regime became so decrepit that it practically abdicated its functions, they prepared to take over the government. In September, 1922, Mussolini began to talk openly of revolution and raised the cry, "On to Rome." In October he presented an ultimatum to the government, demanding new elections, a vigorous foreign policy, and five positions in the cabinet for himself and his followers. When the

[3] Schneider, *Making the Fascist State*, p. 51.

Premier and Parliament ignored these demands, the march on Rome began. On October 28 an army of about 50,000 Fascist militia oc- cupied the capital. The Premier resigned, and the following day Victor Emmanuel III invited Mussolini to form a cabinet. Thus without firing a shot the blackshirted legions had gained control of the Italian government. The explanation is to be found, not in the strength of Fascism, but in the chaos created by the war and in the lack of any firm devotion by the Italian people to constitutional government.

This, however, was but the first stage of the Fascist revolution; for Fascism involved not merely personal control of the political machinery, but sweeping changes extending to the very foundations *The Fascist* of the political and economic structure. In July, 1923, Mussolini *revolution* forced through Parliament a new electoral law, providing that the party which received the most votes in a national election should automatically be entitled to two-thirds of the seats in the Chamber of Deputies. In the first election held under this law the Fascists received, not simply more votes than any other party, but two-thirds of the ballots cast. When the new Parliament convened in May, 1924, the Socialist leader Matteotti accused the Fascist politicians of dishonesty and violence in the recent election. On June 10 he was kidnaped and murdered by Blackshirt gangsters upon orders emanating from members of the cabinet. The crime produced a violent reaction, accompanied by vigorous demands that the Fascists relinquish their power. But at length the storm subsided, and Mussolini was able to proceed with radical alterations of the political system. In 1925 he deprived all anti-Fascist lawyers of their licenses to practice and abolished local self-government in the cities and towns. The following year he capped the climax by declaring all political parties illegal except the one of which he was the head, and by formally abolishing the cabinet system. Henceforth the Premier was to be responsible solely to the king, while the duties of Parliament were to be restricted to ratifying decrees.

The political and economic system in Fascist Italy was officially known as the corporate state. This meant, first of all, that the government rested upon an economic basis. The people were repre- *The corporate* sented in the government, not as citizens inhabiting definite districts, *state* but in their capacity of producers. But the corporate state also included the idea that individual and class interests must be subordinated to the interests of the state. There must be no class war between capital and labor; strikes and lockouts were strictly prohibited. In case of a conflict between workers and employers, the state had the final authority to intervene and impose a settlement. The corporate principle also involved the complete repudiation of *laissez faire*. Though private ownership was still largely preserved, and though the capitalists were recognized as "a socially productive class," the time-honored principles of classical economics were thrown on the scrap heap. Every economic activity of the citizen was subject to regulation, and any industrial or commercial enterprise might be taken over by the government if the interests of the nation required it.[4]

The philosophy of Fascism

The idea of the corporate state was an exceedingly important element in Fascist theory, but it was by no means the only one. The other leading doctrines may be summarized as follows:

(1) Totalitarianism. The state incorporates every interest and every loyalty of its members. There must be "nothing above the state, nothing outside of the state, nothing against the state." Since the state can get nowhere except in so far as its members identify themselves with a common purpose, there can be only a *Fascist* party, a *Fascist* press, and a *Fascist* education.

(2) Nationalism. The nation is the highest form of society ever evolved by the human race. It has a life and a soul of its own apart from the lives and souls of the individuals who compose it. There can never be a real harmony of interests between two or more distinct peoples. Internationalism is therefore a gross perversion of human progress. The nation must be made strong and great, through self-sufficiency, a powerful army, and a rapidly increasing birth rate.

Other major doctrines of Fascism

(3) Idealism. The philosophy of Fascism was an idealist philosophy in the sense that it renounced the materialistic interpretation of history. The nation, according to Mussolini, could become anything it willed to become; its fate was not sealed for all time by its geographic position or by the extent of its natural resources. Idealism was developed primarily as a protest against the defeatism of Italy's former rulers, who argued that since their country has no coal it was doomed to remain a third-rate power.

(4) Romanticism. Reason can never be an adequate instrument for the solution of great national problems. Intellect needs to be supplemented by mystic faith, by self-sacrifice, and by worship of heroism and strength. "The Fascist spirit is will, not intellect."

(5) Authoritarianism. The sovereignty of the state is absolute. The citizen has no rights but simply duties. What nations need is not liberty, but work, order, prosperity. Liberty is "a putrefying corpse," an outworn dogma of the French Revolution. The state should be governed by an *élite*, which has demonstrated its right to rule by its strength and by its superior understanding of the national ideals.

(6) Militarism. Strife is the origin of all things. Nations which do not expand eventually wither and die. War exalts and ennobles man and regenerates sluggish and decadent peoples.

No unprejudiced person would deny that the Fascist regime in Italy had a few achievements to its credit. By June, 1940, when Italy

[4] According to a report of the Institution for Industrial Reconstruction, the state had acquired by 1939 a controlling interest in 25 per cent of Italian industry. *New York Times*, May 5, 1939.

entered World War II, the government had reduced illiteracy, effected what appeared to be a satisfactory settlement of the old quarrel with the papacy,[5] and obliterated the Mafia, or Black Hand organizations, in Sicily. It had succeeded also in making a number of improvements in the economic sphere. By instructing the peasants in scientific farming, it had increased the productivity of the soil by about 20 per cent. Subsidies and protective tariffs had greatly expanded industrial production, particularly of such commodities as silk, rayon, and automobiles. Between 1923 and 1933 Italy almost doubled her hydroelectric power resources. In addition, much progress had been made in reclaiming swamps, in the construction of public works, and in rescuing banks and business corporations from the ravages of the depression.

Achievements of the Fascist regime

But the ledger had also a debit side. The attempt to make Italy self-sufficient had resulted in much higher prices for certain commodities. While business and employment conditions were undoubtedly more stable than in the years just after World War I, there was no evidence that the lot of the workers had materially improved. Wage rates had indeed gone up, but on account of the advances in prices and the movement to spread the work, it was open to serious doubt that there had been any actual increase in real wages. Furthermore, the Italians had been compelled to purchase their stability and order at the price of a deadly uniformity of thought and action—a condition which Mussolini himself described in 1914 as "boredom and imbecility." [6] It should be mentioned also that Fascist rule had involved two costly ventures into foreign war: the conquest of Ethiopia in 1935–1936 and intervention in the Spanish civil war in 1936–1939. There was little to indicate that the Italian people welcomed either one of these exploits, or that the benefits to the country would repay the sacrifices.

The debit side of the ledger

2. The Nazi Triumph in Germany

Germany succumbed to fascism much later than Italy, mainly for the reason that the forces of nationalism and militarism were temporarily discredited as a result of her defeat in World War I. From 1918 to 1933 Germany was a republic. The revolution which overthrew the Kaiser in November, 1918, brought into power a coalition of Socialists, Centrists, and Democrats. In 1919 the leaders of these parties drafted the Weimar Constitution, an instrument of government remarkable for its numerous progressive features. It

The era of the republic in Germany

[5] By a treaty with Pius XI in 1929 the Fascist government abrogated the 1871 Law of Papal Guaranties (see p. 703) and recognized the complete independence of the Vatican City. The agreement also provided that Roman Catholicism should be the official religion of the state, that religious instruction should be given in the schools, and that the laws of the church should be enforced by the government.

[6] Gaudens Megaro, *Mussolini in the Making*, p. 329.

provided for universal suffrage; the cabinet system of government; and for a bill of rights, guaranteeing not only the traditional civil liberties but the right of the citizen to employment, to an education, and to protection against the hazards of an industrial society. But the republic set up under this constitution was beset with troubles from the start. Reactionaries and other extremists plotted against it. The suffering and chaos resulting from the defects of the peace would have shattered confidence in almost any regime. Added to all this was the fact that the German people had had little experience with democratic government. The Weimar republic did not spring from the desires of a majority of the nation. Instead it was born of a revolution forced upon Germany in her hour of defeat.

Causes of the triumph of German fascism: (1) defeat in the war

The factors which led to the eventual triumph of German fascism were many and various. First was the sense of humiliation arising from defeat in the war. Between 1871 and 1914 Germany had risen to lofty heights of political and cultural prestige. Until 1900, at least, she was the leading power on the European Continent. Her universities, her science, her philosophy, and her music were known and admired all over the world. She had likewise attained a fabulous prosperity, and by 1914 she had surpassed even Britain and the United States in several fields of industrial production. Then came the crushing blow of 1918. She was toppled from her pinnacle and left at the mercy of her powerful enemies. It was too much for the German people to understand. They could not believe that their invincible armies had really been worsted in battle. Quickly the legend grew that the nation had been "stabbed in the back" by Socialists and Jews in the government. There was, of course, little truth in this charge, but it helped to salve the wounded pride of German patriots.

(2) the inflation of 1923

A second important factor leading to the growth of the Nazi movement was the runaway inflation of 1923. This was largely a product of the invasion and occupation of the Ruhr valley by a French army in January of that year. The French maintained that the Germans were deliberately evading reparations payments, and that the only way to compel them to keep up with the schedule was to march an army into their country. With the encouragement of the German government, the coal miners and steel workers of the Ruhr basin went on strike. The government attempted to support them by printing huge quantities of paper money. No policy could have been more disastrous. The German mark had already depreciated on account of reparations payments and the steady depletion of gold reserves, but now it started on a veritable toboggan slide. By the first of August, 1923, over 1,000,000 marks were required to purchase $1 of American currency as compared with the pre-war value of 4.2 to the dollar. The decline continued at a fantastic rate, until by November the German paper mark was utterly worthless. It was quoted in Berlin at two and a half trillion to the dollar. Since farmers would no longer accept it in payment for produce, there was only one thing for the government to do, and that was to issue a new currency backed by tangible wealth. This was done late in 1923, and the new marks were exchanged for the old at a ratio of one to one trillion. The effects of this inflation followed by repudiation were disastrous in the extreme for certain classes. Members of the lower bourgeoisie who derived their living from salaries or from fixed-income investments found themselves impoverished. Many home-owners were compelled to sacrifice their property in order to get money for food. On the other hand, thousands of shrewd speculators got rich—in some cases by gambling on the fluctuations of the mark; in others, by making a small payment on valuable business or industrial property and then paying off the balance at a future time in depreciated currency. Some of these wizards of sharp practice were Jews, but there were plenty of full-blooded Germans engaged in it also. No matter by whom it was perpetrated, it had a powerful effect in stirring up discontent among the lower middle class.

A few other causes of the rise and growth of National Socialism may also be mentioned. There was the fact that Germany had always been a military state, imbued with traditions of discipline and order. To many of the people the army was the symbol not merely of security but of national greatness. The qualities of obedience and regimentation, which the military life represented, were virtues most dear to the German heart. As a consequence, many patriotic citizens were seriously disturbed by the laxity and irresponsibility which appeared to distinguish the republican regime. It was alleged that Berlin had displaced Paris as the most frivolous and immoral city of Europe. Another cause of more than minor importance was the fear of Bolshevism. The followers of this philosophy in Germany originally called themselves Spartacists. Subsequently they changed their name to Communists. In the Presidential election of 1932 the Communist party polled about 6,000,000 votes, or over one-seventh of the total. As had happened in Italy, a number of capitalists and property owners took alarm at what they regarded as a growing danger of Bolshevik revolution and secretly gave their support to the triumph of fascism as the lesser of two evils.

(3) militarism and fear of Bolshevism

It seems clear that the major factor which implemented and hastened the ultimate triumph of the Nazis was the Great Depression. This is evidenced by the fact that the party was never able to win more than 32 seats in the Reichstag prior to the election of 1930. Whereas in the early days the movement had drawn its converts chiefly from dissatisfied and uprooted members of the lower middle class and from former army officers unable to adjust to civilian life, after 1929 it received the additional support of farmers, university students, and millions of the unemployed. Farmers flocked to the party in the hope of gaining relief from the collapse of

(4) effects of the depression

agricultural prices and from their crushing burdens of debt and taxes. University students, whose numbers had increased by 60 per cent since 1914, turned to the movement because it seemed utterly hopeless that they should ever have a chance to make use of their training. All of the professions were overcrowded, and were getting more so with each passing year. The millions of unemployed who enlisted under the Hitler banner were conspicuously of the younger generation. Youths who had never had jobs, and who therefore found it difficult to obtain unemployment compensation, fell an easy prey to the smooth promises of the Nazi charlatans. Older men also became victims in considerable numbers, especially those who had formerly held jobs as unskilled or white-collar workers. These constituted a class of "forgotten men," since most of them were unorganized and therefore had no means of exerting pressure upon the government. By 1932 the registered unemployed in Germany numbered 6,000,000; the actual total was undoubtedly higher. By the end of that year trade and production had slowed almost to a halt. Members of all classes were groping in bewilderment and terror. Never in the history of the nation had the future appeared so dark. The majority were not yet Nazis, but their despair was so great as to induce them to accept almost any messiah who promised to deliver them from confusion and fear. To most of them the loss of political and intellectual liberty was a small sacrifice to make in order to gain the priceless boon of economic security.

The founding of the Nazi party; the early career of Hitler

The origins of German fascism go back to 1919 when a little group of seven men met in a beer hall in Munich and founded the National Socialist German Workers' party.[7] Presently the most obscure of the seven emerged as their leader. His name was Adolf Hitler, and he was born in 1889, the son of a petty customs official in the Austrian civil service. His early life was unhappy and maladjusted. Rebellious and undisciplined from childhood, he seems always to have been burdened with a sense of frustration. He wasted his time at school drawing pictures and finally decided that he would become an artist. With this purpose in view he went to Vienna in 1909, hoping to enter the Academy. But he failed the required examinations, and for the next four years he was compelled to eke out a dismal existence as a casual laborer and a painter of little sketches and water-colors which he sometimes managed to sell to the humbler art shops. Meanwhile he developed some violent political prejudices. He became an ardent admirer of certain Jew-baiting politicians in Vienna; and since he associated Judaism with Marxism, he hated that philosophy also. He likewise became a convert to extreme Nordicism, doting on the qualities of the proud German nation and despising Austria-Hungary for its lack of racial unity. When World War I broke out, Hitler was living in Munich, and

[7] The name of the party was soon abbreviated in popular usage to Nazi.

though an Austrian citizen, he immediately enlisted in the Bavarian army. He served through the four years of fighting with enough distinction to be awarded the Iron Cross and a promotion as corporal. He was wounded and gassed at least twice; and it was while recuperating in a hospital just before the armistice that he resolved to become a politician.

The Nazi revolution began in what appeared to be a quite harmless fashion. During the summer of 1932 the parliamentary system broke down. No Chancellor could retain a majority in the Reichstag; for the Nazis declined to support any cabinet not headed by Hitler, and the Communists refused to collaborate with the Socialists. In January, 1933, a group of reactionaries—industrialists, bankers, and Junkers—prevailed upon President von Hindenburg to designate Hitler as Chancellor, evidently in the belief that they could control him. It was arranged that there should be only three Nazis in the cabinet, and that Franz von Papen, a Catholic aristocrat, should hold the position of Vice Chancellor. But the sponsors of this plan failed to appreciate the tremendous resurgence of national feeling back of the Nazi movement. Hitler was not slow in making the most of his new opportunity. He proceeded to overawe as many of his opponents as possible by suppressing the trade unions and by taking vigorous measures against Socialists and Communists. He persuaded von Hindenburg to dissolve the Reichstag and to order a new election on March 5. The voting took place in the midst of intense excitement. Just a few days before, the Reichstag chamber was gutted by a fire, which Hitler contended was of Communist origin. But in spite of this attempt to frighten the nation by conjuring up the specter of Bolshevism, the Nazis won less than a majority of the popular vote and only 288 seats out of the total of 647 in the Reichstag. Nevertheless, with the fifty-two members chosen by their allies, the Nationalists, they did have a slight majority. When the new Reichstag assembled on March 21, it voted to confer upon Hitler practically unlimited powers. Soon afterward the flag of the Weimar Republic was hauled down and replaced by the swastika banner of National Socialism. The new Germany was proclaimed to be the Third Reich, the successor of the Hohenstaufen empire of the Middle Ages and of the Hohenzollern empire of the Kaisers.

The Nazi revolution

The Reichstag fire

Of course, these events marked only the initial stage of the Nazi revolution. Within a very few months, other and more sweeping changes were added. Germany was converted into a highly centralized state with the destruction of the federal principle. All political parties except the Nazi party were declared illegal. A totalitarian control was extended over the press, over education, the theater, the cinema, radio, and many branches of production and trade. Drastic penalties were imposed upon the Jews: they were eliminated from government positions, deprived of citizenship, for-

*Consolidation of
Nazi rule*

bidden to engage in the theatrical and publishing businesses, and practically excluded from the universities. As the work of remaking the country progressed, the radicals in the party were emboldened to demand that more attention should be given to the *socialist* aspects of the Nazi program. A faction under the leadership of Ernst Roehm began criticizing the government for its conservatism;

Hitler in 1936. Germany at this time was rapidly rearming and had remilitarized the Rhineland, the first steps toward her objective of European domination.

whereupon Hitler accused Roehm of plotting to overthrow him. The result was the celebrated Blood Purge of June 30, 1934, in which Roehm and at least 100 others were murdered by Hitler, Goering, and the secret police. But this did not mean a permanent victory for the conservatives. With the passing of the years, the entire regime seemed to shift more and more in a radical direction. The new tendency approached its climax in 1938 with the extension of party control over the army, with the elimination of Hjalmar Schacht (a banker of somewhat conservative views) from his position as economic dictator, and with the institution of a fanatical crusade against the Jews to expel them from the Reich or to annihilate them entirely.

So far as its philosophy was concerned, German fascism resembled in a great many of its essentials the Italian variety. Both were collectivistic, authoritarian, nationalistic, militaristic, and romantic (in the sense of being anti-intellectual). Yet there were some outstanding differences. Italian fascism never had a racial basis. True, after the formation of the Rome-Berlin Axis, Mussolini issued some anti-Jewish decrees; but most of them appear not to have been enforced very strictly. By contrast, National Socialism made the factor of race a central pillar of its theory. The Nazis argued that

*German
fascism com-
pared with the
Italian variety:
racism*

the so-called Aryan race, which was supposed to include the Nordics as its most perfect specimens, was the only one ever to have made any notable contributions to human progress. They contended further that the accomplishments and mental qualities of a people were actually determined by blood. Thus the achievements of the Jew forever remained Jewish, or Oriental, no matter how long he might live in a Western country. It followed that no Jewish science or Jewish literature or Jewish music could ever truly represent the German nation. Obviously, most of this racial doctrine was mere rationalization. The real reason why the Nazis persecuted the Jews seems to have been that they needed a scapegoat upon whom they could place the blame for the nation's troubles.

There were also other differences, both in theory and in practice. Despite the fact that Germany was one of the most highly industrialized countries in the world, National Socialism had a peculiar *Blood and soil* peasant flavor which Italian Fascism did not possess. The key to Nazi theory was contained in the phrase *Blut und Boden* (blood and soil). The word *soil* typified not only a deep reverence for the beautiful homeland but an abiding affection for the peasants, who were considered to embody the finest qualities of the German race. No class of the population was more generously treated by the Nazi government. This high regard for country folk came partly no doubt from the circumstance that they were the most prolific of the nation's citizens and therefore the most valuable for military reasons; but it was explainable also by the reaction of the Nazi leaders against everything that the city stood for—not only intellectualism and radicalism but high finance and the complicated problems of industrial society. As upstarts of obscure origin, the *The state and* Nazis strove to compensate for their sense of inferiority by glorifying the simple life. Still another difference between the German and Italian varieties of fascism was the fact that under the former the corporate state was not fully developed. To be sure, both involved the abolition of the right to strike and the complete subjection of economic activities to political control; but in Germany there was no direct representation of economic interests in the government. Members of the Reichstag continued to be chosen from geographic districts, and the state retained its exclusively political character. Finally, it may be said that National Socialism was more frenzied and fanatical than Italian Fascism. It was comparable to a new religion, not only in its dogmatism and its ritual, but in its fierce intolerance and its zeal for expansion.

Despite the profound changes in theory, several of the forms of the old German government were allowed to remain. Technically the nation was still a republic. As long as von Hindenburg lived, *The govern-* his position as President was not disturbed. When he died in August, *ment of the* 1934, Hitler added the authority of the President to that which he *Third Reich* already possessed as Chancellor. With the consent of the nation expressed through a plebiscite, he adopted the new title of *Fuehrer und Reichskanzler* (Leader and Chancellor of the Reich). The German Parliament was also preserved, at least in name. However, it was now a unicameral body consisting of the Reichstag exclusively. When the principle of states' rights was destroyed, the upper chamber, or Reichsrat, which represented the states, was rendered superfluous. Accordingly, in 1934, it was abolished. But actually this change was of little significance, for even the Reichstag was now seldom convoked and had practically no power. It was hardly much more than a sounding board for Hitler's speeches.

The complex significance of fascism

The significance of fascism, whether German or Italian, is still a subject of controversy among students of modern history. Some argue that it was simply the enthronement of force by big capitalists in an effort to save their dying system from destruction. But this does not square with all of the facts. Neither Italian Fascism nor National Socialism showed any inclination in the beginning to protect the interests of monopolies or of speculative finance. Indeed, if we can judge from their original platforms, their purpose was just the opposite. It is true, however, that the success of both movements in gaining control of the government depended in some measure upon support from great landowners and captains of industry. A second interpretation of fascism would explain it as a reaction of debtors against creditors, of farmers against bankers and manufacturers, and of small businessmen against high finance and monopolistic practices. Still other students of the movement interpret it as a revolt against communism, a reversion to primitivism, a result of the despair of the masses, a protest against the weaknesses of democracy, or a supreme manifestation of chauvinism. Probably fascism was all of these things combined and a good many others besides. At least we can be sure that it was a more complicated species of Caesarism than any that had appeared hitherto. Like its predecessors, it was a product of national pride and of a demand for strength and efficiency in solving the problems of a chaotic society; but it had been vastly complicated by the Second Industrial Revolution and by the disillusionment and economic collapse following in the wake of World War I.

3. The Communist Regime in Russia

Causes of the revolution in Russia

Although Russia fought in World War I on the side of the powers that eventually triumphed, she was the first of the belligerent nations to be engulfed by revolution. The reasons for this are not far to seek. The Russian government's conduct of the war was distinguished by wholesale corruption and utter incompetence. The senile Premier was unable to control the greed of plundering contractors or to curb the selfish ambitions of his subordinates. The weak-willed Tsar came more and more under the influence of the super-

stitious Tsarina, who was putty in the hands of an infamous "holy
man," Rasputin. Soldiers were sent to the front without rifles and
were inadequately supplied with shoes, warm clothing, and blankets.
The wounded sometimes froze to death or died of gangrene because
there were not enough surgeons or hospital facilities to take care
of them. The Russian railway system broke down, producing a
shortage of food not only in the army but in the congested cities as
well. Added to these troubles was a series of crushing defeats suffered at the hands of the enemy. Though Russia mobilized 15,000,-
000 men, she was unable to hold up her end of the fight on the
Eastern Front. By 1915 the Germans had penetrated far into her
territory, and by the end of the following year her power of
resistance had practically collapsed.

The revolution in Russia followed a succession of stages somewhat similar to those of the great French Revolution of 1789. The
first of these stages began in March, 1917, with the forced abdication of the Tsar. For this the principal cause was disgust with the
conduct of the war. But there were also many other factors—the
inflation and consequent high prices, the scarcity of food and of
coal in urban areas, the influx of peasants who overcrowded the
cities, the preaching of radicals, and the legacy of bitterness left
by the revolt of 1905. With the overthrow of the Tsar, the authority
of the government passed into the hands of a provisional ministry
organized by leaders in the Duma in conjunction with representatives of the Petrograd workers. The most important members of
the new cabinet were the Premier, Prince Lvov; the Foreign Minister, Paul Milyukov; and the Minister of Justice, Alexander Kerensky. With the exception of Kerensky, who was a Social Revolutionary, nearly all of the ministers were bourgeois liberals. Their
conception of the revolution was mainly to transform the autocracy
into a constitutional monarchy, modeled after that of Great Britain.
In accordance with this aim they issued a proclamation of civil
liberties, released thousands of prisoners, granted permission for
political exiles to return to the country, and made plans for the
election of a constituent assembly.

*The overthrow
of the Tsar*

But the provisional government committed the fatal blunder of
attempting to force Russia to continue the war. On March 18
Milyukov issued a declaration that his government would honor
the "international obligations" contracted by the Tsar and would
carry on the fight to a victorious conclusion. He and the majority
of his colleagues were just as imperialistic as the old regime. They
hoped to get Constantinople and everything else that had been
promised in the secret treaties. But the masses of the people were
desperately weary of the years of hardship and struggle. All that
they wanted was peace and a chance to return to a normal life.
Consequently, in May, when Milyukov reiterated his pledge of
support for the Allies, criticism was so strong that he was obliged

*The downfall
of Milyukov
and the rise of
Kerensky*

857

to resign. The government was then reorganized with Kerensky as Minister of War and with the addition of a number of Socialists. In July Kerensky became Premier at the head of a cabinet composed primarily of moderate Marxists and Social Revolutionaries. He begged the Allies to consent to a peace on the basis of no annexations and no indemnities; and when that failed, he insisted that Russia must continue the war. He stirred up opposition also by restoring the death penalty in the army and by announcing that the government would not recognize any seizures of land by the peasants. In September he attempted to establish a dictatorship and thereby alienated his moderate followers. From that point on his doom was sealed.

The triumph of the Bolsheviks

The downfall of Kerensky's regime marked the end of the first stage of the Russian revolution. The second began immediately after with the accession of the Bolsheviks to power on November 7, 1917. The Bolsheviks were originally members of the Social Democratic party, but in 1903 this party had split into two factions: a majority or Bolshevik faction of Marxist revolutionists and a minority faction of Mensheviks, who contended that the time for revolution was not yet ripe. Soon after the overthrow of the Tsar the Bolsheviks began laying plans for a socialist revolution. They wormed their way into the Petrograd Soviet, or Council of Workers' and Soldiers' Deputies, and eventually wrested control of it from the Mensheviks and Social Revolutionaries. They organized an armed Red Guard and took possession of strategic points throughout the city. By November 7 everything was ready for the grand *coup*. Red Guards occupied nearly all the public buildings and finally arrested the members of the government, though Kerensky himself escaped. Thus the Bolsheviks climbed to power with scarcely a struggle. Their easy victory was made possible by the utter collapse of Kerensky's authority. Besides, their slogan of "Peace, Land, and Bread" made them heroes to the soldiers disgusted with the war, to the peasants hungry for land, and to the poor of the cities suffering from the shortage of food.

Vladimir Lenin

The two chief actors in the Bolshevik drama were Vladimir Lenin and Leon Trotsky. The former, whose real name was Vladimir Ulianov, was born in 1870. His father was an inspector of schools and a State Counsellor and therefore entitled to rank in the petty nobility. An older son, Alexander, was hanged for participating in a plot to assassinate the Tsar; but this does not seem to have placed any stigma upon the family, for in the very same year of Alexander's execution, Vladimir was admitted to the University of Kazan. However, he was soon afterward expelled for engaging in radical activity. Later he was admitted to the University of St. Petersburg and in 1891 obtained a degree in law. From then on he devoted his entire life to the cause of socialist revolution. From 1900 to 1917 he lived principally in Germany and England, acting much of the time as editor of the Bolshevik journal *Iskra* (*The Spark*). Like most of the Russian revolutionists, he wrote under a pseudonym, signing his articles N. Lenin.[8] When the revolution broke out in March, 1917, he was living in Switzerland. With the aid of the Germans he made his way back to Russia and immediately assumed leadership of the Bolshevik movement. Lenin had all of the qualities necessary for success as a revolutionary figure. He was an able politician and an exceedingly effective orator. Absolutely convinced of the righteousness of his cause, he could strike down his opponents with the

Lenin Addressing a Crowd in Red Square, Moscow, Two Years after the Revolution.

zeal and savagery of a Robespierre. On the other hand, he cared nothing for the fleshpots of wealth or of personal glory. He lived in two rooms in the Kremlin and dressed little better than an ordinary workman. His expensive marble mausoleum in Moscow, where his body has been kept in a glass case since his death in 1924, stands out in bold contrast to the simplicity of his life.

The most prominent of Lenin's lieutenants was the brilliant but erratic Leon Trotsky. Originally named Lev Bronstein, he was born in 1879 of middle-class Jewish parents in Ukrainia. He seems *Leon Trotsky* to have been the stormy petrel of revolutionary politics during most of his life. Before the revolution he refused to identify himself with any particular faction, preferring to remain an independent Marxist. Though he collaborated with Lenin in editing *The Spark*, he did not become a Bolshevik until 1917. For his part in the revolutionary movement of 1905 he was exiled to Siberia; but he escaped, and then for some years led a roving existence in various European capitals. He was expelled from Paris in 1916 for pacifist activity and took refuge in the United States. Upon learning of the overthrow of the Tsar, he attempted to return to Russia. Captured by British agents at Halifax, he was eventually released upon the plea of Kerensky. He arrived in Russia in April and immediately began

[8] The "N." did not stand for anything in particular, though many people have assumed that it was a symbol for Nikolai.

plotting for the overthrow of the provisional government and later of Kerensky himself. His part in the Bolshevik triumph consisted in organizing and disciplining the Red Guard and in ousting the Mensheviks and Social Revolutionaries from control of the Petrograd Soviet. He became Minister of Foreign Affairs in the government headed by Lenin and subsequently Commissar for War.

Revolutionary political and economic changes

No sooner had the Bolsheviks come into power than they proceeded to effect some drastic alterations in the political and economic system. They proclaimed their own rule to be the dictatorship of the proletariat; and when elections for a constituent assembly returned a majority of opposition delegates, they dissolved the assembly by force. On November 8 Lenin decreed nationalization of the land and gave the peasants the exclusive right to use it. On November 29 control of the factories was transferred to the workers, and a month later it was announced that all except the smallest industrial establishments would be taken over by the government. Banks also were nationalized soon after the Bolshevik victory. But the problem of greatest urgency was termination of the war. After vain attempts to induce the Allies to consent to a peace without annexations or indemnities, Trotsky signed an armistice with Germany on December 15. This was followed by the peace of Brest-Litovsk in March, 1918, which officially ended the war so far as Russia was concerned. The terms of the treaty were drastic. Russia was required to evacuate Estonia and Finland, to recognize the independence of the Ukraine, and to allow the Central Powers to determine the status of Poland, Latvia, and Lithuania "in agreement with their populations." These losses, of course, were substantial, but it should be remembered that the provinces surrendered were not sympathetic to Bolshevism, and the new government could scarcely have held them. Furthermore, Russia was assessed with an indemnity of only $1,500,000,000 as compared with a sum twenty-two times as great levied upon Germany at Versailles.

The civil war between Whites and Reds

Scarcely had the Bolsheviks concluded the war with the Central Powers than they were confronted with a desperate civil war at home. Landlords and capitalists did not take kindly to the loss of their property. Besides, the Allies were determined to punish Russia and accordingly sent troops into the country to support the armies of reactionary generals. The result was a prolonged and bloody combat between the Reds, or Bolsheviks, on the one side, and the Whites, or reactionaries, and their foreign allies on the other. Both sides were guilty of horrible brutality. The Whites massacred the inhabitants of captured villages—women and children as well as men. The Reds, in order to exterminate spies and counter-revolutionists, instituted a reign of terror. An extraordinary commission known as the Cheka was set up to arrest and punish suspected persons without a trial. No one knows the exact number of its victims, but authorities agree that there were thousands. At times the Cheka resorted to mass executions, as was done in August, 1918, after a Social Revolutionary had attempted to assassinate Lenin. But at length the terror abated. By the end of 1920 the civil war was practically over. The Bolsheviks had driven nearly all of the foreign soldiers from the country and had forced the reactionary generals to abandon the struggle.

The civil war was accompanied by an appalling economic breakdown. In 1920 the total industrial production was only 13 per cent of what it had been in 1913. To make up for the shortage of goods the government abolished the payment of wages and distributed supplies among the workers in the cities in proportion to their absolute need. All private trade was prohibited, and everything produced by the peasants above what they required to keep from starving was requisitioned by the state. This system was not pure communism, as is often alleged, but was mainly an expedient for crushing the bourgeoisie and for obtaining as much food as possible for the army in the field. It was soon abandoned after the war had ended. In 1921 it was superseded by the New Economic Policy (NEP), which Lenin described as "one step backward in order to take two steps forward." The NEP authorized private manufacturing and private trade on a small scale, reintroduced the payment of wages, and permitted the peasants to sell their grain in the open market. The new policy continued in force until 1928 when the first of the famous Five-Year Plans was adopted. By 1939 two of these plans had been completed and a third was under way. Their purposes were mainly to complete the process of socialization, to make Russia a great industrial country, and to further the evolution of a classless, communist society.

Economic breakdown and the NEP

In the meantime, the death of Lenin in January 1924 precipitated a titanic struggle between two of his lieutenants to inherit his mantle of power. Outside of Russia it was generally assumed that Trotsky would be the man to succeed the fallen leader. But soon it was revealed that the fiery commander of the Red Army had a formidable rival in the shaggy and mysterious Joseph Stalin. Born in 1879, the son of a peasant shoemaker in the province of Georgia, Stalin received part of his education in a theological seminary. But he was expelled at the age of seventeen for "lack of religious vocation" and thereafter dedicated his career to revolutionary activity. He was exiled no fewer than six times to the frozen wastes of the north; five times he managed to escape, and after the sixth he was released by the provisional government. In 1917 he became Secretary-General of the Communist party, a position through which he was able to build up a party machine. The battle between Stalin and Trotsky was not simply a struggle for personal power, but fundamental issues of political policy were also involved. Trotsky maintained that socialism in Russia could never be entirely successful until capitalism was overthrown in surrounding countries. There-

The struggle between Trotsky and Stalin

fore he insisted upon a continuous crusade for world revolution. Stalin was willing to abandon the program of world revolution, for the time being, in order to concentrate upon building socialism in Russia itself. His strategy for the immediate future was essentially nationalist. The outcome of the duel was a complete triumph for Stalin. In 1927 Trotsky was expelled from the Communist party, and two years later he was driven from the country. It is interesting to note that Lenin did not hold either of the two rivals in very lofty esteem. In a "testament" written shortly before his death, he criticized Trotsky for "far-reaching self-confidence" and for being too much preoccupied with administrative detail. But he dealt far less gently with Stalin, condemning him as "too rough" and "capricious" and urging that the comrades "find a way" to remove him from his position at the head of the party.[9]

*The third stage
of the Russian
revolution*

About 1934 the Bolshevik regime entered a new and in some ways more conservative phase, which should perhaps be considered as the third stage of the Russian revolution. It was characterized by a number of significant developments. First, there was the revival of such capitalist devices as the payment of interest on savings accounts and the issuance of bonds to which premiums were attached. Second, the disparity of wage payments was greatly increased. Some menial workers received as little as 100 rubles a month, while skilled employees in the heavy industries and certain administrative officials were permitted to enjoy monthly salaries as high as 6000 rubles.[10] No longer were members of the Communist party limited to incomes of $1500 per year as was the case when Lenin was in power. Third, the laws of marriage and divorce were made more stringent, and women were being urged to bear more children. The original ideal of abolishing the bourgeois family seemed now to be definitely a thing of the past. Fourth, there was a revival of militarism, of nationalism, and of an interest in playing the game of power politics. The army was more than doubled in size and was reorganized in accordance with the Western model. Patriotism, which the older strict Marxists despised as a form of capitalist propaganda, was exalted into a Soviet virtue. In like manner, there was a growing tendency to discard the internationalism of Marx, to strive to make Russia self-sufficient, and to play an active part in old-fashioned diplomacy. With Nazism firmly established in Germany, the rulers in the Kremlin seemed to have decided that Russia needed friends. Along with their efforts to build up a great army and to make their own country self-sufficient, they

[9] The Testament of Lenin is contained in Leon Trotsky, *The Real Situation in Russia*, Supplement I. The authenticity of the document was implicitly admitted by Stalin in a session of the party Central Committee in October, 1927. W. H. Chamberlin, *Soviet Russia: a Living Record and a History*, p. 93n. In an effort to discredit Stalin, Nikita S. Khrushchev distributed the full text of this Testament at the Twentieth Party Conference in February, 1956.

[10] The ruble was officially worth about 25 cents.

adopted a policy of co-operation with the Western powers. In 1934 they entered the League of Nations, and in 1935 they exchanged ratifications of a military alliance with France. It is apparent, however, that the real purpose of these moves was to drive a wedge between Germany on the one side and Britain and France on the other. At any rate, when the Soviet leaders became suspicious in 1938–1939 that Britain and France were encouraging Hitler to expand eastward, they did not hesitate to conclude a nonaggression pact with the Nazi government.[11]

The original philosophy of Bolshevism, now more popularly known as communism, was developed primarily by Lenin. It was not supposed to be a new body of thought but a strict interpretation of the gospel of Marx. Nevertheless, from the beginning there were various departures from the master's teachings. Whereas Marx had assumed that a capitalist stage must prepare the way for socialism, Lenin denied that this was necessary and insisted that Russia could leap directly from a feudal to a socialist economy. In the second place, Lenin emphasized the revolutionary character of socialism much more than did its original founder. Marx did believe that in most cases revolution would be necessary, but he was inclined to deplore the fact rather than to welcome it. Furthermore, in his Amsterdam speech of 1872 he had stated that "there are certain countries such as England and the United States in which the workers may hope to secure their ends by peaceful means." Last of all, Bolshevism differs from Marxism in its conception of proletarian rule. There is nothing to indicate that Marx ever envisaged a totalitarian workers' state as arbitrary and oppressive in its methods of governing as fascism. True, he did speak of the "dictatorship of the proletariat"; but he meant by this a dictatorship of the whole working class over the remnants of the bourgeoisie. Within the ranks of this class, democratic forms would prevail. Lenin, however, set up the ideal of the dictatorship of an *élite*, a select minority, wielding supremacy not only over the bourgeoisie but over the bulk of the proletarians themselves. In Russia this *élite* is the Communist party whose membership has varied from 1,500,000 to 6,300,000.

The philosophy of Bolshevism

Since the Bolshevik revolution Russia has had three constitutions. The first was the constitution of the R.S.F.S.R. (Russian Soviet Federated Socialist Republic), adopted in 1918. This provided for a form of government for all of the territory then under Bolshevik control—chiefly Great Russia and western Siberia. The government was constructed in the form of a pyramid with soviets of workers and peasants at the base and a Council of People's Commissars at the apex. In the years that followed, Bolshevik sympathizers gained control of the governments in the Ukraine and in White Russia as well as in Azerbaijan, Russian Armenia, and Georgia. The result was the formation in 1923 of the U.S.S.R. (Union of Soviet Socialist

The governments of the R.S.F.S.R. and the U.S.S.R.

[11] See p. 907.

Republics). The constitution of the U.S.S.R., adopted in the same year, simply extended the form of government of the R.S.F.S.R. to the entire union. Each republic had its own Soviets and its own Council of Commissars. Surmounting the whole structure was an All-Union Congress of Soviets, a Central Executive Committee elected by the Congress, and a Union Council of Commissars elected by the Central Committee.

The constitu-
tion of 1936

In 1936 a new constitution was drafted. It was adopted by popular vote the following year and went into effect January 1, 1938. The constitution of 1936 is in many ways quite different from the ones it superseded. To begin with, it provides for a union of eleven republics [12] instead of five (later seven) under the constitution of 1923. Much more important is the fact that the new constitution abolishes the system of indirect election and the limited franchise formerly in effect. It provides universal suffrage for all citizens eighteen years of age and over. They vote not only for the local soviets but for members of a national parliament. Moreover, the voting is done by secret ballot. The highest organ of state power is the Supreme Soviet of the U.S.S.R., composed of two chambers— the Soviet of the Union and the Soviet of Nationalities. The former has 600 members elected by the people for four-year terms. The Soviet of Nationalities has about 400 members chosen for similar terms by the governments of the several republics. Both chambers have equal legislative powers. To represent it between sessions, the Supreme Soviet elects a committee of thirty-seven members known as the Presidium. This body also has power to issue decrees, to declare war, and to annul the acts of administrative officials which do not conform to law. The highest executive and administrative agency is the Council of Ministers, likewise elected by the Supreme Soviet. Each Minister is head of a department, such as War, Foreign Affairs, Railways, Heavy Industry, Light Industry, and so forth.[13] Finally, the constitution of 1936 contains a bill of rights. Citizens are guaranteed the right to employment, the right to leisure, the right to maintenance in case of old age or disability, and even the traditional privileges of freedom of speech, of the press, of assemblage, and of religion.

The Party the
real power in
Russia

By many people, both inside and outside the Soviet Union, the constitution of 1936 was hailed as an evidence that Stalin and his brethren had turned over a new leaf of liberal democracy. On paper the provisions for universal suffrage, for direct election, for the secret ballot, and for a bill of rights undoubtedly looked progressive. But in practice there was nothing to indicate that the Bolshevik

[12] During 1939–1940 the number of republics was increased to sixteen as a result of the conquest of territory from Poland and Finland, the taking of Northern Bukovina and Bessarabia from Rumania, and the annexation of Estonia, Latvia, and Lithuania. In 1956 the Karelo-Finnish Republic was incorporated in the R.S.F.S.R.

[13] Before 1946 the Ministers were called Commissars.

leopard had changed its spots. Citizens of the U.S.S.R. had no more freedom of speech or of the press than they had before. The fundamental reason, of course, for the failure of the constitution to provide anything more than nominal benefits is the fact that the real power in the Soviet Union remained in the hands of the Communist Party, the only party allowed to exist. The organs of the government were and still are little more than the vocal mechanisms through which the Party expresses its will. It is noteworthy also that the very period in which the constitution was being put into effect witnessed a new wave of mass arrests and executions of persons alleged to be "Trotskyists, spies, and wreckers."

Perhaps enough has been said already to indicate that the Bolshevik upheaval was not merely political in character but had profound economic and social results. By 1939 private manufacturing and private trade had been almost entirely abolished. Factories, mines, railroads, and public utilities were exclusively owned by the state. Stores were either government enterprises or producers' and consumers' co-operatives. Agriculture also had been almost completely socialized. State farms included about 10 per cent of the land; and collective farms, organized on a co-operative basis, occupied nearly all of the remainder. No less revolutionary were the developments in the social sphere. Religion as a factor in the lives of the people declined to a place of small importance. To be sure, Christianity was still tolerated; but churches were reduced in number, and were not permitted to engage in any charitable or educational activities. Furthermore, members of the Communist Party were required to be atheists. Communism not only renounces all belief in the supernatural but attempts to cultivate a new ethics. The primary aim is to create a *positive* morality, based upon duty to society, in place of the old negative morality, founded upon a notion of personal sin. The cardinal virtues in this positive morality are industry, respect for public property, willingness to sacrifice individual interests for the good of society, and loyalty to the Soviet fatherland and to the socialist ideal at all times. The gulf which separates communist morality from that of bourgeois countries is illustrated by the dedication of a monument in Moscow in 1939 to a twelve-year-old boy who reported his own father to the secret police for shielding some enemies of Stalin.

Economic and social results of the Bolshevik upheaval

Regardless of one's attitude toward the communist philosophy, he can scarcely deny that the Bolshevik regime has certain accomplishments to its credit. Among the principal ones may be mentioned the following: (1) the reduction of illiteracy from a proportion of at least 50 per cent to less than 20 per cent; (2) a notable expansion of industrialization, especially when compared with the levels to which the national economy had sunk at the end of the civil war; (3) the establishment of a planned economy, which at least operates successfully enough to prevent unemployment; (4)

Accomplishments of the Bolshevik regime

the opening of educational and cultural opportunities to larger numbers of the common people; and (5) the establishment of a system of government assistance for working mothers and their infants and free medical care and hospitalization for most of the citizens.

On the other hand, it cannot be overlooked that these accomplishments were purchased at a very high price. The program of socialization and industrialization was pushed at so dizzy a pace that the good of individual citizens was almost forgotten. For example, the overemphasis upon heavy industry and upon armaments manufacture under the Five Year Plans resulted in a scarcity of consumers' goods and consequently in fantastic prices. It must not be forgotten either that the Bolshevik regime fastened upon Russia a tyranny just as extreme as that of the Tsar. Indeed, the number of its victims sentenced to slave-labor camps probably exceeds the number consigned by the Tsars to exile in Siberia. And it is significant that nearly all the old Bolsheviks who took a leading part in the uprising of November, 1917, were subsequently shot or driven into exile.

*The price
of revolution*

4. The Democracies between Two Wars

By 1939 only three of the chief powers—Great Britain, France, and the United States—remained in the list of democratic countries. Among the lesser states democracy survived in Switzerland, Holland, Belgium, Finland, the Scandinavian countries, a few of the republics of Latin America, and the self-governing dominions of the British Commonwealth. Nearly all of the rest of the world had succumbed to despotism of one form or another. Italy, Germany, and Spain were fascist; Russia was communist; Hungary was dominated by a landowning oligarchy; while Poland, Turkey, China, and Japan were essentially military dictatorships. For the most part, this cleavage represented a division between the so-called Have and Have-not nations—the former including the democracies, and the latter the dictatorships. Great Britain, France, and the United States were sated countries, comparatively rich in territorial empire and in mineral resources. Italy, Germany, and Japan were hungry nations, lacking both markets and raw materials to keep their industrial establishments operating successfully. This was not a natural condition. Had it not been for tariffs and other import restrictions, the markets of India would have been just as accessible to Germany or Japan as they were to Britain, and the raw materials of North Africa would have been no less available to Italy than they were to France. But given the tariff barriers, it was impossible for Germany to buy the iron ore of Lorraine since France would not take her exports, and without the sale of exports she could not obtain the money to buy imports. What Germany did, therefore,

*Division of the
world into de-
mocracies and
dictatorships*

was to enter into special barter agreements with such countries as Sweden and Spain. In return for the purchase from Germany of specified quantities of manufactures, Germany would agree to buy from Sweden or Spain iron ore of an equivalent value. These arrangements were cumbersome and seldom produced satisfactory results. At the same time it should be remembered that the democratic countries themselves were not always enjoying halcyon days of security and plenty. Many of them were harassed by debt, unemployment, and business stagnation almost continuously from World War I.

It will be impossible to describe the history of all the democracies between the two wars or even to analyze minutely internal developments in any one of them. In general, there were three main *Stages in* periods: first, a period of acute depression from 1918 to 1923; *the post-war* second, a period of relative prosperity from 1923 to 1929; and third, *history of the* a period of chronic depression after 1929. During the first two *democracies* of these periods efforts were made to continue the policies in vogue before 1914, though naturally some adjustments were necessary. But the era of chronic depression witnessed departures that were much more extreme. Nearly everywhere there was a trend in the direction of planned production, with an increasing amount of governmental intervention in economic affairs and a tendency to consolidate the power of the state.

The oldest and most powerful of the democracies in Europe found herself in a critical position at the end of World War I. For much of Great Britain's foreign commerce had been destroyed. *The critical po-* She was heavily indebted to the United States, and the money she *sition of Great* had advanced to her European allies could not be collected. More- *Britain* over, the demand for British manufactured goods had declined sharply as a result of the fact that, during the war, cotton mills had been established in Japan and in India, and Australians were weaving their own wool. By taking over the German merchant marine, Britain only punished herself; for now the shipyards of the Clyde had nothing to do. There was also a reduced demand for British coal, since the French were collecting millions of tons from Germany. As a consequence of such factors, Great Britain soon found that 1,000,000 of her workers were unable to obtain employment and would have to be supported by the government. By 1921 this number had increased to 2,000,000.

The coalition cabinet formed during the war under the leadership of David Lloyd George did little to remedy Britain's economic ailments except to establish a dole for the unemployed and to impose *The first Labor* limited tariffs on the products of a few key industries. In 1922 the *government* Conservatives forced Lloyd George to resign and organized a new cabinet under Stanley Baldwin. In the election of 1923 the Conservatives lost their majority to the Labor party, whose leader, Ramsay MacDonald, had campaigned on a platform urging nationalization of mines and railways, government subsidies for housing, and a capital levy on fortunes in excess of £5000, or $25,000. MacDonald's term as Prime Minister lasted only ten months. Dependent for a majority upon the support of the Liberals, he was unable to accomplish much, beyond the enactment of a bill providing for government aid for the construction of thousands of houses to rent at 9 shillings, or $2.25 per week. In October, 1924, he was defeated in the House of Commons on a charge of being friendly

The First British Labor Government, 1924. Fifth from the left in the front row is the Prime Minister, Ramsay MacDonald. Third from the left is Philip Snowden, Chancellor of the Exchequer. Last on the right is Arthur Henderson, Foreign Secretary.

toward communism. The ensuing election gave a majority of over 200 seats to the Conservatives, though they actually received only a minority of the popular vote.

The Conservative regime of 1924–1929

Backed by so overwhelming a majority in the House of Commons, the Conservatives were able to continue in power until 1929. Baldwin was again Prime Minister at the head of a cabinet of stodgy industrialists, monocled aristocrats, and hard-bitten politicians of the old school. The period of their supremacy was an era of comparative prosperity. Trade picked up, there was a modest boom in light industry, and unemployment declined by nearly 50 per cent. But coal mining, shipbuilding, and the construction industry were still in the doldrums. In May, 1926, the miners went on strike, and the workers in most of the heavy industries and in transportation walked out in sympathy with them. This was the famous "general strike" which threw such a scare into the possessing classes. It lasted for nine days and in the end was worse than a failure. Not only did the workers receive no positive benefits, but the government stirred up the people against them through the publicly owned broadcasting system and in 1927 enacted a stringent Trade Union and Trade Disputes Act. The Act made general strikes unlawful,

Water, Charles Sheeler (1883–). Sheeler, a Philadelphian, idealizes the industrial scene, which he detaches from humanity. (MMA)

Sea and Gulls, John Marin (1870–1953). A native of New Jersey, Marin was a gifted abstract painter. His objects are sometimes recognizable, sometimes not. He painted not the likeness of nature, but *about* nature. (MMA)

Barricade, José Clemente Orozco (1883–1949). The Mexican muralist Orozco was one of the most celebrated of contemporary painters with a social message. His themes were revolutionary fervor, satire of aristocracy and the Church, and deification of the common man. (Mus. Mod. Art)

The Persistence of Memory, Salvador Dali (1904–). The Spaniard Dali is the outstanding representative of the surrealist school. Many objects in his paintings are Freudian images. (Mus. Mod. Art)

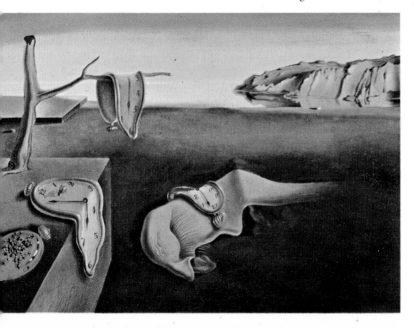

The Gulf Stream, Winslow Homer (1836–1910) Homer is most widely known for his marines. Though his genius was expressed particularly in watercolor, this oil won him great renown. (MMA)

Max Schmitt in a Single Scull, Thomas Eakins (1844–1916). A native of Philadelphia, Eakins painted with superb talent the places and people familiar to him. His work is warm and inspiring, but not profound. (MMA)

Roasting Ears, Thomas Hart Benton (1889–). Benton is one of a group of regional painters who portray scenes of the Midwest and South. (MMA)

Spring in Central Park, Adolf Dehn (1895–). Dehn is one of the most distinguished of American landscape painters. He paints indoors from sketches in order to escape the literalness of nature and to allow freedom for balance and rhythm. (MMA)

Portrait of Myself When Young, Ben Shahn (1898–). A native of Russia who grew up in Brooklyn, Shahn is concerned with communicating ordinary experience. His work combines the precision of photography with startling effects of proportion and size. (Mus. Mod. Art)

John Brown, John Steuart Curry (1897–1946). Born on a farm in Kansas, Curry depicted the beauty and majesty of his native region. *John Brown* is a portion of a large mural in the state capitol at Topeka. A prairie fire and a tornado in the background add fury to the fanaticism of the abolitionist, and symbolize the coming civil conflict. (MMA)

forbade picketing, and practically prohibited the collection of trade-union funds for political purposes. With respect to some other matters, the Baldwin government had a more constructive record. It extended provisions for widows', orphans', and old-age pensions and granted the vote to all women who had not been enfranchised by the Reform Act of 1918.

In the election of 1929 the Conservatives were defeated, and then for a second time Ramsay MacDonald became Prime Minister of Great Britain. As in 1924 he was dependent for a majority in the House of Commons upon the remnant of Liberals who still managed to be elected to that body. Consequently he was again unable to accomplish much. He did succeed in abolishing grants for military training in the schools and in restoring conscientious objectors to civil rights, but he was unable to achieve anything in the direction of socialism, or even to repeal the anti-labor legislation of the Baldwin regime. The Labor party contrived to remain in power until the summer of 1931. By that time England was sinking deep into the quagmire of the Great Depression. In August the level of unemployment rose to 2,700,000. The gold reserve was rapidly dwindling, while a budgetary deficit of nearly £40,000,000 ($200,-000,000) was in prospect by the end of the fiscal year. Faced with this crisis, MacDonald and a few of his colleagues determined to cut unemployment relief, together with all salaries and pensions, in the hope of saving the nation's credit. But unable to win the support of a majority in his own cabinet, the Prime Minister resigned on August 25, 1931. The next day he formed a so-called National Government composed of representatives of all three parties but including a majority of Conservatives.

MacDonald at the helm again

The National Government thus established continued in office through the worst stages of the depression and finally brought England to a substantial recovery. From 1931 to 1935 it was headed by MacDonald and during the next two years by Baldwin. The policies followed by these men were relatively conservative, but they still represented a considerable departure from well-beaten paths. In September, 1931, gold payments were suspended, as a consequence of foreign withdrawals from the Bank of England at the rate of millions of pounds per day. By this act Great Britain abandoned the gold standard, and most of the other nations of the world soon followed her example. Early in 1932 MacDonald inaugurated a system of protectionism, providing for tariffs as high in some cases as 100 per cent. Beginning in 1933 efforts were made to revive the prosperity of British agriculture. A series of Marketing Acts was passed designed to improve the price levels of agricultural products. The Acts empowered two-thirds of the producers of any commodity to plan the quantity and price of their product. Their plan would then be approved and enacted into law by Parliament. In addition to these various expedients, the National Government

The National Government and its efforts to combat the depression

extended subsidies for shipbuilding and housing, reduced interest rates on public and private loans, and increased the rates and lowered the exemptions for taxes on incomes. By the fiscal year 1935–1936 the budget had been brought into balance. Except for the Marketing Acts, the adoption of protective tariffs, and the abandonment of the gold standard, the majority of the cabinet's policies were entirely in line with orthodox economics. No attempt was made to raise prices by monetary inflation or to stimulate prosperity by deficit spending. Nor was there any effort to keep everybody employed at government expense. The aim was rather to create an atmosphere of stability and confidence which would stimulate the flow of private investment into productive channels.[14] Perhaps a fair measure of the success of these policies is to be found in the fact that unemployment was reduced from 2,400,000 in 1933 to 1,130,000 in July, 1937.[15]

During most of the time from 1918 to 1939, the domestic as well as the foreign policies of France were dictated alternately by two powerful groups. The first was made up of finance capitalists, great bankers, and members of the *Comité des Forges,* as the French association of iron and steel manufacturers was called. They believed in strong government and hated every form of economic radicalism. Their fondest ambition after the war was to unite the coal and coke of the Saar and the Ruhr with the iron of Lorraine; for without the former, the latter is of limited value. They were strong exponents also of the alliances with Poland and with the nations of the Little Entente, perhaps partly because these provided for loans of French money and for contracts to buy French munitions. The other group was composed of petty industrialists and shopkeepers and members of the class of *rentiers,* who lived on the income from small investments. The passionate longing of this group was for security. They did not want their nation to expand; they were not even interested in getting rich; but what they desired above everything else was a chance to hold on to what they had. They disliked big business and looked upon the speculative financier as no less an enemy than the communist.

*Conservatives
and moderates
in France*

From 1918 to 1924 the first of these groups was in power, under the leadership for a time of President Poincaré and Premier Clemenceau.[16] These men and their followers upheld the punitive peace and hoped to make Germany pay the whole cost of the war. As we have seen, it was Poincaré who sent troops into the Ruhr valley in 1923. There is a strong suspicion that his object was not simply to punish Germany for her default on reparations but actually to

*The failures of
both factions*

[14] See William Koren, Jr., "Britain's Economic Recovery," *Foreign Policy Reports,* July 31, 1935.

[15] *League of Nations Monthly Bulletin of Statistics.*

[16] The two men were in office together until 1920, when Poincaré's term as President expired and Clemenceau resigned. From 1922 to 1924 Poincaré was Premier.

annex the district to France. Whatever the purpose, the project was a failure and Poincaré was forced out of office. He was suc- ceeded in 1924 by Édouard Herriot, leader of the Radical Socialists, who represented better than any other party the interests of small business and of the *rentier* class. But the tenure of Herriot and his moderates was brief. The conservatives had impaired the credit of the government by borrowing heavily to pay for the war and for reconstruction of the invaded areas. It was expected that the burden could be shifted to Germany, and when this turned out to be a vain hope, the franc began to decline. When Herriot failed to offer any proposals acceptable to the rich for saving the franc, he was thrown out of office. In 1926 Poincaré returned as Premier and restored the government's credit by ruthless economies. The franc consequently rose until it was worth about a fifth of its prewar value. At this level it was stabilized in 1928.

France was not seriously affected by the Great Depression until long after most other countries were ready to be sold under the hammer. The reason lay in the balanced economic life of the French nation. The population was almost evenly divided between urban and agricultural pursuits. Business was mainly small enterprise, and millions of the people were self-employed. Nevertheless, France was not able to withstand the shock indefinitely. When it finally came in 1932, a period of political chaos ensued. Cabinets followed each other with startling rapidity, and communists and fascists rioted in the streets. At length in 1936 a combination known as the Popular Front succeeded in winning a national election. It was composed of the three parties of the left—Radical Socialists, Socialists, and Communists. Its leader at this time was Léon Blum, a member of the Socialist party and a distinguished intellectual.

France succumbs to the depression

The government of the Popular Front is noted especially for its economic reforms and also for its reorientation of foreign policy. It nationalized the munitions industry and reorganized the Bank of France so as to deprive the 200 largest stockholders of their monop- olistic control over credit. It established a forty-hour week with compulsory annual vacations for all urban workers. It canceled the reductions of government salaries, initiated a program of public works, reorganized the coal industry, and devalued the franc by about 30 per cent. For the benefit of the farmers it established a Wheat Office to fix the price and regulate the distribution of grain. In the sphere of foreign policy it entered into a firm alliance with Great Britain and submitted to British leadership in all European questions. Every one of these accomplishments was the work of Léon Blum, who served as Premier from June, 1936, to June, 1937. His policies were continued in slightly modified form by Camille Chautemps until March, 1938. Soon afterward the regime of the Popular Front came to an end with the accession of Édouard Daladier. Though a Radical Socialist, Daladier showed little interest

The regime of the Popular Front

in economic reform. Contending that more labor was necessary to speed up preparations for national defense, he revoked the forty-hour week. Later, as the international crisis deepened, he obtained the consent of Parliament to govern the country by emergency decrees.

Of all the democracies, none had a history between the wars so varied and climactic as the United States. No one of them rose to dizzier economic heights, and few sank to lower depths. At the end of World War I, America was the richest and most powerful nation in the world. While the states of Europe had been mauling each other on the battlefield, she was capturing their markets, penetrating their fields of investment, and expanding her own industry and agriculture enormously. Whereas, before the war, the United States owed Europe about $3,000,000,000, now she was Europe's creditor to the tune of about $11,000,000,000. All of this made for a golden age of power and prosperity in the United States. True, it was interrupted in 1920–1921 by a sharp depression; but this little unpleasantness was soon over, and the forward march was resumed. From 1922 to 1929 America enjoyed seven of the fattest years in any nation's history. The standard of living of her people was the highest in the world. By 1930 one out of every five of her entire population was the owner of an automobile. There were over 13,000,000 radios in American homes and more telephones than in the rest of the world put together. Fortunately not all of the new wealth was expended for conveniences and luxuries. In 1929, publication of books amounted to 10,200 titles, compared with 5700 in 1919, despite an increase in population of only 16 per cent. Appropriations for public education rose from about $500,000,000 on the eve of World War I to over $2,300,000,000 in 1930.

Yet to a large extent the postwar prosperity of the United States rested upon foundations of sand. It was artificially stimulated in the beginning by the high prices of the war era. Farmers in the mid-West went head over heels into debt to purchase land in the arid regions of western Nebraska, eastern Colorado, and western Oklahoma, in the expectation that wheat would always be selling for more than $2.00 a bushel. When the price dropped to 93 cents in 1923, they found themselves stuck with their mortgages. But farmers were not the only ones who had been tempted into over-expansion by fantastic prices; many more coal mines and factories were opened than were necessary to supply the normal demand. A second weakness in American prosperity was the fact that it was unevenly distributed. The profits of the rich increased by a much higher ratio than the incomes of the masses. While the value of manufactured goods increased by some $10,000,000,000 from 1923 to 1929, wages advanced by only $600,000,000. A third of the flimsy foundations of American prosperity was foreign loans. Because of war profits, many United States citizens in 1919 had a surplus of

The U.S. skims the cream of the world

The flimsy foundations of prosperity in the U.S.

capital to invest. Most of it went for the expansion of domestic industry, but a considerable proportion was shipped abroad. By 1930 American private loans in foreign countries amounted to about $16,000,000,000. Much of this money was not really invested at all, but was used for the purchase of American goods. When the loans were called on account of uncertain conditions in Europe, this market dried up.

In 1929 the great bubble burst. About the middle of September speculators on the New York Stock Exchange began selling their holdings. The market stopped rising, fluctuated uneasily for a time, and then, on October 24, crashed in a wild tumult of selling. Some

The bubble bursts

Stock Market Crash, October 24, 1929. Crowds milling outside the New York Stock Exchange on the day of the big crash.

business and political leaders attempted to reassure the public, but everyone who knew much about the financial history of the country realized that this was the end. The causes of the debacle still defy an absolutely satisfactory explanation, but the underlying ones would appear to be closely related to the impetus given to speculation and to overexpansion by World War I. A second factor, perhaps equally important, was the refusal of most capitalists to pass on a sufficient percentage of the benefits of mass production to the consumers in lower prices, or to the workers in higher wages. A third was the disastrous tariff policy of the United States government, which encouraged retaliatory tariffs elsewhere and almost destroyed international trade. Even as late as 1930 President Hoover, against the advice of more than 1000 economists, signed the Hawley-Smoot bill, which raised the duties on many commodities to the highest levels in the nation's history. The effect of this was undoubtedly to deepen the crisis. Most of the other actions of the Hoover administration to check the economic decline were more commendable. It encouraged the appropriation of large sums for public works. It secured a moratorium on intergovernmental debts and reparations from July 1, 1931, to June 30, 1932. It established a Reconstruction Finance Corporation with authority to lend **873** money to banks and to the railroads, and eventually to the States for public relief. None of these expedients, however, seemed to do much good, and in November, 1932, Hoover was defeated for re-election by the Democratic candidate, Franklin D. Roosevelt.

The New Deal

The Roosevelt administration proceeded to carry out such radical alterations in the United States economic picture that some people considered the results as little short of a revolution. Its leader was interested not merely in rescuing the nation from panic but in effecting a New Deal, which would bring a more abundant life to the mass of "forgotten men." His first objectives, however, were not so much reform as relief and recovery. With the banking system in a state of collapse, with at least 15,000,000 workers unemployed, and with wheat selling at the lowest level since the time of Elizabeth I, there seemed no alternative but to shore up what was left of the economic structure in the hope that the skies would brighten in the not too distant future. The initial efforts in this direction took the form of financial measures. A bank holiday was proclaimed throughout the nation and an embargo placed on the export of gold and silver. Next the hoarding of gold and gold certificates was prohibited, and soon afterward all redemptions of paper money in gold were abandoned. Convinced that a rise in prices was necessary to save the producers of raw commodities from ruin, Roosevelt obtained authority from Congress to inflate the currency by the issuance of $3,000,000,000 of paper money. When this failed he reduced the gold content of the dollar to 59¢. Measures were adopted also to eliminate financial abuses. To prevent recurrent epidemics of bank failures Congress established the Federal Deposit Insurance Corporation to provide insurance of bank deposits up to $5000. Severe restrictions were placed upon the use of bank credit for speculative purposes; commercial banks were ordered to divest themselves of their securities affiliates; and a Securities and Exchange Commission was created to regulate the stock and commodity exchanges, to eliminate pools and other devices for manipulating the markets, and to supervise the issuance of new securities.

*Relief
and recovery;
the NRA*

An equally urgent problem was to provide work for the millions of unemployed. Billions of dollars were appropriated for slum clearance, soil erosion work, reforestation, rural electrification, educational and professional projects, and for the construction of highways, schools, power plants, and hospitals. The foundation for many of these projects was provided for in the National Industrial Recovery Act of 1933. This act was designed not only to spread the work by reducing hours of employment in every industry but also to stimulate business and thereby to create new jobs. It set up a National Recovery Administration (NRA) to assist industrial producers in working out codes which would regulate production, hours of labor, and wages in each of the several industries. Its

874 main objective was to prevent excessive competition and overproduction and thereby to enable the business man to earn a fair profit and to pay high wages. The cardinal assumptions underlying it were that the United States economy had reached a stage of maturity, that the problem of production had been solved, and that the major concern of the future should be a more equitable distribution of purchasing power to the great mass of the citizens. The advent of NRA was hailed with great enthusiasm. Effigies of "Old-Man Depression" were publicly burned, and it is estimated that within a year more than 4,000,000 unemployed were reabsorbed into industry. But in 1935 a unanimous Supreme Court found the National Industrial Recovery Act unconstitutional. The technical ground was the delegation of legislative power to administrative agencies, but it is conceivable that the unfortunate effects of the Act in strengthening monopoly (since it suspended the anti-trust laws) had more than a little to do with the Court's decision.

Relief for the farmer was also considered a capital necessity by the Roosevelt administration. As noted, currency inflation was to be one means of accomplishing this purpose. But the President also *The AAA* believed that agriculture suffered in even greater degree than industry from overproduction. In the spring of 1933, therefore, he induced Congress to pass the Agricultural Adjustment Act. Its most significant provisions authorized the Secretary of Agriculture to enter into compacts with farmers whereby, in return for government subsidies, they would agree to reduce the acreage planted in staple commodities. The acreage of some crops was actually reduced by almost one-third. Prices rose by an even greater proportion, since the revenue for the subsidies was obtained from a processing tax, which the processors passed on to the consumers. The Act also provided for the removal of millions of acres of marginal land from cultivation and for the resettlement of their cultivators on more fertile soil elsewhere. No more than for industry did the Roosevelt administration assume that there was any room for an expansion of agricultural production. It was taken for granted that foreign markets were largely relics of the past, and that agriculture in the United States would have to be conducted henceforth mainly on a basis of self-sufficiency. Only in the State Department, where Cordell Hull was striving to establish closer economic ties between nations by Reciprocal Trade Agreements, was much confidence shown in the possibility of expanding international trade. In 1936 the same Supreme Court which struck down the NIRA declared the AAA unconstitutional. This time the decision was by a vote of 6 to 3. Perhaps for this reason the administration did not humble itself in defeat, but induced Congress to pass a new act which accomplished by different methods the same results as the old.

The theory has been advanced in some quarters that there were really two New Deals—the first extending from 1933 to 1935 and concerned primarily with relief and recovery; and the second from

DICTATORSHIP
AND
DEMOCRACY

*Reform; the
Second New
Deal*

1935 to 1939 devoted chiefly to reform.[17] While no sharp dividing line can actually be drawn, there is a measure of truth in this theory. By 1935 recovery was substantial though by no means complete, and relief had been provided on so lavish a scale that no family needed to fear the wolf at the door. Moreover, enough obstacles had arisen within the government itself to make the necessity of reform appear more urgent. One of the first of the measures designed to effect radical changes was the Wagner Act, guaranteeing the right of collective bargaining in industry and authorizing the majority of the workers in each plant to determine which union should serve as the collective bargaining agency for the whole body of workers. A second was the Wheeler-Rayburn Act establishing Federal regulation of the production and transmission of electric power in interstate commerce, and providing a "death sentence" for all non-integrated holding companies in the public-utility industry. A third was the Social Security Act providing for unemployment insurance, old-age pensions, and benefit payments to the blind, to dependent mothers and children, and to crippled children. A fourth was the Fair Labor Standards Act, abolishing child labor and providing for a minimum hourly wage and a maximum working week of forty hours by 1940. Still another reform measure was developed throughout the first and second New Deals. This was the application of the principle of power production by public authorities in order to achieve a "yardstick" of costs against which the charges of privately owned utility companies could be measured. The original project for this purpose was the Tennessee Valley Authority (TVA) started in 1933. Others included the Grand Coulee Dam in the state of Washington and the Bonneville Dam on the lower Columbia River.

*Results of
the Roosevelt
program*

Few historians would deny that the New Deal was one of the most significant events in the history of modern nations. Since its results were mainly in the direction of preserving rather than destroying capitalism, it can scarcely be called a revolution. Nevertheless, it probably did more for the farmer and the wage earner than any of the so-called revolutions in American history. The incomes of these classes had increased nearly 100 per cent since the depth of the depression. Perhaps more important, they had gained a degree of economic security which they had never known before. On the other hand, a number of crucial problems remained unsolved. The most serious was unemployment. In 1939, after six years of the New Deal, the United States still had more than 9,000,000 jobless workers —a figure which exceeded the combined unemployment of the rest of the world. Why this was so is a question almost impossible to answer. Perhaps it was because the governments of most other industrialized nations had emphasized recovery rather than reform.

[17] Richard Hofstadter, *The American Political Tradition: and the Men Who Made It*, pp. 328–34.

Fontana Dam, TVA. The TVA, established in 1933, for the public production of power was one of the characteristic reform achievements of the New Deal. The dam shown here, located on the Little Tennessee River, is the highest east of the Rocky Mountains.

Perhaps it was due also to the fact that the United States had experienced a much greater expansion in the 1920's than Britain, France, or Germany, and that consequently recovery to the levels of 1929 was more difficult for her than for them.

SELECTED READINGS—FASCIST ITALY

Ebenstein, William, *Fascist Italy*, New York, 1939
Haider, Carmen, *Capital and Labor under Fascism*, New York, 1930
Megaro, Gaudens, *Mussolini in the Making*, New York, 1939
Prezzolini, Giuseppe, *Fascism*, New York, 1927
Schneider, H. W., *Making the Fascist State*, New York, 1928

—NAZI GERMANY

Carr, E. H., *German-Soviet Relations Between the Two World Wars, 1919–1939*, Baltimore, 1951
Clark, R. T., *The Fall of the German Republic*, New York, 1935
deWilde, J. C., *Building the Third Reich*, New York, 1939
Ebenstein, William, *The Nazi State*, New York, 1943
Heiden, Konrad, *Der Fuehrer*, New York, 1944
Hitler, Adolf, *Mein Kampf*, New York, 1939
Neumann, Franz, *Behemoth, The Structure and Practice of National Socialism*, New York, 1942
Pinson, K. S., *Modern Germany: Its History and Civilization*, New York, 1954
Pollock, J. K., and Thomas, Homer, *Germany in Power and Eclipse*, New York, 1952
Roberts, S. H., *The House That Hitler Built*, New York, 1938
Rothfels, H., *The German Opposition to Hitler*, Hinsdale, Ill., 1948

Schuman, F. L., *The Nazi Dictatorship; A Study in Social Pathology*, New York, 1935
Valentin, Veit, *The German People*, New York, 1946

—Soviet Russia

Chamberlin, W. H., *Soviet Russia: A Living Record and a History*, Boston, 1931
Citrine, Sir Walter, *I Search for Truth in Russia*, New York, 1937
Crankshaw, Edward, *Cracks in the Kremlin Wall*, New York, 1951
Curtiss, J. S., *The Russian Revolutions of 1917*, New York, 1957
Dallin, D. J., *Soviet Russia's Foreign Policy, 1939–1942*, New Haven, 1942
——, *Soviet Russia and the Far East*, New Haven, 1948
Deutscher, Isaac, *Stalin; A Political Biography*, London, 1949
Fainsod, Merle, *How Russia Is Ruled*, Cambridge, Mass., 1953
Florinsky, M. T., *Toward an Understanding of the U.S.S.R.*, New York, 1939
Hindus, M. G., *Humanity Uprooted*, New York, 1930
——, *The Great Offensive*, New York, 1933
Lenin, Vladimir, *The State and Revolution*, New York, 1926
Lyashchenko, Peter I., *History of the National Economy of Russia to the 1917 Revolution*, New York, 1949
Pares, Sir Bernard, *A History of Russia*, New York, 1953
Seton-Watson, Hugh, *From Lenin to Malenkov*, New York, 1953
Shub, David, *Lenin*, New York, 1948
Taracouzio, T. A., *War and Peace in Soviet Diplomacy*, New York, 1940
Trotsky, Leon, *The History of the Russian Revolution*, New York, 1932, 3 vols.
Wolfe, B. D., *Three Who Made a Revolution*, New York, 1948

—The Democracies

Beard, C. A., and M. R., *America in Midpassage*, New York, 1939
Brinton, Crane, *The United States and Britain*, Cambridge, Mass., 1945
Brogan, D. W., *France Under the Third Republic*, New York, 1940
Burns, J. M., *Roosevelt: The Lion and the Fox*, New York, 1956
Clarke, C. F. O., *Britain Today: A Review of Current Political and Social Trends*, Cambridge, Mass., 1951
Friedel, Frank, *Franklin D. Roosevelt: The Triumph*, Boston, 1956
Fusfield, D. R., *The Economic Thought of Franklin D. Roosevelt and the Origins of the New Deal*, New York, 1956
Guérard, Albert, *France, a Short History*, New York, 1946
Hacker, L. M., *American Problems of Today*, New York, 1938
Hayes, C. J. H., *France: a Nation of Patriots*, New York, 1930
Heaton, Herbert, *The British Way to Recovery*, Minneapolis, 1934
Hill, Helen D., *The Spirit of Modern France*, New York, 1934
Hirst, F. W., *The Consequences of the War to Great Britain*, New Haven, 1934

Hofstadter, Richard, *The American Political Tradition: and the Men*
  Who Made It, New York, 1948
Jackson, J. H., *The Post-War World*, Boston, 1939
Marriot, J. A. R., *Modern England, 1885–1932*, London, 1934
Mitchell, Broadus, *Depression Decade; from New Era through New Deal,*
  1929 to 1941, New York, 1947
Mowat, C. L., *Britain between the Wars, 1918–1940*, Chicago, 1955
Nevins, Allen, *The United States in a Chaotic World*, New Haven, 1950
Roosevelt, F. D., *On Our Way*, New York, 1934
Siegfried, André, *France; a Study in Nationality*, New Haven, 1930
Spitz, David, *Patterns of Anti-Democratic Thought*, New York, 1949
Wecter, Dixon, *The Age of the Great Depression, 1929–1941*, New York,
  1948
Wolfers, Arnold, *Britain and France between Two Wars*, New York,
  1940

SOURCE MATERIALS

Columbia University, *Introduction to Contemporary Civilization in the
  West*, Vol. II, pp. 1062–66, 1077–86, Soviet Constitution of 1936 and
  Weimar Constitution
Hitler, Adolf, *Mein Kampf*, especially Vol. I, Chs. II, IV, XI; Vol. II,
  Chs. II, XIII, XIV
Lenin, Vladimir, *The State and Revolution*
Rocco, Alfredo, *The Political Doctrine of Fascism*
Roosevelt, F. D., *On Our Way*
——, *Public Papers*
Stalin, Joseph, *Leninism*, 2 vols.
——, *Problems of Leninism*
Trotsky, Leon, *History of the Russian Revolution*, 3 vols.

The Return to International Anarchy

The disappointing results of victory and prosperity

Neither the victory of the Allies in 1918 nor the fevered prosperity of the 1920's brought peace and freedom to an agonized world. Perhaps, in the final analysis, both were obstacles to any such desirable results. The Allies did not heed the lessons of the terrible ordeal from which they had emerged victorious. By succumbing to temptations of power and greed they threw their victory away. The prosperity of the 1920's rested upon such freakish foundations and was so badly distributed that economic catastrophe was almost inevitable. By 1939 modern civilization was confronting another great test of its ability to survive in the race with disaster.

1. The Failure of the Wilsonian Peace

Why the peace failed

After a tragically brief interval of less than two decades, the peace which had been concluded in 1919–1920 lay in ruins. It had turned out to be only an armistice, and again the world was marching rapidly down the highroad to war. The causes of the collapse of the peace are now reasonably clear. To begin with, some provisions of the treaties were unnecessarily harsh or, at least, extremely unwise. The makers of the treaties paid little regard to the Fourteen Points or to other pledges which had led the Germans to believe that the peace would have a unique foundation of justice and liberality. The reparations settlement was in flat violation of the pre-Armistice agreement of November 5, 1918, in which it was clearly stated that Germany was to pay compensation only for "damage done to the civilian population of the Allies and their property." Article 231 of the Treaty of Versailles, which held Germany and her allies solely guilty of causing the war, was historically inaccurate and psychologically unsound. Because the Germans were forced to admit their guilt, it became a point of honor with them to rebel against the accusation and to seek vengeance against those who made it. Equally serious was the mistake of the statesmen at the Paris Conference in treating both Germany and Russia as outcast nations. It would have been bad enough to have made one of them a pariah, but to relegate both to that category was to court disaster. Misery loves company among nations as well as among individuals. Consequently, the two countries began to solicit each other's favor as early as 1922 when they signed the Treaty of Rapallo granting each other diplomatic recognition, establishing trade relations, and canceling prewar debts and claims. Even the accession of Hitler did not destroy for some months the friendly regard of the Russian government for Germany.

As we look back upon it now with the wisdom of hindsight, it appears that there was something in the very nature of the Wilsonian peace which practically doomed it to failure. The treaties of 1919–1920 were obsolete in many respects before the ink of the signatures had dried. Essentially, they were treaties which attempted to provide a nineteenth-century solution for a twentieth-century problem. In accordance with the doctrine of the self-determination of peoples, they split Europe into an even larger number of independent political units than had existed in 1914. The result was to encourage bickerings, rivalries, and trade and armaments competition on a greater scale than ever. What Europe needed in 1919 was not a larger number of competing and potentially hostile states but some program for greater unity. Steps at least should have been taken to prevent tariff wars and a mad striving for self-sufficiency which could have no other effect than a drastic impairment of standards of living. It was a fatal defect of the treaties that the solution of economic problems was so largely ignored.

Other causes of the failure

But even if the Wilsonian peace had approached perfection, it might still have failed eventually. The logic of such a conclusion is to be found in the fact that the two powers most strongly committed to upholding it could not agree as to the policies they should follow. The British had one idea, the French something altogether different. About all they were united upon was the desirability of keeping Bolshevism from spreading. Obsessed with a fear that Germany might recover her strength and seek revenge for her defeat, the French were determined upon rigid fulfillment of the terms of the treaties. They were more interested in the security of their own nation than they were in the economic recovery of Europe. To achieve that security they were not content to rely exclusively upon the League of Nations. They attempted to supplement the security offered by the League with a new system of alliances designed to encircle the defeated nations with a band of steel. Between 1919 and

The disagreement of Britain and France

1927 France entered into partnerships with Belgium, Poland, and the members of the Little Entente (Czechoslovakia, Yugoslavia, and Rumania). The governments of all of these countries were encouraged to maintain large armies, to borrow money from France, and to keep careful watch upon the activities of Germany and her former satellites.

The conflict of policies

The policy of Britain with respect to maintaining the peace in these fateful years was almost the opposite of that of France. Separated from the rest of Europe by the English Channel, the British felt that they did not have to worry so much about national security. Moreover, as a trading nation they were vitally interested in the economic recovery of Europe. Germany, in fact, had been one of Britain's best customers before the war. Consequently, as unemployment increased in the industrial areas of the United Kingdom, the British government turned more and more toward a policy of reconciliation with the former enemy. Reparations payments were to be reduced or deferred and perhaps ultimately canceled in order that Germany might recover and once again provide an excellent market for British exports. Britain was interested also in reviving the old system of the balance of power. Germany must therefore be made strong in order to curb the ambitions of France as well as to provide a bulwark against the rising tide of communism. The conflict between British and French policies was dramatically illustrated in 1923 when Premier Poincaré sent a French army to occupy the Ruhr valley as a punishment for a German default on reparations. The British refused to support the move, and the result was dissolution of the Entente Cordiale. Britain and France did not again become allies until 1936.

The refusal of the U.S. to ratify the treaty

Some authorities on recent history emphasize the refusal of the United States to ratify the Treaty of Versailles as a cause of the failure of the peace. It is alleged that in rejecting the treaty the United States Senate betrayed the cause of internationalism and turned back the clock of progress for a hundred years. Although such a conclusion is undoubtedly too sweeping, it is possible to argue that America's adoption of an isolationist policy encouraged the revival of power politics in Europe. If the United States had accepted the treaty and had joined the League of Nations, Britain and France might have been inspired to place more confidence in the League, and perhaps would have been less inclined to turn to old-fashioned, balance-of-power methods of preserving peace. France, in particular, might not have been so adamant in her determination to keep Germany in a state of helpless subjection. Less preoccupied with her own security, she might have been able to take more interest in healing the wounds of Europe.

The reasons why the United States rejected the treaty her own President had negotiated are not always clearly perceived. Many

882 people believe that it was exclusively the work of die-hard reac-

League of Nations Buildings, Geneva, Switzerland. Since the dissolution of the League in 1946, its main building has been occupied by the International Labor Office.

tionaries and incorrigible nationalists. But senators as progressive as Robert M. LaFollette and George W. Norris voted against ratification, while periodicals as internationally minded as *The Nation* and *The New Republic* condemned the treaty. They condemned it, of course, not because of its internationalism, but because they regarded it as unjust and a breeder of new and more terrible wars in the future. There was a general reaction throughout the country against both the war and the peace. The feeling spread that Uncle Sam had got his fingers burned. He had entered the war for noble and idealistic reasons. European nations, however, had shown that they were unable to free themselves from their old habits of carving up their neighbors' territory, making secret bargains, and stabbing each other in the back. It would be better that Uncle Sam should wash his hands of the whole business and have nothing to do with such unregenerate people in the future.

Why the U.S. rejected the treaty

But this does not exhaust the list of causes. To a large extent partisan politics played a role in the rejection of the treaty. In October, 1918, President Wilson had made the mistake of appealing to the American people to confirm his policies by choosing a Democratic Congress in the coming election. Although a later analysis revealed that a majority of the people in the nation as a whole did vote Democratic, the votes were so distributed that the Republicans captured control of both the Senate and the House. As a result, certain Republican leaders denied that Wilson had any right henceforth to speak in the name of the nation. Even so, the treaty might still have been ratified, had not the President suffered a complete breakdown while on a speaking tour across the country. For nearly eight months he did not meet his Cabinet, and only the most important documents were submitted to him. Although his illness was really of the nature of a paralytic stroke, rumors spread that he was insane. Unfortunately, he refused to delegate leadership of the fight for the treaty to anyone else. As a consequence, the campaign was

Congressional opposition and Wilson's illness

883

delayed, and the opposition strengthened its forces. Yet another factor that worked to defeat the treaty was Wilson's refusal to accept reservations to the League Covenant, beyond the few already made before the treaty of which it was a part had been signed. When the final vote was taken in March, 1920, forty-nine Senators voted *in favor* of ratification with reservations and thirty-five against. Since the affirmative votes were less than the two-thirds majority required for approval, the treaty was rejected. Wilson, however, was in a difficult position. He argued that if he accepted further reservations, he would have to return to Paris to get the approval of the remaining signatories; and, since other nations would almost certainly demand reservations of their own, the whole task of negotiating the treaties would have to be done over again.

2. Efforts to Save the Peace

*The Locarno
Agreements*

During the 1920's several attempts were made to save the peace, which did not yet appear hopelessly lost. The first of importance were the Locarno Agreements. In 1925 the statesmen of Europe acted on the suggestion of the German Foreign Minister, Gustav Stresemann, that Germany and France pledge themselves to respect the Rhine frontiers as established in the Versailles Treaty. The outcome was a series of new treaties negotiated in October, 1925, by delegates from Germany, France, Belgium, Great Britain, Italy, Poland, and Czechoslovakia. The first three nations agreed that they would forever respect their mutual frontiers and would never go to war against each other except in "legitimate defense." Great Britain and Italy signed as guarantors of this agreement. Germany pledged that she would never attempt to revise a treaty by force of arms, and that she would settle by peaceful means all future disputes with France, Belgium, Czechoslovakia, and Poland. The Locarno Agreements were widely acclaimed as the heralds of a new era. Statesmen and journalists poured out effusions of praise for the "spirit of Locarno" as if it were a patent medicine which would quickly cure all the ills of Europe. The French were desirous of creating the impression that Germany had at last acknowledged the justice of the peace settlement, and that she would never attempt to revise it. But this did not square with all of the facts. Germany made no commitment to abide by the arrangement of her eastern frontiers, with which she was actually more dissatisfied than with the settlement in the west. Further, she pledged herself to a peaceful solution of future problems only. About all that the Locarno Agreements did was to safeguard temporarily the Rhine frontiers. That, to be sure, was an achievement of definite value, but it did not eliminate the danger of a new European war.

Similar in purpose and in results to the Locarno Agreements was the celebrated Pact of Paris, or Briand-Kellogg Pact. The origins of this pact grew out of an American movement for the outlawry of war, founded about 1925. Influential leaders were S. O. Levinson, a Chicago lawyer, Dr. C. C. Morrison, editor of the *Christian Century*, and Senator William E. Borah, of Idaho. They believed that the best way to abolish war would be to induce as many nations as possible to outlaw it as something criminal and sinful. In the spring of 1927 Professor James T. Shotwell of Columbia University conveyed some of these ideas to Foreign Minister Briand of France. Soon afterward Briand issued an appeal to the American people

Signing of Kellogg-Briand Pact (Pact of Paris), 1928. In the center, about to affix his signature, is Aris- tide Briand, Foreign Minister of France.

recommending that the United States and France join in an agreement mutually renouncing war. Three weeks later President Nicholas Murray Butler of Columbia University wrote a letter to the *New York Times* challenging the United States government to act on the French proposal. The result was an avalanche of American opinion favoring not merely Briand's suggestion but a broader program for renunciation of war by all nations. Nearly every peace organization lent its support, and the government was deluged with petitions bearing two million signatures. The pressure became so strong that Secretary of State Frank B. Kellogg was forced to take action. Late in 1927 he sent a note to Paris recommending that France and the United States invite all nations to adhere to a pact condemning war. In August, 1928, the representatives of fifteen nations assembled in Paris and affixed their signatures to a pact renouncing war as "an instrument of national policy" and providing that the settlement of international disputes "of whatever nature or of whatever origin" should never be sought "except by pacific means." Within a comparatively short time nearly all of the countries of the world had announced their adherence to this agreement.

Regrettably, however, the Pact of Paris was little more than a pious gesture. If its provisions could have been taken at their face value, it would have given the nations the security they demanded, and it would have brought the ideal of a warless world close to reality. But the circumstances under which it was adopted made such results impossible. With the approval of Secretary Kellogg, the Foreign Relations Committee of the United States Senate issued an interpretation declaring that nothing in the treaty impaired the right of the United States to wage war in self-defense. The British Government asserted full liberty of action in certain regions in which they insisted Britain had vital interests essential to her "peace and safety." Since other powers made similar interpretations, the effect was to reduce the Pact to meaningless generalities. There is hardly a war conceivable which both sides would not seek to justify as an action in self-defense or for the protection of vital interests.

3. *The Failure of Disarmament*

Another development which hastened the return to international anarchy was the failure of disarmament. This failure came as a shock to the generation which had fought for a lasting peace during World War I. It had been generally assumed that one of the essential ingredients of such a peace would be a drastic reduction of armaments. President Wilson gave expression to this sentiment in Point Four of the Fourteen Points, which called for arms limitation to the lowest minimum consistent with domestic safety. The Peace Conference declined to accept this proposal as stated, deciding instead to incorporate in the Covenant of the League of Nations a declaration that the members of the League recognized the desirability of reducing armaments to the lowest point "consistent with national safety and the enforcement by common action of international obligations." The Council of the League was given the responsibility of formulating plans for such reduction.

The first moves toward arms limitation after World War I were not initiated by the League of Nations but by the United States government. The reasons were based largely upon self-interest. The war had left Japan the strongest naval power in the Far East. With Russia and Germany temporarily crippled, there were no counterweights left against Nipponese aggrandizement. China was almost at Japan's mercy, and United States interests might well be threatened. Unless the United States should build a huge navy to operate off the coast of Asia, there would be no possibility of restoring the balance of power in the Far East. But the United States government was reluctant to incur the expense of such naval expansion. Accordingly, in 1921, President Warren G. Harding issued an invitation to a conference on naval disarmament and the Far East to be held in Washington. Nine nations sent delegates—the United States, Great Britain, France, Italy, Japan, China, the Netherlands, Belgium, and Portugal. The conference assembled in November, 1921, and completed its work in February of the following year.

THE FAILURE OF DISARMAMENT

On the surface, at least, the Washington Naval Conference was an outstanding success. It established a maximum tonnage for battleships and heavy cruisers and fixed a ratio in such vessels of 5:5:3 for Great Britain, the United States, and Japan, respectively. In addition, no new construction of capital ships was to be allowed for a period of ten years. The delegates also agreed to the conclusion of certain treaties for the protection of their interests in the Far East. One was a Four-Power Treaty by which the United States, Britain, France, and Japan pledged themselves to respect each other's insular possessions in the Pacific. The other was a Nine-Power Treaty by which all of the nations represented at the conference agreed to respect the independence and territorial integrity of China and to observe the principle of the Open Door. On the other hand, the conference did nothing to limit competition in other than capital ships. Largely on account of opposition from France, the ratios for battleships and heavy cruisers were not applied to light cruisers, destroyers, submarines, or other craft. Comprehensive naval limitation was a much more difficult problem than reducing the number of such fighting craft as battleships, whose value under conditions of modern warfare many experts were beginning to doubt.

The limited achievements of the Washington Conference

In the years that followed, some further attempts were made to limit naval armaments by direct agreement among nations, but with little result. A conference called at Geneva in 1927 was a total failure, because Italy and France refused to send delegates, and because Britain and the United States were unable to agree on the types of armaments that should be limited. At the London Conference of 1930 the tactics of Italy, France, Japan, and the United States produced such an atmosphere of distrust that several of the powers inserted "escalator" clauses in the agreements they signed which permitted them to raise their tonnage in case some other power threatened to exceed the limits agreed to.

The London Conference of 1930

The most tragic of all the disarmament conferences was the one which assembled at Geneva in February, 1932. This conference differed from its predecessors in two respects. First, it was held under the auspices of the League of Nations. Secondly, its purpose was not merely naval disarmament but reduction of weapons of every category. Delegates from sixty-one countries attended the conference, and more than 300 different proposals were submitted for consideration. The French delegation proposed that all bombing aircraft be turned over to the League of Nations, and that other "offensive" weapons be placed at the League's disposal. The British recommended that "offensive" weapons be abolished. On behalf of

The Geneva Conference of 1932–1934

President Hoover, the United States delegates proposed the abolition of all bombing planes, large mobile guns, and weapons of chemical warfare and a one-third reduction of all existing land forces in excess of 100,000 men. Maxim Litvinov, representing the Soviet Union, demanded total destruction of all weapons, insisting that "the way to disarm is to disarm." But not a single one of these recommendations could attract the support of more than a handful of delegates. Finally, when it became clear that Germany would be satisfied with nothing less than arms equality with her former enemies, negotiations collapsed.

*Failure of the
Geneva Con-
ference*

The Geneva Conference never officially disbanded. Instead, the delegations straggled homeward as hopes of a settlement faded and vanished. In October, 1933, the German delegates withdrew. A few feeble efforts were made to induce them to return; but in vain, for the Nazi Revolution of the preceding March had brought into power in Berlin a regime that was interested not in disarmament but in *rearmament*. By the summer of 1934 the conference had come to a full stop. The Nazi military budget, announced in April, seemed to many to be an evil portent of Germany's determination to flout all the arms restrictions of the Versailles Treaty. Talk of a preventive war spread through France. A few years later nearly all the powers were engaged in an armaments race which surpassed anything Europe had seen since 1918.

4. The Failure of Economic Recovery

*The depression
of 1929*

Aside from the failure of disarmament, perhaps nothing contributed more to international anarchy between the two wars than the failure of the world to recover from the Great Depression. Recovery from the depressions of the nineteenth and early twentieth centuries had been almost automatic. Sometimes an increase in the supply of gold, due to the discovery of new deposits, had helped, but no tinkering with currencies or government spending for public works had been regarded as necessary. Moreover, when business decline had run its course and recovery had set in, it was invariably found that production had mounted to new levels higher than any previously attained. But the depression which started in 1929 was different. The deflationary spiral seemed almost endless. Governments resorted to drastic expedients to halt the decline. Embargoes were placed on the redemption of paper money in gold. Imports were all but prohibited. To provide employment and stimulate business huge amounts were appropriated in some countries for construction of roads, bridges, dams, sewers, airports, and fortresses. When budgets became badly unbalanced, special measures were sometimes devised to conceal from the people the terrifying size of the national debt.

But none of these expedients seemed to do much good. Though a

Hunger Marchers Advance on Washington, 1931. Hunger marches and bread lines were familiar scenes during the mournful years of the depression. The photograph shows a delegation of jobless workers marching to the Capitol to present a demand for unemployment insurance.

partial recovery did set in about 1935, it never went far enough, prior to the outbreak of World War II, to restore the high levels of 1929. The reason is not easy to discover, but the depression of the 1930's was unique in several respects. Markets destroyed or lost during World War I had never been fully regained. On account of war and revolution, the world was still full of danger areas where the threat of explosive incidents kept the nerves of entire continents on edge. The collection of reparations and war debts disorganized national currencies and upset the distribution of the world's gold. Two-thirds of it eventually became concentrated in the United States, and a large part of the remainder in France. Most serious of all, economic nationalism with its high tariffs, import quotas, exchange controls, and barter agreements made the recovery of international trade virtually impossible. By 1933 it had declined in value to barely one-fourth of the pre-depression figure. In 1918 President Wilson had proclaimed as one of the objectives of the peace the removal of economic barriers and the establishment of an equality of trade conditions among the nations of the world. Fifteen years later economic barriers were higher than ever, and equality of trade conditions seemed like a Utopian dream.

The failure of expedients for recovery

As early as the fall of 1931 the situation of the industrialized world was becoming desperate. In May of that year the Creditanstalt, the largest and most reputable banking firm in Vienna, was found to be insolvent. Soon afterward the great Darmstädter Bank in Germany closed its doors. The Berlin Stock Exchange suspended operations, and dozens of German business firms went into bankruptcy. Panic spread through central and western Europe and quickly reached the British Isles. By the middle of September the Bank of England was losing gold at the rate of about £18,000,000 a day. All over the world nations began battening down the hatches against what they feared would be even more violent storms in the

The storm breaks

889

future. On September 21, as was previously stated, the British government prohibited the redemption of paper currency in gold. By the end of 1936 not a state in the world had a freely convertible gold basis for its currency. Governments did not stop with abolishing the gold standard, but adopted every ingenious device they could think of to make their own countries secure against troubles from without. France and Belgium, for example, put most of their imports on a quota basis. In 1932 Great Britain abandoned her time-honored policy of free trade and made attempts to weld her empire into a close economic union by a system of imperial preference tariffs. Japan and Italy sought to carve out empires for themselves by the sword, the former in Manchuria and northern China and the latter in Ethiopia. In both cases the motives were largely to gain control of economic resources and thereby reduce the dependence of the home countries upon foreign supplies.

*Efforts to
prevent chaos*

It is necessary to add that some steps were taken during the 1930's to avert the utter chaos which was bound to result from the attempts of each nation to solve its own problems at others' expense. On June 21, 1931, President Hoover proposed a one-year moratorium on all intergovernmental payments, including debts and reparations. Unfortunately France showed little enthusiasm for the scheme, and it was not until July 6 that arrangements were completed. By that time Germany was on the verge of a banking crisis which destroyed any beneficent results the moratorium might have had. In June and July, 1932, representatives of Britain, France, Belgium, Italy, Germany, and Japan met at Lausanne, Switzerland, and concluded an agreement which practically abolished reparations. Again it was an action too long delayed. If it had been taken at least two years earlier, it might have prevented a financial crisis in central Europe. Administered when Germany was in a state of near-collapse, and when the Nazi wolves were howling at the gates, its results were nil.

*The World
Economic
Conference of
1933*

The last of the efforts to bring some semblance of economic order out of chaos was the convoking of the World Economic Conference, which met in London in June and July, 1933. The initiative came partly from the League of Nations and partly from Ramsay MacDonald, Prime Minister of Great Britain, who had a sublime faith in the efficacy of conferences to cure the world's ills. Delegates from sixty-six nations, including all the Great Powers, attended. It was generally understood, in Europe at least, that three major subjects would constitute the program for discussion. The first would be intergovernmental debts; the second, tariffs; and the third, stabilization of currencies. Concerning the last, however, there was no basis of agreement. France, the leader of the countries still on gold, urged the restoration of the international gold standard. Britain advocated immediate stabilization of currencies in terms of each other, with an ultimate restoration of the gold standard. The

position of the United States, for a time, was obscure. As late as
May 16, President Roosevelt made a public declaration in favor of
stabilization. But an attempt soon afterward of British and American experts to freeze the value of the pound and the dollar at current levels was followed by a break in United States stock and commodity prices. Mr. Roosevelt then seems to have changed his mind.
Fearful that his entire program for an inflationary boost of prices
in the United States would be jeopardized, he addressed a sharp
rebuke to the London Conference. He declared that the United
States government's effort to raise prices was the "most important
contribution" it could make. "The sound internal economic system
of a nation," he asserted, "is a greater factor in its well-being than
the price of its currency in changing terms of the currencies of
other nations." This message threw a dash of cold water on the
hopes of the conference. On July 27, it adjourned without a solid
achievement to its credit. The nations were now free to follow
whatever currency and tariff policies they pleased. But freedom
with respect to such matters was another name for economic
anarchy.

5. The Road to Munich

Historians of the future will probably look back upon the 1930's
as one of the most critical periods in world history. During this
period most of the powers adopted profound changes of foreign
policy which produced havoc on the international scene and led to
the bitter ordeal of the 1940's. The disgruntled powers resorted to
policies of "dynamism," which meant blustering or bullying or outright aggression. The satisfied powers abandoned the program of
collective security, which had been built upon support of the
League of Nations, and substituted for it the disgraceful policy of
"appeasement." Appeasement may be defined as a policy of granting concessions to an aggressive and unscrupulous nation from motives of fear or indolence. Invariably, the concessions are made at
the expense of some weaker country. The appeaser himself sacrifices nothing; in fact, his usual motive for action is the desire to
avoid having to give up anything of value. Appeasement had occasionally been used before the 1930's. It was employed in 1913
when Britain and Germany supported Austria in browbeating
Serbia into relinquishing her claims to Albania. It was resorted to
again in 1919 when President Wilson allowed Japan to keep the
former German concessions in China for fear that Japanese nationalists would reject the League of Nations. Appeasement should
be distinguished clearly from a policy of conciliation. The latter
represents an attempt to placate an enemy by acts of benevolence
and justice. Though appeasement may be benevolent from the
standpoint of the beneficiary, it has nothing to do with justice.

*The turn
to appeasement*

891

*The appease-
ment of Japan
in the Manchu-
rian crisis*

The first notable example of appeasement between the two wars occurred in connection with the Manchurian crisis. For years Japan had coveted the rich province of Manchuria, technically a part of China, for its deposits of oil shale, coal, and iron and for its fertile soil adapted to the production of soybeans and wheat. In 1931 she determined to strike. A pretext was found in the Mukden Incident of September 18, involving an explosion on the South Manchurian Railroad owned by Japanese capitalists. Responsibility for the deed has not been fixed to this day, but the Japanese immediately accused Chinese soldiers. Though the damage inflicted was trifling—about 30 inches of track destroyed—Japanese officers in Manchuria set their whole military machine in motion. Mukden was captured after a brief battle and a large portion of the province was soon occupied. The Chinese government appealed to the League of Nations, and the result was the appointment of an investigating commission headed by Lord Lytton, a former Viceroy of India. The commission proceeded at a leisurely pace in completing its task. Five months passed before it reached the Far East, and six more months were consumed in collecting evidence. By the itme it published its report, mildly condemning the aggression, Japan was not only firmly entrenched in Manchuria but had annexed additional portions of northeastern China.

None of the powers except the United States took any steps to restrain or punish Japan. And the United States government confined its action to issuance of the Stimson Doctrine declaring that the United States would refuse to recognize any situation in the Far East brought about in violation of the Briand-Kellogg Pact. No military or economic penalties were proposed, and probably none would have been considered. The prevailing attitude of the other powers was indifference. The British Foreign Office at this time was directed by Sir John Simon, a right-wing Liberal, who had never shown much interest in collective security. Some of the Conservative politicians hoped to revive the Anglo-Japanese Alliance which had been terminated under Canadian and United States pressure in 1922. Fearful of Russia and distrustful of the Chinese, they dreamed of using Japan as a counterweight against both. Moreover, any punitive action against Japan would almost certainly involve retaliation against Britain's extensive interests in the Far East. But probably the chief reason for British indifference was the financial crisis in their own country. In September, 1931, Britain entered the most serious stage of the depression. On September 21, just three days after the Mukden Incident, she was compelled to abandon the gold standard. Weighted down by anxiety for the future, her citizens were in no mood to take on additional troubles outside the Empire. France at this time was deeply absorbed in maintaining her own security. Worried over German demands for armament equality, she was even less inclined than Britain to assume international responsibilities in distant regions.

No further instances of flagrant appeasement occurred until 1935. In the fall of that year Benito Mussolini sent an army to invade Ethiopia. The Ethiopian king appealed to the Council of the League of Nations, which was fortunately in session. With promptness unusual under the circumstances, the Council branded Italy as an aggressor and decided to apply economic sanctions against her. These were to include an arms embargo and the prohibition of loans and the sale of certain commodities to the Italian nation. Britain and France now became thoroughly alarmed. Convinced that the United States would not co-operate, they feared that the effort to punish Italy would fail, and that they would then have incurred Italian enmity for nothing. France, especially, was concerned lest Italy be lost as a potential ally in case of trouble with Germany. Accordingly, the statesmen of London and Paris saw to it that economic sanctions did not include prohibition of the sale of oil and oil products. This was almost the equivalent of guaranteeing a victory for Italy, since her armies were partly mechanized, while those of her opponent had only primitive equipment. But still the generosity of British and French politicians was not exhausted. Late in 1935 Sir Samuel Hoare, British Foreign Secretary, and Pierre Laval, Premier of France, agreed secretly to a plan whereby Mussolini would be permitted to keep two-thirds of Ethiopia in return for giving that unhappy country a narrow corridor to the Red Sea. Though the plan never went into effect, because of an outburst of public wrath in Britain and France against it, further efforts to curb or punish Italy were quietly abandoned. In May, 1936, Mussolini completed his conquest of the Lion of Judah and proclaimed the establishment of the Italian Empire.

Mussolini attacks and conquers Ethiopia

With Mussolini so successful in flouting the regime of international law and order, it could be expected that Hitler would take a turn at winning victories by bold defiance. He began by tearing up the disarmament provisions of the Treaty of Versailles. In 1935 he publicly announced the revival of conscription and the return to universal military training. By threatening the creation of a huge air force he hoodwinked the British into signing a naval agreement permitting Germany to build war vessels up to 35 per cent of the strength of Britain's navy. By the end of 1936 he had a conscript army of over 800,000 men and 108 naval vessels already built or under construction. His next most important step of defiance was to send troops into the Rhineland in March, 1936, to occupy the area demilitarized by the Treaty of Versailles. By so doing he violated not only the Versailles Treaty but the Locarno Agreements as well. As a pretext for this move he alleged that the recently negotiated Franco-Soviet alliance had destroyed the validity of the Locarno

The German rearmament and remilitarization of the Rhineland

893

treaties. Despite the strong legal case against him, Great Britain and France did virtually nothing to prevent him from achieving his aims. The French protested vigorously, but the British refused to get excited. And without British help, France could not act, since she was almost paralyzed at home by strikes and class warfare.

Appeasement of the dictators in the Rhineland and in Ethiopia practically liquidated all that was left of collective security.

The end of collective security

Though the League made a bold display of courage in branding Italy as an aggressor against Ethiopia, this was due chiefly to the pressure of public opinion and to the influence of the smaller nations. The attitude of those governments which would have to provide the economic, military, and naval power to back up the decisions of the League was lukewarm and half-hearted. After the remilitarization of the Rhineland, even the smaller nations became discouraged over the breakdown of collective efforts to maintain the peace. Switzerland and the Scandinavian states announced that in the future they would decline to be committed automatically under the League system of applying sanctions against an aggressor. Belgium persuaded Britain and France to allow her to withdraw from all her obligations under the Locarno Agreements in order to make possible a return to her traditional position of neutrality. Canada, also, was seeking to restrain Britain from taking on commitments which might involve the Empire in war. Both inside and outside the League, nations were developing a primary concern for their own safety, as fear of a new holocaust gripped the hearts of rulers and peoples.

Until 1936 there was little evidence of collaboration between the dictators in defying the satisfied powers. Indeed, as late as April,

The civil war in Spain

1935, Mussolini had united with Great Britain and France in the so-called Stresa Front pledging support of Austrian independence and the Locarno treaties and denouncing German rearmament. But the outbreak of civil war in Spain in the summer of 1936 changed the whole picture. For more than a century Spain had been divided into hostile groups of reactionaries, monarchists, and clericals on the one side and bourgeois liberals, anti-clericals, and socialists on the other. In 1931 a bloodless revolution had resulted in the establishment of a republic and in the enactment of some drastic legislation against the army, the great landlords, and the church. In July, 1936, counterrevolution broke out under the leadership of disaffected generals and with secret encouragement from the fascist rulers of Italy and Germany. Each of these dictators had a direct interest in the outcome. Mussolini saw a chance to gain control of the Balearic Islands and to twist the British lion's tail at Gibraltar. Domination of Spain and the western Mediterranean would also enable him to cut France's line of communications with her north African empire. Hitler's stakes in a victory for the Spanish rebels were just as high. He could weaken the position of France by establishing an-

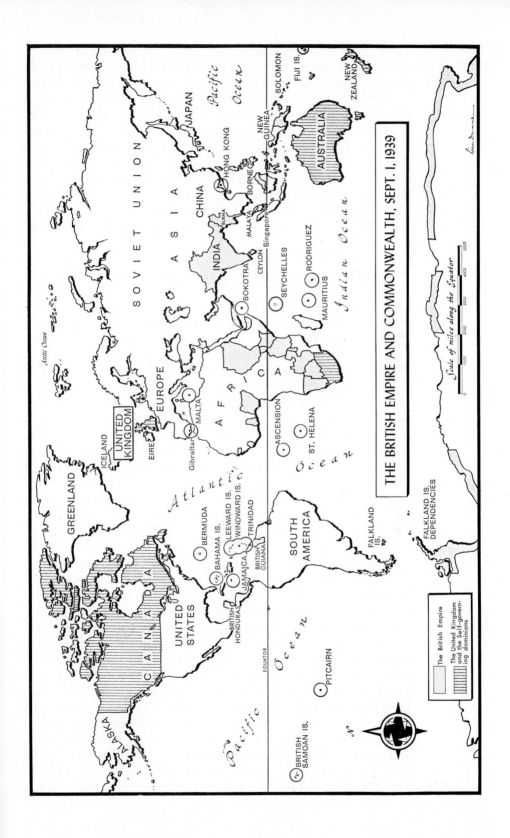

THE BRITISH EMPIRE AND COMMONWEALTH, SEPT. 1, 1939

The British Empire

The United Kingdom
and the Self-govern-
ing dominions

Scale of miles along the Equator

*Again appease-
ment*

*The back-
ground of crisis
in Czechoslo-
vakia*

other fascist state on her borders. He could gain access to the copper and iron resources of the Bilbao region, and he could use Spain
as a proving ground for some of his new weapons. With these ends
in view, the dictators began a period of close collaboration which
continued until the fall of Mussolini in World War II. In October,
1936, they announced the formation of the Rome-Berlin Axis, and
the following year Mussolini signed the Anti-Comintern Pact, to
which Germany and Japan were already parties.

The Spanish civil war raged through three bloody years, and cost
the lives of almost 1,000,000 men. Throughout it had aspects of an
international struggle, since Soviet Russia gave money, weapons,
and technical assistance to the Republicans, or Loyalists, while Germany and Italy provided more generous aid for General Franco's
Insurgents. The war led to further appeasement on the part of the
democratic powers. Seized with fear lest the Spanish civil strife
expand into a world conflict, Britain and France sponsored a policy
of nonintervention. They hoped that all interested powers would
co-operate, but when this failed, they closed their eyes to the active
intervention of Germany and Italy. Fear of a new world war was
not, however, their only motive. British conservatives were suspicious of the radicalism of some of the Loyalists and fearful that
Russia might gain a predominant influence in Spanish affairs. The
attitude of France was determined by a complexity of factors.
Premier Blum, at the head of a Popular Front government, undoubtedly would have preferred a victory for the Loyalists. But he
was not a free agent. He had been swept into power on a platform
of social and economic reforms. To achieve these, it was necessary
not to antagonize the Right too bitterly. Besides, he needed the support of Great Britain against the constant threat from across the
Rhine. In April, 1939, nearly all the powers, including the United
States, accorded diplomatic recognition to the Franco government
set up by the victorious Insurgents.

Even before the Spanish struggle had come to its lamentable end,
the appeasement policy had reached its climax in a different area of
Europe. For years Hitler and his Nazis had been casting greedy and
venomous glances toward Czechoslovakia. They denounced that
state as a dagger pointing at the heart of Germany, but they also
coveted its industries and its mountain bastion controlling a pathway to the East. In the spring of 1938 they launched their campaign of conquest. To make their path easier they decided first to
complete the annexation of Austria. Since World War I there had
been a strong movement in both countries for an *Anschluss*, or
union, of Germany and Austria, but the peace treaties had forbidden
its consummation. On March 15, 1938, Hitler marched into Vienna
and proclaimed the absorption of Austria with scarcely a word of
protest from any official quarter. Czechoslovakia was now almost
surrounded by German territory. Next the Nazis intensified pres-

sure upon the Czech government. An excuse was conveniently at hand. The western portion of Czechoslovakia (the Sudetenland) was inhabited by Germans, who constituted a disgruntled minority. Hitler espoused the cause of this group, offered them a home in the Reich, and fanned the flames of discontent. Events almost came to a crisis in May, 1938, after the Sudeten Germans had presented to Prague a list of demands for complete autonomy and abrogation of the Czech alliances with Russia and France. But the Czech government mobilized its army, and Hitler decided that his hour of destiny had not yet arrived.

During the summer of 1938 Great Britain decided to intervene to force a solution of the Sudeten problem. Convinced that the dispute with Czechoslovakia would plunge all Europe into the maelstrom of war, Prime Minister Neville Chamberlain determined to leave nothing undone to pacify the German dictator. He sent Lord

Toward the surrender at Munich

"Peace in Our Time." On September 30, 1938, Prime Minister Chamberlain returned to London from his conference with Hitler at Munich. To the crowd which had gathered to meet him he waved a copy of the Munich Agreement, proclaiming it a pledge of "peace in our time." The event was the supreme irony of the prewar years.

Runciman to Prague in August, ostensibly as a mediator, but actually to exercise his powers of persuasion upon the Czech government. As events raced toward a crisis, Europe and America were swept by a panic of fear lest a new world war break out. Frantic appeals were addressed to Hitler to negotiate, one of them coming from President Roosevelt. Prime Minister Chamberlain of Great Britain flew to confer with the German Chancellor at Berchtesgaden and later at Godesberg, promising to exert pressure upon the Czechs **897** to comply with Hitler's "reasonable" demands. At length after Britain had mobilized her fleet, and after a telephone conversation with Mussolini, the Fuehrer agreed on September 28 to meet with Chamberlain, Premier Daladier of France, and Mussolini in a four-power conference at Munich. The result was a complete surrender to the violent, browbeating Chancellor. In the early days of October the Sudeten provinces of Czechoslovakia were annexed to Nazi Germany.

*Results
of the Munich
settlement*

The Munich settlement had consequences which can be described only as momentous. It transferred to Germany one-fifth of the area of Czechoslovakia, including valuable minerals and the Skoda Works, one of the largest munitions factories in Europe. It reduced Czechoslovakia to helplessness, since her strategic frontier was gone, and her alliances with supposedly powerful friends had proved worthless. In March, 1939, Hitler pounced upon what was left of the unfortunate republic. He separated the Czech provinces of Bohemia and Moravia from Slovakia and annexed them to Germany. At the same time he established a protectorate over Slovakia and soon afterward permitted Hungary to absorb the Carpatho-Ukraine, at the eastern tip of the Czech republic. But this did not complete the effects. The U.S.S.R. was deeply offended by what looked like an attempt to solve behind her back problems in which she was vitally interested. The Soviet leaders were positive that the Munich settlement was a diabolical plot by Britain and France to save their own skins by diverting Nazi expansion eastward. This multiplied Moscow's suspicions of the West, and undoubtedly was a prime factor responsible for the Nazi-Soviet Pact of August 23, 1939, which gave Hitler the green light for an attack upon Poland. The game of international double-dealing was one at which two could play. Since Britain and France, in going to Munich, had thought of nothing but their own interests, Russia would now look to hers.

SELECTED READINGS

Arndt, H. W., *The Economic Lessons of the 1930's*, New York, 1944
Bailey, T. A., *The Great Betrayal*, New York, 1945
———, *Woodrow Wilson and the Lost Peace*, New York, 1944
Benns, F. L., *Europe since 1914 in Its World Setting*, New York, 1945
Brenan, Gerald, *The Spanish Labyrinth*, New York, 1943
Cattell, David T., *Communism and the Spanish Civil War*, Berkeley, 1955
Dean, Vera M., *Europe in Retreat*, New York, 1941
Gedye, G. E. R., *Betrayal in Central Europe*, New York, 1939
Haines, C. G., and Hoffman, R. J. S., *The Origins and Background of the Second World War*, revised edition, New York, 1947
Hall, W. P., *Iron out of Calvary*, New York, 1946
———, *World Wars and Revolutions*, New York, 1943

Holborn, Hajo, *The Political Collapse of Europe*, New York, 1951
Hutton, Graham, *Survey after Munich*, Boston, 1939
Lattimore, Owen, *Manchuria, Cradle of Conflict*, New York, 1935
Lee, D. E., *Ten Years: The World on the Way to War*, Boston, 1942
May, A. J., *Europe and Two World Wars*, New York, 1947
Orton, William, *Twenty Years' Armistice, 1918–1938*, New York, 1938
Perkins, Dexter, *The American Approach to Foreign Policy*, Cambridge, Mass., 1952
Simonds, F. H., and Emeny, Brooks, *The Great Powers in World Politics*, New York, 1939

SOURCE MATERIALS

Chamberlain, Neville, *In Search of Peace*
Churchill, W. S., *While England Slept*
Dodd, W. E., Jr., and Martha, *Ambassador Dodd's Diary*
Henderson, Sir N., *Failure of a Mission*
Roussy de Sales, Raoul de, ed., *Adolf Hitler: My New Order*

World War II

In September, 1939, Europe plunged again over the rim of the abyss. The peace of 1919–1920 had turned out to be only an armistice, and millions of people were now locked in a conflict which surpassed in dreadfulness any that had occurred heretofore. The name by which this conflict is generally known is something of a misnomer. It was not the *second* world war in history but one of a series dating back to the beginnings of the modern state system. Professor Arthur M. Schlesinger of Harvard has said that it was actually the ninth. Certainly such conflicts as the Thirty Years' War, the Seven Years' War, and the Napoleonic Wars were world wars in everything but name. World Wars I and II involved more nations, but this was due largely to the fact that Europeanization of the globe had been completed over a greater area, and, consequently, the European state system was more widely extended.

1. Underlying Causes

To a certain extent World Wars I and II had identical causes. This was true of nationalism and of what has already been discussed as the condition of international anarchy. The peace of 1919–1920 had been designed to correct both of these evils. Actually it did little to abate either. In fact, it is possible to argue that by stressing the right of the self-determination of peoples, and by creating new minorities problems, the peace made nationalism a more virulent force than ever. The League of Nations, if it had been permitted to function in accordance with the dreams of its founders, might conceivably have provided a remedy for international anarchy. But there is no certainty of this, for it was founded upon principles which severely limited its capacity to maintain universal law and order. It was a league of governments, not a federation of peoples.

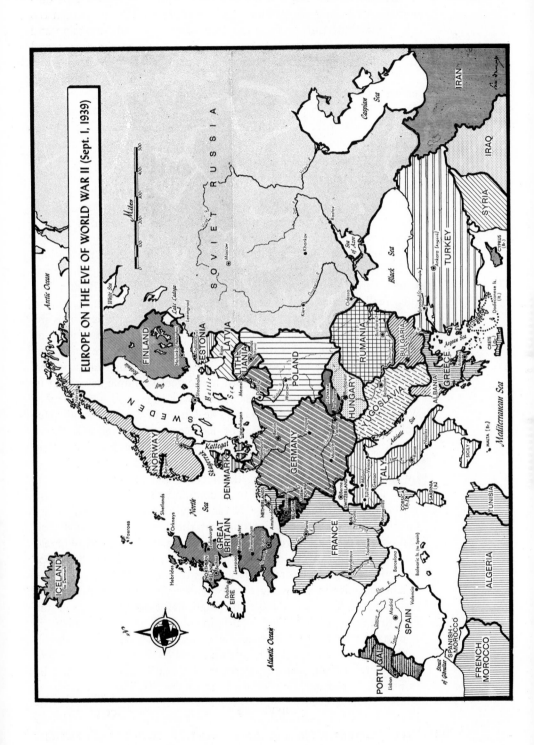

EUROPE ON THE EVE OF WORLD WAR II (Sept. I, 1939)

Essentially, it was not much more than another conference of diplomats, a standing conference, a bit more highly organized than the old Concert of Europe. The member states were still sovereign and independent, with freedom to maintain and use armed forces and to conduct their foreign policies about as they liked.

Struggles over the balance of power were another underlying cause of both wars. But the power struggle which brought on *Squabbles over* World War II was considerably different from the one that had *the balance of* raged before 1914. World War I had profound effects in changing *power* the equilibrium or lack of equilibrium among states. It reduced Germany and Russia temporarily to the level of second-rate powers and eliminated Austria-Hungary from the list entirely. It gave an uneasy primacy to Britain and France in Europe, and it greatly strengthened the position of the United States. It made America the world's chief creditor nation and enabled her to expand her trade into areas formerly dominated by Britain and Germany.

Perhaps most important of all, World War I divided the nations of the world into Have and Have-not powers. The former included *The revolt of* Great Britain, the United States, France, and Russia. Britain had *the Have-not* the smallest homeland, but her empire extended over 13,000,000 *powers* square miles, one fourth of the land area of the earth, and was inhabited by 500,000,000 people, or one-fourth of the population of the globe. France had a total empire of 4,000,000 square miles and 100,000,000 inhabitants. Neither the United States nor Russia owned vast overseas possessions, but both had extensive home areas rich in natural resources. The former ruled over 3,735,000 square miles with a population of 130,000,000. The Union of Soviet Socialist Republics extended over an area of 8,000,000 square miles and was inhabited by no fewer than 170,000,000 people. The position of the Have-not powers—Germany, Italy, and Japan—seemed poor indeed by comparison. The three of them combined had an area of less than 1,500,000 square miles, to accommodate a home population which exceeded the total for Great Britain and the United States. German patriots could point out that the average German citizen had only .004 of a square mile of living space at his disposal, whereas the average Briton could draw upon the wealth and economic opportunities of almost three square miles of imperial territory.

The fallacies in this view of the matter were seldom noticed. It seemed sufficient for the German nationalist to reflect upon the *Fallacies in the* fact that standards of living in Britain were higher than in his own *viewpoint of the* country to prove to him that the existing division of the earth's *Have-not* surface was unjust. He was therefore ready to disrupt the *status quo* *powers* by any means in his power. Perhaps diplomatic cunning would be sufficient, but if not, he would resort to war. Italians and Japanese seemed to have even weightier evidence of the injustice of the existing order, since standards of living in their countries were lower than in Germany. None of them appeared to recognize the fact that living standards in some small European countries, totally or almost completely lacking colonial empires, were just about equal to the average in Britain. This was true of Switzerland and Sweden and possibly also of Denmark and Norway. In fact there probably is no real connection between the size of a nation's empire and its level of prosperity—unless, of course, there are severe restrictions upon international trade, such as those which had been adopted during the Great Depression. But Germany, Italy, and Japan had a sense of grievance for a number of reasons, and presenting themselves before the world as Have-not nations helped to justify their bellicose foreign policies.

No account of the underlying causes of World War II would be complete without consideration of the role played by the Second Industrial Revolution. As was shown in a previous chapter, that movement had disturbing and far-reaching effects upon modern society. It promoted the growth of monopolies, mergers, cartels, holding companies, chain stores, and other instruments of a giant capitalism which imposed upon the small businessman competitive conditions he was frequently unable to withstand. It created a huge white-collar class made up of clerical workers, salesmen, technicians, and employees of service enterprises such as advertising, accounting, and insurance. Unorganized and frequently underpaid, these people became easy victims of demagogues, who promised to save them not only from their capitalist exploiters, but likewise from socialists, who threatened to destroy their means of livelihood and force them to become manual workers. The Second Industrial Revolution also produced technological unemployment, on a scale hitherto unknown. And lastly, it resulted from time to time in a production of goods far in excess of the effective demand. This overproduction led not simply to depressions but to desperate expedients to save the economic system from complete collapse. Prices were fixed for innumerable commodities. Merchants were forbidden to undersell each other. Farmers were required to limit the production of both crops and livestock to restricted quotas. European governments forced producers of basic commodities like iron, steel, and coal to form cartels in order to prevent competitive overproduction. Such methods were familiar elements in the trend toward autarchy, or economic nationalism. In so far as they reduced international trade and sharpened antagonism between nations, they helped to make war inevitable.

Effects of the Second Industrial Revolution

Doubtless the most serious economic cause of World War II was the Great Depression. The depression contributed to the coming of the war in several ways. First and foremost, it intensified economic nationalism. Baffled by problems of unemployment and business stagnation, governments resorted to high tariffs in a frenzied attempt to preserve the home market for their own producers. When tariffs proved insufficiently effective, they turned to cur-

The Great Depression as a cause of the war

rency controls, bilateral trade agreements, and outright prohibitions of imports. By 1934 every important country in the world had abandoned the gold standard in the hope of gaining some temporary advantage in export markets. None of these methods achieved its purposes for more than a brief interval. The ultimate results were indescribable confusion, a partial strangulation of trade, and a deepening of antagonism between nations.

Other effects of the Depression

The Depression also had other effects perhaps more difficult to assay. For one thing, it was responsible for a marked increase in armaments. Armaments expansion, on a large scale, was first undertaken by Germany about 1935. The results in a few years were such as to dazzle the rest of the world. Unemployment disappeared and business boomed. It would have been too much to expect that other dissatisfied nations would not copy the German example. Similarly, the Depression resulted in a new wave of militant expansionism, directed toward the conquest of neighboring territories as a means of solving economic problems. Japan took the lead in 1931 with the invasion of Manchuria. A primary cause was the decline of Japanese exports of raw silk and cotton cloth. Since the nation as a consequence was unable to pay for needed imports of coal, iron, and other minerals, Nipponese militarists were furnished with a convenient pretext for seizing Manchuria, where supplies of these commodities could then be purchased for Japanese currency.

The Depression primarily responsible for the Nazi Revolution

Finally, the Great Depression had results closely related to the factors which directly precipitated the war. The Czechoslovakian crisis might never have occurred, for instance, had it not been for badly depressed economic conditions in the Sudetenland. The Sudeten area being highly industrialized, its inhabitants were victims of unemployment to a greater extent than the remainder of the people of Czechoslovakia. Most important of all, the Depression was primarily responsible for the triumph of Nazism in Germany. The Nazi party would probably have remained weak and ineffectual had it not been for the influx of millions of followers from the ranks of the farmers and the unemployed and from frightened members of the white-collar classes. The whirling spiral of economic decline had overwhelmed these people with a sense of despair. Convinced that capitalism, socialism, and democracy had all failed, they were ready to grasp at almost any straw that would save them from sinking deeper into the quicksands of depression. Some members of the upper classes had also reached the conclusion that the Nazi party was the only party that could save the nation from political and economic breakdown. According to Konrad Heiden, the little group that persuaded President von Hindenburg to appoint Hitler Chancellor believed that the Nazi leader alone had a chance to govern the country with the support of a majority in the Reichstag. They assumed that they could control him, since one of their number, von Papen, was to be Vice Chancellor, and the cabinet was to include only three Nazis in a total membership of about ten.[1]

It may be well before leaving this subject of underlying causes of the war to look at the matter from the standpoint of a different interpretation. According to an important school of thought, which may be called the power-politics school, only a few of the factors mentioned above deserve more than slight consideration. Doubtless leaders of this school would accept the economic causes, but most of the others they would dismiss as inconsequential. They place nearly all of the emphasis upon power politics. They maintain that power rivalries and power struggles have been the real causes of international wars since the beginning of modern history. Such forces as nationalism, militarism, and imperialism have simply been instruments for achieving the ends of a quest for power. The seventeenth century, they point out, was marked by a great power struggle between France and Austria, in which France was victorious. During the eighteenth century a primary struggle raged between Britain and France and culminated in the Seven Years' War, with a decisive victory for Britain. The French attempted to recover their power during the wars of the Revolution and under Napoleon, but the effort failed, and Britain gradually emerged as the dominant nation on the earth. Toward the end of the nineteenth century, however, Germany rose to challenge British supremacy, and the result was World War I. After the war conflicting ambitions among the victors permitted a revival of Teutonic power, with the consequence that, by 1939, Germany was ready to challenge again the ability of the dominant nations to continue ruling the world. The fact that Germany and her allies had fascist governments had little to do with the case. According to the power-politics theorists, fascism was simply a by-product of an age-old struggle among nations to gain advantages at their neighbors' expense.[2]

That there is much truth in the foregoing hypothesis seems almost indisputable. The existence of the modern state system practically guarantees that nations shall be engaged in either white or red wars nearly all of the time. For this so-called system is not really a system at all, but a condition of anarchy. Under it the relation among states is the same as that among individuals in the supposed state of nature, which philosophers like Locke and Rousseau believed to have existed before the formation of political society. In other words, there is no law or order except that which results from agreements between sovereign units. In making these agreements, the units retain their full sovereignty, and therefore may repudiate them whenever they choose. Another element in the hypothesis which is difficult to

[1] *Der Fuehrer*, pp. 531-37.

[2] This theory is implicit in the writings of the so-called geopoliticians, especially in such books as N. J. Spykman, *America's Strategy in World Politics*. See also Herman Finer, *America's Destiny*; and Erno Wittman, *History: A Guide to Peace*.

refute is the contention that ideologies are not fundamental causes of wars. If British politicians had been gravely concerned about the evils of fascism, they could never have pursued their policy of appeasement, since they must have known that its effect would be to strengthen Italy and Germany. Indeed, there is evidence that Neville Chamberlain was perfectly willing to collaborate with fascist governments for his own purposes. One of his chief reasons for going to Munich was to bring Germany, Italy, France, and Britain into a four-power alliance to determine the destinies of Europe. It is significant also that Germany and the Soviet Union became allies in 1939, despite the fact that, shortly before, Hitler had described the Bolsheviks as "scum of the earth," while Stalin had referred to the Nazis as "bloody assassins of the workers." The power-politics hypothesis would appear to suffer, not from inaccuracy, but, like most specialized theories, from a failure to give proper recognition to all of the factors. If nationalism and militarism are not originally primary causes of wars, they often become so as international tension increases.

2. The Outbreak of Hostilities

Immediate causes of the war: (1) the destruction of Czechoslovakia

It seems possible to discover at least two immediate causes which led to the outbreak of World War II. The first was Hitler's destruction of what was left of Czechoslovakia in March of 1939. This act was a direct violation of the Munich Agreement, and gave clear indication that Nazi ambitions were not confined to the acquisition of territories inhabited by German nationals but included a much broader program of expansion. Most important of all, it led to an almost immediate abandonment of the appeasement policy. Even Prime Minister Chamberlain was now convinced that Hitler's word could no longer be trusted. Accordingly, when the Fuehrer began to threaten Poland, demanding the abolition of the Corridor and the return of the free city of Danzig [3] to Germany, Chamberlain announced that Britain would give Poland armed assistance. Soon afterward he declared that his government would come to the aid of *any* country that felt itself menaced by Hitler's ambitions. In the weeks that followed, definite guaranties were extended by both the British and the French to Greece, Rumania, and Turkey. By the middle of July a military alliance had been completed between Britain and France on the one side and Poland on the other. Its terms were sweeping. The British and the French bound themselves to give military aid to Poland in the event of any aggression which the Poles might consider a clear threat to their independence. The only limitation was the requirement that the Poles themselves must resist the aggression—which, in view of the powerful backing promised, was hardly a limitation at all.

[3] For the status of Danzig under the Treaty of Versailles, see p. 836.

Why were such strong pledges of military action insufficient to hold Hitler in check? One reason was his evident belief that he still had trump cards up his sleeve. He was apparently confident that he could outwit the democracies and reduce their pledges to empty gestures. This leads us to consideration of the Nazi-Soviet Pact, which may be regarded as the second immediate cause of World War II. It is now obvious that one reason why Hitler plunged ahead so recklessly in his demands against Poland was the fact that he had strong hopes of cementing some kind of friendly agreement with the Soviet Union. This he finally accomplished on August 23, 1939, when his foreign minister, Joachim von Ribbentrop, flew to Moscow and signed a five-year pact of nonaggression and neutrality with Commissar Vyacheslav M. Molotov of the Soviet Union. By means of this agreement, Hitler split the U.S.S.R. off from the Western powers and prevented her from giving them any assistance. He was apparently certain that he could now attack Poland without fear of the consequences, for Britain and France would be almost powerless to help her. Moreover, documents published since the war by the U.S. State Department indicate that the Nazi-Soviet Pact was accompanied by a secret protocol providing for the division of Poland between Germany and the U.S.S.R. and giving the latter a free hand in Latvia, Estonia, and Bessarabia.

It should be noted that Britain and France also made efforts to win Russia to their side. While the Nazis and the Soviets were carrying on their secret flirtation, representatives of the British and French governments were conferring with Russian officials in Moscow. But an attitude of distrust dogged the footsteps of the negotiators from the beginning. Chamberlain had little enthusiasm for a Russian alliance but had been goaded into seeking one by the pressure of public opinion. The Soviets themselves were still smarting from the rebuff they had received at Munich. They looked upon Chamberlain's surrender to the dictators as an attempt to dump Hitler on Russia's doorstep. In addition, they had apparently decided that Germany had more to offer than they could ever hope to get from the West. Finally, from the Soviet viewpoint, a pact with Germany would have the definite advantage of dividing the capitalist powers, thereby making it impossible for Britain and France to use Germany as the spearhead for a capitalist assault upon the Soviet Union. The danger of such an eventuality still seemed very real to the men in the Kremlin, despite all the assertions of friendship from Paris and London.

After the signing of the Nazi-Soviet agreement, German relations with Poland came quickly to a climax. For some weeks there had been reports from both countries of monster demonstrations and "frontier incidents." Nazi newspapers were hurling recriminations and threats in the most violent language. On August 24, Hitler made ready to take possession of Danzig by requiring the Senate of the free city to appoint the local Nazi leader Chief of State. Soon afterward the German Fuehrer repeated his demands to the Western powers in regard to Danzig and the Corridor, insisting that these problems must be solved immediately, without compromise, and that Britain must abandon her alliance with Poland. Such terms Chamberlain refused to accept, and he continued to urge Hitler not to resort to force, in the hope that a satisfactory solution might yet be negotiated. Finally, on the morning of September 1, the

The Beginning of World War II. A long line of German tanks speeding into Poland.

Fuehrer announced that military action against Poland had begun. In justification for ordering the army to move, he alleged the following: (1) that Poland had already mobilized and had committed hostile acts against Germany; and (2) that the "barbarous persecution" of German men, women, and children in the Corridor could no longer be endured by a great nation.

Although Hitler avowed that he would fight until the situation had been rendered "acceptable to Germany," and that he would *Britain* "win or die," his government did not issue a declaration of war. *and France* The action against Poland was described merely as a "counter-*enter the war* attack with pursuit." Perhaps he really believed that, by negotiating a pact with Russia, he had outmaneuvered the Western powers so completely that they would perceive the futility of trying to rescue Poland, and therefore no general war would result. If these were his thoughts, he was soon disillusioned. Upon learning of the attack upon Poland, Britain and France sent a joint warning to Germany that she must cease her aggression. To this there was no reply. At nine o'clock on the morning of September 3, the British ambassador in Berlin delivered an ultimatum informing the German officials that unless they prepared to withdraw their troops within two hours, Great Britain would declare war. Then at eleven o'clock came the voice of Neville Chamberlain—the voice of a tired and disappointed man—announcing that his country was at war with Germany. He spoke of the "bitter blow" it was to him that his "long struggle for peace" had failed. He concluded by invoking the blessing of God upon his people and asserted that it was "evil things" the British nation would be fighting against—"brute force, bad faith, injustice, oppression, and persecution." At five o'clock in the afternoon of the same day, France also entered the war.

The German war against Poland proved to be a brief encounter. In less than three weeks the Polish armies had been routed, Warsaw had been captured, and the chiefs of the Polish government had fled to Rumania. With the Poles crushed beyond hope of resistance, it was almost universally believed that Germany would unloose a *Blitzkrieg* against England and France. But nothing of the sort took place. Instead, the war in the west resolved itself into a kind of siege, a "phony war" as many people in the democracies called it. Such fighting as did occur, during the remainder of 1939, was largely confined to submarine warfare, to airplane raids on naval bases, and to occasional encounters between cruisers at sea. The strategy of Germany's enemies was mainly to wear her down by a blockade and by the sheer weight of their economic resources. The Germans themselves were diligently increasing their own strength in preparation for the delivery of a crushing blow with the coming of spring.

The Sitzkrieg
or "phony war"

The spring of 1940 had scarcely begun when the Germans transformed the war of siege on the Western front into a violent war of bloody encounter. They began by invading Denmark and Norway on April 9. In taking this action they were motivated by two main purposes. One was to protect the route by which much of their supply of iron ore was shipped by rail from Sweden to Narvik and thence down the Norwegian coast, and the other was to safeguard their northern flank in preparation for an attack upon the Low Countries and upon France. The Danes capitulated to the invaders almost immediately, but the Norwegians resolved to fight. Though the British rushed troops and warships to Norway, the Germans managed to overrun the greater part of the country. Three weeks after the invasion Prime Minister Chamberlain admitted that the British effort to keep Norway from falling under German domination was a failure.

From Sitzkrieg
to Blitzkrieg

On May 10, 1940, the world was stunned by the news that an avalanche of German troops had swept into the Netherlands and Belgium. The Dutch were overwhelmed within five days and forced to lay down their arms. The Belgians, with the assistance of about 400,000 Britons and Frenchmen, fought on for a while longer. Meanwhile, a second horde of Nazi invaders crashed through the northern extension of the Maginot Line and raced down the valley of the Somme to Abbeville on the Channel Coast. On May 28 King Leopold of Belgium decided that further resistance was useless and surrendered the bulk of his army. The British and French, with a remnant of the Belgian forces, retreated into western Flanders, where they were gradually surrounded at Dunkerque and threatened with annihilation by the Germans. Eventually, after

*The attack
upon the Netherlands and Belgium*

days of horror and anguish, all but about 65,000 of them were successfully evacuated by the British navy, with the help of the air force, the merchant marine, and every conceivable craft that would float.

The invasion of France

In the meantime, another horde of Nazi invaders had crashed through the extension of the Maginot Line in the vicinity of Sedan and had swarmed into France. Despite all the efforts of the French soldiers and the solemn commands of their generals to "conquer or die," the German advance could seldom be checked for more than a day at a time. Inspired by the fierce ardor of revenge for 1918 and armored with the zeal of a revolutionary philosophy, Hitler's soldiers fought like crusaders. Equipped with tanks, flame-throwers, armored transport, and dive-bombing airplanes, they concentrated all of their energies upon conquering the enemy by a frightful *Blitzkrieg*. Soon the French army had been pounded into a condition of terror and helplessness. Positions which the Allies had held during World War I for months now crumbled like houses of sand. By June 11, four weeks after the campaign had started, the Nazis had reached the Marne. The French government took refuge in Tours and soon afterward, in order to avert destruction, proclaimed Paris an "undefended city." On June 14 the City of Light was in German hands, and the hated emblem of the hooked cross flew from the Eiffel Tower.[4]

The conquest of France

Though for a time it appeared as if the armies of France might continue the struggle, the government decided that the cause was lost. On June 17 Marshal Pétain, who the day before had become Premier, announced that resistance would cease and appealed to Hitler "as one soldier to another" for peace with honor. Four days later representatives of the French Republic met with Hitler and other officials of the victorious Reich to receive the terms of an armistice. By order of the Nazi Fuehrer the meeting was held in the same railway car at Compiègne in which Marshal Foch had dictated the terms of the armistice of November 11, 1918, to the Germans. The truce now imposed by Hitler required the French to submit to occupation of about half of their country, to demobilize and disarm their military and naval forces, to release all German prisoners of war, and to surrender all armaments and war materials in the occupied territory. By another temporary settlement on June 24 the Italians, who had entered the war on the side of Germany fourteen days previously, received the port of Jibuti in French Somaliland, full control over the railway leading from Jibuti to

---

[4] There is evidence that the defeat of the French was due in part to weakness and incompetence in the government and to the activities of German spies and fifth-column agents in sowing dissension and fear. Mainly, however, it was due to antiquated notions of warfare, to a static defense strategy, and to the fact that France had only half the population of Germany and an even smaller proportion of the industrial strength.

Addis Ababa, and the right to occupy a portion of southeastern France.

With France rendered helpless and forced to submit to the will of her conquerors, the war entered a new stage. Germany was supreme on the Continent, and, among her opponents, only the British Empire was in a position to continue the struggle. Whether the British would ultimately be crushed under the wheels of the Nazi juggernaut or whether they would survive to duplicate their achievement in the wars of Napoleon, or at least to limit Hitler's victory, remained to be seen. The attitude of the government indicated a readiness to face any emergency. In a radio address on June 17, Prime Minister Winston Churchill, who had succeeded Neville Chamberlain on May 10, declared that Britain would "fight on unconquerable until the curse of Hitler is lifted from the brows of men."

To the surprise of many people, the Germans did not attempt an invasion of Britain immediately after the fall of France. Perhaps they thought it would not be necessary since Britain, with all her allies defeated, would sooner or later be forced to capitulate. More likely, they were deterred by military and geographic realities. Time was required for the establishment of bases in northern France and for the collection of thousands of barges and other vessels of transport. The British Navy was still the most powerful on earth. The English Channel was an effective barrier against the use of the very types of mechanized warfare which had been largely responsible for the defeat of France. Not to be dismissed from consideration either was the fact that the Royal Air Force had given a good account of itself as a defensive arm at Dunkerque.[5]

The Germans made their first large-scale air attacks on Britain on August 8, 1940. On that date Goering's *Luftwaffe* began a series of mass raids which continued with increasing fury for two weeks. Hundreds of planes smashed at British ports, industrial centers, and at air defenses throughout the country. In September, the Germans concluded that daylight raids against R.A.F. opposition were too costly, and resorted to night bombing. The result for Britain was a long period of indescribable horror. Thousands of houses were damaged or destroyed in many parts of the country, and entire sections of cities were laid in ruins. Most appalling were the casualties among civilians. From August, 1940, to June, 1941, when large-scale bombings practically ceased, more than 40,000 citizens of Britain were killed in air attacks.

If Hitler and Goering believed that Britain would be crippled

[5] According to the diary of Count Ciano, Hitler was fearful also of Russia and the United States. He was afraid that if he invaded Britain, the United States would come to her rescue, and that Russia would take advantage of any difficulties Germany might encounter in the west to spring a surprise attack in the east.

London during the Blitz. This picture gives a vivid impression of the agony which the British capital suffered during the Battle of Britain, from August, 1940, to June, 1941. Back of the tumbling ruins brought down by fire bombs is St. Paul's Cathedral.

Refuge from the Blitz. Residents of London sought refuge, during the Battle of Britain, in underground shelters, including the subways, as shown in this picture.

Britain takes steps for defense and retaliation

beyond recovery or terrorized into surrendering, they were disillusioned. Churchill's government took swift and effective steps for defense and retaliation. An Emergency Powers Act was rushed through Parliament as soon as it appeared that France might fall. This act empowered the Cabinet to exercise absolute authority over the lives and properties of British subjects. It permitted the requisitioning of any industry and the conscription of wealth and labor for the service of the state. As the danger to the nation increased, actions were taken to frustrate any such tactics as the Germans had employed in the Netherlands and Belgium. A local Defense Force, or Home Guard, was organized and armed for the purpose of dealing with parachute troops. Beaches were strung with barbed wire, and the army was trained in constructing road blocks and in protecting landing fields against hostile planes. More important, the Royal Air Force was far from idle. Even before the *Luftwaffe* had launched its full-scale assault, the R.A.F. had begun the systematic bombing of specific targets in Germany.[6] The objectives at first were communications and troop concentration points. Later the main effort was to demolish port facilities, aircraft and munition factories, and synthetic oil plants. Some of these raids extended as far as Berlin, and hundreds of planes participated in them. The bulk of the Air Force, however, was used to fight off the German marauders. In this action the British pilots and planes

[6] Edgar McInnis, *The War, First Year*, p. 245.

demonstrated a marked superiority. The Air Ministry claimed that during the period when the battle was at its height, nearly three German planes were destroyed for every one lost by the British.[7] Churchill expressed the pride of the nation in the R.A.F. when he declared: "Never in the field of human conflict was so much owed by so many to so few."

The expansion of the conflict

Before the Battle of Britain had come to an end, the war had spread into new areas. In September, 1940, the Italians, anxious to demonstrate their value to their Axis partner, started a drive across North Africa for the capture of Suez. The prize to be gained was nothing less than the severance of Britain's line of communication with her empire. Though initially they won a few spectacular victories, in less than six months they had lost nearly all of their African possessions to the British, and their troops had had to be rescued by the Germans. In the meantime, Mussolini had found a pretext for attacking Greece. Again the results were almost ruinous. Confident of an easy victory, the Fascist generals had made wholly inadequate preparations for the kind of campaign they were forced to fight. In scarcely more than a month the Greeks had driven every single Italian invader from their country.

The conquest of Yugoslavia and Greece

With Italy thus facing catastrophe, it was inevitable that Hitler would take a hand in the war in the Balkans. Besides, he had reasons of his own for wishing to tie the remaining independent countries of southeastern Europe to the German chariot. All of them were valuable as sources of raw materials and as steppingstones to the Near East. Moreover, there was danger that Greece, especially, might be used as a base of operations by the British. On March 1, 1941, German troops occupied Sofia, the capital of Bulgaria, and on April 6 armies of the Fuehrer invaded Yugoslavia and Greece. Since British reinforcements were sent to help the Greeks, the war in the Balkans was now completely merged with the larger struggle. But disaster seemed to stalk Britain and her allies from the beginning. By the end of May, 1941, all organized opposition to the German conquest had been crushed. Britain was left once more to fight the war alone, without a single ally or even a foothold on the European Continent.

The attack on Russia

On June 22, 1941, the World War of 1939 entered its third stage, when Hitler launched a mighty attack upon the Soviet Union. Why he undertook such a gamble while still involved in a war with Britain may never be fully explained. A few of the reasons, however, are fairly obvious. For years he had looked with covetous eyes upon the riches of the U.S.S.R. In the first edition of *Mein Kampf*, published in 1925, he had declared that Germany should

[7] After the war it was revealed that the R.A.F. had been greatly aided by the development of radar (radio detection and range). This invention made possible the detection of enemy planes while they were still a hundred miles or more from their targets. On September 15, 1940, the R.A.F., with the aid of this invention, destroyed no fewer than 180 German planes.

expand, by and large, "only at the expense of Russia." [8] Addressing his party comrades at Nuremberg in 1936, he had described how Germans would "swim in plenty" if their country could gain possession of the wheat lands and minerals of the Ukraine. Faced now with the prospect of a long war against the British, he stood in urgent need of the oil, manganese, and other resources of the Soviet Union if he expected to win. Hitler was also influenced by reasons of strategy. To conquer Britain it was becoming apparent that a colossal invasion would have to be launched. But this would be exceedingly dangerous with the Soviet armies at Germany's back. Finally, there was increasing friction over the division of eastern Europe into spheres of influence which had been made by the Secret Protocol of 1939. Dissatisfied with her original share, the Soviets demanded Lithuania and Northern Bukovina, which they incorporated along with Estonia, Latvia, and Bessarabia into their Union.

The drive to the gates of Moscow

Without the formality of a declaration of war or even an ultimatum Hitler plunged into his fateful effort to conquer the U.S.S.R. The attack was begun before daylight on June 22, 1941, along the entire frontier between the two countries. Within a few days Italy, Hungary, Rumania, and Finland joined the Germans and, still later, Bulgaria and Slovakia. For week after week the Nazi mechanized legions rolled relentlessly onward. By the end of November they had advanced as far as Rostov at the mouth of the Don and Kerch in the Crimea. In the meantime they had been making rapid progress in northern Russia. By September 8 they had reached the banks of the Neva and had begun the siege of Leningrad. On the central front their progress was slower. Three months were required to hack their way from Smolensk to Mozhaisk, a distance of less than 200 miles. Here their advance was momentarily halted. About November 20, however, they started a new offensive which threatened the encirclement of Moscow. Nazi columns penetrated within sight of the capital, and one desperate thrust was made to the very outskirts of the city. Yet Moscow did not fall. So strenuous was the Russians' resistance that as early as December 8 the Germans admitted the failure of their offensive.

How the Russians withstood the German onslaught

How were the Russians able to check the Nazi onslaught where most other nations had failed? To begin with, the Red Army commanders were able to take advantage of the vast space of their country, to draw the Germans farther and farther from their supply bases and at the same time to build up the strength of their own forces for a powerful counteroffensive. They benefited also from the mistakes of the Nazis. Hitler admitted that he had greatly underestimated the strength of the Soviets. Besides, the strategy of his entire campaign was conceived in such a way as seriously to limit his chances of victory. Instead of concentrating his power upon a few vital objectives, he dispersed his forces along an 1800-mile frontier. But these were not the only factors. The Soviet leaders

[8] Reynal and Hitchcock edition, Vol. I, p. 182.

had been preparing for war for a long time. The Five-Year Plans
had been designed, in considerable measure, to increase military
potential. During the period of the Nazi-Soviet Pact the Stalin
government had been able to speed up the construction of industrial
plants in the Ural Mountains and in the mineral producing regions
of Siberia. As a result, the conquest of the western Ukraine was
prevented from being disastrous. In addition, the Russians had had
time to learn a great deal about Nazi military methods and to profit
from the lessons taught by the defeat of other countries. As a
consequence, their armies did not become frightened and surrender
as soon as they found themselves "hopelessly encircled." Instead,
they counterattacked whenever possible and frequently fought
their way out of the trap.

"The Day That Will Live in In-
famy." Damage inflicted upon the
United States Navy by Japanese
bombers at Pearl Harbor, December 7, 1941.

3. The War Becomes a Global War

Prior to December 7, 1941, two great wars had been raging on
the face of the earth. One was the European war which had grown
out of Hitler's attack upon Poland on September 1, 1939. The *The attack*
other was the war between Japan and China which had begun on *at Pearl Harbor*
July 7, 1937.[9] On December 7, 1941, these wars were merged into
one when Japanese planes bombed the great naval base of the
United States at Pearl Harbor, destroying or damaging about 20

[9] The underlying cause of the Far Eastern conflict was the ambition of Japanese militarists to detach the northern provinces of China from the Chinese Republic. They would then be organized as a Japanese puppet state and would
thereby supplement the scanty natural resources of the Japanese Empire.

American war vessels and some 250 planes, and causing the deaths of approximately 3000 persons. A few hours afterward the Japanese government declared war against both the United States and Great Britain. Declarations of war multiplied rapidly after that. On December 8 the United States Congress recognized a state of war with Japan, by a vote of 82 to 0 in the Senate and 388 to 1 in the House of Representatives. On December 11 Germany and Italy declared war upon the United States. Within the next two days Rumania, Hungary, and Bulgaria took similar action. Several of the Latin-American countries followed the United States into the war, among them Cuba, Panama, Honduras, Guatemala, Haiti, Costa Rica, and Nicaragua. During 1942 Brazil and Mexico also joined the Allies, and in subsequent years all of the remaining nations of the Western Hemisphere. While only Brazil and Mexico sent detachments of troops to the fighting fronts, the other Latin-American countries made contributions in the form of moral support, and by producing strategic and basic materials for Great Britain and the United States.

Japan's alliance with Germany and Italy

The sudden eruption of Japanese violence against the West on December 7, 1941, was not an isolated event. Ever since September, 1940, Japan had been allied with Germany and Italy. The pact of alliance provided that Japan recognized "the leadership of Germany and Italy in the establishment of a new order in Europe," and that Germany and Italy recognized the leadership of Japan in the accomplishment of a similar purpose "in Greater East Asia." On the other hand, there is no proof that the Axis allies co-operated closely in planning the Pearl Harbor assault. Indeed, it is probable that Hitler at that time would have much preferred that Japan attack the U.S.S.R. Nevertheless, he carried on activities against the United States which were certain to arouse American enmity. He sent agents into South America to promote sympathy for fascism and for the Axis cause. He maintained a great fleet of U-boats in the Atlantic to prey upon United States commerce, in the hope of preventing shipments of supplies from this country from reaching his enemies. Six months before Pearl Harbor, one of his U-boats had gone so far as to sink a United States freighter, the *Robin Moor*, with a cargo of steel rails and automobiles for South Africa.

The United States abandons neutrality

But these activities were not unrelated to the foreign policy of the United States government. That policy had long since ceased to be one of neutrality. In September, 1940, President Roosevelt had arranged for the transfer of fifty "over-age" destroyers from the United States Navy to the British in exchange for the right to lease naval and air bases in certain British possessions in the Western Hemisphere. In March, 1941, Congress passed, at the request of the President, the celebrated Lend-Lease Act, which empowered the Executive to render to the governments fighting the Axis almost every form of material aid "short of war." During the summer of 1941 the United States Navy began convoying the American freighters and even the freighters of other nations part way across the Atlantic. This led almost inevitably to an undeclared naval war between Germany and the United States. On October 17 the U.S. destroyer *Kearny* was torpedoed off the coast of Iceland while engaged in a battle with one or more submarines. Two weeks later another United States vessel on convoy duty, the destroyer *Reuben James,* was not only torpedoed but sunk, and 100 lives were lost. In the meantime, President Roosevelt was making his own attitude toward Germany's war in Europe crystal clear. Speaking at Hyde Park on September 1, 1941, he declared categorically that we would do "everything in our power to crush Hitler and his Nazi forces." [10] In his Navy Day speech on October 27, 1941, he informed the American people that "the shooting" had "started." [11]

During all of these critical months the militarists of Japan were apparently giving little attention to the events of the war in Europe. Their major aim now seemed to be to conquer an empire in the *The reasons for* southwest Pacific. Bogged down in their war against China, they *Japanese ag-* needed the tin and rubber of Malaya and the oil of the Netherlands *gression* Indies if they hoped to win victory. But conquest of these latter territories would not only cut off American supplies of valuable raw materials but would constitute a threat to the Philippines and would therefore arouse the antagonism of the United States. Previous to the autumn of 1940 the attitude of the Washington government toward the war in the Far East had been somewhat ambiguous. Though professing sympathy for China, the State Department had permitted the shipment of many vital war commodities to Japan. But when the Empire of the Rising Sun began to threaten both Indo-China and the Netherlands Indies, there was a definite reversal of policy. On September 4, 1940, Secretary Hull warned the Japanese that aggressive moves against either of these territories would have "an unfortunate effect" upon American opinion. When, three weeks later, Japan obtained permission from the Vichy government of France to send troops and supplies through Indo-China, Washington placed an embargo upon shipments of scrap iron and steel.

But neither a policy of appeasement nor its opposite seemed to restrain Japan. Her militarists and imperialists were determined to establish Japanese domination over all of East Asia. The United *The deadlock* States was just as determined to frustrate this ambition. She was no *leading to war* more anxious to see the destruction of the balance of power in the Far East than she was to welcome its overthrow in Europe. The result was a deadlock which seemed almost to make war inevitable. In October, 1940, the Japanese Foreign Minister, Matsuoka, de-

[10] *New York Times,* Sept. 2, 1941.
[11] *Ibid.,* Oct. 28, 1941.

clared that if the United States continued to stick "blindly and stubbornly to the *status quo* in the Pacific," Japan would make war upon her. Nevertheless, both governments kept up the pretense of negotiating, perhaps largely for the purpose of gaining time. In the spring of 1941, Secretary Hull began a series of parleys with the Japanese Ambassador in Washington, which continued through the summer and fall. In November the Nipponese government sent a special envoy, Saburo Kurusu, to supplement the efforts of the Ambassador. But never was it possible to reconcile the views of the two governments. The Japanese insisted upon their right to organize East Asia for their own benefit, while the United States demanded that Japan respect the sovereignty and territorial integrity of China, withdraw her forces from China and Indo-China, and recognize the Chinese National government at Chungking. The situation deteriorated rapidly during the summer of 1941 as the Japanese armies increased their encroachments in Indo-China, as Lend-Lease was extended to China, and as oil shipments to Japan were abruptly terminated. By November 29 events had reached such a critical stage that the outlook appeared to Cordell Hull as almost hopeless. He declared on that date that "the diplomatic part of our relations with Japan is almost over and that the matter will now go to the officials of the Army and Navy." [12] The Japanese emissaries, however, did not break off relations. They continued the mockery of negotiating until December 7. Not till 2:20 P.M. on that Sunday in Washington did they inform the State Department of their flat rejection of the United States proposals. Exactly one hour before, at dawn in Hawaii, the planes of their own country had begun their attack on Pearl Harbor.

The immediate result of the outbreak of global war was a series of military and naval disasters for the Allies. In some cases the cause *Japan's light-* was bewilderment or unpreparedness. In others it was overcon-*ning conquests* fidence, a tendency especially to regard the Japanese as inferior soldiers. This last illusion was soon dispelled. On the same day that they bombed Pearl Harbor, the Nipponese delivered smashing blows at Wake, Guam, Midway, and Hong Kong. Midway was defended successfully, but Guam succumbed almost immediately. Wake held out until December 23 and Hong Kong two days longer. On December 10 Japanese dive-bombers and torpedo planes sank the new British battleship *Prince of Wales* and the battle cruiser *Repulse*, the only Allied capital ships in the southwest Pacific. On January 2, 1942, Manila fell to Japanese troops, and on February 15 the great fortress of Singapore was surrendered. The fall of Singapore opened the way to conquest of the Netherlands Indies, and in quick succession one after another of the rich prizes of Java, Sumatra, Borneo, the Celebes, and New Guinea fell to the

---

[12] United States Department of State, *Peace and War: United States Foreign Policy, 1931-1941*, p. 138.

Mikado's soldiers. In the meantime other Japanese forces had moved against Burma and had driven the defending armies over the mountains into China and India. At the end of three months the Japanese had conquered a vast empire of 1,500,000 square miles (equivalent to about half the area of the United States) and including 125,000,000 inhabitants. More important, they had gained control of the rubber, tin, oil, and other essential raw materials which would enable them to prolong the war for an indefinite time.

The years 1941 and 1942 marked the high tide of Axis advance for the period of the war. Several battles may be considered turning points. One was the stubborn defense of Moscow by the Russians in November and early December, 1941. Though Hitler had boasted shortly before that "Russia was crushed and would never rise again," it was the last time his armies ever came within striking distance of

The turning points of the war

The Battle of Stalingrad, 1943. Red Army troops advancing to a position for the defense of the city. The Battle of Stalingrad was a turning point of World War II. In a vain attempt to capture the city, the Germans lost an entire army. No further efforts were made to conquer the Soviet Union.

the Soviet capital. In 1942 his generals decided upon a limited offensive in the southern part of the U.S.S.R. with the hope of smashing through to the Volga and the Caspian Sea. If successful, they could cut northern Russia off from the food-producing region of the Ukraine and from the oil resources north and south of the Caucasus. The defeat at Stalingrad, however, in which the Germans lost about 300,000 men, put an end to this scheme. The turning points in the Pacific war came during the spring of 1942 with the defeat by the United States Navy of Japanese forces in the battles of the Coral Sea and of Midway. These defeats spelled the doom of Japanese attempts to capture Australia and the Hawaiian Islands and thereby deprive the United States of advance bases for a counteroffensive against Japan.

During the remainder of the war the initiative, nearly all the time, was in the hands of the United Nations.[13] In late 1942 and early 1943 a concerted attack of Britons from the east and Americans

[13] The term United Nations came into use after January 2, 1942, when representatives of 26 nations, including Great Britain, the United States, the U.S.S.R., and China, signed a document which came to be known as the United Nations Declaration. See p. 924.

from the west succeeded in driving all Germans and Italians from North Africa. This made possible the invasion of Italy and contributed to the overthrow of Mussolini and to the final surrender of the Italian government on September 3, 1943. Meanwhile, the Russians had seized the initiative from the Germans and managed to hold it almost continuously afterward. By the spring of 1944 the only large Soviet cities left in German hands were Minsk and Odessa. But the offensive power of the United Nations could not be considered complete until after a "second front" had been established in the west. This was accomplished on June 6 (D-Day), 1944, when 5000 Allied ships swarmed across the English Channel and landed their cargoes of soldiers and mechanized equipment on the Normandy coast of France. More than 100,000 troops were landed the first day, and over 2,000,000 by the following September.

It was now possible for the Allies to exert pressure upon Hitler's European fortress from three directions. In the south, Britons and Americans were still fighting in Italy, not against Italians but against the Germans, who had occupied most of the country soon after the overthrow of Mussolini. The conquest of the mountainous terrain of Italy proved a formidable undertaking and was not completed until virtually the end of the war. Soviet pressure from the east kept the Germans on the run until they reached Berlin. By the spring of 1945 Soviet armies had advanced to the banks of the Oder and were boasting that the doom of Hitler's Reich was but a matter of weeks. On April 21 they hammered their way into the suburbs of Berlin. During the next ten days a savage battle raged amid the ruins and heaps of rubble. The Nazi leaders entrenched themselves in underground shelters and goaded their followers into a fanatic defense of every street. But the hour of doom had struck. On May 2 the heart of the city was captured, and the Soviet red banner flew from the ruins of the Brandenburg Gate. A few hours earlier Adolf Hitler, Fuehrer of a state which was supposed to last for a thousand years, killed himself in the bombproof shelter of the Chancellery. Propaganda Minister Goebbels followed the example of his master. Other high Nazi leaders fled from the city, to destroy themselves later or to be taken as prisoners by the victorious armies.

Meanwhile, equally heavy pressure upon Germany was coming from the Allies in the west. Beachheads established on the Normandy coast had been gradually widened and large wedges cut out of Nazi-occupied territory in northern France. On August 25, 1944, Allied troops liberated Paris, and by September advance detachments had driven to the Rhine. In December the Germans attempted to sweep their opponents off their feet by a carefully planned surprise attack, aimed at capturing Liége and Namur and splitting the Allied forces in two. It was a desperate gamble and perhaps foredoomed to failure, but Hitler's generals managed to hammer a large "bulge" into Allied territory before they were stopped. In the late winter and spring of the following year the Allies resumed the offensive. In March they effected several crossings of the Rhine. By April 1 they had encircled the Ruhr valley, thereby cutting Germany off from some of her most valuable industrial centers. On April 25 soldiers of the American Ninth Army joined hands with Russian troops at Torgau near Leipzig, on the Elbe River. Germany was now cut in two. In the meantime, Allied planes, equipped with incendiary bombs and "block busters," had been raining death and destruction upon German cities. The final surrender occurred on May 7. At 2:41 A.M., in a schoolhouse in Reims, France, representatives of the German High Command signed a document of unconditional capitulation. Hostilities were to cease on all fronts at 12:01 A.M., May 9 (6:01 P.M., May 8, New York time). Peace had come to an exhausted Europe after five years and eight months of slaughter and barbarism.

The war in the Far East continued for three months after the end of the conflict in Europe. Following the battles of the Coral Sea and of Midway, the Allies were preoccupied with penetrating the outer and inner defenses of the great empire Japan had conquered. By the end of 1943 the outer defenses were pretty well

The approaching doom of Japan

The Battle of Tarawa. United States Marines establish a beachhead on the island of Tarawa, known as the "Gibraltar of the Pacific."

shattered. In 1944 bases were established close to Japan's inner defense line when Guam, Saipan, and Tinian were captured. In October of the same year a United States victory in the great battle of Leyte Gulf virtually eliminated Japan as a naval power and opened the way for the reconquest of the Philippines. Early in April, 1945, United States marines completed the bloody conquest of Iwo Jima, and in June, after 82 days of the most desperate fighting, Okinawa was taken. The Americans now had footholds less than 500 miles from the Japanese homeland. Such conquests were of exceeding value as bases from which to bomb by air Japan's **921** cities and industries. By early July Nipponese leaders were nervously anticipating an invasion and calling upon the citizens for supreme endeavors to meet the crisis.

The end of the war in the Pacific occurred with the same dramatic suddenness that had marked the collapse of Germany. On July 26 the heads of the United States, British, and Chinese governments issued a joint proclamation calling upon Japan to surrender or be destroyed. For a period of days the Tokyo government made no reply. But early in August a succession of events impelled the Nipponese war lords to change their minds. On August 3 United States naval authorities announced that they had succeeded in mining every Japanese harbor, thereby practically cutting the country off from outside sources of supply. On August 6 a single atomic bomb was dropped on Hiroshima, completely obliterating about 60 per cent of the city. On August 8 Soviet Russia entered the war, for the announced purpose of shortening hostilities and facilitating the restoration of "universal peace." It seems certain, however, that the Russians were influenced also by a desire to recover the position in the Far East which they had lost to Japan in the war of 1904–1905. On August 9, 1945, a second atomic bomb was dropped, this time on Nagasaki. That night President Truman warned that the United States would continue to use the deadly new weapon as long as might be necessary to bring Japan to her knees. The warning apparently had some effect, though it is probable that the Tokyo military leaders had realized for some time that defeat was inevitable. At any rate, the next day the Japanese government offered to accept the surrender ultimatum of July 26, with the understanding that the powers of the Emperor "as a sovereign ruler" should be left untouched. The Allies replied that the Emperor would be allowed to keep his position as a nominal sovereign but must be subject to the orders of the commander-in-chief of the occupying armies. For three agonizing days the world held its breath while the rulers of Nippon made their decision. At 6:10 P.M. on August 14 the answer was received in Washington. It was an unconditional acceptance of the Allied demands. That night there were riotous celebrations in the cities of the victorious nations. Millions of people danced and cheered and paraded in the streets amid the screaming of horns and the shrieking of sirens. Some of the more thoughtful assembled in churches the following day to give thanks that the terrible ordeal was over. And well they might, for the costliest and the most brutal and lawless of wars had passed into history.[14]

---

[14] The formal surrender was signed on September 2, 1945, on board the U.S.S. *Missouri*. General Douglas MacArthur accepted the surrender for the Allied governments. Foreign Minister Shigemitsu signed for Japan. The two-week delay occurred because of the time required to induce Japanese forces on distant islands and in other remote places to lay down their arms.

4. War Aims and Peace Plans

The professed war aims of belligerent nations usually undergo expansion as the military conflict proceeds. The situation in World War II was no exception. For example Hitler, in announcing his attack upon Poland on September 1, 1939, made no reference to plans for the conquest of Europe or of any territory outside of Europe. Instead, he described his purpose as simply to solve the problem of Danzig and the Corridor, both of which he maintained were German. He expressly denied any hostile intent toward Britain and France. Germany's "western wall," he declared, was "for all time the frontier of the Reich in the West." By January 30, 1940, however, he had begun to talk in a different vein. In his anniversary speech of that date he affirmed that it could "no longer be tolerated that the British nation of 44,000,000 souls should remain in possession of fifteen and a half million square miles of the world's surface" while Germany with 80,000,000 souls possessed only 230,000 square miles. Not until late in 1940 did he place much stress upon a conflict of ideologies. Speaking to munitions workers in Berlin on December 10, he referred to the war as a clash between two opposing worlds. The world of his enemies he described as the world of unrestricted capitalism, of the gold standard, of unlimited profits for the rich, and of unemployment and misery for the masses. Germany, he declared, had achieved a "socialist" economy, with restrictions upon greed, with equality of sacrifices, and with rewards apportioned according to work.[15] After the attack upon Russia in June, 1941, it became necessary for Hitler to expand still further his interpretation of the conflict. The war was now a struggle against "Asiatic Bolshevism." The rulers of Russia were partners with the powerful figures behind the capitalist governments in a Jewish world plot to crush the life out of Germany.

The evolution of Hitler's war aims

The first major formulation of Allied war and peace aims was the Atlantic Charter, issued by President Roosevelt and Prime Minister Churchill on August 14, 1941. Its principles, reduced to their essentials, were as follows:

Allied war aims and peace plans:

(1) Britain and the United States seek no aggrandizement, territorial or otherwise.

(1) The Atlantic Charter

(2) There should be no territorial changes that do not accord with the freely expressed wishes of the peoples concerned.

(3) The right of all peoples to choose the form of government under which they will live should be respected.

(4) All states, great or small, victor or vanquished, should enjoy access, on equal terms, to the trade and raw materials of the world.

---

[15] This conception of a war against bourgeois capitalism was also stressed by Hitler in his last important speech on January 30, 1945.

923

(5) Collaboration should be fostered among all nations with the object of securing, for all, improved labor standards, economic advancement, and social security.

(6) The peace to be established should afford to all nations the means of dwelling in safety within their own borders, and should afford assurance to all men that they may live out their lives in freedom from fear and want.

(7) The peace should enable all men to traverse the high seas without hindrance.

(8) Pending the establishment of a permanent system of general security, all nations which threaten or may threaten aggression should be disarmed.

(2) the United Nations Declaration

At the time of its issuance the Atlantic Charter committed no government except the British; the United States was still technically not a belligerent even though she was providing valuable assistance for the enemies of the Axis. The Charter acquired a broader significance on January 2, 1942, when the United Nations Declaration was issued. Twenty-six nations signed this Declaration, including Great Britain, the United States, the Soviet Union, and China. Subsequently about fourteen others added their signatures. Not only did each government dedicate its entire resources to the war and promise never to make a separate peace, but all of them affirmed their adherence to the Atlantic Charter.

(3) the Cairo Declaration

As the war progressed, high officials of the leading United Nations met in various conferences for the purpose of solving problems of strategy and determining the conditions of peace. The first of outstanding importance was the conference which met in Cairo in November, 1943, to discuss the fate of the Japanese Empire. The participants were President Roosevelt, Prime Minister Churchill, and Generalissimo Chiang Kai-shek. They agreed that all of the territories taken by Japan from China, with the exception of Korea (Chosen), were to be restored to the Chinese Republic. Korea, they declared, was to become, "in due course," free and independent. They agreed, further, that Japan was to be stripped of all the islands in the Pacific which she had seized or occupied since 1914, and of "all other territories which she had taken by violence or greed." What disposition was to be made of these islands and territories was not specified. The three statesmen declared, however, that their nations coveted "no gain for themselves" and had "no thought of territorial expansion."

(4) the Teheran Declaration

The second of the major conferences took place in December, 1943, when Churchill, Roosevelt, and Stalin met in Teheran, capital of Iran. Although no great ideas emerged from this conference, it was significant nevertheless as the first meeting of the heads of government of the Big Three. The three rulers expressed their determination that their nations should work together both in the

924

THE COST OF MODERN WAR

THE TOTAL COST OF WORLD WAR II, ESTIMATED AT $1,384,900,000,000,* WOULD HAVE BEEN SUFFICIENT TO PAY FOR ALL OF THE FOLLOWING:

A $20,000 house for every family in the United States, Britain, Belgium, and Portugal.

A $10,000,000 library for every city of 200,000 inhabitants and over in the United States, Great Britain, and the U.S.S.R.

A $50,000,000 university for each of these cities.

A $2500 automobile for every family in the United States, and Great Britain.

The salaries of 50,000 teachers and an equal number of nurses at $6000 a year for 100 years.

A free college or vocational education (at an estimated cost of $9000) for every high school graduate in the United States from 17 to 21 years of age.

*From an estimate prepared by James H. Brady and the American University

war and in the peace. They recognized the supreme responsibility resting upon them and upon all the nations to make a peace which would command good will from the peoples of the world and "banish the scourge and terror of war for many generations." They looked with confidence to the day "when all the peoples of the world may live free lives untouched by tyranny and according to their varying desires and their own consciences."

(5) the Yalta Agreement

After the Teheran meeting there were no further conferences of great importance until 1945. In February of that year Roosevelt and Churchill traveled to the sunny slopes of the Crimea to confer with Stalin. The parleys were held in the luxurious palace of the last of the Tsars near the resort town of Yalta. The outcome was agreement on a large number of troublesome issues. A formal report issued at the close of the conference declared that the Big Three had agreed upon plans for the defeat of Germany, upon the unconditional surrender terms to be imposed upon Germany, upon methods of controlling the Axis nations and their satellites after the war, and upon the establishment of a United Nations Organization with a veto power for each of the Big Five. It was announced, in addition, that agreement had been reached on several of the thorny problems of eastern Europe. The boundary between Poland and the Soviet Union was fixed at a line originally suggested in 1919 by Lord Curzon, British Foreign Secretary, and tentatively approved by the victorious Allies. The U.S.S.R. was thus permitted to keep approximately the same territory she had already incorporated in the Soviet Union as a result of the Ribbentrop-Molotov agreement of September, 1939. Poland was to be compensated for

The Big Three at Teheran, November, 1943. Stalin, Roosevelt, and Churchill on the portico of the Russian Embassy in the Iranian capital.

The Yalta Conference, February, 1945. Standing directly behind the Big Three are Anthony Eden, British Foreign Secretary; Edward R. Stettinius, United States Secretary of State; and Vyacheslav M. Molotov, Soviet Foreign Minister. The exhaustion of President Roosevelt in the 15 months since the Teheran Conference is clearly evident.

her losses in the east by "substantial accessions of territory" in the north and west—to be taken, of course, from Germany. The existing government of Poland, set up under Soviet auspices, was to be "reorganized on a broader democratic basis with the inclusion of democratic leaders from Poland itself and from Poles abroad." The government of Yugoslavia also was to be broadened, and the Big Three pledged themselves to act in concert when formulating policies for the liberated countries of Europe, including those formerly satellites of the Axis. Regarding the Far East, it was agreed secretly that Russia should enter the war against Japan two or three months after the defeat of Germany and receive as her reward, in the event of victory, all the territories and concessions taken from her by Japan in the war of 1904–1905.

The collapse of Germany on May 8, 1945, seemed to require yet another conference of the leading powers. On July 17 Joseph Stalin, Winston Churchill, and Harry S. Truman, who had succeeded Franklin D. Roosevelt as President of the United States on April 12, met in Potsdam, suburb of Berlin and historic center of Prussian militarism. Before the conference had finished its work, Churchill was replaced by Clement Attlee, the new Labor Prime Minister of Great Britain. The Potsdam Conference was not a peace conference; several of its decisions were announced as temporary. Some of them, however, have so radically changed conditions in Europe that they can probably be regarded as permanent. The most important provisions of the formal Declaration, issued by the conference on August 2, were the following: (1) Germany to be deprived of extensive portions of her territory: East Prussia to be divided into two parts, the northern part including the city of Koenigsberg to go to the Soviet Union, and the southern part to be assigned to Poland; Poland also to receive the former free city of Danzig; all German territory east of the Oder and Neisse rivers to be administered by Poland pending a final settlement; (2) the military power of Germany to be totally destroyed; (3) the industrial power of Germany to be drastically reduced; the economic system to be decentralized by abolishing trusts and cartels; the production of chemicals, metals, machinery, and other items necessary to a war economy to be rigidly controlled and restricted; primary emphasis to be given, in reorganizing the German economy, to the development of agriculture and "peaceful domestic industries"; (4) Germany to pay extensive reparations in kind, in the form of machinery, minerals, manufactured products, productive equipment, and merchant ships; (5) Germany to be divided into four occupation zones, to be governed, respectively, by the U.S.S.R., Great Britain, the United States, and France.

Despite the great number and variety of decisions adopted at these conferences, there was by no means a complete solution of postwar problems. The chief powers had not been able to agree on the

(6) the Potsdam Declaration

fundamental principles of the peace. They were just as far apart on the solution of specific problems. They had reached no agreement on control of atomic energy or on such problems as what should be done with Austria, with the city of Trieste, with the Ruhr valley, with the Dardanelles and Bosporus, with the problem of how Germany should be governed, or with the territorial demands of the Greeks against Albania, or the Yugoslavs against Austria. No better results had been achieved with respect to the problems of Asia. The ultimate fate of such territories as Burma, Indo-China, Hong Kong, and the Netherlands Indies remained a mystery. Despite the provisions of the Cairo Declaration, the status of Korea and of Manchuria was also in considerable doubt. A few of these issues were settled by later negotiation. Some were solved by the self-aggrandizement of interested nations. But many of them remained as sources of discord and danger for the incalculable future.

Selected Readings

Armstrong, H. F., *Chronology of Failure: The Last Days of the French Republic*, New York, 1940
Beard, C. A., *Whither Mankind*, New York, 1928
Buell, R. L., *Poland: Key to Europe*, New York, 1939
Dean, Vera M., *Why Europe Went to War*, New York, 1939
Feis, Herbert, *The Road to Pearl Harbor*, Princeton, 1950
Finer, Herman, *America's Destiny*, New York, 1947
Gantenbein, James W. ed., *Documentary Background of World War II, 1931 to 1941*, New York, 1948
Gedye, G. E. R., *Betrayal in Central Europe*, New York, 1939
Haines, C. G., and Hoffman, R. J. S., *The Origins and Background of the Second World War*, New York, 1943
Heiden, Konrad, *Der Fuehrer*, Boston, 1944
Henderson, Sir N., *Failure of a Mission*, New York, 1940
Hutton, Graham, *Survey after Munich*, Boston, 1939
Jackson, J. H., *Finland*, New York, 1940
Machray, Robert, *The Poland of Pilsudski*, New York, 1937
McInnis, Edgar, *The War*, New York, 1940–1944, 4 vols.
Mitchell, Broadus, *Depression Decade; from New Era through New Deal, 1929 to 1941*, New York, 1947
Orton, William, *Twenty Years' Armistice*, New York, 1938
Randall, J. H., Jr., *Our Changing Civilization*, New York, 1929
Reves, Emery, *The Anatomy of Peace*, New York, 1945
Schuman, F. L., *Europe on the Eve*, New York, 1939
Spengler, Oswald, *The Decline of the West*, one-volume edition, New York, 1932
Spykman, N. J., *America's Strategy in World Politics*, New York, 1942
Trevor-Roper, H. R., *The Last Days of Hitler*, New York, 1947
Wittman, Erno, *History: A Guide to Peace*, New York, 1948

Churchill, W. S., *Blood, Sweat, and Tears*
——, *The Second World War*, 6 vols.
Grew, J. C., *Report from Tokyo*
Hambro, C. J., *I Saw It Happen in Norway*
Kleffens, E. N. van, *Juggernaut over Holland*
Lochner, L., ed., *The Goebbels Diaries*
Marshall, G. C., Arnold, H. H., and King, E. J., *The War Reports*
Maurois, André, *Tragedy in France: An Eyewitness Account*
United States Department of State, *Peace and War, U. S. Foreign Policy,
    1931–1941*

The World that Victory Made

The tragic character of the postwar world

The world that emerged from the crucible of World War II bore little resemblance to the dreams of idealists set forth during the early days of the conflict. Over vast areas it was a world of hunger and fear, of ashes and rubble, of hopelessness, misery, and violence. Scarcely anywhere was it possible to find evidence that the Four Freedoms or the provisions of the Atlantic Charter were about to be realized. The hopes of the masses in all nations that security and peace would automatically result when the carnage was over were badly shattered. The revival of power politics and the fear of a new war, to be fought with atomic bombs and bacteriological poisons, made the decade of the 1930's by comparison seem almost serene and orderly. Yet the postwar world was not hopelessly mired in pessimism. Some idealism still existed; but during the first few years, at least, it made difficult headway against bitterness, defeatism, and a longing to smash any obstacle that stood in the way of a return to prewar conditions.

1. The Revolution of Our Age

Origin and nature of the revolution

One of the least obvious but nonetheless important consequences of World War II was to accelerate the world revolution that forms so significant a part of the history of our time. This revolution did not spring upon us overnight. It had its origins in the dying years of the nineteenth century. It was a fundamental factor in producing the two world wars of the twentieth century, and it underlay both fascism and communism. Its nature is not easy to define, but in a general way it resembles the events which marked the transition from the Middle Ages to the modern era or the death of the Old Regime in eighteenth-century France. In short, it is the kind of pattern of developments which has always occurred when an old world is dying and a new one is struggling to be born.

A basic factor in the revolution of the contemporary world has been a declining confidence in the economic system which grew up under the Industrial Revolution. We can refer to this economic system as capitalism, provided we understand by the term the system of free enterprise, free competition, and production for profit which flourished in the nineteenth and early twentieth centuries. Loss of faith in this system did not result because of its failure to raise standards of living or to function efficiently in exploiting the resources of the earth. On the contrary, with respect to both of these factors its record has been astonishingly successful. Despite increases in prices, the wages of workers, since 1850 at least, have shown a substantial advance. Moreover, the economic system of capitalist nations has demonstrated a phenomenal capacity for production, with the result of making available, even to families of modest income, an increasing profusion of goods.

Economic aspects: declining faith in capitalism

The decline of faith in capitalism was not universal. The system has retained popular acceptance in recent years in countries like the United States which rode the crest of the prosperity wave after 1945. But in some areas of Asia and Africa, where the per capita income scarcely exceeded $50 a year, and where infant mortality was five times as high as in the United States, there was a tendency on the part of many to wonder whether some other economic system might not do more to lift the masses out of the mire of starvation and hardship. Capitalism seemed to many, as they looked back upon its history, a most inefficient system for keeping the production and consumption of goods in balance. Every second decade or so a considerable portion of the economy of the industrial nations had had to be put through the wringer. Not until after a sufficient number of bankruptcies, foreclosures, and business failures had taken place could the wheels of production resume turning. Meanwhile, millions of people would have lost their property or suffered the humiliation of unemployment and dependence upon charity or public relief. Perhaps unemployment, overproduction, and insecurity would be recurrent or permanent. These melancholy reflections were relieved only by the outbreak of war in 1939 and the "prosperity" which resulted from the wholesale destruction and waste. Even so, a few skeptics still wondered what would happen when peace returned and brought a cessation of orders for planes, tanks, and jeeps and the steel and aluminum with which to make them.

Declining faith not universal but widespread

Doleful predictions, however, did not come true. The pent-up demand for new cars, refrigerators, television sets, and other durable consumers' goods proved so strong that the years from 1945 to 1957, in the western countries at least, were among the most prosperous in history. The intensification of the cold war and the

Effects of the cold war and war in Korea

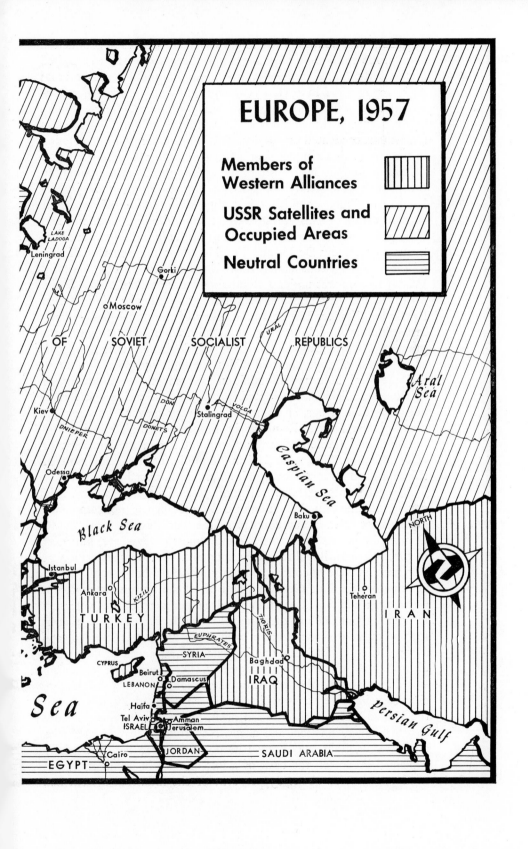

beginning of hostilities in Korea gave such an impetus to production as to make the 1920's seem almost like depression. In the United States, for example, the index of industrial production rose from 48 in 1930 to 121 in 1951. Eventually with the progress of reconstruction, a substantial revival of trade occurred. Great Britain, West Germany, the Netherlands, and ultimately France enjoyed an almost unprecedented prosperity. The index of industrial production in the United States underwent a further rise to 141 in 1955.

The growth of collectivism

A second important feature of the revolution of our time has been the growth of collectivism. This, of course, has been closely related to declining confidence in capitalism. It has manifested itself in such diverse forms as the welfare state, fascism, socialism, and communism. Characteristic expressions of the first were the achievements of the New Deal under Franklin Roosevelt and the reforms of the Popular Front under Léon Blum in France. After World War II fascism was under a cloud almost everywhere except Spain, Portugal, and Argentina, but socialism took on new life in Great Britain and France. The decisive victory of the British Labor Party in the elections of July, 1945, was followed by an extensive program of collectivization. The Bank of England was nationalized, and also the railways, the coal mines, the light and power industry, and the steel industry. In addition, a comprehensive scheme of socialized medicine was adopted, providing free medical attention, hospitalization, drugs, and nursing for every citizen. The government of the Fourth Republic in France, controlled mainly by Socialists and Catholic liberals, also went far in the direction of collectivization. The mines, railways, public utilities, and most of the banks and insurance companies were taken over by the state.

The appeal of communism

A much more extreme form of collectivist movement is, of course, communism. When World War II began, no communist government ruled in any country of the world except the U.S.S.R. Communist parties were to be found almost everywhere, but most of them were small and relatively impotent. Ten years after the war Communists were in control, not only of Russia, but also of Poland, Czechoslovakia, East Germany, and of all the Balkan states except Greece. In addition, they numbered 22 per cent of the voters in Italy and about one out of four in France. It was estimated that in Europe outside of the Russian orbit there were at least 11,000,000 avowed Communists. Communism had also advanced in China and ultimately engulfed the entire country. The spread of communism was due in part to the overshadowing might of the Soviet Union, especially in those states which had been assigned by Britain and the United States to the Russian orbit. It was due in some measure also to hunger, inflation, and chaos. Nevertheless, in such countries as Germany, Italy, and France its popularity can hardly be fully explained except on the basis of a loss of faith in capitalism. Even in Czechoslovakia about 65 per cent of the industrial system had been nationalized *before* the Communists seized control of the government in February, 1948.

It was by no means certain, however, that extreme collectivisim would become a permanent feature of modern civilization. Perhaps it would in some parts of Asia and in Eastern Europe where traditions of freedom and individualism have never been strong. Probably even in Western Europe many elements of socialism will survive for the indefinite future, regardless of what parties control the governments. This trend was exemplified when the Conservatives returned to power in Britain in 1951. Under Winston Churchill and Anthony Eden, who succeeded him in 1955, they contented themselves with denationalizing the steel industry and making slight modifications in the national health program. In the United States the forces of individualism and free enterprise have been able to muster strong opposition to any but a comparatively moderate brand of collectivism. In the Presidential campaign of 1948 the most radical of the leading candidates found it expedient to declare himself an exponent of "progressive capitalism," and this in spite of the fact that he had the support of the Communists. The successful candidate, Harry S. Truman, promised that the New Deal would be revived and that it would be extended and completed by a Fair Deal. His promises, however, were more ambitious than Congress would accept, and the Fair Deal remained only partly realized. In 1953 the Republicans came back into power, after a lapse of twenty years, and installed Dwight D. Eisenhower in the White House. The new administration announced that it would abolish all price controls, substitute credit controls for inflation of the currency, sell the synthetic rubber factories to private companies, and restore the off-shore oil lands to the states. The acceptance of these policies seemed to indicate that the nation had grown weary of the reform enthusiasm of Roosevelt and Truman, although there was still no strong disposition to return to the individualism of the 1920's.

Still another element in the contemporary world revolution has been the rebellion against imperialism, or colonialism, as it is now more commonly called. For more than a century Great Britain, France, and the Netherlands had succeeded in imposing their rule upon a large proportion of the teeming hordes of Southeast Asia, India, the Middle East, and Africa. The superior weapons and technology of the rulers caused them to think of themselves as superior peoples with a God-given mission to carry the blessings of civilization to benighted natives. In some cases the civilizing process was merely a disguised exploitation, though it can scarcely be doubted that benefits in the form of increased education and improved sanitation did flow, in some measure, to the subjugated peoples. So long as the latter saw little hope of changing their status they accepted the rule of the European with no more than feeble protests. World War I transformed this attitude. The spectacle of the great Christian nations mauling each other on the battlefield destroyed their proud boasts of superior virtue. The war also made possible the triumph of communism in Russia and the dissemination of its appeal to the subjects of capitalist powers to throw off their oppressors. World War II had even more startling effects. Britain and France were seriously weakened, while the colonial empires of Italy and Japan ceased to exist. As a result of her part in the defeat of Hitler, the prestige of the U.S.S.R. was higher than ever. These developments inevitably combined to produce in the colonial dependencies a spirit of revolt. Influential also was the gradual discovery by the colonial natives of a better way of life than the cycle of famine, poverty, filth, and disease handed down by their ancestors.

Independence movements in Asia

Independence movements among subject peoples gathered momentum even before the end of World War II, and were ready to burst into open revolt with the signing of the armistice. Five days after V-J Day, nationalists in Indonesia proclaimed their country a republic. Four years of intermittent warfare had to be waged, however, before the Dutch were willing to sign agreements transferring sovereignty to the new government. In February, 1947, the British Labor Government yielded to pressure from Hindu and Moslem nationalists by announcing its intention to withdraw from India and to partition the country into two dominions. In August of that year the Hindu provinces were organized as the Union of India and entered the British Commonwealth of Nations as a self-governing dominion. In 1950 India became a sovereign republic, remaining a member of the Commonwealth of Nations, but with the word "British" omitted. Meanwhile, the Moslem provinces had been organized as the Dominion of Pakistan, which in 1956 also became an independent republic and a member of the Commonwealth of Nations. The other most important Asiatic territories to gain independence were the Philippines and Palestine. The former was proclaimed a republic by the United States in 1946, in accordance with a promise contained in an Act of Congress in 1934. When World War II ended, Palestine was still a British mandate. In response to Zionist pressure and a decision of the United Nations Assembly to partition the country between Arabs and Jews, Britain surrendered its mandate. In 1948 the Jewish portion of Palestine was organized as the Republic of Israel. Its history ever since has been a record of turmoil and strife. The surrounding Arab states resent its establishment, and have plagued its existence by repeated raids across its borders.

The anticolonial revolt in North Africa

From Western Asia the revolt against colonialism spread to North Africa. The French soon found themselves in a welter of trouble in Tunisia, Algeria, and Morocco. Despite recurring waves of terrorism against French officials, farmers, and merchants, only Morocco and Tunisia had gained independence by 1957. The new

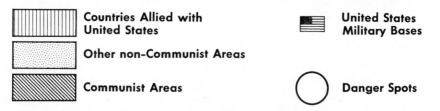

DANGER SPOTS IN THE FAR EAST

Countries Allied with United States

United States Military Bases

Other non-Communist Areas

Communist Areas

Danger Spots

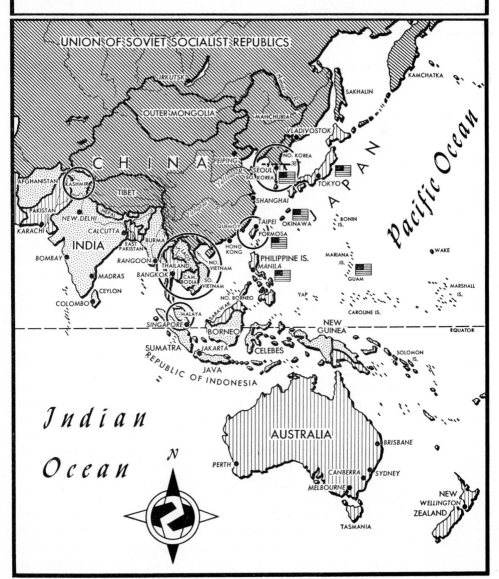

UNION OF SOVIET SOCIALIST REPUBLICS

IRKUTSK

KAMCHATKA

SAKHALIN

OUTER MONGOLIA

MANCHURIA

VLADIVOSTOK

NO. KOREA

PEIPINGS

C H I N A

SEOUL

SO. KOREA

38

TOKYO

J A P A N

AFGHANISTAN

KASHMIR

TIBET

SHANGHAI

BONIN IS.

PAKISTAN

NEW DELHI

NEPAL

QUEMOY

TAIPEI

OKINAWA

KARACHI

CALCUTTA

BURMA

FORMOSA

WAKE

INDIA

EAST PAKISTAN

HONG KONG

MARIANA IS.

BOMBAY

RANGOON

THAILAND

LAOS

NO. VIETNAM

PHILIPPINE IS.

MANILA

MADRAS

BANGKOK

CAM-BODIA

SO. VIETNAM

GUAM

CEYLON

NO. BORNEO

YAP

COLOMBO

MALAYA

SARAWAK

CAROLINE IS.

NEW GUINEA

EQUATOR

SINGAPORE

BORNEO

SUMATRA

JAKARTA

CELEBES

SOLOMON IS.

JAVA

REPUBLIC OF INDONESIA

Pacific Ocean

MARSHALL IS.

Indian

Ocean

N

AUSTRALIA

BRISBANE

PERTH

CANBERRA

SYDNEY

MELBOURNE

NEW WELLINGTON ZEALAND

TASMANIA

The Israeli-Arab Conflict. An Israeli farmer, constantly under threat of attack from border raiders, keeps a rifle within easy reach as he works his land.

status in both came largely as a concession to conciliatory nationalist leaders who helped to restrain their followers. In 1956 one other North African territory achieved independence, not from France but from Britain and Egypt. This was the Sudan, formerly called the Anglo-Egyptian Sudan. The climax of the anticolonial revolt in North Africa, however, was the nationalist revolution in Egypt and the seizure of the Suez Canal. In 1952 a military junta, under the nominal leadership of Major-General Mohammed Naguib, deposed the corrupt and extravagant King Farouk, who was alleged to be subservient to the British. The government was made into a republic with Naguib as President and Premier. It soon became apparent that the real ruler was a fiery lieutenant-colonel, Gamal Abdel Nasser, and in 1956 Nasser became President and virtual dictator. Though the Naguib-Nasser regime initiated various reforms for the benefit of its 20,000,000 poverty-stricken subjects, its major ambition seems to have been to rid the country of foreign domination. In 1954 its leaders browbeat the British into signing an agreement for the withdrawal of British troops from Egyptian territory. In 1956 President Nasser nationalized all British and French banks in his country. He precipitated an international crisis in the same year by seizing the Suez Canal. In retaliation the British and French apparently encouraged the Republic of Israel to invade Egypt, and followed the invasion two days later with an attack of their own. They bombed cities in the Canal region and airfields throughout the country. The fighting ended five days later when the participants accepted a U.N. appeal for a cease-fire, in response to pressure from the United States and threats from the Soviet Union.

The Suez Crisis of 1956

The Suez Crisis was fraught with such grave possibilities that it is still quite difficult to appraise their significance. It resulted, first of all, in serious disaffection among the Western Powers. The United States was offended because Britain and France launched

938 their attack upon Egypt without even informing the government in Washington. The British and the French, on their part, were annoyed with the vacillation of the American State Department, and alleged that the blundering of Secretary Dulles had made drastic action against Egypt the only alternative. The crisis had as a second result the downfall of Anthony Eden as Prime Minister of Britain. Though he was succeeded by a member of his own party, so much

On the Eve of the Suez Crisis. Cairo celebrates the news that British troops are to leave the Suez Canal Zone.

Oil in the Middle East. Long stretches of pipe line carry crude oil from desert fields to Mediterranean seaports and to refineries on the Persian Gulf. United States interests control most of the oil of Saudi Arabia, while that of Iraq and Iran is exploited jointly by both European and American companies.

opposition had developed within the country to what many regarded as a revival of the "gunboat diplomacy" of the nineteenth century that the days of Conservative rule appeared to be numbered. But the most serious of all the consequences of the Suez Crisis was the threatened intrusion of the Soviet Union into the Middle East. For many years Russia had looked with covetous eyes upon the famous land bridge connecting the three continents. Arab nationalism and fanatical hatred of Western imperialists seemed to provide the U.S.S.R. with a golden opportunity. If the Soviets could accomplish nothing more, they might hope to cut off the West from the rich oil resources in the region of the Persian Gulf. Here are located more than half of the proved petroleum reserves of the entire world, and without them the economy of Western Europe would be badly crippled. So ominous had the situation become that in January, 1957, President Eisenhower recommended to Congress the adoption of a policy that would commit the United States to provide military aid to any state of the Middle East threatened by **939** the direct aggression of a Communist power. Despite strong criticism, the policy was approved with slight modifications by overwhelming votes in both Senate and House.

2. New Power Relationships

The shifting positions of the Great Powers

Prior to 1914 the list of World Powers included no fewer than eight states. Of these, the six European nations—Great Britain, France, Germany, Austria-Hungary, Russia, and Italy—were the most powerful and generally were the real arbiters of world affairs. The United States and Japan were newcomers whose position did not count too heavily in the international scale. After World War I the number of Great Powers shrank to five. Austria was eliminated permanently and Germany and Russia for a period of years. On the other hand, the United States and Japan rose to positions much higher than they had previously occupied, while the British Empire sank a bit lower. The effects of World War II upon power relationships were far more upsetting. Germany, Italy, and Japan were defeated so overwhelmingly that it did not seem possible that for many years they could again be first-rank nations. Officially, the list of World Powers still included five states—the U.S.S.R., the United States, Great Britain, China, and France. These were the famous Big Five, who held the dominant position in the United Nations and whose representatives were given authority to draft the treaties of peace. However, China was soon overwhelmed by communist revolution, while Britain and France became increasingly dependent upon the United States and seldom exerted much influence of their own in world affairs.

Power vacuums after World War II

But World War II had at least one other momentous effect. This was to create what diplomats call "power vacuums" in various parts of the world. To illustrate, the annihilation of Germany as a Great Power left a gaping void in central Europe. Whether one likes to admit it or not, Germany during the 1930's was the economic and political hub of a large portion of the European Continent. The trade relations of the Low Countries, of Scandinavia, and the Balkans were more extensive with her than with any other country in the world. Her military power helped to preserve a kind of balance between Britain and France in the west and Russia in the east. But with Germany hopelessly crushed, that balance was gone and in its place was a vacuum which strong and ambitious powers would strive to fill. Similarly, the conquest of Japan removed that power as a counterweight against the Soviets in the Far East, with the result that a vacuum was created in such territories as Manchuria, Korea, and China. Finally, the weakening of Britain as a consequence of the war opened up a number of her colonies and spheres of influence to pressure from powerful rivals. Within a short time Russian, or at least communist, penetration had occurred in the

Middle East, in the Malay Peninsula, and in Greece. Some authorities go so far as to argue that this struggle over power vacuums has been the fundamental cause of nearly all the international friction since World War II. They maintain that as soon as these vacuums are filled—by their own nation or its allies—stability and peace will return to the earth.

No matter how we may interpret the international friction after World War II, there can be no doubt that plenty of it existed. Indeed, the relationship between Britain and the United States, on the one side, and the U.S.S.R., on the other, most of the time was an armed truce, or what has been more commonly called a cold war. For a brief period it appeared that a more cordial atmosphere was going to prevail. In December, 1945, a council of the foreign ministers of the Big Three met in Moscow and, after a week of toasts and banquets and friendly banter, announced that agreement "in principle" had been reached on a large number of difficult issues. Even such questions as control of the atomic bomb and the administration of Japan and Korea were not excluded. Nearly everywhere the announcement was hailed with great rejoicing, in the belief that the problems of the world were as good as solved. However, it was a false dawn. Though representatives of the Powers met many times thereafter, their accomplishments were comparatively few and not generally of major importance. About all they could claim credit for by the twelfth anniversary of the end of the war was the organization of Trieste as a free territory under the Security Council of the United Nations and the adoption of treaties with Japan, with Austria, and with the five smaller Axis satellites. The more serious problems, such as peace with a united Germany, the control of atomic and thermonuclear energy, and disarmament, were as far from solution as ever.

Big Three negotiations

The five treaties for the Axis satellites—Italy, Bulgaria, Rumania, Hungary, and Finland—derive such importance as they have mainly from the fact that they altered the map of Europe. The Italian treaty provided for the cession of Briga and Tenda to France; Venezia Giulia, with the exception of the Free Territory of Trieste, to Yugoslavia; and the Dodecanese Islands to Greece. Hungary was required to surrender the eastern half of Transylvania to Rumania. Rumania was forced to acquiesce in the loss of Bessarabia and Northern Bukovina to the Soviet Union and a portion of the Southern Dobrudja to Bulgaria. Finland was obliged to hand over the province of Petsamo, with its valuable nickel mines, to the U.S.S.R. All of the treaties provided for demilitarization and for reparations penalties, ranging from $70,000,000 to be paid by Bulgaria to $360,000,000 levied upon Italy. The treaty with Austria, signed in 1955, freed the country from Allied occupation, prohibited union with Germany, and required the maintenance of democracy.

The five minor peace treaties

The treaty with Japan was adopted in September, 1951, at a conference in San Francisco attended by delegates from fifty-two nations. Although supposedly a treaty of reconciliation, it deprived Japan of all the territory she had acquired since 1854—in other words, her entire overseas empire. She gave up the Kuriles and the southern half of Sakhalin Island to the Soviets, and the Bonins and Ryukyus to control by the United States. She also renounced all rights to Formosa, which was left in a status still undefined. In return for these concessions she was allowed to recover her sovereignty and to rearm for her own defense. By a separate agreement the United States obtained the right to continue military installations in Japan until the latter was able to defend herself. The treaty went into effect in April, 1952, against the stubborn opposition of the Russians, who had hoped that Japan would be crippled by drastic punishments and thereby left an easy prey to communism. Five years later the United States government announced the withdrawal of all its ground combat troops and the progressive reduction of other forces as Japan increased its capacity for its own defense.

*Reasons for the
disharmony be-
tween East and
West*

Why were the chief powers not more successful in solving the problems of the peace, and why in particular did so much disharmony exist between the Western nations on the one side and the U.S.S.R. on the other? One reason was the fact that their wartime alliance had been simply a marriage of convenience. Each side had been perfectly willing to use the other, but there had been no bond of mutual trust or respect to hold them together. As late as 1940 Churchill had described the Soviet system as one which "rots the soul of a nation" and makes it "abject and hungry in peace" and "base and abominable in war." A second and more important reason was the fundamental conflict of aims between the Soviet Union and the Western powers. Britain and the United States, the latter particularly, had visions of reconstructing the world in accordance with the pattern of 1939, except for the destruction of the military and economic power of the Axis nations. They planned a decentralized government for Germany, the internationalization of the Ruhr, and a redistribution of the colonial possessions of Italy and Japan in such a way as to give to themselves a large measure of control. The Soviet rulers had altogether different ambitions. In general, they appeared to have made only minor changes in their long-term plan for promoting the spread of communism over the entire world. They contended for a share of control of the Bosporus and the Dardanelles and for territorial revisions at the expense of Turkey and China. As a great continental nation, they aspired to freer access to the open seas—to the Mediterranean and Baltic Seas and to the Indian and Pacific Oceans. Further, the Russians were concerned about the danger of a new attack upon the Soviet motherland. Though the Red Army had given an excellent account of itself in the war against Germany, they were afraid that some new combination of capitalist powers, probably under the leadership of the United States, might succeed in a deadly assault upon the home of communism. They therefore proceeded to form a Soviet bloc in eastern Europe, extending as far west as Berlin, and to entrench themselves in such strategic localities in the Far East as Dairen, Port Arthur, and Northern Korea. They also increased their aid and encouragement of native Communists in the efforts of the latter to conquer China, Korea, Indo-China, and some countries of the Middle East.

3. The United States as a World Power

One of the most impressive results of World War II was the emergence of the United States as the most powerful nation in the world. Except for the Soviet Union, there was not a country anywhere on earth that could throw down a challenge to her. For a brief period at the end of the war the United States had the largest army in the world, while her navy was equal to the combined navies of all the other powers. Her tonnage in aircraft carriers alone just about matched the total tonnage of the entire British navy. Though both her land and naval forces were substantially reduced by 1950, she still had impressive strength. From the standpoint of economic power, also, she had far outdistanced the rest of the nations. Since 1939 her people had doubled their national income and quadrupled their savings. Though they constituted only 7 per cent of the world's population, Americans enjoyed over 30 per cent of the world's estimated income. For the first time in her history the United States was in a position to be the arbiter of the destinies of at least half of the earth. Japan was virtually her colony; she controlled both the Atlantic and Pacific Oceans, policed the Mediterranean, and shaped the development of international policy in Western Europe. But it must not be imagined that her people had found for themselves an earthly paradise. The national debt in 1945 stood at $260,000,000,000. More money was required to pay the interest on this debt than had been necessary to defray the entire cost of government before the war. By 1948 the cost of living had risen to 172 per cent of the 1935–1939 average, and one family out of every four was spending in excess of its earnings. Moreover, despite her sacrifice of billions of dollars and 350,000 lives, the United States had not gained security. For years after the war, her citizens lived in as much dread of a new attack as they had felt at almost any time while the war was in progress.

The U.S. on top of the world

With the end of World War II comparatively little evidence was to be found of a desire on the part of the United States to retreat into the kind of isolationism that followed the victory in the previous war. At least this was true of the government. In 1945 the United States Senate ratified the Charter of the United Nations

The decline of isolationism

almost unanimously. Little clamor was raised in Congress or else-where for repayment of the sums advanced by the United States under Lend-Lease. Instead, there was an almost universal disposition to treat those loans as gifts. Eventually about nine-tenths of the amount was written off, and in 1946 a new loan of about $4,000,-000,000 for economic recovery was made to Great Britain, the chief beneficiary under Lend-Lease. Although there was some grumbling by extreme isolationists, Congress appears to have approved these actions in the belief that they would be contributions to world recovery. Hardly anyone believed any longer that the United States could go her own way and prosper and leave the rest of the world to the dogs.

The Truman foreign policy

The most vigorous leadership in inducing the United States to live up to her new obligations of power and responsibility came naturally from the executive branch of the government. In 1947, in an address to Congress, President Truman enunciated the first of a series of important policy statements on foreign affairs. It soon became known as the Truman Doctrine. Pointing to the spread of communism in eastern Europe, the President declared that the United States must go to the aid of any country whose "freedom and independence" were threatened by aggression from within or without. Referring specifically to Soviet pressure against Greece and Turkey, he avowed that the survival and independence of these countries was essential to preserve the integrity of the Middle East. Accordingly, he requested the appropriation of $400,000,000 to send weapons and economic aid to both nations and to provide them with military and naval advisory commissions from the United States. Two months later a bill appropriating the sum requested was passed by bipartisan majorities in both houses of Congress.

The Marshall Plan

The second of the policy statements coming from the executive branch was the Marshall Plan, or European Recovery Program. This program was first suggested in a speech at Harvard University, June 5, 1947, by George C. Marshall, Secretary of State. Marshall said that if the states of Europe would come to an agreement on what they needed to cover the costs of reconstruction, the United States would see what it could do to help them. He declared that United States policy was not directed "against any country or doctrine but against hunger, poverty, desperation, and chaos." At the same time, he issued a warning that any government attempting to block recovery to perpetuate human misery for its own profit would receive no help. Secretary Marshall's proposal aroused an enthusiastic response by European nations. Even the U.S.S.R. participated in a preliminary conference of the Big Three to see what could be done. But this conference ended in deadlock when Molotov demanded that the United States should give up the idea of a combined program for all of Europe and provide for the needs of each nation individually. Apparently he feared that a combined plan might be used as an instrument for organizing Europe under United States control.

To a considerable extent the Marshall Plan and the Truman Doctrine were related programs. Both were elements in a broad strategy of "containing" Soviet Russia. In the development of the Truman Doctrine, open avowals were made of the need to keep Greece and Turkey in the Anglo-American sphere of influence. Control of them was held to be necessary to the protection of British and United States interests in the Middle East. It was argued also that if either or both of them should fall under the sway of Communists, the Soviet power would expand into the Mediterranean. In other words, the two countries were considered almost exclusively from the standpoint of their being pawns in a gigantic struggle for power. It may be doubted that the Marshall Plan as originally conceived was intended as a weapon against the U.S.S.R. The United States was certainly interested in the economic recovery of Europe as a contribution to peace and also as an aid to maintaining her own prosperity. Nevertheless, the supporters of the Plan occasionally used arguments which created the impression that the major interest Americans had in assisting European recovery was to prevent the spread of communism. The Soviets, at any rate, tended to interpret both the Truman Doctrine and the Marshall Plan as maneuvers in a cold war or war of nerves against them.

The Marshall Plan and the Truman Doctrine

Whatever her methods and specific purposes, the United States will undoubtedly continue to play an increasingly important role in world affairs. Britain and the states of Continental Europe have been undergoing decline since 1914. They have suffered appalling losses of manpower and resources in two world wars. They have been drained of their gold and foreign exchange by the United States. The sun of their empires has been slowly setting with the spread of nationalism and industrialization to colonial areas. That the United States and Soviet Russia will fall heir to these empires is by no means certain. The pressure for national independence in most of the colonial areas is too strong to facilitate that. Nevertheless, both powers are likely to push their way into regions where "vacuums" exist. Though the United States government underwent a change of political control in 1953, no fundamental revision of foreign policy was clearly apparent. For a brief period there was talk of "liberating" the Soviet satellites in Eastern Europe and "unleashing" Chiang Kai-shek for an attack upon the Chinese mainland, but the Republican administration soon reverted to the "containment" policy of its Democratic predecessor. This became evident especially in 1957 with the issuance of the Eisenhower Doctrine against communist inroads in the Middle East. Though couched in vaguer language, it did not differ essentially from the Truman Doctrine for Greece and Turkey in the 1940's. Both

New empires for old

were designed to prevent Soviet expansion into areas where the West could claim vital interests. If the pursuance of either doctrine were to require temporary or permanent occupation of the endangered territories, there was scarcely any doubt that occupation would be undertaken.

4. The U.S.S.R. as a Great Power

The U.S.S.R. after World War II

Soviet Russia emerged from World War II as the second strongest power on earth. Though her navy was small, her land army and possibly her air force by 1948 were the largest in the world. Her population was climbing rapidly toward 200,000,000 and this in spite of the loss of 7,000,000 soldiers and about 8,000,000 civilians during the war. In mineral wealth her position compared favorably with that of the richest countries. Her territory contained about 20 per cent of the world's coal deposits and more than 50 per cent of the supply of iron. As a result of the discovery of rich oil reserves in the Urals in 1946, she claimed a large percentage of the world supply of petroleum. On the other hand, there can be no doubt that her industrial machine had been badly crippled by the war. According to estimates of her own statisticians, no fewer than 1700 of her cities and towns had been totally destroyed and also 40,000 miles of railway and 31,000 factories. Stalin declared in 1946 that it would probably require at least six or seven years to repair the damage and rebuild the devastated areas.

Explanation of Russian attitudes

It seems reasonable to suppose that many of the peculiar attitudes displayed by the U.S.S.R. in her dealings with other nations were attributable in some measure to the losses she sustained during the war. Resentful of the fact that she had been compelled to make such sacrifices, she became obsessed with security as a goal that must be attained regardless of the cost to her neighbors. Fearful that poverty and hardship might make her own people rebellious, her rulers adopted a chip-on-the-shoulder attitude in their foreign policy. Soviet citizens must be led to think that their country was in imminent danger of an attack by capitalist powers. For similar reasons they must be induced to believe that their rulers were entitled to a kind of worship hitherto reserved for divine-right monarchs. On the thirtieth anniversary of the Bolshevik revolution, Stalin was hailed as "the sun of the entire universe." In accordance with a new nationalism designed to bolster the people's courage, the Russians laid claim to a majority of the inventions and scientific discoveries of modern times—from the electric light and wireless telegraphy to penicillin.

Scarcely had the hostilities of World War II ended than the U.S.S.R. became involved in a so-called cold war with Great Britain and the United States. Indeed, there were some evidences of growing animosity as far back as the spring of 1945. Who started the squabbling is a question impossible to answer. Perhaps it began when the Soviet Union, soon after the war, gave clear indications of a desire to dominate such countries as Rumania, Bulgaria, Yugoslavia, and Poland. Although these countries had been placed in the Soviet orbit by the Yalta Agreement, the Western powers probably did not intend that the U.S.S.R. should do more than establish "friendly" governments there. In addition, the United States refused to recognize the absorption of Estonia, Latvia, and Lithuania into the Soviet Union, which had been carried out in 1940.

However it began, the cold war raged with increasing fury during the succeeding years. Early in 1946 the U.S.S.R. became embroiled in a dispute with Iran. The Iranian government accused Moscow of refusing to permit troops to be sent from Teheran for the suppression of a revolt in the northern Iranian province of Azerbaijan. The real issue was the claim that the U.S.S.R. was attempting to separate Azerbaijan from Iran and incorporate it in the Soviet Union. The Iranian government appealed to the Security Council of the United Nations, where British and United States representatives vigorously condemned Soviet action. Finally, with world opinion strongly against her, the Soviet Union withdrew the troops she had sent for the protection of the separatist movement in Azerbaijan. Meanwhile, Soviet leaders had been infuriated by the issuance of the Truman Doctrine. Western statesmen were accused of villainous plots to force the U.S.S.R. into war in the hope that they could conquer her with atomic weapons and then divide up the world to suit themselves.

By 1947–1948 the cold war between the U.S.S.R. and the democracies had reached a new stage of intensity. In June, 1947, a communist minority in Hungary seized control of the government and brought that state into close alliance with the Soviet Union. An even more sensational development was the communist seizure of power in Czechoslovakia in February, 1948. To people in Western countries this event was altogether too reminiscent of Hitler's methods in the 1930's. There were bold assertions now that Stalin was no better than Hitler, or perhaps that he was even worse. A United States cabinet member avowed that Russian communism was a far greater menace than German Nazism ever had been. The eminent South African statesman and general, Jan Christiaan Smuts, expressed the opinion that actual warfare would be preferable to continued tolerance by the Western powers of the outrageous system in the U.S.S.R.

A more serious crisis began during the summer and autumn of 1948. In the spring of that year the United States government had intiated plans for consolidating the United States, British, and French zones of Germany into a single west German state. Consideration had also been given to the organization of a Western European Union (originally a British scheme), to be composed of

Beginning of the cold war with Britain and the U.S.

The cold war continues

Climactic events in the cold war

The struggle for Germany

947

Air Lift over Berlin. In 1948, as the result of a dispute over Germany, Russian occupation forces began a blockade of Berlin. The United States and Britain broke the blockade by a system of airplane transport of food and vital materials into the city.

Britain, France, Belgium, Luxembourg, and the Netherlands and to be backed by military aid from the United States. The U.S.S.R. replied to these schemes by attempting to force the Western powers out of Berlin. The issue was the basic one of who should control Germany. The United States government seemed to be convinced that the economic recovery of Europe could not be successful without the development and use of the resources of the Ruhr and of other areas of western Germany. Moreover, a strong West German state would be a bulwark for the containment of Russia. The Soviets were determined to prevent the organization of a compact state in western Germany under Anglo-American auspices. They feared its attractive power for the eastern zone under their own control. Besides, from their viewpoint, there was always the danger that it might be developed into a base of operations for an attack upon Soviet territory. For both the East and the West, Germany was the key to the control of Europe, and the control of Europe was regarded by each side as another name for security. The Soviet blockade of Berlin was eventually relaxed, but the struggle for Germany continued, and the curtain which separated East from West was drawn more tightly than ever.

The objective of Soviet foreign policy, many observers contended, was nothing less than world conquest. They could cite the famous assertion of Lenin that "it is inconceivable that the Soviet republic should continue to exist for a long period side by side with imperialist states." [1] They could also quote Stalin to the effect that the final stage of socialism in the Soviet Union could not be achieved until workers' regimes had been established in at least several other countries.[2] In addition, they could point to the Russian dictator's statement in 1926 that "the Soviet power (and only the Soviet

Objectives of Soviet foreign policy

[1] V. I. Lenin, *Selected Works*, ed. A. Fineberg, Moscow, n.d., Vol. VIII, p. 33. Russian edition, 1932, Vol. XXIV, p. 122.

[2] *Problems of Leninism*, p. 64.

power) is able to withdraw the army from bourgeois command, and to change it from an instrument for the oppression of the people into an instrument for freeing the people from the yoke of the bourgeoisie at home and abroad." [3]

Confirmation of these views seemed to be provided by the outbreak of war in Korea on June 25, 1950. To most people in the West this appeared to be an obvious extension of the cold war into a hot war. The conflict in Korea began suddenly when troops from the Soviet-dominated northern portion of the country crossed the 38th parallel to attack the non-communist republic of South Korea. At the instigation of the United States the Security Council of the United Nations condemned the invasion as "armed aggression" in open defiance of the interest and authority of the United Nations, and called upon the North Koreans to cease hostilities and withdraw their troops. The invaders ignored this demand. Two days after the attack President Truman sent armed assistance to the South Koreans. On July 7 the Security Council authorized the United States to establish a unified command of the United Nations forces in Korea. A short time earlier the first United States troops had gone into action in a vain attempt to check the Red invasion. Weak in numbers and lacking heavy equipment, they were slowly pushed back into a small area surrounding the port of Pusan near the tip of the peninsula. Here they accumulated strength for a counteroffensive. So successful were their efforts that they drove the North Koreans back across the 38th parallel, captured their capital (Pyongyang), and were advancing rapidly toward the Yalu River. Late in October the United Nations commander, General Douglas MacArthur, announced that the war was coming to an end, and that a complete United Nations victory was only a matter of days.

The outbreak of war in Korea

These dreams were rudely shattered when MacArthur's armies found themselves confronted by huge forces from Communist China that had come to the rescue of the North Koreans. Soon the opponents of aggression were once again retreating southward. By the end of 1950 they had lost more than half of the territory conquered in their counteroffensive. Thereafter the two sides alternated in retreating and assuming the offensive. But by the spring of 1951 the war had reached a stalemate, with the line of battle almost stabilized just north of the 38th parallel. In June, 1951, the Communists aroused hopes for an early termination of the conflict when they proposed negotiation for a truce. For more than a year representatives of the two sides struggled to reach an agreement. The chief stumbling block was the repatriation of prisoners. The Communists demanded that all prisoners be returned immediately to their country of origin, regardless of their own wishes. The government of the United States insisted upon voluntary repatriation

The intervention of Communist China

[3] *Leninism*, Vol. I, pp. 120–21.

EASTERN AND WESTERN
POWER COMBINATIONS, 1957

War in Korea. On a bleak hillside in Korea, U.S. Marines pour rifle and machine gun fire into a Chinese Communist roadblock.

only, arguing that it would be an international crime to force soldiers converted from communism to return to North Korea or China where they would be almost certainly shot as traitors. In October, 1952, after more than 100 sessions, the representatives of the United States broke off the negotiations.

Hopes for a reconciliation between East and West

Hopes for an end of the war and for a reconciliation between East and West were suddenly revived in March, 1953, when Joseph Stalin, dictator of the Soviet Union for 29 years, succumbed to a stroke. He was succeeded within twenty-four hours by Georgi M. Malenkov, a dominant figure in the party apparatus. Malenkov indicated, almost immediately, a desire to change some of his predecessor's policies. Perhaps he had fears for the stability of the new regime and thought it necessary to placate the discontented. Perhaps also he was more keenly aware than Stalin that the war in Korea might involve the U.S.S.R. as the ally of China in a deadly conflict with the United States. At any rate, soon after his elevation to power, he announced widespread reductions in the prices of consumers' goods and canceled the indictments brought against a number of Jewish physicians for plotting the deaths of Soviet officials. More significant, he declared in a speech in Moscow that there was no dispute or unresolved question between the Soviet Union and any other nation which could not be settled by "mutual agreement of the interested countries." In pursuance of this statement his government endorsed the proposal of the Chinese Foreign Minister that all prisoners in the Korean war who "insisted on repatriation" be returned immediately and that the others be "handed over" to a neutral country. Soon afterward the U.S.S.R. surprised the world when she and her satellites joined the West in giving unanimous support to a U.N. Assembly resolution expressing hope for a quick termination of the Korean war. These evidences of an apparent change in policy finally bore fruit in a cease-fire agreement concluded by representatives of China, North Korea, and the United States in July, 1953.

Even more extravagant hopes for better relations between the U.S.S.R. and the West were kindled in February, 1955, when

Malenkov resigned as Soviet Premier and was succeeded by Marshal Nikolai Bulganin, with Nikita S. Khrushchev as Secretary of the Communist Party. Khrushchev and Bulganin took several more postive steps than did their predecessor to create the impression that

Farm Dwellings in Soviet Central Asia, 1953. Some of the homes on the collective farm "Rays of the East," near Alma Ata; about 10,000 people lived on this farm.

the Soviet government was ready to repent of the error of its ways. They denounced Stalin for his paranoid suspicions of everyone around him and for his brutal tyranny. They apologized to Yugoslavia for discrimination against her in the past and announced their approval of the doctrine of "more than one road to socialism." They concluded a treaty of peace with Austria and withdrew their occupying troops. They returned the Porkkala naval base to Finland. So impressive were these evidences of a New Look in Soviet attitudes that the governments of Great Britain, France, and the United States sent identical notes to Moscow proposing a "conference at the summit" to be held in Geneva. The conference met in July, 1955, with President Eisenhower, Prime Minister Anthony Eden, Premier Edgar Faure of France, and Premier Bulganin as chief participants. The utmost cordiality prevailed, and repeated pledges of trust and friendship were given by both sides. But the conference had scarcely concluded its sessions when signs of discord again became rife. On such issues as disarmament, the control of atomic weapons, and the unification of Germany, conflicts appeared to be as sharp as ever. Antagonism reached a new peak of intensity when it was revealed that the Soviet government had authorized the transfer of arms to Egypt from the Skoda munitions works in Czechoslovakia. On December 15, 1955, Secretary of State Dulles expressed the opinion that the cold war between the U.S.S.R. and the West had been revived. The mythical character of the alleged transformation in Soviet attitudes became

The New Look and the "summit conference," followed by revival of the cold war

953

even more evident in 1956 with the suppression of revolts in Poland and Hungary. The Poles were let off rather lightly when they promised to remain within the Soviet orbit in return for permission to establish their own brand of socialism. The Hungarians

Revolt in Hungary. By 1956 discontent with Soviet domination manifested itself in several of the satellite states. Violent revolt broke out in Poland and Hungary. The photograph indicates the extent of the violence in Budapest. In the center is a gun turret blown off a Red Army tank on the right.

were repressed with bloody violence when they attempted not merely to change the economic system but to break all ties with the Soviet Union.

5. Nationalism versus Internationalism

Nationalism after World War II

Nationalism both gained and lost as a result of World War II. It made a definite gain during the long night of Nazi occupation of most of Europe when Resistance movements were organized in such countries as France, Yugoslavia, the Netherlands, Poland, and Greece. These movements functioned almost entirely underground, and though their methods were not those sanctioned by "orthodox" warfare, they gave new courage and hope of liberation to peoples under the heel of a foreign conqueror. In other parts of the world, however, nationalism seemed, as a result of the war, to be a less potent force than it had been before 1939. This appeared to be the situation in Germany, in Italy, in Great Britain, and even to a considerable extent eventually in France. Perhaps the people of these countries were more deeply disillusioned with the fruits of nationalism than was true elsewhere. Possibly they had come to realize that their day of greatness as nations was finally over. The old Europe, which these states had dominated for so many years, had suffered an eclipse, and the future seeemed to belong to the "peripheral" powers—the Soviet Union, the United States, and possibly India.

Nationalism received a setback also from the growth of internationalist sentiment during and after the war. While the fighting was still going on, it was almost universally acknowledged that some new form of international organization must be established to take the place of the defunct League of Nations. The idea was incorporated in the Atlantic Charter, which called for the creation of "a permanent system of general security." Finally, at the Yalta meeting of the Big Three, in February, 1945, it was agreed that a conference of all the United Nations to complete plans for a world organization should be convoked for April 25 in San Francisco. Despite the tragic death of President Roosevelt two weeks earlier, the conference met as scheduled. A charter was ultimately adopted on June 26 providing for a world organization to be known as the United Nations and to be founded upon the principle of "the sovereign equality of all peace-loving states." Its important agencies were to be: (1) a General Assembly composed of representatives of all the member states; (2) a Security Council composed of representatives of the United States, Great Britain, the U.S.S.R., China, and France, with permanent seats, and of six other states chosen by the General Assembly to fill the non-permanent seats; (3) a Secretariat, consisting of a Secretary-General and a staff of subordinates; (4) an Economic and Social Council composed of 18 members chosen by the General Assembly; (5) a Trusteeship Council; and (6) an International Court of Justice.

The Charter adopted at San Francisco provided a program for world peace which no one regarded as perfect but which almost everyone hoped would prove effective. By far the most important functions of the new organization are assigned by the Charter to the Security Council. This agency has the "primary responsibility for the maintenance of international peace and security." It has authority to investigate any dispute between nations, to recommend methods for settlement, and, if necessary to preserve the peace, to employ diplomatic or economic measures against an aggressor. If, in its judgment, these have proven, or are likely to prove, inadequate, it may "take such action by air, naval, or land forces" as may be required to maintain or restore international order. The member states are required by the Charter to make available to the Security Council, on its call, armed forces for the maintenance of peace, and to hold in readiness national air-force contingents for the immediate use of the Council in urgent situations.

Despite the great powers entrusted to the Security Council, it was so organized as to give almost a monopoly of authority to its permanent members. It was the belief of the Big Three who assembled at Yalta, and of President Roosevelt especially, that the peace of the world depended upon harmony among the states primarily responsible for winning the war. Accordingly, they agreed that when the Security Council should be set up, no action of any kind could be taken without the unanimous consent of Great Britain, France, the United States, China, and the Soviet Union, and two other members besides. Even the Charter of the United Nations itself was not to be amended except with the approval of every one of the perma-

The growth of internationalism: the United Nations

The Security Council

The veto power of the Big Five

ORGANS OF THE UNITED NATIONS

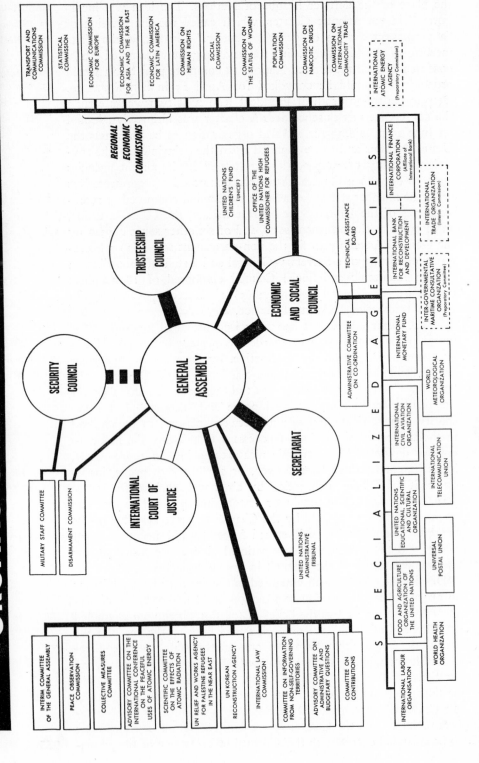

The Security Council of the United Nations. In this beautiful air-conditioned room the Security Council holds its meetings. The spectators in the foreground listen to the proceedings through earphones in the language of their choice.

nent members. This absolute veto given to each of the principal states had none of the hoped-for effects. Instead of bolstering the peace of the world, its chief result was to cripple the U.N. and to render it helpless in the face of emergencies. The primary cause was the growth of distrust between Soviet Russia and the West. Each has opposed the demands of the other with respect to disarmament, the control of atomic energy, and the admission of new states.

Compared to the powers of the Council, the authority of most of the other U.N. agencies is limited. The General Assembly was originally intended to be largely an advisory body. It could initiate studies, make recommendations, and call the attention of the Council to situations likely to endanger peace. It was planned as a place where the little nations could air their grievances while the big powers in the Security Council ran the world. It was not even permitted to make recommendations on any dispute being considered at the time by the Council. In the fall of 1950, however, the General Assembly took steps to remedy this defect. It adopted a series of resolutions providing that if a veto prevents the Security Council from discharging its responsibilities of curbing aggression, the General Assembly may be convened in an emergency session within twenty-four hours, either at the request of seven of the members of the Security Council or by a majority of members of the United Nations. The Assembly then has the power, by a two-thirds vote, to make recommendations for collective action even to the extent of

The General Assembly

using force. In October, 1950, these resolutions were adopted by the
Assembly by an overwhelming vote, with only the Soviet Union
and its satellites opposing.

*Other agen-
cies of the U.N.*

The remaining agencies of the U.N. have a wide variety of functions. The Secretariat, composed of a Secretary-General and a
numerous staff, is chiefly an administrative authority. Its duties,
though, are by no means routine, for the Secretary-General may
bring to the attention of the Security Council any matter which,
in his opinion, may threaten international peace. The Trusteeship
Council exercises supervision over the trust territories, or non-
self-governing territories, administered directly by various nations
under the authority of the U.N. The functions of the Economic
and Social Council are the most varied of all. Composed of eighteen
members elected by the General Assembly, it has authority to
initiate studies and make recommendations with respect to international social, economic, health, educational, cultural, and related
matters, and may perform services within such fields at the request
of U.N. members. Under its jurisdiction are such specialized agencies as the following: the United Nations Educational, Scientific,
and Cultural Organization (UNESCO), whose purpose is to promote international cooperation through education, science, and
culture "in order to further respect for justice, for the rule of law,
and for the human rights and fundamental freedoms of all"; the
World Health Organization (WHO), which works to control
epidemics and to assist backward nations in stamping out cholera,
typhus, and venereal disease and in raising standards of health and
sanitation; and the Food and Agriculture Organization (FAO),
which seeks to promote increases in food production by finding
remedies for agricultural depressions, for plant and animal diseases and insect pests, and by projecting plans for mechanizing
small farms and for the more efficient distribution of food.

*Achievements
of the U.N.*

During the first twelve years of its history the achievements of
the U.N. constituted a modestly impressive record. It had induced
Soviet Russia to withdraw her troops from Iran, and Britain and
France to take their forces out of Syria and Lebanon. It had appointed a commission to investigate the infiltration of foreign Communists into Greece. It had terminated a bloody war between Dutch
and native forces in Indonesia. It had induced the British to agree
to the partition of Palestine, and it had persuaded the warring Jews
and Arabs to conclude a truce. It had assisted in arranging a cease-
fire agreement between India and Pakistan, which prevented war
from inundating some 400 million people. But against these accomplishments must be recorded several failures. It failed completely
in its efforts to establish control of atomic weapons. Despite the
specific requirements of Article 26 of the Charter, it did nothing to
provide for a general reduction of armaments. It failed also to curb
the increasing friction between the U.S.S.R. and the United States,

which was certainly a threat to international peace, and it was unable even to prevent a recurrence of some fighting in Palestine in the midst of the truce. It was powerless in the face of Soviet suppression of the Hungarian revolt in 1956, and its efforts to cope with the Suez crisis of the same year were also unsuccessful. It should be noted, however, that not all of these failures could be ascribed to defects of the U.N. Many resulted from the suspicion and distrust that existed between Soviet Russia and her Western opponents. Each side feared that the other might gain some advantage if vigorous action were taken by the U.N. to prevent or terminate a war.

In the light of conditions obtaining after World War II, it was perhaps inevitable that internationalism should assume a number of forms. Some thoughtful observers criticized the United Nations as a mere replica of the old League of Nations, which had been formally dissolved at a final session held in Geneva, April 18, 1946. Both, it was said, were leagues of governments, not federations of peoples. Those who felt this way argued for nothing less than a world federal republic similar in structure to the United States, with an actual transfer of sovereign powers to a central government. They believed that the government of this republic should include not merely a court to hear disputes and a world executive with police authority, but, above all, a world parliament representing peoples rather than governments and capable of enacting laws which would apply directly to individuals. It was not argued that the functions of the world state should entirely supersede those of national governments. On the contrary, only such sovereign powers as control over armaments, tariffs, and colonial areas should be transferred to the central authority; the rest would be reserved to the national units.

Other forms of internationalism: (1) the movement for a world republic

Less idealistic statesmen and publicists held to the belief that the U.N. should be supplemented by military and political alliances. Convinced that the U.S.S.R. was bent upon world conquest, they could think only in terms of a combination of force for the "containment" of Soviet power. Such was the opinion of President Truman and his advisers in the United States, and they seem to have converted to similar views most of the governments of the Atlantic region. At any rate, in April, 1949, representatives of Canada, Denmark, Portugal, Iceland, Britain, France, Italy, the Netherlands, Norway, Belgium, Luxembourg, and the United States signed an agreement providing for the establishment of the North Atlantic Treaty Organization (NATO). Subsequently Greece, Turkey, and West Germany were added as members. The purposes of the organization were declared to be the protection of the "freedom, common heritage, and civilization" of the Atlantic peoples and the promotion of the stability and well-being of the Atlantic area. The treaty declared that an armed attack against any one of

(2) NATO

the signatory parties would be regarded as an attack against all, and that they would combine their armed strength to whatever extent necessary to repel the aggressor. At a conference held in Lisbon in February, 1952, the NATO members agreed to set up a permanent organization, with a Council and a Secretariat, and a permanent headquarters in Paris. It was decided also that the joint military command, or NATO army, established in 1950, should be increased from thirty to fifty divisions in 1953, and that West Germany should be rearmed and invited to contribute twelve of the divisions. It was thereby hoped that NATO would be ready for any emergency that might arise as a consequence of the expansionist policies of Soviet Russia. By 1956, however, the strength of the alliance had been seriously impaired by disharmony between Britain and France, on the one side, and the United States on the other, and by the deployment of most of France's military strength for the defense of her empire.

(3) the coal and steel community

Internationalism may be said to have made some progress also on a more limited geographic scale. About 1950 Robert Schuman, Foreign Minister of France, conceived the idea of bringing the coal, iron, and steel industries of Western Europe under a supranational authority. No tariff barriers or other international restrictions would exist; instead, each industry regardless of country would have equal access to markets and to sources of raw materials. The plan would also have the advantage of preventing the industries of the Ruhr from ever being used as a foundation for German militarism. After months of negotiation France, West Germany, Belgium, the Netherlands, Luxembourg, and Italy agreed to the plan, and it went into operation in August, 1952. Officially known as the European Coal and Steel Community, it represented a significant step on the long and difficult road toward European federation. So confident were its leaders of the importance of their project that they embarked almost immediately upon the drafting of a constitution for a union of Western Europe.

Further steps toward unity: Western European Union, Euratom, and Euromarket

The most that could be accomplished, however, was the adoption of a plan for bringing Great Britain and West Germany into a close association with the other states of Western Europe. Britain agreed to maintain part of her armed forces on the European Continent as long as a majority of her allies considered it necessary. In return for a restoration of sovereignty and full membership in NATO, West Germany promised to refrain from manufacturing atomic, biological, and chemical weapons, guided missiles, warships larger than 3,000 tons, and bomber aircraft. The association—composed of France, Italy, Belgium, the Netherlands, and Luxembourg, together with West Germany and Britain—was given the name Western European Union. In 1957 the six Continental nations took the further step of agreeing to pool their nuclear-energy resources and to introduce gradually, over a period of twelve to seventeen years, a common tariff-free market, or customs union, for all commodities. When finally established, this union will undoubtedly constitute an important milestone in the long struggle of Western Europe for economic and political security.

6. Changes in Constitutions and Governments

Several European countries made significant changes in their constitutions and governments after World War II. In 1949 the Labor Government of Great Britain cut in half the two-year suspensive veto of the House of Lords provided for by the Parliament Act of 1911. In 1946 the French nation finally agreed, after long dispute, upon a constitution for the Fourth Republic. It differed from that of the Third Republic in three major respects: (1) The cabinet was made responsible to the lower house exclusively instead of to both the Senate and the Chamber of Deputies. (2) A Constitutional Committee was established composed of the President of the Republic, the presiding officers of the two houses, and ten members elected from outside Parliament. The Committee is supposed to serve as a check upon unconstitutional legislation. It functions, however, only upon the joint appeal of the upper house and the President of the Republic and has acted thus far primarily as a guardian of the rights of the upper house. (3) The Constitution of 1946 also includes a provision designed to reduce instability of cabinets, which had been such a notorious feature of the Third Republic. The new instrument provides that Parliament may not be dissolved within eighteen months after a national election. But if a cabinet is forced to resign twice within any subsequent eighteen-month period, by reason of a vote of lack of confidence or censure, the National Assembly or lower house may be dissolved. The provision has had little effect. Since every French cabinet is a coalition cabinet, it can be no more stable than the combination of parties of which it is composed. When one or more elements of the combination become discontented, the cabinet falls without any vote of lack of confidence.

Changes in the governments of Britain and France

The most sweeping constitutional changes were those in the German Federal Republic. Following the collapse of 1945, Germany was divided into occupied zones. The eastern zone became the Russian sphere and was eventually organized into a Soviet puppet state with the label of German Democratic Republic. West Germany was divided into British, French, and American zones and governed by military-occupation authorities until 1949. With the establishment of civil government in the latter year, the West German leaders put into effect for the German Federal Republic a new constitution, which is one of the most ingenious and enlightened the world has yet seen. It contains an extensive Bill of Rights, with the traditional guaranties of freedom of speech, press, assembly, and

Constitutional changes in Germany

961

religion. Such rights are not protected, however, for those who would abuse them to impair or abolish democracy. Enforcement of the Bill of Rights is made the specific duty of the Federal Constitutional Court, which, in fulfillment of this duty, can declare laws of Parliament unconstitutional. Supreme power in the central government is vested in the Chancellor, or Premier, the President being a figurehead like the President of France. The Chancellor is responsible to the Bundestag, or lower house of Parliament, exclusively. But even if he receives a vote of no confidence, he does not resign unless the Bundestag is able to elect a new Chancellor by an absolute majority of its members. By this device the West German government is given a stability not common to most other cabinet systems. It is significant that the German Federal Republic has had but a single Chancellor, Konrad Adenauer, since its founding in 1949.

Recent changes in the Soviet Union

Changes in the Soviet Union were not so much constitutional or governmental as they were political. The only formal change in the Constitution after 1945 was a reduction in the number of republics from 16 to 15 by incorporating the Karelo-Finnish Republic into the Russian Soviet Federated Socialist Republic, the main republic of the Soviet Union. In 1952 the Politburo of the Communist Party was abolished and replaced by a Presidium of 25 (later 15) members. Elected by the Central Committee of the Party, the Presidium is composed of the most powerful men in the country and determines the basic policies which the government is to carry out. Like the old Politburo, however, it follows the leadership of the Secretary of the Party, who is the real dictator of the U.S.S.R. Since the death of Stalin in 1954, this position has been held by Nikita S. Khrushchev. Though he occupies no office in the government, he is more powerful even than the Premier. Nevertheless, he has posed as an advocate of collective leadership and denounced Stalin in 1956 for developing a "cult of personality," or one-man rule. A year later he condemned economic centralization and vested control of all but the key industries in the separate republics. He also relaxed the censorship of books and newspapers, opened the borders of Soviet Russia to foreign travelers, and increased the wages of workers in the lower brackets. But all these changes were simply concessions to allay discontent and could be revoked at any time by the same authority that granted them. The absolutism of Khrushchev and his colleagues was confirmed and strengthened in July 1957, when they ousted from both the Presidium and the government Georgi M. Malenkov and Vyacheslav M. Molotov, whom they alleged to be sympathizers with Stalinist policies and opponents of the new party leadership, with its plans for reducing international tension and elevating standards of living for the Russian masses.

962   The United States has what is commonly considered the most

CHANGES IN
CONSTITU-
TIONS AND
GOVERNMENTS

*Constitutional
amendments in
the U.S.*

rigid constitution in the Western world. Only four amendments were added to the country's organic law during the entire nineteenth century, and three of these resulted directly from conditions created by the Civil War. The idealism and moral fervor generated by the Progressive movement were responsible for the addition of the Sixteenth, Seventeenth, Eighteenth, and Nineteenth Amendments, providing respectively for the income tax, the direct election of United States Senators, the prohibition of intoxicating liquors, and woman suffrage. No further alterations were made until the nation was engulfed by the depression. In 1933 the Twentieth Amendment, energetically sponsored for many years by Senator Norris of Nebraska, became part of the Constitution. It fixed January 20 instead of March 4 as the date for the beginning of the term of the President, and it abolished the "Lame Duck" Congress. (That is, it provided that Congressmen elected in November should take their seats the following January 3. Under the original Constitution Senators and Representatives did not begin their terms until March 4. Since Congress was required to assemble on the first Monday in December, members who had been defeated the preceding November constinued as "Lame Ducks" to represent their constituents until the following March.) The year 1933 also witnessed the adoption of the Twenty-first Amendment, which repealed the Eighteenth. Enforcement of the Prohibition amendment had been largely a failure. In addition, many people believed that revival of the brewing and distilling industries would give a necessary fillip to economic recovery. In 1951, the nation adopted the Twenty-second, or anti-third-term, Amendment. Henceforth, no person could be lawfully elected President more than twice, and no person succeeding to the office of President for more than two years could subsequently be elected President more than once. The Twenty-second Amendment was prompted largely by resentment against the breaking of the anti-third-term tradition by Franklin D. Roosevelt, and by fear that his achievement might be duplicated by others.

As in most countries, however, constitutional changes effected by formal amendments do not tell the whole story. Equally important are informal changes, accomplished by modifications of custom and tradition or by the development of new usages and practices. Every informed person knows that in Great Britain the system of Cabinet government is almost unknown to the written law. It developed through precedents and usages, or what the British call "conventions," over a period of more than two centuries. Informal change has brought similar momentous results in the United States. The Fathers of the Constitution had no conception of the important role which political parties would come to play in our system of government. They envisaged the selection of the President as a process in which the people would not participate directly but

*Informal
changes in the
U.S. system of
government*

would vote merely for Electors, who in turn would choose the President. They foresaw a distribution of powers between the Federal government and the states which would leave most of the authority to be exercised by the latter. In recent years, however, the balance has shifted radically. As a result of new interpretations of the general-welfare clause and the development of the grant-in-aid system, very few areas remain in which the Federal government cannot supersede the states. Congress now appropriates money for building highways within the states, for old-age pensions and unemployment insurance, and for various forms of agricultural and vocational education. Wages-and-hours legislation and the maintenance of labor's right to bargain collectively are now considered legitimate functions of the national government. In addition, the Federal Bureau of Investigation has come to the aid of the states in apprehending criminals and largely supplants the local authorities in the enforcement of certain laws. Though government in the United States is far from the consolidated form characteristic of Britain and France, it still represents a wide departure from the federal system conceived by the founders.

SELECTED READINGS

Barghoorn, F. C., *Soviet Russian Nationalism*, New York, 1956
Buck, P. W., and Travis, M. B., Jr., eds., *Control of Foreign Relations in Modern Nations*, New York, 1957
Beloff, Max, *The Foreign Policy of Soviet Russia*, New York, 1947
Brinton, Crane, *The Temper of Western Europe*, Cambridge, Mass., 1953
Crankshaw, Edward, *Russia and The Russians*, New York, 1948
Dallin, D. J., *The Changing World of Soviet Russia*, New Haven, 1956
Dean, V. M., *The Four Cornerstones of Peace*, New York, 1946
———, *The United States and Russia*, New York, 1948
Dolivet, Louis, ed., *The United Nations: a Handbook*, New York, 1946
Drucker, P. F., *The End of Economic Man*, New York, 1939
Fitzgerald, Walter, *The New Europe*, New York, 1946
Hammer, E. J., *The Struggle for Indochina*, Stanford, 1954
———, *The Struggle for Indochina Continues, Geneva to Bandung*, Stanford, 1955
Holborn, Hajo, *The Political Collapse of Europe*, New York, 1951
Hoskins, H. L., *The Middle East*, New York, 1954
Kahin, G. M., *The Asian-African Conference*, Ithaca, 1956
Kahn, A. E., *Great Britain in the World Economy*, New York, 1946
Laski, H. J., *Reflections on the Revolution of Our Time*, New York, 1943
Lenczowski, George, *The Middle East in World Affairs*, Ithaca, 1956
Lie, Trygve, *In the Cause of Peace: Seven Years with the United Nations*, New York, 1954
Low, Francis, *The Struggle for Asia*, New York, 1956

McCune, Shannon, *Korea's Heritage: A Regional and Social Geography*,
Tokyo, 1956

Mannheim, Karl, *Diagnosis of Our Time*, New York, 1944

Meyer, Cord L., *Peace or Anarchy*, Boston, 1947

Neumann, Sigmund, *The Future in Perspective*, New York, 1943

Patterson, E. M., *An Introduction to World Economics*, New York, 1947

Reves, Emery, *The Anatomy of Peace*, New York, 1945

Russian Institute, *The Anti-Stalin Campaign and International Communism*, New York, 1956

Schapiro, J. S., *The World in Crisis*, New York, 1950

Schuman, F. L., *International Politics*, fourth edition, New York, 1948

Ward, Barbara, *The West at Bay*, New York, 1948

Wertheim, W. F., *Indonesian Society in Transition*, New York, 1956

Williams, Philip, *Politics in Post-War France*, London, 1954

Wilmot, Chester, *The Struggle for Europe*, New York, 1952

Wilson, C. M., *Oil across the World*, New York, 1946

Zinkin, Maurice, *Development for Free Asia*, Fair Lawn, New Jersey, 1956

SOURCE MATERIALS

Dolivet, Louis, *Handbook of the United Nations*, Charter of the United Nations

Proposed Constitution for a World Republic, *Saturday Review of Literature*, Vol. 31 (April 3, 1948)

Roosevelt, F. D., "The Four Freedoms," *Congressional Record*, Vol. 87, pp. 46–47

U. N. Dept. of Public Information, *Yearbook of the United Nations*

Werner, M. R., *Stalin's Kampf*

Contemporary Culture
since 1918

Earlier chapters have presented an account of chaotic political and economic developments in the years that followed World War I. These years constituted one of the most critical periods since the Protestant Revolution. Institutions and ideals which seemed almost impregnable were torn from their moorings and threatened with destruction. Democracy, liberalism, rationalism, and individualism almost went under in a devastating flood of barbarism and unreason. It was inevitable that cultural trends should reflect these political and economic tendencies. We should expect, therefore, that philosophy, literature, and the arts would be characterized by pessimism and bewilderment, accompanied in some instances by despair and in others by an earnest groping for a way of escape. At the same time, it should be pointed out that some cultural influences themselves were partly responsible for the prevailing chaos. A number of scientific theories, for example, tended to impair man's confidence in reason as an instrument for gaining knowledge. More serious was the influence of certain ideologists who developed a cult of the non-rational, denied the possibility of democracy, and justified the rule of force.

1. Revolutionary Developments in Science

Most of the foundations of contemporary science were laid at the end of the nineteenth century and the beginning of the twentieth. It was during that period that the atom was portrayed as a miniature solar system instead of a solid particle, that the phenomenon of radioactivity was discovered, that the ether hypothesis was exploded, and that time and space were shown to be relative. It was during the same period that psychoanalysis was founded, that the germ theory of disease was fully confirmed, and that the laws of heredity were formulated. Scientific development during the years 1918–1958 was distinguished by equally revolutionary achievements, and none more revolutionary than the achievements in physics. By 1958 it had been discovered that the conception of the sub-atomic world as a miniature solar system was much too simple. The atom was found to contain not only positively charged protons and negatively charged electrons, but *positrons*, or positively charged electrons; *neutrons*, which carry no electric charges; and *mesons*, which may be either negative or positive. Mesons, it was discovered, not only exist within the atom (for about two millionths of a second) but are major components of the cosmic rays which are constantly bombarding the earth from somewhere in outer space. A recent hypothesis assumes the existence of a *neutral* meson which has a "life" of only one one-hundredth of a sextillionth of a second, but which, in disintegrating, is converted into the energy which holds the universe together.

Even before the discovery of neutrons, positrons, and mesons the world within the atom had ceased, for many scientists, to be a world whose actions could be predicted on the basis of natural laws. In 1927 the German physicist Werner Heisenberg worked out his famous *principle of indeterminacy*, based upon his discovery that individual electrons do not appear to follow any definite laws of cause and effect, but jump from one orbit to another without apparent reason. He seemed therefore to be suggesting that the old mechanistic principle of universal causation was no longer entirely valid. The phenomena of the sub-atomic world could not be predicted with certainty but could be dealt with only in terms of *probability*, in essentially the same way as a life insurance company compiles actuarial statistics for millions of people. With the gradual acceptance of this hypothesis, the atom was reduced to a kind of "lawless abstraction" of which it was almost impossible to form a mental image.[1]

The principle of indeterminacy

Several of the developments in physics outlined above helped to make possible one of the most spectacular achievements in the history of science, the splitting of the atom to release the energy contained within it. Ever since it became known that the atom is composed primarily of electrical energy, physicists had dreamed of unlocking this source of tremendous power and making it available for man. As early as 1905 Dr. Einstein became convinced of the equivalence of mass and energy and worked out a formula for the conversion of one into the other, which he expressed as follows: $E = mc^2$. E represents the energy in ergs, m the mass in grams, and c the velocity of light in centimeters per second. In other words,

Releasing the energy within the atom

---

[1] It is noteworthy, however, that among the scientists who rejected this hypothesis was Dr. Einstein. He was reported, shortly before his death, to have expressed confidence that a new principle could be discovered which would reduce the whole universe to order and harmony.

Calder Hall, the World's First Atomic Power Plant. Completed by the British in 1956, Calder Hall uses atomic energy to produce electricity for factories and homes. The British plan to construct at least 16 of these power-generating stations by 1965.

the amount of energy locked within the atom is equal to the mass multiplied by the square of the velocity of light. But no practical application of this formula was possible until after the discovery of the neutron by Sir James Chadwick in 1932. Since the neutron carries no charge of electricity, it is an ideal weapon for bombarding the atom. It is neither repulsed by the positively charged protons nor absorbed by the negatively charged electrons. Moreover, in the process of bombardment it produces more neutrons, which hit other atoms and cause them in turn to split and create neutrons. In this way the original reaction is repeated in an almost unending series.

Atomic fission

In 1939 two German physicists, Otto Hahn and F. Strassman, succeeded in splitting atoms of uranium by bombarding them with neutrons. The initial reaction produced a chain of reactions, in much the same way that a fire burning at the edge of a piece of paper raises the temperature of adjoining portions of the paper high enough to cause them to ignite. The potential of the neutrons employed in the splitting was only one-thirtieth of a volt, but the potential released was 200,000,000 volts. It was soon revealed that not all forms of uranium are equally valuable for the production of energy. Only the isotope 235, which forms only a tiny fraction of natural uranium, will split when bombarded with neutrons. Uranium 238, which constitutes over 99 per cent of the world supply, absorbs the neutrons and transmutes itself into neptunium and plutonium. The latter, however, behaves very much like uranium 235. That is, it does split and release great quantities of energy. More recently, the practice has developed of manufacturing plutonium in a structure known as an atomic pile, in which large quantities of uranium 238 are exposed to neutrons from uranium 235.

Atomic weapons

It is a sad commentary on modern civilization that the first use made of the knowledge of atomic fission was in the preparation of an atomic bomb. The devastating weapon was the achievement of a galaxy of scientists working for the War Department of the United

States. Some were physicists who had been exiled by Nazi or Fascist oppression. By 1945 their work was completed, and in July of that year the first atomic bomb was exploded in a test conducted in the New Mexican desert near the War Department laboratory at Los Alamos. On August 6 the first atomic bomb used in warfare was dropped on the Japanese city of Hiroshima. A second bomb was unloaded on Nagasaki on August 9. The deadly effects of the new weapon almost passed belief. It was estimated that a single bomb had the explosive force of 20,000 tons of TNT. More than 100,000 people were killed in the two cities, large portions of which were literally wiped from the map. Man had at last acquired control over the basic substance of the universe, but whether he had created a Frankenstein's monster which might ultimately destroy him, no one could predict. Doleful queries were raised about what would happen in the future when the ability to produce atomic weapons would be no longer a monopoly of Anglo-Americans. This monopoly was brought to an end in the fall of 1949, when the U.S.S.R. exploded an atomic bomb.

Even more disturbing were the first tests of a hydrogen bomb by the United States Atomic Energy Commission in November, 1952. The tests were conducted at Eniwetok Atoll in the South Pacific, *The hydrogen* and according to reports an entire island disappeared after burning *bomb*

Test Explosion of a Hydrogen Bomb, Marshall Islands, 1952. The "mushroom" rose to a height of 10 miles and spread to a width of 100 miles. It eventually fell back into the ocean as radioactive rain, though some of it was distributed by winds over large areas.

brightly for several hours. The hydrogen bomb, or H-bomb, is based upon fusion of hydrogen atoms, a process which requires the enormous heat generated by the splitting of uranium atoms to start the reaction. The fusion results in the creation of a new element, helium, which actually weighs less than the sum of the hydrogen atoms. The "free" energy left over provides the tremendous explosive power of the H-bomb. The force of hydrogen bombs is measured in *megatons*, each of which represents 1,000,000 tons of TNT. Thus a 5-megaton H-bomb would equal 250 times the power of the A-bombs dropped on Hiroshima and Nagasaki. By 1957 both the Soviet Union and the United States had exploded numerous hydrogen bombs in experimental tests. Great Britain, also, had conducted at least two test explosions.

The exploration of space

On October 4, 1957, the government of the Soviet Union inaugurated a new stage in man's control of his physical environment by rocketing into space the first artificial satellite, which began circling the earth at a speed of about 18,000 miles an hour. Though it weighed nearly 200 pounds, it was propelled upward higher than 500 miles. This Russian achievement gave the English language a new word— *sputnik*, the Russian for *satellite* or *fellow traveler*. A month later the Soviet scientists surpassed their first success by sending a new and much larger sputnik to an altitude of approximately 1000 miles. Sputnik II weighed more than half a ton and contained elaborate scientific instruments and even a live dog. These sputniks were doubtless the forerunners of dozens of others to be perfected by the scientists of various nations. In some quarters their launching was considered a development as significant as the voyage of Columbus to the Western Hemisphere. From the most favorable viewpoint they promised vast improvement in our knowledge and would prepare the way for exploration of the moon and eventually of distant planets. But they also had sinister aspects. In Western Europe and the United States the fact that the Russians had launched them loomed as a threat to the peace of the world. Obviously, the U.S.S.R. had rockets of tremendous power, which could be used to propel intercontinental ballistic missiles. The immediate future was thus dark with forebodings of increased competition in the armaments race between East and West.

Advances in biology

Notable advances in the biological sciences also occurred during the period since World War I. An outstanding one was the discovery of the viruses. Viruses are organisms so small that they pass through ordinary filters. Only by means of special filters made of collodion films, or by the use of ultraviolet or electron microscopes, can their presence be detected. They are the cause of a multitude of dread diseases, including smallpox, measles, infantile paralysis, influenza, rabies, yellow fever, and the common cold. No one has yet been able to say whether they should be classified as animate or inanimate objects. In some ways they appear to have the properties of living creatures, including the capacity to reproduce. But they are closely dependent upon their living host, and remain completely dormant except when they come into contact with living tissue. They seem to occupy a kind of intermediate stage between the inorganic and organic worlds, and are sometimes referred to as "the bridge between Life and Death." Perhaps Aristotle was right more than twenty-two centuries ago when he wrote: "Nature makes so gradual a transition from the inanimate to the animate kingdom that the boundary lines which separate them are indistinct and doubtful."

From time to time during the history of medicine, discoveries have been made which can justifiably be described as epochal, in the sense that they open up new and much greater possibilities for the conquest of disease. One example was the discovery of vaccination for smallpox by Sir Edward Jenner in 1796. Another was the development and proof of the germ theory of disease by Louis Pasteur and Robert Koch about 1881. After 1918 a series of such epochal discoveries laid the foundations for another new era of medical progress. In 1935 a German named Gerhard Domagk discovered the first of the sulfa drugs, which he called sulfanilamide. Soon others were added to the list. Each was found to be marvelously effective in curing or checking such diseases as rheumatic fever, gonorrhea, scarlet fever, and meningitis. About 1930 Sir Alexander Fleming described the first of the antibiotics, which came to be known as penicillin. Antibiotics are chemical agents produced by living organisms and possessing the power to check or kill bacteria. Many have their origin in molds, fungi, algae, and in simple organisms living in the soil. Penicillin was eventually found to be a kind of miracle drug producing spectacular results in the treatment of pneumonia, syphilis, peritonitis, tetanus, and numerous other maladies hitherto frequently fatal. About 1940 the second most famous of the antibiotics—streptomycin—was discovered by Dr. Selman A. Waksman. Streptomycin seems to hold its greatest promise in the treatment of tuberculosis, though it has been used for numerous other infections which do not yield to penicillin, including the bubonic plague and tularemia, or rabbit fever. More recently streptomycin has been partly supplanted in the treatment of tuberculosis by isoniazid, a derivative of nicotinic acid. Still other antibiotics are neomycin, also discovered by Dr. Waksman; aureomycin, effective against Rocky Mountain fever; chloromycetin, valuable in the treatment of typhus and typhoid fever; and terramycin, an efficient specific against undulant fever.

Antibiotics

Of almost equal importance with the discovery of new drugs has been the development of means of preventing disease. For the most part these have taken the form of vaccination. A characteristic example has been the development of vaccination against poliomyelitis, or infantile paralysis. The process was discovered in 1953 by Dr. Jonas E. Salk, and its use thus far indicates highly successful results. During World War II a remarkable insecticide was perfected which gives promise of the ultimate elimination of two of the most ancient enemies of mankind, malaria and typhus. Popularly known as DDT, it destroys the lice and mosquitoes which transmit these diseases. Recent years have witnessed also the development

Preventive medicine

and wide though not universal acceptance of the fluoridation process for preventing tooth decay in young people. It consists of the simple expedient of adding sodium fluoride to the water supply of municipalities. So impressive has been the progress in these and other aspects of preventive medicine that some scientists have predicted that in the comparatively near future every infectious disease

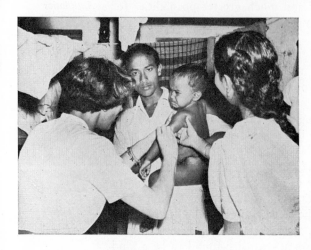

Preventive Medicine on an International Scale. A technician of the United States Foreign Operations Administration inoculates a child against cholera in Pakistan.

known to man will have been finally and completely conquered.

Other medical achievements

No account of medical achievements since 1918 would be complete without mention at least of the following: the development of insulin by the Canadian scientist Frederick Banting for the treatment of diabetes; the perfection of radiation treatments for cancer; the discovery of new methods of detecting cancer and other diseases by the use of radioactive isotopes as "tracers"; the development of techniques for storing blood and blood plasma for transfusions; the introduction of insulin shock, electrical shock, and "tranquillizing" drugs in the treatment of mental ailments; the discovery of a large number of new vitamins; the synthesization of cortisone (originally derived from the cortex of the adrenal gland) and its use in the treatment of rheumatoid arthritis; the discovery of the hormone ACTH and its application to asthma and to inflammatory diseases of the eye; the discovery of atabrine as a substitute for quinine in the treatment of malaria; and the development of psychosomatic medicine based upon a recognition of the importance of anxiety, fear, and other psychological factors in causing ulcers, asthma, high blood pressure, and diseases of the heart. By 1958 the people of the world ought to have enjoyed the most abundant health since the dawn of medicine. Statistically, perhaps they did, taken as a whole. But many parts of the world still suffered from the health problems associated with war, social upheaval, poverty, and famine. Improved medical resources are of little immediate value to people who do not have money to buy them or doctors to apply them. The discovery by research scientists of some new member of the vitamin B complex introduces no immediate improvement into the nutrition of a family that must live on a few handfuls of rice or millet a day.

2. Philosophy in the Contemporary World

The history of philosophy since 1918 presents in large part a record of pessimism and confusion. To the majority of thinkers who lived during this period the events taking place around them justified the deepest anxiety. World War I seemed like the beginning of a new Dark Age. Later the onrush of fascism and the plunge into a second world conflict appeared to leave little hope that civilization would ever recover. To be sure, few of the philosophers gave way to despair, but an increasingly large number lost confidence in the ability of man to save himself without the support of authority or the aid of supernatural powers. George Santayana fled from the materialist world in disgust and established himself for his declining years in the Convent of the Blue Nuns in Rome. He became more and more indifferent to the efforts of men to solve their social problems and to the great intellectual and political battles raging around him. An even more spectacular change of views was accomplished by the English philosopher C. E. M. Joad. Agnostic, advocate of polygamy and euthanasia, and author of the Oxford Oath, which pledged its signers never to fight under any circumstances for king and country, he turned before his death in 1953 into a staunch upholder of original sin and a defender of the Christian faith as a light to live by in a darkening world.

Characteristics of contemporary philosophy

One of the most important of the philosophies which tended to give a pessimistic view of man and his world was the Neo-Orthodoxy of the Swiss-German theologian Karl Barth and the American Reinhold Niebuhr. In form a system of theology, it presented profound philosophical conclusions concerning the nature of life and the destiny of man. Doctors Barth and Niebuhr discussed the universe and its problems in something approaching Calvinist terms. They believed the world to be governed by an all-powerful Deity, who controls all things for His own inscrutable purposes. They considered man to be a moral being, created in the divine image, and responsible to God for the use that he makes of this life. Above all, they emphasized what they regarded as the fundamental fact of sin in the world. Although man is capable of sympathy and benevolence, his nature is sadly corrupted by pride and self-love. These commonly take the form of a will to power, which is the primary source of war, race conflict, tyranny, and exploitation. Sin can be conquered only as men humble themselves before God, acknowledge the evil in their own natures, and accept the redeeming power of the Christian religion. By such means alone can they

Neo-Orthodoxy

973

Neo-Scholasti-cism

achieve that love and respect for others which are the essence of democracy. The fatherhood of God is the essential foundation of the brotherhood of man.

Similar in purpose to Neo-Orthodoxy but altogether different in form and content was the Neo-Scholasticism or Neo-Thomism of Jacques Maritain and his followers. This movement was not new but, in the main, was a continuation of the Neo-Scholasticism of the nineteenth century. Whereas Neo-Orthodoxy was exclusively Protestant, Neo-Scholasticism was predominantly Catholic. Both, however, came close to each other in their views of the two religions. Niebuhr deplored the excessive freedom of conscience permitted by Protestantism, while Maritain criticized the Catholic tendency to rely too much on authority. Maritain and his disciples turned back to the Scholasticism of St. Thomas Aquinas, which they held had the supreme value of exalting reason and giving wholeness and purpose to life. Nothing was left at loose ends by that philosophy to become a source of conflict and exasperation. The universe was governed by intelligent purpose, and everything could be explained by reason. But in the fourteenth century Scholasticism decayed; Nominalism rapidly took its place, and the way was opened for the growth of individualism, materialism, and skepticism. Such concepts eventually destroyed man's confidence in himself as a reasoning creature, dethroned God as the ruler of the universe, and left little but anarchy and chaos. Man ever since has been at odds with himself, a restless and exasperated being who strives to conquer the world at the sacrifice of his soul.

The need for a return to faith

For the Neo-Scholastics, then, the salvation of the world depended upon the development of a Christian culture based on the wisdom of St. Thomas Aquinas. Nothing less, they believed, can give dignity to human nature and meaning to human life. Only by a return to faith in God as the creator and upholder of a rational universe can we escape the mood of despair so relentlessly pressing upon us. The time for this Christian revival, though, is not yet. Five centuries of human history cannot be liquidated in a single night. But it is to be hoped that some day the present period of agony and wretchedness will come to an end, and that a new era will dawn which will be guided by the spirit of the Angelic Doctor of the thirteenth century. Despite its medieval flavor, Neo-Scholasticism attracted many thinkers of the contemporary world. At one time or another it numbered among its followers such diverse intellects as G. K. Chesterton; Etienne Gilson, of the University of Paris; and Mortimer J. Adler, of the University of Chicago.

Existentialism

The depths of pessimism in philosophy were reached by a movement known as Existentialism, the most popular form of which originated in France about 1938. Founded by Jean-Paul Sartre, a teacher of philosophy in a Paris lycée and subsequently a leader of the Resistance against the Germans, it takes its name from its doctrine that the *existence* of man as a free individual is the fundamental fact of life. But this freedom is of no help to man; instead, it is a source of anguish and terror. Realizing however vaguely that he is a free agent, morally responsible for all his acts, the individual feels himself a stranger in an alien world. He can have no confidence in a benevolent God or in a universe guided by purpose, for, according to Sartre, all such ideas have been reduced to fictions by modern science. His only way of escape from forlornness and despair is the path of "involvement," or active participation in human affairs. It should be noted that in addition to the atheistic Existentialism of Sartre, there was also an older, Christian form which had its origin in the teachings of Sören Kierkegaard, a Danish theologian of the middle nineteenth century. Incidentally, the doctrines of Kierkegaard also influenced the Neo-Orthodoxy of Karl Barth. After 1930 the leading exponent of Christian Existentialism was Karl Jaspers, philosophy professor of the University of Heidelberg.

At least two philosophers of the contemporary age retained their optimism amid the welter of gloom and uncertainty. One was Alfred North Whitehead. Born in England, the son of a clergyman of the Church of England, he spent the most fruitful years of his life as Professor of Philosophy at Harvard. Originally a mathematician, he turned to philosophy in an effort to harmonize modern thinking with the revolutionary discoveries of the new age of science. The system of thought he rapidly developed owed much to Plato, Kant, and Einstein. Like the first two, at least, he regarded intuition as just as valid a method of knowing as reason or sensory experience. He rebuked the hardheaded positivists who heaped scorn upon the mystic, the artist, and the romantic poet. A liberal in politics and in social theory, he had a firm belief in the certainty of progress. He had an abiding faith also in a benevolent God. But he refused to think of this God as a divine autocrat handing down tables of laws and punishing men eternally for trespassing against them. Instead, he conceived Him as a God of love, as "the poet of the world, with tender patience leading it by his vision of truth, beauty, and goodness." [2] The defect of most religions, Christianity included, has been to represent God as a God of power. God is not omnipotent, or else He would be the author of evil. His primary function is to save human beings from the evil which necessarily arises in connection with their struggle for the good. Such was Whitehead's conception of a friendly universe in which God and man are partners in striving toward perfection.

The optimistic philosophy of Whitehead

The second of the philosophers whose thinking was basically optimistic was the American John Dewey. Born in 1859, Dewey had already achieved renown before 1918 as a philosopher of Pragmatism. He never abandoned his allegiance to that movement, but after World War I he gave more and more attention to specific

The Humanism of John Dewey

[2] *Process and Reality* (American edition), p. 526.

human problems. In his celebrated *Reconstruction in Philosophy*, published in 1920, he urged that philosophy should abandon its dealings "with Ultimate and Absolute Reality" and "find compensation in enlightening the moral forces that move mankind." [3] Unlike most of his contemporaries, he retained a healthy confidence in the powers of the human intellect. He believed that man, making use of the resources acquired by reason and experience, could solve his own problems without any assistance from the supernatural. In common with the humanists of the past, he considered human beings to be the most important creatures in the universe, and he refused to concede that their nature was corrupt or depraved. Amid the rising tide of totalitarian oppression in the 1930's, he stressed increasingly the importance of freedom. This, together with a belief in equality and in the capacity of men to form intelligent judgments when guided by experience and education, he held to be the essence of democracy.

Antirationalist and antidemocratic philosophies

Included in the social and political philosophy of the time were the theories of some who despised democracy and therefore contributed to the deepening crisis. Foremost among them were the Italian Vilfredo Pareto and the German Oswald Spengler. Their forerunner was the Frenchman Georges Sorel, who has already been discussed as the founder of Syndicalism. For the most part, all of them agreed in their contempt for the masses, in their belief that democracy was impossible, in their anti-intellectual viewpoint, and in their admiration for strong and aggressive leaders. Spengler went farther, perhaps, than any of the others. Although he completed about 1918 an erudite and in some respects brilliant philosophy of history, which he entitled *The Decline of the West*, his later writings were as full of prejudice as the books of the Nazis. In his *Hour of Decision*, published in 1933, he fulminated against democracy, pacifism, internationalism, the lower classes, and the colored races. He sang the praises of those "who feel themselves born and called to be masters," of "healthy instincts, race, the will to possession and power." He despised the cold, analytical reasoning of urban intellectuals and called upon men to admire the "deep wisdom of old peasant families." Human beings, he maintained, are "beasts of prey," and those who deny this conclusion are simply "beasts of prey with broken teeth."

The new conservatism

The years following World War II witnessed an increasing popularity of conservative political and social philosophy. The creeping shadow of communism was undoubtedly largely responsible, but the trend had been initiated while the U.S.S.R. was still an ally of the West. The paternity of the new movement should perhaps be ascribed to Frederick A. Hayek, an Austrian political economist who had taken up residence in London. In *The Road to Serfdom*, Hayek condemned all forms of collectivist interference with capi-

[3] Pp. 26–27.

talism, on the ground that they would lead to socialism and eventually to communism or fascism. Destruction of economic freedom, he contended, must surely lead to the destruction of all freedoms, for the right of the individual to unhampered choice in the pursuit of tastes and interests is the very essence of freedom. A more strictly political variety of the new conservatism is exemplified by the work of Peter Viereck, Russell Kirk, and Eric Voegelin. All three espouse a philosophy essentially reactionary and antirational. Viereck, for example, describes himself as one who "distrusts human nature and believes (politically speaking) in Original Sin which must be restrained by the ethical traffic lights of traditionalism." According to Voegelin, Western society can be saved by venerating its tradition-rooted institutions and by abandoning the belief that knowledge, rather than faith, is the greatest good. Russell Kirk demands a revival of family piety, the defense of property, and a recognition that a "divine intent rules society" and that "Providence is the proper instrument for change."

3. Literature in the Contemporary World

Literary movements during the period of the depression and the two world wars showed tendencies very similar to those in philosophy. Indeed, in many instances, it was difficult to tell where philosophy ended and literature began. The major novelists, poets, and dramatists were deeply concerned about social and political problems and about the hope and destiny of man. Like the philosophers, they were disillusioned by the brute facts of World War I and by the failure of the victory to fulfill its promises. Many were profoundly affected also by the revolutionary developments in science and especially by the probings of the new psychology into the hidden secrets of the mind. Instead of a being created by God just "a little lower than the angels," man seemed now to be a creature just a bit higher than the apes. Finally, of course, literary men were influenced by the Great Depression and by the return to war in 1939. Both these developments led to a searching of methods and, among many writers, to a partial revision of objectives.

Major tendencies in literature

Each of the three decades after 1918 might almost be considered a literary period of its own, although the boundaries between them were far from distinct. The prevailing moods of the 1920's were disenchantment, cynicism, and preoccupation with the tragic fate of individuals. It was the period of the so-called "lost generation," of young men who had come out of the war with shattered ideals. Its literary tone was set by the early novels of Ernest Hemingway and John Dos Passos, by the poetry of T. S. Eliot, and by the dramas of Eugene O'Neill. In *A Farewell to Arms* (1929) Hemingway gave to the public one of its first insights into the folly and meanness of war and set a pattern which other writers were soon to follow. In

The 1920's: an age of cynicism and disenchantment

such novels as *1919* Dos Passos portrayed the bitterness and cynicism resulting from the failure of the peace. T. S. Eliot, in his poem *The Waste Land* (1922), presented a philosophy that was close to despair. Once you are born, he seemed to be saying, life is a living death to be ground out in boredom and frustration. The pessimism of Eugene O'Neill appeared to be somewhat different from that of his contemporaries. His tragedies depicted man not so much as a victim of the defects of society but rather as the pitiable slave of his own abnormal nature. Most critics would probably agree that O'Neill's greatest dramas were *Strange Interlude* (1927) and *Mourning Becomes Electra* (1931). In the former he revived the Elizabethan device of the aside, by which each character was made to express what he really thought, in addition to the conventional remark intended for others to hear.

*Other
tendencies
of the 1920's*

Literary achievements during the 1920's also included important works by such writers as Aldous Huxley, Erich Remarque, Theodore Dreiser, Sinclair Lewis, Thomas Mann, and James Joyce. All except the first two were novelists with established reputations when the decade began. Aldous Huxley in *Point Counter Point* (1928) epitomized the cynicism and frustration of the jazz age. In *All Quiet on the Western Front* (1929) Erich Remarque portrayed the brutality and pointlessness of war perhaps even more effectively than Hemingway. The great realist, Theodore Dreiser, brought his rigidly deterministic philosophy to a climax in *An American Tragedy* (1925). Sinclair Lewis scored triumphs with *Main Street* (1920) and *Babbitt* (1922), the former a savage portrayal of the mean and narrow in small-town society, and the latter a pungent satire on the intellectual poverty of moneygrubbers. Thomas Mann won universal acclaim for his *Magic Mountain* (1924), a psychological study of illusion and distortion of values by an artificial and decadent society. The work of the renowned Irish novelist, James Joyce, was devoted almost entirely to an analysis of the mind. Deeply influenced by psychoanalysis, he became the leading exponent of stream-of-consciousness writing. His greatest novel, *Ulysses* (1922), analyzed the thoughts and experiences of a motley aggregate of characters during a single day in Dublin. It was largely a study of reverie rather than of action.

*The 1930's give
birth to litera-
ture with a
serious purpose*

During the 1930's contemporary literature entered a new phase. The Great Depression forced a re-examination of the methods and purposes of literature. In the midst of economic collapse and threats of fascism and war, it seemed that authors should find something better to write about than the frustrations of idle women or the suppressed desires of psychological misfits. The writers of the 1920's were now often, and in some cases unjustly, accused of negativism and irresponsibility. The theory evolved that literature must have a serious purpose, that it should indict meanness, cruelty, and barbarism and point the way to a society more just. The new trend was symbolized by the works of a diversity of writers. John Steinbeck in *The Grapes of Wrath* depicted the sorry plight of impoverished farmers fleeing from the "dust bowl" to the fabulous land of California, only to find that all the good earth had been monopolized by corporations that exploited their workers. His novel has been described as an *Uncle Tom's Cabin* of the underprivileged. Pervading some of the plays of Robert Sherwood and the novels of André Malraux was the strong suggestion that man's struggle against tyranny and injustice is the chief thing that gives meaning and value to life. Sherwood's *There Shall Be No Night* idealized the struggle of the Finns against Russian aggression in 1939–1940. André Malraux in *Man's Hope* glorified the selflessness of Loyalist heroes in the struggle against fascism in Spain. A somewhat similar theme may be said to have characterized Ernest Hemingway's *For Whom the Bell Tolls* (1940). Here also was the strong implication that the individual in sacrificing himself for the cause of the people gives a meaning and dignity to life which can be achieved in no other way.

A quality of optimism permeated much of the literature of the 1930's. Seldom, however, was it unrestrained. Most of the great writers saw plenty of meanness, tragedy, and suffering, but on occasions, at least, they were able to discover a purpose behind it, so that *Optimism, restrained and unrestrained* life did not have to be a tale told by an idiot. A few found beauty in everything, even in tragedy and death. Such was the philosophy of Thomas Wolfe, who had one of the keenest perceptive intellects of any writer of his time. In such sprawling novels as *Of Time and the River* (1937) and *You Can't Go Home Again* (1940), he wrote with sharp awareness of himself, of America and its relation to the world, of fascism, sex, and death. Despite his fiery protest against many of the things he saw and experienced, he retained his confidence that the America he loved would some day find herself and discover the true meaning of democracy. A much more effervescent optimism was expressed by Carl Sandburg, who entitled one of his volumes of poems *The People, Yes* (1937). Finally, a few writers had sufficient confidence in the future to portray the outlines of a new world which they believed might emerge from the sorrow and pain of the present. A notable example was Thomas Mann, who embodied in a series of novels based upon the Biblical story of Joseph in Egypt the concept of a world society of the brotherhood of man founded upon the Hebrew-Christian heritage.

The years after 1940 witnessed a continuation of many of the trends of the previous decades. Warm sympathy for the plain folk of rural New England was expressed by Robert Frost, greatly *The trends* beloved American poet. Nobel-prize winner William Faulkner *of more recent* devoted superb artistic talents to portrayal of crude elemental be- *years* havior in backward areas of the Deep South. The tragedy of World War II brought a series of novels dealing with the conflict itself, **979** with the heroism of those who resisted Nazi tyranny, or with the brutality and inefficiency of military systems. Foremost among such writings were Norman Mailer's *The Naked and the Dead* and James Jones' *From Here to Eternity*. Both portrayed the coarseness and cruelty of military life with a realism more ruthless than any to be found in the early works of Hemingway or Remarque. But along with these trends toward warm sympathy and stark realism as means of conveying hatred of injustice and oppression, there were also some new manifestations. One was a turning to religion to compensate for a sense of overwhelming tragedy or to prevent calamities which seemed certain to flow from allowing science to get out of control. Aldous Huxley, erstwhile prophet of the age of cynicism and sophistication, turned to Hindu mysticism in such novels as *After Many a Summer Dies the Swan* and *Time Must Have a Stop*. T. S. Eliot, who in the 1920's had found the universe a barren wasteland with no fruits but boredom and despair, now discovered that life could be meaningful when ennobled by the ageless truths of the church. His new mood was exemplified by *Murder in the Cathedral* and *The Cocktail Party*. But in spite of the different directions of their thinking, most of the writers of the 1940's and '50's seemed to have much in common. They were expressing with one voice their concern over the loneliness of man. They saw human beings in an age of mass thinking and mass actions as helpless and pitiable creatures. Embracing religion or lashing injustice and stupidity were simply different means of accomplishing the rescue of modern man from utter destruction by the forces around him.

4. Contemporary Art and Music

Attitudes of pessimism, disillusionment, and revolt were also revealed in the numerous artistic movements which flourished after World War I. Until about 1930 painting was dominated largely by various expressions of the modern or post-impressionist tradition. Futurism lingered for a time from the prewar era, but was soon eclipsed in importance by other movements no less extreme in character. Perhaps the most significant was *expressionism*, exemplified by the work of the German painter, George Grosz. The exclusive object of expressionist painting is to convey meaning—to portray especially the intense feeling of the artist himself. Consequently, form is despised, and distortion is practiced to whatever extent the artist may consider necessary for representing "the state of his soul." It should be added that the later expressionists were noteworthy also as social satirists. An even more violent movement of rebellion against accepted standards of art and of life was *surrealism*, whose high priest was the Spaniard Salvador Dali. Originating about 1918 under the combined influence of the war and psycho-

*Disillusionment
and revolt
in the arts*

*See color
pictures at
pages 868,
869*

analysis, surrealism flourished during the age of nihilism that followed the armistice. The aim of its followers was not to represent the world of nature but to portray the reactions of the human mind. For this purpose they delved into the subconscious and attempted to depict the content of dreams and the weird impressions of reverie. This commonly resulted in a technique quite different from that of traditional art. In general, the surrealists paid little attention to the conventional standards of beauty and form. They argued that, in the light of the new psychology, naturalism was impossible, if art were to have any value as an accurate expression of meaning.

After 1930 the bizarre and anarchic painting of the extreme modernist schools suffered a considerable decline. Its place was taken to a large extent by a virile and popular art of the common man. Among the chief representatives of the new movement were the Mexicans, Diego Rivera and José Clemente Orozco, and the United States painters Thomas Benton, Adolph Dehn, William Gropper, and Grant Wood. The fundamental aim of these artists was to depict the social conditions of the modern world and to present in graphic detail the hopes and struggles of peasants and toilers. While they scarcely adhered to any of the conventions of the past, there was nothing unintelligible about their work; it was intended to be art which anyone could understand. At the same time, much of it bore the sting or thrust of social satire. Orozco, in particular, delighted in pillorying the hypocrisy of the church and the greed and cruelty of plutocrats and plunderers.

The new art of the common man

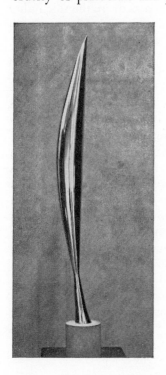

Bird in Space, by Constantin Brancusi. A characteristic example of modern abstract sculpture, in which natural form is subordinated to interpretation.

981

It was inevitable that music should reflect the spirit of disillusionment which reached a climax following World War I. The more original developments were closely parallel to those in painting. Most fundamental of all was the revolt against the romantic tradition, especially as it had culminated in Wagner. Many, although by no means all, composers went so far as to repudiate the aesthetic ideal entirely, relying upon complexity and novelty of structure or a sheer display of energy to supply interest to their works.

Deviations from the classical and romantic formulas have been generally of two types, designated broadly as impressionism and expressionism. The former seeks to exploit the qualities of musical sound to suggest feelings or images. The latter is concerned more with form than with sensuous effects and tends toward abstraction. The most perfect exponent of impressionism was Debussy, its originator, whose work has been described in an earlier chapter. Even in France impressionism did not prove to be an enduring school. With Maurice Ravel (1875–1938), most celebrated of the composers who reflected Debussy's influence, it became less poetic and picturesque, and acquired a degree of cold impassivity together with greater firmness of texture.

Expressionism, more radical and more influential than impressionism, comprises two main schools: *atonality*, founded by the Viennese, Arnold Schoenberg (1874–1951), and *polytonality*, best typified by the Russian, Igor Stravinsky (1882–   ). Atonality implies the repudiation of the concept of fixed tonal relationships; it abolishes *key*. In this type of music, dissonances are the rule rather than the exception, and the melodic line commonly alternates between chromatic creeping and strange unsingable leaps. In short, the ordinary principles of composition are reversed. However, emancipation from the bonds of tradition has enabled the atonalists to give undivided attention to the development of their own subjective ideas with the utmost originality. They attempt, with some success, to let musical sound become, not an object admirable in itself, but a vehicle for expressing the inner meaning and elemental structure of things. Odd as it may appear, some atonal works are deeply emotional in effect. They betray a kinship with symbolism and also show the influence of the theories of the subconscious derived from psychoanalysis. Most of the distinctive features of the atonal school are vividly incorporated in Schoenberg's *Pierrot Lunaire*, the setting of a symbolist text from the Belgian poet, Albert Giraud. This fantasy, in which the singer intones her part in a special "song-speech," somewhat between singing and reciting, has been described as creating "a whole world of strange fascination and enchantment, of nameless horrors and terrible imaginings, of perverse and poisonous beauty . . . of a searing and withering mockery and malicious, elfish humor." [4]

[4] Cecil Gray, *A Survey of Contemporary Music*, p. 176.

Polytonality, of which Stravinsky is the most famous exponent, is essentially a radical kind of counterpoint, deriving its inspiration partly from Bach and the earlier polyphonists. However, it is not content simply to interweave independent melodies which together form concord, but undertakes to combine separate keys and unrelated harmonic systems, with results which are highly discordant. It is thus another example of revolt against the European harmonic heritage and differs from atonality more in technique than in ultimate aim. But while the atonalists, through their emotional expressiveness, have retained elements of romanticism, the polytonalists have tried to resurrect the architectural qualities of pure form, movement, and rhythm, stripping away all sentimentality and sensuous connotations. Stravinsky affirmed that his intention was to produce music in which acoustic properties were the only consideration and which would appeal to the physical ear alone. His coldly detached, anti-aesthetic experiments have much in common with cubism and similar tendencies in modern painting. In spite of this, however, Stravinsky's first really characteristic and widely heralded creations were composed in Paris for the Russian Ballet, a species of theatrical art which not only appeals to other senses than that of hearing but which also is intended to delineate human character and emotions. The application of his theories to such a medium conveys the sardonic impression of human beings who are mere automatons, manipulated by their own physical urges or by the grim hand of a mechanical fate. Stravinsky's style and interests have undergone successive changes; in recent years he has turned from the theater to more distinctly concert forms. Without sacrificing his intense individuality, he has achieved an increasing clarity of expression and an almost classical integration of structural design.

5. Epilogue

We have now come to the end of a long survey of the history of Western man and his civilizations from their earliest beginnings to the present. It is an appropriate time to ask ourselves a number of questions. What is the meaning of history? Do we learn anything of value from the study of history? Does history repeat itself? What is the fate of our own civilization? Is it destined to decay and disintegrate, to succumb to barbarian invasions, either from within or from without, and to be replaced by a new Dark Age?

Ever since the eighteenth century it has been fashionable in some quarters to be cynical about the meaning of history and to scoff at the value of studying it. For Herbert Spencer history was "worthless gossip." To Napoleon it was a "fable agreed upon." To Edward Gibbon it appeared at times to be "little more than a register of the crimes, follies, and misfortunes of mankind." The German philosopher Hegel maintained, in one of his darker moments, that "the only thing that peoples and governments learn from the study of history is that they learn nothing from the study of history." Actually, however, no one seems to take much stock in any of these disparaging doctrines. Every person who lives much above the animal level has constant recourse to the lessons of history. For all experience, whether recorded or merely remembered, is in reality history. In treating diseases the modern physician makes use of *historical* medicine. He may at times experiment with new remedies, but for the most part he relies upon treatments previously developed by research scientists or tested by past experience. The lawyer in defending his client and the judge in deciding cases turn back to the precedents established in similar litigation over a period of decades or even through centuries. The businessman, if he is to avoid severe losses, must take into account the trends of the market and the fluctuations of the economic cycle over a period of considerable length. All of these people and countless others would be as helpless as a ship without rudder or sails if it were not for the "lessons" of history.

The growth and decline of civilizations

But does history repeat itself sufficiently to enable us to predict the future? Thucydides thought that events do "repeat themselves at some future time—if not exactly the same, yet very similar." A large proportion of the philosophers of history have conceived of a uniform pattern characterizing the growth and decline of civilization over thousands of years. Toynbee attributes the growth primarily to a condition of adversity and the decline to such factors as militarism and war, barbarization from within, and the rise of an "internal proletariat." By the last term he means a class like the city mob of ancient Rome who are "in" but not "of" a given society. Despised and disinherited, they nurse grievances against the society and gradually undermine it. Oswald Spengler saw the growth and decay of civilizations, or cultures as he called them, paralleling the four seasons or the life of an organism. Each had its spring or youth phase, its summer or early maturity phase, its autumn or late maturity phase, and its winter or senility phase.

Causes of decline

Even in periods of the brightest optimism writers who have done much thinking about the meaning of history have generally assumed that decay and disintegration will follow prosperity and progress. For example, the Founding Fathers in the United States viewed the future of their own country with grave misgivings. So long as the nation remained predominantly agricultural, with an abundance of cheap land, all would be well. But increasing population in a few generations would result in the growth of large cities, with their slums, corrupt politicians, and a dependent mob ready to sell its votes to the highest bidder. The ultimate outcome would be the rise of Catilines and Caesars, who would seek, with the support of the proletariat, to overthrow the republic. In the late nineteenth

century, when the age of science and industry in the United States was still facing the rising sun, Brooks Adams and his brother Henry described with accents of gloom the ultimate decay of Western culture. The former contended that every civilization passes through two stages, one dominated by fear and the other by greed. Fear stimulates the imagination and results in artistic production and great systems of religion. Greed subordinates everything to economic considerations. Marriage is avoided or postponed, the birth rate declines, and originality is stifled by an atmosphere of caution. Henry Adams sought to interpret civilization in terms of a scientific law—the second law of thermodynamics, or the law of the dissipation of energy. He predicted that the civilization of Western man would expend its vital force and die of exhaustion by 1932.

There seems little doubt that civilizations do grow old and die from a number of causes. A major one apparently is urbanization, carried to the point where a large proportion of the population is crowded into huge metropolitan areas. This condition adds so much to the complexity of social problems that human intelligence is unable to solve them. Crime, disease, boredom, insanity, corruption, poverty in the midst of plenty are only a few of these critical problems. Excessive concentration of industry results in overproduction and leads to depressions and to exhaustion of natural resources. Whether our own civilization has reached this stage is a question impossible to answer. There are, of course, some ominous portents, but there are also signs of hope. Disease, at least in the form of the great pestilences, seems well on the way toward extinction. If crime and corruption have not been eliminated, their nature and causes are better understood. Poverty is still with us, but standards of living for most of the masses have improved, and more adequate provision is made for those who may suffer from want. Imperialism, at least of the type imposed by external conquest, seems on the wane, as exemplified by the freedom gained in recent years by India, Israel, Ceylon, Pakistan, Libya, Ghana, Indonesia, Morocco and the Sudan.

The fate of our own civilization

The most serious threat to civilization wherever it exists is war. Throughout history its principal fruits have been inflation, impoverishment, revolution, and chaos. It has destroyed the best blood of nation after nation and left the physical and mental weaklings to become the fathers of the new generation. But even war must not be regarded as an insoluble problem. With the development of atomic and hydrogen weapons it is coming to be regarded in widening circles as a logical monstrosity. Signs have multiplied that neither of the two great antagonists among the nations desires war or would deliberately take steps to make it inevitable. Despite all the prophets of doom, sanity has not been completely extinguished. Although progress is slow and faltering, the world does move. It is barely twenty centuries since human sacrifice was practiced by such a "civilized" people as the Carthaginians. It is less than one

The threat and the hope

century since slavery was abolished in the United States and serf-dom in Russia. If we have not been able to solve all of our problems, we at least know what we ought to do to dispose of a good many of them. The expansion of knowledge and the application of intelligence will provide us with the means of conquering the remainder.

SELECTED READINGS

Beach, J. W., *The Twentieth Century Novel*, New York, 1933
Bruun, Geoffrey, *The World in the Twentieth Century*, New York, 1948
Colum, Mary, *From These Roots: the Ideas That Have Made Modern Literature*, New York, 1944
Copland, Aaron, *Our New Music*, New York, 1941
Craven, Thomas, *Modern Art: the Men, the Movement, the Meaning*, New York, 1934
Gray, Cecil, *A Survey of Contemporary Music*, London, 1924
Hecht, Selig, *Explaining the Atom*, New York, 1947
Hogben, L. T., *Science for the Citizen*, New York, 1938
Jeans, Sir James, *The Universe around Us*, New York, 1944
Lang, Paul, *Music in Western Civilization*, New York, 1941
Machlis, Joseph, *The Enjoyment of Music*, New York, 1955
Pritchett, V. S., *The Living Novel*, New York, 1947
Randall, J. H., Jr., *Our Changing Civilization*, New York, 1929
Roucek, J. S., ed., *Twentieth Century Political Thought*, New York, 1946
Runes, D. D., *Twentieth Century Philosophy*, New York, 1943
Salazar, Adolfo, *Music in Our Time*, New York, 1946
Schneider, H. W., *A History of American Philosophy*, New York, 1946
Shapiro, J. S., *The World in Crisis*, New York, 1950
Slochower, Harry, *No Voice Is Wholly Lost*, New York, 1945
Ward, Harold, *New Worlds in Medicine*, New York, 1946
Wittels, Fritz, *Freud and His Time*, New York, 1948

SOURCE MATERIALS

Baumer, F. L. V., *Main Currents of Western Thought*, New York, 1952
Dewey, John, *Reconstruction in Philosophy*
———, *Liberalism and Social Action*
Niebuhr, Reinhold, *The Children of Light and the Children of Darkness*
Spengler, Oswald, *The Decline of the West*, Introduction
Whitehead, A. N., *Science and the Modern World*

Rulers of Principal European States since 700 A.D.

The Carolingian Dynasty

Pepin, Mayor of the Palace, 714
Charles Martel, Mayor of the Palace, 715–741
Pepin I, Mayor of the Palace, 741; King, 751–768
Charlemagne, King, 768–814; Emperor, 800–814
Louis the Pious, Emperor, 814–840

WEST FRANCIA

Charles the Bald, King, 840–877; Emperor, 875
Louis II, King, 877–879

Louis III, King, 879–882
Carloman, King, 879–884

MIDDLE KINGDOMS

Lothair, Emperor, 840–855
Louis (Italy), Emperor, 855–875
Charles (Provence), King, 855–863
Lothair II (Lorraine), King, 855–869

EAST FRANCIA

Ludwig, King, 840–876
Carloman, King, 876–880
Ludwig, King, 876–882
Charles the Fat, Emperor, 876–887

Holy Roman Emperors

SAXON DYNASTY

Otto I, 962–973
Otto II, 973–983
Otto III, 983–1002
Henry II, 1002–1024

FRANCONIAN DYNASTY

Conrad II, 1024–1039
Henry III, 1039–1056
Henry IV, 1056–1106

Henry V, 1106–1125
Lothair II (of Saxony), King, 1125–1133; Emperor, 1133–1137

HOHENSTAUFEN DYNASTY

Conrad III, 1138–1152
Frederick I (Barbarossa), 1152–1190
Henry VI, 1190–1197
Philip of Swabia, 1198–1208 ⎱ Rivals
Otto IV (Welf), 1198–1215 ⎰

Frederick II, 1220–1250
Conrad IV, 1250–1254

INTERREGNUM, 1254–1273

EMPERORS FROM VARIOUS DYNASTIES
Rudolf I (Hapsburg), 1273–1291
Adolf (Nassau), 1292–1298
Albert I (Hapsburg), 1298–1308
Henry VII (Luxemburg), 1308–1313
Ludwig IV (Wittelsbach), 1314–1347
Charles IV (Luxemburg), 1347–1378
Wenceslas (Luxemburg), 1378–1400
Rupert (Wittelsbach), 1400–1410
Sigismund (Luxemburg), 1410–1437

HAPSBURG DYNASTY

Albert II, 1438–1439
Frederick III, 1440–1493

Maximilian I, 1493–1519
Charles V, 1519–1556
Ferdinand I, 1556–1564
Maximilian II, 1564–1576
Rudolf II, 1576–1612
Matthias, 1612–1619
Ferdinand II, 1619–1637
Ferdinand III, 1637–1657
Leopold I, 1658–1705
Joseph I, 1705–1711
Charles VI, 1711–1740
Charles VII (not a Hapsburg), 1742–1745
Francis I, 1745–1765
Joseph II, 1765–1790
Leopold II, 1790–1792
Francis II, 1792–1806

Rulers of France from Hugh Capet

CAPETIAN KINGS

Hugh Capet, 987–996
Robert II, 996–1031
Henry I, 1031–1060
Philip I, 1060–1108
Louis VI, 1108–1137
Louis VII, 1137–1180
Philip II (Augustus), 1180–1223
Louis VIII, 1223–1226
Louis IX, 1226–1270
Philip III, 1270–1285
Philip IV, 1285–1314
Louis X, 1314–1316
Philip V, 1316–1322
Charles IV, 1322–1328

HOUSE OF VALOIS

Philip VI, 1328–1350
John, 1350–1364
Charles V, 1364–1380
Charles VI, 1380–1422
Charles VII, 1422–1461
Louis XI, 1461–1483
Charles VIII, 1483–1498
Louis XII, 1498–1515
Francis I, 1515–1547
Henry II, 1547–1559

Francis II, 1559–1560
Charles IX, 1560–1574
Henry III, 1574–1589

BOURBON DYNASTY

Henry IV, 1589–1610
Louis XIII, 1610–1643
Louis XIV, 1643–1715
Louis XV, 1715–1774
Louis XVI, 1774–1792

AFTER 1792

First Republic, 1792–1799
Napoleon Bonaparte, First Consul, 1799–1804
Napoleon I, Emperor, 1804–1814
Louis XVIII (Bourbon dynasty), 1814–1824
Charles X (Bourbon dynasty), 1824–1830
Louis Philippe, 1830–1848
Second Republic, 1848–1852
Napoleon III, Emperor, 1852–1870
Third Republic, 1870–1940
Pétain regime, 1940–1944
Provisional government, 1944–1946
Fourth Republic, 1946–

Rulers of England

ANGLO-SAXON KINGS

Egbert, 802–839
Ethelwulf, 839–858
Ethelbald, 858–860
Ethelbert, 860–866
Ethelred, 866–871
Alfred the Great, 871–900
Edward the Elder, 900–924
Ethelstan, 924–940
Edmund I, 940–946
Edred, 946–955
Edwy, 955–959
Edgar, 959–975
Edward the Martyr, 975–978
Ethelred the Unready, 978–1016
Canute, 1016–1035 (Danish Nationality)
Harold I, 1035–1040
Hardicanute, 1040–1042
Edward the Confessor, 1042–1066
Harold II, 1066

ANGLO-NORMAN KINGS

William I (the Conqueror), 1066–1087
William II, 1087–1100
Henry I, 1100–1135
Stephen, 1135–1154

ANGEVIN KINGS

Henry II, 1154–1189
Richard I, 1189–1199
John, 1199–1216
Henry III, 1216–1272
Edward I, 1272–1307
Edward II, 1307–1327
Edward III, 1327–1377
Richard II, 1377–1399

HOUSE OF LANCASTER

Henry IV, 1399–1413
Henry V, 1413–1422
Henry VI, 1422–1461

HOUSE OF YORK

Edward IV, 1461–1483
Edward V, 1483
Richard III, 1483–1485

TUDOR SOVEREIGNS

Henry VII, 1485–1509
Henry VIII, 1509–1547
Edward VI, 1547–1553
Mary, 1553–1558
Elizabeth I, 1558–1603

STUART KINGS

James I, 1603–1625
Charles I, 1625–1649

COMMONWEALTH AND PROTECTORATE, 1649–1659

LATER STUART MONARCHS

Charles II, 1660–1685
James II, 1685–1688
William III and Mary II, 1689–1694
William III alone, 1694–1702
Anne, 1702–1714

HOUSE OF HANOVER

George I, 1714–1727
George II, 1727–1760
George III, 1760–1820
George IV, 1820–1830
William IV, 1830–1837
Victoria, 1837–1901

HOUSE OF SAXE-COBURG-GOTHA

Edward VII, 1901–1910
George V, 1910–1917

HOUSE OF WINDSOR

George V, 1917–1936
Edward VIII, 1936
George VI, 1936–1952
Elizabeth II, 1952–

Prominent Popes

Silvester I, 314–335
Leo I, 440–461
Gelasius I, 492–496

Gregory I, 590–604
Nicholas, I, 858–867
Silvester II, 999–1003

Leo IX, 1049–1054
Nicholas II, 1058–1061
Gregory VII, 1073–1085
Urban II, 1088–1099
Paschal II, 1099–1118
Alexander III, 1159–1181
Innocent III, 1198–1216
Gregory IX, 1227–1241
Boniface VIII, 1294–1303
John XXII, 1316–1334
Nicholas V, 1447–1455
Pius II, 1458–1464
Alexander VI, 1492–1503
Julius II, 1503–1513

Leo X, 1513–1521
Adrian VI, 1522–1523
Clement VII, 1523–1534
Paul III, 1534–1549
Paul IV, 1555–1559
Gregory XIII, 1572–1585
Gregory XVI, 1831–1846
Pius IX, 1846–1878
Leo XIII, 1878–1903
Pius X, 1903–1914
Benedict XV, 1914–1922
Pius XI, 1922–1939
Pius XII, 1939–

Rulers of Austria and Austria-Hungary

*Maximilian I (Archduke), 1493–1519
*Charles I (Charles V in the Holy Roman Empire), 1519–1556
*Ferdinand I, 1556–1564
*Maximilian II, 1564–1576
*Rudolph II, 1576–1612
*Matthias, 1612–1619
*Ferdinand II, 1619–1637
*Ferdinand III, 1637–1657
*Leopold I, 1658–1705
*Joseph I, 1705–1711
*Charles VI, 1711–1740
Maria Theresa, 1740–1780
*Joseph II, 1780–1790

*Leopold II, 1790–1792
*Francis II, 1792–1835 (Emperor of Austria as Francis I after 1804)
Ferdinand I, 1835–1848
Francis Joseph, 1848–1916 (after 1867 Emperor of Austria and King of Hungary)
Charles I, 1916–1918 (Emperor of Austria and King of Hungary)
Republic of Austria, 1918–1938 (dictatorship after 1934)
Republic restored, under Allied occupation, 1945–1956
Free Republic, 1956–

* Also bore title of Holy Roman Emperor.

Rulers of Prussia and Germany

*Frederick I, 1701–1713
*Frederick William I, 1713–1740
*Frederick II (the Great), 1740–1786
*Frederick William II, 1786–1797
*Frederick William III, 1797–1840
*Frederick William IV, 1840–1861
*William I, 1861–1888 (German Emperor after 1871)
Frederick III, 1888

William II, 1888–1918
Weimar Republic, 1918–1933
Third Reich (Nazi Dictatorship), 1933–1945
Allied occupation, 1945–1952
Division into Federal Republic of Germany in west and German Democratic Republic in east, 1949–

* Kings of Prussia.

Rulers of Russia

Ivan III, 1462–1505
Basil III, 1505–1533
Ivan IV, 1533–1584
Theodore I, 1584–1598
Boris Godunov, 1598–1605
Theodore II, 1605
Basil IV, 1606–1610
Michael, 1613–1645
Alexius, 1645–1676
Theodore III, 1676–1682
Ivan V and Peter I, 1682–1689
Peter I (the Great), 1689–1725
Catherine I, 1725–1727

Peter II, 1727–1730
Anna, 1730–1740
Ivan VI, 1740–1741
Elizabeth, 1741–1762
Peter III, 1762
Catherine II (the Great), 1762–1796
Paul, 1796–1801
Alexander I, 1801–1825
Nicholas I, 1825–1855
Alexander II, 1855–1881
Alexander III, 1881–1894
Nicholas II, 1894–1917
Soviet Republic, 1917–

Rulers of Italy

Victor Emmanuel II, 1861–1878
Humbert I, 1878–1900
Victor Emmanuel III, 1900–1946

Fascist Dictatorship, 1922–1943 (maintained in northern Italy until 1945)
Humbert II, May 9–June 13, 1946
Republic, 1946–

Rulers of Spain

Ferdinand { and Isabella, 1479–1504
and Philip I, 1504–1506
and Charles I, 1506–1516
Charles I (Holy Roman Emperor Charles V), 1516–1556
Philip II, 1556–1598
Philip III, 1598–1621
Philip IV, 1621–1665
Charles II, 1665–1700
Philip V, 1700–1746
Ferdinand VI, 1746–1759
Charles III, 1759–1788

Charles IV, 1788–1808
Ferdinand VII, 1808
Joseph Bonaparte, 1808–1813
Ferdinand VII (restored), 1814–1833
Isabella II, 1833–1868
Republic, 1868–1870
Amadeo, 1870–1873
Republic, 1873–1874
Alfonso XII, 1874–1885
Alfonso XIII, 1886–1931
Republic, 1931–1939
Fascist Dictatorship, 1939–

Index

Guide to Pronunciation

The sounds represented by the diacritical marks used in this Index are illustrated by the following common words:

āle	ēve	īce	ōld	ūse	bōot
ăt	ĕnd	ĭll	ŏf	ŭs	fŏŏt
fâtality	êvent		ôbey	ûnite	
câre			fôrm	ûrn	
ärm					
ȧsk					

Vowels that have no diacritical marks are to be pronounced "neutral," for example: Aegean = ê-jē'an, Basel = bäz'el, Basil = bă'zil, common = kŏm'on, Alcaeus = ăl-sē'us. The combinations ou and oi are pronounced as in "out" and "oil."

993

3   4   5   6   7   8   9

ATLANTIC OCEAN

ICELAND

A R C S NO

Norwegian Sea

SVALBARD

FRANZ JOSEPH LAND

PORTUGAL
Lisbon

IRELAND
Dublin

GREAT BRITAIN

London

North Sea

NETH.

NORWAY
Oslo

SWEDEN

Barents Sea

NOVAYA ZEMLYA

Kara Sea

DENMARK

Stockholm

FINLAND

Casablanca
MOROCCO

Madrid
SPAIN
Gibraltar

Brussels
Bordeaux
Amsterdam
FRANCE
GER.
Bonn
FED. Berlin
REP.

Copenhagen
Baltic Sea

Helsinki

Tallin

Arkangelsk

Dvina R.

Marseilles
Bern
SW.
Paris

GER.DEM.REP.

Leningrad

Kotlas

Algiers
ALGERIA

SARDINIA

Naples

BALEARIC IS.
CORSICA

ITALY

AUST.
Vienna
CZECH.

Prague
POLAND
Warsaw

Minsk

UNION · OF · SOVIET · SOCIAL

Tunis
TUNISIA

SICILY

Rome
HUNG.

Budapest

Dniester R.

Kiev

Moscow

Gorki

Kazan

Sverdlovsk

Yer

Tripoli

Belgrade
YUGOSLAVIA ?
ALB.
Sofia
BULG.

RUMANIA
Bucharest

Odessa

Don R.

Stalino

Sevastopol Rostov

Volga R.

Saratov

Kuibyshev

Stalingrad

Ob R.

Magnitogorsk

Tomsk

Omsk

Nov

Barn

LIBYA

GREECE
Athens
CRETE

Mediterranean Sea

Black Sea

Istanbul

Ankara

TURKEY

CYPRUS

Astrakan

Caspian Sea

Ural R.

Semipalat

Aral Sea

Syr Darya

Lake Balkash

Semipalat

EGYPT

Nile R.

Beirut
SYRIA
Tel Aviv Damascus
Jerusalem
Amman
JOR.

Euphrates

Tigris

IRAQ
Baghdad

Tehran

Ashkhabad

Amu Darya

Samarkand

Tashkent

Alma Ata

Soche

ANGLO - EGYPTIAN

Khartoum

SUDAN

Red Sea

Medina

Mecca

Kuwait

QATAR

SAUDI

ARABIA

Abadan

IRAN

Persian Gulf

Sharja

Matra
OMAN

AFGHANISTAN
Kabul

PAKISTAN

Indus R.

Amritsar
Lahore

Karachi

Delhi

NEPAL

T I B E

Khat

Ganges R.

ERITREA

YEMEN
San'a
ADEN
Aden
Djibouti FR. SOMALILAND

BELG.
CONGO

ETHIOPIA

BR. SOMALILAND

Arabian Sea

INDIA

Bombay

Godavari R.

Hyderabad

Bangalore

Madras

Calcutta

Bay

Ben

I N D I A N O C E

Colombo

CEYLON

Countries in the Western Orbit

U. S. S. R. and satellite states

Neutral

Miles

0   200   400   600   800   1000